FROMMER'S

COMPREHENSIVE TRAVEL GUIDE

ITALY '92

by Darwin Porter
Assisted by Danforth Prince

PRENTICE HALL TRAVEL

NEW YORK • LONDON • TORONTO • SYDNEY • TOKYO • SINGAPORE

FROMMER BOOKS
Published by Prentice Hall General Reference
A division of Simon & Schuster Inc.
15 Columbus Circle
New York, NY 10023

ISBN 0-13-334913-6
ISSN 1044-2170

Design by Robert Bull Design
Maps by Geografix Inc.

Manufactured in the United States of America

FROMMER'S ITALY '92
Editor-in-Chief: Marilyn Wood
Senior Editors: Judith de Rubini, Alice Fellows
Editors: Paige Hughes, Sara Raveret, Lisa Renaud, Theodore Stavrou
Assistant Editors: Peter Katucki, Lisa Legarde
Contributing Editors: David Branton, Eve Novick, Allegra Shapiro
Managing Editor: Leanne Coupe

CONTENTS

1 GETTING TO KNOW ITALY 1

1. Geography, History & Politics 1
2. Art, Architecture, Literature & Music 14
3. Language, Religion & Folklore 19
4. Sports & Recreation 22
5. Food & Drink 24
6. Recommended Books, Films & Recordings 28

SPECIAL FEATURES
● *Did You Know . . . ? 2*
● *Dateline 6*

2 PLANNING A TRIP TO ITALY 34

1. Information, Entry Requirements & Money 34
2. When to Go—Climate, Holidays & Events 37
3. Health & Insurance 42
4. What to Pack 43
5. Tips for the Disabled, Seniors, Singles, Families & Students 44
6. Alternative/Adventure Travel 46
7. Getting There 49
8. Getting Around 57
9. Where to Stay 63
10. Where to Dine 65
11. What to Buy 67

SPECIAL FEATURES
● *What Things Cost in Rome 36*
● *What Things Cost in Naples 37*
● *Italy Calendar of Events 38*
● *Rome Calendar of Events 41*
● *Frommer's Smart Traveler: Airfares 54*
● *Suggested Itineraries 62*
● *Fast Facts: Italy 68*

3 INTRODUCING ROME 73

1. Orientation 73
2. Getting Around 79
3. Networks & Resources 84

SPECIAL FEATURES
● *What's Special About Rome 74*
● *Fast Facts: Rome 81*

4 WHERE TO STAY & DINE IN ROME 86

1. Accommodations 86
2. Dining 109

SPECIAL FEATURES
● *Frommer's Smart Traveler: Hotels 87*
● *Frommer's Cool for Kids: Hotels 108*
● *Frommer's Smart Traveler: Restaurants 113*
● *Frommer's Cool for Kids: Restaurants 129*

5 WHAT TO SEE & DO IN ROME   133

1. Attractions   134
2. Sports & Recreation   172
3. Savvy Shopping   173
4. Evening Entertainment   185
5. Easy Excursions   193

SPECIAL FEATURES
- *Suggested Itineraries 133*
- *Did You Know . . . ? 134*
- *Frommer's Favorite Rome Experiences 147*
- *Walking Tour—Imperial Rome 156*
- *Walking Tour—Roman Forum & Palatine Hill 160*
- *Walking Tour—From Piazza Barberini to Piazza del Popolo 166*
- *Walking Tour—The Spanish Steps to Quirinale 169*

6 INTRODUCING FLORENCE (FIRENZE)   206

1. Orientation   207
2. Getting Around   212
3. Networks & Resources   215

SPECIAL FEATURES
- *What's Special About Florence 207*
- *Fast Facts: Florence 213*

7 WHERE TO STAY & DINE IN FLORENCE   216

1. Accommodations   216
2. Dining   239

SPECIAL FEATURES
- *Frommer's Smart Traveler: Hotels 217*
- *Frommer's Cool for Kids: Hotels 239*
- *Frommer's Smart Traveler: Restaurants 240*
- *Frommer's Cool for Kids: Restaurants 254*

8 WHAT TO SEE & DO IN FLORENCE   256

1. Attractions   257
2. Special & Free Events   280
3. Sports & Recreation   281
4. Savvy Shopping   282
5. Evening Entertainment   288
6. Easy Excursions   291

SPECIAL FEATURES
- *Suggested Itineraries 256*
- *Did You Know . . . ? 257*
- *Walking Tour—The Heart of Florence 273*
- *Walking Tour—In the Footsteps of Michelangelo 277*
- *Frommer's Favorite Florentine Experiences 282*

9 SIENA, PISA & THE HILL TOWNS 294

1. Siena 294
2. San Gimignano 305
3. Pisa 308
4. Perugia 312
5. Assisi 317
6. Spoleto 321

SPECIAL FEATURE
● What's Special About Siena, Pisa & the Hill Towns 295

10 BOLOGNA & EMILIA-ROMAGNA 325

1. Bologna 326
2. Ferrara 338
3. Modena 342
4. Parma 345
5. Ravenna 349

SPECIAL FEATURE
● What's Special About Bologna & Emilia-Romagna 326

11 INTRODUCING VENICE 355

1. Orientation 355
2. Getting Around 361
3. Networks & Resources 364

SPECIAL FEATURES
● What's Special About Venice 356
● Fast Facts: Venice 362

12 WHERE TO STAY & DINE IN VENICE 365

1. Accommodations 365
2. Dining 384

SPECIAL FEATURES
● Frommer's Smart Traveler: Hotels 366
● Frommer's Cool for Kids: Hotels 379
● Frommer's Smart Traveler: Restaurants 385
● Frommer's Cool for Kids: Restaurants 400

13 WHAT TO SEE & DO IN VENICE 402

1. Attractions 403
2. Special & Free Events 421
3. Sports & Recreation 422
4. Savvy Shopping 423
5. Evening Entertainment 428
6. Easy Excursions 432

SPECIAL FEATURES
● Suggested Itineraries 402
● Did You Know . . . ? 403
● Frommer's Favorite Venice Experiences 413
● Walking Tour—Piazza San Marco to the Grand Canal 417

14 VERONA, PADUA (PADOVA) & VICENZA 437

1. Verona 437
2. Padua (Padova) 447
3. Vicenza 452

SPECIAL FEATURE
● What's Special About
Verona, Padua &
Vicenza 438

15 TRIESTE, THE DOLOMITES & SOUTH TYROL 457

1. Trieste 458
2. Cortina d'Ampezzo 466
3. Bolzano 472
4. Merano 475
5. Trent (Trento) 478

SPECIAL FEATURE
● What's Special About
Trieste, the Dolomites &
South Tyrol 458

16 THE LAKE DISTRICT 481

1. Lake Garda 482
2. Lake Como 492
3. Lake Maggiore 498

SPECIAL FEATURE
● What's Special About the
Lake District 482

17 MILAN & LOMBARDY 504

1. Milan 504
2. Bergamo 538
3. Cremona 541
4. Mantua (Mantova) 543

SPECIAL FEATURE
● What's Special About
Milan & Lombardy 505

18 PIEDMONT & THE VALLE D'AOSTA 547

1. Turin (Torino) 547
2. Aosta 557
3. Courmayeur & Entrèves 560

SPECIAL FEATURE
● What's Special About
Piedmont & the Valle
d'Aosta 548

19 GENOA & THE ITALIAN RIVIERA 567

1. San Remo 568
2. Genoa (Genova) 574
3. Rapallo 583
4. Santa Margherita Ligure 586
5. Portofino 590

SPECIAL FEATURE
● What's Special About
Genoa & the Italian
Riviera 568

20 NAPLES & POMPEII 594

1. Naples (Napoli) 596
2. The Environs of Naples 618
3. Pompeii 621

SPECIAL FEATURE
● What's Special About
Naples & Pompeii 595

21 THE AMALFI COAST & CAPRI 625

1. Sorrento 626
2. Positano 632
3. Amalfi 636
4. Ravello 640
5. Paestum 644
6. Capri 645

SPECIAL FEATURE
- *What's Special About the Amalfi Coast & Capri 626*

22 SICILY 657

1. Palermo 662
2. Segesta 673
3. Selinunte 674
4. Agrigento 675
5. Syracuse (Siracusa) 678
6. Taormina 682

SPECIAL FEATURE
- *What's Special About Sicily 658*

APPENDIX 692

A. Basic Vocabulary 692
B. Italian Menu Savvy 693
C. Glossary of Architectural Terms 696
D. Metric Measures 697

INDEX 699

General Information 699
Destinations 700

LIST OF MAPS

ITALY 4-5

ROME

Orientation   76-77
Accommodations   88-89
Dining   110-111
Attractions   136-137
Walking Tour—Imperial
    Rome   157
Walking Tour—Roman Forum &
    Palatine Hill   161

Walking Tour—From Piazza
    Barberini to Piazza del
    Popolo   167
Walking Tour—The Spanish
    Steps to Quirinale   171
Easy Excursions   195

FLORENCE

Orientation   208-209
Accommodations   218-219
Accommodations in the Heart of
    Florence   222-223
Dining in the Heart of
    Florence   242-243

Attractions   260-261
Walking Tour—The Heart of
    Florence   274-275
Walking Tour—In the Footsteps
    of Michelangelo   278-279

VENICE

Orientation   358-359
Accommodations   368-369
Dining   386-387
Attractions   404-405

Walking Tour—From the Piazza
    San Marco to the Grand
    Canal   419
Easy Excursions from
    Venice   433

REGIONAL & OTHER CITY MAPS

Siena, Pisa & the Hill
    Towns   296-297
Bologna & Emilia-
    Romagna   327
Bologna   329
Verona, Padua & Vicenza   439
Trieste, the Dolomites & South
    Tyrol   459

Milan   507
Piedmont & the Valle
    d'Aosta   549
The Italian Riviera   569
Genoa   575
Naples   597
The Amalfi Coast   627
Sicily   661

INVITATION TO THE READERS

In researching this book, I have come across many wonderful establishments, the best of which I have included here. I am sure that many of you will also come across appealing hotels, inns, restaurants, guesthouses, shops, and attractions. Please don't keep them to yourself. Share your experiences, especially if you want to comment on places that have been included in this edition that have changed for the worse. You can address your letters to:

Darwin Porter
Frommer's Italy '92
c/o Prentice Hall Travel
15 Columbus Circle
New York, NY 10023

A DISCLAIMER

SAFETY ADVISORY

Whenever you're traveling in an unfamiliar city or country, stay alert. Be aware of your immediate surroundings. Wear a moneybelt and keep a close eye on your possessions. Be particularly careful with cameras, purses, and wallets, all favorite targets of thieves and pickpockets.

CHAPTER 1

GETTING TO KNOW ITALY

1. GEOGRAPHY,
   HISTORY & POLITICS
   - DID YOU KNOW . . . ?
   - DATELINE
2. ART, ARCHITECTURE,
   LITERATURE &
   MUSIC
3. LANGUAGE,
   RELIGION &
   FOLKLORE
4. SPORTS &
   RECREATION
5. FOOD & DRINK
6. RECOMMENDED
   BOOKS, FILMS &
   RECORDINGS

Conquerors, scholars, artists, and saints, as well as curious travelers, have felt the siren call of Italy for centuries. Across turbulent seas and stormy mountains, they came for a look, even risking their lives to see Italy. Getting there by plane, sea, rail, or car is considerably easier today, but the age-old attractions remain.

Some have been fascinated by its people, including the novelist E. M. Forster, who wrote that the Italians were "more marvellous than the land." Others have been drawn to Italy's artistic treasures left by its geniuses, who have included Leonardo da Vinci and Michelangelo.

Although ancient, Italy is still a relatively modern country in terms of political unity. As late as the 19th century, the Austrian Count Metternich dismissed it as no more than a "geographical expression." Unlike the rest of Europe, Italy was late in developing a national identity. It wasn't until 1870 that the country's 20 regions were united under one central government.

Although Italy may be a late bloomer among European nations, its culture has been known since antiquity, and no country in the world has as many reminders of that culture as does Italy. They range from Rome's Colosseum to Sicily's Greek ruins.

Other visitors come to Italy for the landscapes. As any Italian will confide, "Italy is the world's most beautiful country," encompassing cypress-studded landscapes, coastal coves, jagged Dolomite peaks, spellbinding corniche roads, fishing ports, sandy beaches, and elegant little hill towns.

Many travelers visit Italy just to have fun, and with that country's sense of *La Dolce Vita,* that goal is almost guaranteed. Other, more serious visitors come here to spend their time plumbing the depths of its history and culture, and most of them leave thinking Italy is one of the world's most rewarding targets in travel.

1. GEOGRAPHY, HISTORY & POLITICS

GEOGRAPHY

The entire country, if it were cut up and pieced together to form a contiguous landmass, would be about the size of the state of Arizona. The actual formation, however, gives visitors the impression of a much larger area; the ever-changing sea coast contributes to this feeling, while its large islands, Sicily and Sardinia, only add to this effect.

Bordered on the northwest by France, on the north by Switzerland and Austria, and on the east by Yugoslavia, it is still a sea-girt land.

? DID YOU KNOW . . . ?

- The quintessential Italian vegetable, the tomato, was brought to Europe from North America in the 16th century.
- Sixty percent of Italy's historic and artistic treasures are not on view, but kept in storerooms and warehouses.
- The Italian government began an inventory of the country's cultural objects, buildings, and ruins a century ago. Art experts still consider the list incomplete.
- UNESCO estimates that nearly 80% of all European architecture and visual art—deemed worthy of preservation—lies in Italy.
- Spaghetti, that most famous of Italian dishes, was introduced from China by Marco Polo.
- The wife of slain dictator Mussolini ran a trattoria in northern Italy for many years after the end of World War II.
- Italy's greatest actress, Eleanora Duse—known as *La Dusa*— was destroyed personally, and professionally, by her love for the poet and revolutionary, D'Annunzio.
- Every 30 or 40 minutes— somewhere in Italy—some historical trophy or work of art disappears.

The Ligurian Sea, by the port of Genoa and the Italian Riviera, is on the northwest along the country's curving coast. Southward, still on the west side of the peninsula, is the Tyrrhenian Sea, between southern Italy and Sardinia. Little islands, such as Elba, of the Tuscan archipelago, and the magnificent Bay of Naples with Capri and the steep Sorrento promontory are in the Tyrrhenian coastal waters, which extend all the way to the northern shores of Sicily.

The Ionian Sea laps the east Sicilian coast and the toe, instep, and inner heel of the Italian boot. Dividing the back of the boot from Yugoslavia on the east is the Adriatic, the arm of the Mediterranean that was the highway of the ships that gave Venice, on its northern reaches, a rich and powerful place in history. Along the eastern shores of the Adriatic at the far north, Trieste and its harbor are the only Italian possessions.

Two areas within the boundaries of Italy but not under its government are the State of Vatican City and the Republic of San Marino. The 109 acres of Vatican City in Rome were established by a treaty signed by Mussolini in 1929, which also gave the Roman Catholic religion special status in the country. The pope is the sovereign of the State of Vatican City, which has its own legal system and its own post office.

San Marino is also totally surrounded by Italian land, occupying about 24 square miles in the Tuscan Apennines. It lies on the slopes and peak of Monte Titano (2,421 feet).

So far as the appearance of Italian people is concerned, it is impossible to say that one particular type is unquestionably Italian. Because of the geography of the country, which in the prehistoric and even historic eras often discouraged or prevented interaction from section to section of the land, there is often little similarity between one Italian native and another. This is evident when you meet a blond, blue-eyed northern Italian in company with a sloe-eyed, raven-haired native from another part of the country. However, there are people from Mediterranean stock who are likely to be short of stature and dark of complexion, others who are from Iberian ancestry, hereditary legacies from Greeks, Teutonic races, and even from as far back as the Carthaginians.

As races mixed in various areas, so did cultures, and you will find in Italy today, especially in rural sections, many interesting customs that have come down over centuries. Colorful costumes vary from village to village, and handcrafts are turned out as they were by ancestral families. In Sardinia, Sicily, and the interior mountain country of the mainland, shepherds wear the same kind of clothing, tend their flocks in the same way, and exhibit the same independence of spirit as did their forebears. The custom of having large families and keeping in close touch with relatives still holds, especially in rural Italy.

I have always found the Italian people, whether in small or large towns, as friendly and helpful to visitors as the language barrier may allow. Smiles are acceptable in any language.

THE REGIONS IN BRIEF

Abruzzi   Known for its crafts and its folklore, Abruzzi is the region of Italy bordering the eastern edge of Latium, whose center is Rome. A land of coastal and mountain health resorts, it has as its chief cities l'Aquila (the capital) and Pescara.

Aosta Valley   Located at the northwestern corner of Italy, bordering France, it's surrounded by the towering peaks of the Alps, including Europe's most famous peaks, Mont-Blanc and the Matterhorn. Its resorts of Breuil-Cervinia and Courmayeur are havens for winter sports, although summer skiing and hill climbing are also possible.

Apulia   Also known as Le Puglie and Puglia, Apulia is a great agricultural region, forming the heel of the Italian boot, which is called the Gargano peninsula. The "trulli" houses of Alberobello are known for their unique cylindrical style and conical roofs. Major cities include Bari (the capital) and Brindisi (gateway to Greece).

Basilicata   The smallest region of Italy's Deep South, Basilicata is the poorest part of the peninsula, a mountain region with two coastlines, the Ionian Sea and the Tyrrhenian Sea. It has been called a "strap-shaped wedge" lying between the Apulia heel of the Italian boot and its Calabrian toe.

Calabria   The extreme southwestern region of Italy, lying between the Ionian and Tyrrhenian seas, is a land of plains and mountain ranges, with many recently opened beach resorts. This region is divided into the provinces of Catanzaro, Cosenza, and Reggio di Calabria.

Campania   Set to the south of Italy's western shoreline, this region includes the city of Naples (the region's capital) as well as the city's bay and the world-famous resorts nearby. These include the Amalfi coastline (plus Sorrento), the island of Capri, and such ancient historical sights as Pompeii, Herculaneum, and Mount Vesuvius. Confusingly, the region is divided into five different provinces: Avellino, Benevento, Caserta, Naples, and Salerno.

Emilia-Romagna   Known for its medieval cathedrals and castles, Emilia-Romagna is also the breadbasket of Italy. It forms a kind of buffer zone between the industrial north and the central and southern lands, stretching for some 14,000 square miles, all the way from the Po River to the Apennines, from the Adriatic to Liguria. Its capital, Bologna, contains Europe's oldest university and is said to set the best table. Ravenna—known for its Byzantine mosaics—is the region's artistic highlight, and Rimini is its chief seaside resort on the Adriatic.

Friuli-Venezia Giulia   Bordering the northern edge of the Adriatic Sea, this northeastern region, whose capital is Trieste, was dominated by the non-Italian powers, including the Austrian Hapsburgs, during most of the 18th and 19th centuries. Its landscape is characterized by saltwater lagoons, alpine peaks, and richly fertile plains. Other major cities include Udine, Gorizia, and Pordenone. The area is filled with artistic treasures from the Roman, Byzantine, and Romanesque-Gothic eras, and the buildings of some cities (including Trieste) show the long-ago influence of Austria.

Latium   The region of Latium is dominated by its capital, Rome, location of Vatican City. Containing vast inventories of the world's artistic treasures, Latium is a land of legend. Much of the civilized world was once dominated from here, going back to the days when Romulus and Remus are alleged to have founded Rome on April 21, 753 B.C. Ancient Romans, believing they were deified, felt they were

---

IMPRESSIONS

Italy: A paradise inhabited with devils.
—SIR HENRY WOTTON, LETTER TO LORD ZOUCHE, 1592

Italy is so tender—like cooked macaroni—yards and yards
of soft tenderness, ravelled round everything.
—D. H. LAWRENCE, *SEA AND SARDINIA*, 1923

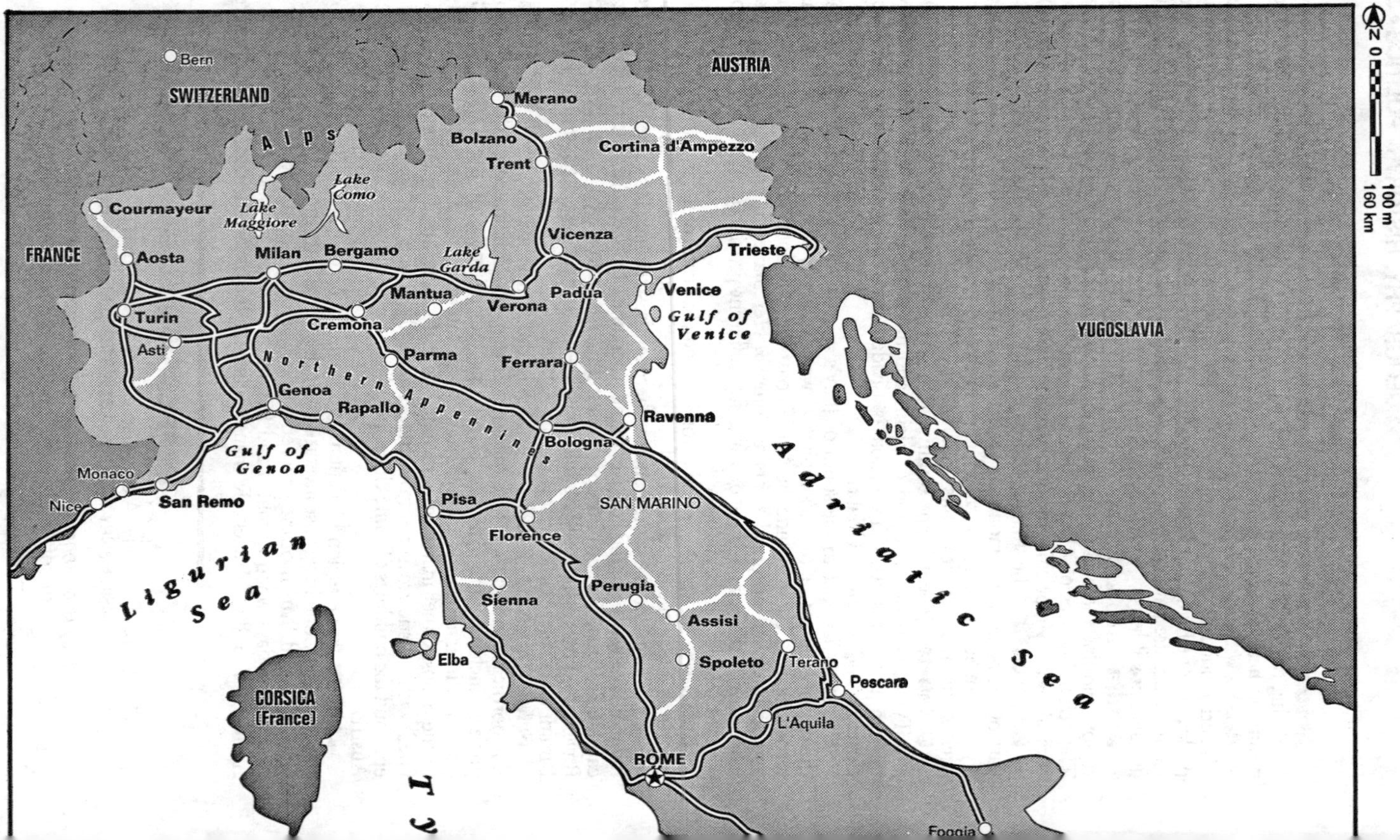

100 m
160 km
N 0
Bern
SWITZERLAND
AUSTRIA
FRANCE
YUGOSLAVIA
Alps
Merano
Bolzano
Cortina d'Ampezzo
Trent
Lake Como
Lake Maggiore
Courmayeur
Vicenza
Lake Garda
Trieste
Aosta
Milan
Bergamo
Mantua
Verona
Padua
Venice
Gulf of Venice
Turin
Cremona
Asti
Parma
Ferrara
Northern Appennines
Genoa
Rapallo
Ravenna
Bologna
Gulf of Genoa
Monaco
Nice
San Remo
Pisa
SAN MARINO
Florence
Ligurian Sea
Adriatic Sea
Perugia
Sienna
Assisi
Elba
Spoleto
Terano
Pescara
CORSICA (France)
L'Aquila
ROME
Foggia

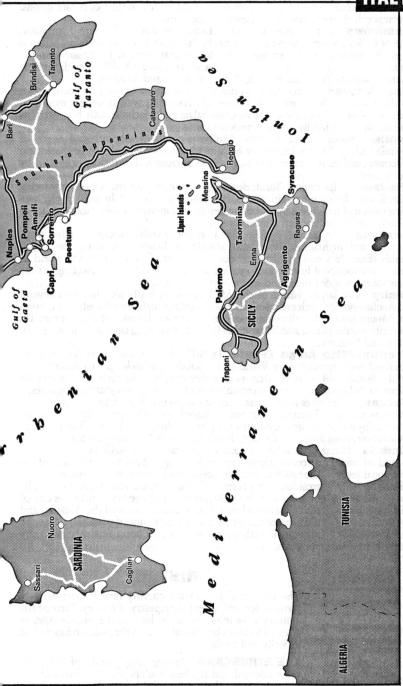

are ripe with charter companies. The desk manager of any reputable seaside hotel usually has at least an idea of where you could rent a boat, but for more information, you can contact the **Federazione Italiana Vela,** viale Brigate Bisagno 2, Genova 16129 (tel. 010/565723). A similar organization in Rome is the **Agenzia Nautica Altura,** via Mecenate 22B, 00184 Roma (tel. 06/733242).

SKIING An array of alpine resorts, following in the stylish leads of resorts in Austria, Switzerland, and France, is now strung across the northern tier of Italy, from the Val d'Aosta to the German-speaking Alto Adige. One of Europe's most famous resorts, Breuil-Cervinia, sits directly atop the southern slopes of the famous Matterhorn (a peak which Italians refer to as Monte Cervino). Several of the finest and most interesting resorts are covered in this guidebook. These include the previously mentioned Breuil-Cervinia as well as the glamorous hideaways of Cortina d'Ampezzo and Courmayeur. More information on individual resorts can be obtained by writing directly to the tourist offices of the specific resorts (see "Essentials" in the individual city sections).

TENNIS The sport has gained great popularity since *La Dolce Vita* made afternoon tennis followed by before-dinner cocktails and a bit of lovemaking *de rigueur* for the smart set. Tennis enthusiasts accustomed to the respectful hush of tennis at, say Forest Hills or Wimbledon, might be unnerved by the background noises at Italian tennis tournaments, although professionals consider this nothing more than an expression of enthusiasm for the game. Most venues for the game occur in the precincts of private tennis courts which may or may not—depending on management policies—accept foreign visitors. Many hotels, however, especially those in Italian resorts, maintain their own courts. Many of the courts are clay, and proper attire (whites and appropriate shoes) is usually a prerequisite for playing. For general information about tennis in Italy, and a list of the various tennis clubs, contact the **Italian Tennis Federation,** viale Tiziano 70, 00100 Roma (tel. 06/321-9897).

5. FOOD & DRINK

Many North American visitors erroneously think of Italian cuisine as limited. Of course, everybody has heard of minestrone, spaghetti, chicken cacciatore, and spumoni. But Italian chefs hardly confine themselves to such a limited repertoire. Incidentally, except in the south, Italians don't use as much garlic in their food as many foreigners seem to believe. Most Italian dishes, especially those in the north, are butter based. Spaghetti and meatballs, by the way, is not an Italian dish, although certain restaurants throughout the country have taken to serving it "for homesick Americans."

FOOD

Rome might be the best place to introduce yourself to the cookery of Italy, as it has specialty restaurants that represent all the culinary centers such as Bologna and Genoa. Throughout your Roman holiday, you'll encounter such savory viands as *zuppa di pesce* (a soup or stew of various fish, cooked in white wine and herb flavored), *cannelloni* (tube-shaped pasta baked with any number of stuffings), *riso col gamberi* (rice with shrimp, peas, and mushrooms, flavored with white wine and garlic), *scampi alla griglia* (grilled prawns, one of the best-tasting, albeit expensive, dishes in the city), *quaglie col risotto e tartufi* (quail with rice and truffles), *lepre alla cacciatore* (hare flavored with white wine and herbs), *zabaglione* (a cream made with sugar, egg yolks, and marsala), *gnocchi alla romana* (potato-flour dumplings with a sauce made with meat and covered with grated cheese), *abbacchio* (baby spring lamb, often roasted over an open fire), *saltimbocca alla romana* (literally "jump-in-your-mouth"—thin slices of veal with sage, ham, and cheese), *fritto alla romana* (a mixed fry that's likely to include everything from brains to artichokes), *carciofi alla romana*

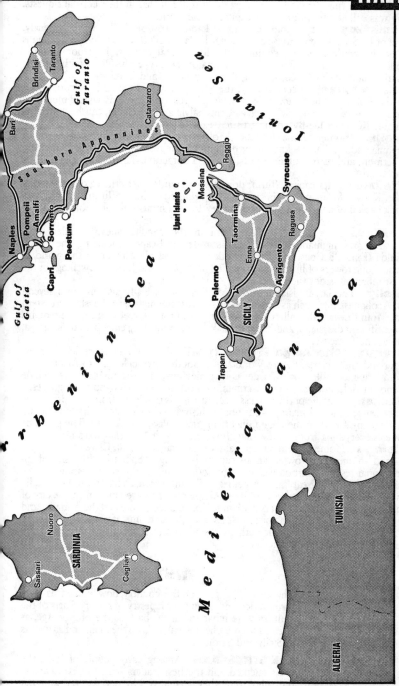

ITALY

preordained to rule the world, and they did just about that in their constant quests. Rome was called *caput mundi*, or capital of the world.

Lombardy   Just as Rome dominates Latium, so does Milan run Lombardy. Home of La Scala Opera House and Leonardo da Vinci's *The Last Supper*, Milan is one of the world's leading commercial and cultural centers. Its Duomo is the third-largest church in Europe. Other major cities—each filled with artistic treasures—include Bergamo, Brescia, Pavia, Cremona, and Mantua.

The Marches   In central Italy, the Marches, whose capital is Ancona, open onto the Adriatic. The region possesses seaside resorts as well as winter mountain resorts. Ruins of ancient cities, such as Urbis Salvia and Macerata, can be visited, as can many Romanesque-Byzantine artistic treasures.

Molise   Bordering the Adriatic, Molise is south of Abruzzi and north of Campania and Apulia. It is known for both its seaside resorts, such as Campomarino and Termoli, and its mountain resorts, such as Capracotta. The region is favored by Italian tourists.

Piedmont   Its capital, Turin, dominates this northwestern region, bordering France. Known for its mountain resorts, it is centered mainly at Turin. The city was the first capital of a united Italy and is the keystone of industrial Italy, home of Italy's fortress of capitalism, the Fiat autoworks.

Sardinia   The second-largest island in the Mediterranean is filled with mountains and highlands, along with seaside landscapes, including the Costa Smeralda (Emerald Coast), which is about the chicest place to be in the world in August. Cone towers of huge stones—called *nuraghi*—and fortified dwellings of the earliest inhabitants dot the island whose capital is Cagliari.

Sicily   The largest island of the Mediterranean, Sicily also includes several small Aeolian islands, such as Stromboli. Rising threateningly over the island's eastern coast, Mount Etna is the tallest active volcano in Europe. Greek and Roman remains are plentiful on the island, and its capital is Palermo. Other big cities include Messina, Catania, and Syracuse.

Trentino/Alto Adige (South Tyrol)   This mountain region borders Switzerland and Austria. Before World War I, South Tyrol belonged to Austria, and the old influence still remains. Trent is its major city, and the chief resorts include Merano. In Bolzano, Italian and German are both officially recognized languages.

Tuscany   Cradle of the Renaissance, Tuscany is rich in art from the 13th to the 16th century, centered mainly—but not exclusively—in Florence. The famous hill towns occupy a part of the region, including Siena, Pisa, and Arezzo. The province embraces everything from the Leaning Tower of Pisa to Michelangelo's *David*.

Umbria   Home of such famous saints as St. Francis and St. Clare of Assisi, this is a land of medieval towns whose capital is Perugia. Spoleto is the site of an international festival. Umbria lies north of Latium and southeast of Tuscany.

Veneto   Many great Italian art cities, including Verona, Vicenza, and Padua, lie in the Veneto region of northeastern Italy. All are overshadowed by Venice, the city of canals and lagoons. Built on marshy islands, Venice once dominated the Adriatic, and today is one of the world's major tourist meccas. Reserve time, if possible, to see the Palladian villas of Vincenza, or perhaps attend Verona's opera festival held every summer in its Roman amphitheater.

HISTORY

The checkered past of the country now known as Italy forms a rich and often gory tapestry of history. Parts of the country were inhabited as far back as the Bronze Age, as attested to by archeological finds on the mainland as well as in Sicily and Sardinia.

THE ETRUSCANS   Among early people of Italy, the most talented and the best leaders were the Etruscans—but who were they, actually? No one knows, and the many inscriptions they left behind—mostly on graves—are of no help, since the Etruscan language has never been deciphered by modern scholars. The date of their arrival on the east coast of Umbria has been figured as several centuries before Rome was built, which was around 800 B.C. Their religious rites and architecture show an obvious contact with Mesopotamia; the Etruscans may have been refugees from Asia Minor who traveled westward about 1200–1000 B.C. The fact that they came from the Near East is further suggested by some 13th-century B.C. monuments whose inscriptions describe raids on the Nile delta by a warlike people called the "Turuscha." We know that they arrived in Italy in large numbers and within 2 centuries had subjugated Tuscany and Campania and the Villanova tribes who lived there. They forced the peninsula's indigenous Latin tribes to work the land for them and support them as an aristocratic class of princes. Their sphere of influence eventually extended from the southern boundaries of Rome as far north as Tuscany's Arno River on the western side of the Apennines.

While the Etruscans built temples at Tarquinia and Caere (present-day Cerveteri), the few nervous Latin tribes who remained outside their sway gravitated to Rome, which was at the time little more than a sheep-herding village in a strategic position. As its power grew, however, Rome, to an increasing degree, profited from the strategically important Tiber crossing where the ancient Salt Way (via Salaria) turned northeastward toward the Central Apennines.

From their base at Rome, the Latins remained free of the Etruscans until about 600 B.C., thanks mainly to the presence of Greek colonies on the Italian coast, which tended to hold back Carthaginians (Phoenicians) on one side and Etruscans on the other. But the Etruscan advance was as inexorable as that of the later Roman Empire, and by 600 B.C. there was an Etruscan stronghold in the hills above Rome. The frightened tribes concentrated their forces at Rome for a last stand, but were swept away by the sophisticated Mesopotamian conquerors. When the new overlords took charge, they not only introduced gold tableware and jewelry, bronze urns and terra-cotta statuary, and the best of Greek and Asia Minor art and culture, but they made Rome the government seat of all Latium. Roma is an Etruscan name, and the kings of Roma had Etruscan names: Numa, Ancus, Tarquinius, even Romulus.

Under the combined influences of the Greek and Mesopotamian east, Roma grew enormously. A new port was opened at Ostia. Artists from Greece carved statues of Roman gods looking like Greek divinities. The "Servian" army was established, and since soldiers had to provide their own horses and armor, the result was that the richest citizens carried the heaviest burden of protection. It is easy to see how this classification by wealth, which also affected voting and lawmaking, stemmed from a democratic concept of the army but led to an undemocratic concept of society.

- **1000 B.C.** Arrival and organization of large colonies of Etruscans settle in Tuscany and Campania, who quickly subjugate many of the Latin inhabitants of the Italian peninsula.
- **800 B.C.** Rome begins to take shape, evolving from a strategically located shepherd's village into a magnet for Latin tribes fleeing the Etruscans.
- **600 B.C.** Etruscans occupy Rome, designating it the capital of their empire; the city grows rapidly and a major seaport opens at Ostia.
- **510 B.C.** The Latin tribes, still centered in Rome, revolt against the Etruscans; alpine Gauls attack from the north; Greeks living in Sicily destroy the Etruscan navy.
- **250 B.C.** The Romans, allied to the Greeks, Phoenicians, and native Sicilians, defeat the Etruscans; Rome flourishes and begins the accumulation of a vast empire.
- **49 B.C.** Italy (through Rome) controls the entire Mediterranean world.
- **44 B.C.** Julius Caesar assassi- *(continues)*

DATELINE

nated; his successor, Augustus, transforms Rome from a city of brick to a city of marble.

- **3rd century A.D.** Rome declines under a series of incompetent and corrupt emperors.
- **4th century A.D.** Rome is fragmented politically as administrative capitals are established in such cities as Milan and Trier, Germany.
- **A.D. 395** The Empire splits; Constantine establishes a "New Rome" at Constantinople (Byzantium); Goths, successfully invade Rome's northern provinces.
- **410–455** Rome is sacked by barbarians—Alaric the Goth, Attila the Hun, and Gaiseric the Vandal.
- **475** Rome falls, leaving only the primate of the Catholic church in control; the pope slowly adopts many of the responsibilities and prestige once reserved for the Roman emperor.
- **800** Charlemagne is crowned Holy Roman Emperor by Pope Leo III; Italy dissolves into a series of small warring kingdoms.

(continues)

THE ROMAN REPUBLIC Gauls from the alpine regions invaded the northern Etruscan territory around 600 B.C., and the Romans revolted in about 510 B.C., toppling the rulers from their power bases and setting the southern boundary of Etruscan influence at the Tiber. Greeks from Sicily ended Etruscan sea power in 474 B.C. in the battle of Cumae off the coast just north of Naples. By 250 B.C. the Romans and their Campania allies had vanquished the Etruscans, wiping out their language and religion. However, manners and beliefs of the former rulers were respected and maintained by Rome, and in many cases assimilated into the culture. Even today, certain Etruscan customs and bloodlines are believed to still exist in Italy, especially in Tuscany.

Meanwhile, Greeks had been colonizing the Ionian coast and western Sicily from around 730 B.C., following the Greek city-state design and founding Naples and towns in southern Italy. Romans supported the Greeks against the Etruscans, the Phoenicians from Carthage, and other warriors. The Sicilians of the time were an aboriginal Mediterranean people who were thought by the Greeks to be of Iberian stock, from Spain. The Phoenicians challenged the Greeks in Sicily and dominated the western part of the island from the latter part of the 6th century to the mid-3rd century B.C.

The Romans increased their powers through conquest of neighboring communities in the highlands and became allied with other Latins of the lowlands, with whose people they easily became the dominant group. They gave to their Latin allies, and then to conquered peoples, part or complete Roman citizenship, with the obligation of military service. Citizen colonies were set up as settlements of Roman farmers. Many of the famous cities of Italy today originated as colonies. Later, as seen in the history of Britain and the continent, colonies were established far outside Italy. The colonies were for the most part fortified, and they were linked to Rome by military roads.

The stern Roman republic was characterized by belief in the gods, the necessity of learning from the past, strength of the family, education through books and public service, and most important, obedience. R. H. Barrow, in his book *The Romans*, points out that "through obedience comes power," and the Roman dedication to the ideal of a worthy life led to a vast empire. The all-powerful Senate presided as Rome defeated rival powers one after the other and grew to rule the Mediterranean. The Punic Wars with Carthage in the 3rd century B.C. cleared away a major obstacle to Rome's growth, although people said later that Rome's breaking of its treaty with Carthage (leading to total destruction of that city) put a curse on the Italian city.

THE ROMAN EMPIRE By 49 B.C., Italy ruled all of the Mediterranean world either directly or indirectly, with all political, commercial, and cultural pathways leading directly to Rome. The possible wealth and glory to be found in Rome lured many there, but drained other Italian communities of human resources, while foreign imports, particularly in the field of agriculture, hurt local farmers and landowners. Municipal governments faltered and civil wars ensued. Public order was restored by the Caesars (planned by Julius, but brought to fruition under Augustus). By the time of the death of Julius Caesar, on the eve of the birth of Christ, Rome was a mighty empire whose general had brought the Western world under the sway of Roman law and civilization.

The emperors, whose succession started with Augustus's principate after the death of Julius Caesar, brought Rome to new, almost giddy, heights. Augustus transformed the city from brick to marble—much the way Napoléon III transformed Paris centuries later. But success led to corruption. The Roman Empire was supposed to have been a republic, but autocratic power of the emperors became the custom, and the colorful centuries witnessed a steady decay in the ideals and traditions upon which the empire had been founded. The army became a fifth column of barbarian mercenaries, the tax collector became the scourge of the countryside, and for every good emperor (Augustus, Trajan, Vespasian, Hadrian, to name a few), there were three or four incredibly corrupt and debased heads of state (Caligula, Nero, Domitian, Caracalla, and more).

The Roman citizen in the capital either lived on the public dole and spent his days at gladiatorial games and imperial baths, or was a disillusioned patrician at the mercy of emperors who might murder him for his property. The 3rd century A.D. saw so many emperors that it was common, as H. V. Morton tells us, to hear in the provinces of the election of an emperor together with a report on his assassination. The 4th-century A.D. reforms of Diocletian held the empire together, but at the expense of its inhabitants, who were reduced to tax units. He reinforced imperial power but paradoxically at the same time weakened Roman dominance and prestige by establishing administrative capitals of the empire at such outposts as Milan, Trier in Germany, and elsewhere, a practice followed by Constantine when he built his "New Rome," Constantinople. (Also known as Byzantium, it was many centuries later renamed Istanbul by the Ottoman Turks.) Constantine, however, didn't establish this stronghold merely as a subsidiary of the capital of the empire—he moved the administrative functions away from Rome altogether, partly because the menace of possible barbarian attack in the West had increased greatly.

With him to the new capital, Constantine took the best of the artisans, politicians, and public figures of Rome, creating a city renowned for its splendor, intrigue, jealousies, and passion.

THE EMPIRE FALLS   The eastern and western sections of the Roman Empire split in A.D. 395, leaving Italy without the support it had formerly received from east of the Adriatic. When the Goths moved toward Rome in the early 5th century, citizens in the provinces, who had grown

DATELINE

- **Late 11th century** The popes function like secular princes with private armies.
- **1065** The Holy Land falls to the Muslim Turks; the Crusades are launched.
- **1303–77** Papal Schism; the pope and his entourage move from Rome to Avignon.
- **1377** The papacy returns to Rome.
- **1443** Brunelleschi's dome caps the Duomo in Florence as the Renaissance ("rebirth") bursts into full bloom in this city-state.
- **1469–92** Lorenzo "Il Magnifico" rules in Florence as the Medici patron of Renaissance artists.
- **1499** *The Last Supper* is completed by Leonardo da Vinci in Milan.
- **1508** Ordered by the pope, Michelangelo begins work on the Vatican's Sistine Chapel.
- **1527** Rome is attacked and sacked by Charles V, who is crowned Holy Roman Emperor the following year.
- **1796–97** Napoleon's series of invasions arouses Italian nationalism.
- **1861** Establish-
(continues)

DATELINE

ment of the King-
dom of Italy.
* **1929** Signing of
a Concordat be-
tween the Vatican
and the Italian gov-
ernment delineates
the rights and re-
sponsibilities of
both parties.
* **1935** Italian in-
vasion of Abyssinia
(Ethiopia).
* **1941** Italian in-
vasion of Yugo-
slavia.
* **1943** General
Patton lands in Sic-
ily and soon con-
trols the island.
* **1945** Mussolini
is killed by a mob
in Milan.
* **1946** Establish-
ment of the Repub-
lic of Italy.
* **1960s** Rise of
left-wing terrorist
groups; flight of
capital from Italy;
continuing prob-
lems of the impov-
erished south.
* **1980s** *Il Sor-
passo* imbues
the country with
dreams of an eco-
nomic rebirth.

to hate and fear the cruel bureaucracy set up by Diocletian and followed by succeeding emperors, welcomed the invaders. And then the pillage began.

Rome was sacked by Alaric in 410, and after more than 40 troubled years, Attila the Hun laid siege to the once-powerful capital. He was followed in 455 by Gaiseric the Vandal, who engaged in a 2-week spree of looting and destruction. The empire of the west lasted for only another 20 years; finally, the sacking and chaos ended it in A.D. 476, and Rome was left to the popes. The empire was terminated by Odovacar, a barbarian chief, who opened areas of Italy to Teutonic settlement. The fortified cities of the country were not much disturbed by this change in the fundamental basis of Italy's government.

Christianity, a new religion which created a new society, was probably founded in Rome around 10 years after Christ's crucifixion. Gradually gaining strength despite early persecution, it moved through the stages of toleration and was finally accepted as the official religion of the empire. But by the end of the power of Rome in 476, the popes of Rome were under the nominal auspices of an exarch from Byzantium (Constantinople).

THE HOLY ROMAN EMPIRE After the fall of the Western Empire, the pope took on more and more of the powers of the emperor, although there was no political unity in the country. Decades of rule by barbarians and then Goths were followed by takeovers in different parts of the country by various strong warriors, such as the Lombards. Italy was thus divided into several spheres of control. In 731, Pope Gregory II renounced Rome's dependence on Constantinople, and thus ended the twilight era of the Greek exarch who had nominally ruled Rome. Papal Rome turned forever toward Europe, and in A.D. 800 a king of the barbarian Franks was crowned Holy Roman Emperor by Pope Leo III. The new emperor's name was Charlemagne. The capital that he established at Aachen (known today to the French as Aix-la-Chapelle) lay deep within territory known to the Romans a half millennium ago as the heart of the barbarian world. Although Charlemagne pledged allegiance to the church and looked to Rome and its pope as the final arbiter in most religious and cultural affairs, he launched northwestern Europe on a course of what would eventually become bitter political opposition to the meddling of the papacy in temporal affairs.

The establishment of the new empire defined the end of the Dark Ages, but it ushered in a period of long and bloody warfare as well. The Saracens (a nomadic tribe of Muslim warriors originating somewhere between Syria and Arabia) invaded Sicily, a land which had already been under Muslim control for 2½ centuries. At the opposite end of Italy, from strongholds near Milan, Lombard leaders battled Franks. Magyars from Hungary invaded northeastern Lombardy and were in turn defeated by the increasingly powerful Venetians. Eventually, aggressive Normans with administrative abilities gained military control of Sicily in the 11th century, divided it completely from the rest of Italy, and altered forever both the island's racial and ethnic makeup as well as its architecture.

As Italy dissolved into an increasingly fragmented collection of city-states, the feudal landowners of Rome gained control of the papacy, and a series of questionably religious pontiffs endured a diminishment of their power. Eventually, even the selection process for determining the choice of the popes fell into the hands of the increasingly Germanic Holy Roman Emperor, although this power balance would very soon shift.

Rome during the Middle Ages was a quaint, rural town. Narrow lanes with overhanging buildings filled many of what were originally built as showcases of ancient imperial power, including the Campus Martius. Great basilicas were built and embellished with golden-hued mosaics. The forums, mercantile exchanges, temples, and great theaters of the imperial era slowly disintegrated and collapsed. The decay of ancient Rome was assisted by periodic earthquakes, centuries of neglect, and, in particular, the growing need for building materials. Until it eventually emerged as a rapacious lion eager to profit from the changing power politics of the Italian peninsula, Rome receded into a dusty provincialism. The seat of the Catholic church, it was a state almost completely controlled by priests, with an insatiable need for new churches and convents.

By the end of the 11th century, the popes shook off control of the Roman aristocracy, rid themselves of what they considered the excessive influence of the emperors at Aachen, and began an aggressive expansion of church influence and acquisitions. The deliberate and conscious organization of the church into a format modeled on the hierarchies of the ancient Roman Empire put the church on a collision course with the empire and the other temporal leaders of Europe, resulting in an endless series of not-very-flattering power struggles.

THE RENAISSANCE The story of Italy from the dawn of the Renaissance to the Age of Enlightenment in the 17th and 18th centuries is as varied and fascinating as that of the rise and fall of the empire. The papacy soon became essentially a feudal state, and the pope was a medieval (later Renaissance) prince engaged in many of the worldly activities that brought criticism upon the church in later centuries. The fall of the Holy Land to the Turks in 1065 catapulted the papacy into the forefront of world politics, primarily because of the Crusades, most of which were judged military and economic disasters, many of which the popes directly caused or encouraged. During the 12th and 13th centuries, the bitter rivalries that rocked the secular and spiritual bastions of Europe took their toll on the stability of the Holy Roman Empire, which grew weaker as city-states buttressed by mercantile and trade-related prosperity grew stronger, and as France emerged as a potent nation in its own right. Each investiture of a new bishop to any influential post became a cause of endless jockeying for power among many factions.

These conflicts achieved their most visible impasse in 1303 with the full-fledged removal of the papacy to the French city of Avignon. For more than 70 years, until 1377, viciously competing popes (one in Rome, another under the protection of the French kings in Avignon) made simultaneous claims to the legacy of St. Peter, underscoring as never before the degree to which the church was both a victim and a victimizer in the temporal world of European politics.

The seat of the papacy was eventually returned to Rome, where a series of popes were every bit as interesting as the Roman emperors they replaced. The great families—Barberini, Medici, Borgia—enhanced their status and fortunes impressively when one of their sons was elected pope.

Despite the civilizing effects of the Renaissance, and the centuries that had passed since the collapse of the Roman Empire, the age of siege was not yet over. In 1527 Charles V carried out the worst sack ever. To the horror of Pope Clement VII (a Medici), the entire city was brutally pillaged by the man who was to be crowned Holy Roman Emperor the next year.

During the years of the Renaissance, Reformation, and the Counter-Reformation, Rome underwent major physical changes. The old centers of culture reverted to pastures and fields, while great churches and palaces were built with the stones of ancient Rome. This building boom, in fact, did far more damage to the temples of the Caesars than did any barbarian sack. Rare marbles were stripped from the imperial baths and used as altarpieces or sent to lime kilns. So enthusiastic was the papal destruction of Imperial Rome that it's a miracle anything is left.

A UNITED ITALY The 19th century witnessed the final collapse of the Renaissance city-states, which had existed since the end of the 13th century. These units, eventually coming under control of a *signore* (lord), were, in effect, regional states, with mercenary soldiers, civil rights, and assistance for their friendly neighbors. Some had attained formidable power under such signori as the Este family in Ferrara, the Medici in Florence, and the Visconti and the Sforza families in Milan.

During the 17th, 18th, and 19th centuries, decades of turmoil in Italy had lasted through the many years of succession of different European dynasties; Napoleon made a bid for power in Italy beginning in 1796, fueling his war machines with what was considered a relatively easy victory. During the Congress of Vienna which followed Napoleon's defeat, Italy was once again divided among many different factions: Austria was given Lombardy and Venetia, and the Papal States were returned to the pope. Some duchies were put back into the hands of their hereditary rulers, and southern Italy and Sicily went to a Bourbon dynasty. One historic move, which eventually assisted in the unification of Italy, was the assignment of the former republic of Genoa to Sardinia (which at the time was governed by the House of Savoy).

Political unrest became a fact of Italian life, at least some of it encouraged by the rapid industrialization of the north, and the almost total lack of industrialization in the Italian south. Despite these barriers, in 1861, thanks to the brilliant diplomacy and insider maneuvering of Cavour and Garibaldi, the Kingdom of Italy was proclaimed and Victor Emmanuel of the House of Savoy, King of Sardinia, became head of the new monarchy.

Although the hope, pushed by Europe's theocrats and some of its devout Catholics, of attaining one empire ruled by the pope and the church, had long ago faded away, there was still a fight followed by generations of hard feelings when the Papal States, a strategically and historically important principality under the temporal jurisdiction of the pope, were confiscated by the new Kingdom of Italy.

The establishment of the kingdom, however, did not signal a complete unification of Italy, because the city of Rome was still under papal control and Venetia was still held by Austria. This was partially resolved when Venetia joined the rest of Italy after the Seven Weeks' War of 1866 between Austria and Prussia in 1866, and Rome became the capital of the newly formed country in 1871. The Vatican, however, did not yield its territory to the new order, despite guarantees of nonintervention proffered by the Italian government, and relations between the pope and the country of Italy remained rocky until 1929.

At that time, Mussolini defined the divisions which, until now, have separated the Italian government and the Vatican by signing a Concordat that granted political and fiscal autonomy to the Vatican City. It also made Roman Catholicism the official state religion of Italy, although this designation was removed through revision of the Concordat in 1978.

WORLD WAR II AND THE AXIS Mussolini's support of the Fascists during the Spanish Civil War helped encourage the formation of the "Axis" between Italy and Nazi Germany. Despite its outdated military equipment, Italy added to the general horror of the era by invading Abyssinia (Ethiopia) in 1935, supposedly to protect Italian colonial interests there. In 1941 Italy invaded neighboring Yugoslavia, and in 1942 sent thousands of Italian troops to assist Hitler in his disastrous campaign along the Russian front. In 1943 General Patton, leading American and (with General Montgomery) British troops, controlled all of Sicily within a month of their first attack.

Faced with this defeat and humiliation, Mussolini was overthrown by his own cabinet (Grand Council). The Allies made a separate deal with Italy's king, Vittorio Emanuele III, who had more or less gracefully collaborated with the Fascists during the previous two decades, and who now shifted allegiances without too much of a visible fuss. A politically divided Italy watched as battalions of fanatical German Nazis moved south to resist the Allied march northward up the Italian peninsula. The Nazis released Mussolini from his Italian jail cell to establish the short-lived Republic of Salo, headquartered on the edge of Lake Garda, hoping for a groundswell of

IMPRESSIONS

The trouble with Italy is that we have never allowed its inhabitants to leave the stage. Italian has to be the language of rhetorical superlatives—a language full of exaggerated gestures. Italy taught Europe how to act and how to sing in opera. Consequently, every Italian is a primo tenore who advances to the footlights and tickles the ears of the groundlings by his florid voice; or else he is always some poor devil of a Harlequin playing for ever the part of the clown.
—WALTER STARKIE, *THE WAVELESS PLAIN*, 1938

popular opinion in favor of Italian fascism. Events quickly proved this nothing more than a futile dream.

In April 1945, with almost half a million Italians rising in a mass demonstration against him and the German war machine, Mussolini was captured by Italian partisans as he fled to Switzerland. With his mistress, Claretta Petacci, and several others of his intimates, he was shot and strung up upside down from the roof of a gasoline station in piazzale Loreto, a few blocks east of the central railway station of Milan.

MODERN ITALY   The Republic of Italy was formed in 1946, and dominated by the moderate Christian Democrats until 1953 thanks to a series of flexible and frequently mutating coalitions. Though stripped of all its overseas colonies in the aftermath of World War II, in the 1950s Italy became one of the leading industrialized nations of the world, a giant in the manufacture of automobiles and office equipment. It also regained its enviable position as an agricultural breadbasket.

In the 1960s, an increasingly powerful socialist party spearheaded by Aldo Moro (who was later assassinated by a left-wing terrorist group) enjoyed growing popularity and power, much to the consternation of Italy's wealthy. Continually plagued by economic inequities between the prosperous and industrialized north and the economically depressed *Mezzogiorno* (southern Italy), Italy suffered an unprecedented flight of capital (frequently aided by Swiss banks only too willing to accept discreet deposits from wealthy Italians) and an increase in bankruptcies, inflation (almost 20% during much of the 1970s), and unemployment.

During the late 1970s and early 1980s, Italy was rocked by the rise of terrorism instigated both by right-wing neofascists and by left-wing intellectuals from the socialist-controlled universities of the north.

Today, after many upheavals and intense power politicking among the varied political parties, Italy maintains a delicate balance between socialists, the Communists, the radicals, the more moderate Social Democrats, and the constant corruption and destablization caused by the Mafia and its underground economies.

Besides football (soccer), the family, and affairs of the heart, the national obsession of Italy today is *Il Sorpasso*, a term which describes Italy's surpassing of its archrivals France and Britain in economic indicators. Economists disagree about whether or not

IMPRESSIONS

The Italian way of life down the centuries attracted people who wanted to take a holiday from their national virtues. In the heart of every man, whenever he is born, whatever his education and tastes, there is one small corner which is Italian, that part that finds regimentation irksome, the dangers of war frightening, strict morality stifling, that part which loves frivolous and entertaining art, admires larger-than-lifesize solitary heroes, and dreams of an impossible liberation from the strictures of a tidy existence.
—LUIGI BARZINI, *THE ITALIANS*, 1964

Il Sorpasso has happened, and statistics (complicated by the presence of Italy's vast underground economy) vary widely from source to source. As part of an almost universal opinion shared by virtually every Italian, all levels of Italian society are actively engaged to some degree in withholding funds from the government. Today, Italy's underground economy (*economia sommersa*) competes on a monumental scale with the official economy, with participation by all sorts of otherwise respectable businesses and individuals. Complicating Italy's problems for economists, the police, and politicians is the constant interference of the Mafia, whose methods—despite numerous more or less heartfelt crackdowns—continue today even more ruthlessly than ever.

Despite these burdensome problems, Italy today is well entrenched as one of Europe's superpowers, eager to play a role in an increasingly complicated global economy.

POLITICS

A democratic government was established in Italy in 1946. The Italian Parliament is composed of the Chamber of Deputies and the Senate of the Republic. The Republic of Italy is divided into 20 regions comprising 94 provinces and more than 8,000 communes. The president of the Republic is elected by the members of both chambers of Parliament, who vote by secret ballot. The average foreign visitor who commits no infraction of the law will not come into contact or have trouble from the authorities (chances are). Italy is a rather free-wheeling land where restrictions are kept to a minimum.

Political parties in Italy are numerous, and party loyalty fluctuates, since it is difficult for any one group to round up sufficient votes for election victory without gathering support from other organizations. The Christian Democrats have been strongest for some time, but they are closely pursued by the Communists, Socialists, Liberals, and Social Democrats, among others.

2. ART, ARCHITECTURE, LITERATURE & MUSIC

ART & ARCHITECTURE

The mysterious Etruscans, whose earliest origins lay probably somewhere in Mesopotamia, brought the first truly impressive art and architecture to mainland Italy. Little remains of their architecture, but historical writings by the Romans themselves record their powerful walls, bridges, and aqueducts which were very similar to the Mycenaean architecture of Crete. The handful of remaining Etruscan murals was discovered in tombs. More numerous are the finely sculpted sarcophagi, many of

IMPRESSIONS

Their smiles and laughter are due to their habit of thinking pleasurably aloud about the pleasures of life. They have humanity rather than humour, and the real significance of the distinction is seldom understood.
—PETER NICHOLS, *ITALIA, ITALIA*, 1973

By 1948 the Italians had begun to pull themselves together, demonstrating once more their astonishing ability to cope with disaster which is so perfectly balanced by their absolute inability to deal with success.
—GORE VIDAL, MATTERS OF FACT AND FICTION, 1977

which rest today in Italian museums. The best collection is at the National Museum of the Villa Giulia in Rome. Several of the most frequently visited of these tombs can be visited on day trips from Rome (see "Easy Excursions" in Chapter 5).

As Rome asserted its own identity and overpowered its Etruscan masters, it borrowed heavily from themes already established by Etruscan artists and architects. In time, however, the Romans discovered Greek art, fell in love with that country's statuary, and looted much of it. Partly because of the admiration of the Romans, the Hellenistic tradition, launched so bravely in the eastern Mediterranean, continued in somewhat altered (some say corrupted) form in the West.

It was in architecture, however, that Rome flourished magnificently, advancing in size and majesty far beyond the architectural examples set by the Greeks. Part of this was because of the development of a primitive form of concrete, but even more important was the fine-tuning of the arch, which was used with a logic, rhythm, and ease never before seen. Monumental buildings were erected, each an embodiment of the strength, power, and careful organization of the empire itself. Examples include forums and baths scattered across the Mediterranean world (the greatest of which were Trajan's Forum and Caracalla's Baths, both in Rome). Equally magnificent were the Colosseum and a building that later greatly influenced the Palladians during the Renaissance, Hadrian's Pantheon, both erected in Rome.

Of course, these immense achievements were made possible by two major resources: almost limitless funds pouring in from all regions of the empire, and an unending supply of slaves captured during military campaigns abroad.

The aesthetic and engineering concepts of the Roman Empire eventually evolved into early Christian and Byzantine art. More concerned with moral and spiritual values than with the physical beauty of the human form or the celebration of political grandeur, early Christian artists turned to the supernatural and spiritual world for their inspiration, often glorifying churches rather than pagan temples. Basilicas and churches were lavishly decorated with mosaics and colored marble, while painting depicted the earthly suffering (and heavenly rewards) of martyrs and saints. Unlike the Etruscans, the Christians depicted death as a beginning (of either salvation or damnation), and God as all-powerful, omniscient, and (according to the artist's depiction) either loving or wrathful.

The art and architecture in the centuries that followed the collapse of Rome became known as early medieval or Romanesque. In its many variations, it flourished between A.D. 1000 and A.D. 1200, although in isolated pockets away from Europe's commercial mainstreams, it continued for several centuries later. Supported by monasteries or churches, it was almost wholly concerned with ecclesiastical subjects, often with the intention of educating the worshipers who studied it. Biblical parables were carved in stone or painted into frescoes, often useful teaching aids for a church eager to spread its messages.

As the appeal of the Romanesque faded, the Gothic or late medieval style encouraged a vast increase in both the quantities and preconceptions of Italian art and architecture. The Italians interpreted Gothic into their own particular style, which was much different from the version manifested by the French. Although the Gothic age continued to be profoundly religious, many secular buildings, including an array of palaces intended to show off the increasing prestige and wealth of Italy's ruling families, were erected. Artists such as Cimabue and Giotto blazed new trails and brought emotional realism into their work in what was later seen as complete breaks from Byzantine gloom and rigidity, and an early harbinger of the Renaissance.

The Italian Renaissance was born in Florence during the 15th century, where members of the powerful Medici family emerged as some of the greatest art patrons in history. The Renaissance began with great artistic events: Ghiberti defeated Brunelleschi in a contest to design bronze doors for the Baptistery of the Cathedral of Florence. (The original doors were recently removed to the Duomo Museum for safekeeping and replaced by copies.) But Brunelleschi designed a dome for the cathedral which has been hailed ever since as "a miracle of design." In Rome, Urbino-born Donato Bramante worked with others on St. Peter's Basilica, the most significant and imposing building of the High Renaissance. (Venice during this period grew prosperous, but differed from Florence in that its architecture adhered steadfastly to Gothic features and influences from Byzantium.)

Sculpture took on a renewed importance during the Renaissance as many great artists, including Michaelangelo, dazzled the world with new and uniquely individual versions of pietàs and Davids. Perhaps it was in painting, however, that the Renaissance excelled. Leonardo da Vinci, whose all-encompassing skill in everything from painting to engineering has defined him as "the epitome of the Renaissance man," gave the world such works as *The Last Supper* and *Mona Lisa*. Urbino-born Raffaello Santi was another giant of the Renaissance. In Rome, he was commissioned to fresco the apartments of Pope Julius II. Simultaneously, Michelangelo painted the ceiling frescoes of the Sistine Chapel, an assignment that took 4 back-breaking years of his life to complete.

The period known as the High Renaissance was said to last for only about 25 years, beginning in the early 16th century. Despite the subtle differences between the stages of the Renaissance, Italy remained Europe's artistic leader for nearly 200 years.

The transitional period between the Renaissance and the baroque came to be called "Mannerism." Out of this period emerged such great artists as Tintoretto, whose major work was the cycle of frescoes for the Scuola di San Rocco in Venice (it took 23 years to finish); Verona-born Paolo Veronese; and perhaps the most sensitive, and some say the finest, of the Mannerists, Parmigianino, who was born in Parma in 1503.

In the early 17th century and into the 18th century, the baroque (meaning absurd or irregular) movement swept Europe, including Italy. The development of the baroque movement was linked to the much-needed reforms and restructuring of the Catholic church that followed the upheavals of the Protestant Reformation. Many great Italian churches and palazzi were constructed during this period. Great artists emerged, including Bernini, who became renowned both as a sculptor and as a painter, and Borromini, one of the great architects of his age. The two painters who best represented the movement were Carracci, who decorated the Roman palace of Cardinal Farnese, and Caravaggio, one of the pioneers of baroque painting. The even more flamboyant rococo grew out of the baroque style.

In the 19th century, the great light had gone out of art in Italy. (The beacon was picked up instead by France.) Neoclassicism—a return to the aesthetic ideals of ancient Greece and Rome whose ideals of patriotism were resonant with the growing sense of pan-Italian patriotism—swept through almost every aspect of the Italian arts.

The 20th century witnessed the birth of several major Italian artists whose works once again captured the imagination of the world. De Chirico and Modigliani (the latter's greatest contribution lay in a new concept of portraiture) were only two among many. The Bolognese painter of bottles and jugs, Morandi, also became known around the world. The greatest Italian sculptor of the 20th century was Medardo Rosso, who died in 1928, and the leading figure in Italian architecture was Pier Luigi Nervi, born in 1891 in Milan. His best-known commission is probably the Palazzo della Sport in Rome, which he designed for the 1960 Olympics.

Since then Italy has been a European leader in sophisticated and witty interpretations of buildings, paintings, fashion, industrial design, and decor. Many modern Italian artists have infused Italian flair into the lines of workaday and utilitarian objects whose quality, humor, and usefulness has become legendary.

LITERATURE

The Italian writer most familiar to readers today is probably Umberto Eco, whose fascinating novel, *The Name of the Rose,* was translated in 1983 and whose English version became a runaway bestseller. Eco follows in the train of a long, long line of literary figures of note who use the Tuscan dialect–based Italian language with outstanding effect.

Since the institution of the Nobel Prize for Literature in 1901, five Italians have been recipients of the coveted prize: Giosuè Carducci, poet and professor of Italian

IMPRESSIONS

The more I see of them the more struck I am
with their having no sense of the ridiculous.
—HENRY JAMES, LETTER TO MRS. FANNY KEMBLE, MARCH 24, 1881

It is not impossible to govern Italians. It is merely useless.
—BENITO MUSSOLINI

literature at the University of Bologna, in 1906; Grazia Deledda, Sardinia-born writer who used her native island as the subject of her work, in 1926; Luigi Pirandello, Sicily-born dramatist, in 1934; Salvadore Quasimodo, a poet, also a native of Sicily, in 1959; and Eugenio Montale, poet, in 1975.

In the days of Rome's glory—shortly before and after the birth of Christ—mighty men of letters included Cicero, Julius Caesar, Virgil, Horace, Ovid, and Livy. When the people's thoughts turned heavenward, which was inevitable when the Christian faith became accepted by the majority of Romans and other Italians, Christian Latin literature became the order of the day. Such writers as St. Augustine, St. Ambrose, and St. Jerome gained repute for their writings and are remembered as among the few voices heard during the Dark Ages.

Medieval Italian literature was represented by religious poetry (St. Francis of Assisi), secular lyric poetry (Provençal troubadour musical tributes), and sonnets as produced by the Sicilian school of verse.

Arguably the greatest period in Italian literature was ushered in during the 14th century, with world-acclaimed works that made the Tuscan dialect the literary language of Italy. Immortals such as Dante, Petrarch, and Boccaccio flourished in this era. *The Divine Comedy* by Dante is called the first masterpiece of the then-modern national language. Petrarch is hailed as the forerunner of humanism, and scholars say that Boccaccio, best known for the *Decameron,* did for Italian prose what Dante did for its poetry.

The term "Renaissance man" is applied to those who excelled in many fields of endeavor in that era. Among these, shining examples are Michelangelo, who wrote sonnets in addition to all his other talents; Leonardo da Vinci, writer, inventor, artist, astronomer, whatever; and even Lorenzo de' Medici (Lorenzo the Magnificent), who is credited with establishing the Tuscan dialect as the national speech of Italy. Machiavelli in the 16th century, Goldoni in the 18th century, and D'Annunzio in the early 20th century, are other names connected with Italian literary achievement. I have mentioned a few. You perhaps have other names to remember in the long annals of literature of Rome and Italy.

MUSIC

Though the ultimate expression of Italian musicality would not reveal itself until the operatic tradition of the 18th and 19th centuries, music has always been a part of Italian life.

Late in the 900s, a Benedictine monk from Arezzo named Guido Monaco invented a musical scale which was used within monasteries for the notation of single-melody, unharmonized religious chanting known as Gregorian chants.

Many of these medieval traditions were reformed by Palestrina during the 1500s, but a truly idiosyncratic version of Italian music only began to be defined in the late 1600s. At that time, Corelli (1653–1713) originated a musical form known as the *concerto grosso* and founded a particular and highly colorful style of violin playing. Scarlatti (1660–1725) refined thematic development of musical scores, popularized the concept of chromatic harmonies, and helped to define the makeup of the operatic orchestra. A few generations later, Boccherini (1743–1805) contributed greatly to sophisticated applications of the chamber orchestra, defining appropriate musical contexts for string quartets at some of the most influential gatherings of Europe.

Especially important was Vivaldi (1678–1741), the Venice-born composer (and ordained priest) who was considered one of the most influential European composers of his day. An innovator in form and orchestration (and composer of more than 700 musical works), he developed techniques that greatly influenced the compositions of Bach.

As mentioned earlier, however, most musicologists best remember Italy for its opera (a drama or comedy in which music is the essential factor, with showcases for both instruments and individual voices). Italy and opera are linked by marriage, and, in fact, many visitors to Italy consider it one of the country's prime touristic attractions. (The opera season in Italy begins in early December and continues through mid-April.)

Jacopo Peri's *Dafne* (first performed in 1597, inspired by the recitative style of ancient Greek dramas and commissioned by the Medicis) is now regarded as the world's first opera. A leading figure in what is considered the musical revolution of the 16th century, Claudio Monteverdi (1567–1643), however, is viewed as the father of modern opera. Developing new styles of operatic oratorios, his masterpiece was *L'Incoronazione di Poppea* (1642). From its origins in Florence, opera moved to Venice before catching on, around 1650, with the audiences of Naples. Even the previously mentioned Vivaldi, although best remembered for his orchestral works, composed 43 different operas, the most famous of which is *Armida al campo d'Egitto* (1718).

From this rich musical tradition arose the *bel canto* (beautiful singing) method of the 18th and early 19th centuries. The movement's most famous adherent was Vincenzo Bellini (1801–35), whose masterpiece, *Norma* (composed just 4 years before his early death) is considered a *tour de force* of the melodic line, and with dozens of famous and challenging arias for coloratura soprano. Opera, particularly its Neapolitan versions, spread around the world. Bellini was followed in the bel canto tradition by Rossini (1792–1868). He moved to Paris in 1823 and remained there for most of the rest of his life. His operas retain both the Italian-inspired *opera buffa* comedic tradition (he's considered the last of the masters of that particular form) as well as a series of brilliant crescendos which express great emotional power. Rossini is best known for his sparkling and witty *The Barber of Seville*.

Romantic opera also flowered, particularly in the works of Donizetti, best known for his *Lucia di Lammermoor,* which many years later brought Joan Sutherland fame at New York's Metropolitan Opera.

It was Giuseppe Verdi (1813–1901) who became the greatest Italian operatic composer, credited (with Richard Wagner) with developing opera into a fully integrated art which combined many different disciplines into a coherent whole. In all, Verdi produced 26 operas, many of which are widely performed today, including *Il Trovatore, La Traviata, Rigoletto, Un Ballo in Maschera,* and *Aïda.*

Verdi's musical heir was Giacomo Puccini (1858–1924), who trained in what had become the operatic headquarters of Italy (Milan). Greatly influenced by Wagner, his music was melodious and romantic, revolving around plots based on tragic love themes. Set in deliberately exotic settings, his most popular operas included *Madama Butterfly, La Bohème, Tosca,* and the incomplete *Turandot* (completed after Puccini's death by his musical disciple, Franco Alfano).

Enrico Caruso (1873–1921), one of the most famous operatic tenors of all time, based his career on his interpretations of Puccini operas, performing some of them for the first time in concert halls from Buenos Aires to San Francisco. Since Verdi and Puccini, however, no Italian composer has entered this exclusive pantheon of the musical greats.

Despite its potency and influence on formal musical compositions around the world, none of the above-mentioned composers or works gives credit to the richness and diversity of Italian popular song. In the early 1900s Italy had one of the wealthiest traditions of folk music in the world, with strongly defined differences in musical traditions among the country's various districts. (Naples had always been particularly fertile—both in childbearing and in music—producing such globally popular songs as "O sole mio" and "Funicule Funicula.")

The effect of television, radio, and cultural inroads from the rest of the world has obliterated at least some of these musical traditions, although musical output in one form or another is still one of Italy's greatest exports to the world. (You're far more likely to hear someone break into spontaneous song in Italy than in almost any other country in Europe.) In the 1950s and early 1960s, Ornella Vanoni and Gino Paoli, Domenico Modugno ("Volaré"), Mina, and Peppino di Capri provided much of the music for the sybaritic but fleeting moment known ever after as *La Dolce Vita*. Then, Italy never seemed as carefree, stylish, and romantic as it enjoyed an economic boom and the devoted patronage of the world's most beautiful people. During this era there developed a greater consciousness of what such singers as Frank Sinatra and Peggy Lee were doing (musically) in America, and an increased awareness of musical trends in both the U.S. and Britain.

Today, jazz, rock, blues, folk music, and (to a lesser degree) heavy metal flourish in Italy in patterns that frequently parallel similar developments in the U.S. and the rest of Europe. Italy, a nation which has always appreciated showmanship, always manages, however to infuse the barrage of outside influences with its own particular expression of style, laughter, and wit, seducing musical forms as well as casual visitors with its highly idiosyncratic and potent charms.

3. LANGUAGE, RELIGION & FOLKLORE

LANGUAGE

Italian, of course, is the official language, and it's spoken all over the country, with many regional dialects. The purest form of Italian is said to be spoken in Tuscany. Italian is probably more directly derived from Latin than many of the other romance languages, which also include French, Spanish, and Romanian.

In the 14th century the dialect of Tuscany became the literary language of Italy. Dante did more than anyone to promulgate the language, although he was aided by such other Tuscan writers as Petrarch and Boccaccio.

Linguists consider Italian the most "musical" and mellifluous language in the West. In fact, it has always been a puzzle why Casanova chose to write his racy memoirs in French instead of Italian, as he was born in Venice. Some critics have suggested that the memoirs would have had even more of an effect had they been written in Italian.

The Italian language easily lent itself to librettos and operas. Many English people have to draw upon Italian words, especially musical terms, such as *basso profundo*, to describe various items. *Prima donna, la dolce vita* (aided in part by the Fellini film), and *inamorata* are just a few Italian words widely used around the world.

The language is a phonetic one. That means you pronounce a word the way it is written, unlike many languages, including English. It has been said that if an Italian sentence sounds "off key," it is because the grammar is incorrect.

IMPRESSIONS

Why are Italians at this day generally so good poets and painters? Because every man of any fashion amongst them hath his mistress. . . . Germany hath not so many drunkards, England tobacconists, France dancers, Holland mariners, as Italy alone hath jealous husbands.
—ROBERT BURTON, *ANATOMIE OF MELANCHOLIE*, 1621

There is no Italian word for privacy.
—PETER NICHOLS, *ITALIA, ITALIA*, 1973

I am very witty in Italian, though a little violent; and I need space.
—DYLAN THOMAS, LETTER TO JOHN DAVENPORT, MAY 29, 1947

The Italian alphabet is not as extensive as the one in English in that it doesn't use such letters as *J, K, W, X,* and *Y.* Italians discovered the *J* with the advent of jeans in the postwar era, although they often pronounce the word "yeans."

Since the coming of television—mainly in the 1950s—more and more Italians speak the language with similarity. Even in World War II many Italian soldiers couldn't understand each other, as some men spoke only in dialect.

A lot of so-called Americanisms have now infiltrated the Italian language, largely because of the success of U.S.-made films in Italy. The films also did much to popularize a Sicilian phrase now known around the world: *Mafia.* Although it menacingly evokes an international crime organization, it literally means "I'll beat you so hard you'll dance with pain."

RELIGION

Few regions on earth have been as religiously prolific as Italy, and few other regions have influenced Christianity the way Italy has done.

Even before the Christianization of the Roman Empire, the ancient Romans artfully (and sometimes haphazardly) mingled their allegiance to the deities of ancient Greece with whatever religious fad happened to be imported at the moment. After its zenith, ancient Rome resembled a theological hodgepodge of dozens of religious and mystical cults which found fertile soil amid the splendor, neuroses, cruelties, and decadence of a crumbling empire. Eastern (especially Egyptian) cults became especially popular, and dozens of emperors showed no aversion to defining themselves as gods and enforcing worship by their subjects.

In A.D. 313 the Emperor Constantine signed the edict of Milan, stopping the hitherto merciless persecution of Christians. (He also converted to Christianity himself.) Since that eventful moment, Italy has adhered rigorously to Catholicism, enforcing its status as the spiritual center of the legacy of St. Peter, and the definer of the wishes of God as defined by the bulwark of the Catholic church's theological doctrines and traditions.

Today the huge majority (99%) of Italians describe themselves as Roman Catholic, although their form of allegiance to Catholicism varies widely according to individual conscience. Despite the fact that only about one-third of the country attends mass with any regularity, and only about 10% claim to receive the sacrament at Easter, the country is innately—to its very core—flavored by the Catholic tradition. That does not always mean that the populace follows the dictates of the Vatican. An example of this is that, despite the pressure by the Holy See against voting in favor of Communist party members (in 1949, the Vatican threatened to excommunicate—*ipso facto*—any Italian who voted for Communist or Communist-inspired candidates), the Communist platform in Italy has during certain elections received up to 33% of the popular vote.

Modern Italy's adherence to Catholicism is legally stressed by a law enacted in 1848 by the Kingdom of Sardinia (and which was later reaffirmed by the Lateran Treaty) which states: "The Catholic apostolic and Roman religion is the sole religion of the (Italian) State." The same treaties, however, give freedom of worship to other religions, but identifies Rome as "the center of the Catholic World and a place of pilgrimage," and confer onto the State of Italy the responsibility of helping to safeguard such Catholic institutions as the security of the pope and his emissaries, and to respect church property and church law in the treatment of matters which include, among others, requests for divorces or annulments.

Significantly, throughout history Italy has produced more upper-echelon leaders to staff the Vatican than any other country in the world. Only recently, with the election of a Polish-born pope (John Paul II), has a pattern of almost complete domination of the papacy by Italian prelates been altered. Because of the sometimes-inconvenient juxtaposition of the Vatican within the administrative capital of Italy, the Lateran Treaty of February 11, 1929, which was confirmed by Article 7 of the constitution of the Italian republic, recognizes the Vatican City State as an independent and sovereign state and establishes and defines its relationship to the Italian State.

Italy's principal religious minorities are for the most part clustered into parts of Calabria and Sicily. There, local Catholic populations adhere to the Byzantine (or Greek) rites, while remaining in communion with the See at Rome. The adherents of these doctrines are for the most part descendants of Albanian refugees from the 15th and 16th centuries (the Italo-Albanesi) or of Greek colonists who arrived even earlier.

A handful of Protestants lie scattered amid the northern hills of the Piedmont, adhering to a rite established during the Reformation in France. Known as the Waldensians, they adhere to a French-based Calvinism, and until late in the 19th century, conducted most of their services in French. Italy also has communities of Jews, about a third of whom live in Rome and the remainder of whom lie scattered throughout the industrial cities of the north; handfuls of Lutherans near the Swiss border; and many expatriates from other parts of Europe and from North America, many of whom are Protestant.

FOLKLORE

Perhaps the most formal manifestation of folk rituals in all of Italy is the Commedia dell'Arte. Although it greatly influenced theatrical styles of France in the 17th century, it is unique to Italy and so engrained in the consciences of modern Italians that they can identify at the glance the stock characters who, behind masks and stylized costumes, perform broadly satirical improvisations. The plots almost always develop and resolve an imbroglio where the beautiful wife of an older curmudgeon dallies with a handsome swain, against the advice of her maid, and much to the amusement of the husband's valet. The art form's grandiose, sometimes bizarre costumes are reflected in the annual carnivals at Venice, when thousands of residents take to the streets and private parties in enigmatic 18th-century costumes and masks.

Italy, even before the Christian era, was a richly religious land ripe with legends and myths. Modern Italy blends superstition, ancient myths and fables, and Christian symbolism in richly folkloric ways and sometimes unnerving ways. Throughout Italy, rites of passage such as births, first communions, marriages, and deaths are linked to endless rounds of family celebrations, feasts, and gatherings. Faithful Italians might genuflect in front of a church, when entering a church, when viewing an object of religious veneration (a relic of a saint, for example), or when hearing a statement which might tempt the Devil to meddle in someone's personal affairs.

Though they are practiced throughout the country, the density and complexity of folkloric rituals are the most pronounced in the high-altitude valleys of the Piedmont, and amid the hot and sun washed hills of Italy's southern regions of Calabria, Sicily, the city of Naples, and the mysterious and remote island of Sardinia. Although there are marked contrasts between the folk customs practiced within these regions, each of the rituals and belief patterns mingles pagan with Christian superstition, a yearning for some manifestation of communal feeling, and, often, a willingness to become a part of this or that inexpressible mystery.

The miracles associated with this or that medieval saint are too numerous to recount, but one example of a folkloric ritual includes Naples's festival of San Gennaro. Held twice a year in its city of origin, it is celebrated nostalgically as far away as Manhattan's Little Italy, usually with feasting and fireworks. The blood of the martyred Saint Gennaro, kept dry in a flask for hundreds of years within the cathedral at Naples, is supposed to liquefy at the dramatic height of the festival, and unless it does, disaster will befall the city.

Though Naples has among the most extreme examples of folkloric oddities, it is not alone within Italy. In Florence, Easter is observed by an armada of floats accompanied by processions of doves, and Ascension Day is the time of a ritualized cricket hunt (crickets being a symbol of good fortune) in the nearby fields. (In recent times, in lieu of actually hunting for crickets, many Florentines opt instead to buy the insects from street vendors.)

Ritualized festivals in Sicily are at their height in Taormina in late May, when local costumes and parades celebrate the unique folklore of Sicily. A similar event takes place in Sardinia around May 4 every year, during the festival of Sant'Efisio.

No one can omit July's ritualized horse race in the heart of medieval Siena, the Palio, when virtually everyone in town invests quantities of money and time in equestrian teams which represent the prestige of 17 different neighborhoods (and the extended families who live in them) of Siena. A similar race is held every year in nearby Pisa, with stiff competition for the most authentic and/or glamorous manifestation of 16th-century costumes, and a thousand shared memories of the folkloric events that occurred during these races the year, the decade, or the half century before.

Folkloric rituals are at their height during Holy Week. In Calabria, until fairly recently, Good Friday processions used to include penitents who flogged themselves until they drew blood. Less extreme incidents include belief still in the destructive powers of the Evil Eye (the malediction that could befall someone by the ill will, for example, of a neighbor), and the dozens of rituals and events associated with a bride and a groom during their transformation into the basic unit of the Italian society—the family.

4. SPORTS & RECREATION

SPORTS

In Italy, a sportsperson is anyone who enjoys watching sports, and not necessarily playing them, and practically no other nation throws itself so wholeheartedly into occasionally fanatical allegiance to favorite **football (soccer)** teams. Originally imported from England, soccer first came to Italy in 1898, when about a hundred spectators on a ragged field near Turin came to blows over the much-disputed outcome of the country's first match. The combined contributions by that historic match's spectators totaled 197 lire, an insignificant amount compared to the trillions of lire amassed in the name of Italian soccer ever since. Today the sport attracts millions of Italian devotees, and is taken so seriously that heart attacks by spectators (both in stadiums or in front of television sets), major riots that have often led to multiple deaths, and endless traffic jams and car accidents have occurred because of it.

Soccer is a fast game played by two teams of 11 men for 90 minutes (two halves of 45 minutes). They are allowed to use only their feet and their heads to move the ball, and score goals by kicking it between two fixed goal posts. At least part of the popularity of soccer was encouraged by Mussolini and the Fascists, who used it to increase the patriotic feelings of Italians, especially by stressing Italy's sports victories over other nations. Today, in a game that seems to renew its modernity with every match, intense competition (and staggeringly large betting pools) accompany matches between Italian villages, Italian cities, and Italian districts. Many famous Italian architects have based their reputations on their designs for sports stadiums. On Sunday afternoon in Italy (the traditional time for the beginning of a match is 2:30pm), all traffic seems to lead in or out of stadium parking lots, all televisions seem to be tuned in to the televised match, and even the most outwardly staid citizens become enmeshed in what has been defined as a regularly scheduled manifestation of national hysteria.

Although not as overwhelmingly popular as soccer, competitive **bicycle races** also draw enthusiastic crowds. Races, which cover widely different terrains, are sponsored by corporations, cities, or investment-minded individuals. Events are arranged either as relays or as showcases for only one racer. Regardless of the weather, crowds invariably gather at finish lines to watch the outcome. The most important Italian cycling event is a 3-week competition held during May or June called Il Giro d'Italia. It covers over 2,400 miles of alpine terrain, including many of the steepest roads in Italy.

After soccer and cycling, **other popular sports** include automobile racing, rugby, motorcycle racing, basketball, downhill skiing in the Italian Alps, boxing, and—to a lesser degree—horse racing. Other sports imported from other parts of the world, such as baseball and ice hockey, are less popular.

RECREATION

BICYCLING Bicycles are forbidden on most motorways, and in view of the dangers of the narrow and fast-paced Italian roads, and the unpredictability of most Italian drivers, it's probably safe only in the most isolated of areas. The country's mountains and rugged terrain almost completely eliminate flat and easy pedaling, yet, nonetheless, the sport has dozens of avid followers. Also, a bicycle might allow the most nimble of enthusiasts to avoid delays in the endless traffic jams of Italy's cities. Ride carefully, and never pedal anywhere without a helmet. If you're really enthusiastic, an Italian-language newspaper designed especially for cyclists is called *La Gazzetta Sportiva*. It and more information can be obtained through the **Federazione Ciclistica Italiana,** via L. Franchetti 2, 00196 Roma (tel. 06/368-5725).

CAMPING Catering to the needs of its citizens for affordable vacations, Italy is now dotted with campgrounds set in regions of natural beauty. If camping appeals to you, be sure to camp only in authorized campsites, many of which require membership in one of Italy's camping associations. For more information, write to the **Federazione Italiana del Campeggio,** Casella Postale 649, 50100 Florence. The organization publishes a directory (the *Guide Camping Italiana*).

FRESH- AND SALTWATER FISHING Freshwater game fish can be pursued in the Alps, Lombardy, Piedmont, Emilia-Romagna, and Venetia, as well as in the sparkling lakes of Como, Garda, and Maggiore. Abundant species include brown and tiger trout, pike and pike-perch, whitefish, carp, and an occasional sturgeon. Fishing licenses, obtainable at most city halls for around $8 each, are usually required before a visitor can fish in the waters of an Italian town. To avoid fines and embarrassments, contact the **F.I.P.S. (Italian Fishing Federation)**, viale Tiziano 70, Roma (tel. 06/36851). This organization describes the legalities of bait and tackle, the allowable weight of any game fish, and the duration of fishing seasons (the limits for each of these categories can vary from region to region). Also, the organization owns the fishing rights to several abundantly stocked streams and lakes in northern Italy, although only members of the organization can fish in them legally.

One Italian-language publication that avid anglers might find useful is *Pescare,* available at newsstands throughout the country, or directly from the publishers; contact Editoriale Olimpia, viale Milton 7, Firenze 50129 (tel. 055/473843).

A similar organization exists for saltwater sports fishing. If you're interested, contact the **Federazione Italiana Pesca Sportiva e Attività Subacquea (F.I.P.S.),** viale Tiziano 70, Roma (tel. 06/394754).

GOLF Although golf is an imported (from Britain) sport, the country boasts about a hundred golf courses, which often are stunningly beautiful. Greens fees usually run about $50 on weekdays, slightly more on weekends when the courses are much more crowded. Membership in a U.S. golf or country club often justifies reciprocal privileges at many Italian golf courses. Otherwise, the desk clerks at most of Italy's finer hotels can arrange for a guest to play in the neighborhood if circumstances are favorable. For more information about golf in Italy, contact the **Italian Golf Federation,** via Flaminia 388, Roma (tel. 06/394641).

HORSEBACK RIDING Despite their romance with the automobile, the Italians trace their love of horses back to the Roman Empire, and have traditionally depicted many of their military and political heroes atop horses. Like-minded Italian enthusiasts can provide lists of the country's stables and riding itineraries if you contact **A.N.T.E. (National Association for Equestrian Tourism)**, via Alfonso Borelli 5, 00161 Roma (tel. 06/494-0969).

SAILING The prowess of Italian sailors is legendary, and few of the world's oceans or seas is as evocative as the richly historic Mediterranean. Virtually every port in Italy contains someone willing to rent a sailboat to a qualified stranger—with or without an attendant crew—and the great resorts along the Riviera, Amalfi, Sicily, or Sardinia are ripe with charter companies. The desk manager of any reputable seaside hotel usually has at least an idea of where you could rent a boat, but for more information, you can contact the **Federazione Italiana Vela,** viale Brigate Bisagno 2, Genova 16129 (tel. 010/565723). A similar organization in Rome is the **Agenzia Nautica Altura,** via Mecenate 22B, 00184 Roma (tel. 06/733242).

SKIING An array of alpine resorts, following in the stylish leads of resorts in Austria, Switzerland, and France, is now strung across the northern tier of Italy, from the Val d'Aosta to the German-speaking Alto Adige. One of Europe's most famous resorts, Breuil-Cervinia, sits directly atop the southern slopes of the famous Matterhorn (a peak which Italians refer to as Monte Cervino). Several of the finest and most interesting resorts are covered in this guidebook. These include the previously mentioned Breuil-Cervinia as well as the glamorous hideaways of Cortina d'Ampezzo and Courmayeur. More information on individual resorts can be obtained by writing directly to the tourist offices of the specific resorts (see "Essentials" in the individual city sections).

TENNIS The sport has gained great popularity since *La Dolce Vita* made afternoon tennis followed by before-dinner cocktails and a bit of lovemaking *de rigueur* for the smart set. Tennis enthusiasts accustomed to the respectful hush of tennis at, say Forest Hills or Wimbledon, might be unnerved by the background noises at Italian tennis tournaments, although professionals consider this nothing more than an expression of enthusiasm for the game. Most venues for the game occur in the precincts of private tennis courts which may or may not—depending on management policies—accept foreign visitors. Many hotels, however, especially those in Italian resorts, maintain their own courts. Many of the courts are clay, and proper attire (whites and appropriate shoes) is usually a prerequisite for playing. For general information about tennis in Italy, and a list of the various tennis clubs, contact the **Italian Tennis Federation,** viale Tiziano 70, 00100 Roma (tel. 06/321-9897).

5. FOOD & DRINK

Many North American visitors erroneously think of Italian cuisine as limited. Of course, everybody has heard of minestrone, spaghetti, chicken cacciatore, and spumoni. But Italian chefs hardly confine themselves to such a limited repertoire. Incidentally, except in the south, Italians don't use as much garlic in their food as many foreigners seem to believe. Most Italian dishes, especially those in the north, are butter based. Spaghetti and meatballs, by the way, is not an Italian dish, although certain restaurants throughout the country have taken to serving it "for homesick Americans."

FOOD

Rome might be the best place to introduce yourself to the cookery of Italy, as it has specialty restaurants that represent all the culinary centers such as Bologna and Genoa. Throughout your Roman holiday, you'll encounter such savory viands as *zuppa di pesce* (a soup or stew of various fish, cooked in white wine and herb flavored), *cannelloni* (tube-shaped pasta baked with any number of stuffings), *riso col gamberi* (rice with shrimp, peas, and mushrooms, flavored with white wine and garlic), *scampi alla griglia* (grilled prawns, one of the best-tasting, albeit expensive, dishes in the city), *quaglie col risotto e tartufi* (quail with rice and truffles), *lepre alla cacciatore* (hare flavored with white wine and herbs), *zabaglione* (a cream made with sugar, egg yolks, and marsala), *gnocchi alla romana* (potato-flour dumplings with a sauce made with meat and covered with grated cheese), *abbacchio* (baby spring lamb, often roasted over an open fire), *saltimbocca alla romana* (literally "jump-in-your-mouth"—thin slices of veal with sage, ham, and cheese), *fritto alla romana* (a mixed fry that's likely to include everything from brains to artichokes), *carciofi alla romana* (tender artichokes cooked with such herbs as mint and garlic, and flavored with white wine), *fettuccine all'uovo* (egg noodles served with butter and cheese), *zuppa di cozze* (a hearty bowl of mussels cooked in broth), *fritti di scampi e calamaretti* (baby squid and prawns fast fried), *fragoline* (wild strawberries, in this case from the Alban Hills), and *finocchio* (fennel, a celerylike raw vegetable, with the flavor of licorice, often eaten as a dessert).

From Rome, it's on to **Florence** and **Siena** where you'll encounter the hearty, rich cuisine of the Tuscan hills (for comments on that cuisine, refer to the introduction to the dining section of Chapter 7).

The next major city to visit is **Venice,** where the cookery is typical of the Venetia district. It has been called "tasty, straightforward, and homely" by one long-ago food critic, and I concur. One of the most typical dishes is *fegato alla veneziana* (liver and onions), as well as *risi e bisi* (rice and fresh peas). Seafood figures heavily in the Venetian diet, and grilled fish is often served with the bitter red radicchio, a lettuce that comes from Treviso.

In **Lombardy,** of which Milan is the center, the cookery is more refined and tasty, in my opinion. No dish here is more famous than *cotoletta alla milanese* (cutlets of tender veal, dipped in egg and breadcrumbs, and fried in olive oil until it's a golden brown). The Viennese called it Wiener Schnitzel. *Ossobuco* is the other great dish of Lombardy. This is cooked with the shinbone of veal in a ragoût sauce and served on a bed of rice and peas. *Risotto alla milanese* is also a classic Lombard dish. This is rice which can be dressed in almost any way, depending on the chef's imagination. It's often flavored with saffron and butter, to which chicken giblets have been added. It's always served, seemingly, with heaps of parmesan cheese. *Polenta,* a cornmeal mush that's "more than mush," is the staff of life in some parts of northeastern Italy and is eaten in lieu of pasta.

The cooking in **Piedmont,** of which Turin is the capital, and the Aosta Valley is different from that in the rest of Italy. Its victuals are said to appeal to strong-hearted men returning from a hard day's work in the mountains. You get such dishes as *bagna cauda,* which is a sauce made with olive oil, garlic, butter, and anchovies in which you dip uncooked fresh vegetables. *Fonduta* is celebrated: It's made with melted Fontina cheese, butter, milk, egg yolks, and, for an elegant touch, white truffles.

In the **Trentino–Alto Adige area,** whose chief towns are Bolzano, Merano, and Trent, the cooking is naturally influenced by the traditions of the Austrian and Germanic kitchens. South Tyrol, of course, used to belong to Austria, and here you get such tasty pastries as strudel.

Liguria, whose chief town is Genoa, turns to the sea for a great deal of its cuisine, as reflected by its version of bouillabaisse, a *buridda* flavored with spices. But its most famous food item is *pesto,* a sauce made with fresh basil, garlic, cheese, and walnuts. It not only dresses pasta or fish, but many dishes such as *gnocchi* (little dumplings).

Emilia-Romagna, with such towns as Modena, Parma, Bologna, Ravenna, and Ferrara, is one of the great gastronomic centers of Italy. Rich in produce, its school of cooking produces many notable pastas that are now common around Italy. They include *tagliatelle, tortellini,* and *cappelletti* (larger than tortellini and made in the form of "little hats"). Tagliatelle, of course, are long strips of macaroni, and tortellini are little squares of dough that have been stuffed with chopped pork, veal, or whatever. Equally as popular is *lasagne,* which by now nearly everybody has heard of. In Bologna it's often made by adding finely shredded spinach to the dough. The best-known sausage of the area is *mortadella,* and equally as famous is a *cotoletta alla bolognese* (veal cutlet fried with a slice of ham or bacon). The distinctive and famous cheese, *parmigiana,* is a product of Parma and also Reggio Emilia. *Zampone* (stuffed pig's foot) is a specialty of Modena.

Much of the cookery of **Naples**—spaghetti with clam sauce, pizzas, and so forth—is already familiar to North Americans because so many Neapolitans moved to the New World and opened restaurants there. *Mozzarella* or buffalo cheese is the classic cheese of this area. Mixed fish fries, done a golden brown, are a staple feature of nearly every table.

Sicily has a distinctive cuisine, with good strong flavors and aromatic sauces. A staple of the diet is *maccheroni con le sarde* (spaghetti with pine seeds, fennel, spices, chopped sardines, and olive oil). Fish is good and fresh in Sicily (try swordfish). Among meat dishes, you'll see *involtini siciliani* on the menu (rolled meat with a stuffing of egg, ham, and cheese cooked in bread crumbs). A *caponata* is a special way of cooking eggplant in a flavor-rich tomato sauce. The desserts and homemade pastries are excellent. The *cannoli* is a cylindrical pastry case stuffed with ricotta and candied fruit (often chocolate). Their ice creams, called *gelati,* are among the best in Italy.

Sardinia is a land unto itself. Game such as wild boar often appears on the Sardinian table, as does *porceddi* (roast suckling pig prepared using methods a thousand years old). It's cooked in an open-air pit under myrtle branches. *Malloreddus* are little dumplings of corn flour flavored with saffron and served in a spicy sauce (everything sprinkled with goat cheese), and cassola is a highly spiced fish stew.

WINES & OTHER DRINKS

Italy is the largest wine-producing country in the world; as far back as 800 B.C. the Etruscans were vintners. It is said that more soil is used in Italy for the cultivation of grapes than for food. Many Italian farmers produce wine just for their own consumption or for their relatives in a big city. However, it wasn't until 1965 that laws were enacted to guarantee regular consistency in winemaking. Wines regulated by the government are labeled DOC (*Denominazione di Origine Controllata*). If you see DOCG on a label (the "G" means *guarantita*), that means even better quality control.

REGIONAL WINES Coming from the volcanic soil of Vesuvius, the wines of **Campania (Naples)** have been extolled for 2,000 years. Homer praised the glory of Falerno, which is straw yellow in color. Neapolitans are fond of ordering a wine known as Lacrima Christi or "tears of Christ" to accompany many seafood dishes. It comes in amber, red, or pink. With meat dishes, try the dark mulberry-colored Gragnano, which has a faint bouquet of faded violets. Also, the red and white wines of Ischia and Capri are justly renowned.

The heel of the Italian boot, **Apulia (Puglia),** produces more wine than any other part of Italy. Try Castel del Monte, which comes in shades of pink, white, and red.

Latium (Rome) is a major wine-producing region of Italy. Many of the local wines come from the Castelli Romani, the hill towns around Rome. Horace and Juvenal sang the praises of Latium wines even in imperial times. These wines, experts agree, are best drunk when young, and they are most often white, mellow, and dry (or else "demi-sec"). There are seven different types, including Falerno (yellowish straw in color) and Cecubo (often served with roast meat). Try also Colli Albani (straw yellow with amber tints and served with both fish and meat). The golden-yellow wines of Frascati are famous, produced both in a demi-sec and sweet variety, the latter served with dessert.

The wines of **Tuscany (Florence and Siena)** are famous, and they rank with some of the finest reds in France. Chianti is the best known, and it comes in several varieties. The most highly regarded is Chianti Classico, a lively ruby-red wine mellow in flavor with a bouquet of violets. A good label is Antinori. A less known, but remarkably fine Tuscan wine is Brunello di Montalcino, a brilliant garnet red that's served with roasts and game. The ruby-red, almost-purple Vino Nobile di Montepulciano has a rich rugged body; it's a noble wine that is aged for 4 years.

The sparkling Lambrusco of **Emilia-Romagna** is by now best known by Americans, but this wine can be of widely varying quality. Most of it is a brilliant ruby red. Be more experimental and try such wines as the dark ruby-red Sanglovese (with a delicate bouquet) and the golden-yellow Albana, which is somewhat sweet. Trebbiano, generally dry, is best served with fish.

From the **Marches** (capital: Ancona) comes one major wine, Verdicchio dei Castelli di Jesi, which is amber straw in color, clear and brilliant. Some have said that it's the best wine in Europe "to marry with fish."

From **Venetia** (Venice and Verona) in northeastern Italy, a rich breadbasket of the country, come such world-famous wines as Bardolino (a light ruby-red wine often served with poultry), Valpolicella (produced in "ordinary quality" and "superior dry," and best served with meats), and Soave, so beloved by W. Somerset Maugham, which has a pale-amber yellow color with a light aroma and a velvety flavor. Try also one of the Cabernets, either the ruby-red Cabernet di Treviso (ideal with roasts and game) or the even-deeper ruby-red Cabernet Franc, which has a marked herbal bouquet and is also served with roasts.

The **Friuli–Venezia Giulia area,** whose chief towns are Trieste and Udine, attract those who enjoy a "brut" wine with a trace of flint. From classic grapes comes Merlot, deep ruby in color, and several varieties of Pinot, including Pinot Grigio, whose color ranges from straw yellow to gray pink (good with fish). Also served with fish, the Sauvignon has a straw-yellow color and a delicate bouquet.

The **Trentino–Alto Adige area,** whose chief towns are Bolzano and Trent, produces wine influenced by Austria. Known for its vineyards, the region has some 20 varieties of wine. The straw-yellow, slightly pale-green Riesling is served with fish, as is the pale greenish-yellow Terlano. Santa Maddalena, a cross between a garnet and a ruby in color, is served with wild fowl and red meats, and Traminer, straw yellow in color, has a distinctive aroma and is served with fish. A Pinot Bianco, straw yellow with greenish glints, has a light bouquet and a noble history, and is also served with fish.

The wines of **Lombardy (Milan)** are justly renowned, and if you don't believe me, would you then take the advice of Leonardo da Vinci, Pliny, and Virgil? These great men have sung the praise of this wine-rich region which is bordered by the Alps to the north and the Po River to the south. To go with the tasty, refined cuisine of the Lombard kitchen, add such wines as Frecciarossa (a pale straw yellow in color with a delicate bouquet; order with fish), Sassella (bright ruby-red in color; order with game, red meat, and roasts), and the amusingly named Inferno (a deep ruby-red in color with a penetrating bouquet; order with meats).

The finest wines in Italy, mostly red, are said to be produced on the vine-clad slopes of the **Piedmont** district (Turin), the word translated literally as "at the foot of the mountain." Of course, Asti Spumante, the color of straw with an abundant champagnelike foam, is considered the prototype of Italian sparkling wines. While traveling through this area of northwestern Italy, you'll want to sample Barbaresco (brilliant ruby-red with a delicate flavor; order with red meats), Barolo (also brilliant ruby-red, best when it mellows into a velvety old age), Cortese (pale straw yellow with green glints; order with fish), and Gattinara (an intense ruby-red beauty in youth that changes with age). Piedmont is also the home of Vermouth, a white wine to which aromatic herbs and spices, among other ingredients, have been added. It's served as an apéritif.

Liguria, which includes Genoa and the Italian Riviera, doesn't have as many wine-growing regions as other parts of Italy, yet produces dozens of different grapes. These are made into such wines as Dolceacqua (lightish ruby-red, served with hearty food) and Vermentino Ligure (a pale yellow in color with a good bouquet; often served with fish).

The wines of **Sardinia** are usually heavy, but many find them satisfying. They include Canonau, a light garnet-red color, served with desserts; Vermentino di Gallura, straw yellow in color, produced in both dry and sweet varieties; and one of the several versions of Torbato, classified as extra, passito, and secco.

The wines of **Sicily,** called a "paradise of the grape," were extolled by the ancient poets, including Martial. Caesar himself lavished praise on Mamertine when it was served at a banquet honoring his third consulship. Marsala, of course, an amber-yellow wine served with desserts, is the most famous wine of Sicily. It's velvety and fruity and is sometimes used in cooking, as in veal marsala. The wines made from grapes grown in the volcanic soil of Etna come in both red and white varieties. Try also the Corvo Bianco di Casteldaccia (straw yellow in color, with a distinctive bouquet) and the Corvo Rosso di Casteldaccia (ruby-red in color, almost garnet in tone, full-bodied and fruity).

I've only cited a few popular wines. Rest assured that there are hundreds more you may want to discover for yourself.

OTHER DRINKS Italians drink other libations as well. Perhaps their most famous drink is **Campari,** bright red in color and herb flavored, with a quinine bitterness to it. It's customary to serve it with ice cubes and soda.

Beer is also made in Italy and, in general, it is lighter than that served in Germany. If you order beer in a bar or restaurant, chances are it will be an imported beer, for which you will be charged accordingly unless you specify otherwise. Some famous names in European beer making now operate plants in Italy where the brew has been "adjusted" to Italian taste.

High-proof **Grappa** is made from the "leftovers" after the grapes have been pressed. Many Italians drink this before or after dinner (some put it into their coffee). To an untrained foreign palate, it often appears rough and harsh. Some say it's an acquired taste.

Italy has many **brandies** (according to an agreement with France, it is not supposed to use the word "cognac" in labeling them). A popular one is Vecchia Romagna.

Other popular drinks include several **liqueurs,** to which the Italians are addicted. Try herb-flavored Strega, or perhaps an Amaretto tasting of almonds. One of the best known is Maraschino, taking its name from a type of cherry used in its preparation. Galliano is also herb flavored, and Sambucca (anisette) is made of aniseed and is often served with a "fly" (coffee bean) in it. On a hot day, an Italian orders a vermouth, Cinzano, with a twist of lemon, ice cubes, and a squirt of soda water.

6. RECOMMENDED BOOKS, FILMS & RECORDINGS

BOOKS

GENERAL & HISTORY

Luigi Barzini's *The Italians* (Macmillan, 1964) should almost be required reading for anyone contemplating a trip to Italy. The section on Sicily alone is worth the price of the book. Critics have hailed it as the liveliest analysis yet of the Italian character.

Edward Gibbon's *The History of the Decline and Fall of the Roman Empire* is published in six volumes, but Penguin issues a passable abridgment. Gibbon issued the first volume in 1776. It has been hailed as a masterpiece and considered one of the greatest histories ever written. No one has ever recaptured the saga of the glory that was Rome the way that Gibbon did.

Giuliano Procacci surveys the spectrum in his *History of the Italian People* (Harper & Row, 1973), which provides an encompassing look at how Italy became a nation.

If you like your history short, readable, and condensed, try *A Short History of Italy,* edited by H. Hearder and D. P. Waley (Cambridge University Press, 1963).

One of the best books on the long history of the papacy—detailing its excesses, its triumphs and its defeats, and its most vivid characters—is Michael Walsh's *An*

IMPRESSIONS

Whoever seeks to convince instead of persuade an Italian will find he has been employed in a Sisyphean labour; the stone may roll to the top, but is sure to return and rest at his feet who had courage to try the experiment. Logic is a science they love not, and, I think, steadily refuse to cultivate; nor is arguement a style of conversation they naturally affect.
—HESTER LYNCH THRALE/PIOZZI, *OBSERVATIONS AND REFLECTIONS IN THE COURSE OF A JOURNEY,* 1789

Illustrated History of the Popes: Saint Peter to John Paul II (St. Martin's Press, 1980).

The roots of modern Italy are explored in Christopher Hibbert's *Garibaldi and His Enemies: The Clash of Arms and Personalities in the Making of Italy* (Penguin, 1989).

In the 20th century, the most fascinating period in Italian history was the rise and fall of Fascism, as detailed in countless works. Try Vittorio De Fiori's *Mussolini, The Man of Destiny: Studies in Fascism, Ideology and Practice* (AMS Press, 1982). One of the best and most recent biographies of Il Duce is Denis M. Smith's *Mussolini: A Biography* (Random House, 1983). Eugen Weber writes of *Varieties of Fascism: Doctrines of Revolution in the Twentieth Century* (Krieger, 1982). Stein Larsen edited *Who Were the Fascists? Social Roots of European Fascism* (Oxford University Press, 1981).

One subject that's always engrossing is the Mafia, and that sinister organization is detailed in Pino Arlacchi's *Mafia Business: The Mafia Ethnic and the Spirit of Capitalism* (Routledge, Chapman, & Hall, 1987). The Mafia from yet another point of view is described in Norman Lewis's *The Honoured Society: The Sicilian Mafia Observed* (Hippocrene Books, 1985).

William Murray's *The Last Italian: Portrait of a People* (Prentice Hall, 1991) is the writer's second volume of essays on his favorite subject—Italy, its people and civilization. *The New York Times* called it "partly a lover's keen, observant diary of his affair."

ART & ARCHITECTURE

Michael Baxandall provides a primer in the social history of the pictorial style in *Painting & Experience in Fifteenth Century Italy* (Oxford University Press, 1988).

In art, the Renaissance period in Italy seems to capture the public's imagination more than any other time, and one of the best accounts is provided in Peter Murray's *The Architecture of the Italian Renaissance* (Schocken, 1986). The same subject is covered by Frederick N. Hartt in his *History of Italian Renaissance Painting* (Abrams, 1987).

Giorgio Vasari's *The Lives of the Most Eminent Italian Architects, Painters, and Sculptors* was originally published in 1550 and was enlarged in 1568. In spite of some fanciful inventions, it remains the definitive work on Renaissance artists, from Cimabue to Michelangelo. Penguin Classics issues a paperback abridged version, called *Lives of the Artists* (1985).

Michael Levey has produced two engrossing books: *Early Renaissance* (Penguin, 1967) and *High Renaissance* (Penguin, 1975) both available in paperback. From a somewhat scholarly point of view, J. R. Hale edited the *Concise Encyclopedia of the Italian Renaissance* (Thames & Hudson, 1981), an exemplary reference book.

T. W. Potter provides one of the best accounts of *Roman Italy* (University of California Press, 1987), which is also illustrated.

Rudolf Wittkower covers *Art and Architecture in Italy 1600–1750* (Penguin, 1980) rather exhaustively.

FICTION & BIOGRAPHY

Both foreign and domestic writers have tried to capture the peculiar nature of Italy—each seen from a completely different angle—in such notable works as Thomas Mann's *Death in Venice* (Random House, 1965); E. M. Forster's *Room with a View* (Random House, 1923), the subject of a famous movie in the 1980s, and Ernest Hemingway's *A Farewell to Arms* (Macmillan, 1929), which remains one of the most enduring novels of World War I. Fred M. Stewart's books are so popular they're sold in supermarkets, and he spins a lively tale in his *Century* (NAL, 1981), tracing the saga of several generations of an Italian family.

All sorts of adventure and mystery novels use the rich, florid background of Italy as a setting for their thrillers—notably Daphne Du Maurier's *The Flight of the Falcon* (Avon, 1965), Ann Cornelisen's *Any Four Women Could Rob the Bank of Italy* (Penguin, 1984), and Helen MacInnes's *The Venetian Affair* (Fawcett, 1963).

John Hersey's Pulitzer Prize winner *A Bell for Adano* (Knopf, 1944) has now entered the realm of a classic and is frequently reprinted. It is a well-written and disturbing story of the American invasion of Italy.

Benvenuto Cellini's *Autobiography,* also available in Penguin Classics, was first printed in Italy in 1728, although Cellini lived from 1500 to 1571. It's a Renaissance romp, filled with gossip and interesting details, so much so that it has been compared to a novel. It launched the tide of the romantic movement.

Irving Stone's *Agony and Ecstasy* (Doubleday, 1961), which was filmed with Charlton Heston playing Michelangelo, is the easiest to read and the most pop version of the life of this great artist. Yet it contains much useful information, with a rather brilliant section on the creation of Michelangelo's most famous statue, *David.*

Dante's *The Divine Comedy* is famed throughout the world. It is a brilliant synthesis of the medieval Christian world view. *The Inferno* in Volume I was issued by Penguin in 1984, and *Purgatory* in Volume II was published by Penguin in 1985.

Giovanni Boccaccio (1313–75) has delighted readers ever since the publication of his *Decameron* (Norton, 1983), a collection of romantic and often racy tales.

Giorgio Bassani, born in 1916, provides the bourgeois milieu of a Ferrara Jewish community under Mussolini in *The Garden of the Finzi-Contini* (Harcourt Brace Jovanovich, 1977).

The novels of Alberto Moravia, born in 1907, are classified as Neo-Realism. Moravia is one of the best-known Italian writers read in English. Notable works include *Roman Tales* (Farrar, Straus, and Cudahy, 1957), *The Woman of Rome* (Penguin, 1957; also available in the Playboy paperback series), and *The Conformist* (Greenwood Press, 1975).

When Giuseppe Tomasi Di Lampedusa (1896–1957) began meditating on the effects of the unification of Italy on his native Sicily, the result was *The Leopard* (Collins, 1958), a novel published posthumously and later made into a film starring Burt Lancaster.

First published in 1959, when it caused a scandal, Pier Paolo Pasolini's *A Violent Life* (Pantheon Books, 1991) is a novel written by the controversial filmmaker. Once viewed with disdain, it is now considered a classic of postwar Italian fiction.

One of the best of the recent novelists of Italy is Leonardo Sciascia (1912–89), who used Sicily as his "metaphor of the world." One critic said he "redefined" the historical novel. Works include *Sicilian Uncles* (Carcanet, 1986) and *The Wine Dark Sea* (Carcanet, 1985).

One of the best-read novels of the 1980s was Umberto Eco's *The Name of the Rose* (Warner Books, 1986), a sort of monastic detective story.

For the most recent look at one of the movers and shakers in Italy, read Alan Friedman's *Agnelli and the Network of Italian Power* (Harrap, 1989).

TRAVEL

H. V. Morton's *A Traveler in Italy* (Methuen, 1964) is a towering work by one of the world's most widely read travel writers who has a rare sense of history and is at his best in describing great centers of culture such as Florence and Venice.

Many great writers—when faced with the challenge of Italy—decided to become travel writers. These have included Charles Dickens who wrote *Pictures from Italy* (Ecco Press, 1988), a classic 19th-century account of the Grand Tour, going from Tuscany to Naples via Rome. Wolfgang Goethe's *Italian Journey* (Penguin, 1982) devotes more attention to Roman antiquities, and Henry James's *Italian Hours* (1909) is young James at his best, capturing the special atmosphere of Italy. It is currently issued by Ecco Press.

D. H. Lawrence and Italy (Viking Press, 1972) is three classic Italian travelogs collected in a single volume which includes *Sea and Sardinia* and *Twilight in Italy.* It also includes *Etruscan Places,* which was published posthumously. Lawrence writes of a way of life that was disappearing even as he wrote the work.

Mary McCarthy gave Italian travel literature two distinguished works, *The Stones of Florence* (Harcourt Brace Jovanovich, 1959) and *Venice Observed* (Penguin, 1972). "The lady of the barbs" pulls no punches in observing these two famed tourist meccas with a sharp eye for detail. These two works were definitely researched on the streets and not in some library.

Kate Simon's *Italy: The Places in Between* (Harper & Row, 1960), explores a lot of the towns overlooked as one races between Rome, Florence, and Venice, including Ferrara, Gubbio, Spoleto, and Padua.

ABOUT FLORENCE   The city of the Renaissance is one of the most written about in the world—from many points of view. Peter Burke's *Culture and Society in Renaissance Italy 1420–1540* received acclaim (published in London by Batsford, 1972, it's often available in libraries). Florence is a backdrop for much of R. Couglan's *The Life and Times of Michelangelo 1475–1564* (Time-Life International, 1975).

J. H. Phumb wrote *The Penguin Book of the Renaissance* (Penguin, 1964), which offers a lively account of the era, as does B. Pullan's *A History of Early Renaissance Art* (St. Martin's Press, 1972). N. Rubinstein also provides an interesting portrait of those patrons of the arts, the Medicis, in *The Government of Florence Under the Medici 1434–1494* (Oxford University Press, 1966).

ABOUT VENICE   Other than London, Venice is perhaps one of the most written about cities in the world. John Ruskin wrote a definitive version in his *The Stones of Venice,* first published in 1853 and in print by Little Boston (1981). Although Ruskin may have come to Venice to debunk (he, for example, found San Giorgio Maggiore "contemptible"), his work has many notable sections, including "The Nature of Gothic."

Peter Lauritzen published *Venice, a Thousand Years of Culture and Civilization* (Atheneum, 1978), and John J. Norwich traces a *History of Venice* (Knopf, 1982). Oliver Logan's *Culture and Society in Venice 1470–1790* is a well-researched work, often available in libraries (London: Batsford, 1972).

A more recent work is George Bull's *Venice, the Most Triumphant City* (St. Martin's, 1982).

FILMS

Italian films have never regained the glory enjoyed in the postwar era. The "golden oldies" are still the best (often found in the classics section of your local video store and still shown on TV).

Roberto Rossellini's *Rome, Open City* (1946) influenced Hollywood's *films noirs* of the late 1940s. Set in a poor section of occupied Rome, the film tells the story of a partisan priest and a Communist who aid the resistance.

Vittorio De Sica's *Bicycle Thief* (1948) achieved world renown. Also set in one of Rome's poor districts, it tells of the destruction of a child's illusions and the solitude of a steel worker.

The Leopard (1963), set in Sicily, gained a world audience for Luchino Visconti and was the first major Italian film made in color. Visconti first came to the attention of cinema audiences with his 1942 *Ossessione* (Obsession).

Frederico Fellini burst into Italian cinema with his highly individual style, beginning with *La Strada* (1954) and going on to such classics as *Juliet of the Spirits* (1965), *Amarcord* (1974), and *The City of Women* (1980). *La Dolce Vita* (1961) helped to define an era.

Marxist, homosexual, and practicing Catholic, Pier Paolo Pasolini was the most controversial of Italian film makers until his mysterious murder in 1975. Explicit sex scenes in *Decameron* (1971) made it a world box-office hit.

Bernardo Bertolucci, once an assistant to Pasolini, achieved fame with such films as *The Conformist* (1970), based on the novel by Moravia. His *1900* is an epic spanning 20th-century Italian history and politics. One of his biggest international films was *Last Tango in Paris* (1971), starring Marlon Brando.

Michelangelo Antonioni swept across the screens of the world with his films of psychological anguish, including *La Notta* (1961), *L'Avventura* (1964), and *The Red Desert* (1964).

A Neapolitan director, Francesco Rosi became known for semidocumentary films, exploring such subjects as the Mafia in *Salvatore Giuliano* (1962) and the army in *Just*

Another War (1970). His *Three Brothers* (1980) examines three different political attitudes, as the brothers have a reunion at their mother's funeral in Apulia.

Current Italian directors include the Taviani brothers. Their *Padre Padrone* (1977) takes place in Sardinia and their *Kaos* (1984) is set in Sicily and is an adaptation of a Pirandello story. Their late '80s film, *Good Morning, Babylon,* brought them worldwide acclaim.

Although directors more than stars have dominated Italian cinema, three actors have emerged to gain worldwide fame, including Marcello Mastroianni, star of such hits as *La Dolce Vita* (1961), and Sophia Loren, whose best film is considered *Two Women* (1961). Mastroianni was Fellini's favorite male actor and he starred him once again in 8½.

Anna Magnani not only starred in Italian films, but made many American films as well, including *The Rose Tattoo* (1955), with Burt Lancaster, and *The Fugitive Kind* (1960), with Marlon Brando.

RECORDINGS

MEDIEVAL & RENAISSANCE MUSIC

Although the medieval Benedictine, Guido Monaco of Arezzo, was a musical theorist rather than a composer, his notational system was widely adopted by monasteries throughout medieval Italy. A recording that might expose you to the fruit of his labors is *Sunday Vespers/Vespers of the Madonna,* recorded by S. Giorgio Maggiore Schola Choir, G. Ernetti, conductor (Cetra Records LPU 0046). Religious music was greatly enhanced several centuries later by the compositions of Palestrina, whose work is admirably recorded in *Missa de Beata Virgine (Three Motets),* sung by the Spandauer Kantorei, conducted by Martin Behrmann (Turnabout TV 34-309).

Very few (if any) recordings of what is regarded as the world's first opera *Dafne* are easily available, but a more popular choral work by the same Renaissance composer, Jacopo Peri, is *Euridice,* sung by the Milan Polyphonic Chorus (I Solisti di Milano), conducted by Angelo Ephrikian (Orpheus Recordings OR 344-345-S).

One well-received interpretation of Monteverdi's famous choral work *L'Incoronazione di Poppea* was recorded by the Concentus Musicus Wien, conducted by Nicholas Harnoncourt (Telefunken 6.35-247 HB). By the same composer, but in a different genre, is Monteverdi's *Seventh Book of Madrigals,* sung by an Italian vocal quartet known as the Ensemble Concerto (Tactus TAC 560 31103).

An excellent collection of the late Renaissance's sonatas, canzonettas, and madrigals, played on original Renaissance instruments, is entitled *Music from the Time of Guido Reni* (Guido Reni, born 1575 and died 1642, was a Renaissance painter who probably caused more public discord because of his philandering and political intrigues than any other in Italian history. He was eventually exiled from Rome in 1622.) This particular musical collection of works by this artist's musical contemporaries was recorded by the Aurora Ensemble (Tactus TAC 56012001).

A good collection of Italian cantatas composed by masters of the 18th century is *Il Lamento d'Olympia.* This includes vocal selections by Scarlatti and Bononcini, sung by mezzo-soprano Gloria Banditelli (Tactus TAC 67012001).

ORCHESTRAL & OPERATIC WORKS

The musical output of Italian composers greatly increased, and its orchestration grew more complex, beginning around 1700. One excellent (and exhaustive) overview of the work of Corelli is his *Complete Works,* recorded by the Academia Byzantina, conducted by Carlo Chiarappa (Europa Musica Eur 350-202).

Italy has produced stellar virtuoso performers who have become world-class experts on specific instruments, changing forever the way that instrument is perceived and played. (Paganini, born 1782, on his violin; Bottesini, born 1821, on his double bass; and Cherubini, born 1760, on his harpsichord are good examples.) Bottesini's *Virtuoso Works for Double-Bass and Strings,* performed by I Solisti Agilani and conducted by Vittorio Antonelli (Nuova Era NUO 6810) might be one of the finest showcases for the not frequently showcased double bass anywhere. Cherubini's

Harpsichord Sonatas Nos. 1–6, performed by Laura Alvini, provides a highly genteel and attractively restrained insight into the work of a conservative Italian classicist who served for several years as court composer to King George III of England.

The best way for most novices to begin an appreciation of opera is to hear an assemblage of great moments of opera accumulated onto one record. A good example contains works by the most evocative and dramatic singer who ever hit a high "C" on the operatic stage, Maria Callas. *La Voce: Historic Recordings of the Great Diva* (Suite SUI 5002) brings together "La Callas's" spectacular arias from *Lucia di Lammermoor, La Traviata, Norma,* and *The Barber of Seville.*

Recordings of complete and unedited operas are even more rewarding: Excellent examples include the following: Bellini's *Norma,* featuring the divine and legendary Maria Callas, accompanied by the Orchestra and the Chorus of Milan's La Scala, is considered one of the world's great operatic events; Tullio Serafin conducts (Angel Records 3517C/ANG 35148-35150). Giuseppe Verdi's genius can be appreciated through *Nabucco,* performed with Placido Domingo by the Rydl Choir and Orchestra of the Dutch National Opera, conducted by Giuseppe Sinopoli (Deutsche Gramophone DDD 410 512-2-GH2). Also insightful for the vocal techniques of Verdi are his *Complete Songs,* recorded by Renata Scotto (soprano) and Paolo Washington (bass), accompanied by Vicenzo Scalera (piano) (Nuova Era NUO 6855). Rossini's great opera *Il Barbiere di Siviglia* and Puccini's *Tosca,* both recorded in their complete versions by the Turin Opera Orchestra and Chorus, are both conducted by Bruno Campanella (Nuova Era NUO 6760 and Foyer FOY 2023, respectively).

RECENT RELEASES

Only a handful of other countries can compete with Italy for richness of popular musical traditions. Although these traditions have been influenced by popular music from the U.S. and Britain, Italy still retains its distinctive musical flair. Some good examples of the peninsula's (musical) charm can be heard on recordings which include *Musical Greetings from Italy;* this tuneful collection of Italian folk and folk-dance music is played by the Nordini Musette Orchestra (Standard Colonial Records COL 808). Specific regions of Italy are featured on other recordings, which include *From Sicily with Love (Favorite Sicilian Songs),* sung by local singers and recorded in Italy (Philips 4118); from Tuscany comes *Le Canzoni di Firenze (Traditional Songs of Florence),* by Odoardo Spadaro (RCA NL33027).

Within the field of jazz, Italy also competes effectively. Recorded in Milan, Chet Baker and Italian-born Mike Melillo, with an assemblage of Italian backup musicians, perform a haunting combination of piano and horn on *Symphonically* (Soul Note SN 11 34C). Another notable recording is the *Twin Peaks Soundtrack* by Italian native Angelo Badalamenti and David Lynch. Despite its original destiny as the musical accompaniment for a film, it survives beautifully without its cinematic visuals. It features what was described by critics as a "magical arrangemental blend" including lazy saxophone tracts imposed over finger-snapping rhythms (Warner Bros 7599-26316-1).

Italian pop is well defended in Alice Elisir's album *Alice Elisir* (EMI 64/74-87-014). Her torchy voice and upbeat modern tempos and arrangements evoke fire, tears, and laughter. Nino Buonocore is Italy's latest emotional heartthrob, bringing a brooding and undeniably sexy male charm to *Le Cite Tra Le Mani* (EMI 64/79-02-044). Finally, an album well suited to appeal to both Italian and American audiences is Jerry Vale's *Italian Album,* sung by Italian-American Jerry Vale and including such smile-inducing standbys as "Amore scusa mi" and "Oh Marie" (Columbia C12 30389).

CHAPTER 2

PLANNING A TRIP TO ITALY

1. **INFORMATION, ENTRY REQUIREMENTS & MONEY**
- **WHAT THINGS COST IN ROME**
- **WHAT THINGS COST IN NAPLES**
2. **WHEN TO GO— CLIMATE, HOLIDAYS & EVENTS**
- **ITALY CALENDAR OF EVENTS**
- **ROME CALENDAR OF EVENTS**
3. **HEALTH & INSURANCE**
4. **WHAT TO PACK**
5. **TIPS FOR THE DISABLED, SENIORS, SINGLES, FAMILIES & STUDENTS**
6. **ALTERNATIVE/ ADVENTURE TRAVEL**
7. **GETTING THERE**
- **FROMMER'S SMART TRAVELER: AIRFARES**
8. **GETTING AROUND**
- **SUGGESTED ITINERARIES**
9. **WHERE TO STAY**
10. **WHERE TO DINE**
11. **WHAT TO BUY**
- **FAST FACTS: ITALY**

This chapter is devoted to the where, when, and how of your trip—the advance-planning issues required to get it together and take on the road.

After deciding where to go, most people have two fundamental questions: What will it cost? and How do I get there? This chapter will answer both these questions and also resolve other important issues such as when to go, what pretrip preparations are needed, where to obtain more information about the destination, and much more.

1. INFORMATION, ENTRY REQUIREMENTS & MONEY

INFORMATION

Tourist information may be obtained by writing directly (in English or Italian) to the provincial or local tourist boards of the places concerned. These provincial tourist boards (known as **Ente Provinciale per il Turismo**) operate in the principal towns of the provinces. The local tourist boards (known as **Azienda Autonoma Soggiorno**) operate in all places of tourist interest, and a list can be obtained from the Italian government tourist offices.

ENTRY REQUIREMENTS

U.S., Canadian, British, Australian, New Zealand, and Irish citizens with a valid passport do not need a visa to enter Italy if they do not expect to stay more than 90 days and do not expect to work there. Those who, after entering Italy, find that they would like to stay more than 90 days, can apply for a permit for an additional stay of 90 days, which as a rule is granted immediately.

MONEY

There are no restrictions as to how much foreign currency you can bring into Italy, although visitors should declare the amount brought in. This proves to the Italian Customs Office that the currency came from outside the country and therefore the same amount or less can be taken out. Italian currency taken into or out of Italy may not exceed 200,000 lire in denominations of 50,000 lire or lower.

The basic unit of Italian currency is the **lira** (plural: **lire**). Because of fluctuations in relative values of world currencies, I suggest that you get in touch with any bank for the latest official exchange rate before going to Italy.

Coins are issued in denominations of 10, 20, 100, 500, and 1,000 lire, and bills come in denominations of 1,000 lire, 5,000 lire, 10,000 lire, 100,000 lire, and 500,000 lire.

For the best exchange rate, go to a bank, not to hotels or shops. Currency and traveler's checks (for which you'll receive a better rate than cash) can be changed at the airport and some travel agencies, such as American Express and Thomas Cook. Note the rates; it can sometimes pay to shop around.

TRAVELER'S CHECKS

Traveler's checks are the safest way to carry cash while traveling. Most banks will give you a better rate on traveler's checks than for cash. The following are the major issuers of traveler's checks:

American Express (tel. toll free 800/221-7282 in the U.S. and Canada) charges a 1% commission. Checks are free to members of the American Automobile Association.

Bank of America (tel. toll free 800/227-3460 in the U.S. or 415/624-5400, collect, in Canada) issues checks in U.S. dollars for a 1% commission everywhere but California.

THE LIRE & THE DOLLAR

At this writing $1 = approximately 1,275 lire, and this was the rate of exchange used to calculate the dollar values given in this book (rounded to the nearest nickel). This rate fluctuates from day to day and may not be the same when you travel to Italy. Therefore the following table should be used only as a general guideline.

Lire	U.S.$	Lire	U.S.$
50	.04	15,000	11.75
100	.08	20,000	15.70
300	.24	25,000	19.65
500	.39	30,000	23.55
700	.55	35,000	27.45
1,000	.79	40,000	31.40
1,500	1.18	45,000	35.35
2,000	1.55	50,000	39.25
3,000	2.35	100,000	78.50
4,000	3.15	125,000	98.15
5,000	3.95	150,000	117.75
6,000	4.70	200,000	157.00
7,500	5.90	250,000	196.25
10,000	7.85	500,000	392.50

Citicorp (tel. toll free 800/645-6556 in the U.S. or 813/623-1709, collect, in Canada) issues checks in U.S. dollars, pounds, or German marks.

MasterCard International (tel. toll free 800/223-9920 in the U.S., or 212/974-5696, collect, in Canada) issues checks in about a dozen currencies.

Barclays Bank (tel. toll free 800/221-2426 in the U.S. and Canada) issues checks in both U.S. and Canadian dollars and British pounds.

Thomas Cook (tel. toll free 800/223-7373 in the U.S., or 212/974-5696, collect, in Canada) issues checks in U.S. or Canadian dollars or British pounds. It's affiliated with MasterCard.

Each of these agencies will refund your checks if they are lost or stolen, provided you produce sufficient documentation. When purchasing checks ask about refund hotlines; American Express and Bank of America have the greatest number of offices around the world.

CURRENCY EXCHANGE

Many hotels in Italy will simply not accept a dollar-denominated check, and if they do, they'll certainly charge for the conversion. In some cases they'll accept counter-signed traveler's checks, or a credit card, but if you're prepaying a deposit on hotel reservations, it's cheaper and easier to pay with a check drawn upon an Italian bank.

This can be arranged by a large commercial bank or by a specialist like **Ruesch International,** 1350 Eye Street, Washington, DC, 20005 (tel. 202/408-1200, or toll free 800/424-2923), which performs a wide variety of conversion-related tasks, usually for only $2 U.S. per transaction.

WHAT THINGS COST IN ROME	U.S. $
Taxi (from the central rail station to piazza di Spagna)	6.00
Subway or public bus (from any point within Rome to any other point)	.65
Local telephone call	.15
Double room at the Hassler (deluxe)	439.60
Double room at the Columbus (moderate)	164.85
Double room at the Hotel Portoghesi (budget)	90.30
Continental breakfast (cappuccino and croissant at most cafés and bars)	1.75
Lunch for one at Da Pancrazio (moderate)	28.25
Lunch for one at del Giglio (budget)	19.65
Dinner for one, without wine, at Relais de Jardin (deluxe)	86.35
Dinner for one, without wine, at Eau Vive (moderate)	35.35
Dinner for one, without wine, at Colline Emiliane (budget)	29.05
Pint of beer	3.75
Glass of wine	1.45
Coca-Cola	1.25
Cup of coffee	.75
Roll of color film, 36 exposures	5.80
Admission to the Vatican Museums and Sistine Chapel	6.30
Movie ticket	6.55
Theater ticket at the Terme di Caracalla	35.00

WHAT THINGS COST IN NAPLES	U.S. $
Taxi (from the rail station to the port)	7.20
Public bus	.72
Local telephone call	.15
Double room at the Excelsior (deluxe)	232.35
Double room at the Jolly (moderate)	149.15
Double room at the Rex (budget)	74.60
Continental breakfast (cappuccino and croissant)	1.35
Lunch for one at Giuseppone a Mare (moderate)	25.90
Lunch for one at Brandi (budget)	22.00
Dinner for one, without wine, at La Sacrestia (deluxe)	74.60
Dinner for one, without wine, at Don Salvatore (moderate)	31.40
Dinner for one, without wine, at Dante e Beatrice (budget)	22.75
Pint of beer	3.50
Glass of wine	1.25
Coca-Cola	1.10
Cup of coffee (cappuccino)	.65
Roll of color film, 36 exposures	5.60
Admission to the Museo Nazionale Archeologico	4.70

If you need a check payable in lire, call Ruesch's toll-free number, describe what you need, and note the transaction number given to you. Mail your dollar-denominated personal check (payable to Ruesch International) to their office in Washington, D.C. Upon receipt, the company will mail a check denominated in lire for the financial equivalent, minus the $2 charge. The company also sells traveler's checks denominated in lire, and can help you with many different kinds of wire transfers and conversion of VAT (Value-Added Tax) refund checks. They'll mail brochures and information packets upon request.

2. WHEN TO GO — CLIMATE, HOLIDAYS & EVENTS

CLIMATE

It's warm all over Italy in summer. The high temperatures (measured in degrees Celsius) begin in Rome in May, often lasting until some time in October. Rome experiences its lowest average monthly temperatures in January, 49°F; its highest in July, 82°F.

Winters in the north of Italy are cold with rain and snow, but in the south the weather is warm all year, averaging 50°F in winter (summers tend to be very hot, especially inland).

For the most part, it is drier in Italy than in North America. High temperatures, therefore, don't seem as bad since the humidity is lower. In Rome, Naples, and the south, temperatures can stay in the 90s for days, but nights are most often comfortably cooler.

Italy's Average Temperatures & Rainfall

		Jan	Feb	Mar	Apr	May	June	July	Aug	Sept	Oct	Nov	Dec
FLORENCE	Temp. (°F)	45	47	50	60	67	75	77	70	64	63	55	46
	Rainfall "	3	3.3	3.7	2.7	2.2	1.4	1.4	2.7	3.2	4.9	3.8	2.9
NAPLES	Temp. (°F)	50	54	58	63	70	75	83	79	74	66	60	52
	Rainfall "	4.7	4	3	3.8	2.4	.8	.8	2.6	3.5	5.8	5.1	3.7
ROME	Temp. (°F)	49	52	57	62	70	77	82	78	73	65	56	47
	Rainfall "	2.3	1.5	2.9	3.0	2.8	2.9	1.5	1.9	2.8	2.6	3.0	2.1
VENICE	Temp. (°F)	43	48	53	60	67	72	77	74	68	60	54	44
	Rainfall "	2.3	1.5	2.9	3.0	2.8	2.9	1.5	1.9	2.8	2.6	3.0	2.1

HOLIDAYS

Offices and shops in Italy are closed on the following dates: January 1 (New Year's Day), Easter Monday, April 25 (Liberation Day), May 1 (Labor Day), August 15 (Assumption of the Virgin), November 1 (All Saints' Day), December 8 (Feast of the Immaculate Conception), December 25 (Christmas Day), and December 26 (Santo Stefano).

Closings are also observed in the following cities on feast days honoring their patron saints: Venice, April 25 (St. Mark); Florence, Genoa, and Turin, June 24 (St. John the Baptist); Palermo, July 15 (Santa Rosalia); Naples, September 19 (St. Gennaro); Bologna, October 4 (St. Petronio); Cagliari, October 30 (St. Saturnino); Trieste, November 3 (San Giusto); Bari, December 6 (St. Nicola); and Milan, December 7 (St. Ambrose).

ITALY
CALENDAR OF EVENTS

For more information about these and other events, contact the various tourist offices throughout Italy. Dates often vary from year to year.

JANUARY

☐ **Viareggio Carnival,** highlight of the Tuscan Riviera, with fireworks, pageants, parades, and a flower show. Dates vary.

☐ **Epiphany Celebrations,** when all cities, towns, and villages in Italy stage Roman Catholic Epiphany observances (usually January 5–6). One of the most festive celebrations is the Epiphany Fair at Rome's piazza Navona.

☐ **Festival of Italian Popular Song,** a 3-day festival taking place in late January at San Remo (the Italian Riviera). Major artists perform the latest Italian song releases.

☐ **Foire de Saint Ours,** Aosta, Val d'Aosta, in late January has been a tradition for 10 centuries. Artisans from the mountain valleys come together to display their wares—often made of wood, lace, wool, or wrought iron—created during the long winter months.

FEBRUARY

✪ *CARNEVALE IN VENICE* *Carnevale is a riotous time in Venice. Theatrical presentations and masked balls cap the festivities.*
Where: Throughout Venice and on the islands in the lagoon. When: The week before Lent. How: The balls are by invitation, but the street events and fireworks are open to everyone. More information is available from the Venice Tourist Office, San Marco Ascensione 71C (tel. 041/5226356).

MARCH

☐ **Good Friday Processions,** usually the end of March, are held throughout Italy. The most notable one is in Rome (see "Rome Calendar of Events," below).

APRIL

☐ **Scoppio del Carro** (Explosion of the Cart), on Easter Sunday in Florence, is an ancient observance: a cart laden with flowers and fireworks is drawn by three white oxen to the Duomo where at noon mass a mechanical dove detonates it from the altar.

☐ **Easter Week** observances throughout Italy begin 4 days before Easter Sunday. Processions and age-old ceremonies—some from pagan days, some from the Middle Ages—are staged. The best are in Sicily.

MAY

✪ *MAGGIO MUSICALE ("Musical May")* *Italy's oldest and most prestigious festival takes place in Florence, the venue for opera, ballet performances, and concerts.*
Where: Various locations, including piazza della Signoria and the Pitti Palace courtyard. When: Often from late April into July. How: Schedule and ticket information available from Maggio Musicale Fiorentino, Teatro Comunale, Corso Italia, Firenze 50123 (tel. 055/2779236).

☐ **La Corsa dei Ceri,** at Gubbio, honors patron saint, Ubaldo, on May 15, a procession of Brobdingnagian candles to the top of Mount Ingino.

JUNE

☐ **L'Infiorata,** Genzano, Lazio, is a religious procession along streets carpeted with flowers in splendid designs, often copies of famous artworks. Details available from Azienda Autonoma di Soggiorno e Turismo dei Laghi e Castelli Romani, via Olivella 2, Albano Laziale 00041 (tel. 06/9305798).

☐ **San Ranieri e Gioco del Ponte,** Pisa, is the night (June 16) when Pisa honors its own saint, with candlelit parades followed the next day by eight-rower teams in 16th-century costumes competing.

✪ *FESTIVAL DEI DUE MONDI,* *dating from 1957, the creation of Maestro Gian Carlo Menotti. International performers convene for 3 weeks of dance, drama, opera, concerts, and art exhibits.*
Where: Spoleto, an Umbrian hill town north of Rome. When: Begins mid-June and lasts 3 weeks. How: Tickets and information available from Festival dei Due Mondi, via Beccaria 18, Roma 00195 (tel. 06/3210288).

JULY

⊕ *IL PALIO* *Palio fever grips the Tuscan hill town of Siena for a wild and exciting horse race from the Middle Ages. Pageantry, costumes, and the celebrations of the victorious contrada mark the well-attended spectacle. It's a "no rules" event: Even a horse without a rider can finish in the money.*
Where: The piazza del Campo at Siena. When: July 2 to August 16. How: Details available by writing Autonoma di Soggiorno e Turismo, via di Città 43, Siena 53100 (tel. 0577/42209).

☐ **Arena of Outdoor Opera Season** brings cultural buffs to the 20,000-seat Roman amphitheater at Verona. Season lasts from early July to mid-August.
☐ **La Festa del Redentore** (The Feast of the Redeemer), in Venice, marks the lifting of the plague in July of 1578. Fireworks, pilgrimages, and boating on the lagoon mark this event between the third Saturday and Sunday in July.
☐ **Festival Internazionale di Musica Antica**, Urbino, is a cultural extravaganza, as international performers converge on Raphael's birthplace. It is the most important Renaissance and baroque music festival in Italy. Annually in late July. Details available from the Società Italiana del Flauto Dolce, via Confalonieri 5, Roma 00195 (tel. 06/354441).

AUGUST

⊕ *VENICE INTERNATIONAL FILM FESTIVAL* *Ranking after Cannes, this film festival at Venice brings together stars, directors, producers, and filmmakers from all over the world. Films are shown both day and night to an international jury.*
Where: Palazzo del Cinema on the Lido. When: Late August to early September. How: Write to the Venice Tourist Office for exact dates for 1992. The office is at San Marco Ascensione 71C, Venezia 30100 (tel. 041/5226356).

SEPTEMBER

☐ **Regatta Storica,** on the Grand Canal in Venice, first Sunday in September. All seaworthy gondolas in Venice participate in this maritime spectacular.

OCTOBER

☐ **Sagra del Tartufo** honors the expensive truffle in Alba (Piedmont), the truffle capital of Italy, with contests, truffle-hound competitions, and tastings of this ugly fungus. For details, write to Azienda di Promozione Turistica, piazza Medford, Alba 12051 (tel. 173/35833).
☐ **Vendemmia del Nonno,** Castagnole Monferrato, Piedmont, takes place the second Sunday of October when villagers enact an age-old grape harvest. After trampling the grapes with bare feet, a day's-end feast follows with plenty of the robust local wines. For details, write to Pro Loco, Castagnole Monferrato 14030 (tel. 141/292136).

DECEMBER

☐ **The Opera Season,** the most important in Europe, is launched at Teatro alla Scala, in Milan, the premier opera and ballet house in the country. The season lasts from December until May.

ROME
CALENDAR OF EVENTS

JANUARY

☐ **Carnival** in piazza Navona marks the last day of the children's market and lasts until dawn of the following day. Usually January 5.
☐ **Festa di Sant'Agnese,** an ancient ceremony in which two lambs are blessed and shorn. Their wool is then used later for palliums. It's at Sant' Agnese Fuori le Mura. Usually January 17.

MARCH

☐ **Festa di Santa Francesca Romana** is a blessing of cars at piazzale del Colosseo near the Church of Santa Francesco Romana in the Roman Forum. Usually March 9.
☐ **Festa di San Guiseppe,** in the Trionfale Quarter, north of the Vatican, when the heavily decorated statue of the saint is brought out at a fair with food stalls, concerts, and sporting events. Usually March 19.

APRIL

☐ **Festa della Primavera.** The Spanish Steps are decked out with banks of flowers, and later orchestral and choral concerts are presented in Trinità dei Monto. Dates vary.
☐ **Holy Week.** The most notable procession is led by the pope, passing the Colosseum and the Roman Forum up to Palatine Hill. A torchlit parade caps the observance. Sometimes at the end of March, but often in April.
☐ **Easter Sunday.** In an event broadcast around the world, the pope gives his blessing from a balcony of St. Peter's.

MAY

☐ **International Horse Show,** held the first 10 days in May, at the piazza di Siena in the Villa Borghese.

JUNE

☐ **Son et Lumière** begins in early June (lasting until the end of September) when the Roman Forum and Tivoli are dramatically lit at night.
☐ **Festa di San Pietro,** the most significant Roman religious festival, is observed with solemn rites in St. Peter's, usually around June 29.

JULY

☼ *LA FESTA DI NOIANTRI Trastevere, the most colorful quarter of Old Rome, becomes a gigantic outdoor restaurant, as tons of food and drink are consumed at tables lining the streets. Merrymakers and musicians provide the entertainment.*
    Where: Trastevere. When: Mid-July. How: After reaching the quarter, find the first empty table and try to get a waiter. But guard your valuables. Details available from Ente Provinciale per il Turismo, via Parigi 11, Roma 00185 (tel. 06/461851).

AUGUST

☐ **Festa delle Catene.** The relics of St. Peter's captivity go on display in the Church of San Pietro in Vincoli on August 1.

SEPTEMBER

☐ **Sagra dell'Uva,** a harvest festival in the Basilica of Maxentius in the Roman Forum. Musicians in ancient costumes entertain, and grapes are sold at reduced prices. Dates vary, usually early September.

NOVEMBER

☐ **Opera season** in Rome begins at Teatro dell'Opera, lasting until June.

DECEMBER

☐ **Festa della Madonna Immacolata** at the piazza di Spagna. Floral tributes to the Madonna by papal and government envoys. Usually December 8.
☐ **Midnight Mass** on December 24 at Santa Maria Maggiore, with veneration of metal and wood relics of the holy crib.
☐ **Blessing of the Pope** is delivered at noon on December 25 from a balcony of St. Peter's. It's broadcast around the world.

3. HEALTH & INSURANCE

HEALTH

You will encounter few health problems traveling in Italy. The tap water is safe to drink, the milk pasteurized, and health services good. Occasionally the change in diet may cause some minor diarrhea so you may want to take some antidiarrhea medicine along.

Carry all your vital medicine in your carry-on luggage and bring enough prescribed medicines to last you during your stay. Bring along copies of your prescriptions that are written in the generic—not brand-name—form. If you need a doctor, your hotel can recommend one or you can contact the American embassy or consulate. You can also obtain a list of English-speaking doctors before you leave from the **International Association for Medical Assistance to Travelers (IAMAT)** in the United States at 417 Center Street, Lewiston, NY 14092 (tel. 716/754-4883); in Canada at 40 Regal Road, Guelph, ON N1K 1B5 (tel. 519/836-0102).

If you suffer from a chronic illness, talk to your doctor before taking the trip. For such conditions as epilepsy, diabetes, or a heart condition, wear a Medic Alert Identification Tag, which will immediately alert any doctor to your condition and provide the number of Medic Alert's 24-hour hotline so that a foreign doctor can obtain medical records for you. For a lifetime membership, the cost is $30. Contact the **Medic Alert Foundation,** P.O. Box 1009, Turlock, CA 95381-1009 (tel. toll free 800/432-5378).

INSURANCE

Before purchasing any additional insurance, check your homeowner's, automobile, and medical insurance policies as well as the insurance provided by credit-card companies and auto and travel clubs. You may have adequate off-premises theft coverage or your credit-card company may even provide cancellation coverage if the ticket is paid for with a credit card.

Remember, Medicare only covers U.S. citizens traveling in Mexico and Canada.

Also note that to submit any claim you must always have thorough documentation, including all receipts, police reports, medical records, etc.

If you are prepaying for your vacation or are taking a charter or any other flight that has cancellation penalties, look into cancellation insurance.

The following companies will provide further information:

Travel Guard International, 1145 Clark Street, Stevens Point, WI 54481 (tel. toll free 800/826-1300), which offers a comprehensive 7-day policy that covers basically everything, including emergency assistance, accidental death, trip cancellation and interruption, medical coverage abroad, and lost luggage. It costs $52. There are restrictions, however, which you should understand before you accept the coverage.

Travel Insurance Pak, Travelers Insurance Co., 1 Tower Square 15 NB, Hartford, CT 06183-5040 (tel. 203/277-2318, or toll free 800/243-3174), offers illness and accident coverage, costing from $10 for 6 to 10 days. For lost or damaged luggage, $500 worth of coverage costs $20 for 6 to 10 days. You can also get trip-cancellation insurance for $5.50.

Mutual of Omaha (Tele-Trip), 3201 Farnam Street, Omaha, NE 68131 (tel. 402/345-2400, or toll free 800/228-9792), charges $3 a day (with a 10-day minimum) for foreign medical coverage up to $50,000, which features global assistance and maintains a 24-hour "hotline." The company also offers trip-cancellation insurance, lost or stolen luggage coverage, the standard accident coverage, and other policies.

HealthCare Abroad (MEDEX), 243 Church Street NW, Suite 100D, Vienna, VA 22180 (tel. 703/255-9800, or toll free 800/237-6615), offers a policy, good for 10 to 90 days, costing $3 a day, including accident and sickness coverage up to $100,000. Medical evacuation is also included, along with a $25,000 accidental death or dismemberment compensation. Trip cancellation and lost or stolen luggage can also be written into this policy at a nominal cost.

WorldCare Travel Assistance Association, 605 Market Street, Suite 1300, San Francisco, CA 94105 (tel. 415/541-4991, or toll free 800/666-4993), features a 9- to 15-day policy, costing $105, including trip cancellation, lost or stolen luggage, legal assistance, and medical coverage and evacuation.

Access America, 600 Third Avenue (P.O. Box 807), New York, NY 10163-0807 (tel. 212/949-5960, or toll free 800/955-4002), has a 24-hour hotline in case of an emergency, and offers medical coverage for 9 to 15 days costing $49 for $10,000. If you want medical plus trip cancellation, the charge is $89 for 9 to 15 days. A comprehensive package for $111 grants 9- to 15-day blanket coverage, including $50,000 worth of death benefits.

4. WHAT TO PACK

Always pack as lightly as possible. Sometimes it's hard to get a porter or a baggage cart in train stations and airports. Also, airlines are increasingly strict about how much luggage you can bring, both carry-on and checked items. Checked baggage should not be more than 62 inches (width plus length plus height), or weigh more than 70 pounds. Carry-on luggage shouldn't be more than 45 inches (width plus length plus height) and must fit under your seat or in the bin above.

Note, also, that conservative middle-aged Italians tend to dress up rather than down, and that they dress very well indeed, particularly at theaters and concerts. Nobody will bar you for arriving in sports clothes, but you may feel awkward, so include at least one smart suit or dress in your luggage.

Some restaurants demand that men wear ties and that women not wear shorts or jogging attire, but those are the only clothing rules enforced.

Pack clothes that "travel well" because you can't always get pressing done at hotels. Be prepared to wash your underwear, etc., in your bathroom and hang it up to dry overnight.

The general rule of packing is to bring four of everything. For men, that means four pairs of socks, four pairs of slacks, four shirts, and four sets of underwear. At least two of these will always be either dirty or in the process of drying. Often you'll have to wrap semiwet clothes in a plastic bag as you head for your next destination. Women can follow the same rule.

Take at least one outfit for chilly weather and one outfit for warm weather. Even in the summer, you may experience suddenly chilly weather. Always take two pairs of walking shoes in case you get your shoes soaked and need that extra pair.

5. TIPS FOR THE DISABLED, SENIORS, SINGLES, FAMILIES & STUDENTS

FOR THE DISABLED

Before you go, there are many agencies that can provide advance-planning information.

For example, contact **Travel Information Service,** Moss Rehabilitation Hospital, 1200 West Tabor Road, Philadelphia, PA 19141-3099 (tel. 215-456-9900). It charges $5 per package, which will contain names and addresses of accessible hotels, restaurants, and attractions, often based on firsthand reports of travelers who have been there.

You may also want to subscribe to *The Itinerary,* P.O. Box 2012, Bayonne, NJ 07002-2012 (tel. 201/858-3400), for $10 a year. This travel magazine, published bimonthly, is filled with news about travel aids for the handicapped, special tours, information on accessibility, and other matters.

You can also obtain a copy of *Air Transportation of Handicapped Persons,* published by the U.S. Department of Transportation. It's free if you write to Free Advisory Circular No. AC12032, Distribution Unit, U.S. Department of Transportation, Publications Division, M-4332, Washington, DC 20590.

You may also want to consider joining a tour for disabled visitors. Names and addresses of such tour operators can be obtained by writing to the **Society for the Advancement of Travel for the Handicapped,** 347 Fifth Avenue, New York, NY 10016 (tel. 212/447-7284). Annual membership dues are $40, or $25 for senior citizens and students. Send a stamped, self-addressed envelope.

The **Federation of the Handicapped,** 211 West 14th Street, New York, NY 10011 (tel. 212/206-4200), also operates summer tours for members, who pay a yearly fee of $4.

For the blind, the best information source is the **American Foundation for the Blind,** 15 West 16th Street, New York, NY 10011 (tel. toll free 800/232-5463).

FOR SENIORS

Many senior discounts are available, but note that some may require membership in a particular association.

For information before you go, write to **"Travel Tips for Senior Citizens"** (publication no. 8970), distributed for $1 by the Superintendent of Documents, U.S. Government Printing Office, Washington, DC 20402 (tel. 202/783-5238). Another booklet—and this one is distributed free—is called **"101 Tips for the Mature Traveler,"** available from Grand Circle Travel, 347 Congress Street, Suite 3A, Boston, MA 02210 (tel. 617/350-7500, or toll free 800/221-2610).

SAGA International Holidays, 120 Boylston Street, Boston, MA 02116 (tel. toll free 800/343-0273), runs all-inclusive tours for seniors, preferably for those 60 years old or older. Insurance is included in the net price of their tours. Membership is $5 a year.

In the United States, the best organization to join is the **American Association of Retired Persons (AARP),** 1909 K Street NW, Washington, DC 20049 (tel.

202/872-4700), which offers members discounts on car rentals, hotels, and airfares. AARP travel arrangements, featuring senior citizen discounts, are handled by American Express. Call toll free 800/927-0111 for land arrangements, toll free 800/745-4567 for cruises. Flights to and from various destinations are handled by both numbers.

Information is also available from the **National Council of Senior Citizens,** 1331 F Street NW, Washington, DC 20004 (tel. 202/347-8800), which charges $12 per person to join (couples pay $16) for which you receive a monthly newsletter, part of which is devoted to travel tips. Reduced discounts on hotel and auto rentals are available.

Elderhostel, 75 Federal Street, Boston, MA 02110 (tel. 617/426-7788), offers an array of university-based summer educational programs for senior citizens throughout the world, including Italy. Most courses last around 3 weeks and are remarkable values, considering that airfare, accommodations in student dormitories or modest inns, all meals, and tuition are included. Courses include field trips, involve no homework, are ungraded, and emphasize liberal arts.

Participants must be over 60, but each may take an under-60 companion. Meals consist of solid, no-frills fare typical of educational institutions worldwide. The program provides a safe and congenial environment for older single women, who make up some 67% of the enrollment.

FOR SINGLE TRAVELERS

Unfortunately for the 85 million single Americans, the travel industry is far more geared toward couples and singles often wind up paying the penalty. It pays to travel with someone, and one company that resolves this problem is **Travel Companion,** which matches single travelers with like-minded companions. It's headed by Jens Jurgen, who charges between $36 and $66 for a 6-month listing in his well-publicized records. People seeking travel companions fill out forms stating their preferences and needs and receive a minilisting of potential travel partners. Companions of the same or opposite sex can be requested. For an application and more information, contact Jens Jurgen, Travel Companion, P.O. Box P-833, Amityville, NY 11701 (tel. 516/454-0880).

Singleworld, 401 Theodore Fremd Avenue, Rye, NY 10580 (tel. 914/967-3334, or toll free 800/223-6490), is a travel agency that operates tours for solo travelers. Some, but not all, are for people under 35. Annual dues are $25.

FOR FAMILIES

Advance planning is the key to a successful overseas family vacation. If you have very small children you should discuss your vacation plans with your family doctor and take along such standard supplies as children's aspirin, a thermometer, Band-Aids, and the like.

On airlines, a special menu for children must be requested at least 24 hours in advance, but if baby food is required, bring your own and ask a flight attendant to warm it to the right temperature. Take along a "security blanket" for your child—a pacifier, a favorite toy or book, or, for older children, something to make them feel at home in different surroundings—a baseball cap, a favorite T-shirt, or some good luck charm.

Make advance arrangements for cribs, bottle warmers, and car seats if you're driving anywhere.

Ask the hotel if it stocks baby food, and, if not, take some with you and plan to buy the rest in local supermarkets.

Draw up guidelines on bedtime, eating, keeping tidy, being in the sun, even shopping and spending—they'll make the vacation more enjoyable.

Baby-sitters can be found for you at most hotels, but you should always insist, if possible, that you secure a baby-sitter with at least a rudimentary knowledge of English.

Family Travel Times is a newsletter about traveling with children. Subscribers to the newsletter, which costs $35 for 10 issues, can also call in with travel questions, but Monday through Friday only from 10am to noon eastern standard time. Contact **TWYCH,** which stands for Travel With Your Children, 80 Eighth Avenue, New York, NY 10011 (tel. 212/206-0688).

Italians adore *bambini,* especially their own, but they are most tolerant of other people's youngsters. Even on shopping expeditions, store owners are fond of giving children candy while parents make their purchases. In many cities, such as Venice, I don't have a special children's section because young ones usually find the canals, the buildings of the city, its narrow humped bridges, and motorboats an experience comparable to visiting an antique Disneyland. So definitely take your children along to Italy, providing you warn them repeatedly to stay out of the way of cars.

You may find that it's worth a detour to visit the tiny town of **Collodi,** 22 miles northeast of Pisa. Collodi was the hometown of the author of the famous Pinocchio story, Carlo Lorenzini. Today the people of the town operate Pinocchio Park, which is "dedicated to the happiness of children everywhere," to honor the memory of the author. The park, with many attractions, is dominated by a statue of Pinocchio with the "Blue Fairy."

FOR STUDENTS

The largest travel service for students is the **Council on International Education-al Exchange (CIEE),** 205 East 42nd Street, New York, NY 10017 (tel. 212/661-1414), providing details about budget travel, study abroad, working permits, and insurance. It also sells a number of helpful publications, including the *Student Travel Catalogue* ($1) and issues International Student Identity Cards (ISIC) for $10 to bonafide students.

For real budget travelers it's worth joining the **International Youth Hostel Federation (IYHF).** For information, write AYH (American Youth Hostels), P.O. Box 37613, Washington, DC 20013-7613 (tel. 202/783-6161). Membership costs $25 annually, except that under-18s pay $10.

6. ALTERNATIVE/ADVENTURE TRAVEL

Mass tourism of the kind that has transported vast numbers of North Americans to the most obscure corners of the globe has been a byproduct of the affluence, technology, and democratization that only the last half of the 20th century was able to produce.

There has emerged a demand for specialized travel experiences whose goals and objectives are clearly defined well in advance of an actual departure. There is also an increased demand for organizations that can provide like-minded companions to share and participate in increasingly esoteric travel plans.

Caveat: Under no circumstances is the inclusion of an organization in this section a guarantee either of its creditworthiness or its competency. Information about the organizations is presented only as a preliminary preview, to be followed by your own investigation should you be interested.

ALTERNATIVE TRAVEL
PROMOTING INTERNATIONAL UNDERSTANDING

About the only thing the following organizations have in common is reflected in that heading. They not only promote trips to increase international understanding, but they also often encourage and advocate what might be called "intelligent travel."

The Friendship Force, 575 South Tower, 1 CNN Center, Atlanta, GA 30303 (tel. 404/522-9490), is a nonprofit organization existing for the sole purpose of fostering and encouraging friendship among disparate people around the world. Dozens of branch offices exist throughout North America and can arrange for en masse visits, usually once a year. Because of group bookings, the price of air transportation to the host country is usually less than what volunteers would pay if they bought an APEX ticket individually. Each participant is required to spend 2 weeks in the host country. One stringent requirement is that a participant must spend 1 full week in the home of a family as a guest. Most volunteers spend the second week traveling in the host country.

Servas (translated from the Esperanto, it means "to serve"), 11 John Street, Room 407, New York, NY 10038 (tel. 212/267-0252), is a nonprofit, nongovernment, international, interfaith network of travelers and hosts whose goal is to help build world peace, goodwill, and understanding. They do this by providing opportunities for deeper, more personal contacts among people of diverse cultural and political backgrounds. Servas travelers are invited to share living space with members of communities worldwide, normally staying without charge for visits lasting a maximum of 2 days. Visitors pay a $45 annual fee, plus pay a $15 deposit for access to lists of international hosts, fill out an application, and are interviewed for suitability by one of more than 200 Servas interviewers throughout the country. They then receive a Servas directory listing the names and addresses of Servas hosts who will allow (and encourage) visitors within their homes.

International Visitors Information Service, 733 15th Street NW, Suite 300, Washington, DC 20005 (tel. 202/783-6540). For $5.95 this organization will mail anyone a booklet listing opportunities for contact with local residents in foreign countries. Europe is heavily featured. For example, if you want to find lodgings with an Italian-speaking family whose members raise grapes and produce wine, this booklet will tell you how. Checks should be made out to Meridian House IVIS, but confirm the latest publication price.

HOME EXCHANGES

Italy doesn't have an established "Meet the Italians" program, but cities and most towns have an official tourist office (called either Ente Provinciale per il Turismo or Azienda Autonoma di Soffiorno e Turismo) that might arrange for you to stay with or just meet an Italian family. Such arrangements are usually made for those staying for several weeks or more in an Italian city, not for brief visits. Requests for such attention should be sent several months before your trip to Italy by writing to the official tourist office of the town.

For home exchanges that can be fun and save money, contact the following:

World Wide Exchange, 1344 Pacific Avenue, Suite 103, Santa Cruz, CA 95060 (tel. 408/425-0531), will list your home and also send you three booklets of listings.

Vacation Exchange Club, 12006 111th Avenue, Suite 12, Youngstown, AZ 85363 (tel. 602/972-2186), with many Italian listings, charges $24.70 to list your home in their spring and winter listings. Subscribers pay $16 for the listings only.

International Home Exchange Service, P.O. Box 190070, San Francisco, CA 94119 (tel. 415/435-3497), charges $35 for three directories annually. The fee includes a listing in one of them. Seniors get 20% off.

OPERA TOURS

On a cultural note, **Dailey-Thorp,** 330 West 58th Street, Suite 6K, New York, NY 10019 (tel. 212/307-1555), in business since 1971, is probably the best-regarded organizer of music and opera tours operating in the U.S. Because of its "favored" relations with European box offices, it's often able to purchase blocks of otherwise unavailable tickets to such events as the Salzburg Festival, the Vienna, Milan, Paris, and London operas, or the Bayreuth Festival in Germany. Tours range from 7 to 21 days and include first-class or deluxe accommodations and meals in top-rated European restaurants.

SENIOR-CITIZEN VACATIONS

One of the most dynamic organizations of postretirement studies for senior citizens is **Elderhostel,** 75 Federal Street, Boston, MA 02110 (tel. 617/427-7788), established in 1975. Elderhostel maintains an array of programs throughout Europe, including

Italy. Most courses last for around 3 weeks and represent good value, considering that airfare, hotel accommodations in student dormitories or modest inns, all meals, and tuition are included. Courses involve no homework, are upgraded, and are especially focused in liberal arts. This is not a luxury vacation, but rather an academic fulfillment of a type never possible for senior citizens until several years ago. Participants must be at least 60 years of age. However, if two members go as a couple, only one needs to be 60. At this writing, Elderhostel offered Italian experiences that included a historic and artistic overview of Sicily from headquarters in the fishing village of Mondello (near Palermo), and an introduction to the art and architecture of Umbria and Tuscany, with detailed overviews of the attractions of Assisi, Perugia, and Siena. Anyone interested in participating in one of Elderhostel's programs should write for the free catalog and a list of upcoming courses and destinations.

One company that has a reputation based exclusively on its quality tours for senior citizens is **SAGA International Holidays,** 120 Boylston Street, Boston, MA 02116 (tel. toll free 800/343-0273). Established in the 1950s, they prefer that participants be at least 60 years of age or older. Insurance and airfare are included in the net price of any of their tours, all of which encompass dozens of locations in Europe and usually last for an average of 17 nights.

At presstime, SAGA's grand tour of Italy takes participants by deluxe motorcoach (leaving the driving and parking hassles to professionals), and staying at four-star hotels in about eight different cities within the peninsula over a duration of 15 nights.

ADVENTURE/WILDERNESS TRAVEL

The Italian countryside has always been legendary for its beauty and architectural richness. Several companies specialize in exposing their clients to its wonders, usually through participation in hill treks and mountain climbing. One of the best recommended of these companies is **Mountain Travel–Sobek,** 6420 Fairmount Avenue, El Cerrito, CA 94530 (tel. toll free 800/227-2384 in the U.S.), which is known as a wilderness specialist formed by a 1991 union between two of California's largest adventure-tour operators.

Mountain Travel–Sobek offers at least three different hill-climbing itineraries through the hills and valleys of Italy. In order of difficulty, the least strenuous is a 12-day hike through the fields and vineyards of Tuscany. Traversing most of the width of the district, the tours explore a region richly studded with centuries of architectural monuments. With three departures every year (in April, September, and October), the price of $2,200 per person, double occupancy, includes all meals, transfers, and guide services, and overnight accommodations in renovated farmhouses, country inns, and an occasional monastery. A similar tour (13 days) exists for treks through the Piedmont (which includes 10 days of "moderate to strenuous hiking") for around $2,000 per person, double occupancy. Most challenging of all, the company offers an 8-day ramble through the Dolomites. Classified as "strenuous" and for experienced and in-shape hikers only, it departs in July and again in August, costs $1,000 per person, and includes an optional climb of one of the region's peaks, 10,355-foot Piz Boe.

Some travelers prefer to visit Tuscany in a style popularized by everyone from the Etruscans to the soldiers and *condotierri* of the Renaissance: on horseback. One company that can help you combine a trek through the Italian countryside with equestrian panache is **Equitour,** P.O. Box 807, Dubois, WY 82513 (tel. toll free 800/545-0019 in the U.S.). Established in 1983 from a base in northwestern Wyoming, this company markets highly organized horseback-riding holidays throughout the world, including tours to such faraway places as Botswana, Iceland, and the Altai region of Soviet Asia. In Italy, Equitour represents at least two separate outfits, both highly reputable, which specialize in equestrian treks through Tuscany. Only English tack is used for tours that are limited to between 8 and 14 participants and last for 8 days each and usually include 6 days of riding. Depending on the itinerary, riders might remain within the vicinity of a single stable (with overnight accommodations within a historic inn) for day trips through the nearby countryside. Another attractive option involves traversing most of the breadth of Tuscany, spending each night in a different farmhouse or inn. Prices for both treks cost around $1,500, double occupancy, and include all meals and accommodations, all horseback riding, and guide fees.

EDUCATIONAL/STUDY TRAVEL
LEARNING THE LANGUAGE

Courses for foreign students are available at several centers covering not only the Italian language and literature but also the country's history, geography, and fine arts. You can write to any of the following addresses for information. Among these are language courses in Florence at the **Università Centro di Cultura per Stranieri,** via Vittorio Emmanuel 64, 50134 Firenze; **Società Dante Alighieri,** Centro Linguistico Italiano, via de Bardi 12, 50125 Firenze; **Eurocentro,** piazza S. Spirito 9, 50125 Firenze; and the **British Institute,** Palazzo Lanfredini, lungarno Guicciardini 9, 50125 Firenze. In Rome, language and literature centers are **Centro Linguistico Italiano,** via B. Marliano 4, 00162 Roma; and **Società Dante Alighieri,** piazza Firenze 27, 00186 Roma.

COOKING CLASSES

The **International Cooking School of Italian Food and Wine,** 300 East 33rd Street, Suite 10J, New York, NY 10016 (tel. 212/779-1921), combines cooking classes in *cucina Italiana* with excursions and restaurant dining. Classes are conducted in English in a 17th-century villa, and students are taught directly by Italy's top chefs and restaurateurs. The course includes a private estate tour of a winery and a wine tasting, and gastronomy shops and produce markets of Bologna are visited. Topping off these events is a full day in Venice exploring and eating. More information and dates of the classes can be obtained by writing Mary Beth Clark at the address above.

COURSES IN ENGRAVING & CERAMICS

Summer courses, which take place from the beginning of July to the beginning of August and which last 30 days, are sponsored in Urbino. For information, write to **Segreteria dei Corsi Internazionali,** Centro Internazionale Artistico Culturale, 61029 Urbino (tel. 0722/329695). The courses, organized by the Raphael Academy, include separate sections on xylography, chalcography, and lithography. Courses also cover many aspects of ceramic design and restoration of ceramics. No more than 20 students are admitted to each course.

7. GETTING THERE

BY PLANE

"All roads lead to Rome" in ways the emperors never dreamed of—by super-fast autostrada, ships, freighters, and, last but certainly not least, by jet plane. Indeed, of all various ways of reaching Italy, the airplane is the best . . . and for the U.S.-to-Italy run, the cheapest.

If you're already in Europe, visiting some other capitals such as Paris and London, and then planning to fly on to Rome, you will have relatively little problem making airline connections. Both Rome and Milan are considered lucrative and essential destinations by the dozens of European carriers that service them. Alitalia flies to all the major capitals of Europe, and all the national carriers of the various countries (such as Air France, British Airways, and Lufthansa) fly to Rome or to Milan. The only problem is that it's expensive to book these fares once you're in Europe. It's better to have Rome or Milan written into your ticket when you book your flight to Europe from North America. You'll save a lot of money that way.

THE MAJOR AIRLINES

At presstime, the airline industry is in upheaval, and comments made here may be hopelessly dated by the time of your actual flight. For last-minute conditions, even a rundown on carriers flying to Italy, check with a travel agent or the individual airlines.

Here is a rundown on the current status:

American Airlines (tel. toll free 800/433-7300) was among the first of the newcomers to receive permission to fly into Italy. From one of the world's busiest hubs, Chicago's O'Hare Airport, American flies nonstop every day to Milan. During the lifetime of this edition American will almost certainly gather even more routes into Italy, probably at heavily discounted promotional fares.

TWA (tel. toll free 800/221-2000) offers daily flights in summer from its New York hub to both Rome and Milan. In winter, several of these flights might be combined, taking passengers first to one, then to the other, of the cities. TWA also has connections to Rome (either one or two per day, depending on the schedule) through Paris from Washington, D.C., and Boston. Its lowest fare from New York to Rome, nonrefundable and requiring a 21-day advance booking and a stopover of between 6 and 30 days, costs $736 round-trip for flights Monday through Thursday, with a $50 surcharge for flights Friday through Sunday. Round-trip flights to Milan usually cost around $85 less than those to Rome.

Delta (tel. toll free 800/221-1212) had applied for permission before presstime for nonstop routes between its headquarters in Atlanta to Rome, with continuing service to Milan. It had also agreed in principle (pending the approval of at least three government bureaucracies) to acquire the bankrupt Pan Am's routes between New York and both Rome and Milan. If these requests are approved, Delta will strengthen its already well-established role as a major force on the transatlantic air routes. Of special interest to travelers is the precedent Delta has established for promoting new routes—low-cost promotional fares.

Finally, for anyone interested in combining a trip to Italy with a stopover in, say, Britain or Germany along the way, there are sometimes attractive deals offered by **British Airways** (tel. toll free 800/247-9297) and **Lufthansa** (tel. toll free 800/645-3880). Depending on any special promotions being offered (and with the understanding that all segments of a flight would be booked simultaneously from within North America), flights into Rome might be attractively priced and offer a few days' holiday in London, Manchester, Munich, or Frankfurt along the way. British Airways, for example, maintains three and four flights a day from London to Rome and Milan, respectively, and often offers promotional deals to London that are appealingly inexpensive.

The airline industry's shakeup coupled with the increased competition has breathed new life into one well-known Italian specialist, **Alitalia** (tel. toll free 800/223-5730). Alitalia flies nonstop to either Rome or Milan (and sometimes both) from five different North American cities. From New York, Alitalia flies two or three times a day, depending on the season, to Italy. Flights depart in the evening nonstop for both Rome and Milan. The schedules are carefully designed to facilitate easy transfers into such cities as Venice, Palermo, and Florence.

Alitalia also flies nonstop to Rome and Milan from Chicago six and three times a week, respectively, and to either one or the other of the cities from Los Angeles (five times a week), Toronto (three times a week), Boston (biweekly), and Miami (four times a week). At presstime, a special promotion allowed up to two young people aged 12 to 24, if accompanied by an adult, to receive a 33⅓% discount off the adult APEX fare.

Be warned that Alitalia's (and most other airlines') cheapest tickets are nonrefundable. Alitalia's sole exception to this rule is in the event of your hospitalization or the death of someone in your close family. Travel in both directions between Monday and Thursday will save you money, since there is a surcharge for weekend (Friday, Saturday, and Sunday) travel.

Sometimes it's hard to reach an airline directly, because of the great demand for plane tickets to Italy. Rather than arranging flights yourself, you may prefer the services of a reputable travel agent instead.

REGULAR FARES

Most of the major airlines that fly to Rome charge approximately the same fare, but if a price war should break out over the Atlantic (and industry sources hint that these are almost always brewing over the most popular routes), fares could change overnight, usually in the consumer's favor. Specific fares, of course, should be discussed with your travel agent when you eventually make your plans.

If seeking a budget fare is uppermost in your mind, the key to getting one is "advance booking"—a process that involves a willingness to make your travel plans, and to purchase your tickets, as far ahead as possible. Moreover, since the number of seats allocated to low-cost "advance-purchase" fares is severely limited (sometimes to less than 25% of the capacity of a particular plane), it will often be the early bird who obtains not the worm, but the low-cost seat, although this may not always be the case.

If your travel plans can possibly permit it, a large number of discounts are available for passengers who can travel either midweek or midwinter in either direction. Many travelers, depending on their interests, prefer the respite from the summertime crowds, and there may be no reason why your itinerary couldn't begin and end, say, on a Tuesday instead of a weekend.

High season on most airlines' routes to Rome usually stretches from June 1 until September 15 (this could vary), and it is both the most expensive and most crowded time to travel. If your schedule will permit it, you should try to plan your departure for the low season, which falls into the period between September and May.

All the major carriers offer an **APEX ticket,** which is generally their cheapest way to fly over. Usually such a ticket must be purchased 21 days in advance and a stopover in Italy must last at least 6 days but not more than 30. Changing the date of departure from North America within 21 days of departure will bring a penalty of $100. Many of the travelers who opt for this method of travel find that sticking to their predetermined dates doesn't present any real hardship.

Most of the airlines, including Alitalia, American, and TWA, offer an even more attractive "Super APEX" fare that will save you an additional $100 or so over the cost of a less-restrictive regular APEX fare. Although it carries additional restrictions (including a no-refund clause except under the most dire health emergencies), many travelers opt for the increased savings. You'll have to pay for your ticket 14 to 21 days before departure, depending on the season, and limit your stay abroad to between 6 and 30 days.

Another attractive option is called the **excursion fare.** No advance purchase is necessary and an open return is possible, giving many travelers the freedom they want to choose a return date once they arrive in Italy. It is, however, required that you wait between 7 and 180 days before using the return half of your ticket. Stopovers at other cities within Europe that lie along a more-or-less direct path of your homeward flight are usually allowed for a surcharge of about $50 per stopover, depending on the airline and the routing.

Another option, which most casual visitors might want to avoid, is the **regular economy fare.** This offers the same seating and the same services as passengers using an excursion ticket, but is usually purchased by those who need to return to North America before spending their obligatory 7 days in Europe, the number required for an excursion ticket.

If comfort is your primary objective, you might want to avail yourself of the more luxurious services offered by all the major carriers. In **business class** you often get seats as wide as in first-class seating. It is ideal for business travelers or long-legged passengers who prefer wide, roomy comfort, free drinks, and savory meals served on fine linen and china. The ultimate relaxing service, of course, is available in **first class,** where the extra-wide seats (usually limited to four across the entire width of the plane) convert into sleepers.

OTHER GOOD-VALUE CHOICES

Alitalia clusters the prices of tickets to its destinations within Italy into approximately four zones. Each zone is centered around the hubs at Milan, Rome, Naples, or

Palermo. If you intend to fly from North America to local airports at, say, Genoa, Venice, Palermo, Rimini, or any of the towns of Sardinia or Sicily, you can do so from the hubs for no additional charge. (Alitalia calls these **"common rated" fares,** meaning that it costs no more to fly to Venice from New York than it would have cost to fly to Rome from New York.) Considering the distance between Rome and Venice, and the extra expense you'd have encountered on the train or highway, it's an attractive offer.

And for students, or anyone aged 12 to 24, special extensions are granted on the length of time a passenger can stay abroad. Alitalia's **youth fare** permits a stay abroad of between 14 days and 1 year. The round-trip fare from New York to Rome, depending on the season and the day of the week, ranges from $736 to $1,075. With the year-long validity of the return half of the ticket, a North American student could, say, complete two full semesters at the University of Bologna and still fly home at a substantial savings over equivalent fares on some other airlines.

BUCKET SHOPS   The name originated in the 1960s in Britain, where mainstream airlines gave that (then-pejorative) name to resalers of blocks of unsold tickets consigned to them by major transatlantic carriers. "Bucket shop" has stuck as a label, but it might be more polite to refer to them as "consolidators." They exist in many shapes and forms. In its purest sense, a bucket shop acts as a clearinghouse for blocks of tickets that airlines discount and consign during normally slow periods of air travel.

Charter operators (see below) and bucket shops used to perform separate functions, but their offerings in many cases have been blurred in recent times. Many outfits perform both functions.

Tickets are sometimes—but not always—priced at up to 35% less than the full fare. Perhaps your reduced fare will be no more than 20% off the regular fare. Terms of payment can vary—say, anywhere from 45 days prior to departure to last-minute sales offered in a final attempt by an airline to fill an empty aircraft.

Since dealing with unknown bucket shops might be a little risky, it's wise to call the Better Business Bureau in your area to see if complaints have been filed against the company from which you plan to purchase a fare.

Bucket shops abound from coast to coast, but to get you started, here are a few listings:

Maharaja Travel, 393 Fifth Avenue, 3rd Floor, New York, NY 10016 (tel. 212/213-2020, or toll free 800/223-6862), has been around for some 20 years, offering tickets to 400 destinations worldwide, including Rome and Milan.

Access International, 101 West 31st Street, Suite 1104, New York, NY 10001 (tel. 212/465-0707, or toll free 800/825-3633), may be the country's biggest consolidator. It specializes in thousands of discounted tickets to the capitals of Europe, including Rome and Milan. Flights are usually on regularly scheduled U.S.-based airlines.

Out west, you can try **Sunline Express Holidays, Inc.,** 607 Market Street, San Francisco, CA 94105 (tel. 415/541-7800, or toll free 800/877-2111), or **Euro-Asia, Inc.,** 4203 East Indian School Road, Suite 210, Phoenix, AZ 85018 (tel. 602/955-2742, or toll free 800/525-3876).

Travel Avenue, 180 North Des Plaines, Chicago, IL 60661 (tel. toll free 800/333-3335), is a national agency whose headquarters are in Chicago. Its tickets are often cheaper than most shops and it charges the customer only a $25 fee on international tickets, rather than taking the usual 10% commission from an airline. Travel Avenue rebates most of that back to the customer—hence, the lower fares.

CHARTER FLIGHTS   Strictly for reasons of economy (and never for convenience), some travelers are willing to accept the possible uncertainties of a charter flight to Italy.

In a strict sense, a charter flight occurs on an aircraft reserved months in advance for a one-time-only transit to some predetermined point. Before paying for a charter, check the restrictions on your ticket or contract. You may be asked to purchase a tour package and pay far in advance. You'll pay a stiff penalty (or forfeit the ticket entirely) if you cancel. Charters are sometimes canceled when the plane doesn't fill up. In some cases, the charter-ticket seller will offer you an insurance policy for your own legitimate cancellation (hospital certificate, death in the family, whatever).

There is no way to predict whether a proposed flight to Rome will cost less on a charter or less in a bucket shop. You'll have to investigate at the time of your trip.

Some charter companies have proved unreliable in the past. Among charter flight operators is a name possibly remembered from one's younger days, the **Council on International Educational Exchange (Council Charters),** 205 East 42nd Street, New York, NY 10017 (tel. 212/661-0311, or toll free 800/800-8222). This outfit can arrange "charter seats on regularly scheduled aircraft."

One of the biggest New York charter operators is **Travac,** 989 Sixth Avenue, New York, NY 10018 (tel. 212/563-3303), which operates charters from New York to European destinations.

REBATORS To confuse the situation even more, rebators also compete in the low-cost airfare market. These outfits pass along to the passenger part of their commission, although many of them assess a fee for their services. Most rebators offer discounts that range from 10% to 25% (but this could vary from place to place), plus a $20 handling charge. They are not the same as travel agents, although they sometimes offer similar services, including discounted land arrangements and car rentals.

Rebators include: **Travel Avenue,** 641 West Lake Street, Suite 201, Chicago, IL 60606-3691 (tel. 312/876-1116, or toll free 800/333-3335); **The Smart Traveller,** 3111 SW 27th Avenue, Miami, FL 33133 (tel. 305/448-3338, or toll free 800/226-3338 in Florida and Georgia only); and **Blitz Travel,** 8918 Manchester Road, St. Louis, MO 63144 (tel. 314/961-2700).

STANDBYS A favorite of spontaneous travelers with absolutely no scheduled demands on their time, standby fares leave your departure to the whims of fortune, and the hopes that a last-minute seat will become available. Most airlines don't offer standbys, although some seats are available to London and to Vienna, from which you will have to go by train, plane, or other means to Italy. Vienna is, of course, a lot closer to Italy than London. From Vienna, there is good and frequent rail service to such cities as Milan and Rome. These fares are generally offered from April to November only.

Virgin Atlantic Airways (tel. toll free 800/862-8621) features both a day-of-departure and a day-prior-to-departure standby fare from New York to London. **Tarom Romanian Airlines** (tel. 212/687-6013 in New York) offers a year-round standby from New York to Vienna.

GOING AS A COURIER This cost-cutting technique may not be for everybody. You travel as a passenger and courier, and for this service you'll secure a greatly discounted airfare or sometimes even a free ticket.

You're allowed one piece of carry-on luggage only; your baggage allowance is used by the courier firm to transport its cargo (which by the way, is perfectly legal). As a courier, you don't actually handle the merchandise you're "transporting" to Europe, you just carry a manifest to present to Customs.

Upon arrival, an employee of the courier service will reclaim the company's cargo. Incidentally, you fly alone, so don't plan to travel with anybody. (A friend may be able to arrange a flight as a courier on a consecutive day.) Most courier services operate from Los Angeles or New York, but some operate out of other cities, such as Chicago or Miami.

Courier services are often listed in the *Yellow Pages* or in advertisements in travel sections of newspapers.

For a start, check **Halbert Express,** 147-05 176th Street, Jamaica, NY 11434 (tel. 718/656-8189 from 10am to 3pm daily); or **Now Voyager,** 74 Varick Street, Suite 307, New York, NY 10013 (tel. 212/431-1616). Call daily from 11:30am to 6pm (at other times you'll get a recorded message announcing last-minute special round-trip fares).

FROMMER'S SMART TRAVELER: AIRFARES

1. Take off-peak flights. That means not only autumn to spring departures, but Monday through Thursday for those midweek discounts.
2. Avoid any last-minute change of plans (if you can help it), and that way you'll also avoid penalties airlines impose for changes in itineraries.
3. Keep checking the airlines and their fares. Timing is everything. A recent spot check of one airline revealed that in just 7 days it had discounted a New York to Rome fare by $195.
4. Shop all airlines that fly to your destination.
5. Always ask for the lowest fare, not just a discount fare.
6. Ask about frequent-flyer programs to gain bonus miles when you book a flight.
7. Check ''bucket shops'' for last-minute discount fares that are even cheaper than their advertised slashed fares.
8. Ask about air/land packages. Land arrangements are often cheaper when booked with an air ticket.
9. Fly free or at a heavy discount as a ''courier.''

BY TRAIN

If you plan to travel heavily on the European and/or British railroads, you will do well to secure the latest copy of the ***Thomas Cook European Timetable of Railroads.*** This comprehensive, 500+ page timetable documents all of Europe's mainline passenger rail services with detail and accuracy. It is available exclusively in North America from **Forsyth Travel Library,** P.O. Box 2975, Shawnee Mission, KS 66201 (tel. toll free 800/FORSYTH), at a cost of $21.95 plus $4 postage priority airmail to the U.S. and $5 (U.S.) for shipments to Canada.

EURAILPASS

Many travelers to Europe have for years been taking advantage of one of its greatest travel bargains, the Eurailpass, which permits unlimited first-class rail travel in any country in Western Europe except the British Isles, and also includes Hungary in Eastern Europe. Oddly, it does *not* include travel on the rail lines of Sardinia, which are organized independently of the rail lines of the rest of Italy. Passes are purchased for periods as short as 15 days or as long as 3 months.

Here's how it works: The pass is sold only in North America. Vacationers in Europe for 15 days can purchase a Eurailpass for $390; and a pass for 21 days costs $498; a 1-month pass costs $616; 2 months, $840, and 3 months, $1,042. Children under 4 travel free providing they don't occupy a seat (otherwise, they must pay half fare); children under 12 pay half fare. If you're under 26, you can purchase a **Eurail Youthpass,** which entitles you to unlimited second-class travel for 1 or 2 months, costing $425 or $560, respectively.

The advantages are tempting. No tickets, no supplements—simply show the pass to the ticket collector, then settle back to enjoy the scenery. Seat reservations are required on some trains. Many of the trains have couchettes (sleeping cars), for which an additional fee is charged. Obviously, the 2- or 3-month traveler gets the greatest economic advantages; the Eurailpass is ideal for such extensive trips. Passholders can visit all of Italy's major sights, from the Alps to Sicily, then end their vacation in Norway, for example.

Fourteen-day or 1-month voyagers have to estimate rail distance before determining if such a pass is to their benefit. To obtain full advantage of the ticket for 15 days or 1 month, you'd have to spend a great deal of time on the train.

Eurailpass holders are entitled to considerable reductions on certain buses and ferries. You'll get a 20% reduction on second-class accommodations from certain companies operating ferries between Naples and Palermo, or for crossings to Sardinia and Malta.

Travel agents in all towns, and railway agents in such major cities as New York, Montréal, or Los Angeles, sell all these tickets. A Eurailpass is available at the North American offices of CIT Travel Service, the French National Railroads, the German Federal Railroads, and the Swiss Federal Railways.

Eurail Saverpass is a money-saving ticket which offers discounted 15-day travel, but only if groups of three people travel constantly and continuously together between April and September, or if two people travel constantly and continuously together between October and March. The price of a Saverpass, valid all over Europe, good for first class only, is $298 for the 15 days.

Eurail Flexipass allows passengers to visit Europe with more flexibility. It is valid in first class and offers the same privileges as the Eurailpass. However, it provides a number of individual travel days which can be used over a much longer period of consecutive days. That makes it possible to stay in one city and yet not lose a single day of travel. There are three passes: 5 days within 15 days for $230, 9 days within 21 days for $398, and 14 days within 1 month for $498.

With many of the same qualifications and restrictions as the previously described Flexipass is a **Youth Flexipass.** Sold only to travelers under age 26, it allows 15 days of travel within 3 months for $340, or 30 days of travel within 3 months for $540.

BY BUS

This is not a popular means of transport for reaching Italy, but some limited services are available. **Eurolines,** 13 Regent Street, London SW1Y 4LR (tel. 071/730-0202), operates a weekly bus service to Rome, taking 2½ days and cutting through France. From June to September, service is increased to three times a week. Buses depart year round on Sunday, or in summer on Sunday, Wednesday, and Friday.

BY CAR

If you're already on the continent, particularly in a neighboring country such as France or Austria, you may want to drive to Italy. However, arrangements should be made in advance with your car-rental company.

It is also possible to drive from London to Rome, a distance of 1,124 miles via Calais/Boulogne/Dunkirk or 1,085 miles via Oostende/Zeebrugge, not counting Channel crossings. Milan is some 400 miles closer to Britain than Rome. If you cross over from England and arrive at one of the continental ports, you still face a 24-hour drive. Most drivers play it safe and budget 3 days for the journey.

Most of the roads from western Europe leading into Italy are toll free, with some notable exceptions. If you use the Swiss superhighway network, you'll have to purchase a special road sticker at the frontier. You'll also pay to go through the St. Gotthard Tunnel into Italy. Crossings from France can be through the Mont Blanc Tunnel, for which you'll pay, or else you can leave the French Riviera at Menton (France) and drive directly into Italy along the Italian Riviera in the direction of San Remo.

If you don't want to drive such distances, ask a travel agent to book you on a Motorail arrangement where the train carries your car. This service, however, is good only to Milan, as there are no car and sleeper expresses running the some 390 miles south to Rome.

ORGANIZED TOURS

Many questions arise for people planning their first European trip, whether to Italy or elsewhere: How do I plan my trip to be sure of seeing the most outstanding sights of the country? How much of a problem will I have in trying to get from place to place, complete with luggage? Am I too old to embark on such a journey? How will I cope with a foreign language?

With all the features provided by a good tour group, you can know ahead just what your visit will cost. Perhaps best of all, you won't be bothered with having to arrange your own transportation in places where language might be a problem, looking after your own luggage, coping with reservations and payment at individual hotels, and facing other "nuts and bolts" requirements of travel that can make or break your enjoyment of a European journey. Although a sampling of three of the best-rated tour companies follows, you should consider consulting a good travel agent for the latest offerings and advice.

There are many different tour operators eager for a share of your business, but one that seems to meet with consistent approval from its participants has been a family-operated company for three generations named **Perillo Tours** (tel. toll free 800/431-1515). Since it was established in 1945, it has sent over a million travelers to Italy in luxurious circumstances. As one of the world's largest Italy operators, it uses more first-class hotel rooms in Italy than any other company in America. Known and well respected for the value it offers, Perillo's tours cost much less than the assembled elements of each tour if each component had been arranged separately. Accommodations are within deluxe or superior first-class hotels, and guides tend to be well qualified, well informed, and sensitive to the needs of tour participants.

Perillo operates hundreds of departures year round. Between April and October, five different itineraries are offered, ranging from 10 to 14 days, covering broadly different regions of the peninsula. Between November and April, the Off-Season Italy tour covers three of Italy's premier cities during a season when they're likely to be less densely filled with other visitors. All tours include airfare from North America (usually on Delta), overnight accommodations in first-class or deluxe hotels, breakfast and dinner daily, and all baggage handling, and taxes. Also included are all sightseeing fees, transfers, and tours by deluxe motorcoach. Each bus contains its own lavatory. Tours begin at $1,659 per person, double occupancy, for one of the off-season short tours, to $2,800 for a 2-week visit to Rome, Florence, and Venice, Italy's most-visited (and most expensive) cities.

Another possibility is offered by a Chicago-based company named **Abercrombie and Kent**, 1520 Kensington Road, Oak Brook, IL 60521 (tel. 708/954-2944, or toll free 800/323-7308). Established 30 years ago, the company specializes in deluxe 9-day tours of Italy which use rail transport between the touristic highlights of Italy. These tours, considering the extra benefits they include, still cost a lot less than comparable visits which travelers arrange themselves. The Great Italy Express offers first-class rail transport between such cities as Florence, Assisi, San Gimignano, Venice, Siena, Perugia, and Rome. Abercrombie is especially capable in handling ailing, elderly, or infirm guests. All luggage is transported by truck from one destination to the next, and all itineraries are accompanied by skilled and multilingual guides. Hotels are chosen for their charm and comfort, and, while not necessarily the most expensive in any given city, they are among the top rated, most unusual, and often the most historic.

The Great Italian Express costs around $4,500 per person, double occupancy, without airfare, focuses on the glamorous, and includes all breakfasts, many meals, tips, and extra benefits.

A third contender for package-tour business is the company selected by Alitalia Airlines as its personal representative to the U.S. travel market. **Italiatour,** 666 Fifth Avenue, New York, NY 10102 (tel. toll free 800/237-0517), works closely with Alitalia to offer an array of appealing tours. Italiatour's programs come in five different degrees of supervision, each designed to satisfy the touring needs of a wide range of clients. These include everything from scheduled, structured tours with the constant presence of a well-trained guide, to a loosely structured series of hotel reservations with no prearranged schedule of any kind. The most closely monitored, all-inclusive packages (known by Italiatour as simply an "escorted tour") includes commentary, accompaniment, and guidance from morning till night. "Semi-escorted tours" and the even more unstructured "hosted tours" leave much greater amounts of free time, including half-day breaks from the tour and many free evenings for restaurant visits on your own. "Independent tours" sell preselected blocks of hotel nights in carefully screened hotels, perhaps a rental car if you request it, and a handful of escorted transfers through and between cities. For the most free-at-heart, Italiatour sells prereserved hotel accommodations which, because of their volume purchases, are usually less expensive than if you had reserved the hotel rooms yourself. There is a strong incentive to book air passage from North America at the same time, and because of its close dialogue with Alitalia, the prices quoted for air passage are among the most reasonable in the industry.

The shortest tour offered by the company is a 1-day city tour of up to 25 different cities in Italy, including Rome, Venice, Florence, or Palermo. (These day tours must be sold simultaneously with at least 1 night's prereserved hotel accommodation. The longest tour is a 22-day escorted jaunt through the major art cities of Italy. Prices are determined by the length of your tour, the degree of supervision you want, and the category of hotel that you select. For example, a closely supervised 11-day/9-night tour of Rome, Florence, and Venice, with all transfers, breakfasts, tours, and guide fees included, can range from $890 to $1,065 per person, double occupancy, in midsummer depending on whether you request accommodations in three-star hotels or in four-star hotels. In the summer, a 9-day/7-night tour called "Treasures of Sicily" includes hotel accommodations, breakfasts, 13 meals, all guide fees, and the safety and convenience of an air-conditioned bus, for between $719 and $819 per person, double occupancy, depending on the hotels and the season you select. In winter, these prices are reduced to as low as $419 per person, double occupancy.

These and an array of other introductions are waiting at Italiatour, along with facilities for booking flights to Italy on Alitalia. For reservations and information, call either Alitalia (tel. toll free 800/223-5730) or Italiatour (tel. toll free 800/237-0517).

8. GETTING AROUND

BY PLANE

Italy's domestic air network, on **Alitalia** and **ATI Domestic Service,** is one of the largest and most complete in Europe. There are some 40 airports serviced regularly from Rome, and most flights are under an hour. Fares vary, but some discounts are available. For those passengers 2 to 12 years old, all tickets are discounted 50%; for passengers 12 to 22 years old, there's a 30% discount. And anyone can get a 30% reduction by taking domestic flights that depart at night.

BY TRAIN

This can be a medium-priced means of transportation, even if you don't buy the Eurailpass or special Italian Railway tickets (see below). A typical one-way adult fare—Intercity, Diretto, or Eurocity (the terms are interchangeable)—between Rome and Florence, would be $36 in first class, dropping to $24 in second class. Between Florence and Venice, the one-way charge is $29 in first class, $19 in second class. The one-way fare from Rome to Naples is $25 in first class, $16 in second class.

In a land where mamma and bambini are highly valued, children aged 4 to 12 receive a discount of 50% off the adult fare, while children under 4 travel free with their parents. If an adult travels with a family of four or more people, he or she receives a discount of 30% off the regular fare.

Senior citizens traveling on Italy's rails get a break. A **Senior Citizen's Silver Card (*Carta d'Argento*)** can be bought by women 60 and over and by men 65 and over, but it must be purchased in Italy (it is not sold in North America) upon presentation of proof of age at any railway station. It will allow a 30% discount off the price of any ticket between points on the Italian rail network. It's good for 1 year and costs 15,000 lire ($11.80). It is not valid on Friday, Saturday, or Sunday between late June and late August or anytime during Christmas week.

An **Italian Railpass** (known within Italy as a BTLC Pass) allows non-Italian citizens to ride as much as they like within the entire rail network of Italy. (As previously mentioned, the rail systems of Sardinia are administered by a separate entity and are not included in this or any of the other passes mentioned.) In the rest of Italy, however, a supplement must be paid to ride on certain very rapid trains. These are designated as ETR-450 trains. (Also known as "Pendolino" trains, their high-speed technology is based on the principle of a pendulum, enabling trains to safely negotiate the sharp curves of Italy's railway tracks at high speeds.) Buy the pass in the U.S., have it validated the first time you use it at any railway station in Italy, and ride as frequently as you like within the time validity of your pass. An 8-day pass costs $206 in first class, $136 in second class; a 15-day pass costs $258 in first class, $172 in second class; a 21-day pass costs $298 in first class, $198 in second class; and a 30-day pass costs $380 in first class, $240 in second class.

More flexible and adaptable to the individual schedule of a traveler is the **Italian Flexirail Card,** which entitles its holder to a predetermined number of days of travel on any rail line of Italy within a certain period of validity. It's ideal for passengers who plan in advance to spend several days sightseeing before boarding a train for another city. A pass giving 4 valid travel days out of a block of 9 days costs $154 in first class, and $104 in second class; a pass for 8 travel days stretched over a 21-day period costs $226 in first class and $148 in second class; and a pass for 12 travel days within a time frame of 30 days costs $284 in first class and $190 in second class.

In addition, the **Kilometric Ticket** is valid for 2 months on regular trains. However, it can also be used on special train rides if you pay a supplement. The ticket is valid for 20 trips, providing that your total riding distance does not exceed 1,875 miles. The price is $238 in first class, dropping to $140 in second class.

With the exception of the Carta d'Argento (which must be purchased in Italy), any of the special discount cards mentioned above can be bought at any North American travel agency, or at CIT Italian State Railways, 594 Broadway, Suite 307, New York, NY 10012 (tel. 212/274-0590 for information).

Warning: Many irate readers have complained about train service in Italy; they have found the railroads dirty, unreliable, and with little regard for schedules. As you may have heard, strikes plague the country, and you never know as you board a train when it'll reach your destination.

BY SHIP

Some of Italy's most seasoned travelers recognize that traffic snarls and road congestion often detract from the country's glamour. An obvious answer to this dilemma is a tour of Italy by a mode of transportation that centuries ago made the Mediterranean the cradle of civilization—sea travel. There are several reputable companies plying the touristic waters for business, but the one offering one of the most attractive options is **Ocean Cruise Lines,** 1510 SE 17th Street, Fort Lauderdale, FL 33316 (tel. toll free 800/556-8850 in the U.S. and Canada).

Its Italian-built flagship, *Ocean Princess,* advertises itself as an intimate, four-star luxury liner. With berths for only 460 passengers (considerably smaller than mega-ships), the yachtlike vessel is capable of berthing in shallow waters, close to the action of harbor life, where larger vessels cannot go.

In the spring and fall, the company offers 10 11-day cruise/tours highlighting the Italian Riviera. The Venice–Nice cruise calls at Sorrento (for Capri or Pompeii), Elba, Taormina, and Portofino, plus Malta, Corfu, and Dubrovnik, depending on the direction. Another itinerary, from Nice to Nice, visits Palermo, Naples, Livorno, and Portofino, as well as Malta. The 11-day per-person rates (based on double occupancy), including the cruise, round-trip airfare from New York, and hotel stays before and/or after the cruise, begin at a reasonable $2,150 for the Venice–Nice cruise and $1,995 for the Nice–Nice itinerary. This is considerably less than one would pay for first-class hotels, meals, and intra-Europe transits if each of the components were purchased separately.

BY BUS

Italy has an extensive and intricate bus network, covering all regions of the country. Because most Italians regard rail travel as inexpensive, the bus is not the preferred method of travel.

ANAC, piazza Esquilino 29, in Rome (tel. 06/463383), blankets the country with air-conditioned coaches. You can pick up a copy of the company's timetable at the address above.

SITA, viale dei Cadorna 105, in Florence (tel. 055/278611), operates a service much like that of ANAC, and its schedule is also available at the address cited in Florence. Sometimes tourist offices also have schedules of these companies if you prefer travel by bus.

Where these nationwide services leave off, local bus companies operate in most regions, particularly in the hill sections and in the alpine regions where travel by rail is not possible. For more information about these services, refer to the "By Bus" sections, listed under "Getting There" under the various city, town, and village headings.

BY TAXI

Taxi service is readily available throughout Italy, in all towns and tourist resorts. Generally they wait in special taxi stands at railway stations and main parts of a city, but one can always be called by phone. Meters are provided and fares are displayed. Fares vary considerably from place to place. Find out the starting rate that is legal in the city or town you visit, and be sure that that's the amount showing on the meter when you embark, or you might find yourself paying for someone else's ride. Taxi trips outside the town area will have a supplemental charge.

BY CAR

U.S. and Canadian drivers are requested to carry an International Driver's License when touring Italy. Drivers without such a license may obtain from the Automobile Club d'Italia a declaration, entitling them to drive on Italian roads, upon presentation of a valid U.S. or Canadian driver's license. The declaration is available from any ACI frontier or provincial office. U.S. and Canadian licenses are valid in Italy if accompanied by an official translation.

The **Automobile Club d'Italia (ACI)** (tel. 06/4462117 or 06/4663370) is the equivalent of the AAA (American Automobile Association). It has offices throughout Italy, including the head office, via Marsala 8, 00185 Rome (tel. 06/49981).

RENTALS

Many say that the best way to see the country is by car, and I heartily agree with them. Many of the most charming landscapes—the same ones seen by Leonardo da Vinci—lie away from the main cities, far away from the train stations. For that, and for the sheer convenience that train travel will never match, you'll find that renting a car is usually the best way to travel if you plan to explore part of the country.

Renting a car is easy. All drivers in Italy must have nerves of steel, a sense of humor, a valid driver's license, a valid passport, and in most cases, must be between the ages of 21 and 70. In all cases, payment and paperwork are simpler if you present a valid credit card with your completed rental contract. If that isn't possible, the payment of a substantial cash deposit will probably be required in advance. Insurance on all vehicles is compulsory in Italy. A *Carta Verde* or "green card" is valid for 15, 30, or 45 days and should be issued to cover your car before your trip to Italy. Beyond 45 days, you must have a regular Italian insurance policy.

You'll find a bewildering assortment of car-rental kiosks at the airports and railway stations of many Italian cities, including the airports of Rome and Milan when you arrive. Especially prominent are the facilities of **Avis** (tel. toll free 800/331-2112), **Budget** (tel. toll free 800/472-3325), and **Hertz** (tel. toll free 800/654-3001), as well as several local car-rental companies. Although there are several reputable European-based car-rental companies, including the Italy-based Maggiore, I have usually found that billing errors are more easily resolved if you stick to an affiliate of one of North America's larger companies. If you do want to try **Maggiore,** they have offices at the Rome and Milan airports, as well as Roman headquarters at piazza della Repubblica 57 (tel. 06/463715).

Budget Rent-a-Car, referred to within Italy as "Italy by Car," sometimes charges less for weekly rentals than its major competitors. Also, except for its most expensive cars, Budget doesn't charge anything if you want to drop the rental car off in an Italian city different from the one where you originally picked it up. (Budget has about 36 locations in Italy, including offices in Sardinia and Sicily.) Many visitors use this option to begin and end their vacations at opposite ends of the peninsula.

All the major companies will quote two tiers of rental prices which either include or do not include collision-damage insurance. This extra protection will eliminate all financial responsibility to a renter in the event of an accident. Each of the companies, for an additional charge of between $11 and $16 a day (the amount varies with the value of the car), will sell a renter a collision-damage waiver (CDW). This policy will eliminate the renter's liability for any or all damage, including damage caused by attempted break-ins while the car is parked. Without the waiver, a renter at any of the companies is liable for up to the first $1,600 to $3,000 worth of damage, depending on the value of the car.

Each of the companies calculates its rates based on a complicated schedule which factors in the appropriate insurance coverage, often with specific discounts for members of certain organizations. Avis, for example, grants 10% discounts to members of both the American Automobile Association (AAA) and the American Association of Retired Persons (AARP). Without their insurance waivers included, the week-long rental of a Fiat Panda works out to $193 per week at Budget, $245 per week at Hertz, and $229 per week at Avis. (Special promotions might apply by the time of your rental, so it pays to make separate calls to each of the companies before your trip.) To these rates is added the unavoidable 19% government tax, plus the cost of any optional medical insurance you opt for at the time of rental.

Despite the appeal of extra insurance, many renters nonetheless decline it and save themselves the equivalent of between $77 and $120 per week in insurance charges. Even for drivers who always select the most comprehensive policies, declining this extra insurance is not as foolish as it sounds. Certain credit-card companies, including American Express, offer to pay the cost of any deductible damage to a rented car in certain countries *if the imprint of the credit card is made on the original rental contract*. The details of this arrangement with the credit-card companies, however, change frequently, so you must check with them before you decide to handle your coverage in this way. If you rely on the guarantee of your credit-card company to reimburse you for the value of the deductible damages to your car, be fully aware that you will first have to pay out a cash or credit-card settlement for the value of the damage to your car (this is usually, but not always, limited to around $3,000), file certain forms with the credit-card company, then wait for some time before the money is reimbursed or until the extra charges on your credit card are voided. But even if you pay up front for the extra insurance, Budget is often less expensive than its competitors.

Most vacationers who opt for a rental car in Italy usually keep it for a week or more to enjoy the freedom of wheels and the Italian countryside. Some visitors, however, who only want a car for a 2- or 3-day visit to the countryside, use Rome or perhaps Milan as their base. If you want just a short holiday in the countryside, try to plan your visit for a weekend, when some companies, most notably Hertz, offer values for short-term weekend rentals. At presstime, neither Budget nor Avis made similar arrangements through their North American network, although some Budget or Avis branches advertise certain weekend specials from their countertops in Italy.

Hertz defines a weekend as any time between 9am on Friday on 9am and Monday. The weekend rental of a Fiat Panda or a Peugeot 205, with few frills and manual transmission, costs about $58 for the full weekend, with unlimited mileage, pending availability, and must be returned to the same location. Insurance is not included, and the 19% government tax is extra.

These prices can—and almost certainly will—change by the time of your arrival in Rome. One thing is certain, however: The best prices are available at any company for clients who reserve their car at least 2 business days in advance from a telephone in North America.

GASOLINE

Gasoline is expensive in Italy, as are autostrade tolls. Carry enough cash if you're going to do extensive motoring. Gasoline discount coupons are part of a package of concessions offered to foreign motorists planning to tour Italy. Besides the gasoline coupons, the packages also offer free breakdown service, free motorway toll vouchers, and provision of a replacement car free for up to 10 days if the package participant's car is under repair for at least 12 hours. The packages must be paid for in foreign currency and may be purchased only outside Italy, at the main European automobile and touring clubs, at the offices of the Italian Government Tourist Office (ENIT) in Europe, and at any ACI or ENIT terrestrial and maritime border offices. These packages are available only to tourists driving their own cars (diesel-fueled vehicles excluded) with a non-Italian registration. The tourist purchases a "Tourist Incentive Package." Gasoline coupons in general yield a savings of approximately 15% compared to pump prices.

Gas prices vary throughout Italy, but count on spending more than $4 per U.S. gallon, although this is shaved by about 15% if you use one of the tourist discount vouchers. Gas stations on autostrade are open 24 hours a day, but on regular roads gas stations are rarely open on Sunday, many close between noon and 2pm for lunch, and most of them shut down after 7pm. Make sure the pump registers zero before an attendant starts refilling your tank. A popular scam, particularly in the south, is to fill your tank before resetting the meter so that you pay not only your bill but the charges run up by the previous motorist who'd already paid them.

DRIVING RULES

The Italian Highway Code follows the Geneva Convention, and Italy uses international road signs. Driving is on the right, passing on the left. Violators of the highway code are fined; serious violations may also be punished by imprisonment. In cities and towns, the speed limit is 50 kilometers per hour (kmph) or 31.25 miles per hour (m.p.h.). For all cars and motor vehicles on main roads and local roads, the limit is 90kmph or 56.25 m.p.h. For the autostrade (national express highways), the limit is 130kmph or 81.25 m.p.h. Seat belts are compulsory.

ROAD MAPS

The best touring maps are published by the **Automobile Club d'Italia (ACI)** and the **Italian Touring Club,** or you can purchase the maps of the **Carta Automobilistica d'Italia** covering Italy in two maps on the scale of 1:800,000 (1cm = 8km). These two maps should fulfill the needs of most motorists. If you plan to explore one region of Italy in depth, then consider one of 15 regional maps (1:200,000; 1cm = 2km), published by **Grande Carta Stradale d'Italia.**

All maps mentioned are sold at certain newsstands and at all major bookstores in Italy, especially those with travel departments. Many travel bookstores in the U.S. also carry them. If U.S. outlets don't have these maps, they often offer Michelin's red map (no. 988) of Italy which is on a scale of 1:1,000,000 (1cm = 10km). This map covers all of Italy in some detail.

BREAKDOWNS/ASSISTANCE

In case of car breakdown and for any tourist information, foreign motorists can call 116 (nationwide telephone service). For road information, itineraries, and all sorts of travel assistance, call 06/4212 (ACI's information center). Both services operate 24 hours a day.

BY FERRY

Ferries are used primarily in the south. Driving time from **Naples to Sicily** is cut considerably by taking one of the vessels operated by Tirrenia Lines, Molo Angioino, Stazione Maritime, in Naples (tel. 081/5512181). Departures are daily at 8:30pm for the 10½-hour trip to Palermo. Frequent ferry services and hydrofoils also depart from Naples for the offshore islands of Capri and Ischia.

From many ports on the Italian mainland, it's possible to reach the island of **Sardinia.** The most popular crossing is from Civitavecchia to Olbia (Sardinia). Departures from Civitavecchia are daily at 11pm for the 7-hour sea trip. In July and

August, one should book 2 weeks in advance. This can be done through a travel agent. The Tirrenia office in Civitavecchia is at Stazione Marittima (tel. 0766/500580).

The least expensive way to reach **Elba** is by ferry from Piombino Marittima which goes to Portoferraio, the largest city on Elba. Two companies, Toremar (tel. 0565/31100) and Navarma (tel. 0565/39775), both at piazzale Premuda in Piombino Marittima, operate these vessels.

HITCHHIKING

In Italy, it is illegal to hitch a ride on the autostrade, mainly because it's dangerous for a car to stop to take on a passenger. Savvy hitchhikers take the primary road systems instead. The less you're burdened by luggage and possessions, of course, the better your chances of getting a ride. Write your destination on a sign with large letters—it helps. Use the Italian name for a city, not the English one (Firenze instead of Florence, for example). Women should hitch in pairs, if at all, because sexual harrassment—or worse—is commonly reported. One Italian male driver confided that he considered any woman hitching a ride "fair game," and such attitudes are prevalent. Of course, young men traveling alone are also subject to propositions, and should take precautions. For example, don't let your baggage be stored in a locked trunk should you decide to make a hasty departure from the vehicle.

SUGGESTED ITINERARIES

IF YOU HAVE 1 WEEK

Days 1–3: Fly to Rome and spend most of the day recovering. If it's summer, view the floodlit Roman Forum at sunset from the balcony of the Campidoglio. Have a drink and dinner near the Spanish Steps and turn in early for a big day of sightseeing tomorrow. Your second day, take in the Colosseum and Forum and visit St. Peter's. On the morning of the third day, explore some of the highlights of the Vatican before going outside Rome to see the gardens at Tivoli and Hadrian's Villa.

Days 4 & 5: Transfer to Florence and soak up as much of the city of the Renaissance as time allows.

Days 6 & 7: Transfer to Venice where so many attractions await you that you will promise yourself a return visit when you have more time.

IF YOU HAVE 2 WEEKS

Most visitors fly into Rome or Milan. I've begun this tour in Rome, but it can be reversed if you fly into Milan instead. It takes in the four most visited (by North Americans) cities of Italy—Rome, Florence, Venice, and Milan—with some diversions along the way.

Days 1–4: Rome, Rome, and more Rome, and you can't begin to take it all in. The first day will be spent recuperating from jet lag and finding a hotel or reaching your reserved room through Rome's traffic. The most important sights are outlined in Chapter 5. If you're thinking you've allowed too much time for Rome, remember that it takes a whole day just to see a part of St. Peter's and the treasure-filled Vatican museums. Your final day might be spent visiting Tivoli and Hadrian's Villa in the environs.

Day 5: Drive north to Florence on the autostrada, veering east and inland (the road is marked) to either Assisi or Perugia, where you can spend the night. If there is time, try to visit both towns; otherwise, read the commentaries and make a choice.

Days 6–8: From Perugia, drive northwest toward the Tuscan capital, but spend most of the day exploring Siena before heading for Florence, where the average American stays 3 nights and 2 days. That will, of course, be shockingly little time to see some of the glories of the Renaissance, but it may be all the time you have.

Day 9: Drive on the autostrada toward Bologna to spend the night in the gastronomic center of Italy. If time is limited, skip a stopover in Bologna and drive directly to Venice.

Days 10–12: A minimum of 3 days is needed just to find your way around the narrow streets and waterways of this once-great maritime republic of the Adriatic. When you leave Venice, you will have seen only a fraction of its attractions.

Day 13: Drive west to Verona, city of Romeo and Juliet, where you can spend a busy day sightseeing and then stay overnight.

Day 14: Continue west to Milan, where you may have just enough time to view the Duomo before winging your way back home the next day.

IF YOU HAVE 3 WEEKS

Days 1–14: Spend your first 2 weeks as outlined above.

Days 15 & 16: To save time, fly on a domestic flight to Naples, as the wonders of Campagnia open up. You can explore once-buried Roman towns and ancient centers of Magna Graecia. You can be in Naples for lunch and afternoon sightseeing. The next morning, I'd catch the hydrofoil to Capri and spend the day there, to visit the Blue Grotto and many other attractions, before returning to Naples for the night.

Days 17 & 18: Leave Naples in the morning, and head south to Sorrento or one of the other resorts along the Amalfi Drive, including Amalfi itself or, better yet, Positano. Spend the rest of the day enjoying one of these resorts and get to bed early so you'll be prepared for a strenuous day of sightseeing. Either on your own or via an organized tour, make the traditional visits to the two towns that Vesuvius destroyed, Herculaneum and Pompeii. If time remains in your day, you can even go up to Mount Vesuvius itself to see the crater from which came the violent eruption. Return to Sorrento or one of the other towns for the night.

Day 19: Head down the coast to Paestum to see its three Doric temples before returning to Naples in the early evening to board a boat for Palermo, the capital of Sicily. If you don't have time for Sicily, you can break the tour here, returning to Rome for your flight back home. If you're going on to Sicily, you'll spend the night aboard the boat in a rented cabin, arriving in Palermo in the early hours of morning.

Day 20: Spend the day in Palermo, exploring its monuments and museums, and save time to visit the Church of Monreale in the hills. Overnight in Palermo.

Day 21: Drive west from Palermo and stop over in Erice, Trapani, or Marsala for lunch. However, don't linger too long in any place, as your major goal should be the ruins of Selinunte on the southern coast. Arrive in Agrigento for an overnight stop and drive through the "Valley of the Temples" at night (the ruins are floodlit).

9. WHERE TO STAY

HOTELS The Italians are never simple. If you aren't aware of that now, you soon will be as you find yourself coping with the myriad Italian hotel prices and classifications. A handy computer or a brain-trust accountant would be ideal to carry along with you.

Cardinal rule: If you want to enjoy average, "middle-class" comfort while keeping your wallet fairly intact, patronize the top-rated second-class hotels and their equivalents, the first-class pensiones. Patronage of a second- or even a third-class hotel does not reflect your social standing. In fact, many of the more cultivated of the world's social, literary, and artistic colony have habitually frequented unheralded small establishments in Italy not because of financial need but because of the charm and atmosphere they found there.

Italy controls the prices of its hotels, designating a minimum and a maximum rate. The difference between the two may depend either on the season, the location of the room, or even its size. Hotels are classified by stars in Italy, indicating their category of comfort: five stars for deluxe, four stars for first class, three stars for second class, two stars for third class, and one star for fourth class. Government ratings do not depend on sensitivity of decoration or on frescoed ceilings but rather on facilities such as elevators and the like. Many of the finest hostelries in Italy are rated second class because they only serve breakfast (a blessing really, for those seeking to escape the board requirements).

Hotels in Italy today are divided on the question of whether breakfast is included in the room price. Usually the more expensive establishments charge extra for this meal, which most often consists of cappuccino (coffee with milk) and croissants, with fresh butter and jam. First-class and deluxe establishments serve what is known as either an English breakfast or an American breakfast—meaning ham and eggs—but this must nearly always be ordered from the à la carte menu. Many smaller hotels and pensiones do not offer such a heavy breakfast, serving only the continental variety. Sometimes fresh juice such as orange is included in the continental breakfast; in other hotels you must pay extra. If you're really watching your lire, and if breakfast is included in the room price, always determine exactly what is included and what is extra. For example, mineral water, if ordered at breakfast, is nearly always à la carte.

Reservations are advised, even in the so-called slow hotel-booking months from November to March. Tourist travel to Italy peaks from May to October, when moderate and budget hotels are full. Only the most adventurous show up without a reservation.

It's easiest to reserve with a chain via their representatives in North America (and toll-free 800 numbers), but they might not be the type of accommodations you're seeking.

For hotels without representatives in North America, write or call. If you write, send an International Reply Coupon, available at post offices. When seeking reservations, give alternative dates if possible. If a hotel accepts your request, you may be asked to send 1 night's deposit. At small places in Italy, many readers reported great difficulty or even complete failure in getting their deposit returned if they were forced to cancel their reservations suddenly.

If you call a hotel right before your arrival, you may be lucky enough to secure a room because of a last-minute cancellation.

Like airlines, hotels traditionally overbook, counting on last-minute cancellations. When everybody shows up, however, they face irate customers shouting at the desk, waving a confirmed reservation. To avoid this, give the hotel a credit-card number and authorize management to add the cost to your bill even if you don't show up.

PENSIONES The *pensione* is generally more intimate and personal than a hotel—in one, the nature and quality of the welcome depend largely on the host or hostess, who might also be the cook and chief maid. As a general rule, a first-class pensione in Rome is the equivalent of a second-class hotel. A third-class hotel is the equivalent of a second-class pensione. In most of these pensiones, you'll be asked to take half-board arrangements, although not always.

ALPINE HUTS The **Club Alpino Italia,** via Ugo Foscolo 3, 20122 Milan, owns about 600 huts in mountain districts and publishes annually a book with a map and information on access, equipment, and tariffs for each one according to its classification. You can write—not call—for information.

BED & BREAKFAST In Italy, these establishments are commonplace, and they offer the best accommodation value. Finding a suitable one, however, may be tricky. Often B&B places are family homes or apartments, so don't count on hotel services, or even private baths. Sometimes, however, B&Bs are in beautiful private homes, lovely guesthouses, or restored mansions. Prices range from $15 to $35 per person nightly, including breakfast. Sometimes arrangements can be made for you to order an evening meal. Reservations organizations can book you into these establishments.

A good source is **Bed & Breakfast Reservations Services Worldwide, Inc.,** P.O. Box 39000, Washington, DC 20016 (tel. toll free 800/842-1486 in the U.S.), providing a listing of its members for $1.

HOME EXCHANGES An increasingly popular and economical way to travel is to exchange your home with that of an Italian family, often with a car included, provided you extend the same privilege. Several U.S.-based organizations specialize in this unique form of vacationing. Two of them, **International Home Exchange Service** and **Vacation Exchange Club,** are detailed in "Alternative/Adventure Travel," above.

RELAIS & CHATEAUX Most member hotels of this association are in France, but many of these prestigious (and invariably expensive) hotels also exist in Italy, about two dozen in all. If you travel the Relais & Châteaux route, it will invariably be deluxe. But instead of sterile modern hotels, you'll frequently get places steeped in atmosphere and quality, often palaces or ancient castles converted to receive guests.

Prices for a double room in these places can range anywhere from $150 to $500 a night. To qualify for membership, all participating hotels must have first-class food and service.

For an illustrated catalog of these establishments, send $5 to Relais & Châteaux, 2200 Lazy Hollow, Suite 152D, Houston, TX 77063. Catalogs are also available through David B. Mitchell & Co., 200 Madison Avenue, New York, NY 10016 (tel. 212/696-1323, or toll free 800/372-1323).

RELIGIOUS INSTITUTIONS Convents, monasteries, and other religious institutions in Italy offer accommodations, generally of the fourth-class hotel or *pensioni* category. Some are just for men; others are for women only. Many, however, accept married couples. Italian tourist offices generally have abbreviated listings of these accommodations, or you can write directly to the archdiocese (Archidiocesi di Roma, for example) in cities in which you desire such an accommodation.

VILLAS AND APARTMENTS For information on renting villas or apartments, you may write directly to the local tourist board or the provincial tourist office in the city or town you expect to stay. For addresses, refer to "Essentials" under the individual city or town listings. In Italy, information on villas and apartments is also available in daily newspapers or through local real-estate agents. The following organizations deal in the rental of villas or apartments in Italy.

At Home Abroad, Inc., 405 East 56th Street, New York, NY 10022 (tel. 212/421-9165). They're strong on Tuscany and Veneto, with excellent villas on the Italian Riviera and the Amalfi Coast. For a $50 registration fee, you get photographs of the properties and a newsletter.

Rent a Vacation Anywhere (RAVE), 328 Main Street East, Suite 526, Rochester, NY 14604 (tel. 716/454-6440), offers reasonably priced to deluxe apartments in Florence and Rome, plus a few listings for Milan. Vacation villas are also arranged from the Italian Riviera to Lake Como, and some Tuscan farmhouses are also available.

Hideaways International, 15 Goldsmith Street (P.O. Box 1270), Littleton, MA 01460 (tel. 508/486-8955, or toll free 800/843-4433), offers a good listing of private homes, villas, and apartments in Tuscany (Florence) and the Italian Riviera.

YOUTH HOSTELS The Italian Youth Hostel Association operates more than 50 hostels throughout Italy, and they are likely to be overcrowded in summer, particularly at popular tourist meccas. Reservations can be made by writing directly to the individual youth hostel. The headquarters, **Associazione Italiana Alberghi per la Gioventu,** via Cavour 44, 00184 Roma (tel. 06/462342), provides details. You must be a member. In the U.S. you can join before you go by contacting American Youth Hostels (AYH), P.O. Box 37613, Washington, DC 20013-7613 (tel. 202/783-6161). Membership is $25. If you're under 18 the charge is $10, and if you're over 54 it's $15.

10. WHERE TO DINE

Some restaurants offer a tourist menu or *menu turistico* at an inclusive price. The tourist menu includes soup (nearly always minestrone) or pasta, followed by a meat dish with vegetables, topped off by dessert (fresh fruit or cheese), as well as a quarter liter of wine or mineral water, along with the bread, cover charge, and service (you'll still be expected to tip something extra).

If you order from the tourist menu, you'll avoid the array of added charges that the restaurateur likes to tack on. You won't get the choicest cuts of meat, nor will you always be able to order the specialties of the house, but you'll probably get a quite good, filling repast if you pick and choose your restaurants carefully. But be warned. Even though a restaurant owner offers such a menu, the staff is often reluctant to serve it, since it is their least profitable item. Often the owner will advertise a tourist menu in the window, but it won't be featured on the menu you're shown by the waiter. You'll have to ask for it in most cases, and you won't win any "most beloved patron" contests when you do.

What about the *prezzo fisso*? A confused picture. A fixed-price meal might even undercut the tourist menu, offering a cheaper meal of the *casa*. On the other hand, it might not include wine, service, bread, or cover charge—for which you'll be billed extra. If you're on the most limited of budgets, make sure you understand what the prezzo fisso entails so as to avoid misunderstandings when you settle the tab.

The distinction between expensive and moderate restaurants in Italy is often blurred. For example, if you order a pasta, a fresh salad, and perhaps a selection of fresh fruit, along with a carafe of the house wine, the restaurant is likely to be a less expensive choice. However, should you prefer a heaping plate of antipasti, a separate pasta course, followed by bottled wine and a Florentine beefsteak, perhaps topped off by dessert, then your bill is likely to be in the more expensive category. So it depends a great deal on how much you want to eat. In many places, most vegetable courses are priced separately.

Most restaurants will charge you a *pane e coperto* (bread and cover) charge which is unavoidable. It's a charge restaurants impose for the privilege of your patronizing their establishment. This charge ranges from about 1,000 lire to 2,000 lire (80¢ to $1.55) per person. A tip (*servizio*), ranging from 10% to 15%, is usually added to your bill, but it is customary to leave some small change as an extra reward, especially if the service has been good.

Here's how to order a full meal in Italy. Begin with a *primo piatto* or first course, which is usually a pasta dish. It is also possible to order *antipasti* (hors d'oeuvres) as a first course. The *secondo piatto* (second course) consists of fish, meat, or poultry, often with a side dish of vegetables or a salad. The main course is called *contorno*. If you're still hungry, you can ask for a *dolce* (dessert). Restaurants almost insist that diners order at least a first and second course. Owners highly disapprove of foreign visitors who come in and order pasta as a main course, perhaps a salad, and then leave. Pressure, subtle or otherwise, is often applied for one to order both a first and a second plate of food. Otherwise, the restaurant figures it loses money on your patronage.

Restaurants owners have a ready response to those visitors who protest they don't want "so much food." If you want only a plate of spaghetti or something light, you need not reserve a table in a proper restaurant, but can patronize any number of cafeterias, *rosticcerias*, or *tavola caldas*. Regardless of what name they come under, these are usually low-priced establishments serving fast-food orders. Often their offerings are behind glass display cases. You don't pay a cover charge, and you can order as much or as little as you wish. You can also go to one of hundreds of pizzerias if you want only a light meal or snack. Many bars or café-bars, as the case may be, also offer both hot and cold food throughout the day. If you're lunching light in the heat, ask for a variety of sandwiches. Called *panini*, they are usually rolls stuffed with meat. *Tramezzini* are white-bread sandwiches with the crust trimmed. It's also possible to go into one of hundreds of general food stores throughout the country (called *alimentari*) and have sandwiches prepared on the spot, or else purchase the makings for a picnic lunch to be enjoyed in a park.

As a final caveat, phone numbers of restaurants often aren't valid for more than a year or two. For reasons known only to the restaurateurs themselves, opening hours, even days of closing, are changed frequently. So, if possible, always check the specific details with the restaurant of your choice before heading there. If the staff doesn't speak English and you need a confirmed reservation (always a good idea), ask someone at your hotel reception desk to make a reservation for you.

11. WHAT TO BUY

BEST BUYS

Considering the influences of ancient Rome and the visual breakthroughs of the Renaissance, the Italian aesthetic has probably exerted more power on the definition of beauty for Westerners than any other culture.

Because of the Italians' consummate skill as manufacturers and designers, it is no surprise that consumers from all over the world flock to Italy's shops, trade fairs, and design studios to see what's new, hot, and saleable back home.

Most obvious is **fashion,** which since World War II has played a major part in the economy of Milan, whose entrepreneurs view Rome as a principal distribution center. There are literally hundreds of famous designers for both men and women, most of whom make eminently wearable and stylish garments. Materials include silks, leathers, cottons, synthetics, and wools, often of the finest quality.

Italian design influences everything from typewriter keyboards to kitchen appliances to furniture. The Italian studios of Memphis-Milano and Studio Alchimia are two of the leaders in this field, and many of their products (and many copies of their products by derivative companies) are now highly visible in machines and furnishings throughout the world. Many of Italy's new products and designs can be previewed by reading a copy of *Domus,* a monthly magazine which reports, with photographs, on many different aspects of the country's design scene.

Food and wine never go out of style, and many gourmets import to North America the sophisticated gastronomic entities that somehow always taste better in Italy. Many shops sell chocolates, pastries, liqueurs, wines, and limited-edition olive oils. Be alert to restrictions in North America against importing certain food products. Italian wines, of course, include many excellent vintages, and bottles of liqueurs (which are sometimes distilled from herbs and flowers) make charming and unusual gifts.

The **glassware** of Italy (and especially of Venice) is famous throughout the world. Elegant homes from Florida to California benefit greatly from the addition of a glass chandelier from Murano, for example, or a set of wine goblets. Shipping is a problem, but for a price, any object—no matter how fragile or elaborate—can be packed, shipped, and insured.

The **porcelain** of Italy is elegant and sought-after, but I personally prefer the hand-painted rustic plates and bowls of thick-edged **stoneware.** Done in strong and clear glazes, and influenced by their rural origins, the bowls and plates are both charming and humorous, and are often used at the most formal dinners for their originality and style. The **tiles and mosaics** of Italy are also charming, whether used individually as drink coasters or decorative ornaments, or in groups set into masonry walls.

Lace was, for many years, made in convents by nuns in cloisters. Venice became the country's headquarters. Handmade Italian lace is beautiful and justifiably expensive, crafted into an amazing array of tablecloths, napkins, clothing, and bridal veils. Beware of machine-made imitations, although with a bit of practice you'll soon be able to recognize the shoddy copies.

Paper goods, writing stationery, and beautifully bound books, prints, and engravings are specialties of Italy. The engraving you find amid stacks of dozens of others will invariably look beautiful when hanging—framed—on a wall back home.

Fabrics, especially silk, are made in the district of Lake Como, in the foothills of the Italian Alps. Known for their supple beauty and their ability to hold color for years (the thicker the silk, the more desirable), these silks are rivaled only by the finest of

India, Thailand, and China. Their history in Italy goes back to the era of Marco Polo, and possibly much earlier.

Finally, ranging from inspirational to grossly tasteless, Rome is the home to a **religious objects** industry which supplies virtually everything a conservative Catholic might want as a religious aid. Centered in Rome around the streets near the Church of Santa Maria Sopra Minerva are dozens of shops selling pictures, statues, and reliefs of most of the important saints, the Madonna, Jesus, and—a perennial favorite—John the Baptist.

TAX REBATES

Visitors to Italy are sometimes appalled at the high taxes and add-ons that seem to influence so many of the bottom-line costs of their trip. Those taxes (totaling as much as 19% for certain luxury goods), which apply to big-ticket purchases of more than 625,000 lire ($490.65), can be refunded if you plan ahead and perform a bit of sometimes tiresome paperwork. At the time of your purchase (of the antique, vase, or garment you couldn't live without), collect a formal receipt from the vendor. When you leave Italy, find an Italian Customs agent at the airport (or at the point of your exit from the country if you're traveling by train, bus, or car). The agent will want to see the item you've bought, confirm that it is physically leaving Italy, and stamp the vendor's receipt.

You should then mail the stamped receipt (keeping a photocopy for your records) back to the original vendor. The vendor will, sooner or later, send you a refund of the tax you paid at the time of your original purchase. Reputable stores view this as a matter of ordinary paperwork and are very businesslike about it. Less honorable stores might lose your dossier. It pays to deal with established vendors on purchases of this size.

FAST FACTS ITALY

American Express Offices are found in Rome at piazza di Spagna 38 (tel. 06/722801), in Florence at via Guicciardini 49R (tel. 055/278751), in Venice at San Marco 1471 (tel. 041/520-0844), in Naples at Ashiba Travel, piazza Municipio 1 (tel. 081/551-5303), and in Milan at via Brera 3 (tel. 02/85571).

Business Hours Regular business hours are Monday through Friday from 9am (sometimes 9:30am) to 1pm and 3:30 (sometimes 4) to 7 or 7:30pm. In July or August, offices may not open in the afternoon until 4:30 or 5pm. **Banks** in Italy are open Monday through Friday from 8:30am to 1 or 1:30pm, and 2 or 2:30 to 4pm; closed all day Saturday, Sunday, and on national holidays. Traveler's checks can be exchanged for Italian currency at most hotels and at the foreign-exchange offices in main railway stations and at airports. Most **stores** are open from 9am to 1pm year round. Shops in Rome in summer reopen at 3:30 or 4pm, doing business until 7:30 or 8pm. Grocery stores are likely to reopen at 5pm. This siesta is observed in Rome, Naples, and most cities of southern Italy; however, in Milan and other northern and central cities the siesta is not faithfully observed and has been completely abolished by some merchants. Most shops are closed on Sunday, except for certain barbershops open Sunday morning. However, hairdressers are closed on Sunday and Monday. If you're traveling in Italy in summer and the heat is intense, I suggest that you learn the custom of the siesta, too.

Camera/Film U.S.-brand film is available in Italy but it's expensive. Take in as much as Customs will allow if you plan to take a lot of pictures.

Cigarettes Seek out stores called *tabacchi*. Some bars also sell cigarettes. For a package of U.S. cigarettes in your familiar brand, you'll pay more than for an Italian variety. However, the taste may be unfamiliar and may require some getting used to. American and British contraband cigarettes are sold freely on the streets for much less than you'll pay in the shops. Although purchasing them is illegal, it seems to be the custom.

Climate See "When to Go" in this chapter.

Crime See "Safety," below.

Currency See "Information, Entry Requirements & Money" in this chapter.

Customs Most items for personal use can be brought duty free into Italy. This includes clothing (new and used), books, camping and household equipment, fishing tackle, a sporting gun and 200 cartridges, a pair of skis, two tennis racquets, a portable typewriter, a record player with 10 records, a tape recorder or Dictaphone, baby carriage, two ordinary hand cameras with 10 rolls of film, a movie camera with 10 rolls of film, binoculars, personal jewelry, a portable radio set (subject to a small license fee), 400 cigarettes (two cartons) or a quantity of cigars or pipe tobacco not exceeding 500 grams (1.1 lbs.).

A maximum of two bottles of alcoholic beverages per person can be brought in duty free. Specifically, overseas tourists arriving in Italy, after having visited other countries, will be allowed to carry with them, without any special formality except a verbal declaration, travel souvenirs purchased in said countries up to a total lira value equivalent of $500 (U.S.), including fine perfumes up to half a liter.

Upon leaving Italy, citizens of the United States who have been outside the country for 48 hours or more are allowed to bring back to their home country $400 worth of merchandise duty free—that is, if they have claimed no similar exemption within the past 30 days. If you make purchases in Italy, it is important to keep your receipts.

Documents Required See "Information, Entry Requirements & Money" in this chapter.

Driving Rules See "Getting Around" in this chapter.

Drug Laws Penalties are severe and could lead to either imprisonment or deportation. Selling drugs to minors is dealt with particularly harshly.

Drugstores At every drugstore (*farmacia*), there is a list of those that are open at night and on Sunday. This list rotates.

Electricity The electricity in Italy varies considerably. It's usually alternating current (A.C.), varying from 42 to 50 cycles. The voltage can be anywhere from 115 to 220. It is recommended that any visitor carrying electrical appliances obtain a transformer either before leaving the U.S. or Canada or in any electrical appliance shop in Italy. Check the exact local current with the hotel where you are staying. Plugs have prongs that are round, not flat; therefore an adapter plug is needed.

Embassies/Consulates The **American Embassy** in Rome is at via Vittorio Veneto 19A (tel. 06/488741). U.S. consulates are in Florence at lungarno Amerigo Vespucci 46 (tel. 055/298276); in Genoa at Banca d'America è Italia Building, piazza Portello 6 (tel. 010/282741); in Milan at piazza della Repubblica 32 (tel. 02/652841); in Naples at piazza della Repubblica (tel. 081/660966); and in Palermo at via Vaccarini 1 (tel. 091/291532). The U.S. Consulate General's office has a list of doctors and dentists who speak English.

Consular and passport services for **Canada** are in Rome at via Zara 30 (tel. 06/440-3028), open Monday through Friday from 10am to noon and 2 to 4pm (from mid-July until the end of August, hours are 10am to 2pm). For the **United Kingdom,** offices in Rome are at via XX Settembre 80A (tel. 06/475-5441), open Monday through Friday from 9:30am to 12:30pm and 2 to 4pm. Consular and passport services for **Australia** are in Rome at via Alessandria 215 (tel. 06/832721), open Monday through Thursday from 9am to noon and 1 to 4pm and on Friday from 9am to noon. For **New Zealand,** the office in Rome is at via Zara 28 (tel. 06/440-2928), and hours are Monday through Friday from 8:30am to 12:45pm and 1:45 to 5pm. In case of emergency, embassies have a 24-hour referral service.

Emergencies Dial 113 for an **ambulance, police, or fire.** In case of a **breakdown** on an Italian road, dial 116 at the nearest telephone box; the nearest Automobile Club of Italy (ACI) will be notified to come to your aid.

Etiquette Women in sleeveless dresses and men with bare chests are not welcome in the best bars and restaurants of Italy and may be refused service. Also, persons so attired are ordered to cover up when they visit museums and churches.

Gasoline See "Getting Around" in this chapter.

Hitchhiking See "Getting Around" in this chapter.

Holidays   See "When to Go" in this chapter.

Information   See "Information, Entry Requirements & Money" in this chapter, and specific city for local information offices.

Language   The official language of Italy, of course, is Italian, a Romance tongue derived from Latin, although it bears little resemblance to the Latin you may have studied in school. The language spoken today also is based on the Tuscan dialect. Numerous dialects were common throughout parts of Italy until the Tuscan dialect became Italy's literary language in the 14th century. Other Latin-based dialects will be heard in various areas, such as a language called Romansh in Friuli–Venezia Giulia in the north and in some Dolomite regions. In Sardinia, many people still speak the ancient Roman language called Sardinian. In the Italian Tyrol, German is spoken, and French is the language in the Pennine alpine valley of Aosta.

Laundry   All deluxe and first- and second-class hotels have laundry and dry-cleaning facilities. Prices are usually moderate, and a small service charge is added to the actual cost. If a hotel doesn't provide these services, the desk clerk can direct you to the nearest *tintoria* (shop), or you can look in the classified telephone directory under *tintorie* (cleaning and pressing) and *lavanderie* (laundry).

Legal Aid   The consulate of your country is the place to turn, although offices cannot interfere in the Italian legal process. They can, however, inform you of your rights and provide a list of attorneys. You'll have to pay for the attorney out of your pocket, however, as there is no free legal assistance. If you're arrested for a drug offense, about all the consulate will do is notify a lawyer about your case and perhaps inform your family.

Liquor Laws   Wine with meals has been considered a normal part of family life for hundreds of years in Italy. Children are exposed to wine at an early age, and alcoholic consumption is not considered anything out of the ordinary. There is no legal drinking age for buying or ordering alcohol. Alcohol is sold day and night throughout the year, as there is almost no restriction on the sale of wine or liquor in Italy.

Lost Property   Report the loss to the nearest police station. For large cities, such as Rome, refer to "Fast Facts" under individual city listings.

Mail   At post offices, General Delivery service is available in Italy. Correspondence can be addressed c/o the post office by adding *Fermo Posta* to the name of the locality. Delivery will be made at the local central post office upon identification of the addressee by passport. In addition to all post offices, you can purchase stamps at little *tabacchi* (tobacco) stores throughout the city.

Mail delivery in Italy is notoriously bad. One letter from a soldier, postmarked in 1945, arrived in his home village in 1982. Letters sent from New York, say, in November, are often delivered (if at all) the following year. If you're writing for hotel reservations, it can cause much confusion on both sides. Many visitors arrive in Italy long before their hotel deposits. Fax machines speed up the process tremendously.

Maps   See "Getting Around" in this chapter. Also see certain map recommendations under city listings for such cities as Rome, Florence, and Venice.

Newspapers/Magazines   In major cities, it is possible to find the *International Herald Tribune* as well as other English-language newspapers and magazines at hotels and news kiosks, including *Time* and *Newsweek*.

Pets   A veterinarian's certificate of good health is required for dogs and cats, and should be obtained by owners before entering Italy. Dogs must be on a leash or muzzled at all times. Other animals must undergo examination at the border or port of entry. Certificates for parrots or other birds subject to psittacosis must state that the country of origin is free of disease. All documents must be certified first by a notary public, then by the nearest Italian Consulate.

Police   The all-purpose number for police emergency assistance in Italy is **113.**

Radio/TV   Most radio and television broadcasts are on RAI, the Italian state radio and TV network. Occasionally, especially during the tourist season, the network will broadcast special programs in English. Announcements are made in the radio and TV guide sections of local newspapers. Vatican Radio also carries foreign-language religious news programs, often in English. Shortwave transistor radios pick up broadcasts from the BBC (British), Voice of America (United States), and CBC (Canadian). RAI television and private channels broadcast only in Italian. More expensive hotels often have TV sets in the bedrooms with cable subscriptions to the CNN news network.

Rest Rooms   All airport and railway stations have rest rooms, often with attendants, who expect to be tipped. Bars, nightclubs, restaurants, cafés, and all hotels have facilities as well. Public toilets are also found near many of the major sights.

Safety   Whenever you're traveling in an unfamiliar city or country, stay alert. Be aware of your immediate surroundings. Wear a moneybelt and don't sling your camera or purse over your shoulder. This will minimize the possibility of your becoming a victim of crime. Every society has its criminals. It's your responsibility to be aware and be alert even in the most heavily touristed areas.

Taxes   As a member of the European Common Market, Italy imposes a tax on most goods and services. It is a "value-added tax," called IVA in Italy. For example, the tax affecting most visitors is that imposed at hotels, which ranges from 9% in first- and second-class hotels and pensions to 18% in deluxe hotels.

Telegram/Telephone/Telex/Fax   For telegrams, ITALCABLE operates services abroad, transmitting messages by cable or satellite. Both internal and foreign **telegrams** may be dictated over the phone (dial 186).

A **public telephone** is always near at hand in Italy, especially if you're near a bar. Local calls from public telephones require the use of tokens (*gettone*) or coins. To make your call, deposit a 200-lira token in the slot but don't release it until after the number has been dialed and the party has answered. Tokens can be purchased at all tobacco shops and bars.

Thanks to ITALCABLE, **international calls** to the U.S. and Canada can be dialed directly. Dial 00 (the international code from Italy), then the country code (1 for the U.S. and Canada), the area code, and the number you are calling. Calls dialed directly are billed on the basis of the call's duration only. A reduced rate is applied from 11pm to 8am Monday through Saturday and all day Sunday.

If you wish to make a **collect or credit-card call,** dial 170. An ITALCABLE operator will come on and will speak English. If you make a **long-distance call** from a public telephone, there is no surcharge. *However, hotels have been known to double or triple the cost of the call, so be duly warned.*

Chances are your hotel will send or receive a **telex or fax** for you.

Time   In terms of standard time zones, Italy is 6 hours ahead of eastern standard time in the United States. Daylight saving time goes into effect in Italy each year from May 22 to September 24.

Tipping   This custom is practiced with flair in Italy—many people depend on tips for their livelihoods. In **hotels,** the service charge of 15% or 18% is already added to a bill. In addition, it's customary to tip the chambermaid 1,000 lire (80¢) per day; the doorman (for calling a cab), 1,000 lire (80¢); and the bellhop or porter, 1,500 lire ($1.20) per bag. A concierge expects 3,000 lire ($2.35) per day, as well as tips for extra services performed, which could include help with long-distance calls, newspapers, or stamps.

In **restaurants,** 15% is added to your bill to cover most charges. An additional tip for good service is almost always expected. Know that it is customary in certain fashionable restaurants in Rome, Florence, Venice, and Milan to leave an additional 10%, which, combined with the assessed service charge, is a very high tip indeed. The sommelier expects 10% of the cost of the wine. Checkroom attendants now expect 1,500 lire ($1.20), although in simple places Italians still hand washroom attendants 100 lire to 300 lire (10¢ to 25¢), more in deluxe and first-class establishments. Restaurants are required by law to give customers official receipts.

In **cafés and bars,** tip 15% of the bill, and give a **theater** usher 1,500 lire ($1.20). **Taxi drivers** expect at least 15% of the fare.

Tourist Offices   See "Information, Entry Requirements & Money" in this chapter, and also specific city chapters.

Visas   See "Information, Entry Requirements & Money" in this chapter.

Water   It is generally considered safe to drink. However, if you venture into the south of Italy, particularly the Naples region, it is best to stick to bottled water.

Yellow Pages   Unless you're fluent in Italian, better forget these. Ask at your hotel for assistance if you're seeking a particular establishment, such as the nearest dry-cleaning store.

CHAPTER 3

INTRODUCING ROME

1. ORIENTATION
- WHAT'S SPECIAL
  ABOUT ROME
2. GETTING AROUND
- FAST FACTS: ROME
3. NETWORKS &
  RESOURCES

The population of Rome is composed mainly of the Romans and the visitors—the two are virtually inseparable. Paris remains indubitably French, even with its hordes of aliens. But in Rome the visitor and the local people become entwined. The city almost seems at times to exist as a host to its never-ending stream of sightseers. It wines them, dines them, and entertains them.

Rome is also a city of images, beginning at dawn, which, in my view, is best seen from Janiculum Hill if you get up early enough or stay up late enough. With its bell towers and cupolas, the silhouette of Rome comes into view. It is a city of sounds, as the first peal of bells calls the faithful to an early-morning mass. As the city wakes up, office-workers rush into cafés for their first cappuccinos of the day, often passing by fruit and vegetable stands (the Romans like their produce fresh).

By 10am the tourists are on the street battling city traffic in their quest for a contact with art and history. Renaissance palaces and baroque facades give way eventually to what is left from the ruins of antiquity, the heritage of a once-great empire.

In Chapter 5, I'll take you on seemingly endless treks through ancient monuments and basilicas. But monuments are not the total picture. In Rome, you'll find yourself embracing life with intensity. In other words, "When in Rome. . . ."

1. ORIENTATION

ARRIVING

BY PLANE Chances are that you'll arrive in Italy at Rome's **Leonardo da Vinci International Airport** (tel. 06/60121), popularly known as Fiumicino, from the town located adjacent to the airport, 18½ miles from the center of the capital. Domestic flights arrive at one terminal, international ones at the other. (If you're flying by charter, you might arrive at Ciampino Airport.)

The least expensive way into Rome from Fiumicino is via a small train departing from the terminal in front of the airport and taking you in about 20 minutes to Ostiense, a suburban rail station. Departures are about every 30 minutes, and the cost is 5,000 lire ($3.95). You can insert a 5,000-lira ($3.95) note in a machine which makes change and gives you the ticket. At Ostiense, you can connect on the lower level with Metropolitan Line B, Piramide station, of the subway system which will take you to Roma Termini at the center of Rome.

Should you arrive on a charter flight at **Ciampino** (tel. 06/724241), take an ACOTRAL bus, departing every 30 minutes or so, which will deliver you to a stop of Metropolitana Line A which will take you into the center.

Taxis from Fiumicino are quite expensive—60,000 lire ($47.10) and up—and therefore not recommended for the trip from the airport.

If you arrive at Ciampino, you're nearer the city, which is usually reached in less than half an hour. Because of the shorter distance, you pay the amount shown on the meter if you go by taxi (not double, as some drivers may insist).

Rome is serviced by many international carriers, among them **TWA,** via Barberini

WHAT'S SPECIAL ABOUT ROME

Ancient Monuments

- ☐ Foro Romano (Roman Forum), ringed by the Palatine and Capitoline hills, the hub of a great imperial city.
- ☐ The Colosseum, symbol of classical Rome, built in A.D. 80 by 20,000 slaves—Byron called it "the gladiator's bloody circus."
- ☐ Ostia Antica, the long-buried city at the mouth of the Tiber, once the seaport and naval base of ancient Rome.
- ☐ The Pantheon, the best-preserved monument of ancient Rome, constructed by order of Emperor Hadrian around A.D. 120.

Religious Shrines/Museums

- ☐ St. Peter's, the world's greatest basilica, spiritual home for millions of Catholics.
- ☐ Basilica of San Giovanni in Laterano, the seat of the archibishop of Rome and the cathedral of Rome.
- ☐ The Vatican, papal residency for 600 years and setting for 4½ miles of art, including Michelangelo's Sistine Chapel.

Parks & Gardens

- ☐ Villa Borghese, a public park with open-air cafés and the Borghese Gallery.
- ☐ Villa d'Este, at Tivoli, outside Rome, with one of the wonders of Italy—its 16th-century fountains.

Ace Attractions

- ☐ The Spanish Steps, the eternal center for tourists and expatriates, everybody from Keats to Wagner.
- ☐ Piazza Navona, the finest of Rome's squares, the former stadium of Domitian, now filled with visitors ringing Bernini's Fountain of the Four Rivers.

Film Locations

- ☐ Not only monuments, but three films helped put Rome on the postwar tourist map: *Roman Holiday*, Fellini's *La Dolce Vita*, and *Three Coins in the Fountain*, which launched the tradition of tossing a coin over your shoulder to assure a return visit to Rome.

---

38 (tel. 06/47211), and **British Airways,** via Bissolati 54 (tel. 06/479991). The national carrier, **Alitalia,** is at via Bissolati 13 (tel. 06/46881).

BY TRAIN Trains arrive in the center of old Rome at the **Stazione Termini,** piazza dei Cinquecento (tel. 4775), the train and subway transportation hub for all of Rome. Many hotels lie within the radius of the station, and you can walk to your hotel if you don't have too much luggage. Otherwise, an array of taxi, bus, and subway lines await you.

If you're taking the Metropolitan (Rome's subway network), follow the illuminated M sign in red which points the way. To catch a bus, go straight through the outer hall of the termini and enter the sprawling bus lot of the piazza dei Cinquecento. Taxis are also found here.

The termini is filled with services. At a branch of the Banca Nazionale delle Communicazioni (between Tracks 8–11 and Tracks 12–15) you can exchange money. Information on rail travel to other parts of Italy is dispensed as Informazioni Ferroviarie, in the larger outer hallway. There is also a Tourist Information Booth here, along with baggage services, barbershops, day hotels, gift shops, restaurants, and bars. But beware of pickpockets, perhaps young children.

BY BUS Arrivals are at the **Stazione Termini** (see above), where all the same facilities awaiting train passengers are also available to bus passengers. Information on buses is dispensed at a booth operated by ATAC, the city bus company, at piazza dei Cinquecento, which is open daily from 7:30am to 7:30pm. The main office of ATAC is at via Volturno 65 (tel. 06/46951).

BY CAR From the north the main access route is the **AI (Autostrada del SoD,** cutting through Milan and Florence, or you can take the coastal route, SSI Aurelia, from Genoa. If you're driving north from Naples, you take the southern lap of the **Autostrada del Sole (A2).** All these autostrade join with the **Grande Raccordo Anulare,** a ring road that encircles Rome, channeling traffic into the congested city. Long before you reach this ring road, you should study a map carefully to see what part of Rome you plan to enter and mark your route accordingly. Route markings along the ring road tend to be confusing.

TOURIST INFORMATION

Tourist information is available at the **Ente Provinciale per il Turismo,** via Parigi 11, 00185 Roma (tel. 06/4883748), open daily from 8:15am to 7:15pm. There's another **information bureau** at the Stazione Termini (tel. 06/4871270), open daily from 8:30am to 7pm.

CITY LAYOUT

Your feet will probably first touch Roman soil at **Leonardo da Vinci International Airport,** near the mouth of the Tiber River, 18½ miles from the center of Rome. The drive in to the city is rather uneventful until you pass through the city wall, the still remarkably intact **Great Aurelian Wall,** started in A.D. 271 to calm Rome's barbarian jitters. Suddenly, ruins of imperial baths loom on one side, great monuments can be seen in the middle of blocks, and you have the shock of recognition that you're really in Rome—not simply looking at pictures. Inside the walls you'll find a city designed for a population that walked to get where it was going. Parts of Rome actually look and feel more like an oversize village than the former imperial capital of the Western world.

The Stazione Termini faces a huge piazza, **piazza dei Cinquecento,** which in many ways is an embodiment of the city. It's named after 500 Italians who died heroically in a 19th-century battle in Africa. There are certainly many more attractive sites in Rome, but this piazza has several noteworthy aspects. First, it is next to the modern railroad station. Immediately next to the sculptured-concrete cantilevered roof of the station facade is a remnant of the Servian Wall, built nearly 6 centuries before the birth of Christ by an ancient Roman king. If that isn't enough, the far side of the piazza is bordered by the ruins of the Baths of Diocletian, a former bastion of imperial luxury whose crumbling brick walls were once covered with the rarest of colored marbles and even now enclose marble and bronze statuary.

Most of the old city and its monuments lie on the east side of the **Tiber River (Fiume Tevere),** which meanders through town between 19th-century stone embankments. However, several important monuments are on the other side: **St. Peter's Basilica** and the **Vatican,** the **Castel Sant' Angelo** (formerly the tomb of the Emperor Hadrian), and the colorful section of town known as **Trastevere.** The bulk of ancient, Renaissance, and baroque Rome lies across the Tiber from St. Peter's on the same side as the Stazione Termini. The various quarters of the city are linked by large boulevards (large at least in some places) that have mostly been laid out since the late 19th century.

Starting from the **Victor Emmanuel monument,** a highly controversial pile of snow-white Brescian marble whose quarrying and construction must have employed whole cities, there's a street running practically due north to the **piazza del Popolo** and the city wall. This is **via del Corso,** one of the main streets of Rome—noisy, congested, always crowded with buses and shoppers, called simply "Corso." Again from the Victor Emmanuel monument, the major artery going west (and ultimately across the Tiber to St. Peter's) is **corso Vittorio Emanuele.** To go in the other direction, toward the Colosseum, you take **via dei Fori Imperiali,** named for the excavated ruins of the imperial forums that flank this avenue. This road was laid out in the 1930s by Mussolini, who was responsible for much of the fine archeological work in Rome, if perhaps for the wrong reasons. Yet another central conduit is **via Nazionale,** running from **piazza della Repubblica** (also called the piazza

ROME

American Express,
  piazza di Spagna ③
Città del Vaticano ⑬
Corso Vittorio
  Emanuele II ⑫
EPT information office ⑧
Information Bureau,
  Stazione Termini ⑥
Piazza dei Cinquecento ⑤
Piazza della Repubblica ④
Piazza del Popolo ②
Piazza di Spagna ③
Piazza Venezia ⑨
Stazione Termini ⑦
Tiber River
  (Fiume Tevere) ①
Via dei Fori Imperiale ⑩
Via del Corso ⑧
Via Nazionale ⑪

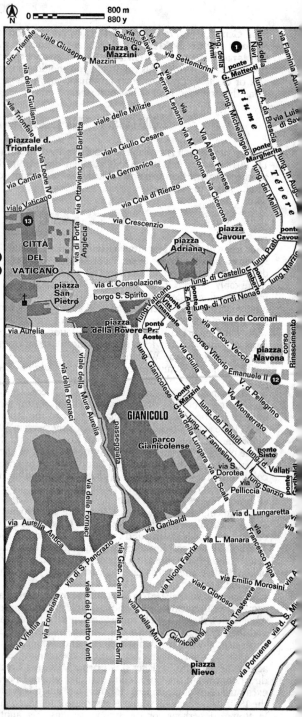

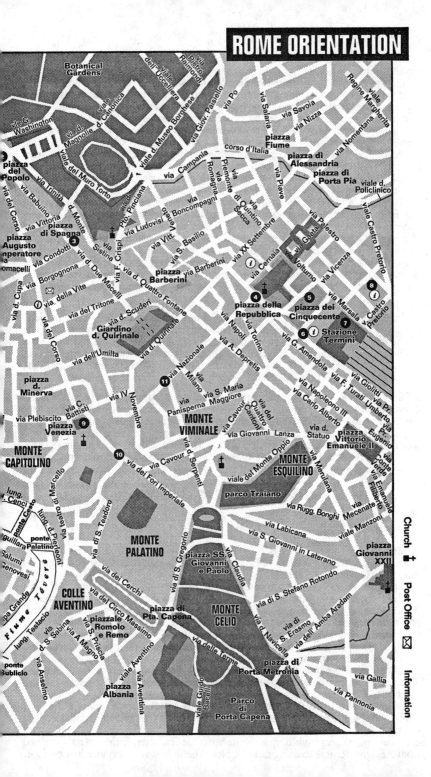

ROME ORIENTATION

Esedra), ending again right by the Victor Emmanuel monument at **piazza Venezia,** which lies in front of it.

For the 2½ millennia before these boulevards were built, the citizens had to make their way through narrow byways and curves that defeated all but the best senses of direction. These streets—among the most charming aspects of the city—still exist in large quantities, mostly unspoiled by the advances of modern construction. However, this tangled street plan has one troublesome element: automobiles. The traffic in Rome is awful! When the claustrophobic street plans of the Dark Ages open unexpectedly onto a vast piazza, every driver accelerates full throttle for the distant horizon, while groups of peripatetic tourists and Romans flatten themselves against marble fountains for protection or stride with firm jaws right into the thick of the howling traffic.

The traffic problem in Rome is nothing new. Julius Caesar was so exasperated by it that he banned all vehicular traffic during the daylight hours. Sometimes it's actually faster to walk than to take a bus, especially during any of Rome's four daily rush hours (that's right, *four:* to work, home for lunch/siesta, back to work, home in the evening). The hectic crush of urban Rome is considerably less during the month of August, when many Romans are out of town on holiday. If you visit at any other time of year, however, be prepared for the general frenzy that characterizes your average Roman street.

FINDING AN ADDRESS Finding an address in Rome can be a problem because of the narrow, often cobbled streets of old Rome and the little, sometimes "hidden" piazzas or squares. Numbers usually run consecutively, with odd numbers on one side of the street and even numbers on the other side. However, in the old districts a different system is sometimes followed, although it is rare. These ancient streets begin their numbering on one side, running in order until the end, then running back in the opposite direction on the other side. Therefore, no. 50 could be opposite no. 308.

STREET MAPS Arm yourself with a detailed street map, not the general overview often handed out free at tourist offices. Even if you're in Rome for only a day or two, and plan to see only the major monuments, you'll still need a detailed street map to find such attractions as the Trevi Fountain. The best ones are published by **Falk,** and they're available at most newsstands and kiosks in Rome. The best selections of maps are sold in the travel departments of various bookstores. See "Bookstores" under "Fast Facts: Rome," below.

NEIGHBORHOODS IN BRIEF

Here are the main districts of interest, and some of their more important attractions. Often a district will be named for a major square or monuments, such as the piazza di Spagna or the piazza Navona district.

Ancient Rome This is the district that most visitors come to Rome to explore, taking in the Colosseum, Palatine Hill, the Roman Forum, the Fori Imperiali (Imperial Forums), and Circus Maximus.

Appian Way Via Appia Antica is a 2,300-year-old road that has witnessed much of the history of the ancient world. By 190 B.C. it extended from Rome to Brindisi, and its most famous sights today are the catacombs, the graveyards of patrician families. It was here that Christ had the famous exchange with St. Peter ("Lord, whither goest thou?"). Christ explained that he was returning to Rome to be crucified again, since Peter had abandoned the Christians in their hour of need. Peter returned to Rome and his own martyrdom.

Città del Vaticano [Vatican City] is a small "city-state" but its influence extends around the world. The Vatican Museums and St. Peter's take up most of the land area and the popes have lived here for 6 centuries.

Medieval Rome [piazza Navona and Pantheon] One of the most alluring areas of Rome centers around the piazza Navona and the Pantheon. The district is a maze of narrow streets and alleys from the Middle Ages and is filled with churches and palaces built during the Renaissance era, often with materials stripped from Ancient Rome, including rare marbles. The only way to explore it is on foot.

Monte Mario   On the northwest precincts of Rome, this residential area offers magnificent views over the eternal city, especially from Villa Madama, which was launched by Raphael but is closed to the public. Monte Mario is the site of the deluxe Cavalieri Hilton where you can stop in for a drink.

Parioli   This is the most elegant residential section of Rome, framed by the green spaces of Villa Borghese to the south and Villa Glori and Villa Ada to the north. It is a setting for some of the city's finest restaurants, hotels, and nightclubs.

Piazza di Spagna   Ever since the 17th century these steps—former site of the Spanish ambassador's residence—have been the center of tourist Rome. Keats lived in a house opening onto the steps, and some of Rome's most prestigious shopping streets fan out from it, including via Condotti.

Prati   Known only to the connoisseurs of Rome, this district is really a middle-class suburb, lying north of Castel Sant'Angelo and Vatican City. It is becoming increasingly patronized by budget travelers because of its low-cost *pensioni* (boarding houses). The flower market in the Trionfale Quarter to the west is worth the trip.

Renaissance Rome   South of corso Vittorio Emanuele, many buildings in this district were constructed in Renaissance times as private homes. Much of the section centers around the Palazzo Farnese. Walk via Giulia with its antiques stores, interesting hotels, and modern-art galleries.

Stazione Termini   adjoins the piazza della Repubblica, and, for many, this is their introduction to Rome. Much of the area is seedy and filled with gas fumes from all the buses and cars, but there is still much here to interest the visitor, including the Basilica da Santa Maria Maggiore and the Baths of Diocletian. Many good hotels remain.

Trastevere   is the most authentic district of Rome, lying "across the Tiber," and its people are of mixed ancestry, including Jewish, Roman, and Greek, and speak their own dialect. The area centers around the ancient churches of Santa Cecilia in Trastevere and Santa Maria in Trastevere.

Via Veneto   In the 1950s and early '60s this was the haunt of the *La Dolce Vita* set, as King Farouk of Egypt and Swedish actress Anita Ekberg paraded up and down the boulevard to the delight of the aggressive cameramen. The street is still there, still the site of luxury hotels, elegant cafés, and restaurants, although it no longer has the allure it did in its heyday.

2. GETTING AROUND

BY PUBLIC TRANSPORTATION

BY SUBWAY   The **Metropolitana,** or **Metro** for short, is the fastest means of transportation in Rome. It has two underground lines: Line A goes from via Ottaviano, near St. Peter's, to Anagnina, stopping at piazzale Flaminio (near piazza del Popolo), piazza Vittorio Emanuele, and piazza San Giovanni in Laterano. Line B connects the Rebibbia district with via Laurentina, stopping at via Cavour, piazza Bologna, Stazione Termini, the Colosseum, Circus Maximus, the Pyramid of C. Cestius, St. Paul's Outside the Walls, the Magliana, and the E.U.R. A big red letter M indicates the entrance to the subway. The price is 700 lire (55¢), but, of course, you'll have to pay more to go to the farther reaches of the underground. A booklet of 10 tickets costs 6,000 lire ($4.70).

Tickets are available from vending machines at all stations. These machines accept 50-lira, 100-lira, and 200-lira coins. Some stations have managers, but they will not make change. Booklets of tickets are available at *tabacchi* (tobacco) shops and in some terminals. Some machines change 1,000-lira (80¢) notes into coins.

Building an underground system for Rome has not been easy, since every time workers start digging, they discover an old temple or other archeological treasure and heavy earth-moving has to cease for a while.

BY BUS/TRAM   Roman buses are operated by an organization known as **ATAC,** or **Azienda Tramvie e Autobus del Comune di Roma** (tel. 46951 for information).

For only 800 lire (65¢), you can ride to most parts of Rome (but not the outlying districts) on quite good bus hookups. The ticket is valid for 1½ hours, and you can get on many buses during that time period, using the same ticket. At the Stazione Termini, you can purchase a special **tourist bus pass,** costing 2,800 lire ($2.20) for 1 day or 10,000 lire ($7.85) for a week. This allows you to ride on the ATAC network without bothering to purchase individual tickets. Never ride the trams when the Romans are going to or from work, or you'll be mashed flatter than fettuccine. When bus tickets have outlived their validity, they are destroyed by a small machine at the entrance to the bus.

Buses and trams stop at areas marked FERMATA, and in general they are in service from 6am to midnight daily. After that and until dawn, service, on main-line stations only, is very marginal. It's best to take a taxi in the wee hours—if you can find one.

At the bus information booth at piazza dei Cinquecento, in front of Stazione Termini, you can purchase a directory complete with maps summarizing the particular routes. Ask there about where to purchase bus tickets, or buy them in a tobacco shop or at a bus terminal. You must have your ticket before boarding the bus, as there are no ticket machines on the vehicles.

Take extreme caution riding the overcrowded buses of Rome. Pickpockets abound!

BY TAXI

If you're accustomed to hopping a cab in New York or London, then do so in Rome. If not, take less expensive means of transport. Avoid paying your fare with large bills—invariably, taxi drivers don't have change. The driver will also expect a 10% tip. Don't count on hailing a taxi on the street or even getting one at a stand. If you're going out, have your hotel call one. At a restaurant, ask the waiter or cashier to dial for you. If you want to phone yourself, try one of these numbers: 3570, 4994, or 8433.

The meter begins at 6,400 lire ($5), plus another 1,000 lire (80¢) for every kilometer. On Sunday a 1,000-lira (80¢) supplement is assessed, plus another 3,000-lira ($2.35) supplement from 10pm to 6am. There's yet another 500-lira (40¢) supplement for every suitcase. From Fiumicino Airport to town, you pay the price on the meter, plus another 30,000 lire ($23.55) for the taxi's return trip. The driver might be heading home for dinner, but you pay the supplement regardless.

BY CAR

For general information, see "Getting Around" in Chapter 2.

Hertz has its main office near the parking lot of the Villa Borghese, via Veneto 156 (tel. 321-6886). The **Budget** headquarters are at via Boncompagni 14C (tel. 482-0966). The downtown **Avis** office, which is usually considered closest to most of Rome's hotels, is at via Sardegna 38A (tel. 470-1228). **Maggiore,** an Italian company, has an office at piazza della Repubblica 57 (tel. 463715).

DRIVING & PARKING   All roads may lead to Rome if you're driving, but don't count on much driving once you get there. Since reception desks of most Roman hotels have at least one English-speaking person, it is wise to call ahead to find out the best route into Rome from whichever point you're at.

Find out if the hotel has a garage. If not, you are usually allowed to park your car in front of the hotel long enough to unload your luggage. Someone at the hotel—a doorman, if there is one—will direct you to the nearest garage or place to park.

To the neophyte, Roman drivers will appear like the chariot race in *Ben Hur.* When the light says green, go forth with caution. Many Roman drivers are still going through the light even though it has turned red. Roman drivers in traffic gridlock move bravely on, fighting for every inch of the road until they can free themselves from the tangled mess.

To complicate matters, many zones, such as that around piazza di Spagna, are traffic free, and other traffic zones are being tried out in various parts of Rome.

In other words, try to get your car into Rome as safely as possible, park it, and proceed on foot or by public transportation from then on.

BY BICYCLE, MOTORSCOOTER & MOTORCYCLE

St. Peter Moto Renting & Selling, via di Porto Castello 43 (tel. 687-5714), open Monday through Saturday from 9am to 7pm, rents bicycles, motorscooters, and motorcycles. Rates range from 40,000 lire ($31.40) for a standard bicycle to 90,000 lire ($70.65) per day for a two-person Suzuki or Honda motorcycle. Motorized bikes require deposits, ranging from 300,000 lire to 700,000 lire ($235.50 to $549.50). For the latter, the minimum age for a renter is 18, and a valid driver's license is required. Take the Metro to Ottaviano.

ON FOOT

Much of the inner core of Rome is traffic free—so you'll need to walk whether you like it or not. Walking is the perfect way to see Rome, especially the ancient narrow cobbled streets of Old Rome. If you're going to another district—and chances are that your hotel will be outside of Old Rome—you can take the bus or Metro. For such a large city, Rome is covered amazingly well on foot, because so much of what will interest a visitor lies in various clusters.

FAST FACTS ROME

American Express   The offices of American Express are at piazza di Spagna 38 (tel. 67-641). The travel service is open Monday through Friday from 9am to 6pm and on Saturday from 9am to 12:30pm. Hours for the financial and mail services are Monday through Friday from 9am to 5pm and on Saturday from 9am to noon. The tour desk is open during the same hours as those for travel services and also on Saturday afternoon from 2 to 2:30pm and on Sunday and holidays from 9 to 9:30am and 2 to 2:30pm.

Area Code   The telephone area code for Rome and its environs is 06. For other telephone information, see "Fast Facts: Italy," in Chapter 2.

Baby-sitters   Most hotel desks in Rome will help you secure a baby-sitter. You should ask for an English-speaking sitter if available. Or you can call a local agency, **Al Circula dei Bambini,** via Ricci Curbastro 34 (tel. 558-2916).

Bookstores   See "Savvy Shopping" in Chapter 5.

Business Hours   In general, **banks** are open Monday through Friday from 8:30am to 1:30pm and 3 to 4pm. Some banks keep afternoon hours ranging from 2:45 to 3:45pm. The American Service Bank is at piazza Mignanelli 5 (tel. 678-6815). Two other favorite U.S. banks are Chase Manhattan, via Michele Mercati 39 (tel. 866361), and Citibank, via Boncompagni 26 (tel. 4713). **Shopping** hours are governed by the siesta. Most stores are open year round Monday through Saturday from 9am to 1pm and then 3:30 or 4pm to 7:30 or 8pm. Most shops are closed on Sunday, except for some barbershops that are open Sunday morning. Hairdressers are closed Sunday and Monday.

Car Rentals   See "Getting Around" in this chapter.

Climate   See "When to Go" in Chapter 2.

Crime   See "Safety," below.

Currency Exchange   This is possible at all major rail and airline terminals in Rome, including the Stazione Termini where the *cambi* (exchange booth) beside the rail information booth is open daily from 8am to 8pm. At some cambi you'll have to pay commissions, often 1.5%. Banks, likewise, often charge commissions. One outfit that doesn't is **Frama,** via Torino 21B (tel. 475-7632), off via Nazionale near Stazione Termini. It's open Monday through Friday from 8:30am to 7pm and on Saturday from 9am to 1:30pm. Many so-called money changers will approach you on the street, but often they're pushing counterfeit lire, and they offer very good rates for their fake money!

Dentist   To secure a dentist who speaks English, call the U.S. Embassy in Rome, via Veneto 121 (tel. 488791). You may have to call around in order to get an appointment.

Doctor   Call the American Embassy (see "Dentist," above), which provides you with a list of doctors who speak English. All big hospitals in Rome have a 24-hour first-aid service (go to the emergency room). You'll find English-speaking doctors at the privately run **Salvator Mundi International Hospital,** viale delle Mura Gianicolensis 67 (tel. 586041). For medical assistance, the **International Medical Center** is on 24-hour duty at via Amendola 7 (tel. 462371).

Drugstores   A reliable pharmacy is **Farmacia Internazionale,** piazza Barberini 49 (tel. 4825456), open day and night. Most pharmacies are open from 8:30am to 1pm and 4 to 7:30pm. In general, pharmacies follow a rotation system so that several are always open on Sunday.

Embassies/Consulates   The consular and passport services of the **United States** are at via Vittorio Veneto 119A (tel. 488741), open Monday through Friday from 8:30am to 4:30pm; for **Canada,** at via Zara 30 (tel. 440-3028), open Monday through Friday from 10am to noon and 2 to 4pm. For the **United Kingdom,** offices are at via XX Settembre 80A (tel. 482-5441), open Monday through Friday from 9:30am to 12:30pm and 2 to 4pm; the **Australian Embassy,** at via Alesandria 215 (tel. 832721), is open Monday through Thursday from 8:30am to 12:30pm and 1:30 to 5:30pm, and on Friday from 8:30am to 1:15pm. The Australia Consulate is around the corner in the same building at corso Trieste 25. For **New Zealand,** the office is at via Zara 28 (tel. 440-2928), and hours are Monday through Friday from 8:30am to 12:45pm and 1:45 to 5pm. In case of emergency, embassies have a 24-hour referral service.

Emergencies   The police "hot line" number is 212121. Usually, however, dial **112** for the police, to report a fire, or summon an ambulance.

Eyeglasses   Try **La Barbera,** via Barberini 74 (tel. 483628), which has been in business since 1837. For more details, see "Eyeglasses" in "Savvy Shopping" in Chapter 5.

Hairdressers/Barbers   Romans are considered great hair stylists for both men and women. Sometimes large hotels have these services on the premises, and all neighborhoods have them. Just ask at the reception desk of your hotel for a good one. Otherwise, women can patronize **Gracia,** via Frattina 75 (tel. 679-2046). An excellent men's hair stylist is **Camp 2,** via Margutta 18C (tel. 361-4106). Both these establishments are in the center of Rome.

Hospitals   An expensive private clinic with English-speaking doctors is **Salvator Mundi,** viale delle Mura Gianicolensis 67 (tel. 586041). One of the major hospitals of Rome is **Ospedale Policlinico Universitario Gemelli,** largo Gemelli 8 (tel. 33051).

Hotlines   Dial **113,** which is a general SOS to report any kind of danger, such as a rape attack. You can also dial **112,** the police emergency number. For a personal crisis, call **Samaritans,** Chiesa di San Silvestro, piazza San Silvestro (tel. 678-9227), daily from 1:30 to 10:30pm.

Laundry/Dry Cleaning   First-class and deluxe hotels provide this service, often on the same day, but you'll pay for the extra convenience. All neighborhoods in Rome have laundries (not self-service) and dry-cleaning establishments. Most laundries have minimum-load requirements ranging from 3 to 4kg. A central laundry is found at **Ianari,** piazza Campo de Fiori 4 (tel. 6869213). For dry cleaning, try **Bologna,** via delle Lungaro 141 (tel. 6875762).

Libraries   The **American Library,** in the American Embassy, is at via Veneto 62 (tel. 46742481). It's open on Monday, Tuesday, Thursday, and Friday from 1 to 5:30pm; on Wednesday, hours are 1:30 to 7pm. There's also the **British Council Library,** via Quattro Fontane 20 (tel. 4826641), open on Monday from 2 to 6pm and Tuesday through Friday from 10am to 8pm.

Lost Property   Usually lost property is gone forever. But you might try checking at **Ogetti Rinvenuti,** via Nicolo Bettoni 1 (tel. 551-6040), which is open daily from 9am to noon. A branch at the Stazione Termini off Track 1 (tel. 473-0682) is open daily from 7am to midnight.

Luggage Storage/Lockers   These are available at the Stazione Termini, piazza dei Cinquecento.

Mail   Post office boxes in Italy are red and are attached to walls. One slot is for letters intended just for the city (on the left). On the right is a slot for letters for all other destinations. Vatican City post office boxes are blue, and you can buy special stamps at the Vatican City Post Office. It is said that letters mailed at Vatican City reach North America far quicker than does mail sent from within Rome.

The Vatican post office is adjacent to the information office in St. Peter's Square. It is open Monday through Friday from 8:30am to 7pm and on Saturday from 8:30am to 6pm.

Packages weighing more than 1 kilo (2.2 lbs.) must be firmly wrapped and taken to one of the larger post offices that takes packages (some of the smaller post offices don't accept them). One post office that does is the most central one, near the Stazione Termini on via della Terme di Diocleziano, at the corner of piazza dei Cinquecento. It is open Monday through Friday from 8:30am to 2pm and on Saturday from 8:30am to noon. Stamps (*francobolli*) can be purchased at *tabacchi* (tobacconists). But before posting stamps on your letters, ask at your hotel for current rates, as they are constantly rising. See, also, "Post Office," below.

Newspapers/Magazines   Most major newsstands, especially those along via Vittorio Veneto, carry copies of the *International Herald Tribune,* as well as certain British newspapers and magazines in English. The English-language daily published in Rome is the ***International Daily News,*** and in addition to its news coverage (with an emphasis on Europe, of course), it also provides several lists of local events and services that the foreign visitor should find helpful. Local newsstands carry European editions of *Time* and *Newsweek.*

Police   See "Emergencies," above.

Post Office   The **central post office** is on piazza San Silvestro, behind the Rinascente department store on piazza Colonna (tel. 672225). It's open Monday through Friday from 8:30am to 7:50pm for mail service, to 1:50pm for money service. Both are open from 8:30am to noon on Saturday. Mail addressed to you c/o that central office, with FERMO POSTA written after the name and address of the post office, will be given to you upon identification by passport.

Radio/Television   In both radio and television, RAI, the Italian state radio and TV network, dominates the broadcast waves. RAI has three radio stations broadcasting from Rome, and the Vatican Radio has its own station, often carrying religious news in English. RAI also has three national television channels broadcasting from Rome. There are also several private TV channels, which have more liberal telecasts.

Religious Services   Catholic churches abound in Rome and throughout Italy. Several of these conduct services in English, including **San Silvestro,** piazza San Silvestro 1 (tel. 679775), and **Santa Susana,** via XX Settembre 14 (tel. 4571510). The **American Episcopal Church** is St. Paul's, via Napoli 58 at via Nazionale (tel. 488-3339). The Jewish temple, **Sinagoga Ebraica,** is at lungotevere dei Cenci (tel. 656-4648).

Rest Rooms   Facilities are found near many of the major sights, often with attendants, as are those at bars, nightclubs, restaurants, cafés, and hotels, plus the airports and the railway station. You're expected to leave 200 lire to 500 lire (15¢ to 40¢) for the attendant. If you're not checking into a hotel in Rome but going on by train elsewhere, you can patronize the **Albergo Diurno,** a hotel without beds at the Stazione Termini. It has baths, showers, and well-kept toilet facilities.

Safety   Purse-snatching is commonplace in Rome. Young men on Vespas or whatever ride through the city looking for victims. To avoid trouble, stay away from the curb and hold on tightly to your purse. Don't lay anything valuable on tables or chairs where it can be grabbed up easily. Gypsy children are a particular menace. You'll often virtually have to fight them off, if they completely surround you. They'll often approach you with cartoon boxes hiding their stealing hands.

Shoe Repair   Many department stores have these services, and each Rome neighborhood has its favorite shoe-repair place. Ask at your hotel reception desk, or go to **Il Calzolaio,** via Cesare Fracassini 17A (tel. 361-5367).

Taxes A value-added tax (called IVA in Italy) is added to all consumer products and most services, including restaurants and hotels.

Taxis See "Getting Around" in this chapter.

Telegrams/Telex/Fax You can send **telegrams** from all post offices during the day and from the telegraph office at the central post office in piazza San Silvestro, off via della Mercede, at night. Your hotel will probably send a **telex or fax** for you. If your hotel doesn't have a fax, go to Capitalexpress, via Bresadola 55 (tel. 258-5404), Monday through Friday from 8:30am to 6:30pm. See, also, "Fast Facts: Italy" in Chapter 2.

Transit Information For airport information at Leonardo da Vinci International Airport, phone 601121; for Ciampino airport, phone 724-0297. For bus information, phone 46951, and for rail information, call 4775.

Water Rome is famed for its drinking water, which is generally safe, even from its outdoor fountains. If it isn't there's a sign reading ACQUA NON POTABILE. Nevertheless, Romans traditionally order bottled mineral water in restaurants, but mostly they prefer wine with their meals.

3. NETWORKS & RESOURCES

FOR STUDENTS The Rome center for budget student travel is **Centro Turistico Studentesco (CTS),** via Genova 16 (tel. 446791), off via Nazionale. Air, sea, train, and bus discounts are available here, and you can pick up a helpful brochure, "Young Rome." An accommodation-booking service is also available, including low-cost hotels in other Italian cities. On the bulletin board young people post notices offering or seeking rides (which is a better arrangement than hitchhiking). The office is open Monday through Friday from 9am to 1pm and 4 to 7pm, and on Saturday from 9am to 1pm.

FOR GAY MEN AND LESBIANS Before you go to Italy, men can order *Spartacus,* the international gay guide ($24.95), from **Giovanni's Room,** 1145 Pine Street, Philadelphia, PA 19107 (tel. 215/923-2960, or toll free 800/222-6996 outside Pennsylvania). *Rome Gay News,* via Einaudi 33 (tel. 935748), publishes a local and international gay news monthly, strong on gay activities in Rome.

The gay male liberation center is **Circolo Mario Mieli,** via Ostiense 202 (tel. 832-2315), a center where gay men meet. There's a bar, and shows are occasionally presented, including HIV-screenings. Hours are Monday through Friday from 6 to 8pm.

The lesbian center is **Centro Femminista Separatista,** via San Francesco di Sales 1A. Since they have no phone, you can obtain information about their activities at the feminist bookstore (see "For Women," below).

Before women go to Italy, they might also purchase a copy of *Gaia's Guide* ($11.95), an international lesbian guide available at many feminist bookstores or from **Robin Tyler Productions,** 15842 Chase Street, Sepulveda, CA 91343 (tel. 818/893-4075).

FOR WOMEN A feminist bookstore and a clearinghouse for "what's happening" is **Al Tempo Ritrovato,** piazza Farnese 103 (tel. 654-3749). Here you'll find an array of international publications appealing to women's interests. It's open Tuesday through Sunday from 10am to 1:30pm and 3:30 to 8pm.

FOR SENIORS Every city of Italy, including Rome, has slightly different guidelines for senior-citizen discounts, so it's a good idea to visit the tourist office in Rome (see "Tourist Information" in "Orientation," above). Ask about any special discounts that might be available on transportation, hotels, cultural events, and museums for older travelers. Many senior-citizen discounts are possible in Italy, although it's often not convenient or possible for short-term travelers to take full advantage of them. Nevertheless, it always pays to ask if there are special rates for senior citizens at various cultural events and national monuments.

CHAPTER 4

WHERE TO STAY & DINE IN ROME

- **1. ACCOMMODATIONS**
- • **FROMMER'S SMART TRAVELER: HOTELS**
- • **FROMMER'S COOL FOR KIDS: HOTELS**
- **2. DINING**
- • **FROMMER'S SMART TRAVELER: RESTAURANTS**
- • **FROMMER'S COOL FOR KIDS: RESTAURANTS**

There are more than 500 hotels in Rome. Decisions on which to recommend were based on whether they offered good value—regardless of their price range—and special considerations, such as charm, comfort, and convenience of location.

All the hotels recommended serve breakfast, and many of them, as will be noted, also have good restaurants. Some of the deluxe hotels have among the finest restaurants in Rome.

Most well-recommended hotels in Rome have private baths, although some of the inexpensive or budget choices do not. If you don't mind the inconvenience of sharing a bath with other visitors, these will be your best bets for economy.

Nearly all hotels are heated if you're planning a visit in the cooler months; however, not all hotels are air-conditioned. The deluxe and first-class ones are, but after that it's a toss-up. Air conditioning could be vitally important to you if you're planning to visit Rome during the months of July and August. Many hotels will grant winter discounts—usually no more than 10%. These discounts are not necessarily published, but some negotiation on your part at the reception desk may get you an off-season discount.

Hotels are divided on the question of whether breakfast is included in the room rate or is extra. Always determine this when checking in—it can make a difference on your final bill. If breakfast is included, it is of the continental variety—that is, cappuccino and croissants, along with jam and butter. American-type breakfasts of bacon and eggs always cost extra.

Nearly all hotels today quote an inclusive rate, including service and value-added taxes. Again, to be doubly certain and to avoid any misunderstanding when time comes to pay the bill, ask when checking in if service and tax are included in the rate you are being quoted, or if they will be added to your final bill. It is rare for Roman hotels to have private garages. Hotel reception desks will advise about nearby garages, where fees usually range from 10,000 lire to 25,000 lire ($7.85 to $19.65).

Rome is one of the world's great capitals for dining. From elegant, deluxe palaces with lavish trappings to little trattorias opening onto hidden piazzas deep in the heart of Old Rome, the city abounds with good restaurants in all price ranges.

1. ACCOMMODATIONS

The city isn't cheap and hasn't been for a very long time. The days when a $5 bill could purchase a lot have gone the way of *La Dolce Vita* along via Vittorio Veneto.

In hotels rated very expensive, you can spend $350 to $500 for a double room. Hotels judged expensive charge $250 to $350 for a double room; those in the moderate category ask $145 to $250. Anything under $145 is considered inexpensive by Roman standards, and if you can get a double for as little as $75 or less you're definitely in the budget category. All prices indicated are for double rooms with private bath.

NEAR PIAZZA DI SPAGNA

VERY EXPENSIVE

HASSLER, piazza Trinità dei Monti 6, 00187 Roma. Tel. 06/6792651.
Fax 06/6789991. 100 rms (all with bath), 15 suites. A/C MINIBAR TV TEL **Metro:**
Piazza di Spagna. **Bus:** 497 from Stazione Termini.

$ Rates: 360,000–380,000 lire ($282.60–$298.30) single; 520,000–590,000 lire ($408.20–$463.15) double; from 1,200,000 lire ($942) suite. Breakfast 24,000 lire ($18.85) extra. AE, DC, MC, V.

The Hassler, the only deluxe hotel in this old part of Rome, uses the Spanish Steps as its grand entrance. The original 1885 Hassler was rebuilt in 1944, and used as headquarters of the American Air Transport Command for the last year of World War II. In 1947 the hotel reopened its doors and became an immediate success, regaining its original glory. Through the years its reputation has become

---

(F) FROMMER'S SMART TRAVELER: HOTELS

VALUE-CONSCIOUS TRAVELERS SHOULD ASK ABOUT THE FOLLOWING:

1. The price you pay in inexpensive hotels depends on the plumbing. Rooms with showers are cheaper than rooms with private baths. For a bath, you'll have to use the corridor bathroom, but you'll save a lot of money.
2. Consider a package tour (or book land arrangements with your air ticket). You'll often pay at least 30% less than individual "rack" rates (off-the-street, independent bookings).
3. If Rome hotels are full, forget it. But if they're not, a little on-the-spot bargaining can bring down the cost of a hotel room. Be polite. Ask if there's a "businessperson's rate," or if schoolteachers get a discount. This is a face-saving technique. Sometimes it works and sometimes it doesn't—but you can try. The technique is best at night, when the hotel faces up to 40% vacancy and wants to fill some of those empty rooms.
4. At cheaper hotels that take credit cards, ask if payment by cash will get you a reduction.
5. If you're going to spend at least a week in Rome, ask about long-term discounts.

QUESTIONS TO ASK IF YOU'RE ON A BUDGET

1. Is there a garage? What's the charge?
2. Is there a surcharge on either local or long-distance calls? There usually is in some places, and it might be an astonishing 40%. Make your calls at the nearest post office.
3. Is service included? This means, Does the hotel include service charge in the rates quoted, or will it be added on at the end of your stay?
4. Are all hotel and city taxes included in the price or will they be added on?
5. Is breakfast (continental) included in the rates?

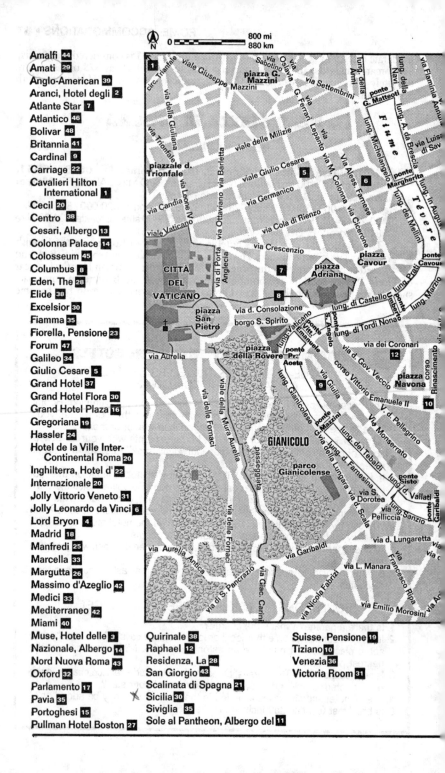

Amalfi 44
Amati 29
Anglo-American 39
Aranci, Hotel degli 2
Atlante Star 7
Atlantico 46
Bolivar 48
Britannia 41
Cardinal 9
Carriage 22
Cavalieri Hilton
  International 1
Cecil 20
Centro 38
Cesari, Albergo 13
Colonna Palace 14
Colosseum 45
Columbus 8
Eden, The 28
Elide 38
Excelsior 30
Fiamma 35
Fiorella, Pensione 23
Forum 47
Galileo 34
Giulio Cesare 5
Grand Hotel 37
Grand Hotel Flora 30
Grand Hotel Plaza 16
Gregoriana 19
Hassler 24
Hotel de la Ville Inter-
  Continental Roma 20
Inghilterra, Hotel d' 22
Internazionale 20
Jolly Vittorio Veneto 31
Jolly Leonardo da Vinci 6
Lord Bryon 4
Madrid 18
Manfredi 25
Marcella 33
Margutta 26
Massimo d'Azeglio 42
Medici 33
Mediterraneo 42
Miami 40
Muse, Hotel delle 3
Nazionale, Albergo 14
Nord Nuova Roma 43
Oxford 32
Parlamento 17
Pavia 35
Portoghesi 15
Pullman Hotel Boston 27

Quirinale 38
Raphael 12
Residenza, La 28
San Giorgio 43
Scalinata di Spagna 21
Sicilia 30
Siviglia 35
Sole al Pantheon, Albergo del 11

Suisse, Pensione 19
Tiziano 10
Venezia 36
Victoria Room 31

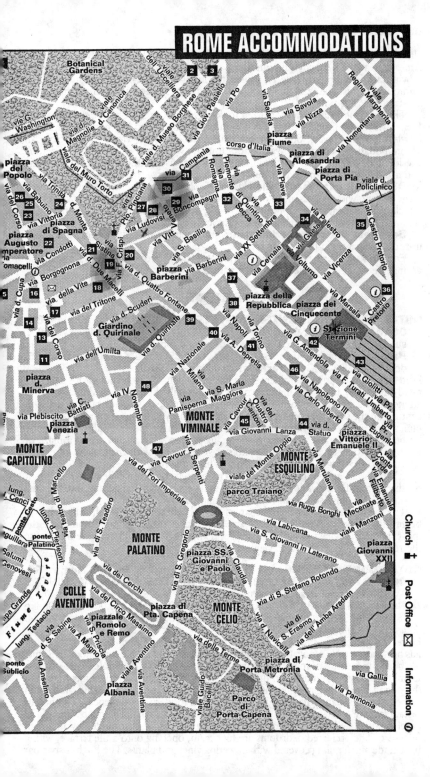

ROME ACCOMMODATIONS

almost legendary. This lush hotel, with its ornate decor, has been favored by such Americans as the Kennedys, Eisenhowers, and Nixons—and by titled Europeans and movie stars. The brightly colored rooms, the lounges with a mixture of modern and traditional furnishings, and the bedrooms with their "Italian Park Avenue" trappings, all strike a 1930s note.

The bedrooms have a personalized look—Oriental rugs, tasteful draperies at the French windows, brocade furnishings, comfortable beds, and (the nicest touch of all) bowls of fresh flowers. Some rooms have balconies with views of the city. All accommodations contain private bath, usually with two sinks and a bidet. A Presidential Suite (next to the restaurant) and a Paradise Penthouse are also available, and are, of course, more expensive.

Dining/Entertainment: The Hassler Roof Restaurant, on the top floor, is a great favorite with visitors and Romans alike for its fine cuisine and lovely view. The Hassler Bar is ideal for an apéritif or a drink; in the evening, it has piano music. In summer, breakfast and lunch are served in a charming, flower-bedecked courtyard.

Services: Room service (until 11:30pm), telex and fax services, limousine, in-room massages, in-house laundry.

Facilities: There is parking in front for only two cars (always taken), so arrangements can be made at a nearby garage.

EXPENSIVE

HOTEL DE LA VILLE INTER-CONTINENTAL ROMA, via Sistina 69, 00187 Roma. Tel. 06/67331. Fax 06/678-4213. 195 rms (all with bath), 7 suites. A/C MINIBAR TV TEL **Metro:** Piazza di Spagna.
$ **Rates** (including breakfast): 317,000 lire ($248.85) single; 410,000 lire ($321.85) double. AE, DC, MC, V. **Parking:** 20,000 lire ($15.70).

Hotel de la Ville Inter-Continental Roma looks deluxe (even though it's officially rated first class) from the minute you walk through the revolving door, which is attended by a smartly uniformed doorman. Once inside this palace built in the 19th century on the site of the ancient Lucullus's Gardens, you'll see Oriental rugs, marble tables, brocade-covered furniture, and a smiling staff that speaks English in correctly hushed tones. There are endless corridors leading to what at first seems a maze of ornamental lounges, all elegantly upholstered and hung with their quota of crystal lighting fixtures. Some of the public rooms have a sort of '30s elegance. Others are strictly baroque, and in the middle of it all is an open courtyard. The Patio Restaurant on the second floor overlooks the garden and serves both Italian and international cuisine. The hotel also has an American piano bar.

The bedrooms and the public areas have been completely rehabilitated in a beautifully classic and yet up-to-date way. The higher rooms with balconies have the most spectacular views of Rome to be found anywhere, and all guests are free to use the roof terrace with the same view.

HOTEL D'INGHLITERRA, via Bocca di Leone 14, 00187 Roma. Tel. 06/672161. Fax 06/684-0828. 102 rms (all with bath), 12 suites. A/C MINIBAR TV TEL **Metro:** Piazza di Spagna.
$ **Rates:** 275,000–280,000 lire ($215.90–$219.80) single; 355,000–390,000 lire ($278.50–$306.15) double; from 450,000 lire ($353.25) suite. Breakfast 22,000 lire ($17.25) extra. AE, DC, MC, V.

Hotel d'Inghliterra nostalgically holds onto its traditions and heritage, even though it has been completely renovated. Considered the most fashionable small hotel in Rome, it's been the favorite of many a discriminating "personage"—Anatole France, Ernest Hemingway, Alec Guinness. (In the 19th century, the king of Portugal met here with the pope.) The bedrooms have mostly old pieces—gilt and much marble, along with mahogany chests and glittery mirrors, as well as modern conveniences. The hotel's restaurant, the Roman Garden, serves excellent Roman dishes. The main salon of the hotel is dominated by an impressive gilt mirror and console, surrounded by Victorian furniture. The preferred bedrooms are higher up, opening onto a tile terrace, with a balustrade and a railing covered with flowering vines and plants. The English-style bar is a favorite gathering spot in the evening, with its paneled walls, tip-top tables, and old lamps casting soft light.

MODERATE

CARRIAGE, via delle Carrozze 36, 00187 Roma. Tel. 06/679-3312. Fax 06/678-8279. 24 rms (all with bath). A/C MINIBAR TV TEL **Metro:** Piazza di Spagna.
$ Rates (including continental breakfast): 180,000 lire ($141.30) single; 205,000 lire ($160.95) double. AE, DC, MC, V. **Parking:** 20,000 lire ($15.70).
The aptly named Carriage caters to the "carriage trade," which in today's sense means staff members of the British and French embassies, plus an occasional movie star or film director. The severely dignified 18th-century facade covers some charming, although small, accommodations (if you reserve, ask for one of the two rooftop bedrooms). Antiques have been used tastefully, creating a personal aura, even in the bedrooms with their matching bedcovers and draperies. Each bedroom has a radio and other amenities. To meet your fellow guests, head for the Renaissance-style salon that is called an American bar or the roof garden. There is no dining room in the hotel.

HOTEL GREGORIANA, via Gregoriana 18, 00187 Roma. Tel. 06/679-4269. Fax 06/678-4258. 38 rms (all with bath or shower). A/C TV TEL **Metro:** Piazza di Spagna.
$ Rates (including breakfast): 140,000 lire ($109.90) single; 205,000 lire ($160.95) double. No credit cards. **Parking:** 30,000 lire ($23.55).
The Hotel Gregoriana is a small, elite hotel favored by members of the Italian fashion industry who book rooms here for visiting friends from out of town. The ruling matriarch of an aristocratic family left the building to an order of nuns in the 19th century, but they eventually retreated to other quarters. Today there might be a slightly more elevated spirituality in Room C than in the rest of the hotel, as it used to be a chapel. Throughout the establishment, however, the smallish rooms provide comfort and Italian design. The elevator cage is a black-and-gold art deco fantasy, and the door to each accommodation has a reproduction of an Erté print whose fanciful characters indicate the letter designating that particular room. You'll pay the bill in the tiny, rattan-covered lobby.

HOTEL INTERNAZIONALE, via Sistina 79, 00187 Roma. Tel. 06/678-4686. Fax 06/678-4764. 42 rms (all with bath), 2 suites. A/C MINIBAR TV TEL **Bus:** 492 from Stazione Termini.
$ Rates (including breakfast): 160,000 lire ($125.60) single; 225,000 lire ($176.65) double; from 600,000 lire ($471) suite. AE, MC, V.
The Hotel Internazionale emerged from the combination of several old palaces, and traces of their past splendor can be seen in a few of the public rooms. Just half a block from the top of the Spanish Steps, the Internazionale has been a favorite of knowledgeable travelers since the 1920s. The atmosphere is like that of a small inn, and service is both friendly and efficient. The rooms are furnished with old wooden pieces that couldn't really be called antiques, yet are substantial and comfortable. Accommodations facing the narrow and often-noisy via Sistina now have double windows. Bits and pieces of former elegance remain, especially in the dining room or Sala de Pranzo, whose ceiling is charmingly paneled.

HOTEL MADRID, via Mario dei Fiori 94-95, 00187 Roma. Tel. 06/679-1243. Fax 06/684-0998. 26 rms (all with bath), 7 suites. A/C MINIBAR TV TEL **Metro:** Piazza di Spagna.
$ Rates (including breakfast): 180,000 lire ($141.30) single; 240,000 lire ($188.40) double; from 260,000 lire ($204.10) suite for three, from 280,000 lire ($219.80) suite for four. AE, DC, MC, V.
The Hotel Madrid evokes *fin-de-siècle* Roma. The interior has been redone, and many modern comforts have been added. The hotel appeals to the individual traveler who wants a good standard of service. Guests often take their breakfast amid ivy and

blossoming plants on the roof terrace. The view of the rooftops and the distant dome of St. Peter's is beautiful. Some of the doubles are really quite large, equipped with small scatter rugs, veneer armoires, and shuttered windows. All accommodations contain a radio. The hotel is an ocher building with a shuttered facade on a narrow street practically in the heart of the boutique area centering around via Frattina, near the Spanish Steps.

MANFREDI HOTEL, via Margutta 61, 00187 Roma. Tel. 06/320-7676. Fax 06/320-7736. 15 rms (all with bath). A/C MINIBAR TV TEL **Metro:** Piazza di Spagna.

$ Rates (including American breakfast): 169,000 lire ($132.70) single; 220,000 lire ($172.70) double. AE, MC, V.

The newly renovated Manfredi is only a few yards away from the Spanish Steps. All rooms are provided with excellent facilities and comforts. This cozy but refined hotel is on the third floor of a stately building on a street known for its art galleries.

SCALINATA DI SPAGNA, piazza Trinità dei Monti 17, 00187 Roma. Tel. 06/679-3006. Fax 06/684-0598. 14 rms (all with bath or shower). A/C MINIBAR TV TEL **Metro:** Piazza di Spagna.

$ Rates (including breakfast): 170,000 lire ($133.45) single; 230,000 lire ($180.55) double; 290,000 lire ($227.65) triple. MC, V.

Scalinata di Spagna was the most appealing pension in the area of the Spanish Steps before its conversion in 1988 into a three-star hotel. It's right at the top of the steps, directly across the small piazza from the deluxe Hassler. This is a delightful little building—only two floors are visible from the outside—done up in mustard-yellow and burgundy-red paint and nestled between much larger structures. You'll recognize the four relief columns across the facade and the window boxes with their bright blossoms. The interior is like an old inn—the public rooms are small with bright print slipcovers, old clocks, and low ceilings.

The decorations vary radically from one room to the next; some have low, beamed ceilings and ancient-looking wood furniture, while others have loftier ceilings and more average appointments. Everything is spotless and most pleasing to the eye. In season, breakfast is served on the roof garden terrace with its sweeping view of the dome of St. Peter's across the Tiber. Reserve well in advance.

BUDGET

HOTEL PENSIONE PARLAMENTO, via delle Convertite 5, 00187 Roma. Tel. 06/678-7880. 22 rms (14 with bath or shower). TEL **Metro:** Piazza di Spagna. **Bus:** 492 from Stazione Termini.

$ Rates: 46,000 lire ($36.10) single without bath; 65,000–90,000 lire ($51–$70.65) double with bath or shower. Extra bed 25,000 lire ($19.65) per person. Breakfast 10,000 lire ($7.85) extra. No credit cards.

The Hotel Pensione Parlamento, three flights upstairs, accepts visitors with warmth and hospitality. Near piazza di Spagna and piazza del Parlamento, it is within walking distance of many of Rome's major sights. The building was constructed in the 17th century with a courtyard. The bedrooms are clean, well maintained, and generally quiet. The hotel has a TV lounge and roof garden.

PENSION SUISSE, via Gregoriana 56, 00187 Roma. Tel. 06/678-3649. Fax 06/678-1258. 35 rms (15 with bath). TEL **Metro:** Piazza di Spagna.

$ Rates (including breakfast): 63,000 lire ($49.45) single without bath; 94,000 lire ($73.80) double without bath, 118,000 lire ($92.65) double with bath. No credit cards.

Pension Suisse is excellent, although small. It's run with efficiency and panache by Signora Jole Ciucci, who has been in the business for about 50 years, the last 30 of which have been here on via Gregoriana. The Suisse is a sparkling-clean affair, with rooms spread out over the fourth and fifth floors of an old building. Halls and lobbies are in muted beige, with high ceilings, leather chairs, and occasional throw rugs on glistening tile floors. There's also a charming writing room with parquet floors, overstuffed leather easy chairs, and a Victorian chandelier. Furnished either in blond-toned modern pieces or antiques, the rooms are big, simple, and comfortable.

ON OR AROUND VIA VITTORIO VENETO

VERY EXPENSIVE

THE EDEN, via Ludovisi 49, 00187 Roma. Tel. 06/474-3551. Fax 06/482-1584. 119 rms (all with bath), 17 suites. A/C MINIBAR TV TEL **Metro:** Piazza Barberini.

$ Rates: 297,000–360,000 lire ($233.15–$282.60) single; 430,000–510,000 lire ($337.55–$400.35) double; from 950,000 lire ($745.75) suite. Breakfast 23,000 lire ($18.05) extra. AE, DC, MC, V.

The Eden is in an enviable location at the entrance to the Borghese Gardens and via Vittorio Veneto. It was originally built in the 1890s, but it has undergone frequent renovations, inside and out, since its original construction. While not exactly dripping with the baroque details you might admire in comparable hotels, it still has rich trappings and furnishings that give it distinction. In the chic Ludovisi district, it is surrounded by the gardens of the Villa Ludovisi, the old Convent of S. Isidoro, and the Villa Medici. The carpeting and lavish use of marble in the entrance hall are befitting such a deluxe hotel. The rooms are of good size and elegantly furnished.

Dining/Entertainment: There is a spectacular penthouse restaurant and bar, offering a panoramic view of Rome which stretches from the Colosseum to the Pincio. At the restaurant, La Terrazza dell'Eden, you can dine for around 100,000 lire ($78.50). Arrive early for dinner so you can enjoy a drink in the bar, with its tufted sofas and armchairs.

Services: Room service, baby-sitting, laundry and valet service.

Facilities: Beauty salon, car-rental desk, currency-exchange center, safe-deposit boxes.

EXCELSIOR, via Vittorio Veneto 125, 00187 Roma. Tel. 06/4708. Fax 06/482-6205 327 rms (all with bath), 45 suites. A/C MINIBAR TV TEL **Metro:** Piazza Barberini.

$ Rates: 275,000–320,000 lire ($215.90–$251.20) single; 350,000–490,000 lire ($274.75–$384.65) double; from 920,000 lire ($722.20) suite. Breakfast 23,000 lire ($18.05) extra. 19% IVA extra. AE, DC, MC, V.

The Excelsior (pronounced "Ess-*shell*-see-or") is a limestone palace whose baroque corner tower, which looks right over the U.S. Embassy, is a landmark in Rome. Guests enter a string of cavernous reception rooms of the same design as the Grand Hotel a few blocks away. That means thick rugs, marble floors, gilded garlands and pilasters decorating the walls, and Empire furniture (supported by winged lions and the like).

The rooms come in two basic varieties: new (the result of a major renovation) and traditional. Doubles are spacious and elegantly furnished, often with antiques and silk curtains. The furnishings in singles are also of high quality. Most of the bedrooms are different, many with a sumptuous Hollywood-style bath—marble-walled with separate bath and shower, sinks, bidet, and a mountain of fresh towels.

The palatial hotel once attracted some of the stellar lights of the "Hollywood on the Tiber" era—notably Shelley Winters, Vittorio Gassman, Ingrid Bergman, and Roberto Rossellini. Nowadays, you're more likely to bump into international financiers and Arab princesses.

Dining/Entertainment: The Excelsior Bar, open daily from 10:30am to 1am, is perhaps the most famous on via Veneto, and La Cupola is known for its national and regional cuisine, with dietetic and kosher food prepared on request.

Services: Room service, baby-sitting service, laundry and valet service.

Facilities: Beauty salon, barber shop, sauna.

EXPENSIVE

GRAND HOTEL FLORA, via Vittorio Veneto 191, 00187 Roma. Tel. 06/497821. Fax 06/482-0359. 175 rms (all with bath), 7 suites. A/C MINIBAR TV TEL **Metro:** Piazza Barberini.

$ Rates (including breakfast): 220,000–260,000 lire ($172.70–$204.10) single; 280,000–350,000 lire ($219.80–$274.75) double; from 600,000 lire ($471) suite. AE, DC, MC, V.

The Grand Hotel Flora, a "grand hotel" styled like a palazzo, stands at the gateway to the Borghese Gardens. The public rooms are furnished with well-selected reproductions and antiques, with Oriental carpets and crystal chandeliers. All accommodations are well furnished and well maintained. A focal point of social get-togethers is the Empire Bar. Room service, laundry, and valet are provided.

JOLLY VITTORIO VENETO, corso d'Italia 1, 00198 Roma. Tel. 06/8495. Fax 06/884-1104. 203 rms (all with bath), 3 suites. A/C MINIBAR TV TEL **Bus:** 910.

$ Rates (including American breakfast): 230,000–255,000 lire ($180.55–$200.18) single; 330,000–375,000 lire ($259.05–$294.40) double; from 450,000 lire ($353.25) suite. AE, DC, MC, V. **Parking:** 37,000 lire ($29.05).

The Jolly Vittorio Veneto lies between the Villa Borghese Gardens and via Veneto. Totally ignoring the traditional, the hotel's architects opted for modern in metal and concrete, with bronze-tinted windows. Try to get a room with a garden view. To register, you descend a grand staircase, arriving at a sunken lobby. The rooms here are bold in concept, compact in space, and contemporary in furnishings. Room service is offered to 11pm.

VICTORIA ROMA, via Campania 41, 00187 Roma. Tel. 06/473931. Fax 06/487-1890. 110 rms (all with bath), 4 suites. A/C MINIBAR TV TEL **Bus:** 910.

$ Rates (including breakfast): 180,000–220,000 lire ($141.30–$172.70) single; 280,000–320,000 lire ($219.80–$251.20) double; from 330,000 lire ($259.05) suite. AE, DC, MC.

The Victoria Roma will fool you. As you sit on wrought-iron chairs on its roof garden, drinking your apéritif in a forest of palms and potted plants—all overlooking the Borghese Gardens—you'll think you're at a country villa. But via Vittorio Veneto's just across the way. Even the lounges and living rooms retain that country-house decor, with soft touches that include high-backed chairs, large oil paintings, bowls of freshly cut flowers, provincial tables, and Oriental rugs. The Swiss owner, Alberto H. Wirth, has set unusual requirements of innkeeping (no groups), and has attracted a fine clientele over the years—diplomats, executives, artists. The bedrooms are well furnished and maintained. Meals can be taken à la carte in the elegant grill room, which serves the best of Italian and French cuisine.

MODERATE

HOTEL OXFORD, via Boncompagni 89, 00187 Roma. Tel. 06/482-8952. Fax 06/481-5349. 58 rms (all with bath), 2 suites. A/C MINIBAR TV TEL **Bus:** 3, 56, 58, or 62.

$ Rates (including breakfast): 150,000 lire ($117.75) single; 220,000 lire ($172.70) double; from 250,000 lire ($196.25) suite. AE, DC, MC, V.

The centrally located Hotel Oxford, off via Veneto, is adjacent to the Borghese Gardens. Recently renovated, the Oxford is now air-conditioned, centrally heated, and fully carpeted throughout. There is a pleasant lounge and a cozy bar (which serves snacks), plus a dining room offering a good Italian cuisine. The hotel is on the American Embassy's preferred list of moderately priced hotels in Rome that can be confidently recommended to U.S. visitors.

PULLMAN HOTEL BOSTON, via Lombardia 47, 00187 Roma. Tel. 06/473951. Fax 06/482-1019. 128 rms (all with bath). A/C MINIBAR TV TEL **Metro:** Piazza Barberini or Piazza di Spagna.

$ Rates (including breakfast): 250,000 lire ($196.25) single; 300,000 lire ($235.50) double. AE, DC, MC, V. **Parking:** 25,000 lire ($19.65).

The Pullman Hotel Boston, just three blocks from via Vittorio Veneto and about a 5-minute walk from the Spanish Steps, has been entirely renovated and upgraded. Across the street from the Villa Borghese, it is a choice address for conservative-minded readers on a Roman holiday. Each bedroom is comfortably fitted and often filled with furniture reproductions of Victorian pieces. The hotel has several sedate lobbies on different levels, with brown marble and velvet-covered pieces. The bar continues the theme with its carved wood and smoked mirrors. The hotel also has a good-size restaurant, filled with plush chairs.

LA RESIDENZA, via Emilia 22-24, 00187 Roma. Tel. 06/488-0789. Fax 06/485721. 27 rms (all with bath or shower), 6 suites. A/C MINIBAR TV TEL **Metro:** Piazza Barberini.
$ Rates (including breakfast): 115,000 lire ($90.30) single; 200,000 lire ($157) double; from 230,000 lire ($180.55) suite. No credit cards. **Parking:** 5,000 lire ($3.95).

La Residenza successfully combines the intimacy of a generously sized town house with the elegant appointments of a well-decorated hotel. The location is superb—in the neighborhood of via Vittorio Veneto, the American Embassy, and the Villa Borghese. The converted villa has an ocher-colored facade, an ivy-covered courtyard, a quiet location, and a labyrinthine series of plushly upholstered public rooms. These contain Oriental rugs, Empire divans, oil portraits, and warmly accommodating groupings of rattan chairs with cushions. Each bedroom has a radio in addition to other amenities. A series of terraces is scattered strategically throughout the hotel, which combines to make this one of my favorite stopovers in the city.

INEXPENSIVE

AMATI, via Vittorio Veneto 155, 00187 Roma. Tel. 06/482-1875. Fax 06/494-1403. 38 rms (all with bath). TEL **Metro:** Piazza Barberini.
$ Rates (including breakfast): 75,000 lire ($58.90) single; 120,000 lire ($94.20) double. AE, MC, V.

The Amati is a reasonably priced, pleasant place to stay right in the middle of via Vittorio Veneto. It's scattered over two floors of a substantial stone building whose elevator will take you to the second-floor reception area. An adjacent sitting room is outfitted with light-grained oak paneling, carpeting, a baronial staircase, and a comfortable series of overstuffed divans. Many of the attractively simple units face an inner courtyard, which, while not offering a monumental view of the boulevard below, will be a lot quieter. Although small, the bedrooms are equipped with modern Italian-inspired furniture. All is colorful and compact, including the very compressed bathrooms. Breakfast is offered family style in a corner room furnished with antique chairs.

HOTEL SICILIA, via Sicilia 24, 00187 Roma. Tel. 06/482-1913. Fax 06/482-1913. 92 rms (all with bath or shower). TEL **Bus:** 492.
$ Rates (including breakfast): 105,000 lire ($82.45) single; 150,000 lire ($117.75) double. AE, DC, V.

At the corner of via Vittorio Veneto is the Hotel Sicilia, a three-star hotel near the American Embassy. The interior of the classic 18th-century building is completely renovated and contains a bar and restaurant. Rooms are furnished with sleek modern styling. It's important to reserve well in advance if you want to stay here.

MONTE MARIO

VERY EXPENSIVE

CAVALIERI HILTON INTERNATIONAL, via Cadlolo 101, 00136 Roma. Tel. 06/31511. Fax 06/315-12241. 373 rms (all with bath), 17 suites. A/C MINIBAR TV TEL **Transportation:** Free hotel shuttle bus goes back and forth to the city center.
$ Rates: 300,000–320,000 lire ($235.50–$251.20) single; 450,000–550,000 lire ($353.25–$431.75) double; from 850,000 lire ($667.25) suite. Breakfast 30,000 lire ($23.55) extra. AE, DC, MC, V. **Parking:** Free outdoors, 20,000 lire ($15.70) indoors.

The Cavalieri Hilton International combines all the advantages of a resort hotel with the convenience of being a 15-minute drive from the center of Rome. Overlooking Rome and the Alban Hills from its perch on top of Monte Mario, it is set in 15 acres of trees, flowering shrubs, and stonework. Its facilities are so complete that many visitors (obviously not first-timers to Rome) never leave the hotel grounds. The entrance leads into a marble lobby, whose sculpture, 17th-century art, and winding staircases are usually flooded with sunlight from the massive windows.

The guest rooms and suites, many with panoramic views, are designed to fit contemporary standards of comfort, quality, and style. Soft furnishings in pastel colors are paired with Italian furniture in warm-tone woods. Each unit has a keyless electronic lock, independent heating and air conditioning, color TV with in-house movies, radio, and bedside control for all electric apparatus in the room, as well as a spacious balcony. The bathrooms, sheathed in Italian marble, are equipped with large mirrors, hairdryer, international electric sockets, vanity mirror, piped-in music, and phone.

Dining/Entertainment: There are two accommodating bars, and the Pergola, one of the best restaurants in Rome. There's a garden restaurant and pool veranda in summer—the Trattoria del Cavalieri—serving well-prepared meals of almost any degree of formality, and a constantly changing international clientele that is usually only about 25% American.

Services: A 24-hour concierge service is there to provide you with solutions to "whatever your problems," including a free hotel bus that makes frequent runs to via Vittorio Veneto and the Spanish Steps; room service, laundry, valet.

Facilities: Tennis courts, jogging path, Turkish bath, sauna with massage, indoor arcade of shops, outdoor swimming pool; facilities for disabled guests.

NEAR PIAZZA NAVONA

EXPENSIVE

HOTEL RAPHAEL, largo Febo 2, 00186 Roma. Tel. 06/650881. Fax 06/687-8993. 51 rms (all with bath). A/C MINIBAR TV TEL **Bus:** 64, 70, or 492.
$ Rates (including breakfast): 230,000 lire ($180.55) single; 360,000 lire ($282.60) double. AE, DC, MC, V.
This tasteful hotel is known to the discerning who prefer a palace hidden in the heart of Old Rome. It lures guests with its sophisticated, restful atmosphere. International celebrities check in and out unobtrusively. The bedrooms, some of which have their own terraces, are individually decorated, simply done with wood-grained built-ins.

In the lounges are fine antiques, excellent art, ornate gilt mirrors, and high-backed chairs. The dining room has a log fireplace, and the bar carries its liquor inside a gilded baroque cabinet. But the special delight is the multilevel rooftop terrace where you can have drinks and enjoy the vista of tile rooftops on nearby buildings.

MODERATE

CARDINAL HOTEL, via Giulia 62, 00186 Roma. Tel. 06/654-2719. Fax 06/678-6376. 73 rms (all with bath or shower). A/C MINIBAR TV TEL **Bus:** 23, 46, 64, or 881.
$ Rates (including breakfast): 131,000 lire ($102.85) single; 219,000 lire ($171.90) double. AE, DC, MC, V.
Like many of the constructions in this part of town, about a block from the Tiber, west of piazza Navona, and on the city's most beautiful Renaissance street, this particular building has had a long and complicated history. Built by Bramante in the 15th century with stones hauled from the Roman Forum, it was intended as a courthouse but later became the center of the Armenian church in Rome. You can see the original stonework in the exposed walls of the bar and the breakfast room, as well as the chiseled inscription of a Sabine tomb built into the red walls of a sitting area. There two inner courtyards are dotted with statues, comfortable leather couches, and interior decor almost entirely done in shades of scarlet. The sunny bedrooms are clean

and well furnished; from the upper floors, they offer interesting views of Renaissance Rome.

INEXPENSIVE

HOTEL PORTOGHESI, via dei Portoghesi 1, 00186 Roma. Tel. 06/686-4231. Fax 06/687-6976. 27 rms (all with bath or shower), 2 suites. A/C TV TEL **Bus:** 492.
$ Rates (including breakfast): 85,000 lire ($66.75) single; 130,000 lire ($102.05) double; from 165,000 lire ($129.55) suite. MC, V. **Parking:** 20,000 lire ($15.70).
In the heart of Old Rome, on a street that intersects via Scrofa between piazza Navona and the Mausoleum of Augustus, is the Hotel Portoghesi. The Portoghesi is in the middle of a perfect tangle of streets that look medieval thanks to the presence of an ancient tower across from the hotel—the type of tower into which warring families retreated during the periodic civil chaos that engulfed Rome every time a pope died. Whether the Portoghesi dates from those days is uncertain, but today the pleasant hotel is modern. Taking its name from the Portuguese Church of St. Anthony, it boasts a scattering of antiques along its upper floors and freshly renovated bedrooms.

NEAR STAZIONE TERMINI
VERY EXPENSIVE

LE GRAND HOTEL, via Vittorio Emanuele Orlando 3, 00185 Roma. Tel. 06/4709. Fax 06/482-3867. 170 rms (all with bath), 30 suites. A/C MINIBAR TV TEL **Metro:** Piazza della Repubblica.
$ Rates: 350,000 lire ($274.75) single; 500,000 lire ($392.50) double; from 1,200,000 lire ($942) suite. Breakfast 23,000 lire ($18.05) extra. 19% IVA tax extra. AE, DC, MC, V. **Parking:** 50,000 lire ($39.25).

The Grand Hotel, just off piazza della Repubblica, is one of the great hotels in Europe. When it was inaugurated by its creator, César Ritz, in 1894, Escoffier, the world's greatest chef, presided over a lavish banquet, and the note of grandeur that was then struck has never died away. Its roster of guests has included some of the greatest names in European history, including royalty, of course, and such New World moguls as Henry Ford and J. P. Morgan. Only a few minutes from via Vittorio Veneto, the Grand looks like a large, late Renaissance palace, its five-floor facade covered with carved loggias, lintels, quoins, and cornices. Inside, the floors are covered with marble and Oriental rugs, the walls are a riot of baroque plasterwork, and crystal chandeliers, Louis XVI furniture, potted palms, antique clocks, and wall sconces complete the picture.

The spacious bedrooms are lavishly decorated with matching curtains and carpets, and equipped with dressing room and fully tiled bath. Every accommodation is different. While most are traditional, with antique headboards and Venetian chandeliers, some are stylishly modern. Every room is soundproof.
Dining/Entertainment: The hotel's Le Grand Bar is an elegant meeting place for the elite. Tea is served every afternoon, accompanied by harp music. At Le Pavillon, a buffet, you can enjoy quick meals amid potted plants, or try Le Restaurant, the hotel's more formal dining room. Dietetic and kosher foods can be arranged with advance notice. Service is first rate.
Services: Room service, baby-sitting, laundry and valet service.
Facilities: Beauty salon, garage available.

EXPENSIVE

HOTEL MEDITERRANEO, via Cavour 15, 00184 Roma. Tel. 06/488-4051. Fax 06/474-4105. 280 rms (all with bath), 7 suites. A/C MINIBAR TV TEL **Metro:** Stazione Termini.
$ Rates (including breakfast): 232,000 lire ($182.10) single; 327,000 lire ($256.70) double; from 440,000 lire ($345.40) suite. AE, DC, MC, V. **Parking:** 32,000 lire ($25.10).
Hotel Mediterraneo is one of Rome's most vivid manifestations of Italian art deco

styling. Because of the war, it wasn't completed until 1944, but its blueprints were executed from 1936 to 1938 in anticipation of the hoped-for World's Fair of 1942. Because its position lay beside what Mussolini planned as his triumphant passageway through Rome, each of the local building codes was deliberately violated, and approval was granted for the creation of an unprecedented 10-floor hotel. Its height, coupled with its position on one of Rome's hills, provides panoramic views from its roof garden and bar, which is especially charming at night.

Mario Loreti, one of Mussolini's favorite architects, was the genius who planned for an interior sheathing of gray marble, the richly allegorical murals of inlaid wood, and the art deco friezes ringing the ceilings of the enormous public rooms. Don't overlook the gracefully curved bar, crafted from illuminated cut crystal, or the ships' figureheads that ring the ceiling of the wood-sheathed breakfast room. The lobby is also decorated with antique busts of Roman emperors, part of the Bettoja family's collection. Each bedroom is spacious and pleasantly furnished, containing lots of exposed wood, solidly dependable furniture, and radio.

HOTEL QUIRINALE, via Nazionale 7, 00184 Roma. Tel. 06/4707. Fax 06/482-0099. 208 rms (all with bath), 13 suites. A/C MINIBAR TV TEL **Metro:** Piazza della Repubblica.

$ Rates (including breakfast): 250,000–265,000 lire ($196.25–$208) single; 330,000–350,000 lire ($259.05–$274.75) double; from 400,000 lire ($314) suite. AE, DC, MC, V.

The Hotel Quirinale was originally built a century ago by the same architect who designed Rome's Teatro dell'Opera. The royal family of Vittorio Emmanuel gathered periodically in its soaring lobby for drinks before moving through a private entrance to the opera. Since then, the Quirinale has hosted more opera stars and composers than any other establishment in Rome. Maria Callas was fond of the hotel, and Giuseppe Verdi stayed here on April 13, 1893, during the première of *Falstaff*. The hotel is set a few paces from the huge fountains of piazza della Repubblica.

Its soaring reception area has the predictable forest of marble columns, as well as barrel vaulting painted in imperial tones of gold and terra-cotta. Units facing the traffic of via Nazionale have soundproof windows. Those fortunate enough to secure a room overlooking the garden can listen to the sound of a splashing fountain or perhaps enjoy a rehearsal of *La Traviata* from the opera across the way. Each accommodation contains a fully accessorized (and often very spacious) bathroom, and deeply comfortable, often Empire-inspired furniture. Several of the rooms offer a Jacuzzi bathtub, as well as satellite TV reception.

Dining/Entertainment: In a setting of trailing vines and ornate statuary, guests can enjoy afternoon coffee in the garden; later, try the hotel's restaurant, which is of a high international standard. Drinks are served amid the antiques and oil paintings of the enormous lounge, but my favorite hideaway is the alcove-style bar decorated with vintage car prints and medallions of leading automobile clubs throughout the world.

Services: Room service, laundry and valet service, baby-sitting.

Facilities: Business center, car-rental desk, shopping boutiques.

MODERATE

HOTEL ATLANTICO, via Cavour 23, 00184 Roma. Tel. 06/485951. Fax 06/482-4976. 82 rms (all with bath). A/C MINIBAR TV TEL **Metro:** Stazione Termini.

$ Rates (including breakfast): 154,000 lire ($120.90) single; 220,000 lire ($172.70) double. AE, DC, MC, V. **Parking:** 30,000 lire ($23.55).

The comfortable Hotel Atlantico, a leading selection in its price bracket, has an old-fashioned aura but has been considerably modernized and updated, making it one of the finer properties within a few blocks of the railway station. This is one of the smaller hotels of the family-run Bettoja chain, so if it's full, one of the polite employees will direct you to another of their nearby hotels. There's a pleasant lobby and comfortable, spacious bedrooms filled with upholstered furniture. The hotel connects with the Mediterraneo "21" Restaurant, and is air-conditioned throughout. It is sensitive to American tastes.

BRITANNIA HOTEL, via Napoli 64, 00184 Roma. Tel. 06/488-3153. Fax
06/488-2343. 32 rms (all with bath). A/C MINIBAR TV TEL **Bus:** 57, 64, or 75.
$ Rates (including breakfast): 188,000 lire ($147.60) single; 226,000 lire ($177.40)
double. AE, DC, MC, V. **Parking:** Free.

The Britannia Hotel takes its name from its location next to an Anglican church on a
street right off via Nazionale, within walking distance of the main railroad station. Its
elaborately detailed Victor Emmanuel facade is graced with plant-filled upper
terraces, each of which adds a note much like that of a private garden. Inside is one of
the neighborhood's most stylish renovations. The bar contains a labyrinth of
banquettes, each padded with plush cushions and amplified with mirrors and lots of
plants. Upstairs, the bedrooms are outfitted in monochromatic schemes of gray, blue,
or pink, and filled with carpeting and modern paintings. Each unit has a radio,
personal safe, fire alarm, and a bath with radio, hairdryer, scales, and a sunlamp. Some
of the rooms have wide private terraces.

HOTEL CENTRO, via Firenze 12, 00184 Roma. Tel. 06/482-8002. Fax
06/482-8002. 38 rms (all with bath), 3 suites. A/C TV TEL **Metro:** Stazione
Termini.
$ Rates (including breakfast): 122,000–142,000 lire ($95.75–$111.45) single;
169,500–189,500 lire ($133.05–$148.75) double; from 220,000 lire ($172.70)
suite. AE, DC, MC, V. **Parking:** 25,000 lire ($19.65).

The Hotel Centro, on a quiet street near busy via Nazionale, facing the Opera House,
offers reasonably priced accommodations and pleasant surroundings. Each of its
comfortable rooms contains a safe and radio, among other amenities. The hotel has
its own parking garage nearby. Room service, laundry, and valet service are available.

HOTEL MARCELLA, via Flavia 106, 00187 Roma. Tel. 06/474-6451. Fax
06/481-5832. 70 rms (all with bath). A/C MINIBAR TV TEL **Metro:** Piazza
Barberini.
$ Rates (including breakfast): 145,000 lire ($113.85) single; 210,000 lire ($164.85)
double. AE, DC, MC, V. **Parking:** 25,000 lire ($19.65).

The Hotel Marcella is a most attractive hotel in a residential and commercial
neighborhood. After renovations, it won a prize from the Rome Tourist Board. The
lattices of its garden-style lobby create a lush decor. Many of the often-stylish
bedrooms contain separate sun alcoves raised on a dais, as well as radios. A popular
area is the flowery rooftop sun terrace, with a distant panorama of St. Peter's. The
hotel has a bar but no restaurant.

**HOTEL MASSIMO D'AZEGLIO, via Cavour 18, 00184 Roma. Tel. 06/
488-0646.** Fax 06/482-7386. 210 rms (all with bath). A/C MINIBAR TV TEL
Metro: Stazione Termini.
$ Rates (including breakfast): 202,000 lire ($158.55) single; 284,000 lire ($222.95)
double. AE, DC, MC, V. **Parking:** 32,000 lire ($25.10).

The Hotel Massimo d'Azeglio is the up-to-date hotel near the train station and
opera that was established as a small restaurant by one of the founders of an
Italian hotel dynasty more than a century ago. In World War II it was a refuge
for the king of Serbia and also a favorite with Italian generals. Today this centrally
located hotel is the "Casa Madre," or Mother House, of the Bettoja chain. Run by
Angelo Bettoja and his charming wife, who hails from America's southland, it offers
clean, comfortable accommodations, plus an adjacent bar and a well-trained staff. Its
facade is one of the most elegant neoclassical structures in the area, and its lobby has
been renovated, with light paneling. Its restaurant is covered separately in the dining
section.

**NORD NUOVA ROMA, via G. Amendola 3, 00185 Roma. Tel. 06/488-
5441.** Fax 06/481-7163. 165 rms (all with bath). A/C MINIBAR TV TEL **Metro:**
Stazione Termini.
$ Rates (including breakfast): 142,000 lire ($111.45) single; 200,000 lire ($157)
double. AE, DC, MC, V. **Parking:** 32,000 lire ($25.10).

The Nord Nuova Roma, near the railway station, is the best bargain in the family-run

Bettoja chain. It has garage parking for 150 cars, and a small, intimate bar. Its well-maintained and most comfortable rooms are standard and modernized, making the hotel a good family choice. A most satisfying table d'hôte lunch or dinner can be arranged at the nearby Massimo d'Azeglio Restaurant, beginning at 40,000 lire ($31.40).

SAN GIORGIO, via G. Amendola 61, 00185 Roma. Tel. 06/482-7341.
   Fax 06/488-3191. 186 rms (all with bath). A/C MINIBAR TV TEL **Metro:** Stazione Termini.
$ Rates (including breakfast): 172,000 lire ($135) single; 242,000 lire ($189.95) double. AE, DC, MC, V. **Parking:** 32,000 lire ($25.10).

A four-star first-class hotel built in 1940, the San Giorgia is constantly being improved by its founders, the Bettoja family (in 1950 it became the first air-conditioned hotel in Rome, and is now also soundproof). The San Giorgio is connected to the Massimo d'Azeglio, so guests can patronize that establishment's fine restaurant without having to walk out on the street. The hotel is ideal for families, as many of its corner rooms can be converted into larger quarters. Each bedroom has a radio, along with other amenities which often lie behind wood-veneer doors. Breakfast is served in a light and airy room. The staff is most helpful in easing your adjustment into the Italian capital.

HOTEL SIVIGLIA, via Gaeta 12, 00185 Roma. Tel. 06/444-1197. Fax
   06/444-1195. 40 rms (all with bath). A/C MINIBAR TV TEL **Metro:** Stazione Termini.
$ Rates (including breakfast): 135,000 lire ($106) single; 205,000 lire ($160.95) double. AE, DC, MC, V.

The Hotel Siviglia was built as a private villa late in the 19th century in a Victor Emmanuel style of cream-colored pilasters and neoclassical detailing. Inside is a combination of antique grandeur and modern comfort. Bronze lampbearers ornament the stairs leading to the simply furnished but high-ceilinged bedrooms, a few of which have sun terraces. Breakfast is served either in a tavernlike basement dining room or in a small side garden under the shade of a venerable palm.

INEXPENSIVE

FIAMMA, via Gaeta 61, 00185 Roma. Tel. 06/482-4083. Fax 06/889371.
   80 rms (all with bath or shower). TV TEL **Metro:** Stazione Termini.
$ Rates (including breakfast): 100,000 lire ($78.50) single; 150,000 lire ($117.75) double. AE, DC, MC, V. **Parking:** 30,000 lire ($23.55).

The Fiamma, on the far side of the Baths of Diocletian, is a renovated old building, with five floors of shuttered windows and a ground floor faced with marble and plate-glass windows. The lobby is long and bright, filled to the brim with a varied collection of furnishings, including overstuffed chairs, blue enamel railings, and indirect lighting. On the same floor (made of marble, no less) is a monklike breakfast room. Air conditioning is available in some of the comfortably furnished bedrooms.

HOTEL GALILEO, via Palestro 33, 00185 Roma. Tel. 06/444-1207. Fax
   06/444-1208. 39 rms (all with bath). A/C TV TEL **Metro:** Stazione Termini.
$ Rates (including breakfast): 120,000 lire ($94.20) single; 175,000 lire ($137.40) double. AE, DC, MC, V.

S The Hotel Galileo, renovated in 1985, receives high honors in its category for good value, comfortable accommodations, and a desirable location. Its entrance lies to the side of a buff- and cream-colored 19th-century palace, at the end of a cobblestone passage whose pavement is set into patterns of papyrus leaves. Inside, an intimate bar stands a few steps from the stylishly modern reception area. An elevator leads to the often-sunny and very clean bedrooms, each a bit larger than you might expect and filled with angular but attractive furniture. A few units offer private terraces. No meals are served other than breakfast, which in inclement weather is offered on a flower-garden terrace several floors above street level.

MEDICI, via Flavia 96, 00187 Roma. Tel. 06/482-7319. Fax 06/474-0767.
   69 rms (all with bath). MINIBAR TV TEL **Metro:** Piazza della Repubblica.

$ Rates (including breakfast): 100,000 lire ($78.50) single; 160,000 lire ($125.60) double. AE, DC, MC, V. **Parking:** 23,000 lire ($18.05).

The Medici, built in 1906, is a substantial hotel which has easy access to the railway terminal and the shops along via XX Settembre. Many of its better rooms overlook an inner patio garden, with Roman columns and benches, and posts holding up greenery and climbing ivy. This miniature refuge is favored by guests for breakfast or afternoon refreshments. The lounge, with its white coved ceiling, has many nooks, all connected by wide white arches. Furnishings are traditional, with lots of antiques. Likewise, the generous-size bedrooms are also attractively furnished.

HOTEL MIAMI, via Nazionale 230, 00184 Roma. Tel. 06/485827. Fax 06/484562. 22 rms (all with bath). MINIBAR TV TEL **Metro:** Piazza della Repubblica.

$ Rates (including breakfast): 130,000 lire ($102.05) single; 187,000 lire ($146.80) double. MC, V.

The Hotel Miami, a former duchess's palace, is squarely and conveniently situated in the heart of a major shopping artery. What used to be a fifth-floor pension is now nicely done over with warmly tinted marble floors, olive-green wall coverings, and comfortable, low-slung chairs in the conservatively elegant sitting room. From the high-ceilinged street-level lobby, you'll ride an elevator up to the reception area. The spacious and simple bedrooms are filled with lots of sunlight, warm colors, and chrome accents, and each has a handsome tiled bath. The quieter rooms get a little less sunlight, as they look out on a courtyard. Air conditioning is available in the rooms for an additional 20,000 lire ($15.70).

HOTEL PAVIA, via Gaeta 83, 00185 Roma. Tel. 06/483801. Fax 06/481-9090. 50 rms (all with bath or shower). A/C MINIBAR TV TEL **Metro:** Stazione Termini.

$ Rates (including breakfast): 90,000–149,000 lire ($70.65–$116.95) single; 120,000–180,000 lire ($94.20–$141.30) double. AE, DC, MC, V. **Parking:** 18,000 lire ($14.15).

The Hotel Pavia is a popular choice on this quiet street near the gardens of the Baths of Diocletian and the railway station. You'll pass through a wisteria-covered passageway that leads to the recently modernized reception area of what used to be a private villa. The public rooms are tastefully covered in light-grained paneling with white lacquer accents and carpeting. The staff is attentive. Each room is quiet, often with a good view and attractively furnished with simple, modern wood furniture and calming colors.

HOTEL VENEZIA, via Varese 18, 00185 Roma. Tel. 06/446-3687. Fax 06/495-7687. 61 rms (all with bath or shower). TV TEL **Metro:** Stazione Termini.

$ Rates (including breakfast): 129,000 lire ($101.25) single; 187,000 lire ($146.80) double. AE, DC, MC, V. **Parking:** 30,000 lire ($23.55).

The Hotel Venezia, near the intersection of via Marghera, is the type of place that restores one's faith in moderately priced hotels. The location is good—three blocks from the railroad station, in a part-business, part-residential area dotted with a few old villas and palm trees. The Venezia had a total renovation some years ago, transforming it into a good-looking and cheerful hostelry, with a charming collection of lobby-sitting rooms. The floors are brown marble. The rooms are bright, furnished with light-wood pieces and papered in stripes or floral patterns. All units have Murano chandeliers, and almost all are air-conditioned. Some accommodations have a minibar and a balcony for surveying the action on the street below. The housekeeping is superb—the management really cares.

READERS RECOMMEND

Albergo-Gabriele, via Principe Amedeo, 76, 00185 Roma Tel. 06/4884434. "Jean Pierre Le Fosse and Annette Kopp, owner-managers, run a modest and friendly pensione, 2 blocks from *the train station. Rooms are clean, tours can be arranged, as well as pickup service from the station. Singles, doubles, and triples (all with baths) cost between $50 to $75."*—Donald Neil Johnson, San Francisco, CA.

BUDGET

HOTEL PENSIONE ELIDE, via Firenze 50, 00184 Roma. Tel. 06/488-3977. 14 rms (9 with bath or shower). TEL **Metro:** Piazza della Repubblica.

$ Rates: 55,000 lire ($43.20) single without bath, 65,000 lire ($51) single with shower; 75,000 lire ($58.90) double without bath, 85,000 lire ($66.75) double with bath or shower. Breakfast 8,000 lire ($6.30) extra. V. **Parking:** 23,000 lire ($18.05).

The Hotel Pensione Elide, just off via Nazionale and near the Opera House, is a simple and attractive pensione whose entrance is one floor above ground level. Owned by Roma Giovanni, it's quiet for an establishment so close to the center of town, with an added calm for rooms facing the inner courtyard. You register in what you might consider a depressingly plain lobby, but then you proceed down papered hallways to clean, well-maintained bedrooms scattered over three floors of the 19th-century building. The rooms without private bath are close to quite adequate facilities a few steps away, and the three floors are connected by a winding marble staircase. Room 18 has what may be the most elaborately gilded ceiling of any pensione in Rome. Its design is repeated in the ceiling of the unpretentious breakfast room, whose workaday furniture provides an amusing contrast to the opulence of another era.

NEAR ST. PETER'S
EXPENSIVE

HOTEL ATLANTE STAR, via Vitelleschi 34, 00193 Roma. Tel. 06/687-3233. Fax 06/687-2300. 80 rms (all with bath), 10 suites. A/C MINIBAR TV TEL **Metro:** Ottaviano. **Bus:** 64, 81, or 492.

$ Rates (including breakfast): 260,000–295,000 lire ($204.10–$231.60) single; 330,000–380,000 lire ($259.05–$298.30) double; from 420,000 lire ($329.70) suite. AE, DC, MC, V. **Parking:** 50,000 lire ($39.25).

The Hotel Atlante Star is a first-class hotel a short distance from St. Peter's Basilica and the Vatican. The tastefully renovated lobby is covered with dark marble, chrome trim, and lots of exposed wood, while the upper floors somehow give the impression of being inside a luxuriously appointed ocean liner. This stems partly from the lavish use of curved and lacquered surfaces, walls upholstered in freshly colored printed fabrics, modern bathrooms, and wall-to-wall carpeting. Even the door handles are art deco–inspired. These doors open into small but posh accommodations outfitted with all the modern comforts. There's also a royal suite with a Jacuzzi. The hotel has the most striking views of St. Peter's of any hotel in Rome. If there is no room at this inn, the owner will try to get you a room at his nearby Atlante Garden.

The restaurant has double rows of windows, plantings, and terra-cotta floors accented with white-painted garden furniture. A meal here begins at 90,000 lire ($70.65).

MODERATE

HOTEL COLUMBUS, via della Conciliazione 33, 00193 Roma. Tel. 06/686-4874. Fax 06/686-4874. 105 rms (all with bath or shower), 4 suites. A/C MINIBAR TV TEL **Bus:** 64.

$ Rates (including breakfast): 130,000–155,000 lire ($102.05–$121.70) single; 185,000–215,000 lire ($145.25–$168.80) double; from 340,000 lire ($266.90) suite. AE, DC, MC, V. **Parking:** Free.

In an impressive 15th-century palace, built some 12 years before its namesake set off for America, is the Hotel Columbus, a few minutes' walk from St. Peter's. It was once the private home of a wealthy cardinal who later became Pope Julius II, who tormented Michelangelo into painting the Sistine Chapel. The building looks much as it must have those long centuries ago—a severe time-stained facade, small windows, and heavy wooden doors leading from the street to the colonnades and arches of the inner courtyard. The cobbled entranceway leads to a reception hall with castlelike furniture, then on to a series of baronial public rooms. Note especially the main salon with its walk-in fireplace, oil portraits, battle scenes, and Oriental rugs. The hotel is conveniently located on the triumphal boulevard built by Mussolini in the 1930s to "open up" the Vatican after the Lateran Treaty of 1929 which created the Vatican State.

The bedrooms are considerably simpler than the tiled and tapestried salons, done in soft beiges and furnished with comfortable and serviceable modern pieces. All accommodations are spacious, but a few are enormous and still have such original details as decorated wood ceilings and frescoed walls.

ON VIA DEL CORSO
MODERATE

GRAND HOTEL PLAZA, via del Corso 126, 00186 Roma. Tel. 06/ 672101. Fax 06/684-1575. 250 rms (all with bath), 4 suites. A/C TV TEL **Bus:** 2, 81, 90, or 115.
$ Rates: 185,000 lire ($145.25) single; 260,000 lire ($204.10) double; from 450,000 lire ($353.25) suite. AE, DC, MC, V. **Parking:** 15,000 lire ($11.80).

The Empress Carlotta of Mexico received Pope Pius IX here in 1866, and in 1933 Pietro Mascagni composed his opera *Nerone* in one of its bedrooms. Vincent Price always stayed here while making "all those bad movies," and when you see the slightly faded but very grand decor, you'll understand why. The public rooms are vintage 19th century and contain stained-glass skylights, massive crystal chandeliers, potted palms, inlaid marble floors, and a life-size stone lion guarding the entrance to the ornate stairway leading upstairs. The bar seems an interminable distance across the parquet floor of the opulent ballroom.

The hotel contains well-furnished bedrooms, many quite spacious, and four suites. Some rooms have been modernized and others are old-fashioned. Many rooms have minibars. There is no restaurant.

IN THE QUARTIERE PRATI
EXPENSIVE

GIULIO CESARE, via degli Scipioni 287, 00192 Roma. Tel. 06/321- 0751. Fax 06/321-1736. 86 rms (all with bath). A/C MINIBAR TV TEL **Bus:** 280.
$ Rates (including breakfast): 260,000 lire ($204.10) single; 360,000 lire ($282.60) double. AE, DC, MC, V. **Parking:** Free.

Located in a sedate part of Rome, across the Tiber from piazza del Popolo, is the tasteful Giulio Cesare, an elegant villa which was the former house of Countess Paterno Solari. In the guest salon, where the countess once entertained diplomats from all over the globe, are mostly antique furnishings and Oriental carpets. In the public rooms are tapestries, Persian rugs, mirrors, ornate gilt pieces, and crystal chandeliers. In yet a smaller salon, guests gather for drinks in an atmosphere of fruitwood paneling and 18th-century furnishings.

The carpeted bedrooms look like part of a lovely private home; some contain needlepoint-covered chairs. Other facilities include a garden where a breakfast is served, a snack bar, a piano bar, and parking space in the courtyard for 10 cars.

JOLLY LEONARDO DA VINCI, via dei Gracchi 324, 00192 Roma. Tel. 06/39680. Fax 06/361-0138. 245 rms (all with bath), 7 suites. A/C MINIBAR TV TEL **Metro:** Lepanto.
$ Rates (including breakfast): 205,000 lire ($160.95) single; 280,000 lire ($219.80) double; from 500,000 lire ($392.50) suite. AE, DC, MC, V. **Parking:** 30,000 lire ($23.55).

The Jolly Leonardo da Vinci stands in the Quartiere Prati, on the Vatican side of the Tiber (across the bridge from piazza del Popolo). This modern hotel has large public lounges furnished with leather-covered, deep armchairs. The buffet breakfast is called *buongiorno Jolly*. Politicians and film and TV stars who live in Rome are regular clients of the outstanding men's hair stylist, Amleto, at this hotel.

Dining/Entertainment: The hotel has a pleasant American bar, a restaurant, a grill, and a snack bar. Meals in the restaurant start at 50,000 lire ($39.25).

Services: Room service, laundry and valet service.

Facilities: Men's and women's hairdresser, underground garage.

NEAR THE PANTHEON
EXPENSIVE

ALBERGO DEL SOLE AL PANTHEON, piazza della Rotonda 63, 00186 Roma. Tel. 06/678-0441. Fax 06/684-0689. 26 rms (all with bath). A/C MINIBAR TV TEL **Bus:** 64, 70, 75, or 492.

$ **Rates:** 230,000 lire ($180.55) single; 350,000 lire ($274.75) double. AE, DC, MC, V. **Parking:** 20,000 lire ($15.70).

The Albergo del Sole al Pantheon, overlooking the Pantheon, is an absolute gem. The present-day albergo is one of the oldest hotels in the world; the first records of it as a hostelry appear in 1467. Long known as a retreat for emperors and sorcerers, the hotel has hosted such guests as Frederick III of the Hapsburg family. Mascagni celebrated the première of *Cavalleria Rusticana* here. Later, it drew such distinguished company as Jean-Paul Sartre and his companion, Simone de Beauvoir. Today the rooms are exquisitely furnished and decorated with period pieces and stylized reproductions. The hotel staff will direct you to a nearby garage.

IN THE PARIOLI DISTRICT
VERY EXPENSIVE

HOTEL LORD BYRON, via G. de Notaris 5, 00197 Roma. Tel. 06/322-0404. Fax 06/322-0405. 50 rms (all with bath), 10 suites. A/C MINIBAR TV TEL **Metro:** Piazzale Flaminio. **Bus:** 52.

$ **Rates** (including breakfast): 350,000 lire ($274.75) single; 470,000–520,000 lire ($368.95–$408.20) double; from 650,000 lire ($510.25) suite. AE, DC, MC, V.

The Hotel Lord Byron is an art deco villa set on a residential hilltop in Parioli, an area of embassies and exclusive town houses at the edge of the Villa Borghese. From the curving entrance steps off the staffed parking lot in front, you'll notice design accessories that attract the most sophisticated clientele in Italy. In a niche in the reception area is an oval Renaissance urn in chiseled marble. Flowers are everywhere, the lighting is discreet, and everything is on a cultivated small scale that makes it seem more like a well-staffed (and extremely expensive) private home than a hotel.

Each of the rooms is different, most often with lots of mirrors, upholstered walls, spacious bathroom with gray marble accessories, big dressing room/closet, and all the amenities.

Dining/Entertainment: On the premises is one of Rome's best restaurants, covered separately in the dining section.

Services: Room service, laundry and valet service, concierge desk.

Facilities: Car-rental desk.

INEXPENSIVE

HOTEL DELLE MUSE, via Tommaso Salvini 18, 00197 Roma. Tel. 06/808-8333. Fax 06/808-5749. 61 rms (all with bath or shower). TV TEL **Bus:** 4.

$ **Rates** (including breakfast): 93,000 lire ($73) single; 136,000–147,000 lire ($106.75–$115.40) double. AE, DC, MC, V. **Parking:** 20,000 lire ($15.70).

The Hotel delle Muse, a three-star establishment, is not far from the Villa Borghese. It's run by the efficient, English-speaking Giorgio Lazar. Furnishings are modern in a wide range of splashy colors. In the summer Mr. Lazar operates a restaurant in the garden, where you can obtain a complete meal for 25,000 lire

($19.65). A bar is open 24 hours a day in case you get thirsty at 5am. There's also a TV room, plus a writing room and two dining rooms, along with a garage for your car. A bus that stops nearby runs to all parts of the city.

NEAR PIAZZA COLONNA

EXPENSIVE

ALBERGO NAZIONALE, piazza Montecitorio 131, 00186 Roma. Tel. 06/678-9251. Fax 06/678-6677. 87 rms (all with bath), 15 suites. TV TEL **Bus:** 95.

$ Rates (including breakfast): 220,000 lire ($172.70) single; 350,000 lire ($274.75) double. AE, DC, MC, V.

The Albergo Nazionale faces one of Rome's most historic squares, piazza Colonna, with its Column of Marcus Aurelius, the Palazzo di Montecitorio, and the Palazzo Chigi. Because of its location next to the Parliament buildings, the albergo is frequently used by government officials and members of diplomatic staffs. In fact, it maintains the atmosphere of a gentleman's club, although women are welcome, too. There are many nooks conducive to conversation in the public lounges. The lobbies are wood-paneled, and there are many antiques throughout the hotel. Rooms are usually spacious, decorated in a traditional style, either carpeted or floored with marble.

COLONNA PALACE HOTEL, piazza Montecitorio 12, 00186 Roma. Tel. 06/678-1341. Fax 06/674496. 110 rms (all with bath). A/C MINIBAR TV TEL **Bus:** 492 from Stazione Termini.

$ Rates: 260,000 lire ($204.10) single; 345,000 lire ($270.85) double. AE, DC, MC, V. **Parking:** 30,000 lire ($23.55).

The Colonna Palace Hotel is housed in a stately five-story building within sight of both the Italian Parliament and the newspaper offices of *Il Tempo*. Despite its Renaissance facade, the hotel's busy interior is stylishly modern, with a lobby where politicians and journalists can talk intimately while seated on leather sofas. The keys that open the bedrooms, each well furnished, are attached to brass replicas of the soaring obelisk standing a few steps from the entrance to the hotel. Each room has free in-house movies and a radio, as well as other amenities. The hotel has an American piano bar and an elegant breakfast room.

INEXPENSIVE

ALBERGO CESARI, via di Pietra 89A, 00186 Roma. Tel. 06/679-2386. Fax 06/679-0882. 50 rms (40 with bath or shower). A/C TV TEL **Bus:** 492 from Stazione Termini.

$ Rates: 110,000 lire ($86.35) single without bath, 130,000 lire ($102.05) single with bath; 133,500 lire ($104.80) double without bath, 153,500 lire ($120.50) double with bath. Breakfast 15,000 lire ($11.80) extra.

The Albergo Cesàri, on a quiet street in the old quarter of Rome, has been around since 1787. Its overnight guests have included Garibaldi and Stendhal. Its well-preserved exterior harmonizes with the Temple of Neptune and many little antiques shops nearby. The completely renovated interior has mostly functional modern pieces in the bedrooms, although there are a few traditional trappings as well to maintain character. Breakfast (which costs extra) is the only meal available.

NEAR THE COLOSSEUM

EXPENSIVE

HOTEL FORUM, via Tor de Conti 25-30, 00184 Roma. Tel. 06/679-2446. Fax 06/678-6479. 80 rms (all with bath), 6 suites. A/C TV TEL **Bus:** 27, 81, 85, or 87.

$ Rates (including breakfast): 180,000–295,000 lire ($141.30–$231.60) single; 280,000–440,000 lire ($219.80–$345.40) double; from 500,000 lire ($392.50) suite. AE, DC, MC, V. **Parking:** 25,000 lire ($19.65).

The Hotel Forum, built around a medieval bell tower off the Fori Imperiali, offers an elegance that savors the drama of Old Rome, as well as tasteful, sometimes opulent accommodations. The bedrooms, which look out on the sights of the ancient city, are well appointed with antiques, mirrors, marquetry, and Oriental rugs. The hotel's lounges are conservatively conceived as a country estate, with paneled walls and furnishings that combine Italian and French provincial styles. Dining is an event in the roof-garden restaurant. During the season, you can enjoy an *aperitivo* at the hotel's bar on the roof, surveying the timeless Roman Forum. Reserve well in advance.

MODERATE

HOTEL DEGLI ARANCI, via Barnaba Oriani II, 00197 Roma. Tel. 06/ 870202. Fax 06/870704. 42 rms (all with bath and shower), 2 suites. A/C MINIBAR TV TEL **Bus:** 3 from Stazione Termini.
$ Rates (including breakfast): 150,000 lire ($117.75) single; 240,000 lire ($188.40) double; from 450,000 lire ($353.25) suite. AE, MC, V. **Parking:** Free.

The Hotel Degli Aranci is a former private villa on a tree-lined residential street, surrounded by similar villas now used, in part, as consulates and ambassadorial town houses. Most of the accommodations have tall windows opening onto city views, and are filled with provincial furnishings or English-style reproductions. The public rooms have memorabilia of ancient Rome scattered about, including bisque-colored medallions of soldiers in profile, old engravings of ruins, and classical vases highlighted against the light-grained paneling. A marble-top bar in an alcove off the sitting room adds a relaxed touch. From the glass-walled breakfast room, at the rear of the house, you can see the tops of orange trees.

INEXPENSIVE

COLOSSEUM HOTEL, via Sforza 10, 00184 Roma. Tel. 06/482-7228. Fax 06/482-7285. 50 rms (all with bath). TEL **Metro:** Cavour.
$ Rates (including breakfast): 102,000 lire ($80.05) single; 159,000 lire ($124.80) double. AE, DC, MC, V. **Parking:** 18,000 lire ($14.15).

Not far from the Santa Maria Maggiore Basilica, the Colosseum Hotel offers baronial living on a miniature scale. Someone with insight and lira notes designed this hotel, which opened in 1965, in excellent taste, a reflection of the best in Italy's design heritage. The bedrooms are furnished with well-conceived antique reproductions (beds of heavy carved wood, dark-paneled wardrobes, leatherwood chairs)—and all with monklike white walls. Air conditioning is available on request for 20,000 lire ($15.70). TV is also available for 10,000 lire ($7.85). The drawing room, with its long refectory table, white walls, red tiles, and provincial armchairs, invites lingering. The reception room, with its parquet floors, arched ceilings, and Savonarola chair, makes a good impression.

NEAR PIAZZA VENEZIA

MODERATE

HOTEL TIZIANO, corso Vittorio Emanuele 110, 00186 Roma. Tel. 06/687-5087. Fax 06/683-3827. 45 rms (all with bath), 4 suites. A/C MINIBAR TV TEL **Bus:** 26, 64, 95, or 492.
$ Rates (including breakfast): 130,000 lire ($102.05) single; 185,000 lire ($145.25) double; from 250,000 lire ($196.25) suite. AE, DC, MC, V. **Parking:** 25,000 lire ($19.65).

The Hotel Tiziano, a former palace on the main thoroughfare between piazza Venezia and St. Peter's, has been entirely renovated and improved, resulting in a more comfortable and functional structure. The changes complement the unique style of the Palace Pacelli (the family home of Pope Pius XII), while maintaining the atmosphere suggested by the classic architecture. The Tiziano is one of the few hotels in the center of Rome that keeps its restaurant open all year. There is a private garage where patrons may park their cars at an extra charge.

NEAR THE QUIRINAL PALACE
MODERATE

HOTEL BOLIVAR, via della Cordonato 6, 00187 Roma. Tel. 06/679-1025. Fax 06/679-1025. 29 rms (all with bath). A/C MINIBAR TV TEL **Bus:** 64, 70, 75, or 81.
$ Rates (including breakfast): 132,000 lire ($103.60) single; 193,000 lire ($151.50) double. AE, DC, MC, V. **Parking:** Free.
The Hotel Bolivar lies only a few blocks from the presidential palace, but its location on an isolated cul-de-sac makes it seem like something in a rural corner of Tuscany. Designed in the palazzo style of symmetrical windows and overhanging roofs, it was built in 1900 on a hilltop looking out over the domes of Old Rome. The modernized interior still contains a staircase wide enough for a Volkswagen and the high ceilings of its original design. Some of the bedrooms are more stylish than others, but each is clean and relatively spacious.

NEAR THE BARBERINI PALACE
MODERATE

ANGLO-AMERICAN, via Quattro Fontane 12, 00184 Roma. Tel. 06/472941. Fax 06/474-6428. 120 rms (all with bath). A/C MINIBAR TV TEL **Metro:** Piazza Barberini.
$ Rates (including breakfast): 150,000 lire ($117.75) single; 200,000 lire ($157) double. AE, DC, MC, V. **Parking:** 25,000 lire ($19.65).
The Anglo-American is next door to the Barberini Palace, half a block from piazza Barberini and half a dozen blocks from the Fontana di Trevi. A total renovation, which included upholstering the entire interior, converted this 1888 hotel into a modern hostelry. Walls are in blue, floors are done in red, chairs and couches in the lobby are covered with black leatherette, and the carpeted rooms are covered from floor to ceiling in pastel-colored fabrics. The overall effect is hushed and smart—these somewhat small rooms are probably some of the best in Rome.

HOTEL CECIL, via Francesco Crispi 55A, 00187 Roma. Tel. 06/679-7998. Fax 06/679-7996. 41 rms (all with bath or shower). TV TEL **Metro:** Piazza Barberini.
$ Rates (including breakfast): 120,000 lire ($94.20) single; 185,000 lire ($145.25) double. V.
The Hotel Cecil is where Henrik Ibsen lived in the 1860s while writing *Peer Gynt* and *Brand*. Today it's an attractively streamlined hotel with bedrooms which, despite their simple furnishings, are clean and comfortable. Many units contain parquet floors and patterned wallpapers. The location is not far from via Sistina, which runs into the top of the Spanish Steps.

NEAR PIAZZA DEL POPOLO
INEXPENSIVE

HOTEL MARGUTTA, via Laurina 34, 00187 Roma. Tel. 06/679-8440. 21 rms (all with bath). **Metro:** Flaminio.

FROMMER'S COOL FOR KIDS
HOTELS

Cardinal Hotel (see page 96) Deep in the heart of Renaissance Rome, this hotel gives both parents and kids a chance to stay in a palace built by Bramante in the 15th century with stones from the Roman Forum. It's an easy stroll to piazza Navona where you can buy your child a tartufo ice-cream treat from Tre Scalini.

Hotel Venezia (see page 101) At this good, moderately priced family hotel near the Stazione Termini, rooms are renovated and most are large enough for extra beds for children.

Cavalieri Hilton International (see page 95) This hotel is like a resort at Monte Mario, with a swimming pool, gardens, and plenty of grounds for children to run and play, yet they're only 15 minutes from the center of Rome, reached by the hotel shuttle bus.

Massimo d'Azeglio (see page 99) Near the Stazione Termini, this has long been a family favorite. Rooms are large, well kept, and comfortable, and the well-trained staff is solicitous of children.

$ Rates (including breakfast): 115,000 lire ($90.30) single or double. AE, DC, MC, V.

The Hotel Margutta, on a cobblestone street, offers attractively decorated rooms, often in a riot of contrasting fabrics and patterns, and a helpful staff. Located off the paneled lobby with a black stone floor is a simple breakfast room with framed lithographs. There are only double rooms; ask for one of the top-floor rooms with a view.

BUDGET

PENSIONE FIORELLA, via del Babuino 196, 00187 Roma. Tel. 06/361-0597. 8 rms (none with bath). **Metro:** Flaminio.
$ Rates (including breakfast): 30,000 lire ($23.55) single; 52,500 lire ($41.20) double. No credit cards.

A few steps from piazza del Popolo is the Pensione Fiorella. Antonio Albano and his family are one of the best reasons to visit this unstylish but comfortable pensione. They speak little English, but their humor and warm welcome make renting one of their well-scrubbed bedrooms a lot like visiting a lighthearted relative. The bedrooms open onto a high-ceilinged hallway.

NEAR SANTA MARIA MAGGIORE
INEXPENSIVE

HOTEL AMALFI, via Merulana 278, 00185 Roma. Tel. 06/474-4313. Fax 06/48020575. 18 rms (16 with bath). MINIBAR TV TEL **Metro:** Cavour.
$ Rates (including breakfast): 94,600 lire ($74.25) single without bath, 125,000 lire ($98.15) single with bath; 184,000 lire ($144.45) double with bath. AE, DC, MC, V. **Parking:** 18,000 lire ($14.15).

In an offbeat but interesting section of Rome lies the Hotel Amalfi, only a short block from the Basilica of Santa Maria Maggiore. It stands behind a narrow and modernized storefront on a busy street. A pleasantly paneled reception area leads to well-scrubbed bedrooms. For the luxury of air conditioning, you pay a 20,000-lira ($15.70) supplement. Mimmo Nigro and his brother, Donato, are the helpful owners. On the premises is a cozy breakfast room and bar.

2. DINING

The largest task confronting guidebook writers is to compile a list of the best restaurants in such cities as Rome and Paris. Everybody—locals, expatriates, even those who have chalked up only one visit—has favorites ("What . . . you don't know about that little trattoria three doors down from piazza Navona?")

What follows is not a list of all the best restaurants of Rome, but simply a running commentary on a number of personal favorites. For the most part, I've chosen not to document every deluxe citadel known to all big spenders. Rather, I've tried to seek out equally fine (or better) establishments often patronized by some of the finest palates in Rome (but not necessarily by the fattest wallets).

Rome's cooking is not subtle, but its kitchen is among the finest in Italy, rivaling anything the chefs of Florence or Venice can turn out. Another feature of Roman restaurants is their skill at borrowing—and sometimes improving upon—the cuisine of other Italian regions. Throughout the capital you'll come across Neapolitan, Bolognese, Florentine, even Sicilian specialties. These dishes carry such designations as alla genovese, alla milanese, alla napolitana, alla fiorentina, and alla bolognese, to cite only a few. And if you don't like the food, you may enjoy the view—of piazza Navona, the Spanish Steps, or via Vittorio Veneto.

One of the oldest sections of the city, Trastevere is a gold mine of colorful streets and, for our purposes, restaurants with inspired cuisine. Although across the Tiber, it's rather far from St. Peter's. It's adjacent to the old ghetto, whose synagogue can be seen across the river between the spires of the island called Tibertina.

In general, lunch is served from 1 to 3pm and dinner from 8 to around 10:30pm. August, when the most tourists are in town, is the most popular month for closing.

Meals rated "Very Expensive" usually cost more than 100,000 lire ($78.50); "Expensive," 60,000 lire to 100,000 lire ($47.10 to $78.50); "Moderate," 30,000 lire to 60,000 lire ($23.55 to $47.10); and anything under 30,000 lire ($23.55) is considered "Inexpensive." These prices are computed on the basis of a three-course meal (not the most expensive items on the menu), including a carafe of the house wine, service, and taxes.

NEAR PIAZZA DI SPAGNA

VERY EXPENSIVE

EL TOULA, via della Lupa 29. Tel. 687-3498.
   Cuisine: ROMAN. **Reservations:** Essential at dinner. **Bus:** 26, 90, or 913.
$ Prices: Appetizers 15,000–22,000 lire ($11.80–$17.25); main courses 38,000–55,000 lire ($29.85–$43.20); fixed-price menu 95,000 lire ($74.60). AE, DC, MC, V.
   Open: Lunch Mon–Sat 1–3pm; dinner Mon–Sat 8–11pm. **Closed:** Aug.
El Toulà offers the quintessence of the Roman haute cuisine with a creative flair. The elegant setting, attracting the international set, is one of vaulted ceilings and large archways which divide the rooms. Guests stop in the charming bar to order a drink while deciding on their food selections from the impressive menu. Main courses include grilled squab with a pungent and well-seasoned sauce of crushed green peppercorns, or a plate of perfectly flavored grilled scampi. I also like filet of beef roasted in a bag with fresh Roman artichokes. The selection of sherbets depends on the availability of fruits—the cantaloupe and fresh strawberry sherbets are celestial concoctions. You can request a mixed plate if you'd like to sample several of them. El Toulà usually isn't crowded at lunchtime. The menu changes every month.

Abruzzi 56
Albanese, Trattoria L' 54
Alberto Ciarla 43
Alfredo alla Scrofa 28
Alvaro al Circo Massimo 49
Ambasciata d'Abruzzo
Angelino a Tormargana 52
Archeologia, Hostaria L' 50
Aurora 10 da Pino il Sommelier 12
Babington's Tea Rooms 10
Battoccio, Il 57
Bibo Astoria '73 5
Birreria Viennese 26
Bolognese, Dal 7
Cabanon, Le 48
Canto del Riso, Il 55
Casa del Tramezzino, La 44
Ceppo, Al 2
Cisterna, La 45
Colline Emiliane 23
Cose Fritte 8
Cowboy, The 11
Domiziano Il 35
Drappo, Il 33
Eau Vive, L' 37
Elettra, Trattoria 19
Flavia di Mimmo, Taverna 16
George's 13
Giardinaccio 32
Giggetto, Da 50
Giglio, Ristorante del 22
Girrerrosto Toscano 14
Jardin, Relais Le 4
Maiella, La 29
Margutta Vegetariano 9
Mario, Da 24
Maschere, Le 39
Massimo d'Azeglio 21
Mastrostefano
Matriciano, Il 6
McDonald's 10
Mejo Pastasciutta der Monno,
   Taverna La 5
Monte Arci 17
Montevecchio 34
Nino 25
Osteria Margutta 9
Pallaro, der 38
Pancrazio, da
Papa Giovanni 36
Passetto 30
Patrizia E Roberto
   del Pianeta Terra 40
Pergola, La 1
Piccolo Abruzzo 15
Pierdonati 31
Quirino 59
Ranieri 24
Ristorante 34 24
Romolo 41
Sabatini I 42
Sans Souci 13
Satyricon 18
Scoglio di Frisio 20
Sora Lella
Tartufo, Er 58
Toula, El 27
Tre Scalini 35
Ulpia 53
Vecchia Roma 51
Vincenzo, Trattoria 47

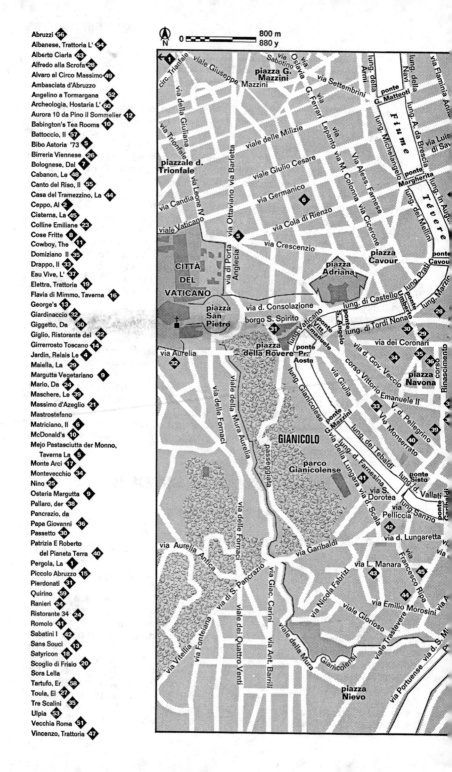

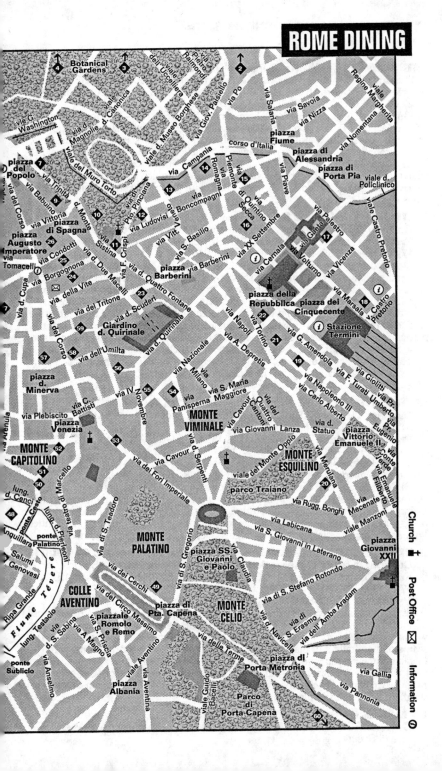

ROME DINING

MODERATE

OSTERIA MARGUTTA, via Margutta 82. Tel. 323-1025.

Cuisine: ROMAN. **Reservations:** Recommended. **Metro:** Piazza di Spagna.

$ Prices: Appetizers 10,000–12,000 lire ($78.50–$94.20); main courses 18,000–22,000 lire ($14.15–$17.25). AE, DC, MC, V.

Open: Lunch Mon–Sat 12:30–3pm; dinner Mon–Sat 7:30–10:30pm.

Osteria Margutta is on a street that traditionally has housed the nucleus of Rome's art colony. It's most fun to visit on Sunday, when art shows are staged along the street, but you can visit the galleries and antiques shops any day of the week. Should you get hungry during your stroll, drop in at this rustic tavern, where art posters provide added style. You'll pass by tables of tempting antipasti, which are priced according to your choice. Dishes include roast beef, lamb with green peppercorns, and various kinds of pasta.

RISTORANTE NINO, via Borgognona 11. Tel. 679-5676.

Cuisine: TUSCAN. **Reservations:** Recommended. **Metro:** Piazza di Spagna.

$ Prices: Appetizers 8,000–12,000 lire ($6.30–$9.40); main courses 15,000–17,000 lire ($11.80–$13.34). AE, DC, MC, V.

Open: Lunch Mon–Sat 12:30–3pm; dinner Mon–Sat 7:30–11pm. **Closed:** Aug.

Ristorante Nino, off via Condotti a short walk from the Spanish Steps, is a tavern mecca for writers, artists, and an occasional model from one of the nearby high-fashion houses. Nino's enjoys deserved acclaim for its Tuscan dishes—everything from "devilish done chicken" to "entrails and paw after the Florentine cuisine." The cooking is hearty and completely unpretentious. The restaurant is particularly known for its steaks shipped in from Florence and charcoal broiled—and these are priced according to weight. A plate of cannelloni Nino is one of the chef's specialties. Other good dishes include grilled veal liver, two deviled quail, fagioli cotti al fiasco, codfish alla livornese, and zampone. For dessert, I suggest the Florentine cake called castagnaccio.

RISTORANTE RANIERI, via Mario de' Fiori 26. Tel. 679-1592.

Cuisine: INTERNATIONAL. **Reservations:** Recommended. **Bus:** 52, 53, 56, 81, or 90.

$ Prices: Appetizers 7,000–22,000 lire ($5.50–$17.25); main courses 15,000–30,000 lire ($11.80–$23.55). AE, DC, MC, V.

Open: Lunch Mon–Sat 12:30–3pm; dinner Mon–Sat 7:30–11pm.

Ristorante Ranieri, off via Condotti, is well into its second century (it was founded in 1843). Neapolitan-born Giuseppe Ranieri, for whom the restaurant is named, was the chef to Queen Victoria. Long a favorite dining place of the cognoscenti, Ranieri still maintains its Victorian trappings. Nothing ever seems to change here. Many of the dishes on the good menu reflect the restaurant's ties with royalty: veal cutlet l'Impériale, mignonettes of veal à la Regina Victoria, and tournedos Enrico IV.

IL RISTORANTE 34 (also AI 34), via Mario de' Fiori 34. Tel. 679-5091.

Cuisine: ROMAN. **Reservations:** Required. **Metro:** Piazza di Spagna.

$ Prices: Appetizers 9,500–11,000 lire ($7.45–$8.65); main courses 12,000–17,000 lire ($9.40–$13.35). AE, DC, MC, V.

Open: Lunch Tues–Sun 12:30–3pm; dinner Tues–Sun 7:30–10:30pm.

Il Ristorante 34 is a very good and increasingly popular restaurant close to the most famous shopping district of Rome. Its long and narrow interior is sheathed in scarlet wallpaper, ringed with modern paintings, and capped with a vaulted ceiling. In the rear, stop to admire a display of antipasti proudly exhibited near the entrance to the bustling kitchen. Your meal might include noodles with caviar and salmon, risotto with chunks of lobster, pasta-and-lentil soup, meatballs in a sauce with fat mushrooms, two kinds of entrecôte, or pasta in a pumpkin-flavored cream sauce. The spaghetti with clams is among the best in Rome.

DA MARIO, via della Vite 55-56. Tel. 678-3818.

Cuisine: ROMAN/FLORENTINE. **Reservations:** Recommended. **Metro:** Piazza di Spagna.

**FROMMER'S SMART TRAVELER:
RESTAURANTS**

VALUE-CONSCIOUS TRAVELERS SHOULD
TAKE ADVANTAGE OF THE FOLLOWING:

1. When available, order a fixed-price menu where everything—including tax, service, and cover charge—is included.
2. Watch the booze—tabs mount quickly. It's cheaper to ask for a carafe of the house wine.
3. Pastas, pizzas, and rice dishes (risottos) are exceptional bargains.
4. Standing up and eating at a café or rosticceria is less expensive than sitting down.
5. Make picnic lunch and save the extra money for a really good dinner.

$ Prices: Appetizers 8,000–9,000 lire ($6.30–$7.05); main courses 11,000–15,000 lire ($8.65–$11.80). AE, DC, MC, V.
Open: Lunch Mon–Sat 12:30–3pm; dinner Mon–Sat 7:30–11pm. **Closed:** Aug.
Da Mario is noted for its moderately priced game specialites. Mario also does excellent Florentine dishes, although the typical beefsteak is too costly these days for most budgets. You can dine in air-conditioned comfort on the street level or descend to the cellars. A good beginning is a wide-noodle dish, pappardelle, best when served with a game sauce (caccia). Capretto (kid) is served in the Florentine fashion, although you may prefer two roasted quail with polenta. I heartily recommend the gelato misto, a selection of mixed ice cream.

ON OR AROUND VIA VITTORIO VENETO

VERY EXPENSIVE

GEORGE'S, via Marche 7. Tel. 484575.
   Cuisine: INTERNATIONAL. **Reservations:** Imperative. **Metro:** Piazza Barberini.
$ Prices: Appetizers 12,000–16,000 lire ($9.40–$12.55); main courses 30,000–40,000 lire ($23.55–$31.40). AE, DC, MC, V.
   Open: Lunch Mon–Sat 12:30–3pm; dinner Mon–Sat 7:30pm–midnight.
   Closed: Aug.
George's has been a favorite of mine ever since Romulus and Remus were being tended by the she-wolf. Right off via Vittorio Veneto, it's not run by George, but by Michele Pavia, maître d' here for a quarter of a century before becoming its owner. Many guests drop in for a before-dinner drink, enjoying the music in the piano bar. They then proceed to an elegantly decorated and raised dining room with a tented ceiling. There is a relaxed clublike atmosphere, and English is spoken, of course. Oysters are a specialty, served in every form from fritters to "angels on horseback." The kitchen has an uncompromising dedication to quality, as reflected by such dishes as marinated mussels, smoked Scottish salmon, and sole Georges; many veal and steak dishes are offered as well. From June to October, depending on the weather, the action shifts to the garden, suitably undisturbed because it is in the garden of a papal villa.

SANS SOUCI, via Sicilia 20. Tel. 482-1814.
   Cuisine: FRENCH. **Reservations:** Required. **Metro:** Piazza Barberini.
$ Prices: Appetizers 20,000–22,000 lire ($15.70–$17.25); main courses 45,000–48,000 lire ($35.35–$37.70). AE, DC, MC, V.
   Open: Dinner only, Tues–Sun 8pm–1am. **Closed:** Aug 10–30.

⭐ Sans Souci is the most elegant and sophisticated dining choice in Rome, and it also serves some of the finest food. With this unbeatable combination, it's no wonder that it has a chic—and frequently famous—clientele. An additional plus is its location—right off via Veneto. To begin your evening, you'll enter the dimly lit small lounge/bar to the right at the bottom of the steps. Here, amid tapestries and glittering mirrors, the maître d' will present you with the menu, and you can leisurely make selections while sipping a drink. The menu is ever changing, as "new creations" are devised. But you are likely to be offered "Beggar's Purse" crêpes filled with seasonal delicacies such as porcini mushrooms or fresh spring asparagus, and blended with ricotta and served with a white-truffle sauce. Fresh goose liver is sautéed with black truffles, and sea bass is grilled with fresh herbs. Salt-marsh lamb from Normandy appears en croûte with a thyme sauce. The dessert soufflés are sensational, made with seasonal fresh fruit. The waiters pay special attention to a chic clientele, including well-known models. In all, Sans Souci is the most elegant spot in Rome for dinner.

MODERATE

AURORA 10 DA PINO IL SOMMELIER, via Aurora 10. Tel. 484747.

Cuisine: ITALIAN. **Reservations:** Recommended. **Metro:** Piazza Barberini.
$ Prices: Appetizers 10,000–18,000 lire ($7.85–$14.15); main courses 16,000–22,000 lire ($12.55–$17.25). AE, DC, MC, V.
Open: Lunch Tues–Sun noon–3pm; dinner Tues–Sun 7–11:15pm.

Established in 1981 a few paces from the top of via Vittorio Veneto, this restaurant lies within the vaulted interior of what was originally a Maronite convent. Its manager (and namesake) is Pino Salvatore, whose high-energy direction and attentive staff have attracted some of the capital's most influential diplomats and a scattering of film stars. The place is especially noted for its awesome array of more than 250 kinds of wine, collectively representing every province of Italy. Unusual for Rome, the place features a large soup menu, along with a tempting array of freshly made antipasti. You can begin with a selection of your favorite pasta or risotto, then follow with perhaps a Florentine beefsteak or fondue bourguignonne.

GIRARROSTO TOSCANO, via Campania 29. Tel. 482-1899.

Cuisine: TUSCAN. **Reservations:** Required. **Bus:** 90B, 95, 490, or 495.
$ Prices: Appetizers 10,000–12,000 lire ($7.85–$9.40); main courses 20,000–25,000 lire ($15.70–$19.65). AE, DC, MC, V.
Open: Lunch Thurs–Tues 12:30–3pm; dinner Thurs–Tues 7:30pm–12:30am.

Girarrosto Toscano, facing the walls of the Borghese Gardens, draws a coterie of guests from via Veneto haunts, which means that you may have to wait. Under vaulted ceilings in a cellar setting, some of the finest Tuscan specialties in Rome are served. Begin by enjoying an enormous selection of antipasti, which the waiters bring around: succulent little meatballs, vine-ripened melon with prosciutto, an omelet, mozzarella, and especially delicious Tuscan salami. You're then given a choice of pasta, such as fettuccine in a cream sauce. Priced according to weight, the bistecca alla fiorentina is the best item to order, although it's expensive. This is a grilled steak seasoned with oil, salt, and pepper. Oysters and fresh fish from the Adriatic are served every day. For dessert, I'd recommend what everybody has—an assortment of different flavors of ice cream, called gelatio misto.

PICCOLO ABRUZZO, via Sicilia 237. Tel. 482-0176.

Cuisine: SEAFOOD. **Reservations:** Highly recommended. **Bus:** 490 or 495.
$ Prices: Appetizers 10,000–14,000 lire ($7.85–$10.95); main courses 20,000–30,000 lire ($15.70–$23.55). AE, MC, V.
Open: Lunch Mon–Fri 12:45–3pm; dinner Mon–Sat 8:30pm–midnight.

An imaginative array of antipasti and copious portions make Piccolo Abruzzo, a good stroll from via Vittorio Veneto, one of the most popular restaurants in its neighborhood. Many habitués plan a meal either early or late to avoid the jam, as the place is small and popular. Full meals are priced according to what you take from the groaning antipasti buffet. You can follow with a pasta course which might be samples of three different versions, followed by a meat course, then cheese and dessert. All this lively scene takes place in a brick- and stucco-sheathed room perfumed with hanging cloves of garlic, salt-cured hams, and beribboned bunches of Mediterranean herbs.

NEAR PIAZZA NAVONA
VERY EXPENSIVE

PAPA GIOVANNI, via dei Sediari 4. Tel. 686-5308.
   Cuisine: ROMAN. **Reservations:** Required, as far in advance as possible. **Bus:** 64 or 70.
$ **Prices:** Appetizers 15,000–38,000 lire ($11.80–$29.85); main courses 22,000–48,000 lire ($17.25–$37.70). MC, V.
   Open: Lunch Mon–Sat 12:30–2:30pm; dinner Mon–Sat 8–11pm. **Closed:** Aug.

Papa Giovanni, a short walk from piazza Navona, is run by Renato Sentuti, who conducts it as if he were an orchestra leader. I've followed this restaurant's history for years, even back when Giovanni Sentuti (the original papa), a wine carter, opened this little *osteria* which soon attracted the attention of the senators from the Palazzo Madama nearby. Roman cuisine has always been served here, but the food is light—not heavy or fat-laden.

It is a tiny restaurant of narrow rooms, with a whimsical decor of rows of wine bottles and picture postcards. In this informal tavern atmosphere, some of the upper crust of Rome society shows up. Your smiling waiter is likely to recommend various courses for the day, so you can dispense with the menu. One of the restaurant's secrets is "truffles with everything." However, tiny shavings of that delicious morsel will cost you extra. The mushroom salad with dandelions is one of the best I've ever sampled. For an apéritif, try uva fracola ("strawberry grapes"), and then perhaps small ravioli with truffles, followed by roast baby lamb flavored with marsala and cocoa. For dessert, try a fresh juice sorbet. The wine cellar is exceptional in scope, and many bottles are reasonable in price.

EXPENSIVE

ALFREDO ALLA SCROFA, via della Scrofa 104. Tel. 686-4519.
   Cuisine: ROMAN/INTERNATIONAL. **Reservations:** Recommended. **Metro:** Piazza di Spagna.
$ **Prices:** Appetizers 12,000–20,000 lire ($9.40–$15.70); main courses 18,000–30,000 lire ($14.15–$23.55). AE, DC, MC, V.
   Open: Lunch Wed–Mon 12:30–3pm; dinner Wed–Mon 7:30–11pm.

Oak panels on the walls contain gold-framed photographs of famous personages who have visited the restaurant. All first-time visitors order the maestose fettuccine al triplo burro, where the waiters make choreography out of whipping butter and cheese. The main-course specialty is filetto di tacchino dorato (breast of turkey, sautéed in batter and covered with thin slices of Piemontese white truffles). You might finish with an Irish coffee.

MONTEVECCHIO, piazza di Montevecchio 22. Tel. 686-1319.
   Cuisine: ROMAN/ITALIAN. **Reservations:** Required. **Bus:** 70 or 492.
$ **Prices:** Appetizers 14,000–22,000 lire ($11–$17.25); main courses 24,000–30,000 lire ($18.85–$23.55). AE, DC, MC, V.
   Open: Lunch Tues–Sun 1–3pm; dinner Tues–Sun 8–11:30pm. **Closed:** Aug 10–25.

To visit, you must negotiate the winding streets of one of Rome's most confusing neighborhoods, in the vicinity of piazza Navona. The heavily curtained restaurant on this Renaissance piazza is where both Raphael and Bramante created many of their masterpieces and where Lucrezia Borgia spun many of her intrigues. The entrance opens onto a high-ceilinged, not particularly large room filled with rural mementoes and bottles of wine. Your meal might begin with a strudel of fungi porcini (mushrooms) followed by the invariably good pasta of the day. Then select roebuck with polenta, roast Sardinian goat, or one of several veal dishes (on one occasion, served with salmon mousse).

MODERATE

IL DRAPPO, vicolo del Malpasso 9. Tel. 687-7365.

Cuisine: SARDINIAN. **Reservations:** Required. **Bus:** 46, 62, or 64.

$ Prices: Fixed-price menu 60,000 lire ($47.10). AE.

Open: Dinner only, Mon–Sat 8:15pm–1am. **Closed:** Aug.

Il Drappo, on a hard-to-find, narrow street off a square near the Tiber, is operated by brother-sister team Paolo and Valentina. The facade is graced with a modernized trompe-l'oeil painting above the stone entrance, which is flanked with potted plants. Inside, you'll have your choice of two tastefully decorated dining rooms festooned with yards of patterned cotton draped from supports on the ceiling. Flowers and candles are everywhere. Fixed-price dinners may include a wafer-thin appetizer called *carte di musica* (sheet music), which is topped with tomatoes, green peppers, parsley, and olive oil, followed by fresh spring lamb in season, a fish stew made with tuna caviar, or a changing selection of strongly flavored regional specialties that are otherwise difficult to find in Rome. Service is personal.

LA MAIELLA, piazza Sant'Apollinare 45. Tel. 686-4174.

Cuisine: ABRUZZI. **Reservations:** Recommended for dinner. **Bus:** 70, 81, 87, or 492.

$ Prices: Appetizers 10,000–15,000 lire ($7.85–$11.80); main courses 20,000–30,000 lire ($15.70–$23.55). AE, DC, MC, V.

Open: Lunch Mon–Sat 12:30–3pm; dinner Mon–Sat 8pm–midnight.

La Maiella, on the corner of a little square between the Tiber and piazza Navona, specializes in the foods of Abruzzi, and stays open all year. The restaurant draws the great and near-great, who mingle with tourists, dining outdoors under big umbrellas in summer and in the indoor dining area in winter. Before his elevation to the papal throne, Polish Cardinal Karol Wojtyla, who became Pope John Paul II, liked to come here. Traditional dishes, expertly prepared and served, include such Abruzzi mountain foods as partridge and venison with polenta, suckling pig, and baby lamb. A chef's specialty is green risotto with champagne, but I also like the risotto with zucchini flowers or wild mushrooms.

PASSETTO, via Giuseppe Zanardelli 14. Tel. 654-0569.

Cuisine: ROMAN/INTERNATIONAL. **Reservations:** Recommended. **Bus:** 70, 87, or 492.

$ Prices: Appetizers 10,000–20,000 lire ($7.85–$15.70); main courses 16,000–30,000 lire ($12.55–$23.55). AE, DC, MC, V.

Open: Lunch Tues–Sat 12:30–3:30pm; dinner Mon–Sat 8–11pm. **Closed:** Feb.

Passetto, dramatically positioned at the north end of the landmark piazza Navona, draws patrons with its reputation for excellent Italian food. The surroundings are stylish—three rooms, one containing frosted-glass cylinder chandeliers, which maintains the tradition of the past. In summer, however, it's better to try one of the outside tables on the big terrace looking out on piazza Sant'Apollinare. Formally dressed waiters, crisp white linen, and heavy silverware add a touch of luxury. Pastas are exceptional, including penne alla Norma. One recommended main dish is orata (sea bass) al cartoccio (baked in a paper bag with tomatoes, mushrooms, capers, and white wine). Another house specialty is rombo passetto (a fish similar to sole) cooked in a cognac-and-pine-nut sauce. Meals can be accompanied by a selection of fresh varied salads personally chosen from a service trolley. Fresh vegetables are abundant in summer, and a favorite dessert is seasonal fruits, such as lingonberries, raspberries, or blackberries with fresh thick cream.

INEXPENSIVE

IL DOMIZIANO, piazza Navona 88. Tel. 687-9647.

Cuisine: ROMAN. **Reservations:** Not accepted. **Bus:** 70, 87, or 492.

$ Prices: Appetizers 6,500–7,000 lire ($5.10–$5.50); main courses 10,000–12,000 lire ($7.85–$9.40). AE.

Open: Lunch daily 12:30–2:30pm; dinner daily 6:30pm–midnight. **Closed:** Thurs Sept–June.

S Il Domiziano is a pizzeria and beer cellar, serving all types of antipasti, pasta, meat dishes, and pizzas. It faces a little street called corsa Agonale, leading right into the square where you can admire the statuary in the piazza. The name "Domiziano" commemorates piazza Navona's former use as a stadium of Emperor Domitian used for chariot races (note the intact original pillar dating back to Domitian). Reasonably priced and well-prepared antipasti and pizzas are served, and many guests order saltimbocca, grilled lamb, or chicken. Dining is outside at sidewalk tables, in the main street-level dining room, or in the cellar.

LE MASCHERE, via Monte della Farina 29. Tel. 687-9444.
   Cuisine: CALABRIAN. **Reservations:** Recommended. **Bus:** 26, 44, 60, 70, or 75.
$ Prices: Appetizers 8,000–12,000 lire ($6.30–$9.40); main courses 10,000–17,000 lire ($7.85–$13.35). AE, DC, MC, V.
   Open: Dinner only, Tues–Sun 7:30pm–midnight.

Le Maschere, near largo Argentina, and within walking distance of piazza Navona, specializes in the fragrant, often-fiery cookery of Calabria's Costa Viola. That means lots of fresh garlic and wake-up-your-mouth red peppers. The restaurant, decorated in regional artifacts of Calabria, occupies a cellar from the 1600s with small outside tables in summer overlooking a tiny little piazzas deep in the heart of Rome. Begin with a selection of antipasti calabresi. There are many different preparations of eggplant. Others prefer the pasta dishes, one made with broccoli, and one flavored with devilish red peppers, garlic, breadcrumbs, and more than a touch of anchovy. The chef also grills meats and also fresh swordfish caught off the Calabrian coast. For dessert, finish with a sheep cheese of Calabria or a fresh fruit salad. If you don't want a full meal, you can just visit for pizza and beer.

NEAR STAZIONE TERMINI
MODERATE

SCOGLIO DI FRISIO, via Merulana 256. Tel. 734619.
   Cuisine: NEAPOLITAN. **Reservations:** Recommended. **Bus:** 93 from Stazione Termini.
$ Prices: Appetizers 10,000–15,000 lire ($7.85–$11.80); main courses 15,000–20,000 lire ($11.80–$15.70). AE, DC, MC, V.
   Open: Dinner only, daily 7:30–11pm.

S Scoglio di Frisio is the choice *suprême* to introduce yourself to the Neapolitan kitchen. While there, you should get reacquainted with pizza (pizza pie is redundant), by abandoning your Yankee concepts so you can begin to appreciate the genuine article. At night, you can begin with a plate-size Neapolitan pizza (crunchy, oozy, and excellent) with clams and mussels. After devouring the house specialty, you may then settle for chicken cacciatore or hunter's style, or veal scaloppine. Scoglio di Frisio also has entertainment—so it makes for an inexpensive night on the town. All the fun, cornball "O Sole Mio" elements spring forth in the evening—a guitar, mandolin, and a strolling tenor who is like Mario Lanza reincarnate. The decor's nautical in honor of the top-notch fish dishes—complete with a high-ceilinged grotto with craggy walls, fishermen's nets, crustaceans, and a miniature three-masted schooner hanging overhead. It lies on a broad street, south of the Stazione Termini.

INEXPENSIVE

MONTE ARCI, via Castelfidardo 33. Tel. 494-1347.
   Cuisine: ROMAN/SARDINIAN. **Reservations:** Recommended. **Bus:** 36 from Stazione Termini.
$ Prices: Appetizers 6,000–8,000 lire ($4.70–$6.30); main courses 12,000–16,000 lire ($9.40–$12.55). AE, DC.
   Open: Lunch Thurs–Tues noon–2:30pm; dinner Thurs–Tues 7–10pm.

Monte Arci, on a cobblestone street not far from the railway station, is set behind a sienna-colored facade which also shelters a stately but faded apartment building. The restaurant features low-cost Roman and Sardinian specialties (you'll spend less money if you have pizza). Typical dishes include maloreddus (a regional form of gnocchetti), spaghetti with clams, seafood antipasti, grilled fish, and veal dishes.

RISTORANTE DEL GIGLIO, via Torino 137. Tel. 488-1606.

    Cuisine: ROMAN. **Reservations:** Recommended. **Metro:** Stazione Termini.

$ **Prices:** Appetizers 6,000–8,000 lire ($4.70–$6.30); main courses 6,800–15,500 lire ($5.35–$12.15). AE, DC, MC, V.

    Open: Lunch Mon–Sat 12:30–3pm; dinner Mon–Sat 6:30–10pm.

Ristorante del Giglio, an old-fashioned dining room near the Teatro dell'Opera, is a restaurant and pizzeria that has been offering a savory Roman cuisine longer than anyone cares to remember. English is not a common language around here, but you'll get by fine. You can first select antipasti such as marinated artichokes or Tuscan-style white beans. You might follow with bolliti misti (assorted boiled meats) or Florentine beefsteak. Everything tastes better when served with one of the wines of Frascati.

SATYRICON, via Marsala 56. Tel. 491824.

    Cuisine: ROMAN. **Reservations:** Not usually required. **Metro:** Stazione Termini.

$ **Prices:** Appetizers 6,000–8,000 lire ($4.70–$6.30); main courses 6,000–15,000 lire ($4.70–$11.80). AE, DC.

    Open: Wed–Mon 8:30am–11:30pm.

Satyricon lies on the left side of the railroad station and does a thriving trade. Specialties, served by uniformed waiters at the small but immaculate tables, include lasagne, pennette with a vodka-flavored cream sauce, risotto with scampi, pappardelle with spinach, and a selection of veal, beef, and chicken dishes.

TRATTORIA ELETTRA, via Principe Amedeo 74. Tel. 474-5397.

    Cuisine: ROMAN/ITALIAN. **Reservations:** Not needed. **Metro:** Stazione Termini.

$ **Prices:** Appetizers 5,000–8,000 lire ($3.95–$6.30); main courses 10,000–16,000 lire ($7.85–$12.55). AE, DC, MC, V.

    Open: Lunch Sun–Fri noon–3:30pm; dinner Sun–Fri 7–11:30pm.

Trattoria Elettra is a well-run family-style trattoria, offering good food at reasonable prices between the Stazione Termini (about three blocks away) and the Basilica of Santa Maria Maggiore, quite close to via Manin. The place is bright and cheerfully unpretentious. The pasta is good, like the ravioli stuffed with ricotta, spinach, and salmon. You might also prefer risotto with asparagus in a cream sauce followed by one of the main meat or poultry dishes of the day, including ossobuco.

NEAR ST. PETER'S
MODERATE

IL MATRICIANO, via dei Gracchi 55. Tel. 321-2327.

    Cuisine: ROMAN. **Reservations:** Needed, especially for dinner. **Metro:** Lepanto.

$ **Prices:** Appetizers 9,000–10,000 lire ($7.05–$7.85); main courses 13,000–25,000 lire ($10.20–$19.65). AE, DC, MC, V.

    Open: Lunch daily 1–2:30pm; dinner daily 8–11pm. **Closed:** Wed off-season, Sat mid-June to mid-Sept.

Il Matriciano is a family restaurant with a devoted set of habitués. Its location near St. Peter's makes it all the more distinguished. The food is good, but it's only country fare—nothing fancy. The decor, likewise, is kept to a minimum. In summer, try to get one of the sidewalk tables behind a green hedge and under a shady canopy. The luncheon clientele seems to linger a long time, perhaps out of reluctance to get back to their offices. For openers, you might prefer a zuppa di verdura or ravioli di ricotta. The preferred choice, however, is tagliolini con tartufi. From many dishes, I recommend scaloppa alla valdostana, abbacchio (baby lamb) al forno, and trippa (tripe) alla romano.

RISTORANTE PIERDONATI, via della Conciliazione 39. Tel. 654-3557.

Cuisine: ROMAN. **Reservations:** Not needed. **Bus:** 64 from Stazione Termini.
$ Prices: Appetizers 8,000–18,000 lire ($6.30–$14.15); main courses 12,000–24,000 lire ($9.40–$18.85). AE, MC, V.
Open: Lunch Fri–Wed noon–3:30pm; dinner Fri–Wed 7–10:30pm. **Closed:** Aug.

Ristorante Pierdonati has been serving wayfarers to the Vatican since 1868. In the same building as the Hotel Columbus (see my hotel recommendation in "Accommodations," above), this restaurant was the former home of Cardinal della Rovere. Today it's the headquarters of the Knights of the Holy Sepulchre of Jerusalem, and the best restaurant in the gastronomic wasteland of the Vatican area. Its severely classical facade is relieved inside by a gargoyle fountain spewing water into a basin. You'll dine beneath a vaulted ceiling. Try the calves' liver Venetian style, the stewed veal with tomato sauce, or ravioli bolognese. It can get rather crowded here on days that see thousands upon thousands flocking to St. Peter's.

INEXPENSIVE

RISTORANTE GIARDINACCIO, via Aurelia 53. Tel. 631367.
Cuisine: MOLISIAN. **Reservations:** Recommended, especially on weekends.
Bus: 46, 62, or 98.
$ Prices: Appetizers 6,000–9,000 lire ($4.70–$7.05); main courses 10,000–15,000 lire ($7.85–$11.80). AE, DC, MC, V.
Open: Lunch Wed–Mon 12:15–3:30pm; dinner Wed–Mon 7:15–11pm.

This popular restaurant, operated by Nicolino Mancini, is only 200 yards from St. Peter's; unusual for Rome, it offers Molisian specialties (a provincial region of Italy). It's rustically decorated in the country-tavern style with dark wood and exposed stone. Flaming grills provide succulent versions of perfectly done quail, goat, and other dishes, but perhaps the mutton goulash would be more adventurous. Many versions of pasta are featured, including taconelle, a homemade pasta with lamb sauce. Vegetarians and others will like the large self-service selection of antipasti.

TAVERNA LA MEJO PASTASCUITTA DER MONNO, piazza Risorgimento 5. Tel. 317345.
Cuisine: ROMAN. **Reservations:** Recommended. **Bus:** 64 from Stazione Termini.
$ Prices: Appetizers 7,000–8,000 lire ($5.50–$6.30); main courses 10,000–11,000 lire ($7.85–$8.65). AE, DC, MC, V.
Open: Lunch Wed–Mon noon–3pm; dinner Wed–Mon 7–11pm.

This taverna is one of the finest of the family-run trattorie in the area. It overlooks the walls of the Vatican on this famous square of Rome, which at first appears as though it belongs more to Naples. Nella and Amanda welcome you; they specialize in many unusual types of pasta such as bucatini (a fat spaghetti) al padellaccio or la mejo pastaciutta der monno. Everything is neat and tidy, and you can also enjoy several meat dishes such as grilled beefsteak. The restaurant is a 5-minute walk from St. Peter's. It's best to call to reserve a table.

NEAR THE PANTHEON
MODERATE

L'EAU VIVE, via Monterone 85. Tel. 654-1095.
Cuisine: FRENCH/INTERNATIONAL. **Reservations:** Recommended. **Bus:** 64 or 78.
$ Prices: Fixed-price menus 20,000 lire ($15.70), 25,000 lire ($19.65), and 50,000 lire ($39.25). AE, MC, V.
Open: Lunch Mon–Sat noon–2:30pm; dinner Mon–Sat 8–9:30pm. **Closed:** Aug.

Dining at L'Eau Vive qualifies as an offbeat adventure, an unusual experience for many people. It is run by lay missionaries who wear the dress or costumes of their native countries. In this formal atmosphere, at 10 o'clock each evening, the waitresses chant a religious hymn and recite a prayer. Your gratuity for service will be turned over for religious purposes. Pope John Paul II used to dine here when he was still archbishop of Cracow, and it's a popular place with overseas monsignors on a visit to the Vatican.

Specialties include hors d'oeuvres and frogs' legs. An international dish is featured daily. The restaurant's cellar is well stocked with French wines. Main dishes range from guinea hen with onions and grapes in a wine sauce to couscous. A smooth finish is the chocolate mousse. Under vaulted ceilings, the atmosphere is deliberately kept subdued, and the place settings—with fresh flowers and good glassware—are tasteful. However, some of the most flamboyant members of international society have adopted L'Eau Vive as their favorite spot. Located on a narrow street in Old Rome, it's hard to find, but it's near the Pantheon.

INEXPENSIVE

IL BARROCCIO, via dei Pastini 13-14. Tel. 679-3797.
   Cuisine: ROMAN. **Reservations:** Recommended. **Bus:** 64 or 78.
$ **Prices:** Appetizers 8,000–9,000 lire ($6.30–$7.05); main courses 12,000–14,000 lire ($9.40–$11). AE, DC, MC, V.
   Open: Lunch daily 12:30–3pm; dinner daily 7:30–11pm.
Il Barroccio, serving generous portions of reasonably priced Roman food, attracts a loyal following who crowd into the restaurant and grab a table in one of several small salons. The parade of dishes is served against a typical backdrop of horseshoes on the wall, dried corn, wagon-wheel lights, and bronze lanterns. In these busy surroundings, you'll often get haphazard service, but no one seems to mind, especially when itinerant musicians arrive to entertain you and then pass the hat. A la carte items range from a simple but good bean soup to the more elaborate seafood antipasto. At night, pizza is a specialty, as is an array of boiled mixed meats, served with a herb-flavored green sauce.

IN THE PARIOLI DISTRICT
VERY EXPENSIVE

RELAIS LE JARDIN, in the Hotel Lord Byron, via dei Notaris 5. Tel. 322-4541.
   Cuisine: ROMAN. **Reservations:** Required. **Bus:** 52.
$ **Prices:** Appetizers 25,000–40,000 lire ($19.65–$31.40); main courses 40,000–55,000 lire ($31.40–$43.20). AE, DC, MC, V.
   Open: Lunch Mon–Sat 1–3pm; dinner Mon–Sat 8–10:30pm. **Closed:** Aug.
Relais Le Jardin is one of the best places to go in Rome for both a traditional and creative cuisine. On the ground floor of one of the most elite small hotels of the capital (see my hotel recommendation in "Accommodations," above), the decor is almost aggressively lighthearted, combining white lattice with cheerful pastel colors. Many of the cooks and service personnel were trained at foreign embassies or diplomatic residences abroad. Classified as a Relais & Châteaux, the establishment serves a frequently changing array of dishes that might include seafood crêpes, noodle pie with salmon and asparagus, or fresh salmon with asparagus. Dessert may be a charlotte kiwi royal or "the chef's fancy."

MODERATE

AMBASCIATA D'ABRUZZO, via Pietro Tacchini 26. Tel. 807-8256.
   Cuisine: ABRUZZI. **Reservations:** Recommended. **Bus:** 3, 26, 52, 53, or 168.
$ **Prices:** Appetizers 10,000–15,000 lire ($7.85–$11.80); main courses 14,000–30,000 lire ($11–$23.55). AE, DC, MC, V.
   Open: Lunch Mon–Sat 1–3:30pm; dinner Mon–Sat 7–11:30pm. **Closed:** Aug.
If you like ambitious portions on an all-you-can-eat basis, and tasty, well-cooked food that's a good value for the money, then strike out for this little, hard-to-find restaurant in the Parioli district. It's both superb value and great fun, providing you are ravenously hungry and enjoy bountiful dining. It accomplishes the seemingly impossible, not skimping on quality or quantity. The atmosphere is exceedingly informal, and you may have to stand in line if you didn't reserve a table.

It's in the true tavern style, with strings of sausages, peppers, and garlic. The culinary parade commences with a basket overflowing with assorted sausages which is placed on your table; even a herb-flavored baked ham is presented, resting on a cutting board with a knife. Help yourself—but go easy, as there's more to come. Another wicker basket holds moist, crunchy peasant-style bread. Next, a hearty mass of spaghetti vongole (with baby clams) is placed before you. Then proceed to an overloaded antipasto table with selections including marinated artichokes, salads, whatever. Later, those still at the table are served a main dish such as grilled fish. Then comes the large salad bowl, mixed to your liking, followed by an assortment of country cheeses, plus a basket brimming with fresh fruit. You're even given your choice of a dessert. A pitcher of the house wine is at your disposal, and the price not only includes coffee, but an entire bottle of Sambuca as well.

AL CEPPO, via Panama 2. Tel. 841-9696.
    Cuisine: ITALIAN. **Reservations:** Highly recommended. **Bus:** 52 or 53.
$ Prices: Appetizers 12,000–15,000 lire ($9.40–$11.80); main courses 15,000–25,000 lire ($11.80–$19.65). AE, DC, MC, V.
    Open: Lunch Tues–Sun 1–3pm; dinner Tues–Sun 7:45–11pm. **Closed:** Aug.
Al Ceppo greets you with a glittering antipasto tray, including such delectables as stuffed yellow and red peppers, finely minced cold spinach blended with ricotta, and at least two dozen other dishes, many of which taste good either hot or cold. Because of its somewhat-hidden location (although it's only two blocks from the Villa Borghese, near piazza Ungheria), the clientele is likely to be Roman rather than foreign. "The Log" (its name in English) features an open fireplace that is fed with wood on which the chef does lamb chops, even quail, liver, and bacon, to charcoal perfection. The beefsteak, which hails from Tuscany, is also succulent. Other dishes on the menu include linguine monteconero; a filet of swordfish filled with grapefruit, parmesan cheese, pine nuts, and dry grapes; and a fish carpaccio (raw sea bass) with a green salad, onions, and green pepper.

NEAR PIAZZA COLONNA

MODERATE

ER TARTUFO, vicolo Sciarra 59. Tel. 678-0226.
    Cuisine: ROMAN. **Reservations:** Recommended. **Bus:** 85, 87, or 90B.
$ Prices: Appetizers 7,000–8,000 lire ($5.50–$6.30); main courses 12,000–15,000 lire ($9.40–$11.80). No credit cards.
    Open: Lunch Mon–Sat 12:30–3pm; dinner Mon–Sat 7–11pm.
While shopping in the area of piazza Colonna, you may want to escape the roar of traffic along the corso by dining at this informal, hidden-away "truffle" in a charming location on a crooked street. It's a cozy, neighborhood setting with fast service and good, mouth-watering food. The decor in the dining room includes a wine keg set in the wall. The restaurateurs, Signori Cesaretti, are most hospitable. A specialty of the house is a plate of truffles, an expensive treat. You might want to try filet of beef with truffles, rosetta di vitello modo nostro (veal "our style"), or spiedino alla siciliana (rolls of veal with ham and cheese inside, onions and bay leaves outside, grilled on a skewer).

NEAR THE COLOSSEUM

INEXPENSIVE

TRATTORIA L'ALBANESE, via dei Serpenti 148. Tel. 474-0777.
    Cuisine: ROMAN. **Reservations:** Recommended on weekends. **Metro:** Cavour.
$ Prices: Appetizers 7,000–8,000 lire ($5.50–$6.30); main courses 9,000–10,000 lire ($7.05–$7.85). DC, MC, V.
    Open: Lunch Wed–Mon noon–3pm; dinner Wed–Sun 6:30–10:30pm.

For years visitors found it difficult to locate a good, inexpensive restaurant while exploring the core of Imperial Rome. Trattoria l'Albanese, however, is a fine choice. It has a garden in the rear where you can order lunch. Sample such dishes as the cannelloni or ravioli di ricotta. The location is between via Nazionale and via Cavour.

NEAR PIAZZA VENEZIA

EXPENSIVE

IL CANTO DEL RISO, via della Cordonata 21-22. Tel. 678-6227.
Cuisine: VENETIAN. **Reservations:** Essential. **Bus:** 64, 70, or 85.
$ Prices: Appetizers 15,000–20,000 lire ($11.80–$15.70); main courses 18,000–25,000 lire ($14.15–$19.65). AE, DC, MC, V.
Open: June–Sept, lunch daily noon–3pm; dinner daily 7pm–1am. Oct–May, lunch Tues–Sun noon–3pm, dinner Tues–Sat 7–11pm.

Il Canto del Riso is chic, sophisticated, and flippantly named ("Song of Rice" in English). Ring a doorbell to gain entrance to a candle-illuminated interior where Romans gather at a small bar to wait for a table to clear. Dozens of well-framed paintings range from Indian love scenes to Italian moderno. The restaurant enjoys a popular vogue; who knows *who* is likely to show up? Housed in a stately Renaissance-inspired building on a quiet, almost-hidden square, the restaurant, in honor of its name, offers rice dishes flavored with you name it—asparagus, artichokes, creamed red peppers, apples, or strawberries. You can order a rice dish as an opening course, then follow with one of the main dishes such as straccetti (filet of beef cooked into thin strips), served with either asparagus, artichokes, or spinach. The menu, inked onto a moveable board, also features many vegetarian dishes as well. The location is between piazza Venezia and piazza del Quirinale.

In summer the dining room remains open, but business is also funneled to a moored barge in the Tiber where fresh seafood is featured. Meals here are also priced at 50,000 lire ($39.25). The barge is near Ponte Cavour. To get there, head down lungotevere Mellini to the Tiber on the Vatican side (phone 361-0430 for a table).

INEXPENSIVE

ABRUZZI, via de Vaccaro 1. Tel. 679-3897.
Cuisine: ABRUZZI. **Reservations:** Recommended. **Bus:** 64, 70, or 75.
$ Prices: Appetizers 8,000–10,000 lire ($6.30–$7.85); main courses 10,000–15,000 lire ($7.85–$11.80). V.
Open: Lunch Sun–Fri 12:30–3pm; dinner Sun–Fri 7:30–10:30pm. **Closed:** Aug.

Abruzzi takes its name from a little-explored region to the east of Rome known for its haunting beauty and curious superstitions. The restaurant is located at one side of piazza SS. Apostoli, just a short walk from piazza Venezia. Many young people have selected this restaurant as their enduring favorite—probably because they get good food here at reasonable prices. The chef is justly praised for his satisfying assortment of cold antipasti. You can make your own selection from the trolley cart. With your beginning, I suggest a liter of garnet-red wine; I once had one whose bouquet was suggestive of the wildflowers of Abruzzi. If you'd like a soup as well, you'll find a good stracciatella (made with a thin batter of eggs and grated parmesan cheese poured into a boiling chicken broth). A typical main dish is saltimbocca, the amusing name ("jump-in-the-mouth") for tender slices of veal that have been skewered with slices of ham, sautéed in butter, and seasoned with marsala.

NEAR THE BARBERINI PALACE

MODERATE

COLLINE EMILIANE, via Avignonesi 22. Tel. 481-7538.
Cuisine: EMILIANA ROMAGNOLA. **Reservations:** Needed in winter. **Metro:** Piazza Barberini.

$ Prices: Appetizers 8,000–10,000 lire ($6.30–$7.85); main courses 18,000–22,000 lire ($14.15–$17.25). No credit cards.
Open: Lunch Sat–Thurs 12:30–2:45pm; dinner Sat–Thurs 7:30–10:45pm.
Closed: Aug.

Colline Emilane is a small restaurant right off piazza Barberini, serving the *classica cucina bolognese*. It's a family-run place where everybody helps out. The owner is the cook, and his wife makes the pasta, which, incidentally, is about the best you'll encounter in Rome. The house specialty is an inspired tortellini alla panna (cream sauce) with truffles. You might prefer one of the less expensive pastas, however, and all of them are excellent and handmade—maccheroncini al funghetto and tagliatelle alla bolognese. As an opener for your meal, I suggest culatello di Zibello, a delicacy from a small town near Parma that is known for having the finest prosciutto in the world. Main courses include braciola di maiale, boneless rolled pork cutlets which have been stuffed with ham and cheese, breaded, and sautéed. To finish your meal, I'd recommend budino al cioccolato, a chocolate pudding that is baked like flan.

NEAR PIAZZA DEL POPOLO
EXPENSIVE

DAL BOLOGNESE, piazza del Popolo 1-2. Tel. 361-1426.
Cuisine: BOLOGNESE. **Reservations:** Required. **Metro:** Flaminio.
$ Prices: Appetizers 13,000–16,000 lire ($10.20–$12.55); main courses 20,000–25,000 lire ($15.70–$19.65). AE, DC, V.
Open: Lunch Tues–Sun 12:45–3pm; dinner Tues–Sat 8:15–11pm. **Closed:** Aug.

If *La Dolce Vita* were being filmed now, director Federico Fellini would probably use this restaurant as a backdrop. It is one of those rare dining spots that's not only chic, but noted for its food as well. Young actors, shapely models, artists from the nearby via Margutta, even industrialists on an off-the-record evening on the town show up here, quickly booking the limited sidewalk tables. To launch your repast, I suggest the savory Parma ham or perhaps the melon and prosciutto if you're feeling extravagant (try a little freshly ground pepper on the latter). For your main course, specialties include lasagne verdi, tagliatelle alla bolognese, and a most recommendable cotolette alla bolognese. Instead of lingering in the restaurant, you may want to cap your evening by calling on the Rosati next door (or its competitor, the Canova, across the street), and enjoying one of the tempting pastries.

IN TRASTEVERE
VERY EXPENSIVE

ALBERTO CIARLA, piazza San Cosimato 40. Tel. 581-8668.
Cuisine: SEAFOOD. **Reservations:** Necessary, especially on weekends. **Bus:** 44, 75, or 170.
$ Prices: Appetizers 15,000–18,000 lire ($11.80–$14.15); main courses 25,000–32,000 lire ($19.65–$25.10). AE, DC, MC, V.
Open: Dinner only, Mon–Sat 8:30pm–12:30am.

Alberto Ciarla is one of the best and most expensive restaurants in Trastevere. Some critics consider it one of the finest restaurants in all of Rome. Contained in a building set into an obscure corner of an enormous square, it serves some of the most elegant fish dishes in Rome. You'll be greeted at the door with a cordial reception and a lavish display of seafood on ice. A dramatically modern decor plays shades of brilliant light against patches of shadow for a result which a Renaissance artist might have called chiaroscuro. Specialties include a handful of ancient recipes subtly improved by Signor Ciarla (an example is the soup of pasta and beans with seafood). Original dishes include a delectable salmon Marcel Trompier, and other delicacies feature a well-flavored sushi, spaghetti with clams, ravioli di pesce, and a full array of shellfish.

EXPENSIVE

SABATINI I, piazza Santa Maria in Trastevere 10. Tel. 582026.

Cuisine: ROMAN/SEAFOOD. **Reservations:** Recommended. **Bus:** 44, 75, or 170.

$ Prices: Appetizers 13,000–22,000 lire ($10.20–$17.25); main courses 16,000–30,000 lire ($12.55–$23.55). AE, DC, MC, V.

Open: Lunch Thurs–Tues noon–3pm; dinner Thurs–Tues 8pm–midnight. **Closed:** 2 weeks in Aug (dates vary).

Sabatini I, owned by the Sabatini brothers, is one of the most popular dining spots in Rome. At night, piazza Santa Maria—one of the settings used in Fellini's *Roma*—is the center of the liveliest action in Trastevere, a favorite with celebrities. In summer, tables are placed outside on this charming square, and you can look across at the floodlit golden mosaics of the church on the piazza. If you can't get a table outside, you may be assigned to a room inside under beamed ceilings, with stenciled walls, lots of paneling, and framed oil paintings. So popular is this place that you may have to wait for a table even if you have a reservation. You can choose from a large table of antipasti. Fresh fish and shellfish, especially grilled scampi, may tempt you. The spaghetti with "fruits of the sea" is excellent. For a savory treat, try pollo con pepperoni, chicken cooked with red and green peppers. The meal price will rise if you order grilled fish or the Florentine steaks. For wine, if it goes with what you ordered, try a white Frascati or an Antinori chianti in a hand-painted pitcher.

MODERATE

LA CISTERNA, via della Cisterna 13. Tel. 582543.

Cuisine: ROMAN. **Reservations:** Recommended. **Bus:** 44, 75, or 170.

$ Prices: Appetizers 8,500–15,000 lire ($6.65–$11.80); main courses 15,000–18,000 lire ($11.80–$14.15). AE, DC, MC, V.

Open: Dinner Mon–Sat 7pm–midnight.

La Cisterna lies deep in the heart of Trastevere. For the last 50 years or so it has been run by the Simmi family, who are genuinely interested in serving only the best as well as providing a good time for all guests. The Cistern in the name comes from an ancient well discovered in the cellar, dating from Imperial Rome. When the weather's good, you can dine outside at sidewalk tables. If it's rainy or cold, you can select from one of a series of inside rooms decorated with murals, including the *Rape of the Sabine Women*. In summer you can inspect the antipasti—a mixed selection of hors d'oeuvres—right out on the street before going in. Recommended are roasted meat dishes such as veal, and fresh fish.

LE CABANON, vicolo della Luce 4-5. Tel. 581-8106.

Cuisine: NORTH AFRICAN/FRENCH/ITALIAN. **Reservations:** Strongly recommended. **Bus:** 23, 75, 170, or 280.

$ Prices: Appetizers 9,000–12,000 lire ($7.05–$9.40); main courses 20,000–22,000 lire ($15.70–$17.25). No credit cards.

Open: Dinner only, Mon–Sat 8:30pm–2am. **Closed:** Aug.

Le Cabanon is lost on a tiny street in the midst of Trastevere. This brick-lined and vaulted restaurant adds musical entertainment to a cuisine derived from the far edges of the Mediterranean. It is owned by a Tunisian-born Italian, Enzo Rallo, whose cook and staff for the most part have the same origins. Around 10 or 10:30pm, a series of singers from around the Mediterranean as well as South America add music to your evening. Typical dishes might include truffled crêpes, onion soups, and filet of sole stuffed with cream and fresh salmon. North African dishes include couscous, shish kebabs, and spicy Tunisian sausages on a brochette. There's a wide array of Sicilian, Neapolitan, Tunisian, and French desserts.

ROMOLO, via Porta Settimiana 8. Tel. 581-18284.

Cuisine: ROMAN. **Reservations:** Recommended at dinner. **Bus:** 23 or 280.

$ Prices: Appetizers 8,000–9,800 lire ($6.30–$7.70); main courses 14,000–22,000 lire ($11–$17.25). AE, DC, V.

Open: Lunch Tues–Sun noon–3pm; dinner Tues–Sun 7:30pm–midnight.
Closed: Aug 5–25.

Romolo is a Trastevere gem established in 1848. You can sit in a Renaissance garden that once belonged to Raphael's mistress, della Fornarina (the baker's daughter), who posed for some of his madonnas. Now it's been patronized by everybody from Kirk Douglas to Clare Boothe Luce. To begin your meal, try the fettuccine with meat sauce, followed by scaloppine al marsala or deviled chicken. A fresh garden salad is extra. For dessert, try a "charlotte"—a sponge cake lathered with whipped cream and topped by a decorative motif. If the garden isn't in use, you'll like the cozy interior, with its bric-a-brac of copper, wood, and silver.

INEXPENSIVE

TRATTORIA VINCENZO, via della Lungaretta 173. Tel. 589-2876.
    Cuisine: SEAFOOD. **Reservations:** Not needed. **Bus:** 23.
$ Prices: Appetizers 10,000–14,000 lire ($7.85–$11); main courses 18,000–22,000 lire ($14.15–$17.25). AE, DC, MC, V.
    Open: Lunch Tues–Sun noon–2:45pm; dinner Tues–Sat 7:30–10:30pm.

Trattoria Vincenzo is surrounded by far more expensive restaurants in the Trastevere district. It has never wasted the cost of an anchovy on fancy trappings; instead, it serves some of the best-prepared dishes—particularly seafoods—in this colorful section of the city. Small, popular (always crowded with flea marketeers at Sunday lunch), the Vincenzo serves a zuppa di pesce, a stew that is as good as the most savory bouillabaisse. Meat items include saltimbocca alla romana (veal with ham and sage). Sample the ravioli di ricotta e spinaci (ravioli with cottage cheese and spinach) or the spaghetti alla carbonara.

IN THE ROMAN GHETTO

EXPENSIVE

VECCHIA ROMA, via della Tribuna di Campitelli 18. Tel. 686-4604.
    Cuisine: ITALIAN/VEGETARIAN. **Reservations:** Recommended. **Bus:** 64.
$ Prices: Appetizers 12,000–13,000 lire ($9.40–$10.20); main courses 17,000–25,000 lire ($13.35–$19.65). AE, DC, MC, V.
    Open: Lunch Thurs–Tues 1–3:30pm; dinner Thurs–Tues 8–11:30pm. **Closed:** Aug 4–19.

Vecchia Roma is a charming, moderately priced trattoria in the heart of the ghetto (a short walk from Michelangelo's Campidoglio). Head in the direction of the Theater of Marcellus, but turn right at the synagogue. Movie stars have frequented the place, sitting at the crowded tables. The room in the back, with a bas-relief, is more popular. The owners are known for their "fruits of the sea." Their antipasti marini with fresh sardines and anchovies is exceptional, and you may get tiny octopus, shrimp, mussels, and sea snails. In the Jewish ghetto tradition of Rome, they offer batter-dipped, deep-fried artichokes. If you want meat, try the veal kidneys or veal chop, or perhaps roasted goat, another specialty.

MODERATE

ANGELINO A TORMARGANA, piazza Margana 37. Tel. 678-3328.
    Cuisine: ROMAN. **Reservations:** Not needed. **Bus:** 64, 70, 170, or 710.
$ Prices: Appetizers 7,000–10,000 lire ($5.50–$7.85); main courses 12,000–20,000 lire ($9.40–$15.70). V.
    Open: Lunch Mon–Sat noon–3:30pm; dinner Mon–Sat 7–9pm.

Angelino a Tormargana, about three blocks from piazza Venezia, is housed in Goethe's historic inn. In this setting of old palazzi and charmingly ancient cobblestone squares, you can dine al fresco at tables hedged with greenery. At night the colored lanterns are turned on. A somewhat-elegant clientele is attracted to the inn, and the atmosphere is sophisticated. The food is very much in the typical Roman trattoria style—not exceptionally imaginative, but good for what it is. I'd recommend the eggplant parmigiana, followed by chicken with peppers.

DA GIGGETTO, via del Portico d'Ottavia 21A. Tel. 686-1105.
    Cuisine: ROMAN. **Reservations:** Recommended. **Bus:** 62, 64, 75, or 170.
$ Prices: Appetizers 8,000–9,000 lire ($6.30–$7.05); main courses 15,000–18,000 lire ($11.80–$14.15). AE, DC.
    Open: Lunch Tues–Sun 12:30–3:30pm; dinner Tues–Sun 7:30–10:30pm.
    Closed: July 15–31.

Da Giggetto, in the old ghetto, is a short walk from the Theater of Marcellus. Not only is it right next to ruins, but old Roman columns extend practically to its doorway. The Romans flock to this bustling trattoria for their special traditional dishes. None is more typical than carciofi alla giudia, the baby-tender fried artichokes—thistles to make you whistle with delight. This is a true delicacy. The cheese concoction, mozzarella in carrozza, is another delight.

NEAR THE TREVI FOUNTAIN
MODERATE

QUIRINO, via delle Muratte 84. Tel. 679-4108.
    Cuisine: ROMAN. **Reservations:** Not needed. **Metro:** Piazza Barberini.
$ Prices: Appetizers 8,000–12,000 lire ($6.30–$9.40); main courses 14,000–20,000 lire ($11–$15.70). V.
    Open: Lunch Mon–Sat 12:30–3:30pm; dinner Mon–Sat 7:30–10:30pm.
    Closed: Aug 4–26.

Quirino is a good place to dine right after you've tossed your coin into the Trevi Fountain. The atmosphere inside is typically Italian, with hanging chianti bottles, a beamed ceiling, and muraled walls. The food is strictly in the "home-cooking" style of Roman trattorie. At times you can enjoy fresh chicory that is perfumed and bitter at the same time. All the ritual dishes of the Roman kitchen are here, including brains in butter. I'm also fond of a mixed fry of tiny shrimp and squid rings which resemble onion rings. For an opening course, I recommend risotto, Milanese style, or spaghetti with clams. For dessert, a basket of fresh fruit will be placed on your table.

NEAR THE VILLA BONAPARTE
EXPENSIVE

TAVERNA FLAVIA DI MIMMO, via Flavia 9. Tel. 474-5214.
    Cuisine: ROMAN/INTERNATIONAL. **Reservations:** Recommended. **Metro:** Piazza della Repubblica.
$ Prices: Appetizers 9,000–14,000 lire ($7.05–$11); main courses 16,000–40,000 lire ($12.55–$31.40). AE, DC, MC, V.
    Open: Lunch Mon–Sat 1–3pm; dinner Mon–Sat 7:30–11:30pm.

Taverna Flavia di Mimmo, just a block from via XX Settembre, is a robustly Roman restaurant where during the heyday of *La Dolce Vita* movie people used to meet over tasty dishes. The restaurant still serves the same food that used to delight Frank Sinatra and the "Hollywood on the Tiber" crowd. Specialties include a risotto with scampi and spaghetti al whisky. A different regional dish is featured daily, which might be Roman-style tripe. Exceptional dishes include ossobuco with peas, a seafood salad, and fondue with truffles.

NEAR THE CIRCUS MAXIMUS
EXPENSIVE

ALVARO AL CIRCO MASSIMO, via dei Cerchi 53. Tel. 678-6112.
    Cuisine: INTERNATIONAL. **Reservations:** Required. **Metro:** Circo Massimo.
$ Prices: Appetizers 12,000–30,000 lire ($9.40–$23.55); main courses 25,000–35,000 lire ($19.65–$27.50). No credit cards.
    Open: Lunch Tues–Sun 12:30–3:30pm; dinner Tues–Sat 7–11:30pm. **Closed:** Aug.

Alvaro al Circo Massimo is the closest thing in Rome to a genuine provincial inn. It's at the edge of the Circus Maximus, which brings back memories of *Ben Hur*. Here is all the decor associated with Italian taverns, including corn on the cob hanging from the ceiling and rolls of fat sausages. You can begin with the antipasti or one of the fine pasta dishes, such as fettuccine. Meat courses are well prepared, and there is an array of fresh fish. A basket of fresh fruit rounds out the repast. Try to linger longer and make an evening of it—the atmosphere is mellow.

ON THE ISLAND OF TIBERINA

SORA LELLA, via dei Ponte Quattro Capi 16. Tel. 686-1601.
   Cuisine: ROMAN. **Reservations:** Required. **Bus:** 23, 97, or 789.
$ **Prices:** Appetizers 10,000–16,000 lire ($7.85–$12.55); main courses 18,000–25,000 lire ($14.15–$19.65). No credit cards.
   Open: Lunch Mon–Sat 1–3pm; dinner Mon–Sat 8–10:30pm. **Closed:** July 27–Aug 31.

Sora Lella, somewhat of a dining curiosity, is recommended primarily for its medieval location, on the boat-shaped island of Tiberina, right in the middle of the river. It's housed in a tower at the foot of a bridge, with busy traffic hurrying by, and regionally decorated with hanging lanterns, tavern tables, and a cozy fireplace. Here you get a flavorsome Roman cuisine, including involtini, ossobuco, and roast lamb with artichokes. Soups are rich and nutritious, and the pasta dishes are homemade, served with savory sauces. Meat courses are also well prepared. A basket of fresh fruit may end your meal.

NEAR PIAZZA DI CAMPIO DEI FIORI

VERY EXPENSIVE

PATRIZIA E ROBERTO DEL PIANETA TERRA, via dell'arco del Monte 95. Tel. 686-9893.
   Cuisine: ITALIAN. **Reservations:** Essential. **Bus:** 64, 75, 170, or 492.
$ **Prices:** Appetizers 16,000–22,000 lire ($12.55–$17.25); main courses 38,000–45,000 lire ($29.85–$35.35). AE, DC, MC, V.
   Open: Dinner only, Tues–Sun 8–11pm. **Closed:** Aug.

Patrizia e Roberto del Pianeta Terrace used to be a secret address but now all the world—at least, those who can secure a reservation—comes to the door of "The Planet Earth" (its English name). Elegant and traditional, this restaurant lies in the heart of Rome, in an ancient palazzo with a reception room on the ground level and a classy dining room with very limited seating on the second floor. Robert and Patrizia Minnetti bring sophistication and flair to their "new Italian style" cookery. Roberto has been acclaimed one of the most imaginative chefs of Rome, and one food critic called his kitchen a "laboratory." Out of this laboratory emerges some of the best food in Rome, beginning, perhaps, with stuffed ravioli served in a pistachio sauce and followed by saffron-flavored risotto with baby zucchini, or roast pigeon and figs. Pigeons might also be stuffed with shellfish. The menu is always changing, but you get the idea. Desserts might be a medley, with everything from a rhubarb-flavored sherbet to a carrot cake with almonds and chocolate. The wine list is vast, and the staff will offer helpful guidance.

MODERATE

RISTORANTE DA PANCRAZIO, piazza del Biscione 92. Tel. 686-1246.
   Cuisine: ROMAN. **Reservations:** Recommended. **Bus:** 46 or 62.
$ **Prices:** Appetizers 10,000–11,000 lire ($7.85–$8.65); main courses 15,000–16,000 lire ($11.80–$12.55). AE, DC, MC, V.
   Open: Lunch Thurs–Tues noon–3pm; dinner Thurs–Tues 7pm–midnight. **Closed:** Aug 10–20.

Ristorante de Pancrazio is a dining oddity. It serenely occupies the ruins of Pompey's ancient theater. The lower section of the theater and the rugged stone-vaulted cellar have been converted into a restaurant that is a national monument whose walls have witnessed 2,000 years of history. A tavern decoration sets the informal mood in several of the dining halls. The main room, however, is more dignified, with tall marble columns and a coffered ceiling. An especially good opener for your meal is risotto alla pescatora (with an assortment of fruits of the sea). Main courses include saltimbocca and baked lamb with potatoes. The fish dishes are also good, especially the mixed fish fry and the scampi. For dessert, try torte Saint-Honoré.

INEXPENSIVE

RISTORANTE DEL PALLARO, largo del Pallaro 15. Tel. 654-1488.

Cuisine: ROMAN. **Reservations:** Recommended for dinner on weekends. **Bus:** 46, 70, or 492.

$ Prices: Fixed-price menu 25,000 lire ($19.65). No credit cards.

Open: Lunch Tues–Sun 1–3pm; dinner Tues–Sun 8–11:30pm.

The cheerful and kind-hearted woman in white who emerges with clouds of steam from this establishment's bustling kitchen is the owner, Paola Fazi. With her husband, Mario, she maintains a simple duet of very clean dining rooms where price-conscious Romans go for good food at bargain price. No à la carte meals are served, but the fixed-price menu has made the place famous. As you sit down, the first of eight courses will appear, one following the other, until you've had more than your fill. You begin with antipasti, then go on to such dishes as the pasta of the day, which might be spaghetti, rigatoni, or pappardelle. The meat courses include roast veal, white meatballs, or (only on Friday) dried cod. Potatoes and eggplant are offered. For your final courses, you're served mozzarella cheese, cake with custard, and fruit in season. The meal also includes bread, a liter of mineral water, and half a liter of the house wine.

ALONG THE APPIAN WAY
MODERATE

HOSTARIA L'ARCHEOLOGIA, via Appia Antica 139. Tel. 788-0494.

Cuisine: ROMAN. **Reservations:** Recommended, especially on weekends. **Bus:** 118.

$ Prices: Appetizers 9,000–14,000 lire ($7.05–$11); main courses 15,000–20,000 lire ($11.80–$15.70). DC.

Open: Lunch Fri–Wed 12:30–3:30pm; dinner Fri–Wed 8–10:30pm.

Hostaria l'Archeologia, on the historic Appian Way, is only a short walk from the catacombs of St. Sebastian. The family-run restaurant is like an 18th-century village tavern with lots of atmosphere, strings of garlic and corn, oddments of copper hanging from the ceiling, earth-brown beams, and sienna-washed walls. In summer, guests dine in the garden out back, sitting under the spreading wisteria. For the chilly months, there are two separate dining rooms on either side of a gravel walkway. The Roman victuals are first rate; you can glimpse the kitchens from behind a partition from the exterior garden parking lot. Many Roman families visit on the weekend, sometimes as many as 30 diners in a group. A joie de vivre permeates the place.

Of special interest is the wine cellar, excavated in an ancient Roman tomb. Wines dating back to 1800 are kept there. You go through an iron gate, down some stairs, and into the underground cavern. Along the way, you can still see the holes once occupied by funeral urns.

SPECIALTY DINING
A TEA ROOM/BRUNCH

BABINGTON'S TEA ROOMS, piazza di Spagna 23. Tel. 678-6027.

Cuisine: ANGLO-AMERICAN. **Reservations:** Not needed. **Metro:** Piazza di Spagna.

$ Prices: Main courses 18,000–30,000 lire ($14.15–$23.55); brunch 40,000 lire ($31.40). AE, DC, MC, V.

Open: Wed–Mon 9am–8pm.

When Victoria was on the English throne, an Englishwoman named Anne Mary Babington arrived in Rome and couldn't find a place for "a good cuppa." With stubborn determination, she opened her own tea rooms near the foot of the Spanish Steps, and the rooms are still going strong. You can order everything from Scottish scones to a club sandwich to Ceylon tea to American coffee. Brunch is served at all hours.

GELATO

TRE SCALINI, piazza Navona 28-32. Tel. 687-9148.
Cuisine: ROMAN. **Reservations:** Not needed. **Bus:** 64 or 70.
$ Prices: Tartufo 4,000–8,000 lire ($3.15–$6.30). No credit cards.
Open: Thurs–Tues 9am–11pm.
If you're in the area, stroll over to Tre Scalini's *gelateria* and try its tartufo (bittersweet chocolate-coated ice cream with cherries and whipped cream). If you order two to take out, they'll cost 4,000 lire ($3.15) each. If you eat at one of the sidewalk tables, the charge is 8,000 lire ($6.30) each.

FAST FOOD

MCDONALD'S, piazza di Spagna 46. Tel. 4679-3382.
This McDonald's practically caused a riot when it was plunked down in the midst of chic boutiques. But today this U.S.-based food emporium has found its place and is popular, even among Romans shopping in the area. The "Big Mac" here costs 4,200 lire ($3.30), and it can be devoured from 10am to midnight 7 days a week. Other fast-food eateries are listed below. Take bus no. 75, or no. 70 from Stazione Termini.

COSE FRITTE, via di Ripetta 3. Tel. 321-9257.
Cuisine: ITALIAN. **Reservations:** Not needed. **Metro:** Flaminio.
$ Prices: Pizza 2,500 lire ($1.95). No credit cards.
Open: Mon–Sat 8:30am–10pm.
Cose Fritte will satisfy an urge for fried food. Near piazza del Popolo, the kitchen provides a wide selection of food items; nothing is more delectable than the deep-fried zucchini blossoms. But almost anything is dipped into the batter and hot oil, including eggplant, codfish, even slices of fruit such as apple. Their pizza, called al taglio, is not your typical fare either; it's deep-fried, cut, and weighed. The place has no tables, so you stand and eat your food or take it outside. The staff will remain later than closing time if there are hungry clients still pouring in.

 FROMMER'S COOL FOR KIDS
RESTAURANTS

Il Matriciano *(see page 118)* This is a safe, clean, and reasonably priced family restaurant in the vicinity of St. Peter's. It's good country fare—nothing fancy.

Taverna La Mejo Pastasciutta der Monno *(see page 119)* One of the best family-type trattorie in the vicinity of the Vatican, this restaurant overlooks one of the most famous squares in Rome. Kids love the "fat spaghetti" called *bucatini*.

Ambasciata d'Abruzzo *(see page 120)* This all-you-can-eat place is recommended for its lively excitement as much as for its hearty cuisine. Your children can pick and choose what they want from a wide assortment of food.

McDonald's *(see page 129)* Even in Rome, kids get hungry for the Big Mac. They're also offered an array of freshly made salads (far better than most of those back home).

BIRRERIA VIENNESE, via della Croce 21-22. Tel. 679-5569.

　　Cuisine: MIDDLE EUROPEAN/ITALIAN. **Reservations:** Not needed. **Metro:** Piazza di Spagna.

$　**Prices:** Appetizers 4,000–6,000 lire ($3.15–$4.70); main courses 7,000–12,000 lire ($5.50–$9.40). AE, DC, MC, V.

　　Open: Thurs–Tues noon–midnight. **Closed:** July 15–Aug 15.

Birreria Viennese has been feeding hungry tourists since before World War II. It has a cozy atmosphere, with rustic Austrian decoration. The kitchen produces all kinds of Middle European dishes, such as Wiener Schnitzel, Hungarian goulash, and over-stuffed sausage and sauerkraut. Three kinds of beer on draft are served here, and few diners object to that final meal tab because it's so reasonable. Those with gargantuan appetites ask for the Transylvania plate, with three kinds of meat, served with vegetables, potatoes, even sausage and bacon (for two or more people). There's no need to reserve a table. The location is between the shopping artery, via del Corso, and one of Rome's "living rooms," piazza di Spagna.

DINING WITH A VIEW

LA PERGOLA, in the Cavalieri Hilton, via Cadlolo 101. Tel. 31511.

　　Cuisine: ITALIAN/INTERNATIONAL. **Reservations:** Required. **Bus:** 907, 913, or 999.

$　**Prices:** Appetizers 20,000–22,000 lire ($15.70–$17.25); main courses 38,000–45,000 lire ($29.85–$35.35); menu dégustation 110,000 lire ($86.35). AE, DC, MC, V.

　　Open: Dinner only, Mon–Sat 7:30pm–midnight.

You'll enjoy a view of Renaissance and ancient Rome from the panoramic windows of this restaurant set on the uppermost level of this deluxe hotel. It's considered by some cuisine critics to be one of the best restaurants in Italy. Its glamorous clientele, good service, and relaxing ambience would make it a sought-after rendezvous in any event.

　　You'll ride to the dramatically lit entrance vestibule in an elevator and emerge facing two snarling porcelain panthers. The maître d' or his assistant will give you a warm but formal greeting before escorting you to your table amid window-walls of glass, intimate lighting, unusual modern paintings, and a stylish decor with accents of glittering brass, silver, and black. Clients have included virtually all the political leaders of Italy, as well as many film stars.

　　The restaurant offers a frequently changing list of seasonal specialties, as well as the popular carpaccio with slivers of parmesan and country salad, risotto with shrimp, filets of chicken, giant prawns in white wine sauce, roast rack of lamb in pepper sauce, and tenderloin of beef in red wine with bone marrow.

RISTORANTE MASTROSTEFANO, piazza Navona 94. Tel. 654-2855.

　　Cuisine: ROMAN. **Reservations:** Recommended. **Bus:** 70, 87, or 492.

$　**Prices:** Appetizers 10,000–18,000 lire ($7.85–$14.15); main courses 18,000–22,000 lire ($14.15–$17.25). AE, DC, MC, V.

　　Open: Lunch Tues–Sun noon–3:30pm; dinner Tues–Sun 7:30pm–midnight.

The world comes to the door of Ristorante Mastrostefano, if not for the food, then for the view of Bernini's *Fountain of the Four Rivers,* of which sidewalk tables offer a ringside view. The restaurant is considered more desirable than its major competitor, Tre Scalini, across the way. You can order such dishes as smoked or marinated salmon, a fritti di verdure (vegetable fry) in the Roman culinary style, and very fresh fish, followed by a range of tempting ice creams and desserts.

RISTORANTE ULPIA, via del Foro Traiano 2. Tel. 678-9980.

　　Cuisine: INTERNATIONAL. **Reservations:** Recommended. **Bus:** 64 or 70.

$　**Prices:** Appetizers 10,000–12,000 lire ($7.85–$9.40); main courses 15,000–18,000 lire ($9.40–$14.15); fixed-price menu 25,000 lire ($19.65). AE, DC, MC, V.

　　Open: Lunch Mon–Sat noon–3pm; dinner Mon–Sat 7–11pm.

Ristorante Ulpia sits on a terrace above the sprawling excavations of what used to be Trajan's Market, where the produce of much of ancient Rome was bought and sold. Today you can dine by candlelight on the restaurant's sheltered balcony while reflecting on the fate of faded empires. You might also take a look at the interior, where a statue of Ulpia, goddess of the marketplace, seems to complement the fragments of ancient bas-reliefs, copies of Roman frescoes, Etruscan-style balustrades, and fresh flowers. Your meal might include sole meunière, stewed chicken with peppers, or other straightforward, flavorful dishes.

HOTEL DINING

MASSIMO D'AZEGLIO, via Cavour 18. Tel. 488-0646.
   Cuisine: ROMAN. **Reservations:** Recommended. **Metro:** Stazione Termini.
$ Prices: Appetizers 12,000–14,000 lire ($9.40–$11); main courses 25,000–28,000 lire ($19.65–$22). AE, DC, MC, V.
   Open: Lunch Mon–Sat 12:30–3pm; dinner Mon–Sat 7–11pm.
Massimo d'Azeglio, in a hotel but with a separate entrance, has dispensed Roman cuisine since 1875. Built near the Stazione Termini, which was a fashionable address in the 19th century, it was named after a famous Savoy-born statesman who helped Garibaldi unify Italy. Today the restaurant is adorned with oil portraits of distinguished Italians. It's run by Angelo Bettoja, whose great-great-grandfather was the founder. Menu items include an excellent version of penne with vodka, trout Cavour (with pine nuts), grilled swordfish, plus an array of grilled meats.

BREAKFAST

BIBO ASTORIA '73, via Cola di Rienzo 60-62. Tel. 687-4185.
   Cuisine: INTERNATIONAL/ITALIAN. **Reservations:** Required. **Bus:** 70, 81, 492, or 910.
$ Prices: Appetizers 5,500–17,000 lire ($4.30–$13.35); main courses 6,500–14,000 lire ($5.10–$11). AE, MC, V.
   Open: Restaurant, Mon–Sat noon–midnight; bar, Mon–Sat 7am–midnight.
Bibo Astoria '73, at the intersection of piazza del Risorgimento and via Cola di Rienzo, is a bar and restaurant, with both an Italian and international kitchen. It is an especially good choice for breakfast, with omelets beginning at 6,500 lire ($5.10). Breakfast is served throughout the day, beginning at 7am in the bar. The caffè is known for its covered winter garden, which is like a veranda. Most visitors come here at night to order the delectable and savory pizzas that emerge bubbling hot from the ovens. However, you can also settle for a plate of spaghetti, and no one faints if you ask for just a hamburger. Nothing is fancy here; the service, like the food, is informal. But you get good value and you don't need to dress up in a Valentino wardrobe to patronize the joint.

VEGETARIAN

MARGUTTA VEGETARIANO, via Margutta 119. Tel. 678-6033.
   Cuisine: VEGETARIAN. **Reservations:** Recommended. **Metro:** Piazza di Spagna.
$ Prices: Appetizers 10,000–16,000 lire ($7.85–$12.55); main courses 12,000–18,000 lire ($9.40–$14.15). AE, DC, MC, V.
   Open: Lunch Mon–Sat 1–3pm; dinner Mon–Sat 7:30–10:30pm.
Margutta Vegetariano, one of the few vegetarian restaurants in Rome, is a favorite haunt of film stars and TV personalities from nearby studios. The stone detailing of its maroon facade is known to those who ignore the riches of traditional Italian cuisine in favor of a simple list of frequently changing high-fiber items whose names are written on a blackboard. There's a vast selection of pasta dishes with a Mediterranean flavor, as well as a soup, a mixed salad, a melange of fried vegetables, a collection of crudités, risotto, and fresh desserts. Eggplant parmigiana is a perennial favorite. The restaurant has a large selection of wines and ciders.

LATE-NIGHT SNACKS

LA CASA DEL TRAMEZZINO, viale Trastevere 81. Tel. 582118.
    Cuisine: SANDWICHES. **Reservations:** Not needed. **Bus:** 23, 26, 44, 75, or 170.
$ Prices: Appetizers 5,000–8,000 lire ($3.95–$6.30); main courses 6,000–9,000 lire ($4.70–$7.05). AE, DC, MC, V.
    Open: Wed–Mon 7:30am–2am. **Closed:** Aug.

La Casa del Tramezzino, deep in Trastevere, is called a "snack bar all'Americana." It's a good place for a snack at almost any time of the day or night. The staff will gladly prepare at least 64 different types of sandwiches. Sometimes the fillings are ordinary; other times they are exotic. Take your pick, and if you stay in Rome long enough, try to work through the entire repertoire. You can also order salads and cold dishes when your taste for sandwiches has been satisfied. Two sandwiches, washed down by a beer, with coffee to follow, costs 11,000 lire ($8.65) and up.

THE COWBOY, via Francesco Crispi 68. Tel. 474-5328.
    Cuisine: AMERICAN/ITALIAN. **Reservations:** Not required. **Bus:** 56.
$ Prices: Appetizers 4,000–8,000 lire ($3.15–$6.30); main courses 6,000–14,000 lire ($4.70–$11). AE, MC, V.
    Open: Lunch Mon–Sat noon–3pm; dinner daily 7:30pm–2:30am. **Closed:** Aug.

The wandering *griglia* can try the Cowboy for a taste of home. It's the best corral in Rome for those with a hankering for the vittles of Texas, offering chili, southern fried chicken with french fries, and Texas-burgers with cheese. The Italian specialty is cannelloni. For dessert you can order a homemade apple pie with ice cream, followed by American-style coffee. This place is popular with Americans, who like the good beer and get a laugh from the satirical western mural inside. After midnight, the prices go up by 15%.

PICNIC SUPPLIES & WHERE TO EAT THEM

Although Rome bounds in delicatessens and food stores—several in every neighborhood—it's much more fun to get the makings for a picnic lunch at one of the open-air daily **food markets** of Rome. The biggest and most plentifully stocked is the one at piazza Vittorio Emanuele, near the Stazione Termini. One of the most characteristic food markets is at the piazza Campo dei Fiori, south of piazza Navona.

Romans prefer to go to **specialty shops** for their supplies instead of a general food market (American-type supermarkets are rare). Cheese, yogurt, and other milk products are sold at a *latteria*. Vegetables are sold at an *alimentari* (actually a small grocery store), and delilike cold cuts are available at a *salumeria*. For your bread, go to a *panetteria*. For dessert, visit a *pasticceria*, and, if you want something to drink (wine, that is), patronize a *vinatteria*.

The best place for a picnic is the **Villa Borghese,** the only park in the center of Rome, beginning at the top of via Vittorio Veneto. To picnic here is doing it in style.

CHAPTER 5

WHAT TO SEE & DO IN ROME

- **SUGGESTED ITINERARIES**
- **DID YOU KNOW . . . ?**
1. **ATTRACTIONS**
- **FROMMER'S FAVORITE ROME EXPERIENCES**
- **WALKING TOUR— IMPERIAL ROME**
- **WALKING TOUR— ROMAN FORUM & PALATINE HILL**
- **WALKING TOUR— FROM PIAZZA BARBERINI TO PIAZZA DEL POPULO**
  WALKING TOUR— THE SPANISH STEPS TO QUIRINALE
2. **SPORTS & RECREATION**
3. **SAVVY SHOPPING**
4. **EVENING ENTERTAINMENT**
5. **EASY EXCURSIONS**

Rome is studded with ancient monuments that silently evoke its history as one of the greatest centers of Western civilization. In the millennium of the Eternal City's influence, all roads led to Rome with good reason. It became one of the first cosmopolitan cities in the world, importing slaves, gladiators, great art—even citizens—from the far corners of the Empire.

With all its carnage, and with all its mismanagement, it left a legacy of law and an uncanny lesson in how to conquer an enemy by absorbing his culture. Rome's pantheon of gods became a galaxy.

But Ancient Rome is only part of the spectacle. The Vatican has had a major effect in making the city a center of world tourism. Although Vatican architects stripped down much of the glory of the past, they created great Renaissance treasures, occasionally incorporating the old—as Michelangelo did in turning the Baths of Diocletian into a church.

In the years that followed, Bernini adorned the city with the wonders of the baroque, especially the fountains. The modern sightseer even owes a debt (as reluctant as one may be to acknowledge it) to Mussolini, who did much to dig out the past, particularly at the Imperial Forum. Today, besides being the Italian capital, Rome, in a larger sense, belongs to the world.

SUGGESTED ITINERARIES

IF YOU HAVE 1 DAY Far too brief—after all, Rome wasn't built in a day and you aren't likely to see it in a day either, but make the most of your limited time. You'll basically have to decide on the legacy of imperial Rome—mainly the Roman Forum, the Imperial Forum, and the Colosseum, or else St. Peter's and the Vatican. Walk along the Spanish Steps at sunset.

IF YOU HAVE 2 DAYS If you elected to see the Roman Forum and the Colosseum, then spend the second day exploring St. Peter's and the Vatican Museum (or vice versa).

❓ DID YOU KNOW . . . ?

- Along with miles of headless statues and acres of paintings, Rome has 913 churches.
- Some Mongol khans and Turkish chieftains pushed westward to conquer the Roman Empire after it had ceased to exist.
- At the time of Julius Caesar and Augustus, Rome's population reached the million mark, the largest city in the Western world. Some historians claim that by the year A.D. 500 only 10,000 inhabitants were left.
- Pope Leo III sneaked up on Charlemagne and set an imperial crown on his head, a surprise coronation that launched a precedent of Holy Roman Emperors being crowned by popes in Rome.
- More than 90% of Romans live in private apartments, some rising 10 floors without elevators.
- The bronze of Marcus Aurelius, one of the world's greatest equestrian statues, escaped being melted down because the early Christians thought the statue was of Constantine.
- The Theater of Marcellus incorporated a gory realism in some of its stage plays: Condemned prisoners were often butchered before audiences as part of the plot.
- Christians were not fed to the lions at the Colosseum, but in 1 day 5,000 animals were slaughtered (one about every 10 seconds). North Africa's native lions and elephants were rendered extinct.

IF YOU HAVE 3 DAYS Spend your first 2 days as above. Go in the morning to the Pantheon in the heart of Old Rome, then try to explore two museums after lunch: Castel Sant'Angelo and the Etruscan Museum. Have dinner at a restaurant on piazza Navona.

IF YOU HAVE 5 DAYS Spend your first 3 days as above. On Day 4 head for the environs, notably Tivoli, where you can see the Ville d'Este and Hadrian's Villa. On Day 5 explore the ruins of Ostia Antica, return to Rome for lunch, and visit the Galeria Borghese and Basilica di San Giovanni in Laterano in the afternoon. Go to the Trevi Fountain and toss a coin in to ensure your return to Rome, as you didn't get to see it all.

1. ATTRACTIONS

In addition to the top attractions in the city itself, there are several places in the environs of Rome worth visiting before leaving this part of the country. It would be a shame to strike out for Naples or Florence without having at least visited Hadrian's Villa and the Villa d'Este, not to mention Palestrina and Ostia Antica (see "Easy Excursions" in this chapter).

THE TOP ATTRACTIONS

ST. PETER'S BASILICA

As you stand in Bernini's **piazza San Pietro** (St. Peter's Square), you'll be in the arms of an ellipse dominated by St. Peter's (tel. 698-4466). Like a loving parent, the Doric-pillared colonnade reaches out to embrace the faithful. Holding 300,000 is no problem for this square. To reach it, take bus no. 23, 30, 32, 49, 51, or 64.

In the center of the square is an Egyptian obelisk, brought from the ancient city of Heliopolis on the Nile Delta, and used to adorn Nero's Circus, which was nearby. Flanking the obelisk are two 17th-century fountains—the one on the right (facing the basilica) by Carlo Maderno, who designed the facade of St. Peter's, was placed there by Bernini himself; the other is by Carlo Fontana.

Inside, the size of this famous church (open daily from 7am to 7pm April through August, daily from 7am to 6pm September through March) is awe-inspiring—although its dimensions are not apparent at first. Guides like to point out to Americans that the basilica is like two football fields joined together. St. Peter's is said to have been built over the tomb of the crucified saint. Originally, it was erected on the order of Constantine, but the present structure is essentially Renaissance and baroque; it showcases the talents of some of Italy's greatest artists: Bramante, Raphael, Michelangelo, and Maderno.

In a church of such grandeur—overwhelming in its detail of gilt, marble, and mosaic—don't expect subtlety. But the basilica is rich in art. The truly devout are prone to kiss the feet of the 13th-century bronze of St. Peter, attributed to Arnolfo di Cambio (at the far reaches of the nave, against a corner pillar on the right). Under Michelangelo's dome is the celebrated *baldacchino* by Bernini, resting over the papal altar. The canopy was created in the 17th century—in part, so it is said, from bronze stripped from the Pantheon. However, analysis of the bronze seems to contradict that.

In the nave on the right (the first chapel) is the best-known piece of sculpture, the *Pietà* that Michelangelo sculpted while still in his early 20s. In one of the worst acts of vandalism on record, a madman screaming "I am Jesus Christ" attacked the *Pietà*, battering the Madonna's stone arm, the folded veil, her left eyelid, and nose. Now restored, the *Pietà* is protected by a wall of reinforced glass.

Much farther on, in the right wing of the transept near the Chapel of St. Michael, rests Canova's neoclassic sculptural tribute to Pope Clement XIII.

In addition, you can visit the sacristy and treasury, filled with jewel-studded chalices, reliquaries, and copes. One robe worn by Pius XII strikes a simple note in these halls of elegance. It costs 2,000 lire ($1.55) to visit the **Historical-Artistic Museum,** which is open daily from 9am to 6pm in summer, daily from 9am to 5:30pm from October to March. Later you can make a visit underground to the **Vatican grottoes,** with their tombs—ancient and modern (Pope John XXIII gets the most adulation). They are open daily from 7am to 6pm April to September, daily from 7am to 5pm October to March.

To go even farther down, to the area around **St. Peter's tomb,** you must apply several days beforehand to the excavations office (tel. 698-5318). Open daily from 9am to noon and 2 to 5pm, it is reached by passing under the arch to the left of the facade of St. Peter's. For 5,000 lire ($3.95), you'll take a guided tour of the tombs that were excavated in the 1940s, 23 feet beneath the floor of the church.

The grandest sight is yet to come: the climb to **Michelangelo's dome,** which towers about 375 feet high. Although you can scale the steps for 2,000 lire ($1.55), I recommend the elevator for as far as it'll carry you. The cost is 3,000 lire ($2.35). The dome is open daily from 8am to 6:15pm April to September, and daily from 8am to 4:45pm October to March. You can walk along the roof, for which you'll be rewarded with a magnificent view of Rome and the Vatican.

Note: To be admitted to St. Peter's, women are advised to wear longer skirts or pants—anything that covers the knees. Men in shorts are not allowed in. Sleeveless tops are a no-no for either gender.

Papal Audiences Private audiences with the pope are not normally a possibility and procedures would in any case begin at local ecclesiastical or nunciature levels. Public audiences with the pope are given each Wednesday morning except when the pope is absent from Rome. Even when in residence at Castelgandolfo in the summer the pope comes down to Rome for the weekly audience. The audience begins at 11am, but sometimes in the summer period, because of the heat, it begins at 10am. The general audience takes place in the Paul VI Hall of Audiences, although to accommodate very large attendances, the Basilica of St. Peter's and St. Peter's Square may also be used. Anyone is welcome.

To attend a general audience, you can obtain a free ticket from the office of the Prefecture of the Papal Household (tel. 698-3865), accessible from St. Peter's Square by the Bronze Door, situated where the right-hand colonnade begins, as one looks toward the basilica. Hours are 9am to 1:30pm and on Monday and Tuesday the entrance cards for the audience are immediately available. Often on the Wednesday before the audience the office is not accessible, although if there is space one can go to the audience even without a ticket.

Prospective visitors should write to the Prefecture of the Papal Household, 00120

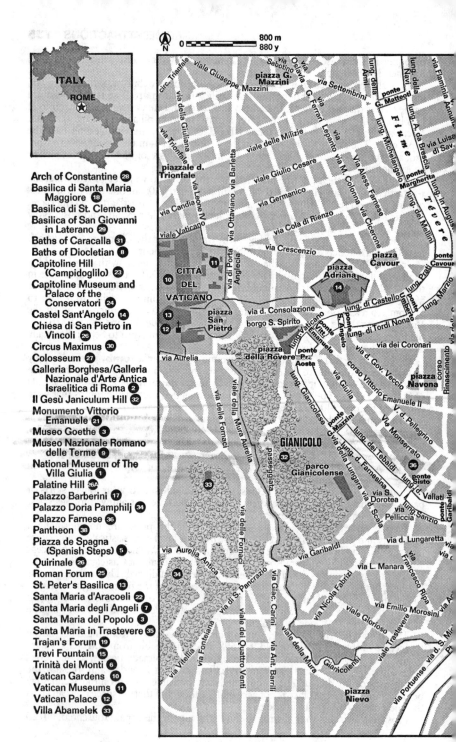

Arch of Constantine

Basilica di Santa Maria Maggiore

Basilica di St. Clemente

Basilica of San Giovanni in Laterano

Baths of Caracalla

Baths of Diocletian

Capitoline Hill (Campidoglilo)

Capitoline Museum and Palace of the Conservatori

Castel Sant'Angelo

Chiesa di San Pietro in Vincoli

Circus Maximus

Colosseum

Galleria Borghesa/Galleria Nazionale d'Arte Antica Israelitica di Roma

Il Gesù Janiculum Hill

Monumento Vittorio Emanuele

Museo Goethe

Museo Nazionale Romano delle Terme

National Museum of The Villa Giulia

Palatine Hill

Palazzo Barberini

Palazzo Doria Pamphilj

Palazzo Farnese

Pantheon

Piazza de Spagna (Spanish Steps)

Quirinale

Roman Forum

St. Peter's Basilica

Santa Maria d'Aracoeli

Santa Maria degli Angeli

Santa Maria del Popolo

Santa Maria in Trastevere

Trajan's Forum

Trevi Fountain

Trinità dei Monti

Vatican Gardens

Vatican Museums

Vatican Palace

Villa Abamelek

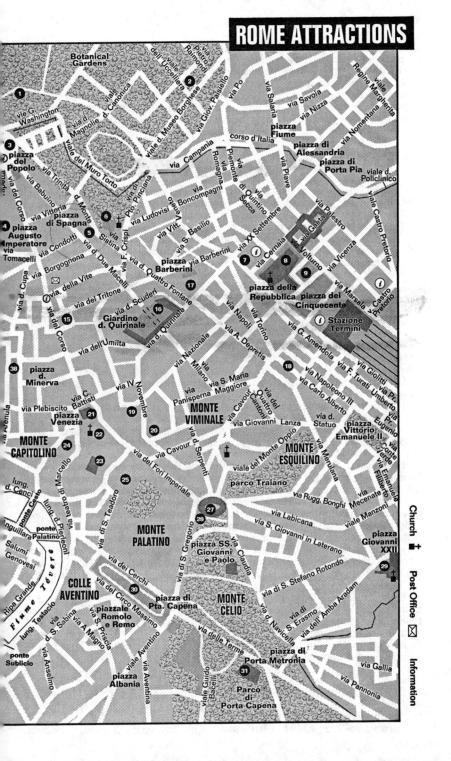

ROME ATTRACTIONS

Botanical Gardens

piazza del Popolo

piazza Augusto Imperatore

piazza di Spagna

piazza Barberini

piazza Fiume

piazza di Alessandria

piazza di Porta Pia

piazza della Repubblica

piazza dei Cinquecento

Stazione Termini

Giardino d. Quirinale

piazza d. Minerva

piazza Venezia

MONTE CAPITOLINO

MONTE VIMINALE

MONTE ESQUILINO

parco Traiano

piazza Vittorio Emanuele II

piazza Giovanni XXIII

MONTE PALATINO

piazza SS. Giovanni e Paolo

MONTE CELIO

COLLE AVENTINO

piazzale Romolo e Remo

piazza di Pta. Capena

piazza Albania

piazza di Porta Metronia

Parco di Porta Capena

Church

Post Office

Information

Vatican City, indicating the language, the dates of their visit, the number of persons in the party and, if possible, the hotel in Rome to which the cards would be sent by hand on the afternoon preceding the audience.

At noon on Sunday the pope speaks briefly from his study window and gives his blessing to the visitors and pilgrims gathered in St. Peter's Square. From about mid-July to mid-September the Angelus and blessing takes place at the summer residence at Castelgandolfo, some 16 miles out of Rome and accessible by Metro and bus.

THE VATICAN & THE SISTINE CHAPEL

In 1929 the Lateran Treaty between Pope Pius XI and the Italian government created Vatican City, viale Vaticano (tel. 6982), the world's smallest independent state, located in Rome.

This state may be small, but it contains a gigantic repository of treasures from antiquity and the Renaissance housed in labyrinthine galleries. The Vatican's art collection reaches its apex in the Sistine Chapel (save this for last, as everything else will be anticlimatic after seeing Michelangelo's frescoes).

The Vatican museums (a house of museums) comprise a series of lavishly adorned palaces and galleries built over the centuries. The entrance is on viale Vaticano, a long walk around from St. Peter's Square. Take bus no. 23, 30, 32, 49, 51, or 64; or the Metro to the Ottaviano station; or a taxi. The museums are open Monday through Saturday (except religious holidays) from 8:45am to 1:45pm, 8:45am to 4:45pm from July to the end of September and during Easter week. Ticket sales stop 1 hour before closing time. The admission price may seem high—8,000 lire ($6.30) for adults and 5,000 lire ($3.95) for children—but it's reasonable when you see what's inside. Entrance is free on the first Sunday of each month. A cafeteria is open to visitors from 8:45am to 2:45pm (to 4:45pm from July to the end of September and during Easter week).

Visitors to the Vatican museums can follow one of four itineraries—A, B, C, or D—according to the time they have at their disposal and their special interests. Determine your choice by consulting large-size panels placed at the entrance; then follow the letter and color of the itinerary chosen. Facilities for disabled visitors are available.

Obviously, 1, 2, or even 20 trips will not be enough to see the wealth of the Vatican, much less digest it. With that in mind, I've previewed only a representative sampling of masterpieces. A dozen museums and galleries should be inspected.

Pinacoteca (Picture Gallery) After climbing the spiral stairway, keep to the right; this path will take you to the Pinacoteca, where some of the most enduring works of art from the Byzantine to the baroque are displayed. For a break with the Byzantine, see one of the Vatican's finest artworks—the *Stefaneschi Polyptych* (six panels) by Giotto and his assistants. You'll also see the works of Fra Angelico, the 15th-century Dominican monk who distinguished himself as a miniaturist (his *Virgin with Child* is justly praised—look for the microscopic eyes of the Madonna).

In the Raphael salon you'll find three paintings by that giant of the Renaissance—including the *Virgin of Foligno* and *The Transfiguration* (completed by assistants following his death). There are also 10 tapestries made by Flemish weavers from cartoons by Raphael. Seek out Leonardo da Vinci's masterful—but uncompleted—*St. Jerome with the Lion*, as well as Giovanni Bellini's *Entombment of Christ*. One of Titian's greatest works, the *Virgin of Frari*, is also displayed. Finally, feast your eyes on one of the masterpieces of the baroque period, Caravaggio's *Deposition from the Cross*.

Egyptian-Gregorian Museum Review the grandeur of the Pharaohs by studying sarcophagi, mummies, statues of goddesses, vases, jewelry, sculptured red-granite queens, and hieroglyphics.

Etruscan-Gregorian Museum With sarcophagi, a chariot, bronzes, urns, jewelry, and terra-cotta vases, this gallery affords remarkable insight into a mysterious people. One of the most acclaimed exhibits is the Regolini-Galassi tomb, unearthed at Cerveteri (see "Easy Excursions" in this chapter) in the 19th century. It shares top honors with the *Mars of Todi*, a bronze sculpture that probably dates from the 5th century B.C.

Pius Clementinus Museum Here you'll find Greek and Roman sculptures, many of which are immediately recognizable masterpieces. In the rotunda is a large gilded bronze of *Hercules* that dates from the time of Christ. Other major works of sculpture are under porticoes in rooms that open onto the Belvedere courtyard. Dating from the 1st century B.C., one sculpture shows *Laocoön* and his two sons locked in an eternal struggle with the serpents (the original statue is broken in parts; the completed version nearby is a copy). The incomparable *Apollo of Belvedere* (Roman reproduction of an authentic Greek work from the 4th century B.C.) has become the symbol of classic male beauty. The rippling muscles of the *Torso of Belvedere*, a partially preserved Greek statue (1st c. B.C.), reveal an intricate knowledge of the human body which predated Michelangelo by centuries, but equaled his achievements.

Chiaramonti Museum You'll find a dazzling array of Roman statuary and copies of Greek originals in these galleries, including *The Nile*, a magnificent reproduction of a long-lost Hellenistic original, and one of the most remarkable pieces of sculpture from antiquity. The imposing statue of Augustus presents him as a regal commander.

Vatican Library The Library is so richly decorated and frescoed that it detracts from its treasures—manuscripts under glass. In the Sistine Salon are sketches by Michelangelo, drawings by Botticelli to illustrate *The Divine Comedy,* and a Greek Bible from the 4th century A.D.

The Stanze of Raphael While still a young man, Raphael was given one of the greatest assignments of his short life: the decoration of a series of rooms for Pope Julius II, who saw to it that Michelangelo was busy in the Sistine Chapel. In these works Raphael achieves the Renaissance aim of blending classic beauty with realism. In the first chamber, the Stanza dell'Incendio, you'll see much work of Raphael's pupils, but little of the master—except in the fresco across from the window. The figure of the partially draped man rescuing an older comrade (to the left of the fresco) is also Raphael's.

Raphael reigns supreme in the next and most important salon, the Stanza della Segnatura, where you'll find the majestic *School of Athens,* one of the artist's best-known works, which depicts such figures as Aristotle and Plato (even Raphael himself). Another well-known masterpiece, the *Disputà* (Disputation), is across from it. The Stanza d'Eliodoro, also by the master, manages to flatter Raphael's papal patrons (Julius II and Leo X) without compromising his art (although one rather fanciful fresco depicts the pope driving Attila from Rome). Finally, there's the Sala di Constantino, which was completed by his students after Raphael's death. And the loggia, frescoed with more than 50 scenes from the Bible, was designed by Raphael, although the actual work was done by his loyal students.

The Borgia Apartments These apartments, frescoed with biblical scenes by Pinturicchio of Umbria and his assistants, were designed for Pope Alexander VI (the famous Borgia pope). The rooms, although generally badly lit, have great splendor and style. At the end of them is the Chapel of Nicholas V, an intimate interlude in a field of museums. The chapel was frescoed by the Dominican monk Fra Angelico, probably the most saintly of all Italian painters.

The Museum of Modern Art This museum represents the American artists' first invasion of the Vatican. Before the Museum of Modern Art opened in 1973, the church limited its purchases to European art, and usually did not exhibit any works created after the 18th century. But Pope Paul's hobby changed all that. Of the 55 galleries in the new museum complex, at least 12 are devoted solely to American artists. All the works chosen for the museum were judged on the basis of their "spiritual and religious values," but religious groups outside the Vatican are represented as well. Among the American works is Leonard Baskin's 5-foot bronze sculpture of *Isaac*. Modern Italian artists such as de Chirico and Manzù are also displayed, and there's a special room for the paintings of the French artist Georges Rouault.

The Sistine Chapel   The story of Michelangelo painting the ceiling of the Sistine Chapel was dramatized by Irving Stone in *The Agony and the Ecstasy;* Charlton Heston did the neck-craning in the film version and thus earned a worldwide audience for one of the classic stories of art history. Michelangelo, of course, considered himself a sculptor, not a painter. While in his 30s, he was virtually commanded by Julius II to stop work on the pope's own tomb and to devote his considerable talents to painting ceiling frescoes—an art form of which the Florentine master was contemptuous.

Michelangelo labored for 4 years over this epic project, which was so physically taxing that it permanently damaged his eyesight. All during the task, he had to contend with the pope's incessant urgings to hurry up; at one point, Julius threatened to topple Michelangelo from the scaffolding—or so Vasari relates.

It is ironic that a project undertaken against the artist's wishes would form his most enduring legend. Glorifying the human body as only a sculptor could, Michelangelo painted nine panels, taken from the pages of Genesis, the panels surrounded by prophets and sibyls. The most notable panels detail the expulsion of Adam and Eve from the Garden of Eden, and the creation of man—where God's outstretched hand imbues Adam with spirit.

The Florentine master was in his 60s when he began to paint the masterly *Last Judgment* on the altar wall. Again working against his wishes, Michelangelo presents a more jaundiced view of people and their fate; God sits in judgment, and sinners are plunged into the mouth of hell.

A master of ceremonies under Paul III, Monsignor Biagio, protested to the pope against the "shameless nudes" painted by Michelangelo. Michelangelo showed he wasn't above petty revenge by painting the prude with the ears of a jackass in hell. When Biagio complained to the pope, Paul III maintained that he had no jurisdiction in hell. However, Daniele de Volterra was summoned to drape clothing over some of the bare figures—thus earning for himself a dubious distinction as a haberdasher.

On the side walls are frescoes by other Renaissance masters such as Botticelli, Luca Signorelli, Pinturicchio, Cosimo Rosselli, and Ghirlandaio. I'd guess that if these paintings had been displayed by themselves in other chapels, they would be the object of special pilgrimages. But since they have to compete unfairly with the artistry of Michelangelo, they're virtually ignored by the average visitor.

The History Museum   This museum, founded by Pope Paul VI, was established to tell the history of the Vatican. It exhibits arms, uniforms, and armor, some of which dates back to the early days of the Middle Ages. The carriages on display are those used by popes and cardinals in religious processions. Among the showcases of dress uniforms are the colorful outfits worn by the Pontifical Army Corps, which was discontinued by Pope Paul VI.

The Ethnological Museum   The Ethnological Museum is an assemblage of works of art and objects of cultural significance from all over the world. The principal route is a half-mile walk through 25 geographical sections, which display thousands of objects covering 3,000 years of world history. The section devoted to China is especially interesting and worthwhile.

The Vatican Gardens   Separating the Vatican from the secular world on the north and west are 58 acres of lush, carefully tended gardens filled with winding paths, brilliantly colored flowers, groves of massive oaks, and ancient fountains and pools. In the midst of this pastoral setting is a small summer house, the Villa Pia, built for Pope Pius IV in 1560 by Pirro Ligorio.

On the left side of piazza San Pietro, near the Arco delle Campane, is the **Vatican Tourist Office** (tel. 698-4466), open daily from 8:30am to 6:30pm, where you can buy a map of the Vatican and have your questions answered about St. Peter's or the Vatican museums. Tours of the Vatican gardens, which must be arranged in advance, run March to October, Monday through Saturday at 10am; November to February, tours are conducted only on Tuesday, Thursday, and Saturday at 10am. Tickets, which cost 14,000 lire ($11) per person, are available here at the Tourist Office. In summer, arrange tours as far in advance of departure as your schedule permits; the size of the tour group is limited to 33 people, and no reservations are taken on the phone.

THE ROMAN FORUM

When it came to cremating Caesar, raping Sabine women, purchasing a harlot for the night, or sacrificing a naked victim, the ✪ Roman Forum, via dei Fori Imperiali (tel. 679-0333), was where the action was hot. Traversed by via Sacra, it was built in the marshy land between the Palatine and the Capitoline hills. It flourished as the center of Roman life in the days of the Republic, before it gradually lost prestige to the Imperial Forum.

Be warned: Expect only fragmented monuments, an arch or two, and lots of overturned boulders. That any semblance of the Forum remains today is miraculous, as it was used for years, like the Colosseum, as a quarry. Eventually it reverted to what the Italians call a *campo vaccino* (cow pasture). But excavations in the 19th century began to bring to light one of the world's most historic spots.

By day, the columns of now-vanished temples and the stones from which long-forgotten orators spoke are mere shells. Bits of grass and weed grow where a triumphant Caesar was once lionized. But at night, when the Forum is silent in the moonlight, it isn't difficult to imagine that Vestal Virgins still guard the sacred temple fire. (Historical footnote: The function of the maidens was to keep the temple's sacred fire burning—but their own flame under control. Failure to do the latter sent them to an early grave . . . alive!)

You can spend at least a morning wandering alone through the ruins of the Forum. If you're content with just looking at the ruins, you can do so at your leisure. But if you want the stones to have some meaning, you'll have to purchase a detailed plan, as the temples are hard to locate otherwise.

Some of the ruins are more important than others, of course. The best of the lot is the handsomely adorned Temple of Castor and Pollux, erected in the 5th century B.C. in honor of a battle triumph. The Temple of Faustina, with its lovely columns and frieze (griffins and candelabra), was converted into the San Lorenzo in Miranda Church.

The senators used to meet and walk on the Curia's marble floors. Diocletian reconstructed the Senate, and it was later transformed into a medieval church. Across from the Curia is the "Lapis Niger," a black marble slab said to be the tomb of Romulus, legendary founder of the city (you can go downstairs).

The Temple of the Vestal Virgins is a popular attraction. Some of the statuary, mostly headless, remains. The Temple of Saturn was rebuilt in the days of the Republic in the 1st century B.C.

The Temple of Julius Caesar was ordered constructed by Octavian, in honor of the place where Caesar's body was cremated following his assassination. Rather oddly placed is the Church of Santa Maria Antiqua, with Christian frescoes that go back to the 7th century A.D.

Finally, the two arches are memorable: the Arch of Septimius Severus, erected in A.D. 203 with bas-reliefs, and the Arch of Titus, with much better carving, commemorating a victory in Jerusalem.

The Roman Forum can be reached by taking bus no. 27, 30, 85, 87, or 88, or the Metro to the Colosseo station. The forum is open on Sunday and Tuesday year round from 9am to 2pm. It is open Monday and Wednesday through Saturday on the following dates: June 1 to July 15, 9am to 7pm; May and July 16 to August 15, 9am to 6:30pm; April 16 to April 30 and August 16 to August 31, 9am to 6pm; March 16 to April 15, 9am to 5:30pm; February 16 to March 15 and October, 9am to 5pm; November through January 15, 9am to 4:30pm. It is closed from January 16 to February 15. Last admission is always 1 hour before it closes. Admission costs 10,000 lire ($7.85) for adults, free for children under 12 if accompanied by adults.

THE PALATINE HILL

A long walk up from the Roman Forum leads to the Palatine Hill, one of the seven hills of Rome. Your ticket from the Forum will admit you to this attraction (it's open the same hours). The Palatine, tradition tells us, was the spot on which the first settlers built their huts, under the direction of Romulus. In later years the hill became a patrician residential district which attracted such citizens as Cicero. In time, however, the area was gobbled up by imperial palaces, and it drew a famous and infamous roster of tenants such as Caligula (who was murdered here), Nero, Tiberius, and Domitian.

Only the ruins of its former grandeur remain today, and you really need to be an archeologist to make sense of them, as they are more difficult to understand than those in the Forum. But even if you're not interested in the past, it's worth the climb for the magnificent sweep of both the Roman and Imperial Forums, as well as the Capitoline Hill and the Colosseum.

Of all the ruins to inspect, none is finer than the so-called **House of Livia** (the "abominable grandmother" of Robert Graves's I, Claudius). Actually, recent archeological research indicates that the house was in fact that of her husband, Augustus. Livia used to slip him maidens noted for their discretion. A guard who controls the gate will show you the mythological frescoes reminiscent of those discovered at Herculaneum and Pompeii.

Domitian lived in the Imperial Palace—the **Domus Augustana**—which is an easy walk away, in the virtual heart of the Palatine. In the middle of the once-lavish estate—now stripped to the brick—is a large peristyle with a fountain. Domitian also ordered the building of the Palatine Stadium or **Hippodrome,** below, as well as a once-remarkable structure, the **Palace of Flavii,** which has a triclinium or great hall. When not overseeing real estate construction, Domitian was ensuring that his name became immortal in the history of vice.

When the glory that was Rome has completely overwhelmed you, you can enjoy a respite in the cooling **Farnese Gardens,** laid out in the 16th century, which incorporate some of the designs of Michelangelo.

THE COLOSSEUM

In spite of the fact that it's a mere shell, the Colosseum, piazzale del Colosseo, via dei Fori Imperiali (tel. 700-4261), remains the greatest architectural inheritance from Ancient Rome. Take the Metro to Colosseo.

Vespasian ordered the construction of the elliptically shaped bowl, called the Amphitheatrum Flavium, in A.D. 72; it was inaugurated by Titus in A.D. 80 with a many-weeks-long bloody combat between gladiators and wild beasts. At its peak, under the cruel Domitian, the Colosseum could seat 50,000 spectators. The Vestal Virgins from the temple screamed for blood, as more and more exotic animals were shipped in from the far corners of the empire to satisfy jaded tastes (lion vs. bear, two humans vs. hippopotamus). Not-so-mock naval battles were staged (the canopied Colosseum could be flooded), in which the defeated combatants might have their lives spared if they put up a good fight. One of the most enduring legends linked to the Colosseum—that is, that Christians were fed to the lions here—is considered to be without foundation by some historians.

Long after it ceased to be an arena to amuse sadistic Romans, the Colosseum was struck by an earthquake. Centuries later it was used as a quarry, and its rich marble facing was stripped away to build palaces and churches.

On one side, part of the original four tiers remain; the first three levels were constructed in Doric, Ionic, and Corinthian styles to lend it variety.

Admission to the Colosseum at street level is free; it costs 6,000 lire ($4.70) to visit the upper levels. It is open on Wednesday and holidays from 9am to 2pm. It is also open Monday, Tuesday, and Thursday through Saturday on the following dates: June 1 to July 15, 9am to 7pm; May and July 16 through August 15, 9am to 6:30pm; April 16 through April 30 and August 16 through August 31, 9am to 6pm; March 16 through April 15 and September, 9am to 5:30pm; February 16 through March 16 and October, 9am to 5pm; November through January 15, 9am to 4:30pm. It is closed from January 16 through February 15.

A highly photogenic memorial (next to the Colosseum on piazzale del Colosseo), the **Arch of Constantine** was erected in honor of Constantine's defeat of the pagan Maxentius (A.D. 306). It is a landmark in every way, physically and historically. Physically, it's beautiful, perhaps marred by the aggravating traffic that zooms around it at all hours, but so intricately carved and well preserved that you almost forget the racket of the cars and buses. Many of the reliefs have nothing whatsoever to do with Constantine or his works, but tell of the victories of earlier Antonine rulers—they were apparently lifted from other, long-forgotten memorials.

Historically, the arch marks a period of great change in the history of Rome, and therefore the history of the world. Rome, which had been pagan since the beginning, now had a Christian emperor, Constantine. Converted by a vision on the battlefield, he led his forces to victory, and officially ended the centuries-long persecution of the Christians. By Constantine's time, many devout followers of the new religion had been put to death (oftentimes horribly) for the sake of their religion, and the new emperor put an end to it. While he did not ban paganism (which survived officially until the closing of the temples more than half a century later), he interceded on an imperial level to stop the persecutions. And by espousing Christianity himself, he began the inevitable development that culminated in the conquest of Rome by the Christian religion. The arch is a tribute to the emperor erected by the Senate in A.D. 315.

After visiting the Colosseum, it is also convenient to look at the site of the **Domus Aurea,** or the Golden House of Nero, on via Labicana on the Esquiline Hill; it faces the Colosseum and is adjacent to the Forum. The Domus Aurea is one of the most sumptuous palaces of all time, and was constructed by Nero after a disastrous fire swept over Rome in A.D. 64. Not much remains of its former glory, but once the floors were made of mother-of-pearl and the furniture of gold. The area that is the Colosseum today was an ornamental lake, which reflected the grandeur and glitter of the Golden House. The hollow ruins—long stripped of their lavish decorations—lie near the entrance of the Oppius Park.

During the Renaissance, painters such as Raphael chopped holes in the long-buried ceilings of the Domus Aurea to gain admittance. Once there, they were inspired by the frescoes and the small "grotesques" of cornucopia and cherubs. The word "grotto" came from this palace, as it was believed to have been built underground. Remnants of these original almost-2,000-year-old frescoes and fragments of mosaics remain. All interiors are currently closed for renovation.

THE CAPITOLINE HILL [CAMPIDOGLIO]

Of the Seven Hills of Rome, Campidoglio, piazza del Campidoglio, is considered the most sacred—its origins stretch way back into antiquity (an Etruscan temple to Jupiter once stood on this spot). The most dramatic approach to the Capitoline Hill is to walk from piazza Venezia, the center of Rome, to via di Teatro Marcello.

On your left, you can climb the steps designed by Michelangelo. At the top of the approach is the perfectly proportioned square of piazza del Campidoglio, also laid out by the Florentine artist.

Michelangelo positioned the bronze equestrian statue of Marcus Aurelius in the center, but it has now been moved inside to be protected from pollution.

One side of the piazza is open; the others are bounded by the **Senatorium** (Town Council), the statuary-filled **Palazza dei Conservatori,** and the **Capitoline Museums** (see "Museums & Galleries," below). The Campidoglio is dramatic at night (walk around to the back for a regal view of the floodlit Roman Forum). On your return, head down the small steps on your right. You'll pass two caged wolves, a commemorative gesture to the "Capitoline Wolf," who is said to have suckled Romulus and Remus, legendary founders of Rome. If you care to climb the other steps adjoining Michelangelo's approach, they'll take you to Santa Maria d'Aracoeli (see "Churches," below). Take bus no. 46, 89, or 92.

CASTEL SANT'ANGELO

This overpowering structure, in a vantage landmark position on the Tiber, at largo Castello (tel. 687-5036), was originally built in the 2nd century A.D. as a tomb for the

Emperor Hadrian; it continued as an imperial mausoleum until the time of Caracalla. It is an imposing and grim castle with thick walls and a cylindrical shape. If it looks like a fortress, it should, as that was its function in the Middle Ages (it was built over the Roman walls and linked by an underground passageway to the Vatican, which was much used by the fleeing papacy, who escaped from unwanted visitors like Charles V, during his sack of the city in 1527).

In the 14th century it became a papal residence, enjoying various connections with Boniface IX, Nicholas V, even Julius II, patron of Michelangelo and Raphael. But its legend rests largely on its link with Pope Alexander VI, whose mistress bore him two children—Cesare and Lucrezia Borgia.

Of all the women of the Italian Renaissance, Lucrezia is the only one who commands universal recognition in the Western world; her name is a virtual synonym for black deeds such as poisoning. But popular legend is highly unreliable: Many of the charges biographers have made against her (such as incestuous involvements with her brother and father) may have been only successful attempts to blacken her name. In addition to being part of an infamous family, she was a patroness of the arts and a devoted charity worker, especially after she moved to Ferrara. Her brother, Cesare, of course, is without defense—he was a Machiavellian figure who is remembered accurately as a symbol of villainy and cruel spite.

Today the highlight of the castle is a trip through the Renaissance apartments with their coffered ceilings and lush decoration. Their walls have witnessed plots and intrigues that make up some of the arch treachery of the High Renaissance. Later, you can go through the dank cells that once rang with the screams of Cesare's victims of torture, such as Astorre Manfredi of Faenza, who was finally relieved of his pain by being murdered.

Perhaps the most famous figure imprisoned here was Benvenuto Cellini, the eminent sculptor and goldsmith, remembered chiefly for his classic, candid *Autobiography*. Cellini kept getting into trouble—murdering people, whatever—but was jailed here on a charge of "peculation" (embezzlement of public funds). He escaped, was hauled back to jail, but was finally freed.

Now an art museum, the castle halls display the history of the Roman mausoleum, along with a wide-ranging selection of ancient arms and armor. Don't fail to climb to the top terrace for another one of those dazzling views of the Eternal City. The museum, which can be visited on your way to St. Peter's, is open Tuesday through Saturday from 9am to 2pm and on Sunday from 9am to 1pm. Admission is 8,000 lire ($6.30) for adults, free for children. Take bus no. 23, 62, 64, or 87.

THE APPIAN WAY & THE CATACOMBS

Of all the roads that led to Rome, the **Appia Antica**—built in 312 B.C.—was the reigning leader. It eventually stretched all the way from Rome to the seaport of Brindisi, through which trade with the colonies in Greece and the East was funneled. According to the Christian tradition, it was on the Appian Way that an escaping Peter encountered the vision of Christ, which caused him to go back into the city to face subsequent martyrdom.

Along the Appian Way the patrician Romans built great monuments above the ground, while the Christians met in the catacombs beneath the earth. The remains of both can be visited today. In some dank, dark grottoes (never stray too far from either your party or one of the exposed lightbulbs), you can still discover the remains of early Christian art.

Only someone wanting to write a sequel to *Quo Vadis* would visit all the catacombs. Of those open to the public, the Catacombs of St. Calixtus and those of St. Sebastian are the most important. Both can be reached by taking bus no. 118, which leaves from near the Colosseum close to the Metro station.

The **Tomb of St. Sebastian,** called the Catacombs di San Sebastiano, is at via Appia Antica 136 (tel. 788-7035). Today the tomb of the martyr is in the basilica (church), but his original tomb was in the catacomb under the basilica. From the reign of Emperor Valerian to the reign of Emperor Constantine, the bodies of Saint Peter and Saint Paul were hidden in the catacomb. The big church was built here in the 4th century. None of the catacombs, incidentally, is a grotto; all are dug from tufo, a soft volcanic rock. This is the only Christian catacomb in Rome that is always open.

The tunnels here, if stretched out, would reach a length of 7 miles. In the tunnels and mausoleums are mosaics and graffiti, along with many other pagan and Christian objects from centuries even before the time of Constantine. Visiting hours are 9am to noon and 2:30 to 5pm Friday through Wednesday, and admission is 4,000 lire ($3.15). Children under 10 are admitted free. The catacombs are closed on Thursday.

To quote the words of Pope John XXIII, the **Catacombs of St. Calixtus** (Catacombe di San Callisto), via Appia Antica 110 (tel. 513-6725), "is one of the oldest and the most ancient of the Christian sanctuaries." The name comes from the deacon Calixtus, who was in charge of the church wealth in the 3rd century; Calixtus himself, however, is buried in the Cemetery of Calepodius on via Aurelia.

The Catacombs of St. Calixtus were the first official Christian burial place, comprising a complex of underground crypts and galleries, rediscovered in 1852, that extend for more than 15 miles. Visitors are conducted by a guide to the Crypts of the Popes (9 of the 16 popes of the 3rd century who were interred in the area are buried here) and to the Cubiculum of St. Cecilia (patron saint of music), an early Christian martyr. Cecilia received three ax strokes on her neck, the maximum number allowed by Roman law, which failed to kill her outright. She reportedly died after 3 days of agonizing pain and bleeding. Farther along, visitors will notice the Crypts of the Sacraments, named for the original frescoes (2nd c. A.D.) which allude to the Holy Eucharist, Baptism, Penance, and a variety of early Christian symbols, including the fish. The catacombs were a resting place for the dead and a place of worship and meeting (not homes or hiding places, as some believe) for the living. Visiting hours are 8:30am to noon and 2:30 to 5:30pm Thursday through Tuesday in summer, closing at 5pm in winter. Admission is 4,000 lire ($3.15) for adults, free for children under 10. They're open all year except on Wednesday, January 1, Easter, and Christmas. Take bus no. 118 at St. John in Lateran, the Colosseum, or Circus Maximus, or bus no. 218 from St. John in Lateran to Fosse Ardeatine. Ask the driver to drop you at the Catacombs of St. Calixtus.

Of the Roman monuments, the most impressive is the **Tomb of Cecilia Metella,** on via Appia Antica, within walking distance of the catacombs. The cylindrically shaped tomb honors the wife of one of Julius Caesar's military commanders from the Republican era. Why such an elaborate tomb for such an unimportant person in history? Cecilia Metella happened to be singled out for enduring fame because her tomb remained and the others decayed.

THE PANTHEON

Of all the great buildings of Ancient Rome, only the Pantheon ("All the Gods"), at piazza della Rotunda (tel. 369831), remains intact today. It was built in 27 B.C. by Marcus Agrippa, and later reconstructed by Emperor Hadrian in the first part of the 2nd century A.D. This remarkable building is among the architectural wonders of the world because of its dome and its concept of space. Byron described the temple as "simple, erect, austere, severe, sublime."

The Pantheon was once ringed with white marble statues of pagan gods, such as Jupiter and Minerva, in its niches. Animals were sacrificed and burned in the center, and the smoke escaped through the only means of light, an opening at the top 27 feet in diameter. The Pantheon is 142 feet wide, 142 feet high. Michelangelo came here to study the dome before designing the cupola of St. Peter's (whose dome is 2 feet smaller than the Pantheon's).

Other statistics are equally impressive. The walls are 25 feet thick, and the bronze doors leading into the building weigh 20 tons each. The temple was converted into a church in the early 7th century.

About 125 years ago, the tomb of Raphael was discovered in the Pantheon (fans still bring him flowers). Victor Emmanuel II, king of Italy, was interred here.

The Pantheon can be reached by bus no. 87 or 94. It's open (admission is free)

Tuesday through Saturday from 9am to 1pm and 2 to 5pm, and on Sunday from 9am to 1pm; from October to April it's open only in the afternoon.

PIAZZA DI SPAGNA [SPANISH STEPS]

The Spanish Steps were the last part of the outside world that Keats saw before he died in a house at the foot of the stairs (see "Keats-Shelley Memorial," below). The steps—filled, in season, with flower vendors, young jewelry dealers, and photographers snapping pictures of tourists—and the square take their names from the Spanish Embassy, which used to have its headquarters here.

At the foot of the steps is a nautically shaped fountain that was designed by Pietro Bernini (papa is not to be confused with his son, Giovanni Lorenzo Bernini, who proved to be a far greater sculptor of fountains). About 2 centuries ago, when the foreign art colony was in its ascendancy, the 136 steps were covered with young men and women who wanted to pose for the painters—men with their shirts unbuttoned to show off what they hoped was a Davidesque physique, and women consistently draped like Madonnas.

At the top of the steps is a good view and the 16th-century church of Trinità dei Monti, built by the French, with twin towers. Take the Metro to piazza di Spagna.

THE FOUNTAINS OF ROME

Rome is a city of fountains—a number of which are so exceptionally beautiful that they're worth a special pilgrimage. Some of the more famous ones are the Four Seasons and Bernini's Triton Fountain at piazza Barberini, but the two that hold the most enduring interest are the Fountains of Trevi and the waterworks at piazza Navona.

Piazza Navona, surely one of the most beautifully baroque sites in all of Rome, is like an ocher-colored gem, unspoiled by new buildings or even by traffic. The shape results from the ruins of the Stadium of Domitian, which lie underneath the present constructions. Great chariot races, some of which were rather unusual, were once held here. In one, for instance, the head of the winning horse was lopped off as he crossed the finish line and carried by runners to be offered as a sacrifice by Vestal Virgins on top of the Capitoline Hill. Historians note that in medieval times the popes used to flood the piazza to stage mock naval encounters. Today the most strenuous activities are performed by occasional fire-eaters who go through their evening paces before an interested crowd of Romans and visitors.

Beside the twin-towered facade of the Church of Saint Agnes (17th century), the piazza boasts several other baroque masterpieces. In the center is Bernini's ✪ **Fountain of the Four Rivers,** whose four stone personifications symbolize the world's greatest rivers—the Ganges, Danube, della Plata, and Nile. It's fun to try to figure out which is which (hint: the figure with the shroud on its head is the Nile, so represented because the river's source was unknown at the time the fountain was constructed). The fountain at the south end, the **Fountain of the Moor,** is also by Bernini and dates from the same period as the church and the Fountain of the Four Rivers. The **Fountain of Neptune,** which balances that of the Moor, is a 19th-century addition. During the summer there are outdoor art shows in the evening, but visit during the day—it's the best time to inspect the fragments of the original stadium under a building on the north side of the piazza. If you're interested, walk out at the northern exit and turn left for a block. It's astonishing how much the level of the ground has risen since ancient times.

As you elbow your way through the summertime crowds around the ✪ **Fontana di Trevi (Trevi Fountain)** at piazza di Trevi, you'll find it hard to believe that this little piazza was nearly always deserted before *Three Coins in the Fountain* brought the tour buses. Today it's a must on everybody's itinerary. The fountain is an 18th-century extravaganza of baroque stonework presided over by a large statue of Neptune. While some of the statuary is the work of other artists, the man who gets credit for the entire project is Nicolo Salvi. The tradition of throwing coins into the fountain is an evolution of earlier customs. At one time visitors drank water from the fountain; later they would also make an offering to the spirits of the place. Nowadays, no one dares to drink the water, but many still make the offering. To do it properly, hold your lira coin in the right hand, turn your back to the fountain, and toss the coin over your shoulder (being careful not to bean anyone behind you). Then the spirit of the fountain will see to it that you return to Rome one day—or that's the tradition, at least.

Piazza Barberini lies at the foot of several Roman streets, among them via Barberini, via Sistina, and via Veneto. It would be a far more pleasant spot were it not for the considerable amount of traffic swarming around its principal feature, Bernini's **Fountain of the Triton.** For more than 3 centuries, the strange figure sitting in a vast open clam has been blowing water from his triton. Off to one side of the piazza is the clean aristocratic side facade of the Palazzo Barberini, named for one of Rome's powerful families. The Renaissance Barberini reached their peak when a son was elected pope (Urban VIII). This Barberini pope encouraged Bernini and gave him great patronage.

As you go up via Veneto, look for the small fountain on the right-hand corner of piazza Barberini, which is another of Bernini's works, the small **Fountain of the Bees.** At first they look more like flies, but they are the bees of the Barberini, the crest of that powerful family complete with the crossed keys of St. Peter above them (the keys were always added to a family crest when a son was elected pope).

MORE ATTRACTIONS

THE BATHS OF CARACALLA

Named for the Emperor Caracalla, the ✪ **Terme di Caracalla** (tel. 575-8302) were completed in the early part of the 3rd century. The richness of decoration has faded and the lushness can only be judged from the shell of brick ruins that remain.

 ## FROMMER'S FAVORITE
ROME EXPERIENCES

Fountain Hopping Rome abounds in Renaissance and baroque fountains—lavish, theatrical, spectacular—none more so than the Trevi Fountain. They're fed by an abundant freshwater supply. A tour of them will lock in your memory. See "The Fountains of Rome" under "Top Attractions," above.

The Campidoglio at Night Climb steps designed by Michelangelo to the back of the square to see a sound-and-light summer spectacle. Suddenly, you hear marching legions, glaring trumphets, rumbling drums—all the sounds needed to convince you you're back in the days of Ancient Rome, with soldiers, soothsayers, and Vestal Virgins.

Opera at the Baths of Caracalla In the gigantic ruins of a former Roman bath house, open-air opera is presented, none more spectacular than *Aïda.* An army of extras people the stage, and elephants or braces of horses come charging in near curtain time.

Flea-Market Shopping Every Sunday morning (until 1pm) make your way to the flea market of Rome, stretching for 2 miles from Porta Portese to the Trastevere rail station. Barter, bargain, buy, or "window shop"—this array of merchandise, everything from fake antiques to illegally cut tapes, from "oddities" from the attic to portraits of Mussolini, will equal one of the shopping adventures of a lifetime.

These imperial baths at via delle Terme di Caracalla can be visited for an admission fee of 3,000 lire ($2.35). Visiting hours April through September, are Tuesday through Saturday from 9am to 6pm and on Sunday and Monday from 9am to 1pm; from October through March, Tuesday through Saturday from 9am to 3pm and on Sunday and Monday from 9am to 1pm.

Viewing the baths during the day is one experience. Even more spectacular, however, is to attend an opera here, perhaps a spectacular version of Verdi's *Aïda* (see "Evening Entertainment" in this chapter). Take bus no. 93 from the Stazione Termini.

CEMETERIES

PYRAMID OF CAIUS CESTIUS, piazzale Ostiense.

Dating from 12 B.C., the Pyramid of Caius Cestius, about 120 feet high, looks as if it belongs to the Egyptian landscape. The pyramid can't be entered, but it's fun to circle and photograph. Who was Caius Cestius? A rich magistrate in Imperial Rome whose tomb is more impressive than his achievements. It can be visited at any time. **Bus:** 30.

CIMITERO MONUMENTALE DEI PADRI CAPPUCINI, in the Church of the Immaculate Conception, via Vittorio Veneto 27.

This cemetery, Rome's most macabre sight, is a short walk from piazza Barberini. You enter from the first staircase on the right of the church, at the entrance to the friary. Guidebooks of old used to rank this sight along with the Forum and the Colosseum as one of the city's top attractions. Qualifying as one of the most horrifying sights in all Christendom, it is a cemetery of skulls and crossbones woven into "works of art." To make this allegorical dance of death, the bones of more than 4,000 Capuchin brothers were used. Some of the skeletons are intact, draped with Franciscan habits. The creator of this chamber of horrors? The tradition of the friars is that it was the work of a French Capuchin. Their literature suggests that the cemetery should be visited keeping in mind the historical moment of its origins, when Christians had a rich and creative cult for their dead, when great spiritual masters meditated and preached with a skull in hand. Those who have lived through the days of crematoriums and other such massacres may view the graveyard differently, but to many who pause to think, this macabre sight of death has a message. It's not for the squeamish.

Admission: Free (donation requested).
Open: Apr–Sept, daily 9am–noon and 3–6:30pm; Oct–Mar, daily 9:30am–noon and 3–6pm. **Metro:** Piazza Barberini.

CHURCHES

St. Peter's is not the only church you should see in Rome. The city's hundreds of churches—some built with marble stripped from ancient monuments—form a major sightseeing treasure. I've highlighted the best of the lot, including four patriarchal churches of Rome that belong to the Vatican. Others are equally worth viewing, especially one designed by Michelangelo.

BASILICA OF SAN GIOVANNI IN LATERANO, piazza di San Giovanni in Laterano 4. Tel. 698-6433.

This church is the seat of the archbishop of Rome (St. John's—not St. Peter's—is the cathedral of Rome). Originally built in the 4th century by Constantine, the cathedral has suffered the vicissitudes of Rome, and was badly sacked and forced to rebuild many times. Only fragmented parts of the baptistery remain from the original structure.

The present building is characterized by its 18th-century facade by Alessandro Galilei (statues of Christ and the Apostles ring the top). Borromini gets the credit (some say blame) for the interior, built for Innocent X. It is said that in the misguided attempt to redecorate, frescoes by Giotto were destroyed (remains believed to have been painted by Giotto were discovered in 1952 and are now displayed). In addition, look for the unusual ceiling, the sumptuous transept, and explore the 13th-century cloisters.

The popes used to live next door at the **Lateran Palace** before the move to Avignon in the 14th century. But the most unusual sight is across the street at the "Palace of the Holy Steps," called the **Santuario della Scala Sancta**, piazza San Giovanni in Laterano (tel. 759-4619). It is alleged that these were the actual steps that Christ climbed when he was brought before Pilate. These steps are supposed to be climbed only on your knees, which you're likely to see the faithful doing throughout the day.

Admission: Free.
Open: Daily 7am–6pm. **Bus:** 93.

BASILICA DI SANTA MARIA MAGGIORE (Saint Mary Major), piazza di Santa Maria Maggiore. Tel. 483195.

This great church was founded in the 5th century and later rebuilt. Its campanile, erected in the 14th century, is the loftiest in the city. Much doctored in the 18th century, the church's facade is not an accurate reflection of the treasures inside. The basilica is especially noted for the 5th-century Roman mosaics in its nave, as well as for its coffered ceiling, said to have been gilded with gold brought from the New World. In the 16th century Domenico Fontana built a now-restored "Sistine Chapel." In the following century Flaminio Ponzo designed the Pauline (Borghese) Chapel in the baroque style. The church contains the tomb of Bernini, Italy's most important architect during the flowering of the baroque in the 17th century. Ironically, the man who changed the face of Rome with his elaborate fountains was buried in a tomb so simple it takes a sleuth to track it down (to the right near the altar).

Admission: Free.
Open: Apr–Sept, daily 7am–8pm; Oct–Mar, daily 7am–7pm. **Metro:** Stazione Termini.

SAN PAOLO FUORI LE MURA (Basilica of St. Paul Outside the Walls), via Ostiense. Tel. 541-0341.

The Basilica of St. Paul, whose origins go back to the time of Constantine, is the fourth great patriarchal church of Rome. It burned in the 19th century and was subsequently rebuilt. This basilica is believed to have been erected over the tomb of St. Paul (St. Peter's was built over the tomb of that saint). Once inside, its windows may appear at first to be stained glass, but they are alabaster—the effect of glass is created by the brilliant light shining through. With its forest of single-file columns and its mosaic medallions (portraits of the various popes), it is one of the most streamlined and elegantly decorated churches in Rome. Its single most important treasure is a 12th-century candelabrum designed by Vassalletto, who is also responsible for the remarkable cloisters—in themselves worth the trip "outside the walls." The Benedictine monks and students sell a fine collection of souvenirs, rosaries, and bottles of Benedictine. The gift shop is open every day except Sunday and religious holidays.

Admission: Free.
Open: Cloisters, Mon–Sat 9–11:45am; basilica, Mon–Sat 9am–1pm and 3–6pm. **Metro:** San Paolo Basilica. **Bus:** 23, 318, or 673.

CHIESA DI SAN PIETRO IN VINCOLI (Saint Peter in Chains), piazza di San Pietro in Vincoli 4A, off via degli Annibaldi. Tel. 462865.

From the Colosseum, head up a "spoke" street, via degli Annibaldi, to a church founded in the 5th century A.D. to house the chains that bound St. Peter in Palestine. The chains are preserved under glass. But the drawing card is the tomb of Julius II, with one of the world's most famous pieces of sculpture, *Moses* by Michelangelo. As readers of Irving Stone's *The Agony and the Ecstasy* know, Michelangelo was to have carved 44 magnificent figures for Julius's tomb. That didn't happen, of course, but the pope was given one of the greatest consolation prizes—a figure intended to be "minor" that is now numbered among Michelangelo's masterpieces. Of the stern, father symbol of Michelangelo's *Moses,* Vasari, in his *Lives of the Artists,* wrote: "No modern work will ever equal it in beauty, no, nor ancient either."

Admission: Free.

Open: Mon–Sat 7am–12:30pm and 3:30–6pm, Sun 7–11:45am and 3–7pm.

Metro: Piazza Cavour.

SANTA MARIA DEGLI ANGELI, piazza della Repubblica 12. Tel. 460812.

On this site, which adjoins the National Roman Museum near the railway station, once stood the "tepidarium" of the 3rd-century Baths of Diocletian. But in the 16th century, Michelangelo—nearing the end of his life—converted the grand hall into one of the most splendid churches in Rome. Surely the artist wasn't responsible for "gilding the lily"—that is, putting trompe-l'oeil columns in the midst of the genuine pillars. The church is filled with tombs and paintings, but its crowning treasure is the statue of St. Bruno by the great French sculptor Jean-Antoine Houdon. His sculpture is larger than life and about as real.

Admission: Free.

Open: Daily 9:30am–noon and 4:30–6:30pm. **Metro:** Piazza della Repubblica.

BASILICA DI ST. CLEMENTE, piazza di San Clemente, via Labicana 95. Tel. 731-5723.

From the Colosseum, head up via di San Giovanni in Laterano, which leads to the Basilica of Saint Clement. This isn't just another Roman church—far from it! In this church-upon-a-church, centuries of history peel away like stalks of the fennel that Romans eat for dessert. In the 4th century a church was built over a secular house of the 1st century A.D., beside which stood a pagan temple dedicated to Mithras (god of the sun). Down in the eerie grottoes (which you can explore on your own—unlike the catacombs on the Appian Way), you'll discover well-preserved frescoes from the 1st through the 3rd century A.D. After the Normans destroyed the lower church, a new one was built in the 12th century. Its chief attraction is its bronze-orange mosaic (from that period) which adorns the apse, as well as a chapel honoring St. Catherine of Alexandria (murals are by Masolino de Panicale, who decorated the Branacacci Chapel in the Church of Carmine in Florence in the 15th century).

Admission: Church, free; grottoes, 2,000 lire ($1.55).

Open: Mon–Sat 9am–noon and 3:30–6pm, Sun 10am–noon and 3:30–6pm.

Metro: Colosseo.

SANTA MARIA IN COSMEDIN, piazza della Verità 18. Tel. 678-1419.

This charming little church was founded in the 6th century, but subsequently rebuilt—and a campanile was added in the 12th century in the Romanesque style. The church is ever popular with pilgrims drawn not by its great art treasures but by its "Mouth of Truth," a large disk under the portico. According to tradition, it is supposed to chomp down on the hand of liars who insert their paws (although Audrey Hepburn escaped with her mitt untouched in *Roman Holiday*). On my last visit to the church, a little woman, her hand draped in black, sat begging a few feet from the medallion. A scene typical enough—except this woman's right hand was covered with bandages.

Admission: Free.

Open: Daily 9am–noon and 3–6pm. **Bus:** 57, 95, or 716.

SANTA MARIA D'ARACOELI, piazza d'Aracoeli.

Sharing a spot on Capitoline Hill, this landmark church was built for the Franciscans in the 13th century. According to legend, Augustus once ordered a temple erected on this spot, where a sibyl, with her gift of prophecy, forecast the coming of Christ. In the interior of the present building, you'll find a nave and two aisles, two rows with 11 pillars each, a Renaissance ceiling, and a mosaic of the Virgin over the altar in the Byzantine style. If you're sleuth enough, you'll also find a tombstone carved by the great Renaissance sculptor Donatello. The church is reached by a long flight of steep steps. However, if you're on piazza del Campidoglio, you can reach it by crossing the piazza and climbing steps on the far side of the Museo Capitolino.

Admission: Free.

Open: Daily 7am–noon and 3:30pm–sunset. **Bus:** 46, 89, or 92.

JANICULUM HILL [GIANICOLO]

From many vantage points in the Eternal City the views are magnificent. Scenic gulpers, however, have traditionally preferred the outlook from the Janiculum Hill (across the Tiber), not one of the "Seven Hills" but certainly one of the most visited (and a stopover on many bus tours). The view is seen at its best at sundown, or at dawn when the skies are often fringed with mauve. The Janiculum was the site of a battle between Giuseppe Garibaldi and the forces of Pope Pius IX in 1870—an event commemorated today with statuary. To reach "Gianicolo" without a private car, take bus no. 41 from Ponte Sant'Angelo.

MUSEUMS & GALLERIES

MUSEO NAZIONALE ROMANO (National Roman Museum), via E. De Nicola 79. Tel. 482-4181.

Located near piazza dei Cinquecento, which fronts the railway station, this museum occupies part of the 3rd-century A.D. Baths of Diocletian and a section of a convent that may have been designed by Michelangelo. It houses one of Europe's finest collections of Greek and Roman sculpture and early Christian sarcophagi.

The Ludovisi Collection is the apex of the museum, particularly the statuary of the Gaul slaying himself after he has done in his wife (a brilliant copy of a Greek original from the 3rd century B.C.).

Another prize is a one-armed Greek Apollo. A galaxy of other sculptured treasures include *The Discus Thrower of Castel Porziano* (an exquisite copy); *Aphrodite of Cirene* (a Greek original); and the so-called *Hellenistic Ruler,* a Greek original of an athlete with a lance. A masterpiece of Greek sculpture, *The Birth of Venus,* is in the Ludovisi throne. The *Sleeping Hermaphrodite* (Ermafrodito Dormiente) is an original Hellenistic statue. Don't fail to stroll through the cloisters, filled with statuary and fragments of antiquity, including a fantastic mosaic.

Admission: 4,000 lire ($3.15).

Open: Tues–Sat 9am–2pm, Sun and hols 9am–1pm. **Metro:** Piazza della Repubblica.

NATIONAL MUSEUM OF THE VILLA GIULIA (Etruscan), piazzale di Villa Giulia 4. Tel. 320-1706.

A 16th-century papal palace in the Villa Borghese Gardens shelters this priceless collection of art and artifacts of the mysterious Etruscans, who predated the Romans. Known for their sophisticated art and design, the Etruscans left a legacy of sarcophagi, bronze sculptures, terra-cotta vases, and jewelry, among other items.

If you have time only for the masterpieces, head for Sala 7, which has a remarkable *Apollo* from Veio from the end of the 6th century B.C. (clothed, for a change). The other two widely acclaimed pieces of statuary in this gallery are *Dea con Bambino* (a goddess with a baby) and a greatly mutilated, but still powerful, *Hercules* with a stag. In the adjoining room, Sala 8, you'll see the lions' sarcophagus from the mid-6th century B.C. which was excavated at Cerveteri, north of Rome.

Finally, one of the world's most important Etruscan art treasures is the bride and bridegroom coffin from the 6th century B.C., also dug out of the tombs of Cerveteri (in Sala 9). Near the end of your tour, another masterpiece of Etruscan art awaits you in Sala 33: the *Cista Ficoroni,* a bronze urn with paw feet, mounted by three figures, which dates from the 4th century B.C.

Admission: 8,000 lire ($6.30) adults, free for children under 18.

Open: Tues–Sat 9am–7pm, Sun 9am–1pm. **Bus:** 30.

GALERIA BORGHESE, piazzale del Museo Borghese, off via Pinciano. Tel. 854-8577.

The gallery, housed in a handsome villa, contains some of the finest paintings in Rome; there's a representative collection of Renaissance and baroque masters, along with important Bernini sculpture. Among these is the so-called *Conquering Venus* by Antonio Canova, Italy's greatest neoclassic sculptor. Actually, this early-19th-century work created a sensation in its day, because its model was Pauline Bonaparte Borghese, sister of Napoleon (if the French dictator didn't like to see his sister naked, he was even more horrified at Canova's totally nude version of himself). In the rooms that follow are three of Bernini's most widely acclaimed works: *David, Apollo and Daphne* (his finest piece), and finally, *The Rape of Persephone.*

The paintings form a display of canvases almost too rich for one visit. If you're pressed for time, concentrate on three works by Raphael (especially the young woman holding a unicorn in her lap and the *Deposition from the Cross*).

Works of Caravaggio (1571–1610), leader of the realists, are on view, including the *Madonna of the Palafrenieri.* Rubens's favorite theme, the elders lusting after Susanna, is displayed. Titian's *Sacred and Profane Love* is exhibited, along with three other works of his.

After visiting the gallery, you may want to join the Italians in their strolls through the **Villa Borghese,** replete with zoological gardens and small bodies of water. Horse shows are staged at piazza di Siena.

Admission: 4,000 lire ($3.15).

Open: Tues–Sat 9am–2pm, Sun 9am–1pm. **Bus:** 910 from Stazione Termini.

CAPITOLINE MUSEUM AND PALACE OF THE CONSERVATORI, piazza del Campidoglio. Tel. 678-2862.

⭐ These two museums house some of the greatest pieces of classical sculpture in the world. The **Capitoline Museum,** or Musei Capitolini, was built in the 17th century, based on an architectural sketch by Michelangelo. It originally housed a papal collection which was founded by Sixtus IV in the 15th century.

In the first room is *The Dying Gaul,* a work of majestic skill that brings worldwide instant recognition. It's a copy of a Greek original that dates from the 3rd century B.C. And in a special gallery all her own is *The Capitoline Venus,* who demurely covers herself; this statue was the symbol of feminine beauty and charm down through the centuries (this one is a Roman copy of the Greek original from the 3rd century B.C.). Finally, *Amore* (Cupid) and *Psyche* are up to their old tricks.

The famous equestrian statue of *Marcus Aurelius* that stood for years in the middle of the piazza was unveiled after a restoration; it had been a victim of pollution. Now it is located in the museum for greater protection. This is the only bronze statue to have survived from ancient Rome, and it survived only because it had been tossed into the Tiber by marauding barbarians. For centuries after its discovery it was thought to be a statue of Constantine the Great; this mistake protected it further, since Papal Rome respected the memory of the first Christian emperor. It's a beautiful statue even though the perspective is rather odd—it was originally designed to sit on top of a column, hence the foreshortened effect. The emperor's stirrups, by the way, are not missing—they were simply unknown in classical times, and Roman horsemen never used them. The statue is found in a glassed-in room on the street level called Cortile di Marforio; it's a kind of Renaissance greenhouse, surrounded by windows.

The **Palace of the Conservatori** across the way was also based on an architectural plan by Michelangelo. It is rich in classical sculpture and paintings. One of the most notable bronzes—a work of incomparable beauty—is the *Spinario* (the little boy picking a thorn from his foot), a Greek classic which dates from the 1st century B.C. In addition, you'll find *Lupa Capitolina* (the Capitoline Wolf), a rare Etruscan bronze that may go back to the 6th century B.C. (Romulus and Remus, the legendary twins that the wolf suckled, were added at a later date). The palace also contains a "Pinacoteca"—mostly paintings from the 16th and 17th centuries. Notable canvases include Carvaggio's *Fortune-Teller* and his curious *John the Baptist,* the *Holy Family* by Dosso Dossi, *Romulus and Remus* by Rubens, and Titian's *Baptism of Christ.*

Admission (for museum and palace): 5,000 lire ($3.95).

Open: Apr–Sept, Tues 9am–2pm and 5–8pm, Wed–Fri 9am–2pm, Sat 9am–2pm and 8–11pm, Sun 9am–1:30pm; Oct–Mar, Tues and Sat 9am–1:30pm and 5–8pm, Wed–Fri 9am–1:30pm, Sun 9am–1pm. **Bus:** 46, 89, or 92.

NATIONAL GALLERY OF MODERN ART, viale delle Belle Arti 131. Tel. 322-4151.

The National Gallery of Modern Art is in the Villa Borghese Gardens, a short walk from the Etruscan Museum. With its neoclassic and romantic paintings and sculpture, it's a dramatic change from the glories of the Renaissance and the Romans. Its 75 rooms house the largest collection in Italy of 19th- and 20th-century artists, including a comprehensive collection of modern Italian paintings.

Also included are important works of Balla, Boccioni, de Chirico, Morandi, Manzù, Marini, Burri, Capogrossi, and Fontana, and a large collection of Italian optical and pop art.

Look for Modigliani's *La Signora dal Collaretto* and the large *Nudo*. Several important sculptures, including one by Canova, are on display in the museum's gardens. The gallery also houses a large collection of foreign artists, including French impressionists Degas, Cézanne, and Monet, and the postimpressionist van Gogh. Surrealism and expressionism are well represented in works by Klee, Ernst, Braque, Miró, Kandinsky, Mondrian, and Pollock. You'll also find sculpture by Rodin. The collection of graphics, the storage rooms, and the department of restoration can be visited by appointment Tuesday through Friday.

Admission: 8,000 lire ($6.30).
Open: Tues–Sat 9am–2pm, Sun 9am–1pm. **Bus:** 19 or 30.

PALAZZO DORIA PAMPHILJ, piazza dei Collegio Romano 1A. Tel. 482-7224.

Located off via del Corso, the museum offers visitors a look at what it's really like to live in an 18th-century palace. The mansion, like many Roman palaces of the period, is partly leased to tenants (on the upper levels), and there are even shops on the street level, but all this is easily overlooked after you enter the grand apartments of the historic princely Doria Pamphilj family, which traces its line to before the great 15th-century Genoese admiral Andrea Doria. The regal apartments surround the central court and gallery of the palace. The 18th-century decor pervades the magnificent ballroom, drawing rooms, dining rooms, and even the family chapel. Gilded furniture, crystal chandeliers, Renaissance tapestries, and portraits of family members are everywhere. The Green Room is especially rich in treasures, with a 15th-century Tournay tapestry, paintings by Memling and Filippo Lippi, and a semi-nude portrait of Andrea Doria by Sebastiano del Piombo. The Andrea Doria Room is dedicated to the admiral and to the ship of the same name. It contains a glass case with mementoes of the great maritime disaster.

Skirting the central court is a picture gallery with a memorable collection of frescoes, paintings, and sculpture. Most important among a number of great works are the portrait of *Innocent X* by Velázquez, called one of the three or four best portraits ever painted; *Salome* by Titian; and works by Rubens and Caravaggio. Notable also are *Bay of Naples* by Pieter Brueghel the Elder and Raphael's portrait of Principessa Giovanna d'Aragona de Colonna (who looks remarkably like Leonardo's *Mona Lisa*). Most of the sculpture came from the Doria country estates. It includes marble busts of Roman emperors, bucolic nymphs, and satyrs. Even without the paintings and sculpture, the gallery would be worth a visit—just for its fresco-covered walls and ceilings.

Admission: 5,000 lire ($3.95) each for the gallery and the apartments.
Open: Tues and Fri–Sun 10am–1pm. **Metro:** Flaminio.

MUSEUM OF THE PALAZZO VENEZIA, piazza San Marco 49. Tel. 679-8865.

The Museum of the Palazzo Venezia, in the geographic heart of Rome, is the building that served until the end of World War I as the seat of the Embassy of Austria. During the Fascist regime (1928–43), it was the seat of the Italian government. The balcony from which Mussolini used to speak to the Italian people was built in the 16th century during the reign of Paulus III Farnese. Standing on part of the Capitoline Hill and overlooking the piazza is the 19th-century monument to Victor Emmanuel II, king of Italy, a lush work that has often been compared to a birthday cake. Here you'll find the Tomb of the Unknown Soldier which was created in World War I. Less known is the museum, founded in 1916 in the former papal residence that dates back to the 15th century. You can now visit the rooms and halls

containing oil paintings, porcelain, tapestries, ivories, ceramics, and arms. No one particular exhibit stands out—it is the sum total that adds up to a major attraction.
Admission: 8,000 lire ($6.30) adults, free for children under 18.
Open: Tues–Sat 9am–2pm, Sun 9am–1:30pm. **Bus:** 64, 75, 85, or 170.

GALLERIA NAZIONALE D'ARTE ANTICA, via Quattro Fontane 13. Tel. 482-4184.

The Palazzo Barberini, right off piazza Barberini, is one of the most magnificent baroque palaces in Rome. It was begun by Carlo Maderno in 1627 and completed in 1633 by Bernini, whose lavishly decorated rococo apartments, called the Gallery of Decorative Art, are on view. The palace houses the Galleria Nazionale.

The bedroom of Princess Cornelia Costanza Barberini and Prince Giulio Cesare Colonna di Sciarra still stands just as it was on their wedding night, and many household objects are displayed in the decorative art gallery. In the chambers, which have frescoes and hand-painted silk linings, you can see porcelain from Japan and Bavaria, canopied beds, and a baby carriage made of wood.

On the first floor of the palace, a splendid array of paintings includes works that date back to the 13th and 14th centuries, most notably the *Mother and Child* by Simone Martini. Also praiseworthy are paintings by Florentine artists from the 15th century, including art by Beato Angelico and Filippo Lippi. Some salons display 15th- and 16th-century paintings by such artists as Andrea Solario and Francesco Francia. Il Sodoma (Giovanni Antonio Bazzi) has some brilliant pictures here, including *The Rape of the Sabines* and *The Marriage of St. Catherine.* One of the best-known paintings is Raphael's beloved *La Fornarina,* of the baker's daughter who was his mistress and who posed for his Madonna portraits. Titian is represented by a portrait of Philip II. Other artists exhibited include Tintoretto, El Greco, and Holbein the Younger. Many visitors come here just to see two magnificent Caravaggios: *St. John the Baptist* and *Narcissus.*
Admission: 6,000 lire ($4.70) adults, free for children under 18.
Open: Mon–Tues 9am–2pm, Wed–Sat 9am–7pm, Sun 9am–1pm. **Metro:** Piazza Barberini.

MUSEO DI ARTE EBRAICO DELLA COMUNITA ISRAELITICA DI ROMA (Jewish Museum), lungotevere Cenci (Tempio). Tel. 687-5051.

This museum of Hebraic art houses a permanent exhibition of the Roman Jewish community. It contains Jewish ritual objects and scrolls from the 17th to the 19th century as well as copies of tombstones, paintings, prints, and documents that illustrate 2,000 years of Jewish history in Rome. The collection of silver ceremonial objects is important, as is a selection of ancient ceremonial textiles. Documents of Nazi domination are of exceptional interest.
Admission: 4,000 lire ($3.15).
Open: Mon–Thurs 9:30am–2pm and 3–5pm, Fri 9:30am–1:30pm, Sun 9:30am–12:30pm. **Bus:** 56 or 60.

MUSEO DELLA CIVITA ROMANA, piazza Giovanni Agnelli. Tel. 592-6135.

This museum of Roman civilization houses Fiat-sponsored reproductions that recapture life in Ancient Rome. Its major exhibition is a plastic representation in miniature of what Rome looked like at the apex of its power. You'll see the impressive Circus Maximus, the intact Colosseum, the Baths of Diocletian—and lots more.
Admission: 5,000 lire ($3.95).
Open: Tues–Sat 9am–1:30pm (plus Thurs 4–7pm), Sun 9am–1pm. **Metro:** Linea B to E.U.R. Fermi.

PARKS & GARDENS

The **Villa Borghese** in the heart of Rome covers a land mass of 3½ miles in circumference. One of the most elegant parks in Europe, it was created by Cardinal Scipione Borghese in the 1600s. Umberto I, king of Italy, acquired it in 1902 and presented it to the city of Rome, renaming it Villa Umberto I. However, Romans preferred their old name, which has stuck. A park of landscaped vistas and wide-open "green lungs," the greenbelt is crisscrossed by roads. But you can escape from the traffic and seek a shaded area—usually pine or oak—where you can enjoy the makings of a picnic. In the northeast of the park is a small zoo, and the park is also host to the Galleria Borghese, one of the finest museums of Rome, with many masterpieces by Renaissance and baroque artists.

COOL FOR KIDS

Rome has lots of other amusements for children when they tire of ancient monuments, although they're usually fond of wandering around the **Colosseum** and the **Forum** (see above). Many children also enjoy the climb to the top of **St. Peter's.** The **Fun Fair (Luna Park),** along via delle Tre Fontane (tel. 592-5933), at E.U.R., is one of the largest in Europe. It's known for its "big wheel" at the entrance, and there are merry-go-rounds, miniature railways, and shooting galleries, among other attractions. Admission is free, but you pay for each ride. It is closed Tuesday.

A **children's cabaret** gives occasional performances at via Morosini 16 (tel. 582049 for more information). There's also Maria Accettella's **Marionette Theater,** via Tripolitania 195 (tel. 832254 for information), which stages shows for children. The **Puppet Theater** on Pincio Square in the Villa Borghese gardens has "Punch and Judy" performances nearly every day. While there, you might also like to take your children through the park (it's closed to traffic). Children enjoy the fountain displays and the lake, and there are many wide spaces in which they can play. Boats can be hired at the **Giardino del Lago.** A trip to the **zoo** in Rome is also possible, as it lies in the Villa Borghese, at viale del Giardino Zoologico 20 (tel. 870564). It's open daily all year from 8:30am to sunset.

At 4pm every day, you can take your child to the **Quirinale Palace,** piazza del Quirinale, the residence of the president of Italy. There's a military band and a parade at that time, as the guards change shifts.

SPECIAL-INTEREST SIGHTSEEING
FOR THE LITERARY ENTHUSIAST

KEATS-SHELLEY MEMORIAL, piazza di Spagna 26. Tel. 678-4235.
At the foot of the Spanish Steps is this 18th-century house where Keats died of consumption on February 23, 1821. "It is like living in a violin," wrote Italian author Alberto Savinio. The apartment where Keats spent his last months, carefully tended by his close friend Joseph Severn, shelters a museum and research library, with a strange death mask of Keats as well as the "deadly sweat" drawing by Severn and many other mementoes of Keats, Shelley, and Byron. For those interested in the full story of the involvement of Keats and Shelley in Italy, books are sold on the premises.
Admission: 4,000 lire ($3.15).
Open: July–Sept, Mon–Fri 9am–1pm and 2:30–5:30pm; Oct–June, Mon–Fri 9am–1pm. **Metro:** Piazza di Spagna.

PROTESTANT CEMETERY, Caio Cestio 6. Tel. 574-1141.
Near St. Paul's Station, in the midst of a setting of cypress trees, lies the old cemetery where John Keats was buried. In a grave nearby, Joseph Severn, his "deathbed" companion, was interred beside him 6 decades later. Dejected, and feeling his reputation as a poet diminished by the rising vehemence of his critics, Keats asked that the following epitaph be written on his tombstone: "Here lies one whose name was writ in water." A great romantic poet Keats certainly was, but a prophet, thankfully not.
Shelley, author of *Prometheus Unbound*, drowned off the Italian Riviera in 1822, before his 30th birthday. His ashes rest alongside those of Edward John Trelawny, fellow romantic and man of the sea. Trelawny maintained—but this was not proved—that Shelley may have been murdered, perhaps by petty pirates bent on robbery. While you're here, you may want to drop in at the neighboring Pyramid of Caius Cestius (see "Cemeteries," above).
Admission: Free, but a 1,000-lira (80¢) offering is customary.

Open: Apr–Sept, daily 8–11:30am and 3:30–5:30pm; Oct–Mar, daily 8–11:30am and 2:30–4:30pm. **Metro:** St. Paul's.

FOR THE ARCHITECTURE ENTHUSIAST

At the height of Mussolini's power, he launched a complex of modern buildings—many of them in cold marble—to dazzle Europe with a scheduled world's fair. But Il Duce got strung up, and **E.U.R.**—the area in question—got hamstrung. E.U.R. is an Italian acronym for Universal Exposition of Rome. The new Italian government that followed inherited the uncompleted project, and decided to turn it into a center of government and administration. It has also developed into a residential section of fairly deluxe apartment houses. Most of the cold granite edifices fail to escape the curse of "Il Duce moderno," but the small "city of tomorrow" is softened considerably by a man-made lagoon, which you can row across in rented boats.

Italy's great modern architect, Milan-born Pier Luigi Nervi, designed the **Palazzo della Sport** on the hill. One of the country's most impressive modern buildings, it was the chief site of the 1960 Olympics. Another important structure is the **Palazzo dei Congressi** in the center, an exhibition hall with changing displays of industrial shows which is well worth a stroll. You'll also spot architecture reminiscent of Frank Lloyd Wright and a building that evokes the design of the United Nations in New York. E.U.R. is reached by Metro Line B to the E.U.R.–Marconi stop.

For still another look at Mussolini's architectural achievements, head across the river from E.U.R. to the **Foro Italico.** Shades of 1932! This complex of sports stadiums blatantly honors Il Duce. At the entrance to the forum, an obelisk bears the name MVSSOLINI so firmly engraved that to destroy the lettering would be to do away with the monument. It stands defiantly. Visitors on a sunny day walk across the mosaic courtyard with DVCE in the pavement more times than they can count. The big attraction of this freakish site is the "Stadium of Marbles," encircled with 50 marble nude athletes—draped discreetly so as not to offend the eyes of the Golden Madonna on the hill beyond. Take bus no. 1 from piazza del Popolo.

WALKING TOUR —— Imperial Rome

Start: Colosseum.
Finish: Circus Maximus.
Time: 2 hours.
Best Time: Any sunny day.
Worst Time: Morning or early-evening rush hours.

Even in the days of the Republic, the population explosion was a problem. Julius Caesar saw the overcrowding and began to expand, starting what were known as the Imperial Forums in the days of the empire. After the collapse of Rome and during the Dark Ages, the Forums were lost to history, buried beneath layers of debris, until Mussolini set out to restore the grandeur of Rome by reminding his compatriots of their glorious past. Take the Metro to the Colosseo stop for the:

1. **Colosseum,** a good starting point, as you get your bearings with the traffic at the piazza del Colosseo. The Colosseum is the greatest monument of ancient Rome, and visitors are impressed with its size and majesty. Either visit it now or return later.
   With your back to the Colosseum, begin your walk up the:
2. **Via dei Fori Imperiali,** keeping to the right side of the street. It was Mussolini who ordered Roman workers to cut through the years of debris and junky buildings to carve out this boulevard, linking the Colosseum to piazza Venezia. Excavations began at once, and much was revealed. Today the boulevard makes for one of the most fascinating walks in Rome. All the Imperial Forums can be seen from street level.

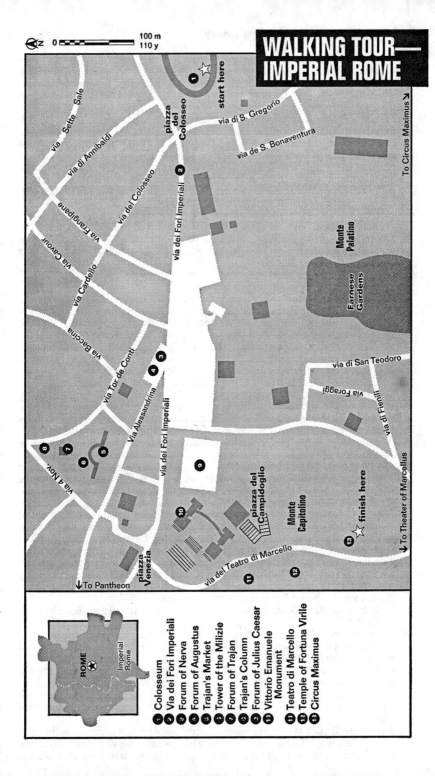

WALKING TOUR—
IMPERIAL ROME

100 m
0
110 y

start here

1

piazza del Colosseo

via di S. Gregorio

via de S. Bonaventura

To Circus Maximus →

2

via dei Fori Imperiali

via di Annibaldi

via di Sette Sale

via dei Colosseo

via Frangipane

via Cavour

via Cardello

via Baccina

via Tor de Conti

via Alessandrina

Monte Palatino

Farnese Gardens

via di San Teodoro

via Foraggi

via di Fienili

3

4

5

6

7

8

via 4 Nov.

9

via dei Fori Imperiali

10

piazza del Campidoglio

Monte Capitolino

finish here

13

→ To Theater of Marcellus

11

via del Teatro di Marcello

12

piazza Venezia

↓ To Pantheon

ROME

Imperial Rome

1 Colosseum
2 Via dei Fori Imperiali
3 Forum of Nerva
4 Forum of Augustus
5 Trajan's Market
6 Tower of the Milizie
7 Forum of Trajan
8 Trajan's Column
9 Forum of Julius Caesar
10 Vittorio Emanuele
   Monument
11 Teatro di Marcello
12 Temple of Fortuna Virile
13 Circus Maximus

The ruins across the street are what's left of the colonnade that once surrounded the Temple of Venus and Roma. Next to it, you'll see the back wall of the Basilica of Constantine. Shortly, you'll come to a large outdoor restaurant, where via Cavour joins the boulevard you're on. Just beyond the small park across via Cavour are the remains of the:

3. **Forum of Nerva,** built by the emperor whose 2-year reign (A.D. 96–98) followed that of the paranoid Domitian. The Forum of Nerva is best observed from the railing that skirts it on via dei Fori Imperiali. You'll be struck by just how much the ground level has risen in 19 centuries. The only really recognizable remnant is a wall of the Temple of Minerva with two fine Corinthian columns. This forum was once flanked by that of Vespasian, which is now, however, completely gone. It's possible to enter the Forum of Nerva from the other side, but you can see it just as well from the railing.

REFUELING STOP   **Il Gladiatore** is rather well named as it faces the Colosseum—site of gladiator contests of yore—at piazza del Colosseo 15. It's a good place for a refreshing drink in the hot sun or a reasonably priced lunch. The restaurant closes on Wednesday.

The next forum you approach is the:

4. **Forum of Augustus,** built before the birth of Christ to commemorate the emperor's victory over the assassins Cassius and Brutus in the Battle of Philippi (42 B.C.). Fittingly, the temple that once dominated this forum—and whose remains can still be seen—was that of Mars Ultor, or Mars the Avenger. In the temple once stood a mammoth statue of Augustus, which has unfortunately completely vanished. Like the Forum of Nerva, you can enter the Forum of Augustus from the other side (cut across the wee footbridge).

Continuing along the railing, you'll see next the vast semicircle of:

5. **Trajan's Market,** via Quattro Novembre 95 (tel. 710-3613), whose teeming arcades stocked with merchandise from the far corners of the Roman world long ago collapsed, leaving only a few ubiquitous cats to watch after things. The shops once covered a multitude of levels, and you can still wander around many of them. In front of the perfectly proportioned semicircular facade—designed by Apollodorus of Damascus at the beginning of the 2nd century—are the remains of a great library, and fragments of delicately colored marble floors still shine in the sunlight between stretches of rubble and tall grass. While the view from the railing is of interest, Trajan's Market is worth the descent below street level. To get there, follow the service road you're on until you reach the monumental Trajan's Column on your left, where you turn right and go up the steep flight of stairs that leads to via Nazionale. At the top of the stairs, about half a block farther on the right, you'll see the entrance to the market. From April to September it is open Tuesday through Saturday from 9am to 1:30pm, and also on Tuesday, Thursday, and Saturday in the afternoon from 4 to 7pm; Sunday hours are 9am to 1pm. From October to March, it operates Tuesday through Saturday from 9am to 1:30pm and on Sunday from 9am to 1pm. Admission is 2,000 lire ($1.55) for adults and 1,000 lire (80¢) for children.

Before you head down through the labyrinthine passageways, you might like to climb the:

6. **Tower of the Milizie,** a 12th-century structure that was part of the medieval headquarters of the Knights of Rhodes. The view from the top (if it's open) is well worth the climb. From the tower, you can wander where you will through the ruins of the market, and admire the sophistication of the layout and the sad beauty of the bits of decoration that still remain. When you've examined the brick and travertine corridors, head out in front of the semicircle to the site of the former library; from here, scan the retaining wall that supports the modern road and look for the entrance to the tunnel that leads to the:

7. **Forum of Trajan (Foro Traiano),** entered on via 4 Novembre near the steps of via Magnanapoli. Once through the tunnel, you'll emerge in the newest and most beautiful of the Imperial Forums, designed by the same man who laid out

the adjoining market. There are many statue fragments, and pedestals which bear still-legible inscriptions, but more interesting is the great Basilica Ulpia, whose gray marble columns rise roofless into the sky. You wouldn't know it to judge from what's left, but the Forum of Trajan was once regarded as one of the architectural wonders of the world. Constructed between 107 and 113, it was designed by the Greek architect Apollodorus of Damascus.

Beyond the Basilica Ulpia is:

 8. Trajan's Column, already mentioned, which is in magnificent condition, with intricate bas-relief sculpture depicting Trajan's victorious campaign (although from your vantage point you'll only be able to see the earliest stages). The emperor's ashes were kept in a golden urn at the base of the column. If you're fortunate, someone on duty at the stairs next to the column will let you out there. Otherwise, you'll have to walk back the way you came.

The next stop is the:

 9. Forum of Julius Caesar, the first of the Imperial Forums. It lies on the opposite side of via dei Fori Imperiali, the last set of sunken ruins before the Victor Emmanuel Monument. While it's possible to go right down into the ruins, you can see everything just as well from the railing. This was the site of the Roman stock exchange, as well as of the Temple of Venus, a few of whose restored columns stand cinematically in the middle of the excavations. From here, retrace your last steps until you're in front of the white Brescian marble monument around the corner on piazza Venezia, where the:

10. Vittorio Emanuele Monument dominates the piazza. The most flamboyant landmark in Italy, it was constructed in the late 1800s to honor the first king of Italy. It has been compared to everything from a frosty birthday cake to a Victorian typewriter. An eternal flame burns at the Tomb of the Unknown Soldier. The interior of the monument has been closed to the public for many years.

Keep close to the monument and walk to your left, in the opposite direction from via dei Fori Imperiali. You might like to pause at the fountain that flanks one of the monument's great white walls and splash some icy water on your face. There is another fountain just like this one on the other side of the monument, and they're both favorite spots for tired visitors. Stay on the same side of the street, and just keep walking around the monument. You'll be on via del Teatro Marcello, which takes you past the twin lions that guard the sloping stairs and on along the base of Capitoline Hill.

Keep walking along this boulevard until you come to the:

11. Teatro di Marcello, on your right. You'll recognize the two rows of gaping arches, which are said to be the models for the Colosseum. Julius Caesar is the man credited with starting the construction of this theater, but it was finished many years after his death (in 11 B.C.) by Augustus, who dedicated it to his favorite nephew, Marcellus. You can stroll around the 2,000-year-old arcade, a small corner of which has been restored to what presumably was the original condition. Here, as everywhere, there are numerous cats stalking around the broken marble.

The bowl of the theater and the stage were adapted many centuries ago as the foundation for the Renaissance palace of the Orsini family. Walk around the theater to the right. The other ruins belong to old temples. Soon you'll walk up a ramp to the street, and to the right is the Porticus of Octavia, dating from the 2nd century B.C. Note how later cultures used part of the Roman structure without destroying its original character. There's another good example of this on the other side of the theater. There you'll see a church with a wall which completely incorporates part of an ancient colonnade.

Returning to via del Teatro Marcello, keep walking away from piazza Venezia for two more long blocks, until you come to piazza Bocca della Verità. The first item to notice in this attractive piazza is the rectangular:

12. Temple of Fortuna Virile. You'll see it on the right, a little off the road. Built a century before the birth of Christ, it's still in magnificent condition. Behind it is another temple, dedicated to Vesta. Like the one in the forum, it is round, symbolic of the prehistoric huts where continuity of the hearthfire was a matter of survival.

About a block to the south, you'll pass the facade of the church of Santa Maria in Cosmedin, set on the piazza Bocca della Verità. Even more noteworthy, a short walk to the east, is the:

13. Circus Maximus, whose elongated oval proportions and ruined tiers of benches might remind visitors of the setting for *Ben Hur*. Today a formless and dusty ruin, the victim of countless raids upon its stonework by medieval and Renaissance builders, the remains of the once-great arena lie directly behind the church. At one time 250,000 Romans could assemble on the marble seats, while the emperor observed the games from his box high on the Palatine Hill.

The circus lies in a valley formed by the Palatine Hill on the left and the Aventine Hill on the right. Next to the Colosseum, it was the most impressive structure in Ancient Rome, located certainly in one of the most exclusive neighborhoods. Emperors lived on the Palatine, while the great palaces of patricians sprawled across the Aventine, which is still a rather nice neighborhood. For centuries the pomp and ceremony of imperial chariot races filled this valley with the cheers of thousands.

When the dark days of the 5th and 6th centuries fell on the city, the Circus Maximus seemed a symbol of the complete ruination of Rome. The last games were held in 549 on the orders of Totila the Goth, who had seized Rome in 546 and established himself as emperor. He lived in the still-glittering ruins on the Palatine and apparently thought that the chariot races in the Circus Maximus would lend credence to his charade of empire. It must have been a pretty miserable show, since the decimated population numbered something like 500 when Totila had recaptured the city. The Romans of these times were caught between Belisarius, the imperial general from Constantinople, and Totila the Goth, both of whom fought bloodily for control of Rome. After the travesty of 549, the Circus Maximus was never used again, and the demand for building materials reduced it, like so much of Rome, to a great dusty field.

To return to other parts of town, head for the bus stop adjacent to the Santa Maria in Cosmedin Church, or walk the length of the Circus Maximus to its far end and pick up the Metro to Stazione Termini.

WALKING TOUR —— Roman Forum & Palatine Hill

Start: Via Sacra.
Finish: Orti Farnesiani.
Time: 2½ hours.
Best Time: Any sunny day.
Worst Time: When the place is overrun with tour groups.

THE ROMAN FORUM The entrance to the Roman Forum is off via dei Fori Imperiali, right at the intersection with via Cavour. Take the Metro to the Colosseo stop.

As you walk down the ramp from the entrance, you'll be heading for the via Sacra, the ancient Roman road that ran through the Forum connecting the Capitoline Hill to your right, with the Arch of Titus (1st c. A.D.), way off to your left. During the Middle Ages when this was the *campo vaccino* and all these stones were underground, there was a dual column of elm trees connecting the Arch of Titus, off to your left, with the Arch of Septimius Severus (A.D. 200) to your right.

Arriving at the via Sacra, turn right. The random columns on the right as you head toward the Arch of Septimius Severus belong to the:

1. Basilica Emilia, formerly the site of great meeting halls and shops all maintained for centuries by the noble Roman family who gave it its name. At the

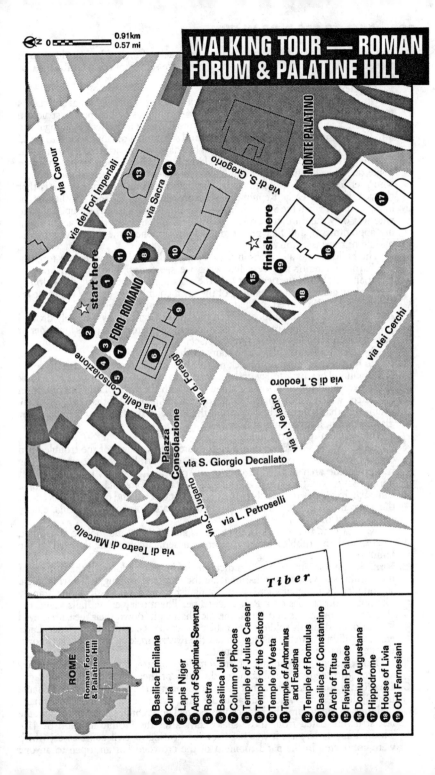

WALKING TOUR — ROMAN FORUM & PALATINE HILL

0.91km
0.57mi

via Cavour

via dei Fori Imperiali

via Sacra

MONTE PALATINO

via di S. Gregorio

start here

FORO ROMANO

finish here

via dei Cerchi

via della Consolazione

via di S. Teodoro

via d. Foraggi

via d. Velabro

Piazza Consolazione

via S. Giorgio Decallato

via C. Jugario

via L. Petroselli

via di Teatro di Marcello

Tiber

ROME

Roman Forum & Palatine Hill

1 Basilica Emiliana
2 Curia
3 Lapis Niger
4 Arch of Septimius Severus
5 Rostra
6 Basilica Julia
7 Column of Phocas
8 Temple of Julius Caesar
9 Temple of the Castors
10 Temple of Vesta
11 Temple of Antoninus and Faustina
12 Temple of Romulus
13 Basilica of Constantine
14 Arch of Titus
15 Flavian Palace
16 Domus Augustana
17 Hippodrome
18 House of Livia
19 Orti Farnesiani

corner nearest the Forum entrance are some traces of melted bronze decoration that fused to the marble floor during a great fire set by invading Goths in A.D. 410.

The next important building is the:

2. Curia, or Senate house—it's the large brick building on the right that still has its roof. Romans had been meeting on this site for centuries before the first structure was erected, and that was still centuries before Christ. The present building is the fifth (if one counts all the reconstructions and substantial rehabilitations) to stand on the site. Legend has it that the original building was constructed by an ancient king, with the curious name of Tullus Hostilius. The tradition he began was a noble one indeed, and our present legislative system owes much to the Romans who met in this hall. Unfortunately, the high ideals and inviolate morals that characterized the early Republican senators gave way to the bootlicking of imperial times, when the Senate became little more than a rubber stamp. Caligula, who was only the third emperor, had his horse appointed to the Senate (it was a life appointment), and that pretty much sums up where the Senate was by the middle of the 1st century A.D.

The building was a church until 1937, when the Fascist government tore out the baroque interior and revealed what we see today. The original floor of Egyptian marble and the tiers that held the seats of the senators have miraculously survived. In addition, at the far end of the great chamber we can see the stone on which rested the fabled golden statue of Victory. Originally installed by Augustus, it was finally disposed of in the late 4th century by a fiercely divided Senate, whose Christian members convinced the emperor that it was improper to have a pagan statue in such a revered place.

Outside, head down the Curia stairs to the:

3. Lapis Niger, the remains of black marble blocks that reputedly mark the tomb of Romulus. They bask today under a corrugated roof. Go downstairs for a look at the excavated tomb. There's a stone here with the oldest Latin inscription in existence, which unfortunately is nearly unintelligible. All that can be safely assumed is that it genuinely dates from the Rome of the kings. Remember, they disappeared in a revolution in 509 B.C.

Across from the Curia, the:

4. Arch of Septimius Severus was dedicated at the dawn of the troubled 3rd century to the last decent emperor who was to govern Rome for some time. The friezes on the arch depict victories over Arabs and Parthians by the cold but upright Severus and his two dissolute sons, Geta and Caracalla. Severus died on a campaign to subdue the unruly natives of Scotland at the end of the first decade of the 3rd century. Rome unhappily fell into the hands of young Caracalla, chiefly remembered today for his baths.

Walk around to the back of the Severus arch, face it, and look to your right. There amid the rubble can be discerned a semicircular stair that led to the famous:

5. Rostra, the podium from which dictators and caesars addressed the throngs of the Forum below. One can just imagine the emperor, shining in his white toga, surrounded by imperial guards and distinguished senators, gesticulating grandly like one of the statues on a Roman roofline. The motley crowd falls silent, the elegant senators pause and listen, the merchants put down their measures, even the harlots and unruly soldiers lower their voices in such an august presence. Later emperors didn't have much cause to use the Rostra, making their policies known through edict and assassination instead.

Now, facing the colonnade of the Temple of Saturn, once the public treasury and going to the left, you'll come to the ruins of the:

6. Basilica Julia, again little more than a foundation. The basilica gets its name from Julius Caesar, who dedicated the first structure in 46 B.C. Like many buildings in the Forum, the basilica was burned and rebuilt several times, and the last structure dated from those shaky days after the Gothic invasion of 410. Throughout its history, it was used for the hearing of civil court cases, which were conducted in the pandemonium of the crowded Forum, open to anyone who happened to pass by. The building was also reputed to be particularly hot in the summer, and it was under these sweaty and unpromising circumstances that Roman justice, the standard of the world for a millennium, was meted out.

Walking back down the ruined stairs of the Basilica Julia and into the broad area whose far side is bounded by the Curia, you'll see the:

7. Column of Phocas. Probably lifted from an early structure in the near vicinity, this was the last monument to be erected in the Roman Forum, and it commemorates the Byzantine emperor Phocas's generous donation of the Pantheon to the pope of Rome, who almost immediately transformed it into a church.

Now make your way down the middle of the Forum nearly back to the ramp from which you entered. The pile of brick with the semicircular indentation that stands in the middle of things was the:

8. Temple of Julius Caesar, erected some time after the dictator was deified. Judging from the reconstructions, it was quite an elegant building. As you stand facing the ruins, with the entrance to the Forum on your left, you'll see on your right three columns belonging originally to the:

9. Temple of the Castors. This temple perpetuated the legend of Castor and Pollux, who appeared out of thin air in the Roman Forum and were observed watering their horses at the fountain of Juturna (still visible today), just as a major battle against the Etruscans turned in favor of Rome. Castor and Pollux, the heavenly twins—and the symbol of the astrological sign Gemini—seem a favorite of Rome.

The next major monument is the circular:

10. Temple of Vesta, wherein dwelt the sacred flame of Rome, and the Atrium of the Vestal Virgins. A vestal virgin was usually a girl of good family who signed a contract for 30 years. During that time, she lived in the ruin we're standing in right now. Of course, back then it was an unimaginably rich marble building with two floors. There were only six vestal virgins during the imperial period, and even though they had the option of going back out into the world at the end of their 30 years, few did. The cult of Vesta came to an end in 394, when a Christian Rome secularized all its pagan temples. A man standing on this site before then would have been put to death immediately.

Stand in the atrium with your back to the Palatine and look beyond those fragmented statues of former vestals to the:

11. Temple of Antoninus and Faustina. It's the building with the free-standing colonnade just to the right of the ramp where you first entered the Forum. Actually, just the colonnade dates from imperial times; the building behind is a much later church dedicated to San Lorenzo.

After you inspect the beautifully proportioned Antoninus and Faustina temple, head up via Sacra away from the entrance ramp in the direction of the Arch of Titus. Pretty soon, on your left, you'll see the twin bronze doors of the:

12. Temple of Romulus. It's the doors themselves that are really of note here—they're the original Roman doors, and swing on the same massive hinges they were originally mounted on in A.D. 306. In this case, the temple is not dedicated to the legendary cofounder of Rome, but to the son of its builder, the emperor Maxentius, who gave Romulus his name in a fit of antiquarian patriotism. Unfortunately for both father and son, they competed with a general who deprived them of their empire and lives. That man was Constantine, who, while camped outside Rome during preparations for one of his battles against Maxentius, saw the sign of the Cross in the heavens with the insignia IN HOC SIGNO VINCES (In This Sign Shall You Conquer). Raising the standard of Christianity above his legions, he defeated the (pagan) Emperor Maxentius and later became the first Christian emperor.

At the time of Constantine's victory (A.D. 306) the great:

13. Basilica of Constantine (marked by those three gaping arches up ahead on your left) was only half finished, having been started by the unfortunate Maxentius. However, Constantine finished the job and affixed his name to this, the largest and most impressive building in the Forum. To my taste, the more delicate, Greek-influenced temples are more attractive, but you have to admire the scale and the engineering skill that erected this monument. The fact that portions of the original coffered ceiling are still intact is amazing. The basilica once held a statue of Constantine so large that his little toe was as wide as an average man's waist. You can see a few fragments from this colossal thing—the remnants were found in 1490—in the courtyard of the Conservatory Museum on the Capitoline Hill. As far as Roman emperors went, Christian or otherwise, ego knew no bounds.

From Constantine's basilica, follow the Roman paving stones of via Sacra to the:

14. Arch of Titus, clearly visible on a low hill just ahead. Titus was the emperor who sacked the great Jewish temple in Jerusalem, and the bas-relief sculpture inside the arch shows the booty of the Jews being carried in triumph through the streets of Rome, while Titus is crowned by Victory, who comes down from heaven for the occasion. You'll notice in particular the candelabrum, for centuries one of the most famous pieces of the treasure of Rome. In all probability, it now lies at the bottom of the Busento River in the secret tomb of Alaric the Goth.

THE PALATINE HILL   When you've gathered your strength in the shimmering hot sun, head up the Clivus Palatinus, the road to the palaces of the Palatine Hill. With your back to the Arch of Titus, it's the road going up the hill to the left.

It was on the Palatine Hill that Rome first became a city. Legend tells us the date was 753 B.C. The new city originally consisted of nothing more than the Palatine, which was soon enclosed by a surprisingly sophisticated wall, remains of which can still be seen on the Circus Maximus side of the hill. As time went on and Rome grew in power and wealth, the boundaries were extended and later enclosed by the Servian Wall. When the last of the ancient kings was overthrown (509 B.C.), Rome had already extended onto several of the adjoining hills and valleys. As Republican times progressed, the Palatine became a fashionable residential district. So it remained until Tiberius—who, like his predecessor, Augustus, was a bit too modest to really call himself "emperor" out loud—began the first of the monumental palaces that were to cover the entire hill.

It's difficult today to make sense out of the Palatine. The first-time viewer might be forgiven for suspecting it to be an entirely artificial structure built on brick arches. Those arches, which are visible on practically every flank of the hill, are actually supports that once held imperial structures. Having run out of building sites, the emperors, in their fever, simply enlarged the hill by building new sides on it. The road goes only a short way, through a small sort of valley filled with lush, untrimmed greenery. After about 5 minutes (for slow walkers), you'll see the ruins of a monumental stairway just to the right of the road. The Clivus Palatinus turns sharply to the left here, skirting the monastery of San Bonaventura, but we'll detour to the right and take a look at the remains of the:

15. Flavian Palace. As you walk off the road and into the ruins, you'll be able to discern that there were once three rooms here. But it's really impossible for anyone but an archeologist to comprehend quite how splendid these rooms were. The entire Flavian Palace was decorated in the most lavish of colored marbles, sometimes inlaid with precious silver. The roofs were, in places, even covered with gold. Much of the decoration survived as late as the 18th century, when the greedy Duke of Parma removed most of what was left. The room closest to the Clivus Palatinus was called the Lararium, and held statues of the divinities that protected the imperial family. The middle room was the grandest of the three. It was the imperial throne room, where sat the ruler of the world, the emperor of Rome. The far room was a basilica, and as such was used for miscellaneous court functions, among them audiences with the emperor. This part of the palace was used entirely for ceremonial functions. Adjoining these three rooms are the remains of a spectacularly luxurious peristyle. You'll recognize it by the hexagonal remains of a fountain in the middle. Try, if you can, to imagine this fountain surrounded by marble arcades, planted with mazes, and equipped with mica-covered walls. On the opposite side of the peristyle from the throne rooms are several other great reception and entertainment rooms. The banquet hall was here, and beyond it, looking over the Circus Maximus, are a few ruins of former libraries. Although practically nothing remains except the foundations, every now and again you'll catch sight of a fragment of colored marble floor, in a subtle, sophisticated pattern.

The imperial family lived in the:

16. Domus Augustana, the remains of which lie in the direction of the Circus Maximus, and slightly to the left of the Flavian Palace. The new building that stands here—it looks old to us, but in Rome it qualifies as a new building—is a museum (usually closed). It stands in the absolute center of the Domus Augustana. In the field adjacent to the Stadium well into the present century stood the Villa Mills, a gingerbread Gothic villa of the 19th century. It was quite a famous place. Owned by a rich Englishman who came to Rome from the West Indies, Villa Mills was the scene of many fashionable entertainments in Victorian times, and it's interesting to note, as H. V. Morton pointed out, that the last dinner parties that took place on the Palatine Hill were given by an Englishman.

Heading across the field parallel to the Clivus Palatinus, you come to the north end of the:

17. Hippodrome, or Stadium of Domitian. The field was apparently occupied by parts of the Domus Augustana, which in turn adjoined the enormous stadium. The stadium itself is worth examination, although sometimes it's difficult to get down inside it. The perfectly proportioned area was usually used for private games, staged for the amusement of the imperial family. As you look down the stadium from the north end, you can see, on the left side, the semicircular remains of a structure identified as Domitian's private box. I'll note at this point that some archeologists claim the "stadium" was actually an elaborate sunken garden, and perhaps we'll never know exactly what it was.

The aqueduct that comes up the wooded hill used to supply water for the Baths of Septimius Severus, whose difficult-to-understand ruins lie in monumental piles of arched brick at the far end of the stadium.

Returning to the Flavian Palace, leave the peristyle on the opposite side from the Domus Augustana and follow the signs for the:

18. House of Livia. They take you down a dusty path to your left, from which entrance to the house is made. Although legend says that this was the house of Augustus's consort, it actually was Augustus's all along. The place is notable for some rather well-preserved murals showing mythological scenes. But more interesting is the aspect of the house itself—it's smallish, and there never were any great baths or impressive marble arcades. Augustus, even though he was the first emperor, lived simply compared to his successors. His wife, Livia, was a fiercely ambitious aristocrat who divorced her own husband to marry the emperor (the ex-husband was made to attend the wedding, incidentally) and according to some historians was the true power behind Roman policy between the death of Julius Caesar and the ascension of Tiberius. She even controlled Tiberius, her son, since she had engineered his rise to power through a long string of intrigues and poisonings.

After you've examined the frescoes in Livia's parlor, head up the steps that lead to the top of the embankment to the north. Once on top, you'll be in the:

19. Orti Farnesiani, the 16th-century addition of a Farnese cardinal. They are built on the top of the Palace of Tiberius, which, you'll remember, was the first of the great imperial palaces to be put up. It's impossible to see any of it, but the gardens are cool and nicely laid out. You might stroll up to the promontory above the Forum and admire the view of the ancient temples and the Capitoline heights off to the left.

When you've seen this much, you've seen the best of the Forum and the Palatine. To leave the archeological area, you should now continue through the Orti Farnesiani, keeping the Forum on your left. Soon you'll come to a stairway that leads to the path from the Arch of Titus. There is an exit just behind the arch, but since it's usually closed, you'll probably have to exit up the ramp you entered by.

WALKING TOUR —— From Piazza Barberini to Piazza del Popolo

Start: Piazza Barberini.
Finish: Piazza del Popolo.
Time: 2 leisurely hours.
Best Time: Any sunny day.
Worst Time: Morning or late-afternoon rush hours.

1. **Piazza Barberini** (also the Metro stop) lies at the foot of several important Roman streets: via Barberini, via Sistina, via Quattro Fontane, and via del Tritone. It would be a far more pleasant spot were it not for the considerable amount of traffic swarming around its principal feature, Bernini's Fontana del Tritone (Triton Fountain). Day and night for more than 3 centuries, the strange figure sitting in a vast open clam has been blowing water from his triton. Above it is the clean aristocratic side facade of the Palazzo Barberini. Rome has always been a city of powerful families. The Renaissance Barberini reached their peak when a son was elected Pope Urban VIII. And it was this Barberini pope who encouraged Bernini and gave him so much patronage.

   As you start up via Vittorio Veneto directly north of the square, look for the small fountain on the right-hand corner of piazza Barberini. There you'll see another of Bernini's many works, the small Fontana delle Api or "fountain of the bees." At first they look more like flies, but they are the bees of the Barberini, the crest of that powerful family complete with the crossed keys of St. Peter above them (the crossed keys were added to a family crest when a son was elected pope). Before you survey the attractions of via Vittorio Veneto, you might stop first at the:

2. **Cimitero Monumentale dei Padri Cappucini,** in the Church of the Immaculate Conception, via Vittorio Veneto 27, a short walk from piazza Barberini, where the bones of 4,000 monks have been artistically arranged in various geometric and representational patterns. There is, appropriately, a design that shows the "grim reaper" amid a sea of skulls and thighbones. You'll find it just below the church.

   After leaving the church, the posh, tree-lined:

3. **Via Vittorio Veneto** awaits you. It doesn't look as elegant as it did in the 1950s when it reached its peak. Those *La Dolce Vita* days, when Middle Eastern businessmen in fezzes and sunglasses sat surrounded by bevies of blonde beauties in the sidewalk cafés, when movie stars promenaded with rich old men in monocles, are gone, although admittedly you can still see scenes of the above sort on rare occasions.

   Via Vittorio Veneto makes a large S-curve, and just where it straightens out for the last time, you'll see the swank U.S. Embassy, whose Consular Division is in a rose-colored palace where the queen of Italy once lived. From the embassy on up to the Aurelian Wall are the chicest of the cafés, which still carry on a thriving business despite the depletion of the celebrity roster. These cafés, with their brightly colored umbrellas and awnings, are perfectly designed for people-watching. They straddle the sidewalk, and there's no way to stroll up via Vittorio Veneto without going through the middle of half a dozen of them.

   The end of via Veneto comes with a final burst of plush hotels and Harry's Bar.

REFUELING STOPS   At the top of via Vittorio Veneto, **Harry's Bar,** at no. 148 is everybody's perennial favorite. The IBF—International Bar Flies—are there in constant attendance. You can enjoy a drink or a complete meal, depending on your taste and pocketbook. The two most famous cafés along the boulevard are

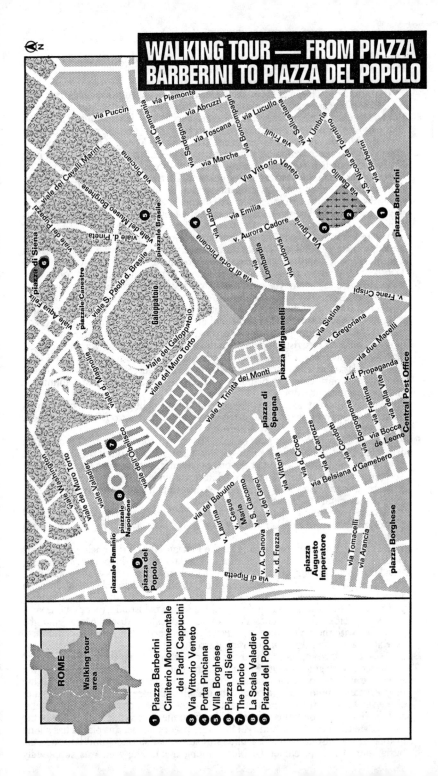

WALKING TOUR — FROM PIAZZA BARBERINI TO PIAZZA DEL POPOLO

ROME
Walking tour area

1. Piazza Barberini
2. Cimiterio Monumentale dei Padri Cappucini
3. Via Vittorio Veneto
4. Porta Pinciana
5. Villa Borghese
6. Piazza di Siena
7. The Pincio
8. La Scala Valadier
9. Piazza del Popolo

Gran Caffè Doney, via Vittorio Veneto 139-143, and **Caffè de Paris,** via Vittorio Veneto (see "Evening Entertainment," below).

Right in front of you is the hulking brickwork of the Aurelian Wall, begun in A.D. 271. The gate, however, is a bit newer:

4. Porta Pinciana derives its name from the Pincian Hill. It was built in A.D. 546 by the Byzantine general Belisarius, who was, at the time, seeking to assert the rule of Eastern Rome over the fallen capital of Western Rome. The city was in a shambles after more than a century of barbarian assaults, which had looted it of nearly all its ancient treasure. The last emperor of the West had long fallen (A.D. 476), and the pope was the real power in Rome. Even the pope was gone, however, the city being depopulated as a result of the constant upheaval. The leader of the goths was Totilla, and though he initially defeated Belisarius, Belisarius won in the end, eventually laying the dead Goth at the feet of his emperor in Constantinople.

While Belisarius was building the Pincian Gate, the land just outside was the sometime campground of Totilla. All traces of the Goths have long ago been smoothed away, and today we see a perfectly exquisite (albeit well used) 17th-century country estate, with the addition of modern roads. It is today the:

5. Villa Borghese, one of the most magnificent parks and gardens in Europe. The land was developed by Cardinal Scipio Borghese, a high churchman belonging to another of Rome's mighty families. In later years a Borghese prince was to marry Napoleon's sister, Pauline. The most striking feature of the Villa Borghese (aside from the palace, whose museum is described above) are its trees—stark and eerie looking, their trunks rising some 50 or more feet into the air without a single branch, only to burst forth in an evergreen canopy high above. Few activities are quite as pleasant as a slow stroll through the Villa Borghese on a sunny afternoon, pausing to admire carefully planned 17th-century vistas, ornamental fountains, and the magnificent trees.

From the Pincian Gate, cross the street and bear right down the path through the trees. Soon you'll see the equestrian statue of King Umberto I. That statue faces the:

6. Piazza di Siena, through a bit of intermediate territory. The piazza is a perfect oval ring, lined with elegant pines—a fine place for a picnic if you have time. Beyond the road at the far end of the piazza lies another section of the park whose iron fence you'll have to follow (to the left) for a while. Turn right at the gate and walk straight in. Soon you'll come to a delightful small lake, complete with Greek temple and rental rowboats.

Retrace your steps to the road and turn right. A walk the equivalent of several blocks brings you to another tract of gardening, this one dating from the 19th century.

7. The Pincio, stands on the summit of the Pincian Hill on the ancient site of the gardens of Lucullus. This formal garden was laid out by Napoleon's architect, Valadier. There are almost as many busts here as there are trees—almost all with new noses, since it seems a favorite sport to chip off the old marble ones. The main attraction of the Pincio is a wide terrace that overlooks the city from a vantage point high above piazza del Popolo. From the ornate balustrade, there's a fine view across the Tiber that includes the wooded slopes of Monte Mario and the Janiculum with the white dome of St. Peter's in between. It's a most romantic view, especially at sunset. And for an evening stroll, take:

8. La Scala Valadier, the stairs to the right that lead down the hill, past several fountains lit with golden-orange lights at night, until finally you arrive below at the:

9. Piazza del Popolo. Aside from the Pincio, this exquisitely balanced piazza is the only Roman reminder of the once-considerable influence of Napoleon. Valadier chose the sites for the central fountain, the flanking semicircular retaining walls, and the hillside of fountains. The matching baroque churches on either side of the Corso date from the 17th century. Like every part of Rome, this piazza has a long history. It was also a part of Lucullus's estate—a lavish one—and later was the burial site of several emperors, Nero among them. The area was supposedly haunted by that imperial ghost until a medieval pope tore down the tomb and consecrated the site. The obelisk is thousands of years old. It originally was Roman booty from the Egyptian city of Heliopolis and once stood in the Circus Maximus. It's surrounded today by four marble lions, carved with the initials of 19th-century tourists. At night, the thin sheets of water from the lions' mouths are illuminated by spotlights hidden in the marble basins below. A fashionable meeting place these days, piazza del Popolo boasts two sidewalk cafés—Canova, and the much better known Rosati—which are ideal for watching expensive Italian cars full of rich Italians doing expensive things.

There are buses from piazza del Popolo straight down the Corso to piazza Venezia and other points in town.

WALKING TOUR —— The Spanish Steps to Quirinale

Start: Scalinata di Spagna.
Finish: Quirinale.
Time: 2 hours.
Best Time: Sunday morning.
Worst Time: Morning and afternoon rush hours.

1. **The Scalinata di Spagna (Spanish Steps)** and the adjoining piazza di Spagna both take their name from the Spanish Embassy, which was in a palace here during the 19th century. The Spanish, however, had nothing to do with the construction of the steps. They were built by the French, and lead to the French church in Rome, Trinità dei Monti, and that's why they're called "Scala Della Trinità Dei Monti." There is nothing Spanish in their real Italian name. "Spanish Steps" is just an easy way of referring to them in English. The twin-towered church behind the obelisk at the top of the steps is early 16th century. The steps themselves are early 18th century. The French are in the church to this day, and the adjoining Villa Medici is now a French school.

   The Spanish Steps are at their best in spring, when the many flights are filled with flowers. You'll see a wide variety of types of people, most of them young, sitting around here anytime of the year. In the fall and winter, the population is much sparser, with only an occasional Roman soaking up a few of the sun's warming rays. It is a rare visitor who hasn't sat for a while on one of the landings—there's one every 12 steps—perhaps to read a letter from home or observe the other sitters. It's interesting to note that in the early 19th century the steps were famous for the sleek young men and women who lined the travertine steps flexing muscles and exposing ankles in hopes of attracting an artist and being hired as a model. The Barcaccia fountain at the foot was designed by Bernini's father at the end of the 16th century.

   There are two nearly identical houses at the foot of the steps on either side. One is the home of Babington's Tea Rooms (see refueling stop); the other was the house where the English romantic poet John Keats lived—and died.
2. **The Keats-Shelley Memorial,** at piazza di Spagna 26, has been bought by English and American contributors and turned into a museum. The rooms where Keats lived are chock-full of mementoes of the poet.

REFUELING STOP Babington's Tea Rooms, piazza di Spagna 23, was opened in 1896 by Miss Anna Maria Babington, and it has been serving homemade scones and muffins—along with a "good cuppa"—ever since, based on her original recipes. Celebrities and thousands upon thousands of tourists have stopped off here. Prices are high, however.

In the past the piazza di Spagna area was a favorite of English lords, who rented palaces hereabouts and parked their coaches on the streets. Americans predominate in the 20th century, especially since the main office of American Express is right on piazza di Spagna and dispenses all those letters (and money) from home. There's a street called:

3. Via della Croce that intersects the northern end of piazza di Spagna perpendicularly from the left. Follow this street for four blocks, passing vendors selling the choicest and most expensive fruit in town between parked cars, and small workrooms filled with dust, where old men are repairing 16th-century gilt frames, until you come to via del Corso. Continue straight across the Corso, where the street takes a sharp turn to the left. At the first intersection, turn right, and across the piazza is your next stop, the:

4. Mausoleo Augusteo (Augustus Mausoleum). This seemingly indestructible pile of bricks along via di Ripetta has been here for 2,000 years, and will probably remain for another 2,000. Like the larger tomb of Hadrian across the river, this was once a circular, marble-covered affair with tall cypress trees on the earth-covered dome. Many of the emperors of the 1st century had their ashes deposited in golden urns inside this building, and it was probably due to the resultant crowding that Hadrian decided to construct an entirely new tomb for himself. The imperial remains stayed intact until the 5th century, when invading barbarians smashed the bronze gates and stole the golden urns, probably emptying the ashes on the ground outside. The tomb was restored in the 1930s. You cannot enter, but you can walk around looking inside.

Across via di Ripetta, the main street on the far side of the tomb, is an airy glass-and-concrete building right on the banks of the Tiber 'at Ponte Cavour. Within it is one of the treasures of antiquity, the:

5. Ara Pacis (Altar of Peace), built by the Senate during the reign of Augustus as a tribute to that emperor and the peace he had brought to the Roman world. On the marble walls can be seen portraits of the imperial family—Augustus, Livia (his wife), Tiberius (Livia's son and the successor to the empire), even Julia (the unfortunate daughter of Augustus, exiled by her father for her sexual excesses). The altar was reconstructed from literally hundreds of fragments scattered in museums for centuries. A major portion came from the foundations of a Renaissance palace on the Corso. The reconstruction—quite an archeological adventure story in itself—was executed by the Fascists during the 1930s. The Ara Pacis (tel. 710-2071) is open April through September on Tuesday, Thursday, and Saturday from 9am to 1:30pm and 4 to 7pm; October to March, on Tuesday, Thursday, and Saturday from 9am to 2pm. Admission of 2,000 lire ($1.55) is charged.

Continuing south, take via del Corso, a shopping artery leading to piazza Colonna, and its Marcus Aurelius Column, which dominates the piazza. Here is the Palazzo Chigi, official residence of the Italian prime minister, and the Bernini-designed Palazzo di Montecitorio, east of the Italian legislature, the Chamber of Deputies (closed to the public).

From via del Corso, walk up the right side of via del Tritone and then follow the signs to the:

6. Fontana di Trevi. At piazza di Trevi, the Trevi Fountain is the most famous one in all of Rome. Tourists come here and toss a coin in the fountain, which according to legend ensures their return. Supplied by water from the Acqua Vergine aqueduct, it was based on the design of Nicolo Salvi and completed in 1762.

On one corner of the piazza, you'll see an ancient church with a strange claim to fame. In it are contained the hearts and viscera of several centuries of popes. This was the parish church of the popes when they resided at the Quirinal Palace on the hill above, and for many years each pontiff willed those parts of his body to the church.

To reach the Quirinal, take via Lucchesi from the church for two blocks, where it intersects with via Doloria. Turn left and straight ahead and you'll see the steps to the:

7. Palazzo de Quirinale. At the top of the stairs, you'll be in a wide pink piazza, piazza del Quirinale, with the palace of the president of Italy on your left. Until the end of World War II the palace was the home of the king of Italy, and before that it was the residence of the pope. In antiquity this was the site of Augustus's Temple

WALKING TOUR — THE SPANISH STEPS TO QUIRINALE

1. The Scalinata di Spagna (SpanishSteps)
2. The Keats-Shelley Memorial
3. Via della Croce
4. Mausoleo Augusteo (Augustus Mausoleum)
5. Ara Pacis (Altar of Peace)
6. Fontana di Trevi
7. Palazzo de Quirinale

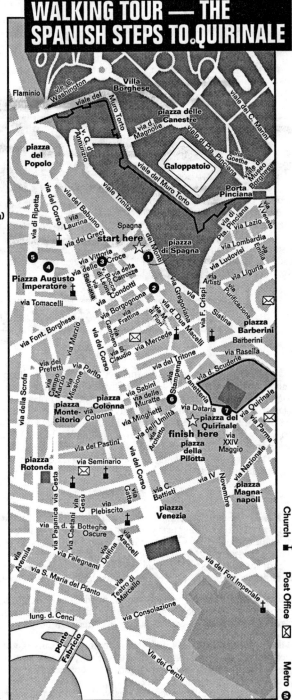

Church ✝   Post Office ✉   Metro Ⓜ

of the Sun. The steep marble steps that lead to Santa Maria d'Aracoeli on the Capitoline Hill once led to that temple. The great baths of Constantine also stood nearby, and that's the origin of some of the fountain statuary.

From here, your closest public transportation is on via Nazionale, reached by taking via della Consulta between the Palazzo della Consulta and the little park.

ORGANIZED TOURS

Because of the sheer volume of artistic riches, some visitors prefer to begin their stay in Rome with an organized tour. While few things can really be covered in any depth on these "overview tours," they are sometimes useful for getting the feel and geography of a complicated city. One of the leading tour operators (among the zillions of possibilities) is **American Express,** piazza di Spagna 38 (tel. 67641).

One of the most popular tours, which lasts 3 hours, is an orientation tour of Rome and the Vatican which costs 45,000 lire ($35.35) per person. Times of departure depend on the time of the year. For the same price, you can go on a "Rome of the Caesars" tour. One 3-hour tour takes visitors to the Sistine Chapel and Vatican Museum at a cost of 50,000 lire ($39.25). The major excursion outside Rome is to Tivoli, with its Villa d'Este and Villa Adriana, costing 60,000 lire ($47.10). You can also go farther afield, on a 1-day tour to Pompeii, Naples, and Sorrento, at a cost of 150,000 lire ($117.75) per person. But you'll need a lot of stamina, as the tour departs Rome at 7am, and returns at 11pm to your hotel.

2. SPORTS & RECREATION

SPORTS

SOCCER Soccer is one of the three or four all-consuming passions of thousands of Italians, richly intertwined with their image of the country. Rome boasts two intensely competitive teams, Lazio and Roma, which tend to play either against each other or against visiting teams from other parts of the world every Sunday afternoon. Matches are held at the **Olympic Stadium,** Foro Italico, viale dei Gladiatori (tel. 396-4661), originally built by Mussolini as a nationalistic (Fascist) statement. Thousands of tickets are sold during the 2 or 3 hours before each game. The players usually take a break during June, July, and August, beginning the season with something approaching pandemonium in September.

RECREATION

BIKING The traffic is murderous, and the pollution might make your head spin, but there are quiet times (early mornings and Sunday) when a spin beside the Tiber or through the Borghese Gardens might prove highly appealing. It's highly advisable to wear a helmet when bicycling, even if the local Vespa riders don't.

For itineraries especially engineered for cyclists in Italy, contact the **Federazione Ciclistica Italiana,** via Leopoldo Franchetti 2, 00194 Rome (tel. 06/36851).

BOWLING One of the city's largest bowling complexes, whose hordes of participants provide a spectacle almost more interesting than the game itself, lies at **Bowling Brunswick,** lungotevere Acqua Acetosa (tel. 396-6697).

GOLF Rome boasts at least three different golf courses, each of which will usually welcome members of other golf clubs. Each, of course, will be under the greatest pressure on Saturday and Sunday, so as a nonmember it would be best to schedule your arrival for a weekday.

One of the capital's newest courses, with a clubhouse set within a villa built during the 1600s and fairways designed by Robert Trent Jones, is the **Country Club Castelgandolfo,** via Santo Spirito 13, Castelgandolfo (tel. 931-3084). An older, more entrenched, and probably more prestigious course is the **Circolo del Golf Roma,** via Acqua Santa 3 (tel. 783407), about 8½ miles from the center of Rome. Near the Appian Way, about 12 miles from the center of town, lies the **Olgiata Golf Club,** largo Olgiata 15, off via Cassia (tel. 378-9141).

HORSEBACK RIDING   The most convenient of Rome's several riding clubs is the **Associazione Sportiva Villa Borghese,** via del Galoppatoio 23 (tel. 360-6797). Other stables are in the **Circolo Ippico Olgiata,** largo Olgiata 15 (tel. 378-8792), near Cassia, and the **Società Ippica Romana,** via Monti della Farnesina 18 (tel. 378-8792). Tack and equipment are English style.

JOGGING   Not only does jogging provide a moving view of the city's monuments, but it might improve your general health as well. Beware of the city's heat, however, and be alert to speeding traffic. Several possible itineraries include the park of the **Villa Borghese,** where the series of roads and pathways, some of them beside statuary, provide a verdant oasis within the city's congestion. The best places to enter the park are at piazza del Popolo or at the top of via Vittorio Veneto. The **Cavalieri Hilton International,** via Cadlolo 101, Monte Maria (tel. 31511), offers a jogging path (measuring a third of a mile) through the trees and flowering shrubs of its landscaping. The grounds that surround the **Villa Pamphilj** contain three running tracks, although they might either be locked or in use by local sports teams during your exercise period. Certain roads beside the Tiber might provide an almost-uninterrupted stretch for runners. A final possibility, not recommended for jogging after dark, is the rounded premises of the **Circus Maximus.** Built by the ancient Romans, and now reduced to dust and grandiose rubble, it contains a footpath inside its ruined walls, and an outward perimeter (ringed with roaring traffic) which measures about a half mile.

SWIMMING   One of the busiest all-year pools is the **Roman Sport Center,** via del Galoppatoio 33 (tel. 360-1667), which lies adjacent to the parking lot on the grounds of the Villa Borghese. Open to the public, it contains two large swimming pools, squash courts, a gym, and saunas. In another part of town, the **Piscina della Rose,** viale America (tel. 378-9141), is an Olympic-size pool open to the public (and crowded with teenagers and *bambini*) between June and September. More sedate, set in lushly landscaped gardens, and open to nonresidents, is the pool in the resort-inspired premises of the **Cavalieri Hilton International,** via Cadlolo 101 (tel. 31511).

TENNIS   The best tennis courts are at private clubs, many of which are within a handful of suburbs. Players are highly conscious of proper tennis attire, so be prepared to don your most sparkling whites and your best manners. One of the city's best-known clubs is the **Tennis Club Parioli,** largo de Morpurgo 2, via Salaria (tel. 839-0392).

3. SAVVY SHOPPING

Rome offers temptations of every kind, but this section will try to focus for you the urge to shop that sometimes overcomes even the most stalwart of visitors. You might find hidden oases of charm and value in hitherto unpublicized streets and districts, but what follows is a listing and description of certain streets known throughout Italy for the desirability of their shops. The monthly rental of floor space on these famous streets is very high, and some of those costs will almost certainly be passed on to the consumer. Nonetheless, a stroll down some of these streets usually presents a cross section of the most desirable wares in Italy.

Cramped urban spaces and a well-defined sense of taste has encouraged most

Italian stores to elevate the boutique philosophy to its highest levels. A boutique, at least in theory, is a smallish space filled with a well-defined congregation of specifically chosen merchandise for a specific type of client. The theory is that if you like what you see in a shop window, you'll find it duplicated, in spirit and style, inside. Lack of space, and definition of a merchandising program, usually restrict an establishment's merchandise to one particular style, degree of formality, or mood. Therefore, browse at will, and let the allure of the shop window communicate the mood and style of what you're likely to find inside.

Caveat: I won't pretend that Rome is Italy's finest shopping center (Florence and Venice are), or that its shops are unusually inexpensive—many of them aren't. But even on the most elegant of Rome's thoroughfares, there are values mixed in with the costly boutiques.

THE SHOPPING SCENE

I don't know who numbered Rome's streets—doubtless it was done centuries ago—but many times you'll find that the numbers start on one side of the street, run all the way down that side in sequence to the far end of the street, then change sides and run all the way back. Therefore, no. 500 is sometimes across the street from no. 1. Thus warned, you're ready to begin strolling.

Via Borgognona Beginning near piazza di Spagna, both the rents and the merchandise are chic and very, very expensive. Like its neighbor, via Condotti, it's a mecca for wealthy well-dressed women from around the world. Its architecture, and its storefronts, have retained their baroque or neoclassical facades.

Via Condotti Easy to find because it begins at the base of the Spanish Steps, this is probably the poshest and the most visible upper-bracket shopping street in Rome, and probably the best example in Europe of a certain kind of avidly elegant consumerism. Even the recent incursion of some less elegant stores hasn't diminished the allure of this street as a consumer's playground for the rich and the very, very rich.

Via del Corso Not attempting the stratospheric image (or prices) of via Condotti or Borgognona, the styles here tend to be aimed at younger consumers. There are, however, some gems scattered amid the shops selling jeans and sporting equipment. These you'll identify according to your particular tastes. This street had most of its automobile traffic diverted for some of its length, a lucky change that improved merchandising considerably. The most interesting shops are on the section nearest the fashionable cafés of piazza del Popolo.

Via Francesco Crispi Most shoppers reach this street by following via Sistina (see below) one long block from the top of the Spanish Steps. Near the intersection of these streets are several shops well suited for unusual and less expensive gifts.

Via Frattina Running parallel to via Condotti, it begins, like its more famous sibling, at piazza di Spagna. Part of its length is closed to traffic. Here, the concentration of shops is denser, although some aficionados claim that its image— and its prices—are slightly less chic and slightly less expensive than its counterparts on via Condotti. It is usually thronged with shoppers who appreciate the lack of motor traffic.

Via Nazionale The layout here recalls 19th-century grandeur and ostentatious beauty, but the traffic is horrendous; crossing via Nazionale requires a good sense of timing and a strong understanding of Italian driving patterns. It begins at piazza della Repubblica (with its great *Fountain of the Naiads* in front of the Baths of Diocletian) and runs down almost to the 19th-century monuments of piazza Venezia. There is an abundance of leather stores—more reasonable than in many other parts of Rome—many different apartment buildings, and a welcome handful of stylish boutiques.

Via Sistina Beginning at the top of the Spanish Steps, via Sistina runs from that point (the Trinità dei Monte) into piazza Barberini. Shops are small, stylish, and based on the personalities of their owners. Pedestrian traffic is less dense than on other major streets. It's convenient to combine a visit to this street with the aforementioned via Francesco Crispi.

Via Vittorio Veneto and via Piazza Barberini   Evocative of *La Dolce Vita* fame, via Vittorio Veneto is filled these days with expensive hotels and cafés and an array of relatively expensive stores selling shoes, gloves, and leather goods. Although it's considered a desirable address by day, this street can be rough at night, and motor traffic is always both dense and noisy.

SHOPPING A TO Z
ANTIQUES

Some visitors to Italy consider the trove of saleable antiques the country's greatest treasures. Long gone are the days when you could find priceless treasures for pocket change. The value of almost any antique has risen to alarming levels as increasingly wealthy Europeans have outbid one another in frenzies of acquisitive lust. You might remember that any antiques dealer who risks the high rents of central Rome to open an antiques store is probably acutely aware of the value of almost everything ever made, and will probably recognize anything of value long before his or her clients. Beware of fakes, remember to insure anything you have shipped home, and for larger purchases—anything over 625,000 lire ($490.65)—keep your paperwork in order to obtain your eventual tax refund. (See "What to Buy" in Chapter 2.)

If you love to shop for antiques, one street that you should not miss is **via dei Coronati.** Buried in a colorful section of the Campus Martius (Renaissance Rome), via dei Coronati is an antiquer's dream, literally lined with magnificent vases, urns, chandeliers, breakfronts, chaises, refectory tables, candelabra—you name it. You'll find the entrance to the street just north of piazza Navona. Turn left outside the piazza, past the excavated ruins of Domitian's Stadium, and the street will be just ahead of you. There are more than 40 antiques stores in the next four blocks, and on my last trip I saw in the windows inlaid secretaries, marble pedestals, claw and ball tables, gilded consoles, and enamel clocks, among countless other treasures. Bring your pocket calculator with you (and know how to use it), and keep in mind that stores are frequently closed between 1 and 4pm.

GALLERIA CORONARI, via dei Coronati 59. Tel. 686-9917.
Galleria Coronari is a desirable shop which might be used as a starting point to many other shops nearby. Many of its antiques are nostalgia-laden bric-a-brac small enough to fit into a suitcase, including jewelry, dolls, paintings, and elaborately ornate picture frames from the 19th century. Also represented is furniture from the 18th, 19th, and early 20th centuries, and such oddities as a completely furnished dollhouse, accurate even down to the miniature champagne bottles in the miniature pantry. Open on Monday from 3:30 to 7:30pm and Tuesday through Saturday from 10am to 1pm and 3:30 to 7:30pm.

ALBERTO DI CASTRO, piazza di Spagna 5. Tel. 679-2269.
One of Rome's most extensive antiques-dealing families is the di Castro family. Their main shop, established originally by the family's patriarch, Alberto di Castro, is located at the bottom of the frequently visited Spanish Steps. Many of the brothers, nephews, sisters, and nieces of Alberto di Castro run other shops, all named "di Castro's," which stretch along the length of via del Babuino, between piazza di Spagna and piazza del Popolo. Open on Monday from 3:30 to 7pm and Tuesday through Friday from 9am to 1pm and 3:30 to 7pm.

ART

GALLERIA D'ARTE SCHNEIDER, rampa Mignanelli 10. Tel. 678-4019.
Located near the Spanish Steps, this art gallery is named for a well-known American professor of art, Robert E. Schneider. It's worth a visit to see its changing exhibitions. Open Monday through Saturday from 4:30 to 7:30pm (closed August 15–30).

GIOVANNIA B. PANATTA FINE ART SHOP, via Francesco Crispi 117. Tel. 679-5948.
Giovanni B. Panatta Fine Art Shop, in business since 1890, is up the hill toward the

Borghese Gardens. Here you'll find excellent prints in color and black-and-white which cover a variety of subjects from 18th-century Roman street scenes to astrological charts. There is also a good selection of reproductions of medieval and Renaissance art that are extremely attractive and reasonably priced. Open Monday from 3:30 to 7:30pm and Tuesday through Saturday from 9:15am to 1pm and 3:30 to 7:30pm.

ALDO DI CASTRO, via del Babuino 71. Tel. 679-4900.

Aldo di Castro is one of the largest dealers of antique prints and engravings in Rome. You'll find rack after rack of depictions of everything from the Colosseum to the Pantheon, each evocative of the best architecture in the Mediterranean world, priced between $20 and $900, depending on the age and rarity of the engraving. Open on Monday from 3:30 to 7:30pm and Tuesday through Saturday from 9am to 1pm and 3:30 to 7:30pm.

IL PONTE, via di San Ignazio 6. Tel. 679-6114.

Il Ponte is one of the city's most tireless promoters of untested, developing artists and sometimes iconoclastic new kinds of art. The gallery specializes in modern sculptures, paintings, engravings, and is well known for sponsoring and commercializing the expositions of American artists, both resident and nonresident of Italy. Open Monday through Friday from 11am to 7pm.

BEAUTY CENTERS

SERGIO VALENTE BEAUTY CENTER, via Condotti 11. Tel. 679-1268.

This beauty center offers every cosmetic indulgence—fashion hair styling, coloring, scalp treatments, facials, manicures, massages, and saunas—in bright, luxurious surroundings. English is spoken. Open Tuesday through Saturday from 9:30am to 6pm.

BOOKSTORES

THE LION BOOKSHOP, via del Babuino 181. Tel. 322-5837.

The Lion Bookshop has U.S. and British books, including a section for children, the whole range of Penguin books, photographic books on Rome and Italy, and the most recent paperback fiction. Open Tuesday through Saturday from 9:30am to 1:30pm and 3:30 to 7:30pm (closed in August, Monday morning in winter, and Saturday afternoon in summer).

ECONOMY BOOK AND VIDEO CENTER, via Torino 136. Tel. 474-6877.

The Economy Book Center sells new and used American and English paperback books, a selection of U.S. magazines, and souvenir or get-acquainted videos on the major Italian cities. This store is one block from the piazza della Repubblica Metro station and numerous bus lines such as no. 64, 75, or 170. Open Monday through Friday from 9:30am to 7:30pm and on Saturday from 9:30am to 1:30pm.

RIZZOLI, largo Chigi 15. Tel. 679-6641.

Rizzoli's collection of Italian-language books is one of the largest in Rome, but if your native language is French, English, German, or Spanish, the interminable shelves of this very large bookstore have a section to amuse, enlighten, and entertain you. Open on Monday from 2:30 to 7:30pm and Tuesday through Saturday from 9am–2pm and 2:30–7:30pm.

DEPARTMENT STORES

COIN, piazzale Appio 15. Tel. 757-3241.

This bustling, workaday store is a Roman staple, known for carrying almost everything. Its selection of clothing is very large. Open on Monday from 4 to 8pm and Tuesday through Saturday from 9am to 1pm and 4 to 8pm.

LA RINASCENTE, piazza Colonna, via del Corso 189. Tel. 679-7691.

The upscale department store La Rinascente offers clothing, hosiery, perfume, cosmetics, housewares, and furniture. It also has its own line of clothing (Ellerre) for men, women, and children. This is the largest of the Italian department-store chains; its name is seen frequently on billboards and in newspaper ads throughout the country. Open on Monday from 2 to 7:30pm and Tuesday through Saturday from 9:30am to 7:30pm.

STANDA, corso Francia 124. Tel. 328-8254.

Rome's six Standa branches could not be considered stylish by any stretch of the imagination, but some visitors find it enlightening to wander—just once—through the racks of department-store staples to see what an average Italian household might accumulate. Other branches are at corso Trieste 200, via Trionfale, via Cola di Rienzo 173, viale Regina Margherita, and viale Trastevere 60. Open on Monday from 3:30 to 7:30pm and Tuesday through Saturday from 9am to 1pm and 2:30 to 7:30pm.

UPIM, piazza Santa Maria Maggiore. Tel. 736658.

Upim will sell you the full line of practical and unfussy department-store necessities that you may have forgotten before you left home. Other branches of this chain of stores are at via Alessandria 160, via Nazionale 211, and via del Tritone 172. Open on Monday from 1 to 7:30pm and Tuesday through Saturday from 9am to 7:30pm.

DISCOUNT SHOPPING

Certain stores that can't move their merchandise at any price often consign their unwanted goods to discounters. In Italy, the original labels are usually still inside the garment (and you'll find some very chic labels strewn in with mounds of other garments). Know in advance, however, that these garments couldn't be sold at higher prices in more glamorous shops, and some garments are either the wrong size, the wrong "look," or a stylistic mistake that the original designer wishes had never been produced.

DISCOUNT SYSTEM, via Viminale 35. Tel. 474-6545.

Discount System sells men's wear by many of the big names (Armani, Valentino, Nino Cerruti) and women's wear by such stars as Fendi and Krizia. It also has stacks and stacks of less noticeable names and, frankly, a great deal of formless, bland, and banal merchandise that will probably never sell at any price. However, don't give up hope: If you find something you like, know that it will be priced at around 50% of its original price tag in its original boutique, and it just might be a cut-rate gem well worth your effort. Open on Monday from 3:30 to 7:30pm and Tuesday through Saturday from 9:30am to 1pm and 3:30 to 7:30pm.

EYEGLASSES

LA BARBERA, via Barberini 74. Tel. 483628.

La Barbera, in business since 1837, has built a substantial reputation in the field of optical equipment. The store also carries a full spectrum of related wares: cameras, films, binoculars, opera glasses, and microscopes. You can have prescription glasses reproduced in 48 hours. For those fashionable hangouts on via Vittorio Veneto and piazza del Popolo, take a look at Barbera's collection of sunglass frames—more than 5,000 varieties. Open on Monday from 3:30 to 7:30pm and Tuesday through Saturday from 9am to 1pm and 3:30 to 7:30pm.

FABRICS

BISES, via del Gesu 93. Tel. 678-0941.

If you've been dreaming of richly ornate draperies, chic upholstery, or fabric for homemade fashion, you might be interested in the hundreds of bolts of cloth in stock at Bises. Most of their "yard goods" are made in Italy. Some bear such prestigious names as Valentino, and some are as stunningly beautiful as anything you're likely to find in all of Europe. Scattered amid the silk moirés are dozens of simple and practical cottons, so don't be daunted by the staggering variety. The store is beneath the frescoed ceilings of the Palazzo Altieri, which lend an undeniable elegance to the sometimes-exhausting business of rifling through hundreds of bolts of cloth. The salespeople can sometimes help to eliminate many hours of searching if you have something specific in mind. The section that inventories fabric for furnishings is open Monday through Friday from 9:30am to 1pm and 3:30 to 7:30pm. The section that stocks fabric for clothing is open on Monday from 3:30 to 7:30pm and Tuesday through Friday from 9:30am to 7:30pm.

FASHION
For Men

VALENTINO, via Mario de' Fiori 22. Tel. 678-3656.

Behind all the chrome and mirrors at via Mario de' Fiori is this swank emporium, which sells the men's clothing of this acclaimed designer. Here you can become the most fashionable man in town (if you can afford the high prices). Valentino's women's haute couture is sold around the corner, in an even bigger showroom at via Bocce di Leone 15 (tel. 679-5862). Open on Monday from 3 to 7pm and Tuesday through Saturday from 10am to 7pm.

GIORGIO ARMANI, via del Babuino 102. Tel. 679-6898.

The couturier who has dressed more movie stars on the screen than practically any other designer sells beautiful men's clothes here for a sometimes-staggering price. (What you pay here, however, is estimated to be 30% less than you'd pay in the U.S.) The less expensive men's line is a few storefronts away, at the Emporio Armani, via del Babuino 140. Open on Monday from 3:30 to 7:30pm and Tuesday through Saturday from 9:30am to 1pm and 3:30 to 7:30pm.

CUCCI, via Condotti 67. Tel. 679-1882.

Cucci—not to be confused with Gucci—has been a leading name in custom tailoring and shirt-making since 1912. Here you'll find beautifully made knitwear, sports shirts, and cashmere sweaters for both women and men. Many original designs are available. Cucci's also features handsome ties and scarves, along with an exclusive line of handmade moccasins. Open on Monday from 3:30 to 7:30pm and Tuesday through Saturday from 9:30am to 1:30pm and 3:30 to 7:30pm.

GIANNI VERSACE UOMO, via Borgognona 36. Tel. 679-5292.

Gianni Versace Uomo is the biggest Roman outlet for the famous designer's men's-wear line. The daring clothes are displayed in a long format of stone floors and white-lacquered walls. Open on Monday from 3:30 to 7:30pm and Tuesday through Saturday from 10am to 1:30pm and 3 to 7:30pm.

GIANFRANCO FERRE, via Borgognona 6. Tel. 679-7445.

This is the Rome outlet for Gianfranco Ferre's world-famous men's line. Open Monday through Thursday from 9:30am to 1pm and 3:30 to 7:30pm and on Friday and Saturday from 9:30am to 7:30pm.

CARLO PALAZZI, via Borgognona 7E. Tel. 678-9143.

Carlo Palazzi, in a 16th-century palazzo near the Spanish Steps, provides the modern man with a wardrobe of beautiful suits and shirts, either off the rack or custom-made. Amid the antique/modern decor and sculptures, you can also choose from a wide selection of knitwear, ties, belts, and whatever else a discerning man wears. Open on Monday from 3:30 to 7:30pm and Tuesday through Saturday from 9:30am to 1pm and 3:30 to 7:30pm (in July and August, closed Saturday afternoon instead of Monday morning).

RIBOT, via Vittorio Veneto 98A. Tel. 483485.

Ribot, in front of the Excelsior Hotel, offers exclusive ties; Peter Scott and Ribot exclusive cashmeres; all Burberry lines, including suits, jackets, and sportswear; plus Italian shoes made by Sutor exclusively for Ribot. Open on Monday from 3:30 to 7:30pm and Tuesday through Saturday from 9:30am to 1:30pm and 3:30 to 7:30pm.

For Women

KRIZIA, piazza di Spagna 77. Tel. 679-3419.

Krizia, near the corner of the famous street but still on the piazza, is the only outlet in Rome for one of Italy's best-received designers. Floor space is breathtakingly small and prices are breathtakingly high, but that won't prevent a crowd of women from struggling to acquire the jewelry, accessories, and silk or knit clothing that has made Krizia one of the very chic names in Italian fashion. Open on Monday from 3:30 to 7:30pm and Tuesday through Saturday from 9:30am to 7:30pm.

VANILLA, via Frattina 37. Tel. 679-0638.

Vanilla, a boutique for women, offers an unusual collection of sometimes offbeat items, including handmade, elaborately decorated sweaters and imaginative accessories. Open on Monday from 3:30 to 7:30pm and Tuesday through Saturday from 9:30am to 7:30pm.

PANCANI, via Sistina 117. Tel. 488434.

Pancani has a wispy, boutique look. The inventory at this small shop (whose ceiling has a fanciful fresco by well-known Roman artist Novella Parigini) includes well-cut clothes in muted pastels, sometimes in cashmere, for younger women. Open on Monday from 3:30 to 7:30pm and Tuesday through Saturday from 9:30am to 1pm and 3:30 to 7:30pm.

MAX MARA, via Frattina 28, at largo Goldoni. Tel. 679-3638.

Max Mara is one of the best outlets in Rome for women's clothing, if you like to look chic and witty. The fabrics are appealing and the alterations are free. Open on Monday from 3:30 to 7:30 pm and Tuesday through Saturday from 10am to 2pm and 3:30 to 7:30pm.

GIVENCHY, via Borgognona 21. Tel. 678-4058.

Givenchy is a Rome outlet for this world-famous Paris fashion house, one of the great couturiers. Open on Monday from 3 to 7pm and Tuesday through Saturday from 10am to 7pm.

SCOTCH HOUSE, via Borgognona 36. Tel. 678-2660.

Scotch House is an attractively cramped women's boutique with helpful saleswomen and a floor-to-ceiling collection of fashions by such European designers as Sonia Rykiel, Pancaldi, and Angelo Tarlazzi. Open on Monday from 3:30 to 8pm, Tuesday from 9:30am to 8pm, Wednesday from 9:30am to 1pm and 3:30 to 8pm, and Thursday through Saturday from 9:30am to 7:30pm.

GIANFRANCO FERRE, via Borgognona 42B. Tel. 679-0050.

Here you can find the women's line of this famous designer whose clothes have been called "adventurous." Open on Monday from 3:30 to 7:30pm and Tuesday through Saturday from 9:30am to 1:30pm and 3:30 to 7:30pm.

BENETTON, via Condotti 19. Tel. 679-0042.

Despite the gracefully arched ceiling of its showroom and its glamorous address on via Condotti, prices at this branch of the worldwide sportswear distributor are about the same as at branches at less glamorous addresses. Famous for woolen sweaters, tennis wear, blazers, and the kind of outfits you'd want to wear on a private yacht, this company has suffered (like every other clothier) from inexpensive Asian copies of its designs. The original, however, is still the greatest. Open on Monday from 3:30 to 7:30pm and Tuesday through Saturday from 9:30am to 7:30pm.

ELSY, via del Corso 106. Tel. 679-2275.

Elsy features women's clothing on two levels of ultramodern, warmly accented floor space. Open on Monday from 3:30 to 8pm and Tuesday through Saturday from 9:30am to 1pm and 3:30 to 8pm.

For Children

BENETTON, via Condotti 19. Tel. 679-0042.

Despite its elegant address (see above), Benetton isn't as expensive as you might expect. This store is an outlet for children's clothes (from infants to age 12) of the famous sportswear manufacturer. You can find rugby shirts, corduroys and jeans, and accessories for junior or your favorite nephews and nieces in a wide selection of colors and styles. Open on Monday from 3:30 to 7:30pm and Tuesday through Saturday from 9:30am to 7:30pm.

BABY HOUSE, via Cola di Rienzo 117. Tel. 321-4291.

Baby House offers what might be the most label-conscious collection of children's and young people's clothing in Italy. With an inventory of clothes suitable for children and adolescents to age 16, they sell clothing by Valentino, Bussardi, and Laura Biagiotti, whose threads are usually reserved for adult, rather than juvenile, playtime. Open on Monday from 3:30 to 7:30pm and Tuesday through Saturday from 9am to 1pm and 3:30 to 7:30pm.

THE COLLEGE, via Vittoria 52. Tel. 678-4073.

The College has everything you'll need to make adorable children more adorable, and less-adorable children at least presentable. Part of the inventory of this place is reserved for adult men and women, but the majority is intended for the infant and early adolescent offspring of the store's older clients. Open on Monday from 3:30 to 7:30pm and Tuesday through Saturday from 9:30am to 1pm and 3:30 to 7:30pm.

FOOD

CASTRONI, via Cola di Rienzo 196. Tel. 687-4383.

Castroni carries an amazing array of unusual foodstuffs from throughout the Mediterranean. If you want herbs from Apulia, pepperoncino oil, cheese from the Valle d'Aosta, or that strange brand of balsamic vinegar whose name you can never remember, Castroni will probably have it. Large, old-fashioned, and filled to the rafters with the abundance of agrarian Italy, it also carries certain foods that are considered exotic in Italy but commonplace in North America, such as taco shells and corn curls. Open Monday through Saturday from 8am to 2pm and 3:30 to 8pm.

GIFTS

A. GRISPIGNI, via Francesco Crispi 59. Tel. 679-0290.

At the corner of via Sistina is A. Grispigni, which has a large assortment of leather-covered boxes, women's purses, compacts, desk sets, and cigarette cases. Many items, like Venetian wallets and Florentine boxes, are inlaid with gold. Open on Monday from 3:30 to 7:30pm and Tuesday through Saturday from 9:30am to 1pm and 3:30 to 7:30pm.

LEMBO, via XX Settembre 25A. Tel. 488-3759.

Lembo is an excellent place to find such gifts as crystal, china, glassware, and sterling. Open Monday through Friday from 9am to 7:30pm and on Saturday from 9am to 2pm and 3:30 to 7:30pm.

ANATRIELLO BOTTEGA DEL REGALO, via Frattina 123. Tel. 678-9601.

Anatriello Bottega del Regalo is chock-full of high-quality gifts such as silver candelabra, elegant table lighters, and tea sets. Open on Monday from 3:30 to 7:30pm and Tuesday through Saturday from 9am to 1pm and 3:30 to 7:30pm (closed August 10–20).

GLOVES

Since the baroque days when grand courtesans outfitted themselves from toenail to fingernail with Italy's finest, gloves and glovemaking have been highly esteemed. Made by fitting oddly shaped pieces of suede, leather, or cloth into a covering for the human hand, wearing Italian gloves has for centuries been considered a high-style fashion statement.

ANTICOLI GLOVES FACTORY, piazza Mignanelli 21. Tel. 679-6873.

Anticoli Gloves Factory, a well-known establishment since 1920, is located conveniently near the bottom of the Spanish Steps. The oldest glove factory in Rome, it also has the largest selection. Since it is a direct factory outlet, it also has—for comparable quality—some of the best prices around. Open Monday through Saturday from 9:30am to 1:30pm and 3 to 7pm.

HATS

BORSALINO, via IV Novembre 157B. Tel. 679-4192.

Borsalino, the most famous hatmaker in Italy (perhaps even in the world) is chock-full of rakish hats reminiscent of the 1930s as well as other styles for both women and men. The store also sells ultra-well-made trousers and suits. Open on Monday from 3:30 to 8pm and Tuesday through Saturday from 9am to 1pm and 3:30 to 8pm.

JEWELRY

Since the ancient Romans imported amethyst and pearls from the distant borders of their empire, and the great trading ships of Venice and Genoa carried rubies and sapphires from Asia, the Italians have loved jewelry. That is still true today, as can be seen by the dozens of jewelry stores throughout Rome. Styles range from the most classically conservative to neo-punk-rock-frivolous, and part of the fun is shopping for styles you might never have considered to be your own.

BULGARI, via Condotti 10. Tel. 679-3876.

Bulgari, the capital's best and most prestigious jeweler, has the kind of shopfront and window displays that simply seem to breathe prosperity. There is very little inexpensive jewelry at Bulgari, and the price of some of the pieces reaches the millions (of dollars, not lire). The shop window, on a conspicuously affluent stretch of via Condotti, is a bit of a visual attraction in its own right; it attracts a minor assemblage of salivating hopefuls. Open on Monday from 3 to 7pm and Tuesday through Saturday from 10am to 7pm.

FEDERICO BUCCELLATI, via Condotti 31. Tel. 679-0329.

Federico Buccellati, one of the best gold- and silversmiths in Italy, sells Neo-Renaissance creations that will change your thinking about the way gold and silver are designed. Here you will discover the tradition and beauty of handmade jewelry and holloware with designs that recall those of Renaissance goldmaster Benvenuto Cellini. Open Tuesday through Saturday from 10am to 1:30pm and 3 to 7pm.

FORNARI, via Condotti 80. Tel. 679-2524.

Fornari specializes in sumptuous small jewelry and gift items for both sexes. The collection includes gold and silver jewelry, striking rings in traditional and modern designs, unusual bracelets, watches, silver key rings, chains, and necklaces, plus an array of charms. Open on Monday from 3:30 to 7:30pm and Tuesday through Saturday from 9:30am to 1:30pm and 3:30 to 7:30pm.

E. FIORE, via Ludovisi 31. Tel. 481-9296.

At E. Fiore, near via Vittorio Veneto, you can choose a jewel and have it set according to your specifications. Or you can make your selection from a rich assortment of charms, bracelets, necklaces, rings, brooches, corals, pearls, and cameos. Also featured are elegant watches, silverware, and goldware. Fiore also does expert repair work on jewelry and watches. Open on Monday from 3:30 to 7:30pm and Tuesday through Saturday from 9am to 1pm and 3:30 to 7:30pm (closed August).

KNITWEAR

MISSONI, via Borgognona 38B. Tel. 679-7971.

Missoni is the main outlet in Rome for this imaginative designer who is known for spectacular knitwear in kaleidoscopic patterns and colors. Open on Monday from 3:30 to 7:30pm and Tuesday through Saturday from 9:30am to 7:30pm.

LEATHER

Italian leather is among the very best in the world; it can attain butter-soft textures more pliable than cloth. You'll find hundreds of leather stores in Rome, many of them excellent.

LIMENTANI FRANCO, via Barberini 78. Tel. 482-7122.

Limentani Franco has a good assortment of such leather goods as handbags, wallets, and gloves; it also sells T-shirts, silk ties, silk scarves, and souvenirs. Open on Monday from 3:30 to 7:30pm and Tuesday through Saturday from 9:30am to 1pm and 3:30 to 7:30pm.

CESARE DIOMEDI LEATHER GOODS, via Vittorio Emanuele Orlando 96-97. Tel. 488-4822.

Cesare Diomedi Leather Goods, located in front of the Grand Hotel, offers one of the most outstanding collections of leather goods in Rome. And leather isn't all you'll find in this small, two-story shop with an attractive winding staircase. There are many other distinctive gift items—small gold cigarette cases, jeweled umbrellas—that make this a good stopping-off point for that last important item. Upstairs is a wide assortment of elegant leather luggage and accessories. Open on Monday from 3:30 to 7:30pm and Tuesday through Saturday 9am to 1pm and 3:30 to 7:30pm.

FENDI, via Gorgognona 36A-39. Tel. 679-7641.

Fendi is mainly known for its leather goods, but it has also furs, stylish purses, ready-to-wear clothing, and a new men's line of clothing and accessories. Gift items, home furnishings, and sports accessories are also sold in Fendi's, which is designated by an "F." Open on Monday from 3:30 to 7:30pm and Tuesday through Saturday from 9:30am to 7:30pm (closed Saturday afternoon from July to September).

PAPPAGALLO, via Francesco Crispi 115. Tel. 678-3011.

At Pappagallo ("Parrot"), a suede-and-leather factory, the staff make all manner of leather goods, including bags, wallets, suede coats. The quality is fine too, and the prices are reasonable. Open on Monday from 3:30 to 7:30pm and Tuesday through Saturday from 9am to 1pm and 3:30 to 7:30pm.

ELENA, via Sistina 81-82. Tel. 678-1500.

Elena is a lesser-known leather store. It has a good selection of handbags and wallets, but doesn't sell shoes or garments. Open on Monday from 3:30 to 7:30pm and Tuesday through Saturday from 10:30am to 7:30pm.

GUCCI, via Condotti 8. Tel. 679-0405.

Gucci, of course, is a legend. An established firm since 1900, its merchandise consists of high-class leather goods, such as suitcases, handbags, wallets, shoes, and desk accessories. It also has departments of elegant men's and women's wear, including beautiful shirts, blouses, and dresses, as well as ties and neck scarves of numerous designs. *La bella figura* is alive and well at Gucci, and prices have never been higher. Among the many temptations is Gucci's own perfume. Open on Monday from 3 to 7pm and Tuesday through Saturday from 10am to 7pm.

LINGERIE

BRIGHENTI, via Frattina 7-8. Tel. 679-1484.

At Brighenti, amid several famous neighbors on via Frattina, you might run across Gina Lollobrigida, Sophia Loren, or several hopeful lookalikes shopping for some "seductive fantasy." It is strictly *lingerie di lusso,* or perhaps better phrased, *haute corseterie.* Open on Monday from 3:30 to 7:30pm and Tuesday through Saturday from 9am to 1pm and 3:30 to 7:30pm (closed August).

TOMASSINI DI LUISA ROMAGNOLI, via Sistina 119. Tel. 488-1909.

Tomassini di Luisa Romagnoli offers delicately beautiful lingerie and negligees, all of which are original designs of Luisa Romagnoli. Her creations of frothy nylon, shimmery Italian silk, and fluffy cotton come either ready to wear or custom-made. Open on Monday from 3:30 to 7:30pm and Tuesday through Saturday 9am to 1pm and 3:30 to 7:30pm.

CESARI, via Barberini 1. Tel. 488-0048.

Cesari is an enormous shop set directly on piazza Barberini which sells lingerie and skillfully embroidered linens, towels, and handkerchiefs. Open on Monday from 3:30 to 7:30pm and Tuesday through Saturday from 9am to 1pm and 3:30 to 7:30pm.

LIQUORS

AI MONASTERI, piazza delle 5 Lune 76. Tel. 654-2783.

Ai Monasteri has one of the city's best selections; there's a treasure trove of liquors (including liqueurs and wines), honey, and herbal teas made in monasteries and convents all over Italy. You can buy excellent chocolates and other candies here as well. You make your selections in a quiet atmosphere which is reminiscent of a monastery, just two blocks from Bernini's *Fountain of the Four Rivers* in piazza Navona. The shop will ship some items home for you. Open Monday through Wednesday and Friday and Saturday from 9am to 1pm and 4:30 to 7:30pm, on Thursday from 9am to 1pm.

MARKETS

At the sprawling **open-air flea market** of Rome held every Sunday morning, every peddler from Trastevere and the surrounding Castelli Romani sets up a temporary shop. The vendors are likely to sell merchandise ranging from secondhand paintings of madonnas (the Italian market is glutted with these) to termite-eaten Il Duce wooden medallions (many of the homes of the lower-income groups still display likenesses of the murdered dictator), to pseudo-Etruscan hairpins, to bushels of rosaries, to 1947 television sets, to books printed in 1835. Serious shoppers can often ferret out a good buy. If you've ever been impressed with the bargaining power of the Spaniard, you haven't seen anything till you've viewed an Italian.

Go to the flea market in Trastevere, near the end of viale Trastevere (bus no. 75 to Porta Portese), then a short walk away to via Portuense, to catch the workday Roman in an unguarded moment. By 10:30am the market is full of people. Some of the vendors get there as early as midnight to get their choice space. As you would at any street market, beware of pickpockets. Open on Sunday from 7am to 1pm.

MOSAICS

Piecing together hundreds of multicolored pieces of stone, tile, or glass to make an image is an art form as old as ancient Rome. One of Italy's most venerated producers of mosaics is listed below.

SAVELLI, via Sant'Ufficio 27. Tel. 654-7017.

The selection here is probably the largest in Rome, and it includes reproductions of ancient mosaics discovered at archeological excavations in Pompeii and Ostia. Prices depend on the size and intricacy of detail, and range from $100 to $20,000 or more for full-blown masterpieces. Savelli will ship your purchase to America, Japan, or Australia, where you can proudly display it as the focal point of your living room, pool cabaña, or whatever. The outlet also has the largest selection of souvenirs in Rome, ranging from key chains to carved marble statues. Open Monday through Saturday from 9:30am to 5:30pm and on Sunday from 9:30am to 1:30pm.

RELIGIOUS ART

MARIA GUADENZI, piazza della Minerva 69A. Tel. 679-0431.

Set in a neighborhood loaded with purveyors of religious art and icons, this shop claims to be the oldest of its type in Rome. If you collect depictions of the Mother of Jesus, paintings of the saints, exotic rosaries, chalices, small statues, or medals, you can feel secure knowing that thousands of pilgrims have spent their money here before you. Whether you view its merchandise as a devotional aid or as bizarre kitsch, this shop has it all. Open on Monday from 3:30 to 7:30pm and Tuesday through Saturday from 9am to 1pm and 3:30 to 7:30pm (closed August 10–20).

SHOES

RAPHAEL SALATO, via Vittorio Veneto 104. Tel. 484677.

The elegant store of Raphael Salato, near the Excelsior Hotel, is where the style-conscious woman goes for the latest in shoe fashions. The selection of unusual and well-crafted shoes is wide. In addition, Raphael Salato stocks an exclusive line of children's shoes, plus bags and leather fashions. Other stores in Rome include via Vittorio Veneto 149 (tel. 482-1816), and piazza di Spagna 30 (tel. 679-5646). Open on Monday from 3:30 to 7:30pm and Tuesday through Saturday from 9:30am to 1:30pm and 3:30 to 7:30pm (closed Saturday afternoon in July and August).

SALVATORE FERRAGAMO, via Condotti 73-74. Tel. 679-8402.

Salvatore Ferragamo sells elegant and fabled footwear, plus women's clothing and accessories in an atmosphere full of Italian style. The name became famous in America when such silent-screen stars as Pola Negri and Greta Garbo began appearing in Ferragamo shoes. Open on Monday from 3 to 7pm and Tuesday through Saturday from 10am to 7pm.

FRAGIACOMO, via Condotti 35. Tel. 679-8780.

Fragiacomo sells shoes for both men and women in a champagne-colored showroom with gilt-painted chairs and big display cases. Open on Monday from 3:30 to 7:30pm and Tuesday through Saturday from 9:30am to 1:30pm and 3:30 to 7:30pm.

BRUNO MAGLI, via Vittorio Veneto 70A. Tel. 488-4355.

Bruno Magli offers dressy footwear for both sexes. There are other stores at via Barberini 94 (tel. 486850), via del Gambero (tel. 679-3802), and via Cola di Rienzo 237 (tel. 372-1972). Open on Monday from 3:30 to 7:30pm and Tuesday through Saturday form 9:30am to 1pm and 3:30 to 7:30pm.

DOMINICI, via del Corso 14. Tel. 361-0591.

Dominici, located behind an understated facade a few steps from piazza del Popolo, shelters an amusing and lighthearted collection of men's and women's shoes in a pleasing variety of vivid colors. The style is aggressively young-at-heart, and the children's shoes are adorable. Open on Monday from 3:30 to 8pm and Tuesday through Saturday from 9:30am to 1pm and 3:30 to 7:30pm.

SILVER

FORNARI, via Frattina 71-72. Tel. 679-2524.

Fornari has been providing fine silver to an international clientele for more than half a century. The showroom has two floors, on which are displayed the precision-crafted items that have earned this establishment the reputation of being the finest silversmith in Rome. Elegant silver trays and boxes, complete tea services, small gift items, handsome silver table settings, and many fine antique pieces, as well as modern gift items, are on display and can be shipped anywhere in the world. It's great fun to browse around inside and inspect the objects in elegantly curved brass-and-glass cases. In addition, the store has added a whole section of dishes and glassware, everything related to wedding listings for brides. Open on Monday from 3:30 to 7:30pm and Tuesday through Saturday from 9am to 1pm and 3:30 to 7:30pm.

TOYS

LA CITTA DEL SOLE, via della Scrofa 65. Tel. 687-5404.

This branch of La Città del Sole is the largest and best stocked of any of the stores in its nationwide chain. Its selection ranges from small and inexpensive toys to baroquely complicated puzzles that will challenge children's gray matter and drive their parents crazy. Also on sale are such rainy-day distractions as miniature billiard tables, tabletop golf sets, and electric train sets. Open on Monday from 3 to 8pm and Tuesday through Saturday from 10am to 7:30pm.

WINES

ENOTECA ROCCHI, via Alessandro Scarlatti 7. Tel. 855-1022.

Rocchi carries one of Rome's largest selection of wines and liqueurs; they'll ship your purchase anywhere. Open Monday through Saturday from 8:30am to 2pm and 4:30 to 8pm (closed August).

TRIMANI, via Goito 20. Tel. 497971.

Trimani, established in 1821, sells wines and spirits from Italy, among other offerings. Purchases can be shipped to your home. Open Monday through Saturday from 8:30am to 1:30pm and 3:30 to 8pm.

4. EVENING ENTERTAINMENT

When the sun goes down, lights across the city bathe palaces, ruins, fountains, and monuments in a theatrical white light. There are actually few evening occupations quite as pleasurable as a stroll past the solemn pillars of old temples or the cascading torrents of Renaissance fountains glowing under the blue-black sky. Of the **fountains,** the *Naiads* (piazza della Repubblica), the *Tortoises* (piazza Mattei), and of course, the *Trevi* are particularly beautiful at night. The **Capitoline Hill** is magnificently lit after dark, with its measured Renaissance facades glowing like jewel boxes. Behind the Senatorial Palace is a fine view of the **Roman Forum.** If you're staying across the Tiber, **piazza San Pietro** (in front of St. Peter's Basilica) is particularly impressive at night without tour buses and crowds. And a combination of illuminated architecture, Renaissance fountains, and, frequently, sidewalk shows and art expositions is at **piazza Navona.** If you're ambitious and have a good sense of direction, try exploring the streets to the west of piazza Navona, which look like a stage set when they're lit at night.

There are no inexpensive nightclubs in Rome, so be duly warned. Another important warning: During the peak of the summer visiting days, usually in August, all nightclub proprietors seem to lock their doors and head for the seashore. Many of them seem to operate alternate clubs at coastal resorts. Some of them close at different times each year, so it's hard to keep up-to-date. Always have your hotel check to see if a club is operating before you make a trek to it. Many of the legitimate nightclubs, besides being expensive, are highlighted by hookers plying their trade. Younger people fare better than some more sedate folk, as the discos open and close with free-wheeling abandon.

But remember that for many Romans, a night on the town means dining late at a trattoria. The local denizens like to drink wine and talk after their meal, even when the waiters are putting chairs on top of empty tables.

THE PERFORMING ARTS

CLASSICAL MUSIC

ACADEMY OF ST. CECILIA, via della Concilia zione. Tel. 654-1044.

Concerts given by the orchestra of the Academy of St. Cecilia take place at piazza di Villa Giulia, site of the Etruscan Museum from the end of June to the end of July (take bus no. 30); in winter they are held in the concert hall on via della Conciliazione.

Prices: Tickets 18,000–42,000 lire ($14.15–$32.95) for symphonic music, 18,000–32,000 lire ($14.15–$25.12) for chamber music.

RAI AUDITORIUM, Foro Italico. Tel. 368-65625.

Classical concerts are given by the RAI Symphony Orchestra on Saturday nights. Some of the concerts are also presented on a Friday afternoon, and many of these are especially designed for young people. You can purchase tickets for these concerts at an

agency, Orbis, piazza Esquilino 37, or at the auditorium at the Foro Italico. At either place you have to show up in person instead of telephoning.
Prices: Tickets 15,000 lire ($11.80).

OPERA

TEATRO DELL'OPERA, piazza Beniamino Gigli 1. Tel. 488-1755.

⭐ If you're in the capital for the opera season, usually from the end of December until June, you may want to attend the historic Rome Opera House, located off via Nazionale. The sale of tickets begins 2 days before a performance is scheduled.
Prices: Tickets 19,000–106,000 lire ($14.90–$83.20).

TERME DI CARACALLA, via delle Terme di Caracalla. Tel. 461755.

⭐ When the Romans stage an event, they like it to be of epic quality. At the Imperial Baths of Caracalla, you can attend summer performances of grand opera, usually from the first of July to the middle of August. Sponsored by the Teatro dell'Opera, the season is likely to include Verdi's *Aïda,* the best selection to employ the grandeur of the setting. The ending of *Aïda* is a smash—the celebrated "double scene," the floodlit upper part representing the Temple of Vulcan; the part underneath, the tomb. And for sheer unrivaled Cecil B. de Mille, it's worth seeing the phalanx of trumpeters enter in the second act, playing the "Grand March." They are followed by Egyptian troops, with banners, chariots, Ethiopian slaves, dancing girls—a spectacular crescendo.

Tickets are on sale at the Teatro dell'Opera (see above). If you don't mind taking along a pair of binoculars, try an unreserved seat.
Prices: Tickets 25,000 lire ($19.65) unreserved seat, 50,000–65,000 lire ($39.25–$51) numbered seat.

BALLET & DANCE

Performances of the **Rome Opera Ballet** are given at the Teatro dell'Opera (see above). The regular repertoire of classical ballet is supplemented by performances of internationally acclaimed guest artists, and Rome is on the major agenda for troupes from around the world, ranging from the United States to Russia. Major performances are at the Teatro dell'Opera, but watch for announcements in the weekly entertainment guides to Rome about other venues, including Teatro Olimpico or even open-air ballet performances. Both modern (such as the Alvin Ailey dancers) or classical dance troupes appear frequently in Rome. Check the entertainment guides to see what's happening at the time of your visit.

DINNER THEATER

FANTASIE DI TRASTEVERE, via di Santa Dorotea 6. Tel. 589-2986.

Roman rusticity is combined with theatrical flair at Fantasie di Trastevere, the "people's theater" where the famous actor Petrolini made his debut. Dressed in regional garb of Italian provinces, the waiters serve with drama. The cuisine isn't subtle, but it's good and bountiful. Such dishes as the classic saltimbocca (ham with veal) are prepared, preceded by tasty pasta (including one with a sauce made with red peppers) and everything is aided by the wines from the Castelli Romani. Accompanying the main dishes is a big basket of warm, country-coarse herb bread (you'll tear off hunks). Expect to pay 70,000–80,000 lire ($54.95–$62.80) for a full meal. If you visit for a drink, the first one will cost 30,000 lire ($23.55). Some two dozen folk singers and musicians in regional costumes perform, making it a festive affair. The theater is open from 8 to 11pm, and the folklore show, featuring both Roman and Neapolitan favorites, is presented from 9:30 to 10:30pm. It's closed Sunday.

THE CLUB & MUSIC SCENE
NIGHTCLUBS

ACROPOLIS, via Giovanni Schiapparelli 29-31. Tel. 322-1360.

Acropolis, entered at via Luciani 52 in spite of what the address says, is rated by many young Romans as the No. 1 disco. At night there are no buses running, so you'll have to rely on a taxi for your transportation. In the first part of the evening you're likely to hear anything from rap music to Bob Marley. But as the night progresses, the tones of these recorded selections grow more soothing. The club is open Tuesday through Sunday from 11pm to 4am.

Admission: 22,000–28,000 lire ($17.25–$22).

DIVINA, via Romagnosi 11A. Tel. 361-1231.

The aptly named Divina is a chic rendezvous, a relaxing piano bar where you just might end up spending the evening. Many people still come here looking for Gil's, a famous club that once stood on this spot which has gone down in Roman nightlife history. What you get today is a romantic evening in one of several small rooms lined with mirrors. It's open Tuesday through Saturday from 11pm to either 4 or 5am.

Admission (including one drink): Tues–Thurs 30,000 lire ($23.55), Fri–Sat 35,000 lire ($27.50). It is important to call for a reservation, as some nights are by invitation only, at which time you can't get in unless you're a "friend of the club" (frequent patron).

LA CABALA, at the Hostaria dell'Orso, via dei Soldati 25. Tel. 686-4221.

In this 14th-century Renaissance palazzo, near piazza Navona, the clientele usually wears stunning (but not formal) clothes. Two guitarists and a pianist entertain, and it's fun to sip and admire the scenery. It's magnificent Roman splendor, and shuts down in July and August. The building housing the hostaria and bar has a rich history. It was once a simple inn, constructed in 1300. Reportedly, St. Francis of Assisi once stayed here, as did Dante during the Jubilee Year. Later, as a hotel, it attracted such guests as Rabelais, Montaigne, and Goethe. It is open Monday through Saturday from 8:30pm to 4am. On the second floor is the Hostaria dell'Orso, one of the most famous restaurants of Rome, and on the first floor is a piano bar, Blue Bar, with live music.

Admission (including one drink): 35,000 lire ($27.50).

ARCILIUTO, piazza Monte Vecchio 5. Tel. 687-9419.

Arciliuto is one of the most romantic candlelit spots in Rome. It was reputedly the former studio of Raphael. From 10pm to 1:30am guests enjoy a musical salon ambience, listening to both a guitarist and flutist. The evening's presentation also includes live Neapolitan songs, old Italian madrigals, even current hits from Broadway or the London's West End. The setting and atmosphere are intimate. This highly recommended establishment is hard to find, but it's within walking distance of piazza Navona. Closed Sunday.

Admission (including first drink): 30,000 lire ($23.55); subsequent drinks are 10,000 lire ($7.85).

GILDA, via Mario dei Fiori 97. Tel. 678-4838.

Gilda is noted for its adventurous combination of nightclub, disco, and restaurant and for the glamorous acts it books. In the past it has hosted Diana Ross and splashy, Paris-type revues, often with young women from England and the United States. The artistic direction assures first-class shows, a well-run restaurant, an attractive bar, and recently released disco music played between the live musical acts. The restaurant opens at 9:30pm and occasionally presents shows. An international cuisine is featured, with meals costing from 85,000 lire ($66.75). The nightclub, opening at midnight, presents music of the 1960s as well as modern recordings. The club stays open daily until 3 or 3:30am.

Admission (including first drink): 35,000 lire ($27.50).

NOTORIOUS, via San Nicola de Tolentino 22. Tel. 474-6888.

Notorious really isn't. It's one of the most popular discos of Rome, open daily from 11pm to 4am. The music is always recorded. Some of the most beautiful people of Rome show up in these crowded confines, often in their best disco finery. But show up late—it's more fashionable.

Admission (including one drink): 30,000 lire ($23.55).

CASANOVA, piazza Rondanini 36. Tel. 654-7314.

Casanova crowds its patrons into two rooms. One room is a normal disco with recorded music. The second room is like a music hall with live music, both rock and disco, played by a group of five musicians. Hours are 11pm to 3:30am daily.

Admission: Sun–Thurs 20,000 lire ($15.70), Fri–Sat 30,000 lire ($23.55).

LE STELLE, via Beccaria 22. Tel. 361-1240.

Le Stelle attracts the "stars" (*le stelle* means stars in Italian) in the Roman nightlife galaxy. Successful since the day it opened, it lures young clients, many of whom are chicly dressed. After 3am the clients who show up are often older. Le Stelle is a slice of ancient Rome, with benches for sitting and stones on the floor. Hours are 11pm to 5am (sometimes 6am) Tuesday through Sunday (closed June to September). Drinks cost 15,000 lire ($11.80).

Admission: 30,000 lire ($23.55).

CABARET

DA MEO PATACCA, piazza dei Mercanti 30. Tel. 582552.

Da Meo Patacca, in Trastevere, would certainly have pleased Barnum and Bailey. On a gaslit piazza from the Middle Ages, it serves bountiful self-styled "Roman country" meals to flocks of tourists. The atmosphere is one of extravaganza—primitive, colorful, theatrical in a carnival sense—good fun if you're in the mood. From the huge open spit and the charcoal grill, many tempting platters are served. Downstairs is a vast cellar, studded with waves of strolling musicians and singers—a smash hit. Utilizing a tavern theme, the restaurant is decked out with wagon wheels, along with garlands of pepper and garlic. And many offerings are as adventurous as the decor: wild boar, wild hare, and quail; but there are also corn on the cob, pork and beans, thick-cut sirloins, and chicken on a spit. The antipasti—many succulent tidbits—are a good opener. Expect to spend 45,000 lire ($35.35) and up for a meal here. In summer, you can dine at outdoor tables. It's open daily from 8 to 11:30pm.

DA CICERUACCHIO, via del Porto 1. Tel. 580-6046.

Located on piazza dei Mercanti, the restaurant was once a sunken jail—the ancient vine-covered walls date from the days of the Roman Empire. Featured here are charcoal-broiled steaks and chops, along with lots of local wine. Bean soup is a specialty. The grilled mushrooms are another good opening, as is the spaghetti with clams. For a main course, I'd recommend scampi with curry or charcoal-broiled meats. You can dine here Tuesday through Sunday from 7:30 to 11:30pm for 30,000 lire to 60,000 lire ($23.55 to $47.10) and up.

AR FIERAMOSCA, piazza dei Mercanti 3A. Tel. 589-0289.

Ar Fieramosca, named after a medieval knight hero, is super-rustic, with large 15th-century fireplaces, waiters dressed as fishermen, and strolling musicians. Charcoal-grilled meats and seafood and a huge buffet are featured, and beer and wines are on tap. The restaurant is also known for its pizzas. Expect to pay at least 40,000 lire ($31.40) for a complete meal. It's open from 7pm to midnight Monday through Saturday.

JAZZ, SOUL & FUNK

MUSIC INN, largo dei Fiorentini 3. Tel. 654-44934.

Music Inn is considered the leading jazz club of Rome. Some of the biggest names in jazz, both European and American, are known to perform here. It's open Thursday through Sunday from 11pm to 3:30am.

Admission (including one drink): 30,000 lire ($23.55).

SAINT LOUIS MUSIC CITY, via del Cardella 13A. Tel. 474-5076.

Saint Louis Music City is another leading jazz venue. In large, contemporary surroundings, it doesn't necessarily attract the big names in jazz. What you get instead are young and sometimes very talented groups beginning their careers. Many celebrities have been known to patronize the place. Soul and funk music are also performed on occasion. You can also dine at a restaurant on the premises, where meals cost 35,000 lire ($27.50) and up. It is open Tuesday through Sunday from 9pm to 2am.

Admission: 15,000 lire ($11.80), plus 7,000 lire ($5.50) for an obligatory first drink.

ALEXANDERPLATZ, via Ostia 9. Tel. 372-9398.

At Alexanderplatz, a leading jazz club, you can hear jazz (not rock) every night except Sunday from 9pm to 2am. Entrance is free, and the price of your evening of listening pleasure depends on what you have to drink. A whisky costs 8,000 lire ($6.30). There is also a restaurant, with a good Italian kitchen, that serves everything from pesto alla genovese to gnocchi alla romana. A full meal begins at 30,000 lire ($23.55).

BIG MAMA, vicolo San Francesco a Ripa 18. Tel. 582551.

Big Mama is a hangout for jazz and blues musicians where you're likely to meet the up-and-coming jazz stars of tomorrow. But sometimes the big names appear as well. The entrance fee, therefore, depends on what's being presented. The club is open nightly from 9pm to 1:30am. Drinks begin at 7,000 lire ($5.50); beer, at 4,000 lire ($3.15).

Admission: 10,000–30,000 lire ($7.85–$23.55), depending on the show.

VELENO, via Sardegna 27. Tel. 482-1838.

Veleno is a Roman nightlife oddity, off via Vittorio Veneto and north of piazza Barberini. Many Romans often show up here in their fashionable finery to enjoy rap, soul, and funk music. It has also been a favorite on the celebrity circuit. It's open Tuesday through Saturday from 10pm to 4am.

Admission (including one drink): Men, Tues–Thurs 20,000 lire ($15.70), Fri–Sat 30,000 lire ($23.55); women, free.

BRAZILIAN MUSIC

Brazilian music is quite the rage in Rome these days. For a sampling of this nightlife diversion, visit the establishment listed below.

FONCLEA, via Crescenzio 82A. Tel. 689-6302.

Fonclea offers live music every night—jazz, Brazilian, or perhaps the sounds from other countries in South America. This is basically a cellar jazz establishment which attracts a cross spectrum of Roman life. The music starts at 10:30pm and usually lasts until 12:30pm. The club is open nightly from 8:30pm to 2:30am (on Friday and Saturday it stays open until 3:30am). There's also a restaurant which features grilled meats, salads, and crêpes. A meal starts at 30,000 lire ($23.55). But if you want dinner, it's best to reserve a table, as the club becomes crowded after 10:30pm. Closed July and August.

Admission: Obligatory first drink 6,000–10,000 lire ($4.70–$7.85).

GAY CLUBS

ANGELO AZZURO, via Cardinal Merry del Val 13. Tel. 580-0472.

Angelo Azzuro is a gay "hot spot," deep in the heart of Trastevere, which is open nightly except Monday from 11pm to 3:30am. No food is served, nor is live music presented. Men dance with men to recorded music, and women are also invited to patronize the club.

Admission (including obligatory first drink): 10,000 lire ($7.85).

L'ALIBI, via Monte Testaccio 44. Tel. 574-3448.

L'Alibi, in the Testaccio sector, away from the heart of Rome, is a year-round venue on many a gay man's agenda. The crowd, however, tends to be mixed, both Roman and international, straight and gay, male and female. One room is devoted to dancing. It's open Tuesday through Sunday from 11pm to 3:30am. Take bus no. 27, 57, 92, or 95 from largo Argentina near the Piramide. Drinks run 10,000 lire ($7.85).

Admission: Tues–Thurs and Sun 10,000 lire ($7.85), Fri 15,000 lire ($11.80), Sat 20,000 lire ($15.70).

THE BAR & CAFE SCENE

Unless you're dead set on making the Roman nightclub circuit, try what might be a far livelier and less expensive scene—sitting late at night on via Vittorio Veneto or piazza del Popolo (see below)—all for the cost of an espresso.

ON VIA VITTORIO VENETO

Back in the 1950s—a decade that *Time* magazine gave to Rome, in the way it conceded the 1960s to London—via Vittorio Veneto rose in fame and influence as the choicest street in Rome, crowded with aspirant and actual movie stars, their directors, and a fast-rising group who were card-carrying members of the so-called jet set. Fashions, of course, are one of the most fickle elements in social culture. Today the *belle gente* (beautiful people), movie stars, and directors wouldn't be caught dead on via Vittorio Veneto—even with night-owl sunglasses. In the course of time, via Vittorio Veneto has moved into the mainstream of world tourism (no first-timer should miss it). It's about as "in" and undiscovered today as pretzels. But you may want to spend some time there.

GRAN CAFFE DONEY, via Vittorio Veneto 139-143. Tel. 482-1788.

Gran Caffè Doney is one of Rome's most enduring cafés. It began in Florence in 1822, and came to Rome in 1884. The via Vittorio Veneto location opened in 1946. Legend has it that only foreigners go there, but they must like it, as they return year after year. In fact, Doney is now considered more fashionable than the Caffè de Paris (see below). While you're eating lunch at a sidewalk table, pedestrians walk right through the maze, inspecting your chicken-salad sandwich. A cup of coffee costs 4,000 lire ($3.15); a two-course light meal, 35,000 lire ($27.50). Service is from 8:30am to 12:30am in the cafeteria, the pastry and chocolate shop, and the bar. From 10am to 12:30am, you can also order light lunch or dinner, as well as items listed above. From 8pm to midnight September to June, piano music is played. If you've got it, flaunt it at the Doney every night except Monday.

CAFFE DE PARIS, via Veneto 90. Tel. 488-5284.

A rival café across the street from Gran Caffè Doney, the Caffè de Paris rises and falls in popularity depending on the decade. In the 1950s it was a haven for the fashionable, and now it's a popular restaurant in summer where you can occupy a counter seat along a bar or select a table inside. However, if the weather's right, the tables spill right out onto the sidewalk, and the passing crowd walks through the maze. A cup of coffee costs 5,000 lire ($3.95) if you sit outside. Hours are 8:30am to 1:30am Thursday through Tuesday.

HARRY'S BAR, via Vittorio Veneto 148. Tel. 474-5832.

Harry's Bar is a perennial favorite. Every major Italian city (Florence and Venice, for example) seems to have one, and Rome is no exception, although the one here has no connection with the others. This haunt of the IBF—International Bar Flies—at the top of via Vittorio Veneto is elegant, chic, and sophisticated. In summer, sidewalk tables are placed outside, but off-season the ambience is more intimate, with walls of tapestry, ornate wood paneling, carved plastering, and Florentine sconces. In back is a small dining room, which serves good but expensive food, meals going for 60,000 lire to 85,000 lire ($47.10 to $66.75). A whisky costs 9,000 lire to 12,000 lire ($7.05 to $9.40). The bar is open from 11:30am to 1:30am; closed Sunday and August 1–10.

PIAZZA DEL POPOLO

The piazza is haunted with memories. According to legend, the ashes of Nero were enshrined here, until 11th-century residents began complaining to the pope about his imperial ghost. The Egyptian obelisk seen here today dates from the 13th century B.C., removed from Heliopolis to Rome during the reign of Augustus (it originally stood at the Circus Maximus). The present piazza was designed in the early 19th century by Valadier, Napoleon's architect. The twin baroque churches also stand on the square, overseeing the never-ending traffic.

CAFE ROSATI, piazza del Popolo 4-5. Tel. 361-1418.

Café Rosati, which has been around since 1923, attracts Fellini and Zeffirelli types, plus an assortment of guys and dolls of all persuasions who drive up in Maseratis and Porsches. It's really a sidewalk café/ice-cream parlor/candy store/confectionery that has been swept up in the fickle world of fashion. The later you go, the more interesting the action. Whisky at a table begins at 9,500 lire ($7.45). It's open daily from 7:30am to 1am (closed Tuesday November through March).

CANOVA CAFE, piazza del Popolo. Tel. 361-2231.

Although management has filled the interior with boutiques that sell expensive gift items, including luggage and cigarette lighters, many Romans still consider this the place to be on piazza del Popolo. The Canova has a sidewalk terrace for pedestrian-watching, plus a snack bar, a restaurant, and a wine shop inside. In summer you'll have access to a courtyard whose walls are covered with ivy and where flowers grow in terra-cotta planters. Expect to spend 1,000 lire (80¢) for a coffee at the stand-up bar. If ordered at a table, coffee costs 5,000 lire ($3.95). A complete fixed-price meal is offered for 30,000 lire ($23.55). Food is served from noon to 3:30pm and 7 to 11pm, but the bar is open from 7am to midnight or 1am. It's closed Monday except from May to October.

NEAR THE PANTHEON

Many visitors to the Eternal City now view piazza della Rotonda, located across from the Pantheon, and reconstructed by the Emperor Hadrian in the first part of the 2nd century A.D., as the "living room" of Rome. This is especially true on a summer night.

DI RIENZO, piazza della Rotonda 8-9. Tel. 686-9097.

Di Rienzo, the most desirable café here, is open daily from 7am to 1:30am. In fair weather you can sit at one of the sidewalk tables (if you can find one free) and contemplate life on the square and the Pantheon. In cooler weather you can retreat inside, where the walls are inlaid with the type of marble found on the Pantheon's floor. You can order a coffee at 3,500 lire ($2.75), or a complete meal, which will cost from 30,000 lire ($23.55). Many types of pasta appear on the menu, as does risotto alla pescatora (fisherman's rice) or several meat courses such as roast veal. You can also order pizzas.

CAFFE SANT'EUSTACHIO, piazza Sant'Eustachio 82. Tel. 686-1309.

Strongly brewed coffee might be considered one of the elixirs of Italy, and many Romans will walk many blocks for what they consider a superior brew. Caffè Sant'Eustachio, one of the most celebrated espresso shops, is on a small square near the Pantheon, where the water supply comes from a source outside Rome, which the Emperor Augustus funneled into the city with an aqueduct in 19 B.C. Rome's most experienced espresso judges claim that the water plays an important part in the coffee's flavor, although steam forced through ground Brazilian coffee roasted on the premises has an important effect as well. Stand-up coffee at this well-known place costs 1,000 lire (80¢); if you sit, you'll pay 2,500 lire ($1.95). Purchase a ticket from the cashier for as many cups as you want, and leave a small tip (about 100 lire, 8¢) for the counterperson when you present your receipt. It's open from 8am to 1am every day except Monday, although on Saturday it stays open until 1:30am.

IN TRASTEVERE

Piazza del Popolo lured the chic and sophisticated from via Vittorio Veneto, and now several cafés in the district of Trastevere, across the Tiber, threaten to attract the same from Popolo. Fans who saw Fellini's *Roma* know what **piazza di Santa Maria in Trastevere** looks like. The square—filled with milling throngs in summer—is graced with an octagonal fountain and a church which dates from the 12th century. On the piazza, despite a certain amount of traffic, children run and play, and occasional spontaneous guitar fests are heard when the weather's good.

CAFE-BAR DI MARZIO, piazza di Santa Maria in Trastevere 14B. Tel. 581-6095.

This warmly inviting place, which is strictly a café (not a restaurant), has both indoor and outdoor tables at the edge of the square with the best view of its famous fountain. Whisky begins at 9,000 lire ($7.05), and a coffee goes for 2,500 lire ($1.95). It's open Tuesday through Sunday from 7am to 2am.

ON THE CORSO

CAFE ALEMAGNA, via del Corso 181. Tel. 678-9135.

The monumental Café Alemagna is usually filled with busy shoppers. You'll find just about every kind of dining facility a hurried resident of Rome could want, including a stand-up sandwich bar with dozens of selections from behind a glass case, a cafeteria, and sit-down area with waiter service. The decor includes high coffered ceilings, baroque wall stencils, globe lights, crystal chandeliers, and black stone floors. Pastries start at 1,000 lire (80¢). It's open Monday through Saturday from 7:30am to 11:50pm.

NEAR THE SPANISH STEPS

ANTICO CAFFE GRECO, via Condotti 86. Tel. 679-1700.

✪ Off and on since 1760, Antico Caffè Greco has been the poshest and most fashionable coffee bar in Rome. Attired in the trappings of the turn of the century, it has for years enjoyed a reputation as the gathering place of the literati. Previous sippers included Stendhal, Goethe, even D'Annunzio. Keats would also sit here and write. Today, however, you're more likely to see dowagers on a shopping binge and American tourists, but there's plenty of atmosphere here. In the front is a wooden bar, and beyond that a series of small salons, decorated in the 19th-century style with oil paintings in gilded frames. You sit at marble-top tables of Napoleonic design, against a backdrop of gold or red damask, romantic paintings, and antique mirrors. Waiters are attired in black tailcoats. A cup of cappuccino costs 5,000 lire ($3.95). The house specialty is a paradiso, made with lemon and orange, costing 6,000 lire ($4.70). The caffè is open Monday through Saturday from 8am to 9pm, closing for 10 days in August (days vary).

ENOTECA FRATELLI ROFFI ISABELLI, via della Croce 76. Tel. 679-0896.

The fermented fruits of the vine have played a prominent role in Roman life since the word "Bacchanalian" was first invented (and that was very early indeed), and one of the best places to taste the wines of Italy is at Enoteca Fratelli Roffi Isabelli. A stand-up drink within its darkly antique confines might be the perfect ending to a visit to the nearby Spanish Steps. Set behind an unflashy facade in a chic shopping district, this is the best repository for Italian wines, brandies, and grappa. You can opt for a postage-stamp table in back, if you desire, or stay at the bar with its impressive display of wines which lie stacked upon shelves in every available corner. It's open daily except Sunday from 8am to 1:30pm and 5 to 8pm. A glass of wine costs 2,000 lire to 8,000 lire ($1.55 to $6.30), depending on its quality. Grappa costs 4,000 lire ($3.15) and up.

NEAR PIAZZA COLONNA

GIOLITTI, via Uffici del Vicario 40. Tel. 678-0410.

For devotees of *gelato* (addictively tasty ice cream), Giolitti is one of the city's most popular nighttime gathering spots; in the evening, it's thronged with strollers with a sweet tooth. To satisfy that craving, try a whipped-cream–topped Giolitti cup of gelato. The ice cream costs from 2,000 lire ($1.55). Some of the sundaes look like Vesuvius about to erupt. During the day, good-tasting snacks are also served. Many people take gelato out to eat on the streets; others enjoy it in the post-Empire splendor of the salon inside. You can have your "coppa" from 7am to 2am every day except Monday. There are many excellent, smaller *gelateria* throughout Rome, wherever you see the cool concoction advertised as *produzione propria* (homemade).

NEAR PIAZZA NAVONNA

BAR DELLA PACE, via della Pace 3. Tel. 686-1216.

Bar della Pace, located near piazza Navona, has elegant neighbors, such as Santa Maria della Pace, a church with sybils by Raphael and a cloister designed by Bramante. The bar dates from the beginning of this century, with wood, marble, and mirrors forming its decor. Along with the chic Hemingway bar (see below), della Pace forms the golden Romulus and Remus on the Roman nightlife circuit. It's open daily except Monday from 9:30am to either 2:30 or 3am. A whisky begins at 7,000 lire ($5.50).

GARDENIA, via del Governo Vecchio 98. Tel. 689-2542.

Gardenia has its admirers. Decorated in a turn-of-the-century style, it's a soothing choice to stop in for a drink in the evening—any time from 9pm to 2am daily except Sunday. While listening to mellow recorded music, you can order cappuccino at 5,000 lire ($3.95), or perhaps a cocktail at 8,000 lire ($6.30). The staff will also serve you crêpes, even a chocolate mousse, at prices beginning at 7,000 lire ($5.50).

HEMINGWAY, piazza delle Coppelle 10. Tel. 654-4135.

Hemingway's discreet door is located off one of the most obscure piazzas in Rome. Inside, the owners have re-created a 19th-century decor beneath soaring vaulted ceilings which shimmer from the reflection of various glass chandeliers. An interior room repeats in scarlet what the first room did with shades of emerald. Evocations of a Liberty-style salon are strengthened by the sylvan murals and voluptuous portraits of reclining odalisques. Assorted painters, writers, and creative dilettantes occupy the clusters of overstuffed armchairs, listening to conversation or classical music. The establishment is open Monday through Saturday from 9am to 3am. Drinks cost 18,000 lire ($14.15).

IRISH PUBS

It's an indication of the diversity of their tastes that young Italians are drawn in large numbers to Irish-style pubs. The two most popular ones are previewed below.

FIDDLER'S ELBOW, via dell'Olmata.

Fiddler's Elbow, in the vicinity of piazza Santa Maria Maggiore near the railway station, is reputedly the oldest pub in the capital. It's open daily except Monday from 5pm to 12:15am; a pint of Guinness is 5,000 lire ($3.95). Sometimes, however, the place is so packed you can't find room to drink it.

DRUID'S DEN, via San Martino Monto 28. Tel. 488-0258.

Druid's Den, an establishment similar to Fiddler's Elbow and equally popular, is open daily from 8:30pm to 1am. Here, while enjoying a pint of beer at 5,000 lire ($3.95), you can listen to recorded Irish music. A group of young Irishmen one night even did the Irish jig in front of the delighted Roman spectators. The "den" is also in the vicinity of piazza Santa Maria Maggiore and the train station.

MOVIES

PASQUINO, vicolo del Piede 19. Tel. 580-3622.

In Trastevere, not too far from piazza di Santa Maria in Trastevere, the little Pasquino draws a faithful coterie of English-speaking fans including Italians and expatriates. It's located on a small street deep in the district, across the Tiber. The average films—usually of recent vintage—cost 6,000 lire ($4.70).

5. EASY EXCURSIONS

Most European capitals are ringed with a number of scenic attractions, and as far as sheer variety, Rome tops all of them. Just a few miles away, you can walk across the cemetery of U.S. servicemen killed on the beaches of Anzio in World War II, or go back to the dawn of Italian history and explore the dank tombs the Etruscans left as their legacy.

You can wander around the ruins of Hadrian's Villa, the "queen of villas of the ancient world," or be lulled by the music of baroque fountains in the Villa d'Este. You can drink the golden wine of the Alban hill towns (Castelli Romani), or turn yourself bronze on the beaches of Ostia di Lido—or even explore the ruins of Ostia Antica, the ancient seaport of Rome.

Unless you're rushed beyond reason, allow at least 3 days for taking a look at the attractions in the environs. I've highlighted the best of the lot below.

TIVOLI

GETTING THERE

The town of Tivoli is 20 miles east of Rome on via Tiburtina—about an hour's drive with traffic. Even if you don't have a car, you won't have to take a guided tour, as a bus leaves from via Volturno, around the corner from via Gaeta in Rome (piazza dei Cinquecento) nearly every 20 minutes. Or you can take an Acotral coach from via Gaeta, in the heart of Rome, one block west of via Volturno, near piazza dei Cinquecento. Buses leave every 20 minutes.

WHAT TO SEE & DO

Tivoli, known as Tibur to the ancient Romans, was the playground of emperors. Today its reputation continues unabated: It's the most popular half-day jaunt from Rome. The ruins of Hadrian's Villa as well as the Villa d'Este, with their fabulous fountains and gardens, remain the two chief attractions of Tivoli—and both should be seen, even if you must curtail your sightseeing in Rome.

Right inside the town, you can look at two villas before heading to the environs of Tivoli and the ruins of Hadrian's Villa.

VILLA D'ESTE, piazza Trento, viale delle Centro Fontane. Tel. 0774/22070.

⭐ Like Hadrian centuries before, Cardinal Ippolito d'Este of Ferrari believed in heaven on earth. In the mid-16th century he ordered this villa built on a hillside. The dank Renaissance structure, with its second-rate paintings, is hardly worth the trek from Rome, but the gardens below—designed by Pirro Ligorio—dim the luster of Versailles.

Visitors descend the cypress-studded slope to the bottom, and on their way are rewarded with everything from lilies to gargoyles spouting water, torrential streams, and waterfalls. The loveliest fountain—on this there is some agreement—is the *Fontana dell'Ovato,* designed by Ligorio. But nearby is the most spectacular achievement—the hydraulic organ fountain, dazzling visitors with its water jets in front of a baroque chapel, with four maidens who look tipsy. The work represents the genius of Frenchman Claude Veanard.

Don't miss the moss-covered, slime-green *Fountain of Dragons,* also by Ligorio, and the so-called *Fountain of Glass* by Bernini. The best walk is along the promenade which has 100 spraying fountains. The garden, filled with rhododendron, is worth hours of exploration, but you'll need frequent rest periods after those steep climbs.

Admission: 10,000 lire ($7.85).

Open: Feb–Oct, daily 9am–6:30pm; Nov–Jan, daily 9am–4pm. **Transportation:** The bus from Rome stops right near the entrance.

VILLA GREGORIANA, largo Sant'Angelo. Tel. 0774/21249.

Whereas the Villa d'Este dazzles with artificial glamour, the Villa Gregoriana relies more on nature. The gardens were built by Pope Gregory XVI in the 19th century. At one point on the circuitous walk carved along a slope, visitors stand and look out onto the most spectacular waterfall (Aniene) at Tivoli. The trek to the bottom on the banks

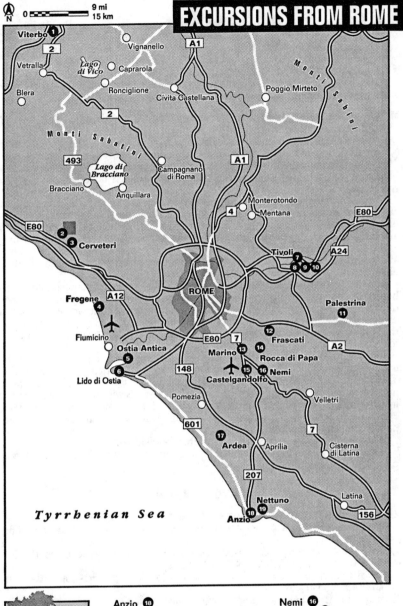

EXCURSIONS FROM ROME

N

0 _____ 9 mi
_____ 15 km

Viterbo ①

Vignanello

A1

② Vetralla

Caprarola

Lago di Vico

Blera

Ronciglione

Civita Castellana

Monti Sabini

Poggio Mirteto

②

Monti Sabatini

493

Lago di Bracciano

Campagnano di Roma

A1

Bracciano

Anquillara

Monterotondo

④

Mentana

E80

E80

② Cerveteri
③

Tivoli ⑦
⑧ ⑨ ⑩
A24

Fregene ④

ROME

Palestrina
⑪

Fiumicino

E80 7

⑫ Frascati

A2

Ostia Antica
⑤

Marino ⑬ ⑭
Rocca di Papa

Lido di Ostia ⑥

148

⑮ ⑯ Nemi
Castelgandolfo

Pomezia

Velletri

601

⑰ Ardea

Aprilia

7

Cisterna di Latina

207

Latina

Tyrrhenian Sea

Nettuno
⑱ ⑲

Anzio

156

Anzio ⑱
Ardea ⑰
Castelgandolfo ⑮
Cerveteri ③
Frascati ⑫
Fregene ④
Hadrian's Villa (Villa Adriana) ⑧
Lido di Ostia ⑥
Marino ⑬
Necropolis of Cerveteri ②

Nemi ⑯
Nettuno ⑲
Ostia Antica ⑤
Palestrina ⑪
Rocca di Papa ⑭
Tivoli ⑦
Villa d'Este ⑨
Villa Gregoriana ⑩
Viterbo ①

ITALY

ROME

of the Anio is studded with grottoes and balconies which open onto the chasm. The only problem is that if you do make the full journey, you may need a helicopter to pull you up again (the climb back is fierce). From one of the belvederes there is an exciting view of the Temple of Vesta on the hill.

Admission: 2,500 lire ($1.95).

Open: Daily 9am to 1 hour before sunset. **Transportation:** The bus from Rome stops near the entrance.

VILLA ADRIANA (Hadrian's Villa), via di Villa Adriana. Tel. 0774/ 530203.

Of all the Roman emperors dedicated to *la dolce vita*, the globe-trotting Hadrian spent the last 3 years of his life in the grandest style. Less than 4 miles from Tivoli he built one of the greatest estates ever erected in the world, and filled acre after acre with some of the architectural wonders he'd seen on his many trips.

Perhaps as a preview of what he envisioned in store for himself, the emperor even created a representation of hell centuries before Dante got around to recording its horrors in a poem. A patron of the arts, a lover of beauty, and even something of an architect, Hadrian directed the staggering feat of constructing much more than a villa—a self-contained world for a vast royal entourage and the hundreds of servants and guards they required to protect them, feed them, bathe them, and satisfy their libidos.

On the estate were erected theaters, baths, temples, fountains, gardens, and canals bordered with statuary. Hadrian filled the palaces and temples with sculpture, some of which now rests in the museums of Rome. In later centuries, barbarians, popes, and cardinals, as well as anyone who needed a slab of marble, carted off much that made the villa so spectacular. But enough of the fragmented ruins remain for us to piece together the story.

For a glimpse of what the villa used to be, see the plastic reconstruction at the entrance. Then, following the arrows around, look in particular for the Marine Theater (the ruins of a round structure with Ionic pillars); the Great Baths, with some intact mosaics; and the Canopus, with a group of caryatids whose images are reflected in the pond, as well as a statue of Mars. For a closer look at some of the items excavated, you can visit the museum on the premises and a museum and visitor center near the villa parking area.

Admission: 8,000 lire ($6.30) adults, free for children.

Open: Daily 9am–sunset (about 7:30pm in summer, 4pm in Nov–Mar). **Bus:** 2 or 4 from Tivoli to the villa gateway.

WHERE TO DINE

LE CINQUE STATUE, via Quintillio Varo 1. Tel. 0774/20366.

Cuisine: ROMAN. **Reservations:** Recommended. **Bus:** The bus from Rome stops nearby.

$ Prices: Appetizers 10,000–12,000 lire ($7.85–$9.40); main courses 15,000–23,000 lire ($11.80–$18.05). AE, DC, MC, V.

Open: Lunch Fri–Wed 12:30–3pm; dinner Mon–Wed and Fri–Sat 7:30–10pm.
Closed: Aug 15–Sept 7.

This restaurant of much comfort is maintained by a single hard-working Italian family, who prepare a honest and unpretentious cuisine without a lot of fuss and bother. Everything is accompanied by the wines of the hill towns of Rome. Begin with such dishes as a pastiche of mushrooms or brains, or make a selection from their excellent antipasti offerings. Try rigatoni with fresh herbs, tripe fried Roman style, or a mixed fry of brains and vegetables. All the pasta is freshly made on the premises. They also have an amazingly wide array of ice creams and fruits.

ALBERGO RISTORANTE ADRIANO, via di Villa Adriana. Tel. 0774/ 529174.

Cuisine: ITALIAN. **Reservations:** Not required. **Bus:** 2 or 4 from Tivoli.

$ Prices: Appetizers 10,000–12,000 lire ($7.85–$9.40); main courses 15,000–22,000 lire ($11.80–$17.25). AE, DC, V.
Open: Lunch Tues–Sun 12:30–3pm; dinner Tues–Sun 8–10pm.

Albergo Ristorante Adriano might be the perfect stopover point either before or after you visit Hadrian's Villa. At the bottom of the villa's hill, in an ocher-colored building a few steps from the ticket office, it offers terrace dining under plane trees or indoor dining in a high-ceilinged room with terra-cotta walls, neoclassical moldings, and Corinthian pilasters painted white. Menu items—everything homemade—include roast lamb, saltimbocca, a variety of veal dishes, deviled chicken, a selection of salads and cheeses, and simple desserts.

OSTIA

GETTING THERE

Ostia Antica is one of the area's major attractions, particularly interesting to those who can't make it to Pompeii. If you want to see ancient and modern Rome, get your bikini and take the Metropolitana (subway) Line B from the Stazione Termini to the Piramide stop. Change there for the Lido train to Ostia Antica, about 16 miles from Rome. Departures are about every half hour, and the trip takes only 20 minutes. The Metro lets you off across the highway that connects Rome with the coast. It's just a short walk to the excavations.

Later, board the Metro again to visit the **Lido di Ostia,** the beach. Italy may be a strongly Catholic country, but the Romans don't allow religious conservatism to affect their bathing attire. This is the beach where the denizens of the capital frolic on the seashore and at times create a merry carnival atmosphere, with dance halls, cinemas, and pizzerias. The Lido is set off best at Castelfusano, against a backdrop of pinewoods. This stretch of shoreline is often referred to as the Roman Riviera.

WHAT TO SEE & DO

OSTIA ANTICA. Tel. 565-0022.

Ostia, located at the mouth of the Tiber, was the port of Ancient Rome. Through it were funneled the riches from the far corners of the empire. It was founded in the 4th century B.C., and became a major port and naval base primarily under two later emperors: Claudius and Trajan.

A thriving, prosperous city developed, full of temples, baths, theaters, and patrician homes. Ostia Antica flourished for about 8 centuries before it began eventually to wither and the wholesale business of carting off its art treasures began. Gradually it became little more than a malaria bed, a buried ghost city that faded into history.

Although a papal-sponsored commission launched a series of digs in the 19th century, the major work of unearthing was carried out under Mussolini's orders from 1938 to 1942 (the work had to stop because of the war). The city is only partially dug out today, but it is believed that all the chief monuments have been uncovered.

All the principal monuments are clearly labeled. The most important spot in all the ruins is piazzale delle Corporazioni, an early version of Wall Street. Near the theater, this square contained nearly 75 corporations; the nature of their businesses was identified by the patterns of preserved mosaics.

Greek dramas were performed at the ancient theater which was built sometime in the early days of the Empire. The classics are still aired here in summer (check with the tourist office for specific listings), but the theater as it looks today is the result of much rebuilding. Every town the size of Ostia had a forum, and during the excavations a number of pillars of the ancient Ostia Forum were uncovered. At one end is a 2nd-century B.C. temple honoring a trio of gods—Minerva, Jupiter, and Juno (little more than the basic foundation remains). In addition, there is a well-lit museum within the enclave, which displays Roman statuary along with some Pompeii-like frescoes. There are perfect picnic spots beside fallen columns or near old temple walls.

Admission: 8,000 lire ($6.30).

Open: Tues–Sun to 1 hour before sunset. **Metro:** Ostia Antica.

CASTELLI ROMANI

For the Roman emperor and the wealthy cardinal in the heyday of the Renaissance, the Castelli Romani (Roman Castles) exerted a powerful lure, and they still do. Of course, the Castelli are not castles, but hill towns—many of them with an ancient history. The wines from the Alban Hills will add a little *feu de joie* to your life. The ideal way to explore the hill towns is by car. But you can get a limited preview by taking one of the buses that leaves every 20 minutes from Rome from the Subaugusta stop of the Metro system (Linea A). For more information about particular routings, call 57531 for information. My selection of the most interesting towns follows.

MARINO

This hillside town, about 14 miles from Rome, out via Appia, is the most easily reached of Rome's satellites. It was the birthplace of the poetess Victoria Colonna, a friend of Michelangelo who greatly influenced his life. In spite of its charming fountains and interesting churches, it has been encroached upon by modern development, which drains much of its charm.

Other towns in the Castelli Romani are for most of the year more intriguing, but at grape-harvesting time in October, Marino is the liveliest spot in all of Italy. The fountains start spouting wine (you can drink all you want—free), and Bacchanalian revelry reigns supreme. The only trick is to avoid the snakelike line of homeward-bound Romans afterward. When stone sober, the Romans drive as if the Madonna were their own special protector. When filled with the golden wine of the Alban Hills, they descend like the Normans in their sack of the city.

CASTELGANDOLFO

Since the early 17th century this resort on Lake Albano, 16 miles from Rome, has been the summer retreat of the popes. As such, it attracts thousands of pilgrims yearly, although the papal residence, Villa Barberini, and its surrounding gardens, are private and open only on special occasions. Interestingly, the pope's summer place incorporates part of Domitian's imperial palace (but the pastimes have changed). Domitian (A.D. 51–96) was one of the most notorious of Roman emperors, reigning from A.D. 81. As he grew more and more despotic, he viciously persecuted his opponents until stabbed to death by a freed man (the instigation came from his wife, Domitia).

On days that the pope grants a mass audience, thousands of visitors—many of whom arrive on foot—stream into the audience hall. Pope Pius XII, worried about the thousands of people who waited out in the rain to see him, built this now air-conditioned structure to protect the faithful from the elements. On a summer Sunday, the pope usually appears on a small balcony in the palace courtyard, reciting with the crowd the noon Angelus prayers.

The seat of the papacy opens onto a little square in the center of the town, where holiday-makers sip their wine—nothing pontifical here. A chair lift transports visitors from the hillside town to the lake, where some of the aquatic competitions were held in the 1960 Olympics. The Church of St. Thomas of Villanova, on the principal square, as well as the fountain, reveal Bernini's hand. If you need to be sold more on visiting Castelgandolfo, remember that it was praised by the eminent guidebook writer Goethe.

ROCCA DI PAPA

Easily approached from Frascati (see below) is Rocca di Papa, the star sapphire in the Castelli Romani crown. Towering over all, the medieval village lies near what was supposedly the campground of Hannibal's legions. The most colorful time to visit is on market day, but any time can be good for those who are athletic. The narrow lanes are filled with kinks, swirls, ups and downs—more suitable for donkeys than those who grew up in the elevator era. The snug little houses hug the slopes like cliff dwellings. A greater peak still—3,130 feet high—is Monte Cavo, which you can drive to (not walk) from Rocca di Papa. It's the most scenic spot in the hill towns.

NEMI

The Romans flock to Nemi in droves, particularly from April through June for the succulent strawberry of the district—acclaimed by some gourmets as the finest in Europe. (In May, there's a strawberry festival.) Nemi was also known to the ancients. A temple to the huntress Diana was erected on Lake Nemi, which was said to be her "looking glass."

In A.D. 37, Caligula built luxurious barges to float on the lake. Mussolini, much later, drained Nemi to find the barges, but it was a dangerous time to excavate them from the lake's bottom. They were senselessly destroyed by the Nazis during their infamous retreat.

What to See and Do

While at Nemi, you can visit the Roman Ship Museum or **Museo delle Navi,** via di Diana (tel. 06/936-8140). The ships destroyed by the Nazis have been replaced by two scale models. The major artifacts on display are mainly copies, as the originals now rest in world-class museums. The museum is open daily from 9am to 2pm, and admission is 2,000 lire ($1.55) for adults, free for children under 18. To reach the museum, unless you're driving, you have to walk from the center of Nemi toward the lake.

The 15th-century **Palazzo Ruspoli,** a baronial estate, is the focal point of Nemi, but the hill town itself invites exploration—particularly the alleyways the local denizens call streets and the houses with balconies jutting out over the slopes. While darting like Diana through the Castelli Romani, try to time your schedule for lunch in Nemi.

Where to Dine

LA TAVERNA, via Nemorense 13. Tel. 06/936-8135.
   Cuisine: INTERNATIONAL. **Reservations:** Required.
$ Prices: Appetizers 6,000–8,000 lire ($4.70–$6.30); main courses 15,000–18,000 lire ($11.80–$14.15). AE, DC, MC, V.
   Open: Lunch Thurs–Tues 12:30–2pm; dinner Thurs–Tues 8–10pm.
Offering a large array of the dishes of the region, as well as a rustic atmosphere, La Taverna is worth the trouble it takes to get there. In April the *fragole* (wild strawberries) signs go out. Spring is also the time to order pappardella al sugo de lepre (large noodles with wild-game sauce), worthy of the goddess of the hunt. For a main dish, I suggest the chef's specialty, arrosto di abbacchio e maiale (it consists of both a pork chop and grilled lamb). If you want to have a Roman feast, accompany your main dish with large roasted mushrooms, priced according to size, and a small fennel salad. To top off the galaxy of goodies, it's traditional to order sambucca, a clear white drink like anisette, "with a fly in it." The "fly," of course, is a coffee bean, which you suck on for added flavor.

FRASCATI

Located about 13 miles from Rome out via Tuscolana, and some 1,073 feet above sea level, is Frascati, one of the most beautiful of the hill towns—known for the wine to which it lends its name and its villas. The town bounced back from the severe destruction caused by bombers in World War II. To get there, take one of the Acotral buses which leave from the Subaugusta stop of the Metro system (Linea A). You can also take a small train which leaves from the Ferrorie Laziali section of the central Stazione Termini in Rome. This train runs only to Frascati.

What to See and Do

Although bottles of Frascati wine are exported—and served in many of the restaurants and trattorie of Rome—tradition holds that the wine is best near the golden vineyards from which it came. Romans drive up on Sunday just to drink *vino*. To sample some of that golden white wine yourself, head for **Cantina Comandini, via E. Filiberto 1** (tel. 06/942-0307), right off piazza Roma. The Comandini family welcomes you to the wine cellar, a regional tavern in which they sell Frascati wine from their own vineyards. You can stop and drink the wine on the spot for only 4,500 lire ($3.55) per liter or 1,000 lire (80¢) per glass. This is not a restaurant, but they sell sandwiches to go with your wine for 3,500 lire ($2.75). They might also take you on a tour of the grottoes, where selected vintage bottles are carefully displayed. The tavern is open Monday through Saturday from 3 to 7pm.

For your other sightseeing, stand in the heart of Frascati, at piazza Marconi, to see the most important of the estates: **Villa Aldobrandini.** The finishing touches to this 16th-century villa were applied by Maderno, who designed the façade of St. Peter's. Only its gardens (free) may be visited. With its grottoes, yew hedges, statuary, and splashing fountains, it makes for an exciting outing. To visit the gardens, which are open only in the morning, go to Azienda di Soggiorno e Turismo, piazza Marconi 1 (tel. 06/942-0331), which is open Tuesday through Saturday from 9am to 1pm.

If you have a car, you can continue past the Villa Aldobrandini to **Tuscolo,** about 3 miles beyond the villa. An ancient spot with the ruins of an amphitheater which date from the 1st century B.C., Tuscolo offers what may be one of Italy's greatest views.

You may also want to go to the bombed-out **Villa Torlonia.** Its grounds have been converted into a public park, whose chief treasure is the "Theater of the Fountains," also designed by Maderno.

Where to Dine

CACCIANI RESTAURANT, via Armando Diaz 13. Tel. 06/942-0378.
  Cuisine: ROMAN. **Reservations:** Required on weekends.
$ **Prices:** Appetizers 10,000–15,000 lire ($7.85–$11.80); main courses 18,000–22,000 lire ($14.15–$17.25). AE, DC.
  Open: Lunch Wed–Mon 12:30–2:30pm; dinner Wed–Mon 7:30–10pm.
  Closed: Jan 6–16 and Aug 15–25.

Cacciani is the choicest restaurant in Frascati, where the competition has always been tough (Frascati foodstuffs once attracted Lucullus, the epicurean). A large, modern restaurant in the center of town, with a terrace commanding a view of the valley, Cacciani has drawn such long-departed celebrities as Clark Gable. The kitchen is exposed to the public, and it's fun just to watch the women wash the sand off the spinach. To get you started, I recommend the pasta specialties, such as fettuccine (thin noodles) or rigatoni alla vaccinara (oxtail in tomato sauce). For a main course, the baby lamb with a special sauce of white wine and vinegar is always reliable. There is a large choice of wines, which are kept in a cave under the restaurant.

PALESTRINA

If you go out via Prenestina for about 24 miles, you'll eventually come to Palestrina, a medieval hillside town which overlooks a wide valley.

WHAT TO SEE & DO

When U.S. airmen flew over in World War II and bombed part of the town, they scarcely realized their actions would launch Palestrina as an important tourist attraction. After the debris was cleared, a pagan temple—once one of the greatest in the world—emerged: the **Fortuna Primigenia,** rebuilt in the days of the empire but dating from centuries before.

Palestrina antedates the founding of Rome by several hundred years. It resisted conquest by the early Romans, and later took the wrong side in the civil war between Marius and Sulla. When Sulla won, he razed every stone in the city except the Temple of Fortune, and then built a military barracks on the site. Later, as a favorite vacation spot for the emperors and their entourages, it sheltered some of the most luxurious villas of the Roman Empire.

In medieval feuds, the city was repeatedly destroyed. Its most famous child was Pier Luigi da Palestrina, who is recognized as the father of polyphonic harmony.

The **Barberini Palace** (tel. 06/955-8100), high on a hill overlooking the valley, today houses Roman statuary found in the ruins, plus Etruscan artifacts, such as urns the equal of those in the Villa Giulia Museum in Rome. But the most famous work—worth the trip itself—is the "Nile Mosaic," a well-preserved ancient Roman work, the most remarkable one ever uncovered. The mosaic details the flooding of the Nile, a shepherd's hut, mummies, ibises, and Roman warriors, among other things. The museum is open daily: November through February, from 9am to 4pm; in March, from 9am to 5pm; in April, from 9am to 6pm; in May, from 9am to 6:30pm; June through August, from 9am to 7:30pm; in September, from 9am to 5:30pm; and in October, from 9am to 5pm. Admission is 6,000 lire ($4.70).

You'll also find a **cathedral** here which dates from 1100, with a mostly intact bell tower. It rests on the foundation of a much earlier pagan temple.

WHERE TO STAY & DINE

ALBERGO RISTORANTE STELLA (Restaurant Coccia), piazza della Liberazione 3, Palestrina, 00036 Roma. Tel. 06/955-8172. Fax 06/757-3360. 15 rms (all with bath), 1 suite. TEL

$ Rates: 35,000 lire ($27.50) single; 55,000 lire ($43.20) double; from 105,000 lire ($82.45) suite. Breakfast 6,500 lire ($5.10) extra. **Parking:** Free.

Albergo Ristorante Stella, a buff-colored hotel set in the commercial center of town, is located on a cobblestone square filled with parked cars, trees, and a small fountain. The simple lobby is filled with warm colors, curved leather couches, and autographed photos of local sports heroes. The restaurant is sunny. There is a small bar where you might have an apéritif before lunch. Meals begin at 30,000 lire ($23.55). The restaurant is open daily from noon to 3pm and 7 to 9pm.

ANZIO & NETTUNO

Motorists can visit Ostia Antica in the morning, then Anzio and Nettuno in the afternoon. Go out via Ostiense until you reach Route 8, which you take to the coast. Once at Lido di Ostia, you can head south along Route 41 to Anzio.

The two towns of Anzio and Nettuno are peaceful seaside resorts today, but to many Americans and English they conjure up bitter memories. On January 22, 1944, an Allied amphibious task force landed the U.S. VI Corps at both towns, as a prelude to the liberation of Rome. Fighting against terrific odds, the Allies lost many lives.

The Italian government presented 77 acres in **Nettuno** to the United States for a cemetery. The graves are visited today by those who lost relatives in the campaign. The cemetery contains graves not only of those who died on the beaches of Anzio and Nettuno (where holiday-makers now revel), but also of those who were killed in the Sicilian campaign.

The fields of Nettuno contain 7,862 American dead—39% of those originally buried (the others have been returned home by their relatives). In Nettuno, a Graves Registry office helps visitors locate the markers of particular servicemen. The neatly manicured fields are peppered with crosses and stars of David, plus the saddest sight of all: 488 headstones that mark the graves of the unknowns. The cemetery is open daily from 8am to 6pm.

In **Anzio,** you can visit the British cemetery filled with war dead. One memorial to B. J. Pownell, a gunner in the Royal Artillery, seems to symbolize the plight of all the young men who died on either side. "He Gave the Greatest Gift of All: His Unfinished Life." Gunner Pownell was struck down on January 29, 1944. He was 20 years old.

Anzio was the birthplace of both Nero and Caligula. Many wealthy Romans once erected villas here at the port said to have been founded by Antias, the son of Circe and Odysseus. In the ruins of Nero's fabulous villa, the world-famous statue of *Apollo Belvedere* was discovered.

FREGENE

The fame of this coastal city north of the Tiber—24 miles from Rome—dates back to the 1600s when the land belonged to the Rospigliosi, a powerful Roman family. Pope

Clement IX, a member of the wealthy family, planted a forest of pine which extends along the shoreline for 2½ miles and half a mile deep to protect the land from the strong winds of the Mediterranean. Today the wall of pines makes a dramatic backdrop for the golden sands and luxurious villas of the resort town. You can take a Civitavecchia-bound train from the Stazione Termini in Rome to Fregene, the first stop.

WHERE TO STAY & DINE

LA CONCHIGLIA, lungomare 4, Fregene, 00050 Roma. Tel. 06/646-0229. 36 rms (all with bath). A/C TV TEL **Bus:** The bus from Rome leaves from Lepanto Metro stop and takes passengers to the center of Fregene.

$ Rates (including full board): 105,000 lire ($82.45) per person. AE, DC, MC, V.
   Parking: Free.

La Conchiglia means "the shellfish" in Italian—an appropriate name for this hotel and restaurant right on the beach, which offers views of the water and of the pine trees. Its circular lounge is painted white, with built-in curving wall banquettes which face a cylindrical fireplace with a raised hearth. It seems like a setting for one of those modern Italian films, with its cubical upholstered chairs. A resort aura, however, is created by the large green plants. The bar in the cocktail lounge, which faces the terrace, is also circular. The rooms are comfortable and well furnished. Some contain a minibar.

It's also possible to stop by for a meal, and the food is good. Try, for example, spaghetti with lobster and grilled fish. Many excellent meat dishes are offered. Meals start at 40,000 lire ($31.40). The restaurant's in the garden, shaded by bamboo. Oleander flutters in the sea breezes. The restaurant is open daily from 1 to 3pm and 7 to 10pm.

ETRUSCAN HISTORICAL SIGHTS

CERVETERI [CAERE]

As you walk through the Etruscan Museum in Rome (Villa Giulia), you'll often see the word *Caere* written under a figure vase or a sarcophagus. This is a reference to the nearby town known today as Cerveteri. Caere was one of the great Etruscan cities of Italy, whose origins may go as far back as the 9th century B.C. Of course, the Etruscan town has long faded, but not the ✪ **Necropolis of Cerveteri.** The effect is eerie; Cerveteri is often called a "city of the dead."

When you go beneath some of the mounds, you'll discover the most striking feature of the necropolis—the tombs are like rooms in Etruscan homes. The main burial ground is called the Necropolis of Banditaccia. Of the graves thus far uncovered, none is finer than the Tomba Bella (sometimes called the Reliefs' Tomb), the burial ground of the Matuna family. Articles such as utensils and even house pets were painted in stucco relief. Presumably these paintings were representations of items the dead family would need in the world beyond. The necropolis is open May to September, Tuesday through Sunday from 9am to 6pm; other months, Tuesday through Sunday from 10am to 4pm. Admission is 8,000 lire ($6.30).

Cerveteri can be reached by bus or car. If you're driving, head out via Aurelia, northwest of Rome, for a distance of 28 miles. By public transportation, take Metro Line A in Rome to the Lepanto stop. From via Lepanto you can take an Actoral coach to Cerveteri; the trip takes about 1 hour and costs 2,300 lire ($1.80). Once at Cerveteri, it's a 1¼-mile walk to the necropolis. Just follow the signs that point the way.

TARQUINIA

If you wish to see tombs even more striking and more recently excavated than those at Cerveteri, go to Tarquinia. The medieval turrets and fortifications atop the rocky cliffs overlooking the sea seem to contradict the Etruscan name of Tarquinia. Actually, Tarquinia is the adopted name of the old medieval community of Corneto, in honor of the major Etruscan city that once stood nearby. The main attraction within the town is the ✪ **Tarquinia National Museum,** piazza Cavour (tel. 0766/856036), which is devoted to Etruscan exhibits and sarcophagi excavated from the necropolis a few miles away. The museum is housed in the Palazzo Vitelleschi, a Gothic palace which dates from the mid-15th century. Among the exhibits are gold jewelry, black vases with carved and painted bucolic scenes, and sarcophagi decorated with carvings of animals and relief figures of priests and military leaders. But the biggest attraction is in itself worth the ride from Rome—the almost life-size pair of winged horses from the pediment of a Tarquinian temple. The finish is worn here and there, and the terra-cotta color shows through, but the relief stands as one of the greatest Etruscan masterpieces ever discovered. The museum is open Tuesday through Sunday from 9am to 7pm May through October and 9am to 2pm in the off-season, and charges 8,000 lire ($6.30) admission.

The same ticket also admits you to the **Etruscan Necropolis** (tel. 0766/856308), which covers more than 2½ miles of rough terrain near where the ancient Etruscan city once stood. Thousands of tombs have been discovered here, some of which have not been explored even today. Others, of course, were discovered by looters, but many treasures remain even though countless pieces were removed to museums and private collections. The paintings on the walls of the tombs have helped historians reconstruct the life of the Etruscans—a heretofore impossible feat without a written history. The paintings depict feasting couples in vivid colors mixed from iron oxide, lapis lazuli dust, and charcoal. One of the oldest tombs (from the 6th century B.C.) depicts young men fishing while dolphins play and colorful birds fly high above. Many of the paintings convey an earthy, vigorous, sex-oriented life among the wealthy Etruscans. The tombs are generally open Tuesday through Sunday from 9am to 6pm (to 2pm November through March). You can reach the grave sites by taking a bus from the Barriera San Giusto to the Cimitero stop. Or try the 20-minute walk from the museum. Inquire at the museum for directions.

To reach Tarquinia by car, take via Aurelia outside Rome, and continue on the autostrada toward Civitavecchia. Bypass Civitavecchia and continue another 13 miles north until you see the exit signs for Tarquinia. As for public transportation, going by train is the preferred choice: a *diretto* train from the Stazione Termini takes 50 minutes. Also, eight buses a day leave from the via Lepanto stop in Rome for the 2-hour trip to the neighboring town, Barriera San Giusto, which is 1½ miles from Tarquinia. Bus schedules are available at the tourist office in Barriera San Giusto (tel. 856384), which is open Monday through Saturday from 8am to 2pm and 5 to 7pm.

VITERBO

The 2,000 years that have gone into the creation of the city of Viterbo, 62 miles north of Rome, make it one of the most interesting day trips from Rome. An hour away by car off the autostrada north (take the Orte exit), Viterbo traces its history back to the Etruscans. The bulk of its historical architecture, however, dates from the Middle Ages and the Renaissance, when the city was a residence—and hideout—for the popes. The old section of the city is still surrounded by thick stone walls that once protected the inhabitants from papal (or antipapal, depending on the situation at the time) attacks.

WHAT TO SEE & DO

The only way to see Viterbo properly is to take a **walking tour** where you wander through the narrow cobbled streets and pause in front of its remarkable structures. Begin at piazza del Plebiscito, which is dominated by the 15th-century town hall, and notice the fine state of preservation of Viterbo's old buildings. The courtyard and attractive fountain in front of the town hall and the 13th-century governor's palace are a favorite meeting place for townfolk and visitors alike.

Just down via San Lorenzo is the **Palazzo San Lorenzo,** the site of Viterbo's cathedral, which sits atop the former Etruscan acropolis. The Duomo, dating from 1192, is a composite of architectures, from its pagan foundations to its Renaissance facade to its Gothic bell tower. Next door is the 13th-century **Palazzo Papale,** built as a residence for the pope, but used as a hideout when the pope was in exile. It was also the site of three papal elections. The exterior staircase and the colonnaded loggia combine to make one of the finest examples of civil Roman architecture from the Gothic period.

The finest example of medieval architecture in Viterbo is the **San Pellegrino Quarter,** reached from piazza San Lorenzo by a short walk past piazza della Morte. This quarter, inhabited by working-class Viterboans, is a maze of narrow streets, arched walkways, towers, steep stairways, and ornamental fountains.

Worth a special visit is the **Convent of Santa Maria della Verità,** which dates from 1100. The church has 15th-century frescoes by Lorenzo da Viterbo, student of Piero della Francesca. But the real reason for visiting the convent is to see the Etruscan collection in the Municipal Museum (Museo Civica).

MUSEO CIVICO (Municipal Museum), piazza Crispi. Tel. 0761/340810.

Among the contents of the museum, which is housed in the cloisters, are several Etruscan sarcophagi, including ones that depict a red-haired woman and a red-faced fat man with a broken nose. The collection also includes sculpture (among them, an excellent Etruscan lion) and pottery. Adjoining the museum is a picture gallery with the best work of Sebastiano del Piombo (a student of Michelangelo), a painting of the dead Christ.

Admission: 6,000 lire ($4.70).

Open: May–Sept, Mon–Sat 8:30am–1:30pm and 3:30–7:30pm, Sun and hols 8:30am–1:30pm; Oct–Apr, Mon–Sat 8:30am–1:30pm and 3:30–6pm, Sun and hols 8:30am–1:30pm.

VILLA LANTE, Bagnaia. Tel. 0761/288-8008.

The English author Sacheverell Sitwell called Villa Lante, located in Bagnaia, a suburb of Viterbo, "the most beautiful garden in Italy"; indeed, it is a worthy contender with Villa d'Este at Tivoli for that title. Water from Mount Cimino flows down to the handsome fountains of the villa, running from terrace to terrace until it reaches the central pool of the magnificent garden, with statues, stone banisters, and shrubbery. Two symmetrical Renaissance palaces make up the villa. The estate is now partly a public park which is open during the day. The gardens that adjoin the villa, however, can only be visited on a guided tour. (The gatekeeper at the guard house will show you through, usually with a group that has assembled.) The interiors of the twin mansions can't be visited without special permission.

Admission: 30-minute garden tour, 4,000 lire ($3.15).

Open: May–Aug, Tues–Sun 9am–7:30pm; Mar–Apr and Sept–Oct, Tues–Sun 9am–5:30pm; Nov–Feb, Tues–Sun 9am–4pm. **Bus:** 6 from Viterbo.

PARCO DEI MOSTRI (Park of the Monsters), villa delle Meravisglie, Bomarzo. Tel. 0761/924029.

About 8 miles east of Bagnaia at Bomarzo lies the Park of the Monsters, which Prince Vicino Orsini had built in a deep valley, and which is overlooked by the Orsini Palace and the houses of the village. On the other side of the valley are stone cliffs. Prince Orsini's park, Bosco Sacro (Sacred Wood), is filled with grotesque figures carved from natural rock. The figures probably date from about 1560 (Annibale Caro, a Renaissance poet, refers to them in a letter he wrote in 1564). They rise mysteriously from the wild Tuscan landscape, covered with strangling weeds and moss. Nature and art have created a surrealistic fantasy: the Mouth of Hell (an ogre's face so big that people can walk into its gaping mouth), a crude Hercules slaying an Amazon, nymphs with butterfly wings, a huge tortoise with a statue on its shell, a harpy, a mermaid, snarling dogs, lions, and much, much more. If you need to refresh yourself after this excursion to the edge of madness, you'll find a snack shop near the entrance.

Admission: 8,000 lire ($6.30) adults, 7,000 lire ($5.50) children under 7.

Open: Daily 8am–dusk. **Bus:** Bomarzo bus from viale Trento in Viterbo.

NEARBY DINING

Instead of dining at Viterbo, I suggest a detour to La Quercia, less than 2 miles from the medieval center of Viterbo. (La Quercia, incidentally, was the seat of the Basilica of the Madonna of Quercia, with a cloister by Bernini, a bell tower by Sangallo, and a ceramic portal by della Robbia.)

AQUILANTI, via del Santuario 4. Tel. 0761/341911.
   Cuisine: ITALIAN. **Reservations:** Recommended. **Bus:** 6 from Viterbo.
$ Prices: Appetizers 12,000–15,000 lire ($9.40–$11.80); main courses 15,000–22,000 lire ($11.80–$17.25).
   Open: Lunch Wed–Mon noon–3pm; dinner Wed–Mon 7:30–10pm.
Aquilanti is the best place to eat in the area. The dining room, with a view of an Etruscan burial ground, does not disappoint those seeking good-quality Italian fare. Specialties include fettuccine allo stennarello, ravioli de ricotta e spinaci all'etrusca, plus vitella (veal) alla montanera, as well as a fabulous array of fruits and vegetables. The wine is from Orvieto.

ARDEA

In the village of Ardea, the **Raccolta Manzù,** via Sant' Antonio 1 (tel. 06/916-1022), is housed in a simple but effective museum. A short drive through the pine- and eucalyptus-studded countryside outside Rome, it is a unique tribute to Giacomo Manzù, a remarkable sculptor who was strongly influenced by the 15th-century works of Donatello and Rosso. His combination of classicism and individuality is especially apparent in his ecclesiastical figures. His portraits of his friend Pope John XXIII (they both came from Bergamo), and especially the huge bronze sculpture of *Il Grande Cardinale,* demonstrate this combination. Look for the oversize pram with the likenesses of the children on it. Also on display are articles of jewelry created by Manzù.
   The collection assembles more than 400 pieces (sculpture, drawings, etchings and lithographs, and gold and silver jewelry) from among the most significant works by Manzù over his half-century-long artistic career. Archives and documents are also collected in this museum. It's open daily from 9am to 7pm, and admission is free. The collection is now a special wing of the National Gallery of Modern Art in Rome. You can reach the museum by coach from Rome (E.U.R. Fermi). Ride the coach to Nettuno, and get off just before Ardea. The museum is nearby.

CHAPTER 6

INTRODUCING FLORENCE (FIRENZE)

- **WHAT'S SPECIAL ABOUT FLORENCE**
- **1. ORIENTATION**
- **2. GETTING AROUND**
- **FAST FACTS: FLORENCE**
- **3. NETWORKS & RESOURCES**

On the banks of the Arno, Florence has been a Roman stronghold since the 1st century B.C., but it was not until after A.D. 1200 that it began to come into its own as a commercial and cultural center. During the 13th century, merchants and tradesmen organized the guilds that controlled the city's economy and government for nearly 150 years. These guilds supervised the construction of several important buildings, and with their newfound wealth, they commissioned works of art that adorned the churches and palaces.

This revival of interest in art and architecture brought about the Italian Renaissance, an amazing outburst of activity between the 14th and the 16th centuries that completely changed the face of the Tuscan town. During its heyday under the benevolent eye (and purse) of the Medicis, the city was lavishly decorated with churches, palaces, galleries, and monuments, making it the world's greatest repository of art treasures. The list of geniuses who lived or worked here reads like a "who's who" in the world of art and literature: Dante, Boccaccio, Fra Angelico, Brunelleschi, Donatello, da Vinci, Raphael, Cellini, Michelangelo, Ghiberti, Giotto, and Pisano.

Efforts to preserve Florence as the "jewel of the Renaissance" have been successful, in spite of the calamities it has suffered during the past 400 years. Wars and floods have damaged some of its treasures. The flood of 1966 temporarily took the glow off the "jewel," but today Florence shines again almost as brightly as it did in the days of Michelangelo.

When the last Renaissance artist capitulated to the baroque and pundits began to evaluate the era, the question was asked, "Why was Florence the city chosen for the 'rebirth'?" Some long-forgotten individual emerged with the opinion that the Renaissance didn't choose Florence, but Florence chose the Renaissance.

The Florentines are a unique lot. A Genoese sailor could persuade Isabella to finance his expedition to the Americas, but it took a Florentine by the name of Amerigo Vespucci to get the country named after himself. The Florentines are the champions of the vigorous life. To adapt another saying, they believe in taking the dilemma by the horns. Thus the Florentine Dante wrote *The Divine Comedy* in the vernacular—and not only persuaded his readers to accept such a "vulgar" work but helped make the Tuscan dialect and language *the* tongue of Italy.

To appreciate Florence, to understand its treasures, we need to know something, however meager, of the boldness and tenacity of its people. So we'll check into our hotel first, look over the city's restaurants, and then set out on our task.

WHAT'S SPECIAL ABOUT FLORENCE

Museums

- ☐ Uffizi Galleries, one of the great art museums of the world, repository of masterpieces of the Renaissance.
- ☐ Pitti Palace, a complex of museums whose Galleria Palatina is second only to the Uffizi in art.
- ☐ Il Bargello, a treasure house of Renaissance sculpture, including works by Michelangelo and Donatello.

Religious Shrines

- ☐ Duomo, one of the largest cathedrals in the Christian world, begun in 1296 and consecrated in 1436, the dome by Brunelleschi.
- ☐ Battistero di San Giovanni, in front of the Duomo, famed for Lorenzo Ghiberti's pair of bronze exterior doors known as the *Gates of Paradise*.

Ace Attractions

- ☐ Piazza della Signoria, the political stage of Florence, set against the background of the Palazzo Vecchio and the statue-filled Loggia della Signoria.

- ☐ Galleria dell'Accademia, proud home of the world's most famous and most reproduced statue: Michelangelo's towering and majestic nude, *David*.
- ☐ Medici Chapels, in the Basilica di San Lorenzo, containing, among others, Michelangelo's tomb for Lorenzo de Medici, with the figures of *Dawn* and *Dusk*.

Shopping

- ☐ Some of the most elegant merchandise in Europe is for sale in the chic, fashion-conscious city of Florence, especially Florentine leather goods.

1. ORIENTATION

ARRIVING

BY PLANE   If you're flying from New York, the best air connection is to Milan where you can board a domestic flight to the **Galileo Galilei Airport** at Pisa (tel. 050/280088), 58 miles to the west of Florence. You can then take an express train to Florence in an hour.

There is also a small domestic airport, **Peretola,** on via del Termine, near the A11 (tel. 370125), which lies 3½ miles northwest of Florence, a 15-minute ride. It is mainly for such domestic destinations as Rome and Milan, and receives 35-seater planes. This airport can be reached by city bus service available on the ATAF line (no. 23C), departing from the main Santa Maria Novella rail terminal. Domestic air service is provided by **Alitalia,** lungarno degli Acciaiuoli 10-12 in Florence (tel. 27889).

BY TRAIN   A major stopover in Europe for holders of the Eurailpass, Florence lies in the heart of Italy. If you're coming north from Rome, count on a 2- to 3-hour trip, depending on your connection. Bologna is just an hour away by train, and if you decide to see Venice first, it's only 4 hours' traveling distance by train. The Santa Maria Novella rail station, in piazza della Stazione, adjoins piazza di Santa Maria Novella, which has one of the great churches of Florence. From here, most of the major hotels are within easy reach, either on foot or by taxi or bus. For railway information, phone 278783.

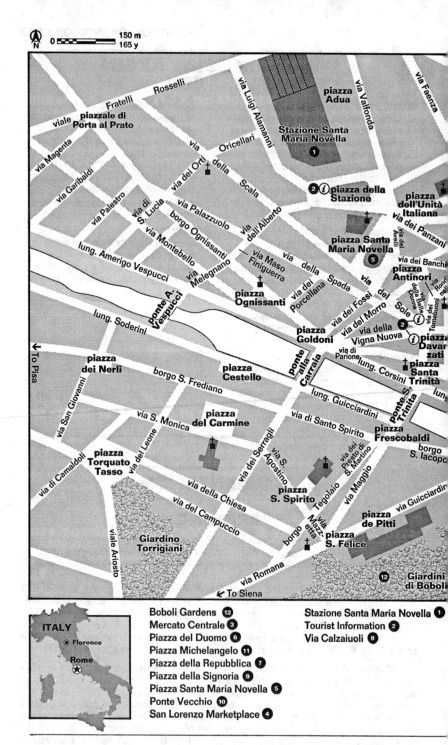

Boboli Gardens ⑫
Mercato Centrale ③
Piazza del Duomo ⑥
Piazza Michelangelo ⑪
Piazza della Repubblica ⑦
Piazza della Signoria ⑨
Piazza Santa Maria Novella ⑤
Ponte Vecchio ⑩
San Lorenzo Marketplace ④

Stazione Santa Maria Novella ①
Tourist Information ②
Via Calzaiuoli ⑧

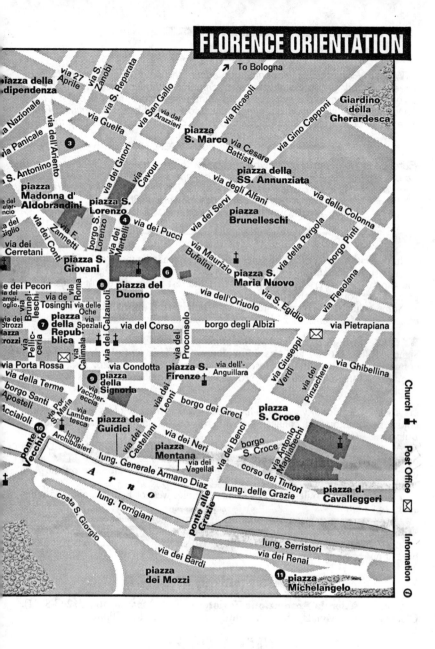

FLORENCE ORIENTATION

To Bologna

piazza della Indipendenza

via 27 Aprile

via S. Zanobi

via S. Reparata

via San Gallo

via dei Arazzieri

via Ricasoli

Giardino della Gherardesca

via Nazionale

via dell'Ariento

via Guelfa

piazza S. Marco

via Cesare Battisti

via Gino Capponi

via Panicale

❸

S. Antonino

via dei Ginori

via Cavour

piazza della SS. Annunziata

via degli Alfani

via della Colonna

piazza Madonna d' Aldobrandini

via del belar-ancio

piazza S. Lorenzo

via dei Servi

piazza Brunelleschi

via della Pergola

borgo Pinti

via F. Zannetti

a del iglio

via dei Conti

borgo S. Lorenzo

via dei Martelli

❹ via dei Pucci

via Maurizio Bufalini

via dei Cerretani

piazza S. Giovani

❽

piazza del Duomo

❻

piazza S. Maria Nuovo

via S. Egidio

via Fiesolana

e dei Pecori

ia dei ampi-oglio

via Brunel-leschi

via de Tosinghi

via Roma

via delle Oche

via delle Spaziali

via dell'Oriuolo

via dei Strozzi

piazza della Repub-blica

via dei Calzauoli

via del Corso

borgo degli Albizi

via Pietrapiana

iazza rozzi

via Pellic-ceria

via Calimala

via del Proconsolo

✉

via Ghibellina

via Porta Rossa

✉

via Condotta

piazza S. Firenze

via dell'-Anguillara

via Giuseppi Verdi

via dei Pinzachere

via della Terme

❾ piazza della Signoria

via Vaccher-eccia

via dei Leoni

borgo dei Greci

piazza S. Croce

borgo Santi Apostoli

via Por S. Maria

via Lamber-tesca

piazza dei Guidici

via dei Castellani

via dei Neri

via dei Benci

borgo S. Croce

via Antonio Magliabechi

Acciaioli

❿ ponte Vecchio

lung. Archibusieri

piazza Mentana

via dei Vagellai

corso dei Tintori

piazza d. Cavalleggeri

A r n o

lung. Generale Armano Diaz

lung. delle Grazie

lung. Torrigiani

ponte alle Grazie

costa S. Giorgio

lung. Serristori

via dei Renai

via dei Bardi

piazza dei Mozzi

⓫ piazza Michelangelo

Church ✝ Post Office ✉ Information ❶

IMPRESSIONS

[When in Florence] it's very popular to admire the Arno. It is a great historical creek with four feet in the channel and some scows floating around. It would be a very plausible river if they could pump some water into it. They all call it a river, and they honestly think it is a river do these dark and bloody Florentines. They even help out the delusion by building bridges over it. I do not see why they are too good to wade.
—MARK TWAIN, *THE INNOCENTS ABROAD,* 1869

Florence is the home of those who cultivate with an equal ardour Mah-jongg and a passion for Fra Angelico. Over tea and crumpets they talk, if they are too old for love themselves, of their lascivious juniors; but they also make sketches in water colour and read the Little Flowers of St. Francis.
—ALDOUS HUXLEY, *ALONG THE ROAD,* 1925

In the station is a bank in the outer hall, which exchanges money Monday through Saturday from 8:20am to 6:30pm. There is also a day hotel, Albergo Diurno, where you can take a shower after a long train ride and rest up. At the top of Track 16 is a place where you can store your luggage.

Some trains into Florence stop at the **Stazione Campo di Marte,** on the eastern side of Florence. A 24-hour bus service runs between the two rail terminals.

BY BUS   Long-distance buses service Florence, run by **SITA,** via Santa Caterina da Siena 15R (tel. 211487), and **Lazzi Eurolines,** via Mercadante 2 (tel. 215154). SITA connects Florence with such Tuscan hill towns as Siena, Arezzo, Pisa, and San Gimignano, and Lazzi Eurolines provides service from such cities as Rome and Naples.

BY CAR   If you're driving, you'll find that Florence, because of its central location, enjoys good autostrada connections with the rest of Italy, especially Rome and Bologna.

Autostrade A1 connects Florence with both the north and south of Italy. Drivers need about an hour to reach Bologna and about 3 hours to reach Rome in the south (or vice versa). The Tyrrhenian coast is only an hour from Florence on the A11 heading west.

Florence lies 172 miles north of Rome, 65 miles west of Bologna, and 185 miles south of Milan.

Use a car only to get to Florence. Don't even contemplate its use once there, as most of the monumental belt of central Florence is closed to all vehicles except those of local residents. For traffic information in Florence, or other questions you might have about bringing your car in, call 577777.

TOURIST INFORMATION

Contact the **Azienda Promozione Turistica,** via A. Manzoni 16 (tel. 247-8141). Offices are open Monday through Saturday from 8:30am to 1:30pm.

CITY LAYOUT

Florence is a city seemingly designed for walking. It's amazing how nearly all the major sights can be discovered on foot. The only problem is that the sidewalks in summer are so crowded that I can only hope you don't suffer from claustrophobia.

The city is split by the **Arno River,** which usually looks serene and peaceful, but can turn ferocious with flood waters on rare occasions. The major part of Florence, certainly its monumental and historical core, lies on the north or "right" side of the river. But the "left" side is not devoid of attractions. Many long-time visitors frequent the left bank for its tantalizing trattoria meals; they also maintain that the shopping here is less expensive. Even the most cursory visitor will want to cross over to the left bank to see the Pitti Palace with its many art treasures and walk through the Giardini di Boboli, a series of formal gardens, the most impressive in Florence. In addition, you'll also want to cross over to the left bank heading for the belvedere piazzale Michelangelo for one of the most panoramic vistas of this city of the Renaissance. To reach it, follow viale Michelangelo up the flank of the hill (one easy way to go is to take bus no. 13 from the train station).

The Arno is spanned by eight bridges, of which the **Ponte Vecchio,** with jewelry stores on either side, is the most celebrated and most central. Many of these bridges were ancient structures until the Nazis, in a hopeless and last-ditch effort, senselessly destroyed them in their "defense" of Florence in 1944. With tenacity, Florence rebuilt its bridges, using, whenever possible, pieces from the destroyed structures. The Ponte S. Trinità is the second most important bridge spanning the Arno. After crossing it, you can continue along **via dei Tornabuoni,** which is the most important right-bank shopping street (don't look for bargains, however). At the Ponte Vecchio you can walk, again on the right bank, along via Por Santa Maria which will become Calimala. This will lead you into the heartbeat **piazza della Repubblica,** a commercial district known for its cafés such as the Caffè Gilli.

From there, you can take via Roma, which leads directly into **piazza di San Giovanni.** There you'll find the baptistery and its neighboring sibling, the larger **piazza Duomo,** with a world-famous cathedral and bell tower by Giotto. From the far western edge of piazza Duomo, you can take via del Proconsolo south to **piazza della Signoria,** to see the landmark Palazzo Vecchio and its sculpture-filled Loggia della Signoria.

High in the hills overlooking Florence is the ancient town of **Fiesole,** with Roman ruins and a splendid cathedral.

NEIGHBORHOODS IN BRIEF

Florence isn't divided into neighborhoods the way many cities are. Most locals refer to either the left bank or the right bank of the Arno—and that's about it, unless they head out of town for the immediate environs, such as Fiesole. The following selection of "neighborhoods"—most of them grouped around a monumental palace, church, or square—is therefore rather arbitrary.

Centro   Called simply that by the Florentines, the Centro could, in effect, be all the historic heart of Florence, but mostly the term is used to describe the area southwest of the Duomo. Most of it has a 19th-century overlay, and its focal point is piazza della Repubblica. On the western part of this old town is via dei Tornabuoni, flanked with palazzi and quality shops selling expensive merchandise.

Piazza della Signoria   The ancient center of city life, this busy square was once the forum of the Republic. It is dominated by the Palazzo Vecchio, Florence's massive fortresslike town hall. To the south of the Palazzo Vecchio are the Uffizi Galleries.

Piazza del Duomo   In the center of Florence, this square is dominated by the Duomo Santa Maria del Fiore, and immediately adjoins piazza San Giovanni, site of the Baptistery, a domed structure on an octagonal plan. The square bell tower was begun in 1334 by Giotto.

Santa Maria Novella   On the northwestern edge of central Florence is the large piazza di Santa Maria Novella with its church of the same name, which dominates this section of Florence. Northwest of Santa Maria Novella lies piazza della Stazione, the main railway terminal of Florence. Southwest of Santa Maria Novella is piazza Ognissanti, opening onto the Arno. On the east side of Santa Maria Novella, via del Melarancio goes a short distance east to San Lorenzo, the first cathedral of Florence. Beyond San Lorenzo, is piazza Madonna degli Aldobrandini, the entrance to the Medici Chapels.

Piazza San Marco   is dominated by its church, now the Museo di San Marco. To the south is the Accademia di Belle Arti, with the Galleria dell'Accademia, at via Ricasoli 52, containing Michelangelo's *David*.

Santa Croce   This section is in the southeastern part of the old town of

Florence, near the Arno, dominated by its Gothic Santa Croce or Holy Cross Church, completed in 1442. A little distance to the north of Santa Croce is Casa Buonarroti, at via Ghibellina 70, which Michelangelo acquired for his nephew.

Ponte Vecchio   Southwest of piazza della Signoria is the Ponte Vecchio (Old Bridge) area. This is the oldest of the bridges of Florence, and it is flanked by jewelry stores. The bridge will carry you across the Arno onto the left bank.

The Palazzo Pitti   area lies to the southwest of Ponte Vecchio, on the slopes of the Colle di Boboli. This fortresslike palace—filled with museums—faces the Giardino di Boboli (Boboli Gardens) to the south, an 11-acre site laid out in 1560.

Fiesole,   although a town in its own right, is treated by some as a neighborhood or suburb of Florence. An ancient town on a hill overlooking Florence, it has splendid views of the city of the Renaissance and the Arno Valley. It was founded by the Etruscans, perhaps as early as the 7th century B.C. Its center is the large piazza Mino da Fiesole.

2. GETTING AROUND

BY PUBLIC TRANSPORTATION   The major sights in the small city of Florence are within walking distance of most hotels, but you might prefer to use the public transportation provided by **buses.** If you do, you must purchase your bus ticket before boarding one of the public vehicles. For 800 lire (65¢), you can ride on any public bus in the city for a total of 70 minutes. Bus tickets can be purchased from tobacconists and news vendors. The local bus station, terminal of ATAF city buses, is at piazza del Duomo 57F (tel. 213301). Bus routes are posted at bus stops, but for a comprehensive map of the Florentine bus network go to the ATAF booth at the rail station. If you're caught riding a bus without a ticket, the fine is 24,000 lire ($18.85).

BY TAXI   Taxis can be found at stands at nearly all the major squares in Florence. If you need a radio taxi, call 4390.

BY CAR   As mentioned, driving a car in Florence is a hopeless undertaking—not only because of the snarled traffic, but because much of the district you've come to see is a pedestrian zone. If your hotel doesn't have a garage, someone on the staff will direct you to the nearest garage after you've parked long enough to unload your luggage. Garage fees for the night average between 15,000 lire and 25,000 lire ($11.80 and $19.65).

You'll need a car to explore Tuscany in any depth, and these are available at **Avis,** borgo Ognissanti 128R (tel. 213629); **Budget,** borgo Ognissanti 113 (tel. 293021); and **Europcar,** borgo Ognissanti 55R (tel. 293444).

BY BICYCLE   Bicycles are a practical means of transport in Florence. You can rent one from **Ciao & Basta,** whose headquarters are at lungarno Pecori Giraldi 3 (tel. 234-6555). You can also rent boats here for tips on the Arno.

ON FOOT   Because Florence is so compact, getting around on foot is the ideal way to do it—at times, the only way because of so many pedestrian zones. In theory at least, pedestrians have the right of way at uncontrolled zebra crossings, but don't count on that should you encounter a speeding Vespa.

Maps   Arm yourself with a map from the tourist office (see "Orientation," above). But if you'd like to see Florence in any depth—particularly those little side streets, ask for a **Falk** map (indexes are included) which give all the streets. These are available at all bookstores and at most newsstands.

FLORENCE

American Express The Florentine branch of American Express is at via Guicciardini (tel. 28875). It's open Monday through Friday from 9am to 5:30pm and on Saturday from 9am to 12:30pm.

Area Code The telephone area code for Florence and Fiesole is 055.

Baby-sitters Most hotel desks will make arrangements for you to have a baby-sitter. If you need an English-speaking sitter, try to make arrangements as far in advance as possible.

Bookstores See "Savvy Shopping" in Chapter 8.

Business Hours From mid-June to mid-September most shops and business offices are open Monday through Friday from 9am to 1pm and 4 to 8pm. Off-season hours, in general, are Monday afternoon from 3:30 to 7:30pm and Tuesday through Saturday from 9am to 1pm and 3:30 to 7:30pm.

Car Rentals See "Getting Around" in this chapter.

Climate See "When to Go" in Chapter 2.

Currency See "Information, Entry Requirements & Money" in Chapter 2.

Currency Exchange Local banks in Florence grant the best rates. Most **banks** are open Monday through Friday from 8:30am to 1:30pm and 2:45 to 3:45pm. The **tourist office** (see "Orientation," above) exchanges money at official rates when banks are closed and on holidays, but the commission here is often 3,000 lire ($2.35) or more. You can also go to the **Ufficio Informazione booth** at the rail station, which is open daily from 7:30am to 7:40pm. The American Express office (see above) also exchanges money.

Dentist For a list of English-speaking dentists, consult your national consulate or contact **Tourist Medical Service,** viale Lorenzo Il Magnifico (tel. 475411).

Doctor Night service is available by calling 477891. Otherwise, contact your national consulate (see below) for a list of English-speaking doctors. You can also contact **Tourist Medical Service,** viale Lorenzo Il Magnifico (tel. 475411).

Drugstores Pharmacy service is available 24 hours a day at **Molteni,** via Calzaiuoli 7R (tel. 289490).

Embassies/Consulates The **U.S. Consulate** is at lungarno Amerigo Vespucci 38 (tel. 239-8276), and hours are Monday through Friday from 8:30am to noon and 2 to 4pm. The **British Consulate** is at lungarno Corsini 2 (tel. 284133), near piazza Santa Trinità, open Monday through Friday from 9:30am to 12:30pm and 2:30 to 4:30pm. Citizens of other English-speaking countries, including Canada, Australia, and New Zealand, should contact their consulates in Rome.

Emergencies For fire, call 222115; for an ambulance, call 212222; for the police, 113, and for road service, 116.

Eyeglasses One of the best places to go is **Salmoinaghi,** which has two branches—at via Calzainoli 73 (tel. 294956) and via Panzani 42 (tel. 215941).

Hairdressers/Barbers Both women and men are fond of **Big Art,** piazza della Repubblica 3 (tel. 212016), right in the center of Florence. Call for an appointment.

Holidays See "When to Go" in Chapter 2.

Hospitals Call the **General Hospital of Santa Maria Nuova,** piazza Santa Maria Nuova 1 (tel. 27581).

Hotlines Call the police at 113.

Information See "Tourist Information" in "Orientation" in this chapter and also "Information, Entry Requirements & Money" in Chapter 2.

Laundry/Dry Cleaning Because of its central location, try **Lavanderia Superlava Splendis,** via del Sole 29R (tel. 218835), off piazza Santa Maria Novella, near the rail station. Hours for this self-service laundry are Monday through Friday from 8am to 7:30pm. Most hotels can arrange for dry cleaning, although you'll pay extra for the convenience. You can also ask at your hotel reception desk for the nearest dry-cleaning establishment in your neighborhood.

Libraries An American studies library of the University of Florence, the

Biblioteca di Storia e Letteratura Nordamericana (American Library), is at via San Gallo 10 (tel. 275-7940), open Monday through Friday from 9am to 1pm.

Lost Property   The lost-and-found office, **Oggetti Smarriti,** is at via Circondaria 19 (tel. 367943), near the rail terminal.

Luggage Storage/Lockers   These are available at Santa Maria Novella Stazione, in the center of the city at piazza della Stazione (tel. 278785). It's open daily from 7am to 9pm.

Newspapers/Magazines   Copies of the *International Herald Tribune* are sold at many first-class and deluxe hotels and at most newsstands, especially in the summer. You can also obtain copies of *Time* and *Newsweek.*

Photographic Needs   One of the best places to patronize is **Bottega della Fotto,** piazza del Duomo 17 (tel. 283006), across from the cathedral in the center of Florence.

Police   Dial 113 in an emergency. English-speaking foreigners who want to see and talk to the police should go to the **Ufficio Stranieri** station at via Zara 2 (tel. 49771), where English-speaking personnel are available daily from 9am to 2pm.

Post Office   The **Central Post Office** is on via Pelliceria off piazza della Repubblica (tel. 216122). A telegram, telex, and fax can be sent from there. You can also send telegrams by phoning 186. Hours are Monday through Friday from 8:15am to 7pm and Saturday from 8:15am to 7pm. If you wish to send packages, go to the rear of the building and enter at via de' Sassetti 4. This department is open Monday through Friday from 8:15am to 7pm and on Saturday from 8:15am to noon. Stamps (*francobolli*) can be purchased at Windows 21–22. If you want your mail sent general delivery (*fermo posta*), have it sent in care of this office and pick up mail at Windows 23–24.

Radio   Although there are some private channels, the air waves are dominated by RAI, the national radio network. In the summer months, RAI broadcasts some news in English. Vatican Radio's foreign news broadcasts (in English) also reach Florence. Shortwave radio reception is also possible, and you can pick up American (VOA), British (BBC), and Canadian (CBC) radio broadcasts. The American Southern European Broadcast Network (SEB) from Vicenza can also be heard on regular AM radio (middle or medium wave).

Religious Services   There is a **Baptist church** at via Borgognissanti 6 (tel. 210537), and a **Jewish synagogue** at via Farini 4 (tel. 245252). Florence also has a **Lutheran church** at via dei Bardi 20 (tel. 234-2775). If you're Catholic, you can walk into virtually any church in the city. The **American Episcopalian church** is St. James, at via Rucellai 9 (tel. 294417).

Rest Rooms   Public toilets are found in most galleries, museums, bars, cafés, and restaurants, as well as bus, train, and air terminals. Usually they are designated as W.C. (water closet) or else DONNE (women) or UOMINI (men). The most confusing designation is SIGNORI (men) and SIGNORE (women). Watch those *I*s and *E*s.

Safety   The most violent crimes are rare in Florence, where crime consists mainly of pickpockets who frequent crowded tourist centers, such as corridors of the Uffizi Galleries. Members of group tours who cluster together are often singled out as victims. Car thefts are relatively common: Don't leave your luggage in an unguarded car, even if it's locked in the trunk. Women should be especially careful in avoiding pursesnatchers, some of whom grab a women's purse while whizzing by on a Vespa, often knocking the woman down. Documents such as passports and extra money are better stored in safes at your hotel if available.

Shoe Repairs   Try **Riparazioni Scarpe Il Ciabattino,** via del Moro 88R, near piazza Santa Maria Novella, a short walk from the main rail terminal. Hours are Monday through Friday from 8:30am to noon and 2:30 to 7:30pm, and on Saturday from 8:30am to noon.

Taxes   A value-added tax (IVA) is added to all consumer products and most services, including those at hotels and restaurants. The tax is refundable if you spend more than 625,000 lire ($490.65) on any item.

Taxis   See "Getting Around" in this chapter.

Telegrams/Telex/Fax   Most of these can be sent at your hotel, or you can go to the post office (see above).

Television   The RAI is the chief television network broadcasting in Italy. Every TV in the country receives these highly politicized channels: RAI-1 for Christian Democrats, RAI-2 for Italian Socialists, and RAI-3 for Italian Communists.

Transit Information   For international flights at Galileo Galilei Airport, dial 050/280088; for domestic flights at Peretola, call 370125; for railway information, dial 278783; for long-distance bus information, call 211487; and for city buses, dial 213301.

Weather   May and September are the ideal time to visit. The worst times to go are the week before and including Easter and June until the first week of September. Florence is literally overrun with tourists, and the city streets, or anything else, weren't designed for mass tourism. Temperatures in July and August hover in the 70s, dropping to a low of 45° or 46° Fahrenheit in December and January, the coldest months.

3. NETWORKS & RESOURCES

FOR STUDENTS   The University of Florence lies between piazza San Marco and the Mercato Centrale. Most of the student activity takes place in and around piazza San Marco. The center for student budget travel is **Centro Turistico Studentesco e Giovanile (CTSG),** via dei Ginori 11R (tel. 263570). It doesn't offer an accommodation service, but can arrange discounts on transportation within Italy. It's open Monday through Friday from 9:30am to 1pm and 4 to 7pm, and on Saturday from 9am to noon. Although they specialize in youth and student fares, they're helpful to budget-minded travelers of all ages.

FOR GAY MEN AND LESBIANS   The local headquarters of gay liberation for men is **Arci Gay,** via Montebello 6 (tel. 210075), which meets Wednesday from 6 to 8pm. This is a good source of information about local gay-related activities.

For women, **Lesbian Line** can be telephoned at 240384, Wednesday through Saturday from 8 to 10:30pm. Someone there (usually English-speaking) has details of lesbian-related activities in the Florence area.

FOR WOMEN   A good feminist bookstore is the **Libreria delle Donne,** via Fiesolana 2B (tel. 240384), which is open Monday through Saturday from 9am to 1pm and 3:30 to 7:30pm. In addition to selling books, it is a clearinghouse for information pertinent to women in Florence.

FOR SENIORS   Go to the **tourist office** (see "Orientation," above) and inquire about any discounts—such as on transportation and museum entrances—that pertain to senior citizens. This data is always changing, so it's best to get the latest information. Also, for some good travel discounts, go to the **Centro Turistico Studentesco e Giovanile (CTSG)**—see "For Students," above—which although essentially a student budget travel agency will also help you with discounts on senior-citizen travel within Italy.

CHAPTER 7

WHERE TO STAY & DINE IN FLORENCE

1. ACCOMMODATIONS
- **FROMMER'S SMART TRAVELER: HOTELS**
- **FROMMER'S COOL FOR KIDS: HOTELS**

2. DINING
- **FROMMER'S SMART TRAVELER: RESTAURANTS**
- **FROMMER'S COOL FOR KIDS: RESTAURANTS**

The days when Aldous Huxley called Florence "under-bathroomed and over-monumented" are past. The monuments are still there, but bathrooms today are plentiful. Even some of the monuments that Huxley obviously referred to have been turned into hotels, with bathrooms installed.

A vast array of hotels—sometimes not enough in the peak tourist months from spring to fall—await today's visitor. They range from deluxe to fourth class, and they are supplemented by an array of *pensioni* (boarding houses) of varying standards, ranked P1 (the best) to P3 (the most modest). Many students and young people from all over the world—especially those interested in art—fill up these pensioni, often for weeks at a time.

The Florentine table has always been set with the abundance provided by the Tuscan countryside. That means the best of olive oil and wine, such as chianti, succulent fruits and vegetables, fresh fish from the coast, and the best of game in season. Meat-lovers all over Italy sing the praise of *bistecca alla fiorentina,* a thick and juicy steak on the bone often served with white Tuscan beans. It is said that you can gauge the cost of a meal in the restaurant before you go in by the price charged per kilo (2.2 lbs.) for the Florentine beefsteak printed on the menu outside. It isn't considered impolite to order one steak for two diners.

1. ACCOMMODATIONS

Florence was always a leader in architecture. Consequently, with the decline and fall of the great aristocratic families of Tuscany, many of the city's grand old villas and palaces have been converted into hotels. For sheer charm and luxury, the hotels of Florence are among the finest in Europe. There are not too many tourist cities where you can find a 15th- or 16th-century palace—tastefully decorated and most comfortable—rated as a second-class pensione (boarding house). Florence is equipped with hotels in virtually all price ranges and of widely varying standards, comfort, service, and efficiency.

However, during the summer there simply aren't enough rooms to meet the demand, and if you arrive without a reservation you may not find a place for the night and will have to drive to nearby Montecatini, where you'll always stand a good chance of securing accommodations.

If you should arrive without a reservation and don't want to wander around town on your own looking for a room, go in person (instead of calling) to the **Consorzio ITA office** in the rail terminal at piazza della Stazione. The office is open daily from 9am to 8:30pm.

Hotels rated "Very Expensive" charge more than 400,000 lire ($314) for a double

FROMMER'S SMART TRAVELER: HOTELS

VALUE-CONSCIOUS TRAVELERS SHOULD ASK ABOUT THE FOLLOWING:

1. The price you pay in inexpensive hotels depends on the plumbing. Rooms with showers are cheaper than rooms with private baths. For a bath, you'll have to use the corridor bathroom, but you'll save a lot of money.
2. Consider a package tour (or book land arrangements with your airline ticket). You'll often pay at least 30% less than individual "rack" rates (off-the-street, independent bookings).
3. At cheaper hotels that take credit cards, ask if payment in cash will get you a reduction.
4. If you're going to spend at least a week in Florence, ask about long-term discounts.

QUESTIONS TO ASK IF YOU'RE ON A BUDGET

1. Is there a garage? What's the charge?
2. Is there a surcharge on either local or long-distance calls? There usually is in some places, and it might be an astonishing 40%. Make your calls at the nearest post office.
3. Is service included? This means, Does the hotel include a service charge in the rates quoted, or will a service charge be added on at the end of your stay?
4. Are all taxes included in the price or will they be added on?
5. Is continental breakfast included in the rates?

room; those considered "Expensive" ask 280,000 lire to 400,000 lire ($219.80 to $314) for a double, "Moderate" means 130,000 lire to 280,000 lire ($102.05 to $219.80) for a double, and "Inexpensive" is anything from 130,000 lire ($102.05). All prices are for a double room with private bath, including tax and service. "Budget" is any double under 70,000 lire ($54.95).

Unless otherwise indicated, Florentine hotels that provide room service do so only from 7am to midnight.

NEAR PIAZZA OGNISSANTI

VERY EXPENSIVE

GRAND HOTEL, piazza Ognissanti 1, 50123 Firenze. Tel. 055/288781. Fax 055/217400. 107 rms (all with bath), 17 suites. A/C MINIBAR TV TEL **Bus:** 6 or 16.

$ Rates: 357,000–404,000 lire ($280.25–$317.15) single; 500,000–595,000 lire ($392.50–$467.10) double; from 800,000 lire ($628) suite. IVA tax 19% extra. Breakfast 23,000 lire ($18.05) extra. AE, DC, MC, V. **Parking:** 40,000 lire ($31.40).

The Grand Hotel is a bastion of luxury, fronting a little Renaissance piazza across from the Excelsior. A hotel of history and tradition, the Grand is known for its halls and salons. Its legend grew under its name as the Continental Royal de la Paix. In both the 19th and 20th centuries it has attracted many famous people. Its rooms and suites have a refined elegance, and the most desirable overlook the Arno. Each bedroom contains all the silks, brocades, and real or reproduction antiques you'd expect from such a highly regarded establishment.

Dining/Entertainment: A highlight of the hotel is the Winter Garden, an enclosed court lined with arches, which has been restored. Here regional and seasonal specialties are served along with an array of international dishes. Guests gather at night in the Fiorino Bar to listen to the piano music.

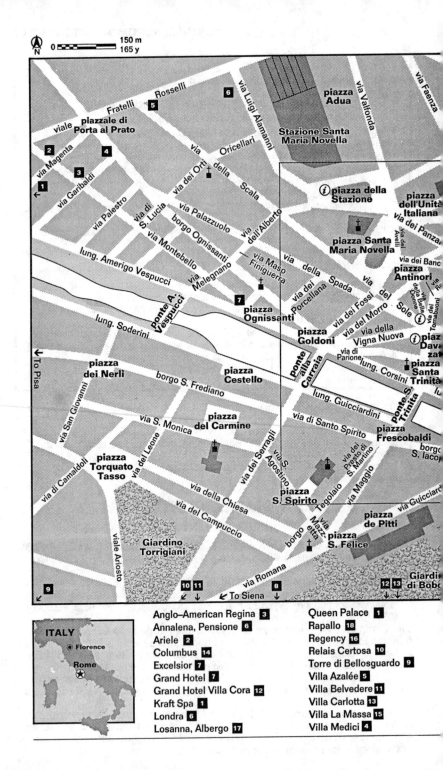

ITALY

● Florence

Rome ★

Anglo–American Regina **3**
Annalena, Pensione **6**
Ariele **2**
Columbus **14**
Excelsior **7**
Grand Hotel **7**
Grand Hotel Villa Cora **12**
Kraft Spa **1**
Londra **6**
Losanna, Albergo **17**

Queen Palace **1**
Rapallo **18**
Regency **16**
Relais Certosa **10**
Torre di Bellosguardo **9**
Villa Azalée **5**
Villa Belvedere **11**
Villa Carlotta **13**
Villa La Massa **15**
Villa Medici **4**

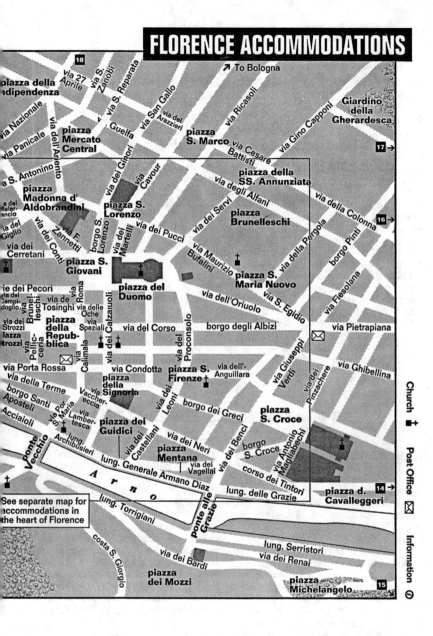

FLORENCE ACCOMMODATIONS

↗ To Bologna

18

piazza della
ndipendenza

via 27
Aprile

via S.
Zanobi

via S. Reparata

via San Gallo

via del
Arazzieri

via Nazionale

via Panicale

Guelfa

via dell'Ariento

piazza
**Mercato
Central**

via Ricasoli

piazza
S. Marco

via Cesare
Battisti

via Gino Capponi

**Giardino
della
Gherardesca**

17 →

a S. Antonino

a del
Melar-
ancio

a del
Giglio

piazza
**Madonna d'
Aldobrandini**

via F.
Zannetti

via dei Conti

via dei Ginori

via Cavour

piazza **S.
Lorenzo**

borgo S.
Lorenzo

via dei
Martelli

via dei Pucci

piazza della
SS. Annunziata

via degli Alfani

via dei Servi

piazza
Brunelleschi

via della Colonna

16 →

borgo Pinti

via dei
Cerretani

piazza **S.
Giovanni**

via
Roma

piazza del
Duomo

via Maurizio
Bufalini

via della Pergola

piazza **S.
Maria Nuovo**

via Fiesolana

ie dei Pecori

ia del
ampi-
doglio.

via de
Tosinghi

via delle
Oche

via
Speziali

via dei Calzauoli

via dell'Oriuolo

via S. Egidio

via dei
Strozzi

azza
trozzi

via
Brunel-
leschi

piazza
**della
Repub-
blica**

via del Corso

borgo degli Albizi

via Pietrapiana

via
Pelli-
ceria

via Calimala

via del
Proconsolo

via Porta Rossa

via Condotta

piazza **S.
Firenze** †

via dell'-
Anguillara

via Ghibellina

via della Terme

piazza
**della
Signoria**

via
Vaccher-
eccie

via dei Leoni

via Giuseppi
Verdi

via dei
Pinzachere

borgo Santi
Apostoli

via Por
S. Maria

via
Lamber-
tesca

borgo dei Greci

piazza
S. Croce

Acciaioli

lung.
Archibusieri

piazza dei
Guidici

via dei
Castellani

piazza
Mentana

via dei Neri

via dei Benci

borgo
S. Croce

via Antonio
Magliabechi

ponte
Vecchio

A   r   n   o

lung. Generale Armano Diaz

via dei
Vagellai

corso dei Tintori

piazza d.
Cavalleggeri

14 →

†

See separate map for
accommodations in
the heart of Florence

lung. Torrigiani

ponte alle
Grazie

lung. delle Grazie

costa S. Giorgio

via dei Bardi

lung. Serristori
via dei Renai

piazza
dei Mozzi

piazza
Michelangelo

15

Church ✝

Post Office ⊠

Information ☉

Services: 24-hour room service, baby-sitting, laundry, valet.
Facilities: Car-rental desk.

HOTEL EXCELSIOR, piazza Ognissanti 3, 50123 Firenze. Tel. 055/ 264201. Fax 055/210278. 205 rms (all with bath), 17 suites. A/C MINIBAR TV TEL **Bus:** 6 or 16.

$ **Rates:** 245,000–310,000 lire ($192.35–$243.35) single; 360,000–450,000 lire ($282.60–$353.25) double; from 750,000 lire ($588.75) suite. IVA tax 19% extra. Breakfast 23,000 lire ($18.05) extra. AE, DC, MC, V. **Parking:** 40,000 lire ($31.40).

The Hotel Excelsior, set on a Renaissance square, is the ultimate in well-ordered luxury during a stopover in Florence. Demand for the elegant bedrooms is so great that during peak season most of the accommodations are reserved many weeks in advance. Once part of the hotel was owned by Carolina Bonaparte, sister of Napoleon. The present hotel was formed in 1927 by the fusion of two other hotels, the De la Ville and the Italie. Several of the bedrooms have terraces, and many open onto views of the Arno. The rooms offer lots of comfortable chairs, well-appointed space, and baths with heated racks, thick towels, and high-ceilinged comfort.

Dining/Entertainment: Il Castello, the hotel's deluxe restaurant, attracts an upper-crust clientele who, in summer, come to drink beside the piano or on the flowered terrace of the roof garden, or to dine under a canopy by candlelight. On the sixth floor, the garden is open from May to October (in winter, it moves back downstairs again), when the hotel closes its downstairs dining room in favor of the garden terrace's breezes and panoramic views of the Arno. Meals are served from noon to 3pm and 7 to 11pm daily. A dinner costs 100,000 lire ($78.50). The cuisine is Mediterranean with Tuscan specialties and a few items that are always "fresh from today's market." Reservations are always imperative.

Services: 24-hour room service, baby-sitting, laundry, valet.
Facilities: Roof garden.

NEAR PIAZZA MASSIMO D'AZEGLIO
VERY EXPENSIVE

HOTEL REGENCY, piazza Massimo d'Azeglio 3, 50121 Firenze. Tel. 055/245247. Fax 055/245247. 38 rms (all with bath), 5 suites. A/C MINIBAR TV TEL **Bus:** 6.

$ **Rates** (including breakfast): 300,000–350,000 lire ($235.50–$274.75) single; 350,000–520,000 lire ($274.75–$408.20) double; from 550,000 lire ($431.75) suite. AE, DC, MC, V. **Parking:** 30,000 lire ($23.55).

The Hotel Regency lies a bit apart from the shopping and sightseeing center of Florence, but it's only a 15-minute stroll to the cathedral. And although its location isn't central (a blessing for tranquility seekers), it is conveniently and quickly reached by taxi. This well-built, old-style villa, a member of Relais & Châteaux, has its own garden across from a park in a residential area of the city. This luxurious hideaway, filled with stained glass, paneled walls, and reproduction antiques, offers exquisitely furnished rooms. There are some special rooms on the top floor with walk-out terraces. The owner, who also has the prestigious Lord Byron in Rome, has a capable staff at the Regency.

Dining/Entertainment: The attractive paneled dining room serves excellent food; you can also take your meals in the well-lit winter garden.
Services: Room service, baby-sitting, laundry, valet.
Facilities: Garden.

INEXPENSIVE

ALBERGO LOSANNA, via Vittorio Alfieri 9, 50121 Firenze. Tel. 055/ 245840. 10 rms (4 with bath). **Bus:** 7 to Mattonaia.

$ **Rates:** 44,500 lire ($34.95) single without bath, 49,500 lire ($38.85) single with bath; 73,500 lire ($57.70) double without bath; 78,500 lire ($61.60) double with bath. Breakfast 12,000 lire ($9.40) extra. No credit cards. **Parking:** 20,000 lire ($15.70).

A good, inexpensive choice, the Albergo Losanna is a tiny family-run place off viale Antonio Gramsci, between piazzale Donatello and piazza Massimo d'Azeglio. It offers utter simplicity and cleanliness. The bus stops a block and a half away. The bedrooms are homey and well kept.

NEAR THE RAILWAY STATION
EXPENSIVE

ATLANTIC PALACE HOTEL, via Nazionale 12, 50123 Firenze. Tel. 055/ 294234. Fax 055/268353. 44 rms (all with bath). A/C MINIBAR TV TEL **Bus:** 19.

$ Rates (including breakfast): 240,000 lire ($188.40) single; 320,000 lire ($251.20) double. AE, DC, MC, V. **Parking:** 35,000 lire ($27.50).

Late in 1985 a group of entrepreneurs transformed a run-down hotel into a four-star model of imaginative design, using the shell of a 17th-century monastery as a foundation. Today this is one of the most alluring hotels in the vicinity of the railway station, a 5-minute walk away. Each of its oversize bedrooms has some kind of memorable ceiling, often with heavy beams crisscrossed with old tiles or with rows of hand-painted panels set into geometric patterns. Accommodations contain reproductions of antiques and private baths. The hotel has a bar and serves breakfast.

GRAND HOTEL MINERVA, piazza S. Maria Novella 16, 50123 Firenze. Tel. 055/284555. Fax 055/268281. 96 rms (all with bath or shower), 3 suites. A/C MINIBAR TV TEL **Bus:** 19.

$ Rates: 220,000 lire ($172.70) single; 295,000 lire ($231.60) double; from 395,000 lire ($310.10) suite. Breakfast 20,000 lire ($15.70) extra. AE, DC, MC, V. **Parking:** 30,000 lire ($23.55).

The Grand Hotel Minerva is one of the most streamlined choices near the railway station. The bedrooms are pleasantly furnished with modern pieces. The most popular feature of the Minerva is its rooftop swimming pool, a choice spot with a view of the city. The hotel is well protected against noise; it bills itself as "the really quietest hotel of the town."

HOTEL CROCE DI MALTA, via della Scala 7, 50123 Firenze. Tel. 055/ 282600. Fax 055/287121. 98 rms (all with bath), 15 duplex suites. A/C MINIBAR TV TEL **Bus:** 31, 32, 36, or 37.

$ Rates (including breakfast): 190,000–245,000 lire ($149.15–$192.35) single; 250,000–330,000 lire ($196.25–$259.05) double; from 380,000 lire ($298.30) duplex suite. AE, DC, MC, V. **Parking:** 35,000 lire ($27.50).

The Hotel Croce di Malta is housed in a stately palace whose soaring interior was modernized in the early 1970s. It's one of the few hotels in Florence with its own swimming pool, whose curved edges are partially shaded by the rear garden's 100-year-old magnolia. The stylish lobby has massive stone columns between which the architects placed rounded doorways you might expect to see on "Star Trek." In sharp contrast, the bedrooms are classically elegant, filled with Florentine furniture and frescoed headboards showing landscapes that might have been done by an artist of the early Renaissance. Some of the more expensive accommodations are duplexes with their own sleeping loft set midway between the floor and high ceilings.

Dining/Entertainment: There's a whimsically decorated restaurant, Il Coccodrillo, which serves well-prepared meals beginning at 50,000 lire ($39.25).

Services: Room service, baby-sitting, laundry, valet.

Facilities: Swimming pool.

HOTEL KRAFT SPA, via Solferino 2, 50123 Firenze. Tel. 055/284273. Fax 055/298267. 73 rms (all with bath). A/C MINIBAR TV TEL **Bus:** 3, 6, 11, 16, 31, or 32.

$ Rates (including breakfast): 160,000–255,000 lire ($125.60–$200.20) single; 295,000–350,000 lire ($231.60–$274.75) double. AE, DC, MC, V.

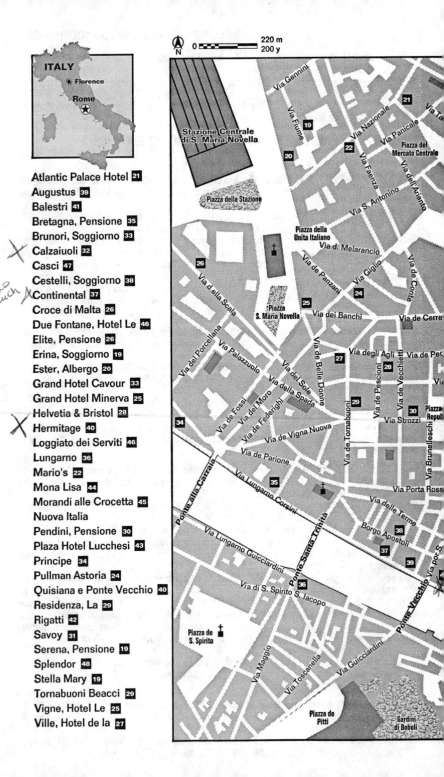

ITALY
Florence
Rome

Atlantic Palace Hotel **21**
Augustus **39**
Balestri **41**
Bretagna, Pensione **35**
Brunori, Soggiorno **33**
Calzaiuoli **32**
Casci **47**
Cestelli, Soggiorno **38**
Continental **37**
Croce di Malta **26**
Due Fontane, Hotel Le **46**
Elite, Pensione **26**
Erina, Soggiorno **19**
Ester, Albergo **20**
Grand Hotel Cavour **33**
Grand Hotel Minerva **25**
Helvetia & Bristol **28**
Hermitage **40**
Loggiato dei Serviti **46**
Lungarno **36**
Mario's **22**
Mona Lisa **44**
Morandi alle Crocetta **45**
Nuova Italia
Pendini, Pensione **30**
Plaza Hotel Lucchesi **43**
Principe **34**
Pullman Astoria **24**
Quisiana e Ponte Vecchio **40**
Residenza, La **29**
Rigatti **42**
Savoy **31**
Serena, Pensione **19**
Splendor **48**
Stella Mary **19**
Tornabuoni Beacci **29**
Vigne, Hotel Le **25**
Ville, Hotel de la **27**

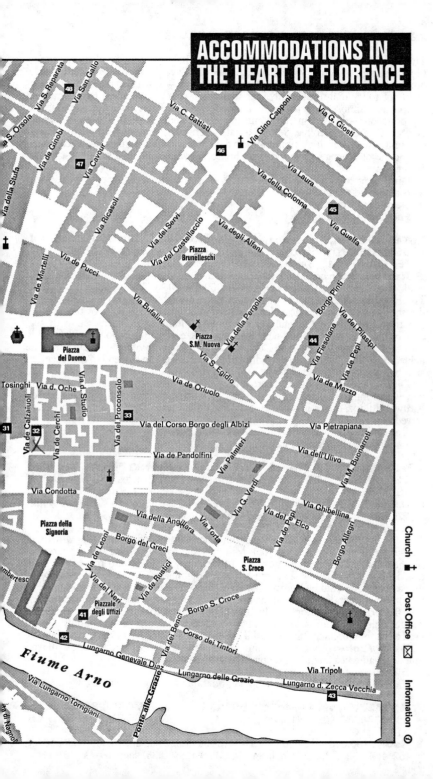

ACCOMMODATIONS IN THE HEART OF FLORENCE

The Hotel Kraft was created by the son of one of Italy's greatest hoteliers (the father, Herman Kraft, of Berne, Switzerland, sparked the Excelsior in the 19th century). The present-day Kraft is far removed from the baroque—instead, it meets the requirements of today quite beautifully. It's at the side of a square, close by the railroad station and almost next to the Arno and the U.S. Consulate. Fine antiques or reproductions are used in the comfortable bedrooms. Many have little terraces, perfect for morning coffee. Several terraces above the dining room is an open-air swimming pool. Imagine swimming with a view of the Duomo, piazzale Michelangelo, and Fiesole. Being so near the opera house, the Kraft is popular with maestros and singing stars.

Dining/Entertainment: The Kraft is crowned with a dining room that opens onto a covered terrace.

Services: Room service, baby-sitting, laundry, valet.

Facilities: Swimming pool.

HOTEL LONDRA, via Jacopo da Diacceto 16-20, 50123 Firenze. Tel. 055/238-2791. Fax 055/210862. 107 rms (all with bath). A/C MINIBAR TV TEL **Bus:** 3, 6, 11, 31, or 32.

$ Rates (including breakfast): 210,000 lire ($164.85) single; 280,000 lire ($219.80) double. AE, DC, MC, V. **Parking:** 25,000 lire ($19.65).

The Hotel Londra is a modern, first-class hotel near the museums and monuments, the shopping areas, and the railroad station. The marble-tile floor of the lobby is beautified by a large Oriental carpet, and the lounges are furnished with big, comfortable chairs. The wood-paneled bedrooms, each with a radio, are comfortably furnished and well lighted, and each bath is complete with bidet and hairdryer. The lighted room numbers beside each door are helpful. You can descend to the reception area by elevator or carpeted stairs.

Dining/Entertainment: There is a small American bar with an adjacent piano bar, where music is played nightly after dinner. The dining room, with a polished hardwood floor, opens in summer onto the walled terrace garden where meals are served amid greenery.

Services: Room service, baby-sitting, laundry, valet.

Facilities: Large private garage.

HOTEL PULLMAN ASTORIA, via del Giglio 9, 50123 Firenze. Tel. 055/239-8095. Fax 055/571070. 90 rms (all with bath), 3 suites. A/C MINIBAR TV TEL **Bus:** 19.

$ Rates (including breakfast): 190,000–240,000 lire ($149.15–$188.40) single; 270,000–340,000 lire ($211.95–$266.90) double; from 450,000 lire ($353.25) suite. AE, DC, MC, V. **Parking:** 35,000 lire ($27.50).

The Hotel Pullman Astoria at one time housed the offices of a now-defunct newspaper. In the 17th century John Milton wrote parts of *Paradise Lost* in one of the bedrooms. Pullman renovated the 14th-century building into one of the most original hotels in Florence. The stylish lobby is illuminated with a skylight that shines into a copy of a mural by Botticelli and a heroic collection of metallic horses more or less on permanent display. From the bedrooms on the upper floors, you'll have a view over the terra-cotta rooftops of Florence. If you choose to stay in one of the stylishly comfortable bedrooms of this hotel, be sure to inspect the conference rooms of what used to be the adjoining Palazzo Gaddi, whose frescoes are filled with chubby cherubs.

Dining/Entertainment: On the premises is a garden-style restaurant with wall murals, beamed ceilings, and Empire lyre-backed chairs.

Services: Room service.

Facilities: Car-rental desk, shopping boutique.

VILLA MEDICI, via il Prato 42, 50123 Firenze. Tel. 055/238-1331. Fax 055/238-1336. 103 rms (all with bath), 14 suites. A/C MINIBAR TV TEL **Bus:** 3, 6, 11, 31, or 32.

$ Rates: 190,000–270,000 lire ($149.25–$211.95) single; 270,000–420,000 lire ($211.95–$329.70) double; from 510,000 lire ($400.35) suite. IVA tax 19% extra.

Breakfast 20,000 lire ($15.70) extra. AE, DC, MC, V. **Parking:** 20,000 lire ($15.70).

The Villa Medici, centrally located between the railway station and the Arno, creates its own world once you walk through its glass doorways. This 1960 luxury hotel has all the trappings and extra services needed to attract the famous and glamorous, even kings and princesses. The super-size, handsomely maintained bedrooms (each with radio) combine both traditional and modern features in decor. Rates depend on whether you request a private bath or shower. The big draw at the Medici is its private garden, with its open-air, onion-shaped swimming pool (for the use of guests at no additional charge) which is complete with poolside tables and changing rooms. On the rooftop terrace you can enjoy a view of Brunelleschi's dome and Giotto's bell tower. In summer, meals are served by the pool.

Dining/Entertainment: Dining is in the Lorenzo de' Medici Restaurant, which offers both international and Florentine cuisine.

Services: Room service, baby-sitting, laundry, valet.

Facilities: Barbershop, hairdressing salon, cleaning and pressing facilities, swimming pool.

MODERATE

HOTEL MARIO'S, via Faenza 89, 50123 Firenze. Tel. 055/216801. Fax 055/212039. 16 rms (all with bath), 1 suite. TV TEL **Bus:** 31 or 32.

$ **Rates** (including breakfast): 85,000–100,000 lire ($66.75–$78.50) single; 115,000–150,000 lire ($90.30–$117.75) double; from 200,000 lire ($157) suite. AE, DC, MC, V.

The spotless Hotel Mario has been completely restored and refurnished in 16th-century Florentine style. Mario Noce is a gracious host, and he and his staff speak English. Although you'll find cheaper inns in Florence, the service, hospitality, and good level of innkeeping make Mario's worth your lire. TV is available upon request.

VILLA AZALEE, viale Fratelli Rosselli 44, 50123 Firenze. Tel. 055/ 214242. Fax 055/268264. 25 rms (all with bath or shower). A/C MINIBAR TV TEL **Bus:** 17.

$ **Rates** (including breakfast): 105,000 lire ($82.45) single; 164,000 lire ($128.75) double. AE, DC, MC, V. **Parking:** 20,000 lire ($15.70).

The Villa Azalee, a handsome structure with a big garden, is a remake of a gracious 19th-century corner villa. The owners have provided a personal touch in both atmosphere and decor. The decorating is tasteful: tall, white-paneled doors with ornate brass fittings, parquet floors, crystal chandeliers, and antiques intermixed with credible reproductions. The lounge is as in a private home, and the bedrooms have distinction (one, in particular, boasts a flouncy canopy bed). The hotel is a 5-minute walk from the rail station.

INEXPENSIVE

HOTEL CASCI, via Cavour 13, 50124 Firenze. Tel. 055/211686. Fax 055/239-6461. 25 rms (all with bath). MINIBAR TV TEL **Bus:** 1, 6, 7, 11, or 17.

$ **Rates** (including breakfast): 48,000 lire ($37.70) single; 75,000 lire ($58.90) double; 105,000 lire ($82.45) triple; 132,000 lire ($103.60) quad. AE, MC, V. **Parking:** 30,000 lire ($23.55).

The Hotel Casci is a well-run little hotel in the historic district, 200 yards from the main railway station. The building dates from the 14th century, and some of the public rooms feature the original frescoes. It also lies 100 yards from piazza del Duomo. The hotel is both traditional and modern, and the English-speaking reception staff looks after guests very well. The bedrooms are comfortably furnished.

NUOVA ITALIA, via Faenza 26, 50123 Firenze. Tel. 055/287508. Fax 055/210941. 20 rms (all with bath). **Bus:** 31 or 32.

$ **Rates** (including breakfast): 60,000 lire ($47.10) single; 75,000 lire ($58.90) double. MC, V.

The Nuova Italia is a renovated hotel in a 17th-century building in the center of Florence. All the bedrooms are pleasantly furnished with pieces by Salvarani, a well-known Italian furniture maker. Some large rooms are particularly suitable for families, to whom the management—the Viti family—grants special reductions. The location is only one block from the railway station, near the San Lorenzo market (the flea market) and the Medici Chapels. A garage is also nearby.

BUDGET

ALBERGO ESTER, largo Fratelli Alinari 15, 50123 Firenze. Tel. 055/212741. 9 rms (2 with bath). **Bus:** 31 or 32.

$ Rates: 29,000 lire ($22.80) single without bath; 44,000 lire ($34.55) double without bath, 54,000 lire ($42.40) double with bath. No credit cards.

The Albergo Ester sits opposite via Fiume, in a middle-class apartment building a 5-minute walk from the railway station. You'll take a creaking elevator to the second floor. The lobby is unpretentious, but several of the rooms are quite spacious and all are clean but basic. No breakfast is served, but there are many cafés in the neighborhood.

PENSIONE ELITE, via della Scala 12, 50123 Firenze. Tel. 055/215395. 8 rms (all with shower). TV TEL **Bus:** 31 or 32.

$ Rates: 38,000 lire ($29.85) single; 68,000 lire ($53.40) double. Breakfast 8,000 lire ($6.30) extra. No credit cards. **Parking:** 25,000 lire ($19.65).

The Elite is a little pensione worthy of being better known. Attractive in scale and appointments, it's about a two-block walk from the main railway station. It's also convenient for exploring most of the major monuments. The owner, Maurizio Maccarini, speaks English and he's a helpful, welcoming host. The pensione rents light and airy bedrooms, divided equally between singles and doubles.

PENSIONE SERENA, via Fiume 20, 50123 Firenze. Tel. 055/213643. 7 rms (1 with shower). **Bus:** 14, 28, or 31.

$ Rates: 45,000 lire ($35.35) single or double without shower, 55,000 lire ($43.20) single or double with shower. Breakfast 10,000 lire ($7.85) extra. V.

The building that houses the Pensione Serena was erected in 1905 as an apartment house. Today it still contains a scattering of stained-glass doors and ornate plaster ceilings, but the furnishings are considerably simpler than they were in the building's heyday. The owner makes guests feel comfortable and welcome as soon as they walk in. All rooms are doubles, and singles are accepted at the double rate. After riding the elevator to the first floor, guests register in the wide hallway and are taken to a spaciously high-ceilinged but dimly illuminated bedroom. The house lies 30 yards from the railway station.

SOGGIORNO ERINA, via Fiume 17, 50123 Firenze. Tel. 055/284343. 7 rms (all with bath). TV **Bus:** 14, 28, or 31.

$ Rates: 55,000 lire ($43.20) single; 70,000 lire ($54.95) double. AE, V.

The Soggiorno Erina is convenient to the railway station, along a street lined with residential buildings. It sits on the third floor of a 19th-century building whose facade is ornamented with sculpted faces peering from above the windows. The wrought-iron elevator requires a coin before it will take you to the hotel's third-floor reception area, or else you can take the stairs. The double bedrooms stretch off a wide central hallway. The place is basic and simple, but newcomers are made to feel welcome.

STELLA MARY HOTEL, via Fiume 17, 50123 Firenze. Tel. 055/215694. Fax 055/301270. 8 rms (all with shower). TEL **Bus:** 14, 28, or 31.

$ Rates (including breakfast): 39,000–51,000 lire ($30.60–$40.05) single; 72,000–96,000 lire ($56.50–$75.35) double. V.

The Stella Mary Hotel is a small but quiet pensione lying 1½ blocks from the train station. The owners are very hospitable, and they operate a clean and comfortable "home in Firenze." All their bedrooms contain toilets, and two of them have TVs. Rooms are cozy and full of light. Breakfast is extra. A sitting room with a TV set is reserved for guests.

AT PIAZZA S. MARIA NOVELLA
INEXPENSIVE

HOTEL LE VIGNE, piazza S. Maria Novella 24, 50123 Firenze. Tel. 055/294449. Fax 055/230-2263 19 rms (16 with bath), 2 suites. A/C TEL **Bus:** 11, 36, or 37.

$ Rates (including breakfast): 63,000 lire ($49.45) single without bath, 55,000 lire ($43.20) single with bath; 87,000 lire ($68.30) double without bath, 100,000 lire ($78.50) double with bath; 139,000 lire ($109.10) triple with bath; from 178,000 lire ($139.75) suite for four people. MC, V. **Parking:** 23,000 lire ($18.05).

The Hotel Le Vigne, which offers comfortably furnished bedrooms, enjoys a prime location on one of the most central squares of Florence. Its sitting room overlooks the square. An Italian family took over this ancient building and restored it, preserving the old features, including frescoes, whenever possible. Some of the rooms, those containing three to six beds, are suitable for families. This small hotel is on the first floor (second, to Americans) of this old-fashioned building. Breakfast is the only meal served. Take your problems to English-speaking Giovanna.

ON OR NEAR VIA TORNABUONI
EXPENSIVE

HOTEL DE LA VILLE, piazza Antinori 1, 50123 Firenze. Tel. 055/238-1805. Fax 055/238-1809. 78 rms (all with bath), 4 suites. A/C MINIBAR TV TEL **Bus:** 31 or 32.

$ Rates (including breakfast): 190,000–232,000 lire ($149.15–$182.10) single; 260,000–331,000 lire ($204.10–$259.85) double; from 520,000 lire ($408.20) suite. AE, DC, MC, V. **Parking:** 40,000 lire ($31.40).

The Hotel de la Ville stands on the most elegant and exclusive street of the historic center, close to the Arno. It has a conservatively contemporary appearance, with a decor that includes flowering plants, mirror-bright marble floors, and many sitting areas. Each bedroom is soundproof. The hotel has an American piano bar, a grill room, a restaurant, and a laundry, as well as a garage and parking area for patrons. The hotel lies 200 yards from the rail station.

MODERATE

TORNABUONI BEACCI, via Tornabuoni 3, 50123 Firenze. Tel. 055/212645. Fax 055/203594. 29 rms (all with bath). A/C MINIBAR TV TEL **Bus:** 31 or 32.

$ Rates (including breakfast): 125,000–140,000 lire ($98.15–$109.90) single; 220,000–250,000 lire ($172.70–$196.25) double. AE, DC, MC, V. **Parking:** 22,000 lire ($17.25).

Near the Arno and piazza S. Trinità, on the city's principal shopping street, is the Tornabuoni Beacci. The pensione occupies the three top floors of a 14th-century palazzo. All its living rooms have been furnished with care, with bowls of flowers, parquet floors, a formal fireplace, old paintings, murals, and rugs. The hotel was completely renovated recently, but it still bears an air of gentility. The roof terrace, surrounded by potted plants and flowers, is for late-afternoon drinks or breakfast. The view of the nearby churches, towers, and rooftops is worth experiencing. The names in the guest book are numerous, including, in days of yore, many personalities such as John Steinbeck, the Gish sisters, and Fredric March. The bedrooms are moderately well furnished. It offers good value, and there's an elevator and a bar.

BUDGET

LA RESIDENZA, via Tornabuoni 8, 50123 Firenze. Tel. 055/284197. Fax 055/284197. 25 rms (21 with bath or shower). TEL **Bus:** 31 or 32.

$ Rates (including breakfast): 74,500 lire ($58.50) single without bath, 92,000 lire

($72.20) single with bath; 117,000 lire ($91.85) double without bath; 143,500 lire ($112.65) double with bath. **Parking:** 28,000 lire ($22).

La Residenza, right in the hub of Florence, is on an elegant shopping street of fashion houses, boutiques, and palaces. It occupies the top floors of a 16th-century Renaissance building, just a few blocks from American Express and the Arno, right next door to the Palazzo Strozzi. The palace housing the pensione belongs to the descendants of the Tornabuoni, the family of Lorenzo de' Medici's mother. The pensione offers freshness, comfort, and style. The elevator is a mahogany-and-glass jewel rising up the interior of the stone stairwell, whose entrance is graced by a statue of a bashful Venus. The dining room is elegant with high ceilings, and antiques are extensively used. The rooms have been redecorated with reproductions and color-coordinated pieces, and some have private balconies. You can have morning coffee in the roof garden, enjoying the wisteria, pots of flowering plants. The bathrooms have been recently renovated.

PIAZZA DELLA REPUBBLICA

EXPENSIVE

SAVOY HOTEL, piazza della Repubblica 7, 50123 Firenze. Tel. 055/ 283313. Fax 055/284840. 101 rms (all with bath), 6 suites. A/C MINIBAR TV TEL **Bus:** 31 or 32.

$ **Rates** (including breakfast): 220,000 lire ($172.70) single; 350,000 lire ($274.75) double. AE, DC, MC, V. **Parking:** 30,000 lire ($23.55).

The dignified Savoy Hotel has a buff-colored facade with neoclassical trim carved from gray stone. It sits in what might be called the commercial center of Florence (also the historic district), in an area filled with fine stores, a few blocks from the Duomo and a 5-minute walk from the railway station. The predictably upper-class interior includes potted plants, patterned carpeting, and coffered ceilings. Rooms have traditional Italian styling.

Dining/Entertainment: The hotel offers a classy Florentine restaurant, with formal service, featuring both a regional and an international cuisine, with meals ranging from 65,000 lire to 105,000 lire ($51 to $82.45). An accommodating bar area has frescoed walls reminiscent of a trompe-l'oeil view from an 18th-century balcony, with jardinières and parrots.

Services: Room service, baby-sitting, laundry, valet.
Facilities: Limited facilities for the disabled.

MODERATE

PENSIONE PENDINI, via Strozzi 2, 50123 Firenze. Tel. 055/211170. 42 rms (all with bath). TEL **Bus:** 31 or 32.

$ **Rates** (including breakfast): 87,000 lire ($68.30) single; 136,000 lire ($106.75) double. DC, MC, V.

Founded in 1879, the family-owned and -run Pensione Pendini offers an old-fashioned environment in a distinguished setting. Your room may overlook the active piazza or front an inner courtyard (more peaceful). One of the oldest pensiones in Florence, it's located on the fourth floor of an arcaded building. The all-purpose lounge is furnished family style with a piano and card tables. The breakfast room is modestly provincial, and some of the bedrooms have quite a lot of character, with reproductions of antiques. The Pendini is not for everyone, but it's one of the long-enduring favorites among pensione devotees visiting Florence. Only breakfast is served.

NEAR THE DUOMO

EXPENSIVE

HOTEL HELVETIA & BRISTOL, via dei Pescioni 2, 50123 Firenze. Tel. 055/287814. Fax 055/288353. 52 rms (all with bath), 12 suites. A/C MINIBAR TV TEL **Bus:** 31 or 32.

$ **Rates:** 240,000–270,000 lire ($188.40–$212) single; 330,000–400,000 lire

($259.05–$314) double; from 490,000 lire ($384.65) suite. IVA tax 19% extra. Breakfast 20,000 lire ($15.70) extra. AE, DC, MC, V. **Parking:** 24,000 lire ($18.85).

The Hotel Helvetia & Bristol is located in the most elegant part of Florence, just a few steps from the Duomo between via Tornabuoni and via degli Strozzi. Constructed in the late 19th century, and reopened in 1988 after a massive restoration, it was once considered the most exclusive hotel in Florence, frequented by noble Florentines and British aristocrats. It has now been restored to its former pedestal. Its guest list has included such notables as Luigi Pirandello, Igor Stravinsky, Giorgio de Chirico, and Gabrielle d'Annunzio. Strict attention was devoted to preserving its original architectural features. Period decoration and furnishings include a famous set of 17th-century paintings which represent the five senses. The bedrooms are attractively decorated and comfortable.

Dining/Entertainment: The Giardino d'Inverno (Winter Garden) is a first-class restaurant, and what was a gathering place for Florentine intellectuals in the 1920s is now a cocktail bar serving light food. The main dining room serves a deluxe cuisine, with meals costing from 75,000 lire ($58.90).

Services: Room service, baby-sitting, laundry, valet.

Facilities: Car-rental desk.

MODERATE

HOTEL MONNA LISA, borgo Pinti 27, 50121 Firenze. Tel. 055/ 2479751. Fax 055/2479755. 20 rms (all with bath). A/C MINIBAR TV TEL **Bus:** 6 or 14.

$ Rates (including breakfast): 150,000–200,000 lire ($117.75–$157) single; 220,000–300,000 lire ($172.70–$235.50) double. **Parking:** 20,000 lire ($15.70).
The Hotel Monna Lisa (yes, that's the right spelling), a well-preserved structure, is a privately owned Renaissance palazzo. Located on a narrow street where carts were once driven, the palace facade is forbiddingly severe, in keeping with the style of its day. But when one enters the reception rooms, the atmosphere is inviting. Most of the great old rooms overlook either an inner patio or the garden in the rear. Each of the salons is handsomely furnished in a restrained way, utilizing many fine antiques and oil paintings. The bedrooms vary greatly. The stamp of owner Countess N. D. Oslavia Ciardi-Dupré's individuality and good taste is everywhere.

BUDGET

SOGGIORNO BRUNORI, via del Proconsolo 5, 50122 Firenze. Tel. 055/289648. 9 rms (4 with bath). **Bus:** 14 or 23.

$ Rates: 42,000 lire ($32.95) double without bath, 53,000 lire ($41.60) double with bath. Breakfast 7,000 lire ($5.50) extra. No credit cards. **Parking:** 15,000 lire ($11.80). **Closed:** Jan–Feb.
About two blocks from piazza del Duomo, the Soggiorno Brunori is an unpretentious little pensione in the center of the historic district. Its comfortably simple bedrooms are outfitted in angular furniture. The management speaks English. There are no singles.

NEAR THE OPERA HOUSE

EXPENSIVE

ANGLO-AMERICAN REGINA HOTEL, via Garibaldi 9, 50123 Firenze. Tel. 055/282114. Fax 055/268513. 107 rms (all with bath or shower), 12 suites. A/C MINIBAR TV TEL **Bus:** 16.

$ Rates (including breakfast): 190,000–240,000 lire ($149.15–$188.40) single; 270,000–330,000 lire ($211.95–$259.05) double; from 390,000 lire ($306.15) suite. AE, MC, V.
The Anglo-American Regina Hotel occupies an old Florentine palace near Cascine Park. Its streetside buildings enclose a covered garden room, lounge, and loggia—springlike all year. The older parts of the hostelry have exquisite architectural features,

as does the dining room, with ornate plaster designs on the walls in pink, red, and white. Crystal chandeliers and towering gilt mirrors grace the public salons. The lobby has draperies covering the sloping skylights. Each room has a radio. The hotel is well placed near the Arno, close to the opera house and the U.S. Consulate. A garage for your car is available nearby.

Dining/Entertainment: There's an elegant dining room with Victorian chairs and an English club–style bar. Piano music is provided every night except Sunday.

Services: Room service, baby-sitting, laundry, valet.

Facilities: Inside garden and loggia.

QUEEN PALACE HOTEL, via Solferino 5, 50123 Firenze. Tel. 055/ 239818. Fax 055/213143. 20 rms (all with bath), 1 suite. A/C MINIBAR TV TEL **Bus:** 13 or 16.

$ Rates (including breakfast): 250,000 lire ($196.25) single; 370,000 lire ($290.45) double; from 450,000 lire ($353.25) suite. AE, DC, MC, V. **Parking:** 25,000 lire ($19.65).

In a quiet, fashionable area in the heart of Florence, near the opera house, the U.S. Consulate, and several big hotels, is the Queen Palace Hotel. The comfortably proportioned rooms, hidden behind an 18th-century palazzo facade, have been fully modernized. A suite for two people has a bedroom and a living room.

MODERATE

ARIELE, via Magenta 11, 50123 Firenze. Tel. 055/211509. Fax 055/ 268521. 40 rms (all with bath or shower). TEL **Bus:** 13 or 16.

$ Rates (including breakfast): 95,000 lire ($74.60) single; 135,000 lire ($106) double; 165,000 lire ($129.55) triple. AE, DC, MC, V. **Parking:** 15,000 lire ($11.80).

Just a block from the Arno is the Ariele, which calls itself "Your Home in Florence." It's an old corner villa that has been converted into a roomy pensione. The building is architecturally impressive, with large salons and lofty ceilings. The furnishings, however, combine antique with functional. The bedrooms are a grab bag of comfort.

INEXPENSIVE

PENSIONE BRETAGNA, lungarno Corsini 6, 50123 Firenze. Tel. 055/ 289618. 18 rms (7 with bath). **Bus:** 32 or 36.

$ Rates (including breakfast): 51,000 lire ($40.05) single without bath, 61,000 lire ($47.90) single with bath; 80,000 lire ($62.80) double without bath, 96,000 lire ($75.35) double with bath. No credit cards.

The Pensione Bretagna is in a palace that was the residence of Louis Napoléon in the 1820s. It's run by a helpful family, most of whom speak English. Offering bed and breakfast only, the pensione is centrally located. Rates depend on the plumbing, as some rooms don't have private bath or shower. Accommodations are furnished in a basic style, but the public rooms of this early Renaissance palace impress with their gilded stucco work, painted ceilings, fireplaces, and a balcony overlooking the Arno.

NEAR PIAZZA SS. ANNUNZIATA

MODERATE

HOTEL LE DUE FONTANE, piazza SS. Annunziata 14, 50122 Firenze. Tel. 055/210987. Fax 055/294461. 48 rms (all with bath). A/C MINIBAR TV TEL **Bus:** 17.

$ Rates (including breakfast): 96,500 lire ($75.75) single; 152,000 lire ($119.30) double. AE, MC, V. **Parking:** 20,000 lire ($15.70).

The Hotel Le Due Fontane is a small neoclassical palace on the best-known

Renaissance square in Florence, right in the heart of the artistic center of the city, within an easy walk of the Duomo. In spite of its antique origins, the little hotel has been completely renovated and modernized. Today it offers simply but tastefully furnished bedrooms. The upper-floor rooms are preferred for those desiring the most tranquil sleep.

LOGGIATO DEI SERVITI, piazza SS. Annunziata 3, 50121 Firenze. Tel. 055/289592. Fax 055/289595. 29 rms (all with bath), 4 suites. A/C MINIBAR TV TEL **Bus:** 1 or 17.

$ Rates (including breakfast): 96,500 lire ($75.75) single; 152,000 lire ($119.30) double; 200,000–400,000 lire ($157–$314) duplex suite for four. AE, DC, MC, V. **Parking:** 40,000 lire ($31.40).

On one of the most quietly elegant squares in Florence, you'll find the Loggiato dei Serviti. Built in the early 1500s as a monastery, it has served as a hotel since the turn of this century. Its entrance lies beneath soaring arcades which face the Renaissance Hospital of the Innocents and an imposing equestrian statue. More than any other hotel in the neighborhood, its bedrooms evoke the aura of an austerely elegant monastery, with vaulted or beamed ceilings, some of which are painted with Renaissance-inspired designs.

INEXPENSIVE

HOTEL MORANDI ALLE CROCETTA, via Laura 50, 50121 Firenze. Tel. 055/234-4747. Fax 055/248-0954. 10 rms (all with bath), 1 suite. A/C MINIBAR TV TEL **Bus:** 1, 7, 10, 11, or 17.

$ Rates: 70,000–85,000 lire ($54.95–$66.75) single; 107,000–128,000 lire ($84–$100.50) double; from 144,000 lire ($113.05) suite. Breakfast 15,000 lire ($11.80) extra. AE, DC, MC, V.

The small, charming Hotel Morandi alle Crocetta is administered by one of the most experienced hoteliers in Florence, a sprightly matriarch, Katherine Doyle, who came to Florence from her native Ireland when she was 12. It contains all the elements needed for a Florentine pensione, lying on a little-visited backstreet near a university building. The structure was built in the 1500s as a convent. The bedrooms have been tastefully and gracefully restored, filled with framed examples of 19th-century needlework, beamed ceilings, and antiques. In the best Tuscan tradition, the tall windows are sheltered from the summer sunlight with heavy draperies. You register in a high-ceilinged and gracefully austere salon filled with Persian carpets. The hotel lies right behind the Archeological Museum and two blocks from the Accademia (which displays Michelangelo's *David*).

OFF PIAZZA DELL'INDIPENDENZA

MODERATE

RAPALLO, via Santa Caterina d'Alessandria 7, 50129 Firenze. Tel. 055/472412. Fax 055/268364 30 rms (20 with bath). A/C MINIBAR TEL **Bus:** 19.

$ Rates: 63,000 lire ($49.45) single without bath, 80,500 lire ($63.20) single with bath; 93,500 lire ($73.40) double without bath, 120,000 lire ($94.20) double with bath. Breakfast 11,000 lire ($8.65) extra. AE, DC, MC, V. **Parking:** 18,000 lire ($14.15).

An "E" for effort is due Rapallo, which has attempted to make its rooms liveable and comfortable. Without succeeding in being typical of Florence, it is, nevertheless, newish (completely revamped), fresh, and inviting. The lounge, ingeniously using small space, is brightened by planters, Oriental rugs, and barrel stools set in the corners for drinking and conversation. The bedrooms are furnished mostly with blond-wood suites, quite pleasant, and all have a private safe, and upon request, a TV.

The twin-bedded rooms have end-to-end beds. The hotel is within walking distance of the railway station.

INEXPENSIVE

HOTEL SPLENDOR, via S. Gallo 30, 50129 Firenze. Tel. 055/483427.
Fax 055/461276. 31 rms (25 with bath or shower). TEL **Bus:** 1, 7, 10, 17, or 25.
$ Rates (including breakfast): 73,000 lire ($57.30) single with bath; 91,000 lire ($71.45) double without bath, 117,000 lire ($91.85) double with bath. MC, V. **Parking:** 22,000 lire ($17.25).

Although the Hotel Splendor is within a 10-minute walk from the Duomo, the residential neighborhood it occupies is a world away from the milling hordes of the tourist district. The hotel has three high-ceilinged floors of a 19th-century apartment building. Its elegantly faded public rooms evoke the kind of family-run pensione which, early in the century, attracted genteel visitors from northern Europe for prolonged art-related visits. This is the domain of the Masoero family, whose rooms contain an eclectic array of semi-antique furniture and much of the ambience of bedrooms in a private house. All the singles have baths. There is no restaurant, but room service is available.

NEAR PIAZZA DELLA SIGNORIA
MODERATE

GRAND HOTEL CAVOUR, via del Proconsolo 3, 50122 Firenze. Tel. 055/287102. Fax 055/218955. 89 rms (all with bath). A/C MINIBAR TV TEL **Bus:** 14 or 19.
$ Rates (including breakfast): 105,500 lire ($117.75) single; 170,000 lire ($133.45) double. AE, DC, MC, V. **Parking:** 20,000 lire ($15.70).

Opposite the Bargello Museum, between via del Proconsolo and via Dante Alighieri, is the Grand Hotel Cavour, an elaborate palace built in the 13th century. The hotel is located on an important corner of the city, near the Badia Church, between the houses of the Cerchi and Pazzi families. It once belonged to the Cerchis, and in the lounge you can see where the old courtyard was laid out. In the basement, a historic well is called Beatrice's Well. The Portinaris, family of Dante's beloved Beatrice, lived nearby, and it is possible that the young woman actually drew water from the well. Such a chore was at least certainly done by Beatrice's nurse, Monna Tessa. The Hotel Cavour came into being when Florence was the capital of Italy (1860–65), and it was nicknamed "The Senators' Hotel" because it was frequented by the members of the highest assembly of the new state.

The Cavour maintains its architectural splendor. The coved main lounge, with its frescoed ceiling and crystal chandelier, is of special interest, as is the old chapel, now used as a dining room. The altar and confessional are still there. The ornate ceiling and stained-glass windows reflect superb crafting. The Cavour attained a curious supremacy in Florence in 1905, when it gained the first elevator in town. Elevators now take you to the traditionally styled and comfortably furnished bedrooms. Each unit has a hairdryer.

ON THE ARNO
EXPENSIVE

PLAZA HOTEL LUCCHESI, lungarno della Zecca Vecchia 38, 50122 Firenze. Tel. 055/264141. Fax 055/248-0921. 97 rms (all with bath), 10 suites. A/C MINIBAR TV TEL **Bus:** 13, 15, 19, 31, or 32.
$ Rates (including breakfast): 240,000 lire ($188.40) single; 340,000 lire ($266.90) double; from 450,000 lire ($353.25) suite. AE, DC, MC, V. **Parking:** 40,000 lire ($31.40).

The Plaza Hotel Lucchesi, one of the most charming and best-managed hotels in Florence, offers many of the facilities and services of the city's famous five-star hotels, but at about half the price. Originally built in 1860, and gracefully renovated many times since then, it lies along the banks of the Arno, a 10-minute walk from the Duomo and a few paces from the imposing Church of Santa Maria della Croce. Its interior decor includes lots of glossy mahogany, acres of marble, and masses of fresh flowers. Each of the handsomely furnished and beautifully kept bedrooms contains all the modern equipment and comfort you'd expect from such a stellar property. About 20 accommodations open onto private terraces or balconies, some with enviable views over the heart of historic Florence.

Dining/Entertainment: In the sunny lobby-level restaurant, La Serra, the site of copious morning breakfast buffets and elegant dinners, diners often enjoy the melodies of a resident pianist/singer. The comfortably appointed bar reigns supreme as the hotel's social center.

Services: 24-hour room service, baby-sitting, laundry, valet.

Facilities: Car-rental desk.

MODERATE

HOTEL AUGUSTUS, vicolo del'Oro 5, 50123 Firenze. Tel. 055/283054.

Fax 055/268557. 67 rms (all with bath or shower), 6 suites. A/C MINIBAR TV TEL **Bus:** 3, 6, 31, or 32.

$ **Rates:** 120,000–185,000 lire ($94.20–$145.25) single; 170,000–240,000 lire ($133.45–$188.40) double; from 360,000 lire ($282.60) suite. Breakfast 18,000 lire ($14.15) extra. AE, DC, MC, V.

The Hotel Augustus is for those who require modern comforts in a setting of historical and monumental Florence. The Ponte Vecchio is just a short stroll away, as is the Uffizi Gallery. The exterior is rather pillbox modern, but the interior seems light, bright, and comfortable. The expansive lounge and drinking area is like an illuminated cave, with a curving ceiling and built-in conversational areas interlocked on several levels. Some of the bedrooms open onto little private balconies with garden furniture.

HOTEL BALESTRI, piazza Mentana 7, 50122 Firenze. Tel. 055/214743.

Fax 055/239-8042. 50 rms (all with bath). TEL **Bus:** 13 or 23.

$ **Rates** (including breakfast): 105,000 lire ($82.45) single; 166,000 lire ($130.30) double. AE, DC, MC, V. **Parking:** 20,000 lire ($15.70).

The buff-colored front of this hotel faces a quiet square, and its side looks out over the Arno and the traffic running along its quay. Built as a private home in 1888 (the date is set into the floor of the entryway in contrasting shades of marble), the hotel has a lobby with vaulted ceilings, red-and-white stone floors, Oriental rugs, and modern paintings. The hotel has been run by the same family for generations, and the reception is helpful. The hotel lies between the Ponte Vecchio and piazza del Duomo. Bedrooms have traditional styling, and half of them contain air conditioners.

HOTEL PRINCIPE, lungarno Vespucci 34, 50123 Firenze. Tel. 055/284848.

Fax 055/283458. 21 rms (all with bath), 2 suites. A/C MINIBAR TV TEL **Bus:** 31 or 32.

$ **Rates:** 160,000–220,000 lire ($125.60–$172.70) single; 190,000–260,000 lire ($149.15–$204.10) double; from 360,000 lire ($282.60) suite. Breakfast 20,000 lire ($15.70) extra. AE, DC, MC, V. **Parking:** 30,000 lire ($23.55).

The Hotel Principe is a real "find." Its facade is dignified, like an old embassy town house, and its bedrooms have been well adapted. Each bedroom is treated differently, reflecting the taste of the owner, who blends antique and modern. Ask for one of the terrace rooms, where tables and chairs are set out for breakfast facing the Arno. Double glass doors protect the bedrooms from street noises. One of the nicest features of the hotel is its little walled garden in back where drinks are served. The hotel serves breakfast only.

LUNGARNO, borgo San Jacopo 14, 50125 Firenze. Tel. 055/264211.

Fax 055/268437. 66 rms (all with bath or shower), 12 suites. A/C MINIBAR TV TEL **Bus:** 31 or 32.

$ **Rates:** 190,000 lire ($149.15) single; 260,000 lire ($204.10) double; from 350,000 lire ($274.75) suite. Breakfast 18,000 lire ($14.15) extra. AE, DC, MC, V. **Parking:** 30,000 lire ($23.55).

As you stand on the banks of the Arno, looking at the facade of the 10 floors of the Lungarno, you'll find it difficult to believe that the hotel was built entirely in the 1960s. It's proof that a modern, comfortable hotel can be created in the old style without sacrificing conveniences of the 20th century. Imagine sitting in a stone tower suite, enjoying a room-long view through a picture window of the rooftops of Florence, including the Duomo and campanile. Throughout the hotel is a collection of contemporary watercolors and oils. Around the fireplace is a "clutter wall" of framed art. On sunny days guests congregate on the upper terrace, enjoying the drinks and a view of the bridges spanning the Arno. The bedrooms are consistently well designed and attractive, each with its own color theme. Singles have showers and doubles have baths. The hotel lies near the Ponte Vecchio on the Palazzo Pitti side. The hotel has no restaurant but does offer a snack bar.

INEXPENSIVE

HOTEL COLUMBUS, lungarno Cristofo Colombo 22A, 50136 Firenze. Tel. 055/677251. Fax 055/669100. 99 rms (all with bath or shower). A/C TEL **Bus:** 14.
$ Rates: 87,500 lire ($68.70) single; 122,000 lire ($95.75) double. Breakfast 10,000 lire ($7.85) extra. AE, DC, MC, V.

The modern Hotel Columbus is built and furnished with good taste. Although set quite a distance from the city's major attractions, it's still only a 20-minute walk from the Ponte Vecchio and can also be reached by bus. The air-conditioned public rooms, with light-inviting windows, have informal furnishings. The dining room has round tables, with ladder-back chairs, potted greenery, and a sense of space. The bedrooms (each with a private balcony) are compact, in the motel fashion, with everything built in: bedside table, lights, and all. TV is available upon request. There's no fussy decor—instead, the tone is severe but restful.

NEAR THE PONTE S. TRINITA

BUDGET

SOGGIORNO CESTELLI, borgo SS. Apostoli 25, 50123 Firenze. Tel. 055/214213. 7 rms (1 with bath). **Bus:** 37.
$ Rates (including breakfast): 40,000 lire ($31.40) single without bath; 68,000 lire ($53.38) double without bath; 70,000 lire ($54.95) double with bath. No credit cards.

A simple pensione, the Soggiorno Castelli has comfortable rooms on the upper floors of a centuries-old palazzo. Set about a block from the Arno on a narrow street in the old city, its rates depend on plumbing in each room. The pensione is located near the Ponte Vecchio, about a 3-minute walk from piazza della Signoria. It's about a 10-minute walk from the central station. Bus no. 37 passes by about every 30 minutes.

NEAR THE PONTE VECCHIO

MODERATE

HOTEL CONTINENTAL, lungarno Acciaiuoli 2, 50123 Firenze. Tel. 055/282392. Fax 055/282392. 61 rms (all with bath or shower), 9 suites. A/C MINIBAR TV TEL **Bus:** 31.
$ Rates: 110,000–150,000 lire ($86.35–$117.75) single; 160,000–230,000 lire ($125.60–$180.55) double; from 280,000 lire ($219.80) suite. AE, DC, MC, V. **Parking:** 30,000 lire ($23.55).

Located at the entrance of the Ponte Vecchio, the Hotel Continental occupies some choice real estate. Through the lounge windows and from some of the bedrooms you can see the little jewelry and leather shops that flank the much-painted bridge over the Arno. Despite its perch in the center of historic Florence, the hotel was created in the 1960s, so its style of accommodation is utilitarian, with functional furniture that is softened by the placement of decorative accessories. You reach your bedroom by the elevator or by climbing a wooden staircase (note that parts of the old stone structure have been retained). The bedrooms are furnished with Italian provincial pieces, color coordinated. The management likes to put up North Americans, knowing they'll be attracted to the roof terrace, a vantage point for viewing piazzale Michelangelo, the Pitti Palace, the Duomo, the campanile, and Fiesole. Artists fight to get the tiny simple rooms up in the tower ("Torre Guelfa dei Consorti").

HERMITAGE HOTEL, vicolo Marzio 1, 50122 Florence. Tel. 055/ 267216. Fax 055/212208. 22 rms (20 with bath or shower). A/C TEL **Bus:** 23.
$ Rates (including breakfast): 90,000 lire ($70.65) single without bath, 100,000 lire ($78.50) single with bath; 147,000 lire ($115.40) double without bath, 157,000 lire ($123.25) double with bath. V.

The offbeat, intimate Hermitage Hotel is a charming place to stay right on the Arno, with a sun terrace on the roof providing a view of much of Florence, including the nearby Uffizi. You can take your breakfast under a leafy arbor surrounded by potted roses and geraniums. The success of the small hotel has much to do with its English-speaking owners, Paolo and Vincenzo Scarcelli, who have made the Hermitage an extension of their home, furnishing it in part with antiques and well-chosen reproductions. Best of all is their warmth toward guests, many of whom keep coming back to enjoy the gatherings in the top-floor living room around the wood-burning fireplace on nippy nights.

The bedrooms are pleasantly furnished, many with Tuscan antiques, rich brocades, and good beds. The tiled baths are superb and contain lots of gadgets. Breakfast is served in a dignified, beam-ceilinged dining room. Rooms overlooking the Arno have the most scenic view, and they've been fitted with double-glass windows, which reduces the traffic noise by 40%.

QUISIANA E PONTE VECCHIO, lungarno Archibusieri 4, 50122 Firenze. Tel. 055/216692. Fax 055/268303. 37 rms (all with bath). **Bus:** 13, 19, 23, 31, or 32.
$ Rates (including breakfast): 91,000 lire ($71.45) single; 142,000 lire ($111.45) double. AE, DC, MC, V.

The Quisiana e Ponte Vecchio stands directly on the Arno, near the Ponte Vecchio and within an easy walk of the Uffizi Gallery. This late 19th-century Florentine pensione, furnished in a homelike fashion, is serviced by an elevator. The pensione's nicest feature is a loggia overlooking the Arno. Some scenes from E. M. Forster's *A Room with a View* were filmed here.

INEXPENSIVE

HOTEL CALZAIUOLI, via Calzaiuoli 6, 50122 Firenze. Tel. 055/212456. Fax 055/268310. 49 rms (all with bath or shower). A/C MINIBAR TV TEL **Bus:** 1, 14, 19, or 23.
$ Rates: 82,000 lire ($64.35) single; 120,000 lire ($94.20) double. Breakfast 11,000 lire ($8.65) extra. AE, DC, MC, V.

The Hotel Calzaiuoli is a 19th-century structure on a pedestrian street connecting piazza del Signoria with the Duomo. The location is one of the city's most desirable in terms of sightseeing, as the major attractions are virtually at your doorstep. Although the building is old, the hotel has been completely modernized, in a rather severe style. Rooms are spacious and furnished with functional pieces. Guests register in a marble-and-teakwood lobby.

NEAR SANTA CROCE

INEXPENSIVE

HOTEL PENSIONE RIGATTI, lungarno Diaz 2, 50122 Firenze. Tel. 055/ 213022. 28 rms (15 with bath). **Bus:** 13, 19, 23, or 32.
$ Rates (including breakfast): 53,000 lire ($41.60) single without bath, 64,000 lire ($50.25) single with shower; 86,000 lire ($67.50) double without bath, 102,000 lire ($80.05) double with bath or shower; 120,000 lire ($94.20) triple without bath, 143,000 lire ($112.25) triple with bath or shower. No credit cards.

$ A rare find in Florence, the Rigatti is an establishment doing what it can to preserve the aura of an elegant private palace studded with many of its original frescoes and antiques. The loyal clientele includes teachers, art historians, and an international collection of friends of the cultivated family running it, the Rigatti. The owners are Gabriella di Benedictus and her brother, Luigi, descendants of the Rigatti family who set up the pensione in 1907 in a 14th-century palazzo. On the banks of a noisy Arno quay, the hotel's entrance is on a narrow sidewalk, through massive wooden doors, and up a small elevator to the second floor. There, a series of elegantly furnished high-ceilinged rooms with rococo lighting fixtures, musical instruments, and 19th-century chairs create a baronial setting that extends into the simple and comfortable bedrooms. The windows of these open onto carved stone columns that look out, depending on the exposure, over the river, a garden filled with azaleas, or a narrow side street of Renaissance buildings. On the upper floor, a covered loggia with views of piazza della Signoria offers a place where guests can sometimes order coffee or drinks.

ON THE LEFT BANK

VERY EXPENSIVE

GRAND HOTEL VILLA CORA, viale Machiavelli 18-20, 50125 Firenze. Tel. 055/229-8451. Fax 055/229086. 48 rms (all with bath), 16 suites. A/C MINIBAR TV TEL **Bus:** 13.
$ Rates (including breakfast): 274,000–363,000 lire ($215.10–$284.95) single; 448,000–648,000 lire ($351.70–$508.70) double; from 648,000 lire ($508.70) suite. AE, DC, MC, V. **Parking:** Free.

★ The Grand Hotel Villa Cora is a grandiose Renaissance neoclassic palace on the hill near piazza Michelangelo above the city. Built by Baron Oppenheim and once lived in by the Italian ambassador to the U.S., the luxury hotel stands in its own formal gardens, with a special recreation area, including an open-air swimming pool. The villa was chosen as a residence for the ex-Empress Eugénie, widow of Napoléon III, to whom Florence gave a warm and deferential welcome. The public rooms have architectural splendor, with drawing rooms that open off the domed circular rotunda. Marble, ornate bronze, white-and-gilt doors, frescoed ceilings, parquet floors, and silk damask walls characterize the decor. The more expensive bedrooms are one-of-a-kind, although the others are well furnished with tasteful reproductions of the 19th-century pieces. Singles have showers and doubles have baths or showers. In warm weather meals are also served in the open air near the swimming pool. From the rooftop solarium, a panoramic view of the rooftops of Florence unfolds.

Dining/Entertainment: In the restaurant, Taverna Machiavelli, you can enjoy fine food. Music is played nightly in the piano bar.

Services: 24-hour room service, free limousine service to and from Ponte Vecchio, laundry, valet.

Facilities: Swimming pool.

INEXPENSIVE

PENSIONE ANNALENA, via Romana 34, 50125 Firenze. Tel. 055/222403. Fax 055/229600. 20 rms (all with bath). TV TEL **Bus:** 13.
$ Rates (including breakfast): 85,000–95,000 lire ($66.75–$74.60) single; 120,000–145,500 lire ($94.20–$114.20) double. AE, DC, MC, V.

In existence since the 15th century, Pensione Annalena has had many owners, including the Medici. Once a convent, in the past three-quarters of a century it has been a haven for artists, poets, sculptors, and writers (Mary McCarthy once wrote of its importance as a cultural center). During a great deal of that period it was the domain of the late sculptor Olinto Calastri. Now it is owned by Claudio Salvestrini, who attracts paying guests sympathetic to the pensione's special qualities. Most of the accommodations overlook a garden. During the war, the Annalena was the center of much of the underground, as many Jews and rebel Italians found safety hidden away in an underground room behind a secret door. The pensione is about a 5-minute walk from the Pitti Palace, 10 minutes from the Ponte Vecchio.

AT GALLUZZO
EXPENSIVE

RELAIS CERTOSA, via Colle Ramole 2, 50124 Firenze. Tel. 055/204-7171. Fax 055/268575. 70 rms (all with bath), 6 suites. A/C MINIBAR TV TEL **Directions:** Take the Rome–Milan expressway to exit A1, "Firenze/Certosa." Go 300 yards, and turn left on a signposted road leading to the hotel. **Bus:** 37 from the center of Florence to Certosa.

$ Rates (including breakfast): 215,000 lire ($168.80) single; 290,000 lire ($227.65) double; from 418,000 lire ($328.15) suite. **Parking:** Free.

The Relais Certosa, a four-star hotel of exceptional merit, is set on 5 acres of land with tennis courts. The relais was originally a guesthouse for the monastery near here, but during the Renaissance it became the villa that stands today. In the 19th century it was a farm. After centuries of use in private hands, it became a hotel in the 1970s, which today could easily become your home in Florence. Convenient for motorists who want to avoid the hysterical city center, it's only 10 minutes from the monumental district and 5 minutes from the Rome–Milan expressway. Open all year, its rooms are well furnished, and each has individual climate control. Somehow the owners, the Bettoja family, have managed to blend Renaissance charm and style with today's comforts. The atmosphere is a special Florentine one. All rooms face a park with views of the Tuscan hills and the Certosa monastery. There's parking space for 200 cars.

Dining/Entertainment: For some of the best Tuscan dining in the area, you can patronize the Greenhouse Restaurant even if you're not a guest of the hotel. It offers regional specialties as well as continental dishes. Guests also enjoy a garden and terrace for drinks and snacks and a bar and piano bar.

Services: Room service, laundry, valet.

Facilities: Heated swimming pool, sauna, solarium, parking.

NEAR PIAZZALE MICHELANGELO
EXPENSIVE

HOTEL VILLA CARLOTTA, via Michele di Lando 3, 50125 Firenze. Tel. 055/233-6134. Fax 055/233-6147. 27 rms (all with bath). A/C MINIBAR TV TEL **Bus:** 11, 13, 36, or 37.

$ Rates (including breakfast): 120,000–240,000 lire ($94.20–$188.40) single; 170,000–340,000 lire ($133.45–$266.90) double. AE, DC, MC, V. **Parking:** Free.

The lavish renovations that the owner poured into her distinguished establishment transformed it into one of the most charming smaller hotels in Florence. It was built during the Edwardian age as a private villa and acquired in the 1950s by Carlotta Buchholz, who named it after herself. When her daughter, Evelina Pagni, took the administrative reins, she enlarged the ground floor with a glassed-in extension, filled it with Persian carpets and family heirlooms, and restored the elaborate plaster detailing of the formal interior. The aura here is still very much like that of a private villa. It's in a residential section of the city, behind a neoclassical facade whose entrance columns are capped with stone lions and flanked with venerable cypresses. In 1985 all bedrooms were upgraded with the addition of a sheathing of pink or blue silk wallpaper, reproduction antiques, silk bedspreads, private safety-deposit boxes, and crystal chandeliers; each also has a view of the surrounding garden. The hotel lies only 10 pedestrian minutes from the Ponte Vecchio; by taxi, it's a 5-minute ride.

Dining/Entertainment: The dining room serves meals ranging from fresh salads to full culinary regalias, always accompanied by top-notch service and personal touches.

Services: Room service, baby-sitting, laundry, valet.

Facilities: Garden, car-rental desk.

AT COLLI

EXPENSIVE

TORRE DI BELLOSGUARDO, via Roti Michelozzi 2, 50125 Firenze. Tel. 055/229-8145. Fax 055/229008. 16 rms (all with bath), 6 suites. A/C MINIBAR TEL **Bus:** 13.

$ Rates: 210,000 lire ($164.85) single; 280,000 lire ($219.80) double; from 380,000 lire ($298.30) suite. Breakfast 18,000 lire ($14.15) extra. AE, DC, MC, V. **Parking:** Free.

This four-star hotel, a 14th-century tower surrounded by a majestic villa, is a little-known treasure which merits a high recommendation. Located on top of a hill about a mile and a half from the city walls with a spectacular view of Florence, the hotel is framed by an avenue of cypresses in the Tuscan style. The tower was once part of a manor house constructed by a Florentine nobleman who was a friend of Dante. Two magnolia trees lead into a sunny veranda. Guests enter a frescoed ballroom. No two bedrooms are alike; your room might have a gilded four-poster bed or a 16th-century rosette-studded ceiling. Family accommodations are available. The garden around the hotel is almost like a park, with a series of terraces stretching toward Florence.

Dining/Entertainment: Breakfast, the only meal served, is offered on a sunny veranda or in the cool dining room. Tasty seasonal fruit comes from the hotel's orchard.

Services: Room service, baby-sitting, laundry, valet.

Facilities: Swimming pool.

VILLA BELVEDERE, via Benedetto Castelli 3, 50124 Firenze. Tel. 055/222501. Fax 055/223163. 27 rms (all with bath). A/C TV TEL **Bus:** 11 or 37 to "Poggio Imperiale."

$ Rates (including breakfast): 155,000 lire ($121.70) single; 220,000–240,000 lire ($172.70–$188.40) double. AE, DC, MC, V. **Parking:** Free. **Closed:** Dec–Feb.

On the edge of Florence, the Villa Belvedere stands on grounds that once belonged to the Medici, although the present building is a reconstruction. It's suitable for those who want a tranquil setting, gardens for sunbathing, a swimming pool for quick dips, and a tennis court for exercise. The bedrooms are efficient and well planned. The villa lies on the Siena–Rome road. Some doubles have a veranda with a panoramic view of Florence. Facilities include a swimming pool and tennis court.

AT CANDELI

VERY EXPENSIVE

VILLA LA MASSA, via La Massa 8, 50010 Candeli. Tel. 055/630051. Fax 055/632579. 42 rms (all with bath). A/C MINIBAR TV TEL

$ Rates (including breakfast): 290,000 lire ($227.65) single; 440,000–490,000 lire ($345.40–$384.65) double. AE, DC, MC, V. **Parking:** Free.

Villa La Massa lies about a 10-minute drive south of the city, 4 miles from the railway station, at Candeli. One of the loveliest spots in all the hill country, the villa is on a projection of parkland with tennis courts that has the Arno snaking around on three sides. This 15th-century home of the Count Giraldi family is favored by numerous celebrities in summer. The spacious and well-adorned drawing rooms, private library, and dining salons open onto a central covered courtyard-lounge, with a surrounding arched passageway. The bedrooms, located on the floor above, open onto this courtyard or the river and gardens and are lavishly furnished with antiques or fine reproductions. Some rooms have hydromassage. In addition, you'll find a sun terrace, flowers, and shade trees.

Dining/Entertainment: The glittery bar was once an altar, and the Corinthian-columned dining room is formal, with a vaulted ceiling and a stone fireplace—ideal for baronial meals. There's another building, near the riverside, where dining is

FROMMER'S COOL FOR KIDS
HOTELS

Hotel Casci (see page 225) This hotel is not only inexpensive in price, but it's well located in the historic district. Many of its bedrooms are rented as triples and quads.

Nuova Italia (see page 225) This 17th-century building near the rail station offers some very large rooms suitable for families, for whom management will make special reductions.

Hotel Pensione Rigatti (see page 235) In a former private palace, under family ownership, this hotel rents many triple rooms and enjoys a good location near the Church of Santa Croce where Michelangelo is buried.

Torre di Bellosguardo (see page 238) This majestic villa, a mile and a half from Florence, enjoys a parklike setting with a garden and swimming pool. Family accommodations are available.

accompanied by dance music. A cellar (Club La Cave) offers an American-style bar and occasional entertainment.

Services: Room service, baby-sitting, laundry, valet.
Facilities: Hotel bus to Florence, swimming pool, tennis courts.

2. DINING

After checking into your hotel you'll begin an even more interesting search—this time for a restaurant that may represent your introduction to Florentine cuisine.

The Tuscan cuisine (except for some of its hair-raising specialties) should please most North Americans, as it's simply flavored, without rich spices, and based on the hearty, bountiful produce brought in from the hills. Florentine restaurants are not generally as acclaimed by gourmets as those of Rome, but many dishes are prepared so well that the Tuscan kitchen is considered among the finest in Italy. Florentines often assert that the cooking in the other regions of Italy "offends the palate."

The case was stated most critically by Mary McCarthy, who wrote: "The food in the restaurants is bad, for the most part, monotonous, and rather expensive. Many of the Florentine specialties—tripe, paunch, rabbit, and a mixture of the combs, livers, hearts, and testicles of roosters—do not appeal to the foreign palate." The statement is funnier than it is true, although I concede the point about some of the specialties. And although I don't know where Ms. McCarthy dined, it's true that Florence has many expensive citadels which dispense viands at "Grand Duke" prices. On the other hand, the city often stuns visitors with the sheer preponderance of good moderately priced eating establishments. And one of the most typical platters, the Florentine beefsteak, is savored by foreigners and locals alike.

The one Italian wine all foreigners recognize, the ruby-red chianti, usually in a straw bottle, comes from Tuscany. Although shunned by some wine snobs, it is a fit complement to many a local repast.

Armed with a knife and fork, we'll eat our way down through the pick of the restaurants. I hasten to point out that the reference to "down" is in price only. Many of my most memorable and top-level dinners have been in some of the completely unheralded trattorie and *buca* (cellar) restaurants of the city.

Restaurants rated "Very Expensive" charge more than 120,000 lire ($94.20) for a meal, "Expensive" restaurants charge between 80,000 lire and 120,000 lire ($62.80 and $94.20), restaurants in the "Moderate" bracket charge 40,000 lire to 80,000 lire

($31.40 to $62.80), and restaurants judged "Inexpensive" charge less than 40,000 lire ($31.40). These prices are per person, for a three-course meal, including house wine, taxes, and service.

NEAR THE RAILWAY STATION

MODERATE

LE FONTICINE, via Nazionale 79R. Tel. 282106.
   Cuisine: TUSCAN/BOLOGNESE. **Reservations:** Recommended for dinner. **Bus:** 19.
$ **Prices:** Appetizers 10,000–15,000 lire ($7.85–$11.80); main courses 15,000–20,000 lire ($11.80–$15.70). AE, V.
   Open: Lunch Tues–Sat noon–3pm; dinner Tues–Sat 7–10:30pm. **Closed:** July 25–Aug 25.

Le Fonticine used to be part of a convent until the gracious owner, Silvano Bruci, converted both it and its adjoining garden into one of the most hospitable restaurants of Florence. Today the richly decorated interior contains all the abundance of an Italian harvest, as well as the second passion of Signor Bruci's life, his collection of original paintings. The first passion, as a meal here reveals, is the cuisine that he and his elegant wife produce from recipes she collected from her childhood in Bologna.

Proceed to the larger of the establishment's two dining areas, and along the way you can admire dozens of portions of recently made pasta decorating the table of an exposed grill. At the far end of the room, a wrought-iron gate shelters the wine collection that Mr. Bruci has amassed, like his paintings, for many years. The food, served in copious portions, is both traditional and delectable. Begin with a platter of fresh antipasti, then follow with samplings of three of the most excellent pasta dishes of the day. This might be followed by fegatina di pollo (chicken), veal scaloppine, or another main dish from a full repertoire of the classic Italian cuisine.

SABATINI, via de' Panzani 9A. Tel. 282802.
   Cuisine: FLORENTINE. **Reservations:** Recommended. **Bus:** 19.
$ **Prices:** Appetizers 10,000–20,000 lire ($7.85–$15.70); main courses 14,000–26,000 lire ($11–$20.40). AE, DC, MC, V.
   Open: Lunch Tues–Sun 12:30–3:30pm; dinner Tues–Sat 7:30–11:30pm.

Despite its unchic location near the railway station, Sabatini has long been extolled by Florentines and visitors alike as the finest of the restaurants characteristic of the city. To celebrate my return visit to this restaurant, I ordered the same main course I had when I originally researched this guide. It was boiled Valdarno chicken with a savory green sauce. Back then I had complained to the

FROMMER'S SMART TRAVELER: RESTAURANTS

VALUE-CONSCIOUS TRAVELERS SHOULD TAKE ADVANTAGE OF THE FOLLOWING:

1. When available, order a fixed-price menu where everything—including tax, service, and cover charge—is included.
2. Watch the booze—tabs mount quickly. It's cheaper to ask for a carafe of the house wine.
3. Pastas, pizzas, and rice dishes (risottos) are exceptional bargains.
4. Standing up at a café or roticceria is less expensive than sitting down.
5. Make lunch a picnic and save the extra money for a really good dinner.

waiter that the chicken was tough. He'd replied, "But, of course!" The Florentine likes chicken with muscle, not the hot-house variety so favored by Americans. Having eaten a lot of Valdarno chicken since those long-ago days back in the 1960s, I was more appreciative of Sabatini's dish. But on a subsequent visit I found some of the other main courses more delectable, especially the veal scaloppine with artichokes. Of course, you can always order a good sole meunière and the classic beefsteak Florentine. American-style coffee is also served, following the Florentine cake, called zuccotto.

AT PIAZZA S. MARIA NOVELLA
MODERATE

RISTORANTE OTELLO, via degli Oricellari 36R. Tel. 215819.
Cuisine: FLORENTINE. **Reservations:** Recommended. **Bus:** 31 or 32.
$ Prices: Appetizers 6,000–8,000 lire ($4.70–$6.30); main courses 14,000–18,000 lire ($11–$14.15). AE, DC, MC, V.
Open: Lunch Wed–Mon noon–3pm; dinner Wed–Mon 7:30–11pm.

Ristorante Otello is a long-established Florentine dining room which serves an animated clientele in comfortably renovated surroundings. Its antipasto Toscano is considered one of the best in town, an array of appetizing hors d'oeuvres that practically becomes a meal in itself. The waiter urges you to "Mangi, mangi, mangi!" ("Eat, eat, eat!") and that's what diners do here, as the victuals at Otello have been known to stir the most lethargic of appetites. The true trencherperson goes on to order one of the succulent pasta dishes, such as spaghetti with small baby clams. The meat and poultry dishes are equally delectable, including sole meunière or veal pizzaiola with lots of garlic.

SOSTANZA, via del Porcellana 25R. Tel. 212691.
Cuisine: FLORENTINE. **Reservations:** Recommended. **Bus:** 31 or 32.
$ Prices: Appetizers 10,000–12,000 lire ($7.85–$9.40); main courses 20,000–22,000 lire ($15.70–$17.25). No credit cards.
Open: Lunch Mon–Fri noon–2:10pm; dinner Mon–Fri 7:30–9:30pm. **Closed:** Aug.

Sostanza is a tucked-away little trattoria where working people have gone for years to get excellent moderately priced food. But in more recent times the invading sophisticates have been pouring in to share tables with them. The small dining room has crowded family tables. The rear kitchen is open, its secrets exposed to diners. When you taste what comes out of that kitchen, you'll know that fancy decor would be superfluous. Specialties include breaded chicken breast and a succulent T-bone steak. You might also want to try tripe here the Florentine way—that is, cut into strips, then baked in a casserole with tomatoes, onions, and parmesan cheese. A fine beginning is the tortellini and a fit ending is Florentine cake.

INEXPENSIVE

LA CARABACCIA, via Palazzuolo 190R. Tel. 214782.
Cuisine: FLORENTINE. **Reservations:** Not needed. **Bus:** 19.
$ Prices: Appetizers 8,000–10,000 lire ($6.30–$7.85); main courses 10,000–15,000 lire ($7.85–$11.80). MC, V.
Open: Lunch Tues–Sat 12:30–2:30pm; dinner Mon–Sat 7:30–10:30pm. **Closed:** Aug.

Two hundred years ago a *carabaccia* was a workaday boat, shaped like a hollowed-out half onion and used on the Arno to dredge silt and sand from the river bottom. The favorite onion soup of the Medici was zuppa carabaccia, which this restaurant still features today. It is a creamy white onion soup served with croutons (and not in the French style, the chef rushes to tell you). Carabaccia is a style of Florentine cuisine that still presents a meat, such as boar, with stewed onions on the side. You can, of course, eat more than onions here. The menu changes every day and is based on the use of fresh local ingredients. There is always one soup, followed by four or five

ITALY
• Florence
Rome ★

Al Lume di Candela ㉑
Antico Fattore, Trattoria ㉖
Bistro, Le ❺
Borga, La ㉕
Buca Mario ⓮
Buca dell'Orafo ㉗
Buca Lapi ⓯
Caffè Voltaire ⑪
Cammillo, Trattoria ㉓
Cantinetta Antinori ⓰
Carabaccia, La ⑬
Cavallino, Il ㉙
Centro Vegetariano Fiorrentino
   Almanacco ❹
Cestello, Il ❸
Cibreo ㊲
Doney ⑰
Fonticine, Le ❼
Ganino, Da ㉚
Garga, Trattoria
Gelateria Vivoli ㉟
Giannino in San Lorenzo ❾
Harry's Bar ⑲
Kenny ㉘
Leo in Santa Croce ㊱
Loggia, La ❻
Mamma Gina ㉓
Mossacce, Le ㉝
Nandina ㉔
Natale ㉒
Otello ❽
Paoli ㉛
Pennello, Da ㉜
Pierot ❶
Sabatini ❿
Sostanza ⑫
Toula-Oliviero ㉑
Trattoria Coco Lezzone ⑳
Vecchia Firenze ㉞
Vittoria, Trattoria ❷

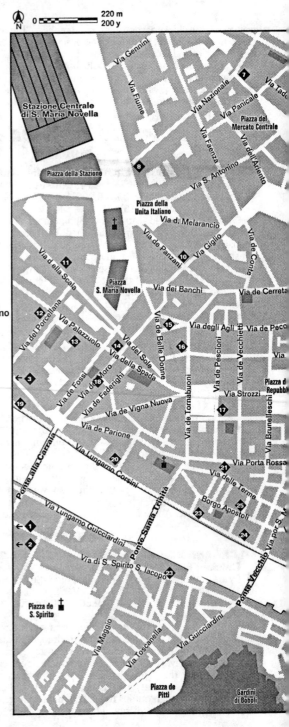

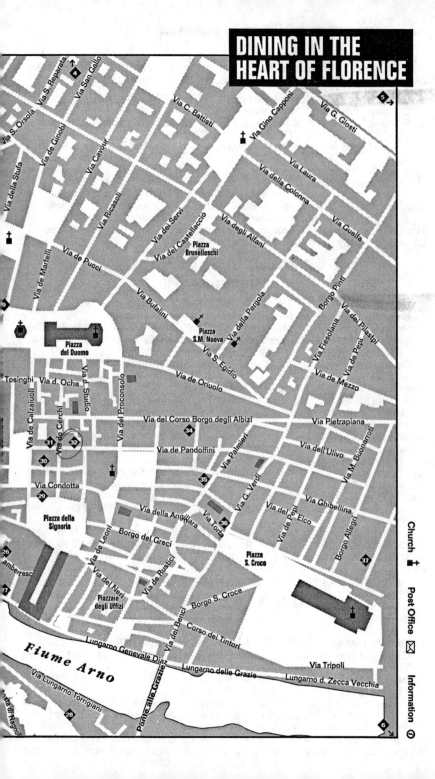

DINING IN THE HEART OF FLORENCE

pastas, including crespelle (crêpe) of such fresh vegetables as asparagus or artichokes. A daily fish dish is also featured. Run by a quartet of Florentine friends, the restaurant features white walls decorated with ceramic and copper objects.

LE MOSSACCE, via del Proconsolo 55R. Tel. 294361.
  Cuisine: TUSCAN. **Reservations:** Not required. **Bus:** 19.
$ Prices: Appetizers 5,000–6,000 lire ($3.95–$4.70); main courses 9,000–9,500 lire ($7.05–$7.45). AE, V.
  Open: Lunch Mon–Sat noon–2:30pm; dinner Mon–Sat 7–9:30pm. **Closed:** Aug.

S Le Mossacce, patronized by a long list of faithful Tuscan devotees, is conveniently located midway between two of the city's most famous monuments, the Bargello and the Duomo. This small 35-seat restaurant was established at the turn of the century. Within its 300-year-old walls, a team of hard-working waiters serve excellent meals, offering selections from a wide range of Florentine and Italian specialties, including ribollita (a thick regional soup), cannelloni, heavily seasoned baked pork, and involtini.

ON OR NEAR VIA TORNABUONI

MODERATE

DONEY, piazza Strozzi 18-19. Tel. 239-8206.
  Cuisine: FRENCH. **Reservations:** Required. **Bus:** 31 or 32.
$ Prices: Appetizers 10,000–12,000 lire ($7.85–$9.40); main courses 14,000–20,000 lire ($11–$15.70); fixed-price meal 25,000 lire ($19.65) at lunch or dinner. AE, DC, MC, V.
  Open: Lunch Mon–Sat 12:30–2:30pm; dinner Tues–Sat 7–10:30pm. **Closed:** Aug 12–18.

Doney used to be the most famous restaurant in Florence. The Doney Café first opened in 1827 and quickly became a favorite with the haut monde and the literati. It attracted such illustrious names as the Duke of Windsor, W. Somerset Maugham, and Ezra Pound, among others. In 1990 designer Giorgio Armani reopened the restaurant and it is now again a staple for Florentine society, who view it as a favorite hangout. (Armani purchased the name of the restaurant and its original furnishings from the previous owners.) The reopened Doney still has an entrance on via Tornabuoni in remembrance of things past. The restaurant is adjacent to one of Armani's larger Italian boutiques, so presumably some of the restaurant's clientele will have just finished shopping or plan to begin shopping after their meal. Gian Carlo Ortelli, a leading Italian architect, redesigned the interior in a style close to that of the original Doney Café.

The chef cooks in the modern Italian style, providing an array of homemade pastas, the freshest of fish, juicy poultry and duck, and crisp fresh salads (models like to dine here). A specialty of the house is grilled Florentine beef served on a bed of arugula (a bitter green) and dressed with five different sauces. To begin, you might try one of the excellent pasta dishes, perhaps tagliata Doney.

NEAR THE DUOMO

MODERATE

GIANNINO IN SAN LORENZO, borgo San Lorenzo 37R. Tel. 212206.
  Cuisine: FLORENTINE/PIZZA. **Reservations:** Required. **Bus:** 6, 11, 14, 17, or 23.
$ Prices: Appetizers 10,000–12,000 lire ($7.85–$9.40); main courses 14,000–24,000 lire ($11–$18.85). AE, DC, MC, V.
  Open: Lunch Fri–Wed 11:30am–2:30pm; dinner Fri–Wed 6:30–11:30pm.

Giannino in San Lorenzo, a short walk from the Duomo, prepares some of the finest steaks and roasts in Florence. Serving diners upstairs and down, Giannino crackles with an open-fire grill, usually chock-full of golden-brown roast chickens turning on the spit—thus its reputation as a *rosticceria*. Many diners come here for a juicy, charcoal-grilled Florentine steak. For starters, tortellini alla panna is a house specialty. To finish, the Florentine cake, zuccotto, will completely destroy your waistline but please your tastebuds. Late at night you may want to drop in for a pizza, as the restaurant's also a pizzeria. The best one I've tried here is the pizza capricciosa, made with ham, mushrooms, and cheese.

TRATTORIA COCO LEZZONE, via del Parioncino 26R. Tel. 287178.
   Cuisine: FLORENTINE. **Reservations:** Not accepted. **Bus:** 27 or 31.
$ Prices: Appetizers 8,000–15,000 lire ($6.30–$11.80); main courses 15,000–35,000 lire ($11.80–$27.50). No credit cards.
   Open: Lunch Mon–Sat noon–3pm; dinner Wed–Mon 7:30–10:30pm. **Closed:** Last week of July through Aug.

In Florentine dialect, the establishment's name refers to the sauce-stained apron of the extroverted chef who established this place more than a century ago. Today, some of the heartiness of the Tuscan countryside can be purchased for the price of a meal at this duet of tile-covered rooms on a backstreet a short walk from the Duomo. Florentine "blue bloods" wait with workers crowding in on their lunch hours for a seat at one of the long tables. Go early before the rush begins if you want a seat in this crowded, bustling trattoria. The fare includes generous portions of boiled meats with a green sauce, pasta fagiole (beans), ossobuco, tripe, or beefsteak Florentine, which is the most expensive item on the menu at 35,000 lire ($27.50).

INEXPENSIVE

VECCHIA FIRENZE, borgo degli Albizi 18. Tel. 234-0361.
   Cuisine: FLORENTINE. **Reservations:** Not required. **Bus:** 31 or 32.
$ Prices: Appetizers 6,000–8,000 lire ($4.70–$6.30); main courses 10,000–12,000 lire ($7.85–$9.40). AE, DC, MC, V.
   Open: Lunch Tues–Sat noon–2:30pm; dinner Tues–Sat 7–10pm.

Ⓢ Vecchia Firenze combines atmosphere and budget meals. Near the Duomo, it's housed in an old palace with an elegant entrance, through high doors. Some of the tables are in the courtyard; others are inside the vaulted dining rooms. The restaurant is lit by a wrought-iron chandelier. It's not elaborately voguish—in fact, it caters to students and the working people of Florence, who eat here regularly and never seem to tire of its offerings. You might begin with a tagliatelle Vecchia Firenze, then follow with a quarter of a roast chicken or sole in butter.

NEAR PIAZZA DELLA SIGNORIA
MODERATE

DA GANINO, piazza dei Cimatori 4. Tel. 214125.
   Cuisine: FLORENTINE/TUSCAN. **Reservations:** Recommended. **Bus:** 31 or 32.
$ Prices: Appetizers 8,000–10,000 lire ($6.30–$7.85); main courses 12,000–25,000 lire ($9.40–$19.65). AE, DC.
   Open: Lunch Mon–Sat 1–3pm; dinner Mon–Sat 8pm–1am.

The well-established Da Ganino is staffed with the kind of waiters who take the quality of your meal as their personal responsibility. This little-known restaurant has vaulted ceilings, glazed walls, and an array of paintings by Florentine artists. Someone will recite to you the frequently changing specialties of the day, including, perhaps, well-seasoned versions of Tuscan beans, spinach risotto, grilled veal liver, grilled veal chops, and Florentine beefsteak on the bone. The cost of your gastronomic sins will be figured on the paper tablecloth. Small and intimate, it lies on a square in the center of town.

DA PENNELLO, via Dante Alighieri 4R. Tel. 294848.
   Cuisine: FLORENTINE/ITALIAN. **Reservations:** Accepted but not necessary. **Bus:** 13, 14, or 23.
$ Prices: Appetizers 5,000–10,000 lire ($3.95–$7.85); main courses 10,000–20,000 lire ($7.85–$15.70). No credit cards.

Open: Lunch Tues–Sun noon–2:30pm; dinner Tues–Sat 7–9:30pm. **Closed:** Aug 1–21 and Dec 25–Jan 3.

At the family-style Da Pennello, the waiters speak some English. The food is top-notch, produced with skill by the women in the kitchen. The informally operated trattoria offers many Florentine specialties on its à la carte menu. A filling and good-tasting dish is spaghetti alla carbonara. Da Pennello is known for its wide selection of antipasti; you can fill your plate with it to make a meal out of these delectable hors d'oeuvres. The ravioli is homemade. To follow, you can have deviled roast chicken. Typically Italian dishes include a plate of mixed roasts and a Florentine beefsteak. The chef posts daily specials, and sometimes it's best to order one of these, as the food offered was bought fresh that day at the market. A Florentine cake, zuccotto, rounds out the meal. The restaurant is on a narrow street, near Dante's house, about a 5-minute walk from the Duomo toward the Uffizi.

IL CAVALLINO, via della Farine 6. Tel. 215818.
Cuisine: TUSCAN/ITALIAN. **Reservations:** Recommended. **Bus:** 31 or 32.
$ Prices: Appetizers 8,000–9,000 lire ($6.30–$7.05); main courses 10,000–15,000 lire ($7.85–$11.80). AE, DC, MC, V.
Open: Lunch Thurs–Tues noon–2:30pm; dinner Thurs–Mon 7–10pm. **Closed:** Aug.

Il Cavallino is the kind of discreetly famous restaurant where Florentines invariably go just to be with one another. It is on a tiny street (which probably won't even be on your map) that leads into piazza della Signoria at its northern end, not far from the equestrian statue. There's usually a gracious reception at the door, especially if you called ahead for a reservation. The walls are dotted with unusual art, and seating is divided into three rooms, two of which have vaulted ceilings and peach-colored marble floors. The main room looks out over the piazza right in the heartbeat of Florence. Menu items are typical Tuscan fare, including an assortment of boiled meats in a green herb sauce, grilled filet of steak, breast of chicken Medici style, a mixed fish fry, grilled sole, and the inevitable Florentine spinach.

PAOLI, via dei Tavolini 12R. Tel. 216215.
Cuisine: TUSCAN/ITALIAN. **Reservations:** Recommended. **Bus:** 14, 19, or 23.
$ Prices: Appetizers 8,000–12,000 lire ($6.30–$9.40); main courses 14,000–18,000 lire ($11–$14.15); fixed-price menu 28,000 lire ($22). AE, DC, MC, V.
Open: Lunch Fri–Wed noon–2:30pm; dinner Fri–Wed 7–10:30pm.

Paoli, between the Duomo and piazza della Signoria, is one of the finest restaurants in Florence. It turns out a host of specialties but it could be recommended almost solely for its medieval-tavern atmosphere, with arches and ceramics stuck into the walls like medallions. The walls are adorned with frescoes. Its pastas are homemade, and the fettuccine alla Paoli is served piping hot. The chef also does a superb rognoncino (kidney) trifolato and a sole meunière. A recommendable side dish is piselli (garden peas) alla fiorentina.

ON THE ARNO

EXPENSIVE

HARRY'S BAR, lungarno Vespucci 22R. Tel. 239-6700.
Cuisine: ITALIAN. **Reservations:** Required. **Bus:** 3.
$ Prices: Appetizers 5,000–19,000 lire ($3.95–$14.95); main courses 12,000–28,000 lire ($9.40–$22). AE, DC, MC, V.
Open: Lunch Mon–Sat noon–3pm; dinner Mon–Sat 7–11pm. **Closed:** Aug 11–18 and Dec 15–30.

Harry's Bar, in a prime position on the Arno, is an enclave of expatriate and well-heeled visiting Yankees that deserves its well-earned reputation. You'll be welcomed at the bar and in the dining room, and you'll soon find that Harry's is the easiest place in Florence to meet your fellow Americans and (at least for a while) escape from some of the glory of the Renaissance. On a recent visit I heard three words of Italian from a frustrated woman from Alabama who was kindly assured by the Tuscan waiter (in English) that she need struggle no more. As if by inner radar, patrons know they'll be able to order from an international menu—small but select, and beautifully prepared. Several soups are featured daily, including cream of green pea or cream of chicken. The gamberetti (crayfish) cocktail is very tempting. Harry has created his own tortellini (stuffed pasta), but Harry's hamburger and his club sandwich are the most popular items. The chef also prepares about a dozen specialties every day: breast of chicken "our way," grilled giant-size scampi, and a lean broiled sirloin steak. An apple tart with fresh cream nicely finishes off a meal.

NEAR THE PONTE S. TRINITA
MODERATE

RISTORANTE NATALE, lungarno Acciaioli 80R. Tel. 213968.
> **Cuisine:** FLORENTINE. **Reservations:** Recommended for dinner. **Bus:** 3, 31, 32, or 37.
> **$ Prices:** Appetizers 6,000–12,000 lire ($4.70–$9.40); main courses 10,000–25,000 lire ($7.85–$19.65). MC, V.
> **Open:** Lunch Wed–Mon noon–3pm; dinner Wed–Mon 7:15–10:30pm. **Closed:** July 15–Aug 15.

Ristorante Natale, between the Ponte Vecchio and the Ponte S. Trinità, is an excellent choice for good food and leisurely dining along the Arno. A big refrigerator case greets you as you enter from the riverside quay. The decor includes paintings and old photos of the street life of Florence, plus wrought-iron chandeliers with dragons and their slayers hanging from the vaulted ceilings. I've found that this restaurant's kitchen is among the best in Florence—and its prices are below those of more-heralded establishments nearby. You might begin with fried squash blossoms in springtime or fresh asparagus and peas. Daily specials include veal piccata, beefsteak Florentine, fried chicken with zucchini, and scampi flambé. A second room in the back offers additional seating.

NEAR THE PONTE VECCHIO
MODERATE

BUCA DELL'ORAFO, via Volta dei Girolami 28. Tel. 213619.
> **Cuisine:** FLORENTINE. **Reservations:** Not needed. **Bus:** 3, 31, or 32.
> **$ Prices:** Appetizers 6,000–10,000 lire ($4.70–$7.85); main courses 10,000–20,000 lire ($7.85–$15.70). No credit cards.
> **Open:** Lunch Tues–Sat 12:30–2:30pm; dinner Tues–Sat 7:30–10:30pm. **Closed:** Aug.

⑤ Buca dell'Orafo is a little dive (one of the many cellars or *buca*-type establishments beloved by Florentines). An *orafo* is a goldsmith, and it was in this part of Florence that the goldsmith trade grew up. The buca, once part of an old goldsmith's shop, stands near the Ponte Vecchio, reached via a street under a vaulted arcade right off piazza del Pesce. The trattoria is usually stuffed with its habitués, so if you want a seat, go early. Over the years the chef has made little concession to the foreign palate, turning out instead genuine Florentine specialties, including tripe and mixed boiled meats with a green sauce and stracotto e fagioli (beef braised in a sauce of chopped vegetables and red wine), served with beans in a tomato sauce. For a savory beginning, try the fennel-flavored salami or asparagus in the spring. Florentine beefsteak is the most expensive item on the menu. There's a feeling of camaraderie among the diners here.

LA NANDINA, borgo SS. Apostoli 684. Tel. 213024.
> **Cuisine:** TUSCAN/INTERNATIONAL. **Reservations:** Recommended. **Bus:** 3, 31, or 32.
> **$ Prices:** Appetizers 8,000–12,000 lire ($6.30–$9.40); main courses 18,000–22,000 lire ($14.15–$17.25). AE, DC, MC, V.

Open: Lunch Mon–Sat noon–3pm; dinner Mon–Sat 7:30–10:30pm. **Closed:** Aug 10–25.

The elegant La Nandina is an old favorite with both Florentines and visitors alike. A family-run restaurant, it's just off the Arno, about a 4-minute walk from the Uffizi (in fact, it's an excellent choice for lunch if you're viewing the galleries). Fresh flowers are placed on the tables under vaulted ceilings and iron chandeliers. If you arrive early, you can have an apéritif in the intimate and plushly upholstered cocktail lounge near the entrance. There is also a 14th-century cellar for dining. The cuisine consists of dishes from the provinces and such cities as Rome, Tuscany, and Venice, and might include taglierini with flap mushrooms, spinach crêpes, curried breast of capon, veal piccatina, several kinds of beefsteak, and a changing array of daily specials.

NEAR SANTA CROCE
MODERATE

CIBREO, via del Macci 118R. Tel. 234-1100.

Cuisine: MEDITERRANEAN. **Reservations:** Recommended in restaurant, not accepted in trattorie. **Bus:** 14 or 49.

$ Prices: Restaurant, appetizers 8,000–10,000 lire ($6.30–$7.85); main courses 18,000–22,000 lire ($14.15–$17.25). Trattoria, appetizers 4,000–6,000 lire ($3.15–$4.70); main courses 9,000–10,000 lire ($7.05–$7.85). MC, V.

Open: Lunch Tues–Sat 12:30–2:20pm; dinner Tues–Sat 8–11:15pm. **Closed:** Aug 27–Sept 5.

Cibreo is a plain little restaurant and trattoria where Fabio and Benedetta Picchi turn out far-from-plain food. The decor consists of flowers in beer mugs and pictures on the walls. The food is served indoors where patrons can watch the activity in the kitchen around the charcoal oven, or at tables placed on the back sidewalk in summer. Here you can observe the shoppers in the big open food market held in the square during the morning. Fabio's soups are special (he serves no pasta); you might choose the potato and chickpea or pumpkin soup. Tuscan dishes are well prepared here, and there are also such international specialties as brains baked en papillote, a Turkish offering. No cocktails are served, but you can have wine with your meal. Prices are lower in the trattoria.

RISTORANTE LEO IN SANTA CROCE, via Torta 7R. Tel. 210829.

Cuisine: ITALIAN/INTERNATIONAL. **Reservations:** Recommended in summer. **Bus:** 14 or 49.

$ Prices: Appetizers 10,000–13,000 lire ($7.85–$10.20); main courses 15,000–25,000 lire ($11.80–$19.65). AE, DC, MC, V.

Open: Lunch Tues–Sun noon–2:30pm; dinner Tues–Sun 7:30–10:30pm.

Ristorante Leo in Santa Croce offers good food in a trio of appealingly decorated dining rooms. It has a convenient location a few paces from the piazza in front of the Church of Santa Croce. An array of watercolors, some of them satirical portraits of past clients, decorate the walls. Menu items might include ravioli with salmon, pappardella with rabbit, fondue bourguignonne, and kidneys flambé. Succulent grills such as steak and chicken are regularly featured as well.

NEAR THE STRAW MARKET
EXPENSIVE

TOULA-OLIVIERO, via delle Terme 51R. Tel. 287643.

Cuisine: TUSCAN/ITALIAN. **Reservations:** Required. **Bus:** 11, 31, or 32.

$ Prices: Appetizers 16,000–18,000 lire ($12.55–$14.15); main courses 24,000–30,000 lire ($18.85–$23.55); fixed-price lunch 40,000 lire ($31.40). AE, DC, MC, V.

Open: Lunch Tues–Sat noon–3pm; dinner Mon–Sat 7:30–11:30pm. **Closed:** Aug 5–26.

Toulà-Oliviero, member of a prestigious chain, operates a small but smart, luxurious dining room. You can arrive here any time after 7:30pm except Sunday and enjoy a drink. From 8pm on, live music entertains guests in the piano bar. The service is elegantly courteous. An excellent beginning to any meal is the chef's crêpes alla fiorentina. Two top-quality main dishes include sogliola (sole) Oliviero and a veal prepared "in the style of the chef." The featured dessert is crêpes Suzette, although I prefer the heavenly, cloudlike soufflé.

MODERATE

AL LUME DI CANDELA, via delle Terme 23R. Tel. 294566.

Cuisine: TUSCAN/RUSSIAN. **Reservations:** Required. **Bus:** 3, 31, or 32.

$ Prices: Appetizers 9,000–10,000 lire ($7.05–$7.85); main courses 18,000–25,000 lire ($14.15–$19.65). AE, DC, MC, V.

Open: Lunch Tues–Sat noon–3pm; dinner Mon–Sat 7:30–11pm. **Closed:** Aug 5–25.

Al Lume di Candela is uniquely located in a 13th-century tower that was partially leveled when its patrician family fell from grace (the prestige of Tuscan families was once reflected in how high their family towers soared). With a tavern decor, the restaurant offers a typically Florentine cuisine, under the deft guiding hand of the padrone in the kitchen. The candlelit atmosphere makes for a romantic dining place and has drawn celebrities in the past. Both Tuscan and Russian specialties are served. Among main-course specialties, I recommend the entrecôte alla Diana or perhaps the veal kidney in a tempting sauce. The most spectacular dessert is the crêpes Suzette, served only for two people. The bistro lies off the major shopping artery, via Por Santa Maria, near the straw market.

NEAR PIAZZA GOLDONI

MODERATE

TRATTORIA GARGA, via del Moro 48R. Tel. 298898.

Cuisine: TUSCAN/SARDINIAN. **Reservations:** Required. **Bus:** 26, 27, or 48.

$ Prices: Appetizers 6,000–25,000 lire ($4.70–$19.65); main courses 12,000–18,000 lire ($9.40–$14.15). AE, DC, MC, V.

Open: Lunch Tues–Fri 1–3pm; dinner Mon–Sat 7pm–2am.

S Some of the most creative cuisine in Florence is served here in an amicably cramped dining room barely large enough for 30 people. The establishment is run by Giuliano Gargani and his Canadian wife, Sharon, a happy combination of personalities that began when a strawberry blonde met "Signor Right." The building's thick Renaissance walls contain paintings by both Florentine and American artists, and the decor is complemented by hanging oil lamps. Operatic arias emerge along with heavenly odors from a postage-stamp-size kitchen. Many of the Tuscan menu items are so unusual that Sharon's bilingual skills are put to good use. You can enjoy a fine array of salads, including a well-dressed combination of artichokes, hearts of palm, fresh lettuce, and parmigiana cheese. Other dishes include tagliatelle with garlic, tomatoes, anchovies, and smoked salmon, along with octopus with chile peppers and garlic, boar with juniper berries, grilled marinated quail, and "whatever strikes the mood" of Giuliano. Call ahead for a table. The location is in the monumental center of Florence, between the Ponte Vecchio and Santa Maria Novella.

AT PIAZZA ANTINORI

MODERATE

BUCA LAPI, via del Trebbio 1R. Tel. 213768.

Cuisine: TUSCAN. **Reservations:** Required for dinner. **Bus:** 31 or 32.

$ Prices: Appetizers 3,000–18,000 lire ($2.35–$14.15); main courses 10,000–20,000 lire ($7.85–$15.70). AE, DC, V.

Open: Lunch Tues–Sat 12:30–2:30pm; dinner Mon–Sat 7:30–10:30pm.

Buca Lapi, a cellar restaurant founded in 1880, is big on glamour, good food, and the almost *gemütlich* enthusiasm of fellow diners. Its decor alone—under the Palazzo Antinori—makes it fun: Vaulted ceilings are covered with travel posters from all over the world. There's a long table of interesting fruits, desserts, and vegetables. The cooks know how to turn out the most classic dishes of the Tuscan kitchen with superb finesse. Specialties include pâté di fegato della casa, a liver pâté; cannelloni; scampi giganti alla griglia, a super-size shrimp; and bistecca alla fiorentina (local beefsteak). In season, the fagioli toscani all'olio—Tuscan beans in the native olive oil—are considered a delicacy by many palates. For dessert, you can order the international favorite, crêpes Suzette, or the local choice, zuccotto, a Florentine cake that's *delicato*. Evenings can be quite festive, as the singing becomes contagious.

BUCA MARIO, piazza Ottaviani 16R. Tel. 214179.
   Cuisine: FLORENTINE. **Reservations:** Required. **Bus:** 6, 9, 17, or 19.
$ Prices: Appetizers 8,000–12,000 lire ($6.30–$9.40); main courses 10,000–60,000 lire ($7.85–$47.10); fixed-price menu 30,000 lire ($23.55). AE, DC, MC, V.
   Open: Lunch Thurs–Tues 12:15–2:30pm; dinner Thurs–Tues 7:15–10:30pm. **Closed:** Aug.

Buca Mario, in business for around a century, is one of the most famous cellar restaurants of Florence. It's located right in the monumental historic center in the 1886 Palazzo Niccolini. Tables are placed beneath vaulted ceilings, and you'll often find that some of the waiters have worked in the States. They might suggest such dishes as an array of Florentine pastas, beefsteak, Dover sole, and beef carpaccio, followed by a tempting selection of desserts.

CANTINETTA ANTINORI, piazza Antinori 3. Tel. 292234.
   Cuisine: TUSCAN. **Reservations:** Recommended. **Bus:** 31 or 32.
$ Prices: Appetizers 9,000–10,000 lire ($7.05–$7.85); main courses 18,000–20,000 lire ($14.15–$15.70). AE, DC, MC, V.
   Open: Lunch daily 12:30–2:30pm; dinner daily 7–10:30pm. **Closed:** Aug.

Hidden behind the severe stone facade of the 15th-century Palazzo Antinori is Catinetta Antinori, one of Florence's most popular restaurants and one of the city's few top-notch wine bars. Small wonder that the cellars should be supremely well stocked since the restaurant is one of the city's showplaces for the vintages of the oldest and most distinguished wine company in Tuscany and Umbria. It has become the preferred rendezvous point for wine lovers who appreciate an overview of the assembled wines of the region, readily available and cheerfully served. Vintages can be consumed by the glass at the stand-up bar or by the bottle as an accompaniment for the Italian meals served at wooden tables. The room is not especially large, and the decorative statement is from the floor-to-ceiling racks of aged and undusted wine bottles set on their sides in wooden racks. The overflow from the ground floor goes up to the overhead balcony. You can eat for less than the full meal price quoted above by sampling only the snacks, such as salads, sandwiches, and other light dishes.

NEAR PIAZZA TADDEO GADDI
MODERATE

PIEROT, piazza Tadeo Gaddei 25R. Tel. 702100.
   Cuisine: SEAFOOD. **Reservations:** Recommended. **Bus:** 1, 2, 9, 13, or 27.
$ Prices: Appetizers 10,000–12,000 lire ($7.85–$9.40); main courses 14,000–22,000 lire ($11–$17.25). AE, DC, MC, V.
   Open: Lunch Mon–Sat noon–3pm; dinner Mon–Sat 7–11:30pm. **Closed:** July 15–31.

Pierot is housed in a 19th-century building constructed during the reign of Vittorio Emmanuel. Before World War II a food store was here, but for at least 40 years Pierot has been a restaurant fixture of Florence. The restaurant is unusual in that it specializes in seafood, and therefore is considered a bit of an oddity in landlocked Florence. The seasonal menu varies with the availability of ingredients, but might include linguine with a creamy crabmeat sauce, pasta with clams, and a succulent version of squid and beets (yes, you heard right).

TRATTORIA VITTORIA, via Fonderia 52R. Tel. 225657.
   Cuisine: SEAFOOD. **Reservations:** Recommended. **Bus:** 6.

$ Prices: Appetizers 12,000–20,000 lire ($9.40–$15.70); main courses 20,000–30,000 lire ($15.70–$23.55). AE, DC, MC, V.
Open: Lunch Thurs–Tues noon–2:30pm; dinner Thurs–Tues 7:30–10:30pm.
Closed: Aug 13–Sept 1.

Trattoria Vittoria is unheralded and untouristy, but it serves some of the finest fish dishes in Florence. This big, bustling trattoria offers you three dining rooms. Service is frenetic. Most of the fresh fish dishes of the day are priced according to weight. Sole is the most expensive, although you can also order equally tempting lower-priced dishes. Two outstanding choices to begin your meal include risotto alla marinara and spaghetti alla vongole (clams). The mixed fish fry gives you a little bit of everything. Desserts are homemade and extremely rich.

INEXPENSIVE

TRATTORIA ANTICO FATTORE, via Lambertesca 1. Tel. 238215.
   Cuisine: TUSCAN. **Reservations:** Recommended. **Bus:** 14, 19, or 23.
$ Prices: Appetizers 7,000–8,000 lire ($5.50–$6.30); main courses 9,000–15,000 lire ($7.05–$11.80). AE, V.
   Open: Lunch Tues–Sat 12:30–2:30pm; dinner Tues–Sat 7:30–10:30pm.
   Closed: Aug 10–20.

Trattoria Antico Fattore, on a backstreet near the Uffizi, is an inviting place where the owners speak English and cook good Tuscan food. As you enter the trattoria, with its dark-wood and marble furniture, you'll be greeted by a tempting array of antipasti, ranging from marinated anchovies to salami to ham. Follow your pasta selection with a Florentine steak or other grilled or roast meats. Local fare, which includes chicken and guinea fowl as well as tasty Tuscan desserts, is all fresh cooked. You can have some of the good regional bread with your meal, or perhaps you'd prefer the chunky rolls called *stinchi* (pronounced "stinky").

ON THE LEFT BANK
MODERATE

MAMMA GINA, borgo S. Iacopo 37. Tel. 239-6009.
   Cuisine: TUSCAN. **Reservations:** Required for dinner. **Bus:** 3.
$ Prices: Appetizers 7,000–8,000 lire ($5.50–$6.30); main courses 15,000–18,000 lire ($11.80–$14.15). AE, DC, MC, V.
   Open: Lunch Mon–Sat noon–2:30pm; dinner Mon–Sat 7–10pm. **Closed:** Aug 5–25.

Mamma Gina is a rustic left-bank restaurant that's a winner for fine foods prepared in the traditional manner. This exceptional trattoria, well worth the trek across the Ponte Vecchio, is a center for hearty Tuscan fare. The chef does an excellent tortellini verde (a green pasta dish). You can follow with any number of fish or meat dishes. Mamma Gina is ideal for lunch after visiting the Pitti Palace.

SPECIALTY DINING
DINING WITH A VIEW

BAR RISTORANTE LA LOGGIA, piazzale Michelangelo 1. Tel. 234-2832.
   Cuisine: FLORENTINE. **Reservations:** Recommended. **Bus:** 13.
$ Prices: Appetizers 8,000–10,000 lire ($6.30–$7.85); main courses 15,000–22,000 lire ($11.80–$17.25). AE, DC, MC, V.
   Open: Lunch Thurs–Tues noon–2:30pm; dinner Thurs–Tues 7–10:30pm.

You shouldn't have any trouble locating this popular restaurant housed in a 100-year-old former art gallery. It occupies one of the most prominent positions in Florence, a panoramic piazza where all first-time visitors appear to drink in the view of the City of the Renaissance. The food is good, too. Service may be a bit chaotic, but when you get to order, you might like to try the giant porcini and ovoli mushrooms, among the favorite antipasti. Florentine steaks are usually tender here, grilled over an open fire. Try such dishes as fresh pasta with four cheeses and an arugula salad, Gorgonzola risotto with pink peppercorns, and fresh fish cartoccio. Technically translated as "bag," cartoccio is a method of cooking fish or meat in a greased and sealed paper bag, which helps to retain the moisture. When the cartoccio is opened at the table, it gives off a delectable aroma. For a perfect finish for your meal, try a herb-flavored liqueur, Amaro Montenegro. Another specialty of the bartender is a heavenly apéritif of champagne and peaches.

HOTEL DINING

IL CESTELLO, in the Hotel Excelsior, piazza Ognissanti 3. Tel. 264201.
   Cuisine: TUSCAN/MEDITERRANEAN. **Reservations:** Essential. **Bus:** 6 or 16.
$ **Prices:** Appetizers 15,000–32,000 lire ($11.80–$25.10); main courses 30,000–40,000 lire ($23.55–$31.40).
   Open: Lunch daily noon–3pm; dinner daily 7:30–11pm.
This deluxe restaurant attracts an upper-crust clientele who, in summer, come either to drink beside the piano or on the flowered terrace of this hotel's roof garden, or else to dine under a canopy by candlelight. On the sixth floor of what is the finest hotel in Florence, the garden is open only from May to October (in winter the restaurant moves back downstairs again). During the summer visitors enjoy gentle breezes and the panoramic views of the Arno from the terrace.

The cuisine is Mediterranean with many Tuscan specialties, such as gnocchetti with Gorgonzola and veal scaloppine with artichokes. Sea bass is sautéed with herbs, or you can regularly order the famed Florentine T-bone steak. A small part of the menu lists those items that are always "fresh from today's market." These include some of the finest fresh vegetables in Florence. My most recent assorted spring salad and fresh asparagus were a true celebration of the season.

LOCAL FAVORITES

TRATTORIA CAMMILLO, borgo S. Iacopo 57. Tel. 212427.
   Cuisine: TUSCAN. **Reservations:** Required. **Bus:** 1, 3, 6, 11, or 36.
$ **Prices:** Appetizers 6,000–30,000 lire ($4.70–$23.55); main courses 12,000–35,000 lire ($9.40–$27.50). AE, DC, MC, V.
   Open: Lunch Fri–Mon noon–2:30pm; dinner Fri–Mon 7–10:30pm. **Closed:** Aug and Dec.
Trattoria Cammillo is one of the most popular—and perhaps the finest—of the left-bank dining spots, housed on the ground floor of a former Medici palace. It's good enough to lure the snobbish owners of the boutiques, who cross the Arno regularly to feast here. They know they'll get such specialties as tortellini alla panna or zuppa alla certosina to begin their feast. The characteristic trattoria also does a scaloppa alla parmigiana and that old standby, beloved by the locals, Florentine tripe. In modest but attractive surroundings, the trattoria is between the Ponte Vecchio and the Ponte S. Trinità. Because of increased business, you're is likely to be rushed through a meal.

VEGETARIAN

CENTRO VEGETARIANO FIORRENTINO ALMANACCO, via della Ruote 30R. Tel. 475030.
   Cuisine: VEGETARIAN. **Reservations:** Not accepted. **Bus:** 31 or 32.
$ **Prices:** Appetizers 3,500–5,000 lire ($2.75–$3.95); main courses 7,000–7,500 lire ($5.50–$5.90). No credit cards.
   Open: Lunch Tues–Fri 12:30–2:30pm; dinner Tues–Sun 7:30–10:30pm. **Closed:** Aug.
S Almanacco is considered more of a private vegetarian club than a traditional restaurant. This popular eating house serves only vegetarian food, in a room filled with wooden tables and basket-shaped lamps. In the cafeteria-style setup an employee ladles out portions onto plates and trays. First-time diners are required to

pay a membership fee of 8,000 lire ($6.30), after which they receive a membership card and access to the brick-floored interior. In Florence alone, this membership card entitles holders entrance to some 20 private clubs—gastronomical, musical, and cultural. Within sight of a waiting cashier, you select your dinner from a chalkboard, filling in the items you want on a preprinted form. Wine is served from a brimming carafe, although some vegetarians feel more comfortable with a bottle of organic, preservative-free Italian wine. Menu items vary with the seasonality of Italy's produce, but typical items include pasta and vegetarian sauces, rice with pumpkin, eggplant parmigiana, and country-derived pizza with thick crusts, along with an array of freshly composed salads.

GELATO

GELATERIA VIVOLI, via Isola delle Stinche 7R. Tel. 292334.
   Cuisine: ICE CREAM. **Reservations:** Not needed. **Bus:** 6 or 16.
$ **Prices:** Gelati 1,500–6,000 lire ($1.20–$4.70). No credit cards.
   Open: Tues–Sat 9am–1am, Sun 10:30am–1:30pm and 4:15pm–1am. **Closed:** Aug 7–31 and Dec 31–Feb 1.

This little establishment serves the finest ice cream I've tasted in Italy. Buy your ticket first and select your flavor from among such delights as blueberry fig, melon, and other fruits in season, as well as chocolate mousse, or even coffee ice cream flavored with espresso. A special ice cream is made from rice. The establishment offers a number of semifreddi concoctions—an Italian ice cream using cream as a base instead of milk. Semifreddi are hardly obtainable outside Italy, and the most popular flavors are almond, marengo (a type of meringue), and zabaglione (eggnog). Other flavors include limoncini alla crema (candied lemon peels with vanilla-flavored ice cream) and aranciotti al cioccolate (candied orange peels with chocolate ice cream). On a backstreet near the church and cloisters of Santa Croce, the establishment has a white marble and chrome interior, spotlights, and palm trees.

LIGHT, CASUAL & FAST FOOD

CAFFE VOLTAIRE, via della Scala 9R. Tel. 218255.
   Cuisine: ITALIAN. **Reservations:** Recommended. **Bus:** 31 or 32.
$ **Prices:** Appetizers 7,000–8,000 lire ($5.50–$6.30); main courses 10,000–12,000 lire ($7.85–$9.40). AE, V.
   Open: Lunch Mon–Fri 12:30–2:30pm; dinner daily 8:30pm–midnight.
Caffè Voltaire isn't exactly a fast-food eatery, but more a place for a light meal or drink. It's like a French bistro, even though the chef is Italian. Every night live music is performed, usually jazz, and you can also enjoy piano-bar entertainment. You drink at a table serviced by a waiter. It's a refined place, what the French would call "high bourgeois." China plates are used, and sometimes champagne is served in an ice bucket. It's really a private club—but anybody can come here. Management gives out a pro-forma card (free) to clients, entitling them to "membership." You can also visit for cocktails at 8,000 lire ($6.30).

KENNY, via dei Bardi 64R. Tel. 212915.
   Cuisine: SANDWICHES/SALADS. **Reservations:** Not accepted. **Bus:** 3, 31, or 32.
$ **Prices:** Appetizers 4,500 lire ($3.55); hamburgers 2,300 lire ($1.80). No credit cards.
   Open: Tues–Sun 11am–1am.
Kenny was the harbinger of "food on the run" eateries in Florence. Although an incongruous oddity when it opened, it is now an accepted part of the culinary life of the city. Choose your food at a counter, pay for it at the cashier, and enjoy it at a table. French fries accompany most orders, and eaters usually wash it down with a beer.

LE BISTRO, via Gabriele d'Annunzio 149B. Tel. 602605.
   Cuisine: ITALIAN. **Reservations:** Recommended. **Bus:** 10 from the center.
$ **Prices:** Appetizers 6,000–10,000 lire ($4.70–$7.85); main courses 9,000–15,000 lire ($7.05–$11.80).

Open: Wed–Mon 11am–midnight. **Closed:** Aug.

Le Bistro, on the outskirts of Florence, is a restaurant/crêperie/pizzeria and, for some sports buffs, a social center. Le Bistro offers two rooms where you can eat. In the biggest, there is a bar and a counter where you can buy cigarettes or pick up certain grocery supplies. In the restaurant, you can order a wide selection of crêpes, both savory and dessert, which cost 8,000 lire to 12,000 lire ($6.30 to $9.40). You might begin with a selection of pâté, then follow with one of their pastas, for which the kitchen is known. These range from penne with an olive sauce to farfalle with salsa dell'amore (love sauce). You can finish with the house pastry, tarte tatin. Meals begin at 25,000 lire ($19.65), and you can order good chianti or white Orvieto wine here, even cider.

SNACK BAR AND RISTORANTE LA BORGA, via Por Santa Maria 55R. Tel. 216109.

Cuisine: TUSCAN. **Reservations:** Not needed. **Bus:** 3, 31, or 32.

$ Prices: Appetizers 4,000–6,000 lire ($3.15–$4.70); main courses 6,000–8,000 lire ($4.70–$6.30). No credit cards.

Open: Mon–Sat 7:30am–midnight. **Closed:** Dec 1–15.

Ristorante La Borsa, under the portico of the Volta dei Mercanti, is the perfect spot for a snack on a hot Tuscan afternoon. They don't cook here but will warm toasts and small pizzas al taglio. Mainly, they serve freshly made salads. Salads cost 5,000 lire to 7,000 lire ($3.95 to $5.50), with a cold-meat dish with vegetables priced at 7,000 lire to 10,000 lire ($5.50 to $7.85).

PICNIC SUPPLIES & WHERE TO EAT THEM

Many visitors, especially those interested in Italian cuisine and the ingredients produced by some of the richest farmlands in Europe, enjoy a firsthand view of the markets that supply the kitchens of Florence. Buying ingredients for a picnic will introduce you firsthand to the fruits of the Tuscan landscape. Large supermarkets are rare in Italy. Ingredients are usually segregated among a wide diversity of food stores, which any Italian shopper knows include *panterria* for bread, *salumeria* for slices of cold meats and sausages, *vinaterria* for wines, *latteria* for cheese and yogurt, and *alimentaria* for canned goods and such staples as salt and sugar.

Because of the many individual transactions necessary for the compilation of a picnic lunch, your foray into the markets will provide as much of a cultural insight as a culinary one. (If your grasp of the Italian language isn't very good, pointing and gesticulating will work wonders.)

FROMMER'S COOL FOR KIDS
RESTAURANTS

Da Pennello *(see page 245)* This family-style trattoria near Dante's house offers filling, tasty, and inexpensive dishes.

La Nandina *(see page 247)* Florentine families frequent this place off the Arno and a 4-minute walk from the Uffizi.

Kenny *(see page 253)* The first fast-food eatery in Florence still dispenses an array of sandwiches, salads, and hamburgers—nearly all orders come with french fries.

Gelateria Vivoli *(see page 253)* After tasting the ice cream here—in virtually every known flavor—your child might agree that this place was worth the trip to Florence.

Florence's largest assemblage of markets lie under the communal roof of the **Mercato Centrale,** via Ariento 12, in the San Lorenzo district between via San Antonio and via Panicale. Covering more than a full square block, and sheltered from the glaring sun with a series of covered passageways, it's open Monday through Saturday from 7am to 2pm, and on Saturday afternoon from 4 to 8pm.

Also within the historic core, near piazza Santa Croce, is **via Neri,** whose edges are lined with dozens of richly stocked food shops.

The fine art of choosing a site for a picnic is arguably as complicated as selecting the perfect ingredients. Florence is filled with richly panoramic or historic possibilities, but several that compete for the attention of picnickers include the formal mannerist verdancy of the **Boboli Gardens,** and the more isolated and less visited sprawl of **La Cascine Park,** which is located a 15-minute walk northwest of the historic core. Other appropriate spots lie scattered throughout the city, wherever your whim, a lack of traffic, and a pleasant view inspire you to stop, reflect, and picnic. Don't litter.

CHAPTER 8

WHAT TO SEE & DO IN FLORENCE

- **SUGGESTED ITINERARIES**
- **DID YOU KNOW . . . ?**
1. **ATTRACTIONS**
- **WALKING TOUR— THE HEART OF FLORENCE**
- **WALKING TOUR— IN THE FOOTSTEPS OF MICHELANGELO**
2. **SPECIAL & FREE EVENTS**
3. **SPORTS & RECREATION**
4. **SAVVY SHOPPING**
- **FROMMER'S FAVORITE FLORENTINE EXPERIENCES**
5. **EVENING ENTERTAINMENT**
6. **EASY EXCURSIONS**

Florence was the fountainhead of the Renaissance, the city of Dante and Boccaccio. Characteristically, it was the city of Machiavelli; uncharacteristically, of Savonarola. For 3 centuries it was dominated by the Medici family, patrons of the arts, masters of assassination. But it is chiefly through its artists that we know of the apogee of the Renaissance: Ghiberti, Fra Angelico, Donatello, Brunelleschi, Botticelli, and the incomparable Leonardo da Vinci and Michelangelo.

In Florence we can trace the change from medievalism to an age of "rebirth." For example, all modern painters owe a debt to an ugly, awkward, unkempt man who died at age 27. His name was Masaccio (Vasari's "Slipshod Tom"). Modern painting began with his frescoes in the Brancacci Chapel in the Church of Santa Maria del Carmine, which you can go see today. Years later Michelangelo painted a more celebrated Adam and Eve in the Sistine Chapel, but even this great artist never realized the raw humanity of Masaccio's Adam and Eve fleeing from the Garden of Eden.

In *The Man of the Renaissance* (1930), Ralph Roeder wrote: "In the broadest sense the Renaissance might be described as one of those recurring crises in the annals of the race when a ferment of a new life, like a rising sap, bursts the accepted codes of morality and men revert to Nature and the free play of instinct and experience in its conduct."

SUGGESTED ITINERARIES

IF YOU HAVE 1 DAY   You face a major dilemma and will have to accept the inevitable that you can see only a fraction of the "must see" attractions. Go to the Uffizi Galleries as soon as they open and concentrate only on some of the masterpieces. Before 1:30pm, visit the Accademia to see Michelangelo's *David* . . . at least that.

Have lunch on piazza della Signoria, dominated by the Palazzo Vecchio, and admire the statues in the Loggia della Signoria. After lunch visit the Duomo and Baptistery, then pay a late-afternoon visit to the open-air straw market, Mercanto San

DID YOU KNOW...?

- Florentines regard themselves as the "most civilized" of all Italians—based on their pure language, their culture, and their position as the cradle of the Renaissance.
- In 1503 both Michelangelo and Leonardo da Vinci won commissions to fresco the walls of the council chamber of the republic. Neither work has survived.
- Some 500 sculptures and 1,000 paintings—considered priceless in the art world—were destroyed in the disastrous flood of 1966.
- In 1865, Florence—not Rome—became the capital of Italy.
- The word *renaissance* to describe the historic and artistic period that swept across Florence did not come into vogue until the publication in 1855 of Jules Michelet's *La Renaissance*.
- Mark Twain, working on *Pudd'nhead Wilson* in the 1890s, claimed that he could write more in 4 months in the Tuscan countryside than he could produce in 2 years at home.
- No dome since antiquity had been raised more than 180 feet above the ground until Brunelleschi created the dome for the Duomo of Florence.
- The oldest bridge in Florence, the Ponte Vecchio, was the only bridge over the Arno spared in August 1944 by the retreating Nazis.

Lorenzo, before crossing the Ponte Vecchio at sunset. Finish a very busy day with a hearty Tuscan dinner in one of Florence's many *bucas* or cellar restaurants.

IF YOU HAVE 2 DAYS Spend your first day in Florence as suggested above.

On Day 2, return to the Uffizi Galleries for a more thorough look at this museum—the most important in Italy. Then in the afternoon visit the Pitti Palace on the other side of the Arno, and wander through the Galleria Palatina, with its 16th- and 17th-century masterpieces, including 11 works by Raphael alone. After a visit, stroll through the adjoining Boboli Gardens. At sunset, stroll again to the Duomo and the Baptistery for a much better look.

IF YOU HAVE 3 DAYS Spend your first two days as suggested above.

In the morning of Day 3, visit the Palazzo Vecchio on piazza della Signoria, then walk nearby to the Palazzo del Bargello which contains the most important works of Tuscan and Florentine sculpture from the Renaissance era. After lunch, visit the Museo dell'Opera del Duomo, with its sculptural masterpieces from the Duomo, including Donatello's *Mary Magdalene*.

IF YOU HAVE 5 DAYS Spend Days 1 through 3 as suggested above.

On the fourth day, continue your exploration of Renaissance masterpieces by visiting the Medici Chapels, with Michelangelo's tomb for Lorenzo de Medici, including the figures of *Dawn* and *Dusk*. Later in the morning go to the Museo di San Marco, a small museum which is a monument to the work of Fra Angelico. Before it closes at 6:30pm, call at the Basilica di Santa Croce, with its two restored chapels by Giotto.

On the fifth day, leave Florence, as fascinating as it is, and head south to yet another fascinating art city, Siena, most important of the Tuscan hill towns.

1. ATTRACTIONS

Readers traveling to Florence on limited time (2 or 3 days) should be there toward the middle or end of the week if possible. Most museums close at 12:30 or 1pm on Sunday and are closed all day Monday, so it's wise to plan your visit accordingly.

THE TOP ATTRACTIONS

In the heart of Florence, at piazza del Duomo and piazza S. Giovanni (named after John the Baptist), is a complex of ecclesiastical buildings that form a triumvirate of top sightseeing attractions.

In addition to the sights listed below, consider visiting **piazza della Signoria**. This square, although never completed, is one of the most beautiful in Italy; it was the center of secular life in the days of the Medici. Through it pranced church robbers, connoisseurs of entrails, hired assassins seeking employment, chicken farmers from Valdarno, book burners, and many great men—including Machiavelli on a secret mission to the Palazzo Vecchio, and Leonardo da Vinci, trailed by his inevitable entourage.

On the square is the *Fountain of Neptune,* the sea god surrounded by creatures from the deep, as well as frisky satyrs and nymphs. It was designed by Ammannati, who later repented for chiseling Neptune in the nude. But Michelangelo, to whom Ammannati owes a great debt, judged the fountain inferior.

Near the fountain is a spot where Savonarola walked his last mile. This zealous monk was a fire-and-brimstone reformer who rivaled Dante in conjuring up the punishment hell would inflict on sinners. Two of his chief targets were Lorenzo the Magnificent and the Borgia pope, Alexander VI, who excommunicated him. Savonarola whipped the Florentine faithful into an orgy of religious fanaticism, but eventually fell from favor. Along with two other friars, he was hanged in the square in 1498. Afterward, as the crowds threw stones, the pyre underneath the men consumed their bodies. It is said that the reformer's heart was found whole and grabbed up by souvenir collectors. His ashes were tossed in the Arno.

For centuries Michelangelo's *David* stood in piazza della Signoria, but it was moved to the Academy Gallery in the 19th century. The work you see on the square today is an inferior copy, commonly assumed by many first-time visitors to be Michelangelo's original.

In the 14th-century **✪ Loggia della Signoria** (sometimes called Loggia dei Lanzi) is a gallery of sculpture which often depicts fierce, violent scenes. The most famous and the best piece is a rare work by Benvenuto Cellini, the goldsmith and tell-all autobiographer. Critics have said his exquisite, but ungentlemanly *Perseus,* who holds the severed head of Medusa, is the most significant Florentine sculpture since Michelangelo's *Night* and *Day.* Two other well-known, although less skilled, pieces are Giambologna's *Rape of the Sabines* and his *Hercules with Nessus the Centaur.* For those on the mad rush, I suggest saving the interior of the Palazzo Vecchio (see "More Attractions," below) for another day.

CAMPANILE (Giotto's Bell Tower), piazza del Duomo. Tel. 213229.

✪ If we can believe the accounts of his contemporaries, Giotto was the ugliest man ever to walk the streets of Florence. Ironically, then, he left to posterity the most beautiful bell tower, or campanile, in Europe, rhythmic in line and form. That Giotto was given the position of "capomastro" and grand architect (and pensioned for 100 gold florins for his service) is remarkable in itself, for he is famous for freeing painting from the confinements of Byzantium. He designed the campanile in the last 2 or 3 years of his life, and he died before its completion.

The final work was admirably carried out by Andrea Pisano, one of the greatest Gothic sculptors in Italy (see his bronze doors on the nearby Baptistery). The 274-foot tower, a "Tuscanized" Gothic, with bands of colored marble, can be scaled for a panorama of the sienna-colored city. The view will surely rank among your most memorable—it encompasses the enveloping hills and Medici villas. If a medieval pageant happens to be passing underneath (a likely possibility in spring), so much the better. After Giotto's death, Pisano and Luca della Robbia did some fine bas-relief and sculptural work, now in the Duomo Museum, at the base of the tower.

Admission: 4,000 lire ($3.15).

Open: Mid-Mar to Sept, daily 9am–7:30pm; Oct to mid-Mar, daily 9am–5:30pm. **Bus:** 1, 6, 11, 17, 19, or 23.

BATTISTERO DI SAN GIOVANNI (Baptistery), piazza S. Giovanni. Tel. 213229.

⭐ Named after the city's patron saint, Giovanni (John the Baptist), the present octagonal Battistero dates from the 11th and 12th centuries. The oldest structure in Florence, the baptistery is a highly original interpretation of the Romanesque style, with its bands of pink, white, and green marble. Visitors from all over the world come to gape at its three sets of bronze doors, although they are copies. Restored panels of the original rest in the Museo dell'Opera del Duomo (see below).

In his work on two sets of doors, Lorenzo Ghiberti reached the pinnacle of his artistry in "quattrocento" Florence. To win his first commission on the north door, the then-23-year-old sculptor had to compete against such formidable opposition as Donatello, Brunelleschi (architect of the dome crowning the cathedral), and Siena-born Jacopo della Quercia. Upon seeing Ghiberti's work, Donatello and Brunelleschi conceded defeat. By the time he completed the work, Ghiberti was around 44 years old. The gilt-covered panels—representing scenes from the New Testament, including the *Annunciation,* the *Adoration,* and Christ debating the doctors in the temple—make up a flowing rhythmic narration in bronze.

After his long labor, the Florentines gratefully gave Ghiberti the task of sculpting the east door (directly opposite the entrance to the Duomo). On seeing the doors, Michelangelo is said to have exclaimed, "The Gateway to Paradise!" Given carte blanche, Ghiberti designed his masterpiece, choosing as his subject familiar scenes from the Old Testament, including Adam and Eve at the creation. This time, Ghiberti labored over the rectangular panels from 1425 to 1452 (he died in 1455).

Shuttled off to adorn the south entrance and to make way for Ghiberti's "gate" to paradise were the oldest doors of the baptistery, by Andrea Pisano, mentioned earlier for his work on Giotto's bell tower. For his subject, the Gothic sculptor represented the "Virtues" as well as scenes from the life of John the Baptist, whom the baptistery honors. The door was completed in 1336. On the interior (just walk through Pisano's doors—no charge), the dome is adorned with 13th-century mosaics, dominated by a figure of Christ. Mornings are reserved for worship.

Admission: Free.

Open: Mon–Sat 1–6pm. **Bus:** 1, 6, 11, 17, 19, or 23.

CATHEDRAL OF SANTA MARIA DEL FIORE (Duomo), piazza del Duomo. Tel. 294514.

⭐ The Duomo, graced by Brunelleschi's dome, is the crowning glory of Florence. But don't rush inside too quickly, as the view of the exterior, with its bands of white, pink, and green marble—geometrically patterned—is, along with the dome, the best feature. One of the world's largest churches, the Duomo represents the flowering of the "Florentine-Gothic" style. Typical of the history of cathedrals, construction stretched over centuries. Begun in 1296, it was finally consecrated in 1436, although finishing touches on the facade were applied as late as the 19th century. The cathedral was designed by Arnolfo di Cambio in the closing years of the 13th century, and the funds were raised in part by a poll tax.

Brunelleschi's efforts to build the dome (1420–36) would make the subject of a film, as did Michelangelo's vexations over the Sistine Chapel. At one time before his plans were eventually accepted, the architect was tossed out on his derrière and denounced as an idiot. He eventually won the commission by a clever "egg trick," as related in Giorgio Vasari's *Lives of the Painters,* written in the 16th century, a book to which I am here indebted (as are all authors of books dealing with Italian Renaissance art). His dome—a "monument for posterity"—was erected without supports. When Michelangelo began to construct a dome over St. Peter's, he paid tribute to Brunelleschi's earlier cupola in Florence: "I am going to make its sister larger, yes, but not lovelier."

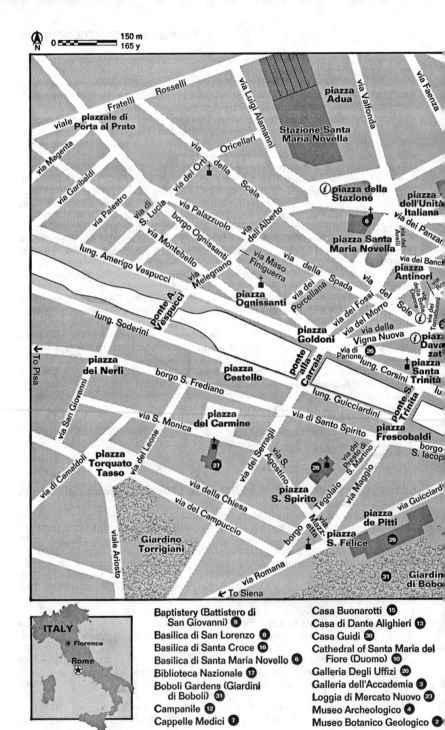

0 ━━━ 150 m
      ━━━ 165 y

N

Rosselli
Fratelli
viale
piazzale di
Porta al Prato
via Luigi Alamanni
via Oricellari
della Scala
piazza
Adua
via Valfonda
via Faenza

Stazione Santa
Maria Novella

via Magenta
via Garibaldi
via di S. Lucia
via Palestro
via dei Orti
via Palazzuolo
borgo Ognissanti
via dell'Alberto

(i) piazza della
Stazione

piazza
dell'Unità
Italiana
via dei Panzar

via Montebello
lung. Amerigo Vespucci
via Melegnano
via Maso
Finiguerra
via della Spada

piazza Santa
Maria Novella

via dei Banch
via dei Avelli

piazza
Antinori

Ponte A. Vespucci
lung. Soderini
piazza
Ognissanti
via dei Porcellana
via dei Fossi
via del Morro
via del Sole

piazza
Goldoni
via della
Vigna Nuova

(i) piaz
Dava
zat

piazza
dei Nerli
borgo S. Frediano
piazza
Cestello
ponte alla Carraia
via di Parione
lung. Corsini

piazza
Santa
Trinità

ponte S. Trinità

lung. Guicciardini
via di Santo Spirito

piazza
Frescobaldi
borgo
S. Iacop

via S. Monica
piazza
del Carmine
via dei Serragli
via S. Agostino
via di Presto S. Martino
via del Leone

piazza
Torquato
Tasso
via di Camaldoli
via della Chiesa
piazza
S. Spirito
Tegolaio
via Maggio
via Guicciard

via del Campuccio
borgo
via Mazz. etta
piazza
de Pitti

viale Ariosto
Giardino
Torrigiani
piazza
S. Felice
via Romana

To Pisa
To Siena
Giardin
di Bobo

ITALY
Florence
Rome

Baptistery (Battistero di
  San Giovanni) 9
Basilica di San Lorenzo 8
Basilica di Santa Croce 16
Basilica di Santa Maria Novello 6
Biblioteca Nazionale 17
Boboli Gardens (Giardini
  di Boboli) 31
Campanile 12
Cappelle Medici 7

Casa Buonarotti 15
Casa di Dante Alighieri 13
Casa Guidi 30
Cathedral of Santa Maria del
  Fiore (Duomo) 10
Galleria Degli Uffizi 20
Galleria dell'Accademia 3
Loggia di Mercato Nuovo 23
Museo Archeologico 4
Museo Botanico Geologico 2

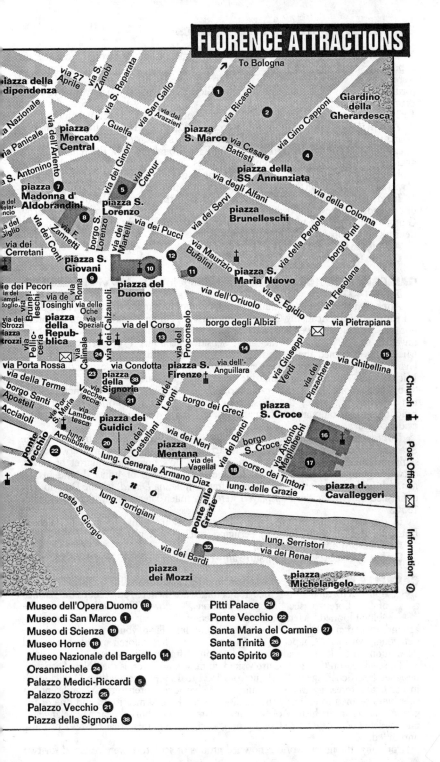

FLORENCE ATTRACTIONS

To Bologna

Giardino della Gherardesca

piazza della Indipendenza

via 27 Aprile

via S. Zanobi

via Nazionale

via Panicale

via dell'Ariento

piazza Mercato Central

via S. Antonino

via S. Reparata

Guelfa

via dei Arazzieri

via San Gallo

piazza S. Marco

via Cesare Battisti

via Ricasoli

via Gino Capponi

❶

❷

piazza della SS. Annunziata

❹

via degli Alfani

via della Colonna

piazza Madonna d' Aldobrandini

❼

via del Melancio

via dei Giglio

via dei Conti

via F. Zannetti

❽

borgo S. Lorenzo

piazza S. Lorenzo

❺

via Cavour

via dei Ginori

piazza Brunelleschi

via dei Servi

via dei Martelli

via dei Pucci

borgo Pinti

via dei Cerretani

piazza S. Giovani

❾

piazza del Duomo

❿

⓬

⓫

via Maurizio Bufalini

piazza S. Maria Nuovo

via della Pergola

via Fiesolana

ie dei Pecori

via del Campidoglio

via de' Tosinghi

via Brunel-leschi

via delle Oche

via Roma

via del Calzaiuoli

via della Spezali

via del Corso

via dell'Oriuolo

via S. Egidio

borgo degli Albizi

via Pietrapiana

piazza della Repub-blica

via dei Strozzi

piazza Strozzi

via Pellic-ceria

via Calimala

⓬

piazza S. Firenze

via dell'-Anguillara

⓮

via Giuseppi Verdi

via Ghibellina

⓯

via Porta Rossa

via della Terme

via Condotta

⓬

piazza della Signoria

⓴

⓳

via del Pinzachere

borgo Santi Apostoli

Acciaioli

Ponte Vecchio

㉒

via Vacchereccia

via Lamber-tesca

via Por S. Maria

lung. Archibusieri

㉑

⓴

piazza dei Guidici

via dei Leoni

via dei Castellani

borgo dei Greci

piazza S. Croce

via dei Neri

via del borgo S. Croce

via Antonio Magliabechi

⓰

⓱

piazza Mentana

via dei Vagellai

⓲

corso dei Tintori

lung. delle Grazie

piazza d. Cavalleggeri

lung. Generale Armano Diaz

ponte alle Grazie

A r n o

costa S. Giorgio

lung. Torrigiani

lung. Serristori

via dei Renai

via dei Bardi

㉜

piazza dei Mozzi

piazza Michelangelo

Church ✠

Post Office ✉

Information ❶

Museo dell'Opera Duomo ⓲
Museo di San Marco ❶
Museo di Scienza ⓳
Museo Horne ⓰
Museo Nazionale del Bargello ⓮
Orsanmichele ㉔
Palazzo Medici-Riccardi ❺
Palazzo Strozzi ㉕
Palazzo Vecchio ㉑
Piazza della Signoria ㊳

Pitti Palace ㉙
Ponte Vecchio ㉒
Santa Maria del Carmine ㉗
Santa Trinità ㉖
Santo Spirito ㉘

Inside, the overall effect of the cathedral is bleak, except when you stand under the cupola, frescoed in part by Vasari. Some of the stained-glass windows in the dome were based on designs by Donatello (Brunelleschi's friend) and Ghiberti (Brunelleschi's rival). If you resisted scaling Giotto's bell tower, you may want to climb Brunelleschi's ribbed dome. And if so, you can, Monday through Saturday from 10:30am to 5pm, for 4,000 lire ($3.15) admission. The view is well worth the trek.

Also in the cathedral are some terra-cottas by Luca della Robbia. In 1432 Ghiberti, taking time out from his "Gateway to Paradise," designed the tomb of St. Zenobius. Excavations in the depths of the cathedral have brought to light the remains of the ancient Cathedral of Santa Reparata (tombs, columns, and floors), which was probably founded in the 5th century, and transformed in the following centuries until it was demolished to make way for the present cathedral.

Incidentally, during some 1972 excavations the tomb of Brunelleschi was discovered, and new discoveries indicate the existence of a second tomb nearby. Giotto's tomb, which has never been found, may be in the right nave of the cathedral, beneath the campanile that bears his name.

Admission: 2,000 lire ($1.55).
Open: Daily 10am–5pm. **Bus:** 1, 6, 11, 17, 19, or 23.

GALLERIA DELL'ACCADEMIA (Michelangelo's David), via Ricasoli 60. Tel. 214375.

After coming out of the entrance to the Duomo, turn to the right, then head down via Ricasoli to the Academy Gallery. This museum contains paintings and sculpture, but it is completely overshadowed by one work, Michelangelo's colossal *David*, unveiled in 1504. One of the most sensitive accounts I've ever read of how Michelangelo turned the 17-foot "Duccio marble" into *David* is related in "The Giant" chapter of Irving Stone's *The Agony and the Ecstasy*. Stone describes a Michelangelo "burning with marble fever" who set out to create a *David* who "would be Apollo, but considerably more; Hercules, but considerably more; Adam, but considerably more; the most fully realized man the world had yet seen, functioning in a rational and humane world." How well he succeeded is much in evidence today.

David once stood in piazza della Signoria but was removed in 1873 to the Academy (a copy was substituted). Apart from containing the masterwork, the sculpture gallery is also graced with Michelangelo's unfinished quartet of slaves, carved around 1520 and intended for the ill-fated tomb of Julius II, and his *St. Matthew,* which he worked on (shortly after completing *David*) for the Duomo. His unfinished *Palestrina Pietà* displayed here is a much later work which dates from 1550.

In the connecting picture gallery is a collection of Tuscan masters, such as Botticelli, and Umbrian works by Perugino (teacher of Raphael).

Admission: 4,000 lire ($3.15).
Open: Tues–Sat 9am–2pm, Sun 9am–1pm. **Bus:** 1, 6, 11, 17, 19, or 23.

★ CAPPELLE MEDICI, piazza Madonna degli Aldobrandini 6. Tel. 213206.

A mecca for all pilgrims, the Medici tombs are sheltered adjacent to the Basilica of San Lorenzo (see "More Attractions," below). The tombs, housing the "blue-blooded" Medici, are actually entered in back of the church by going around to piazza di Madonna degli Aldobrandini. First, you'll pass through the octagonal, baroque "Chapel of the Princes," which has colored marble but a cold decoration. In back of the altar is a collection of Italian reliquaries.

The real reason the chapels are visited en masse, however, is the "New Sacristy," designed by Michelangelo. Working from 1521 to 1534, he created the Medici tomb in a style that foreshadowed the coming of the baroque. Lorenzo the Magnificent—a ruler who seemed to embody the qualities of the Renaissance itself, and one of the greatest names in the history of the Medici family—was buried near Michelangelo's uncompleted *Madonna and Child* group, a simple monument that evokes a promise unfulfilled.

Ironically, the finest, world-renowned groups of sculpture were reserved for two

Medici "clan" members, who (in the words of Mary McCarthy) "would better have been forgotten." Both are represented by Michelangelo as armored, regal, idealized princes of the Renaissance. In fact, Lorenzo II, Duke of Urbino, depicted as "the thinker," was a deranged young man (just out of his teens before he died). Clearly, Michelangelo was not working to glorify these two Medici dukes. Rather, he was chiseling for posterity. The other two figures on Lorenzo's tomb are most often called *Dawn* and *Dusk*, with morning represented as woman, and evening as man.

The two best-known figures—Michelangelo at his most powerful—are *Night* and *Day* at the feet of Giuliano, the Duke of Nemours. *Night* is chiseled as a woman in troubled sleep; *Day* is a man of strength awakening to a foreboding world. These two figures were not the sculptural works of Michelangelo's innocence.

Discovered in a sepulchral chamber beneath the Medici Chapel was Michelangelo's only group of mural sketches. Access is through a trap door and a winding staircase. The walls apparently had been used by the great artist as a giant doodling sheet. Drawings include a sketch of the legs of Duke Giuliano, Christ risen, and a depiction of the Laocoön, the Hellenistic figure group. Fifty drawings, done in charcoal on plaster walls, were found. The public can sometimes view these sketches in the choir.

Admission: 9,000 lire ($7.05).

Open: Tues–Sat 9am–2pm, Sun 9am–1pm. **Bus:** 1, 6, 11, 17, 19, or 23.

GALLERIA DEGLI UFFIZI, loggiato degli Uffizi 6. Tel. 218341.

When the last grand duchess of the Medici family died, she bequeathed to the people of Tuscany a wealth of Renaissance, even classical, art. The paintings and sculpture had been accumulated by the powerful grand dukes in 3 centuries of rule that witnessed the height of the Renaissance. Vasari designed the palace in the 16th century for Cosimo I.

The Uffizi, with the finest collection of art in Italy, ranks along with the Prado and the Louvre as one of the greatest art galleries in the world. To describe all its offerings would fill a very thick volume, and to see and have time to absorb all the Uffizi paintings would take at least 2 weeks. I'll present only the sketchy highlights to get the first-timer through a citadel of madonnas and bambini, mythological figures, and Christian martyrs. The Uffizi is nicely grouped into periods or schools to show the development and progress of Italian and European art.

The first room begins with classical sculpture. You'll then meet up with those rebels from Byzantium, Cimabue and his pupil Giotto, with their madonnas and bambini. Since the Virgin and Child seem to be the overriding theme of the earlier of the Uffizi artists, it's enlightening just to follow the different styles over the centuries, from the ugly, almost midget-faced babies of the post-Byzantine works to the chubby, red-cheeked cherubs that glorified the baroque.

Look for Simone Martini's *Annunciation,* a collaborative venture. The halo around the head of the Virgin doesn't conceal her pouty mouth. Fra Angelico of Fiesole, a 15th-century painter, lost in a world peopled with saints and angels, makes his Uffizi debut with (naturally) a *Madonna and Bambino.* A special treasure is a work by Masaccio, who died at an early age, but is credited as the father of modern painting. In his madonnas and bambini we see the beginnings of the use of perspective in painting. Two important portraits are by Piero della Francesca, the 15th-century painter. Fra Angelico's *Coronation of the Virgin* is also in this salon.

In another room you'll find Friar Fillippo Lippi's far-superior *Coronation,* as well as a galaxy of charming madonnas. He was a rebel among the brethren.

The Botticelli rooms, which contain his finest works, are popular, especially with visitors who contemplate what is commonly referred to as "Venus on the Half-Shell." This supreme conception of life—the *Birth of Venus*—really packs them in. Flora tries to cover the nude goddess, while the gods of the wind puff up a storm. But before being captured by Venus, don't miss *Minerva Subduing the Centaur,* an important painting which brought about a resurgence of interest in mythological subjects. Botticelli's *Allegory of Spring* or *Primavera* is a gem; it's often called a symphony because you can listen to it. Set in a citrus grove, the painting depicts Venus with Cupid hovering over her head. "The Wind" tries to capture a nymph; but the three graces, in a lyrical composition, form the painting's chief claim to greatness. Mercury looks out of the canvas to the left. Before leaving the room, look for Botticelli's *Adoration of the Magi,* in which we find portraits of the Medici (the vain man at the far right is Botticelli). Also here is Botticelli's small allegorical *Calumny.*

Nobody should miss *The Adoration of the Shepherds,* a superbly detailed triptych, commissioned for a once-important Tuscan family and painted by Hugo van der Goes, a 15th-century artist. In another room we come across one of Leonardo da Vinci's unfinished paintings, the brilliant *Adoration of the Magi,* and Verrocchio's *Baptism of Christ,* not a very important painting, but noted because da Vinci painted one of the angels when he was 14 years old. Also in this salon hangs da Vinci's *Annunciation,* which reflects the early years of his genius with its twilight atmosphere and each leaf painstakingly in place. Proof that Leonardo was an architect? The splendid Renaissance palace he designed is part of the background.

The most beautiful room in the gallery with its dome of pearl shells contains the *Venus of the Medici* at center stage; it's one of the most reproduced of all Greek sculptural works. Also displayed are *Apollo* and *The Wrestlers,* from greek originals of the 3rd and 4th centuries B.C.

In the rooms to follow are works by Perugino, Dürer, Mantegna, Giovanni Bellini, Giorgione, and Correggio. Finally, don't miss Michelangelo's *Holy Family,* as well as Raphael's *Madonna of the Goldfinch,* plus his portraits of Julius II and Leo X. There is also what might be dubbed the Titian salon, which has two of his interpretations of Venus (one depicted with Cupid). When it came to representing voluptuous females on canvas, Titian had no rival. In other rooms are important Mannerists: Parmigianino, Veronese, and Tintoretto (*Leda and the Swan*). In the rooms nearing the end are works by Rubens, Caravaggio (*Bacchus*), and Rembrandt.

Admission: 10,000 lire ($7.85).

Open: Tues–Sat 9am–7pm, Sun and hols 9am–1pm (last entrance 45 minutes before closing time).

PITTI PALACE, piazza de' Pitti. Tel. 213440.

The Palatine Gallery, on the left bank (a 5-minute walk from the Ponte Vecchio), houses one of Europe's great art collections, with masterpieces hung one on top of the other, as in the days of the Enlightenment. If for no other reason, it should be visited for its Raphaels alone. The Pitti, built in the mid-15th century (Brunelleschi was the original architect), was once the residence of the powerful Medici family.

There are actually several museums in this complex, including the most important, the **Galleria Palatina,** repository of old masters. Other museums include the **Appartamenti Monumentali,** which the Medici family once called home, and the **Museo degli Argenti,** 16 rooms devoted to displays of the "loot" acquired by the Medici dukes. Others are the **Coach and Carriage Museum** and the **Galleria d'Arte Moderna,** as well as the **Museo della Porcellane** (porcelain) and the **Galleria del Costume.**

After passing through the main door, proceed to the Sala di Venere (the Room of Venus), which appropriately belongs to Titian, who greatly admired his favorite goddess. In it are his *La Bella,* of rich and illuminating color (entrance wall), and his portrait of Pietro Aretino, one of his most distinguished works. On the opposite wall are Titian's *Concert of Music,* often attributed to Giorgione, and his portrait of Julius II.

In the Sala di Apollo (on the opposite side of the entrance door) are Titian's *Man with Gray Eyes*—an aristocratic, handsome romanticist—as well as his *Mary Magdalene* with a plunging décolletage. On the opposite wall are van Dyck portraits of Charles I of England and Henrietta of France.

In the Sala di Marte (entrance wall) is an important *Madonna and Child* by Murillo of Spain, as well as the Pitti's best-known work by Rubens, *The Four Philosophers.* On the left wall is one of Rubens's most tragic and moving paintings, depicting the *Consequences of War*—an early *Guernica.*

In the Sala di Giove (entrance wall) are Andrea del Sarto's idealized John the Baptist in his youth, Fra Bartolomeo's *Descent from the Cross,* and one of Rubens's most exciting paintings (even for those who don't like art), which depicts a romp of nymphs and satyrs. On the third wall (opposite the entrance wall) is the Pitti's second famous Raphael, the woman under the veil, known as *La Fornarina*, his bakery-girl mistress.

In the following gallery, the Sala di Saturno, look to the left on the entrance wall to see Raphael's *Madonna of the Canopy*. On the third wall near the doorway is the greatest Pitti prize, Raphael's *Madonna of the Chair*, his best-known interpretation of the Virgin, and what is in fact probably one of the six most celebrated paintings in all of Europe.

In the Sala dell'Iliade (to your left on the entrance wall) is a work of delicate beauty, Raphael's rendition of a pregnant woman, painted while he was still searching for a personal style. On the left wall is Titian's *Portrait of a Gentleman*, which he was indeed. (Titian is the second big star in the Palatine Gallery.) Finally, as you're leaving, look to the right of the doorway to see one of Velázquez's interpretations of the many faces of Philip IV of Spain.

In the rooms that follow, the drama of the salons remains vivid—enhanced by portraits by Justus Sustermans, who could be almost as devastating as Velázquez.

Major works in the Sala di Prometeo include Filippo Lippi's *Madonna and Child*, and two Botticelli portraits. In the Sala dell'Educazione di Giove hangs Caravaggio's *Sleeping Cupid*, and in the Sala della Giustizia you'll find Tintoretto's *Virgin and Child*, a vintage work by that Venetian master.

Admission: 4,000 lire ($3.15); the modern-art gallery requires a separate 4,000-lira ($3.15) ticket.

Open: Tues–Sat 9am–2pm, Sun 9am–1pm. **Bus:** 3.

★ MUSEO NAZIONALE DEL BARGELLO, via del Proconsolo 4. Tel. 218341.

The National Museum, a short walk from piazza della Signoria, is a 13th-century fortress palace whose dark underground chambers once resounded with the echoing cries of the tortured. Today it's a vast repository of some of the most important sculpture of the Renaissance, including works by Michelangelo and Donatello.

Here you'll see another of Michelangelo's *David*s (referred to in the past as *Apollo*), chiseled perhaps 25 to 30 years after the statuesque figure in the Academy Gallery. The Bargello *David* is totally different—even effete when compared to its stronger brother. The gallery also displays Michelangelo's grape-capped *Bacchus* (one of his earlier works), who is tempted by a satyr. Among the more significant sculptures is Giambologna's *Winged Mercury*.

The Bargello displays two versions of Donatello's John the Baptist—one emaciated, the other a younger and much kinder edition. Donatello, of course, was one of the outstanding and original talents of the early Renaissance. In this gallery you'll learn why. His *St. George* is a work of heroic magnitude. According to an oft-repeated story, Michelangelo, upon seeing it for the first time, commanded it to "March!" Donatello's bronze *David* in this salon is one of the most remarkable figures of all Renaissance sculpture—it was the first "free-standing" nude since the Romans stopped chiseling. As depicted, *David* is narcissistic (a stunning contrast to Michelangelo's latter-day virile interpretation). For the last word, however, I'll have to call back our lady of the barbs, Mary McCarthy, who wrote: "His David . . . wearing nothing but a pair of fancy polished boots and a girlish bonnet, is a transvestite's and fetishist's dream of alluring ambiguity."

Look for at least one more notable work, another *David*—this one by Andrea del Verrocchio, one of the finest of the 15th-century sculptors. The Bargello contains a large number of terra-cottas by the della Robbia clan.

Admission: 6,000 lire ($4.70).

Open: Tues–Sat 9am–2pm, Sun 9am–1pm. **Bus:** 14, 15, 18, 19, or 23.

MUSEO DI SAN MARCO, piazza San Marco. Tel. 218341.

The Museo di San Marco, a state museum, is a handsome Renaissance palace whose cell walls are decorated with frescoes by the mystical Fra Angelico, one of Europe's greatest 15th-century painters. In the days of Cosimo dei Medici, San Marco was built by Michelozzo as a Dominican convent. It originally contained bleak, bare cells, which Angelico and his students then brightened considerably with some of the most important works of this pious artist of Fiesole, who portrayed recognizable landscapes in strong, vivid colors.

One of his better-known paintings found here is *The Last Judgment,* which depicts people with angels on the left dancing in a circle, and lordly saints towering overhead. Hell, as it is depicted on the right, is naïve—Dante-esque—infested with demons, reptiles, and sinners boiling in a stew. Much of hell was created by his students; Angelico's brush was inspired only by the Crucifixion, madonnas and bambini—or landscapes, of course. Here, also, are his *Descent from the Cross* and an especially refined interpretation panel of scenes from the life of Mary, including the *Flight into Egypt.*

In one room are frescoes by Fra Bartolomeo, who lived from 1475 to 1517 and worked with Raphael. Note his *Madonna and Child with Saints.* In the Capitolo is a fading but powerful *Crucifixion* by Angelico.

Turn right at the next door and you'll enter a refectory devoted to the artistic triumph of Domenico Ghirlandaio, the man who taught Michelangelo how to fresco. Ghirlandaio's own *Last Supper* in this room is rather realistic; his saints have tragic faces and silently evoke a feeling of impending doom.

Upstairs on the second floor—at the top of the hallway—is Angelico's masterpiece, *The Annunciation,* a perfect gem of a painting. From here, you can walk down the left corridor to explore the cells of the Dominicans which are enhanced by frescoes by Angelico and his pupils. Most of the frescoes depict scenes from the Crucifixion.

After turning to the right, you may want to skip the remaining frescoes, which appear to be uninspired student exercises. But at the end of the corridor is the cell of Savonarola which was the scene of his arrest. The cell contains portraits of the reformer by Bartolomeo, who was plunged into acute melancholy by the jailing and torturing of his beloved teacher. You'll also find pictures of the reformer on the pyre at piazza della Signoria.

If you retrace your steps to the entrance, then head down still another corridor, you'll see more frescoes, past a library with Ionic columns designed by Michelozzo. Finally, you'll come to the cell of Cosimo dei Medici, with a fresco by Gozzoli, who worked with Angelico.

Admission: 6,000 lire ($4.70).
Open: Tues–Sat 9am–2pm, Sun 9am–1pm. **Bus:** 1, 6, 7, 11, 15, 17, or 20.

MORE ATTRACTIONS
PIAZZALE MICHELANGELO

For a view of the wonders of Florence below and Fiesole above, climb aboard bus no. 13 from the central station and head for piazzale Michelangelo, a 19th-century belvedere overlooking a view seen in many a Renaissance painting. It's best at dusk, when the purple-fringed Tuscan hills form a frame for Giotto's bell tower, Brunelleschi's dome, and the towering hunk of stones which stick up from the Palazzo Vecchio. Another copy of Michelangelo's *David* dominates the square.

Warning: At certain times during the day the square is so crowded with tour buses and peddlers selling trinkets and claptrap souvenirs that the balcony is drained of its chief drama. If you go at these times, often midday in summer, you'll find that the view of Florence is still intact—but you may be run down by a Vespa if you try to enjoy it.

PONTE VECCHIO

Spared by the Nazis in their bitter retreat from the Allied advance in 1944, "The Old Bridge" is the last remaining medieval *ponte* spanning the Arno (the Germans blew up the rest). The bridge was again threatened in the flood of 1966 when the waters of the Arno swept over it and washed away a fortune in jewelry from the goldsmiths' shops that flank the bridge.

Today the restored Ponte Vecchio is closed to traffic except the *pedoni* (pedestrian) type. The little shops continue to sell everything from the most expensive of

Florentine gold to something simple—say, a Lucrezia Borgia poison ring. Florentine hog butchers once peddled their wares on this bridge.

OSPEDALE DEGLI INNOCENTI

At piazza SS. Annunziata 12 is the Hospital of the Innocents (tel. 243670), the oldest of its kind in Europe. The building, and the loggia, with its Corinthian columns, was conceived by Brunelleschi and marked the first architectural bloom of the Renaissance in Florence. In the cortile are terra-cotta medallions done in blues and opaque whites by Andrea della Robbia which depict babes in swaddling clothes.

Still used as a hospital, the building also contains an art gallery. Notable among its treasures is a terra-cotta *Madonna and Child* by Luca della Robbia, plus works by Andrea del Sarto and Filippo Lippi. One of the gallery's most important paintings is an *Adoration of the Magi* by Domenico Ghirlandaio (the chubby Bambino looks a bit pompously at the Wise Man kissing his foot). The gallery is open Thursday through Tuesday from 9am to 2pm (to 1pm on Sunday). Admission is 3,000 lire ($2.35).

CHURCHES

The wealth of architecture, art, and treasures of Florence's churches is hardly secondary, but if you want to see even a sampling of the best, you'll have to schedule an extra day or more in the City of the Renaissance.

BASILICA DI SANTA CROCE, piazza Santa Croce 16. Tel. 244533.

The Pantheon of Florence, this church shelters the tombs of everyone from Michelangelo to Machiavelli, from Dante (he was actually buried at Ravenna) to an astronomer (Galileo) who—at the hands of the Inquisition—"recanted" his concept that the earth revolves around the sun. Just as Santa Maria Novella was the church of the Dominicans, Santa Croce was the church of the Franciscans, said to have been designed by Arnolfo di Cambio.

In the right nave (first tomb) is the Vasari-executed monument to Michelangelo, whose body was smuggled back to his native Florence from its original burial place in Rome. Along with a bust of the artist are three allegorical figures who represent the arts. In the next memorial a prune-faced Dante, a poet honored belatedly in the city that exiled him, looks down. Farther on, still on the right, is the tomb of Machiavelli, whose *The Prince* became a virtual textbook in the art of wielding power. Nearby is a lyrical bas-relief, *The Annunciation* by Donatello.

The "Trecento" frescoes are reason enough for visiting Santa Croce—especially those by Giotto to the right of the main chapel. Once whitewashed, the Bardi and Peruzzi Chapels were "uncovered" in the mid-19th century in such a clumsy fashion that they have had to be drastically restored. Although badly preserved, the frescoes in the Bardi Chapel are most memorable, especially the deathbed scene of St. Francis. The cycles in the Peruzzi Chapel are of John the Baptist and St. John. In the left transept is Donatello's once-controversial wooden *Crucifix*—too gruesome for some Renaissance tastes, including that of Brunelleschi, who is claimed to have said: "You [Donatello] have put a rustic upon the cross." (For Brunelleschi's "answer," go to Santa Maria Novella.) Incidentally, the Pazzi Chapel, entered through the cloisters, was designed by Brunelleschi, with terra-cottas by Luca della Robbia.

Additionally, inside the monastery of this church the Franciscan fathers established the **Leather School** at the end of World War II. The purpose of the school was to prepare young boys technically to specialize in Florentine leather work. The school has flourished and produced many fine artisans who continue their careers here. Stop in and see the work when you visit the church.

Admission: Church, free; cloister and church musuem, 3,000 lire ($2.35) adults, 1,000 lire (80¢) children.

Open: Church, daily 8am–12:30pm and 3–6:30pm; museum and cloister, Thurs–Tues 10am–12:30pm and 2:30–6:30pm. **Bus:** 13, 14, or 19.

BASILICA DI SANTA MARIA NOVELLA, Piazza Santa Maria Novella. Tel. 282187.

Near the railway station is one of Florence's most distinguished churches, begun in 1278 for the Dominicans. Its geometric facade, with bands of white and green marble, was designed in the late 15th century by Leon Battista Alberti, an aristocrat and true Renaissance man (philosopher, painter, architect, poet). The church borrows from and harmonizes the Romanesque, Gothic, and Renaissance styles.

In the left nave as you enter (third large painting) is the great Masaccio's *Trinity,* a curious work that has the architectural form of a Renaissance stage setting, but whose figures—in perfect perspective—are like actors in a Greek tragedy. If you view the church at dusk, you'll see the stained-glass windows in the fading light cast kaleidoscopic fantasies on the opposite wall.

Head straight up the left nave to the Gondi Chapel for a look at Brunelleschi's wooden *Christ on the Cross,* which is said to have been carved to compete with Donatello's same subject in Santa Croce (see above). According to Vasari, when Donatello saw Brunelleschi's completed Crucifix, he dropped his apron full of eggs intended for their lunch. "You have symbolized the Christ," Donatello is alleged to have said. "Mine is an ordinary man." (Some art historians reject this story.)

In the late 15th century Ghirlandaio contracted with a Medici banker to adorn the choir with frescoes which illustrate scenes from the lives of Mary and John the Baptist. Michelangelo, only a teenager at the time, is known to have studied under Ghirlandaio (perhaps he even worked on this cycle).

If time remains, you may want to visit the cloisters, going first to the "Green Cloisters," and then the splendid Spanish Chapel frescoed by Andrea di Bonaiuto in the 14th century (one panel depicts the Dominicans in triumph over heretical wolves).

Admission: Church, free; cloisters, 3,000 lire ($2.35)

Open: Church, daily 9am–2pm; cloisters, Mon–Thurs and Sat 9am–2pm, Sun 9am–1pm. **Bus:** 1, 6, 11, 17, 19, or 23.

BASILICA DI SAN LORENZO, piazza San Lorenzo.

This is Brunelleschi's 15th-century Renaissance church, where the Medici used to attend services from their nearby palace on via Larga, now via Camillo Cavour. Most visitors flock to see Michelangelo's "New Sacristy" with his *Night* and *Day* (see the Medici chapels under "The Top Attractions," above), but Brunelleschi's handiwork deserves some time too.

Built in the style of a Latin cross, the church is distinguished by harmonious grays and rows of Corinthian columns. The Old Sacristy (walk up the nave, then turn left) was designed by Brunelleschi and decorated, in part, by Donatello (see his terra-cotta bust of St. Lawrence).

After exploring the Old Sacristy, go through the first door (unmarked) on your right, then turn right again and climb the steps.

The **Biblioteca Medicea Laurenziana** (tel. 213206) is entered separately at piazza San Lorenzo 9 and was designed by Michelangelo to shelter the expanding library of the Medici. Beautiful in design and concept, and approached by exquisite stairs, the library is filled with some of Italy's greatest manuscripts—many of which are handsomely illustrated.

After a visit here, you may want to wander through the cloisters of San Lorenzo and study their Ionic columns.

Admission: Free.

Open: Library, Mon–Sat 9am–1pm; study room, Mon–Sat 8am–2pm. **Bus:** 1, 6, 11, 17, 19, or 23.

SANTA MARIA DEL CARMINE, piazza Santa Maria del Carmine.

A long walk from the Pitti Palace on the left bank is this baroque church, a result of rebuilding after a fire in the 18th century. Miraculously, the renowned Brancacci Chapel was spared—miraculous because it contains frescoes by Masaccio, who ushered in the great century of "Quattrocento" Renaissance painting. Forsaking the ideal, Masaccio depicted man and woman in their weakness and their glory.

His technique is seen at its most powerful in the expulsion of Adam and Eve from the Garden of Eden. The artist peopled his chapel, a masterpiece of early perspective, with scenes from the life of St. Peter (the work was originally begun by his master, Masolino). Note especially the fresco, *Tribute Money,* and the baptism scene with the nude youth freezing in the cold waters.

No less an authority than Leonardo da Vinci commented on Masaccio's work: "Masaccio showed by his perfect works how those who take for their ideal anything but nature—mistress of all masters—tire themselves in vain." Masaccio did the upper frescoes, but because of his early death, the lower ones were completed by Filippino Lippi (not to be confused with his father, Filippo Lippi, a greater artist).

Admission: Free.

Open: Mar–Oct, daily 7am–noon and 4–6pm; Nov–Feb, daily 7am–noon and 4–5pm. **Bus:** 3.

THE SYNAGOGUE OF FLORENCE, via Farini 4. Tel. 245242.

This synagogue is in the Moorish style, inspired by Constantine's Byzantine church of Hagia Sophia. Completed in 1882, it was badly damaged by the Nazis in 1944 but has been restored to its original splendor. A museum is upstairs.

Admission: 3,000 lire ($2.35) adults, 2,000 lire ($1.55) children.

Open: Sun–Fri; for the exact timetable of visits and prayers, phone the secretary. **Closed:** Jewish hols. **Bus:** 13, 14, or 19.

PALACES

PALAZZO VECCHIO, piazza della Signoria. Tel. 27681.

The secular "Old Palace" is without doubt the most famous and imposing palace in Florence. It dates from the closing years of the 13th century. Its remarkable architectural feature is its 308-foot tower, an engineering feat that required supreme skill. Once home to the Medici, the Palazzo Vecchio (also called Palazzo della Signoria) is occupied today by city employees, but much of it is open to the public.

The 16th-century "Hall of the 500" ("Dei Cinquecento"), the most outstanding part of the palace, is filled with Vasari & Co. frescoes as well as sculpture. As you enter the hall, look for Michelangelo's *Victory.* It depicts an insipid-looking young man treading on a bearded older man (it has been suggested that Michelangelo put his own face on that of the trampled man).

Later you can stroll through the rest of the palace, through its apartments and main halls. You can also visit the private apartments of Eleanor of Toledo, wife of Cosimo I, and a chapel which was begun in 1540 and frescoed by Bronzino. The palace displays the Verrocchio's original bronze putto (from 1476) from the courtyard fountain. This work is called both *Winged Cherub Clutching a Fish* and *Boy with a Dolphin.* The palace also shelters a 16th-century *Portrait of Machiavelli* which is attributed to Santi di Tito. Donatello's famous bronze group, *Judith Slaying Holofernes,* once stood on piazza dei Signoria, but it was brought inside.

The salons, such as a fleur-de-lis apartment, have their own richness and beauty. Following his arrest, Savonarola was taken to the Palazzo Vecchio for more than a dozen torture sessions, including "twists" on the rack. The torturer pronounced him his "best" customer.

Admission: 8,000 lire ($6.30).

Open: Mon–Fri 9am–7pm, Sun 8am–1pm. **Bus:** 14, 15, 19, 23, 31, or 32.

PALAZZO MEDICI-RICCARDI, via Camillo Cavour 1. Tel. 27601.

This palace, a short walk from the Duomo, was the home of Cosimo dei Medici before he took his household to the Palazzo della Signoria. Built by palace architect Michelozzo in the mid-15th century, the brown stone building was also the scene, at times, of the court of Lorenzo the Magnificent. Art lovers visit today chiefly to see the mid-15th-century frescoes by Benozzo Gozzoli in the Medici Chapel.

Gozzoli's frescoes, which depict the *Journey of the Magi,* form his masterpiece—in fact, they are considered a hallmark in Renaissance painting in that they abandoned ecclesiastical themes to celebrate emerging man (he peopled his work with the Medici, the artist's master Fra Angelico, and even himself). Gozzoli's ability as a landscape artist and a distinguished portraitist (each man in the procession is a distinctly identifiable individual—often elaborately coiffed and clothed) is seen at its finest here.

Another gallery, which has to be entered by a separate stairway, was frescoed by Luca Giordano in the 18th century, but his work seems merely decorative. The apartments, where the prefect lodges, are not open to the public. The gallery, incidentally, may also be viewed free.

Admission: Free.

Open: Mon–Tues and Thurs–Sat 9am–1pm and 3–5pm, Sun 9am–noon. **Bus:** 1, 6, 11, 17, 19, or 23.

MUSEUMS & GALLERIES

MUSEO ARCHEOLOGICO, via della Colonna 38. Tel. 247-8641.

The Archeological Museum, a short walk from piazza della SS. Annunziata, houses one of the most outstanding Egyptian and Etruscan collections in Europe. Its Egyptian mummies and sarcophagi are on the first floor, along with some of the better-known Etruscan works. Pause to look at the lid to the coffin of a fat Etruscan (unlike the blank faces staring back from many of these tombs, this overeater's countenance is quite expressive).

One room is graced with three bronze Etruscan masterpieces, among the rarest objets d'art of these relatively unknown people. They include the *Chimera,* a lion with a goat sticking out of its back. The lion's tail—in the form of a venomous reptile—lunges at the trapped beast. The others are a statue of *Minerva* and one of an *Orator.* These pieces of sculpture range from the 5th to the 1st century B.C. Another rare find is an original Greek bronze of a young man, the so-called *Idolino from Pesaro.* The François vase on the ground floor, from the year 570 B.C., is celebrated.

Admission: 3,000 lire ($2.35).

Open: Tues–Sat 9am–2pm, Sun 9am–1pm. **Bus:** 1, 6, 7, 11, 15, 17, or 20.

MUSEO DELL'OPERA DEL DUOMO, piazza del Duomo 9. Tel. 230-2885.

The Museo dell'Opera del Duomo, across the street but facing the apse of Santa Maria del Fiore, is beloved by connoisseurs of Renaissance sculptural works. It shelters the sculpture removed from the campanile and the Duomo—not only to protect the pieces from the weather, but from visitors who wanted samples. A major attraction of this museum is the unfinished *Pietà* by Michelangelo, which is in the middle of the stairs. It was carved between 1548 and 1555 when the artist was in his 70s. In this vintage work, a figure representing Nicodemus (but said to have Michelangelo's face) is holding Christ. The great Florentine intended it for his own tomb, but he is believed to have grown disenchanted with it and to have attempted to destroy it. The museum has a Brunelleschi bust, as well as della Robbia terra-cottas. The museum's premier attraction is four restored panels of Ghiberti's "Doors to Paradise" removed from the Baptistery.

You'll see bits and pieces from what was the old Gothic-Romanesque fronting of the cathedral, with ornamental statues, as conceived by the original architect, Arnolfo di Cambio. One of Donatello's early works, *St. John the Evangelist,* is here—not his finest hour certainly, but anything by Donatello is worth looking at, including one of his most celebrated works, the *Magdalene,* which is in the room with the cantorie (see below). This wooden statue once stood in the Baptistery, and had to be restored after the flood of 1966. Dating from 1454–55, it is stark and penitent.

A good reason for visiting the museum is to see the marble choirs—*cantorie*—of Donatello and Luca della Robbia (the works face each other, and are in the first room you enter after climbing the stairs). The Luca della Robbia choir is more restrained, but it still "Praises the Lord" in marble—with clashing cymbals and sounding brass which constitute a reaffirmation of life. In contrast, all restraint breaks loose in the *cantoria* of dancing cherubs in Donatello's choir. It's a romp of chubby bambini. Of all of Donatello's works, this one is perhaps the most lighthearted. But, in total contrast, don't miss Donatello's *Zuccone,* which some consider to be one of his greatest masterpieces; it was done for Giotto's bell tower.

Admission: 4,000 lire ($3.15).

Open: Mar–Sept, Mon–Sat 9am–8pm; Oct–Feb, Mon–Sat 9am–6pm. **Bus:** 1, 6, 11, 14, 19, or 23.

MUSEO BARDINI, piazza de' Mozzi 1. Tel. 234-2427.

The Bardini Museum grew out of the collections of Stefano Bardini, who died in 1922. In his heyday in the 19th century he was a major art dealer who grew wealthy buying and selling art. He kept a lot of the art for himself, however, as this collection clearly reveals. The only regret I have is that he short-sightedly demolished a 13th-century church to build a palace to house his collection; however, he at least used some of the architectural remnants in his new palace.

This museum seems little visited and even less known, except among art connoisseurs, those who make a point to visit every museum in Florence. Bardini seems to have followed no particular guidelines in his collection, and thus one is likely to get a little bit of everything, from Greek and Roman sculpture, even Etruscan. Antique musical instruments are exhibited along with church altars. Naturally, he was able to acquire some stunning Renaissance furniture, along with paintings by such old masters as Lucas Cranach and Tintoretto. He also collected terra-cotta reliefs, the favorite mother and child theme from the della Robbias.

Admission: 5,000 lire ($3.95).
Open: Mon–Tues and Thurs–Sat 9am–2pm, Sun 8am–1pm. **Bus:** 13, 15, or 23.

HORNE MUSEUM, via dei Benci 6. Tel. 244661.

Herbert Horne, an art historian, immortalized himself upon his death in 1916, having collected the nucleus for this exhibition. A bachelor, and also a prominent figure in the pre–World War I expatriate colony that flourished in Florence, English-born Horne was a great collector. This is even more remarkable when one remembers that he was not wealthy.

But he knew art, and he shopped for "bargains," especially in the art of the Renaissance. He was mainly interested in painting. His greatest acquisition was the Giotto portrait of Saint Stephen, which dates from the early 14th century. Other minor masterpieces were also acquired, including works by Filippo Lippi, Simone Martini, Dosso Dossi, and Masaccio.

Admission: 4,000 lire ($3.15).
Open: Mon, Wed, and Sat 9am–1pm. **Bus:** 13, 14, or 19.

MUSEO STIBBERT, via F. Stibbert 26. Tel. 475520.

This eclectic collection of arms and armor, paintings by major and minor artists, tapestries, furniture, porcelain, and costumes for men and women (particularly the apparel of warriors of many civilizations) was the life interest of Florentine Frederick Stibbert. The collection is often called "worthy of *Citizen Kane*." Stibbert, son of an upper-class English father and a Florentine mother, made his 62-room villa, set in an elegant park, into his own personal museum, which he left to the city on his death in 1906. It is on the Montughi hill just outside the city.

From the entrance into the Malachite Room with red-brocade-covered walls, you go through Louis XV, Louis XVI, and Empire salons, Italian rooms, Turkish corridors, and samurai arsenals. The museum is unusual in that it houses the most extensive collection known of Near Eastern armor, as well as armor of Oriental warriors, and complete sets of the finery that European knights wore during at least 2 centuries. Of special interest are three rooms whose walls and doors are completely covered with embossed and painted leather. The park in which the villa stands is a mixture of English horticulture and exotic flora, with a pond and a little Egyptian pavilion.

Visits are by guided tour only, beginning on the hour. On Sunday, only part of the museum can be visited. It's north of the center off via Bolognese (it's signposted).

Admission: 4,000 lire ($3.15).
Open: Mon–Wed and Fri–Sat 9am–1pm, Sun 9am–12:30pm.

GARDENS

GIARDINI DI BOBOLI (Boboli Gardens), piazza Pitti 1. Tel. 218741.

Behind the Pitti Palace are the Giardini di Boboli, through which the Medici romped. They were originally laid out by Triboli, a great landscape artist, in the 16th century. The Boboli is ever popular for a promenade or an idyllic interlude in a pleasant setting; it's also the scene of the annual open-air Maggio Musicale, the international music festival that draws artists from all over the world in May. The gardens are filled with fountains and statuary, such as a *Venus* by Giambologna in the "Grotto" of Buontalenti. You can climb to the top of the Fortezza di Belvedere for a dazzling view of the city.

Admission: Free.

Open: Apr–Oct, daily 9am–6:30pm; Nov–Mar, daily 9am–4:30pm. **Bus:** 3 or 15.

SPECIAL-INTEREST SIGHTSEEING

FOR THE LITERARY ENTHUSIAST

CASA GUIDI, piazza S. Felice 8. Tel. 284393.

Just beyond the Pitti Palace, not far from the Arno, is the former residence of Elizabeth Barrett and Robert Browning. They chose this location less than a year after their clandestine marriage in London, and it became their home for the remaining 14 years of their life together. Casa Guidi is where their son was born and where they wrote some of their best-known works. Barrett died here in 1861. Her tomb can be visited at the English cemetery in Florence. After her death, a heart-broken Browning left Florence, never to return (he died in Venice in 1889 and is buried in Westminster Abbey in London). The poets' son, Pen, acquired the residence in 1893, intending to make a memorial to his parents; however, he died before completing his plans. The rooms were first opened to the public in 1971 when the Browning Institute, an international charitable organization, acquired the apartment. "White doves in the ceiling" and frescoes of "angels looking down from a cloud," both of which Barrett wrote about, will interest aficionados.

It's admirable what the institute has done to pay homage to the two 19th-century poets who were the center of the Anglo-Florentine community, much as Keats and Shelley were the stars in "English Rome." Elizabeth Barrett Browning wrote regarding Casa Guidi that "the charm of a home is a home to come back to." As such, the institute is maintaining the house for future generations.

Admission: Free (donations accepted).

Open: Feb 2–Dec 14, Mon–Fri 3–6pm, Sat–Sun and hols by appointment; Dec 15–Feb 1, by appointment only. **Bus:** 15.

CASA DI DANTE, via Santa Margherita 1. Tel. 283343.

For those of us who were spoon-fed hell but spared purgatory, a pilgrimage to this rebuilt medieval house may be of passing interest, although it contains few specific exhibits of note. Dante was exiled from his native Florence in 1302 for his political involvements. He never returned, and thus wrote his *Divine Comedy* in exile, conjuring up fit punishment in the *Inferno* for his Florentine enemies. Dante certainly had the last word. The house is reached by walking down via Dante Alighieri.

Admission: Free.

Open: Mon–Tues and Thurs–Sat 9:30am–12:30pm and 3:30–6:30pm, Sun 9:30am–12:30pm. **Closed:** Approximately 3 weeks during July–Aug (dates vary). **Bus:** 14, 15, 18, 19, or 23.

FOR THE ART ENTHUSIAST

CASA BUONARROTI, via Ghibellina 70. Tel. 241752.

Only a short walk from Santa Croce stands the house that Michelangelo managed to buy for his nephew. Turned into a museum by his descendants, the house was restored in 1964. It contains some fledgling work by the great artist, as well as some models by him. Here you can see his *Madonna of the Stairs,* which he did when he was about 17 years old, as well as a bas-relief he did later, depicting *The Battle of the*

Centaurs. The casa is enriched by many of Michelangelo's drawings shown to the public in periodic exhibitions.

Admission: 5,000 lire ($3.95).

Open: Wed–Mon 9:30am–1:30pm. **Bus:** 14.

FOR VISITING AMERICANS

FLORENCE AMERICAN CEMETERY AND MEMORIAL, via Cassia, 50023 Impruneta. Tel. 055/202-0020.

The Florence American Cemetery and Memorial is on a 70-acre site about 7½ miles south of the city on the west side of via Cassia, the main highway connecting Florence with Siena and Rome. One of 14 permanent American World War II military cemetery memorials built on foreign soil by the American Battle Monuments Commission, the memorial is on a site that was liberated on August 3, 1944, and later became part of the zone of the U.S. Fifth Army. It is adjacent to the Greve River and framed by wooded hills. Most of the 4,402 servicemen and women interred here died in the fighting that occurred after the capture of Rome in June 1944.

Admission: Free.

Open: Apr 16–Sept, daily 8am–6pm; Oct–Apr 15, daily 8am–5pm. **Bus:** The SITA city bus stops at the cemetery entrance every 2 hours, except on holidays, when there is usually no bus service. The bus follows via Cassia.

WALKING TOUR — The Heart of Florence

Start: Piazza de' Pitti.

Finish: Ponte Trinità.

Time: 2 hours.

Best Time: Any sunny day.

Worst Times: From 8 to 9:30am and 5 to 7:30pm Monday through Saturday.

This tour begins at piazza de' Pitti, where you may or may not elect to visit the art treasures of the:

1. **Pitti Palace,** or walk through the Boboli Gardens in back of the palace. Head up via di Guicciardini until you reach the ancient, shop-flanked:

2. **Ponte Vecchio,** which spans the river. Pause at the top of the bridge where a vista from the double-sided belvedere offers views of the Arno on both sides. The calm waters you see today belie the unpredictable torrents that are capable of sweeping over sections of the bridge, as they did in 1966.

   After crossing the bridge, turn right and walk alongside the Arno, passing beneath a riverside arcade pierced both longitudinally and latitudinally by a series of arches which open from four directions like a Renaissance study in perspectives. Traffic whizzes beside you, funneling into the tiny piazza del Pesce. The riverside promenade that supports you now changes its name to the lungarno degli Archibusieri, which, a few steps later, gives way to lungarno Anna Maria Luisa de' Medici, just at the end of your sheltering arcade. Note the almost medieval view of the Ponte Vecchio from this spot.

   In about 40 paces you'll come to a soaring canopy of one of the most impressive arcades in Florence. This closes off the Arno side of the three-sided colonnades of the:

3. **Uffizi Gallery,** Italy's greatest museum. Walk between the rhythmically spaced arches of the arcades onto flagstones, which in sunny weather support dozens of hawkers and vendors. The Tower of the Signoria opens to your sight as you approach it. At:

4. **Piazza della Signoria,** stop to admire the sculpture-filled Loggia della Signoria and the Palazzo Vecchio. Pass the *Fountain of Neptune* and turn right just before the equestrian statue. Head to the far corner of the square and take the

ITALY

● Florence

Rome ★

1. Pitti Palace
2. Ponte Vecchio
3. Uffizi Gallery
4. Piazza della Signoria
5. Basilica of Santa Croce
6. Palazzo Bargello
7. Duomo
8. Museo del Duomo
9. The Baptistery
10. Basilica of San Lorenzo
11. Medici chapels
12. Piazza della Santa Maria Novella
13. Via dei Tornabuoni
14. Ponte Trinità

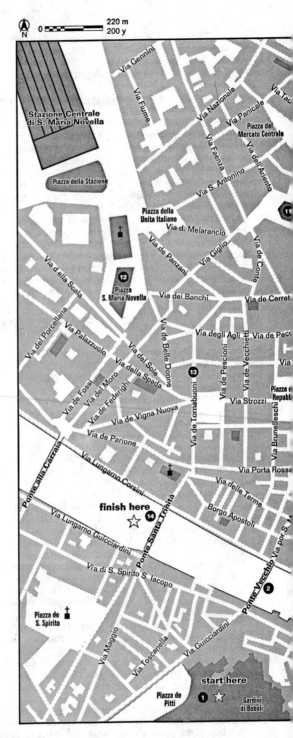

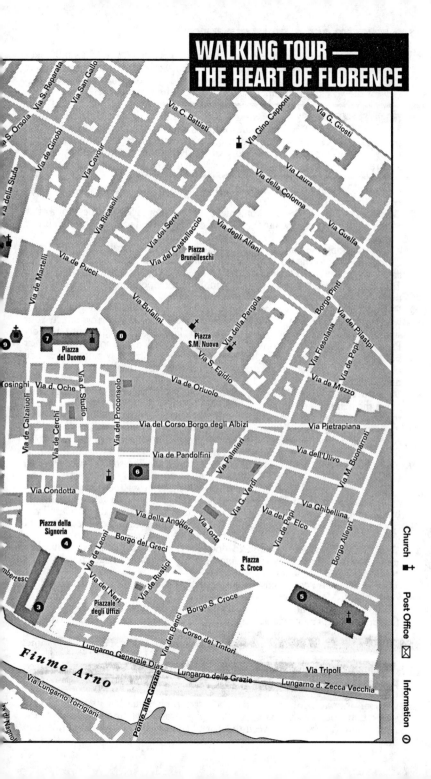

WALKING TOUR —
THE HEART OF FLORENCE

Via S. Orsola
Via S. Reparata
Via S. Gallo
Via de Ginobi
Via Cavour
Via Ricasoli
Via della Stufa
Via de Martelli
Via de Pucci
Via dei Servi
Via del Castellaccio
Via C. Battisti
Via degli Alfani
Via G. Giosti
Via Gino Capponi
Via Laura
Via della Colonna
Via Guelfa
Piazza
Brunelleschi
Via Bufalini
Via della Pergola
Borgo Pinti
Via dei Pilastri
Via Fiesolana
Via de Pepi
Piazza
S.M. Nuova
Via S. Egidio
Piazza
del Duomo
Via de Oriuolo
Via de Mezzo
Tosinghi
Via d. Oche
Via d. Studio
Via de Calzaiuoli
Via de Cerchi
Via del Proconsolo
Via del Corso Borgo degli Albizi
Via Pietrapiana
Via de Pandolfini
Via dell'Ulivo
Via Palmieri
Via M. Buonarroti
Via Condotta
Via della Anguillara
Via G. Verdi
Via del Pel. Elco
Via Ghibellina
Piazza della
Signoria
Via de Leoni
Borgo del Greci
Via Torta
Borgo Allegri
Via del Neri
Via de Rustici
Piazza
S. Croce
mberzesc
Piazzale
degli Uffizi
Via del Bencl
Borgo S. Croce
Lungarno Genevale Diaz
Corso dei Tintori
Via Tripoli
Lungarno delle Grazie
Lungarno d. Zecca Vecchia
Fiume Arno
Ponte alle Grazie
Via Lungarno Torrigiani
di Nagroli

Church ✝

Post Office ⊠

Information ⊙

small street at the side of the Palazzo Vecchio. This street, via de' Gondi, takes you to piazza di San Firenze in one block. Cross this street, climb seven stone steps of the baroque palace in front of you, and turn to contemplate your first view of the very top of Brunelleschi's dome on the Duomo.

REFUELING STOP　At the west end of piazza della Signoria, the most famous square in Florence, **Rivoire** is known for its chocolate, either served hot or else packaged to take with you. A seat at one of its outdoor tables is considered the most ideal way to observe the glory of the Renaissance in the sculpture-filled square.

Proceed down a narrow alley, borgo de' Greci, where a yellow-and-black sign points the way to the:

5. **Basilica of Santa Croce.** You emerge onto piazza di Santa Croce, for a view of the pink, green, and white bands that ornament the facade of the Basilica of Santa Croce.

After visiting the church, take a small street in front of it, called via Torta. Continue along to the first intersection, going along via della Burella, a narrow, flagstone-covered neighborhood street. At the end, you'll come to via dell'Acqua. Turn right and walk a short distance until the foreboding brown stone bulk of the:

6. **Palazzo Bargello** now soars above you. Turn left on via della Vigna Vecchia, which parallels the side of the Bargello. At the end of this narrow street, your sightlines will expand into piazza di San Firenze. Go right onto via del Proconsolo. The sidewalk is very narrow, often crowded, and somewhat a threat because of traffic. But, suddenly, there explodes the intricately patterned facade of what might be Italy's most obvious symbol of the Renaissance, the red-tile dome of the:

7. **Duomo.** Head across the crosswalk and continue more or less in a straight line along the periphery of shops and buildings that ring the edges of the rear side of the Duomo. Stop at piazza del Duomo 9, if you have time, and visit the:

8. **Museo del Duomo.** As you leave the museum, continue to ring the periphery of the piazza until you reach a pedestrian crosswalk, which leads you to a point between the cathedral's entrance and the doors of:

9. **The Baptistery,** which actually sits on its own satellite square, piazza di San Giovanni.

After visiting the Duomo and the Baptistery, cross the same street you approached them from. Turn left as soon as you reach via Martelli and walk 1½ blocks until you turn right at borgo San Lorenzo. Walk a short distance until you reach piazza di San Lorenzo. Pass to the right of the roughly textured facade of the:

10. **Basilica of San Lorenzo** and go along the side of this building. Continue in a crescent-shaped arc, always following the periphery of this huge church. You'll reach the wooden doors leading to the:

11. **Medici chapels,** containing sculpture by Michelangelo. At this point, you'll be on piazza di Madonna degli Aldobrandini.

Take via del Giglio, and walk straight across the busy traffic of via Panzani. Continue straight along via del Giglio until its end, via de Banchi, where you turn right. This will take you to the:

12. **Piazza della Santa Maria Novella** and its famous church of the same name. After visiting the church, take via delle Belle Donne and follow it past a granite column. Cross via del Moro, taking via del Trebbio. Follow this narrow street, past the Buca Lapi restaurant, until you come to piazza degli Antinori. Turn right onto the most famous shopping street of Florence:

13. **via dei Tornabuoni.** Walk along this street, checking out its many elegant shops, until you pass the soaring column of piazza Trinità, up to the banks of the Arno again. At a point between the pair of statues which flank the entrance to the:

14. Ponte Trinità, your tour has ended. Now you can plan your visits to the other treasures of Florence.

WALKING TOUR — In the Footsteps of Michelangelo

Start: Church of Santa Croce.
Finish: Piazzale Michelangelo.
Time: About 2½ hours, not counting interior visits.
Best Times: Early morning or late afternoon.
Worst Times: During the midafternoon heat. If you plan to visit the museums that dot this tour, avoid Monday, when most of them are closed.

Begin in front of the elegant marble geometrics that adorn the facade of the:

1. **Church of Santa Croce,** whose confines contain Michelangelo's tomb. After paying your respects, and admiring the design of what might be Florence's second-most-famous church, head west along borgo de' Greci, begins at the piazza's southwestern corner. It will eventually narrow to become via de' Gondi before opening onto the piazza whose buildings once housed the administration of some of the most famous rulers of the Renaissance:

2. **Piazza della Signoria.** Notice the elaborate *Fountain of Neptune,* close to which lies a brass plaque commemorating the site where the religious fanatic Savonarola was burned at the stake in 1498. (Michelangelo at the time was 23.) The square contains a series of dramatically displayed statues, some of them beneath soaring loggias. The most instantly recognizable statue is a copy of Michelangelo's *David,* the original of which was removed for safekeeping. Exit the piazza from its northeastern corner (take via dei Maggazzini) and follow the signs to the once-fortified walls of one of Florence's most famous galleries, the:

3. **Bargello Museum** (Palazzo del Bargello). Originally built during the 13th century, it contains depictions of David by both Donatello and Verrocchio (both of which Michelangelo studied intensely), as well as many of the greatest art treasures of Florence.

   Continue north along the clearly marked via del Proconsolo for four blocks, passing between the solid stone buildings of one of Florence's oldest neighborhoods, until you arrive at:

4. **Piazza del Duomo.** The architectural ensemble contained within it has changed little (apart from the roaring traffic) since Michelangelo first saw it. The cupola atop the cathedral, designed by Brunelleschi and completed in 1436 after 16 years of construction, inspired Michelangelo in his design of St. Peter's in Rome. (The soaring square bell tower was designed by Giotto.) Constructed of the same pink, green, and white marble as the cathedral itself is the octagonal:

5. **Baptistery,** whose eastern doors (designed by Ghiberti) are considered masterpieces of the metalworker's art. (What you'll see on the Baptistery are excellent copies of originals now in the Museo del Duomo.)

   After your exploration of the famous buildings on the piazza, exit from a point near its northwestern corner, via Ricasoli, and walk 2½ blocks to no. 60, which marks the site of:

6. **The Academy** (Galleria dell'Accademia). Its premises shelter the original of what might be the most famous statue in the world, Michelangelo's *David.* Less famous but immensely intriguing are the artist's *Four Prisoners,* whose forms seem to struggle to be released from the marble that seems to enslave them. The museum also contains a *Pietà,* and Michelangelo's figures of St. Matthew.

   Retrace your path south, walking toward piazza del Duomo, but turn right before you reach it at via dei Pucci. Within one block, at the corner of via Cavour, you'll reach the:

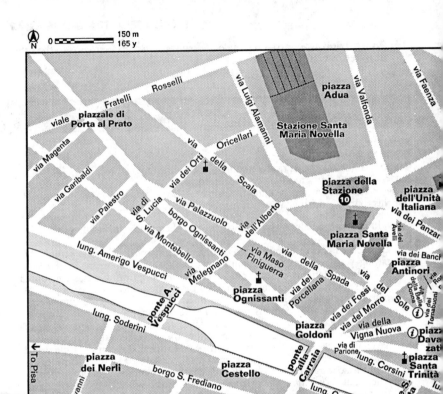

piazza Adua

via Valfonda

via Faenza

Rosselli

via Luigi Alamanni

Fratelli

viale — piazzale di Porta al Prato

via Magenta

via Garibaldi

via Palestro

via Oricellari

via dei Orti

della Scala

Stazione Santa Maria Novella

piazza della Stazione ❿

piazza dell'Unità Italiana

via dei Panzar

via di S. Lucia

borgo Ognissanti

via Palazzuolo

via Montebello

via dell'Alberto

lung. Amerigo Vespucci

via Melegnano

via Maso Finiguerra

piazza Ognissanti

via della Spada

piazza Santa Maria Novella

via dei Avelli

via dei Banch

piazza Antinori

via dei Porcellana

via dei Fossi

via del Sole

via della Belle Donna

via Ror

piazza Davazat

Ponte A. Vespucci

lung. Soderini

piazza Goldoni

via del Morro

via della Vigna Nuova

Ponte alla Carraia

via di Parione

lung. Corsini

ⓘ

ⓘ

piazza Santa Trinità

piazza dei Nerli

borgo S. Frediano

piazza Cestello

lung. Guicciardini

ponte S. Trinità

lu.

via San Giovanni

via S. Monica

piazza del Carmine

via di Santo Spirito

piazza Frescobaldi

borgo S. Iacop

via di Camaldoli

via del Leone

via dei Serragli

via S. Agostino

via del Presto di S. Martino

piazza Torquato Tasso

viale Ariosto

via della Chiesa

piazza S. Spirito

Tegolaio

via Maggio

via Guicciard

via del Campuccio

Giardino Torrigiani

borgo

via Mazzetta

piazza S. Felice

piazza de Pitti

via Romana

↙ To Siena

Giardir di Bobo

← To Pisa

0 ─── 150 m / 165 y

ITALY

● Florence

Rome ★

❶ Church of Santa Croce
❷ Piazza della Signoria
❸ The Bargello Museum
❹ Piazza del Duomo
❺ Baptistery
❻ The Academy

❼ Medici Palace
❽ Church of San Lorenzo
❾ New Sacristy
❿ Piazza Stazione
⓫ Piazzale Michelangelo

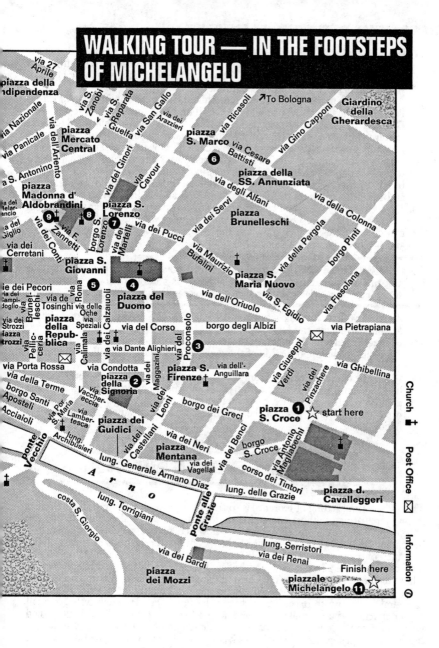

WALKING TOUR — IN THE FOOTSTEPS OF MICHELANGELO

via 27 Aprile

piazza della ndipendenza

via S. Zanobi

via Nazionale

via dell'Ariento

via Panicale

a S. Antonino

piazza Mercato Central

via S. Reparata

via dei Arazzieri

via San Gallo

via Guelfa

via dei Ginori

via Cavour

via Ricasoli

↗ To Bologna

piazza S. Marco

via Cesare Battisti

Giardino della Gherardesca

via Gino Capponi

6

piazza della SS. Annunziata

via degli Alfani

via della Colonna

piazza Madonna d' Aldobrandini

ia del elar ancio

a del iglio

9 ✝

via F Zannetti

8

piazza S. Lorenzo

7

borgo S. Lorenzo

via dei Martelli

via dei Servi

piazza Brunelleschi

via dei Pucci

borgo Pinti

via dei Conti

via dei Cerretani

piazza S. Giovanni

ie dei Pecori

via del ampi oglio

via dei Strozzi

iazza trozzi

via Roma

5

4

piazza del Duomo

via Maurizio Bufalini

✝ piazza S. Maria Nuovo

via dell'Oriuolo

via S. Egidio

via della Pergola

via Fiesolana

via de Tosinghi

via delle Oche

via dei Calzaiuoli

piazza della Repubblica

via Speziali

via dei Pellicceria

✝ via Calimala

✝ via dei

via del Corso

via Dante Alighieri

borgo degli Albizi

via del Proconsolo

3

via Pietrapiana

✉

via Ghibellina

via Porta Rossa

✉

via Condotta

2

piazza della Signoria

piazza S. Firenze ✝

via dell'- Anguillara

via Giuseppi Verdi

via dei Pinzachere

via della Terme

Vaccher- eccia

via dei Lamber- tesca

via Leoni

via Maggazini

piazza dei Guidici

borgo Santi Apostoli

via Por S. Maria

Acciaioli

via dei Castellani

piazza dei Neri

piazza Mentana

borgo dei Greci

1

piazza S. Croce ☆ start here

via Antonio Maglianechi

✝

Ponte Vecchio

lung. Archibusieri

via dei Vagellai

via dei Benci

borgo S. Croce

piazza d. Cavalleggeri

A r n o

lung. Generale Armano Diaz

corso dei Tintori

lung. Torrigiani

costa S. Giorgio

ponte alle Grazie

lung. delle Grazie

✝

lung. Serristori

via dei Renai

via dei Bardi

piazza dei Mozzi

Finish here

piazzale Michelangelo ☆

11

Church ✝   Post Office ✉   Information ⓘ

7. **Medici Palace** (Palazzo Medici-Riccardi). Originally constructed by the founder of the legendary dynasty (Cosimo dei Medici) as the ancestral home for his offspring, it was the birthplace of Lorenzo the Magnificent and the home of young Michelangelo during his art studies with Bertoldo.

One block to the Medici Palace's southwest, along the continuation of via dei Pucci (which changes its name to via Canto de Nelli), you'll arrive at the:

8. **Church of San Lorenzo,** parish church of the Medici family. Within its massive confines lies the Laurentian Library (piazza di San Lorenzo 9), which is sometimes more easily accessible via the church's cloisters. Designed by Michelangelo to contain the Medici family's impressive collection of original manuscripts, it contains what might be the most-photographed staircase (also designed by Michelangelo) in Florence. At the rear of the church, accessible from the small and sun-flooded piazza di Madonna dei Aldobrandini, lies the:

9. **New Sacristy,** designed by Michelangelo and adorned with some of his most evocative sculptures. These include *Dawn, Dusk, Day,* and *Night*. (In the same church is another chapel known as the Old Sacristy, designed by Brunelleschi, and partly decorated by Donatello.)

REFUELING STOP An ideal place for a lunch after all that walking, **La Loggia,** overlooking piazzale Michelangelo, has outdoor tables in summer and serves Florentine classic dishes such as bistecca alla fiorentina. Dress is casual.

After your visit, walk west from the Church of San Lorenzo along via del Melarancio to the city bus station in:

10. **Piazza Stazione.** From there, as part of an optional excursion, take bus no. 13 (or a cab) to the opposite side of the Arno, to the much visited but nonetheless charming:

11. **Piazzale Michelangelo.** From its panorama, you'll have a view over the city like the one that fed the creative juices of Michelangelo. Appropriately, the piazzale's crowning feature is yet another copy of Michelangelo's *David* which overlooks from afar most of the monuments you've already examined close at hand.

2. SPECIAL & FREE EVENTS

The architectural setting of Florence is so richly evocative that many visitors consider it amply rewarding without the added theatricality of seasonal events. Despite the appeal of "everyday Florence," there are, however, several annual events which—depending on your interests—might heighten even further the city's legendary allure.

Much of the innate religiosity of Florence is especially visible during **Holy Week.** Two days after the sobriety of Good Friday, Easter is an extroverted religious event whose highlight is the Scoppio del Carro (Explosion of the Cart). A two-wheeled cart filled with fireworks and flowers is drawn to the historic piazza in front of Florence's cathedral by six white oxen. Then, during the Easter Sunday High Mass, a small rocket attached to a facsimile of a white dove is lit at the cathedral's high altar, then whizzes down the length of the nave along the length of a taut wire high above the heads of the congregation. Simultaneously, displays of flowers—which often continue until June—are shown in the Uffizi and piazza della Signoria.

Throughout the month of May, the city welcomes classical musicians for its **Maggio Musicale** festival of cantatas, madrigals, and concertos, many of which are presented in Renaissance buildings.

Between June and September, don't overlook the many musical events presented in Florence's hillside suburb of **Fiesole.** Its summer festival draws enthusiastic audiences from throughout Italy.

The feast day of Florence's patron saint, John the Baptist, occurs every year on

June 24 during the **Calcio Storico** (also known as the Gioco del Calcio). To celebrate, groups of young Florentine men organized into teams representing the four original parishes of the city compete in a reenactment of a medieval sport which combines elements of both soccer and rugby. Dressed in Renaissance costumes, players face each other at either piazza Santa Croce or piazza della Signoria (and sometimes at both). The contest uses a wooden ball, a minimum of protective padding, and rules which to an observer appear fluid and/or nonexistent. During the evening of the day of the contest, displays of fireworks are shot from piazzale Michelangelo out over the Arno for the benefit of viewers throughout the region. For anyone who missed the first one, these contests are repeated, in somewhat different forms, on June 28.

On **Assumption Day,** August 15, caged crickets are sold throughout the city as part of a modern interpretation of a medieval custom where children ran through the nearby fields catching wild crickets as good luck charms.

On September 7, on the eve of the Nativity of the Virgin, children run through the city's medieval streets carrying colorful paper lanterns as part of the **Festa delle Rificolone (Lantern Day).** The festival continues the following day in processions leading from the Duomo to the Church of Santa Annunziata.

Every September 28, the eve of the **Festival of St. Michael,** Tuscany's official hunting season begins. At the Porta Romana, hunting equipment and caged birds of all kinds (parakeets, falcons, bluebirds, and owls) are assembled and sold to hunters and bird lovers alike.

In October, the collections of the **winter fashions** from the couturiers of Italy are assembled and shown to photographers, fashion editors, and buyers in the Pitti Palace. A similar exposition is held in early March, also in the Pitti Palace, for the spring collections.

Also in October, the **winter musical season** for orchestral and chamber music pieces begin at the Teatro Comunale. This is followed in November by the opening of the **opera season.** These musical divisions continue till mid-December and mid-January, respectively.

3. SPORTS & RECREATION

Of course, your main diversion in Florence will be the perusal of the city's artistic and architectural treasures, but if the urge for exercise and sports should overtake your thirst for culture, here is a list of possibilities:

GOLF   You'll find an 18-hole golf course in the nearby suburb of Impruneta, at via Chiatigiana 3 (tel. 230-1009). Impruneta lies about 9 miles south of the center.

JOGGING   One of the city's finest stretches of uninterrupted pedestrian footpaths is in **La Cascine,** a park west of the center on the north bank of the Arno. Its eastern end begins beside the Ponte della Vittoria, and it includes tennis courts, a racetrack, a public swimming pool, and miles of pedestrian walkways. (You can jog there by following the river to piazza Vittorio Veneto, although bus no. 17 will carry you there from the cathedral.) Another possibility is to jog amid the ornamental walkways of the **Boboli Gardens,** behind the Pitti Palace, although there you might find greater crowds of art lovers. If none of this appeals to you, you might jog along any of the city's **riverside quays** (the best time is early morning if you're up to it), although you'll have to pay close attention to breakneck traffic feeding onto the Arno bridges.

SOCCER   Florence's home-town team is Fiorentina and the city's residents take their games very seriously indeed. To watch them, head for the **Stadio Comunale,** viale Manfredi Fanti 4-6 (tel. 572625), near the Campo di Marte, about 1½ miles northeast of the town's historic center. Games are usually held on Sunday afternoon between September and May, and tickets go on sale at the stadium 2 or 3 hours before

FROMMER'S FAVORITE
FLORENTINE EXPERIENCES

Standing in awe in front of Michelangelo's David   Some one million visitors a year can't be wrong: In spite of countless copies, there is nothing as majestic as seeing the original statue of "The Giant"—carved from a single block of Carrara marble.

A Shopping Spree   Florence, Italy's most fashionable city, dazzles with its array of merchandise—everything from gold jewelry to leather and fashion. Stroll the Ponte Vecchio, via Tornabuoni, via della Vigna Nova, and via Roma.

Having a Campari at piazza della Signoria   In the "living room" of Florence, at an open-air café, enjoy a refreshing drink while surrounded by some of the world's most famous statues—everything from Cellini's *Perseus to Giambologna's Rape of the Sabines.*

Wandering in the Uffizi Galleries   There are those who come to Florence every year with good reason: to explore gallery after gallery of Italy's most important museum, treasure trove of Renaissance masterpieces.

the scheduled beginning. Any hotel receptionist in Florence can give you details for the upcoming week.

If you're interested in practicing your dribble, and perhaps practicing with local enthusiasts, head for the previously mentioned La Cascine Park, beside the river west of town, or to the Campo di Marte, the soccer headquarters of Florence, where a handful of youths will likely be practicing.

SQUASH   The city's squash headquarters lies at the **Centro Squash Firenze,** viale Piombino 24-29 (tel. 710055), about 1½ miles due west of the center.

SWIMMING   There's a public pool at the eastern edge of **La Cascine,** the Piscina Le Pavoniere, viale Degli Olmi (tel. 367506). Another possibility is the **Piscina Bellariva,** lungarno Colombo 6 (tel. 677521). These pools are crowded, however, with lots of bambini, and visitors might prefer the more secluded premises of the pools (if one exists) in their hotels.

TENNIS   Although technically classified as semiprivate clubs, you'll often find an available court at one of a handful of Florentine tennis courts. Be aware of dress codes which might strongly encourage you to dress in tennis court whites with appropriate shoes. Possibilities include **Assi-Giglio-Rosso,** viale Michelangelo 64 (tel. 5812686); **Il Poggetto,** via Michele Mercati 24B (tel. 460127); and the **Circolo Tennis alle Cascine,** viale Viscarno 1 (tel. 687858).

4. SAVVY SHOPPING

Skilled craftsmanship and traditional design unchanged since the days of the Medici have made Florence a goal for the serious shopper. Florence is noted for its hand-tooled **leather goods** and its various **straw merchandise,** as well as superbly crafted **silver jewelry.** Its reputation for fashionable custom-made clothes is no longer what it was, having lost its position of supremacy to Milan.

The whole city of Florence strikes many visitors as a gigantic department store. Entire neighborhoods on both sides of the Arno offer good shops, although those along the medieval Ponte Vecchio (with some exceptions) strike most people as too touristy.

Florence's Fifth Avenue is **via dei Tornabuoni,** with its flagship Gucci stores for leather and Ferragamo for stylish but costly shoes.

The better shops are for the most part along Tornabuoni, but there are many on **via Vigna Nuova, via Porta Rossa,** and **via degli Strozzi.** You might also stroll on the lungarno along the Arno.

SHOPPING A TO Z
ANTIQUES

There are many outlets for antiques in Florence (but those high prices!). If you're in the market for such expensive purchases, or even if you like to browse, try the following:

BOTTEGA SAN FELICE, via Maggio 39R. Tel. 215479.

Bottega San Felice offers many intriguing items from the 19th century, sometimes in the style known as "Charles X," but also sells more modern pieces (those made in this century). Many art deco items are for sale. Open on Monday from 3:30 to 7:30pm and Tuesday through Saturday from 9am to 12:30pm and 3:30 to 7:30pm.

GALLORI TURCHI, via Maggio 14. Tel. 282279.

Gallori Turchi is one of the best antiques stores in Florence for the serious collector—that is, the serious well-heeled collector. Some of its rare items go back to the 1600s. Each item seems well chosen, ranging from polychrome figures to gilded Tuscan pieces. Open on Monday from 4 to 7:30pm and Tuesday through Saturday from 10am to 1pm and 4 to 7:30pm (closed August).

ART

GALLERIA MASINI, piazza Goldoni 6R. Tel. 294000.

Established for more than 300 years, Galleria Masini lies a few minutes' walk from the Hotel Excelsior and other leading hotels. The selection of modern and contemporary paintings by top artists is extensive. Even if you're not a collector, this is a good place to select a picture that will be a lasting reminder of your visit to Italy—and you can take it home duty free. Open Monday through Saturday from 9am to 1pm and 3:30 to 7:30pm (closed August).

BOOKS

LIBRERIA BM BOOK SHOP, borgo Ognissanti 4R. Tel. 294575.

A vast array of books is carried here at one of the finest such stores in Europe. Browsers are encouraged, aided, and informed. Many customers come here just to look over the collection of art books. The bookshop is near the Excelsior Hotel. Open Monday through Saturday from 9am to 1pm and 3:30 to 7:30pm.

PAPERBACK EXCHANGE, via Fiesolana 31R. Tel. 247-8154.

Paperback Exchange has thousands and thousands of books, both fiction and nonfiction, on its shelves. Books are recycled, so you can trade in your old paperbacks, and if they're acceptable, you're granted discounts on the advertised price of any more volumes you purchase. It's very democratic and very cheap if you want to catch up on your reading while in Florence. In addition to the used books, a large stock of paperbacks is also available, including current bestsellers, classics, and the like, as well as modern and contemporary literature with emphasis on Italy, plus travel guides. Open Monday through Saturday from 9am to 1pm and 3:30 to 7:30pm (closed Monday November through March).

CHILDREN'S WEAR

DODO, borgo Santi Apostoli 32R. Tel. 282022.

Dodo, the best place to outfit your child in fine Italian clothing, has an animal motif to amuse and delight children while parents scan the array of clothing. The shop also stocks jewelry for children as well as toys. Open on Monday from 4 to 7:30pm and Tuesday through Saturday from 9:30am to 1pm and 4 to 7:30pm.

DEPARTMENT STORES

STANDA, via Panzani 31R. Tel. 239-8963.

Here you'll find general merchandise, including moderately priced clothing, household goods, and other items. Open on Monday from 2 to 7:30pm and Tuesday through Saturday from 9am to 7:30pm.

UPIM, via Speziali 3R. Tel. 216867.

Upim is a chain of nationwide stores similar to Standa. Open June to September, Monday through Friday from 8:45am to 7:45pm and on Saturday from 8:45am to 7pm; October to May, on Monday from 2 to 7:45pm and Tuesday through Saturday from 8:45am to 7:45pm.

EMBROIDERY

RIFREDI SCHOOL OF ARTISTIC EMBROIDERY, via Carlo Bini 29. Tel. 422-0575.

You'll find superior work at the Rifredi School of Artistic Embroidery. However, it's a 15-minute ride from the center of town (take bus no. 8, 14, 28, or 20). Awaiting your inspection is an array of delicate embroidery or artistic design, including tea and breakfast sets, tablecloths, bed linen, handkerchiefs, and women's lingerie. Open Monday through Saturday from 9am to 1pm and 2 to 7pm.

FABRICS

CASA DI TESSUTI, via de' Pecori 20. Tel. 215961.

In business for more than half a century, Casa di Tessuti is a shop for connoisseurs, those seeking one of the largest and highest-quality selections of materials in linen, silk, wool, and cotton. The Romoli family, longtime proprietors, are proud of their assortment of fabrics, and rightly so, and are known for their selections of design and colors. Open on Monday from 3:30 to 7:30pm and Tuesday through Saturday from 9am to 1pm and 3:30 to 7:30pm.

FASHION (MEN & WOMEN)

MARQUIS EMILIO PUCCI, via de' Pucci 6. Tel. 287622.

The name needs little introduction. In the palazzo near the Duomo you'll find a sampling of high-quality, expensive fashion in the boutique on the second floor. It's on this same floor that his latest fashions are presented to the world in his much-photographed showroom. Open on Monday from 3 to 7pm, Tuesday through Friday from 9am to 1pm and 3 to 7pm, and on Saturday from 9am to 1pm.

ROMANO, piazza della Repubblica. Tel. 239-6890.

In the commercial center of town near the Duomo is Romano, a glamorous clothing store for women. The owners commissioned a curving stairwell to be constructed under the high ornate ceiling. But even more exciting are their well-stocked leather and suede goods, along with an assortment of dresses, shoes, and handbags, many at very high prices if you're willing to pay for quality. Open on Monday from 3:30 to 7:30pm and Tuesday through Saturday from 9:30am to 1pm and 3:30 to 7:30pm.

BELLUCCI ABBIGLIAMENTO, borgo S. Lorenzo 14R. Tel. 213525.

Bellucci Abbigliamento offers good-quality men's clothing, excellent service, and better prices than at many other shops. The ready-to-wear selection, from top Italian manufacturers, specializes in classic jackets, suits, trousers, and seasonal outerwear. There is a custom-made tailoring service, and you can arrange to have the finished garment sent to you at home. Open on Monday from 3:30 to 7:30pm and Tuesday through Saturday from 9:30am to 1pm and 3:30 to 7:30pm.

MARIPOSA, lungarno Corsini 1B-20R. Tel. 284259.

Mariposa offers women's fashions with such famous design labels as Krizia, Fendi, Rocco Barocco, and Mimmina. Foreign customers are often granted a 10% discount. Open Monday through Saturday from 9:30am to 7:30pm.

GIFTS

MENEGATTI, piazza del Pesce—Ponte Vecchio. Tel. 215202.

You'll find a wide selection of items at Menegatti, including pottery from Florence, Faenza, and Deruta. There are also della Robbia reproductions made in red clay like the originals. Items can be sent home if you arrange it at the time of your purchase. Open Monday through Friday from 10am to 6pm.

BALATRESI GIFT SHOP, lungarno Acciaiuoli 22R. Tel. 287851.

Balatresi Gift Shop is presided over by Umberto and Giovanna Balatresi, who have stocked their shop full of treasures. Among them are Florentine mosaics created for them by Maestro Marco Tacconi and Maestro Metello Montelatici, who are arguably the greatest mosaicists alive today. The store also sells original ceramic figurines by the sculptor Giannitrapani, Fabergé reproductions, and a fine selection of hand-carved alabaster and hard stones. Many Americans come into this store every year to do their Christmas shopping. Open Monday through Saturday from 9:30am to 1pm and 3:30 to 7:30pm.

HANDCRAFTS

S.E.L.A.N., via Porta Rossa 113R. Tel. 212995.

S.E.L.A.N., off piazza S. Trinità, is a star choice for traditional designs in Italian ceramics. A wide assortment of merchandise, all made by hand in Italy, is offered. Open on Monday from 3:30 to 7:30pm and Tuesday through Saturday from 9am to 1pm and 3:30 to 7:30pm.

JEWELRY

Buying jewelry is almost an art in itself, so proceed with caution. Florence, of course, is known for its jewelry. You'll find some stunning antique pieces, and if you know how to buy, much good value.

BEFANI & TAI, via Vacchereccia 13R. Tel. 287825.

Befani & Tai is one of the most unusual jewelry stores in Florence—some of its pieces date from the 19th century. Some of their clients even design their own jewelry for special orders. Artisans are skilled at working in gold and platinum. Open mid-June to mid-September, Monday through Friday from 9am to 1pm and 3:30 to 7:30pm; off-season, Tuesday through Saturday from 9am to 1pm and 3:30 to 7:30pm (closed August).

FARAONE-SETTEPASSI, via Tornabuoni 25R. Tel. 215506.

Faraone-Settepassi, one of the most distinguished jewelers of the Renaissance city, draws a well-heeled patronage. Open on Monday from 3:30 to 7:30pm and Tuesday through Saturday from 9:45am to 1pm and 3:30 to 7:30pm (closed August 8–21).

MARIO BUCCELLATI, via Tornabuoni 69-71R. Tel. 239-6579.

Away from the Ponte Vecchio, Mario Buccellati specializes in exquisite hand-crafted jewelry and silver. A large selection of intriguing pieces at high prices is offered. Open June 15 to September 15, Monday through Friday from 9am to 1pm and 3:30 to 7:30pm; off-season, Monday from 3:30–7:30pm, Tuesday through Friday from 9am to 1pm and 3:30 to 7:30pm, and on Saturday from 9am to 1pm (closed August).

AURUM, lungarno Corsini 16R. Tel. 284259.

Aurum sells contemporary 18-karat gold jewelry. Many pieces of the selection are modern, based on designs created exclusively for this store. Others are reproductions of Etruscan designs. Open Monday through Saturday from 9:30am to 7:30pm.

LEATHER

Universally acclaimed, Florentine leather is still the fine product it always was—smooth, well shaped, and vivid in such colors as green and red.

S. LUTI & SON, via Parione 28-32R. Tel. 287047.

S. Luti & Son, offering hundreds of fine-quality articles, has been in the leather-goods business since 1922. It has a large selection of high-fashion women's handbags, as well as many fine gift items and travel articles. Businesspeople can select from a wide range of contemporary attaché cases and well-styled traditional briefcases. The craftsmanship is of top-notch quality. Via Parione, one of the oldest streets in Florence, is in the historical center, perpendicular to via Tornabuoni and parallel to the Arno. Open on Monday from 3:30 to 7:30pm, Tuesday through Friday from 9am to 1pm and 3:30 to 7:30pm, and on Saturday from 9am to 1pm.

JOHN F., lungarno Corsini 2. Tel. 298985.

John F., located near the S. Trinità Bridge, is a high-fashion house of leather in a Florentine palace. The leather clothing is of exclusive design, and the salon shows models from the *crème de la crème* of its collection. Although foreign patronage is high, the shop also dresses some of the chicest Florentine women. Accessories, including handbags and leather articles, made here are well crafted and beautifully styled. Open Monday through Saturday from 9:30am to 7:30pm.

POLLINI, via Calimala 12R. Tel. 214738.

Pollini, one of the leading leather-goods stores of Florence, offers a wide array of stylized merchandise, including shoes, suitcases, clothing, belts, and virtually anything made of leather. It's located in the monumental heart of Florence, near the Ponte Vecchio. Open on Monday from 3:30 to 7:30pm, Tuesday through Friday from 9:30am to 1pm and 5:30 to 7:30pm, and on Saturday from 9:30am to 7:30pm.

BOJOLA, via dei Rondinelli 25R. Tel. 211155.

Bojola is another leading name in leather. Sergio Bojola has distinguished himself in Florence by his selections for many types and tastes, in both synthetic materials and beautiful leathers. Hundreds of customers are always enthusiastic about the variety of items found here, which reflect first-class quality and craftsmanship. Open Monday through Friday from 9am to 1pm and 1:30 to 7:30pm, and on Saturday from 9am to 1pm.

LEONARDO LEATHER WORKS, borgo dei Greci 16A. Tel. 292202.

Leonardo Leather Works concentrates on two of the oldest major crafts of Florence: leather and jewelry. Leather goods include wallets, bags, shoes, boots, briefcases, clothing, travel bags, belts, and gift items, with products by famous designers. No imitations are permitted here. The jewelry department has a large assortment of gold chains, bracelets, rings, earrings, and charms. Open Monday through Saturday from 9am to 7pm.

MARKETS

After checking into a hotel, the most intrepid shoppers head for **piazza del Mercato Nuovo (Straw Market)** of Florence, called Il Porcellino by the Italians because of the bronze statue of a reclining wild boar there (it's a copy of the one in the Uffizi). Tourists pet its snout (which is well worn) for good luck. The market stands in the monumental heart of Florence, an easy stroll from the Palazzo Vecchio. It sells not only straw items but leather goods as well, along with an array of typically Florentine merchandise, such as frames, trays, hand-embroidery, table linens, and hand-sprayed and -painted boxes in traditional designs. Open Monday through Saturday from 9am to 7pm.

However, even better bargains await those who make their way through pushcarts to the stalls of the open-air **Mercato Centrale,** in and around borgo San Lorenzo, in the vicinity of the railway station. If you don't mind bargaining, which is imperative here, you'll find an array of merchandise that includes raffia bags, Florentine leather purses, salt-and-pepper shakers, straw handbags, and art reproductions.

Warning: In some of these markets you may think you've found Puccis, Guccis, and Louis Vuittons selling for peanuts. You can be sure that such low-priced merchandise is imitation. Most often it is easily recognized as fake.

MOSAICS

ARTE MUSIVA, largo Bargellini 2-4. Tel. 241647.
Florentine mosaics are universally recognized for their distinction. Bruno Lastrucci, the director of Arte Musiva, located in the old quarter of Santa Croce, is one of the most renowned living exponents of this art form. In the workshop you can see artisans plying their craft; some of the major mosaicists of Italy are here. In addition to traditional Florentine, modern mosaic has been developed. A selection of the most significant works is permanently displayed in the gallery. These include decorative panels, linings, and tiles. Open Monday through Saturday from 9am to 1pm and 3 to 7pm.

PAPER & STATIONERY

GIULIO GIANNINI & FIGLIO, piazza Pitti 36-37R. Tel. 212621.
Giulio Giannini & Figlio is the leading stationery store in Florence. Much of its merchandise is so exquisite that it's snapped up by foreigners for gift-giving later in the year. The English-speaking staff is helpful. This has been a family business for nearly 140 years. Open Monday through Saturday from 9am to 7:30pm.

PHARMACY

OFFICINA PROFUMO FARMACEUTICA DI SANTA MARIA NOVELLA, via della Scala 16N. Tel. 216276.
This is perhaps the most fascinating pharmacy in Italy. Northwest of the Church of Santa Maria Novella, it opened its doors to the public in 1612, offering a selection of herbal remedies that were created by friars of the Dominican order. Those closely guarded secrets have been retained, and many of the same elixirs are still sold today. You've heard of papaya as an aid to digestion, but what about elixir of rhubarb? A wide selection of perfumes, scented soaps, shampoos, and of course, potpourris, along with creams and lotions, is handsomely presented in these old-fashioned precincts, which almost qualifies as a sightseeing attraction. Open on Monday from 3 to 6:55pm, Tuesday through Friday from 8:30am to 12:25pm and 3 to 6:55pm, and on Saturday from 8:30am to 12:25pm and 3 to 6:30pm.

PRINTS & ENGRAVINGS

GIOVANNI BACCANI, via della Vigna Nuova 75R. Tel. 214467.
Giovanni Baccani has long been a specialist in this field. Everything it sells is old—nothing new here. "The Blue Shop," as it is called, offers a huge array of prints and engravings, often of Florentine scenes. These are found in bins, and you're free to look as long as you want. Tuscan paper goods are also sold. Open on Monday from 3:30 to 7:30pm and Tuesday through Saturday from 8:30am to 1pm and 3:30 to 8pm. Closed: Aug.

SHOES

LILY OF FLORENCE, via Guicciardini 2R. Tel. 294748.
Both men and women can buy shoes in American sizes at Lily of Florence. For women, Lily distributes both her own designs and other well-known names in shoes. Color comes in a wide range, the designs are stylish, and leather texture is of good quality. Open Monday through Saturday from 9:30am to 7:30pm.

SALVATORE FERRAGAMO, via Tornabuoni 16R. Tel. 292123.
Salvatore Ferragamo has long been one of the most famous names in shoes. Although he started in Hollywood just before the outbreak of World War I, the headquarters of this famed manufacturer were installed here in the Palazzo Ferroni, on the most fashionable shopping street of Florence, before World War II broke out. Ferragamo sells shoes for both men and women, along with some of the most elegant boutique items in the city, including scarves, handbags, and other merchandise. But chances are you'll want to visit it for its stunning shoes which are known for their durability and style. Open June 15 to August 1, Monday through Friday from 9:30am

to 7:30pm; August 2 to June 14, on Monday from 3:30 to 7:30pm and Tuesday through Saturday from 9:30am to 7:30pm.

CRESTI, via Roma 9R. Tel. 292377.

Cresti is one of the leading Florentine outlets for high-quality footwear for men, women, and children. The other main store is at via Roma 14R (tel. 214150), and other branches are at via Pietrapiana 73R (tel. 240856), which specializes in shoes for older women, and at via Martelli 42 (tel. 212609), which has shoes for women, men, and children. All branches carry well-made shoes for women. Open on Monday from 3:30 to 7:30pm and Tuesday through Saturday from 9am to 1pm and 3:30 to 7:30pm.

SILVER

PERUZZI BROTHERS, Ponte Vecchio 60. Tel. 292027.

There are many charming little antiques stores clustered around the Ponte Vecchio that sell silverware. I regard Peruzzi Brothers, at the corner of borgo San Jacopo 2-4, as one of the finest silversmiths in the city. The firm, which has been doing business since 1880, specializes in the best Florentine silverware as well as handmade jewelry. Open Monday through Saturday from 9:30am to 1pm and 3:30 to 7:30pm.

STRAW

EMILIO PAOLI, via della Vigna Nuova 24-28R. Tel. 289185.

Emilio Paoli, a display house for the manufacturers of straw and raffia goods, offers women's handbags, hats, skirts, raffia shoes, table mats, baskets, and cane furniture. The exhibits in the showroom are tasteful, and the designs show considerable flair. The shop is likely to be closed for 3 weeks in August. Open on Monday from 3 to 7:30pm and Tuesday through Saturday from 9:30am to 1pm and 3 to 7:30pm.

5. EVENING ENTERTAINMENT

Evening entertainment in Florence is not an exciting prospect unless you simply like to walk through the narrow streets or head up toward Fiesole for a view of the city at night (truly spectacular). The typical Florentine begins an evening early, perhaps at one of the cafés listed below.

For a list of theatrical and concert listings, pick up a free copy of **Welcome to Florence,** available at the tourist office. This helpful publication contains information on recitals, concerts, theatrical productions, and other cultural presentations that are offered at Florence at the time of your visit.

Many cultural presentations are performed in churches. These might include open-air concerts in the cloisters of the Badia Fiesolana in Fiesole (the hill town above Florence), or at the Ospedale degli Innocenti, the foundling "hospital of the innocents" on summer evenings only.

Orchestral offerings—performed by the Regional Tuscan Orchestra—are often presented at the Church of Santo Stefano al Ponte Vecchio.

THE PERFORMING ARTS

TEATRO COMUNALE, corso Italia 16. Tel. 277-9236.

This is the main theater in Florence, with a concert season presented in October and November. The short Florence opera season usually lasts from mid-December to mid-January only. This theater is also the major venue for the Maggio Musicale, or musical May festival of opera, ballet, concerts, and recitals, lasting from May until sometime in July. The box office is open Tuesday through Saturday from 9am to 1pm and 1 hour before the curtain.

Prices: Tickets 10,000–30,000 lire ($7.85–$23.55), but could be higher, depending on the production.

TEATRO DELLA PERGOLA, via della Pergola 32. Tel. 262690.

This is the major legitimate theater of Florence, but you'll have to understand Italian to appreciate its productions. Plays are performed year round except during the Maggio Musicale, when the theater becomes the setting for the many musical presentations of the festival.

THE CLUB & MUSIC SCENE

NIGHTCLUBS

RIVER CLUB, lungarno Corsini 8. Tel. 282465.

The River Club was once the baroque Orsini palace, but it has been converted into one of the poshest and most sophisticated nightclubs in Italy, featuring a disco, a semi-nude floor show, and a piano bar. You can sit at the bar, with its double-barreled baroque fountain and monumental figures of Adam and Eve. The bar stools opposite the fountain are often adorned with "hostesses." To see the floor show at 12:30am, you must go into the adjoining ornate room. A six-piece orchestra plays until dawn on most nights. At the tables, regular whisky costs 20,000 lire ($15.70) for your first drink. The club is open daily from 10pm to 4:30am.

FULL UP, via della Vigna Vecchia 21R. Tel. 293006.

Full Up is a nightclub/disco frequented by a mature crowd who appreciate the subdued atmosphere. Music is generally recorded. In the center of the city, this club in the past attracted upper-crust Florentines, but that could always change. Naturally, in summer it is frequented by more foreigners. Hours are 11pm to 4am Wednesday through Monday.

Admission: 20,000 lire ($15.70).

ROCK

THE RED GARTER, via de' Benci. Tel. 234-4904.

Perhaps nothing could be more unexpected in this city of Donatello and Michelangelo than a club called the Red Garter, right off piazza Santa Croce. The American Prohibition era lives on—in fact, it has been exported. Visitors to the Red Garter can hear a variety of music, ranging from rock to bluegrass. The club attracts young people from all over the world. A mug of Heineken lager on tap goes for 5,000 lire ($3.95), and most tall drinks, made from "hijacked hootch," as it's known here, begin at 9,000 lire ($7.05). The club is open Monday through Thursday from 8:30pm to 1am and Friday through Sunday from 9pm to 1:30am.

DISCOS

MARAGIA, via delle Oche 19R Tel. 213706.

Maragia offers both an upstairs piano bar, which sometimes has a singer, and a downstairs disco, where the music is recorded. The decor has a certain elegance, as reflected by the black marble. There is no restaurant, but if you reserve beforehand you can sometimes enjoy a late-night cold buffet. It's open Tuesday through Sunday from 10pm to 3am. Drinks run about 20,000 lire ($15.70).

Admission: Free.

SPACE ELECTRONIC DISCOTEQUE, via Palazzuolo 37. Tel. 293082.

Space Electronic Discoteque offers a spectacular light-and-sound show. On its ground floor you can have a quiet drink while seated in one of the comfortably secluded flower-shaped booths. There are giant carnival heads, wall-to-wall mirrors, and a unique aquarium with live piranha fish. On the upper level is a large dance floor with up-to-date music, a laser show, and a spaceship that descends and opens to reveal the spotlights that produce the light show. The management and employees help to create a relaxing ambience. The disco is open nightly from 9:30pm to 1:30am.

Admission: 15,000 lire ($11.80), including one drink.

YAB-YUM CLUB, via dei Sassetti 5R. Tel. 282018.

The entrance takes you down an illuminated staircase flanked with Plexiglas columns that contain bubbling water; the decor reflects a sort of blend between the electronic age and neoclassicism. Often entertainers are presented, occasionally including acrobats and costumed dancers. Banquettes are arranged theater style around the dance floor, where tunes include American and British music. Near piazza della Repubblica, the club is open Tuesday through Sunday from 10pm to 4:30am. The first drink costs 25,000 lire ($19.65); the second drink, 10,000 lire ($7.85).

THE BAR & CAFE SCENE
A PIANO BAR

DONATELLO BAR, in the Hotel Excelsior, piazza Ognissanti 3. Tel. 264201.

Donatello Bar lies on the roof garden of this grand hotel. Many of the bar's guests, both residents and nonresidents of the hotel, prefer to visit in the late afternoon or early evening, to enjoy the incomparable view of the Arno. This place is the choicest watering spot in Florence. You are likely to see everyone from Milanese industrialists to French movie stars. In any event, the piano music from 7pm to 1am encourages conviviality that makes the 10,000-lira ($7.85) and up price per drink worth it. The bar is open from 11am to 1:30am every day.

CAFES

CAFE RIVOIRE, piazza della Signoria 5R. Tel. 214412.

Café Rivoire offers a classy, amusing, and interesting old-world ambience with a direct view of the statues of one of my favorite squares in the world. You can sit at one of the metal tables set up on the flagstones outside, or at one of the tables in a choice of inner rooms filled with marble detailing and unusual oil renderings of the piazza outside. If you don't want to sit at all, try the mahogany and green-marble bar, where many of the more colorful characters making the Grand Tour of Europe talk, flirt, or gossip. A member of the staff will serve you espresso for 3,500 lire ($2.75) at a table or a long drink for 10,000 lire ($7.85). There is also a selection of small sandwiches, omelets, and ice creams. The café is noted for its hot chocolate as well. It's open Tuesday through Sunday from 8am to midnight.

GIACOSA, via Tornabuoni 83. Tel. 239-6226.

Giacosa is a deceptively simple-looking café whose stand-up bar occupies more space than its limited number of sit-down tables. Set behind three Tuscan arches on a fashionable shopping street in the center of the old city, it has a warmly paneled interior, a lavish display of pastries and sandwiches, and a reputation as the birthplace of the Negroni. That drink, as you probably know, is a combination of gin, Campari, and red vermouth. Other drinks served here include Singapore slings, Italian and American coffee, and a range of apéritifs. Sandwiches and omelets range upward from 2,300 lire ($1.80), and ice creams, for which the café is famous, begin at 2,000 lire ($1.55) if you stand. Light lunches are served. The café is open Monday through Saturday from 7:30am to 8:30pm.

GILLI, piazza della Repubblica 39R. Tel. 213896.

Gilli, said to be the oldest and most beautiful café in Florence, occupies a desirable position in the center of the city, a few minutes' walk from the Duomo. It was founded in 1733, when piazza della Repubblica had a different name. You can sit at a small, brightly lit table near the bar, or retreat to an intricately paneled pair of rooms to the side and enjoy the flattering light from the Venetian-glass chandeliers. A cappuccino costs 5,000 lire ($3.95) at a table or 1,600 lire ($1.25) if you stand at the bar. Daily specials, sandwiches, toasts, and hard drinks are sold, along with an array of "tropical" libations. Open daily from 8am to midnight.

GIUBBE ROSSE, piazza della Repubblica 13-14R. Tel. 212280.

The waiters of this place still wear the red coats—but only in winter—they did when the establishment was founded in 1888. Originally a beerhall, it is today an elegantly paneled café, bar, and restaurant filled with turn-of-the-century chandeliers and polished granite floors. You can enjoy a drink or cup of coffee which costs from

3,000 lire ($2.35) at one of the small tables near the zinc-top bar. An inner dining room has a soaring vaulted ceiling of reddish brick, and an Italian menu where meals cost 20,000 lire to 50,000 lire ($15.70 to $39.25). Light lunches are a specialty, as well as full American breakfasts. Open Friday through Wednesday from 7am to 1:30am.

MOVIES

CINEMA ASTRO, piazza San Simone. Tel. 222388.

Across from the famous ice-cream emporium, Gelateria Vivoli, this cinema shows English-language films. The schedule changes about twice a week. It's closed Monday and in August.

Prices: Tickets 7,000 lire ($5.50).

GAY NIGHTLIFE

TABASCO, piazza Santa Cecelia 3. Tel. 213000.

The leading disco is Tabasco, near piazza della Signoria in the heart of the city. Renewed in 1989, it is open Tuesday through Sunday from 10pm to 4am (sometimes it closes earlier, depending on business). The club offers two bars, along with video games and X-rated male action movies. You must be 18 to be admitted.

Admission: 12,000–20,000 lire ($9.40–$15.70), including the price of your first drink.

CRISCO, via S. Egidio 43R. Tel. 248-0580.

The No. 1 gay bar is Crisco, which is actually a *club privato* that admits most foreigners without an entrance fee (subject to change, of course). Drinks cost 7,000 lire ($5.50). The club is open Monday and Wednesday through Friday from 10pm to 3am; on Saturday and Sunday it stays open until 6am. It also has a sex shop and features recorded music.

Admission: 10,000 lire ($7.85).

---

6. EASY EXCURSIONS

FIESOLE

For more extensive day trips, you can refer to the next chapter. But Fiesole is a virtual suburb of Florence.

When the sun shines too hot on piazza della Signoria and tourists try to prance bare-backed into the Uffizi, Florentines are likely to head for the hills—usually to Fiesole. But they will probably encounter more tourists, as this town—once an Etruscan settlement—is the most popular outing from the city. Bus no. 7, which leaves from piazza San Marco, will take you there in 25 minutes and give you a fine, breathtaking view along the way. You'll pass fountains, statuary, and gardens strung out over the hills like a scrambled jigsaw puzzle.

WHAT TO SEE & DO

When you arrive at Fiesole, by all means don't sit with the throngs all afternoon in the central square sipping Campari (although that isn't a bad pastime). Explore some of Fiesole's attractions. You won't find anything as dazzling as the Renaissance treasures of Florence, however—the charms of Fiesole are more subtle. Fortunately, all major sights branch out within walking distance of the main piazza, beginning with the **Duomo.** At first this cathedral may seem austere, with its concrete-gray Corinthian columns and Romanesque arches. But it has its own beauty. Dating from A.D. 1000, it was much altered during the Renaissance. In the Salutati Chapel are important sculptural works by Mino da Fiesole.

BANDINI MUSEUM, via Dupre. Tel. 59061.

This ecclesiastical museum, around to the side of the Duomo, belongs to the

Fiesole Cathedral Chapter, established in 1913. On the ground floor are della Robbia terra-cotta works, as well as art by Michelangelo and Nino Pisano. On the top floors are paintings by the best Giotto students, which reflect ecclesiastical and worldly themes, most of them the work of Tuscan artists of the 14th century.

Admission: 2,000 lire ($1.55).

Open: Apr–Sept, daily 9:30am–1pm and 3–7pm; Oct–Mar, Wed–Mon 10am–1pm and 3–6pm. **Bus:** 7.

ROMAN THEATER AND ARCHEOLOGICAL MUSEUM, via Portigiani 1. Tel. 59477.

On this site is the major surviving evidence that Fiesole was an Etruscan city 6 centuries before Christ, and later a Roman town. In the 1st century B.C. a theater was built, the restored remains of which you can see today. Near the theater are the skeletonlike ruins of the baths, which may have been built at the same time. Try to visit the Etruscan-Roman museum, with its many interesting finds which date from the days when Fiesole—not Florence—was supreme (a guide is on hand to show you through).

Admission: 4,000 lire ($3.15).

Open: Apr–Sept, daily 9am–7pm; Oct and Mar, Tues–Sun 9am–6pm; Nov–Feb, Wed–Mon 9am–5pm. **Bus:** 7.

MUSEO MISSIONARIO FRANCES CANO FIESOLE, via S. Francesco 13. Tel. 59175.

The hardest task you'll have in Fiesole is to take the steep goat-climb up to the Convent of San Francesco. You can visit the Franciscan church, in the Gothic style, but it's of routine interest, with mediocre frescoes (some in contemporary dress). In the basement, however, is a museum devoted to objets d'art from China (collected by a father who was sent there as a missionary), along with Etruscan and Roman artifacts, even an Egyptian sarcophagus. But the real reason to make the climb is for the unforgettable view.

Admission: Free (donation expected).

Open: Apr–Sept, daily 10am–noon and 3–6pm; Oct–Mar, daily 10am–noon and 3–5pm. **Bus:** 7.

WHERE TO STAY

VILLA SAN MICHELE, via Doccia 4, Fiesole, 50014 Firenze. Tel. 055/59451. Fax 055/598734. 28 rms (all with bath). A/C TEL **Bus:** 7.

$ Rates (including half board): 450,000–610,000 lire ($353.25–$478.85) single; 750,000–940,000 lire ($588.75–$737.90) double. AE, DC, MC, V. **Parking:** Free. **Closed:** Nov–Mar.

Villa San Michele is an ancient monastery of unsurpassed beauty—the setting is memorable, even breathtaking. On a hill just below Fiesole, and complete with gardens, the monastery was built in the 15th century on a wide ledge. After being damaged in World War II, the villa was carefully restored. It is said that the facade and the loggia were designed by Michelangelo. A curving driveway, lined with blossoming trees and flowers, leads to the entrance. A 10-arch covered loggia continues around the view side of the building to the Italian gardens at the rear. On the loggia, chairs are set out for drinks and moonlight dinners. Most of the bedrooms open onto the view, or the inner courtyard. Each room is unique, some with iron or wooden canopy beds, antique chests, Savonarola chairs, formal draperies, old ecclesiastical paintings, candelabra, and statues—in other words, a stunning tour de force of rich but restrained design. TV and minibar are available upon request. Half board is required. Poets and artists have stayed at the San Michele and sung its praise.

HOTEL AURORA, piazza Mino da Fiesole 39, Fiesole, 50014 Firenze. Tel. 055/59100. Fax 055/59587. 26 rms (all with bath), 2 suites. A/C MINIBAR TV TEL **Bus:** 7.

$ Rates: 100,000–190,000 lire ($78.50–$143.15) single; 160,000–290,000 lire ($125.60–$227.65) double; from 350,000 lire ($274.75) suite. Breakfast 18,000 lire ($14.15) extra. AE, DC, MC, V. **Parking:** Free.

The Hotel Aurora, on the main square of town in a modernized 1890s building, is concealed behind an ocher facade set with green shutters. The terrace of the restaurant in back (closed for 20 days in November) offers typical Italian meals and views of hanging vines and city lights. You can also eat inside. The hotel has a high, beamed reception area and functional furniture. A la carte meals are served in the dining room, averaging around 50,000 lire ($29.25).

PENSIONE BENCISTA, via Benedetto de Maiano 4, Fiesole, 50014 Firenze. Tel. 055/59163. Fax 055/59163. 43 rms (29 with bath). TEL **Bus:** 7.
$ Rates (including half board): 67,700 lire ($53.15) per person without bath, 87,900 lire ($68.29) per person with bath. No credit cards. **Parking:** Free.

Pensione Bencista has been the family villa of the Simoni family for years. It was built around 1300, with an addition made to the existing building about every 100 years after that. In 1925 Paolo Simoni opened the villa to paying guests. Its position, high up on the road to Fiesole, is commanding, with an unmarred view of the city and the hillside villas. The driveway to the formal entrance, with its circular fountain, winds through olive trees. The widely spread-out villa has many lofty old rooms—unspoiled and furnished with family antiques. The bedrooms vary in size and interest; most are without bath and have hot and cold running water only. In chilly weather, guests meet each other in the evening in front of a huge fireplace. The Bencista is suitable for parents who might want to leave their children in the country while they take jaunts into the city. It's a 10-minute bus ride from the heart of Florence.

WHERE TO DINE

LE LANCE AT SAN DOMENICO, via Mantellini 2B. Tel. 599308.
Cuisine: TUSCAN. **Reservations:** Recommended. **Bus:** 7.
$ Prices: Appetizers 8,000–12,000 lire ($6.30–$9.40); main courses 12,000–22,000 lire ($9.40–$17.25). MC, V.
Open: Lunch Wed–Sun 12:30–2pm; dinner Tues–Sun 7:30–10pm. **Closed:** Jan.

For good food in a pleasant ambience, go to Le Lance at San Domenico. The airy and sunny construction of this hillside restaurant could almost be something you'd find in southern California, except for the lights of Florence that stretch below you. The low-lying building has many glass windows and much exposed stone and plants. This restaurant is popular with city residents on summer nights. Dining is either indoors on rush-bottomed chairs, or on a terrace illuminated with carriage lights and surrounded by shrubbery. Menu specialties include mixed Tuscan hors d'oeuvres from a well-stocked table in the center of the room, fresh mozzarella with fresh tomatoes, fresh spinach parmigiana, beefsteak Florentine (priced by the kilogram), cutlets of lamb with artichokes, risotto with champagne, and sole meunière.

TRATTORIA LE CAVE DI MAIANO, via delle Cave 16. Tel. 59133.
Cuisine: TUSCAN. **Reservations:** Required. **Bus:** 7.
$ Prices: Appetizers 7,000–8,000 lire ($5.50–$6.30); main courses 12,000–18,000 lire ($9.40–$14.15). AE, DC, MC, V.
Open: Lunch Fri–Wed noon–3pm; dinner Mon–Wed and Fri–Sat 7:30–10pm. **Closed:** Aug 14–31.

This restaurant, at Maiano, is a mere 15-minute ride from the heart of Florence. It's a family-run establishment, which since the 17th century has been an esoteric address to discerning Florentines. It's imperative, incidentally, that you reserve a table before heading here. The rustically decorated trattoria is a garden restaurant, with stone tables and large sheltering trees, which create a setting for the excellent cooking. Inside, the restaurant is in the tavern style, with a beamed ceiling. I recommend highly the antipasto and the homemade green tortellini. For a main course, there is a golden grilled chicken or perhaps a savory herb-flavored roast lamb. For side dishes, I suggest fried polenta, Tuscan beans, and fried potatoes. As a final treat, the waiter will bring you homemade ice cream with fresh raspberries.

CHAPTER 9
SIENA, PISA & THE HILL TOWNS

1. SIENA

- **WHAT'S SPECIAL ABOUT SIENA, PISA & THE HILL TOWNS**

2. SAN GIMIGNANO

3. PISA

4. PERUGIA

5. ASSISI

6. SPOLETO

The hill towns of Tuscany and Umbria are prized not only for their essential beauty (for example, the unspoiled medieval severity in the heart of Siena and San Gimignano)—but for their spectacular art treasures, created by such "hometown boys" as Leonardo da Vinci. From Florence, you can explore numerous nearby cities, including Pisa and Siena, as well as San Gimignano with its medieval towers.

And if you're traveling between Rome and Florence, why not veer off the autostrada and visit a string of other hill towns such as Spoleto and Perugia that are, in essence, sanctuaries of the past?

SEEING SIENA, PISA & THE HILL TOWNS

SUGGESTED ITINERARY

Day 1 From Rome, head north, stopping first at Spoleto, before continuing to Assisi for the night.

Day 2 Journey to Perugia to see its attractions and stay overnight there.

Day 3 Visit San Gimignano in the morning and stay overnight in Siena.

Day 4 Head for Pisa to see its Leaning Tower and Duomo.

GETTING THERE

Plane arrivals are at either Pisa's Galileo Galilei airport or Florence's Peretola airport. Motorists take the Autostrada del Sole, connecting Florence with Bologna and Florence with Rome. The coastal rail line from Rome to Genoa passes through Pisa and the main rail link from Rome to Bologna goes through Arezzo and Florence, from which other connections can be made for the hill towns. The small towns and villages of Tuscany are connected by bus lines (see individual listings).

---

1. SIENA

21 miles S of Florence, 143 miles N of Rome

GETTING THERE By Plane Fly either to Florence's Peretola airport or Pisa's Galileo Galilei airport.

By Train Trains arrive hourly from both Florence and Pisa.

WHAT'S SPECIAL ABOUT SIENA, PISA & THE HILL TOWNS

Great Towns/Villages

☐ Siena, which after Florence contains the richest artistic heritage in Italy.

☐ Assisi, the goal of both secular visitors and religious pilgrims, as it was the birthplace of St. Francis of Assisi in 1182.

☐ Pisa, a once-great maritime port on the Arno—now visited for its leaning tower, Duomo, and Baptistry.

☐ San Gimignano, the "Manhattan of Tuscany," containing some one dozen of its original 72 medieval towers.

Museums

☐ Pinacoteca Nazionale, Siena, containing the collection of the Sienese school of painting which once rivaled that of Florence.

☐ National Gallery of Umbria, Perugia, housing the most comprehensive collection of Umbrian art from the 13th up to the 18th century.

Religious Shrines

☐ Il Duomo, Siena, dating from the 13th century, with a zebralike interior of black-and-white stripes.

Ace Attractions

☐ The Leaning Tower of Pisa, launched in 1174, and dangerously leaning as the world waits for what may be inevitable.

Festivals

☐ Palio della Contrade, at Siena, beginning the first week of July, a historical pageant and horse-racing tournament.

By Bus SITA, piazza San Domenico 1 (tel. 221221), in Siena, offers bus service to all of Tuscany. Express buses from Florence to Siena cost 6,800 lire ($5.35) one way. You can also go between Rome and Siena on a SITA bus in 3½ hours for a one-way cost of 15,000 lire ($11.80).

By Car Head south from Florence along the Firenze–Siena autostrada, a superhighway that links the two towns, going through Poggibonsi.

ESSENTIALS The Siena **telephone area code** is 0577. The **Tourist Information Office** is at piazza del Campo 56 (tel. 280551).

SPECIAL EVENTS The best time to visit is usually on July 2 or August 16, the occasions of the **Palio delle Contrade,** a historical pageant and tournament known throughout Europe, which draws thousands annually. In the horse race, each bareback-riding jockey represents a *contrada* (the wards into which the city is divided). The race, which requires tremendous skill, takes place on the shell-shaped piazza del Campo, the historic heart of Siena. Before the race, much pageantry evoking the 15th century parades by, with colorfully costumed men and banners. The flag-throwing ceremony, depicted in so many travelog films, takes place at this time. And just as enticing is the victory celebration.

Don't buy expensive tickets for the day of the Palio. It's free to stand in the middle—and a lot more fun. Just get there real early, and bring a book and a Thermos. For a memorable dinner and lots of fun, join one of the 17 *contradas* attending a *cena* (supper) that is held outdoors the night before the race.

After visiting Florence, it's altogether fitting, certainly bipartisan, to call on what has been labeled in the past its natural enemy. In Rome we saw classicism and the baroque; in Florence, the Renaissance; but in the walled city of Siena we stand solidly planted back in the Middle Ages. On three sienna-colored hills in the center of

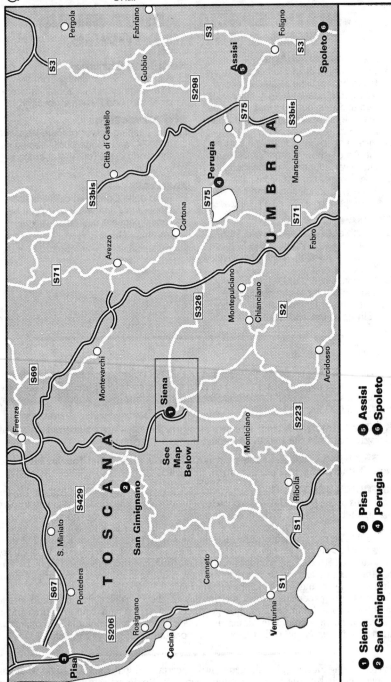

1 Siena
2 San Gimignano
3 Pisa
4 Perugia
5 Assisi
6 Spoleto

SIENA, PISA & THE HILL TOWNS

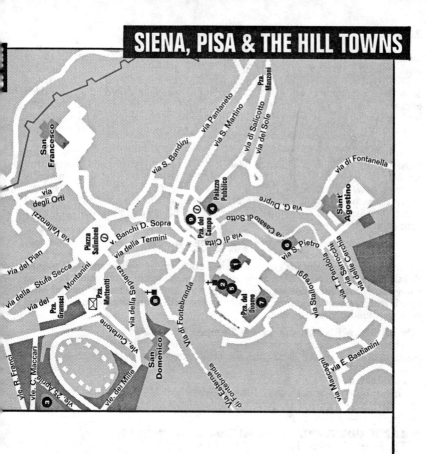

ITALY
Siena, Pisa &
The Hill Towns
★ ROME

Cathedral Museum ❶
Il Duomo ❷
Enoteco Italica Permanente ❸
Palazzo Pubblico ❹
Piccolomini Library ❺
Pinacoteca Nazionale ❻
Opera Metropolitana ❼
Santuario e Casa di Santa Caterina ❽
Torre del Mangia ❾

Tuscany, "Sena Vetus" lies in chianti country. Perhaps preserving its original character more markedly than any other city in Italy, it is a showplace of the Italian Gothic.

William Dean Howells, the American novelist (*The Rise of Silas Lapham*), called Siena "not a monument but a flight." Regrettably too often visited on a quick day's excursion, Siena is a city of contemplation and profound exploration. It is character-ized by Gothic palaces, almond-eyed madonnas, mansions of long-faced aristocrats, letter-writing St. Catherine (patron saint of Italy), narrow streets, and medieval gates, walls, and towers.

Although such a point of view may be heretical, one can almost be grateful that Siena lost its battle with Florence. Had it continued to expand and change after reaching the zenith of its power in the 14th century, chances are it would be markedly different now, influenced by the rising tides of the Renaissance and the baroque (represented today only in a small degree). But Siena retained its uniqueness (I've read that certain Sienese painters were still showing the influence of Byzantium in the late 15th century).

WHAT TO SEE & DO

There's much to see here. Let's start in the heart of Siena, the shell-shaped **⊙ piazza del Campo,** described by Montaigne as "the finest of any city in the world." Pause to enjoy the *Fonte Gaia,* the fountain of joy, with embellishments by Jacopo della Quercia (the present sculptured works are reproductions; the badly beaten original ones are found in the town hall).

TORRE DEL MANGIA, piazza del Campo. Tel. 292111.
The skyline of Siena is characterized by its lithe Torre (tower) del Mangia, on piazza del Campo, which dates from the 14th century and soars to a height of 335 feet.

Admission: 5,000 lire ($3.35).

Open: Nov 16–Mar 14, daily 10am–1:30pm; Mar 15–Apr 15 and Oct 16–Nov 15, daily 10am–5pm; Apr 16–June 15 and Sept 16–Oct 15, daily 10am–6pm; June 16–Sept 15, daily 10am–7pm.

PALAZZO PUBBLICO, piazza del Campo. Tel. 292111.
The Palazzo Pubblico dates from 1288–1309 and is filled with important artworks by some of the leaders in the Sienese school of painting and sculpture. This collection is the Museo Civico. Upstairs in the museum is the Sala della Pace, frescoed from 1337 to 1339 by Ambrogio Lorenzetti; the allegorical frescoes show the idealized effects of good government and bad government. In this depiction, the most notable figure of the Virtues surrounding the king is "La Pace" (Peace). To the right of the king and the Virtues is a representation of Siena in peaceful times.

On the left, Lorenzetti showed his opinion of "ward heelers," but some of the sting has been taken out of the frescoes, as the evil-government scene is badly damaged. Actually, these were propaganda frescoes in their day, commissioned by the party in power, but they are now viewed as among the most important of all secular frescoes to come down from the Middle Ages.

In the Sala del Mappamondo is Simone Martini's *Majesty,* the Madonna enthroned with her Child, surrounded by angels and saints. It is his earliest-known documented work (ca. 1315). The other remarkable Martini fresco (on the opposite wall) is the equestrian portrait of Guidoriccio da Fogliano, general of the Sienese Republic, in ceremonial dress.

Admission: 5,500 lire ($4.30).

Open: Nov 16–Mar 14, daily 9:30am–1:45pm; Mar 15–Nov 15, Mon–Sat 9:30am–7:45pm, Sun 9:30am–1:45pm; hols 9:30am–1:45pm.

IL DUOMO, piazza del Duomo. Tel. 42020.
At piazza del Duomo, directly southeast of piazza del Campo, stands an architectural fantasy. With its colored bands of marble, the Sienese cathedral is an original and exciting building, erected in the Romanesque and Italian Gothic styles and dating from the 12th century. The dramatic facade—designed in part by Giovanni Pisano—dates from the 13th century, as does the Romanesque bell tower.

The zebralike interior, with its black-and-white stripes, is equally stunning. The floor consists of various embedded works of art, many of which are roped off to preserve the richness in design, which depict both biblical and mythological subjects. Numerous artists worked on the floor, notably Domenico Beccafumi. For most of the year, a large part of the cathedral floor is covered to protect it.

The octagonal 13th-century pulpit is by Niccolò Pisano (Giovanni's father), who was one of the most significant Italian sculptors before the dawn of the Renaissance (see his pulpit in the Baptistery at Pisa). The Siena pulpit is considered his masterpiece; it reveals in relief such scenes as the slaughter of the innocents and the Crucifixion. The elder Pisano finished the pulpit in 1268, aided by his son and other artists. Its pillars are supported by four marble lions, again reminiscent of the Pisano pulpit at Pisa.

In the chapel of the left transept (near the library) is a glass-enclosed box with an arm that tradition maintains is John the Baptist's, used to baptize Christ, and Donatello's bronze of John the Baptist. To see another Donatello work in bronze—a bishop's gravemarker—look at the floor in the chapel to the left of the pulpit's stairway. And don't miss the inlaid wooden stalls in the apse, some based on designs by Riccio. A representational blue starry sky twinkles overhead.

Admission: Free.
Open: Nov–Mar 16, daily 7:30am–1:30pm and 2:30pm–sunset; Mar 17–Oct, daily 7:30am–7:30pm.

PICCOLOMINI LIBRARY, inside Il Duomo, piazza del Duomo. Tel. 42020.

Founded by Cardinal Francesco Piccolomini (later Pius III) to honor his uncle (Pius II), the library inside Il Duomo is renowned for its cycle of frescoes by the Umbrian master Pinturicchio. His frescoes are well preserved, even though they date from the early 16th century. In Vasari's words, the panels illustrate "the history of Pope Pius II from birth to the minute of his death." Raphael's alleged connection with the frescoes, if any, is undocumented. In the center is an exquisite *Three Graces,* a Roman copy of a 3rd-century B.C. Greek work from the school of Praxitales.

Admission: 2,000 lire ($1.55).
Open: June–Oct, daily 9am–7:30pm; Nov–May, daily 10am–1pm and 2:30–5pm.

OPERA METROPOLITANA, piazza del Duomo 5. Tel. 283048.

This museum housing paintings and sculptures originally created for the cathedral deserves some attention. On the ground floor you'll find much interesting sculpture, including works by Giovanni Pisano and his assistants. But the real draw hangs on the next floor in the Sala di Duccio: his fragmented *La Maestà,* a Madonna enthroned, painted from 1308 to 1311. The panel was originally an altarpiece by Duccio di Buoninsegna for the cathedral, filled with dramatic moments that illustrate the story of Christ and the Madonna. A student of Cimabue's, Duccio was the first great name in the school of Sienese painting. In the rooms upstairs are the collections of the treasury, and on the very top floor is a display of paintings from the early Sienese school.

Admission: 5,000 lire ($3.95).
Open: Mar 17–Oct, daily 9am–7:30pm; Nov–Dec, daily 9am–1:30pm. **Closed:** Jan–Mar 16.

THE BAPTISTERY, piazza San Giovanni.

The facade of the Baptistery dates from the 14th century. In the center of the interior is the baptismal font by Jacopo della Quercia, which contains some bas-reliefs by Donatello and Ghiberti.

Admission: Free.
Open: Daily 9am–1pm and 3–7pm.

PINACOTECA NAZIONALE (Picture Gallery), in the Palazzo Buon-signori, via San Pietro 29. Tel. 281161.

Housed in the 14th-century palazzo near piazza del Campo is the national gallery's collection of the Sienese school of painting, which once rivaled that of Florence.

Displayed here are some of the giants of the pre-Renaissance. Most of the paintings cover the period from the late 12th century to the mid-16th century.

The principal treasures are on the second floor, where you'll contemplate the artistry of Duccio in the early salons. The gallery is rich in the art of the two Lorenzetti brothers, Ambrogio and Pietro, who painted in the 14th century. Ambrogio is represented by an *Annunciation* and a *Crucifix,* but one of his most celebrated works, carried out with consummate skill, is an almond-eyed *Madonna and Bambino* surrounded by saints and angels. Pietro's most important entry here is an altarpiece—*The Madonna of the Carmine*—made for a church in Siena in 1329. Simone Martini's *Madonna and Child* is damaged but one of the best-known paintings here.

In the salons to follow are works by Giovanni di Paolo (*Presentation at the Temple*) and Sano di Pietro, who seemed to have had an eternal fixation on the Madonna and Child. In one room is a masterpiece of Giovanni Antonio Bazzi (called "Il Sodoma," allegedly because of his sexual interests). It is a picture of Christ at a column, a work of such plastic quality it almost qualifies for publication in a body-beautiful magazine.

Admission: 8,000 lire ($6.30).

Open: Tues–Sat 8:30am–7pm, Sun 8:30am–12:45pm.

SANTUARIO E CASA DI SANTA CATERINA (St. Catherine's Sanctuary), costa di S. Antonio. Tel. 280330.

Of all the personalities associated with Siena, the most enduring legend surrounds that of St. Catherine, acknowledged by Pius XII in 1939 as the patron saint of Italy. The mystic, who was the daughter of a dyer, was born in 1347 in Siena. She was instrumental in persuading the papacy to return to Rome from Avignon. The house where she lived, between piazza del Campo and San Domenico, has now been turned into a sanctuary—it's really a church and oratory, with many works of art, located where her father had his dyeworks. Nearby at the 13th-century Basilica of St. Domenico is a chapel dedicated to St. Catherine, frescoed by Il Sodoma.

Admission: Free, but an offering is expected.

Open: Mon–Sat and hols 9am–12:30pm and 3–6pm.

ENOTECA ITALICA PERMANENTE, Fortezza Medicea. Tel. 288497.

Owned and operated by the Italian government, Enoteca Italica Permanente, which serves as a showcase for the finest wines of Italy, would whet the palate of even the most sophisticated wine devotee. An unusual architectural setting is designed to show bottles to their best advantage. The establishment lies just outside the entrance to an old fortress, at the bottom of an inclined ramp, behind a massive arched doorway. Marble bas-reliefs and wrought-iron sconces, along with regional ceramics, are set into the high brick walls of the labyrinthine corridors, the vaults of which were built by Cosimo dei Medici in 1560. On the premises are several sunny terraces for outdoor wine tasting, an indoor stand-up bar, and voluminous lists of available vintages, which are for sale either by the glass, from 2,000 lire ($1.55), or by the bottle. Count yourself lucky if the bartender will agree to open an iron gate for access to the subterranean wine exposition. There, in the lowest part of the fortress, carpenters have built illuminated display racks containing bottles of recent vintages.

Admission: Free.

Open: Daily 3pm–midnight.

WHERE TO STAY

You'll *definitely* need hotel reservations for the Palio. Make them far in advance, and secure your room with a deposit.

EXPENSIVE

CERTOSA DI MAGGIANO, strada di Certosa 82, 53100 Siena. Tel. 0577/288180. Fax 0577/288189. 5 rms (all with bath), 9 suites. A/C MINIBAR TV TEL **Bus:** Pollicino 6.

$ Rates (including breakfast): 290,000–350,000 lire ($227.65–$274.75) single;

330,000–400,000 lire ($259.05–$314) double; from 440,000 lire ($345.40) suite. AE, DC, MC, V. **Parking:** Free.

⭐ Certosa di Maggiano had been lying in dusty disrepair until 1975, when Anna Grossi Recordati renovated it and began attracting some of the world's social luminaries into its 700-year-old interior. It was built as a monastery by Certosinian monks in the early 13th century, and they maintained their vegetable gardens in an area just beyond the stone walls. These have been transformed into elegant gardens dotted with old masonry, flowering shrubs, and arcaded terraces. The public rooms fill the spaces between what used to be the ambulatory of the central courtyard, and include a stylish and plush collection of intimately proportioned gathering places (including a re-creation of a Renaissance library), filled with antiques and old masonry. A medieval church with a separate entrance adjoins the hotel and still holds mass on Sunday. The entire hotel contains only 14 accommodations, one of which has a private walled garden. It's filled with lighthearted summer furniture, and has attracted such guests as the late Richard Burton, the prime minister of Austria, and the president of Italy. On warm days, breakfast is served in the courtyard, within sight of the ancient well, which adds a decorative note to the otherwise severe stonework. The hotel is not easy to find; it's set away from the center of town on a narrow road barely wide enough for two cars. You might phone for directions before you set out, although the city has made efforts to post signs for general directions.

Dining/Entertainment: The vaulted dining room contains seven tables, a marble fireplace, and entire walls of modern ceramics. It's open to nonresidents who make a reservation. It serves guests a fixed-price lunch for 95,000 lire ($74.60), and a table d'hôte dinner for 135,000 lire ($106). Beverages are extra.

Services: Guide service, massages, room service.

Facilities: Tennis courts, swimming pool.

JOLLY HOTEL EXCELSIOR, piazza La Lizza, 53100 Siena. Tel. 0577/ 288448. Fax 0577/41272. 126 rms (all with bath). A/C MINIBAR TV TEL
$ Rates (including breakfast): 185,000 lire ($145.25) single; 290,000 lire ($227.65) double. AE, DC, MC, V. **Parking:** 35,000 lire ($27.50).

The Jolly Hotel Excelsior, set in the commercial center of the newer section of town near the sports stadium is a distinguished member of this nationwide chain. It is sheltered behind an imposing red-brick facade set with neoclassical stone trim. The renovated lobby is stylishly Italian, with terra-cotta trim and white columns, plus an illuminated bar set up at the far end. The bedrooms offer convenient modern comfort.

Dining/Entertainment: A restaurant is on the premises, serving both regional and international dishes. It is decorated in a modern style. Meals begin at 50,000 lire ($39.25).

Services: Room service, laundry, valet.

PARK HOTEL SIENA, via di Marciano 18, 53100 Siena. Tel. 0577/ 44803. Fax 0577/49020. 70 rms (all with bath), 6 suites. A/C MINIBAR TV TEL
Bus: Hotel shuttle bus to center.
$ Rates: 170,000–215,000 lire ($133.45–$168.80) single; 225,000–300,000 lire ($176.65–$235.50) double; from 490,000 lire ($384.65) suite. Breakfast 19,000 lire ($14.90) extra. 19% IVA tax extra. AE, DC, MC, V. **Parking:** Free.

This is a luxurious hotel whose physical plant was originally commissioned in 1530 by one of Siena's most famous Renaissance architects. A difficult access road leads around a series of hairpin turns (watch the signs carefully) to a buff-colored villa set with a view over green trees and suburbanite houses about a 12-minute drive (1½ miles) southwest of the city center. The landscaped swimming pool, double-glazed windows, upholstered walls, and plush carpeting have set new standards around here. The hotel is well tended, with stylish modern decoration, and a comfortably furnished series of public salons.

Dining/Entertainment: Meals in the hotel restaurant might include wild-mushroom salad with black truffles, tortellini with spinach and ricotta, and a regularly featured series of regional dishes from Tuscany, Umbria, or Emilia-Romagna. Prices begin at 70,000 lire ($54.95).

Services: Room service, laundry, valet.

Facilities: Swimming pool, public salons.

VILLA PATRIZIA, via Fiorentina 58, 53100 Siena. Tel. 0577/50431. Fax 0577/50431. 33 rms (all with bath). MINIBAR TV TEL **Bus:** 10 or 15.
$ Rates: 200,000 lire ($157) single; 300,000 lire ($235.50) double. AE, DC, MC, V. **Parking:** Free.
This is a white-walled villa set into a well-planned park dotted with old trees and sculpture. Outside the city, the hotel is comfortably and attractively furnished, it offers both an outdoor pool and a tennis court.

VILLA SCACCIAPENSIERI, via di Scacciapensieri 10, 53100 Siena. Tel. 0577/41441. Fax 0577/270854. 27 rms (all with bath), 2 suites. A/C MINIBAR TV TEL **Bus:** 8 or 12 into Siena (an 8-minute ride) every 15 minutes.
$ Rates (including breakfast): 130,000–170,000 lire ($102.05–$133.45) single; 170,000–270,000 lire ($133.45–$211.95) double; from 350,000 lire ($274.75) suite. AE, DC, MC, V. **Parking:** Free. **Closed:** Jan–Feb.
This is one of the lovely old villas of Tuscany, where you can stay in a personal and tasteful atmosphere. The hostess, Mrs. Emma Nardi, opened her hotel in the summer of 1934, and it is still run by her family. Standing on the crest of a hill, with a panoramic view of Tuscany's chianti hills and Siena about 2 miles away, the villa is approached by a private driveway under shade trees. The bedrooms are individually designed and exquisitely appointed.
The gardens open onto many vistas. Additions include a completely equipped *villino*, with charming sleeping and sitting areas.
Dining/Entertainment: Evenings in the informal restaurant, Altri Tempi, are worth the trip; guests chat as they gather around the log fire burning on a raised hearth in winter. This restaurant is becoming better known; it offers not only panoramic views, but quality Tuscan food and wine. You can dine here Thursday through Tuesday for about 55,000 lire ($43.20), but it's advisable to call and make a reservation.
Services: Room service, laundry, valet.
Facilities: A handsomely landscaped swimming pool, tennis court.

MODERATE

CASTAGNETO HOTEL, via dei Cappuccini 55, 53100 Siena. Tel. 0577/45103. 11 rms (all with bath). TEL **Bus:** 1.
$ Rates: 95,000 lire ($74.60) double. No credit cards. **Parking:** Free. **Closed:** Dec to mid-Mar.
This is a modestly proportioned brick villa set behind a graveled parking lot, near a garden with birds and trees on the western outskirts of Siena. It was renovated into a hotel in 1973 with unpretentious rooms in clean and functional working order. Only doubles are available.

GARDEN HOTEL, via Custoza 2, 53100 Siena. Tel. 0577/47056. Fax 0577/46050. 140 rms (all with bath or shower). TV TEL **Bus:** 6.
$ Rates (including breakfast): 75,000 lire ($58.90) single; 125,000 lire ($98.15) double. AE, DC, MC, V. **Parking:** Free.
The Garden Hotel is a well-styled country house, built by a Sienese aristocrat in the 16th century. On the edge of the city, high up on the ledge of a hill, it commands a view of Siena and the surrounding countryside which has been the subject of many a painting. The hotel stands formal and serene, with an entrance on the garden side and a long avenue of clipped hedges. There's a luxurious sense of space and an aura of freshness. Some of the rooms are in the old villa, the others in an adjoining building. One hundred rooms contain a minibar and 75 are air-conditioned. An enjoyable spot for morning coffee is the breakfast room, with its flagstone floor, decorated ceiling, and view of the hills. You can take your other meals in an open-air restaurant on the premises. There is also a swimming pool.

PALAZZO RAVIZZA, Pian dei Mantellini 34, 53100 Siena. Tel. 0577/ 280462. Fax 0577/271370. 30 rms (21 with bath), 3 suites. TEL **Bus:** 3.
$ Rates (including half board): 92,000–105,000 lire ($72.20–$82.45) per person. AE, DC, MC, V.

⑤ The Palazzo Ravizza has lots of old-fashioned charm. A first-class pensione in Siena, it's really an old palace, within walking distance of the major attractions. In the front is a formal facade, in the rear a terraced garden with shade trees and benches for viewing the sweeping countryside. For years the home of great Tuscan families, it is owned and managed by sensitive people who have not allowed drastic modernization, except for the installation of water basins and a few private baths. The well-furnished bedrooms, each with a distinct personality, utilize fine old furniture. The living room and drawing rooms of the second floor are furnished with antiques, including a grand piano. All the rooms are interesting architecturally, many with coved ceilings. The pension accepts guests only on the half-board plan.

INEXPENSIVE

ALBERGO CENTRALE, via Cecco Angiolieri 26, 53100 Siena. Tel. 0577/ 280379. 7 rms (all with bath or shower). MINIBAR TV TEL
$ Rates: 79,000 lire ($62) double. Breakfast 8,000 lire ($6.30) extra. No credit cards.
A minute's walk from piazza del Campo, Albergo Centrale is rated two stars by the government, and it's inexpensive and clean. Many students have stayed here who come to Siena to attend the School of Language and Culture, mainly to learn Italian (the Sienese "tongue" is said to be pure—that is, free of dialect). The Centrale is housed in an old building that's in keeping with surrounding structures, and is reached by a stairway (no elevator, of course). They have no singles.

ALBERGO CHIUSARELLI, via Curtatone 11, 53100 Siena. Tel. 0577/ 280562. Fax 0577/271177. 50 rms (all with bath). MINIBAR TEL **Bus:** 3.
$ Rates: 54,000 lire ($42.40) single; 85,000 lire ($66.75) double. Breakfast 8,000 lire ($6.30) extra. V. **Parking:** Free.
The Albergo Chiusarelli is housed in an ocher-colored building with Ionic columns and Roman caryatids which support a second-floor loggia. It looks much older, but the building was constructed around 1900. The interior has been almost completely renovated into a functional format that includes a modern bath and electric hairdryer in each room. The hotel is just at the edge of the old city, and is convenient to the parking areas at the sports stadium a 5-minute walk away. A bar and restaurant on the basement level serve full meals for around 30,000 lire ($23.55).

VILLA TERRAIA, via dell'Ascarello 13, 53100 Siena. Tel. 0577/221108. Fax 0577/280290. 27 rms (24 with bath). MINIBAR TEL **Bus:** 8, 12, or 34.
$ Rates: 40,000 lire ($31.40) single without bath, 57,000 lire ($44.75) single with bath; 68,000 lire ($53.40) double without bath, 91,000 lire ($71.45) double with bath. Breakfast 7,000 lire ($5.50) extra. DC. **Parking:** Free. **Closed:** Nov to mid-Mar.
This three-star is a country villa on a hill about 2 miles from Siena. Both inexpensive and restful, it has long been a haven for artists and musicians. The bedrooms differ in shape, decor, and size, and much of the villa has the aura of a country home. To get there, head out via Simone Martini, cross viale Lippo Memmi, and turn right on viale Sardegna, until you come to via dell'Ascarello, about a 10-minute drive through undulating hills. You can also take a bus.

A NEARBY PLACE TO STAY

VILLA BELVEDERE, Belvedere, 53034 Colle di Val d'Elsa (Siena). Tel. 0577/920966. Fax 0577/271570. 15 rms (all with bath). TEL **Directions:** Exit the autostrada from Florence at Colle di Val d'Elsa and follow the signs.

$ Rates (including half board): 115,000 lire ($90.30) single; 125,000 lire ($98.15) double. AE, DC, MC, V. **Parking:** Free.

The Villa Belvedere, about 7½ miles from Siena and halfway to San Gimignano, is in a villa built in 1795. In 1820 it was the residence of Ferdinand III, Archduke of Austria and Grand Duke of Tuscany, and in 1845 of Grand Duke Leopold II. Surrounded by a large park, the hotel has bar service, a garden with a panorama, and elegant dining rooms, where typical Tuscan and classic Italian dishes are served. The bedrooms, furnished with antiques, all have central heating and overlook the park.

WHERE TO DINE

Even half-day trippers sometimes find themselves in Siena for lunch, and that's a happy prospect, as the Sienese are good cooks, in the best of the Tuscan tradition.

MODERATE

AL MANGIA, piazza del Campo 43. Tel. 281121.
   Cuisine: TUSCAN. **Reservations:** Not needed.
$ Prices: Appetizers 9,000–15,000 lire ($7.05–$11.80); main courses 15,000–23,000 lire ($11.80–$18.05). AE, DC, MC, V.
   Open: Lunch Tues–Sun 12:30–2:30pm; dinner Tues–Sun 7:30–10pm. **Closed:** Feb.

Al Mangia, one of the finest restaurants in the heart of the city, has outside tables which overlook the town hall. The food is not only well cooked, but appetizingly presented. To begin with, the house specialty is cannoli alla Mangia. If you then crave a savory Tuscan main dish, try a bollito di manzo con salsa verde (boiled beef with green sauce). Another excellent course is the ossobuco with artichokes, and in season wild boar is featured. For dessert, there's one specialty that transcends identification with its hometown and is known all over Europe: panforte, made of spicy delights, including almonds and candied fruits.

AL MARSILI (Ristorante Enoteca Gallo Nero), via del Castoro 3. Tel. 47154.
   Cuisine: SIENESE/ITALIAN. **Reservations:** Recommended.
$ Prices: Appetizers 8,000–9,000 lire ($6.30–$7.05); main courses 16,000–18,000 lire ($12.55–$14.15). AE, DC, MC, V.
   Open: Lunch Tues–Sun 12:30–2:30pm; dinner Tues–Sun 7:30–10pm.

This beautiful restaurant, the best in Siena, stands between the Duomo and via di Città in a neighborhood packed with medieval and Renaissance buildings. You dine beneath crisscrossed ceiling vaults whose russet-colored brickwork was designed centuries ago. Specialties of the chef include a rigatoni with zucchini, selections of antipasti from an abundantly stocked table, gnocchi with duck sauce, and a scallop of veal with chive sauce, followed by well-prepared desserts.

DA GUIDO, vicolo Pier Pettinaio 7. Tel. 200042.
   Cuisine: SIENESE/INTERNATIONAL. **Reservations:** Recommended.
$ Prices: Appetizers 6,000–7,000 lire ($4.70–$5.50); main courses 10,000–13,000 lire ($7.85–$10.20). AE, DC, MC, V.
   Open: Lunch daily 12:30–2:30pm; dinner daily 7:30–10pm.

Da Guido is a medieval Tuscan restaurant about 100 feet off the promenade street near piazza del Campo. It's decked out with crusty old beams, time-aged brick walls, arched ceilings, and iron chandeliers. My approval is backed up by the public testimony of more than 300 prominent people, who have left autographed photographs to adorn the walls of three dining rooms—film stars, diplomats, opera singers, and car-racing champions. There's a grill for steaks, chickens, and roasts. You may want to order some of the specialties on the à la carte list. That way, you can have assorted antipasti, which are most rewarding. For a main dish, you may want to stick to the roasts, or try a pasta, tagliata alla Guido. Desserts are good, too.

INEXPENSIVE

NELLO LA TAVERNA, via del Porrione 28. Tel. 289043.
  Cuisine: TUSCAN. **Reservations:** Required. **Bus:** Pollicino 6.
$ **Prices:** Appetizers 2,500–7,000 lire ($1.95–$5.50); main courses 9,000–14,000 lire ($7.05–$11); fixed-price menu 25,000 lire ($19.65). AE, DC, MC, V.
  Open: Lunch Tues–Sun 12:30–2:30pm; dinner Tues–Sat 7:30–10pm. **Closed:** Feb.

Nello La Taverna offers an ambience that's about as typical of the Sienese region as anything you'll find. On a narrow stone-covered street about half a block from piazza del Campo, the establishment, as its name implies, offers a tavern decor that includes brick walls, hanging lanterns, racks of wine bottles, and sheaves of corn hanging from the ceiling. Best of all, you can view the forgelike kitchen with its crew of uniformed cooks busily preparing your dinner from behind a row of hanging copper utensils. Specialties include a salad of fresh radicchio, green lasagne ragoût style, and lamb cacciatore with beans. The best wines, according to the owner, come from the region. Your waiter will gladly suggest a local vintage for you.

GROTTA SANTA CATERINA–DA BAGOGA, via della Galluzza 26. Tel. 282208.
  Cuisine: TUSCAN/INTERNATIONAL. **Reservations:** Recommended. **Bus:** Pollicino C.
$ **Prices:** Appetizers 6,000–8,000 lire ($4.70–$5.60); main courses 9,000–15,000 lire ($7.05–$11.80). AE, V.
  Open: Lunch Tues–Sun 12:30–3pm; dinner Tues–Sat 7:30–10pm. **Closed:** July 10–25.

This restaurant, in a brick building midway up a narrow, steeply inclined cobblestone street, is an unpretentious gathering place popular with local residents. Inside are brick arches, lots of rustic detailing, plants, and wooden chairs. You are served such specialties as eight kinds of scaloppine, beef with truffles, or chicken cooked in beer. Rabbit in champagne is a favorite, and the kitchen will also prepare a wide variety of mixed roast meats, including veal, pork, and lamb. Many dishes are based on 16th century recipes which means no tomatoes and no potatoes, since these vegetables were not in use at the time.

---

2. SAN GIMIGNANO

23 miles NW of Siena, 34 miles SW of Florence

GETTING THERE   By Bus   TRA-IN buses service San Gimignano from Florence with a change at Poggibonsi (trip time: 75 minutes). The one-way fare is 6,200 lire ($4.85). The same company also operates services from Siena, with a change at Poggibonsi. Trip time is 50 minutes, and the one-way cost is 4,300 lire ($3.40).

By Car   From Florence, take the Firenze–Siena autostrada south to Poggibonsi, where you'll need to cut west along a secondary route (no. 324). From Siena, head northwest along the Firenze–Siena autostrada until you reach Poggibonsi, where Route 324 leads west to San Gimignano.

ESSENTIALS   The **telephone area code** is 0577. The nearest **tourist office** is at Siena (see above).

A golden lily of the Middle Ages! Called the Manhattan of Tuscany, the town preserves 13 of its noble brick towers, which give it a skyscraper skyline. The approach to the walled town today is dramatic, but once it must have been fantastic, as San Gimignano in the heyday of the Guelph and Ghibelline conflict had as many as 72 towers. Today its fortresslike severity is softened by the subtlety of its quiet, harmonious squares, and many of its palaces and churches are enhanced by Renaissance frescoes, as San Gimignano could afford to patronize major painters.

WHAT TO SEE & DO

In the center of town is the palazzo-flanked **piazza della Cisterna** (see my hotel recommendations)—so named because of the 13th-century cistern in its heart. Connected with the irregularly shaped square is its satellite, **piazza del Duomo.** The square's medieval architecture—towers and palaces—is almost unchanged, and it is the most beautiful spot in town.

The **Palazzo del Popolo** is a palace designed by Arnolfo di Cambio in the 13th century, with a tower built a few years later that is believed to have been the tallest "skyscraper" (about 178 feet high), and a symbol of the *podestà* or mayor. You can scale this tower, the Torre Grossa (the tallest in town), and be rewarded with a bird's-eye view of this most remarkable town. Hours and admission charges are the same as for the Museo Civico (see below).

IL DUOMO, piazza del Duomo.

The present Duomo dates essentially from the 13th century. Inside, the cathedral is richly frescoed. In the right aisle, panels trace scenes from the life of Christ—the kiss of Judas, the Last Supper, the flagellation, and the Crucifixion—painted by an artist most often known as Barna da Siena. In the left aisle are frescoes by Bartolo di Fredi; this mid-14th-century cycle represents scenes from the Old Testament, including the massacre of Job's servants.

The chief attraction of the cathedral is the Chapel of Santa Fina, designed by Giuliano da Maiano. It was frescoed in about 1475 by Domenico Ghirlandaio, who depicted scenes from the life of Saint Fina, as in the memorable deathbed panel. Ghirlandaio, you may recall, was Michelangelo's fresco teacher.

Admission (including entrance to Museo Civico): 10,000 lire ($7.85) adults, 7,500 lire ($5.90) children.

Open: Daily 8:30am–12:30pm and 3–6pm.

MUSEO CIVICO, in the Palazzo del Popolo, piazza del Duomo 1. Tel. 940340.

Installed upstairs in the Palazzo del Popolo (Comune, or town hall) is the Museo Civico, notably the Sala di Dante, where the Guelph-supporting poet spoke out for his cause in 1300. Look for one of the masterpieces of San Gimignano—the *Maestà,* or Madonna enthroned, by Lippo Memmi (later "touched up" by Gozzoli).

The first large room you enter upstairs contains the other masterpieces of the museum—a *Madonna in Glory,* with Saints Gregory and Benedict, painted by Pinturicchio when perspective was flowering. On the other side of it are two different depictions of the *Annunciation* by Filippino Lippi. On the opposite wall, note the magnificent primitive *Crucifix* by Coppo di Marcovaldo.

Around to the left of the cathedral on a little square (piazza Luigi Pecori) is the **Museum of Sacred Art,** an unheralded museum of at least passing interest for its medieval tombstones and wooden sculpture. It also has an illustrated-manuscript section and an Etruscan section. Admission is with your ticket from the Museo Civico, and hours are the same.

Admission (including entrance to the Chapel of Santa Fina and Museum of Sacred Art): 10,000 lire ($7.85) adults, 7,500 lire ($5.90) children.

Open: Apr–Sept, Tues–Sun 9:30am–12:30pm and 3–6pm; Oct–Mar, Tues–Sun 9:30am–12:30pm and 2:30–5:30pm.

CHURCH OF SANT'AGOSTINO, piazza Sant'Agostino.

This handsome Gothic church was built in the 13th century. It is visited today chiefly by those wanting to see the mid-15th-century cycle of 17 frescoes on the choir by Benozzo Gozzoli. The panels, which depict scenes from the life of St. Augustine, are noted for their backgrounds and for the attention to architectural detail and costumes. You can also explore the cloisters, with their simple but beautiful

architectural lines. It's 200 yards from the Duomo, a pleasant stroll from the town center.
Admission: Free.
Open: Daily 8am–noon and 3–6pm.

WHERE TO STAY

LA CISTERNA, piazza della Cisterna, 53037 San Gimignano. Tel. 0577/940328. Fax 0577/942080. 50 rms (all with bath or shower). TEL
$ Rates: 60,000 lire ($47.10) single; 82,000–90,000 lire ($64.35–$70.65) double. Half board 82,000–90,000 lire ($64.35–$70.65) per person extra; breakfast, 9,000 lire ($7.05). AE, DC, MC, V. **Parking:** 15,000 lire ($11.80).

A second-class hotel, La Cisterna is modernized but still retains its medieval lines (it was built at the base of some 14th-century patrician towers). In its heyday La Cisterna was the palazzo of a Tuscan family of nobility. Many tourists visit it just for the day, and to patronize Le Terrazze restaurant (see "Where to Dine," below). The bedrooms are generally large; some of the more superior lodgings open onto terraces with views of the Val d'Elsa (the hotel rests on a hilltop). Within 2 minutes after leaving the front door, you'll be at all the major sightseeing attractions.

PESCILLE, Località Pescille, 53037 San Gimignano. Tel. 0577/940186. Fax 0577/940186. 33 rms (all with bath), 4 suites. TEL
$ Rates: 58,000 lire ($45.55) single; 91,000 lire ($71.45) double. Half board 94,000 lire ($73.75) per person extra; breakfast 8,000 lire ($6.30). AE, DC, MC, V. **Parking:** Free. **Closed:** Jan–Feb.

This is the most tranquil hotel in the San Gimignano area. It was once a castle before it was converted in time to a monastery. Napoleon came this way in 1812 and chased out the monks. Later in its career the building became a winery, and, finally, in 1971, was turned into a hotel in a setting of olive groves and vineyards. Rooms are furnished in traditional taste. The most desirable accommodation is the two-level Tower Room, opening onto a framed picture view of San Gimignano. Since it costs the same as the other accommodations, this "room with a view" is naturally every guest's first choice. Meals are served daily except Wednesday in the I Cinque Gigli restaurant, and cost 40,000 lire to 56,000 lire ($31.40 to $43.95) per person. The Pescille lies almost 3 miles from the center of town heading toward Volterra, and therefore is best for motorists.

BEL SOGGIORNO, via San Giovanni 41, 53037 San Gimignano. Tel. 0577/940375. Fax 0577/940375. 17 rms (all with bath), 4 suites. TEL
$ Rates: 60,000 lire ($47.10) single; 80,000–90,000 lire ($62.80–$70.65) double; from 139,000 lire ($109.10) suite. Breakfast 8,000 lire ($6.30) per person extra. AE, DC, MC, V. **Parking:** 15,000 lire ($11.80).

The Bel Sorggiorno lies on a narrow street which runs through the town. Its rear bedrooms and dining room open on the lower pastureland and the bottom of the village, providing a splendid view of the Val d'Elsa. The front is in the unspoiled Tuscan style, with an entryway and arched windows. Although rated only three stars by the government, the lodgings offered are far superior to what you might expect. The rooms are small and pleasantly revamped, and they offer excellent views (some have antiques and terraces). All of them were designed in the High Tuscan style by an architect from Milan; eight contain TV and four offer a minibar.

In high season you'll be asked to have your meals here—which is no great hardship as the cuisine is excellent. The dining room opens onto picture-window views. Done in the medieval style, it contains murals depicting the hunting of wild boar. There's a country fireplace with crude chairs. Nonresidents are welcome to come in for meals Tuesday through Sunday.

WHERE TO DINE

RISTORANTE LE TERRAZZE, in La Cisterna Hotel, piazza della Cisterna. Tel. 940328.
Cuisine: TUSCAN. **Reservations:** Required.

$ Prices: Appetizers 8,000–9,000 lire ($6.30–$7.05); main courses 14,000–20,000 lire ($11–$15.80). AE, DC, MC, V.
Open: Lunch Thurs–Mon 12:30–2:30pm; dinner Wed–Sun 7:30–10pm.
Closed: Nov–Mar.

Ristorante Le Terrazze offers a panoramic view through glassed-in windows which open onto the Val d'Elsa. The setting is one of a country inn. The food is an assortment of produce from the surrounding Tuscan farm country. Many soups and pastas make for fine beginnings, and the risotto alla Cisterna is a specialty of the house. In meats, the house specialties are vitello alla Cisterna with beans in butter, breaded lamb cutlet with fried artichokes, and faraona arrosto (roast guinea fowl) with fried potatoes.

3. PISA

47 miles W of Florence, 207 miles N of Rome

GETTING THERE **By Plane** Both domestic and international flights arrive at Pisa's Galileo Galilei airport (tel. 28088 for information). Trains into the center of Pisa make the 5-minute trip for 600 lire (45¢) per person.

By Train Trains link Pisa and Florence at the rate of one every 30 minutes. Trip time is 1 hour, and a one-way fare is 5,300 lire ($4.15). Coastal trains also link Pisa and Rome.

By Bus There is frequent bus service to Florence operated by APT (tel. 501038 in Pisa for more information and schedules).

By Car From Florence, take the autostrada west (A11) to the intersection (A12) going south to Pisa.

ESSENTIALS The **telephone area code** is 050. The **Tourist Information Office** is on piazza del Duomo (tel. 560464).

One of Katherine Anne Porter's best short stories was called "The Leaning Tower."
A memorable scene in that story dealt with a German landlady's sentimental attachment to a 5-inch plaster replica of the Leaning Tower of Pisa, a souvenir whose ribs caved in at the touch of a prospective tenant. "'It cannot be replaced,' said the landlady, with a severe, stricken dignity. 'It was a souvenir of the Italian journey.'" Ironically, the year (1944) Miss Porter published her "Leaning Tower," a bomb fell near the real campanile, but, fortunately, it wasn't damaged.

Few buildings in the world have captured imaginations as much as the Leaning Tower of Pisa. It is probably the single most instantly recognizable building in all the Western world. Perhaps visitors are drawn to it as a symbol of the fragility of people or at least the fragility of their work.

The Leaning Tower is a landmark powerful enough to entice visitors to call, and once there, they usually find other sights to explore as well. I'll survey the top attractions first, as most visitors pass through just for the day.

WHAT TO SEE & DO

In the Middle Ages, Pisa reached the apex of its power as a maritime republic before it eventually fell to its rivals, Florence and Genoa. As is true of most cities at the zenith, Pisa turned to the arts, and made contributions in sculpture and architecture. Its greatest legacy remains at **piazza del Duomo,** which D'Annunzio labeled "Piazza dei Miracoli" (miracles). Here you'll find an ensemble of the top three attractions—original "Pisan-Romanesque" buildings, including the Duomo, the Baptistery, and the Leaning Tower itself. Nikolaus Pevsner, in his classic *An Outline of European Architecture,* wrote: "Pisa strikes one altogether as of rather an alien character—Oriental more than Tuscan."

Construction of the ✪ **Leaning Tower,** an eight-story campanile, began in 1174 by Bonanno, and a persistent legend is that the architect deliberately intended the bell tower to lean (but that claim is undocumented). Another legend is that Galileo let objects of different weights fall from the tower, then timed their descent to prove his theories on bodies in motion.

Unfortunately, the tower is in serious danger of collapse. The government has announced an international competition to solicit plans to save the monument. The tower is said to be floating on a sandy base of water-soaked clay; it leans at least 14 feet from perpendicular. If it stood up straight, the tower would measure about 180 feet.

In 1990 the government suspended visits made inside the tower. In years gone by, one of the major attractions in Europe was to climb the Tower of Pisa—taking all 294 steps. But that is considered too dangerous today, and visitors must be content to observe the tower from the outside—but at a safe distance, of course.

IL DUOMO, piazza del Duomo 17. Tel. 561820.

✪ The cathedral, which dates from 1063, was designed by Buschetto, although Rainaldo in the 13th century erected the unusual facade with its four layers of open-air arches that diminish in size as they ascend. The cathedral is marked by three bronze doors—rhythmic in line—which replaced those destroyed in a disastrous fire in 1596. The south door, considered the most notable, was designed by Bonanno in 1180.

In the restored interior, the chief art treasure is the pulpit by Giovanni Pisano, which was finished in 1310. The pulpit, damaged in the cathedral fire, was finally rebuilt (with bits and pieces of the original) in 1926. The polygonal pulpit is held up by porphyry pillars and column statues that symbolize the Virtues (two posts are supported on the backs of lions). The relief panels depict scenes from the Bible. The pulpit is similar to an earlier one by Giovanni's father, Niccolò Pisano, which is in the Baptistery across the way.

There are other treasures, too—Galileo's lamp (according to unreliable tradition, the Pisa-born astronomer used the chandelier to formulate his laws of the pendulum), mosaics in the apse said to have been designed by Cimabue, the tomb of Henry VII of Luxembourg, a *St. Agnes* by Andrea del Sarto, a *Descent from the Cross* by Il Sodoma, and a *Crucifix* by Giambologna.

Admission: Free.

Open: May–Oct, daily 7:45am–12:50pm and 3–6:50pm; Nov–Apr, 7:45am–12:50pm and 3–4:50pm. **Bus:** 1, 3, or 4.

THE BAPTISTERY, piazza del Duomo. Tel. 560547.

Begun in 1153, the Baptistery is like a Romanesque crown capped by Gothic. Although it's most beautiful on the exterior, with its arches and columns, it should be visited inside to see the hexagonal pulpit made by Niccolò Pisano in 1260. Supported by pillars which rest on the backs of a trio of marble lions, the pulpit contains bas-reliefs of the Crucifixion, the Adoration of the Magi, the presentation of the Christ child at the temple, and the Last Judgment (many angels have lost their heads over the years). Column statues represent the Virtues. At the baptismal font is a contemporary John the Baptist by a local sculptor. The echo inside the Baptistery shell has enthralled visitors for years.

Admission: 5,000 lire ($3.95), including admission to Museo dell'Opera (see below).

Open: May–Oct, daily 9am–12:50pm and 3–6:50pm; Nov–Apr, daily 9am–12:50pm and 3–5pm. **Bus:** 1, 3, or 4.

MUSEO DELL'OPERA, piazza Arcivescovado. Tel. 560547.

Opened in 1986, it exhibits works of art removed from the monumental buildings on the piazza. The heart of the collection, on the ground floor, consists of sculptures spanning the 11th to the 13th century. The most famous exhibit is an ivory *Madonna* and the *Crucifix* by Giovanni Pisano. Also exhibited is the work of French goldsmiths, which was presented by Maria de' Medici to Archbishop Bonciani in 1616. Upstairs are paintings from the 16th to the 18th century. Some of the textiles and embroideries date from the 15th century. Another section of the museum is devoted to Egyptian, Etruscan, and Roman works of art.

Admission: Included in admission price to the Baptistery (see above).

Open: May–Oct daily 9am–12:50pm and 3–6:50pm; Nov–Apr daily 9am–12:50pm and 3–5pm. **Bus:** 1, 3, or 4.

CAMPOSANTO, campo dei Miracoli. Tel. 560547.

This cemetery was originally designed by Giovanni di Simone in 1278, but a bomb hit it in 1944. Recently it has been partially restored. It is said that earth from Calvary was shipped here by the Crusaders on Pisan ships (the city was a great port before its water receded). The cemetery is of interest because of its sarcophagi, statuary, and frescoes. Notable frescoes, badly damaged, were by Benozzo Gozzoli, who illustrated scenes from the Old Testament; he paid special attention to architectural details. One room contains three of the most famous frescoes from the 14th century: the *Triumph of Death,* the *Last Judgment,* and the *Inferno,* with the usual assortment of monsters, reptiles, and boiling caldrons. The *Triumph of Death* is the most interesting, with its flying angels and devils—superb in composition. In addition, you'll find lots of white-marble bas-reliefs, including Roman funerary sculpture.

Admission: 5,000 lire ($3.95).

Open: May–Oct, daily 8am–8pm; Nov–Apr, daily 8am–5pm. **Bus:** 1, 3, or 4.

MUSEO NAZIONALE DI SAN MATTEO, lungarno Mediceo. Tel. 541-1865.

The well-planned Museo Nazionale di San Matteo, near piazza Mazzini, contains a good assortment of paintings and sculpture, many of which date from the 13th and 14th centuries. In the museum are statues by Giovanni Pisano; Simone Martini's *Madonna and Child with Saints,* a polyptych, as well as Nino Pisano's *Madonna del Latte* (milk), a marble sculpture; Masaccio's *St. Paul,* painted in 1426; Domenico Ghirlandaio's two *Madonna and Saints* depictions; works by Strozzi and Alessandro Magnasco; and very old copies of works by Jan and Peter Brueghel. You enter from piazza San Matteo.

Admission: 3,000 lire ($2.35).

Open: Tues–Sat 9am–7pm (until sunset in winter). **Bus:** 1, 3, or 4.

WHERE TO STAY
EXPENSIVE

GRAND HOTEL DUOMO, via Santa Maria 94, 56100 Pisa. Tel. 050/561894. Fax 050/560418. 94 rms (all with bath). A/C MINIBAR TV TEL **Bus:** 1, 3, or 4.

$ Rates (including breakfast): 165,000 lire ($129.55) single; 235,000 lire ($184.50) double. AE, DC, MC, V. **Parking:** 25,000 lire ($19.65).

The Grand Hotel Duomo is a blending of the talents of an architect and decorator who set out to create a streamlined modern hotel in the heart of Pisa, a short walk from the Leaning Tower. Contemporary it is, in a buff-colored stucco, with a covered roof garden for uninterrupted views. Inside, there's a liberal use of marble, crystal chandeliers, even tall murals in the dining room, one of which is an artist's rendering of a verdant, blooming Pisa. A garage is on the premises. The bedrooms are well furnished, with parquet floors, big windows, built-in headrests, and individual lights.

JOLLY HOTEL CAVALIERI, piazza della Stazione 2, 56100 Pisa. Tel. 050/500218. Fax 050/502242. 100 rms (all with bath). A/C MINIBAR TV TEL **Bus:** 1, 3, or 4.

$ Rates: 215,000 lire ($168.80) single; 350,000 lire ($274.75) double. Breakfast 21,000 lire ($16.50) extra. AE, DC, MC, V. **Parking:** 25,000 lire ($19.65).

This is the best hotel in Pisa, with a view over the monumental train station and the piazza in front of it, just 2 miles from Pisa International Airport. It was built in 1948, in a design that emphasizes strong angles and postwar modernity. Since then it has been practically rebuilt from the inside out. Today the rooms are filled with plush furniture, paneling, and large expanses of glass. The hotel has been visited by such personalities as former British Prime Minister Edward Heath, opera star Eduardo de Filippo, and actor Vittorio Gassman. The hotel also hosts dozens of business travelers, who appreciate the serenity of the bar and restaurant for their meetings. Each room has a radio. Parking is often possible in the square in front of the station or, for better security, in the nearby garage.

MODERATE

HOTEL D'AZEGLIO, piazza Vittorio Emanuele II no. 18, 56100 Pisa. Tel. 050/500310. Fax 050/28017. 29 rms (all with bath). A/C MINIBAR TV TEL **Bus:** 1, 3, or 4.
$ Rates (including breakfast): 150,000 lire ($117.75) single; 200,000 lire ($157) double. AE, DC, MC, V. **Parking:** 20,000 lire ($15.70).
This is a first-class hotel in the vicinity of the railway station and the air terminal, in the historic and commercial center of Pisa. On the premises is an American bar and roof garden with a view of the city. A garage is adjacent to the hotel. The rooms are well furnished and comfortable.

BUDGET

HOTEL ARNO, piazza della Repubblica 6, 56100 Pisa. Tel. 050/542958. Fax 050/543441. 30 rms (all with shower). TEL **Bus:** 1, 3, or 4.
$ Rates: 68,000 lire ($53.40) single; 90,000 lire ($70.65) double. AE, DC, MC, V.
This is one of the best of the second-class hotels, conveniently situated in a quiet position in front of the Tribunal. This modern hotel is furnished throughout with pieces of a functional design. Half the bedrooms contain TVs.

ROYAL VICTORIA, lungarno Pacinotti 12, 56126 Pisa. Tel. 050/502130. Fax 050/502189. 42 rms (all with bath). TEL **Bus:** 3.
$ Rates: 75,000 lire ($58.90) single; 105,000 lire ($82.45) double. AE, DC, MC, V. **Parking:** 15,000 lire ($11.80).
The Royal Victoria is conveniently located on the Arno, within walking distance of most of the jewels in Pisa's crown. Its tastefully decorated lounge sets the hospitable scene. Most of the rooms are devoted to the past only through painted ceilings, spaciousness, and the warmth of antiques suitable to contemporary comfort.

WHERE TO DINE

Pisan fare has greatly improved in recent years, particularly since the opening of Ristorante Sergio.

RISTORANTE SERGIO, lungarno Pacinotti 2. Tel. 48245.
Cuisine: TUSCAN. **Reservations:** Required. **Bus:** 1, 3, or 5.
$ Prices: Appetizers 15,000–18,000 lire ($11.80–$14.15); main courses 25,000–28,000 lire ($19.65–$22). AE, DC, MC, V.
Open: Lunch Tues–Sat 12:30–3pm; dinner Mon–Sat 7:30–10pm. **Closed:** July 15–30.
Residents of Pisa flock to Ristorante Sergio, which sits on the banks of the Arno, in a building whose walls are 1,000 years old. In days of yore, when it was an inn, the building sheltered such illustrious guests as Montaigne, Shelley, and Garibaldi. A long bar area is near the entrance, flanked by a massive stone wall that's dotted with medieval wrought-iron keys, wood carvings, and rare wines. Dining is on two levels, on comfortably rustic chairs pulled up to beautifully set tables. The service is impeccable, with help offered at the proper moments by Sergio Lorenzi's gracious wife and daughter. The bouquets, as well as many of the herbs and vegetables, come from the family garden.

All the finest ingredients combine with Sergio's talents to form a unique *cucina Toscana* that has been presented by him on cooking lectures throughout Europe and North America. A *gran menu del giorno* (menu of the day) is offered for 90,000 lire ($70.65), although a smaller luncheon menu is also popular at 75,000 lire ($58.90). My favorite is the 90,000-lira ($70.65) menu dégustation, offered only in the evening, which promises a "taste of everything." It features a portion of many different courses, all of them superb. These might include a rich salad with truffles, a re-creation of an ancient Tuscan recipe for vegetable-and-meat soup, and a range of delicacies that make this the best-rated restaurant in Pisa. The collection of wines is superb, and the waiter will be pleased to help you in selecting one.

AL RISTORO DEI VECCHI MACELLI, via Volturno 49. Tel. 20424.
   Cuisine: TUSCAN. **Reservations:** Required. **Bus:** 1, 3, or 4.
$ Prices: Appetizers 10,000–12,000 lire ($7.85–$9.40); main courses 18,000–25,000 lire ($14.15–$19.65). AE, DC, MC, V.
   Open: Lunch Mon–Tues and Thurs–Sat 12:30–2:30pm; dinner Thurs–Tues 7:30–10pm. **Closed:** 2 weeks in Aug (dates vary).

This is one of the best restaurants in Pisa, set in a comfortably rustic building near piazzetta di Vecchi Macelli. Residents of Pisa claim that the cuisine is prepared with something akin to love, and they prove their devotion by returning frequently. After selecting from a choice of two dozen varieties of seafood antipasti, you can enjoy a homemade pasta with scallops and zucchini or fish-stuffed ravioli in a shrimp sauce. Other dishes include gnocchi with pesto and shrimp and roast veal with a truffle-flavored cream sauce.

BUZZINO, via Cammeo 42. Tel. 562141.
   Cuisine: INTERNATIONAL. **Reservations:** Required. **Bus:** 1, 3, or 4.
$ Prices: Appetizers 8,000–10,000 lire ($6.30–$7.85); main courses 15,000–20,000 lire ($11.80–$15.70). AE, DC, MC, V.
   Open: Lunch Thurs–Tues noon–3pm; dinner Thurs–Tues 7–11pm.

Buzzino is conveniently reached from piazza dei Miracoli (the Square of Miracles, with the Leaning Tower). It slightly resembles a Santa Barbara hacienda, with a clerestory window that filters light down on the interior brick wall and ladderback dining chairs. The waiter will point out specialties on the à la carte menu, among them fresh fish. Although the restaurant resembles "the businessperson's choice," the food is really good. The chef does a nice scaloppine.

EMILIO, via Roma 26–28. Tel. 26028.
   Cuisine: ITALIAN. **Reservations:** Not needed. **Bus:** 1, 3, or 4.
$ Prices: Appetizers 8,000–10,000 lire ($6.30–$7.85); main courses 12,000–14,000 lire ($9.40–$11). AE, DC, MC, V.
   Open: Lunch Tues–Sun 12:30–2:30pm; dinner Tues–Sun 7:30–10pm.

(S) Emilio stands midway between the Arno and the tower. It's convenient for lunch, although dinner is also appetizing. The antipasti buffet is tempting, especially the seafood dishes. The menu features the usual Italian fare, and the food is well prepared and particularly good. With your repast, I suggest a local red wine, Bellavista. The dining room is decorated with a painting collection, and overhead is a pair of glittering globular chandeliers. Fresh flowers are placed on every table.

4. PERUGIA

50 miles SE of Arezzo, 117 miles N of Rome, 96 miles SE of Florence

GETTING THERE   By Train   Perugia enjoys excellent rail connections with central Italy. Daily trains arrive from Rome (trip time: 3 hours), costing 12,200 lire ($9.60) for one-way passage. Daily trains also arrive from Florence (trip time: 2½ hours), costing 9,900 lire ($7.75) for a one-way ticket.

By Bus   Frequent buses arrive from Rome and Florence.

By Car   From either Florence (coming from the north) or Rome (coming from the south) use the A1 autostrada until you reach the junction signposted to Perugia, at which point you head east.

ESSENTIALS   The **telephone area code** is 075. The **Tourist Information Office** is at via IV Novembre no. 3 (tel. 23327).

For one of their greatest cities, the Etruscans chose a setting of remarkable beauty—much like Rome, with a group of hills overlooking the Tiber River Valley. In Perugia we can peel away the epochs. For example, one of the town gates is called the **Arco di Augusto,** or Arch of Augustus. The loggia spanning the arch dates from the Renaissance, but the central part is Roman. Builders from both periods used the reliable Etruscan foundation, which was the work of architects who laid stones to last. Perugia was one of a dozen major cities in the mysterious Etruscan galaxy.

Today the city is the uncrowned capital of Umbria; it has retained much of its Gothic and Renaissance charm, although it has been plagued with wars and swept up in disastrous events. To capture the essence of the Umbrian city, you must head for piazza IV Novembre in the heart of Perugia. During the day the square is overrun, so try to go to the piazza late at night when the old town is sleeping. That's when the ghosts come out to play.

WHAT TO DO & SEE

As the villages of England compete for the title of most picturesque, so the cities of Italy vie for the honor of having the most beautiful square. As you stand on ✪ **piazza IV Novembre,** you'll know that Perugia is among the top contenders for that honor.

In the heart of the piazza is the **Fontana Maggiore** (Grand Fountain), built some time in the late 1270s by a local architect, a monk named Bevignate. The fountain's artistic triumph stems from the sculptural work by Niccolò Pisano and his son, Giovanni. Along the lower basin of the fountain—which is the last major work of the elder Pisano—is statuary that symbolizes the arts and sciences, Aesop's fables, the months of the year, signs of the zodiac, and scenes from the Old Testament and Roman history. On the upper basin (mostly the work of Giovanni) is allegorical sculpture, such as one figure representing Perugia, as well as saints, biblical characters, even local officials of the city in the 13th century.

After viewing the marvels of the fountain, you'll find that most of the other major attractions either open onto piazza IV Novembre or lie only a short distance away.

The exterior of the **Cathedral of San Lorenzo,** piazza IV Novembre, is rather raw-looking, as if the builders were suddenly called away and never returned. The basilica is built in the Gothic style, and dates from the 14th and 15th centuries. Inside, you'll find the *Deposition* of Frederico Barocci. In the museum, Luca Signorelli's *Virgin Enthroned* with saints is displayed. Signorelli was a pupil of della Francesca. It is open daily from 8am to 1pm and 4 to 7:30pm.

On the opposite side of Piazza IV Novembre is the **Palazzo dei Priori (Palace of the Priors),** on corso Vannucci. The town hall, considered one of the finest secular buildings in Italy, dates from the 13th century. Its facade is characterized by a striking row of mullioned windows. Over the main door is a Guelph (member of the papal party) lion and a griffin of Perugia, which hold chains once looted from a defeated Siena. You can walk up the stairway—the Vaccara—to the pulpit. By all means explore the interior, especially the vaulted Hall of the Notaries, frescoed with stories of the Old Testament and from Aesop.

An escalator has been installed to take passengers from the older part of Perugia at the top of the hill and the upper slopes to the lower city. During construction of the escalator the old fortress, **Rocca Paolina,** via Marzia, was rediscovered, along with buried streets. The fortress had been covered over to make the park and viewing area at the end of corso Vannucci in the last century. The old streets and street names have been cleaned up, and the area is well lighted, with an old wall exposed and modern sculpture added. It is open daily from 9am to 1pm and 4 to 7pm. Admission is free. The escalator, with stops at several levels, is a marvel in itself.

GALLERIA NAZIONALE DELL'UMBRIA, upstairs in the Palazzo dei Priori, piazza IV Novembre. Tel. 20316.

⭐ Upstairs in the Palace of the Priors is the National Gallery of Umbria, which houses the most comprehensive collection of Umbrian art from the 13th to the 18th century. Among the earliest paintings of interest is a *Virgin and Child* by Duccio de Buoninsegna, the first important master of the Sienese school. You'll see statuary by the Pisano family, who designed the Grand Fountain out front, and by Arnolfo di Cambio, the architect of the Palazzo Vecchio in Florence.

Tuscan artists are well represented—the pious Fra Angelico's *Virgin and Child* with saints and angels is there, as well as the same subject treated differently by Piero della Francesca and Benozzo Gozzoli.

You'll also see works of native-son Perugino, among them his *Adoration of the Magi*. Perugino, of course, was the master of Raphael. Often accused of sentimentality, Perugino does not enjoy the popularity today that he did at the peak of his career, but he remains a key painter of the Renaissance, who is noted especially for his landscapes.

The gallery also displays art by Pinturicchio, who studied under Perugino, and whose most notable work was the library of the Duomo of Siena. Vasari had few kind words for Pinturicchio: "It seems that fortune's favorites are those who must depend on her alone, unaided by any ability, and of this we have an instance in Pinturicchio of Perugia, whose reputation was far greater than he deserves." In this salon, you can decide for yourself.

Admission: 4,000 lire ($3.15).
Open: Tues–Sat 9am–2pm, Sun 9am–1pm. **Bus:** 26, 27, 29, 32, or 36.

COLLEGIO DEL CAMBIO, corso Vannucci 25. Tel. 61379.

Right off piazza IV Novembre, this medieval exchange building—part of the Palazzo dei Priori—opens onto the main street of Perugia, corso Vannucci (Vannucci was the real name of Perugino). The collegio is visited chiefly by those seeking to view the Hall of the Audience, frescoed by Perugino and his assistants, including a teenage Raphael. On the ceiling Perugino represented the planets allegorically. The Renaissance master peopled his frescoes with the Virtues, sybils, and such biblical figures as Solomon. But his masterpiece is his own countenance. It seems rather ironic that—at least for once—Perugino could be realistic. Another room of interest is the Chapel of S. J. Battista, which contains many frescoes painted by a pupil of Perugino, G. Nicola di Paolo.

Admission: 2,000 lire ($1.55).
Open: Tues–Sat 9am–12:30pm and 2:30–5:30pm, Sun and hols 9am–12:30pm. **Bus:** 26, 27, 29, 32, or 36.

WHERE TO STAY

Suitable accommodations in most price ranges can be found in Perugia. But since the town has so few recommendable hotels, you are always advised to arrive with a reservation.

LOCANDA DELLA POSTA, corso Vannucci 97, 06100 Perugia. Tel. 075/61345. Fax 075/61345. 40 rms (all with bath or shower), 1 suite. A/C MINIBAR TV TEL **Bus:** 26, 27, or 36.

$ Rates (including breakfast): 187,000 lire ($146.80) single; 275,000 lire ($215.90) double; from 425,000 lire ($333.65) suite. AE, DC, MC, V. **Parking:** 20,000 lire ($15.70).

Goethe slept here. So did Hans Christian Andersen. The hotel sits on the main street of the oldest part of Perugia, behind an impressively ornate facade that was originally sculpted in the 1700s. The hotel lies in the center of town, 15 yards from piazza Italia. All buses coming to the center stop at piazza Italia, so it's very convenient if you're depending on public transportation. The hotel, which used to be the only hotel in Perugia, is at the beginning of a pedestrian zone.

HOTEL BRUFANI, piazza Italia 12, 06100 Perugia. Tel. 075/62541. Fax 075/20210. 20 rms (all with bath), 3 suites. A/C MINIBAR TV TEL **Bus:** 33 or 36.
$ Rates: 210,000 lire ($164.85) single; 300,000 lire ($235.50) double; from 400,000 lire ($314) suite. 19% IVA tax extra. Breakfast 15,000 lire ($11.80) extra. AE, DC, MC, V. **Parking:** 20,000 lire ($15.70).

This hotel, at the top of the city, was built by Giacomo Brufani in 1884 on the ruins of the ancient Rocca Paolina. It is placed on a cliff edge of town, only a few yards from the main street of Perugia, corso Vannucci. A view of the Umbrian landscape so beloved by painters is offered in most of the rooms and suites of this five-star hostelry, which was completely renovated in 1984. All rooms are equipped with radio and color TV (with CBS news from the U.S.). The hotel has a good café-restaurant, Mr. Collins (see below), named for the great-grandfather of Mr. Bottelli, who succeeded the original owner, Mr. Brufani, nearly a century ago.

HOTEL LA ROSETTA, piazza Italia 19, 06100 Perugia. Tel. 075/20841. Fax 075/20841. 96 rms (all with bath). TV TEL **Bus:** 26, 27, 32, or 36.
$ Rates: 80,000 lire ($62.80) single; 135,000 lire ($106) double. AE, DC, MC, V. **Parking:** 20,000 lire ($15.70).

Since 1922 when this Perugian landmark was established, it has expanded from a seven-room pensione to a labyrinthine complex. With its frescoed ceiling, Room 55 has been declared a national treasure. (The bullet holes that papal mercenaries shot into the ceiling in 1848 have been artfully preserved.) The other, less grandiose accommodations include decors ranging from slickly contemporary to Victorian to the 1950s era. Each unit is peaceful, clean, and comfortable, regardless of decor. Some units contain minibars. The in-house restaurant is recommended separately (see "Where to Dine," below).

A NEARBY PLACE TO STAY

LE TRE VASELLE, via Garibaldi 48, 06089 Torgiano. Tel. 075/982447. Fax 075/985214. 48 rms (all with bath), 1 suite. A/C MINIBAR TV TEL **Transportation:** Reached by commuter train from Perugia.
$ Rates (including breakfast): 190,000 lire ($149.15) single; 230,000 lire ($180.55) double; from 300,000 lire ($235.50) suite. AE, DC, MC, V. **Parking:** Free.

Some 10 miles from Perugia stands Le Tre Vaselle, which many discriminating guests prefer to make their base for exploring the Umbrian countryside. It stands a 5-minute walk from the train station. Its stucco facade, pierced by arched doorways and shuttered windows, is framed by the greenery of a baroque garden. Inside, the soaring ceilings are capped with hand-hewn timbers or vaulted stonework whose amber-colored reflections highlight the combinations of new and old furniture. Some of the public rooms contain grandly proportioned fireplaces, near which secluded seating areas give guests the chance to relax with a drink. In addition to its up-to-date conference facilities, the establishment contains a modern dining room where regional specialties are carefully prepared. A la carte meals begin at 60,000 lire ($47.10). The cozy bedrooms are comfortable and contemporary, and an occasional antique softens their angular lines. A widely acclaimed wine museum designed to appeal to scholars, wine enthusiasts, and other visitors is on the premises.

WHERE TO DINE

EXPENSIVE

MR. COLLINS, in the Hotel Brufani, piazza Italia 12. Tel. 62541.

Cuisine: UMBRIAN/INTERNATIONAL. **Reservations:** Recommended. **Bus:** 33 or 36.

$ **Prices:** Appetizers 10,000–12,000 lire ($7.85–$9.40); main courses 15,000–20,000 lire ($11.80–$15.70). AE, DC, MC, V.

Open: Daily 12:30–9:30pm.

This is a café-restaurant on the ground floor of the hotel, with a private entrance from piazza Italia. Guests can enjoy an open-air café in front of a small park from May to October. Light snacks are available, and before you go inside, you can study the à la carte menu outside the entrance. You can select anything from a dish of spaghetti to a complete meal of traditional Italian cuisine.

TRATTORIA RICCIOTTO, piazza Dante 19. Tel. 21956.

Cuisine: UMBRIAN. **Reservations:** Recommended.

$ **Prices:** Appetizers 9,000–10,000 lire ($7.05–$7.85); main courses 15,000–18,000 lire ($11.80–$14.15). AE, DC, MC, V.

Open: Lunch Mon–Sat 12:30–2:30pm; dinner Mon–Sat 7:30–10pm. **Closed:** June.

This rustically elegant restaurant is owned and operated by members of the Betti family, who cook, serve the food, uncork the wine, and welcome visitors to Perugia. The restaurant offers a variety of well-prepared specialties. These include, for example, fettuccine with artichokes, a spicy combination of lentils with sausage, suckling pig, baby veal dishes, and a full array of grilled meats and well-prepared vegetables.

MODERATE

IL FAICHETTO, via Bartolo 20. Tel. 61875.

Cuisine: UMBRIAN/ITALIAN. **Reservations:** Not needed. **Bus:** 26, 27, 29, 32, or 36.

$ **Prices:** Appetizers 5,000–10,000 lire ($3.95–$7.85); main courses 9,000–15,000 lire ($7.05–$11.80). AE, DC, MC, V.

Open: Lunch Tues–Sun 12:30–2:30pm; dinner Tues–Sun 7:30–10pm.

Many of the dishes here take traditional themes and have a certain zest that has won critical approval for the medieval-style restaurant the owner works so hard to maintain. Menu items include tagliatelle with truffles, grilled trout, prosciutto several different ways, pasta with chickpeas, and grilled filet of goat. The restaurant is a short walk from piazza Piccinino (where you'll be able to park).

LA ROSETTA, piazza Italia 19. Tel. 20841.

Cuisine: UMBRIAN. **Reservations:** Required, especially in summer. **Bus:** 26, 27, 29, 32, or 36.

$ **Prices:** Appetizers 9,000–10,000 lire ($7.05–$7.85); main courses 9,000–14,000 lire ($7.05–$11). AE, DC, MC, V.

Open: Lunch Tues–Sun 12:30–2:30pm; dinner Tues–Sun 7:30–10pm.

La Rosetta has gained more fame than the hotel in which it's lodged. Food-smart Italian travelers manage to arrive here at mealtime: It's that good and reasonable. You'll find three areas in which to dine: an intimate wood-paneled salon, a main dining area divided by Roman arches and lit by brass chandeliers, and a courtyard enclosed by the walls of the villa-style hotel. Under shady palm trees you can have a leisurely meal. The menu choice is vast, but a few specialties stand out over the rest. To begin, the finest dishes are either spaghetti alla Norcina (with a truffle sauce) or vol-au-vent di tortellini Rosetta. Among the main dishes, the outstanding entry is scaloppine alla Perugina. The vegetable choices are fresh and tasty, and several desserts, such as fresh fruit and ice cream, are the pick of the after-dinner choices.

LA TAVERNA, via delle Streghe 8. Tel. 61028.

Cuisine: UMBRIAN. **Reservations:** Recommended. **Bus:** 26, 27, 29, 32, or 36.

$ Prices: Appetizers 8,000–18,000 lire ($6.30–$14.15); main courses 14,000–20,000 lire ($11–$15.70). AE, DC, MC, V.
Open: Lunch Tues–Sun 12:30–2:30pm; dinner Tues–Sun 7:30–10pm. **Closed:** Jan 16–29 and July 24–31.

The entrance to this provincial tavern is at the bottom of one of the narrowest alleyways in town. Prominent illustrated signs indicate its position off corso Vannucci at the bottom of a flight of steps. You enter a high-ceilinged room filled with overflowing displays of antipasti. Four dining rooms radiate outward from there, each filled with exposed brick and oil paintings. The menu includes arrays of pasta, polentas, soups, and a typical list of fish, meats, and liver.

CAFES

CAFFE DEL CAMBIO, corso Vannucci 29. Tel. 61065.

A local café in Perugia is favored by the town's many university students and stands in the very center. The first room is the most impressive. Capped with a vaulted ceiling, it contains racks of pastries, cases of ice cream, a long stand-up bar, and a handful of tiny tables. The low-ceilinged room in back is smokier, more crowded, and, to some, much livelier. If you stand, a whisky costs 4,000 lire ($3.15); if you sit it's 6,000 lire ($4.70). Open Tuesday through Saturday from 8am to 1am and on Sunday from 9am to 1am.

SANDRI PASTICCERIA, corso Vannucci 32. Tel. 61012.

On the main shopping street of town, Sandri Pasticeria offers drinks, cakes, pastries, sandwiches, and rolls to clients who cluster around the shiny marble-top bar area. If you order Milanese cutlet, Parmesan eggplant, chicken salad, or one of the many other hot or cold dishes, you can perch on a red stool or sit at a small table. Pasta and rice is offered for 7,000 lire ($5.50). Only the finest ingredients are used. You can also buy the city's famous candies and specialties gleaned from many other places displayed on the antique carved wooden shelves. The bar is lit by crystal chandeliers and candles in silver holders. Of course, many patrons come here only for coffee, which costs 1,000 lire (80¢). Open Tuesday through Sunday from 8am to 10pm.

5. ASSISI

110 miles N of Rome, 16 miles E of Perugia

GETTING THERE By Train Assisi lies on the Poligno–Teróntola train line, a 30-minute ride from the terminal at Foligno. The one-way fare from Perugia is 1,800 lire ($1.40). At Teróntola connections are made for Florence and at Poligno for Rome.

By Bus One bus a day arrives from Rome and two from Florence. Local buses also run back and forth between Assisi and Perugia.

By Car From Perugia (see above) continue east on Route 3, continuing east toward Assisi at the junction of Route 147.

ESSENTIALS The **telephone area code** is 075. The **Tourist Information Office** is at piazza del Comune 12 (tel. 812534).

Ideally placed on the rise to Mount Subasio, watched over by the medieval Rocco Maggiore, this purple-fringed Umbrian hill town retains a mystical air. The site of many a pilgrimage, Assisi is forever linked in legend with its native son, St. Francis. The gentle saint founded the Franciscan order and shares honors with St. Catherine of Siena as the patron saint of Italy. But he is remembered by many, even non-Christians, as a lover of nature (his preaching to an audience of birds is one of the legends of his life).

WHAT TO SEE & DO

In addition to the sights listed below, you might also visit the **Church of San Rufino.** Built in the mid-12th century at piazza San Rufino, the Duomo of Assisi is graced with a Romanesque facade, greatly enhanced by rose windows. It's one of the finest churches in the hill towns, as important as the one at Spoleto. Adjoining the cathedral is a bell tower or campanile. Inside, the church has been baroqued, an unfortunate decision that lost the purity that the front suggests. St. Francis and St. Clare were both baptized here. It is open daily from 8am to 1pm and 4 to 8pm.

The **Basilica of Santa Chiara** (Clare), on piazza Santa Chiara (tel. 812282), is dedicated to "the little plant of Blessed Francis," as St. Clare liked to describe herself. Born in 1193 into one of the richest and noblest families of Assisi, Clare was to give all her wealth to the poor and to found, together with St. Francis, the Order of the Poor Clares. She was canonized by Pope Alexander IV in 1255. Pope Pius XII declared her Patroness of Television in 1958. It was decided to entrust to her this new means of social communication on the basis of a vision which she related she had on Christmas Eve of 1252 in which she saw the manger and heard the friars sing in the Basilica of St. Francis while she was bedridden in the Monastery of San Damiano.

The frescoes that once decorated the walls of this basilica were almost completely destroyed by whitewash applied over them in the 18th century. Indeed, only a shortage of funds saved those in the Basilica of St. Francis from a similar fate. In the Chapel of the Crucifix, to the right of the nave, is displayed what is possibly the world's most famous crucifix. According to the testimony of the first biographers of St. Francis, the saint heard a command while in prayer at the foot of this crucifix. "Francis," the voice told him, "go and repair my house, which, as you see, is falling completely into ruin." On the end wall of the same chapel, behind a double grille you may see some of the most important relics extant of St. Clare and St. Francis. A Poor Clare nun of the neighboring Protomonastery of St. Clare offers visitors a brief explanation of them. Downstairs in the crypt, the mortal remains of St. Clare repose on a wooden table inside a simple urn. The church, in Italian Gothic style, built in the 13th century, is characterized by its facade of alternating rose and white decorative stripes.

The closest bus stop to the Basilica of Santa Chiara (Clare) is to be found near Porta Nuova, the eastern gate to the city. The bus in question does not bear a number; it departs from the depot in piazza Matteotti for its first run to the train station at 6:10am and concludes its final run at 9:40pm. Buses arrive at half-hour intervals. Admittance to the basilica is free; however, the custodian turns away visitors in shorts, miniskirts, plunging necklines, and backless attire. It's open November through March, daily from 6am to noon and 1 to 6pm; April through October, daily from 6am to 12:30pm and 2 to 7:15pm.

The **Temple of Minerva** opens onto piazza del Comune, the heart of Assisi. The square is a dream for a lover of architecture from the 12th through the 14th century. A pagan structure, with six Corinthian columns, the Temple of Minerva dates from the 1st century B.C. With Minerva-like wisdom, the people of Assisi let it stand, and turned it into a baroque church inside so as not to offend the devout. Adjoining the temple is the 13th-century Tower of the People, built by Ghibelline supporters.

BASILICA DI SAN FRANCESCO, piazza di San Francesco. Tel. 813098.

⭐ This important church, which consists of both an upper and lower church, houses some of the most important cycles of frescoes in Italy, including works by such pre-Renaissance giants as Cimabue and Giotto. Both churches were built in the first part of the 13th century. The basilica and its paintings form the most significant monument to St. Francis.

Upon entering the upper church through the principal doorway, look to your immediate left to see one of Giotto's most celebrated frescoes, that of St. Francis preaching to the birds. In the nave of the upper church you'll find the rest of the cycle of 27 additional frescoes, some of which are by Giotto, although the authorship of the entire cycle is a subject of controversy. Many of the frescoes are almost surrealistic—in architectural frameworks—like a stage setting that strips away the walls and allows us to see the actors inside. In the cycle we see pictorial evidence of the rise of humanism that lead to Giotto's and Italy's split from the rigidity of Byzantium.

Proceed up the nave to the transept and turn left to find a masterpiece of Cimabue's, the *Crucifixion*. Time has robbed the fresco of its former radiance, but its power and ghostlike drama remain. The cycle of badly damaged frescoes in the transept and apse are other works by Cimabue and his paint-smeared helpers.

From the transept, proceed down the stairs through the two-tiered cloisters to the lower church, which will put you in the south transept. Look for Cimabue's faded but masterly *Virgin and Child* with four angels and St. Francis looking on from the far right. The fresco is badly lit, but is often reproduced in detail as one of Cimabue's greatest works. On the other side of the transept is the *Deposition from the Cross*, a masterpiece by that Sienese artist Pietro Lorenzetti, plus a *Madonna and Child* with St. John and St. Francis (stigmata showing). In a chapel honoring St. Martin of Tours, Simone Martini of Siena painted a cycle of frescoes, with great skill and imagination, which depicts the life and times of that saint. Finally, under the lower church is the crypt of St. Francis.

Admission: Free.
Open: Apr–Oct, daily 8am–7pm; Nov–Mar, daily 8am–noon and 2–6pm.
Bus: 2.

EREMO DELLE CARCERI, via Eremo delle Carceri. Tel. 812301.

The Eremo delle Carceri (Prisons' Hermitage), in a setting 2½ miles east of Assisi (out via Eremo delle Carceri), is from the 14th and 15th centuries. The "prison" is not a penal institution but rather a spiritual retreat. It is believed that St. Francis retired to this spot for meditation and prayer. Out back is a gnarled, moss-covered ilex (or live oak) tree, more than 1,000 years old, where St. Francis is believed to have blessed the birds, after which they are said to have flown in the four major directions of the compass to symbolize that Franciscans, in coming centuries, would spread out from Assisi all over the world. The friary contains some faded frescoes. One of the handful of friars who still inhabit the retreat will show you through. Donations are gratefully accepted to defray the cost of maintenance. In keeping with the Franciscan tradition, the friars at Le Carceri are completely dependent on alms for their support.

Admission: Free (donations accepted).
Open: Daily 6:30am–sunset. **Transportation:** By car, taxi, or foot.

ROCCA MAGGIORE, reached by an unmarked stepped street opposite the basilica.

The Rocca Maggiore (Great Fortress) sits astride a hill overlooking Assisi. It should be visited if for no other reason than for the view of the Umbrian countryside from its ramparts. The present building—now in ruins—dates from the 14th century, and the origins of the structure go back beyond that.

Admission: 3,000 lire ($2.35).
Open: Apr–Oct, daily 9am–noon and 2–6pm.

WHERE TO STAY

Space in Assisi tends to be tight—so reservations are important. Still, for such a small town, Assisi has a good number of accommodations.

HOTEL SUBASIO, via Frate Ella 2, 60081 Assisi. Tel. 075/812206. Fax 075/816691. 70 rms (all with bath), 10 suites. MINIBAR TV TEL **Bus:** 2.

$ Rates (including breakfast): 120,000 lire ($94.20) single; 190,000 lire ($149.15) double; from 300,000 lire ($235.50) suite. AE, DC, MC, V. **Parking:** 20,000 lire ($15.70).

This is a first-class hotel with a decidedly old-fashioned aura. The Subasio has been the unquestioned choice of many a famous visitor—the king and queen of Belgium, the queen of the Netherlands, Charlie Chaplin, Merle Oberon, Marlene Dietrich, and James Stewart. The hotel is linked to the Church of St. Francis by a covered stone arched colonnade, and its dining terrace (with extremely good food) is perhaps the most dramatic in Assisi. Your table will be shaded by a sprawling vine. Dining is also an event on the vaulted medieval loggia. The bedrooms at the front open onto balconies with a good view. The rooms are furnished with Italian flair.

HOTEL GIOTTO, via Fontebella 41, 06082 Assisi. Tel. 075/812732. Fax 075/816479. 70 rms (all with bath), 1 suite. TV TEL **Bus:** 2.

$ Rates (including breakfast): 105,000 lire ($82.45) single; 170,000 lire ($133.45) double; from 285,000 lire ($223.75) suite. AE, DC, MC, V. **Parking:** 15,000 lire ($11.80).

The Hotel Giotto is an up-to-date and well-run hotel, built at the edge of town on several levels. Near the Basilica of St. Francis, and opening onto panoramic views, the Giotto offers little formal gardens and terraces for meals or sunbathing. It has spacious modern public rooms and an elevator, which leads to the well-furnished and comfortable rooms. Bright colors predominate, and there's a Parmeggiani (a modern artist from Bologna) mural over the drinking bar. The hotel is open all year.

UMBRA, via degli Archi 6, 06081 Assisi. Tel. 075/812240. Fax 075/813653. 27 rms (all with bath or shower), 4 suites. TEL **Bus:** 2.

$ Rates (including breakfast): 75,000 lire ($58.90) single; 114,000 lire ($89.50) double; from 159,000 lire ($124.80) suite. AE, DC, MC, V.

Umbra is the most centrally located accommodation in Assisi, in a position right off piazza del Comune with its Temple of Minerva. The outdoor terraced dining room forms an important part of the hotel's entryway. You enter through old stone walls covered with vines and walk under a leafy pergola. The lobby is compact and functional. The bedrooms are efficient, with comfortable beds. Some have a tiny balcony overlooking the crusty old rooftops and the Umbrian countryside; 20 rooms have TV and 17 offer a minibar.

ST. ANTHONY'S GUEST HOUSE, via Galeazzo Alessi 10, 06081 Assisi. Tel. 075/812542. 20 rms (all with bath). **Bus:** 2.

$ Rates (including breakfast): 36,000 lire ($28.25) single; 64,000 lire ($50.25) double. No credit cards.

This special hotel is for those desiring an economical and comfortable accommodation in a medieval villa turned guesthouse. Operated by the Franciscan Sisters of the Atonement (an order that originated in Graymoor, New York), the guesthouse offers the pilgrim/traveler hospitality and a peaceful atmosphere. Located on the upper ledges of Assisi, St. Anthony's Guest House contains its own terraced garden and panoramic view. In all, 35 people can be accommodated. For an additional 16,000 lire ($12.55) a midday meal is served at noon. Meals and companionship are enjoyed in a restored 12th-century dining room. The sisters and their co-workers welcome you, showing you their library with English-language books.

WHERE TO DINE

UMBRA, via degli Archi 6. Tel. 812240.
Cuisine: UMBRIAN. **Reservations:** Recommended. **Bus:** 2.

$ Prices: Appetizers 10,000–13,000 lire ($7.85–$10.20); main courses 15,000–28,000 lire ($11.80–$22). AE, DC, MC, V.

Open: Lunch Wed–Mon noon–2pm; dinner Wed–Mon 7:30–9pm. **Closed:** Jan 15–Mar 15.

The shaded garden of this pleasant restaurant is calm and quiet enough to have pleased St. Francis (well, almost). On a warm day you'll probably hear birds chirping. In the heart of the old city, not far from the basilica, the establishment is the personal statement of the owner and his staff of capable helpers. Umbrian menu items include dishes that range from the fanciful to the classically popular. In any event, ample use is made of truffles. The best cuts of meat are generally used, along with very fresh vegetables.

RISTORANTE BUCA DI SAN FRANCESCO, via Brizi 1. Tel. 812204.

Cuisine: UMBRIAN/ITALIAN. **Reservations:** Recommended. **Bus:** 2.

$ Prices: Appetizers 6,000–9,000 lire ($4.70–$7.05); main courses 8,000–12,000 lire ($6.30–$9.40). AE, DC, MC, V.

Open: Lunch Tues–Sun 12:30–3pm; dinner Tues–Sun 7:30–10pm. **Closed:** July.

This restaurant, set below street level in the basement of an ancient palace, is outfitted with stone walls. The menu changes frequently, according to the availability of ingredients. One of the specialties is spaghetti alla buca, as well as onion soup. Grilled meats are always featured, and sometimes they are served with truffles, which are so popular in the Umbrian countryside.

IL MEDIOEVO, via dell'Arco dei Priori 4. Tel. 813068.

Cuisine: UMBRIAN/INTERNATIONAL. **Reservations:** Required. **Bus:** 2.

$ Prices: Appetizers 7,000–15,000 lire ($5.50–$11.80); main courses 12,000–14,000 lire ($9.40–$11). AE, DC, MC, V.

Open: Lunch Thurs–Tues noon–2:30pm; dinner Thurs–Tues 7:30–9:45pm. **Closed:** July 3–21.

The best place to dine is Il Medioevo, one of the gastronomic staples and architectural oddities of Assisi. The foundations on which the restaurant rests are at least 1,000 years old. During the Middle Ages and again in Renaissance times it was successively enlarged and modified until today it is considered an authentic medieval gem of heavy stonework. Fresh ingredients and skill go into the genuine Umbrian cooking. You might order, for example, roast duck, a fritto misto (mixed fry), several preparations of lamb, and succulent pastas laced with fish and/or vegetables.

LA TAVERNA DELL'ARCO DA BINO, vicolo San Gregorio 8. Tel. 812383.

Cuisine: UMBRIAN. **Reservations:** Required Sat–Sun and hols. **Bus:** 2.

$ Prices: Appetizers 9,000–15,000 lire ($7.05–$11.80); main courses 15,000–20,000 lire ($11.80–$15.70). V.

Open: Lunch Wed–Mon 12:30–2:30pm; dinner Wed–Mon 7:30–9:30pm. **Closed:** Jan 20–30.

Down a walk of old steps, at La Taverna dell'Arco da Bino, you'll find some of the best cuisine to be found outside the hotels. The tavern captures the atmosphere of the 14th century, with original vaulted ceilings and stone walls. In the days of St. Francis, this was the abode of monks. Nowadays it's run by owners known for their good food and wine such as the locally produced Bianco dell'Umbria. Your first plate might be melon and figs. Main dishes include piccione (pigeon), served in a sauce of fresh sage, lemon, capers, olive oil, and black olives, or veal scaloppine in marsala wine. Much of the meat and vegetables come from a farm the family has in the Umbrian countryside. Desserts are homemade and luscious.

6. SPOLETO

80 miles N of Rome, 30 miles S of Assisi

GETTING THERE   By Train   Daily trains arrive from Rome (trip time: 2 hours), with a one-way fare costing 8,700 lire ($6.85). Ten trains arrive from Perugia (trip time: 1 hour), with a one-way fare costing 4,100 lire ($3.20).

By Bus   Spoleto is served by daily buses from Rome. Two buses a day arrive from Perugia and Assisi.

By Car   From Perugia, continue south along Route 3.

ESSENTIALS   The **telephone area code** is 0743. The **Tourist Information Office** is at piazza Libertà 7 (tel. 220311).

SPECIAL EVENTS Dates, programs, and ticket prices change yearly for the Festival dei Due Mondi (Festival of Two Worlds), discussed below. In Spoleto, the general offices of the festival are at piazza del Duomo 7.

Hannibal couldn't conquer it, but Gian-Carlo Menotti did—and how! Before Maestro Menotti put Spoleto on the tourist map, it was known mostly to art lovers, teachers, and students. Today the chic and fashionable, the artistic and arty flood the Umbrian hill town to attend performances of the world-famed **Festival dei Due Mondi (Festival of Two Worlds),** most often held in June and July. Menotti searched and traveled through many hill towns of Tuscany and Umbria before making a final choice. When he saw Spoleto, he fell in love with it. And quite understandably.

Long before Tennessee Williams arrived to première a new play, Thomas Schippers to conduct the opera *Macbeth,* or Shelley Winters to do three one-act plays by Saul Bellow, Spoleto was known to St. Francis and to Lucrezia Borgia (she occupied the 14th-century castle that towers over the town, the Rocca dell'Albornoz). The town is filled with palaces of Spoletan aristocracy, medieval streets, and towers for protection from a time when visitors weren't as friendly as they are today. There are churches, churches, and more churches—some of which, such as **San Gregorio Maggiore,** were built in the Romanesque style in the 11th century.

But the tourist center is **piazza del Duomo,** with its cathedral and **Teatro Caio Melisso (Chamber Theater).** Although a few visitors know it, Mr. Menotti has a small house with a terrace which opens onto the square. The cathedral is a hodgepodge of Romanesque and medieval architecture, with a 12th-century campanile. Its facade is of exceptional beauty, renowned especially for its mosaic by Salsterno. The interior should be visited if for no other reason than to see the cycle of frescoes in the chancel by Filippo Lippi. His son, Filippino, also an artist, designed the tomb for his father. The keeper of the apse will be happy to unlock it for you. These frescoes, believed to have been carried out largely by students, were the elder Lippi's last work; he died in Spoleto in 1469. Vasari writes, "Some said he was poisoned by certain persons related to the object of his love." As friars went in those days, Lippi was a bit of a swinger; he ran off with a nun, Lucrezia Buti, who later posed as the Madonna in several of his paintings.

Spoleto should be visited even when the festival isn't taking place, as it's a most interesting town. It has a number of worthwhile sights, including the remains of a **Roman theater** off piazza della Libertà. Motorists wanting a view can continue up the hill from Spoleto around a winding road (about 5 miles) to **Monteluco,** an ancient spot 2,500 feet above sea level. Monteluco is peppered with summer villas.

WHERE TO STAY

Spoleto offers an attractive range of hotels, but when the "two worlds" crowd in at festival time, the going's rough (last season a group of students bedded down on piazza del Duomo). In an emergency, the tourist office at piazza della Libertà 7 (tel. 0743/220311) can probably arrange for you to stay in a private home—at a moderate price. The office is open only during regular business hours, but it's imperative to telephone in advance for a reservation. Many of the private rooms are often rented well in advance to artists appearing at the festival. Innkeepers are likely to raise all the prices listed below to whatever the market will bear.

GATTAPONE, via del Ponte, 06049 Spoleto. Tel. 0743/36147. Fax 0743/36148. 6 rms (all with bath), 7 suites. MINIBAR TV TEL **Bus:** A, B, or C.
$ Rates: 105,000 lire ($82.45) single; 120,000 lire ($94.20) double; from 180,000 lire ($141.30) suite. Breakfast 15,000 lire ($11.80) extra. AE, DC, MC, V. **Parking:** Free. **Closed:** Nov–Feb.

The Gattapone is more a spectacle than a hotel. Probably the only 13-room hotel in Italy to be rated first class, it's among the clouds, high on a twisting road leading to the ancient castle and the 13th-century Ponte delle Torri, a bridge 250 feet high. The hotel and restaurant occupy two separate stone cottages, which are side by side. The buildings cling closely to the road, and each descends the precipice overlooking the gorge. The hotel's view side is equipped with a two-story picture window and an open spiral stairway which leads from the intimate lounge to the bedrooms. Each of the rooms is individually furnished, with comfortable beds, antiques, and plenty of space.

DEI DUCHI, viale Matteotti 4, 06049 Spoleto. Tel. 0743/44541. 51 rms (all with bath). MINIBAR TV TEL **Bus:** A, B, or C.

$ Rates: 110,000 lire ($86.35) single; 150,000 lire ($117.75) double. Half board 100,000–150,000 lire ($78.50–$117.75) per person. Breakfast 12,000 lire ($9.40) extra. AE, DC, MC, V. **Parking:** Free.

This well-designed, modern hotel is within walking distance of the major sights—yet it perches on a hillside with views and terraces. Near the Roman theater, Dei Duchi is graced with walls of natural brick, open-to-the-view glass, tropical plants, and lounges with modern furnishings and original paintings. Every bedroom has its own balcony, plus brightly colored bed coverings, wood-grained furniture, built-in cupboards—quite a good layout. In high season, half board is required. Half board rates include the room and are obligatory from June 15 to July 20. You have a choice of two dining rooms, each airy, light, and roomy.

CLARICI, piazza della Vittoria 32, 06049 Spoleto. Tel. 0743/46706. Fax 0743/222020. 24 rms (all with bath or shower). A/C MINIBAR TV TEL **Bus:** A, B, or C.

$ Rates: 68,000–70,000 lire ($53.40–$54.95) single; 80,000–95,000 lire ($62.80–$74.60) double. Breakfast 12,000 lire ($9.40) extra. AE, DC, MC, V. **Parking:** Free.

The Clarici is rated only third class, but it's airy and modern. Each accommodation has a private balcony, which opens onto a view. The hotel doesn't emphasize style, but rather the creature comforts: soft low beds, built-in wardrobes, steam heat, an elevator. There's a large terrace for sunbathing or sipping drinks.

HOTEL CHARLESTON, piazza Collicola 10, 06049 Spoleto. Tel. 0743/ 223235. Fax 0743/222010. 18 rms (all with bath or shower). MINIBAR TV TEL **Bus:** A, B, or C.

$ Rates: 70,000 lire ($54.95) single; 95,000 lire ($74.60) double. Breakfast 12,000 lire ($9.40) extra. AE, DC, MC, V.

This tile-roofed, sienna-fronted building was originally built in the 17th century. Today it serves as a pleasantly accessorized hotel, conveniently located in the historic center. Each of the bedrooms has a ceiling accented with beams of honey-colored planking, and comfortable mattresses. On the premises is a sauna, as well as a bar, library, and a sitting room with sofas and a writing table.

WHERE TO DINE

TRIC-TRAC DA GIUSTINO, piazza del Duomo, via dell'Arringo 10. Tel. 44592.

Cuisine: INTERNATIONAL. **Reservations:** Recommended. **Bus:** A, B, or C.

$ Prices: Appetizers 10,000–12,000 lire ($7.85–$9.40); main courses 12,000–18,000 lire ($9.40–$14.15). AE, DC, MC, V.

Open: Thurs–Tues 9am–2am.

This restaurant is frequented by an international clientele at the Festival of Two Worlds. The setting on this landmark square evokes the 16th century. The restaurant as well as Giustino's American Bar is beneath Maestro Menotti's house. The food is well prepared and the service excellent.

IL TARTUFO, piazza Garibaldi 24. Tel. 40236.

Cuisine: UMBRIAN. **Reservations:** Required. **Bus:** A, B, or C.

$ Prices: Appetizers 6,000–16,000 lire ($4.70–$12.55); main courses 20,000–38,000 lire ($15.70–$39.85). AE, DC, MC, V.

Open: Lunch Thurs–Tues 12:30–3pm; dinner Thurs–Tues 7:30–10pm. **Closed:** July 15–Aug 5.

At Il Tartufo, outside the heart of town, near the amphitheater, you may be introduced to the Umbrian tartufo (truffle). This immaculately kept, excellent tavern serves at least nine regional specialties which use the black tartufo of Spoleto. An ever-popular dish—and a good introduction for neophyte palates who may never have tried truffles—is strengozzi al tartufo, a pasta dish with truffles. Alternatively, you may want to start your meal with an omelet—for instance, frittata al tartufo. Main dishes of veal and beef are also excellently prepared. For such a small restaurant, the menu is large.

CHAPTER 10

BOLOGNA & EMILIA-ROMAGNA

- **WHAT'S SPECIAL ABOUT BOLOGNA & EMILIA-ROMAGNA**
1. **BOLOGNA**
2. **FERRARA**
3. **MODENA**
4. **PARMA**
5. **RAVENNA**

L ying in the northern reaches of central Italy, the district of Emilia-Romagna is known for gastronomy and for its art cities, Modena and Parma. Once-great families, including the Renaissance dukes of Ferrara, rose in power and influence, creating courts that attracted painters and poets, notably Tasso and Ariosto.

Bologna, the capital of Emilia, stands at the crossroads between Venice and Florence, and is linked by express highways to Milan and Tuscany. By basing yourself in this ancient university city, you can branch out in all directions: north for 32 miles to Ferrara, southeast for 31 miles to the ceramics-making town of Faenza, northwest for 25 miles to Modena with its Romanesque cathedral, or 34 miles farther northwest to Parma, the legendary capital of the Farnese family duchy in the 16th century. Ravenna, famed for its mosaics, lies 46 miles east of Bologna on the Adriatic Sea.

Most of our sightseeing destinations lie on the ancient Roman road, via Emilia, that began in Rimini and stretched all the way to Piacenza, a Roman colony that often attracted invading barbarians.

This ancient land (known to the Romans as "Æmilia" and to the Etruscans before them) is rich in attractions—the cathedral and baptistery of Parma, for instance—and in scenic beauty (the green plains and the slopes of the Apennines). Emilia is one of the most bountiful farming districts in Italy, and sets a table highly praised in Europe—both for its wines and for its imaginatively prepared pasta dishes.

SEEING BOLOGNA & EMILIA-ROMAGNA

SUGGESTED ITINERARY

There is much to see and do in Emilia-Romagna, but those on the most rushed of schedules confine their visits to the following cities.

Day 1: Spend the entire day in Bologna, sampling its excellent cuisine and viewing its major sights, all in the center.

Day 2: Pay a visit to the city of Ferrara, former seat of the Este dynasty, with many palaces and castles from that era.

Day 3: In Modena, former duchy of the Este family, see its Duomo and Estense Gallery before sampling its regional dishes washed down with Lambrusco.

Day 4: At parma, where you can overnight, visit at least the Duomo and Baptistery before wandering through its National Gallery.

Day 5: After visiting the inland cities, head to the Adriatic Sea in the east and the former imperial city of Ravenna, the Byzantium of the West, for at least an overnight stopover.

WHAT'S SPECIAL ABOUT BOLOGNA & EMILIA-ROMAGNA

Great Towns/Villages

☐ Bologna, gastronomic capital of Italy, a historical city that reached its artistic peak in the 16th century.

☐ Parma, home of Correggio, Il Parmigianino, Bodoni (of type fame), Toscanini, and parmesan cheese.

☐ Ravenna, a city of faded glory, once the capital of the Roman Empire.

Museums

☐ Pinacoteca Nazionale, in Bologna, containing the major works in Bologna from the 14th century to the advent of the baroque.

☐ Galleria Estense, in Modena, with its collection of Emilian works from the 14th through the 18th century.

Religious Shrines

☐ The Duomo at Modena, one of the glories of the Romanesque in northern Italy.

☐ St. Petronius Basilica, in Bologna, launched in 1390, although work was never actually completed.

Ace Attractions

☐ Tomb of Galla Placidia, at Ravenna, offering mosaics famous for their range of coloring, in the oldest structure in Ravenna.

☐ San Domenico, a restaurant in Imola, outside Bologna, considered by many food critics to be the greatest in Italy.

GETTING THERE

The via Emilia, one of the most famous highways of Italy, cuts through the district. Mostly this road is straight and low lying, and it connects all the most interesting towns and cities of the region. The railway, likewise, follows this route, and you can also take private bus services which link all cities, villages, and towns. Bologna is the transportation hub of the region. If you're flying into the region, Bologna is the gateway, with direct flights from many European capitals.

1. BOLOGNA

32 miles S of Ferrara, 59 miles SE of Parma, 94 miles SE of Venice, 227 miles N of Rome

GETTING THERE By Plane The international airport, the **Aeroporto Guglielmo Marconi,** is 4 miles north of the center of town and serviced by such domestic carriers as Aermediterranea and ATI. All the main European airlines have connections through this airport. For information about flights, phone 311578. A frequent bus runs from the airport to the air terminal at the rail station in the center of Bologna.

By Train There is one rail station in Bologna at piazza Medaglie d'Oro (tel. 246490). Trains arrive from Rome every hour (trip time: 3½ hours). Trains arrive from Milan every hour (trip time: 2 hours).

By Bus ATC buses serve the area from their terminal at piazza XX Settembre (tel. 248374 for information). Buses to and from Florence run at the rate of one every hour (trip time: 1½ hours). Buses from Venice also arrive every hour (trip time: 2 hours), and from Milan, also every hour (trip time: 3 hours).

By Car From Florence, continue north along autostrada A1 until you reach the outskirts of Bologna where signs direct you to the center of the city. Coming over the Apennines, the Autostrada del Sole (A1) runs northwest to Milan just before reaching

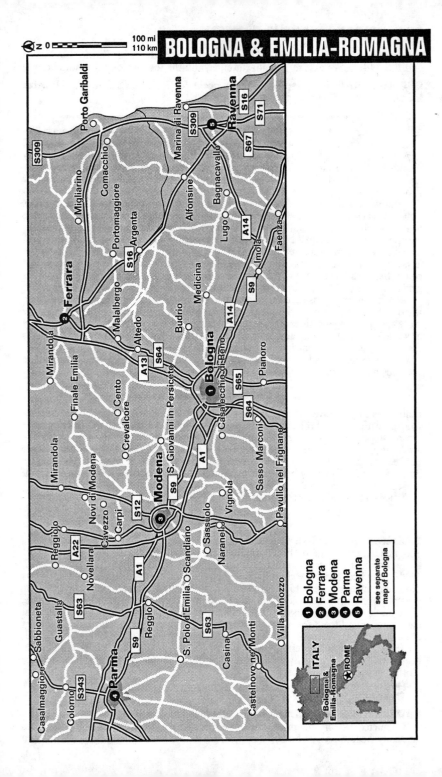

BOLOGNA & EMILIA-ROMAGNA

100 mi
110 km

Porto Garibaldi
Ferrara ❷
Ravenna ❺
Bologna ❶
Modena ❸
Parma ❹

Marina di Ravenna
S16
S71
S309
S67
Bagnacavallo
Alfonsine
Lugo
A14
Faenza
Comacchio
Migliarino
Portomaggiore
Argenta
S16
Medicina
Imola
S9
Malalbergo
Altedo
Budrio
A14
Mirandola
Finale Emilia
Cento
A13
S64
Casalecchio di Reno
Pianoro
S65
S. Giovanni in Persiceto
A1
S64
Mirandola
Crevalcore
Sasso Marconi
Novi di Modena
S9
Sassuolo
Vignola
Pavullo nel Frignano
S12
Carpi
Cavezzo
Reggiolo
A22
Scandiano
Naranel
Novellara
A1
Reggio
S63
S. Polo d'Emilia
S63
Casina
Villa Minozzo
Sabbioneta
Guastalla
Castelnovo ne' Monti
Casalmaggiore
Colorno
S343
S9

see separate
map of Bologna

❶ Bologna
❷ Ferrara
❸ Modena
❹ Parma
❺ Ravenna

ITALY
Bologna &
Emilia-Romagna
★ROME

the outskirts of Bologna. The A13 superhighway cuts northeast to Ferrara and Venice and the A14 dashes east to Rimini, Ravenna, and the towns along the Adriatic.

ESSENTIALS The **telephone area code** for Bologna is 051. The **Tourist Information Office** is at piazza Maggiore 6 (tel. 239660).

The manager of a hotel in Bologna laments: "The Americans! They spend a week in Florence, a week in Venice. Why not 6 days in Florence, 6 days in Venice, and 2 days in Bologna?" That's a good question. Bologna is one of the most sadly overlooked Italian cities—I've found cavernous accommodation space here in July and August, when the hotels in Venice and Florence were packed as tightly as a can of Progresso clam sauce.

"But what is there to see in Bologna?" is also a common question. True, it boasts no Uffizi or Doges' Palace. However, it does offer a beautiful city considered by some to be the most architecturally unified in Europe—a panorama of marbled sidewalks and porticos that, if spread out, would surely stretch all the way to the border.

Filled with sienna-colored buildings, Bologna is the leading city of Emilia. Its rise as a commercial power was almost assured by its strategic location as the geographic center between Florence and Venice. Its university, the oldest in Europe, has for years generated a lively interest in art and culture.

Bologna is also considered the gastronomic capital of Italy. Gourmets flock here just to sample the food—the pasta dishes (tortellini, tagliatelle, lasagne verde), the meat and poultry specialties (zampone, veal cutlet bolognese, tender breasts of turkey in sauce suprême), and, finally, mortadella, the incomparable sausage of Bologna, as distant a cousin to baloney as porterhouse is to the hot dog.

The city seems to take a vacation in August, becoming virtually dead. Everywhere you see the sign proclaiming CHIUSO ("closed").

GETTING AROUND

Bologna is easy to cover on foot, as most of the major sights are in and around piazza Maggiore, the heart of the city. However, if you don't want to walk, **city buses** leave for most points from either piazza Nettuno or piazza Maggiore. Free maps are available at the storefront office of the A.T.C. in the Palazzo del Podesta, right between piazza Nettuno and piazza Maggiore in the heart of town. Tickets can be purchased at one of many booths throughout Bologna. Once on board, however, you must have your ticket validated.

Taxis are on radio call (tel. 534141).

WHAT TO SEE & DO

BASILICA DI SAN PETRONIUS, piazza Maggiore. Tel. 275805.

Sadly, the facade of this enormous Gothic basilica honoring the patron saint of Bologna was never completed. Although the builders went to work in 1390, after 3 centuries the church was still not completed (even though Charles V was crowned emperor here in 1530). However, Jacopo della Quercia of Siena did grace the central door with Renaissance sculpture, which is considered a masterpiece. Inside, the church could accommodate the traffic of Grand Central Terminal. The central nave is separated from the aisles by pilasters shooting upward to the flying arches of the ceiling. Of the 22 art-filled chapels, the most interesting is the Bolognini Chapel, the fourth chapel on the left as you enter. It is embellished with frescoes representing heaven and hell. The purity and simplicity of line represent some of the best of the Gothic in Italy.

Admission: Free.

Open: Daily 7:30am–6:30pm. **Bus:** 25 or 30.

FONTANA DEL NETTUNO, piazza del Nettuno.

Characteristic of the pride and independence of Bologna, this fountain has gradually become a symbol of the city, but it was in fact designed in 1566 by a

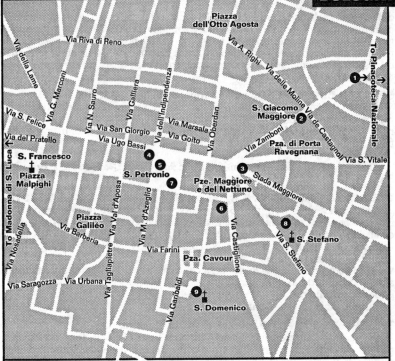

BOLOGNA

Piazza
dell'Otto Agosta

Via Riva di Reno

Via A. Righi — Via delle Moline

Via de Castagnol

To Pinacoteca Nazionale →

Via della Lame

Via G. Marconi

Via N. Sauro

Via Galliera

Via dell'Indipendenza

Via Marsala

Via Oberdan

S. Giacomo
Maggiore ②

① →

Via S. Felice

Via San Giorgio

Via Goito

Via Zamboni

Pza. di Porta
Ravegnana

Via del Pratello

Via Ugo Bassi

To Madonna di S. Luca

✝ S. Francesco
■ Piazza
Malpighi

S. Petronio ④
⑤
⑦

Pze. Maggiore
e del Nettuno

③

Stada Maggiore

Via S. Vitale

⑥

Via Castiglione

⑧
✝ S. Stefano

Via S. Stefano

Via Nosadella

Piazza
Galiléo

Via Barberia

Via Tagliapietre

Via d'Aposa

Via M. d'Azeglio

Via Farini

Pza. Cavour

Via Saragozza

Via Urbana

Via Garibaldi

⑨ ✝
■
S. Domenico

ITALY

Bologna
ROME ✪

Basilica di San Petronius ⑦
Basilica di St. Domenico ⑨
Chiesa di San
  Giacomo Maggiore ②
Fontana del Nettuno ⑤
Leaning Towers ③
Museo Civico Archeologico
Palazzo Communale ④
Pinacoteca Nazionale
  di Bologna ①
Santo Stefano ⑧

Frenchman named Giambologna by the Italians (his fame rests largely on the work he did in Florence). Considered irreverent by some, vulgar by others, and magnificent by more liberal appraisers, this 16th-century fountain depicts Neptune with rippling muscles, a trident in one arm and a heavy foot on the head of a dolphin. Around his feet are four cherubs, also with dolphins. At the base of the fountain nestle four sirens, each spouting five different streams of water from her breasts.
Bus: 25 or 30.

PALAZZO COMUNALE, piazza Maggiore 6. Tel. 203526.

Built in the 14th century, this town hall has seen major restorations, but happily retains its splendor. Enter through the courtyard, then proceed up the steps on the right to the **Comunal Collection of Fine Arts,** which includes many paintings from the 14th- and 19th-century Emilian school.
Admission: Free.
Open: Mon and Wed–Sat 9am–2pm, Sun 9am–1pm. **Closed:** Hols. **Bus:** 25 or 30.

BASILICA DI ST. DOMENICO, piazza San Domenico 13. Tel. 239310.

The basilica dates from the 13th century, but it has seen many alterations and restorations. The church houses the tomb of St. Domenico, in front of the Cappella della Madonna. The sculptured tomb—known as an *arca*—is a Renaissance masterpiece, a joint enterprise of Niccolò Pisano, Guglielmo (a friar), Niccolò dell'Arca, Alfonso Lombardi, and the young Michelangelo. The choir stalls, the second major artistic work in the basilica, were carved by Damiano da Bergamo, another friar, in the 16th century.
Admission: Free.
Open: Daily 7:30am–7pm. **Bus:** 25 or 30.

THE LEANING TOWERS, piazza di Porta Ravegnanna.

These towers keep defying gravity year after year. The Due Torri were built by patricians in the 12th century. In the Middle Ages, Bologna had dozens of these skyscraper towers, anticipating Manhattan by several centuries. They were status symbols: the more powerful the family, the taller the tower. The smaller one, the **Garisenda,** is only 162 feet high, leaning approximately 10½ feet from true perpendicular. The taller one, the **Asinelli** (334 feet high, a walk up nearly 500 steps), inclines almost 7½ feet. Those who scale the Asinelli should be awarded a medal, but instead they're presented with a panoramic view of the tile roofs of Bologna and the hills beyond.
After visiting the towers, take a walk up what must be the most architecturally elegant street in Bologna, strada Maggiore, with its colonnades and mansions.
Admission: 3,000 lire ($2.35).
Open: Daily 9am–6pm. **Bus:** 25 or 30.

SANTO STEFANO, via Santo Stefano. Tel. 223256.

From the leaning towers, head up via Santo Stefano to see a virtual community of churches, linked together like Siamese twins. The first church you enter is the Church of the Crucifix, relatively simple with only one nave and a crypt. It dates from the 11th century. To the left is the entrance to the Church of Santo Sepolcro, its present structure dating principally from the 12th century. Under the altar is the tomb of patron saint Petronius. Continuing left, you enter another rebuilt church, this one honoring Saints Vitale and Agricola. The present building, graced with three apses, also dates from the 11th century. Reentering Sepolcro, take the back entrance this time into the Courtyard of Pilate, onto which several more chapels open. Through the courtyard entrance to the right, proceed into the Romanesque cloisters, dating from the 11th and 12th centuries. The names on the wall of the lapidary honor Bolognese war dead.
Admission: Free.
Open: Daily 7am–noon and 3:30–6pm. **Bus:** 25 or 30.

CHIESA DI SANGIACOMO MAGGIORE, via Zamboni 15. Tel. 225970.

Located on piazza Possini, the Church of St. James was originally a Gothic structure in the 13th century. But, like so many others, it has been altered and restored at the expense of its original design. Still, it is one of Bologna's most interesting churches, filled with art treasures. The Bentivoglio Chapel is the most sacred haunt, even though time has dimmed the luster of its frescoes. Near the altar, seek out a Madonna and Child enthroned, one of the most outstanding works of the artist Francesco Francia. The holy pair are surrounded by angels and saints, as well as a half-naked Sebastian to the right. Nearby is a sepulchre of Antonio Bentivoglio, designed by the Sienese Jacopo della Quercia, who labored so long over the doors to the Basilica of San Petronio. In the Chapel of Santa Cecilia you'll discover important frescoes by Francia and Lorenzo Costa.

Admission: Free.
Open: Daily 7am–noon and 3:30–6:30pm. **Bus:** 14, 25, or 50.

MUSEO CIVICO ARCHEOLOGICO, via dell'Archiginnasio 2. Tel. 233849.

Housed in this museum is one of the major Egyptian collections in Italy, as well as important Etruscan discoveries found in Emilia. As you enter, look to the right in the atrium to see a decapitated marble torso, said to be that of Nero. Upstairs are cases of prehistoric relics, tools, and artifacts. But interest is greater in the Egyptian collection—notably an array of mummies and sarcophagi. The chief attraction among this collection is the cycle of bas-reliefs from Horemheb's tomb. The museum's greatest single treasure is Phidias's head of Athena Lemnia, a copy of a Greek work dating from the 5th century B.C. The relics of the Etruscans comprise the best part of the museum. Look for a highly stylized Askos Benacci, depicting a man on a horse that is perched on yet another animal. Also displayed are an intriguing terra-cotta urn and a vase depicting fighting Greeks and Amazons. A bronze Certosa jar dates from the 6th century B.C.

Admission: 3,000 lire ($2.35) adults, free for children under 18.
Open: Tues–Sat 9am–2pm, Sun 9am–12:30pm **Bus:** 11, 17, or 25.

PINACOTECA NAZIONALE DI BOLOGNA, via Belle Arti 56. Tel. 243222.

The most significant works of the school of painting that flourished in Bologna from the 14th century to the heyday of the baroque have been assembled under one roof in this second-floor pinacoteca. In addition, the gallery houses works by other major Italian artists, such as Raphael's *St. Cecilia in Estasi*. Guido Reni (1575–1642) of Bologna steals the scene with his *St. Sebastian* and his *Pietà*, along with his equally penetrating *St. Andrea Corsini, The Slaying of the Innocents*, and his idealized *Samson the Victorious*. Other Reni works at the National include *The Flagellation of Christ, The Crucifixion*, and his masterpiece—*Ritratto della Madre*—a revealing portrait of his mother that must surely have inspired Whistler. Then, don't miss Vitale de Bologna's (1330–61) rendition of St. George slaying the dragon—a theme in European art that parallels Moby-Dick in America. Also displayed are works by Francesco Francia, and especially noteworthy is a polyptych attributed to Giotto.

Admission: 6,000 lire ($4.70).
Open: Tues–Sat 9am–2pm, Sun 9am–1pm. **Closed:** Hols. **Bus:** 36 or 37.

MUSEO CIVICO MEDIEVALE, via Manzoni 4. Tel. 228912.

Stop in at the 15th-century Palazzo Ghisilardi Fava to see a collection of Gothic sculptures, medieval ivories, glass, and weapons of the Middle Ages, as well as many other artifacts from that era.

Admission: 3,000 lire ($2.35) adults, free for children under 18.
Open: Wed–Mon 9am–2pm, Sun 9am–1pm. **Closed:** Midweek hols. **Bus:** 11, 17, 25, or 27.

WHERE TO STAY
VERY EXPENSIVE

GRAND HOTEL BAGLIONI, via dell'Indipendenza 8, 40122 Bologna. Tel. 051/225445. Fax 055/234840. 125 rms (all with bath), 5 suites. A/C MINIBAR TV TEL **Bus:** 25 or 30.

$ Rates (including breakfast): 310,000 lire ($243.35) single; 465,000 lire ($365) double; from 600,000 lire ($471) suite. AE, DC, MC, V. **Parking:** 30,000 lire ($23.55).

This structure was originally built in the 19th century as the headquarters of a local bishop, the famous and very rich Cardinal Lambertini. It was transformed into a hotel in the early 1900s and thoroughly renovated in the 1980s. Reopened after a decade, it boasts a desirable location in the center of Bologna, near the main square and Neptune's fountain. Its facade is crafted of the same reddish brick that distinguishes many of the city's older buildings. The interior is noted for its wealth of wall and ceiling frescoes, many of which were painted by two of Bologna's most famous 19th-century artists, the Carracci brothers. Each room contains reproductions of antique furniture as well as all the modern conveniences that one would expect in a grand hotel. The suites even have hydromassage in the bathtubs.

Dining/Entertainment: Good-tasting Bolognese cooking is served in the elegant à la carte restaurant, I Carracci. The restaurant—the most fashionable in Bologna—is named after a family of artists who decorated the premises with frescoes depicting the four seasons. It is closed Sunday and in August.

Services: Room service, baby-sitting, laundry, valet.

Facilities: Hairdresser.

ROYAL HOTEL CARLTON, via Montebello 8, 40121 Bologna. Tel. 051/ 249361. Fax 051/249724. 230 rms (all with bath). A/C MINIBAR TV TEL **Bus:** 25 or 30.

$ Rates (including breakfast): 270,000 lire ($211.95) single; 350,000 lire ($274.75) double. AE, DC, MC, V. **Parking:** 13,000–26,000 lire ($10.20–$20.40). **Closed:** Aug.

The Royal Hotel Carlton, only a few minutes' walk from the railway station and many of the national monuments, is L-shaped, rises six stories high, and has a triangular garden. It is in the modern style, with a balcony and picture window for each bedroom. Inside, the decorator infused the establishment with warmth. The large stone-floored lobby contains leather sofas and sculpture, whose futuristic forms increase the impression that this is a stylish hotel well suited for the dozens of businesspeople who stop here on work-related visits to Bologna. The carpeted bedrooms offer all the usual amenities.

Dining/Entertainment: One of the most dramatic staircases in Bologna sweeps from the second floor in an elegant crescent to a point near the comfortable American bar. The grill restaurant serves good food in an ambience of style and comfort.

Services: Room service, baby-sitting, laundry, valet.

Facilities: Limited facilities for the disabled.

EXPENSIVE

INTERNAZIONALE, via dell'Indipendenza 60, 40121 Bologna. Tel. 051/ 245544. Fax 051/249544. 140 rms (all with bath). A/C MINIBAR TV TEL **Bus:** 25 or 30.

$ Rates (including breakfast): 175,000 lire ($137.40) single; 275,000 lire ($215.90) double. AE, DC, MC, V. **Parking:** 16,000–24,000 lire ($12.55–$18.85).

The Internazionale is in a typical classic palace-style building, over an arched sidewalk colonnade, with a contemporary extension. However, its interior has been given the lush Italian-modern look. Lounges are dominated by overscale plastic armchairs and contemporary paintings. All guest rooms have been given that decorator touch. Breakfast is the only meal served.

JOLLY, piazza XX Settembre no. 2, 40121 Bologna. Tel. 051/248921. Fax 051/249764. 176 rms (all with bath), 8 suites. A/C MINIBAR TV TEL **Bus:** 1, 3, 25, 30, or 32.

$ Rates (including breakfast): 200,000 lire ($157) single; 290,000 lire ($227.65) double; from 360,000 lire ($282.60) suite. AE, DC, MC, V.

The Jolly is one of the golden nuggets in this ubiquitous hotel chain. Nicely placed right off piazza Medaglie d'Oro, it avoids much of the deafening noise of the heavy traffic. The guest rooms escape the usual Jolly simplicity; many have mahogany period furniture and Oriental rugs, combined with soft draperies and pastel colors. The drinking lounge, in wood paneling, is a good spot for an apéritif or an after-dinner coffee.

HOTEL MILANO EXCELSIOR, viale Pietramellara 51, 40121 Bologna. Tel. 051/246178. Fax 051/249448. 72 rms (all with bath). A/C MINIBAR TV TEL **Bus:** 25 or 30.
$ Rates: 210,000 lire ($164.85) single; 310,000 lire ($243.35) double. AE, DC, MC, V. **Parking:** 9,000 lire ($7.05).

The Hotel Milano is a first-class hotel near piazza Medaglie d'Oro. It has all the trappings and fringe benefits associated with its class: a private bath in every soundproof room, an American bar, and a restaurant decorated with crystal chandeliers. Frequented largely by a commercial clientele, the Milano Excelsior has a completely modern decor, although a number of its bedrooms have been filled with the traditional designs of the past. The hotel offers excellent service and an unusually attentive staff. The hotel dining room, the Ristorante Felsineo, serves tasty Emilian cookery.

MODERATE

ALEXANDER, viale Pietramellara 47, 40121 Bologna. Tel. 051/247118. Fax 051/249448. 108 rms (all with bath). A/C MINIBAR TV TEL **Bus:** 25 or 30.
$ Rates (including breakfast): 130,000 lire ($102.05) single; 190,000 lire ($149.15) double. AE, DC, MC, V. **Parking:** 9,000 lire ($7.05). **Closed:** Aug.

The Alexander, perhaps the best hotel buy near the main hub of automotive and rail traffic, piazza Medaglie d'Oro, is for the wayfarer who wants maximum comfort at moderate price. Perched near the more expensive Hotel Milano Excelsior, the Alexander tempts with its quite-good bedrooms, which contain brightly painted foyers, compact furnishings, and neat, tidy baths. The thickness of the double glass in the windows helps to blot out street noises. The main lounge is crisply and warmly paneled in wood, with lounge chairs placed on Turkish rugs.

GRAND HOTEL ELITE, via Aurelio Saffi 36, 40131 Bologna. Tel. 051/437417. Fax 051/424968. 86 rms (all with bath), 18 suites. A/C MINIBAR TV TEL **Bus:** 13 or 23.
$ Rates (including breakfast): 178,000 lire ($139.75) single; 242,000 lire ($189.95) double; from 330,000 lire ($259.05) suite. AE, DC, MC, V. **Parking:** 15,000 lire ($11.80). **Closed:** July 25–Aug 25.

The Grand Hotel Elite, on the outskirts of Bologna near Autostrada A1, is highly recommended. It makes a bold architectural and decorative statement, with tastefully applied primary colors contrasting with bone white. Wood paneling creates a warm ambience and the guest rooms are well designed and decorated. Even if you're not staying at the hotel, you may want to patronize the dining room, Cordon Bleu, which features an array of international specialties, plus classic dishes from Emilia. Also popular is an "enoteca" American bar, which has comfortable tufted banquettes.

INEXPENSIVE

REGINA HOTEL, via dell'Indipendenza 51, 40121 Bologna. Tel. 051/248878. Fax 051/224143. 61 rms (all with bath). A/C MINIBAR TV TEL **Bus:** 25 or 30.
$ Rates: 85,000 lire ($66.75) single; 116,000 lire ($91.05) double. Breakfast 15,000 lire ($11.80) extra. AE, DC, MC, V. **Parking:** 30,000 lire ($23.55).

The Regina Hotel has been much improved. It offers attractive rooms and a modern lounge dotted with sofas. The personnel who run the place are helpful, and the maids keep everything clean. The hotel has no restaurant, but there is a pleasant bar. The rooms are small and comfortably furnished. The Regina is located right off piazza dell'Agosto.

TRE VECCHI, via dell'Indipendenza 47, 40121 Bologna. Tel. 051/ 231991. Fax 051/224143. 96 rms (all with bath). A/C MINIBAR TV TEL **Bus:** 25 or 30.

$ Rates: 100,000 lire ($78.50) single; from 150,000 lire ($117.75) double. Breakfast 18,000 lire ($14.15) extra. AE, DC, MC, V. **Parking:** 30,000 lire ($23.55).

The Tre Vecchi is clean and bright, and most of its sections have been recently renovated. It has no restaurant and serves only breakfast, which costs extra. In spite of the location, on a much-traveled street, most of the accommodations are noiseless because of the hotel's isolation. On the floors are several lounges where you can relax and watch television. The hotel lies a 5-minute walk from the railway station, from which many buses depart for the center of the city.

WHERE TO DINE

Even though Bologna is the reigning monarch of Italian cuisine, the city's restaurants do not charge regal prices. And, happily, Bologna—being a university town—has a number of good budget-dining spots catering to a student clientele. I'll begin with the top restaurants, then descend in price.

EXPENSIVE

GRASSILLI, via del Luzzo 3. Tel. 222961.
   Cuisine: BOLOGNESE. **Reservations:** Required. **Bus:** 14, 23, 27, or 45.
$ Prices: Appetizers 15,000–18,000 lire ($11.80–$14.15); main courses 25,000–28,000 lire ($19.65–$22). AE, MC, V.
   Open: Lunch Thurs–Tues 12:30–2:30pm, dinner Thurs–Tues 8–10:15pm.
   Closed: July 15–Aug 15 and Dec 22–Jan 2.

Grassilli is a good bet for conservative regional cooking with few deviations from the time-tested formulas that have made Bolognese cuisine famous. It's located in an ocher building across from an antiques store, on a narrow cobblestone alleyway a short block from the two leaning towers. The restaurant also has a summertime streetside canopy for outdoor dining. At night it can be festive, and your good time will probably be enhanced if you order such specialties as tortellini in a mushroom-cream sauce, the chef's special tournedos, maccheroni with fresh peas and prosciutto, a range of grilled and roasted meats, and many tasty desserts.

RISTORANTE AL PAPPAGALLO, piazza della Mercanzia 3C. Tel. 232807.
   Cuisine: BOLOGNESE. **Reservations:** Required. **Bus:** 25 or 30.
$ Prices: Appetizers 15,000–20,000 lire ($11.80–$15.70); main courses 30,000–32,000 lire ($23.55–$25.10). AE, DC, MC, V.
   Open: Lunch Mon–Sat 12:30–2:30pm; dinner Mon–Sat 8–10:20pm.

This restaurant draws a faithful coterie of gastronomes. Diners have included Einstein, Hitchcock, and Toscanini. It's still going strong, with memories of a glorious past, but competition has long ago buried its former reputation as the finest restaurant in Italy. "The Parrot" is housed on the ground floor of a Gothic mansion, across the street from the landmark 14th-century Merchants' Loggia (a short walk from the leaning towers). Under a beamed ceiling and crystal chandeliers, diners from many lands are introduced to the Bolognese cuisine.

For the best possible introduction, begin your meal with lasagne verde al forno (baked lasagne that gets its green color from minced spinach). And then, for the main course, the specialty of the house: filetti di tacchino, superb turkey breasts baked with white wine, parmigiano cheese, and truffles. With your meal, the restaurant serves the amber-colored Albana wine and the sparkling red Lambrusco, two of the best-known wines from the vineyards of Emilia.

RISTORANTE LE TRE FRECCE, strada Maggiore 19. Tel. 231200.
   Cuisine: BOLOGNESE. **Reservations:** Required. **Bus:** 25 or 30.

$ Prices: Appetizers 12,000–15,000 lire ($9.40–$11.80); main courses 24,000–28,000 lire ($18.85–$22). AE, DC, MC, V.
Open: Lunch Tues–Sun 12:30–2:30pm; dinner Tues–Sat 7:30–10:30pm.
Closed: Aug.

This attractive restaurant, located near the two leaning towers, lies under an arcade of a medieval mansion whose stonework shows the slow weathering of many centuries. The remodeled interior retains its high Gothic ceilings, old portraits, and much of the stonework of the original house. A balcony has been constructed over one of the two rooms for additional seating, and a bar is set on a raised dais with a view over the crowd of contented diners. Service here is excellent, and the menu includes such time-honored favorites as tagliatelle bolognese, green gnocchi with Gorgonzola, salmon with chive sauce, and veal scaloppine with fresh asparagus.

RISTORANTE NOTAI, via dei Pignattari 1. Tel. 228694.
Cuisine: INTERNATIONAL. **Reservations:** Required.
$ Prices: Appetizers 18,000–20,000 lire ($14.15–$15.70); main courses 30,000–35,000 lire ($23.55–$27.50). AE, DC, MC, V.
Open: Lunch Mon–Sat noon–3pm; dinner Mon–Sat 8pm–midnight.

Hidden behind a lattice- and ivy-covered facade next to the cathedral, within view of one of the most beautiful squares in Italy, this popular restaurant draws from a loyal clientele of local residents. In summer sidewalk tables are placed outside. Music lovers and relaxing businesspeople appreciate the upstairs piano bar where low-slung couches and a hi-tech bar blend with posters of Italian and American show-biz types. The decor combines Belle Epoque with Italian flair and includes artwork, hanging Victorian lamps, and clutches of beautifully arranged flowers on each table, all in a subdued color scheme of creams and beiges. The building dates from 1382.

The Notai, owned by a well-known restaurateur and wine expert, Nino Castorina, has been praised by a variety of Italian food critics for having the best food in a town distinguished for its fine restaurants. Specialties include a salad delizia (with scampi, carpaccio, fruit, salad greens, olive oil, lemon, and seasonings), as well as tagliatelle Notai, homemade foie gras, calves' liver Grand Marnier, Florentine beefsteak, and chateaubriand with béarnaise sauce.

TRATTORIA LA BRASERIA, via Testoni 2. Tel. 222839.
Cuisine: BOLOGNESE. **Reservations:** Recommended. **Bus:** 25 or 30.
$ Prices: Appetizers 10,000–12,000 lire ($7.85–$9.40); main courses 25,000–30,000 lire ($19.65–$23.55). AE, DC, V.
Open: Lunch Mon–Sat 12:30–2:30pm; dinner Mon–Sat 7:30–10:30pm.
Closed: Dec 20–Jan 10.

Trattoria La Braseria is a modernized little restaurant with wood paneling and many original paintings. Only a short walk from the basilica, it is often frequented by athletes—footballers, mountain climbers, and swimmers. Typical main dishes include tortellacci al vino rosso (big green ravioli stuffed with meat and served in a red wine sauce), gnocchetti alla monsignore (potato pasta with vegetables and mushrooms), and tagliata di manzu (grilled thin-cut beef with red chicory, artichokes, and truffles, or other ingredients depending on the season). On Thursday and Friday fish is featured.

MODERATE

ANTICA OSTERIA ROMAGNOLA, via Rialto 13. Tel. 263699.
Cuisine: SOUTHERN ITALIAN. **Reservations:** Recommended for dinner. **Bus:** 25 or 30.
$ Prices: Appetizers 8,000–10,000 lire ($6.30–$7.85); main courses 18,000–22,000 lire ($14.15–$17.25). AE, DC, MC, V.
Open: Lunch Wed–Sun 1–2:30pm; dinner Tues–Sun 8–10:30pm. **Closed:** Aug.

In spite of its location in Bologna, this delightful restaurant serves many dishes inspired by recipes from the south. Unusual and well-flavored risottos might launch many a repast. Or you can make a selection of antipasti, as the kitchen puts much effort into a savory selection of dishes. The array of pastas is also impressive, including ravioli with essence of truffles, fusilli with zucchini, or pasta whipped with asparagus tips. You might also select a terrine of ricotta and arugula, the latter considered an aphrodisiac by the ancient Romans. For your main course you might try a springtime specialty of roast goat with artichokes and potatoes or filet mignon prepared with basil.

MONTEGRAPPA DA NELLO, via Montegrappa 2. Tel. 236331.
   Cuisine: BOLOGNESE/INTERNATIONAL. **Reservations:** Recommended for dinner. **Bus:** 25 or 30.
$ **Prices:** Appetizers 10,000–12,000 lire ($7.85–$9.40); main courses 13,000–20,000 lire ($10.20–$15.70). AE, DC, MC, V.
   Open: Lunch Tues–Sun noon–3pm; dinner Tues–Sun 8pm–midnight. **Closed:** July 19–Aug 26.

Montegrappa da Nello has a faithful set of habitués who swear by its pasta dishes. Franco and Ezio Bolini are your hosts, and they insist that all produce be fresh. The restaurant, just a short walk from piazza Maggiore, offers tortellina Montegrappa, a pasta favorite served in a cream-and-meat sauce. The restaurant is also known for its fresh white truffles and mushrooms. You can try these in an unusual salad with porcini, the large wild mushrooms. Another salad I like is made with truffles, mushrooms, parmesan cheese, and artichokes. For a main course, I suggest misto del cuoco—a mixed platter from the chef, featuring a selection of his specialties, including zampone, cotoletta bolognese, and scaloppine with fresh mushrooms.

ROSTERIA DA LUCIANO, via Nazario Sauro 19. Tel. 231249.
   Cuisine: BOLOGNESE. **Reservations:** Recommended. **Bus:** 25 or 30.
$ **Prices:** Appetizers 10,000–15,000 lire ($7.85–$11.80); main courses 15,000–20,000 lire ($11.80–$15.70). AE, DC, MC, V.
   Open: Lunch Thurs–Tues 12:30–2:30pm; dinner Thurs–Mon 7:30–10:30pm. **Closed:** Aug.

Rosteria da Luciano is seriously challenging the competition for supremacy. It serves some of the best food in Bologna. On a side street, within walking distance of the center, it has an art deco style and contains three large rooms with a real Bolognese atmosphere. The front room, opening onto the kitchen, is preferred. As a novelty, there's a see-through window on the street, looking directly into the kitchen.

The chefs not only can't keep any secrets from you, but you get an appetizing preview of what awaits you before you step inside. To begin your gargantuan repast, request the tortellini Petroniani. Well-recommended main dishes include the fritto misto all'Italiana and the scaloppe al cartoccio. A dramatic dessert is crêpes flambés.

INEXPENSIVE

AL CANTUNZIEN, piazza Verdi 4. Tel. 051/238356.
   Cuisine: BOLOGNESE. **Reservations:** Recommended. **Bus:** 25 or 30.
$ **Prices:** Appetizers 8,000–10,000 lire ($6.30–$7.85); main courses 12,000–18,000 lire ($9.40–$14.15). DC, V.
   Open: Lunch Thurs–Tues noon–3pm; dinner Thurs–Tues 7–11pm. **Closed:** July.

⑤ Al Cantunzien occupies a "small corner" on an arcaded piazza with ocher-tinted Renaissance buildings. It faces the Teatro Comunale, 100 yards from the two towers. Behind brass-fitted doors are small and intimate tables set against stucco walls and lots of wood trim.

The chef is especially noted for his many varieties of pasta, including several made with spinach. A local favorite is green noodles al Cantunzian (stuffed with sausages). For a main course, I recommend the cotoletta Eva farcita ("stuffed Eve's rib"), the suprema di pollo (chicken suprême flamed with cognac), followed by a dining oddity, fritto di frutta (a mixed fruit fry). For your wine, I suggest Sangiovese, a dark ruby-red "brut" wine whose name translates as "the blood of Jove."

ROSTARIA ANTICO BRUNETTI, via Canduti di Cefalonia 5. Tel. 234441.
   Cuisine: BOLOGNESE. **Reservations:** Not needed. **Bus:** 25 or 30.

$ Prices: Appetizers 8,000–9,000 lire ($6.30–$7.05); main courses 12,000–13,000 lire ($9.40–$10.20). AE, DC, MC, V.
Open: Lunch Tues–Sun noon–2:30pm; dinner Tues–Sat 7–10:30pm. **Closed:** Aug.

Rostaria Antico Brunetti is sheltered in a 12th-century tower just off piazza Maggiore in the heart of Bologna. The restaurant is reportedly the oldest in town, dating back to 1873. Antico Brunetti has distinguished itself for its gramigna verde alla moda dello chef, green spaghetti with a sauce made with sausage. Other dishes worth trying are the lasagne, a kind of pasta asciutta, made with sheets of green pasta with tomato sauce and cheese inside; and mama's tortellini, those little stuffed squares of dough in a ragoût. With the tortellini, I suggest a bottle of Lambrusco di Sorbara, one of the most straightforward and best-known wines of Italy. It is a brilliant ruby-red and has a natural sparkle. For a main course, I prefer the traditional cotoletta al prosciutto, veal cutlet with a slice of ham and cheese, topped with white truffles. The dessert specialty is chocolate cake.

TRATTORIA DA PIETRO, via Da Falegnami 18A. Tel. 230644.
Cuisine: NORTHERN ITALIAN. **Reservations:** Recommended. **Bus:** 25 or 30.
$ Prices: Appetizers 8,000–10,000 lire ($6.30–$7.85); main courses 12,000–14,000 lire ($9.40–$11). AE, DC, MC, V.
Open: Lunch Tues–Sun noon–2:30pm; dinner Tues–Sat 7:15–10:30pm.
Closed: June 24–July 10.

Trattoria Da Pietro may win you over with its local color, a fit foil for the typical regional dishes served here, including foods from Umbria, Lazio, and Tuscany as well as Bolognese dishes. An elaborate display of foods—fresh strawberries, oranges, sausages, apples, strings of garlic, peppers, green tomatoes, fresh asparagus, cherries—is a Lorelei lure. The lower level has only a few tables. The upper level, by contrast, has several family-style tables, at which you're likely to see a gathering of artists. The English-speaking owner is also likely to say: "Forget about the menu. We'll tell you what we have."

A NEARBY PLACE TO DINE

SAN DOMENICO, via Gaspare Sacchi 1, Imola. Tel. 0542/29000.
Cuisine: ITALIAN. **Reservations:** Essential.
$ Prices: Appetizers 20,000–25,000 lire ($15.70–$19.65); main courses 35,000–40,000 lire ($27.50–$31.40); menu of the day 90,000 lire ($70.65), without wine. AE, DC.
Open: Lunch Tues–Sun 12:30–2:30pm; dinner Tues–Sun 8–10:30pm. **Closed:** First 2 weeks of Jan; July 23–Aug 20.

To an increasing degree, gastronomes from all over Europe and America are traveling to the unlikely village of Imola, which lies 21 miles southeast of Bologna, to savor the cuisine of what some food critics consider the best restaurant in Italy. The restaurant can also be easily reached from Ravenna as well.

The cuisine here is sometimes compared to modern cuisine creations in France. However, owner Gian Luigi Morini claims that his delectable offerings are nothing more than adaptations of festive regional dishes rendered lighter and subtler, then served in more manageable portions. He was born in this rambling stone building whose simple facade faces the courtyard of a neighboring church. For 25 years Signor Morini worked at a local bank, returning home every night to administer his restaurant. Now his establishment is among the primary attractions of Emilia-Romagna.

A tuxedo-clad member of his talented young staff will escort you to a table near the tufted leather banquettes whose dark colors offset the candles, baroque silver, and hanging lamps whose fabric matches that of the tented ceilings. Meals include heavenly concoctions made with the freshest ingredients. You might select goose-liver pâté studded with white truffles, fresh shrimp in a creamy sweet bell-pepper sauce, roast rack of lamb with fresh rosemary, stuffed suprême of chicken wrapped in lettuce leaves, or fresh handmade spaghetti with shellfish. Signor Morini has collected some of the best vintages in Europe for the past 30 years. Men are required to wear a jacket and tie.

2. FERRARA

262 miles N of Rome, 29 miles N of Bologna, 68 miles SW of Venice

GETTING THERE By Train Getting there by train is fast and efficient, as Ferrara lies on the main train line between Bologna and Venice. A total of 33 trains a day pass through here, originating in Bologna. Trip time is 40 minutes, and the cost is 2,900 lire ($2.30) one way. Some 24 trains arrive from Venice (trip time: 1½ hours). A one-way fare is 7,000 lire ($5.50).

By Bus From most destinations, the train is best, but if you're in Modena (see below) you'll find 11 bus departures a day for Ferrara. Trip time is between 1½ and 2 hours, and a one-way ticket costs 4,800 lire ($3.75). In Ferrara, bus information for the surrounding area is available by calling 94178.

By Car From Bologna, take the A13 north. From Venice, take the A4 southwest to Padua and continue along the A13 south until you reach Ferrara.

ESSENTIALS The **telephone area code** for Ferrara is 0532. The **Tourist Information Office** is at piazza Municipale 9 (tel. 209370).

When Papa Borgia, also known as Pope Alexander VI, was shopping around for a third husband for the apple of his eye, darling Lucrezia, his gaze fell on the influential house of Este. From the 13th century, this great Italian family had dominated Ferrara, building up a powerful duchy and a reputation as builders of palaces and patrons of the arts. Alfonso d'Este, son of the shrewd but villainous Ercole I, who was the ruling duke of Ferrara, was an attractive, virile candidate for Lucrezia's much-used hand (her second husband had already been murdered, perhaps by her brother, Cesare, who was the apple of nobody's eye—with the possible exception of Machiavelli).

Although the Este family may have had private reservations (after all, it was common gossip that the pope "knew" his daughter in the biblical sense), they finally consented to the marriage. As the Duchess of Ferrara, a position she held until her death, Lucrezia was to have seven children. But one of her grandchildren, Alfonso II, wasn't as prolific as his forebear, although he had a reputation as a roué. He left the family without a male heir. The greedy eye of Pope Clement VIII took quick action on this, gobbling up the city as his fief in the waning months of the 16th century. The great house of Este went down in history, and Ferrara sadly declined under the papacy.

Incidentally, Alfonso II was a dubious patron of Torquato Tasso (1544–95), author of the epic *Jerusalem Delivered,* a work that was to make him the most celebrated poet of the late Renaissance. The legend of Tasso—who is thought to have been insane, paranoid, or at least tormented—has steadily grown over the centuries. It didn't need any more boosting, but Goethe fanned the legend through the Teutonic lands with his late 18th-century drama *Torquato Tasso.* It is said that Alfonso II at one time made Tasso his prisoner.

Ferrara today is still relatively undiscovered, especially by the globe-trotting North American. The city is richly blessed, with much of its legacy intact. Among the historic treasures remaining are a great cathedral and the Este Castle, along with enough ducal palaces to make for a hysterically frantic day of sightseeing. Its palaces, for the most part, have long been robbed of their lavish furnishings, but the faded frescoes, the paintings not carted off, and the palatial rooms are ghostly reminders of the vicissitudes of power.

WHAT TO SEE & DO

CASTELLO ESTENSE, piazza della Repubblica. Tel. 299279.
A moated, four-towered castle (lit at night), this proud fortress began as a bricklayer's dream near the end of the 14th century, although its face has been lifted and wrenched around for centuries. It was home to the powerful Este family. Here the dukes went about their daily chores: murdering their wives' lovers, beheading or imprisoning potential enemies, whatever. Today it is used for the provincial and prefectural administration offices, and many of its once-lavish rooms may be inspected—notably the Salon of Games, the Room of Games, and the Room of Dawn, as well as a chapel that once belonged to Renata di Francia, daughter of Louis XII.
Admission: 5,000 lire ($3.95).
Open: Tues–Sun 9am–12:30pm and 2:30–5pm. **Bus:** 1, 2, or 9.

IL DUOMO, corso dei Martiri della Libertà. Tel. 32969.
Located only a short stroll from the Este castle, the Duomo weds a delicate Gothic with a more virile Romanesque. The offspring: an exciting marble facade. Behind the cathedral is a typically Renaissance campanile (bell tower). Inside, the massive structure is heavily baroqued, as the artisans of still another era festooned it with trompe l'oeil. The entrance to the **Museo del Duomo** lies to the left of the atrium as you enter. It's worth a visit just to see works by Ferrara's most outstanding painter of the 15th century, Cosmé Tura. Aesthetically controversial, the big attraction here is Tura's St. George slaying the dragon to save a red-stockinged damsel in distress. Opposite is a work by Jacopo della Quercia depicting a sweet, regal Madonna with a pomegranate in one hand and the Child in the other. This is one of della Quercia's first masterpieces. Also from the Renaissance heyday of Ferrara are some bas-reliefs, notably a "Giano bifronte," a mythological figure looking at the past and the future, along with some 16th-century *arazzi,* or tapestries, woven by hand.
Admission: Free.
Open: Apr–Sept, daily 10am–noon and 4–6pm; Oct–Mar, daily 10am–noon and 3–5pm. **Bus:** 1, 2, or 9.

THE SCHIFANOIA PALACE, via Scandiana 23. Tel. 62038.
Housing the **Museo Civico d'Arte Antica,** the first part of the Schifanoia Palace was built in 1385 for Albert V d'Este, and later enlarged by Borso d'Este (1450–71). The museum was founded in 1758 and was transferred to its present site in 1898. The first part of the collection then exhibited, which consisted of coins and medals, was enhanced by donations of archeological finds, antique bronzes, small Renaissance plates and pottery, and other collections.
Art lovers are lured to its Salon of the Months to see the astrological cycle. The humanist Pellegrino Prisciani at court conceived the subjects of the cycle, though Cosmé Tura, the official court painter for the Estes, was probably the organizer of the works. Tura was founder of the Ferrarese School, to which belonged, among others, Ercole de'Roberti and Francesco del Cossa, who painted the March, April, and May scenes. In the wall cycle, which represents the 12 months of the year, each month is subdivided into three horizontal bands: the lower band shows scenes from the daily life of courtiers and people, the middle one the relative sign of the zodiac, and the upper one presents the triumph of the classical divinity for that particular myth. The frescoes form a complex presentation, leading to varying interpretations as to the meaning.
Admission: 5,000 lire ($3.95) adults, free for children under 18.
Open: Daily 9am–7pm. **Closed:** Major hols. **Bus:** 1, 2, or 9.

THE ESTE TOMB, at the Monastery of Corpus Domini, via Pergolato 4. Tel. 207825.
Lucrezia Borgia, the most famous woman of the Renaissance, lies here buried with her secrets. The much-married duchess gave up her wicked ways in Rome when she became the wife of Alfonso I (except for, perhaps, a discreet love affair with the

handsome, romantic Venetian poet Bembo). The woman whose very name has become synonymous with evil lies under a flat slab, a simple tomb. Frankly, it's not much of a sight, but it would be heretical to come all this way and not pay your respects to the seductive enchantress who, dressed in crimson velvet, died on a warm Emilian morning on June 24, 1519, having only days before given birth to a daughter.

Admission: Free (donations accepted).

Open: Mon–Fri 9:30am–noon and 4–5:30pm. **Bus:** 1 or 9.

THE PALACE OF LUDOVIC THE MOOR, via XX Settembre no. 124. Tel. 66299.

This ducal Renaissance palace makes a handsome background for the priceless collection of Etruscan works discovered in the necropolis at Spina (in the environs of Comechio). The **National Archeological Museum,** which is housed in the building, contains the booty unearthed from the Etruscan tomb. Downstairs is a salon with admirable frescoes by Garofalo. In another room are two hand-hewn trees (pirogues) that date from late Roman years. Afterward, you may want to stroll through the gardens behind the palace.

Admission: Free.

Open: Tues–Sun 9am–2pm. **Bus:** 1, 2, or 9.

PALAZZO DEI DIAMANTI, corso Ercole d'Este 21. Tel. 205844.

The Palazzo dei Diamanti, another sparkler to d'Este splendor, is so named because of the diamond-shaped stones on its facade. Of the handful of museums sheltered here, the **National Picture Gallery (Pinacoteca Nazionale)** is the most important, holding the works of the Ferraresi artists—notably the trio of old masters, Tura, del Cossa, and Roberti. The collection covers the chief period of artistic expression in Ferrara from the 14th to the 18th century.

Admission: 6,000 lire ($4.70).

Open: Tues–Sat 9am–2pm, Sun 9am–1pm. **Bus:** 1, 2, or 9.

THE ROMEI HOUSE, via Savonarola 30. Tel. 40341.

This 15th-century palace, Casa Romei, was the property of a rich man, John Romei, a friend and confidant of the fleshy Duke Borso d'Este, who made the Este realm a duchy. John (or Giovanni) was later to marry one of the Este princesses, although we don't know if it was for love or for power or both. In later years, Lucrezia and her gossipy coterie—the ducal carriage drawn by handsome white horses—used to descend upon the Romei house, perhaps to receive Borgia messengers from Rome. The house is near the Este tomb. Its once-elegant furnishings have been carted off, but the chambers—many with terra-cotta fireplaces—remain, and the casa has been filled with frescoes and sculpture.

Admission: 4,000 lire ($3.15).

Open: Tues–Sun 8:30am–2pm. **Bus:** 1, 2, or 9.

LA PALAZZINA MARFISA D'ESTE, corso Giovecca 170. Tel. 36923.

This residence was part of a larger complex of buildings erected for Francesco of Este, and given to his daughter, Marfisa, married in 1578 to Alfonsino of Este and in 1580 to the Marquis Alderano Cybo of Carrara. Legends surrounding this woman, reputedly of exceptional beauty (according to Tasso), have attributed to her a sentimental restlessness, and a house with traps and secrets, inhabited by ghosts. Instead, this was a luxurious noble residence, today no longer connected to the original complex of Este's buildings. The pictorial decorations and floral motifs, together with the hunting scenes in two rooms of the adjoining loggia, are attributed to Ferrarese painters of the late 16th century. Also in the house are exquisite furniture and fittings, a bust of Ercole I by Sperandio of Mantua and numerous paintings.

Admission: 2,000 lire ($1.55).

Open: Mar–Sept, Mon–Sat 9am–12:30pm and 3–6pm, Sun 9am–12:30pm and Oct–Feb, Mon–Sat 9am–12:30pm and 2–5pm, Sun 9am–12:30pm. **Bus:** 1, 2, or 9.

WHERE TO STAY

RIPAGRANDE HOTEL, via Ripagrande 21, 44100 Ferrara. Tel. 0532/

765250. Fax 0532/764377. 20 rms (all with bath), 20 junior suites. A/C MINIBAR TV TEL **Bus:** 1, 2, or 9.
$ Rates (including breakfast): 160,000 lire ($125.60) single; 240,000 lire ($188.40) double; 300,000 lire ($235.50) suite. AE, DC, MC, V. **Parking:** 20,000 lire ($15.70).

The Ripagrande Hotel, one of the most unusual hotels in town, occupies one of the city's Renaissance palaces. Rich coffered ceilings, walls in Ferrarese brickwork, 16th-century columns, and a wide stairway with a floral cast-iron handrail character-ize the broad entrance hall. On the inside are two Renaissance courtyards decorated with columns and capitals. The hotel has 40 rooms, half of which are junior suites equipped with a "cooking corner" and living and sleeping areas connected to an internal stairway. The furnishings are modern and in good taste.

HOTEL-RISTORANTE DUCHESSA ISABELLA, via Palestro 70, 44100 Ferrara. Tel. 0532/202121. Fax 0532/202638. 28 rms (all with bath), 7 suites. A/C MINIBAR TV TEL **Bus:** 1, 2, or 9.
$ Rates (including breakfast): 180,000 lire ($141.30) single; 250,000–300,000 lire ($196.25–$235.50) double; from 457,000 lire ($358.75) suite. AE, DC, MC, V. **Parking:** 15,000 lire ($11.80).

The Hotel-Ristorante Duchessa Isabella is a splendid palace in the heart of the city which has been turned into a five-star hotel with a private garden. Named in honor of Isabella d'Este, the hotel rents sumptuous bedrooms and suites. Rooms, all doubles, aren't numbered but have names instead. Each was individually decorated. Single occupancy of a double room gets a reduced rate (see above).

Dining/Entertainment: The hotel also operates a deluxe restaurant, outfitted with painted wooden ceilings bordered in gold and authentic painted doors from the 15th century. The restaurant has frescoes from the Ferrara school. A selection of Emilia-Romagna specialties is offered. Meals begin at 45,000 lire ($35.35).

Services: A landau, decorated with the image of Isabella d'Este and drawn by a white horse, will take guests on excursions into the historic center; also room service, laundry, valet.

Facilities: Private garden.

ASTRA HOTEL, viale Cavour 55, 44100 Ferrara. Tel. 0532/206088. Fax 0532/47002. 80 rms (all with bath). A/C MINIBAR TV TEL **Bus:** 1, 2, or 9.
$ Rates: 140,000 lire ($109.90) single; 200,000 lire ($157) double. Breakfast 20,000 lire ($15.70) extra. **Parking:** 20,000 lire ($15.70).

The Astra Hotel is one of the most prominent and best-recommended hotels in town. Behind a dignified travertine-and-brick facade, the hotel has a sunny lobby and a conservatively modern interior dotted with comfortable furniture. Bedrooms are clean, comfortable, and well maintained.

HOTEL EUROPA, corso della Giovecca 49, 44100 Ferrara. Tel. 0532/206770. Fax 0532/202638. 45 rms (all with bath). MINIBAR TEL **Bus:** 1, 2, or 9.
$ Rates: 62,000 lire ($48.65) single; 80,000 lire ($62.80) double. Breakfast 15,000 lire ($11.80) extra. AE, DC, MC, V. **Parking:** 15,000 lire ($11.80).

The Hotel Europa is housed in a 17th-century palace said to have been visited by Napoleon, Casanova, and Verdi. It is furnished in part with antiques in the Venetian style and has some old murals. Rooms are comfortably furnished. The hotel also has a solarium.

WHERE TO DINE

BUCA DI SAN DOMENICO, piazza Sacrati 22. Tel. 200018.
Cuisine: INTERNATIONAL/PIZZA. **Reservations:** Required Sat–Sun. **Bus:** 1, 2, or 9.
$ Prices: Appetizers 8,000–9,000 lire ($6.30–$7.05); main courses 15,000–16,000 lire ($11.80–$12.55). DC, V.
Open: Lunch Tues–Sun noon–2:30pm; dinner Tues–Sun 7:30–11pm. **Closed:** Aug.

This restaurant near the Chiesa di San Domenico should have a Neapolitan name, since it specializes in pizza, and serves at least 25 different kinds. You can enjoy your meal against a backdrop of a tavern decor. The soups are good, especially the mushroom and asparagus with fresh vegetables. There is also a wide selection of pasta dishes to begin with, followed by such classic dishes as sole meunière. If you're fond of kidneys, the chef knows how to prepare them in interesting variations. He also serves two types of carpaccio.

GROTTA AZZURRA, piazza Sacrati 43. Tel. 209152.
   Cuisine: NORTHERN ITALIAN. **Reservations:** Required. **Bus:** 3, 6, 9, or 11.
$ **Prices:** Appetizers 7,000–15,000 lire ($5.50–$11.80); main courses 9,500–20,000 lire ($7.45–$15.70). AE, DC, MC, V.
   Open: Lunch Thurs–Tues 12:30–2:30pm; dinner Thurs–Tues 7:30–9:30pm.
   Closed: July.

Behind a classic brick facade on a busy square, Grotta Azzurra seems like a restaurant you might encounter on the sunny isle of Capri, not in Ferrara. However, the cuisine is firmly entrenched in the northern Italian kitchen. It is best to visit in the autumn when favorite dishes include wild boar and pheasant. Usually these dishes are served with the characteristic polenta. Many sausages, served as antipasti, are made with game as well. The chef also prepares esoteric dishes such as a boiled calves' head and tongue. A local favorite is stuffed pork leg, which is also boiled. He's also an expert at grilled meats, especially pork, veal, and beef. If you're rushed, a number of dishes can be prepared in just 15 minutes. You might begin with a tasty helping of creamy lasagne.

LA PROVVIDENZA, corso Ercole 1° d'Este 92. Tel. 205187.
   Cuisine: ITALIAN. **Reservations:** Required. **Bus:** 1, 2, or 9.
$ **Prices:** Appetizers 5,000–12,000 lire ($3.95–$9.40); main courses 10,000–25,000 lire ($7.85–$19.65). AE, DC, MC, V.
   Open: Lunch Tues–Sun noon–2:30pm; dinner Tues–Sun 8–10pm. **Closed:** Aug 14–18.

La Provvidenza stands on the same street as the Palazzo dei Diamanti, a sightseeing attraction already mentioned. It has a farm-style interior, with a little garden where its habitués request tables in fair weather. The antipasti table spread before you is the finest I have seen—or sampled—in Ferrara. It includes fresh anchovies, mozzarella with sweet yellow peppers, fresh asparagus in spring and several kinds of shellfish. Really hearty eaters should order a pasta, such as fettuccine with smoked salmon, before tackling the main course, perhaps perfectly grilled and seasoned veal chops. The dessert choice is wide and luscious. Take a large appetite to this local favorite.

RIPARESTAURANT, via Ripagrande 23. Tel. 765721.
   Cuisine: FERRARESE. **Reservations:** Required. **Bus:** 1, 2, or 9.
$ **Prices:** Appetizers 8,000–15,000 lire ($6.30–$11.80); main courses 9,000–16,000 lire ($7.05–$12.55). AE, DC, MC, V.
   Open: Lunch Tues–Sun 12:30–2:30pm; dinner Tues–Sun 7:30–10pm. **Closed:** July 25–Aug 25.

Riparestaurant is a public room of the previously recommended Ripagrande Hotel, set aside as a restaurant which seats 150 people, double that number when good weather makes it possible to dine in the Renaissance courtyard. In pleasant surroundings diners can taste the Ferrarese cuisine as well as regional and national dishes. Tradition reigns here with the classic Ferrarese bread, the salama da sugo, cappellacci di zucca, and pasticcio di maccheroni. Each dish is accompanied by excellent wines.

3. MODENA

25 miles NW of Bologna, 250 miles N of Rome, 81 miles N of Florence

GETTING THERE   By Train   There are good connections to and from Bologna (one train every 30 minutes). Trip time is 20 minutes, and a one-way fare is 2,000 lire

($1.55). Trains arrive from Parma at the rate of one per hour (trip time: 40 minutes). The one-way fare is 3,500 lire ($2.75).

By Bus The train is better. However, if you're in Ferrara (see above), a local ATCM bus (no. 7) leaves Ferrara for Modena at the rate of one per hour. Trip time is 1 hour, and a one-way fare runs 4,600 lire ($3.60). In Modena, telephone 308800 for bus information, including local connections.

By Car From Bologna, take Autostrada A1 northeast until you see the turnoff for Modena.

ESSENTIALS Modena's **telephone area code** is 059. The **Tourist Information Office** is at via Scudaria 30 (tel. 222482).

After Ferrara fell to Pope Clement VIII, the duchy of the Este family was established at Modena in the closing years of the 16th century. Lying in the Po Valley, the provincial and commercial city possesses a great many art treasures that evoke its more glorious past. And, too, the chefs of Modena enjoy an outstanding reputation in hard-to-please gastronomic circles. Traversed by the ancient Roman road, via Emilia, Modena (pronounced *Mo*-den-ah) is often visited by European art connoisseurs, less frequently by overseas travelers.

Many visitors who care little about antiquities come to Modena just to visit the plants that make the sports cars of Ferrari and Maserati. Ask at the tourist office (see above) for details and a map. Those who can veer from northern Italy's mainline attractions for a few hours will be richly rewarded by a visit to Modena.

WHAT TO SEE & DO

IL DUOMO, via Sant 'Eufemia 6. Tel. 223474.

One of the glories of the Romanesque in northern Italy, the Duomo of Modena was built in a style that will be familiar to those who've been to Lombardy. It was founded in the summer of the closing year of the 11th century, and designed by an architect named Lanfranco, with Viligelmo serving as decorator.

The work was carried out by Campionesi masons from Lake Lugano. The cathedral, consecrated in 1184, was dedicated to St. Geminiano, the patron saint of Modena, a 4th-century Christian and defender of the faith. Towering from the rear is the "Ghirlandina" (so named because of a bronze garland), a 12th- to 14th-century campanile, 285 feet high. Leaning slightly, the bell tower guards the replica of the "Secchia rapita" (stolen bucket), which was garnered as booty from a defeated Bolognese.

The facade of the Duomo features a 13th-century rose window by Anselmo da Campione. It also features Viligelmo's main entryway, with pillars supported by lions, as well as Viligelmo bas-reliefs depicting scenes from Genesis. But don't confine your look to the front. The south door, the so-called Princes' Door, was designed by Viligelmo in the 12th century, and is framed by bas-reliefs that illustrate scenes in the saga of the patron saint. You'll find an outside pulpit from the 15th century, with emblems of Matthew, Mark, Luke, and John.

Inside, there's a vaulted ceiling, and the overall effect is gravely impressive. It was all wisely and prudently restored by the Modenese during the first part of the 20th century, so that its present look resembles the original design. The gallery above the crypt is an outstanding piece of sculpture, supported by four lions. The pulpit, also intriguing, is held up by two hunchbacks. The crypt, where the body of the patron saint was finally taken, is a forest of columns. In it, you'll find Guido Mazzoni's *Holy Family* group in terra-cotta, which was completed in 1480.

After visiting the crypt, head up the stairs on the left, where the custodian (tip expected) will lead you to the **Museum of the Cathedral.** In many ways the most intriguing of the Duomo's art, the metopes displayed here were used to adorn the architecture. Like gargoyles, these profane bas-reliefs are a marvelous change of pace from solemn ecclesiastical art. One, for example, is part bird and part man—with one hoof. But that's not all: He's eating a fish whole.

Admission: Free.
Open: Daily 10am–noon and 3:30–6pm. **Bus:** 7 or 11.

ESTENSE GALLERY AND LIBRARY, Palazzo del Musei, largo Sant'
Agostino 48, off via Emilia. Tel. 235004 for the Estense Gallery, 222145 for
the library.

⭐ The Estense Gallery is noted for its paintings from the Emilian or Bolognese
schools from the 14th to the 18th century. The nucleus of it was created by the
Este family in Ferrara's, and afterward, Modena's heyday as duchies. Some of
the finest work is by Spanish artists, including a miniature triptych by El Greco of
Toledo and a portrait of Francesco I d'Este by Velázquez. Other works of art include
Bernini's bust of Francesco I, plus paintings by Cosmé Tura, Correggio, Veronese,
Tintoretto, Carracci, Reni, and Guercino.

Considered one of the greatest libraries in southern Europe, the **Estense Library**
contains around 500,000 printed works and 13,000 manuscripts. An assortment of
the more interesting volumes are kept under glass for visitors to inspect. Of these, the
most celebrated is the 1,200-page Bible of Borso d'Este, bordered with stunning
miniatures.

Admission: Gallery, 4,000 lire ($3.15) adults, free for children under 18. Library,
free.

Open: Gallery, Tues–Wed and Fri 9am–2pm, Thurs and Sat 9am–7pm, Sun
9am–2pm. Library, Apr–Oct, Mon–Sat 9am–2pm; Nov–Mar, Mon–Fri 9am–8pm,
Sat 9am–2pm. **Bus:** 7 or 11.

WHERE TO STAY

CANALGRANDE HOTEL, corso Canalgrande 6, 41100 Modena. Tel.
059/217160. Fax 059/221674. 74 rms (all with bath), 4 suites. A/C MINIBAR
TV TEL **Bus:** 7 or 11.
$ Rates: 143,000 lire ($112.25) single; 205,000 lire ($160.95) double; from
410,000 lire ($321.85) suite. Breakfast 18,000 lire ($14.15) extra. AE, DC, MC, V.
Parking: 15,000 lire ($11.80).

Located in the old town, the Canalgrande Hotel is housed in a stucco palace. It has
elaborate mosaic floors, voluptuous Victorian-era furniture, intricately carved and
frescoed ceilings, and gilded chandeliers. There's a beautiful garden behind the hotel
whose central flowering tree seems filled with every kind of bird in Modena. Some
visitors might find the monumental oil paintings of the salons too much like a
museum. A tavern lies below the hotel, under the basement's vaulted ceiling.

HOTEL ROMA, via Farini 44, 41100 Modena. Tel. 059/222218. Fax
059/223747. 53 rms (all with bath). MINIBAR TV TEL **Bus:** 7 or 11.
$ Rates: 65,500 lire ($51.40) single; 92,000 lire ($72.20) double. Breakfast 10,000
lire ($7.85) extra. AE, DC, MC, V. **Parking:** 8,000 lire ($6.30).

Ⓢ The Hotel Roma is a buff-and-white neoclassical building about two blocks
from the cathedral. The building dates from the 17th century, when it belonged
to the Duke of Este. It's one of my favorite hotels in its category in Modena,
and is preferred above many others by opera stars who gravitate to Pavarotti's
hometown for concerts and auditions. The windows and doors are soundproof,
presumably so anyone can imitate his or her favorite diva while practicing an aria. The
guest rooms have high ceilings, tasteful colors, and comfortable and attractive
furnishings. The lobby is a long skylit room with an arched ceiling and a bar and a
snack bar at the far end.

WHERE TO DINE

FINI, rua Frati Minori 54. Tel. 214250.
Cuisine: MODENESE/INTERNATIONAL. **Reservations:** Recommended.
Bus: 7 or 11.

$ Prices: Appetizers 12,000–30,000 lire ($9.40–$23.55); main courses 25,000–50,000 lire ($19.65–$39.25). AE, DC, MC, V.

Open: Lunch Wed–Sun 12:30–2:30pm; dinner Wed–Sun 7:30–10pm. **Closed:** July 29–Aug 27.

A visit to this restaurant alone is well worth making the trip to Modena. Proudly maintaining the high reputation of the city's kitchens, Fini is one of the best restaurants you're likely to encounter in Emilia-Romagna. In spite of its modern decor, the restaurant was founded in 1912. This is a favorite restaurant of Pavarotti when he visits Modena.

For an appetizer, try the green lasagne or the tortellini (prepared in six different ways here—for example, with truffles). For a main dish, the gran bollito misto reigns supreme. A king's feast of boiled meats, accompanied by a selection of four different sauces, is wheeled to your table. Included on this board of meats is zampone, the specialty of Modena. As prepared at Fini's, it is stuffed pigs' trotters boiled with beef, a calves' head, ox tongue, chicken, and ham. After all this rich fare, you may settle for the fruit salad for dessert. For wines, Lambrusco is the local choice, and it's superb. The Fini is splashed with Picasso-esque murals and equipped with banquettes.

RISTORANTE DA ENZO, via Coltellini 17. Tel. 225177.

Cuisine: MODENESE. **Reservations:** Recommended. **Bus:** 7 or 11.

$ Prices: Appetizers 8,000–12,000 lire ($6.30–$9.40); main courses 9,000–20,000 lire ($7.05–$15.70). AE, DC, MC, V.

Open: Lunch Wed–Mon 12:30–2:30pm; dinner Wed–Mon 7:30–10pm.

Ristorante Da Enzo is kind to wallets while still alluring to the palate. Four specialties are noteworthy—lasagne verde, tortellini, boiled meats, and zampone. The menu is in English. The restaurant upstairs is closed Tuesday.

---

4. PARMA

284 miles N of Rome, 60 miles SE of Bologna

GETTING THERE   By Train   Parma is conveniently served by the Milan–Bologna rail line, with 20 trains a day arriving from Milan (trip time: 80 minutes). The one-way fare is 7,600 lire ($5.95). From Bologna, 14 trains per day arrive in Parma (trip time: 1 hour). The one-way fare is 5,300 lire ($4.15). There are also seven connections a day from Florence, with a one-way fare of 10,100 lire ($7.95).

By Bus   From major towns or cities in Italy, it's best to go by train because of faster connections. The bus comes into play only if you're planning to visit provincial towns in the Parma area. Information and schedules are available at the terminal at viale Toschi right before the ponte Verdi (tel. 233813).

By Car   From Bologna, head northwest along Autostrada A1.

ESSENTIALS   The **telephone area code** for Parma is 0521. The **Tourist Information Center** is at piazza del Duomo 5 (tel. 234735).

Straddling via Emilia, Parma was the home of Correggio, Il Parmigianino, Bodoni (of type fame), Toscanini, and parmesan cheese. It rose in influence and power in the 16th century as the seat of the Farnese duchy, then in the 18th century came under Bourbon rule. For years Parma has been a favorite of art lovers.

It has also been a mecca for opera lovers such as Verdi, the great Italian composer. Verdi, whose works included *Il Trovatore* and *Aïda,* was born in the small village of Roncole, north of Parma, in 1813. In time, his operas echoed through the opera house, the Teatro Regio, which was ordered constructed by Queen Marie Louise.

Because of Verdi, Parma became a center of music, and even today the opera house is jam-packed in season. It is said that the Teatro Regio is the most "critical Verdi house" in Italy.

WHAT TO SEE & DO
THE TOP ATTRACTIONS

IL DUOMO, piazza del Duomo. Tel. 235886.

✪ Built in the Romanesque style in the 11th century, with 13th-century Lombard lions guarding its main porch, the dusty-pink Duomo stands side by side with a campanile (bell tower)—in the Gothic-Romanesque style—completed in 1294. The facade of the cathedral is highlighted by three open-air loggias. Inside, two darkly elegant aisles flank the central nave. The octagonal cupola was frescoed by the "divine" Correggio. Master of light and color, Correggio (1494–1534) was one of Italy's greatest painters of the High Renaissance. His fresco here, *Assumption of the Virgin*, foreshadows the baroque. The frescoes were painted from 1522 to 1534. In the transept to the right of the main altar is a Romanesque bas-relief, *The Deposition from the Cross* by Benedetto Antelami, which is somber, with each face bathed in tragedy. Made in 1178, the bas-relief is the best-known work of the 12th-century artist, who is considered the most important sculptor of the Romanesque in northern Italy.

Admission: Free.
Open: Daily 7:30am–noon and 3–7pm. **Bus:** 6 or 7.

BAPTISTERY, piazza del Duomo. Tel. 235886.

✪ Among the greatest Romanesque buildings in northern Italy, the Baptistery was the work of Antelami. The project was begun in 1196, although the date of its actual completion is in doubt. Made of salmon-colored marble, it is spanned by four open tiers (the fifth one is closed off). Inside, the Baptistery is richly frescoed with biblical scenes: a *Madonna Enthroned* and a *Crucifixion*. But it is the sculpture by Antelami that forms the most worthy treasure and provides the basis for that artist's claim to enduring fame, especially his portrayal of the "months of the year."

Admission: 3,000 lire ($2.35).
Open: Apr–Jun, daily 9am–noon and 3–6pm; July–Aug, daily 9am–12:30pm and 3:30–7pm; Sept–Mar, Tues–Sun 9am–noon and 3–5pm. **Bus:** 6 or 7.

ABBEY OF ST. JOHN (San Giovanni Evangelista), piazzale San Giovanni. Tel. 39067.

Behind the Duomo is this church of unusual interest. After admiring the baroque front, pass into the interior to see yet another cupola by Correggio. Working from 1520 to 1524, the High Renaissance master depicted the *Vision of San Giovanni*. Vasari liked it so much that he became completely carried away in his praise, suggesting the "impossibility" of an artist's conjuring up such a divine work and marveling that it could actually have been painted "with human hands." Correggio also painted a St. John with pen in hand in the transept (over the doorway to the left of the main altar). Il Parmigianino, the second Parmesan master, also did some frescoes in the chapel at the left of the entrance.

Admission: 3,000 lire ($2.35).
Open: Tues–Sun 9am–7pm. **Bus:** 6 or 7.

ARTURO TOSCANINI'S BIRTHPLACE, via Rodolfo Tanzi 13. Tel. 285499.

This is the house where the great musician and conductor was born in 1867. The Italian orchestral conductor was unquestionably the greatest of the first half of the 20th century, and one of the most astonishing musical interpreters of all time. He spent his childhood and youth in this house, which has been turned into a museum with interesting relics and a record library, containing all the recorded works that he conducted.

Admission: Free.
Open: Mon–Sat 10am–1pm. **Bus:** 1, 7, or 11.

MORE ATTRACTIONS

After viewing Parma's ecclesiastical buildings, you'll find its second batch of attractions conveniently sheltered under one roof at the **Palazzo della Pilotta,** via della Pilotta 5. This palazzo once housed the Farnese family in Parma's heyday as a duchy in the 16th century. Badly damaged by bombs in World War II, it has been restored and turned into a palace of museums.

In addition to the following listings, the **Bodoni Museum** is a collection of graphic arts and rare manuscripts, including a rare edition of Homer's *Iliad.* Also, the **Biblioteca Palatina,** nearby, exhibits works from the fallen House of Bourbon. However, both the museum and library may be closed at the time of your visit; check with the tourist office. Normally, admission is free and operating hours are Monday through Saturday from 9am to noon.

GALLERIA NAZIONALE, in the Palazzo della Pilotta. Tel. 233309.

The most important component of the Palazzo della Pilotta is the National Gallery. Filled with the works of Parmesan artists from the late 15th century to the 19th century—notably paintings by Correggio and Parmigianino—the National Gallery offers a limited but well-chosen selection of art. In one room is an unfinished head of a young woman attributed to da Vinci. Correggio's *Madonna dell Scala* (of the stairs), the remains of a fresco, is also displayed. But his masterpiece—one of the celebrated paintings of northern Italy—is *St. Jerome with the Madonna and Child.* Imbued with a delicate quality, it represents age, youth, love—a gentle ode to tenderness. In the next room is Correggio's *Madonna della Scodella* (with a bowl), with its agonized faces. You'll also see Correggio's *Coronation,* a golden fresco and a work of great beauty, and his less successful *Annunciation.* One of Parmigianino's best-known paintings is here, *St. Catherine's Marriage,* with its rippling movement and subdued colors.

With the same ticket, you're entitled to view **St. Paul's Chamber,** which Correggio frescoed with mythological scenes, including one of Diana. The chamber lies on via Macedonio Melloni. On the same floor as the National Gallery is the **Farnese Theater,** evocative of Palladio's theater at Vicenza. Originally built in 1618, the structure was bombed in 1944 and has been restored.

Admission: 10,000 lire ($7.85) adults, free for children under 18.
Open: Tues–Sat 9am–2pm, Sun 9am–1pm. **Bus:** 1, 7, or 11.

MUSEO ARCHEOLOGICO NAZIONALE, in the Palazzo della Pilotta. Tel. 282787.

This most interesting museum houses Egyptian sarcophagi, Etruscan vases, Roman and Greek-inspired torsos, Bronze Age relics, and its best-known exhibition called "Tabula Alimentaria," a bronze-engraved tablet dating from the reign of Trajan and excavated at Velleia in the province of Piacenza.

Admission: 4,000 lire ($3.15) adults, free for children under 18.
Open: Tues–Sat 9am–2pm, Sun 9am–1pm. **Bus:** 1, 7, or 11.

WHERE TO STAY

The choice of accommodations is limited but adequate.

EXPENSIVE

PALACE HOTEL MARIA LUIGIA, viale Mentana 140, 43100 Parma. Tel. 0521/281032. Fax 0521/231126. 102 rms (all with bath). A/C MINIBAR TV TEL **Bus:** 1, 7, or 11.
$ Rates (including breakfast): 170,000 lire ($133.45) single; 250,000 lire ($196.25) double. AE, DC, MC, V. **Parking:** 16,000 lire ($12.55).

This hotel, located near the station, is a welcome addition to the Parma hotel scene. Bold colors and molded plastic built-ins set the up-to-date mood, and bedrooms are made particularly comfortable by soundproof walls and other amenities. There's a very Italian-looking American bar on the premises. The hotel has one of the best restaurants in Parma, Maxim's, which serves excellent Italian and international specialties daily except Sunday and in August. Dinners range from 45,000 lire ($35.35) and up.

PARK HOTEL STENDHAL, piazzetta Bodoni 3, 43100 Parma. Tel. 0521/ 208057. Fax 0521/285655. 60 rms (all with bath). A/C MINIBAR TV TEL **Bus:** 1, 7, or 11.

$ Rates: 145,000 lire ($113.85) single; 220,000 lire ($172.70) double. Breakfast 15,000 lire ($11.80) extra. AE, DC, MC, V. **Parking:** 13,000 lire ($10.20).

The Park Hotel Stendhal sits on a square near the opera house, a few minutes' walk from many of the city's important sights. The bedrooms are well maintained and furnished with contemporary pieces. There's a traditional American bar and lounge, with comfortable armchairs for before- and after-dinner drinks.

MODERATE

FARNESE INTERNATIONAL, via Reggio 51A, 43100 Parma. Tel. 0521/ 994247. Fax 0521/992317. 76 rms (all with bath). A/C MINIBAR TV TEL **Bus:** 11.

$ Rates (including breakfast): 85,000 lire ($66.75) single; 125,000 lire ($98.15) double. AE, DC, MC, V. **Parking:** Free outdoors, 8,000 lire ($6.30) indoors.

The Farnese International is one of the best choices. The Farnese is located in a quiet area but convenient from the town center, airport, and fairs. Parma specialties are served in the hotel restaurant. Bedrooms are comfortably furnished in Italian marble.

HOTEL BUTTON, strada Vitale 7, 43100 Parma. Tel. 0521/208039. Fax 0521/238783. 41 rms (all with bath). TV TEL **Bus:** 1, 7, or 11.

$ Rates: 62,000 lire ($48.65) single; 95,000 lire ($74.60) double. Breakfast 9,000 lire ($7.05) extra. AE, DC, MC, V.

Closed: July.

The Hotel Button is a local favorite, one of the best bargains in town. This is a family-owned and -run hotel, and you're made to feel welcome. Rooms are simply but comfortably furnished. It stands just off the heartbeat piazza Garibaldi. The hotel doesn't have a restaurant—in Parma this is no problem at all—but will serve you a continental breakfast for an extra charge.

PRINCIPE, via Emilia Est 46, 43100 Parma. Tel. 0521/493847. Fax 0521/242106. 33 rms (all with bath). TV TEL **Bus:** 10.

$ Rates: 62,000 lire ($48.65) single; 92,000 lire ($72.20) double. Breakfast 9,500 lire ($7.45) extra. **Parking:** Free. **Closed:** Aug 4–28.

The Principe is about a 10-minute walk from the center of town and is considered the best bargain hotel in Parma. The place is clean and pleasant, although the front rooms are somewhat noisy. There is frequent bus service from here to the center of Parma and to points of interest. The Principe has a restaurant, which is closed on Sunday from December through March.

WHERE TO DINE

The chefs of Parma are known throughout Italy for the quality of their cuisine. Of course, parmesan cheese has added just the right touch to thousands of Italian dinners, and the word *parmigiana* is quite familiar to American diners.

PARIZZI, strada della Repubblica 71. Tel. 285952.
   Cuisine: PARMIGIANA. **Reservations:** Required. **Bus:** 3, 4, 5, or 8.
$ Prices: Appetizers 8,000–20,000 lire ($6.30–$15.70); main courses 13,000–30,000 lire ($10.20–$23.55). AE, DC, MC, V.
   Open: Lunch Tues–Sun 12:30–2:30pm; dinner Tues–Sat 7:30–10:20pm. **Closed:** July 20–Aug 20.

At Parizzi, under a skylit patio, the people of Parma, known for their exacting tastes and demanding palates, enjoy the rich cuisine for which their town is celebrated. There are those who say that this restaurant serves the best food in town. After you're shown to a table in one of the good-size dining rooms, a trolley cart filled with antipasti is wheeled before you, containing shellfish and salmon among its many delectable offerings. The stuffed vegetables are especially good (try the zucchini). You might begin with the chef's specialty, crêpes alla parmigiana—that is, crêpes stuffed with fontina, Parma ham, and ricotta, or with truffles in September. In May you'll want to try the asparagus fresh from the fields. A good main course is the veal scaloppine with fontina and ham. Desserts include zabaglione laced with marsala.

LA GREPPIA, strada Garibaldi 39. Tel. 233686.
   Cuisine: PARMIGIANA. **Reservations:** Necessary. **Bus:** 3, 4, 5, or 8.
$ Prices: Appetizers 10,000–20,000 lire ($7.85–$15.70); main courses 22,000–24,000 lire ($17.25–$18.85). AE, DC, MC, V.
   Open: Lunch Sat–Wed 12:30–2:30pm; dinner Sat–Wed 7:30–10pm. **Closed:** July and Dec 24–Jan 4.

La Greppia has an unpretentious decor yet it's near the top of every gourmet's list of the finest dining rooms of Parma. Through a plate-glass window at one end of the dining room, you can see the chef at work. My most recent pasta dish came baked with radicchio. Try, if featured in autumn, tortelli stuffed with a spicy pumpkin purée. However, chances are your tortelli will be stuffed with chopped spinach and ricotta, over which a rich butter, a light cream sauce, and, naturally, grated parmesan cheese have been spread. For a main dish, I recently enjoyed the grilled sole, which was excellent, my dining companion preferring thinly sliced raw beef like steak tartare, which the Italians call carpaccio. The tarts made with fresh fruit are succulent desserts. Even better, the chef is known for his compelling chocolate cake, which one reviewer claimed was much better than the famed Sachertorte served at the Hotel Sacher in Vienna.

AL CANON D'OR, via Nazario Sauro 3. Tel. 285234.
   Cuisine: PARMIGIANA. **Reservations:** Needed Sat–Sun. **Bus:** 3, 4, 5, or 8.
$ Prices: Appetizers 9,000–12,000 lire ($7.05–$9.40); main courses 12,000–18,000 lire ($9.40–$14.15). AE, DC, MC, V.
   Open: Lunch Tues–Sun 12:30–2:30pm; dinner Tues–Sun 7:30–10pm. **Closed:** Sat–Sun in July–Aug.

Al Canon d'Or is considerably down the price scale, but known for its quality meals at moderate prices. The owner pays a lot of attention to the food, turning out a worthy cuisine in a city where diners are often hard to please. The menu changes based on the seasons.

5. RAVENNA

46 miles SE of Bologna, 90 miles S of Venice, 227 miles N of Rome

GETTING THERE By Train Ravenna can be visited on a day trip from Bologna as there is frequent service; a one-way fare is 5,300 lire ($4.15). There is also frequent service to Ferrara, costing 4,700 lire ($3.70) for a one-way ticket. At Ferrara, you can make connections to Venice, for 11,000 lire ($8.65) one way.

By Bus Trains are better. Once at Ravenna, however, you'll find both a regional (ATR) system and a municipal (ATM) bus network serving the area. Buses depart from outside the train station. The tourist office (see below) will have bus schedules and more details, depending on where you want to go, or call 35288 for information.

By Car From Bologna, head east along Autostrada A14.

ESSENTIALS Ravenna's **telephone area code** is 0544. The **Tourist Information Center** is at piazza Mameli 4 (tel. 37333).

If Ravenna existed in some remote corner of Italy, chances are it would be overrun by visitors and sprinkled with first-class hotels. But all too often it's relegated to a quick day's jaunt from either Venice or Rimini. Steeped in industry and ravaged by World War II bombings, Ravenna still evokes its illustrious past. But you must follow an inviolable rule: Never decide whether to enter a church just by looking at its exterior.

Like the Alhambra at Granada, many of Ravenna's basilica facades appear unprepossessing, but contain a wealth of Byzantine mosaics inside. Incidentally, the mosaic business—now reactivated—is going strong once more in Ravenna.

Ravenna had the dubious privilege of being the capital of a declining Roman Empire in the West. Flavius Honorius, emperor of the West, moved his court to Milan after the sack of Rome. But, again threatened by barbarian hordes, he set up his capital in Ravenna, near his Adriatic fleet, convenient for a quick getaway should the need arise. The court was graced by the presence of the legendary Galla Placidia, sister of Honorius, who ruled for a time in place of her son, Valentinian III. With the fall of the Roman emperors, Odoacer came to the throne, then the Ostrogothic King Theodoric. King Theodoric converted to Christianity and left many great monuments and reminders of his peaceful reign in Ravenna. He governed for more than 30 years during the late 5th and early 6th centuries. Eventually, Justinian recaptured the city in 539, returning it to the fold of Roman civilization. Ravenna became the outpost of Byzantium in the West. Today, we can explore many of the glories left behind during all these periods.

Ravenna, where Dante Alighieri came to die, is one of Italy's greatest art cities—but different from all the rest. The sea long ago receded and today Ravenna is as landlocked as Pisa. The waters left behind one of the greatest collections of mosaics in the Western world—many created to decorate 5th- and 6th-century basilicas during the flowering of Ravenna's artistic expression within the confines of Byzantine and early Christian art.

WHAT TO SEE & DO

At the tourist office you can purchase a ticket to visit six monuments for a single cost of 7,000 lire ($5.50). These sights include the Battistero Neoniano, Archepiscopal Museum and Church of St. Andrea, Church of San Vitale, Mausoleum of Galla Placidia, the Adrian Baptistery, and Basilica of St. Apollinare Nuovo.

BATTISTERO NEONIANO, piazza del Duomo. Tel. 33696.

The octagonal Baptistery was built in the 5th century. In the center of the cupola is a tablet showing John the Baptist baptizing Christ. The circle around the tablet depicts in mosaics the 12 crown-carrying Apostles, dramatic in deep violet-blues and sparkling golds. The Baptistery originally serviced a cathedral that no longer stands. (The present-day Duomo of Ravenna was built around the mid-18th century and is of little interest except for some unusual pews.) Beside it is a campanile from the 11th century, perhaps earlier.

Admission: 2,000 lire ($1.55).
Open: Daily 9am–7pm. **Bus:** 1 or 11.

ARCHEPISCOPAL MUSEUM AND CHURCH OF ST. ANDREA, piazza Arcivescovado. Tel. 33696.

This twofold attraction is housed in the Archbishop's Palace, which dates mainly from the 6th century. In the museum, the major exhibit is a throne carved out of ivory for Archbishop Maximian, which dates from around the mid-6th century.

In the chapel or oratory dedicated to St. Andrea are brilliant mosaics. Pause a while in the antechamber and look over the entrance for a most intriguing mosaic. Here is an unusual representation of Christ as a warrior, stepping on the head of a lion and a snake. Although haloed, he wears partial armor, evoking "Onward, Christian Soldiers." The chapel—built in the shape of a cross—contains other mosaics that are "angelic," both figuratively and literally. Busts of saints and apostles stare down at you with the ox-eyed look of Byzantine art.

Admission: 3,000 lire ($2.35).
Open: Tues–Sat 9:30am–4:30pm, Sun 9am–1pm. **Bus:** 1 or 11.

CHURCH OF ST. VITALE, via San Vitale. Tel. 33696.

On via San Vitale sits an octagonal domed church that dates from the mid-6th century. Inside, the mosaics—in brilliant greens and golds, lit by poetic light from translucent panels—are among the most celebrated in the Western world. Covering the apse is a mosaic rendition of a clean-shaven Christ, astride the world, flanked by saints and angels. To the right is a mosaic of Empress Theodora and her court, and to the left, the man who married the courtesan-actress, Emperor Justinian, and his entourage. If you can tear yourself away from the mosaics long enough, you might admire the church with its marble decoration. Seven large arches span the temple, but the frescoes of the cupola are unimaginative.

Admission: 3,000 lire ($2.35).
Open: Daily 8:30am–7pm. **Bus:** 1 or 11.

MAUSOLEUM OF GALLA PLACIDIA, via San Vitale. Tel. 33696.

⭐ This 5th-century chapel is so unpretentious that you'll think you're at the wrong place. But inside it contains mosaics of exceptional merit—dripping with antiquity, but not looking it. Translucent panels bring the mosaics alive in all their grace and harmony—rich and vivid with peacock-blue, moss-green, Roman gold, eggplant, and burnt orange. The mosaics in the cupola literally glitter with stars. Popular tradition has it that the cross-shaped structure houses the tomb of Galla Placidia, sister of Honorius, but there is evidence that this claim may be false.

Admission: 3,000 lire ($2.35).
Open: Daily 8:30am–7pm. **Bus:** 1 or 11.

MUSEO NAZIONALE DI RAVENNA, via San Vitale. Tel. 34424.

This museum, adjacent to San Vitale, contains archeological objects from the early Christian and Byzantine periods—icons, fragments of tapestries, medieval armaments and armory, sarcophagi, ivories, ceramics, and bits of broken pieces from the stained-glass windows of St. Vitale.

Admission: 6,000 lire ($4.70) adults, free for children under 18.
Open: Tues–Sat 8:30am–7pm. Sun and hols 8:30am–1:30pm. **Bus:** 1 or 11.

ADRIAN BAPTISTERY, off piazza Ariani. Tel. 33696.

The Baptistery definitely deserves a visit. Dating from the 5th century, the octagonal structure is noted for its mosaics. In the center of the cupola is a portrait of John the Baptist baptizing Christ, and the figure of an old man who represents the Jordan River. Like spokes in a wheel, the 12 Apostles—all haloed—branch out.

Admission: Free.
Open: Spring–fall, daily 9am–7pm; winter 9am–4:30pm. **Bus:** 1 or 11.

BASILICA OF ST. APOLLINARE NUOVO, via di Roma. Tel. 33696.

This church, dating from the 6th century, was founded by Theodoric. In the nave are some of Ravenna's finest mosaics, illustrating the procession of virgins and martyrs, with their typically rounded faces, in brilliant greens, golds, and whites. On the left are 22 haloed virgins, plus the Madonna and her Bambino, as well as three Wise Men and four angels. On the right wall, Christ is depicted seated on his throne with four angels and 26 martyrs carrying crowns. Repetitious in part, the processionals create a stunning effect. At one end of the panel that depicts the martyrs is a representation of the Palace of Theodoric. Supporting the walls are two dozen Corinthian columns. Adjoining the church is an impressive circular campanile (bell tower) of the 10th century.

Admission: 3,000 lire ($2.35).
Open: Spring–fall, daily 9:30am–4:30pm; winter, daily 9:30am–5pm. **Bus:** 1 or 11.

DANTE'S TOMB, via Dante.

The final monument to Dante Alighieri, "the divine poet," isn't much to look at, graced as it is with a bas-relief in marble. But it's a far better resting place than he assigned to some of his fellow Florentines. The author of *The Divine Comedy*, in exile from his hometown of Florence, died in Ravenna on September 14, 1321. To the right of the small temple is a mound of earth in which Dante's urn went "underground" from March 1944 to December 1945—it was feared in Ravenna that his tomb might suffer in the bombings. Near the tomb is the Church of San Francesco, dating from the 5th century, in which the poet's funeral was held.

Admission: Free.
Open: Daily 7am–7pm. **Bus:** 1 or 11.

THEODORIC MAUSOLEUM, via della Industrie. Tel. 34424.

Less than a mile from the above-mentioned attractions, this mausoleum honors Theodoric, king of the Ostrogoths (A.D. 474–526). Although stripped of its art, the two-story tomb, made of Istrian stone, is starkly impressive. In the upper chamber is a porphyry sarcophagus, but the remains of Theodoric have long disappeared, of course.

Admission: 6,000 lire ($4.70) adults, free for children under 18.
Open: Tues–Sun 8:30am–2:30pm. **Bus:** 2 or 22.

BASILICA OF ST. APOLLINARE IN CLASSE, Località Classe. Tel. 527004.

About 3½ miles south of the city (it can be visited on the way to Ravenna if you're heading north from Rimini), this church dates from the 6th century, having been consecrated by Archbishop Maximian. Before the waters receded, Classe was a seaport of Rome's Adriatic fleet. Dedicated to St. Apollinare, the bishop of Ravenna, the early basilica stands side-by-side with a campanile—both symbols of faded glory now resting in a lonely low-lying area. Inside is a central nave flanked by two aisles, the latter containing tombs of ecclesiastical figures in the Ravenna hierarchy. The floor—once carpeted with mosaics—has been rebuilt. Along the central nave are frescoed tablets. Two dozen marble columns line the approach to the apse, where you find the major reason for visiting the basilica. The mosaics are exceptional, rich in gold and turquoise, set against a background of top-heavy birds nesting in shrubbery. St. Apollinaire stands in the center, with a row of lambs on either side lined up as in a processional, the 12 lambs symbolizing the Apostles, of course.

Admission: Free.
Open: Spring–fall, daily 8am–noon and 2–6:30pm; winter, daily 8am–noon and 2–5pm. **Bus:** 4 or 44 from the railroad station (every 30 minutes).

WHERE TO STAY

PARK HOTEL RAVENNA, viale delle Nazioni 181, 48023 Marina di Ravenna. Tel. 0544/531743. Fax 0544/5304030. 144 rms (all with bath), 8 suites. A/C MINIBAR TV TEL **Bus:** A bus bound for Marina di Ravenna leaves from the center of Ravenna every 2 hours.

$ Rates (including breakfast): 140,000 lire ($109.90) single; 205,000 lire ($160.95) double; from 213,000 lire ($167.20) suite. AE, DC, MC, V. **Parking:** Free.

Some visitors prefer a beachside resort after visiting the narrow and crowded streets of Ravenna. The best one in the area is the Park Hotel, located 8 miles from the heart of Ravenna, an oasis with a large swimming pool and many resort activities. Its arching windows are separated from a popular beach by a coppice of evergreens. Inside, public areas range from airy tile-floored lounges to warm re-creations of country taverns. There are two large tennis courts alongside the building.

JOLLY HOTEL, piazza Mameli 1, 48100 Ravenna. Tel. 0544/35762. Fax 0544/39541. 70 rms (all with bath). A/C MINIBAR TV TEL **Bus:** 1 or 11.

$ Rates (including breakfast): 180,000 lire ($141.30) single; 240,000 lire ($188.40) double. AE, DC, MC, V. **Parking:** Free.

This four-story hotel, built in 1950, contains two elevators and a conservative decor that includes a bunkerlike facade, stone floors, and lots of paneling. The Jolly is considered the best hotel in Ravenna, and is usually preferred by traveling business-people. The hotel lies 50 yards from the railway station.

BISANZIO, via Salara 30, 48100 Ravenna. Tel. 0544/27111. Fax 0544/32539. 36 rms (all with bath). A/C MINIBAR TV TEL **Bus:** 1 or 11.

$ Rates (including breakfast): 100,000 lire ($78.50) single; 130,000–170,000 lire ($102.05–$133.45) double. AE, DC, MC, V.

Closed: Jan.

The Bisanzio stands in the heart of town, just a few minutes' walk from many of Ravenna's treasures, such as the Basilica of St. Vitale and the Mausoleum of Galla Placidia. This is a pleasantly coordinated modern hotel with guest rooms that have attractive Italian styling. Wall-to-wall draperies and Oriental carpets brighten the wood paneling. It's ideal for those who want the comfort of a well-organized hotel, with good bedrooms, offering simplicity and compactness. Other amenities include an uncluttered breakfast room with softly draped windows and all the other modern conveniences that travelers have come to expect. Guests also have use of a garden.

HOTEL CENTRALE BYRON, via IV Novembre no. 14, 48100 Ravenna.
 Tel. 0544/22225. 54 rms (all with bath). A/C TV TEL **Bus:** 1 or 11.
$ Rates (including breakfast): 58,000 lire ($45.55) single; 95,000 lire ($74.60) double. AE, DC, MC, V.

The Hotel Centrale Byron is an art deco–inspired hotel a few steps from piazza del Popolo. The lobby is an elegantly simple combination of white marble and brass detailing. The public rooms stretch "railroad style" in a long narrow format past a reception desk, an alcove sitting room, a long hallway, and a combination TV room, bar, and snacking and breakfast-room area. Rooms are simply but comfortably furnished.

WHERE TO DINE

RISTORANTE TRE SPADE, via G. Rasponi 37. Tel. 32382.
 Cuisine: INTERNATIONAL. **Reservations:** Recommended. **Bus:** 1 or 11.
$ Prices: Appetizers 12,000–15,000 lire ($9.40–$11.80); main courses 18,000–20,000 lire ($14.15–$15.70). AE, DC, MC, V.
 Open: Lunch Tues–Sun 12:30–2:30pm; dinner Tues–Sun 7:30–10:30pm.
 Closed: July 21–Aug 31.

Ristorante Tre Spade is an appealing restaurant set behind a rounded set of canopies about a block from piazza del Popolo. You enter a beautifully appointed room with wood detailing, half-paneled walls, lace curtains, a corner bar, and a big antipasti table, along with dozens of culinary accessories and lots of 19th-century military-inspired engravings.

Specialties include an asparagus parfait accompanied by a zesty sauce of bits of green peppers and black olives, and an appetizing assortment of carpaccio (thinly sliced raw meat covered with sliced sheets of parmesan cheese with raw artichoke hearts in olive oil). This might be followed by taglioni with smoked salmon sauce, veal cooked with sage, spaghetti with fruits of the sea (which includes clams in their shells), green gnocchi in Gorgonzola sauce, or roast game in season, plus a good collection of wines. The menu changes frequently, and daily specials are offered according to the market.

BELLA VENEZIA, via IV Novembre. Tel. 22746.
 Cuisine: EMILIA-ROMAGNA. **Reservations:** Required. **Bus:** 1 or 11.
$ Prices: Appetizers 9,000–14,000 lire ($7.05–$11); main courses 18,000–22,000 lire ($14.15–$17.25). AE, DC, MC, V.
 Open: Lunch Mon–Sat noon–2:30pm; dinner Mon–Sat 7–10pm. **Closed:** Dec 22–Jan 22.
Bella Venezia, a few steps from piazza del Popolo, is the kind of well-known restaurant that many of the city's hotel managers recommend to their clients. Located next to the Hotel Centrale Byron, the restaurant offers well-prepared, typically Italian food, which includes a wide range of pasta, vegetable, and meat dishes. Beefsteak Ortolana is a specialty.

RISTORANTE LA GARDELA, via Ponte Marino 3. Tel. 27147.
 Cuisine: EMILIA-ROMAGNA. **Reservations:** Recommended. **Bus:** 1 or 11.
$ Prices: Appetizers 5,000–7,000 lire ($3.95–$5.50); main courses 8,000–12,000 lire ($6.30–$9.40). AE, DC, MC, V.
 Open: Lunch Fri–Wed noon–2pm; dinner Fri–Wed 7:30–9:30pm. **Closed:** Aug 10–25.

Ristorante La Gardela, which is located a few steps from one of Ravenna's most startling leaning towers, is spread out over two levels with paneled walls lined with racks of wine bottles. The waiters bring out an array of typical but savory dishes. These include fried squid, pork liver, veal chops, baked green lasagne, Parma ham, and beefsteak.

SPECIALTY DINING

Ca de Ven is housed in the 16th-century Palazzo Rasponi at via Corrado Ricci, near piazza San Francesco (tel. 30163). It honors the Robin Hood of the region, Passatore. This folk hero of the 19th century was a bearded ferryboat operator whose robbing of the rich to give to the poor was somewhat suspect. Some people said he gave mainly to the poor (but pretty) girls he liked. At any rate, his likeness appears on the neck of the bottles at this wine bar. Food of the region served here includes pizza and the almond cake, marzipane. They don't offer normal meals, but you can order a big crêpe, called a piadina, which is often stuffed with ham like a sandwich, priced at 3,800 lire ($3). A glass of wine costs 1,500 lire ($1.20). The establishment is open Tuesday through Sunday from 10am to 2pm and 5:30 to 10:30pm.

CHAPTER 11

INTRODUCING VENICE

1. ORIENTATION
- **WHAT'S SPECIAL ABOUT VENICE**

2. GETTING AROUND
- **FAST FACTS: VENICE**

3. NETWORKS & RESOURCES

One rainy morning as I was leaving my hotel—a converted palazzo—a decorative stone fell from the lunette, narrowly missing me. For a second it looked as if I was a candidate for the gondola funeral cortège to the island of marble tombs, San Michele. In dismay I looked back at the owner, a woman straight from a Modigliani portrait. From the doorway, she leaned like the Tower of Pisa, mocking the buildings of her city. Throwing up her hands, she sighed: "Venezia, Venezia," then turned and went inside.

Stoically, she had long ago surrendered to the inevitable decay that embraces Venice like moss at the base of the pilings. Venice is a preposterous monument to both the folly and the obstinacy of humankind. It shouldn't exist . . . but it does, much to the delight of thousands upon thousands of tourists, gondoliers, lacemakers, hoteliers, restaurateurs, and glassblowers.

Fleeing the barbarians, centuries ago Venetians left drydock and drifted out to a flotilla of "uninhabitable" islands in the lagoon. Survival was difficult enough, but no Venetian has ever settled for mere survival. The remote ancestors of the present inhabitants created the world's most beautiful city.

However, to your children or their children, Venice may be a legend from the past. It is sinking at a rate of about 2½ inches per decade. It is estimated that one-third of the city's art will have deteriorated hopelessly within the next decade or so if action is not taken to save it. Clearly, Venice is in peril. One headline recently read, "The Enemy's at the Gates."

Working on a campaign to save Venice, John R. McDermott put the case this way: "Venice is under assault by uncontrolled tides, pollution, and old age. Atmospheric acid is eating away its art treasures—stone, bronze, and pigment—and the walls of its buildings are being eroded by floods; industrial waste is polluting its water. Unless these conditions are alleviated and repairs made, some of the loveliest art in the world will be lost forever and eventually the city itself could cease to exist as we know it now."

1. ORIENTATION

ARRIVING

All roads lead not necessarily to Rome, but in this case to the docks on the mainland of Venice. The arrival scene at the unattractive piazzale Roma is filled with nervous expectation, and even the most veteran traveler can become confused. Whether you arrive by train, bus, auto, or airport limousine, there is one common denominator—everyone walks to the nearby docks to select a method of transport to his or her hotel. The cheapest way is by vaporetto, the more expensive by gondola or motor launch (see "Getting Around," below).

If you need help with your luggage to reach a remote accommodation tucked into the inner regions of Venice, the chances are that you'll be dependent on the Venetian

WHAT'S SPECIAL ABOUT VENICE

Museums

☐ Palazzo Ducale, with its Bridge of Sighs, the home of the doges (dukes) who ruled Venice with an iron fist.

☐ Accademia, the definitive treasure trove of Venetian painting from the 13th through the 18th century.

☐ Collezione Peggy Guggenheim, one of Italy's most outstanding modern-art museums created by the late American heiress.

Religious Shrines

☐ Basilica di San Marco, a sumptuous Byzantine confection in the center of Venice with several bulbed domes.

Ace Attractions

☐ Scuola Grande di San Rocco, a vast monument to the work of Tintoretto, the largest collection anywhere.

☐ A gondola ride, symbol of romance and passion—something to try at least once in a lifetime.

Shopping

☐ Venetian glass—known around the world, it's sold on virtually every street or you can buy it on the island of Murano where it's made.

Cool for Kids

☐ Many kids consider "fantasy, fairytale" Venice an Italian extension of Disneyland—and they love those boat rides across the canals.

Events/Festivals

☐ The Carnevale, during the week and a half before Ash Wednesday, a bacchanalian affair when revelers take over the streets.

☐ Venice International Film Festival, in August, second in Europe after the French Riviera's fête at Cannes.

Beaches

☐ The Lido, the most fashionable beachfront in Italy, former stamping ground of everybody from Goethe to Byron to Thomas Mann.

---

porter. The porter can carry your luggage aboard the vaporetto or water taxi (you pay his boat fare), then lead you through the winding narrow streets until he reaches your hotel. In this capacity, he'll double as a guide, eliminating the need to pore over tiny lettering on a map. Some porters, if business is good, will refuse to perform this time-consuming service.

Between two points in the city, give the porter 8,500 lire ($6.65) for one or two pieces of luggage and 2,500 lire ($1.95) for each additional piece. If your hotel lies near one of the public vaporetto stops, you can sometimes struggle with your own luggage until you reach the hostelry's reception area. In any event, the one time-tested rule for Venice-bound travelers is that excess baggage is bad news, unless you're willing to pay dearly to have it carried for you.

The rates stated here are the official fees for porters, but they are valid only at the time of this writing and will surely go up in the lifetime of this edition. If, however, a porter thinks you're unaware of the city's official guidelines, he may try to charge you more—sometimes *much* more. Protests mean little to these battle-toughened veterans who have stood off the most robust of visitors in sirocco winds under the blazing August sun.

BY PLANE You can now fly from North America to Venice via Rome on Alitalia. You'll land at Mestre, with its **Marco Polo Aeroporto.** Boats depart directly from the airport, taking visitors to a terminal near piazza San Marco.

It's less expensive to take a bus from the airport, a trip of less than 5 miles. Cross the Ponte della Libertà to the Stazione di Santa Lucia, the railway station of Venice. You will be at piazzale Roma, where you can make transportation connections to most parts of Venice, including the Lido. It is at this point that first-time visitors encounter the Canal Grande or Grand Canal, a channel leading to the Canale di San Marco, which itself heads directly to the Adriatic.

If you need to find out about flight arrivals or departures at Marco Polo Airport, call 661111.

BY TRAIN Trains pull into the **Stazione di Santa Lucia,** at piazzale Roma. Travel time by train from Milan is 3½ hours; from Florence, 4 hours; and from Bologna, 2 hours. For information about rail connections, dial 715555. The best way—and the least expensive way—to get from the station to the rest of town is to take a vaporetto (see below), which departs near the main entrance to the station.

BY BUS Buses arrive from the points on the mainland of Italy at piazzale Roma. For information about schedules, call the office of ACTV at piazzale Roma (tel. 528-7886). If you're coming from a distant city in Italy, it's better to take the train. But Venice has good bus connections with such nearby cities as Padua. A one-way fare from Venice to Padua (or vice versa) is 3,200 lire ($2.50). After disembarking from the bus in Venice the nearby vaporetto is the cheapest method of reaching the heart of Venice.

BY CAR Venice has autostrada links with the rest of Italy, with direct routes from such cities as Trieste (driving time: 1½ hours); Milan (driving time: 3 hours), and Bologna (driving time: 2 hours). Bologna is 94 miles southwest of Venice; Milan, 165 miles west of Venice; and Trieste, 97 miles to the east. Rome is a distance of 327 miles to the southwest.

If you arrive in Venice by auto, there are multitiered parking areas, **Garage San Marco,** piazzale Roma (tel. 522-8640), near the vaporetto, gondola, and motor-launch docks. You'll be charged 20,000 lire to 32,000 lire ($15.70 to $25.10) per day, depending on the size of your car. However, I must warn you that from spring to fall this municipal car park is nearly always filled, and often people have to park great distances away at Mestre. However, there is one method that always seems to work, even when the dispatchers assure you that there is "not one spot left." Offer a bribe! It usually helps get you parked. Hours are daily from 9am to 8:30pm.

TOURIST INFORMATION

Visitors can get information at the **Ente Provinciale per il Turismo,** piazza San Marco 71C (tel. 522-6356). It's open Monday through Saturday from 9am to 2pm.

CITY LAYOUT

MAIN ARTERIES AND STREETS Venice, lying 2½ miles from the Italian mainland and 1¼ miles from the open seas of the Adriatic, is an archipelago of some 117 islands. Most visitors, however, concern themselves only with piazza San Marco and its vicinity. In fact, the entire city has only one "piazza," which is San Marco. Venice is divided into six quarters which local residents call **sestieri.** These include the most frequented, San Marco, but also Santa Croce, San Paolo, Castello, Cannaregio, and Dorsoduro, the last of which has been compared to New York's Greenwich Village.

Many of the so-called streets of Venice are actually **canals,** 150 in all. A canal is called a *rio,* and a total of 400 bridges span these canals. If Venice has a main street, it is the **Grand Canal,** which is spanned by three bridges: the Rialto, the Academy Bridge, and the stone Railway Bridge (the last dates from the 20th century). The canal splits Venice into two unequal parts.

Get used to a lot of unfamiliar street designations. A street running alongside a canal is called a *fondamenta,* and major thoroughfares are known as *salizzada, ruga,* or a *calle larga.* But what is a *sottoportego?* That's a passageway beneath buildings. You'll often encounter the word *campo* when you come to an open-air area. That is a reference to the fact that such a place was once grassy, and in days of yore cattle grazed there.

South of the section called Dorsoduro, which is south of the Grand Canal, is another major channel, **Canale della Giudecca,** which separates Dorsoduro from

Canale della Giudecca **⑩**
Cannareggio **①**
Castello **④**
Dursoduro **⑧**
La Giudecca **⑪**
Grand Canal (Canal Grande) **⑦**
Isola di San Giorgio Maggiore **⑨**
Isola di San Pietro **⑫**
Murano **⑤**
San Marco **⑥**
San Polo **③**
Santa Croce **②**
Stazione di Santa Lucia **⑬**

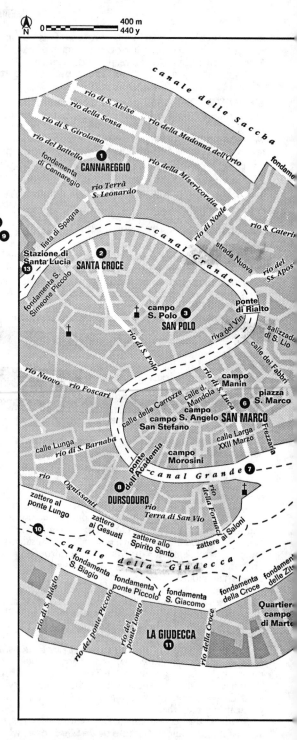

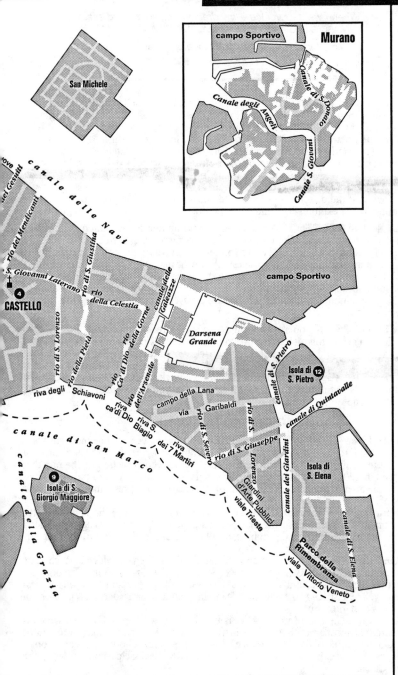

Murano

campo Sportivo

Canale di S. Donato

Canale degli Angeli

Canale S. Giovanni

San Michele

canale delle Navi

nuove

dei Gesuiti

rio dei Mendicanti

rio di S. Giustina

S. Giovanni Laterano

4

CASTELLO

rio della Celestia

canale delle Galeazze

campo Sportivo

rio di S. Lorenzo

rio della Pietà

rio Ca di Dio della Corte

rio dell'Arsenale

Darsena Grande

canale di S. Pietro

Isola di S. Pietro 12

canale di Quintavalle

riva degli Schiavoni

riva ca di Dio

riva S. Biagio

campo della Lana

via Garibaldi

rio di S. Severo

rio di S.

rio di S. Giuseppe

canale dei Giardini

Isola di S. Elena

riva dei 7 Martiri

canale di San Marco

canale della Grazia

9

Isola di S. Giorgio Maggiore

Lorenzo Giardini d'Arte Pubblici

viale Trieste

Parco della Rimembranza

viale Vittorio Veneto

canale di S. Elena

IMPRESSIONS

When I went to Venice—my dream became my address.
—MARCEL PROUST, LETTER TO MADAME STRAUSS, MAY 1906

Wonderful city, streets full of water, please advise.
—ROBERT BENCHLEY

---

the large island of La Giudecca. At the point where Canale della Giudecca flows into the Canale di San Marco, you'll spot the little **Isola di San Giorgio Maggiore,** with a church by Palladio. The most visited islands in the lagoon, aside from the **Lido,** are **Murano, Burano, and Torcello,** each of which we'll visit in due course.

Once you land and explore piazza San Marco and its satellite, piazzetta San Marco, you can head down **Riva degli Schiavoni,** with its deluxe and first-class hotels, or follow the signs along the **Mercerie,** the major shopping artery of Venice, which leads to the Rialto, site of the market area.

But with all the directions in the world and with all the signposts and maps, the best thing for an explorer in Venice is to get lost.

FINDING AN ADDRESS A maniac must have numbered the buildings of Venice at least 6 centuries ago. There seems to be no numbering system. Numbers are completely illogical. Therefore, before you set out on your journey to a specific place, get detailed instructions and have the establishment marked on your map. Instead of depending on street numbers, try to locate the nearest cross street instead and, once there, look for signs posted outside—a hotel, museum, or whatever—instead of searching out a number, many of which have decayed over the ages until they are no longer legible.

STREET MAPS If you really want to tour Venice and find that little hidden trattoria on a nearly forgotten street, you might as well abandon any map that doesn't detail every street and have an index in the back so you can find what you're looking for. The best of the lot is the *Falk* map of Venice. It details everything, and is sold at many news kiosks and at all bookstores. Since it's pocket size, you can open it in the Adriatic winds without having it blow away from you as do many of those big, overblown maps.

NEIGHBORHOODS IN BRIEF

San Marco Everybody goes here: It's the center of Venice. The main square is piazza San Marco, or St. Mark's Square, dominated by St. Mark's Basilica. Just outside the basilica is the campanile, or bell tower, a reconstruction of the one that collapsed in 1902. Around the corner is the Palazzo Ducale or doge's palace. In and around the area of San Marco lie the most expensive hotels, restaurants, cafés, and shops of Venice.

Cannaregio This section basically runs from the Rialto to the Jewish Ghetto and contains much of sightseeing interest, including Ca' d'Oro, housing the Galleria Giorgio Franchetti. Beyond the train station lies the old Jewish Ghetto, the first one established on the continent.

San Polo This is basically a commercial district of Venice, which is reached by crossing the Ponte Rialto (Rialto Bridge) spanning the Grand Canal. Its open-air market is called Erberia, and its center is the Church of San Giacomo di Rialto, oldest in the city. The district also encloses the Scuola Grande di San Rocco, a repository of the works of Tintoretto.

Castello The San Marco district is bordered on its east by Castello, which is considered the most amorphous of the districts of Venice. One of its major attractions is the Gothic church of Santi Giovanni e Paolo, or Zanipolo. This was the Pantheon of the doges of Venice. Its most popular boulevard is Riva degli Schiavoni, bordering the Grand Canal.

Santa Croce Another one of the sestieri, Santa Croce takes its name from an old church which was long ago destroyed. It generally follows the snakelike curve of the Grand Canal from piazzale Roma to a point just short of the Ponte Rialto. At this point it flows into the district of San Polo.

Dorsoduro   This district is compared variously to New York's Greenwich Village or London's Chelsea, although in truth it doesn't resemble either section very much. The least populated of the sestieri, it is filled with old homes and half-forgotten churches. It is the southernmost section of the historic district, and its major attraction is the Gallerie dell'Accademia.

Lido   This slim, sandy island cradles the Venetian lagoon, offering protection against the Adriatic Sea. Italy's most fashionable bathing resort, it is 7½ miles long and about half a mile wide. It was the setting for many famous books, including Thomas Mann's *Death in Venice* and Evelyn Waugh's *Brideshead Revisited*.

Torcello   Lying 6½ miles northeast of Venice, Torcello is called "the mother of Venice," the island having been settled between the 9th and 17th centuries. Once it was the most populous of the islands in the lagoon but since the 18th century it has been nearly deserted. Tourists visit it today to see its cathedral.

Burano   Perched 5½ miles northeast of Venice, Burano is the most populous of the lagoon islands. In the 16th century it produced the finest lace in Europe, and lace is still made here, although nothing like the production of centuries ago.

Murano   This island three-quarters of a mile northeast of Venice has been famed since 1291 for its glassmakers. At its apex in the 16th century, the island had 37 glass factories and a thriving population of 30,000 people. Once a closely guarded secret, Murano glassmaking is now clearly visible to any tourist who wants to visit the island and observe the technique on a guided tour.

2. GETTING AROUND

Since you can't hail a taxi, at least not on land, what you do in Venice is walk and walk and walk. People from North America who get in their cars to drive two blocks back home often find themselves walking for miles and miles in Venice. Of course, such walks can be broken up by vaporetto or boat rides.

It may seem that excessive attention is devoted below to porters, water taxis, vaporetti, and gondoliers, but I've seen too many visits to Venice marred by a hassle that dampens the tourist's enthusiasm for the city at the outset. Providing you can overcome the problem of getting yourself and your luggage transported safely—and without fisticuffs—to your hotel, you'll probably be set to embark on one of the grandest experiences of a lifetime: the exploration of Venice.

BY PUBLIC TRANSPORTATION   Much to the chagrin of the once-ubiquitous gondolier, the motorboats, or **vaporetti,** of Venice provide inexpensive and frequent, if not always fast, transportation in this canal-riddled city. The average fare on the *accelerato* (which makes every stop) is 1,800 lire ($1.40) and it will take you from St. Mark's to the Lido. The average fare on the *diretto* (only express stops) is 2,500 lire ($1.95) for a trip, say, from the railway station to the Rialto Bridge. In summer, the vaporetti are often fiercely crowded.

Discount Passes   Visitors to Venice may avail themselves of 24-hour 10,000-lira ($7.85) **biglietto turistico,** or tourist ticket, which allows them to travel all day long on any of the many routes of the city's boat services. This all-inclusive ticket is a bargain, as is the 3-day ticket allowing unlimited travel for 17,000 lire ($13.35).

BY WATER TAXI / MOTOR LAUNCH   It costs more than the public vaporetto, but you won't be hassled as much when you arrive with your luggage if you hire one of the city's many private motor launches. You may or may not have the cabin of one of these sleek vessels to yourself, since the captains fill all their boats with as many passengers as the law allows before taking off. Your porter's uncanny radar will guide you to one of the inconspicuous piers where a water taxi waits.

You always have to negotiate the fare before getting in. The sailors seem to follow in the footsteps of the most cunning of doges. To their credit, the captains of Venice's motor launches are usually adroit about depositing you, with your luggage, at the canalside entrance to your hotel or on one of the city's smaller waterways within a short walking distance of your destination.

BY GONDOLA In *Death in Venice,* Thomas Mann wrote: "Is there anyone but must repress a secret thrill, on arriving in Venice for the first time—or returning thither after long absence—and stepping into a Venetian gondola? That singular conveyance, come down unchanged from ballad times, black as nothing else on earth except a coffin—what pictures it calls up of lawless, silent adventures in the plashing night; or even more, what visions of death itself, the bier and solemn rites and last soundless voyage!"

Mann reflected the point of view of German romanticism, but he didn't tell all the story. A voyage on a gondola isn't likely to be so "soundless"—at least not when time comes to pay the bill. When riding in a gondola, two major agreements have to be reached: (1) the price of the ride and (2) the length of the trip. If you even vaguely suggest in any way one of Barnum's suckers, you're likely to be taken on both counts. It's a common sight in Venice to see a gondolier huffing and puffing to take his passengers on a "quickie," often reducing the hour to 15 minutes. The gondolier, with his eye on his watch, is anxious to dump his load and pick up the next batch of passengers. Consequently, his watch almost invariably runs fast.

There is an accepted official rate schedule for gondoliers, but I've never known anyone to honor it. The actual fare depends on how effective you are in standing up to the gondolier's attempt to get more money out of you. Many visitors hire a gondolier for 65,000 lire ($51) and *up*—emphasis on the *up*—per 40 minutes. In fairness to the gondoliers, it must be said that they have an awful job, which is romanticized out of perspective by the world. They row boatloads of tourists across hot, smelly canals with such endearments screamed at them as "No sing! No pay!" And these fellows must make plenty of lire while the sun shines, as their work ends when the first cold winds blow in from the Adriatic.

Two major stations at which you can hire gondolas include piazza San Marco (tel. 5200685) and Ponte Rialto (tel. 5224904).

ON FOOT The only way to explore Venice unless you plan to see it from a boat on the Grand Canal. Everybody walks in Venice: There is no other way. The streets are too crowded for bicycles or much else. In summer, the overcrowding is so severe you'll often have a hard time finding room for your feet on the street.

FAST FACTS VENICE

American Express The office of American Express in Venice is at San Mose 1471 (tel. 5200844), in the San Marco area. City tours and mail handling can be obtained here. It is open Monday through Friday from 9am to 5:30pm and on Saturday from 9am to 12:30pm.

Area Code The telephone area code is 041.

Baby-sitters In lieu of a central booking agency, arrangements have to be made individually at various hotels. Obviously, the more advance your notice the better your chances of getting a sitter who speaks English.

Bookstores One of the best ones is **Sansovino-Bacino Orseolo,** San Marco 84 (tel. 5222623).

Car Rentals Obviously you won't need a car in Venice. But you may need one upon departure. You can make arrangements at **Europcar,** piazzale Roma 540 (tel. 5238616), or at Avis, piazzale Roma 496H (tel. 5237377). Offices are open Monday through Saturday from 8am to 7pm and on Sunday from 8am to 1pm. In winter the agencies are closed on Sunday.

Climate See "When to Go" in Chapter 2.

Crime See "Safety," below.

Currency Exchange There are many banks in Venice where you can exchange money. For example, try the **Banca d'America e d'Italia,** San Marco

2216 (tel. 5200766). Many travelers find that **Guetta Viaggi,** San Marco 1289 (tel. 5208711), offers the best rates in Venice.

Dentist   Try **Dr. Hilber,** Castello 5267 (tel. 5228649).

Doctor   You can call for an appointment with **Dr. Zampini,** Castello 4981 (tel. 5238191).

Drugstores   If you need a drugstore in the middle of the night, call 192 for information about one that is open. Pharmacies take turns staying open late.

Embassies/Consulates   There is no U.S. Consul in Venice; the closest is in Milan (tel. 02/652841). The British Consulate is at Dorsoduro 1051 (tel. 5227207), open Monday through Friday from 9am to noon and 2 to 4pm.

Emergencies   Phone numbers are: 113 for **police,** 5230000 for an **ambulance,** and 5222222 to report a **fire.**

Eyeglasses   This service is available at **Querzola,** Castello 2690 (tel. 5228366).

Hairdressers/Barbers   Women can patronize **Bruno,** Cannaregio 3924 (tel. 5285833), and men can go to **Babuin,** Cannaregio 4589A (tel. 5236314). Both places should be called for an appointment.

Holidays   See "When to Go" in Chapter 2.

Hospitals   Get in touch with the **Civili Riuniti di Venezia,** campo Santi Giovanni e Paolo (tel. 5294517).

Information   See "Tourist Information" in "Orientation" in this chapter.

Laundry/Dry Cleaning   Go to **Lavaget,** Cannaregio 1269 (tel. 715976), on fondamenta Pescaria off rio Terà San Leonardo. It is open Monday through Friday from 8:30am to 12:30pm and 3 to 7pm. This is the most convenient self-service laundry to the rail station, only a 5-minute walk away. It also does dry cleaning.

Libraries   The biggest library is **Biblioteca Nazionale Marciana,** San Marco 7 (tel. 5208788).

Lost Property   The central office for recovering lost property is **Ufficio Oggetti Rinvenuti,** an annex to the Municipio (town hall) at San Marco 4134, on calle Piscopia o Loredan, lying off rive del Carbon on the Grand Canal. Open Monday, Wednesday, and Friday from 9:30am to 12:30pm.

Luggage Storage/Lockers   These services are available at the main rail station, **Stazione di Santa Lucia,** at piazzale Roma (tel. 715555).

Newspapers/Magazines   The *International Herald Tribune* is sold at most newsstands and in many first-class and deluxe hotels, as are the European editions (in English) of *Time* and *Newsweek.*

Police   See "Emergencies," above.

Post Office   The major post office is at Fondaco dei Tedeschi (tel. 5289317), in the vicinity of the Rialto Bridge. It is open Monday through Saturday from 8:30am to 7pm.

Radio   The major station is run by RAI, the Italian state radio and TV network, and broadcasts in Italian only (at least you can listen to the music even if you don't speak the tongue). Vatican Radio is received in Venice and often carries English-language news broadcasts. Throughout the night and for part of the day, shortwave radio reception in Venice is excellent, including British (BBC), American (VOA), and Canadian (CBC). At night, the American Armed Forces Network (AFN) from Munich or Frankfurt can be heard on regular AM radio (middle or medium wave).

Religious Services   If you're **Catholic,** you'll find churches all over Venice. There is a **Jewish synagogue** in the Ghetto Vecchio (tel. 715012). A **Methodist** church is at Santa Maria Gormosa 5170 (tel. 5227549), and there's an **Anglican Episcopal church,** St. George's, in Dorsoduro at campo San Vio 870 (tel. 5200571).

Rest Rooms   These are available at piazzale Roma and various other places in Venice, but not as plentiful as they should be. Often you'll have to rely on the facilities of a café, although you should purchase something, perhaps a light coffee, as in theory commercial establishments reserve their toilets for customers only. Most museums and galleries have public toilets. You can also use the public toilets at the Albergo Diurno, on via Ascensione, just behind piazza San Marco. Remember, *Signori* means men and *Signore* is for women.

Safety   The curse of Venice is the pickpocket artist. Violent crime is rare. But because of the overcrowding in vaporetti and even on the small narrow streets, it is easy to pick pockets. Purse snatchers are commonplace as well. A purse snatcher seemingly darts out of nowhere, grabs a purse, and in seconds seems to have disappeared down some narrow alleyway. Secure your valuables, and if your hotel has such amenities, keep them locked in a safe there when not needed.

Shoe Repairs   A shoe-repair shop that never bothered to name itself is found at Dorsoduro 871, on calle Nuova Sant'Agnese. This is the route most visitors travel between the Accademia and the Collezione Peggy Guggenheim.

Taxes   A 19% value-added tax (called IVA) is added to the price of all consumer goods and products and most services, such as those in hotels and restaurants.

Taxis   See "Getting Around" in this chapter.

Telegrams/Telex/Fax   The post office maintains a telegram and fax service 24 hours a day. You can also call Italcable at 170 if you wish to send an international telegram; otherwise, call 186.

Television   The RAI is the chief television network broadcasting in Italy. Every TV in Venice has these highly politicized channels: RAI-1 for Christian Democrats, RAI-2 for Italian Socialists, and RAI-3 for Italian Communists.

Transit Information   For flights, call 661111; for rail information, 715555; and for bus schedules, 5287886.

Useful Telephone Numbers   To check on the time, call 161; for the weather, 191.

3. NETWORKS & RESOURCES

FOR STUDENTS   The center for budget student travel is **Centro Turistico Studentesco (CTS),** Dorsoduro 3252, on fondamenta Tagliapietra (tel. 5205660). The office is near campiello Squellini, lying to the west of campo Santa Margherita, and is reached by going to vaporetto stop San Tomà. Cheap transportation and low-cost lodgings can be arranged here. Hours are Monday through Saturday from 8:30am to 1:30pm.

The tourist office (see above) distributes a free **Venice for the Young" Pass,** which entitles holders to various discounts throughout the city. But takers must be between the ages of 16 and 26 and have photo ID to prove it.

FOR GAY MEN & LESBIANS   There are no gay liberation headquarters or club centers in Venice. There are also no gay bars as such, although this condition could change at any minute. Lesbians have bars, bookstores, and women's centers in some parts of Italy, but not in Venice.

FOR WOMEN   The **Instituto Suore Canossiane,** Giudecca 428, fondamenta del Ponte Piccolo (tel. 5222157), is a 35-bed private Catholic kindergarten which at night becomes a budget hotel for women (usually young women). Guests must vacate the premises by 8:30am, however. The cost is 1,200 lire (95¢) per person per night. An 11pm curfew is imposed.

FOR SENIORS   Go to the tourist office (see above) and inquire about any discounts—such as on transportation and museum admissions—that pertain to senior citizens. This data is always changing, so it's best to get the latest information. Also, for some good travel discounts, go to the Centro Turistico Studentesco (see "For Students," above) which, although essentially a student budget travel agency, may also help you with discounts on senior-citizen travel within Italy.

CHAPTER 12

WHERE TO STAY & DINE IN VENICE

1. ACCOMMODATIONS
- **FROMMER'S SMART TRAVELER: HOTELS**
- **FROMMER'S COOL FOR KIDS: HOTELS**

2. DINING
- **FROMMER'S SMART TRAVELER: RESTAURANTS**
- **FROMMER'S COOL FOR KIDS: RESTAURANTS**

Venice has some of the most expensive hotels in the world within its borders, including the Gritti Palace and the Cipriani. These pockets of posh cosset their guests in ultimate luxury and comfort, but there are also dozens of unheralded and moderately priced places to stay, often on narrow, hard-to-find streets. Venice has never been known, however, as an inexpensive destination. Everything, even a cup of coffee, costs a lot of money here. To combat high prices, many travelers—much to the chagrin of local merchants—have taken to visiting Venice on a day trip (along with their packed lunches).

The cheapest way to live in Venice is to book in a *locanda,* which means a small inn, carrying an even lower rating than the three categories of *pensioni* (boarding houses). Standards are highly variable in these places, many of which are dank, damp, and dark. Rooms even in many second- or first-class hotels are often cramped, as space has always been a problem in Venice.

It is estimated that in this "City of Light," at least half the bedrooms in any category are dark, so be duly warned. Rooms with lots of light opening onto the Grand Canal cost a hefty price. Single rooms are often a horror in Venice. One frequent traveler who goes to Venice at least once a month on business confides that he rents a double room in a third- or fourth-class hotel and finds it better value than a single room in a second- or first-class establishment.

Likewise, restaurants, even the so-called cheap ones, may appear expensive to you, depending on what part of the world you're from. For example, if you come from the state of Missouri, which offers all-you-can-eat buffets for $5.95, you may be horrified to find yourself paying that for a cappuccino in certain Venetian cafés.

Seafood is the specialty of Venice, but it's very expensive, especially fish priced by the weight.

Dining hours tend to be short, lunch starting at either 12:30 or 1pm and ending at 2:30pm. Most restaurants reopen at 8pm and close by 10pm or 11pm. A service charge of 15% to 20% will almost certainly appear on your final bill, and it isn't necessary to tip extra.

1. ACCOMMODATIONS

The most difficult time to find rooms are the busy seasons: the February Carnevale, Easter, and anytime from June through September. Because of the tight hotel

FROMMER'S SMART TRAVELER: HOTELS

VALUE-CONSCIOUS TRAVELERS SHOULD ASK ABOUT THE FOLLOWING:

1. The price you pay in inexpensive hotels depends on the plumbing. Rooms with showers are cheaper than rooms with privates baths. For a bath, you'll have to use the corridor bathroom, but you'll save a lot of money.
2. Consider a package tour (or book land arrangements with your air ticket). You'll often pay at least 30% less than individual "rack" rates (off-the-street, independent bookings).
3. If Venice hotels are full, forget it. But if they're not, a little on-the-spot bargaining can bring down the cost of a hotel room. Be polite. Ask if there's a "businessperson's rate," or if schoolteachers get a discount. This is a face-saving technique. Sometimes it works and sometimes it doesn't, but you can try. The technique is best at night, when the hotel faces up to 40% vacancy and wants to fill some of those empty rooms.
4. At cheaper hotels that take credit cards, ask if payment by cash will get you a reduction.
5. If you're going to spend at least a week in Venice, ask about long-term discounts.

QUESITONS TO ASK IF YOU'RE ON A BUDGET

1. Is there a surcharge on eithe rlocal or long-distance calls? There usually is. In some places, it might be an astonishing 40%. Make your calls at the nearest post office.
2. Is service included? This means, does the hotel include service charges in the rates quoted, or will a service charge be added on at the end of your stay?
3. Are all hotel and city taxes included in the price or will they be added on?
4. Is continental breakfast included in the rates?

situation, advance reservations as far in advance as possible are highly recommended. After those peak times, you can virtually have your pick of rooms, as many travelers avoid the damp, cold, and windy months of winter.

Hotel breakfasts are generally disappointing. Unless your breakfast is included in the rates, you may want to avoid breakfast at your hotel and retreat to a bar or café, which are plentiful in every district.

Be very careful about making long-distance phone calls from your hotel room in Venice: *Many hoteliers impose a 40% phone surcharge.* Go to the post office or use public phones instead.

Most hotels, if you ask at the reception desk, will grant you a 10% to 15% discount in winter (that is, from November until March 15). But getting this discount may require a little negotiation at the desk. A few hotels close in January if there's no prospect of business.

If an elevator is essential for you, always inquire in advance when booking a room if your hotel has one. Many do not have public lounges.

Often facilities normally associated with first-class and deluxe hotels don't exist in Venetian hotels, many of which have floor plans laid out centuries ago. Unless otherwise specified, room service is only from 7am to midnight in Venetian hotels.

Even though Venice doesn't have cars making noise, it does have a lot of boat traffic and the streets are often filled with chattering, noisy people until late at night. If you like to turn in early, a set of earplugs is always helpful.

Should you arrive without a reservation, go to the **AVA (Hotel Association) reservations booth** at the train station, at the airport, or at the municipal parking garage on piazzale Roma. You're required to post a 20,000-lira ($15.70) deposit to secure a room, which is then rebated on your final hotel bill. All three booths are open daily from 9am to 9pm.

Hotels rated "Very Expensive" charge more than 400,000 lire ($314) for a double, those considered "Expensive" ask for 220,000 lire ($172.70) to 400,000 lire ($314), "Moderate" suggests doubles for 120,000 lire to 220,000 lire ($94.20 to $172.70), and "Inexpensive" is anything under 120,000 lire ($94.20). All tariffs quoted are for a standard double room occupied by two people, including tax and service.

ISOLA DELLA GIUDECCA

VERY EXPENSIVE

CIPRIANI, Isola della Giudecca 10, 30133 Venezia. Tel. 041/5207744. Fax 041/5203939. 95 rms (all with bath), 29 suites. A/C MINIBAR TV TEL **Vaporetto:** Zitelle.

$ Rates (including breakfast): 450,000–585,000 lire ($353.25–$459.25) single; 600,000–840,000 lire ($471–$659.40) double; from 1,500,000 lire ($1,177.50) suite. AE, DC, MC, V.

The Cipriani is a select resort villa on a small island across from piazza San Marco. It was conceived as a private residence and guesthouse emphasizing personal comfort. It is the creation of the late Giuseppe Cipriani, the founder of Harry's Bar and the one real-life character in Hemingway's Venetian novel. Nowadays it's owned and run by Venice Simplon Orient Express Hotels. There's even an exclusive Sea Gull Club, reserved for hotel guests.

The guest rooms have different exposures, facilities, and sizes, but all have splendid views, either of the lagoon to the south, the Palladian San Giorgio Maggiore to the east and north, or the vineyards and the domed Redentore and Le Zitelle to the west. Over the years the hotel has hosted guests ranging from Margaret Thatcher to Barbra Streisand.

Dining/Entertainment: In the evening a piano is played for informal dancing in the Gabbiano grill-bar or on terraces overlooking the lagoon. Also, the Cipriani prides itself on serving an authentic Venetian cuisine.

Services: A private launch service ferries guests, at any hour, to and from the hotel's own pier and piazza San Marco; room service, baby-sitting, laundry, valet.

Facilities: Olympic-size swimming pool, tennis, sauna.

NEAR PIAZZA SAN MARCO

VERY EXPENSIVE

HOTEL BAUER GRÜNWALD & GRAND HOTEL, campo San Moisè 1459, 30124 Venezia. Tel. 041/5231520. Fax 041/5207557. 214 rms (all with bath), 4 suites. A/C MINIBAR TV TEL **Vaporetto:** San Marco.

$ Rates (including breakfast): 240,000–285,000 lire ($188.40–$223.75) single; 310,000–405,000 lire ($243.35–$317.95) double; from 890,000 lire ($698.65) suite. AE, DC, MC, V.

The Hotel Bauer Grünwald & Grand Hotel is the combination of an ornate 13th-century palazzo which faces the Grand Canal and a massive concrete wing that was the talk of Venice when it was built back in the 1960s. The entrance is a huge rectangular room with an elegant decor of warm colors and gilt trim. The rather spacious bedrooms range from the opulently antique to the more conservatively decorated units in the newer section. A canalside terrace is dotted with striped gondola tie-ups and a baroque statue of a torch-bearing Amazon jutting out from the corner.

Dining/Entertainment: Guests gather for drinks in the American bar before enjoying both regional and international dishes served on the hotel's terrace restaurant overlooking the Grand Canal. Meals begin at 100,000 lire ($78.50).

Accademia, Pensione  6

Ala 11
American 9
Bauer Grunwald & Grand 16
Bel Sito 11
Belvedere 39
Bisanzio 31
Bonvecchiati 20
Boston 27
Calcina, La 8
Caneva 21
Carpaccio 4
Casanova 18
Cavaletto & Doge Orselo 19
Cipriani 34
Citta di Milano 24
Concordia 26
Da Bruno 22
Danieli 28
Des Bains 37
Do Pozzi 14
Doni Pensione 29
Europa & Regina 14
Excelsior Palace 35
Falier 5
Fenice & Des Artistes, La 12
Gabrielli Sandwirth 33
Giorgione 2
Gritti Palace 11
Helvetia 38
Kette 13
Lisbona 26
Locanda Montin 7
Londra Palace 29
Luna Baglioni 17
Marconi & Milano 29
Metrople 29
Mignon 2
Monaco & Grand Canal 15
Montecarlo 15
Panada 25
Quattro Fontane 36
Residenza, La 32
Rialto 3
Salute "da Cici,"
    Pensione alla 10
San Moisè 13
San Cassiano Ca' Favretto 1
Saturnia-Internazionale 14
Savoia & Jolanda 29
Scandinavia 23
Seguso 8

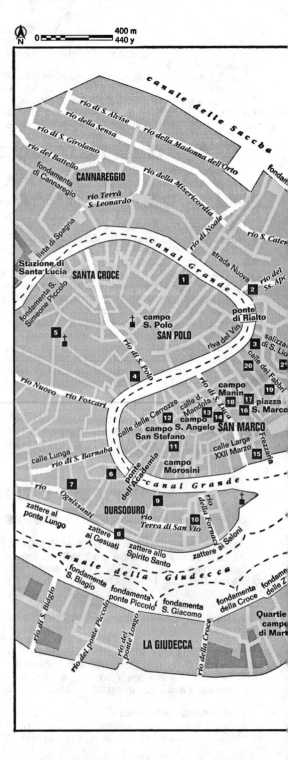

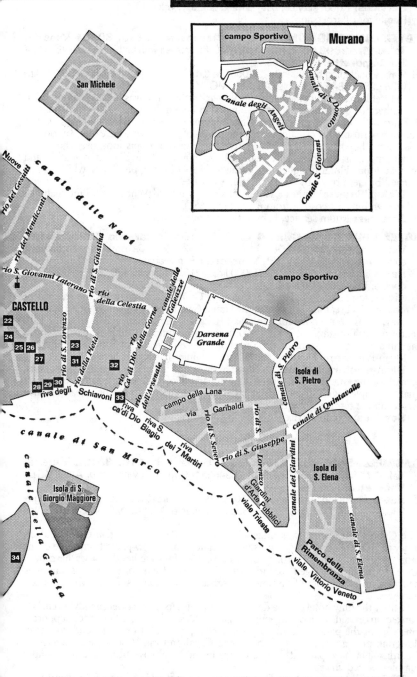

Services: Room service, baby-sitting, laundry, valet.
Facilities: Barbershop.

HOTEL LUNA BAGLIONI, calle dell'Ascensione 1243, 30124 Venezia.
Tel. 041/5289840. Fax 041/5287160. 86 rms (all with bath). A/C MINIBAR TV
TEL **Vaporetto:** San Marco.
$ **Rates** (including breakfast): 220,000 lire ($172.70) single; 450,000–490,000 lire
($353.25–$384.65) double. AE, DC, MC, V.

The Hotel Luna is "the oldest hotel in Venice," although it was long ago modernized
in a rather bland international style. Founded in 1474 as a monastery by the Congrega
di Fratti della Luna, it took in traveling pilgrims on their way through Venice. The
tradition of hospitality remains for the thousands of visitors who have found a room at
this deluxe hotel near piazza San Marco. Some of the rooms look over the Grand
Canal, and most of them have high ceilings, renovated interiors, and marble and
parquet floors. Floral bouquets are in the hallways of the upper floors, which can be
reached by elevator or by a wide marble staircase.

Dining/Entertainment: The hotel serves a refined Venetian and international
cuisine, with meals costing from 65,000 lire ($51).
Services: Room service, baby-sitting, laundry, valet.

HOTEL MONACO & GRAND CANAL, calle Vallaresso 1325, 30124
Venezia. Tel. 041/5200211. Fax 041/5200501. 69 rms (all with bath), 7
suites. A/C MINIBAR TV TEL **Vaporetto:** San Marco.
$ **Rates** (including breakfast): 275,000 lire ($215.90) single; 430,000 lire ($337.55)
double; from 850,000 lire ($667.25) suite. AE, DC, MC, V.

The intimate and refined Hotel Monaco & Grand Canal captures the essence of
Venice with its breathtaking view of the Grand Canal. Harry's Bar is right across from
the way. It has been a hotel for more than 100 years; the structure dates from the 18th
century. This five-star hostelry is a favorite with discriminating Italians, particularly in
the fall and winter seasons. It was the choice place in Venice of Simone de Beauvoir
and Jean-Paul Sartre. More recently, Prince Rainier has stayed here as well.

Dining/Entertainment: The hotel harbors one of the city's leading restaurants,
named for the Grand Canal, where you can partake of Venetian specialties of highest
quality, coupled with impeccable service and a panorama. In season, meals are also
served on the terrace along the canal.
Services: Room service, baby-sitting, laundry, valet.

EXPENSIVE

GABRIELLI-SANDWIRTH, riva degli Schiavoni 4110, 30122 Venezia.
Tel. 041/5231580. Fax 041/5209455. 100 rms (all with bath). A/C TV TEL
Vaporetto: Arsenale.
$ **Rates** (including breakfast): 140,000–195,000 lire ($109.90–$153.10) single;
230,000–370,000 lire ($180.55–$290.45) double. AE, DC, MC, V. **Closed:** Nov
15–Feb 20.

The Gabrielli-Sandwirth was originally built in 1238 as a Venetian-Gothic palace;
today its peach-colored stone-and-stucco facade stands a few paces from some of the
most expensive and glamorous hotels in Venice. Two medieval houses have been
joined to its high-ceilinged core to form a labyrinth of interior courtyards, rambling
hallways, and a number of tastefully conservative bedrooms, some of which contain
minibars.

This is the only hotel on riva degli Schiavoni with its own garden, an idyllic enclave
banked on one side by a canal, with espaliered roses, palm trees, and lattice-supported
vines. From the panoramic rooftop sun terrace, a handful of chairs and dozens of
flowering pots accent views of the Grand Canal and the Venetian lagoon such as
Guardi might have painted. Public rooms in the hotel have beamed ceilings and a
marble-covered charm.

Dining/Entertainment: The dining room, outfitted in a turn-of-the-century art
nouveau, contains three of the most beautiful Murano chandeliers in Venice. It serves
a typically Venetian and international cuisine.

Services: Concierge, room service, baby-sitting, laundry, valet.
Facilities: Solarium.

HOTEL CAVALETTO E DOGE ORSEOLO, calle del Cavaletto 1107, 30124
Venezia. Tel. 041/5200955. Fax 041/5238184. 81 rms (all with bath). A/C
MINIBAR TV TEL **Vaporetto:** San Marco.
$ Rates (including breakfast): 185,000–225,000 lire ($145.25–$176.65) single;
310,000–380,000 lire ($243.35–$298.30) double. AE, DC, MC, V.

Filled with the accumulated charm of its 800-year history, the elegant Hotel Cavaletto
e Doge Orseolo occupies a prime position a few paces from St. Mark's Square. It lies
on a narrow cobblestone street between the arched footbridge and an unused
baroque church in one of the most historic sections of Venice. The hotel was created
by ancestors of its sophisticated owner, Eduardo Mario Masprone, when a trio of
buildings was unified into one well-managed unit in the early 1900s. In the 1100s the
oldest of the three was the private home of one of the most famous of the early
Venetian patriarchs, Doge Orseolo, who, according to plaques on the front, "was
esteemed by Caesars of the East and West." The family trees and names of other
doges connected with the site are proudly displayed in some of the bedrooms. In the
1300s, part of what is now the hotel served as one of the city's first taverns.

Today the Cavaletto is best viewed from its sinuously curved rear, where a flotilla
of moored gondolas use a stone-sided harbor, one of only two such basins in Venice.
A quartet of well-trained concierges seem to have the client's interests at heart. From a
position in the airily comfortable lounge, a metal plaque indicates the position, about
3 feet off the floor, of the high-water flood mark in the 1960s. Each of the hotel's
bedrooms has a radio and is comfortably outfitted with glass chandeliers from nearby
Murano, hardwood floors, and elegant Italian-inspired furniture. Many have views of
canals and ancient stones.

Dining/Entertainment: The hotel has a big-windowed restaurant, with reflected sunlight from the lagoon dappling the high ceiling. Excellent meals of a high
international standard are served here for 55,000 lire ($43.20). There's also a kind of
dolce vita bar where a relaxing cocktail might be the perfect end to a day.

HOTEL EUROPA & REGINA, via XXII Marzo no. 2159, 30124 Venezia.
Tel. 041/5200477. Fax 041/5231533. 189 rms (all with bath). A/C MINIBAR
TV TEL **Vaporetto:** San Marco.
$ Rates: 180,000–250,000 lire ($141.30–$196.25) single; 300,000–390,000 lire
($235.50–$306.15) double. 19% IVA tax extra. Breakfast 21,000 lire ($16.50)
extra. AE, DC, MC, V.

A longtime favorite on the Grand Canal is Hotel Europa & Regina, which can be
reached by motorboat at its canal side or through a courtyard on via XXII Marzo.
The hotel was formed by combining two Venetian palaces, both of which face the
Grand Canal and the Church of La Salute, with a restaurant terrace and a café terrace
between them. This five-star deluxe hotel contains excellent accommodations, the
majority of which offer canal views. They are beautifully furnished, with varying
decor. The most expensive bedrooms open onto a view of the lagoon. Both Venetian
and international food is served in the hotel restaurant.

SATURNIA-INTERNAZIONALE, via XXII Marzo no. 2399, 30124 Vene-
zia. Tel. 041/5208377. Fax 041/5207131. 95 rms (all with bath). A/C
MINIBAR TV TEL **Vaporetto:** San Marco.
$ Rates (including breakfast): 220,000 lire ($172.70) single; 320,000–390,000 lire
($251.20–$306.15) double. AE, DC, MC, V.

The Saturnia-Internazionale is a 14th-century Venetian palazzo near piazza San
Marco, part and parcel of old Venice. Wherever you wander throughout this palace,
you'll find richly embellished beauty—the grand hallway with its wooden staircase,
heavy iron chandeliers, fine paintings, and beamed ceiling. The bedrooms are spacious
and furnished with chandeliers and Venetian antiques and enriched with tapestry
rugs, gilt mirrors, and ornately carved ceilings. Many of these bedrooms overlook the
quiet and dignified garden in the back. The cost of staying here varies according to the
season.

Dining/Entertainment: There's a dining salon with rustic decor, including regal chairs and pillars of bricks. There is also the more intimate dining gallery in a nautical theme. The cuisine is excellent.

Services: Room service, baby-sitting, laundry, valet.

MODERATE

BONVECCHIATI, calle Goldoni 4488, 30100 Venezia. Tel. 041/ 5285017. Fax 041/5285230. 86 rms (74 with bath or shower). TEL **Vaporetto:** San Marco.

$ Rates (including breakfast): 119,500 lire ($93.80) single without bath, 145,000 lire ($113.85) single with bath; 162,000 lire ($127.15) double without bath, 194,000 lire ($152.30) double with bath. AE, DC, MC, V.

The Bonvecchiati, located halfway between the Rialto Bridge and piazza San Marco, stands proudly on its little square, looking much like the private villa of a titled Venetian family. The owner, Giovanni Deana, is a noted collector of modern art. Paintings acquired by him are in most of the lounge halls, corridors and living rooms, and even grace some of the bedrooms. Most of the units are furnished with antiques or good reproductions. Some are air-conditioned; 21 rooms have TV, and 26 offer a minibar.

The interior dining room—all in white and ivory, with fluted columns and a central crystal chandelier—has a balcony for overflow dining. But the favored spot for meals is the outside canopied terrace, which borders the canal and is decorated with potted plants, lanterns, and garden furniture. The drinking bar is warmed by a collection of copper pots hanging from the beamed ceiling. The lounges are more like personalized living rooms, with paintings and Turkish carpets.

BOSTON HOTEL, Ponte dei Dai 848, 30124 Venezia. Tel. 041/5287665. Fax 041/5226628. 42 rms (all with bath). TV TEL **Vaporetto:** San Marco.

$ Rates (including breakfast): 120,000 lire ($94.20) single; 180,000 lire ($141.30) double. AE, DC, MC, V. **Closed:** Nov–Feb.

The Boston Hotel, built in 1962, is just a whisper away from St. Mark's. It's run by an attractive couple, Mario and Adriana Bernardi, who have instilled their good taste here. The hotel was named after an uncle who left to seek his fortune in Boston . . . and never returned. The little living rooms combine the old and the new, containing many antiques and Venetian ceilings. For the skinny guest, there's a tiny, self-operated elevator and a postage-stamp-size street entrance. Most of the bedrooms with parquet floors have built-in features, snugly designed beds, chests, and wardrobes. Fortunately, several have tiny balconies that open onto canals. Some rooms are air-conditioned, and a minibar is available upon request.

GIORGIONE, SS. Apostoli 4586, 30001 Venezia. Tel. 041/5225810. Fax 041/5239092. 56 rms (all with bath), 1 suite. A/C MINIBAR TV TEL **Vaporetto:** Ca' d'Oro.

$ Rates (including breakfast): 130,000–150,000 lire ($102.05–$117.75) single; 170,000–200,000 lire ($133.45–$157) double; from 300,000 lire ($235.50) suite. AE, MC, V.

Giorgione is a glamorized little hotel. In spite of its modernization, its decor is traditionally Venetian. The lounges and dining rooms are equipped with fine furnishings and decorative accessories. Likewise, the bedrooms are designed to coddle guests, as they're very comfortable as well as stylish. The owner hawkeyes the running of the dining room to assure that the cuisine is first rate. The hotel also has a typical Venetian garden. It's rated second class by the government, but the Giorgione maintains higher standards than many of the first-class establishments.

HOTEL BISANZIO, calle della Pietà 3651, 30122 Venezia. Tel. 041/ 5203100. Fax 041/5204114. 39 rms (with bath). A/C MINIBAR TV TEL **Vaporetto:** San Zaccaria.

$ Rates (including breakfast): 110,000–140,000 lire ($86.35–$109.90) single; 140,000–195,000 lire ($109.90–$153.05) double. AE, DC, MC, V.

The Hotel Bisanzio is a three-story hotel with green shutters and a plaque honoring it as the former home of the sculptor Alessandro Vittoria. Near St. Mark's Square and set back from riva degli Schiavoni, the hotel is quieter and cheaper than many of its famous neighbors along the quay. The interior has gray marble floors, a uniformed staff, a bar, and a conservatively modern decor that includes stone floors and lots of exposed wood.

HOTEL CARPACCIO, San Tomà 2765, 30125 Venezia. Tel. 041/5235946. Fax 041/5242134. 18 rms (all with bath). TEL **Vaporetto:** San Tomà.

$ Rates (including breakfast): 123,800 lire ($97.20) single; 185,000 lire ($145.25) double. DC, MC, V.

Don't be put off by the narrow, winding alleyways leading up to the wrought-iron entrance of this second-class hotel—the building was meant to be approached by gondola. Once you're inside, you'll realize that your location in the heart of the oldest part of the city justifies your confusing arrival. This building used to be the Palazzo Barbarigo della Terrazza, and part of it is still reserved for private apartments. Owner Guido Tassotto, who studied in London, maintains tasteful and spacious rooms filled with serviceable furniture. The salon is decorated with gracious pieces, marble floors, and a big arched window whose exterior is crowned with a bearded head of stone looking, along with you, over the Grand Canal. Breakfast is the only meal served.

HOTEL CASANOVA, Frezzeria 1285, 30124 Venezia. Tel. 041/5206855. Fax 041/5206413. 43 rms (all with bath), 3 suites. A/C MINIBAR TV TEL **Vaporetto:** San Marco.

$ Rates (including breakfast): 153,000 lire ($120.10) single; 210,000 lire ($164.85) double; from 250,000 lire ($196.25) suite. AE, DC, MC, V.

The Hotel Casanova, located a few steps from piazza San Marco, was formerly a private home. Today transformed into a hotel, it contains an elegant collection of church art and benches from old monasteries. These sit on flagstone floors near oil portraits. The reception manager will give you a key to a modernized bedroom with comfortably contemporary furnishings.

HOTEL CONCORDIA, calle Larga San Marco 367, 30124 Venezia. Tel. 041/5206866. Fax 041/5206775. 55 rms (all with bath). A/C MINIBAR TV TEL **Vaporetto:** San Marco.

$ Rates (including breakfast): 100,000–215,000 lire ($78.50–$168.80) single; 230,000–330,000 lire ($180.55–$259.05) double. AE, DC, MC, V.

The Hotel Concordia is the only hotel in Venice containing rooms that look out over St. Mark's Square. Completely renovated, the century-old hotel, now a four-star choice, is housed in a five-story russet-colored building with stone-trimmed windows. The name of the hotel is spelled out in mosaics just below your feet as you enter. A series of gold-plated marble steps takes you to the lobby where you'll find a comfortable bar area, friendly service, and elevators to whisk you to the labyrinthine corridors upstairs. All bedrooms are decorated in a Venetian antique style and contain an electronic safe, hairdryer, and radio in addition to other amenities.

Dining/Entertainment: Light meals and Italian snacks are available in the bar. Otherwise, only breakfast is served.

Services: 24-hour room service, baby-sitting, laundry, valet.

Facilities: Business center.

HOTEL DO POZZI, corte do Pozzi 2373, calle XXII Marzo, 30124 Venezia. Tel. 041/5207855. Fax 041/5229413. 29 rms (all with bath). A/C MINIBAR TV TEL **Vaporetto:** San Marco.

$ Rates (including breakfast): 100,000–150,000 lire ($78.50–$117.75) single; 150,000–210,000 lire ($117.75–$164.85) double. AE, DC, MC, V.

The Hotel Do Pozzi is small, modern, and centrally located just a short stroll from the

Grand Canal. More of a little country tavern than a hotel, it opens onto a paved front courtyard with potted greenery. You can arrive via water-taxi, boat, gondola, or vaporetto. The sitting and dining rooms are furnished with antiques (and near antiques)—all intermixed with utilitarian modern decor. Baths have been added, and a major refurbishing has given everything a fresh touch.

HOTEL KETTE, piscina San Moisè 2053, 30124 Venezia. Tel. 041/ 5207766. Fax 041/5228964. 60 rms (all with bath). A/C MINIBAR TV TEL **Vaporetto:** San Marco.

$ Rates (including breakfast): 90,000–120,000 lire ($70.65–$94.20) single; 160,000–200,000 lire ($125.60–$157) double. AE, DC, MC, V.

The Hotel Kette lies a 5-minute walk from piazza San Marco. You'll be welcomed inside by a pleasant receptionist, and will find a decor consisting of copies of Victorian armchairs, Oriental carpets, and a pair of cast-iron columns flanking the stairwell. Each of the compact bedrooms contains an electronic safe, hairdryer, and other amenities.

HOTEL LA FENICE ET DES ARTISTES, campiello de la Fenice 1936, 30124 Venezia. Tel. 041/5232333. Fax 041/5203721. 70 rms (all with bath), 4 suites. TV TEL **Vaporetto:** San Marco.

$ Rates (including breakfast): 156,000–161,000 lire ($122.45–$126.40) single; 200,000 lire ($157) double; from 260,000 lire ($204.10) suite. MC, V.

This hotel offers widely varying accommodations in two buildings. One building is rather romantic in decor, with an architecturally rich staircase leading to beautifully decorated bedrooms (one accommodation was once described as "straight out of the last act of *La Traviata*, enhanced by small gardens and terraces"). Your satin-lined room may have an inlaid desk and a wardrobe painted in the Venetian manner to match a baroque bed frame. Capping the decor are velvet bedcovers, gilt mirrors, and crystal chandeliers. Other chambers are far less glamorous. Both buildings that comprise the hotel are at least 100 years old, and are connected at lobby level. The older of the two has no elevator, and while the newer has an elevator, its modern bedrooms have conservative, rather sterile furniture. These more contemporary rooms have met with little favor from guests, so your reaction to this hostelry will depend entirely on your room assignment. Some 10% of the rooms are air-conditioned. Some more expensive suites are available. This hotel, one of the most famous in Venice, occupies a desirable location behind the opera house.

HOTEL MONTECARLO, calle dei Specchieri 463, 30124 Venezia. Tel. 041/5207144. Fax 041/5207789. 48 rms (all with bath). A/C TV TEL **Vaporetto:** San Marco.

$ Rates (including breakfast): 120,000–150,000 lire ($94.20–$117.75) single; 150,000–250,000 lire ($117.75–$196.25) double. AE, DC, MC, V.

The Hotel Montecarlo, located only a 2-minute walk from St. Mark's Square, was established some years ago in a 17th-century building. It was recently renovated to include modern baths. Your walk to your bedroom leads through upper hallways lined with paintings by Venetian artists. The double rooms are comfortably proportioned and decorated with functional furniture. However, the handful of singles are very, very small. Venetian-glass chandeliers in the rooms add a festive note.

HOTEL PANADA, calle dei Specchieri 646, 30124 Venezia. Tel. 041/ 5209088. Fax 041/5209619. 48 rms (all with bath). A/C TEL **Vaporetto:** San Marco.

$ Rates (including breakfast): 135,000 lire ($106) single; 210,000 lire ($164.85) double. AE, DC, MC, V.

The Hotel Panada lies along a narrow street, a few steps from St. Mark's Square. Its 1981 renovation transformed a run-down 19th-century hotel into a clean, bright, air-conditioned enclave with red-and-white marble floors, a charming bar, and cozy bedrooms. Each of these bedrooms offers a tile bath, gilt-framed mirrors, and

Venetian furniture painted with pastel-colored landscapes or flower arrangements. Some rooms contain TV.

HOTEL SAN CASSIANO CA' FAVRETTO, calle della Rosa 2232, 30145 Venezia. Tel. 041/5241768. Fax 041/721033. 35 rms (all with bath). A/C MINIBAR TV TEL **Vaporetto:** San Stae.

$ Rates (including breakfast): 90,000–160,000 lire ($70.65–$125.60) single; 150,000–202,000 lire ($117.75–$158.55) double. AE, DC, MC, V.

The Hotel San Cassiano Ca' Favretto used to be the studio of the 19th-century painter Giacomo Favretto. The views from the hotel's gondola pier and from the four-arched porch of the dining room encompass the lacy facade of the Ca' d'Oro, which is sometimes considered the most beautiful building in Venice. The hotel was constructed in the 14th century as a palace. The present owner has worked closely with Venetian authorities to preserve the original details, which include a 20-foot beamed ceiling in the entrance area. Today, the architectural plans from the many renovations hang in gilt frames above the antiques in the lobby. Patrons have included George McGovern and guests of the American Embassy. Fifteen of the conservatively decorated rooms overlook one of two canals, and many of them are filled with antiques or high-quality reproductions.

SAN MOISE, piscina San Moisè 2058, 30124 Venezia. Tel. 041/ 5203755. Fax 041/5228550. 16 rms (all with shower). A/C MINIBAR TV TEL **Vaporetto:** San Marco.

$ Rates (including breakfast): 160,000 lire ($125.60) single; 210,000 lire ($164.85) double. AE, DC, MC, V.

Off the beaten track for most visitors, the San Moisè provides much-needed peace and privacy. Located only a short walk from St. Mark's and near the theater, La Fenice, it's on a cul-de-sac, a little canal (Canale dei Barcaroli) overlooking the private garden of a neighboring palace. The hotel's bedrooms have been renovated and partially redecorated in a typical draped Venetian style. The owner suggests arriving by gondola if you can afford it. Breakfast is the only meal served.

INEXPENSIVE

HOTEL CITTA DI MILANO, campiello San Zulian 590, 30124 Venezia. Tel. 041/5227002. Fax 041/5227834. 24 rms (14 with bath). **Vaporetto:** Rialto or San Marco.

$ Rates (including breakfast): 57,500 lire ($45.15) single without bath, 86,500 lire ($67.90) single with bath; 86,500 lire ($67.90) double without bath, 118,000 lire ($92.65) double with bath. AE, MC, V.

You go through a winding series of narrow streets to reach this small hotel 300 feet from St. Mark's Square. However, relatively reliable signs point the way. The hotel is mainly known for its restaurant. Its accommodations are simple, but they are clean and centrally located. The reception area is usually filled with pedestrian traffic from the adjoining restaurant.

HOTEL LISBONA, San Marco 2153, 30124 Venezia. Tel. 041/5286774. Fax 041/5207061. 15 rms (all with bath). A/C MINIBAR TV TEL **Vaporetto:** San Marco.

$ Rates (including breakfast): 90,000 lire ($70.65) single; 120,000 lire ($94.20) double. MC, V.

The Hotel Lisbona is a simple and unpretentious hotel which benefits from its location near St. Mark's Square. It's next door to the far more expensive Hotel Europa & Regina and across a narrow canal from the costly Hotel Bauer Grünwald. Each of the Lisbona's rooms is clean and simply furnished in the style of the year of the hotel's opening (1975).

SAVOIA & JOLANDA, riva degli Schiavoni 4187, 30122 Venezia. Tel.

041/5206644. Fax 041/5207494. 80 rms (all with bath), 3 suites. TEL **Vaporetto:** San Zaccaria.

$ **Rates** (including breakfast): 145,000 lire ($113.85) single; 194,000 lire ($152.30) double; from 270,000 lire ($211.95) suite. AE, MC, V.

The Savoia & Jolanda is in a prize position on Venice's main street, with a lagoon at its front yard. Most of the bedrooms have a view of the boats and the Lido. While its exterior reflects much of old Venice, the interior is somewhat spiritless. However, the staff makes life here comfortable and relaxed. The bedrooms are neutral modern, with plenty of space for daytime living (desk and armchairs). An addition to the hotel contains 20 rooms, each with air conditioning, minibar, and TV.

PENSIONI

DONI PENSIONE, calle de Vin 4656, 30122 Venezia. Tel. 041/ 5224267. 13 rms (none with bath). **Vaporetto:** San Marco.

$ **Rates** (including breakfast): 70,000 lire ($54.95) single or double. No credit cards.

The Doni Pensione sits in a private position, about a 3-minute walk from St. Mark's. Most of its rooms either overlook a little canal, where four or five gondolas are usually tied up, or a garden with a tall fig tree. Simplicity prevails, especially in the pristine and down-to-earth bedrooms, but the level of cleanliness is high.

ON THE LIDO

VERY EXPENSIVE

EXCELSIOR PALACE, lungomare Marconi 41, 30126 Venezia Lido. Tel. 041/5260201. Fax 041/5267276. 196 rms (all with bath), 18 suites. A/C MINIBAR TV TEL **Vaporetto:** Lido; then bus A, B, or C.

$ **Rates** (including breakfast): 357,000–417,000 lire ($280.25–$327.35) single; 452,000–536,000 lire ($354.80–$420.75) double; from 1,190,000 lire ($934.15) suite. **Parking:** 25,000 lire ($19.65). **Closed:** Mid-Oct to Apr 1.

When the mammoth Excelsior Palace was built, it was the biggest resort hotel of its kind in the world. It did much to make the Lido fashionable. At first glance it appears to be a castle or a government building. However, it's a hotel of sweeping magnitude with rooms that range in style and amenities from cozy singles to suites. The Excelsior is a monument to *La Dolce Vita*—the preferred hotel of the film-industry people who, at festival time, book practically every one of the upper-floor rooms. Most of the social life here takes place around the angular swimming pool, which is traversed like lines on a Mondrian painting with two bridges, or on the flowered terraces leading up to the cabañas on the sandy beach. Clients can rent boats from a pier extending far into the Adriatic, the entrance to which passes between two guardian sphinxes. One of these, like the original in Cairo, is missing its nose, although the overall effect is undeniably high-style Italian.

All guest rooms—some of them big enough for tennis games—have been modernized, often with vivid colors that look like reminders of summer, regardless of the season.

Dining/Entertainment: On the premises is one of the most elegant dining rooms on the Adriatic, the Tropicana, with a soaring ceiling, thousands of embellishments, and meals costing around 90,000 lire to 145,000 lire ($70.65 to $113.85). The Blue Bar on the ground floor has piano music and views of the beach.

Services: 24-hour room service, baby-sitting, laundry, valet.

Facilities: Six tennis courts, swimming pool; a private launch makes hourly runs to the other CIGA hotels on the Grand Canal.

EXPENSIVE

HOTEL DES BAINS, lungomare Marconi 17, 30126 Venezia Lido. Tel.

041/5265921. Fax 041/526013. 190 rms (all with bath), 19 suites. A/C MINIBAR TV TEL **Vaporetto:** Lido; then bus A, B, or C.

$ **Rates** (including breakfast): 241,000–271,000 lire ($189.20–$212.75) single; 372,000–380,000 lire ($292–$298.30) double; from 650,000 lire ($510.25) suite. 19% IVA tax extra. Breakfast 21,000 lire ($16.50) extra. AE, DC, MC, V. **Parking:** Free.

⭐ The Hotel des Bains was built in the grand era of European resort hotels. It has its own wooded park and private beach with individual cabañas along with a kind of confectionary facade from the turn of the century. Thomas Mann stayed here several times before making it the setting for his novella *Death in Venice,* and later it was used as a set for the film of the same name. The renovated interior exudes the flavor of the leisurely life of the Belle Epoque era. This is suggested most strongly in its high-ceilinged main salon, the paneling of which is a dignified combination of Gothic with art deco. The hotel, which overlooks the sea, has well-furnished, fairly large rooms.

Dining/Entertainment: Guests can dine in a large veranda room cooled by Adriatic sea breezes. The food is top rate and the service is superior.

Services: A motorboat shuttle back and forth between Venice and the Lido, room service, baby-sitting, laundry, valet.

Facilities: Many resort-type amenities at Golf Club Alberoni (tennis courts, a large swimming pool, a private pier, and a park with shade trees and flowering shrubbery).

MODERATE

HOTEL BELVEDERE, piazzale Santa Maria Elisabetta 4, 30126 Venezia Lido. Tel. 041/5260115. Fax 041/5261486. 30 rms (all with shower). TV TEL **Vaporetto:** Lido.

$ **Rates** (including breakfast): 115,000 lire ($90.30) single; 180,000 lire ($141.30) double. AE, DC, MC, V.

Built in 1857, the Hotel Belvedere is still run by the same family. Restored and modernized, it also offers a popular restaurant (recommended in "Dining," below). The hotel is open all year, which is unusual for the Lido. It offers simply furnished double rooms, each with radio. Some have air conditioning or a view of the St. Mark lagoon. For the Lido, prices are reasonable. The hotel has parking in its garden, and it's located right across from the vaporetto stop.

HOTEL HELVETIA, Gran Viale 4-6, 30126 Venezia Lido. Tel. 041/ 5260105. Fax 041/5268903. 57 rms (all with bath). TEL **Vaporetto:** Lido; then bus A, B, or C.

$ **Rates** (including breakfast): 70,000–145,500 lire ($54.95–$114.20) single; 120,000–195,000 lire ($94.20–$153.10) double. MC, V. **Parking:** 10,000 lire ($7.85). **Closed:** Nov–Mar.

The Hotel Helvetia is a four-story, russet-colored, 19th-century building with stone detailing. It's on a side street near the lagoon side of the island, an easy walk from the vaporetto stop. The hotel is owned by two brothers who acquired it from an earlier Swiss owner who'd named it for his homeland. The quieter rooms face away from the street and rooms in the older wing have Belle Epoque high ceilings and attractively comfortable furniture. The newer wing, dating from around 1950, is more stream-lined, and has been renovated into a style appropriate to the conservative management that maintains this establishment. Breakfast is served, weather permitting, in a flagstone-covered wall garden behind the hotel.

QUATTRO FONTANE, via Quattro Fontane 16, 30126 Venezia Lido. Tel. 041/5260227. Fax 041/5260726. 69 rms (59 with bath). A/C TV TEL **Vaporetto:** Lido; then bus A, B, or C.

$ **Rates** (including breakfast): 170,000–190,000 lire ($133.45–$149.15) single; 230,000–250,000 lire ($180.55–$196.25) double. AE, MC, V. **Parking:** Free. **Closed:** Nov–Mar.

✪ In its price bracket, the Quattro Fontane is one of the most charming hotels on the Lido. The trouble is, a lot of people know that, so it's likely to be booked (and it's only open from April to October). Like a chalet from the Dolomites, this former summer home of a 19th century Venetian family is most popular with the discriminating British. They seem to appreciate the homelike atmosphere, the garden, the helpful staff, the rooms with superior amenities, and the good food served at tables set under shade trees. Many of the rooms are furnished with antiques. The hotel has a private beach and a tennis court.

NEAR THE ACCADEMIA

MODERATE

AMERICAN HOTEL, campo San Vio 628, 30123 Venezia. Tel. 041/5204733. Fax 041/5204048. 29 rms (all with bath). A/C MINIBAR TV TEL **Vaporetto:** Accademia.

$ Rates (including breakfast): 145,000 lire ($113.85) single; 200,000 lire ($157) double; 260,000 lire ($204.10) triple. AE, DC, MC, V.

Set on a small waterway, the American Hotel lies in an ocher building across the Grand Canal from the most heavily touristed areas. The lobby is filled with murals, warm colors, and antiques, and the location is the kind preferred by anyone wanting to avoid the crowds that descend on Venice in summer. Bedrooms are simply but comfortably furnished.

PENSIONI

LOCANDA MONTIN, fondamenta di Borgo 1147, 31000 Venezia. Tel. 041/5227151. 7 rms (none with bath). **Vaporetto:** Accademia.

$ Rates: 35,000 lire ($27.50) single; 50,000 lire ($39.25) double. Breakfast 4,000 lire ($3.15) extra. AE, DC, MC, V.

✪ ⑤ The well-recommended Locanda Montin is an old-fashioned Venetian inn whose adjoining restaurant is one of the most loved and frequented in the area. The hotel is located in the Dorsoduro section, an area across the Grand Canal from the most popular tourist zones. The establishment is officially listed as a fourth-class hotel, but its accommodations are considerably larger and better than that rating would suggest. Reservations are virtually mandatory, because of the reputation of this locanda. Because it has virtually all the business it can handle, the inn is difficult to locate, marked only by a small carriage lamp etched with the name of the establishment, which extends over the pavement.

PENSIONE ACCADEMIA, fondamenta Bollani 1058, in Dorsoduro, 30123 Venezia. Tel. 041/5210188. Fax 041/5239152. 26 rms (22 with bath). TEL **Vaporetto:** Accademia.

$ Rates (including breakfast): 72,000 lire ($56.50) single without bath, 108,000 lire ($84.80) single with bath; 126,000 lire ($98.90) double without bath, 186,000 lire ($146) double with bath. AE, DC, MC, V.

⑤ The Pensione Accademia is the most patrician of the pensioni. It's in a villa whose garden extends into the angle created by the junction of two canals. Iron fences, twisting vines, and neoclassical sculpture are a part of the setting, as are Gothic-style paneling, Venetian chandeliers, and Victorian-era furniture. The building served as the Russian Embassy before World War II, and as a private house before that. There's an upstairs sitting room flanked with two large windows and a formal rose garden, which is visible from the breakfast room. The bedrooms are spacious and decorated with original furniture from the 19th century. Some of the rooms are air-conditioned. The Pensione Accademia was the fictional residence of Katharine Hepburn's character in the film *Summertime*. Incidentally, it was when Hepburn was in Venice for the film that she fell into a canal and got a permanent eye infection.

FROMMER'S COOL FOR KIDS
HOTELS

Quattro Fontane *(see page 377)* Long a Lido family favorite, this hotel guarantees summertime fun. It's somewhat like staying in the big chalet of a Venetian family. There's a private beach, too.

Pensione Accademia *(see page 378)* Considered the best of the pensioni of Venice, this villa has a garden and large rooms. The former Russian embassy was the fictional home of Katharine Hepburn in the film *Summertime*.

American Hotel *(see page 378)* Secluded away from the tourist hordes across the Grand Canal, this is a moderately priced choice where many rooms are rented as triples.

Pensione Seguso *(see page 383)* An antique-filled palace dating from the 15th century, this is a relatively secluded family-type place where the half-board rates are good value.

NEAR THE RIALTO
MODERATE

HOTEL RIALTO, riva del Ferro 5147, 30124 Venezia. Tel. 041/5209166. Fax 041/5238958. 71 rms (all with bath). A/C MINIBAR TV TEL **Vaporetto:** Rialto.

$ Rates (including breakfast): 153,000 lire ($120.10) single; 210,000 lire ($164.85) double. AE, DC, MC, V.

The Hotel Rialto opens right onto the Grand Canal at the foot of the Ponte di Rialto, the famous bridge flanked with shops. Its bedrooms are quite satisfactory. They combine modern or Venetian furniture with the complexities of ornate Venetian ceilings and wall decorations. The beds are comfortable. The hotel has been considerably upgraded to second class, and private baths or showers have been installed in each unit. The most desirable double rooms overlook the Grand Canal, and naturally these go first.

MARCONI & MILANO, riva del Vin 729, 30100 Venezia. Tel. 041/ 5224503. Fax 041/5229700. 28 rms (all with bath or shower). A/C MINIBAR TV TEL **Vaporetto:** Rialto Bridge.

$ Rates (including breakfast): 149,000 lire ($116.95) single; 202,000 lire ($158.55) double. AE, MC, V.

The Marconi & Milano was built in 1500 when Venice was at the height of its naval supremacy. It incorporates a later addition. The older portion, once a wine shop, has been absorbed into the hotel. The drawing-room furnishings would be appropriate for visiting archbishops. The hotel lies less than 50 feet from the much portraited Rialto Bridge. The Maschietto family operates everything efficiently. Only four of the lovely old bedrooms open onto the Grand Canal, and these, of course, are the most eagerly sought after. Meals are usually taken in an L-shaped room with Gothic chairs. In fair weather, one of the sidewalk tables opening on the Grand Canal is preferred by many.

INEXPENSIVE

HOTEL DA BRUNO, salizzada San Lio 5726A, 30122 Venezia. Tel. 041/5230452. Fax 041/5221557. 32 rms (26 with shower). TEL **Vaporetto:** Rialto. **Closed:** Nov–Jan.

$ Rates: 84,000 lire ($65.95) single; 116,000 lire ($91.05) double. MC, V.

The Hotel da Bruno offers a view of Italian locanda life. The bedrooms are quite satisfactory—nicely furnished, compact, and tidy. Ignore the tiny lobby and the lack of a lounge, and concentrate on a good night's sleep. Da Bruno is halfway between the Rialto Bridge and piazza San Marco.

HOTEL MIGNON, SS. Apostoli 4535, 30131 Venezia. Tel. 041/5237388. Fax 041/5208658. 20 rms (15 with bath). TEL **Vaporetto:** Ca' d'Oro.

$ Rates (including breakfast): 59,000 lire ($446.30) single without bath; 88,000 lire ($69.10) double without bath, 115,000 lire ($90.30) double with bath. MC, V.

The Hotel Mignon is a small third-class hotel not far from the Rialto Bridge. After a facelift, it now offers some accommodations with private bath. Fortunately for lone travelers, there are many single rooms, a rarity in Venice. Most of the chambers overlook a private garden where breakfast and afternoon tea is served.

PENSIONI

CANEVA, ramo della Fava 5515, 30122 Venezia. Tel. 041/5228118. 23 rms (12 with bath or shower). **Vaporetto:** Rialto or San Marco.

$ Rates (including breakfast): 20,000 lire ($15.70) single without bath, 55,000 lire ($43.20) single with bath; 40,000 lire ($31.40) double without bath, 90,000 lire ($70.65) double with bath. No credit cards.

The Caneva is located midway between the Rialto Bridge and piazza San Marco. Many of the functional, comfortably furnished bedrooms overlook either the canal or the courtyard with its potted trees and balconies. The owner, Cagnato Gino, keeps his rooms tidy and employs a helpful staff.

RIVA DEGLI SCHIAVONI

VERY EXPENSIVE

DANIELI ROYAL EXCELSIOR, riva degli Schiavoni 4196, 30122 Venezia. Tel. 041/5226480. Fax 041/5200208. 231 rms (all with bath), 9 suites. A/C MINIBAR TV TEL **Vaporetto:** San Zaccaria.

$ Rates (including breakfast): 360,570–431,970 lire ($283.05–$339.10) single; 530,740–649,740 lire ($416.65–$510.05) double; from 1,125,740 lire ($883.70) suite. AE, DC, MC, V.

The Danieli Royal Excelsior was built as a grand showcase by the Doge Dandolo in the 14th century. In 1822 it was transformed into a deluxe "hotel for kings." Placed in a most spectacular position, right on the Grand Canal, it has sheltered not only kings, but princes, cardinals, ambassadors, and such literary figures as George Sand and her 24-year-old lover, Alfred de Musset. The palace has also played host to Charles Dickens, D'Annunzio, and Wagner. The palace fronts the canal with the New Danieli Excelsior, a modern wing. Another palace has been incorporated into this *serenissima* ensemble.

You enter into a four-story-high stairwell, with Venetian arches and balustrades. Throughout the hotel, you can wander in an atmosphere of silk-flocked walls, gilt mirrors, ornate furnishings, marble walls, decorated ceilings, and Oriental carpeting. Even the balconies opening off the main lounge have been illuminated by stained-glass skylights. The bedrooms range widely in price, dimension, decor, and vistas, and those opening onto the lagoon cost more.

Dining/Entertainment: The hotel has a rooftop dining room, giving you an undisturbed view of the canals and "crowns" of Venice, and an intimate cocktail lounge with leather armchairs. Guests gather in the Bar Dandolo in the evening to listen to piano music.

Services: Room service, baby-sitting, laundry, valet.
Facilities: CIGA hotel boat launch to the Lido.

LONDRA PALACE, riva degli Schiavoni 4271, 30122 Venezia. Tel. 041/5200533. Fax 041/5225032. 69 rms (all with bath). A/C MINIBAR TV TEL

Vaporetto: San Zaccaria.

$ **Rates:** 250,000 lire ($196.25) single; 400,000 lire ($314) double. Breakfast 25,000 lire ($19.60) extra. AE, DC, MC, V.

⭐ The Londra Palace is an elegant hotel with 100 windows on the Venetian lagoon. It was formed by two palaces that were joined together about 80 years ago and is now located a few yards from piazza San Marco. The hotel's most famous patron was arguably Tchaikovsky, who wrote his Fourth Symphony in Room 108 in December 1877. He also composed several other works here. The cozy reading room off the main lobby is decorated like a section of an English club, with leaded windows and blowups of some of Tchaikovsky's sheet music set into frames along the paneled walls. Other public rooms contain modern paintings, some showing an apocalyptic end of Venice by flooding. Bedrooms are luxuriously furnished.

Dining/Entertainment: The hotel has a popular piano bar and an excellent restaurant, Les Deux Lions.

Services: Room service, baby-sitting, laundry, valet.
Facilities: Conference hall.

EXPENSIVE

HOTEL METROPOLE, riva degli Schiavoni 4149, 30122 Venezia. Tel. 041/5205044. Fax 041/5223679. 63 rms (all with bath). A/C MINIBAR TV TEL

Vaporetto: San Zaccaria.

$ **Rates** (including breakfast): 255,000 lire ($200.20) single; 299,000–360,000 lire ($234.70–$282.60) double. AE, DC, MC, V.

At the widest part of the Grand Canal is the Hotel Metropole. This was once a house with a small musical chapel where Antonio Vivaldi taught and composed music from 1703 to 1740, and the study where he composed *The Four Seasons* concerto suite. An easy walk from piazza San Marco, this hotel is in a four-story building with green shutters, white trim, and a buff-colored stone facade. As you cross over the red-and-white checkerboard of the lobby's marble floor, you'll pass beneath a red-and-gold depiction of the lion of St. Mark attached to the ceiling.

This is a good hotel, dotted with unusual detailing and craftsmanship, and filled with lots of antiques and personal touches. A bar and grill with a zodiac theme lies just off the lobby. The hotel has an attractive sitting room and even a boat landing on a side canal for water-taxi and gondola embarkations. Built at the beginning of the 17th century, the premises were used as a private residence, then as a military hospital, and finally, in 1909, as a hotel. Totally renovated in 1985, the bedrooms are filled with elegantly conservative furniture, Venetian-glass chandeliers, painted headboards, and marble baths. Many of the accommodations overlook either the lagoon, one of the lesser canals leading into it, or a Venetian garden.

MODERATE

HOTEL SCANDINAVIA, campo Santa Maria Formosa 5240, 30122 Venezia. Tel. 041/5223507. Fax 041/5235232. 29 rms (25 with bath or shower). A/C MINIBAR TV TEL **Vaporetto:** San Zaccaria.

$ **Rates** (including breakfast): 96,500 lire ($75.75) single without bath, 147,500 lire ($115.40) single with bath; 135,000 lire ($106) double without bath, 199,000 lire ($156.20) double with bath. AE, DC, MC, V.

The entrance to the Hotel Scandinavia is set behind a dark-pink facade just off one of the most colorful squares in Venice. You'll have to climb a steep marble staircase to the reception desk, where a nearby window offers a panoramic view of the piazza. The public rooms are filled with copies of 18th-century Italian chairs, Venetian-glass chandeliers, and a re-created rococo decor. The decoration is in the Venetian style, but modern comforts have been added. There is also a bar, and room service is available for drinks 24 hours a day. A lobby lounge overlooks campo Santa Maria Formosa.

CAMPO MARIA DEL GIGLIO

VERY EXPENSIVE

GRITTI PALACE, campo Santa Maria del Giglio 2467, 30124 Venezia.
  Tel. 041/794611. Fax 041/5200942. 92 rms (all with bath), 4 suites. A/C
  MINIBAR TV TEL **Vaporetto:** Santa Maria del Giglio.
$ Rates (including breakfast): 375,000–425,000 lire ($294.40–$333.65) single;
  500,000–600,000 lire ($392.50–$471) double; from 1,150,155 lire ($902.85)
  suite. 19% IVA tax extra. AE, DC, MC, V.

The Gritti Palace, in a stately setting on the Grand Canal, is a renovated palazzo of the 15th-century doge Andrea Gritti. "Our home in Venice" to Ernest Hemingway, it has for years drawn a select clientele of some of the world's greatest theatrical, literary, political, and royal figures—Queen Elizabeth and Prince Philip, Greta Garbo, Herbert von Karajan, and Winston Churchill. The range and variety of the rooms seem almost limitless, from elaborate suites to relatively small singles. But in every case, the stamp of glamour is evident. Antiques are often used in both the bedrooms and the public rooms. For a splurge, ask for Hemingway's old suite or the Doge Suite, once occupied by W. Somerset Maugham. The management is used to catering to the whims of the famous, but it doesn't overlook the needs and desires of first-timers.

Dining/Entertainment: The cuisine served here is among the best in Venice. At Ristorante Club del Doge, an intimate room whose size is more than doubled in summer when tables are placed on a platform over the canal, meals are served daily from 12:30 to 2:30pm and 7:30 to 11:30pm. The cuisine is mainly Mediterranean. Expect to spend 100,000 lire ($78.50) and up per person for a meal.

Services: 24-hour room service, baby-sitting, laundry, valet.
Facilities: Use of Hotel Excelsior facilities on the Lido.

MODERATE

HOTEL ALA, campo Santa Maria del Giglio 2494, 30124 Venezia. Tel.
  041/5208333. Fax 041/5206390. 85 rms (all with bath). A/C MINIBAR TV TEL
  Vaporetto: Santa Maria del Giglio.
$ Rates (including breakfast): 110,000–155,000 lire ($86.35–$121.70) single;
  155,000–210,000 lire ($121.70–$164.85) double. AE, DC, MC, V.

The Hotel Ala has an entrance flanked by a pair of stone lions that look out over the same square that opens onto the Hotel Gritti Palace. Originally constructed as a palace in the 16th century, the establishment was converted into a hotel in the 1960s. It's under the same management as the Raffaele restaurant (see "Dining," below). It has simple lounges, a modest interior decor, and clean bedrooms. It has a flower-filled roof terrace suitable for sunbathing.

HOTEL BEL SITO, campo Santa Maria del Giglio 2517, 30124 Venezia.
  Tel. 041/5223365. Fax 041/5204083. 35 rms (all with bath or shower). A/C
  TEL **Vaporetto:** Santa Maria del Giglio.
$ Rates (including breakfast): 130,000 lire ($102.05) single; 185,000 lire ($145.25)
  double. AE, DC, MC, V.

The Hotel Bel Sito, located near the Gritti Palace Hotel, is considered one of the finest small hotels of Venice. It sits behind a baroque facade with green shutters and a view of the elaborately decorated Church of Santa Maria del Giglio. There's no elevator, so guests walk to the upper floors (four in all) for access to the guest rooms. Four rooms have a TV and 16 offer a minibar. Only breakfast is served.

NEAR THE SALUTE
PENSIONI

LA CALCINA, zattere al Gesuati 780, 30123 Venezia. Tel. 041/ 5206466. Fax 041/5227065. 40 rms (19 with bath or shower). TEL **Vaporetto:** Accademia.

$ Rates (including breakfast): 53,500 lire ($42) single without bath, 81,000 lire ($63.60) single with bath; 76,500 lire ($60.05) double without bath, 110,000 lire ($86.35) double with bath. AE, MC, V.

$ La Calcina lies in what was the English enclave of Venice before the area developed a broader base of tourism. This hotel is located in a less-trampled, secluded, and dignified district of Venice. John Ruskin, who wrote *The Stones of Venice,* stayed here in 1877, and he charted the ground for his latter-day compatriots. This pensione is absolutely clean, and the furnishings are deliberately simple and unpretentious. The rooms are comfortable.

PENSIONE SEGUSO, zattere al Gesuati 779, 30123 Venezia. Tel. 041/ 5222340. Fax 041/5222340. 40 rms (30 with bath or shower). TEL **Vaporetto:** Accademia.

$ Rates (including half board): 100,000 lire ($78.50) single without bath, 126,000 lire ($98.90) single with bath; 164,000 lire ($128.75) double without bath, 196,000 lire ($153.85) double with bath. AE, DC, MC, V. **Closed:** Dec–Feb.

$ The Pensione Seguso is a terra-cotta-colored house whose foundation dates from the 15th century. Set at the junction of two canals, this hotel is located on a less-traveled side of Venice across the Grand Canal from piazza San Marco. Its relative isolation made it attractive to such tenants as Ezra Pound and John Julius Norwich and his mother, Lady Diana Cooper. The interior is furnished with the family antiques of the Seguso family, who have maintained the hotel for the past 70 years. Small tables are set up near the hotel entrance, upon which breakfast is served on sunny days. Half board, obligatory, is served in the elegantly upper-crust dining room, where reproduction antiques, real heirlooms, and family cats vie for the attention of the many satisfied guests.

PENSIONE ALLA SALUTE "DA CICI," fondamenta Ca' Bala 222, in Dorsoduro, 30123 Venezia. Tel. 041/5222271. 50 rms (25 with bath). **Vaporetto:** Salute.

$ Rates (including breakfast): 57,000 lire ($44.75) single without bath, 80,000 lire ($62.80) single with bath or shower; 77,000 lire ($60.45) double without bath, 108,000 lire ($84.80) double with bath. No credit cards.

The Pensione alla Salute "Da Cici" is a centuries-old palazzo in a secluded and charming part of Venice. It avoids the usual mass-tourism features and links itself with the inner image of the city. It can be described as poetically oriented and has served as an offbeat haven for numerous writers and artists, including Ezra Pound at one time. This pensione is situated on a small waterway that empties into the Grand Canal. The "Da Cici" is furnished in a standard way, but most serviceably. The level of cleanliness is good.

NEAR THE ARSENALE
INEXPENSIVE

LA RESIDENZA, Castello 3608, campo Bandiera e Moro, 30122 Venezia. Tel. 041/5285315. Fax 041/5238859. 12 rms (all with bath). MINIBAR TV TEL **Vaporetto:** Arsenale.

$ Rates (including breakfast): 75,000 lire ($58.90) single; 120,000 lire ($94.20) double. AE, DC, MC, V. **Closed:** Nov–Feb.

$ This is one of the most unusual hotel finds in Venice. La Residenza is in a pleasingly proportioned 14th-century building that looks a lot like a miniature version of the Doge's Palace. It's on a residential square where children play soccer and older people feed the pigeons. After gaining access (just press the button outside the entrance), you'll pass through a stone vestibule lined with ancient Roman columns before ringing another bell at the bottom of a flight of stairs. First an iron gate and then a door will open into an enormous salon with elegant antiques, 300-year-old paintings, and some of the most marvelously preserved walls in Venice. Applied in 1750, they swirl to the top of the 20-foot ceilings in flamboyant curves of pink and green, the color contained within, not applied over, the stucco.

The bedrooms are far less opulent than the public salons, and are furnished with contemporary pieces and functional accessories. The choice ones are usually booked far in advance, especially for carnival season.

NEAR PIAZZALE ROMA

INEXPENSIVE

HOTEL FALIER, salizzada San Pantalon 130, 30125 Venezia. Tel. 041/ 5228882. Fax 041/5206554. 19 rms (17 with bath). TEL **Vaporetto:** Piazzale Roma.

$ Rates (including breakfast): 50,000 lire ($39.25) single without bath, 79,500 lire ($62.40) single with bath; 70,000 lire ($54.95) double without bath, 117,000 lire ($91.85) double with bath. AE, DC, MC, V.

The small and tastefully decorated Hotel Falier has an elegant reception area with stone Doric columns, red-and-white marble floors, and lots of paneling. In 1984 the owners combined their back-alley hotel with a streetside shop, and renovated each of the bedrooms to create what eventually became an almost completely new hotel. It's located in a commercial and working-class district of Venice not visited by the average tourist, campo San Rocco. Neighboring streets are lined with shops and local restaurants. Two peaceful and sunny terraces, situated at different levels of the establishment, are dotted with flowers and outdoor furniture. The hotel lies between the Santa Lucia railway station and piazzale Roma.

2. DINING

Although Venice doesn't grow much foodstuff, and is hardly a victory garden, it is bounded by a rich agricultural district and plentiful vineyards in the hinterlands. The city gets the choicest items on its menu from the Adriatic, although the fish dishes, such as scampi, are very expensive. The many rich and varied specialties prepared in the Venetian kitchen will be surveyed in the restaurant recommendations to follow. For Italy, the eating establishments of the city are high priced. However, there are many trattorie that cater to moderate budgets.

In Venice, a meal rated "Very Expensive" costs more than 120,000 lire ($94.20), meals judged "expensive" range from 90,000 lire to 120,000 lire ($70.65 to $94.20), "Moderate" is in the 50,000-lira to 90,000-lira ($39.25 to $70.65) range, and anything under 50,000 lire ($39.25)—at least by the standards of Venice—is judged "Inexpensive." These prices are per person and include three standard courses (but never the most expensive item on the menu, such as scampi or truffles), plus a carafe of the house wine, tax, and service.

NEAR PIAZZA SAN MARCO & LA FENICE

VERY EXPENSIVE

ANTICA MARTINI, San Marco 1983, campo San Fantin. Tel. 5224121.
Cuisine: VENETIAN. **Reservations:** Required. **Vaporetto:** San Marco.

FROMMER'S SMART TRAVELER: RESTAURANTS

VALUE-CONSCIOUS TRAVELERS SHOULD
TAKE ADVANTAGE OF THE FOLLOWING:

1. When available, order a fixed-price menu where everything—including tax, service, and cover charge—is included.
2. Watch the booze—tabs mount quickly. It's cheaper to ask for a carafe of the house wine.
3. Pastas, pizzas, and rice dishes (risottos) are exceptional bargains.
4. Standing up at a café or rosticceria is less expensive than sitting down.
5. Make lunch a picnic and save the extra money for a really good dinner.

$ Prices: Appetizers 12,000–24,000 lire ($9.40–$18.85); main courses 30,000–42,000 lire ($23.55–$32.95). AE, DC, MC, V.
Open: Lunch Thurs–Mon noon–2:30pm; dinner Wed–Mon 7–11:30pm.
Closed: Dec to mid-Mar.

Antico Martini is elegantly situated opposite the Teatro della Fenice. As the city's leading restaurant, it elevates Venetian cuisine to its highest level. It has enjoyed a long list of distinguished patrons, including Lord Olivier, Sir John Gielgud, Leonard Bernstein, Igor Stravinsky, and George Balanchine. Inside, the walls are paneled; elaborate chandeliers glitter overhead and gilt-framed oil paintings adorn the walls. Outside, the courtyard is favored in summer. The restaurant continues in the tradition of a Venetian palazzo. Actually, it was founded in 1720 as a coffeehouse, which served the popular Turkish brew in the heyday of trade with the Ottoman Empire. A wine grower from Tuscany acquired the coffeehouse as a bad debt in 1921. That long-ago proprietor was the father of the present owner, Emilio Baldi, who runs the present Antico Martini with just the right amount of dash and flair.

An excellent beginning is the risotto di frutti di mare, creamy Venetian style with plenty of fresh seafood. For a main dish, try the fegato alla veneziana (best when covered with a liberal sprinkling of freshly ground pepper), which is tender liver fried with onions and served with a helping of polenta, a yellow cornmeal mush praised by Goldoni. The roast baby lamb is also good. The yellow Tocai is an interesting local wine and especially good with fish dishes.

LA CARAVELLA, calle larga XXII Marzo no. 2398. Tel. 5208901.

Cuisine: INTERNATIONAL. **Reservations:** Required. **Vaporetto:** San Marco.
$ Prices: Appetizers 16,000–22,000 lire ($12.55–$17.25); main courses 32,600–46,000 lire ($25.60–$36.10). AE, DC, MC, V.
Open: Lunch Thurs–Tues noon–3pm; dinner Thurs–Tues 7pm–midnight.

La Caravella, next door to the Hotel Saturnia-Internazionale, offers, with its gracious ambience, an elegant pub atmosphere with time-mellowed paneling. Many of the specialties are featured nowhere else in town. For a different beginning, try a smooth gazpacho—the cold "liquid salad" of Andalusia. Standard dishes include chateaubriand for two people and spring chicken cooked in a paper bag. The best item to order, however, is one of the poached-fish dishes, such as bass—all priced according to weight and served with a tempting sauce. The bouillabaisse in the style of Marseilles is also excellent. After all that, the ice cream in champagne is welcome.

HARRY'S BAR, calle Vallaresso 1323. Tel. 5285777.

Cuisine: VENETIAN. **Reservations:** Required. **Vaporetto:** San Marco.
$ Prices: Appetizers 25,000–30,000 lire ($19.65–$23.55); main courses 45,000–50,000 lire ($35.35–$39.25). AE, DC, MC, V.

Alfredo, Alfredo 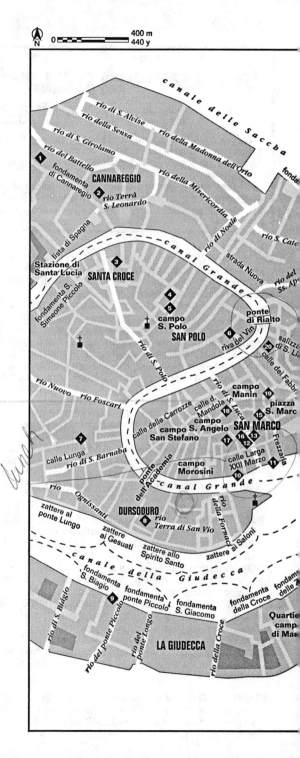 27
All'Angelo 26
Antica Besseta 3
Antica Martini 16
Archimboldo 29
Bar Torino 26
Barbacani, Ai 23
Belvedere 32
Botteghe, Osteria alle 26
Bruno, Da 24
Caravella, La 13
Chat Qui Rit, Le 26
Ciccio, Da 31
Club del Doge 10
Colomba, Trattoria alla 15
Corte Sconta 23
Cortile, Il 13
Dalvo 19
Deux Lions, Les 28
Fenice, Taverna La 17
Fiachetteria Toscana 21
Fiore, Osteria da 4
Forni, Do 28
Franz, Hostaria da 30
Harry's Bar 11
Harry's Dolci 9
Locanda Montin 8
Maddalena 2
Madonna, Trattoria 6
Noemi 14
Nuova Rivetta 27
Patata, Da 5
San Bartolomeo,
    Rosticceria 26
Spade, Cantina do 5
Teatro, Al 16
Tiziano Snack 1
Vecia Cavana, a la 22
Vedova, Alla 1
Vini da Arturo 18

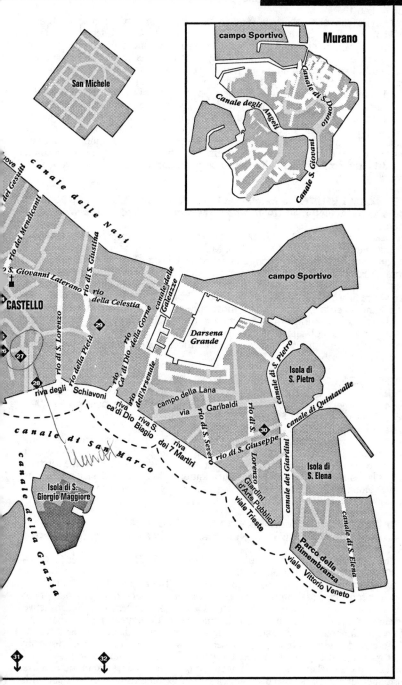

Murano

campo Sportivo

Canale di S. Donato

Canale degli Angeli

Canale S. Giovanni

San Michele

canale dei Gesuiti

canale delle Navi

rio dei Mendicanti

rio di S. Giustina

S. Giovanni Laterano

rio della Celestia

CASTELLO

canale delle Galeazze

campo Sportivo

rio di S. Lorenzo

rio della Pietà

rio Ca' di Dio - della Corte

rio dell'Arsenale

29

Darsena Grande

canale di S. Pietro

Isola di S. Pietro

27

28

riva degli Schiavoni

riva ca di Dio

riva S. Biagio

campo della Lana

via Garibaldi

rio di S. Severo

riva dei 7 Martiri

rio di S. Giuseppe

rio di S.

canale di Quintavalle

30

canale di San Marco

Lorenzo

Giardini d'Arte Pubblici

canale dei Giardini

Isola di S. Elena

Isola di S. Giorgio Maggiore

viale Trieste

viale Vittorio Veneto

Parco della Rimembranza

canale di S. Elena

canale della Grazia

31

32

Open: Lunch Tues–Sun noon–2:30pm; dinner Tues–Sun 7–10:30pm. **Closed:** Jan 4–Feb 15.

Harry's Bar serves the best food in Venice. Its fame was spread by Ernest Hemingway. A. E. Hotchner, in his *Papa Hemingway*, quoted the writer as saying, "We can't eat straight hamburger in a Renaissance palazzo on the Grand Canal." So he ordered a 5-pound "tin of beluga caviar" to, as he said, "take the curse off it." Harry, by the way, is an Italian named Arrigo, son of the late Commendatore Cipriani. Like his father, Arrigo is an entrepreneur extraordinaire known for the standard of his cuisine. His bar is a watering spot for martini-thirsty Americans—the vodka martini is dry and well chilled, but Hemingway and Hotchner always ordered Bloody Marys. Some superb libations are made with the juice of fresh peaches grown in the lagoon—a Bellini, consisting of champagne and fresh peach juice, is truly delectable. The food is good, and you can have your choice of dining in the bar downstairs or the room with a view upstairs. I recommend the Venetian fish soup, followed by the scampi Thermidor with rice pilaf, and topped off by a chocolate mousse.

TAVERNA LA FENICE, campiello de la Fenice 1938. Tel. 5223856.

Cuisine: ITALIAN/VENETIAN. **Reservations:** Required. **Vaporetto:** San Marco.
$ Prices: Appetizers 18,000–20,000 lire ($14.15–$15.70); main courses 20,000–32,000 lire ($15.70–$25.10). AE, DC, MC, V.
Open: Lunch Thurs–Tues noon–2:30pm; dinner Thurs–Tues 7–10:30pm.

Taverna La Fenice is one of the most romantic dining spots in Venice. The interior is elegant, but in summer guests dine outside under a canopy, beside the Teatro La Fenice where Stravinsky introduced *The Rake's Progress*. The service is smooth and efficient, and English is spoken. The most appetizing beginning is a selection of seafood antipasti. The fish in this selection is fresh caught from the Adriatic. You might enjoy the cannoli alla Fenice, rigatoni Fenice, or tagliatelle alle noci di mare (seafood pasta). Main-dish specialties include cartoccio Fenice (fish cooked in a paper bag) and steak Elisabeth cooked at your table.

AI BARBACANI, calle del Paradiso 5746. Tel. 4210234.

Cuisine: SEAFOOD. **Reservations:** Required. **Vaporetto:** San Zaccaria.
$ Prices: Appetizers 12,000–14,000 lire ($9.40–$11); main courses 22,000–35,000 lire ($17.25–$27.50). AE, DC, MC, V.
Open: Lunch Tues–Sun noon–3pm; dinner Tues–Sun 7–10:30pm.

You can enjoy some of the freshest fish in Venice here in a brick-lined series of dining rooms, by the light of flickering candles in the evening. The fish is grilled over a charcoal fire which is unusual for a Venetian restaurant. When you enter, the catch of the day is laid out on ice for your perusal. In addition to fish, a limited meat selection is available, along with an array of antipasti and pastas. The gnocchi a la seppie is definitely worth a try.

IL CORTILE, via XXII Marzo no. 2402. Tel. 5208938.

Cuisine: ITALIAN/VENETIAN. **Reservations:** Recommended. **Vaporetto:** San Marco.
$ Prices: Appetizers 15,000–17,000 lire ($11.80–$13.35); main courses 25,000–35,000 lire ($19.65–$27.50). AE, DC, MC, V.
Open: Lunch Thurs–Tues noon–2:30pm; dinner Thurs–Tues 7–10:30pm.

Il Cortile is connected to the more expensive Caravella Restaurant, which is part of the Hotel Saturnia-Internazionale. Il Cortile uses the same kitchen, but this attractive place charges less and offers just as much atmosphere. In summer, folding chairs are set beneath the abbreviated canopy of the central courtyard, permitting candlelit meals in a garden setting. In colder weather, guests select one of a pair of rustically elegant rooms covered with a painted and paneled ceiling. Bouquets of flowers and wrought-iron chandeliers add to the enjoyment of meals, as does the music of a live pianist. Specialties include osso buco with a saffron-flavored risotto, grilled quail with polenta, a mixed grill of fish, Venetian eel, grilled turbot, and several preparations of lobster, along with sea bass, truffled calves' kidney, and veal piccata. There is a changing array of daily specials derived from local recipes. The large wine list is one of the most impressive in the city.

EXPENSIVE

DO FORNI, calle dei Specchieri 468. Tel. 5237729.
   Cuisine: INTERNATIONAL. **Reservations: Required. Vaporetto:** San Marco.
   $ Prices: Appetizers 12,000–18,000 lire ($9.40–$14.15); main courses 18,000–28,000 lire ($14.15–$22). AE, DC, MC, V.
   Open: Apr–Oct, lunch daily noon–3pm; dinner daily 7–11pm. Nov–Mar, lunch Fri–Wed noon–3pm; dinner Fri–Wed 7–11pm. **Closed:** Nov 22–Dec 5.

Centuries ago, this was the site where bread was baked for some local monasteries, but today it's the most frenetically busy restaurant in Venice—even when the rest of the city slumbers under a wintertime Adriatic fog. It is divided into two sections, separated by a narrow alleyway. The Venetian cognoscenti prefer the front part, decorated in *Orient Express* style. The larger section at the back is like a country tavern, with ceiling beams and original paintings. The English menu is entitled "food for the gods" and lists such specialties as spider crab in its own shell, champagne-flavored risotto, calves' kidney in a bitter mustard, and sea bass in papillotte, to name only a few items.

RISTORANTE NOEMI, calle dei Fabbri 909. Tel. 5225238.
   Cuisine: INTERNATIONAL/VENETIAN. **Reservations:** Recommended. **Vaporetto:** San Marco.
   $ Prices: Appetizers 13,000–15,000 lire ($10.20–$11.80); main courses 18,000–20,000 lire ($14.15–$15.70); fixed-price menus 35,000–45,000 lire ($27.50–$35.35). AE, DC, MC, V.
   Open: Lunch Tues–Sat noon–2:45pm; dinner Mon–Sat 7–10:30pm. **Closed:** Dec 16–Jan.

Ristorante Noemi is a simple but tasteful room whose main decorative feature is a multicolored marble floor pieced into abstract patterns. It stands on a narrow street behind a russet stucco facade with swag curtains covering big glass windows, a short walk from piazza San Marco. Specialties include many items bordering on *nuova cucina*, such as thin black spaghetti with cuttlefish "in their own sauce," fresh salmon crêpes with cheese, shrimp soup in pink spumante, spider crab dressed in its shell, roast shoulder of veal (with chile peppers, olives, bacon, and capers), followed by the special lemon sorbet of the house, made with sparkling wine and fresh mint.

RISTORANTE A LA VECIA CAVANA, rio Terra SS. Apostoli 4624. Tel. 5287106.
   Cuisine: SEAFOOD. **Reservations:** Not needed. **Vaporetto:** San Marco.
   $ Prices: Appetizers 7,000–15,000 lire ($5.50–$11.80); main courses 15,000–25,000 lire ($11.80–$19.65); fixed-price menu 30,000 lire ($23.55). AE, DC, MC, V.
   Open: Lunch Wed–Mon noon–2:30pm; dinner Wed–Mon 7:30–10:30pm.

Ristorante a la Vecia Cavana is off the tourist circuit and well worth the trek through the winding streets to find it. A *cavana* is a place where gondolas are parked, a sort of liquid garage, and the site of this restaurant used to be such a place. When you enter, you'll be greeted with brick arches, stone columns, terra-cotta floors, framed modern paintings, and a photograph of 19th-century fishermen relaxing after a day's work. It's an appropriate introduction to a menu that specializes in seafood. These include a mixed grill from the Adriatic, fried scampi, fresh sole, squid, three different types of risotto (each prepared with seafood), and a spicy zuppa di pesce (fish soup). Another specialty of the house is antipasti di pesce Cavana, which includes an assortment of just about every sea creature.

TRATTORIA ALLA COLOMBA, San Marco-Piscina-Frezzeria 1665. Tel. 5221175.

Cuisine: INTERNATIONAL/VENETIAN. **Reservations:** Required. **Vaporetto:** San Marco.

$ **Prices:** Appetizers 12,000–20,000 lire ($9.40–$15.70); main courses 20,000–30,000 lire ($15.70–$23.55). AE, DC, MC, V.

Open: Lunch daily noon–3pm; dinner daily 7–11pm. **Closed:** Wed Nov–June.

Trattoria Alla Colomba is the leading trattoria of Venice. The restaurant is decorated with a small gallery of modern paintings, including works by well-known Italian and internationally known artists. The popularity of the trattoria is mainly due to the excellence of its cuisine, which includes such specialties as minestre di fagioli (bean soup), risotto di frutti di mare alla pescatora (risotto with seafood), risotto di funghi del Montello (risotto with mushrooms of the local hills of Montello), baccala alla vicentina (milk-simmered dried cod, seasoned with onions, anchovies, and cinnamon, and served with polenta), and granzeola (shellfish of the Adriatic). Fruits and vegetables are produced locally on the islands near Venice.

MODERATE

ALL'ANGELO, calle larga San Marco 408. Tel. 522-2000.

Cuisine: INTERNATIONAL. **Reservations:** Recommended. **Vaporetto:** San Marco.

$ **Prices:** Appetizers 10,000–12,000 lire ($7.85–$9.40); main courses 25,000–30,000 lire ($19.65–$23.55); fixed-price meal 38,000 lire ($29.85). AE, DC, MC, V.

Open: Wed–Mon 11am–midnight.

All'Angelo is the restaurant portion of a small hotel that draws a large clientele of artists, and paintings cover the bare brick walls. Here you can have some of the more popular Venetian specialties. From the à la carte listings, four are especially recommended: the mixed fish fry from the Adriatic, tender calves' liver fried with onions, scaloppine marsala, and sweetbreads, also cooked in marsala. Seafaring tastes may be attracted to the Venetian bouillabaisse or the grilled sturgeon. For those who flunked Italian, the menu's in English. The service is efficient. There's no pretentious drama, but superb victuals are prepared. If the weather's right, aim for a sidewalk table.

DALVO, calle dei Fuseri 1809. Tel. 5285004.

Cuisine: TUSCAN. **Reservations:** Required. **Vaporetto:** San Marco.

$ **Prices:** Appetizers 15,000–25,000 lire ($11.80–$19.65); main courses 20,000–30,000 lire ($15.70–$23.55). AE, DC, MC, V.

Open: Lunch Mon–Sat noon–2:40pm; dinner Mon–Sat 7pm–midnight. **Closed:** Jan 6–31.

Dalvo has such a faithful clientele that you'll think at first that you're in a semiprivate club. The rustic atmosphere is both cozy and relaxing, and your well-set table flickers to the glow of candlelight. A big plate-glass window frames a vista of an offshoot canal by which gondolas and their passengers glide. Homesick Florentines go here for some fine Tuscan cookery from that land of "milk and honey." In season, game, prepared according to ancient traditions, is cooked over an open fire. Of course, Tuscan beef is best, and it's preferred charcoal grilled with a minimum of condiment and sauce, simply seasoned with pepper, salt, and oil. A popular appetizer in Florence is anything prepared on "crostini"—that is, toasted bread. On my latest rounds, my hearty bread was browned to perfection and spread with a pâtélike paste made of chopped chicken livers and anchovies (it's recommended even to people who don't like anchovies). On a cold day one December my heart and plate were warmed when I ordered a homemade tagliatelli. Over it were spread slivers of tartufi bianchi, the pungent white truffle from the Piedmont district that is unforgettable to the palate.

AL GAMBERO, calle dei Fabbri 4685. Tel. 5224384.

Cuisine: ITALIAN/VENETIAN. **Reservations:** Not needed. **Vaporetto:** San Marco.

$ **Prices:** Appetizers 9,000–10,000 lire ($7.05–$7.85); main courses 10,000–20,000 lire ($7.85–$15.70); fixed-price menu 20,000 lire ($15.70). AE, DC, MC, V.

Open: Lunch Fri–Wed noon–2pm; dinner Fri–Wed 6–11:30pm.

Al Gambero, a canalside restaurant with a sidewalk terrace, is one of the best of the appealingly priced dining spots of Venice. The food is good and well prepared, with all sorts of taste treats. One fixed-price menu might include spaghetti or pastina in brodo, followed by Hungarian goulash or calves' liver fried with onions in the Venetian style. Other main dishes are likely to include a veal cutlet milanese or perhaps baked chicken accompanied by roast potatoes and a mixed salad. Afterward, you're faced with the fruit of the season or a selection of Italian cheeses. Many typical Venetian dishes are offered on another, slightly more expensive, menu—spaghetti with onion-and-anchovy sauce, gnocchi al casta (potato dumplings with stewed lamb sauce), casta in tecia (stewed lamb with polenta), stewed cuttlefish, and fresh sardines, marinated with onions and vinegar. Expect to pay a cover charge of 2,000 lire ($1.60) per person if you order à la carte.

RISTORANTE DA RAFFAELE, calle larga 22 Marzo 2347 (fondamenta delle Ostreghe). Tel. 5232317.
> **Cuisine:** ITALIAN/VENETIAN. **Reservations:** Recommended. **Vaporetto:** San Marco.
> **$ Prices:** Appetizers 8,000–12,000 lire ($6.30–$9.40); main courses 15,000–35,000 lire ($3.95–$27.50); fixed-price menu 30,000 lire ($23.55). AE, DC, MC, V.
> **Open:** Lunch Fri–Wed noon–3pm; dinner Fri–Wed 6:30–10:30pm. **Closed:** Dec 10–Jan 25.

Ristorante da Raffaele, a 5-minute walk from piazza San Marco and a minute from the Grand Canal, has long been a favorite canalside restaurant in Venice. The outdoor tables offer the kind of charm and special atmosphere unique to the city. However, the inner rooms are popular with Venetians and visitors alike. The huge inner sanctum has a high-beamed ceiling, 17th- to 19th-century pistols and sabers, exposed brick, wrought-iron chandeliers, a massive fireplace, and copper pots (hundreds of them), all of which contribute to the rustic ambience. If you go to the rest room, you pass through part of one of the kitchens, which is worth a visit in and of itself. The food is excellent, beginning with a choice of tasty antipasti or well-prepared pastas. Seafood specialties include scampi, squid, or a platter of deep-fried fish from the Adriatic. The grilled meats are also succulent and can be followed by rich, tempting desserts. The crowded conviviality is part of the experience.

VINI DA ARTURO, calle degli Assassini 3656. Tel. 5286974.
> **Cuisine:** VENETIAN. **Reservations:** Strongly recommended. **Vaporetto:** San Marco.
> **$ Prices:** Appetizers 8,000–15,000 lire ($6.30–$11.80); main courses 20,000–30,000 lire ($15.70–$23.55). No credit cards.
> **Open:** Lunch daily noon–2:30pm; dinner daily 7–10:30pm.

Vini Da Arturo attracts many devoted habitués, including artists and writers. Here you get some of the most delectable of the local cooking—and not just the standard cliché Venetian dishes. One local restaurant owner, who likes to dine here occasionally instead of at his own place, explained, "The subtle difference between good and bad food is often nothing more than the amount of butter and cream used." Instead of ordering plain pasta, one might try a tantalizingly sophisticated dish called spaghetti alla Gorgonzola. The beef is also good, especially when prepared with a cream sauce flavored with mustard and freshly ground pepper. Salads are made with crisp, fresh ingredients, often in unusual combinations. The place is small and contains only seven tables. The location is between the Fenice Opera House and St. Mark's Square.

INEXPENSIVE

AL TEATRO, campo San Fantin 1917. Tel. 5222446.
> **Cuisine:** ITALIAN. **Reservations:** Not needed. **Vaporetto:** San Marco.
> **$ Prices:** Appetizers 5,000–9,000 lire ($3.95–$7.05); main courses 10,000–19,000 lire ($7.85–$14.90); fixed-price menus 15,000–18,000 lire ($11.80–$14.15). AE, DC, MC, V.

Open: Lunch Thurs–Tues noon–2:30pm; dinner Thurs–Tues 7–11:30pm.

Al Teatro is a ristorante-pizzeria on a piazzetta adjoining the opera house. You can let your mood dictate your dining spot for the evening, as there are several rooms from which to choose. In fair weather, tables are placed out on the charming little square. Downstairs, one can order pizza and several regional dishes, including zuppa d'orzo e fagioli (a soup made with barley in fresh cream of beans). A noodle dish worthy of an award is tortelloni Lucia (made with butter, eggs, cheese, and bits of pork). This is one of the many specialties that the maître d' prepares right at your table. For dessert, try a mixed fresh fruit salad (macedonia) with ice cream or tiramesù, a typical Venetian cake. The upper-floor dining rooms are decorated in a rustic manner.

NUOVA RIVETTA, Castello 4625, campo San Filippo. Tel. 5287302.
Cuisine: SEAFOOD. **Reservations:** Required. **Vaporetto:** San Zaccaria.
$ Prices: Appetizers 6,000–9,000 lire ($4.70–$7.05); main courses 12,000–13,000 lire ($9.40–$10.20). No credit cards.
Open: Tues–Sat 9am–11pm. **Closed:** July 15–Aug 20.

Nuova Rivetta is an old-fashioned Venetian trattoria where you eat well and don't pay much. The restaurant stands close to an old bridge in the monumental heart of the old city. Many find it best for lunch during a stroll around Venice. The most representative dish to order is frittura di pesce, a mixed fish fry from the Adriatic, which includes squid or various other "sea creatures" that turned up at the market on that day. The most typical wine of the house is Prosecco, whose bouquet is refreshing and fruity with a slightly sharp flavor. This is one of the most celebrated wines of the Veneto region, and that's been true for centuries.

EAST OF PIAZZA SAN MARCO

MODERATE

ARCHIMBOLDO, Castello Calle dei Furlani 3219. Tel. 5286569.
Cuisine: VENETIAN/ITALIAN. **Reservations:** Recommended. **Vaporetto:** Arsenale or San Zaccaria.
$ Prices: Appetizers 6,000–14,000 lire ($4.70–$11); main courses 10,000–22,000 lire ($7.85–$17.25). AE, V.
Open: Pub, Wed–Mon 12:30–6pm; restaurant, dinner only, Wed–Mon 8pm–12:30am.

At the corner on which sits the Scuola di San Giorgio degli Schiavoni (containing Carpaccio's celebrated cycle of paintings), turn into a little street and follow a narrow footpath leading deep into Venice's oldest quarter. At the end of the street, you'll stumble upon Archimboldo, one of the city's most charming restaurants and tea rooms. It overlooks a canal and is named for Giuseppe Archimboldo, a famous 16th-century painter who worked at the Hapsburg court. Reproductions of his work line the walls.

The intimate and romantic decor is a fitting backdrop for the traditional Venetian fare served here. Both old and modern dishes are prepared with the excellent fruit and vegetables grown on the neighboring islands. Diners can enjoy Venetian-style antipasti, excellent pasta dishes, and the pick of poultry and meat. Everything is washed down with quality wines. Even though the restaurant is open only at night, an adjoining pub serves small lunches, snacks, and crêpes all afternoon, a light meal costing from 18,000 lire ($14.15).

HOSTARIA DA FRANZ, fondamenta San Isepo 754. Tel. 5227505.
Cuisine: SEAFOOD. **Reservations:** Required. **Vaporetto:** Giardini.
$ Prices: Appetizers 13,000–28,000 lire ($10.20–$22); main courses 18,000–35,000 lire ($14.15–$27.50). MC, V.
Open: Lunch Sat–Sun 12:30–3pm; dinner Wed–Mon 7pm–midnight. **Closed:** Jan.

Much of the experience of this place derives from the promenade required to visit it. It lies a long walk from St. Mark's Square beside a narrow canal whose waters are bordered by children, pets, flapping laundry, and grandiose monuments to 19th-century military heroes. Long ago the troops of the Austro-Hungarian armies used this building as a barracks, but today you'll find a bar, a dining room spanned with weathered beams, and an ebullient reception. In summer, elegant candlelit tables are placed along the river. Your meal might include a pasticcio of fresh fish, fish-flavored gnocchi, and a satisfying choice of fresh seafood. These even include lobster flown in from the waters off North America. The maître d' will recommend one of the local vintages to accompany your meal. Most maps spell this establishment's street name as "rio di S. Giuseppe," although local street signs refer to it as "rio di S. Isepo."

ON THE LIDO

MODERATE

RISTORANTE BELVEDERE, piazzale Santa Maria Elisabetta 4. Tel. 5223088.
   Cuisine: VENETIAN. **Reservations:** Required. **Vaporetto:** Lido.
$ **Prices:** Appetizers 12,000–13,000 lire ($9.40–$10.20); main courses 20,000–22,000 lire ($15.70–$17.25). AE, DC, MC, V.
   Open: Lunch Wed–Mon noon–2:30pm; dinner Wed–Mon 7–9:30pm. **Closed:** Oct 31–Easter.

Outside the big hotels, the best food on the Lido is served at the Ristorante Belvedere. Don't be put off by its location, across from where the vaporetto from Venice stops. In such a location, one might expect a touristy establishment. Actually, the Belvedere attracts some of the finest people of Venice. They often come here as an excursion, knowing that they can get some of the best fish dishes along the Adriatic. Sidewalk tables are placed outside, and there is, as well, a glass-enclosed portion for windy days. The main dining room is attractive, with cane-backed bentwood chairs and big windows. In back, reached through a separate entrance, is a busy café. Main dishes include the chef's special sea bass, along with grilled dorade (or sole), fried scampi, and other selections. You might begin with the special fish antipasti or spaghetti en papillote.

BUDGET

DA CICCIO, via San Gallo 241, Lido di Venezia. Tel. 5265489.
   Cuisine: VENETIAN/SEAFOOD. **Reservations:** Recommended. **Transportation:** See below.
$ **Prices:** Appetizers 3,000–4,000 lire ($2.35–$3.15); main courses 9,000–15,000 lire ($7.05–$11.80). MC.
   Open: Lunch Wed–Mon noon–3:30pm; dinner Wed–Mon 7:30–11pm.

Diners (or drinkers) here can sit either indoors or outside beneath a lovely pergola. This restaurant is located on the main street of the Lido. The atmosphere is decidedly informal. Most guests opt for a platter of fish, often fried, from the Adriatic, washed down with a simple wine from the Veneto area.

To reach the place, take the vaporetto to piazzale Santa Maria Elisabetta. From there, take bus D or G and ask the driver to let you off near the trattoria.

NEAR THE RIALTO

EXPENSIVE

"AL GRASPO DE UA," calle des Bombaseri 5093. Tel. 5200150.
   Cuisine: SEAFOOD. **Reservations:** Required. **Vaporetto:** Rialto Bridge.
$ **Prices:** Appetizers 10,000–20,000 lire ($7.85–$15.70); main courses 15,000–30,000 lire ($11.80–$23.55). AE, DC, MC, V.

Open: Lunch Wed–Sun noon–3pm; dinner Wed–Sun 8–11pm. **Closed:** Dec 20–Jan 8.

⭐ "Al graspo de ua" is one bunch of grapes you'll want to pluck. For that special meal, it's a winner. Decorated in the old taverna style, it offers several air-conditioned dining rooms. One has a beamed ceiling, hung with garlic and copper bric-a-brac. Considered among the best fish restaurants in Venice, "al graspo de ua" has been patronized by such celebs as Elizabeth Taylor, Jeanne Moreau, Rossano Brazzi, even Giorgio de Chirico. You can help yourself to all the hors d'oeuvres you want—known on the menu as "self-service mammoth." You can order the gran fritto dell'Adriatico, a mixed treat of deep-fried fish from the Adriatic. Desserts are good, especially the peach Melba.

MODERATE

FIACHETTERIA TOSCANA, San Giovanni Cristostomo 5719. Tel. 5285281.

Cuisine: VENETIAN. **Reservations:** Recommended. **Vaporetto:** Rialto.
$ **Prices:** Appetizers 9,000–15,000 lire ($7.05–$11.80); main courses 15,000–22,000 lire ($11.80–$17.25). AE, DC, MC, V.
Open: Lunch Wed–Mon 12:30–2:30pm; dinner Wed–Mon 7:30–10:30pm. **Closed:** July.

A street-level dining room spanned by old ceiling beams contains amusing modern art and an impressive display of the day's catch. A country-style wooden staircase leads past marble columns to an upper room and additional tables. Menu specialties mainly consist of different varieties of fish, including an octopus-and-celery salad, spider crab in its own shell, grilled razor clams, seafood risotto with champagne, and baked eel. A red-chicory salad from Treviso is the perfect accompaniment.

INEXPENSIVE

RESTAURANT DA BRUNO, Castello Calle del Paradiso 5731. Tel. 5221480.

Cuisine: VENETIAN. **Reservations:** Not needed. **Vaporetto:** San Marco.
$ **Prices:** Appetizers 8,000–12,000 lire ($6.30–$9.40); main courses 6,000–20,000 lire ($4.70–$15.70). AE, MC, V.
Open: Lunch Thurs–Tues noon–3pm; dinner Thurs–Tues 7–10pm. **Closed:** Jan.

Restaurant da Bruno is like a country taverna in the center of Venice, on a narrow street about halfway between the Rialto Bridge and piazza San Marco. The restaurant attracts its crowds by grilling meats on an open-hearth fire. Get your antipasti at the counter and watch your prosciutto order being prepared—paper-thin slices of spicy flavored ham wrapped around breadsticks (grissini). In the right season, da Bruno does some of the finest game specialty dishes in Venice. If featured, try in particular its capriolo (roebuck) and its fagiano (pheasant). A typical Venetian specialty—prepared well here—is the zuppa di pesce (fish soup). After that rich fare, you may settle for a macedonia of mixed fruit for dessert.

ROSTICCERIA SAN BARTOLOMEO, San Marco 5421-23 (calle della Bissa). Tel. 5223569.

Cuisine: VENETIAN. **Reservations:** Not needed. **Vaporetto:** Rialto.
$ **Prices:** Appetizers 6,000–8,000 lire ($4.70–$6.30); main courses 7,500–13,000 lire ($5.90–$10.20). AE, DC, MC, V.
Open: Lunch Tues–Sun 10am–2:30pm; dinner Tues–Sun 5–9pm.

Ⓢ The Rosticceria San Bartolomeo is the most frequented fast-food eatery in Venice and has long been a haven for budget travelers. Downstairs is a *tavola calda* where you can eat standing up, but upstairs is a budget-level restaurant with waiter service. Typical dishes include baccala alla vicentina (codfish simmered in herbs and milk), deep-fried mozzarella (which the Italians call *in carrozza*), seppie con polenta (squid in its own ink sauce, served with a cornmeal mush), and other dishes. Everything is washed down with typical Veneto wine. Once you leave the vaporetto, take an underpass on your left (that is, with your back facing the bridge). This passageway is labeled "sottoportego della Bissa." The restaurant will be at the first corner, off campo San Bartolomeo.

TRATTORIA MADONNA, calle de la Madonna 594. Tel. 5223824.
   Cuisine: SEAFOOD. **Reservations:** Recommended but not always accepted.
   Vaporetto: Rialto.
$ Prices: Appetizers 6,000–7,000 lire ($4.70–$5.50); main courses 13,000–14,000 lire ($10.20–$11). AE, MC, V.
   Open: Lunch Thurs–Tues noon–3pm; dinner Thurs–Tues 7:15–10pm. **Closed:** Aug 1–15 and Dec 20–Jan 31.

The Trattoria Madonna is one of the most characteristic trattorie of Venice. Unfortunately, it's usually so crowded you can't get in. On a narrow street, it lures customers with its fish specialties. To get you started, I suggest the antipasto frutti di mare (fruits of the sea). At the fish counter, you can inspect the sea creatures that are your potential meal. The mixed fish fry is a preferred dish

NEAR THE ARSENALE

EXPENSIVE

RISTORANTE CORTE SCONTA, calle del Pestrin 3884. Tel. 5227024.
   Cuisine: SEAFOOD. **Reservations:** Required. **Vaporetto:** Arsenale.
$ Prices: Appetizers 10,000–32,000 lire ($7.85–$25.10); main courses 20,000–35,000 lire ($15.70–$27.50). AE, MC, V.
   Open: Lunch Tues–Sat 12:30–2:30pm; dinner Tues–Sat 7:30–9:30pm. **Closed:** July 15–Aug 15 and Jan 7–Feb 7.

Ristorante Corte Sconta is located behind a narrow storefront that you'd probably ignore if you didn't know about this place. On a narrow alley whose name is shared by at least three other streets in Venice (this particular one is near campo Bandiere Moro and San Giovanni in Bragora), the restaurant has a multicolored marble floor, plain wooden tables, hanging metallic lights, and no serious attempt at decoration. It's become well known, however, as a sophisticated gathering place. As the depiction of the satyr chasing the mermaid above the entrance implies, this is a fish restaurant, serving a variety of grilled creatures (much of the "catch" is largely unknown in North America). If you don't like fish, a tender filet of beef is available. The restaurant's specialties include a mixed fish fry from the Adriatic (which includes scampi), a wide selection of grilled fish, Venetian antipasti, a few well-chosen pasta dishes, and both a zuppa di pesce and a risotto di pesce. A good selection of wines adds to the enjoyment of your meal. There's a big stand-up bar in an adjoining room that seems to be almost a private fraternity of the locals.

IN THE DORSODURO

MODERATE

LA FURATOLA, called lunga San Barnaba 2870A. Tel. 5208594.
   Cuisine: SEAFOOD. **Reservations:** Recommended for dinner. **Vaporetto:** Ca' Rezzonico or Accademia.
$ Prices: Appetizers 14,000–15,000 lire ($11–$11.80); main courses 25,000–28,000 lire ($19.65–$22). No credit cards.
   Open: Lunch Fri–Wed noon–2:30pm; dinner Fri–Tues 7–9:30pm. **Closed:** July–Aug.

La Furatola is very much a neighborhood hangout, but it has captured the imagination of Venetian restaurant aficionados. It's located in the Dorsoduro section, along a narrow flagstone-paved street that you'll need a good map and a lot of patience to find. Perhaps you'll have lunch here after a visit to the Church of San Rocco, which is located only a short distance away. You'll push past double glass doors and enter a simple dining room. The specialty is fish brought to your table in a wicker basket so that you can judge its size and freshness. A display of seafood antipasti is set out near the entrance.

LOCANDA MONTIN, fondamenta di Borgo 1147. Tel. 5227151.
   Cuisine: INTERNATIONAL/ITALIAN. **Reservations:** Recommended. **Vaporetto:** Accademia.
$ **Prices:** Appetizers 5,000–8,000 lire ($3.95–$6.30); main courses 12,000–20,000 lire ($9.40–$15.70). AE, DC, MC, V.
   Open: Lunch Thurs–Tues 12:30–2:30pm; dinner Thurs–Mon 7:30–9:30pm.

The Locanda Montin is the kind of rapidly disappearing Venetian inn that virtually every literary and artistic figure in Venice has visited since it opened just after World War II. Famous clients have included Ezra Pound, Jackson Pollock, Mark Rothko, and many of the assorted artist friends of the late Peggy Guggenheim, whose museum is just around the corner. Other luminaries have included Jimmy Carter, who, after a long day at a summit conference, requested dinner at a traditional Venetian restaurant. The inn is owned and run by the Carretins, who have covered the walls with paintings donated by or purchased from their many friends and clients. The building was constructed in the 17th century and used for many years as a storage place for the masses of firewood needed to chase away the chill of a Venetian winter.

Today its arbor-covered garden courtyard is filled with regular clients, many of whom allow their favorite waiter to select most of the items for their meal. The frequently changing menu is printed daily on the back of reproductions of one of the restaurant's paintings. Specialties of the chef include antipasti Montin, which includes a cold assortment of fruits of the sea. There is always an array of fresh pasta, plus a variety of salads, grilled meats, and fish caught in the Adriatic. Dessert might be a semifreddo di fragoline, a tempting chilled liqueur-soaked cake, capped with whipped cream and wild strawberries. The locanda lies in one of the least-trampled sections of Venice, the Dorsoduro, across the Grand Canal from piazza San Marco.

ELSEWHERE

AT SAN POLO

OSTERIA DA FIORE, calle del Scalater 2202. Tel. 721308.
   Cuisine: SEAFOOD. **Reservations:** Essential. **Vaporetto:** Silvestro.
$ **Prices:** Appetizers 12,000–13,000 lire ($9.40–$10.20); main courses 20,000–25,000 lire ($15.70–$19.65). AE, DC, MC, V.
   Open: Lunch Tues–Sat 12:30–2:30pm; dinner Tues–Sat 8–9:30pm. **Closed:** Aug and Dec 25–Jan 6.

The breath of the Adriatic seems to blow through this place, although how the wind finds this little restaurant tucked away in a labyrinth is a mystery. One never knows what's likely to be on the menu. An imaginative and changing fare is offered, depending on the availability of fresh fish and produce. If you have a love of maritime foods, you'll find them here—everything from scampi (a sweet Adriatic prawn, cooked in as many different ways as there are chefs) to granzeola, a type of spider crab. In days gone by, I've sampled everything from fried calamari (cuttlefish) to bottarga (dried mullet roe eaten with olive oil and lemon). For your wine, I suggest Prosecco, which has a distinctive golden-yellow color and a bouquet that's refreshing and fruity. It's been around for centuries, and is in fact one of the best-known wines of Venetia, made with grapes from the Conegliano. The proprietors extend a hearty welcome to match their fare.

TRATTORIA ANTICA BESSETA, calle Savio 1395. Tel. 721687.
   Cuisine: VENETIAN. **Reservations:** Essential. **Vaporetto:** Riva Biasio.

$ Prices: Appetizers 10,000–11,000 lire ($47.85–$8.65); main courses 15,000–16,000 lire ($11.80–$12.55). No credit cards.
Open: Lunch Thurs–Mon 12:30–2:30pm; dinner Thurs–Mon 7:30–9:30pm.
Closed: July 10–Aug 31.

If you manage to find this place (go armed with a good map), you'll be rewarded with true Venetian cuisine at its most unpretentious. Head for campo San Giacomo dell'Orio, then negotiate your way across infrequently visited piazzas and winding alleys. Push through saloon doors into a bar area filled with African masks and modern art. The dining room in back is ringed with paintings and illuminated with wagon-wheel chandeliers. Nereo Volpe, his wife, Mariuccia, and one of their sons are the guiding force, the chefs, the buyers, and even the "talking menus." The food depends on what looked good in the market that morning. The menu could include roast chicken, fried scampi, fritto misto, spaghetti in a sardine sauce, various roasts, and a selection from the day's catch. The Volpe family produces two kinds of their own wine, a pinot blanc and a cabernet.

LA GIUDECCA

HARRY'S DOLCI, fondamenta San Biago, Isola della Giudecca. Tel. 5224844.
Cuisine: INTERNATIONAL. **Reservations:** Recommended, especially Sat–Sun. **Vaporetto:** S. Eufemia.
$ Prices: Appetizers 17,000–18,000 lire ($13.35–$14.15); main courses 25,000–30,000 lire ($19.65–$23.55); fixed-price menus 50,000–53,000 lire ($39.25–$41.60). AE, MC, V.
Open: Lunch Tues–Sun 12:30–3:30pm; dinner Tues–Sun 7:30–10pm. **Closed:** Nov–Feb.

The people at the famed Harry's Bar have established their latest enclave far from the maddening crowds of St. Mark's Square on this little-visited island. From the quayside windows of this chic place, you can watch seagoing vessels, including everything from yachts to lagoon-based barges. White napery and uniformed waiters grace a modern room, where no one minds if you order only coffee and ice cream or perhaps a selection from the large pastry menu (the zabaglione cake is divine). Popular items include carpaccio Cipriani, chicken salad, club sandwiches, gnocchi, and house-style cannelloni. Dishes are deliberately kept simple, but each is well prepared.

SPECIALTY DINING

DINING WITH A VIEW

CLUB DEL DOGE, in the Hotel Gritti Palace, campo Santa Maria del Giglio 2467. Tel. 794611.
Cuisine: ITALIAN/VENETIAN. **Reservations:** Required. **Vaporetto:** Santa Maria del Giglio.
$ Prices: Appetizers 20,000–35,000 lire ($15.70–$27.50); main courses 38,000–65,000 lire ($29.85–$51). AE, DC, MC, V.
Open: Lunch daily noon–3pm; dinner daily 7–11:30pm.

This restaurant comes closer than practically any other restaurant in Venice to re-creating the setting of a doge's palace, as well as presenting some of the finest cuisine in Venice. Contained in a prestigious deluxe hotel, the restaurant has hosted such luminaries as Hemingway, Somerset Maugham, Princess Grace, Princess Margaret, and numerous show-biz figures such as Gregory Peck and Roger Moore.

The restaurant is in an intimate room whose size is more than doubled in summer when tables are placed on an outdoor platform extending over the canal. Indoors, you have a view of the beamed ceilings whose gray, beige, and pink patterns subtly match the colors of the marble floors, but outdoors you have the stone expanse of Santa Maria della Salute spread out just across the water.

The cuisine is essentially Mediterranean, and the chef always presents a limited selection of regional dishes from the Veneto area, including marinated baby sole in a Venetian sour sauce, Adriatic sea crab, and calves' liver with polenta. The menu always includes freshly made antipasti, elegant meats and fish, and other classic Italian dishes with many imaginative touches.

HOTEL DINING

LES DEUX LIONS, in the Londra Palace Hotel, riva degli Schiavoni 4171. Tel. 5200533.
   Cuisine: FRENCH. **Reservations:** Recommended. **Vaporetto:** San Zaccaria.
$ **Prices:** Appetizers 15,000–17,000 lire ($11.80–$13.35); main courses 22,000–33,000 lire ($17.25–$25.90). AE, DC, MC, V.
   Open: Snacks Wed–Mon noon–3pm; dinner Wed–Mon 8–11pm.
Les Deux Lions offers a view of a magnificent 19th-century equestrian statue ringed with heroic women taming lions. The restaurant, on the ground floor of the hotel, is filled with scarlet and gold, a motif of lions patterned into the carpeting, and English pub-style furniture. An adjoining piano bar is a popular nightspot. Menu items include typical French and international specialties. You might begin with foie gras de canard (duck liver), then follow with entrecôte béarnaise or salmon with champagne. The chef also prepares an excellent sole with "fruits of the sea." Summer dining is on an outdoor terrace with a view of the pedestrian traffic from the nearby piazza San Marco. This is a dinner restaurant, as only snacks are served at lunch

LOCAL FAVORITES

CANTINA DO SPADE, San Polo 860. Tel. 5210574.
   Cuisine: VENETIAN. **Reservations:** Recommended. **Vaporetto:** Rialto.
$ **Prices:** Appetizers 6,000–7,000 lire ($4.70–$5.50); main courses 8,000–10,000 lire ($6.30–$7.85); fixed-price menu 25,000 lire ($19.65). No credit cards.
   Open: Lunch Mon–Sat 9am–2:30pm; dinner Mon–Sat 5–8:30pm.
The Cantina Do Spade is an old (1475) and historic wine bar beneath an arcade near the main fish and fruit market of Venice. It was once frequented by Casanova. Venetians refer to it as a *bacaro* instead of a wine bar. It's decorated in the rustic Venetian style. The owner (whose hobby is collecting travel guidebooks) has 220 kinds of wine, which cost 1,000 lire (80¢) to 2,000 lire ($1.55) per glass. It's also a family restaurant, serving typical Venetian fare, including pasta e fagioli (with beans), spaghetti in a savory clam sauce, and other homemade pastas such as ravioli or lasagne. The kitchen also features game dishes such as hare. You can order 300 different kinds of sandwiches if you're eating light. Some sandwiches are made of the meats of boar, deer, or reindeer. Mainly the place is for Venetians, not tourists, but visitors are welcome.

LIGHT, CASUAL & FAST FOOD
Near Piazza San Marco

Le Chat Qui Rit, San Marco 1131 (tel. 5229086), is a self-service cafeteria, which offers Venetian dishes prepared "just like mama made." These might include cuttlefish simmered in stock and served on a bed of yellow polenta. You can also order a steak grilled very simply, flavored with oil, salt, and pepper, perhaps a little garlic and herbs if you prefer. Main-dish platters, which are served rather quickly after you order them, cost 9,000 lire to 12,000 lire ($7.05 to $9.40). It's open Sunday through Friday from 11am to 9:30pm; from July until the end of October it is open daily. Vaporetto: San Marco.
   Alfredo, Alfredo, piazza San Felipe e Giacomi, Castello 4294 (tel. 5225331), might be classified as a coffee shop. Here you can order any number of items, prepared in short order. These include pasta dishes such as spaghetti with a number of sauces, freshly made salads, crêpes, various grilled meats, and omelets. Main courses cost 12,000 lire to 22,000 lire ($9.40 to $17.25). Fixed-price menus are available for 16,000 lire ($12.55), 18,000 lire ($14.15), and 20,000 lire ($15.70). Service is Thursday

through Tuesday from 9am to midnight, so it's convenient to have a light meal at almost any time of the day. Vaporetto: San Zaccaria.

Near the Rialto

Tiziano Snack, Cannaregio 5747 (tel. 5235544) is a tavola calda (literally "hot table"). There is no waiter service. You eat standing at a counter or on one of the high stools. The place is known in Venice for selling pizza by the yard. From noon to 3pm, they serve hot pastas such as rigatoni and cannelloni. But throughout the day you can order sandwiches or perhaps a plate of mozzarella. Hours are 8am to 8pm Sunday through Friday. Main dishes cost 4,000 lire to 5,000 lire ($3.15 to $3.95). Vaporetto: Rialto.

    Bar Torino, San Marco 1501 (tel. 5223914), is ideal for food on the run. Between sightseeing jaunts, you can stop off here for a freshly made sandwich, but no pasta. There is waiter service at the tables. You can order a hamburger for 4,000 lire ($3.15) along with a beer costing from 2,000 lire ($1.55). Hours are 7am to 8:30pm Monday through Saturday. Vaporetto: Rialto.

Near Campo San Polo

Da Patata, San Polo 2741A (tel. 5237238), is what the Venetians call a *bacalo* or wine bar. This is a family-run place by a bridge near the Church of Santa Maria dei Frari. The place has an authentic atmosphere (with nothing gussied up for tourists). From the back emerge tasty treats such as fried potatoes or mozzarella to have with your wine. You might also ask for crisp rings of fried squid, which look like french-fried onion rings. The medley of bar snacks is called *cicchetti* in Italian. A glass of wine costs 500 lire to 1,200 lire (40¢ to 95¢). Ask for Prosecco, a sparkling wine with a distinctive golden-yellow color. It produces a great deal of foam. Hours are 10am to 8:30pm Monday through Saturday. Vaporetto: San Tomà.

Near Campo San Marcuola

Maddalena, Cannaregio 2348 (tel. 720723), is a self-service snack bar where you eat standing. From noon to 3pm you can order hot dishes, including such typical Venetian fare as pasta e fagiolo (with beans), a savory concoction that's a meal unto itself. Perhaps you'll choose the typical platter of Venetian liver and onions. Main dishes cost 8,000 lire to 10,000 lire ($6.30 to $7.85). At other times, you can try freshly made sandwiches, along with various toasts usually covered with some delectable spread. Sandwiches cost 2,000 lire to 3,500 lire ($1.55 to $2.75). This informal place is open Monday through Saturday from 7:30am to 8:30pm. Vaporetto: San Marcuola.

    Alla Vedova, Cannaregio 3912 (tel. 5285324), translates as "the widow's place" in Italian. It's a typically Venetian *osteria* which is 130 years old, with a vine growing inside. It's primarily a wine bar. However, many come to eat as well, although it's not a restaurant. You can feast on hearty Venetian soups, tripe, pesto alla genovese, or pasta all'amatriciana. If you're visiting just to drink the wine, I suggest that you sample a carafe of Marzeminio. You can also order wine by the glass, which costs 500 lire (40¢) and up. That's what many of the locals order. Main dishes begin at 5,500 lire ($4.30). Hours are 11am to 3pm and 5:30pm to midnight. It is closed on Thursday, and on Sunday opens only in the evening. Vaporetto: Ca' d'Oro.

Near Campo San Samuele

Osteria alle Botteghe, San Marco 3454A (tel. 5228181), is an offbeat snack bar featured in many publications, including the *Washington Post,* as a place for a light Venetian meal. It is small and decorated in a modern but classically inspired decor. You can feast on cold main dishes, including delectable eggplant, zucchini, and mushroom concoctions, or order one of the sandwiches made with such items as smoked salmon or truffles. Most diners gravitate to the suckling pig which is raised on a Veneto farm especially for this place. You can order prosciutto as well. Hot sandwiches are also available. Main dishes range from 6,000 lire to 10,000 lire ($4.70

to $7.85). Hours are 8am to 10pm Monday through Saturday. Vaporetto: San Samuele.

PICNIC FARE & WHERE TO EAT IT

Although its labyrinth of canals and lagoons permits restful vistas throughout Venice, there are only a few pockets of verdancy inside the city limits, and many of these are fenced-in and private. Because of that, your search for appropriately isolated picnic spots might require a bit more travel time (and a bit more imagination) than in cities with greater numbers of parks and public gardens.

You won't lack, however, for places to purchase the ingredients you'll need, which almost always taste better because of the tang of salt in the Venetian air. Don't expect an antiseptic and airy supermarket within the Venetian city limits. Virtually everyone in town divides her or his shopping among a variety of small stores, each specializing in a separate type of foodstuff. (Yogurt and cheese, for example, come from a *latteria,* slices of cold ham and salamis from a *salumeria,* wine from a *vinatteria,* bread from a *panneteria,* pastries from a *pasticerria,* and fruits and vegetables from an *alimentaria.*) Although only a handful of these shops are in the vicinity of St. Mark's Square, they appear frequently in virtually every other residential section of Venice. Shopkeepers are by now accustomed to foreign visitors, and even if your language skills aren't very good, pointing and gesticulating will work wonders in making yourself understood.

Venice's shops are supplemented with open-air markets selling every product of the Italian harvest. The biggest of these lies on the **campo Santa Margherita** (usually open Tuesday through Saturday, depending on the individual shopkeepers, till around 1:30pm). Conveniently, food shops tend to appear more frequently in neighborhoods containing these open-air markets, allowing shoppers to supplement their fruits, vegetables, and fish with such staples as cheese, meat, laundry soap, and spices. A similar market also exists near the railway station along the **rio Terrà San Leonardo** (between campiello Anconetta and the Ponte alle Guglie), another in **campo Santa Maria Formosa,** and yet another on **via Giuseppe Garibaldi,** in the eastern sector of the Castello Sestiere district. Most of the outlying islands (including Burano and Murano) also contain their share of small, family-run food shops as well.

Discovering a relatively calm corner might be as easy as locating an unoccupied bench on a quiet square, perhaps the steps of an off-the-beaten-track church, or the stone coping at the edge of an isolated canal. But if a windswept ride on a vaporetto appeals to your sense of seafaring adventure, why not combine your picnic with public transportation that offers a spectacular view of the Venetian lagoon and its many

---

 FROMMER'S COOL FOR KIDS
RESTAURANTS

Le Chat Qui Rit *(see page 398)* This is a self-service cafeteria where children are allowed to select what they want. Lots of pasta dishes.

Alfredo, Alfredo *(see page 398)* For the family on a sightseeing run. Short-order items are served quickly including spaghetti with a number of sauces and freshly made salads.

Tiziano Snack *(see page 399)* Famous for selling "pizza by the yard." You can also order hot pasta dishes and sandwiches.

Maddalena *(see page 399)* Filling fare is served quickly at this self-service snack bar where you stand up. The price is right, too. Introduce your child to pasta e fagiolo (pasta with beans).

architectural treasures? Take vaporetto no. 12 from fondamenta Nuove for a 45-minute ride to the sparsely populated island of Torcello, 6½ miles northeast of Venice. (The island also contains one of the region's oldest and most unusual churches, the Cathedral of Santa Maria Assunta—see Torcello in the next chapter.) There, after visiting the famous church, the trees and grasses of Torcello will beckon you to an isolated corner for a picnic, which, if the weather and your companion(s) are right, might become memorable.

CHAPTER 13

WHAT TO SEE & DO IN VENICE

- **SUGGESTED ITINERARIES**
- **DID YOU KNOW . . . ?**
1. **ATTRACTIONS**
- **FROMMER'S FAVORITE VENICE EXPERIENCES**
- **WALKING TOUR— PIAZZA SAN MARCO TO THE GRAND CANAL**
2. **SPECIAL & FREE EVENTS**
3. **SPORTS & RECREATION**
4. **SAVVY SHOPPING**
5. **EVENING ENTERTAINMENT**
6. **EASY EXCURSIONS**

Venice appears to have been created specifically to entertain its legions of callers. Ever since the body of St. Mark was smuggled out of Alexandria and entombed in the basilica, Venice has been host to a never-ending stream of visitors—famous, infamous, and otherwise—from all over the world.

Venice has perpetually captured the imagination of poets, artists, and travelers. Wordsworth, Byron and Shelley addressed poems to the city, and it has been written about or used as a setting by many contemporary writers.

In the pages ahead, we'll explore the city's great art and architecture. But, unlike Florence, Venice would reward its guests with treasures even if they never ducked inside a museum or church. In the city on the islands, the frame eternally competes with the picture inside.

"For all its vanity and villainy," wrote Lewis Mumford, "life touched some of its highest moments in Venice."

SUGGESTED ITINERARIES

IF YOU HAVE 1 DAY   Get up early in the morning and watch the sun rise over piazza San Marco, as the city wakes up. The pigeons will already be there to greet you. Have an early-morning cappuccino on the square, then visit the Basilica of San Marco and the Palazzo Ducale later. Ride the Grand Canal in a gondola 2 hours before sunset, and spend the rest of the evening wandering the narrow streets of this strangely unreal and most fascinating of the cities of Europe. Apologize to yourself for such a short visit and promise to return.

IF YOU HAVE 2 DAYS   Spend your first day as suggested above. On the second day it's time for more concentrated sightseeing. Begin at piazza San Marco (viewing it should be a daily ritual regardless of how many days you have in Venice), then head for the major museum, the Accademia, in the morning. In the afternoon, visit the Collezione Peggy Guggenheim (modern art) and perhaps the Ca d'Oro and Ca' Rezzonico.

IF YOU HAVE 3 DAYS   Spend your first 2 days as above. Begin in the morning of Day 3 by riding the elevator to the top of the Campanile di San Marco, then visit the Museo Correr later in the morning. In the afternoon, go to the Scuola Grande di San Rocco to see the works of Tintoretto. Spend the rest of the day strolling the streets of Venice. Even if you get lost, you'll eventually return to a familiar landmark, and you

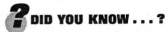

DID YOU KNOW . . . ?

- The Aga Khan owns many of the greatest hotels of Venice, including the Gritti Palace, named for the notorious womanizer, Doge Andrea Gritti.
- John Ruskin once wrote that nothing could have been "more childish in conception, more servile in plagiarism" than Palladio's Church of San Giorgio Maggiore.
- Many famous foreigners have asked to be buried on the cemetery island of San Michele: Lord Byron, John Ruskin, and Ezra Pound among them.
- The Lido, the bathing beach of Venice, was the original "Lido," lending its name to innumerable bathing spots and cinemas the world over.
- In the 16th century, any master glassblower escaping Murano with the secrets of the trade was tracked down by the Venetian republic. For punishment, his hands were cut off or he was murdered.
- The idea of encasing a Jewish settlement into a ghetto is of Venetian origin.
- When Paolo Veronese's *The Last Supper*—filled with "buffoons, drunkards, Germans, dwarfs, and similar indecencies"—brought down the wrath of the Inquisition, he simply retitled it *The banquet in the House of Levi.*
- The dogeship of Venice was the monopoly of old men because a ruler in his 70s would have fewer chances to abuse his position.

can't help but see the signs pointing you back to piazza San Marco. Have dinner in a typical Venetian trattoria.

IF YOU HAVE 5 DAYS Spend Days 1–3 as outlined above. On the fourth day, plan to visit the islands of the lagoon, including Murano, Burano, and Torcello. All three can be covered—at least briefly—on one busy day. On the fifth day, take an excursion to Verona (see Chapter 14).

1. ATTRACTIONS

THE TOP ATTRACTIONS
ST. MARK'S SQUARE

The ✪ **piazza San Marco** was the heartbeat of the Serenissima in the heyday of Venice's glory as a seafaring republic, the crystallization of the city's dreams and aspirations. If you have only 1 day for Venice, you need not leave the square, as the city's major attractions, such as the Basilica of St. Mark and the Doges' Palace, are centered there or nearby.

The traffic-free square, frequented by tourists and pigeons, and sometimes by Venetians, is a constant source of bewilderment and interest. If you rise at dawn, you can almost have the piazza to yourself as you watch the sun come up—the sheen of gold mosaics glisten into a mystic effect of incomparable beauty. At midmorning (9am) the overstuffed pigeons are fed by the city (if you're caught under the whir, you'll think you're witnessing a remake of Hitchcock's *The Birds*). At midafternoon the tourists reign supreme, and it's not surprising in July to witness fisticuffing over a camera angle. At sunset, when the two "Moors" in the Clock Tower strike the end of

another day, lonely sailors begin a usually frustrated search for those hot spots that characterized the Venice of yore but not of today. Deep in the evening the strollers parade by or stop for espresso at the fashionable Florian Caffè and sip while listening to a band concert.

Thanks to Napoleon, the square was unified architecturally. The emperor added the Fabbrica Nuova, thus bridging the Old and New Procuratie. Flanked with medieval-looking palaces, Sansovino's Library, elegant shops and colonnades, the square is now finished—unlike piazza della Signoria at Florence.

BASILICA DI SAN MARCO, piazza San Marco. Tel. 5225697.

The so-called Church of Gold dominates piazza San Marco. This is one of the world's greatest and most richly embellished churches. In fact, it looks as if it had been moved intact from Istanbul. The basilica is a conglomeration of styles, although it is particularly indebted to Byzantium. It incorporates other schools of design, such as Romanesque and Gothic, with free-wheeling abandon. Like Venice, it is adorned with booty from every corner of the city's once far-flung mercantile

Accademia 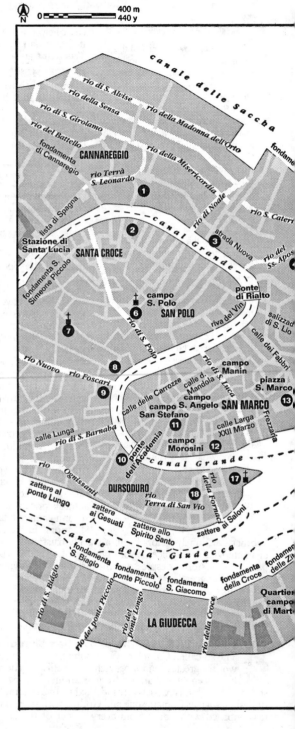⑩

Basilica dei Frari ⑥

Basilica di San
  Giorgio Maggiore ⑲

Basilica di San Marco ⑭

Ca' d'Oro ③

Ca' Foscari ⑧

Ca' Rezzonico ⑨

Collezione Peggy
  Guggenheim ⑱

Fondaco dei Turchi ②

Museo Correr ⑯

Palazzo Ducale ⑮

Palazzo Vendramin ①
  Calergi

Piazza San Marco ⑬

San Moisè ⑫

Santa Maria dei
  Frari ⑥

Santa Maria Formosa ⑤

Santa Maria del Giglio ⑪

Santa Maria dei Miracoli ④

Santa Maria della Salute ⑰

Scuola di San Giorgio
  degli Schiavoni

Scuola di San Rocco ⑦

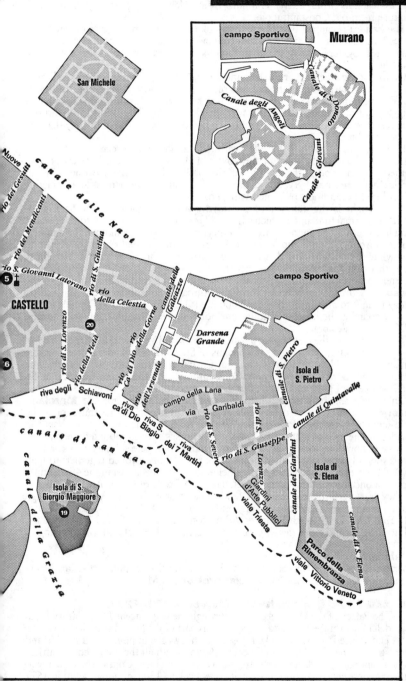

Murano

campo Sportivo

Canale di S. Donato

Canale degli Angeli

Canale S. Giovanni

Canale S. Giovanni

San Michele

Nuove

rio dei Gesuiti

canale delle Navi

rio dei Mendicanti

rio di S. Giustina

rio S. Giovanni Laterano

5

rio della Celestia

canale delle Galeazze

campo Sportivo

CASTELLO

20

rio di S. Lorenzo

rio della Pietà

rio Ca di Dio della Gorne

rio dell'Arsenale

Darsena Grande

canale di S. Pietro

Isola di S. Pietro

6

riva degli Schiavoni

riva ca di Dio

riva S. Biagio

riva dei 7 Martiri

campo della Lana

via Garibaldi

rio di S. Severo

rio di S. Giuseppe

rio S. Lorenzo

Giardini d'Arte Pubblici

viale Trieste

canale dei Giardini

canale di Quintavalle

Isola di S. Elena

canale di San Marco

canale della Grazia

Isola di S. Giorgio Maggiore

19

Parco della Rimembranza

viale Vittorio Veneto

canale di S. Elena

empire—capitals from Sicily, columns from Alexandria, porphyry from Syria, sculpture from old Constantinople.

The basilica is capped by a dome that—like a spider plant—sends off shoots, in this case a quartet of smaller-scale cupolas. Spanning the facade is a loggia, surmounted by replicas of the four famous St. Mark's horses—the *Triumphal Quadriga*.

On the facade are rich marble slabs and mosaics that depict scenes from the lives of Christ and St. Mark. One of the mosaics re-creates the entry of the evangelist's body into Venice, transported on a boat. St. Mark's body, hidden in a pork barrel, was smuggled out of Alexandria in 828 and shipped to Venice. The evangelist dethroned Theodore, the Greek saint who up until then had been the patron of the city that had "outgrown" him.

In the atrium are six cupolas filled with mosaics illustrating scenes from the Old Testament, including the story of the Tower of Babel. Once the private chapel and pantheon of the doges, the interior of the basilica is a stunning wonderland of marbles, alabaster, porphyry, and pillars. Visitors walk in awe across the undulating multicolored ocean floor, patterned with mosaics.

To the right is the admission-free **baptistery,** dominated by the Sansovino-inspired baptismal font, upon which a bronzed John the Baptist is ready to pour water. If you look back at the aperture over the entryway, you can see a mosaic, the dance of Salome in front of Herod and his court. Wearing a star-studded russet-red dress and three white fox tails, Salome dances under a platter holding John's head. Her glassy face is that of a Madonna, not an enchantress.

After touring the baptistery, proceed up the right nave to the doorway to the **treasury** (*tesoro*), open Monday through Saturday from 9:30am to 5:30pm and on Sunday from 2 to 5pm, and charging 2,000 lire ($1.55) for admission. The oft-looted treasury contains the inevitable skulls and bones under glass, plus goblets, chalices, and Gothic candelabra.

The entrance to the **presbytery** is nearby, and admission is 2,000 lire ($1.55). In it, on the high altar, the alleged sarcophagus of St. Mark rests under a green marble blanket and is held up by four sculptured, Corinthian-style alabaster columns. The Byzantine-style **Pala d'Oro,** from Constantinople, is the rarest treasure at St. Mark's—made of gold and studded with precious stones.

On leaving the basilica, head up the stairs in the atrium for the **Marciano Museum** and the Loggia dei Cavalli. The star attraction of the museum is the world-famous Quadriga, four horses looted from Constantinople by Venetian crusaders in the sack of that city in 1204. These horses once surmounted the basilica, but were removed because of damage by pollution. They were subsequently restored. This is the only quadriga (which means a quartet of horses yoked together) to have survived from the classical era. They are believed to have been cast in the 4th century. Napoleon once carted these much-traveled horses off to Paris for the Arc du Carousel, but they were returned to Venice in 1815. The museum is open Monday through Saturday from 10am to 5:30pm and on Sunday from 2 to 4:30pm. Off-season, it closes at 4:45pm Monday through Saturday. Admission is 2,000 lire ($1.55). The museum, with its mosaics and tapestries, is especially interesting, but walk out onto the loggia for a view of piazza San Marco.

Admission: Basilica, free.

Open: Apr–Sept, Mon–Sat 9:30am–5:30pm, Sun 2–5:30pm; Oct–Mar, Mon–Sat 9:30am–4:30pm, Sun 2–4:30pm. **Vaporetto:** San Marco.

PALAZZO DUCALE, piazzetta San Marco. Tel. 5204287.

The Palace of the Doges is entered through the magnificent 15th-century Porta della Carta at the piazzetta. This palace is part of the legend and lore of Venice. The palace is somewhat like a frosty birthday cake in pinkish-red marble and white Istrian stone. The Venetian-Gothic palazzo—with all the architectural intricacies of a paper doily—gleams in the tremulous Venetian light. Considered by many to be the grandest civic structure in Italy, it dates back to 1309, although a fire in 1577 destroyed much of the original building.

If you enter from the piazzetta, past the four porphyry Moors, you'll be right in the middle of the splendid Renaissance courtyard, one of the most recent additions to a palace that has experienced the work of many different architects with widely varying tastes. You can take the "giants' stairway" to the upper loggia—so called because of the two Sansovino statues of mythological figures.

The fire made ashes of many of the palace's greatest masterpieces, and almost spelled doom for the building itself, as the new architectural fervor of the post-Renaissance was in the air. However, fortunately, sanity prevailed. Many of the greatest Venetian painters of the 16th century contributed to the restored palace, replacing the canvases or frescoes of the old masters.

After climbing the Sansovino "stairway of gold," you'll enter some get-acquainted rooms. Proceed to the Anti-Collegio salon, which houses the palace's greatest artworks—notably Veronese's *Rape of Europa*, to the far left on the right-hand wall. One critic called the work "delicious." Tintoretto is well represented with his *Three Graces* and his *Bacchus and Ariadne*. Some critics consider the latter his supreme achievement. In the adjoining Sala del Collegio, you'll find allegorical paintings by Veronese on the ceiling. As you proceed to the right, you'll enter the Sala del Senato o Pregadi, with its allegorical painting by Tintoretto in the center of the ceiling.

In the Sala del Consiglio dei Dieci, with its gloomy paintings, the dreaded Council of Ten (often called "The Terrible Ten" for good reason) used to assemble to decide who was in need of decapitation. In the antechamber, bills of accusation were dropped in the lion's mouth.

Now trek downstairs through the once-private apartments of the doges to the grand Maggior Consiglio, with its allegorical *Triumph of Venice* on the ceiling, painted by Veronese. What makes the room outstanding, however, is Tintoretto's *Paradise,* over the Grand Council chamber—said to be "the largest oil painting in the world." Paradise seems to have an overpopulation problem, perhaps a too-optimistic point of view on Tintoretto's part. Tintoretto was in his 70s when he began this monumental work (he died only 6 years later). The second grandiose hall, entered from the grand chamber, is the Sala dello Scrutinio, with paintings that tell of the past glories of Venice.

Reentering the Maggior Consiglio, follow the arrows on their trail across the **Bridge of Sighs,** linking the Doges' Palace with the Palazzo delle Prigioni, where the cellblocks are found, the ones that lodged the prisoners who felt the quick justice of the "Terrible Ten." The "sighs" in the bridge's name stemmed from the sad laments of the numerous victims led across it to certain torture and possible death. The cells are just dank remnants of the horror of medieval justice.

Admission: 5,000 lire ($3.95).

Open: Easter–Oct, daily 8:30am–6pm; Nov–Easter, daily 8:30am–2pm. **Vaporetto:** San Marco.

CAMPANILE DI SAN MARCO, piazza San Marco. Tel. 5224064.

One summer night back in 1902, the bell tower of the Basilica of St. Mark on piazza San Marco, which was suffering from years of rheumatism in the damp Venetian climate, gave out a warning sound that sent the elegant and fashionable coffee drinkers scurrying from the Florian Caffè in a dash for their lives. But the campanile gracefully waited till the next morning—July 14—before it tumbled into the piazza. The Venetians rebuilt their belfry, and it's now safe to ascend. In campanile-crazed Italy, where visitors must often ascend circuitous stairs, it's good to report that the Venetian version has a modern elevator. You can ride it and get a pigeon's view of the city. It's a particularly good vantage point for viewing the cupolas of St. Mark's Basilica.

Admission: 3,000 lire ($2.35).

Open: June–Aug, daily 9:30am–9:30pm; Sept–Dec and Feb–May, daily 10am–4pm. **Closed:** Jan. **Vaporetto:** San Marco.

TORRE DELL'OROLOGIO, piazza San Marco.

At piazza San Marco is one of the most typical and characteristic of Venetian scenes—the two Moors striking the bell atop the Clock Tower (Torre dell'Orologio). The torre soars over the Old Procuratie. The clock under the winged lion not only tells the time, but is a boon to the astrologer: It matches the signs of the zodiac with the position of the sun. If the movement of the Moors striking the hour seems slow in today's fast, mechanized world, remember how many centuries the poor wretches have been at their task without time off. The "Moors" originally represented two European shepherds. However, after having been reproduced in bronze, they have grown darker with the passing of time. As a consequence, they came to be called Moors by the Venetians. The tower is closed for restoration, but check its status and the price of admission at the time of your visit.

Admission: Not known at press time. At least you can observe its exterior.
Open: See above. **Vaporetto:** San Marco.

PIAZZETTA SAN MARCO

If piazza San Marco is the drawing room of Europe, then its satellite, piazzetta San Marco, is the antechamber. Hedged in by the Doges' Palace, Sansovino's Library, and a side of St. Mark's, the tiny square faces the Grand Canal. One of the two tall granite columns is mounted by a winged lion, which represents St. Mark. The other is topped by a statue of a man taming a dragon, supposedly the dethroned patron St. Theodore. Both columns came from the East in the 12th century.

During the heyday of the Serene Republic, dozens of victims either lost their heads or were strung up here, many of them first being subjected to torture that would have made the Marquis de Sade flinch. One, for example, had his teeth hammered in, his eyes gouged out, and his hands cut off before being strung up. Venetian justice became notorious throughout Europe.

If you stand with your back to the canal, looking toward the south facade of St. Mark's Basilica, you'll see the so-called *Virgin and Child* of the poor baker, a mosaic honoring Pietro Fasiol (also Faziol), a young man unjustly sentenced to death on a charge of murder.

To the left of the entrance to the Doges' Palace are four porphyry figures, which, for want of a better description, the Venetians called "Moors." These puce-colored fellows are huddled close together, as if afraid. Considering the decapitations and torture that have occurred on the piazzetta, I shouldn't wonder. Vaporetto: San Marco.

THE LIDO

Along the white sands of the Lido strolled a hand-holding Eleonora Duse and Gabriele d'Annunzio (*Flame of Life*), Goethe in Faustian gloom, a clubfooted Byron trying to decide with whom he was in love that day, de Musset pondering the fickle ways of George Sand, and Thomas Mann's Gustave von Aschenbach with his eye on Tadzio in *Death in Venice*. But gone is the relative isolation of yore. The de Mussets of today aren't mooning over lost loves—they're out chasing bikini-clad new ones.

Near the turn of the century the Lido began to blossom into a fashionable beachfront resort, complete with deluxe hotels and its Municipal Casino (see "Evening Entertainment," below). Lido prices are usually stratospheric. It is not a haven for budget-minded tourists.

Even if you aren't lodging at the Lido, you may still want to come over for a swim in the Adriatic. And if you don't want to cross the thresholds of the rarefied citadels of hotel beachfront property—with huts lining the beach like those of some tropical paradise—you can try the Lungomare G. d'Annunzio Public Bathing Beach at the end of the Gran Viale (piazzale Ettore Sorger), a long stroll from the vaporetto stop. You can book cabins—called *camerini*—and enjoy the sand. Rates change seasonally.

To reach the Lido, take vaporetto no. 6 (the ride takes about 15 minutes). The boat departs from a landing stage near the Doges' Palace.

THE GRAND CANAL

Peoria may have its Main Street, Paris its Champs-Elysées—but Venice, for uniqueness, tops them all with its ✪ **Canal Grande.** Lined with palazzi—many in the elegant Venetian-Gothic style—this great road of water is today filled with vaporetti, motorboats, and gondolas. Along the canal the boat moorings are like peppermint sticks. It begins at piazzetta San Marco on one side and Longhena's Salute Church on the opposite bank. At midpoint, it is spanned by the Rialto Bridge. Eventually, the canal winds its serpentine course to the railway station. I can guarantee that there's not a dull sight en route.

Of course, the gloriously coiffured ladies Longhi painted have faded with high tide. Many of the lavish furnishings and tapestries that adorned the interiors of the palaces were hauled off to museums or ended up in the homes of the heirs of the rising mercantile class of 2 centuries ago. In the sad decline of their city, the Venetian nobility didn't become less noble; they only went broke.

Some of the major and most impressive buildings along the Grand Canal have been converted into galleries and museums. Others have been turned into cooperative apartments. Venetian housewives aren't as incurably romantic as foreign visitors. A practical lot, these women can be seen stringing up their laundry in front of thousands upon thousands of tourists.

Along this canal one foggy day came Madame Amandine Lucile Aurore Dudevant, née Dupin (otherwise known as George Sand), with her effete, poetic young lover, Alfred de Musset. John Ruskin came this way to debunk and expose in his *The Stones of Venice*. Robert Browning, burnt out from the loss of his beloved Elizabeth and his later rejection at the hands of Lady Ashburton, came here to settle down in a palazzo where he eventually died. More recently, Eleonora Duse came this way with the young poet to whom she had given her heart, Gabriele d'Annunzio. Even Shakespeare came here in his fantasies. Intrepid guides will point out the "Palazzo de Desdemona."

MUSEUMS & GALLERIES

Venice is a city of art. Decorating its palazzi and adorning its canvases were artists such as Giovanni Bellini, Carpaccio, Giorgione, Titian, Lotto, Tintoretto, Veronese, Tiepolo, Guardi, Canaletto, and Longhi, to name just the more important ones. In the museums and galleries to follow, important works by all these artists are exhibited, as well as a number of modern surprises, such as those in the Guggenheim Collection.

Open hours are often subject to major variations, so keep this in mind as you go sightseeing. Many visitors who have budgeted only 2 or 3 days for Venice often express disappointment when, for some unknown reason, a major attraction closes abruptly.

ACCADEMIA, campo della Carità, Dorsoduro. Tel. 5222247.

The pomp and circumstance, the glory that was Venice, lives on in this remarkable collection of paintings which span the 14th to the 18th century. The hallmark of the Venetian school is color and more color. From Giorgione to Veronese, from Titian to Tintoretto, with a Carpaccio cycle thrown in, the Accademia has samples—often their best—of its most famous sons. I'll highlight only some of the most-renowned masterpieces for the first-timer in a rush.

You'll first see works by such 14th-century artists as Paolo and Lorenzo Veneziano, who bridged the gap from Byzantine art to Gothic (see the latter's *Annunciation*). Next, you'll view Giovanni Bellini's *Madonna and Saint* (poor Sebastian, not another arrow), and Carpaccio's fascinating, although gruesome, work of mass crucifixion. As you move on, head for the painting on the easel by the window, attributed to the great Venetian artist Giorgione. On this canvas he depicted the

IMPRESSIONS

A city for beavers.
—RALPH WALDO EMERSON, REFERRING TO VENICE, IN HIS JOURNAL, JUNE 1833

I'm glad to find that you dislike Venice because I thought it detestable when we were there, both times—once it might be due to insanity but not twice, so I thought it must be my fault.
—VIRGINIA WOOLF, LETTER TO VANESSA BELL, APRIL 25, 1913

Madonna and Child, along with the mystic St. Catherine of Siena and John the Baptist (a neat trick for Catherine, who seems to have perfected transmigration to join the cast of characters).

Two of the most important works with secular themes are Mantegna's armored *St. George,* with the dragon slain at his feet, and Hans Memling's 15th-century portrait of a young man. A most unusual *Madonna and Child* is by Cosmé Tura, the master of Ferrara, who could always be counted on to give a new twist to an old subject. The Tuscan master Piero della Francesca is represented by his *St. Jerome.*

The madonnas and bambini of Giovanni Bellini, an expert in the harmonious blending of colors, are the focus of another room. None but the major artists could stand the test of a salon filled with the same subjects, but under Bellini's brush each Virgin achieves her individual spirituality. Giorgione's *Tempest,* displayed here, is the single most famous painting at the Accademia. It depicts a baby suckling from the breast of its mother, while a man with a staff looks on. What might have emerged as a simple pastoral scene on the easel of a lesser artist comes forth as a picture of rare and exceptional beauty. Summer lightning pierces the sky, but the tempest seems to be in the background—far away from the figures in the foreground, who are menaced without knowing it.

The masterpiece of Lorenzo Lotto, a melancholy portrait of a young man, can be seen before you come to a room dominated by Paolo Veronese's *The Banquet in the House of Levi.* This is, in reality, a "Last Supper" that was considered a sacrilege in its day and Veronese was forced to change its name to indicate a secular work. Impish Veronese caught the hot fire of the Inquisition by including in the mammoth canvas dogs, a cat, midgets, blackamoors, Huns, and drunken revelers. Four large paintings by Tintoretto—noted for their swirling action and powerful drama—depict scenes from the life of St. Mark. Finally, painted in his declining years (some have suggested in his 99th year before he died from the plague), is Titian's majestic *Pietà.*

Many other works by Veronese (an epic *Crucifixion,* an *Annunciation,* and *The Battle of Lepanto,* based on a battle in which the Venetians triumphed over the Turks) and by Tintoretto (a golden *Cain and Abel* and an *Adam and Eve*) can be viewed. Tiepolo, the great decorative painter, has figures writhing across one wall, plus two curious 3-D works in the corners.

After a long and unimpressive walk, you can search out Canaletto's *Porticato.* Yet another room is heightened by Gentile Bellini's stunning portrait of St. Mark's Square, back in the days (1496) when the houses glistened with gold in the sunlight. All the works in this salon are intriguing, especially the re-creation of the *Ponte de Rialto,* and a covered wood bridge, by Carpaccio.

The cycle of narrative paintings that Vittore Carpaccio did of St. Ursula for the Scuola (School) of Santa Orsola is displayed. The most famous is no. 578, which shows Ursula asleep on her elongated bed, with a dog nestled on the floor nearby, as the angels come for a visitation. But all the works are excellent virtuoso performances by the artists. Finally, on the way out, look for Titian's *Presentation of the Virgin,* a fit farewell to this galaxy of great Venetian art.

Admission: 4,000 lire ($3.15).

Open: Daily except hols 9am–2pm, hols 9am–1pm. **Vaporetto:** Accademia.

MUSEO CORRER, in the Procuratie Nuove, piazza San Marco. Tel. 5225625.

This museum traces the development of Venetian painting from the 14th to the 16th century. On the second floor are the red-and-maroon robes once worn by the doges, plus some fabulous street lanterns. There is also an illustrated copy of *Marco Polo in Tartaria.* You can see Cosmé Tura's *La Pietà,* a miniature of renown from the genius in the Ferrara School. This is one of his more gruesome works. It depicts a bony, gnarled Christ sprawled on the lap of the Madonna. Farther on, search out a Schiavone *Madonna and Child* (no. 545), my candidate for the ugliest bambino ever depicted on canvas (no wonder the mother looks askance).

One of the most important rooms at the Correr is filled with three masterpieces: *La Pietà* by Antonello da Messina, a *Crucifixion* by the Flemish painter Hugo van der Goes, and a *Madonna and Child* by Dieric Bouts, who depicted the baby suckling his mother in a sensual manner. The star attraction of the Correr is the Bellini salon, which includes works by founding padre Jacopo and his son, Gentile. But the real master of the household was the other son, Giovanni, the major painter of the 15th-century Venetian school (see his *Crucifixion* and compare it with his father's treatment of the same subject).

A small but celebrated portrait of St. Anthony of Padua by Alvise Vivarini is here, plus works by Bartolomeo Montagna. The most important work in the gallery, however, is Vittore Carpaccio's *Two Venetian Ladies*, popularly known as "The Courtesans." A lesser work, *St. Peter,* depicts the saint with the daggers in him, and hangs in the same room. The entrance is under the arcades of Ala Napoleonica at the western end of the square.

Admission: 3,000 lire ($2.35).

Open: Mon and Wed–Sat 10am–6pm, Sun 9:30am–12:30pm. **Vaporetto:** San Marco.

CA' D'ORO, Cannaregio 3931-3932, Ca' d'Oro. Tel. 5238790.

This is one of the grandest and most handsomely embellished palaces along the Grand Canal. Although it contains the important Galleria Giorgio Franchetti, the House of Gold (so named because its facade was once gilded) competes with its own paintings. Built in the first part of the 15th century in the ogival style, it has a lacy Gothic look. Baron Franchetti, who restored the palace and filled it with his own collection of paintings, sculpture, and furniture, presented it to Italy during World War I.

You enter into a stunning courtyard, 50 yards from the vaporetto stop, which has a multicolored patterned marble floor and is filled with statuary. Then proceed upstairs to the lavishly appointed palazzo. One of the gallery's major paintings is Titian's voluptuous *Venus.* She coyly covers one breast, but what about the other?

In a special niche reserved for the masterpiece of the Franchetti collection is Andrea Mantegna's icy-cold *St. Sebastian,* the central figure of which is riddled with what must be a record number of arrows. You'll also find works by Carpaccio. Don't fail to walk out onto the loggia for a view of the Grand Canal.

Admission: 2,000 lire ($1.55).

Open: Mon–Sat 9am–2pm; Sun and hols 9am–1pm. **Vaporetto:** Ca' d'Oro.

CA' REZZONICO, fondamenta Rezzonico, Dorsoduro. Tel. 5224543.

This 17th- and 18th-century palace along the Grand Canal is where Robert Browning set up his bachelor headquarters. Pope Clement XIII also stayed here. It's a virtual treasure house, known for both its baroque paintings and furniture. First, you enter the Grand Ballroom, with its allegorical ceiling, then proceed through lavishly embellished rooms with Venetian chandeliers, brocaded walls, portraits of patricians, tapestries, gilded furnishings, and touches of chinoiserie. At the end of the first walk is the Throne Room, with its allegorical ceilings by Giovanni Battista Tiepolo.

On the first floor you can walk out onto a balcony for a view of the Grand Canal as the aristocratic tenants of the 18th century saw it. After this, another group of rooms follow, including the library. In these salons look for a bizarre collection of paintings. One, for example, depicts half-clothed women beating up a defenseless naked man (one Amazon is about to stick a pitchfork into his neck, another to crown him with a violin). In the adjoining room another woman seems ready to chop off a man's head, and in still another painting a woman is hammering a spike through a man's skull. Enough torture performed by the ladies to please even the most fervent masochist.

Upstairs you'll find a survey of 18th-century Venetian art. As you enter the main room from downstairs, head for the first salon on your right (facing the canal), which contains the best works of all, paintings from the brush of Pietro Longhi. His most famous work, *The Lady and the Hairdresser,* is the first canvas to the right on the entrance wall. Others depict the life of the idle Venetian rich. On the rest of the floor are bedchambers, a chapel, and salons—some with badly damaged frescoes, including a romp of satyrs.

Admission: 3,000 lire ($2.35).

Open: Mon–Thurs 10am–3:30pm, Sat 10am–4pm, Sun 9am–noon. **Vaporetto:** Ca' Rezzonico.

COLLEZIONE PEGGY GUGGENHEIM, Ca' Venier dei Leoni, Dorsoduro 701, calle San Cristoforo. Tel. 5206288.

★ This is one of the most comprehensive and brilliant modern-art collections in the Western world, and it reveals both the foresight and critical judgment of its founder. The collection is housed in an unfinished palazzo, the former Venetian home of Peggy Guggenheim, who died in 1979. In the tradition of her family, Peggy Guggenheim was a lifelong patron of contemporary painters and sculptors. Founder of the Art of This Century Gallery in New York in the 1940s, she created one of the most avant-garde galleries for the works of contemporary artists. Critics were impressed not only by the high quality of the artists she sponsored, but by her methods of displaying them.

As her private collection increased, she decided to find a larger showcase and selected Venice, steeped in a long tradition as a haven for artists. While the Solomon Guggenheim Museum was going up in New York according to Frank Lloyd Wright's specifications, she was creating her own gallery in Venice. Guests can wander through and enjoy art in an informal and relaxed way. Max Ernst was one of Peggy Guggenheim's early favorites, as was Jackson Pollock (she provided a farmhouse where he could develop his painting technique). Displayed here are works not only by Pollock and Ernst, but also by Picasso (see his cubist *The Poet* of 1911), Duchamp, Chagall, Mondrian, Brancusi, Delvaux, Magritte, Dalí, and Moro, and a garden of modern sculpture which includes works by Giacometti. Temporary modern-art shows may be presented during the winter months in place of the permanent collection. Since Peggy Guggenheim's death, the collection has been administered by the Solomon R. Guggenheim Foundation, which also operates the Solomon R. Guggenheim Museum in New York.

Admission: 5,000 lire ($3.95) adults, 4,000 lire ($3.15) children under 17.

Open: Mar–Dec, Sun–Mon and Wed–Fri 11am–6pm, Sat 11am–9pm. **Vaporetto:** Accademia.

MUSEO NAVALE AND ARSENALE, campo San Biasio, Castello 2148. Tel. 5200276.

The Naval Museum of Campo San Biasio **(Museo Storico Navale)** is filled with cannons, ships' models, and fragments of old vessels that date back to the days when Venice was supreme in the Adriatic. The prize exhibit is a gilded model of the *Bucintoro,* the great ship of the doge that surely would have made Cleopatra's barge look like an oil tanker in comparison. In addition, you'll find models of historic and modern fighting ships, of local fishing and rowing craft, and a collection of 24 Chinese junks, as well as a number of maritime *ex voto* from churches of Naples.

If you walk along the canal as it branches off from the museum, you come first (about 270 yards from the museum and before the wooden bridge) to the **Ships' Pavilion** where historic vessels are displayed. Proceeding on along the canal, you soon reach the **Arsenale,** campo del'Arsenale, guarded by stone lions, Neptune with a trident, and other assorted ferocities. You'll spot it readily enough because of its two towers which flank each side of the canal. In its day, the Arsenale turned out galley after galley at speeds usually associated with wartime production.

Admission: 2,000 lire ($1.55).

Open: Sun–Fri 9am–1pm, Sat 9am–noon. **Closed:** Hols. **Vaporetto:** Arsenale.

MUSEO FORTUNY, campo San Benedetto 3780. Tel. 5200995.

The 15th-century Palazzo Pesaro degli Orfei is now the Museo Fortuny. Here you can see the home and work surroundings of Mariano Fortuny, who lived here for almost 50 years. The Spanish-born Fortuny was known for his fabric and dress designs, especially his pleated silk Grecian gowns popular around the turn of the century. However, he was also engaged in theater set design, painting, and photography. In his fabric designs, he used motifs of Islam, France, Greece, Africa, and Italy, as well as pre-Columbian civilizations. In the museum and the artist's former living quarters, you can see murals, fabrics (including a fine Oriental rug simulated on velvet), portraits, his own copies of old masters, and other interesting decorative pieces.

Admission: 5,000 lire ($3.95) adults, 3,000 lire ($2.35) children.
Open: Tues–Sun 9am–7pm. **Vaporetto:** San Angelo.

MORE ATTRACTIONS

SCUOLE & CHURCHES

Much of the great art of Venice lies in its churches and *scuole* (schools). The latter weren't schools in the usual sense, but fraternities or guilds. Most of their members were drawn from the rising bourgeoisie of Venice. Through male bonding, fraternity members were said to have had both their material and spiritual needs fulfilled by these guilds. The members of the scuole, such as that of San Rocco, often engaged in charitable works in honor of the saint for whom their fraternity was named. Many of the greatest artists of Venice, including Tintoretto, were commissioned to decorate these schools with art. Some of the artists created masterpieces which can still be viewed today. Often the lives of the patron saints of the schools were commemorated. Narrative canvases that depicted the lives of the saints were called *teleri*.

SCUOLA DI SAN ROCCO, campo San Rocco, San Polo. Tel. 5234864.

 Of the scuole of Venice, none is as richly embellished as the Scuola di San Rocco, which is filled with epic canvases by Tintoretto. By a clever trick, he won the competition to decorate the darkly illuminated early 16th-century building. He began painting in 1564, and the work stretched on till his powers as an artist waned. The paintings sweep across the upper and lower halls, mesmerizing the viewer with a kind of passion play. In the grand hallway, they depict New Testament scenes, devoted largely to episodes in the life of Mary (the *Flight into Egypt* is among the best). In the top gallery are works that illustrate scenes from both the Old and New Testaments, the most renowned being those devoted to the life of Christ. In a separate room is what is considered Tintoretto's masterpiece—his mammoth *Crucifixion,* one of the world's most celebrated paintings. In it he showed his dramatic scope and sense of grandeur as an artist, creating a deeply felt scene that virtually comes alive—filling the viewer with the horror of systematic execution, thus transcending its original subject matter.

FROMMER'S FAVORITE
VENICE EXPERIENCES

Riding the Grand Canal on a Gondola Just before sunset, order some delectable sandwiches from Harry's Bar and a bottle of chilled Prosecco, then take someone you love on a gondola ride along the Grand Canal for the boat trip of a lifetime.

Sitting on piazza San Marco Select a choice spot on one of the world's most famous and photographed squares, order a cup of cappuccino, listen to the classical music, and absorb the special atmosphere of Venice.

A Day at the Lido The world has seen better beaches, but few sights equal the parade of flesh and humanity of this fashionable beach on a hot summer day. Everybody from Thomas Mann's fictional von Aschenbach to horseback-riding Byron have romped here.

Contemplate Giorgione's *Tempest* If you have time to see only one painting, make it this one at the Accademia. The artist's haunting sense of oncoming menace superimposed over a bucolic setting will become a memory page for you.

Admission: 5,000 lire ($3.95).
Open: Mar 28–Nov 1, daily 9am–1pm and 3:30–6:30pm; Nov 2–Mar 27, Mon–Fri 10am–1pm, Sat–Sun 10am–4pm. **Vaporetto:** San Tomà; from the station, walk straight onto ramo Mondoler, which becomes larga Prima; then take salizzada San Rocco which opens into campo San Rocco.

SANTA MARIA DEI FRARI, campo dei Frari, San Polo. Tel. 5222637.

Known simply as the Frari, this Venetian-Gothic church is only a short walk from the Scuola di San Rocco (vaporetto: San Tomà). The church is filled with some great art. First, the best—Titian's *Assumption* over the main altar is a masterpiece of soaring beauty which depicts the ascension of the Madonna on a cloud "puffed up" by floating cherubs. In her robe, but especially in the robe of one of the gaping saints below, "Titian red" dazzles as never before.

On the first altar to the left as you enter is Titian's second major work here—a *Madonna Enthroned,* painted for the Pesaro family in 1526. Although lacking the power and drama of the *Assumption,* it nevertheless is brilliant in its use of color and light effects. But Titian surely would turn redder than his madonna's robes if he could see the latter-day neoclassical tomb built for him on the opposite wall. The kindest word for it: large.

Facing the tomb is a memorial to Canova, the Italian sculptor who led the revival of classicism. To return to more enduring art, head to the sacristy for a Giovanni Bellini triptych on wood, painted in 1488. The Madonna is cool and serene, one of Bellini's finest portraits of the Virgin. Also see the almost primitive-looking wood carving by Donatello of *St. John the Baptist.*
Admission: 800 lire (65¢).
Open: Mon–Sat 9–11:45am and 2:30–6pm, Sun 3–5:30pm. **Vaporetto:** San Tomà.

SCUOLA DI SAN GIORGIO DEGLI SCHIAVONI, calle Furlani, Castello. Tel. 5228828.

At the St. Antonino Bridge (fondamenta dei Furlani) is the second important school to visit in Venice. Between 1502 and 1509, Vittore Carpaccio painted a pictorial cycle here of exceptional merit and interest. Of enduring fame are his works of St. George and the dragon—these are my favorite art in all of Venice and certainly the most delightful. For example, in one frame St. George charges the dragon on a field littered with half-eaten bodies and skulls. Gruesome? Not at all. Any moment you expect the director to call "Cut!" The pictures relating to St. Jerome are appealing but don't compete with St. George and his ferocious dragon.
Admission: 3,000 lire ($2.35).
Open: Apr–Oct, Tues–Sat 9:30am–12:30pm and 3:30–6:30pm, Sun 9:30am–12:30pm; Nov–Mar, Tues–Sat 10am–12:30pm and 3:30–6pm, Sun 10am–12:30pm. **Vaporetto:** San Zaccaria.

CHIESA MADONNA DELL'ORTO, campo dell'Orto, Cannaregio. Tel. 719933.

This church provides a good reason to walk to this fairly remote northern district of Venice. At the church on the lagoon you'll be paying your final respects to Tintoretto. The brick structure with a Gothic front is famed not only because of its paintings by that artist, but because the great master is buried in the chapel to the right of the main altar. At the high altar are Tintoretto's *Last Judgment* (on the right) and his *Sacrifice of the Golden Calf* (left)—two monumental paintings that curve at the top like a Gothic arch. Over the doorway to the right of the altar is Tintoretto's superb portrayal of the presentation of Mary as a little girl at the temple. The composition is unusual in that Mary is not the focal point—rather, a pointing woman bystander dominates the scene. The first chapel to the left of the main altar contains a masterly work by Cima de Conegliano, showing the presentation of a sacrificial lamb to the saints (the plasticity of St. John's body evokes Michelangelo). Finally, the first chapel on the left (as you enter) is graced with an exquisite Giovanni Bellini *Madonna and Child.* Note the eyes and mouth of both mother and child—they constitute a work of consummate skill. Two other pictures in the apse are *The Presentation of the Cross to*

St. Peter and *The Beheading of St. Christopher* (1551–55). Besides the five paintings in the apse are works by Tintoretto and his school. Two paintings are by Palma the Younger: *The Annunciation* and *The Crucifixion* (where the influence of his master, Tintoretto, can be seen).
Admission: Free.
Open: May–Oct, daily 9:30am–noon and 4–7pm; Nov–Apr, daily 9:30am–noon and 3–4:30pm. **Vaporetto:** Madonna dell'Orto.

CHURCH OF SAN SEBASTIANO, campo San Sebastiano, Dorsoduro.
In a city as rich in art as Venice, this small Renaissance church might easily be overlooked. However, it's well worth a visit, as it contains the only frescoes of Paolo Veronese in Venice (also his first), plus canvases of exceptional beauty, the cycle illustrating the story of San Sebastian and of Esther. The master, who died in 1588, is buried near the side altar on the left. The church also contains paintings by Titian, Tintoretto, and an architectural monument by Sansovino.
The Church of San Sebastiano is not a museum. It is a functioning Catholic church. Regrettably, it keeps erratic hours, so whether it will be open at the time of your visit depends a bit on chance.
Admission: Free.
Open: See above. **Vaporetto:** San Basilio.

CHURCH OF SAN ZACCARIA, campo San Zaccaria, Castello. Tel. 5221257.
Behind St. Mark's Basilica is a Gothic church with a Renaissance facade. The church is filled with works of art, notably Giovanni Bellini's *Madonna Enthroned,* painted with saints (second altar to the left). Many have found this to be one of Bellini's finest madonnas, and it does have beautifully subdued coloring, although it appears rather static. Apply to the sacristan to see the Sisters' Choir, with works by Tintoretto, Titian, Il Vecchio, Anthony van Dyck, and Bassano. The paintings aren't labeled, but the sacristan will point out the names of the artists. In the Sisters' Choir are five armchairs in which the Venetian doges of yore sat. Also, if you save the best for last, you can see the faded frescoes of Andrea del Castagno in the shrine that honors San Tarasio.
Admission: Free.
Open: Daily 10am–noon and 4–6pm. **Vaporetto:** San Zaccaria.

BASILICA DI SAN GIORGIO MAGGIORE, San Giorgio Maggiore, across from piazzetta San Marco. Tel. 5289900.
This church sits on the little island of San Giorgio Maggiore. The building was designed by Palladio, the great Renaissance architect of the 16th century—perhaps as a consolation prize since he was not chosen to rebuild the burnt-out Doges' Palace. The logical rhythm of the Vicenza architect is played here on a grand scale. But inside it's almost too stark since Palladio was not much on gilded adornment. The chief art hangs on the main altar—two epic paintings by Tintoretto, one to the left, the *Fall of Manna,* and then the far more successful *Last Supper* to the right. It's interesting to compare Tintoretto's *Cena* with that of Veronese at the Academy. Afterward, you may want to take the elevator for 2,000 lire ($1.55) to the top of the belfry for a view of the greenery of the island itself, the lagoon, and the Doges' Palace across the way. In a word, it's unforgettable.
Admission: 2,000 lire ($1.55) adults, 1,000 lire (80¢) children.
Open: June–Sept, daily 10am–12:30pm and 2:30–6pm; Oct–May, daily 10am–12:30pm and 2:30–3:30pm. **Transportation:** Take the Giudecca-bound vaporetto (no. 8) or motorboat (no. 5) on riva degli Schiavoni and get off at the first stop, right in the courtyard of the church.

SANTA MARIA DELLA SALUTE, campo della Salute, Dorsoduro.
Like the proud landmark that it is, this church—the pinnacle of the baroque movement in Venice—stands at the mouth of the Grand Canal overlooking piazzetta San Marco. It opens onto campo della Salute, Dorsoduro. One of the most historic churches in Venice, it was built by Longhena in the 17th century as an offering to the Virgin for delivering the city from the grip of the plague. It was erected on enough

pilings to support the Empire State Building (well, almost). Surmounted by a great cupola, the octagonal basilica makes for an interesting visit, as it houses a small art gallery in its sacristy (tip the custodian)—a marriage feast of Cana by Tintoretto, allegorical paintings on the ceiling by Titian, a mounted St. Mark, and poor St. Sebastian with his inevitable arrow. The latter works, however, did not earn for Titian the title of "Il Divino."

Admission: Free.
Open: Daily 8am–noon and 3–6pm. **Vaporetto:** Salute.

CHURCH OF SS. GIOVANNI E PAOLO, campo SS. Giovanni e Paolo.
   This church, also known as Zanipolo, is often called the pantheon of Venice as it houses the tombs of many doges. One of the great Gothic churches of Venice, the building was erected between the 13th and 14th centuries. Inside, it contains artwork by many of the most noted Venetian painters. As you enter (right aisle), you'll find a retable by Giovanni Bellini (which includes a St. Sebastian filled with arrows). In the Rosary Chapel are ceilings by Veronese, depicting New Testament scenes, including *The Assumption of the Madonna*. To the right of the church is one of the world's best-known equestrian statues—that of Bartolomeo Colleoni (paid for by the condottiere), sculpted in the 15th century by Andrea del Verrochio. The bronze has long been acclaimed as his masterpiece, although it was completed by another artist. The horse is far more beautiful than the armored military hero, who looks as if he had just stumbled upon a three-headed crocodile.
   To the left of the pantheon is the Scuola di San Marco, with its stunning Renaissance facade (it's now run as a civic hospital).

Admission: Free.
Open: Apr–Oct, daily 9am–noon and 3–6pm; Nov–Mar, daily 9am–noon and 3–5pm. **Vaporetto:** Rialto or fondamenta Nuove.

THE GHETTO

The Ghetto of Venice, called Ghetto Nuovo, was instituted in 1516 by the Venetian Republic in the Cannaregio district. It stands in what is now the northwestern corner of Venice. Once Venetian Jews were confined to a walled area and obliged to wear distinctive red or yellow marks (cloth circles or hats). The walls were torn down long ago, but much remains of the past. One of the most beautiful synagogues, the **Scola Tedesca,** has been restored with funds from Germany. This is the German *Scola,* one of five synagogues: The others are the Spanish one that is the oldest continuously functioning synagogue in Europe, the Italian, the Levantine-Oriental, and Scola Canton. Tours usually include three synagogues (sometimes two), with the museum and tourist service run by a partnership providing tourists with multilingual guides.
   The tiny **Museo Israelitico** (tel. 715359) is open daily from 10:30am to 1pm and 2:30 to 5pm from mid-March to the end of June, and 9:30am to 5pm from July to the end of October. Admission to the museum is 2,000 lire ($1.55). For more information, get in touch with the museum at Cannaregio 2901, campo di Ghetto Nuovo, where you can also inquire about infrequent tours of the area.
   While in the area, you can explore on your own, seeing houses huddled close together and narrow streets. In all, it represents a complex that is unique in the world. Vaporetto: San Marcuola.

COOL FOR KIDS

Unlike any other city of Europe, Venice seems made for kids. Providing you don't mind issuing a lot of warnings about avoiding the edge of every canal you see (and you'll see plenty), Venice is like wandering around in a Disneyland fantasy for a child, complete with vaporetto rides to yet-unexplored islands. After a day of wandering endless alleyways and crossing dozens of footbridges, most children tire early and few have to be coaxed to turn in.
   The most exciting activity for children is a **gondola ride.** Gondoliers are usually very patient with children, explaining (in Italian) the intricacies of their craft, although

their actual demonstrations are more effective in getting the point across. Later in the day you can take your child to the **glass-manufacturing works** at **Murano** (see below), where the intricacies of the craft of blowing glass will be demonstrated.

The one museum that seems to fascinate children the most is the **Naval Museum and Arsenale** (see above), where the glorious remnants of Venice's maritime past are presented.

To cap the day, you can always purchase a bag of corn from a street vendor so your child can feed the fat pigeons at **piazza San Marco.**

WALKING TOUR — Piazza San Marco to the Grand Canal

Start: Piazza San Marco.
Finish: Grand Canal at the Ponte Rialto.
Time: 2 hours, not including stops.
Best Time: Any sunny day.
Worst Time: Holidays and festivals (streets are too crowded).

There are potentially hundreds of byways, alleyways, and canals stretching across the faded splendor of Venice. This 2-hour walking tour will give you at least an exterior view plus a general orientation to the layout of parts of the city, often showing lesser-known sights, which can best be seen from the outside, on foot. Later, you can pick and choose at your leisure the sights you most want to revisit, especially those requiring interior inspections.

Our tour begins, appropriately enough, at the heartbeat:

1. **Piazza San Marco,** or St. Mark's Square, perhaps the most famous in Italy. Here and on its satellite square, piazzetta San Marco, you can explore the major attractions of the city. These include the:

2. **Basilica di San Marco,** named for St. Mark, whose body was allegedly stolen from his tomb in Alexandria in 828 and brought to Venice. This basilica was built to enshrine the body of the man who became the city's patron saint. Next door is the:

3. **Palazzo Ducale,** with its adjoining Ponte dei Sospiri (Bridge of Sighs), a pink confection that was the home of the doges (dukes) who ruled Venice for years. In front of the palace is the:

4. **Campanile di San Marco,** the bell tower of Venice which visitors climb for a spectacular view of the city and the lagoon.

   The Renaissance mariners who supplied the lifelines that lead to their Adriatic capital realized that the most impressive view of the city was, and perhaps still is, visible only from the water. To better see this unforgettable view, I suggest that you take a brief vaporetto ride across the Grand Canal to the rhapsodically baroque white walls of:

5. **Santa Maria della Salute.** Buy your ticket at either of two vaporetto stops: no. 16 (San Zaccaria), just east of St. Mark's Square, or no. 15 (San Marco), which lies just west of the square along the Grand Canal. Enjoy the short water ride and the view before getting off on the opposite canal at the pier marked "Salute." There you can look back across the Grand Canal at the rows of palazzi, many of which have been turned into glamorous hotels.

   Walk to the right-hand side of the church along campo della Salute, past a pair of wooden bridges, and continue until you reach the third bridge, the only one of the three that is made of stone. Cross this bridge and head onto rio Terradei Catecumeni. After one block, turn left onto calle Constantina. Now walk toward the water, along a wide flagstone-covered walkway divided by a single row of trees which must struggle to survive in the salt air of Venice. The waterway you'll soon reach separates this section of Venice from the rarely visited:

6. **Island of Giudecca,** which lies across the broad and often wind-lathered

Canale di Giudecca. Though you won't visit it as part of this walking tour, you might decide to return to explore its untrammeled streets later during your visit. From this vantage point, you can also admire the cranes of Venice's industrialized mainland sister, Mestre, to the north.

Turn right along the waterfront of a district known to Venetians as Dorsoduro. Much more of a residential neighborhood than the area around piazza San Marco, it has often been compared to New York's Greenwich Village because artists and writers have traditionally been attracted to it. Many, of course, came to avoid the stratospheric prices charged on the opposite side of the Grand Canal. With water to your left and a changing panorama of brick and stone buildings to your right, you'll cross over the high arches of several bridges, always continuing along the canalside walkway which, in characteristically Venetian fashion, will change its name at least three times.

At the third and last bridge, the Ponte della Calcina, at campiello della Calcina, you will notice two of the most famous pensiones of Venice, La Calcina, where John Ruskin stayed, and the Pensione Seguso. The name of the pavement that supports you here is zattere ai Gesuati. You'll notice a pair of wooden platforms, managed by local cafés and separated from one another by drydocked steel-hulled ships. After, perhaps, a coffee, you reach the acanthus-inspired pilasters of the baroque:

7. **Chiesa dei Gesuiti.** After visiting the church, take the street to its right, which is referred to variously as rio Terrà Antonio Foscarini, the rio Terrà Marco Foscarini, or simply rio Terrà Foscarini, and walk northwest. At the side of the church, admire campo Santa Agnese, where tolling bells call the neighborhood to mass.

Now, continue north along rio Foscarini until you reach the Grand Canal and the:

8. **Gallerie dell'Accademia.** You can either visit this great gallery of art or save it for another day. Cross the bridge, and you may notice the German consulate beside the elegant garden to the left. When you step off the bridge, you'll be on campo San Vidal. At this point, the city of Venice has graciously mapped out one of the most logical walking tours in the city by posting prominent yellow signs with black lettering on dozens of appropriate street corners.

Your walk, if you follow the signs, will take you back to St. Mark's Square through dozens of claustrophobic alleys, which are crumbling from exposure to the Adriatic winds, and into gloriously proportioned squares whose boundaries are often ornamented with exquisite detailing. From this point on, follow the signs that say PER S. MARCO. You can afford to ignore your map and lose yourself in the Renaissance splendor in this most unusual city.

At campo San Vidal, the pavement will funnel you in only one possible direction. After several twists and turns, you'll be in the huge expanse of:

9. **Campo San Stefano** (whose southern end is referred to on some maps as campo Francesco Morosini). Keep walking across the square, past a wood-and-iron flagpole capped with the Lion of St. Mark. Midway along the right-hand side of the square, follow the PER S. MARCO sign down a tiny alleyway called calle del Spezier. The alley funnels across a bridge and then changes its name to calle del Piovan. This will open to the wide expanses of:

10. **Campo San Maurizio.** Walk directly across the square, looking for yet another PER S. MARCO sign, which should direct you over another set of bridges.

This square funnels into the narrow calle Zaguri. Cross another canal's arched bridge and enter campiello de la Feltrina. Keep following the signs to San Marco. Soon you'll come to one of the most famous squares of Venice, shaped roughly like a crucifix. One end opens onto the Grand Canal, near the most famous hotel in Venice, the Gritti Palace. The full name of the square is campo Santa Maria Zobenigo O del Giglio, a name usually shortened to:

11. **Campo del Giglio.** The square is dominated by a larger-than-life-size statue, which guards the baroque facade of the Chiesa di Santa Maria del Giglio.

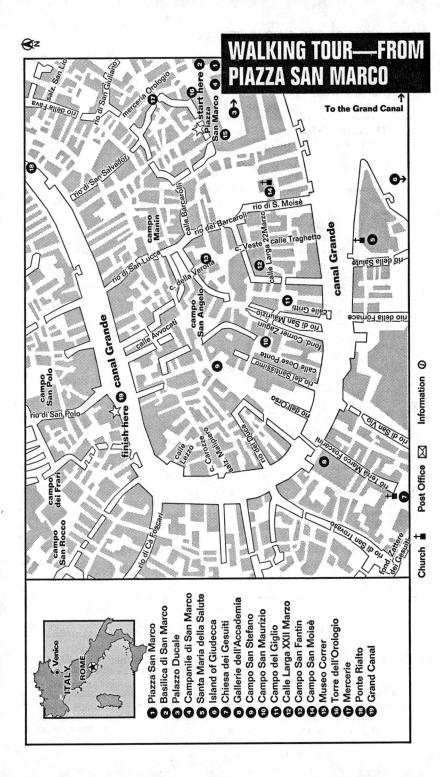

WALKING TOUR—FROM PIAZZA SAN MARCO

To the Grand Canal

start here

Piazza San Marco

merceria Orologio

salz. San Lio

rio della Fava

rio di San Giuliano

rio di San Salvador

calle Barcarolli

rio di S. Moisè

rio dei Barcaroli

campo Manin

c. Veste · Calle Larga 22 Marzo · calle Traghetto

canal Grande

rio di San Luca

c. della Verona

fond. Corner Zaguri

rio di San Maurizio

calle Gritti

campo San Angelo

rio di San Polo

canal Grande

calle Avvocati

rio del Santissimo

calle Dose Ponte

rio della Fornace

campo San Polo

finish here

campo dei Frari

calle Lezzo

Calle Carrozze

salz. Malipiero

rio del Duca

rio dell'Orso

rio terrà Marco Foscarini

rio di San Vio

campo San Rocco

rio di Ca Foscari

rio di San Trovaso

fond. Zattere dei Gesuiti

Church ✝   Post Office ⊠   Information ℹ

Venice

ITALY

ROME

1. Piazza San Marco
2. Basilica di San Marco
3. Palazzo Ducale
4. Campanile di San Marco
5. Santa Maria della Salute
6. Island of Giudecca
7. Chiesa dei Gesuiti
8. Gallerie dell'Accademia
9. Campo San Stefano
10. Campo San Maurizio
11. Campo del Giglio
12. Calle Larga XXII Marzo
13. Campo San Fantin
14. Campo San Moisè
15. Museo Correr
16. Torre dell'Orologio
17. Mercerie
18. Ponte Rialto
19. Grand Canal

Founded in the 9th century, but reconstructed in the 17th, it contains canvases by Tintoretto and Rubens.

As you exit from the church, follow once again the signs to San Marco, going down an alleyway, calle delle Ostreghe. Cross the high arch of a canal-spanning bridge, on the opposite side of which you'll spot your:

REFUELING STOP   Bar Ducale, calle delle Ostreghe, offers professionally made cocktails and sandwiches. The owner once worked at Harry's Bar and learned that restaurant's culinary secrets. The only difference here is not in taste, but in price—the Bar Ducale charges half the price of Harry's Bar. If not a sandwich, then enjoy a cappuccino.

When you exit from the Bar Ducale, follow the street through several twists and turns onto:

12. **Calle Larga XXII Marzo,** whose many shops, cafés, and restaurants make this one of the most-frequented and crowded streets of Venice. In about a block, midway down its length, I recommend a short detour off to the left. Notice the gold, white, and red sign pointing to "al teatro la Fenice." The street this points to is calle del Sartor da Veste. Turn neither to the left or right, but follow it over two bridges, into what is often considered one of the most intimate summertime "living rooms" of Venice:

13. **Campo San Fantin.** In fair weather, the enclosed square is dotted with tables set out by the best restaurant in Venice, Antico Martini, and its lesser rivals. Here you'll find the Teatro La Fenice and the Church of St. Fantin. After visiting the church, retrace your steps along the street you took previously. From the end of the square, its name appears as calle del Cafetier. This walk will take you back over the pair of bridges leading once again to calle larga XXII Marzo.

Head left, in the direction of San Moisè Church. By now the PER S. MARCO signs will lead you through:

14. **Campo San Moisè,** whose ornate facade contrasts oddly with the modern bulk of the Hotel Bauer Grünwald and Grand on your right. Take the street to the left of the church, and note the sign PER S. MARCO as you pass by the American Express office while heading straight along the street which, by now, has changed its name once again, this time to calle Seconda de l'Ascension. Continue straight under an arched tunnel to the sweeping expanses of **Piazza San Marco,** once again, where you may want to visit the:

15. **Museo Correr,** in the Procuratie Nuove, opposite the basilica. This museum traces the development of Venetian painting from the 14th to the 16th century.

REFUELING STOP   Since **Florian,** piazza San Marco 56-59, was established this has been considered "the most Venetian" of all cafés. Its interior rooms drip with a nostalgic 18th-century decor, but if the weather's sunny most guests prefer to sit outside. The Venetians patronized this café during the Austrian occupation, whereas the occupying army brass went to the rival café, the Quadri, across the square.

Later, walk through the square and pass to the left of the Basilica of St. Mark, stopping perhaps to admire a pair of lions carved from red porphyry. As you gaze with the lions back across the wide expanse of the square, notice the arched tunnel that pierces the base of the:

16. **Torre dell'Orologio.** Pass beneath the Moorish bellringers and the zodiac representations of the clock face. Here you will be on the major shopping street of Venice, the:

17. **Mercerie.** Of course, this is the popular name of the street. It actually has many longer names, preceded by the word *merceria*. From now on, your guiding light will be the signs that say PER RIALTO. They will be either formally positioned at strategic corners in yellow or black or scrawled sometimes graffiti-style on the sides of buildings.

Soon you'll reach the:

18. Ponte Rialto, from the Latin *rivo alto,* meaning high bank. The Istrian-stone bridge dates from 1588. The architect, Antonio da Ponte, actually won in a competition against Michelangelo, Palladio, and Sansovino, among others, to design this bridge. Until 1854 the bridge was the only pedestrian crossing on the Grand Canal.

Once at this point, you can board a vaporetto to take you back to piazza San Marco. Along the way you can enjoy the:

19. Grand Canal. A ride along the palazzo-flanked banks of this highly touted waterway is not only one of the grandest experiences in all of Italy, but the entire world. It is the one experience visitors are likely to remember when other monuments have gone hazy.

ORGANIZED TOURS

Tours through the streets and canals of Venice are distinctly different from tours through other cities of Italy because of the complete absence of traffic. You can always wander at will through the labyrinth of streets, but many visitors opt for a guided tour to at least familiarize themselves with the geography of the city.

American Express, San Moisè 1471 (tel. 5200844), which operates from a historic building a few steps from St. Mark's Square, offers an array of guided city tours. Four of their most popular offerings include the following:

Every morning at 9:30am a 2½-hour guided tour of the city departs from in front of the American Express building for a cost of 28,000 lire ($22). Sights include St. Mark's Square, the cathedral, the Doges' Palace, the prison, the bell tower, and a demonstration of the art of Venetian glassblowing.

Every afternoon, between 3 and 5:30pm a 2½-hour guided tour incorporates visits to the exteriors of several palaces along campo San Benetto, and other sights of the city. Clients eventually cross the Grand Canal to visit the Church of Santa Maria del Frari (which contains the *Assumption* by Titian). The tour continues by gondola down the canal to visit the Ca d'Oro and eventually ends at the Rialto Bridge. Cost of the afternoon tour is 32,000 lire ($25.10). A combined purchase of the morning and afternoon tour allows a discount of 10%.

The "Evening Serenade Tour," priced at 30,000 lire ($23.55) per person, allows a nocturnal view of Venice accompanied by the sound of singing musicians in gondolas. May to October there are two daily departures, one at 7:30 and another at 8:30pm, which leave from campo Santa Maria del Giglio. Four to five occupants fit in each gondola as a singer and a handful of musicians sing throughout the Venetian evening.

A "Tour of the Islands of the Venetian Lagoon," priced at 20,000 lire ($15.70), departs twice daily, at 9:30am and again at 2:30pm, and lasts 3 hours. You'll pass the islands of San Giorgio and San Francesco del Deserto, and eventually land at Burano, Murano, and Torcello, for brief tours of their churches and landmarks. This trip departs and returns to the pier at riva del Schiavoni.

2. SPECIAL & FREE EVENTS

Although cities from New Orleans to Rio celebrate their own respective carnivals with their own kinds of panache, the **Carnavale of Venice** might be the oldest, most historic, and most eerily evocative. Continuing a tradition established during the Renaissance, it occupies 10 days in February with sometimes-raucous parties which seem to anticipate the upcoming sobriety of Lent, Good Friday, and Easter. Declared an official holiday by the mayor of Venice in the 1970s, it includes around-the-clock street theater, highly electrified pop concerts, and the presence of thousands of non-Venetians who pour into the city for a series of private and public masked balls. The festival's most famous garb includes three-cornered hats, elaborate wigs, costumes inspired by something out of an opera by Mozart, and blandly enigmatic porcelain masks whose contours and nuances are considered a well-established art form in their own right.

In springtime, on the first Sunday after Ascension Day, Venetians observe **La Vogalonga** ("The Long Row"). Established as late as 1975, it's now one of the best-attended events in the Venetian calendar year. More of an oarsman's marathon than a race, it includes all kinds of oar-powered seacraft whose 20-mile course takes them from the base of St. Mark's Square around Saint-Elena, to points as far away as San Francesco del Deserto and Burano before returning to Venice via the Cannaregio Canal and the Grand Canal. Boats depart around 9:30am, returning (with very tired oarsmen) anytime between 11am and into the early evening. Unlike many other nautical events in Venice's calendar of events, this one is open to any foreigner with a safely outfitted oar-driven craft.

At midsummer, during the crush of the tourist season's third weekend in July, illuminated gondolas, fireworks above the lagoon, and roaming musicians floating on barges contribute to a holiday known as the **Feast of the Redeemer (Festa del Redentore).** A bridge of boats is erected across the Giudecca Canal near the base of the Church of the Redentore, commemorating the end of the plague of 1576, and many Venetians spend most of the festival picnicking from the gunnels of their boats. Many end the festival early the next morning, perhaps on the beaches of the Lido.

In September, one of Italy's most famous nautical events is the **Historic Regatta (Regatta Storica).** Then, richly decorated gondolas, staffed by boatmen in Renaissance costumes, race one another along the Grand Canal. Floating barges and historically important boats carry the music and parties out into the open lagoons in an event that perhaps better than any other evokes the nautical traditions of imperial Venice.

Late in August and early in September, the **International Film Festival** is hosted on the Lido, during which the stars, starlets, producers, directors, salespeople, artists, charlatans, and wannabees of the film industry congregate in a frenzy of exhibitionistic and voyeuristic yearning to promote, titillate (or whatever) the emissaries of the viewing public. Hundreds of films are shown almost around the clock. Ticket costs spiral as the festival progresses.

During alternate (even-numbered) years, between June and October, the **International Exposition of Modern Art,** better known as the **Biennale d'Arte,** adds a modern note to the antique charm of Venice with some of the largest imported collections of contemporary paintings and sculptures in the world. These are displayed in a series of around 35 different exposition spaces, both indoor and outdoor, whose locations are announced as part of each (alternate) year's events. (Most are centered around the vaporetto stop of La Giardini.) Originally established in 1895, the Biennale is one of the most famous art events in Europe.

In November, during a wet and rainy season which attracts what might be the fewest numbers of international visitors, the **opera season** at the theaters of Malibran and Fenice begins, continuing through till mid-May. On November 21, a **religious procession,** ending within the imperious white walls of Santa Maria della Salute (considered the most important baroque building in Venice), remembers the end of the plague of 1630. To commemorate the event, a pair of floating bridges are devised, spanning the Grand Canal for the benefit of the faithful and/or nostalgic.

---

3. SPORTS & RECREATION

Venice is so richly stocked with architectural and artistic riches that few visitors will look for opportunities for sport and conventional recreations. In a city without cars, the labyrinth of pedestrian walkways and steeply inclined bridges offers ample opportunities for walking, with never a dull expanse between landmarks. The densely populated labyrinth of the city itself offers almost no sports facilities within its historic or residential core, but if you insist on diversions, you'll have to head out to the flat and sandy expanses of Venice's playground, the Lido. A selection of this island's offerings include:

GOLF With the salt air whipping in from the Adriatic, a brisk 18 holes of golf might be especially invigorating. At the extreme western end of the Lido you'll find the **Golf Club di Venezia** (tel. 731333). To reach it, take vaporetto no. 11 from riva degli Schiavoni or the C bus from the Lido's main dock at Santa Maria Elisabetta.

JOGGING   The broad thoroughfares of central Venice's riva degli Schiavoni, just east of piazza San Marco, are usually suitable for jogging, except in midsummer when they tend to be jammed with slowly meandering pedestrians. Another possibility includes the lengthy and often less-crowded expanse of paved-over shoreline beside the Giudecca Canal. More suitable in any season is the beach of the Lido.

SAILING   Sailing boats, with or without skippers, can be rented and sailing lessons given, at the **Ciga Yacht Club,** based beside the Excelsior Hotel (tel. 5260201), the most prominent hotel on Venice's Lido.

SOCCER   The season for spectator soccer (by far the best-attended sports event in Venice) lasts from September to May. The city's soccer team, Venezia, welcomes visiting teams from throughout the rest of Europe for games that are usually held on Sunday afternoon at the **Stadio Comunale P.L. Penzo,** San Elena (tel. 5225770). Tickets go on sale at the stadium's box office several hours before play begins. If you want to actually play soccer, you'll have to content yourself with joining a scrimmage or spontaneous pickup game in one of the city's residential squares.

SWIMMING   Because of the polluted waters of Venice itself, all swimming should be confined to the tide-scoured beaches of the Lido, and even then it probably isn't such a great idea. Most of the city's public beaches lie along the Lido's northern end, while beaches fronting the island's southern and central end tends to be reserved for clients of the various hotels that line its shores. There's a public pool, the **Piscina Gandini,** where waters might be somewhat healthier, on the Isola di San Giorgio.

TENNIS   The **Tennis Club,** lungomare Marconi 41D (tel. 5260335), offers a handful of courts which, if not being used by members, can be rented by the hour to players appropriately dressed in tennis whites. You can also try the **Tennis Club Lido,** via Sandro Gallo 163 (tel. 5260954), or the **Henkell Club,** via Malamocco (tel. 5260122). Because of the frequent winter rainfall, all of these tend to close down in winter.

4. SAVVY SHOPPING

Venetian **glass** and **lace** are known throughout the world. However, selecting quality products in either craft requires a shrewd eye. There is much that is tawdry and shoddily crafted in Venetian shops. Some of the glassware hawked isn't worth the cost of shipping it home. Yet other pieces represent some of the world's finest artistic and ornamental glass. Murano is the island where glass is made, and the women of Burano put in painstaking hours turning out lace. If you're interested in some little glass souvenir of your stay, perhaps an animal or a bird, you'll find such items sold in shops all over Venice.

SHOPPING A TO Z

ANTIQUES

ANTICHITA SANTO MARCO, Frezzeria 1504, San Marco. Tel. 5236643.
   This store is for the specialist only—especially the well-heeled specialist. It specializes in antique furniture, books, prints, and coins. Of course, the merchandise is ever-changing, but you are likely to pick up some little "heirloom" item in the midst

of the clutter. Many of the items date from the Venetian heyday of the 1600s. Open on Monday from 3 to 8pm, Tuesday through Saturday from 9:30am to 1pm and 3 to 8pm, and on Sunday from 10am to 1pm. Vaporetto: San Marco.

BRASS OBJECTS

VALESE FONDITORE, calle Fiubera 793, San Marco. Tel. 5227282.
Founded in 1913, Valese Fonditore is located only a short walk away from piazza San Marco. It serves as a showcase outlet for one of the most famous of the several foundries that make their headquarters in Venice. Many of the brass copies of 18th-century chandeliers produced by this company grace fine homes in the United States. Many visitors to Venice invest in these brass castings which eventually become family heirlooms. If you're looking for a brass replica of the sea horses decorating the sides of gondolas, this shop stocks them in five or six different styles and sizes. Open on Monday from 2 to 7:30pm and Tuesday through Saturday from 10:30am to 7:30pm. Vaporetto: San Marco.

CARNIVAL MASKS

LABORATORIO ARTIGIANO MASCHERE, Castello 6657, Barbaria delle Tole. Tel. 5223110.
This shop is one of the best places to purchase carnival masks handcrafted in papier-mâché or leather. The masks carry names and symbols, the best known being the birdlike "luck bringer," called Portafortuna in Italian. Masks are sold all over Venice, but this well-established store has a particularly good selection, including masks that depict characters of the Commedia dell'Arte. Prices begin at 25,000 lire ($19.65), but could range much higher—up to 220,000 lire ($172.70) and way beyond. Open Tuesday through Sunday from 10am to 1pm and 3 to 7pm. Vaporetto: Rialto.

FASHIONS

Children's

MARICLA, calle larga XXII Marzo no. 2401. Tel. 5232202.
Select merchandise is offered here. In Venice, it is called the boutique *per bambini e giovinette,* which means for babies and young girls. The shop also sells clothing for little boys up to 4 years old. It also has a fine collection of lingerie for women, as well as exquisite embroideries. Open on Monday from 2 to 7:30pm and Tuesday through Saturday from 9:30am to 1pm and 2 to 7:30pm. Vaporetto: San Marco.

Men's

LA BOTTEGA DI NINO, San Marco 223, Mercerie dell'Orologio. Tel. 5225608.
This is one of the leading Venetian retail outlets for the elegantly attired male. It features the work of many European designers, even some from England, but it shines brightest in its Italian names, such as Nino Cerruti and Valentino. The prices are also better for the Italian wear. The store also sells a limited selection of clothing for women. Styling is first rate. Open on Monday from 3 to 7pm, Tuesday through Saturday from 10am to 7pm, and on Sunday from 10am to 1pm and 3 to 7pm. Vaporetto: San Marco.

Women's

KRIZIA, calle delle Ostreghe 2359, San Marco. Tel. 5232162.
This line has its devotees of chic women on all continents. Here, at breathtaking

prices, are some of the finest designs in the line, including a selection of jewelry. If you're going to Milan, you'll find lots of Krizia on several floors in a company-owned store. The Venice shop, however, is small but select. The Krizia line earned its reputation for bold knitwear, and is known today for outfits described as "playful." Open on Monday from 3:30 to 7:30pm, Tuesday through Saturday from 9am to 7:30pm, and on Sunday from 10:30am to 6:30pm. Vaporetto: Santa Maria del Giglio.

BETTA SCARPA, Frezzeria 1797, San Marco. Tel. 5287051.
This shop has a well-chosen selection of all-purpose clothing for women, which ranges from bathing suits to evening wear. It also has a good collection of handbags. Accessories are also sold here, along with some good buys in cashmere knitwear. Open on Monday from 3:30 to 7:30pm and Tuesday through Saturday from 9:30am to 7:30pm. Vaporetto: San Marco.

GIFTS

IL PAPIRO, campo San Maurizio 2764. Tel. 5223055.
Il Papiro is mainly noted for its stationery supplies, but it also carries and sells many different textures and colors of writing paper and cards. In addition to hand-printed paper, it sells any number of easy-to-pack gift items, which include wooden animals and copybooks. It's a good bet for those who want to take back small, inexpensive gifts. Open on Monday from 3:30 to 7:30pm, Tuesday through Saturday from 9:30am to 7:30pm, and on Sunday from 10am to 6pm. Vaporetto: Accademia.

GLASS

SALVIATI & CO., San Gregorio 195. Tel. 5224257.
Perhaps the finest and most reliable dealer in Venetian glass in the city is Salviati & Co. It keeps two small shops on St. Mark's Square. If you apply there, you'll be escorted to the main showrooms and to the museum of antique glass on the Grand Canal. Salviati has displays in great museums of the world, including the Vatican and the Museum of Modern Art in New York. Open from April to the end of September, on Monday from 2 to 7:30pm, Tuesday through Saturday from 9am to 7pm, and on Sunday from 9am to 12:30pm; October to March, on Monday from 2 to 7:30pm and Tuesday through Saturday from 9am to 12:30pm and 3 to 6pm. Vaporetto: San Marco.

PAULY & CO., San Marco, Ponte Consorzi. Tel. 5209899.
This award-winning house exports its products all over the world. You can wander through its 21 salons, enjoy an exhibition of artistic glassware, and later see a furnace in full action. There is no catalog offered; Pauly's production, which is mainly made to order, consists of continually renewed patterns, subject to change and alteration based on customer desire. Open Easter through October Monday through Saturday from 9am to 7pm and on Sunday from 9am to 1pm; off-season, on Monday from 3 to 7pm and Tuesday through Saturday from 9am to 12:30pm and 3 to 7pm. Vaporetto: San Zaccaria.

VENINI, piazzetta Leoncini 314, San Marco. Tel. 5224045.
Venini has won collector fans all over the globe for its Venetian art glass. They sell lamps, bottles, and vases, but not ordinary ones. Many are considered works of art, representing the best of Venetian craftsmanship in design and manufacture. Along with the previously recommended Pauly & Co. and Salviati, Venini represents the big triumvirate of Venetian glass-makers. Their best-known glass has a distinctive swirl pattern in several colors, which is called a venature. This shop is known for the refined taste of its glass, some of which appears almost transparent. Much of it is very fragile, but they long ago learned how to ship it anywhere safely. Open on Monday from 3:30

to 7:30pm, Tuesday through Saturday from 9am to 7:30pm, and on Sunday from 9am to 1pm (closed Sunday from November to March). Vaporetto: San Zaccaria.

GRAPHICS

BAC ART STUDIO, campo San Maurizio 2663, San Marco. Tel. 5228171.
This studio sells paper goods, but it's mainly a graphics gallery, noted for its selection of engravings, posters, and lithographs, which represent Venice at carnival time. Many views of Venice parade before you. Items for the most part are reasonably priced as well, and care and selection obviously went into the gallery's choice of its merchandise. Open Monday through Saturday from 10am to 1pm and 3 to 7pm. Vaporetto: Santa Maria del Giglio.

OSVALDO BOHM, San Moisè 1349-1350. Tel. 5222255.
For the right—and light—souvenir of Venice. Osvaldo Bohm has a rich collection of photographic archives specializing in Venetian art as well as original engravings and maps, lithographs, watercolors, and Venetian masks in bronze and leather. Some prints date from the 17th century. Also you can see modern serigraphy by local artists and some fine handcrafted bronzes. Open on Monday from 2 to 7:30pm and Tuesday through Saturday from 9am to 7:30pm. Vaporetto: San Marco.

JEWELRY

NARDI SERGIO, piazza San Marco 68-71. Tel. 5232150.
The most highly refined selection of exquisite Venetian jewelry is found at Nardi Sergio. For old pieces, fine silver, antique jewelry, and new and original designs, it's stunning. Open on Monday from 3 to 7pm and Tuesday through Saturday from 9am to 12:30pm and 3 to 7pm. Vaporetto: San Marco.

JEWISH HANDCRAFTS

SHALOM, Ghetto Vecchio 1218. Tel. 720092.
This is a gift shop that sells Judaica of all kinds (Venetian mosaic, gold, silver, brass, and glass handcrafts). It lies a 5-minute walk from the rail station. Walk up Lista di Spagna, cross the Ponte delle Guglie, turn left and under the sottoportico di Ghetto, then go straight to the shop standing out for its Menorah sign. Open Sunday through Friday from 9am to 7pm. Vaporetto: Piazzale Roma.

LACE

JESURUM, Ponte Canonica 4310, behind St. Mark's Basilica. Tel. 5206177.
For serious purchases, Jesurum is the best place. This elegant shop, a center of noted lacemakers and fashion creators, has been located in a 12th-century church since 1868. You'll find Venetian handmade or machine lace and embroidery on table, bed, and bath linens, hand-printed or -embroidered beach clothes, and bathing suits. Quality and originality are guaranteed, and special orders are accepted. The exclusive linens created here are expensive, but the inventory is large enough to accommodate many budgets. Open Monday through Saturday from 9:30am to 7:30pm. Vaporetto: San Zaccaria.

LEATHER

VOGINI, San Marco Ascensione 1291, 1301, and 1305. Tel. 5287933.
Every kind of leatherwork is offered at Vogini, especially women's handbags, which are exclusive models. There's also a large assortment of handbags in

petit-point, plus men's and women's wear and shoes. The collection of artistic Venetian leather is of the highest quality. The travel-equipment department contains a large assortment of trunks and wardrobe suitcases as well as dressing cases—many of the latest models in luggage. Open April to October, Monday through Saturday from 9am to 7:30pm; November to March, on Monday from 3 to 7:30pm and Tuesday through Saturday from 9am to 12:30pm and 3 to 7:30pm. Vaporetto: San Marco.

FURLA, San Marco 4954, Mercerie. Tel. 5230811.

Furla is a specialist in women's leather bags. It also sells belts and gloves for women. Many of the bags are stamped with molds, making them appear to be alligator, lizard, or some other exotic creature. These bags come in a varied choice of colors, including what the Austrians call "Maria Theresa ocher." Furla also displays a varied selection of costume jewelry. Open October to May, on Monday from 3 to 7:30pm, Tuesday through Saturday from 9:15am to 12:30pm and 3 to 7:30pm, and on Sunday from 10:30am to 1:15pm and 2:15 to 6:30pm; June to September, daily from 9:15am to 7:30pm. Vaporetto: Rialto.

BOTTEGA VENETA, calle Vallaresso 1337, San Marco. Tel. 5228489.

Bottega Veneta is primarily known for its woven leather bags. These bags are sold elsewhere too, but the cost is said to be less at the company's flagship outlet in Venice. In addition, the shop sells shoes for men and women, suitcases, belts, and "everything made of leather." There is also an array of high-fashion accessories. Both men and women will find this store a delight. Men will enjoy the assortment of leather wallets, for example. Open on Monday from 3 to 7:30pm and Tuesday through Saturday from 9:30am to 1pm and 3 to 7:30pm; from June to September, also on Sunday from 11am to 1pm and 2 to 6pm. Vaporetto: San Marco.

MARFORIO, campo San Salvador 5033, San Marco. Tel. 5225734.

Marforio is located in the heart of the city. It's a showroom for high-quality handbags and luggage, along with a wide selection of such useful items as umbrellas and wallets. The shop has been delighting devotees of leather since it opened in 1875. Many of the goods are made in the firm's own workrooms. Open Monday through Saturday from 9am to 7:30pm. Vaporetto: Rialto.

MARKETS

If you're seeking some bargain-basement buys, head not for any basement but to one of the little shops that line the **Rialto Bridge.** The shops there branch out to encompass fruit and vegetable markets as well. The Rialto isn't the Ponte Vecchio in Florence, but, for what it offers, it isn't bad, particularly if your lire are running short. You'll find a wide assortment of merchandise here, from angora sweaters to leather gloves. Quality is likely to vary widely, so plunge in with the utmost discrimination. Vaporetto stop: Rialto.

PAPER

LEGATORIA PIAZZESI, Santa Maria del Giglio 2511. Tel. 5221202.

You can browse or buy at Legatoria Piazzesi, among the displays of patterned, hand-painted paper. You can select paper-covered objects in bright colors as souvenirs of Venice. *Legatoria* means bookbindery, and some of this work is still done on special order, but the shop mainly offers such objects as scrapbooks, address books, diaries, Venetian carnival masks, and paperweights. Of course you can also find writing paper and decorative pieces. Open Monday through Saturday from 9:30am to 12:30pm and 4 to 7:30pm. Vaporetto: San Marco.

SHOES

LA CORTE DELLE FATE, Castello 5690, San Lio. Tel. 5286611.

La Corte delle Fate is the premier place for shoes for women and men. Designs are elegant, and the craftsmanship is high, yet prices remain reasonable. Mostly Italian and French designs are sold. Many of the designs are very imaginative, and there is a notable display of footgear for women to wear at night, including shoes made of rich satin. Open on Monday from 3:30 to 7:30pm and Tuesday through Saturday from 9:30am to 1pm and 3 to 7:30pm. Vaporetto: Rialto.

LA FENICE, calle larga XXII Marzo no. 2255, San Marco. Tel. 5231273.
La Fenice is another major outlet for shoes in Venice. Many of the shoes sold here are by the store's own designers. However, the outlet also stocks the work of some of the "big names of footwear," including Maud Frizon. Informal, casual shoes along with "dressed to kill" evening slippers are sold here. The store also sells a selection of clothing. Open on Monday from 4 to 7:30pm and Tuesday through Saturday from 9:30am to 8pm. Vaporetto: San Marco.

5. EVENING ENTERTAINMENT

For such a fabled city, Venice has some of the most meager nightlife of any of the tourist meccas of Europe. Few patrons seem to want to patronize nightclubs when walking about the city at night is more interesting than any spectacle staged inside. Cafés and bars, however, are well-recommended places to enjoy a brief interlude before you continue your walk of exploration. Venice, although it offers gambling and a few other diversions, is pretty much an early-to-bed town. Most restaurants close at midnight.

The tourist office distributes a free pamphlet (part in English, part in Italian), called *un Ospite di Venezia.* A section of this useful publication lists events, including any music and opera or theatrical presentations, along with art exhibitions and local special events. It's the best guide to "what's happening" at the time of your visit to Venice.

In addition, classical concerts are often featured using various churches, such as the Chiesa di Vivaldi, as a venue. Most of these concerts cost around 15,000 lire ($11.80) for a good seat. To see if any church concerts are being presented at the time of your visit, call 5208722 for information.

THE PERFORMING ARTS

TEATRO LA FENICE, campo San Fantin, San Marco 2549. Tel. 5210161.
One of the most famous theaters in Europe, Teatro La Fenice has existed in its present incarnation from the 19th century (an earlier structure was gutted by fire). To cap the perfect visit, try to attend either a concert or an opera at this theater should it be open at the time of your visit. The box office is open Monday through Saturday from 9:30am to 12:30pm and 4 to 6pm, and also 30 minutes before curtain time. If a Sunday performance is given, the box office will open, closing on Monday instead. Performances are usually presented Tuesday to Saturday at 8pm; sometimes 4pm matinees are offered (check at the box office). The Venetian opera season runs from

---

THE MAJOR CONCERT & PERFORMANCE HALLS

The following is a quick-reference list of major performance spaces in Venice, with box-office telephone numbers. Details are provided in the listings below.

Teatro Goldoni (tel. 5207583).
Teatro La Fenice (tel. 5210161).

December to May. The opera theater, however, presents a year-round repertoire of concerts and ballets—except in August when everybody is on vacation. Vaporetto: San Marco.

Prices: Tickets, 20,000–60,000 lire ($15.70–$47.10).

TEATRO GOLDONI, calle Goldoni near campo San Luca. Tel. 5207583.

This theater, close to the Ponte Rialto in the San Marco district, honors Carlo Goldoni (1707–93), the most prolific—critics say the best—of Italian playwrights. The theater presents a changing repertoire of productions, often plays in Italian, but musical presentations as well. The box office is open daily from 10am to 1pm and 4:30 to 7pm.

Prices: Tickets, 15,000–30,000 lire ($11.80–$23.55).

THE CLUB & MUSIC SCENE

ALLA GROTTA, calle dell'Angelo 407. Tel. 5209299.

Performers alternate between operatic arias and old Venetian love ballads with occasional audience participation. You can drown your own blues in purple wine. The Grotta is incredibly touristy, but that's a characteristic it shares with nearly every other establishment in Venice. It's open daily in season, which usually lasts from April until the end of October. The action with gondolier musicians starts after dinner at 9:30pm, and usually continues to 11:40pm or later. Your second drink costs 7,000 lire ($5.50). Vaporetto: San Marco.

Admission: 15,000 lire ($11.80), including one drink.

THE BAR SCENE

Want more in the way of nightlife? All right, but be warned: The Venetian nightclub owners may sock it to you when they present the bill.

BAR AI SPECI, in the Hotel Panada, calle dei Specchieri 646. Tel. 5209088.

Bar ai Speci is a charming corner bar located only a short walk from St. Mark's Basilica. Its richly grained paneling is offset by dozens of antique mirrors, each different, whose glittering surfaces reflect the rows of champagne and scotch bottles and the clustered groups of Biedermeier chairs. The bar is open to the public every day except Monday when only hotel guests may use it. Open daily from 10am to 2pm and 5pm to 1am. Whisky runs 6,000 lire to 7,500 lire ($4.70 to $5.50). Vaporetto: San Marco.

BAR DUCALE, San Marco 2354 (calle delle Ostreghe). Tel. 5210002.

Bar Ducale occupies a tiny corner of a building near a bridge over a narrow canal. Customers stand at the zinc bar which faces the carved 19th-century Gothic-reproduction shelves. A specialty is the mimosa cocktail, but the sandwiches are also one of the bar's attractions. The ebullient owner learned his craft at Harry's Bar before going into business for himself. Today his small establishment is usually mobbed every day of the week. It's ideal for an early-evening apéritif as you stroll about. Open daily from 7am to 11pm (closed Tuesday in winter). Whisky begins at 5,000 lire ($3.95); beer, 2,500 lire ($1.95). Vaporetto: San Marco.

LES DEUX LIONS, in the Londra Palace Hotel, riva degli Schiavoni 4171. Tel. 5200533.

Les Deux Lions has joined the ranks of piano bars. The hotel's exclusive restaurant has already been recommended (see "Dining" in Chapter 12). Here, the interior is a rich blend of scarlet-and-gold carpeting with a motif of lions, English pub-style furniture, and Louis XVI–style chairs, along with plenty of exposed mahogany. An outdoor terrace is more nautical in feeling, with drinks served at canvas director's chairs surrounded by lots of shrubbery. The view is of a 19th-century bronze statue, of a collection of Amazonian lion tamers, the lagoon, and the foot traffic along the Grand Canal. However, from 8pm (till 1am) daily entertainment takes over, the piano adding musical warmth. A whisky starts at 10,000 lire ($7.85). Vaporetto: San Zaccaria.

LINEA D'OMBRA, fondamenta delle Zattere. Tel. 5285259.

Venice, to the surprise of many of its visitors, has few real nightclubs. However, a good piano bar with a restaurant is found at Linea d'Ombra. It has a terrace that overlooks the Canale della Giudecca. A pianist sings international songs, and if the night is right, it can make for one of the more romantic evenings in Venice. Drinkers and diners are treated to a view of the island of San Giorgio. You should reserve a table if you want to eat. The restaurant is open Monday, Tuesday, and Thursday through Saturday from 12:30 to 2:30pm and 8 to 10:30pm, and on Sunday from 12:30 to 2:30pm; the bar is open daily from 8am to 2am. Meals run 50,000 lire to 70,000 lire ($39.25 to $54.95); drinks are 6,000 lire to 10,000 lire ($4.70 to $7.85). Vaporetto: Salute.

MARTINI SCALA CLUB, calle delle Veste (campo San Fantin). Tel. 5224121.

The Martini Scala Club is an elegant restaurant with a piano bar. You can enjoy its food and wine until 2am, the only kitchen in Venice that stays open that late. You can order such dishes as smoked goose breast with grapefruit and arugula, fresh salmon with black butter and olives, or gnocchi (dumplings) with butter and sage. After 10pm, you can come here to enjoy the piano bar. It's possible to order drinks without having food. The bar stays open nightly except Tuesday until 3:30am. The restaurant is open April to October, Wednesday through Monday from 8pm to 2am; November to March, Wednesday through Monday from 10pm to 2am. Drinks begin at 12,000 lire ($9.40); meals, at approximately 50,000 lire ($39.25). Vaporetto: San Marco.

WINE BARS

VINO VINO, calle del Cafetier 2007A. Tel. 5237027.

This wine bar has a selection of more than 250 Italian and imported wines. Vino Vino attracts a heterogeneous clientele. It wouldn't be unusual to see a Venetian countess sipping Prosecco near a gondolier eating a meal. This place is loved by snobs, young people, and tourists with little money left. It offers wines by the bottle or glass, including Italian grappas. Dishes of Venetian popular cuisine are served, including pastas, beans, baccalà (codfish), and polenta. The two rooms are always jammed like a vaporetto in rush hour, and there is take-away service if you can't find a place. It's open Wednesday through Monday from 10am to 1am. Meals cost 25,000 lire to 30,000 lire ($19.65 to $23.55); wine runs 900 lire to 7,000 lire (70¢ to $5.50) per glass. Vaporetto: San Marco.

ENOTECA AL VOLTO, Di Giancarlo Mersini, calle Cavalli di San Marco. Tel. 5228945.

Enoteca Volto lies off fondamenta del Carbon. The tiny room that shelters this wine bar is unpretentious when you consider the rarity of some of the vintages served. Yet it's also a Venetian institution. It offers more than 2,000 labels, as well as dozens of varieties of beer. There are few places to sit, but that doesn't bother some of the more dedicated drinkers, a few of whom have patronized the place since it was established in 1936. Salty snacks and small pizzas are sold. Open Monday through Saturday from 9am to 1:20pm and 4 to 9pm (closed August). Wine costs 1,000 lire to 10,000 lire (80¢ to $7.85) per glass. Vaporetto: San Marco.

CAFES

FLORIAN, piazza San Marco 56-59. Tel. 5285338.

The most famous café is the Florian. The Florian was built in 1720 and it remains romantically and elegantly decorated—pure Venetian salons with red plush banquettes, intricate and elaborate murals under glass, and art nouveau lighting and lamps. It's considered the most fashionable and aristocratic rendezvous in Venice: The Florian roster of customers has included such figures as Casanova, Lord Byron, Goethe, Canova, de Musset, and Madame de Stael. Special cocktails include a Bellini or a mimosa. Open Thursday through Tuesday from 9am to midnight. An espresso is 4,500 lire ($3.55); long drinks cost 14,000 lire ($11), plus 4,300 lire ($3.40) extra if you drink on the square when music is playing. Vaporetto: San Marco.

QUADRI, piazza San Marco 120-124. Tel. 5289299.
Quadri stands on the opposite side of the square from the Florian. It, too, is elegantly decorated in an antique style. It should be, as it was founded in 1638. Wagner used to drop in for a drink when he was working on *Tristan und Isolde*. Its prices are virtually the same as at the Florian, and it, too, imposes that surcharge on drinks ordered during concert periods. The bar was a favorite with the Austrians during their long-ago occupation. Open October to June, Tuesday through Sunday from 9am to midnight; July to September, daily from 9am to midnight. A whisky costs 14,000 lire ($11); coffee, 4,500 lire ($3.55). There's a music surcharge of 4,300 lire ($3.40). Vaporetto: San Marco.

CAFE LAVENA, piazza San Marco 134. Tel. 5224070.
Café Lavena is a popular but intimate café under the arcades of piazza San Marco. The establishment was frequented by Richard Wagner during his stay in Venice; he composed some of his greatest operas here. It has one of the most beautifully ornate glass chandeliers in town—the kind you'll love even if you hate Venetian glass. They hang from the ceiling between the iron rails of an upper-level balcony. The dozens of maroon glass "Aunt Jemima" heads perched on each of the chandeliers is an example of Italian humor. The most interesting tables are near the plate-glass window in front, although there's plenty of room at the stand-up bar as well. Open daily from 9am to 11pm. Coffee costs 1,100 lire (85¢) if you're standing, 4,500 lire ($3.55) if you're sitting at a table. And there's a music surcharge of 3,500 lire ($2.75).

ICE CREAM

GELATERIA PAOLIN, campo San Stefano 2962A. Tel. 5225576.
For many, strolling to Gelateria Paolin (set in a large colorful square), and ordering some of the tastiest ice cream (gelato) in Venice is nightlife enough. That's the way many a Venetian spends the evening in summer. This ice-cream parlor (gelateria) stands on the corner of the busy square. You can order your ice cream to go or eat it at one of the sidewalk tables. Many interesting flavors are offered, including pistachio. However, you may want to be adventurous and try something known as "Malaga". Open from spring through fall, Tuesday through Sunday from 7:30am to 11:30pm; in winter, Tuesday through Sunday from 7:30am to 8:30pm (closed in January). Ice cream costs 4,500 lire to 8,000 lire ($3.55 to $6.30).

GAMBLING

CASINO MUNICIPALE, lungomare G. Marconi 4. Tel. 5297111.
If you want to risk your luck and your lire, you can take a vaporetto ride on the Casino Express, which leaves from the stops at the railway station, piazzale Roma, and piazzetta San Marco, and delivers you to the landing dock of the Casino Municipale. The Italian government wisely forbids its nationals to cross the threshold unless they work here, so bring your passport. The building itself is foreboding, almost as if it could have been inspired by Mussolini-era architects. However, the action gets hotter once you step inside. At the casino, you can play blackjack, roulette, baccarat, or whatever. You can also dine, drink at the bar, or enjoy a floor show. Open daily from 4pm to 2:30am.

Admission: 15,000 lire ($11.80).

VENDRAMIN-CALERGI PALACE, Cannaregio 2040, Strada Nuova. Tel. 5297111.

From October to May, the casino action moves to the Vendramin-Calergi Palace. Incidentally, in 1883 Wagner died in this house which opens onto the Grand Canal. Open daily from 3pm to 3am. Vaporetto: San Marcuola.

Admission: 15,000 lire ($11.80).

6. EASY EXCURSIONS

MURANO

This is the island where for centuries **glassblowers** have performed oral gymnastics to turn out those fantastic chandeliers (some with porpoise arms) that Victorian ladies used to prize so highly. They also produce heavily ornamented glasses so ruby-red or so indigo-blue you can't tell if you're drinking blackberry juice or pure wood-grain. Happily, the glassblowers are still plying their trade, although increasing competition—notably from Sweden—has compelled a greater degree of sophistication in design.

Murano remains the chief expedition from Venice, but not the most beautiful island. (Burano and Torcello are far more attractive.)

You can combine a tour of Murano with a trip around the lagoon. To reach it, take vaporetto no. 5 at riva degli Schiavoni, a short walk from piazzetta San Marco. The boat docks at the landing platform at Murano where—lo and behold—the first furnace awaits conveniently. It's best to go Monday through Friday from 10am to noon if you want to see some glassblowing action.

WHAT TO SEE & DO

As you stroll through Murano, you'll find that the factory owners are only too glad to let you come in and see their age-old crafts. These managers aren't altogether altruistic, of course. While browsing through the showrooms, you'll need stiff resistance to keep the salespeople at bay. And it's possible to bargain down the initial price quoted. Don't—repeat, *don't*—pay the marked price on any item. That's merely the figure at which to open negotiations.

An exception to that is made-on-the-spot souvenirs, which are turned out at Murano. For example, you might want to purchase a horse streaked with blue. The artisan takes a piece of incandescent glass, huffs, puffs, rolls it, shapes it, snips it, and behold—he has shaped a horse. The showrooms of Murano also contain a fine assortment of Venetian crystal beads, available in every hue of the rainbow. You may find some of the best work to be the experiments of apprentices.

While on the island, you can visit the Renaissance palazzo that houses the **Museo Vetrario di Murano,** via Marche 13, fondamenta Giustinian (tel. 4871400). From April through October, it's open Tuesday through Saturday from 9am to 7pm and on Sunday from 9:30am to 12:30pm; in winter, it closes at 3pm. Admission costs 5,000 lire ($3.95) for adults, 3,000 lire ($2.35) for children. Inside is a spectacular collection of Venetian glass.

The **Church of San Pietro Martire** dates from the 1300s but was rebuilt in 1511. Richly decorated, with paintings by Tintoretto and Veronese, it offers a respite from the glass factories. Its proud possession is a *Madonna and Child Enthroned* by Giovanni Bellini, plus two superb altarpieces by the same master. The church lies right before the junction with Murano's Grand Canal, about 250 yards from the vaporetto landing stage.

Even more notable is **Santi Maria e Donato,** campo San Donato, which is open daily from 8am to noon and 4 to 7pm. This building is a stellar example of the Venetian Byzantine style, in spite of its 19th-century restoration. It dates from the 7th

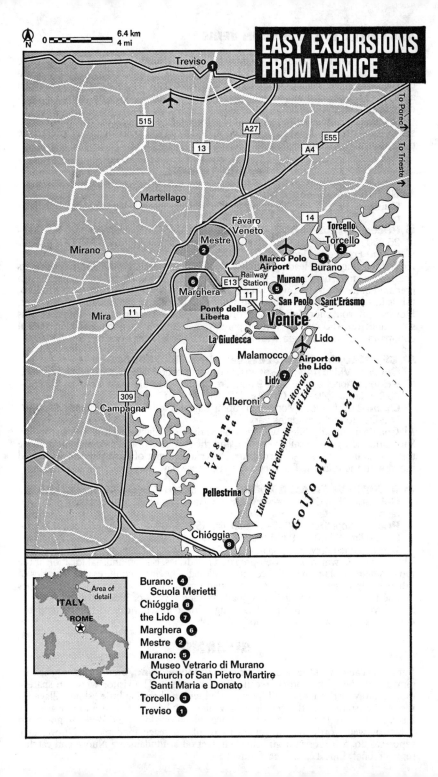

EASY EXCURSIONS FROM VENICE

0 ━━━ 6.4 km
  ━━━ 4 mi
N

Treviso ❶

To Poreč →

To Trieste →

515

A27

13

E55

A4

Martellago

14

Torcello
Torcello ❸

Fávaro
Veneto

Mestre ❷

Marco Polo
Airport

Burano ❹

Mirano

Railway
Station

Murano

E13

Marghera ❻

11

San Paolo ❺

Sant'Erásmo

Mira

11

Ponte della
Liberta

Venice

La Giudecca

Lido

Malamocco

Airport on
the Lido

309

Campagna

Lido ❼

Alberoni

Litorale di Lido

Laguna Veneta

Golfo di Venezia

Pellestrina

Litorale di Pellestrina

Chióggia ❽

Area of
detail

ITALY

ROME ★

Burano: ❹
  Scuola Merietti
Chióggia ❽
the Lido ❼
Marghera ❻
Mestre ❷
Murano: ❺
  Museo Vetrario di Murano
  Church of San Pietro Martire
  Santi Maria e Donato
Torcello ❸
Treviso ❶

century but was reconstructed in the 1100s. The interior is known for its mosaic floor—a parade of peacocks and eagles, as well as other creatures—and a 15th-century ship's-keel ceiling. Over the apse is an outstanding mosaic of the Virgin against a gold background, which dates from the early 1200s. The church is open daily from 8am to noon and 4 to 7pm.

You can take the same ferry back, but why not get off at fondamente Nuove, then slowly stroll through an unheralded section of the city that will bring you closer to the quiet charm and serene beauty of Venice?

WHERE TO DINE

AI VETRAI, fondamenta Manin 29. Tel. 739293.

Cuisine: VENETIAN. **Reservations:** Recommended. **Vaporetto:** 5 to Murano.

$ Prices: Appetizers 6,000–9,000 lire ($4.70–$7.05); main courses 12,000–25,000 lire ($9.40–$19.65); fixed-price menu 28,000 lire ($22). AE, DC, MC, V.
Open: Fri–Wed 11am–7pm.

Ai Vetrai is one of the leading restaurants of Murano. It entertains and nourishes its guests in a large room not far from the Canale dei Vetrai. If you're looking for fish prepared in the local style, with what might be called the widest selection in Murano, this is it. Most varieties of crustaceans and gilled creatures are available on the spot. However, if you phone ahead and order food for a large party, as the Venetians sometimes do, the owners will prepare what they call "a noble fish" on special command. You might begin with spaghetti in a green clam sauce.

AL CORALLO, fondamenta dei Vetrai 73. Tel. 739080.

Cuisine: VENETIAN. **Reservations:** Not needed. **Vaporetto:** 5 to Murano.

$ Prices: Appetizers 6,000–9,000 lire ($4.70–$7.05); main courses 12,000–23,000 lire ($9.40–$18.05). AE, DC, MC, V.
Open: Lunch Wed–Mon noon–3pm; dinner Wed–Mon 7–8:30pm. **Closed:** Mid-Dec to mid-Jan (dates vary).

Al Corallo is usually filled with a wide variety of clients from all walks of life. Specialties here are typically Venetian, and the service is polite. Local clients choose this restaurant for a well-deserved meal after a morning of hard physical work and blend with the tourists. The menu changes every day.

TRATTORIA BUSA ALLA TORRE, campo San Stefano 3. Tel. 739662.

Cuisine: SEAFOOD. **Reservations:** Recommended. **Vaporetto:** 5 to Murano.

$ Prices: Appetizers 9,000–12,000 lire ($7.05–$9.40); main courses 12,000–25,000 lire ($9.40–$19.65). AE, DC, MC, V.
Open: Lunch only, Tues–Sun noon–3pm.

This restaurant, which offers well-prepared fish dishes, is in an unusual location at the top of a flight of stairs in a 13th-century building. The decor conjures up memories of other family restaurants along the Venetian coast. Here, specialties include recipes unique to Murano, including scampi alla Busa, a variety of bluefish, good sardines, and a wide array of fish antipasti, along with a mixed Adriatic fish fry and the ubiquitous fish-flavored risotto and grilled fish.

BURANO

Burano became world famous as a center of **lacemaking**, a craft that reached its pinnacle in the 18th century (recall Venetian point?). The visitor who can spare a morning to visit this island will be rewarded with a charming little fishing village far removed in spirit from the grandeur of Venice, but lying only half an hour away by ferry. Boats leave from fondamente Nuove, which overlooks the Venetian graveyard (which is well worth the trip all on its own). To reach fondamente Nuove, take vaporetto no. 5 from riva degli Schiavoni. Get off at fondamente Nuove and catch a separate boat, Line 12, marked Burano.

WHAT TO SEE & DO

Once at Burano, you'll discover that the houses of the islanders come in varied colors—sienna, robin's-egg or cobalt blue, barn-red, butterscotch, grass green. If you need a focal point for your excursion, it should be the **Scuola Merietti** in the center of the fishing village at piazza Baldassare Galuppi. The Burano School of Lace was founded in 1872 as part of a resurgence movement aimed at restoring the age-old craft that had earlier declined, giving way to such other lacemaking centers as Chantilly and Bruges. By going up to the second floor you can see the lacemakers, mostly young women, at painstaking work, and can purchase hand-embroidered or handmade-lace items.

After visiting the lace school, you can walk across the square to the **Duomo** and its leaning campanile (inside, look for the *Crucifixion* by Tiepolo). However, do so at once, because the bell tower is leaning so precariously it looks as if it may topple at any moment.

WHERE TO DINE

TRATTORIA DE ROMANO, via Baldassare Galuppi 223. Tel. 730030.
   Cuisine: VENETIAN. **Reservations:** Recommended. **Vaporetto:** Line 12 from Murano.
$ Prices: Appetizers 7,000–9,000 lire ($5.50–$7.05); main courses 10,000–18,000 lire ($7.85–$14.15). AE, MC, V.
   Open: Lunch Wed–Mon noon–2:30pm; dinner Wed–Mon 7–8:30pm. **Closed:** Dec 15–Feb 15.

If you're on the island at mealtime, you may want to join a long line of people who have patronized the rather simple-looking *caratteristico* Trattoria de Romano, which is around the corner from the lace school. You can enjoy a superb dinner here, which might consist of risotto di pesce (the Italian version of the Valencian paella), followed by fritto misto di pesce, a mixed fish fry from the Adriatic, with savory bits of mullet, squid, and shrimp. The tab might also include refreshing wine, fresh fruit, and service.

OSTARIA AI PESCATORI, piazza Baldassare Galuppi 371. Tel. 730650.
   Cuisine: SEAFOOD. **Reservations:** Recommended. **Vaporetto:** Line 12 from Murano.
$ Prices: Appetizers 6,000–12,000 lire ($4.70–$9.40); main courses 13,000–30,000 lire ($10.20–$23.55). DC, MC, V.
   Open: Lunch Tues–Sun noon–3pm; dinner Tues–Sun 7–9pm. **Closed:** Jan.

The family that pools its efforts to run this well-known restaurant maintains strong friendships with the local fishermen, who often reserve the best parts of their daily catch for preparation in the kitchen here. The cooking is performed by the matriarch of an extended family. The place has gained a reputation as the preserver of a type of simple and unpretentious restaurant unique to Burano. Locals in dialect call it a *buranello*. Clients often take the vaporetto from other sections of Venice (the restaurant lies close to the boat landing) to eat at the plain wooden tables set up either indoors or on the small square in front. Specialties feature all the staples of the Venetian seaside diet, including fish soup, risotto di pesce, pasta seafarer's style, and a wide range of crustaceans, plus grilled, fried, or baked fish. Your meal might also include a bottle of fruity wine from the region.

TORCELLO

Of all the islands of the lagoon, Torcello—the so-called Mother of Venice—offers the most charm. If Burano is behind the times, Torcello is positively antediluvian. You can follow in the footsteps of Hemingway and stroll across a grassy meadow, traverse an ancient stone bridge, and step back into that time when the Venetians first fled from invading barbarians to create a city of Neptune in the lagoon.

To reach Torcello, take vaporetto no. 12 from fondamenta Nuova on Murano. The trip takes about 45 minutes.

Final warning: If you go on your own, don't listen to the savvy gondoliers who hover at the ferry quay. They'll tell you that both the cathedral and the locanda are "miles away." Actually, they're both reached after a leisurely 12- to 15-minute stroll along the canal.

WHAT TO SEE & DO

Torcello has two major attractions: a church with Byzantine mosaics good enough to make the Empress Theodora at Ravenna turn as purple with envy as her robe, and a *locanda* (inn) that converts trippers into inebriated angels of praise. First the spiritual nourishment before the alcoholic sustenance.

The **Cattedrale di Torcello,** also called the Church of Santa Maria Assunta (tel. 730084), was founded in A.D. 639 and was subsequently rebuilt. It stands in a lonely, grassy meadow beside a campanile which dates from the 11th century. It is visited chiefly because of its Byzantine mosaics. Clutching her child, the weeping Madonna in the apse is a magnificent sight while on the opposite wall is a powerful *Last Judgment.* Byzantine artisans, it seems, were at their best in portraying hell and damnation. At Santa Maria Assunta they do not disappoint. In their Inferno they have re-created a virtual human stew with the fires stirred by wicked demons. Reptiles slide in and out of the skulls of cannibalized sinners. It is open April to October, daily from 10am to 12:30pm and 2:30 to 6:30pm; November to March, daily from 10am to 12:30pm and 2:30 to 5:30pm. Admission costs 1,500 lire ($1.20).

WHERE TO DINE

After a whiff of this Dante-esque nightmare, you'll need one of "Harry's" martinis.

LOCANDA CIPRIANI, piazza S. Fosca 29. Tel. 730150.
  Cuisine: VENETIAN. **Reservations:** Recommended.
$ **Prices:** Appetizers 18,000–25,000 lire ($14.15–$19.65); main courses 27,000–36,000 lire ($21.20–$28.25). AE, DC, MC, V.
  Open: Lunch Wed–Mon noon–3pm; dinner Wed–Mon 7–10pm. **Closed:** Nov 10–Mar 15.

⭐ The Locanda Cipriani, located just across from the church, is an inn extraordinaire. The term *locanda* usually denotes an inexpensive lodging, rated under the lowliest pensione. However, that is not the case at Cipriani. This country inn is well appointed, with an open-air dining loggia. The chef features a number of high-priced dishes, with suggested dinners on the menu. Specialties include cannelloni, a most savory fish soup, and a rice pilaf. For an appetizer, try the gnocchi, a Roman-inspired dish made with a semolina base. Most guests prefer the fresh fish from the Adriatic.

CHAPTER 14

VERONA, PADUA (PADOVA) & VICENZA

1. VERONA
- **WHAT'S SPECIAL ABOUT VERONA, PADUA & VICENZA**
2. PADUA (PADOVA)
3. VICENZA

Tearing yourself away from piazza San Marco is a task for those of iron will. However, Venice doesn't possess a regional monopoly on art or treasures. Of the cities of interest easily reached from Venice, three tower above the rest. They are Verona, the home of the eternal lovers, Romeo and Juliet; Padua, the city of Mantegna, with frescoes by Giotto; and Vicenza, city of Palladio, with streets of Renaissance palazzi and villa-studded hills. The miracle of all these cities is that Venice did not siphon off their creative drive completely, although the Serene Republic dominated them for centuries.

SEEING VERONA, PADUA & VICENZA

SUGGESTED ITINERARY

Day 1: Leave Venice (as hard as that is to do) and spend a full day taking in the artistic treasures of the ancient city of Padua.

Day 2: Too often ignored, Vicenza is an architectural treasure trove of the works, either original or inspired, of Palladio.

Day 3: Not enough time, but most visitors allow only a day to try to cover the highlights of the beautiful city of Verona and its many monuments and gardens.

GETTING THERE

The nearest airport is outside Venice, with domestic flights offered by Alitalia. If you're dependent on public transportation, use Verona as your center, as it lies at the crossroads of the main north-south rail links connecting Munich with Rome. It has easy connections also to Venice, Vicenza, and Padua. Once in Verona, you'll find easy bus connections to all the major towns in the province. Buses in Padua and Vicenza are also mainly used for destinations within their different provinces. For motorists, the main highway that connects the region is A4, linking Verona, Padua, and Venice.

---

1. VERONA

71 miles W of Venice, 312 miles NE of Rome

GETTING THERE **By Train** A total of 37 trains a day make the 2-hour run between Venice and Verona, costing 7,000 lire ($5.50) for a one-way ticket. If you're in

WHAT'S SPECIAL ABOUT VERONA, PADUA & VICENZA

Great Towns/Villages

☐ Verona, forever associated with the legend of Romeo and Juliet, one of the most romantically beautiful of all northern Italian cities.

☐ Padua, in 1406 part of the Venetian empire, an art-filled city with Italy's second-oldest university.

☐ Vicenza, the home of Palladianism, the most influential building style in the history of Western architecture.

Architectural Highlights

☐ Piazza dei Signori, at Vicenza, a classical square partially designed by Palladio, the open-air "living room" of the city.

☐ Piazza delle Erbe, Verona, the "square of herbs," a former Roman forum, where an architectural farra-go of old houses and towers line the square.

Ancient Monuments

☐ Tombs of the Scaligere, Verona, an artistic treasure, mostly 14th cen-tury.

☐ Roman Arena, Verona, completed in A.D. 30, the third largest and one of the best-preserved Roman amphi-theaters extant.

Churches

☐ Cappella degli Scrovegni, Padua, visited by art lovers from all over the world because of its remarkable cy-cle of 35 frescoes by Giotto begun around 1305.

---

the west—say, at Milan, there are even more connections, some 40 trains a day, taking 2 hours to reach Verona at a cost of 8,200 lire ($6.45) for a one-way ticket. Six trains make the 6-hour run north from Rome, costing 31,900 lire ($25.05) for a one-way ticket.

By Bus   APT buses depart from the Porta Nuova FS Station (tel. 8004129) in Verona, serving the province and fanning out to such cities as Brescia, Mantua, and Lake Garda. If you're coming from Venice, it's better to take the train.

By Car   From Venice, take the autostrada (A4) west all the way until you see the signposted cutoff for Verona.

ESSENTIALS   The **telephone area code** is 045. The **Tourist Information Office** is at piazza delle Erbe 42 (tel. 8006997).

The home of a pair of star-cross'd lovers, Verona was the setting for the most famous love story in the English language, Shakespeare's *Romeo and Juliet*. A long-forgotten editor of an old volume of the bard's plays once wrote: "Verona, so rich in the associations of real history, has even a greater charm for those who would live in the poetry of the past." It's not known if a Romeo or a Juliet ever existed, but the remains of Verona's recorded past are much in evidence today. Its Roman antiquities, for example, are unequaled north of Rome.

In the city's medieval golden age under the despotic, cruel Scaligeri princes, Verona reached the pinnacle of its influence and prestige, developing into a town that, even today, is considered among the great cities of Italy. The best-known member of the ruling Della Scala family, Cangrande I, was a patron of Dante. His sway over Verona has often been compared to that of Lorenzo the Magnificent over Florence.

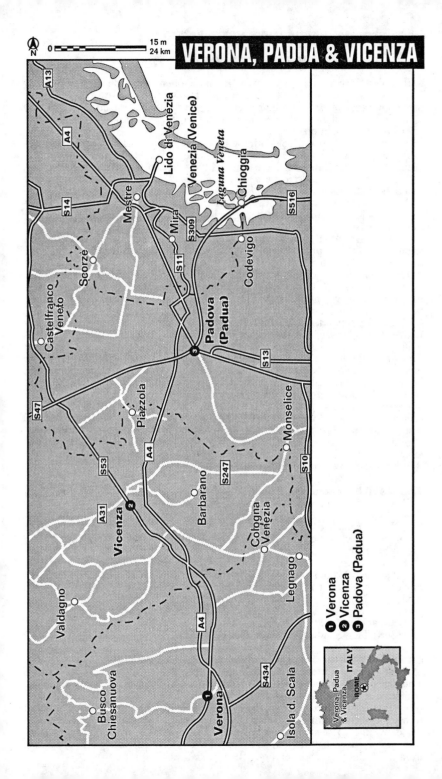

VERONA, PADUA & VICENZA

0 ⊨ 15 m
24 km
N

A13
A4
S14
S11
S309
S516
S47
S53
A31
A4
A4
S13
S247
S10
S434

Lido di Venézia
Venézia (Venice)
Laguna Veneta
Chioggia
Mestre
Mira
Codevigo
Scorzè
Castelfranco Veneto
Padova (Padua) ❸
Piazzola
Monselice
Barbarano
Cologna Venézia
Legnago
Valdagno
Vicenza ❷
Busco Chiesanuova
Verona ❶
Isola d. Scala

❶ Verona
❷ Vicenza
❸ Padova (Padua)

Verona, Padua & Vicenza
ITALY
ROME

WHAT TO SEE & DO

Verona lies alongside the Adige River. It's most often visited on a quick half-day excursion (easily reached on the autostrada), but Verona deserves more time. It's meant for wandering and for contemplation. If you're rushed, head first to the old city to begin your explorations. In addition to the sights listed below, there are other attractions that might merit a visit.

Opening onto Piazza dei Signori, the handsomest in Verona, is the **Palazzo del Governo,** where Cangrande extended the shelter of his hearth and home to that fleeing Ghibelline, Dante Alighieri. The marble statue in the center of the square, whose expression is as cold as a Dolomite icicle, is of the "divine poet" but unintimidated pigeons perch on his pious head. Facing Dante's back is the late 15th-century **Loggia del Consiglio,** surmounted by five statues. The most attractive building on the square, the loggia is frescoed. Five different arches lead into **piazza dei Signori,** the innermost chamber of the heart of Verona.

The **Arche Scaligere** are outdoor tombs surrounded by highly decorative wrought iron that form a kind of open-air pantheon of the Scaligeri princes. One tomb, that of Cangrande della Scala, rests directly over the door of the Santa Maria Antica Church which dates from the 12th century. The mausoleum contains many Romanesque features. It is crowned by a copy of an equestrian statue (the original is now at the Castelvecchio). The tomb nearest the door is that of Mastino II; the one behind it—and the most lavish of all—that of Cansignorio.

The ✪ **piazza delle Erbe** is a lively, palace-flanked square that was formerly a Roman forum. Today, it is the setting of the fruit and vegetable market as well as milling Veronese, both shoppers and vendors. In the center of the square is a fountain dating from the 14th century and a Roman statue dubbed *The Virgin of Verona.* The pillar at one end of the square, crowned by a chimera, symbolizes the many years that Verona was dominated by the Serenissima. Important buildings and towers include the **House of Merchants,** which dates from the early years of the 14th century. Other interesting structures include the **Gardello Tower,** built by one of the Della Scala princes; the restored former city hall and the **Lamberti Tower,** soaring about 260 feet; the **Maffei Palace,** in the baroque style; and finally, the **Casa Mazzanti.**

From the vegetable market, you can walk down **via Mazzini,** the most fashionable street in Verona, to **piazza Brà,** with its neoclassical town hall and the Renaissance palazzo, the Gran Guardia.

THE ARENA, piazza Brà. Tel. 8003204.

The elliptical amphitheater on piazza Brà, which resembles the Colosseum in Rome, dates from the 1st century A.D. Standing today are four arches of the "outer circle" and a complete "inner ring." For nearly half a century it has been the setting of a summer opera house, usually from mid-July to mid-August. More than 20,000 people are treated to Verdi or Mascagni, for example.

Reservations can be made and tickets purchased at the box office of the arena daily from 9am to 12:20pm and 3 to 5:30pm. Reservations can also be made by letter: Enclose a bank draft or money order and indicate the date of performance, the section, and the number of tickets desired. Write to Ente Lirico Arena di Verona, piazza Brà 28, 37100 Verona (tel. 045/590109). Phone orders are not accepted.

Admission: 5,000 lire ($3.95).

Open: Tues–Sun 8am–6:45pm. **Bus:** 2 or 5.

CASTELVECCHIO, corso Castelvecchio 2. Tel. 594734.

Built under the order of Cangrande II in the 14th century, the Old Castle is alongside the Adige River (reached by heading out via Roma). It stands near the Ponte Scaligero, the bridge bombed by the Nazis in World War II and subsequently reconstructed. The former seat of the Della Scala family, the restored castle has been turned into an **art museum,** with important paintings from the Veronese school and works by other masters of northern Italy. On the ground floor are displays of 14th- and 15th-century sculpture, and on the upper floor you'll see masterpieces of painting from the 15th to the 18th century.

In the Sala Monga is Jacopo Bellini's *St. Jerome,* in the desert with his lion and crucifix. Two sisterlike portraits of Saint Catherina and Veneranda by Vittore Carpaccio grace the Sala Rizzardi Allegri. The Bellini family is also represented here by a lyrical *Madonna con Bambino* painted by Giovanni, the master of that subject.

Between the buildings is the most charming equestrian statue I've ever seen, that of Cangrande I, grinning like a buffoon, with a dragon sticking out of his back like a projectile. In the Sala Murari dalla Corte Brà is one of the most beguiling portraits in the castle—Giovanni Francesco Caroto's smiling red-haired boy. In the Sala di Canossa are paintings by Tintoretto, a *Madonna Nursing the Child* and a *Nativity,* and by Veronese, a *Deposition from the Cross* and the *Pala Bevilacqua Lazise.*

In the Sala Bolognese Trevenzuoli is a rare self-portrait of Bernardo Strozzi, and in the Sala Avena, among paintings by the most famous Venetian masters such as Gianbattista and Giandomenico Tiepolo and Guardi, hangs an almost satirical portrait of an 18th-century patrician family by Longhi.

Admission: 5,000 lire ($39.25) adults, 3,000 lire ($2.35) children.
Open: Tues–Sun 8am–6:45pm. **Bus:** 2, 3, 7, or 20.

CHURCH OF SAN ZENO MAGGIORE, piazza San Zeno. Tel. 8006120.

This near-perfect Romanesque church and campanile is graced with a stunning entrance—two pillars supported by puce-colored marble lions and surmounted with a rose window. On either side of the portal are bas-reliefs depicting scenes from the Old and New Testaments, as well as a mythological story portraying Theodoric as a huntsman lured to hell (the king of the Goths defeated Odoacer in Verona). The panels on the bronze doors, nearly 50 in all, are a remarkable achievement of primitive art, sculpted perhaps in the 12th century. They reflect, of course, a naïve handling of their subject matter—see John the Baptist's head resting on a platter. The artists express themselves with such candor that they achieve the power of a child's storybook. Inside, the church is divided into a central nave and two aisles. Somber and severe, it contains a major Renaissance work at the main altar, a triptych by Andrea Mantegna, which shows the Madonna and Child enthroned with saints. Although not remarkable in its characterization, it reveals the artist's genius for perspective.

Admission: Free.
Open: Daily 8am–12:30pm and 4–7pm. **Bus:** 2 or 5.

CHURCH OF SANT'ANASTASIA, piazza Sant'Anastasia. Tel. 8004325.

This church dates from the 13th century. Its facade isn't complete, yet nevertheless it is considered the finest representation of Gothic design in Verona. Many artists in the 15th and 16th centuries decorated the interior, and few of the works seem worthy of being singled out for special mention. The exception, however, is the Pellegrini Chapel, with the reliefs in terra-cotta by the Tuscan artist Michele. The interior consists of one nave flanked by two aisles, and the overall effect is impressive, especially the patterned floor. As you enter, look for two hunchbacks.

Admission: Free.
Open: Apr–Oct, daily 8am–12:30pm and 4–7pm; Nov–Mar, daily 9am–noon and 3–5:30pm. **Bus:** 2 or 5.

IL DUOMO, piazza del Duomo. Tel. 595627.

The cathedral of Verona is less interesting than San Zeno Maggiore, but it still merits a visit. A blend of the Romanesque and Gothic styles, its facade contains (lower level) 12th-century sculptured reliefs by Nicolaus that depict scenes of Roland and Oliver, two of the legendary dozen knights attending Charlemagne. In the left aisle (first chapel) is an *Assumption* by Titian. The other major work of art is the rood screen in front of the presbytery, with Ionic pillars, designed by Samicheli.

Admission: Free.
Open: Apr–Oct, daily 9am–noon and 3–6pm; Nov–Mar, daily 9am–noon and 3–5:30pm. **Bus:** 2 or 5.

CHIESA DI SAN FERMO, piazza San Fermo. Tel. 8007287.

This Romanesque church, which dates from the 11th century, forms the foundation of the 14th-century Gothic building that surmounts it. Through time it has been used by both the Benedictines and the Franciscans. The interior is unusual, with a single nave and a splendid roof constructed of wood and exquisitely paneled. The most important work inside is Pisanello's frescoed *Annunciation,* to the left of the main entrance (at the Brenzoni tomb). Delicate and graceful, the work reveals the artist's keen eye for architectural detail and his bizarre animals.

Admission: Free.

Open: Apr–Oct, daily 9am–noon and 3–6pm; Nov–Mar, daily 9am–noon and 3–5:30pm. **Bus:** 2 or 5.

TEATRO ROMANO [ROMAN THEATER] AND MUSEUM, via Rigaste Redentorre 2A. Tel. 8000360.

The **Teatro Romano,** originally built in the 1st century A.D., now stands in ruins at the foot of St. Peter's Hill. For nearly a quarter of a century, a Shakespearean festival has been staged here on certain dates in July and August, and, of course, a unique theater-going experience is to see *Romeo and Juliet* or *Two Gentlemen of Verona* in this setting. The theater is across from the Adige River (take the Ponte di Pietra).

After seeing the remains of the theater, you can take a rickety elevator to the 10th-century Santa Libera Church towering over it. In the cloister of St. Jerome is the **Roman Archeological Museum** (same phone), which has interesting mosaics and Etruscan bronzes.

Admission: Theater and museum, 5,000 lire ($3.95).

Open: Theater and museum, Nov–Mar, Tues–Sun 8:30am–1:30pm; Apr–Oct, Tues–Sun 8am–6pm. **Bus:** 2 or 5.

GIARDINO GIUSTI, via Giardino Giusti. Tel. 38029.

One of the oldest and most famous gardens in Italy, the Giardino Giusti was created at the end of the 14th century. These well-manicured Italian gardens, studded with cypress trees, form one of the most relaxing and coolest spots in all of Verona for strolls. You can climb all the way to the "monster balcony" for an incomparable view of the city. The romantic Arcadians of the 18th century met here in a setting appropriate to their idealized beliefs.

What we see today is the layout given the gardens by Alessandro Vittoria, who worked with Palladio. All of its 16th-century characteristics—the grottoes, the statues, the fountains, the mascarons, the box-enclosed flower garden, and the maze—have remained intact. In addition to the flower displays, you can admire the statues by Lorenzo Muttoni and Alessandro Vittoria, interesting Roman remains, and the great cypress mentioned by Goethe.

These gardens have been visited by the illustrious over the centuries, including Addison, De Brosses, Mozart, Goethe, and Emperor Joseph II. The gardens, with their adjacent 16th-century palazzo, form one of Italy's most interesting urban complexes. The maze, constructed with myrtle hedges, faithfully reproduces the 1786 plan of the architect Trezza. Its complicated pattern and small size make it one of the most unusual in Europe.

The gardens lie near the Roman Theater, only a few minutes' walk from the heart of the city.

Admission: 4,000 lire ($3.15).

Open: Daily 9am–sunset. **Bus:** 20.

TOMBA DI GIULIETTA, via Luigi da Porto 5. Tel. 8000361.

The so-called Juliet's Tomb is sheltered in a Franciscan monastery entered on via Luigi da Porto, off via del Pontiere. "A grave? O, no, a lantern. . . . For here lies Juliet, and her beauty makes this vault a feasting presence full of light." Don't you believe it! Still, the cloisters, in the vicinity of the Adige River, are graceful. Adjoining the tomb is a museum of frescoes, dedicated to G. B. Cavalcaselle.

Admission: 4,000 lire ($3.15).

Open: Tues–Sun 8am–6:45pm. **Bus:** 2 or 5.

CASA GIULIETTA, via Cappello 23. Tel. 38303.
Juliet's house is a small home with a balcony and a courtyard. With a little bit of imagination it's not difficult to hear Romeo saying: "But, soft! what light through yonder window breaks? It is the east, and Juliet is the sun!"
   Admission: 3,500 lire ($2.75).
   Open: Tues–Sun 8am–7pm. **Bus:** 2 or 5.

SHOPPING

Verona attracts devotees of antiques. Around corso Santa Anastasia, via Massalongo, via Sottoriva, and adjacent streets you'll find any number of shops selling porcelain, furniture, ornaments, tapestries, paintings, and prints. In addition, the historic center of Verona, particularly via Cappello and via Mazzini, is full of shops, ranging from fashionable boutiques to handcraft shops and department stores. The already-previewed piazza delle Erbe, of course, sells every conceivable kind of item.

WHERE TO STAY

Verona boasts a deluxe hotel, the Due Torri. After that, a selection in various price levels follows. Hotel rooms tend to be scarce during the Country Fair in March and the opera and theater season in July and August.

VERY EXPENSIVE

HOTEL DUE TORRI, piazza Sant'Anastasia 4, 37121 Verona. Tel. 045/595044. Fax 045/595044. 100 rms (all with bath). A/C MINIBAR TV TEL **Bus:** 2 or 5.
$ Rates (including breakfast): 295,000 lire ($231.60) single; 410,000 lire ($321.85) double. AE, DC, MC, V. **Parking:** 25,000 lire ($19.65).

The Hotel Due Torri is almost a sightseeing attraction. It was rebuilt in 1958 in the original style and it hides secret glamour behind a streamlined facade. Originally, the Due Torri belonged to the Scaligeri dynasty and has sheltered such notables as Mozart, Goethe, and Tsar Alexander I of Russia. Enrico Wallner did a brilliant job of creating one of the most unusual luxury hotels in Italy. To attain the perfection he sought, he launched a massive antiques hunt for fine pieces of the 18th and 19th centuries.

When you check in, the concierge will show you color photographs of what the rooms are like, and you can choose your own theme. The range is splendid—Directoire, Empire, Louis XVIII, even the Germanic Biedermeier. Few hotels in Europe have such tasteful and well-thought-out rooms. These impressive bedchambers have central heating and most are soundproof. The old oil paintings inserted in ceiling panels make for a floating art gallery. The little salons available on each floor are equally distinguished.

Dining/Entertainment: If you order dinner, expect to pay 70,000 lire ($54.95) for a gourmet meal, served in the restaurant, All'Aquila. Menus are based on typical local and light cuisine. This is one of the most distinguished restaurants of Verona, and even if you're not a guest of the hotel you can visit for a meal. Food is served daily from 12:30 to 2:30pm and 7:30 to 10pm.

Services: Room service, baby-sitting, laundry, valet.

EXPENSIVE

COLOMBA D'ORO, via C. Cattaneo 10, 37121 Verona. Tel. 045/595300. Fax 045/594974. 51 rms (all with bath), 2 suites. A/C MINIBAR TV TEL **Bus:** 2 or 5.
$ Rates (including breakfast): 136,000–151,000 lire ($106.75–$118.55) single; 188,000–210,000 lire ($147.60–$164.85) double; from 428,000 lire ($336) suite. AE, DC, MC, V. **Parking:** 20,000 lire ($15.70).
The Colomba d'Oro is an old villa in the center of town, with moss-green shutters and balconies. Inside, it is efficiently organized to accommodate voyagers in an atmosphere that hovers between semitraditional and contemporary. The bedrooms are nicely

furnished with matching fabrics and comfortable pieces. The hotel's service is good. Only breakfast is served.

HOTEL ACCADEMIA, via Scala 12, 37121 Verona. Tel. 045/596222. Fax 045/596222. 97 rms (all with bath). A/C MINIBAR TV TEL **Bus:** 2 or 4.

$ Rates: 145,000–185,000 lire ($113.85–$145.25) single; 185,000–255,000 lire ($145.25–$200.20) double. Breakfast 15,000 lire ($11.80) extra. AE, DC, MC, V. **Parking:** 20,000 lire ($15.70).

The Hotel Accademia is an elegant, centrally located hotel whose marble-floored lobby contains Oriental rugs, a medieval tapestry, and two marble columns which flank the polished stone stairwell leading to the bedrooms. There's a warmly paneled, modern bar at the far end of the lobby, just past the elevator and a monochromatic mural of old Verona. The hotel has a covered garage and a full-service restaurant.

MODERATE

MILANO HOTEL, vicolo Tre Marchetti 11, 37121 Verona. Tel. 045/596011. Fax 045/8011299. 50 rms (all with bath). A/C MINIBAR TV TEL **Bus:** 2 or 5.

$ Rates (including breakfast): 98,600 lire ($77.40) single; 133,000 lire ($104.40) double. AE. **Parking:** 15,000 lire ($11.80).

The Milano Hotel is located approximately 1 minute from the Roman arena. Its public rooms are furnished in a functional style. The bedrooms are neatly laid out with utilitarian simplicity but are restful, although some are too small. Facilities include a garage and an elevator. Only breakfast is served.

GIULIETTA E ROMEO, vicolo Tre Marchetti 3, 37121 Verona. Tel. 045/8003554. Fax 045/8010862. 30 rms (all with bath or shower). A/C MINIBAR TV TEL **Bus:** 1, 8, or 10.

$ Rates (including breakfast): 100,000 lire ($78.50) single; 141,700 lire ($111.25) double. AE, MC, V.

The Giulietta e Romeo has two balconies on the street facade for the Romeo and Juliet of today. By leaning out either balcony, you can see the Roman arena. The hotel has a slight formality to it with a fumed oak lobby. Bedrooms are simply but comfortably furnished.

HOTEL DE' CAPULETI, via del Pontiere 26, 37122 Verona. Tel. 045/8000154. Fax 045/32970. 36 rms (all with shower). A/C MINIBAR TV TEL **Bus:** 21.

$ Rates (including breakfast): 108,000 lire ($84.80) single; 145,700 lire ($114.35) double. AE, DC, MC, V. **Parking:** Free.

The Hotel de' Capuleti is an attractively pristine little hotel, conveniently located a few steps from Juliet's (supposed) Tomb and the chapel where she is said to have been married. The reception area has stone floors and leather-covered couches, along with a tastefully renovated decor that's reflected upstairs in the comfortable bedrooms.

HOTEL SAN LUCA, vicolo Volto San Luca 8, 37122 Verona. Tel. 045/591333. Fax 045/8002143. 41 rms (all with bath). A/C MINIBAR TV TEL **Bus:** 2 or 5.

$ Rates (including breakfast): 117,000 lire ($91.85) single; 180,000 lire ($141.30) double. AE, DC, MC, V. **Parking:** 18,000 lire ($14.15).

The Hotel San Luca is a contemporary hotel whose entrance is below a covered passage leading into a major boulevard, corso Porta Nuova, just beyond the city walls. The well-maintained lobby has two-tone marble floors and lots of sunlight. Bedrooms are well maintained and furnished.

INEXPENSIVE

AURORA, piazza delle Erbe 2, 37121 Verona. Tel. 045/594717. Fax 045/8080860. 22 rms (17 with bath or shower). TEL **Bus:** 4 or 5.

$ Rates (including breakfast): 43,600 lire ($34.25) single without shower; 78,000–88,000 lire ($61.25–$69.10) double with bath or shower; 114,500 lire ($89.90) triple with shower. MC, V.

The Aurora is a tower-size building—three rooms on each landing—stacking up six flights and serviced by an elevator. This hotel opens off piazza delle Erbe, the center of the city. It's modest, immaculate, and comfortable. Many of the rooms overlook the market square. Each floor has its own toilet and bath, and each room is equipped with an individual water basin. Six accommodations also have a TV.

WHERE TO DINE

RISTORANTE IL DESCO, via Dietro San Sebastiano 7. Tel. 8349990.
   Cuisine: ITALIAN. **Reservations:** Strongly recommended. **Bus:** 2 or 5.
$ Prices: Appetizers 12,000–22,000 lire ($9.40–$17.25); main courses 30,000–35,000 lire ($23.55–$27.50); menu dégustation 85,000 lire ($66.75). AE, DC, MC, V.
   Open: Lunch Mon–Sat 12:30–2pm; dinner Mon–Sat 7–10pm. **Closed:** Jan 1–7.

Ristorante il Desco is a handsome restaurant, one of the best in Verona. It's located in the city's historic center, inside a tastefully renovated palazzo that's one of the civic prides of the city. The restaurant is ably directed by Elia Rizzo. The menu steers closer to the philosophy of nouvelle cuisine à l'italienne than anything else in town. Specialties make use of the freshest ingredients, including a purée of shrimp, taglierini with crabmeat, calamari salad with shallots, tortellini with sea bass, risotto with radicchio and truffles, and tagliolini with fresh mint, lemon, and oranges. The wine cellar is superb, and your sommelier will help you with a choice if you're unfamiliar with regional vintages. The cheese selection is wide ranging, featuring choices from France.

NUOVO MARCONI, via Fogge 4. Tel. 591910.
   Cuisine: ITALIAN. **Reservations:** Required. **Bus:** 2 or 5.
$ Prices: Appetizers 15,000–25,000 lire ($11.80–$19.65); main courses 26,000–35,000 lire ($20.40–$27.50); fixed-price lunch 70,000 lire ($54.95). AE, DC, MC, V.
   Open: Lunch Mon–Sat noon–2:30pm; dinner Mon–Sat 7:30–11pm.

Nuovo Marconi is one of the most glamorous restaurants in Verona. It's in an ocher-colored villa with canopies on a narrow street just around the corner from piazza dei Signori. The exterior doors are covered with an art nouveau wrought-iron grill, and the interior has stone columns, silk-shaded lamps, lots of framed paintings, and some of the best food in Verona (many claim the best). The restaurant is the winner of many culinary prizes. The menu reflects the best of traditional and regional dishes, many of which change daily, depending on the availability of ingredients at the market. The kitchen uses only fresh products, whether it be pasta, fish, or meat. In season, the chef likes to specialize in game dishes. The wine list is updated every 6 months. Dining is on two levels, and the service is agreeable.

AL BRAGOZZO, via del Pontiere 13. Tel. 30035.
   Cuisine: SEAFOOD. **Reservations:** Recommended. **Bus:** 2 or 5.
$ Prices: Appetizers 12,000–20,000 lire ($9.40–$15.70); main courses 10,000–30,000 lire ($7.85–$23.55). AE, DC, MC, V.
   Open: Lunch Tues–Sun noon–2:30pm; dinner Tues–Sun 7–10pm. **Closed:** June 26–July 17.

Al Bragozzo lies at the edge of the historic district, a short walk from the river and Juliet's so-called tomb. It is also across the street from one of Verona's more popular hotels, De' Capuleti. This restaurant lies behind a crumbling stucco facade whose windows are topped with canopies. It is arguably the best fish restaurant in the city, serving a fresh array of crustaceans and Adriatic fish, which can be baked, grilled, or fried, according to your preference. The calamari are very good, as are the scampi, usually priced by the gram.

RISTORANTE 12 APOSTOLI, vicolo Corticella San Marco 3. Tel. 596999.
  Cuisine: ITALIAN. **Reservations:** Recommended. **Bus:** 2 or 5.
$ **Prices:** Appetizers 12,000–15,000 lire ($9.40–$11.80); main courses 25,000–28,000 lire ($19.65–$22). AE, DC, MC, V.
  Open: Lunch Tues–Sun 12:30–2:30pm; dinner Tues–Sat 7:30–10pm. **Closed:** Jan 2–8 and June 15–July 5.

This restaurant is the oldest eating place in Verona, in business for 2 centuries. It's a festive place, steeped in tradition, with frescoed walls and two dining rooms separated by brick arches. It's operated by the two Gioco brothers. Giorgio, the artist of the kitchen, changes his menu daily in the best tradition of great chefs, while Franco directs the dining room.

Just consider some of these delicacies: salmon baked in a pastry shell (the fish is marinated the day before, seasoned with garlic and stuffed with scallops); or chicken stuffed with shredded vegetables and cooked in four layers of paper. To begin, I recommend the tempting antipasti alla Scaligera. Another specialty is cotoletta 12 Apostoli. Even the spaghetti alla salmi d'olive is superb. For dessert, try the homemade cake.

RISTORANTE RE TEODORICO, piazzale di Castel San Pietro. Tel. 8349990.
  Cuisine: ITALIAN/INTERNATIONAL. **Reservations:** Recommended. **Bus:** 2 or 5.
$ **Prices:** Appetizers 15,000–18,000 lire ($11.80–$14.15); main courses 20,000–25,000 lire ($15.70–$19.65). AE, DC, MC, V.
  Open: Lunch Thurs–Tues noon–3pm; dinner Thurs–Tues 7–10pm. **Closed:** Nov.

Ristorante Re Teodorico is perched in a choice scenic position, high on a hill at the edge of town, with a panoramic view of Verona and the Adige River. From its entrance, you descend a cypress-lined road to a ledge-hanging restaurant, which is somewhat suggestive of a lavish villa. Tables are set out on a wide flagstone terrace edged with a row of classical columns and an arbor of red and yellow rose vines.

Specialties on the à la carte menu include fondue bourguignonne, filet of sole cooked in white wine, and rognone di vitello (calves' kidneys). The desserts are as heavenly as the view. The zabaglione in marsala wine or a banana flambé with Cointreau are good choices.

TORCOLOTI, via Zambelli 24. Tel. 8006777.
  Cuisine: INTERNATIONAL. **Reservations:** Not needed. **Bus:** 2, 8, or 32.
$ **Prices:** Appetizers 10,000–18,000 lire ($7.85–$14.15); main courses 15,000–18,000 lire ($11.80–$14.15). AE, DC, MC, V.
  Open: Lunch Mon–Sat 12:30–2:30pm; dinner Tues–Sat 7:30–10:30pm. **Closed:** Dec 23–Jan 2.

Torcoloti offers an elegant, refined atmosphere and has one of the best reputations in the city for turning out skillfully prepared specialties. Menu items include gnocchi verde with Gorgonzola, Italian antipasti (which includes smoked salmon), tortellini with ricotta and fresh spinach, grilled filet of pork, tournedos, pasta with mushrooms, and filet of veal castellana (stuffed with fresh mushrooms and prosciutto).

VERONANTICA, via Sottoriva 10. Tel. 8004124.
  Cuisine: INTERNATIONAL. **Reservations:** Recommended. **Bus:** 2 or 5.
$ **Prices:** Appetizers 5,000–18,000 lire ($3.95–$14.15); main courses 18,000–23,000 lire ($14.15–$18.05); fixed-price menu 35,000 lire ($27.50). MC, V.
  Open: Lunch Sun–Fri 12:15–2:30pm; dinner Mon–Sat 7:30–10:30pm.

VeronAntica is a distinguished local restaurant housed on the ground floor of a five-story town house. It lies a short block from the river, across from a cobblestone arcade similar to the ones used in the film *Romeo and Juliet*. This is an establishment that attracts the locals—not just tourists. It's made even more romantic at night by a hanging lantern that dimly illuminates the street. The chef knows how to prepare all the classic Italian dishes as well as some innovative ones, too. Try his seafood risotto or turbot with thyme. He also prepares excellent veal escalopes with wild mushrooms.

2. PADUA (PADOVA)

25 miles W of Venice, 50 miles E of Verona, 145 miles E of Milan

GETTING THERE   By Train   The train is best if you're coming from such major transportation hubs as Venice and Milan. Padua lies on the main rail lines between Venice and Milan and Venice and Bologna. Trains depart for or arrive from Venice at the rate of one per 30 minutes (trip time: 30 minutes), costing 2,400 lire ($1.90) one way. Trains from Milan arrive or depart every hour (trip time: 1½ hours), costing 13,400 lire ($10.50) one way.

By Bus   Buses from Venice arrive every 30 minutes (trip time: 45 minutes), costing 3,600 lire ($2.80) for a one-way fare. There are also connections to Vicenza every 30 minutes (trip time: 30 minutes), costing 3,600 lire ($2.80) for a one-way fare. The local bus station in Padua is at via Trieste 40 (tel. 775759), near piazza Boschetti, 5 minutes from the rail station.

By Car   Take the autostrada A4 west from Venice.

ESSENTIALS   The **telephone area code** is 049. The **Tourist Information Center** is at piazzale Boschetti (tel. 8206867).

Padua no longer looks as it did when Burton tamed shrew Taylor in the Zeffirelli adaptation of Shakespeare's *The Taming of the Shrew,* which was set in old Padua. However, it remains a major art center of Venetia. Shakespeare called Padua a "nursery of arts."

Padua is sometimes known as "La Città del Santo" (the city of the saint), a reference to St. Anthony of Padua, who is buried at a basilica that the city dedicated to him. "Il Santo" was an itinerant Franciscan monk who should not be confused with St. Anthony of Egypt, the monastic hermit who could resist all the temptations of the Devil.

WHAT TO SEE & DO

A university that grew to fame throughout Europe was founded here as early as 1222 (Galileo and the poet Tasso attended). Petrarch also lectured here, and the University of Padua has remained one of the great centers for learning in Italy. Today its buildings are scattered throughout the city. The historic main building of the university is called **Il Bo,** which was the name of an inn with an ox as its sign. The chief entrance to Palazzo Bo is on via Otto Febbraio (tel. 651400). Incidentally, Il Bo was the major font of learning in the heyday of the Venetian Republic. Of particular interest is an anatomy theater, which dates from 1594 and was the first of its kind in Europe. Guided tours of the university are conducted Monday through Friday from 9am to noon and 3 to 5pm, and on Saturday from 9am to noon.

If you're on a tight schedule when you visit Padua, then I recommend that you confine your sightseeing to the Cappella degli Scrovegni (Giotto frescoes) and the Basilica di San Antonio.

CAPPELLA DEGLI SCROVEGNI (also Arena Chapel), in the public gardens off corso Garibaldi. Tel. 650845.

☆ This modest (on the outside) chapel is the best reason for visiting Padua. Sometime around 1305 and 1306 Giotto did a cycle of more than 35 (remarkably well-preserved) frescoes inside, which, along with those at Assisi, form the basis of his claim to fame. Like an illustrated storybook, the frescoes unfold biblical scenes. The third bottom panel (lower level on the right) depicts Judas kissing a most skeptical Christ and is perhaps the most reproduced and widely known panel in the cycle. On the entrance wall is Giotto's *Last Judgment,* in which hell wins out in sheer fascination. The master's representation of the *Vices and Virtues* is bizarre; it reveals the depth of his imagination in personifying the nebulous evil or the elusive good. One of the most dramatic of the panels depicts the raising of Lazarus from the dead. This is a masterly balanced scene, rhythmically ingenious for its day. The swathed and cadaverous Lazarus, however, looks indecisive as to whether or not he'll rejoin the living.

Admission: 5,000 lire ($3.95) (same ticket as for the Cappella degli Scrovegni).

Open: Apr–Sept, Mon–Sat 9am–7pm, Sun 9:30am–12:30pm; Oct–Mar, Mon–Sat 9am–5pm, Sun 9:30am–12:30pm. **Bus:** 3, 8, or 18.

CHIESA DEGLI EREMITANI, piazza Eremitani 9. Tel. 8756410.

One of the tragedies of Padua is that this church was bombed during World War II. Before that time it housed one of the greatest art treasures in Italy, the Ovetari Chapel frescoed by Andrea Mantegna. The cycle of frescoes was the first significant work by Mantegna (1431–1506). The church was rebuilt, but unfortunately, one can't resurrect 15th-century frescoes. Inside, to the right of the main altar, are fragments left after the bombing, a glimpse of what we lost of Mantegna's work. The most interesting fresco saved is a panel depicting the dragging of St. Christopher's body through the streets. Note also the *Assumption of the Virgin.* Mantegna is recommended even to those who don't like "religious painting." Like da Vinci, the artist had a keen eye for architectural detail.

Admission: Free (donations accepted).

Open: Apr–Sept, Mon–Sat 8:15am–noon and 3:30–6:30pm, Sun and religious hols 9am–noon and 3:30–5:30pm; Oct–Mar, Mon–Sat 8:15am–noon and 3:30–5:30pm, Sun and religious hols 9am–noon and 3:30–5:30pm. **Bus:** 8, 9, 10, 11, 12, or 13.

BASILICA DI SAN ANTONIO, piazza del Santo. Tel. 663944.

✪ This building was constructed in the 13th century and dedicated to St. Anthony of Padua, who is interred within. The basilica is a synthesis of styles, with mainly Romanesque and Gothic features. It has eight cupolas. Campanili and minarets combine to give it an Eastern appearance. Inside, it is richly frescoed and decorated, and usually filled with pilgrims devoutly touching the saint's marble tomb. One of the more unusual relics is in the treasury—the 7-centuries-old, still-uncorrupt tongue of St. Anthony.

The greatest art treasures are the Donatello bronzes at the main altar, with a realistic *Crucifix* towering over the rest. Seek out, too, the Donatello relief depicting the removal of Christ from the cross, a unified composition that expresses in simple lines and with an unromantic approach, the tragedy of Christ and the sadness of the mourners.

In front of the basilica is one of Italy's best-known statues—this one by Donatello. Donatello broke with the regimentation and rigidity of medievalism in the 15th century by sculpting an undraped *David.* Likewise, in the work in front of the basilica, he restored the lost art of the equestrian statue. Though the man it honors—called Gattamelata—is of little interest to art lovers, the statue is of prime importance. The large horse is realistic, as Donatello was a master of detail. He cleverly directs the eye to the forceful, commanding face of the Venetian military hero. Gattamelata was a dead ringer for Lord Laurence Olivier.

Admission: Free.

Open: Apr–Sept, daily 6:30am–7:45pm; Oct–Mar, daily 6:30am–7pm. **Bus:** 8, 12, 18, or 22.

MUSEO CIVICO, piazza Eremitani. Tel. 662512.

This picture gallery is important. It's filled with minor works by major Venetian artists, some of which date from the 14th century. Look for a wooden *Crucifix* by Giotto and two miniatures by Giorgione (Leda and her amorous swan, and a mother and child in a bucolic setting). Other works include Giovanni Bellini's *Portrait of a Young Man* and Jacopo Bellini's miniature *Descent into Limbo,* with its childlike devils. The 15th-century Arras tapestry is also on display. Other works are Veronese's *Martyrdom of St. Primo and St. Feliciano,* plus Tintoretto's *Supper in Simone's House* and his *Crucifixion* (the latter is probably the finest single painting in the gallery).

Admission: 5,000 lire ($3.95) (same ticket as for the Capella degli Scrovegni).
Open: Tues–Sun 9am–7pm. **Bus:** 3, 8, or 18.

PALAZZO DELLA REGIONE, via 8 Febbraio, between piazza delle Erbe and piazza dell Frutta. Tel. 8205006.

This "Palace of Law," which dates from the early 13th century, is among the remarkable buildings of northern Italy. Ringed with loggias, and with a roof shaped like the hull of a sailing vessel, it sits in the marketplace of Padua. Climb the steps and enter the grandiose Salone, an assembly hall that's about 270 feet long. In the hall is a gigantic wooden horse that dates from the 15th century. The walls are richly frescoed with symbolic paintings in place of the frescoes by Giotto and his assistants that were destroyed in a fire in 1420.

Admission: 8,000 lire ($6.30) adults, 4,000 lire ($3.15) children under 12.
Open: Tues–Sun 9:30–7:30pm. **Bus:** 3, 8, or 18.

WHERE TO STAY
EXPENSIVE

HOTEL PLAZA, corso Milano 40, 35139 Padova. Tel. 049/656822. Fax 049/661117. 142 rms (all with bath or shower). A/C MINIBAR TV TEL **Bus:** 3, 8, or 18.
$ Rates (including breakfast): 120,000 lire ($94.20) single; 175,000 lire ($137.40) double. AE, DC, MC, V. **Parking:** 20,000 lire ($15.70).

The Hotel Plaza is a commercially oriented hotel with brown ceramic tiles and cement-trimmed square windows in pairs. The entrance is under a modern concrete arcade, which leads into a contemporary lobby. Its angular lines are softened with an unusual Oriental needlework tapestry, brown leather couches, and a pair of gilded baroque cherubs. The rooms are comfortable and well decorated. The bar, which you can reach through a stairwell and an upper balcony dotted with modern paintings, is a relaxing stopover place for a drink. There is also a restaurant on the premises, plus a parking garage.

MAJESTIC HOTEL TOSCANELLI, piazzetta dell'Arco 2, 35122 Padova. Tel. 049/663244. Fax 049/8760025. 32 rms (all with bath), 6 suites. A/C MINIBAR TV TEL **Bus:** 5, 7, 8, 16, or 18.
$ Rates: 130,000 lire ($102.05) single; 165,000 lire ($129.55) double; from 220,000 lire ($172.70) suite. AE, DC, MC, V. **Parking:** 20,000 lire ($15.70).

The Majestic Hotel Toscanelli is in a pastel-pink building on a cobblestone square in the heart of town. Wrought-iron balconies protect the French windows, whose edges are trimmed with stone. There's even a Renaissance well and dozens of potted shrubs in front. Inside, you'll find an octagonal bar whose walls are shingled with nostalgic mementos. The lobby has white marble floors, Oriental rugs, and a format that includes an upper balcony and a comfortable mishmash of old and new. There's also a restaurant in the basement called the Toscanelli (see my recommendation in "Where to Dine," below). Rooms are well furnished, comfortable, and well maintained. Furnishings are traditional. Parking is on the premises.

MODERATE

HOTEL LEON BIANCO, piazzetta Pedrocchi 7, 35122 Padova. Tel. 049/8750814. Fax 049/31059. 22 rms (all with bath). A/C MINIBAR TV TEL **Bus:** 7, 8, 16, or 18.
$ Rates: 75,000 lire ($58.90) single; 107,000–118,000 lire ($84–$92.65) double. Breakfast 13,000 lire ($10.20) extra. AE, DC, MC, V. **Parking:** 20,000 lire ($15.70).

The Hotel Leon Bianco is a small, tasteful hotel that has been recently modernized and restructured. Its rooms are simple but comfortable. It's located across from the historic Caffè Pedrocchi and sits in the center of a pedestrian zone. In good weather, breakfast—the only meal served here—may be taken in the roof garden.

HOTEL DONATELLO, piazza del Santo, 35123 Padova. Tel. 049/ 8750634. Fax 049/8750829. 42 rms (all with bath). A/C MINIBAR TV TEL **Bus:** 7, 8, 16, or 18.

$ Rates: 90,000 lire ($70.65) single; 140,000 lire ($109.90) double. Breakfast 12,000 lire ($9.40) extra. AE, DC, MC, V. **Parking:** 25,000 lire ($19.65).

The Hotel Donatello is a renovated hotel with an ideal location near the Basilica of St. Anthony. Its buff-colored facade is pierced by an arched arcade, and the oversize chandeliers of its lobby combine with the checkerboard marble floor for a hospitable ambience. To prepare you for the eventual sight of Padua's famed wooden horse, the management has placed a big illuminated photo of it in the lobby. On the premises is one of my preferred restaurants, the Sant'Antonio (see my recommendation in "Where to Dine," below). The rooms are well furnished.

EUROPA-ZARAMELLA, larga Europa 3, 35137 Padova. Tel. 049/ 661200. Fax 049/661508. 59 rms (all with bath). A/C MINIBAR TV TEL **Bus:** 7, 8, 16, or 18.

$ Rates (including breakfast): 85,000–95,500 lire ($66.75–$74.95) single; 110,000–127,000 lire ($86.35–$99.70) double. AE, DC, MC, V. **Parking:** 20,000 lire ($15.70).

The Europa-Zaramella was built in the 1960s and remains inviting today. It is located near the Padua post office. The tasteful bedrooms are compact and serviceable and have pastel walls and built-in furnishings. The rooms open onto small balconies. Public rooms are enhanced by cubist murals, free-form ceramic plaques, and furniture placed in conversational groupings. The American bar is popular, as is the dining room. The Zaramella Restaurant features a good Paduan cuisine, with an emphasis on seafood dishes from the Adriatic. Meals begin at 40,000 lire ($31.40).

WHERE TO DINE

RISTORANTE EL TOULA, via Belle Parti 11. Tel. 875-1822.
  Cuisine: INTERNATIONAL/ITALIAN. **Reservations:** Required. **Bus:** 6, 7, or 10.

$ Prices: Appetizers 15,000–22,000 lire ($11.70–$17.25); main courses 25,000–38,000 lire ($19.65–$29.85). AE, DC, V.
  Open: Lunch Tues–Sat 12:30–2:30pm; dinner Mon–Sat 8–10:30pm. **Closed:** Aug.

Ristorante El Toulà is the most elegant and best-rated dining place in Padua. It was established in 1982 in a building that had housed an earlier restaurant for 200 years, under ceiling beams that are at least 400 years old. The age of the physical plant, however, did not stop a team of designers from creating a sensual decor of Italian style at its best. The ground-floor level includes a slick black bar, near an equally black piano, which provides music for diners savoring an apéritif on the leather couches or for the late-night crowd who drop in for an evening drink at closing time. The main dining area offers the kind of excellent service that this most sophisticated of nationwide restaurant chains is eager to provide.

The palate-pleasing menu items change monthly, but might on any given day include blinis with caviar, crostino (a flaky appetizer) with mozzarella, sweet peppers, and anchovy sauce, or asparagus milanese, five kinds of homemade pasta, five kinds of risotto (one with caviar and fresh salmon), Westphalian salmon with capers, along with a wide assortment of veal, beef, and chicken, topped off by freshly baked pastries and dessert crêpes. A meal here is a regalia by anyone's standards.

RISTORANTE DOTTO, via Squarcione 23. Tel. 8751490.
  Cuisine: PADUAN. **Reservations:** Not needed. **Bus:** 6, 7, or 10.

$ Prices: Appetizers 10,000–15,000 lire ($7.85–$11.80); main courses 16,000–30,000 lire ($12.55–$23.55). AE, DC, MC, V.

Open: Lunch Tues–Sun noon–2pm; dinner Tues–Sat 8–10:15pm. **Closed:** Aug.
Ristorante Dotto takes its name from the *dottori* (doctors) of the university for which
Padua is famous. The discreet, elegant restaurant is in the heart of the city, suitable
not only for an academic or business meal but also for an intimate tête-à-tête dinner.
Try their pasta e fagioli, grilled sole, risotto made with fresh asparagus, or the chef's
pâté. You could top all this off with a feathery dessert soufflé, the most elaborate of
which must be ordered at the beginning of a meal.

TOSCANELLI, piazzetta dell'Arco 2. Tel. 663244.

Cuisine: SEAFOOD/INTERNATIONAL. **Reservations:** Not needed. **Bus:** 5, 7,
8, 16, or 18.
$ **Prices:** Appetizers 15,000–18,000 lire ($11.80–$14.15); main courses 20,000–
25,000 lire ($15.70–$19.65). AE.
Open: Lunch Mon–Sat 12:30–2:30pm; dinner Mon–Sat 7pm–midnight.
Toscanelli is connected to the Majestic Hotel Toscanelli (see "Where to Stay," above),
but reachable through a separate entrance from under an arcade. The decor includes
warm colors and ceiling beams, lots of exposed brick, and a kitchen that is visible
from behind a plate-glass window. There's even an open grill for the proper
preparation of fish, scampi, and meats. Many of the specialties are Tuscan, although
dishes also include international recipes such as fondue bourguignonne and sauerkraut Alsatian style. The zuppa di pesce (fish soup) is especially recommendable.

RISTORANTE SANT'ANTONIO, in the Hotel Donatello, piazza del Santo. Tel. 8750634.

Cuisine: PADUAN. **Reservations:** Not needed. **Bus:** 7, 8, 16, or 18.
$ **Prices:** Appetizers 7,000–9,000 lire ($5.50–$7.05); main courses 15,000–
20,000 lire ($11.80–$15.70). AE, DC, MC, V.
Open: Lunch Thurs–Tues 12:30–2:30pm; dinner Thurs–Tues 7:30–9:30pm.
Closed: July 7–Aug and Dec 15–Jan 15.
Ristorante Sant'Antonio offers a rewarding view of Saint Anthony's Basilica. A series
of outdoor tables are set up in summer, although the L-shaped interior is pleasant as
well, outfitted with tones of white, beige marble floors, and bentwood chairs. All the
standard Italian dishes are served here, many of them so familiar to foreign visitors
that they may not need to ask for the English menu. However, it's available if you
want it.

TRATTORIA DA PLACIDO, via Santa Lucia 59. Tel. 8752252.

Cuisine: VENETIAN. **Reservations:** Recommended. **Bus:** 3, 8, or 18.
$ **Prices:** Appetizers 4,500–6,000 lire ($3.55–$4.70); main courses 8,000–16,000
lire ($6.30–$12.55). No credit cards.
Open: Lunch Mon–Sat 12:30–2:30pm; dinner Mon–Fri 7:30–9:30pm. **Closed:**
Aug.
The Trattoria da Placido is one of the most reliable choices for good food at
moderate prices in Padua. It doesn't spend its money on decor, although the
ambience is warm and inviting. You dine here on traditional Italian fare,
including bollito misto (a mixed selection of boiled meats with a green herbal sauce),
fettuccine alla boscaiola, baccala (dried codfish) alla vicentina, and cuttlefish alla
veneziana. However, the chef will surprise you and serve a salad, for example, of
radicchio that is commonplace in Italy, but a gourmet treat in North America.

A FAMOUS COFFEEHOUSE

CAFFE PEDROCCHI, piazzetta Pedrocchi 6. Tel. 8752020.

Caffè Pedrocchi, located off piazza Cavour, is a neoclassical landmark. It was
opened by Antonio Pedrocchi in 1831 and was hailed at the time as the most
elegant coffeehouse in Europe. Its green, white, and red rooms reflect the
national colors of Italy. On sunny days you might want to sit under one of the two
stone porches, architectural oddities in themselves, and in winter you'll have plenty to
distract you inside. There, the sprawling bathtub-shaped travertine bar has a brass top

and brass lion's feet. The velvet banquettes have maroon upholstery, red-veined marble tables, and Egyptian Revival chairs. And if you tire of all this 19th-century outrageousness, you can retreat to a more conservatively decorated English-style pub on the premises, whose entrance is under a covered arcade a few steps away. Coffee costs 1,100 lire (85¢) at the stand-up bar, 2,000 lire ($1.55) at a table. Although drinks cost more than they would in a lesser café, you haven't heard the heartbeat of Padua until you've been at the Pedrocchi. It's open Tuesday through Sunday from 7:30am to 1am.

---

3. VICENZA

126 miles E of Milan, 32 miles NE of Verona

GETTING THERE By Train Most visitors arrive from Venice (trip time: 50 minutes), a one-way ticket costing from 4,100 lire ($3.20). Trains also arrive frequently from Padua (trip time: 25 minutes), costing 2,400 lire ($1.90) one way. There are also frequent connections from Milan (trip time: 2½ hours), costing 11,600 lire ($9.10) one way.

By Bus It's best to arrive by train. Once at Vicenza, however, you'll find good bus connections for the province of Vicenza if you'd like to tour the environs. The service is operated by FTV, viale Milano 7 (tel. 544333), to the left as you exit from the rail station.

By Car From Venice, take the autostrada (A4) west in the direction of Verona, bypassing Padua.

ESSENTIALS The **telephone area code** is 0444. The **Tourist Information Center** is at piazza Matteotti 12 (tel. 320854).

In the 16th century, Vicenza was transformed into a virtual laboratory for the architectural experiments of Andrea Palladio, a Paduan who arrived there in 1523. One of the greatest architects of the Renaissance, he was inspired by the classical art and architecture of ancient Greece. Palladio peppered the city with palazzi and basilicas, and the surrounding hills with villas for patrician families.

The architect was particularly important to England and America. In the 18th century Robert Adam was especially inspired by him, as reflected by many country homes in England today. Then, through the influence of Adam and others even earlier, the spirit of Palladio was imported across the waves to America (examples include Jefferson's Monticello or plantation homes in the antebellum South). Palladio even lent his name to this style of architecture—"Palladianism"—identified by regularity of form, massive, often-imposing size, and an adherence to lines established in ancient Greece and Rome.

WHAT TO SEE & DO

To introduce yourself to the "world of Palladio," head for ○ **Piazza dei Signori.** In this classical square stands the **Basilica Palladiana**, partially designed by Palladio. The loggias consist of two levels, the lower tier with Doric pillars, the upper with Ionic. In its heyday, this building was much frequented by the aristocrats among the Vicentinos, who lavishly spent their gold on villas in the neighboring hills. They met here in a kind of social fraternity, perhaps to talk about the excessive sums being spent on Palladio-designed or -inspired projects. Originally, the basilica was in the Gothic style, and served as the Palazzo della Ragione (justice). The roof collapsed following a 1945 bombing, but has been subsequently rebuilt. To the side is the Tower of the Piazza, which dates from the 13th century and soars approximately 270 feet high. Across from the basilica is the **Loggia del Capitanio** (guard), designed by Palladio in his waning years. On the square are two pillars, one supporting a chimera, another a saint.

TEATRO OLIMPICO [Olympic Theater], piazza Matteotti. Tel. 323781.

The masterpiece and last work of Palladio—ideal for performances of classical plays—is one of the world's greatest theaters still in use. It was completed in 1585, 5 years after Palladio's death, by Vincenzo Scamozzi, and the curtain went up on the Vicenza première of Sophocles' *Oedipus Rex*. The arena seating area, in the shape of a half moon, is encircled by Corinthian columns and balustrades. The simple proscenium is abutted by the arena. What is ordinarily the curtain in a conventional theater is here a permanent facade, U-shaped, with a large central arch and a pair of smaller ones flanking it. The permanent stage setting represents the ancient streets of Thebes, combining architectural detail with trompe l'oeil. Above the arches (to the left and right) are rows of additional classic statuary on pedestals or in niches. Over the area is a dome, with trompe-l'oeil clouds and sky, giving the illusion of an outdoor Roman amphitheater.

Admission: 5,000 lire ($3.95) (includes the Museo Civico).

Open: Mar 16–Oct 15, Mon–Sat 9:30am–12:20pm and 3–5:20pm, Sun 9:30am–12:15pm; Oct 16–Mar 15, daily 9:30am–12:20pm and 2–4:30pm. **Bus:** 1 or 7.

MUSEO CIVICO [City Museum], in the Palazzo Chiericati, piazza Matteotti. Tel. 321348.

This museum is housed in one of the most outstanding buildings by Palladio. Begun in the mid-16th century, it was not finished until the late 17th century, during the baroque period. Today the palazzo is visited chiefly for its excellent collection of Venetian paintings on the second floor. Works by lesser-known artists—Paolo Veneziano, Bartolomeo Montagna, and Jacopo Bassano—are displayed alongside paintings by such giants as Tintoretto, Veronese, and Tiepolo. Notable items include Tintoretto's *Miracle of St. Augustine,* Veronese's *The Cherub of the Balustrade* and his *Madonna and Child,* and Tiepolo's *Time and Truth.*

Admission: 5,000 lire ($3.95) (includes the Olympic Theater).

Open: Tues–Sat 9:30am–noon and 2:30–5pm, Sun 10am–noon. **Bus:** 1 or 7.

TEMPIO DI SANTA CORONA, via Santa Corona. Tel. 323644.

This church was founded in the mid-13th century, designed in the Gothic style. Much altered over the centuries, it should be visited if for no other reason than to see Giovanni Bellini's *Baptism of Christ* (fifth altar on the left). In the left transept, a short distance away, is another of Vicenza's well-known works of art—this one by Veronese, depicting the three Wise Men paying tribute to the Christ child. The high altar with its intricate marble work is also of interest. A visit to Santa Corona is more rewarding than a trek to the Duomo (cathedral), which is only of passing interest.

Admission: Free.

Open: Mon 3:30–6pm, Tues–Sun 9:30am–12:15pm and 3:30–6pm. **Bus:** 1 or 7.

BASILICA OF MONTE BERICO, viale 10 Giugno no. 87. Tel. 320999.

This basilica is located high on a hill overlooking the town and the surrounding villas and serves as the Sacré-Coeur of Vicenza. Lit at night, the church is reached by car or a hike up a colonnaded street. But the real reason for climbing the hill is to walk out onto the belvedere near the church. You'll see the town spread beneath your feet—a sight of splendor day or night.

Admission: Free.

Open: Apr–Oct, daily 8am–noon and 2:30–7:30pm; Nov–Mar, daily 8am–noon and 2:30–6pm. **Bus:** 1 or 7 to the center; then walk.

LA ROTONDA, stradella della Rotonda. Tel. 321793.

On the southeastern border of the town, past the Arco delle Scalette (the landmark "arch of the tiny steps" from the late 16th century) is another of the most famous creations of that maestro, Palladio. Like the Olympic Theater, the Rotonda was started by Palladio but completed by his pupil, Scamozzi. Many great estates in Europe and America found their inspiration in this elegantly domed villa. The Rotonda is a private residence.

Admission: Residence, 5,000 lire ($3.95); grounds, 3,000 lire ($2.35).
Open: Residence, Mar 15–Nov 15, Tues–Thurs 10am–noon and 3–6pm; grounds, Tues–Sun 10am–noon and 3–6pm. **Bus:** 8 or 13 from the rail station.

A NEARBY ATTRACTION

VILLA VALMARANA, via Tiepolo. Tel. 543976.

This villa is a mile southeast of the center of Vicenza. Called "Dwarf's Villa," it comprises two buildings, the villa and the guesthouse. These are not creations of Palladio but were built as a private estate at the end of the 17th century. It is visited today for its beautiful frescoes by Giambattista Tiepolo in the villa and by Giandomenico Tiepolo in the guesthouse, painted in the last half of the 18th century.
Admission: 5,000 lire ($3.95) adults, 3,000 lire ($2.35) children.
Open: Mar 15–Oct, Tues and Fri 3–6pm, Wed–Thurs and Sat 10am–noon and 3–6pm, Sun 10am–noon. **Bus:** 8.

WHERE TO STAY

HOTEL CAMPO MARZIO, viale Roma 21, 36100 Vicenza. Tel. 0444/545700. Fax 0444/320495. 35 rms (all with bath). A/C MINIBAR TV TEL **Bus:** 1 or 7.
$ Rates (including breakfast): 135,000 lire ($106) single; 205,000 lire ($160.95) double. AE, DC, MC, V. **Parking:** Free.
This contemporary hotel is ideally situated in a peaceful part of the historic center of Vicenza, adjacent to a park. The hotel has undergone complete renovation. The sunny lobby has a conservatively comfortable decor that extends into the bedrooms. A cozy restaurant offers regional dining Monday through Friday.

HOTEL EUROPA, viale San Lazzaro 11, 36100 Vicenza. Tel. 0444/564111. Fax 0444/564382. 122 rms (all with bath). A/C MINIBAR TV TEL **Bus:** 1.
$ Rates (including breakfast): 105,000 lire ($82.45) single; 150,000 lire ($117.75) double. AE, DC, MC, V. **Parking:** Free.
The Hotel Europa is a good stopover. The interior of this roadside hotel is nicer than its boxy facade implies. The most modern hotel in Vicenza (built in 1980), lying 1¼ miles southwest of the center on the road to Verona, is a favorite of business travelers who use it during the winter, tourists who come in summer, and high-ranking officers of the nearby American military base who appreciate the leather-accented bar during off-hours. Each room has a radio, among other amenities.

HOTEL CRISTINA, corso San Felice 32, 36100 Vicenza. Tel. 0444/323751. Fax 0444/543656. 34 rms (all with bath or shower). A/C MINIBAR TV TEL **Bus:** 1.
$ Rates: 80,000 lire ($62.80) single; 100,000 lire ($78.50) double. Breakfast 10,000 lire ($7.85) extra. AE, DC, MC, V. **Parking:** 10,000 lire ($7.85).
The well-maintained, contemporary Hotel Cristina is a cozy place near the city center, with an inside courtyard where visitors can park. The decor consists of large amounts of marble and parquet flooring and lots of exposed paneling, coupled with comfortable furniture in the public rooms. The high-ceilinged bedrooms are also well furnished, although some are small. A breakfast buffet (which costs extra) is the only meal served.

CONTINENTAL, viale Trissino 89, 36100 Vicenza. Tel. 0444/505478. Fax 0444/513319. 55 rms (all with bath). MINIBAR TV TEL **Bus:** 3.
$ Rates: 74,000–85,000 lire ($58.10–$66.75) single; 93,000–107,000 lire ($73–$84) double. Breakfast 12,000 lire ($9.40) extra. AE, DC, MC, V. **Parking:** Free.
The Continental is among the best choices for an overnight stopover in a town not known for its hotels. It has been renovated in a modern style and offers comfortably appointed bedrooms. About 70% of the rooms are air-condi-

tioned. The hotel has a good restaurant where meals begin at 30,000 lire ($23.55). However, there is no meal service on Saturday, Sunday, or in August. There is a solarium on the premises.

WHERE TO DINE

CINZIA E VALERIO, piazzetta Porta Padova 65. Tel. 512796.
Cuisine: SEAFOOD. **Reservations:** Required. **Bus:** 1 or 7.
$ Prices: Appetizers 10,000–15,000 lire ($7.85–$11.80); main courses 25,000–40,000 lire ($19.65–$31.40). AE, DC, V.
Open: Lunch Tues–Sun noon–2:30pm; dinner Tues–Sun 7:30–9:30pm. **Closed:** Aug.

By most accounts, this is the best (and perhaps the most beautiful) restaurant in Vicenza. You'll be greeted by a polite staff and views of masses of seasonal flowers before being ushered into the elegant dining rooms. The house fish specialties are time-tested recipes that originated on the Adriatic coastline. In this particular restaurant, the chef is a woman named Cinzia, and the maître d'hôtel a man named Valerio—this combination gave the restaurant its name. Your meal might begin with mollusks and shellfish arranged into an artfully elegant platter. Other dishes might include risotto flavored with squid and squid ink, a collection of crab and lobster that might surprise you by its size and weight, and an endless procession of fish that arrives cooked any way you prefer, from Cinzia's ovens.

SCUDO DI FRANCIA, contra Piancoli 4. Tel. 320898.
Cuisine: VICENTINO. **Reservations:** Recommended. **Bus:** 1 or 7.
$ Prices: Appetizers 8,000–10,000 lire ($6.30–$7.85); main courses 15,000–18,000 lire ($11.80–$14.15). AE, DC, MC, V.
Open: Lunch Tues–Sun 12:30–2:30pm; dinner Tues–Sat 8–10pm. **Closed:** Aug 10–25.

This Venetian-style palace is a short walk from piazza dei Signori. The restaurant has a sunny decor accented with gilt wall sconces, high ceilings, and a garden visible through its rear windows. Menu choices change frequently, but are likely to include filet of beef with green peppercorns, Venetian-style liver, osso buco with polenta, fettuccine with fresh spring peas, and risotto with fresh asparagus, plus a range of fresh antipasti such as artichoke salad with parmesan cheese and smoked salmon.

RISTORANTE PEDAVENA, viale Verona 93. Tel. 563064.
Cuisine: VICENTINO. **Reservations:** Recommended. **Bus:** 1 or 7.
$ Prices: Appetizers 7,000–8,000 lire ($5.50–$6.30); main courses 10,000–15,000 lire ($7.85–$11.80). AE, DC, MC, V.
Open: Lunch Tues–Sun 12:30–2:30pm; dinner Tues–Sun 7:30–10pm. **Closed:** Aug 18–31 and Jan 1–12.

Ristorante Pedavena, on a four-lane highway on the road leading to Verona, is one of the better dining spots in town. It's housed in a chalet stucco building with stone-trimmed wrought-iron accents. There's a parking lot in front, plus a summer beer garden sheltered from the busy street with a wall and a row of leafy trees. There's a wide assortment of pasta, along with such selections as arrosti misti (mixed roast meats), scaloppine with asparagus, entrecôte, and an array of fresh salads.

RISTORANTE GRANDCAFFE GARIBALDI, piazza dei Signori 5. Tel. 544147.
Cuisine: VICENTINO/INTERNATIONAL. **Reservations:** Not needed. **Bus:** 1 or 7.
$ Prices: Appetizers 8,000–9,000 lire ($6.30–$7.05); main courses 14,000–15,000 lire ($11–$11.80). AE, DC, MC, V.
Open: Lunch Thurs–Tues 12:30–2:30pm; dinner Thurs–Mon 7:30–10pm.

The most impressive café in town has a design worthy of the city of Palladio. In the heartbeat center, it has a wide terrace and an ornate ceiling, marble tables, and a long glass case of sandwiches from which you can make a selection before you sit down (the waitress will bring them to your table). Prices are slightly lower if you stand at the bar. On the premises is an upstairs restaurant, with trays of antipasti and arrangements of fresh fruit set up on a central table. The menu's array of familiar Italian specialties is among the best in town.

ANTICA TRATTORIA TRE VISI, contra Porti 6. Tel. 324868.

Cuisine: VICENTINO/INTERNATIONAL. **Reservations:** Required. **Bus:** 1 or 7.

$ Prices: Appetizers 8,000–10,000 lire ($6.30–$7.85); main courses 18,000–20,000 lire ($14.15–$15.70). AE, DC, MC, V.

Open: Lunch Tues–Sun 12:30–2:30pm; dinner Tues–Sat 7:30–10:30pm. **Closed:** July 8–Aug 8.

The Antica Trattoria Tre Visi deserves to be better known. It's on the ground floor of a Venetian-style palazzo that dates from 1483. The decor is in the rustic style, with a fireplace, ceramic wall decorations, baskets of fresh fruit, and tavern chairs. You can see the kitchen from the main dining area. Together with the rich choice of international dishes, you can enjoy a good selection of wines of the Vicenza region. The owner, Luigi Barbiero, will be pleased to suggest and help you with your choice.

CHAPTER 15

TRIESTE, THE DOLOMITES & SOUTH TYROL

- **WHAT'S SPECIAL ABOUT TRIESTE, THE DOLOMITES & SOUTH TYROL**
- **1. TRIESTE**
- **2. CORTINA D'AMPEZZO**
- **3. BOLZANO**
- **4. MERANO**
- **5. TRENT (TRENTO)**

The limestone Dolomites are a peculiar mountain formation of the northeastern Italian Alps. Some of their peaks soar to a height of 10,500 feet. One of Europe's greatest natural attractions, the Dolomites are a year-round pleasure destination, with two high seasons: in midsummer, and then in winter when the skiers slide in.

At times the Dolomites form fantastic shapes, combining to create a landscape that looks primordial, with chains of mountains that resemble a giant dragon's teeth. Clefts descend precipitously along jagged rocky walls, while at other points a vast flat tableland—spared by nature's fury—emerges.

The provinces of Trent and Bolzano (Bozen in German) form the Trentino–Alto Adige region. The area is rich in health resorts, attracting many German-speaking visitors to its alpine lakes and mountains. Many of its waters—some of which are radioactive—are said to have curative powers.

South Tyrol is surrounded by the Dolomite Alps. Until 1919 South Tyrol was part of Austria, and even though it today belongs to Italy, it is still very much Tyrolean in character, both in its language (German) and in its dress.

Today the Trentino–Alto Adige region functions with a great deal of autonomy.

Before I proceed to details, readers with an extra day or so to spare may first want to postpone their Dolomite or Tyrolean adventure for a detour to Trieste.

SEEING TRIESTE, THE DOLOMITES & SOUTH TYROL

SUGGESTED ITINERARY

Day 1: From Venice, head northeast to the port of Trieste, former port of the Hapsburg Empire.

Days 2–3: From Trieste, head northwest into the Dolomites for a 2-day holiday in Cortina d'Ampezzo, taking in its natural attractions. It is both a summer and a winter resort.

Day 4: From Cortina, continue the 68-mile drive along the Great Dolomite Road heading west. It's one of the most scenic drives in all of Europe. Overnight in Bolzano.

Day 5: Leave Bolzano and head north for an overnight in Merano, most interesting center for exploring South Tyrol.

☑ WHAT'S SPECIAL ABOUT TRIESTE, THE DOLOMITES & SOUTH TYROL

Great Towns & Villages
- ☐ Cortina d'Ampezzo, a splendid mountain town that is the leading ski resort of the Dolomites.
- ☐ Trieste, the former major port of the Hapsburg Empire, a city that basks in its long-ago reputation as the cultural and commercial center of the Adriatic.
- ☐ Merano, an old-fashioned spa town, with a rich Tyrolean character, a most interesting base for South Tyrol.

Religious Shrines
- ☐ Duomo, at Trent (meeting place of the Council of Trent in 1545), a majestic building in the Lombard Romanesque style.

Architectural Highlights
- ☐ Piazza dell'Unità d'Italia, Trieste, a neoclassic square of perfect proportions, the only one in Italy fronting the sea.

Ace Attractions
- ☐ Tondi di Faloria, a cable car in Cortina d'Ampezzo that offers the grandest panorama of the Dolomites from its summit at 10,543 feet.
- ☐ Grotta Gigante, 9 miles from Trieste, an enormous cavern, considered Italy's most interesting phenomena of speleology.

Museums & Palaces
- ☐ Miramare, outside Trieste, former home of Archduke Maximilian, the Hapsburg ruler who became emperor of Mexico.

Day 6: Return south to other centers on the Italian mainland, but budget an overnight stopover if possible in the historic center of Trent.

GETTING THERE

The only commercial airport in the region is Ronchi dei Legionari, 21½ miles northwest of Trieste. Most visitors travel the region by rail or private car. The Brenner–Bolzano–Trent–Verona rail line is part of the international Trans-European Express (TEE) which runs north to Innsbruck (Austria) and Munich (Germany). Rail travel to Cortina is via Venice and on to Calalzo di Cadore. For motorists, the most important route in the region is A22, connecting the north-south autostrada of Italy with continental Europe via the Brenner Pass. The A22 runs between Balzano and Trent.

1. TRIESTE

72 miles NE of Venice, 414 miles NE of Rome, 253 miles E of Milan

GETTING THERE   By Plane   Trieste is serviced by an airport at **Ronchi dei Legionari,** 21½ miles northwest of the city. Daily flights on Alitalia connect the airport with Linate airport in Milan (trip time: 50 minutes) and Leonardo da Vinci in Rome (trip time: 1 hour 10 minutes). For airport information, call 0481/7731.

By Train   Trieste lies on a direct rail link from Venice. Trip time to Venice is 2½

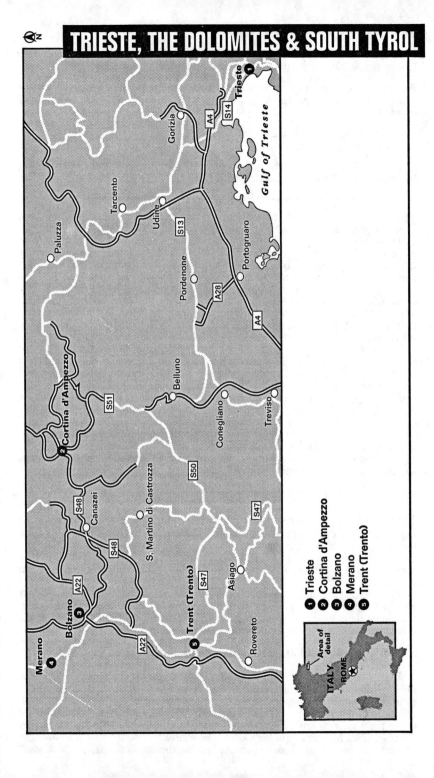

TRIESTE, THE DOLOMITES & SOUTH TYROL

N

Trieste ①

Gulf of Trieste

A4

S14

Gorizia

Tarcento

Udine

S13

Paluzza

Pordenone

A28

Portogruaro

A4

Cortina d'Ampezzo ②

S51

Belluno

Conegliano

Treviso

S50

Canazei

S48

S. Martino di Castrozza

S48

S47

A22

Asiago

Trent (Trento) ⑤

S47

Bolzano ③

A22

Rovereto

Merano ④

① Trieste
② Cortina d'Ampezzo
③ Bolzano
④ Merano
⑤ Trent (Trento)

Area of detail

ITALY

ROME ✪

hours and a one-way ticket goes for 9,300 lire ($7.30). Trains pull into piazza della Libertà (tel. 418207), northwest of the historic center.

By Bus   It's better to fly, drive, or take the train to Trieste. Once there, you'll find a network of local buses servicing the region at corso Cavour (tel. 370160 for schedules).

By Car   From Venice, continue northeast along autostrada A4 until you reach the end of the line at Trieste.

ESSENTIALS   The **telephone area code** for Trieste is 040. The **Tourist Information Office** is at Castello di San Giusto, colle di San Giusto (tel. 420182).

On the half-moon Gulf of Trieste, opening into the Adriatic, Trieste is perched at a remote point in Italy, a shimmering, bright city with many neoclassical buildings.

As an Adriatic seaport, Trieste has had a long history, with many changes of ownership. The Hapsburg emperor, Charles VI, declared it a free port in 1719, but by the 20th century it was an ocean outlet for the Austro-Hungarian Empire. Came the war and a secret deal among the Allies, and Trieste was ceded to Italy in 1918. In the late summer of 1943 Trieste again fell to foreign troops—this time the Nazis. The arrival of Tito's army from Yugoslavia in the spring of 1945 changed its destiny once more. A postwar attempt to turn it into a free territory failed. In 1954, after much hassle, the American and British troops withdrew as the Italians marched in, with the stipulation that the much-disputed Trieste would be maintained as a free port.

Trieste has known many glamorous literary associations, particularly in the pre–World War II years. As a stopover on the *Orient Express,* it became a famed destination. Dame Agatha Christie came this way, as did Graham Greene. As part of his elopement with Nora Barnacle, James Joyce arrived in Trieste in 1904. Out of both work and money, Joyce got a job teaching at the Berlitz School. He was to live here for nearly 10 years. He wrote *A Portrait of the Artist as a Young Man* here, and may have begun his masterpiece, *Ulysses,* here also.

Author Richard Burton, known for his *Arabian Nights* translations, lived in Trieste from 1871 until he died, about 20 years later.

The Teatro Verdi, the opera house, enjoys a deserved reputation throughout Italy, and many compare it favorably with La Scala.

WHAT TO SEE & DO

The heart of Trieste is the neoclassic ✪ **piazza dell'Unità d'Italia,** said to be the largest in Italy fronting the sea. Opening onto the square is the town hall with a clock tower, the Palace of the Government, and the main office of the Lloyd Triestino ship line. Flanking the square are numerous cafés and restaurants, popular at night with the denizens of Trieste who sip an apéritif, then later promenade along the seafront esplanade.

After visiting the main square, you may want to view Trieste from an even better vantage point. If so, head up the hill for another cluster of attractions. You can take an antiquated tram, leaving from piazza Oberdan, getting off at Obelisco. There, at the belvedere, the city of the Adriatic will spread out before you.

CATHEDRAL OF SAN GIUSTO, colle Capitolino, piazzale San Giusto. Tel. 302874.

Dedicated to the patron saint (St. Just) of Trieste, who was martyred in A.D. 303, the basilica atop Colle di San Giusto was consecrated in 1330, incorporating a pair of churches that had been separate until then. The front is in the Romanesque style, enhanced by a rose window. Inside, the nave is flanked by two pairs of aisles. To the left of the main altar are the best of the Byzantine mosaics in Trieste (note especially the blue-robed Madonna and her Child). The main altar and the chapel to the right contain less interesting mosaics. To the left of the basilica entrance is a small campanile from the 14th century, which you can scale on foot for a view of Trieste and its bay. At its base are preserved the remains of a Roman temple from the 1st century A.D. I prefer to take a taxi to the top, then walk back down, allowing a leisurely 15 minutes. From the basilica you can walk to the nearby Castle of San Giusto.

Admission: Free.
Open: Daily 8am–12:30pm and 3–6pm. **Bus:** 24.

CASTLE OF SAN GIUSTO, piazza Cattedrale 3. Tel. 309298.

Constructed in the 15th century by the Venetians on the site of a Roman fort, this fortress maintained a sharp eye on the bay, watching for unfriendly visitors arriving by sea. From its bastions, panoramic views of Trieste unfold. Inside is a **museum** (tel. 308686) with a collection of arms and armor.

In July and August, open-air performances—Hungarian dancers, for instance—are staged at the castle. An elegant tavern in the castle complex, Bottega del Vino, caps your exploration within the city proper.

Admission: Museum, 4,000 lire ($3.15).
Open: Museum, Tues–Sun 9am–1pm. **Bus:** 24.

MIRAMARE, viale Miramare, Grignano. Tel. 224143.

Overlooking the Bay of Grignano, this castle was erected by Archduke Maximilian, the brother of Franz Joseph, the Hapsburg emperor of Austria. Maximilian, who married Princess Charlotte of Belgium, was the commander of the Austrian navy in 1854. In an ill-conceived move, he and "Carlotta" sailed to Mexico in 1864, where he became the emperor in an unfortunate reign. He was shot in 1867 in Querétaro, Mexico. His wife lived until 1927 in a château outside Brussels, driven insane by the Mexican episode. You may remember the movie, probably on late at night, about Maximilian and Carlotta, called *Juárez*, starring Bette Davis, Paul Muni, and Brian Aherne. On the ground floor of the castle, you can visit the bedroom of Maximilian (built like a ship's cabin) and that of Charlotte, as well as an impressive receiving room and more parlors, including a chinoiserie salon.

Enveloping the castle are magnificently designed park grounds (Parco di Miramare), ideal for pleasant strolls. In summer, a sound-and-light presentation in the park of the castle depicts Maximilian's tragedy in Mexico. Tickets to the presentation, staged in July and August, begin at 6,000 lire ($4.70).

Admission: Castle, 4,000 lire ($3.15) adults, free for children under 12; grounds, free.
Open: Castle, Mon–Sat 9am–1:30pm, Sun and hols 9am–12:30pm; grounds, till sunset. **Bus:** 6 from center of town to the end of the line; then transfer to no. 36.

THE GIANT CAVE

In the heart of the limestone plateau called Carso that surrounds the city, you can visit the ✪ **Grotta Gigante** (tel. 327312), an enormous cavern and one of the most interesting phenomena of speleology. First explored in 1840 via the top ceiling entrance, this huge room, some 446 feet deep, was opened to the public in 1908. It's the biggest single-room cave ever opened to tourists and one of the world's largest underground rooms. A visit can be made only with a guide and takes nearly an hour. Near the entrance is the **Man and Caves Museum,** opened in 1963 and unique in Italy.

Tours of the cave are given Tuesday through Sunday: in March and October, Sunday, every 30 minutes from 9am to noon and 2 to 5pm; November to February, every hour from 10am to noon and 2:30 to 4:30pm; April to September, every 30 minutes from 9am to noon and 2 to 7pm. Tours cost 7,000 lire ($5.50) for adults, 5,000 lire ($3.95) for children 6 to 12. April to Sept you can purchase a "Troll to the Cave" ticket for 8,000 lire ($6.30), including a return ride on the typical troll cars of transit line no. 2 to the suburb of Villa Opicina, a round-trip ride to the cave on bus no. 45, and an entrance ticket to the cave, allowing a substantial saving. If you're driving, take Strada del Friuli beyond the white marble Victory Lighthouse as far as Prosecco. On the freeway you can take the exit at Prosecco.

WHERE TO STAY

VERY EXPENSIVE

SAVOIA EXCELSIOR PALACE, riva del Mandracchio 4, 34124 Trieste. Tel. 040/7690. Fax 040/77733. 154 rms (all with bath). A/C MINIBAR TV TEL **Bus:** 8, 9, or 11.
$ **Rates** (including breakfast): 205,000–215,000 lire ($160.95–$168.80) single; 250,000–290,000 lire ($196.25–$227.65) double. AE, DC, MC, V. **Parking:** 30,000 lire ($23.55).

This leading choice stands proudly next to the headquarters of the Lloyd Triestino shipping palazzo, right off piazza dell'Unità. Fronting the water, the hotel has witnessed much of the pageantry of Trieste. The rooms in this first-class hotel are equipped with radio and other amenities, and many are furnished in bold modern designs. In respect to the past, there's a tea room, but an American bar adds a contemporary touch. The hotel has an excellent restaurant.

JOLLY HOTEL, corso Cavour 7, 34132 Trieste. Tel. 040/7694. Fax 040/362699. 180 rms (all with bath). A/C MINIBAR TV TEL **Bus:** 8, 9, or 11.
$ **Rates** (including breakfast): 190,000 lire ($149.15) single; 250,000 lire ($196.25) double. AE, DC, MC, V. **Parking:** 20,000 lire ($15.70).

The Jolly rises from a convenient spot in the center of town behind a two-tone concrete facade 200 yards from the railway station. The public rooms are decorated in a conservatively plush decor that includes velvet armchairs and appealing colors; the conference rooms are frequently used for local gatherings and social celebrations. The bedrooms include a radio, as well as comfortable bedding and an up-to-date bath.

HOTEL DUCHI D'AOSTA, piazza dell'Unità d'Italia 2, 34121 Trieste. Tel. 040/7351. Fax 040/366092. 52 rms (all with bath), 2 suites. A/C MINIBAR TV TEL **Bus:** 8, 9, or 11.
$ **Rates** (including breakfast): 228,000 lire ($179) single; 270,000 lire ($211.95) double; from 480,000 lire ($376.80) suite. AE, MC, V. **Parking:** 30,000 lire ($23.55).

⭐ This now-glamorous hotel began about 200 years ago as a restaurant for the dock workers who toiled at the nearby wharves. In 1873 one of the most beautiful facades in Trieste was erected to cover the existing building in a white neoclassical shell with delicate carving, arched windows, and a stone crown of heroic sculptures. The design is a lot like that of an 18th-century palace, an effect enhanced by views over the fountains and lamps of the major square of Trieste and the sea beyond it. The hotel was practically rebuilt from the inside in the 1970s. Today the bedrooms are a favorite with business travelers, who appreciate the food in the ground-floor restaurant (see my recommendation for Harry's Grill in "Where to Dine," below) and the 19th-century ambience of the Victorian-style public rooms. Each accommodation has a well-stocked minibar concealed behind panels, antiqued walls, built-in radio, and tasteful furniture.

MODERATE

HOTEL AL TEATRO, capo di piazza G. Bartoli 1, 34100 Trieste. Tel. 040/366220. 47 rms (28 with bath or shower). TEL **Bus:** 4, 8, or 30.
$ **Rates:** 54,000 lire ($42.40) single with shower; 46,000–60,000 lire ($36.10–$47.10) double without bath, 85,000 lire ($66.75) double with shower. Breakfast 10,000 lire ($7.85) extra. No credit cards.

$ The theatrical mask carved into the stone arch above the entrance is an appropriate symbol of a hotel favored by many of Trieste's visiting opera stars. Behind a beige neoclassical facade, a few steps from the seaside panorama of piazza dell'Unità d'Italia and about a 10-minute walk from the station, the hotel has comfortable rooms reached by a stone stairwell. The simply furnished and slightly old-fashioned rooms have parquet floors, lots of space, and comfortable but minimal furniture. The hotel was built in 1830 as a private house and later served as a headquarters of the British army in the aftermath of World War II.

HOTEL CITTA DI PARENZO, via Artisti 8, 34100 Trieste. Tel. 040/ 630119. Fax 040/367510. 43 rms (all with bath). TEL **Bus:** 4, 8, or 30.
$ Rates: 39,000 lire ($30.60) single; 67,000 lire ($52.60) double. Breakfast 12,000 lire ($9.40) extra. AE, MC, V.

This is the economy special of Trieste. On a narrow street in the 19th-century business district, it is relatively secluded from the major traffic artery, although overnight guests may still hear the inevitable sounds of a Vespa. The marble wall covering of the lobby extends into the hall. The simple bedrooms are furnished YMCA style. The reception is English-speaking. No meals are served, but breakfast is available at a little café across the street. The hotel is named after an old seaport about 30 miles from Trieste, a favorite destination of the former owners.

WHERE TO DINE

VERY EXPENSIVE

RISTORANTE HARRY'S GRILL, in the Hotel Duchi d'Aosta, piazza dell'Unità d'Italia 2. Tel. 7351.
Cuisine: INTERNATIONAL. **Reservations:** Recommended. **Bus:** 8, 9, or 11.
$ Prices: Appetizers 13,500–15,000 lire ($10.60–$11.80); main courses 25,000–35,000 lire ($19.65–$27.50). AE, DC, MC, V.
Open: Lunch daily 12:30–3pm; dinner daily 7:30–10pm.

For good food, go to Harry's Grill. The adjoining bar is one of the most popular rendezvous spots in town, particularly for the business community (although it's not related to any of the many other Harry's restaurants or bars scattered throughout Italy). The big lace-covered curtains complement the paneling, the polished brass, and the chandeliers of blue glass from Murano. In summer, tables are set up in the central traffic-free piazza dell'Unità d'Italia. Illuminated with light from the carriage lamps set into the stonework of the hotel, the outdoor terrace, with a separate area for bar clients, is sheltered by a canopy to protect clients from the Adriatic winds that sometimes sweep in from the sea.

The Mediterranean-inspired cuisine includes fresh shrimp with oil and lemon, pasta and risotto dishes, boiled salmon in sauce, veal in madeira sauce, butter-fried calves' liver with onions, and an array of beef and fish dishes.

EXPENSIVE

ANTICA TRATTORIA SUBAN, via Comici 2 (at San Giovanni). Tel. 54368.
Cuisine: ITALIAN/YUGOSLAVIAN. **Reservations:** Recommended. **Bus:** 8, 9, or 11.
$ Prices: Appetizers 8,000–14,000 lire ($6.30–$11); main courses 18,000–22,000 lire ($14.15–$17.15). AE, DC, MC, V.
Open: Lunch Wed–Sun 12:30–2:30pm; dinner Wed–Mon 7:30–10pm. **Closed:** Aug 1–15.

In 1865 the founder established a country tavern with a spacious terrace opening onto a view of the hills near Trieste. Today the surrounding landscape contains glimpses of the industrial age, but the brick and stone walls, the terrace, and the country feeling are still intact. The cuisine is both hearty and delicate. The chefs concoct specialties from fresh ingredients gathered from surrounding farmlands. Specialties include a flavorful risotto with herbs, basil-flavored crêpes, beef with garlic sauce, a perfectly prepared chicken Kiev, and veal croquettes with parmesan and egg yolks. The chef's handling of grilled meats, with some recipes derived from neighboring Yugoslavia, is adept, and the rich pastries are worth the extra calories.

AL BRAGOZZO, riva Nazario Sauro 22. Tel. 303001.

Cuisine: SEAFOOD. **Reservations:** Required. **Bus:** 8, 9, 10, 11, or 30.
$ **Prices:** Appetizers 10,000–15,000 lire ($7.85–$11.80); main courses 18,000–25,000 lire ($14.15–$19.65); fixed-price menu 60,000 lire ($47.10). DC, MC, V.
Open: Lunch Tues–Sat 11am–3pm; dinner Tues–Sat 6pm–midnight. **Closed:** June 20–July 10.

This is one of the best-known fish restaurants at the port. The outdoor tables, sheltered by a canopy, are popular in summer, although the paneled dining room is better during inclement weather. Serving meals for 36,000 lire ($28.25) and up, it offers calamari, a well-prepared Adriatic fish fry, risotto with seafood, zuppa di pesce, a few meat dishes, and a variety of dessert crêpes.

ELEFANTE BIANCO, riva Tre Novembre 3. Tel. 365784.

Cuisine: INTERNATIONAL. **Reservations:** Required. **Bus:** 8, 9, or 11.
$ **Prices:** Appetizers 12,000–14,000 lire ($9.40–$11); main courses 20,000–22,000 lire ($15.70–$17.25). AE, DC, MC, V.
Open: Lunch Mon–Fri 1–3pm; dinner Mon–Sat 8–11:30pm.

To get a table at this talked-about "white elephant," reserve early before the crowds form. Its reputation has caught on with the fashionable set of Trieste. The location is on a busy street fronting the harbor, behind lattices and a semicircular wooden platform. The centerpiece of the garden-style interior is an abundantly stocked table of fruit and antipasti above a white porcelain elephant festooned with trailing ivy. The young and cooperative waiters serve a light and healthy cuisine, including such temptations as pasta with truffles or salmon, tagliolini with shrimp, grilled beef with fresh rosemary, grilled shrimp marinated with oranges and champagne, and well-prepared beefsteak flavored with herbs.

MODERATE

AI DUE TRIESTINI, via Cadorna 10. Tel. 303759.

Cuisine: ITALIAN/AUSTRIAN. **Reservations:** Not necessary. **Bus:** 8 or 9.
$ **Prices:** Appetizers 3,000–5,000 lire ($2.35–$3.95); main courses 6,000–10,000 lire ($4.70–$7.85). No credit cards.
Open: Lunch only, Mon–Sat noon–2:30pm.

ⓢ For one of the best bargains in Trieste, I suggest this tavern behind piazza dell'Unità. Run by a husband-and-wife team, the little trattoria covers its tablecloths with plastic and doesn't even bother to print a menu. Some of the cookery leans heavily on the influence of neighboring Austria. Try, for example, spezzatino, chunks of beef in a goulash ragoût, with fresh peas and potatoes. The Hungarian goulash is quite good, as is a rich strudel in the tradition of Budapest. Many diners order beer with their meals, and others come in for a glass of wine, served from one of the casks that line a wall. It's in the center near the sea, near the Stazione Marittima.

AL GRANZO, piazza Venezia 7. Tel. 306788.

Cuisine: SEAFOOD. **Reservations:** Recommended. **Bus:** 8, 9, 10, or 30.
$ **Prices:** Appetizers 6,000–9,000 lire ($4.70–$7.05); main courses 12,000–15,000 lire ($9.40–$11.80). AE, DC, MC, V.
Open: Lunch Thurs–Tues 12:30–3pm; dinner Mon–Tues and Thurs–Sat 7:30–10pm.

This is one of the leading seafood restaurants of Trieste. Try to get a seat on its waterfront terrace facing the fish market. Here you might order a brodetto, a traditional bouillabaisse spiced with saffron and other herbs, or vermicelli with black mussels, or perhaps a risotto with fruits of the sea. For your main course, I recommend the fish of the day. You can make your own choice from a wagon where the fish are displayed on a bed of ground ice. Good with fish is a local Tocai Friulano, which is aromatic, harmonious, and somewhat tart in flavor, its color a lemon yellow tending to pale green.

BOTTEGA DEL VINO DI SAN GIUSTO, Castello di San Giusto, piazza Cattedrale 3. Tel. 309142.

Cuisine: TRIESTINE/INTERNATIONAL. **Reservations:** Required. **Bus:** 24.

$ Prices: Appetizers 6,500–10,000 lire ($5.10–$7.85); main courses 10,000–20,000 lire ($7.85–$15.70); fixed-price menu 24,000 lire ($18.85). AE.

Open: Wed–Mon 6:30pm–2am. **Closed:** Jan.

Bottega del Vino is a rustic, medieval-style wine cellar inside the Castle of San Giusto, whose view encompasses most of Trieste. The entrance is a massive arched door set into an ivy-covered wall leading off the central courtyard. An upper floor is often used for private parties, while the heavily timbered lower level is dotted with wooden tables for tasting a large selection of Italian wines. Amid a setting of massive stone columns, 1,000-year-old walls, and iron wall sconces, guests can also enjoy full meals beginning at 40,000 lire ($31.40)—all the classic Italian dishes, such as veal piccata, risotto with scampi and curry or with champagne, a few pasta dishes, and a limited selection of fish. The most elaborate offering is chateaubriand with béarnaise sauce, which could be accompanied by one (or two) of the establishment's large selection of red and white Italian wines. These include Asti Spumanti, and even champagne if you're feeling extravagant. Evening music is provided.

INEXPENSIVE

BUFFET BENEDETTO, via XXX Ottobre no. 19. Tel. 61655.

Cuisine: ITALIAN/TRIESTINE. **Reservations:** Recommended. **Bus:** 8 or 9.

$ Prices: Appetizers 6,500–7,000 lire ($5.10–$5.50); main courses 12,000–18,000 lire ($9.40–$14.15). AE, DC, MC, V.

Open: Lunch Tues–Sun noon–3pm; dinner Tues–Sun 7–10pm. **Closed:** Aug.

Buffet Benedetto is a good example of the kind of establishment that's popular in Trieste. Near the front door is a high-ceilinged room crowded with jars of local produce, wine, and regional foodstuffs, as well as a crowd of stand-up diners, many elbow to elbow, who order a plate of food from behind a glass display case. Many diners prefer to pass through the deli-buffet section into one of two inner rooms (there might be a wait at lunchtime). There, a uniformed waiter will recite menu items to you in rapid Italian—you'll probably understand some of the more commonly known specialties. The antipasti, when I was last there, consisted of a cold salad of fresh shrimp mixed with squid and served with a lemon and mild creamy sauce. Other menu items include thinly sliced prosciutto, a huge bowl of rigatoni with tomato sauce, baked lasagne, Florentine steaks, saltimbocca, eggplant parmigiana, and several kinds of beef. Full meals at the tables begin at 32,000 lire ($25.10). Stand-up meals at the buffet cost substantially less, and no one will mind if you have only a dish of pasta as a main course.

DA PEPI, via Cassa di Risparmio 3. Tel. 366858.

Cuisine: AUSTRIAN/HUNGARIAN. **Reservations:** Not accepted. **Bus:** 10, 11, 17, or 18.

$ Prices: Main courses 5,000–18,000 lire ($3.95–$14.15). No credit cards.

Open: Lunch Mon–Sat noon–2pm; dinner Mon–Sat 7–9pm. **Closed:** July.

If you're intrigued with the idea of a buffet, you might try Da Pepi, with a groaning counter display of "the works." Try, in particular, a long, thinnish sausage known as luganiga, sometimes broiled with tomato sauce. The boiled beef called Rindfleisch in Vienna is simmered to perfection, and the sauerkraut is distinctive in flavor. No appetizers are served. For your drink, select either a liter of the robust local wine or a beer, perhaps an import from Czechoslovakia or Austria. A hearty meal here is likely to cost 28,000 lire ($22).

A CAFÉ

At the center of Trieste is **Caffè degli Specchi**, piazza dell'Unità d'Italia 7 (tel. 365777). You can sit at a sidewalk table with a view of a sunset over the open sea on one side and the rhythmically neoclassical buildings of the most important piazza in Trieste on the other. In summer, the sidewalk tables face one of the liveliest congregations of people in town. However, when the cold Adriatic wind blows, everybody retreats behind the giant plate-glass windows. With its contemporary iciclelike chandeliers and its wide selection of clients, the café has very much an Eastern European aura. You can have a coffee here for 1,100 lire (85¢) if you stand at the counter. Bus no. 9 or 10 will take you there.

2. CORTINA D'AMPEZZO

100 miles N of Venice, 82 miles E of Bolzano, 255 miles NE of Milan

GETTING THERE   By Train   Frequent trains run between Venice and Calalzo di Cadore (trip time: 2 hours 20 minutes), 19 miles south of Cortina. You proceed the rest of the way by bus. For information about schedules, call 0435/32300 in Calalzo.

By Bus   About 14 to 16 buses a day connect Calalzo di Cadore with Cortina. Buses arrive at the Cortina bus station on viale Marconi (tel. 0436/2741 for information about schedules).

By Car   Take Route 13 north from Venice via Treviso, continuing north along Route 51 all the way to Cortina d'Ampezzo.

ESSENTIALS   The **telephone area code** for Cortina d'Ampezzo is 0436. The **Tourist Information Office** is at piazzetta San Francesco (tel. 3231). They can assist you in arranging accommodations (see "Where to Stay," below).

This fashionable resort is your best center for exploring the snowy Dolomites. Its reputation as a tourist mecca dates back to before World War I, but its recent growth has been phenomenal. Cortina d'Ampezzo draws throngs of nature lovers in summer and both Olympic-caliber and neophyte skiers in winter. It's a hotel owner's Shangri-la, charging maximum prices in July and August as well as in the 3 months of winter.

The town *signora* of propaganda once insisted: "Just say Cortina has everything." Statements of propaganda chiefs, even when they come from charming Italian ladies, are suspect—but in this case she's nearly right. "Everything," in the Cortina context, means—first and foremost—people of every shape and hue: New York socialites rub elbows in late-night spots with frumpy Bremen hausfraus. Young Austrian men, clad in Loden jackets and stout leather shorts, walk down the streets with feathers in their caps and gleams in their eyes. French women in red ski pants sample Campari at café tables, while the tweedy English sit at rival establishments drinking "tea like mother made."

Then, too, "everything" means location. Cortina is in the middle of a valley ringed by enough Dolomite peaks to cause Hannibal's elephants to throw up their trunks and flee in horror. Regardless of which road you choose for a motor trip, you'll find the scenery rewarding. Third, "everything" means good food. Cortina sets an excellent table, inspired by the cuisine of both Venice and Tyrol. Fourth, "everything" means summer and winter sporting facilities—chiefly golf, horseback riding, curling, tennis, fishing, mountain climbing, skiing, skating, and swimming. The resort not only has an Olympic ice stadium, but an Olympic bobsled track and ski jump (the 1956 Olympics were held at Cortina, publicizing the resort all over the world). In addition, it has a skiing school, an Olympic-size ice-skating rink, a large indoor swimming pool, an Olympic downhill track, and a cross-country track.

Finally, "everything" means top-notch hotels, pensiones, private homes, and even mountain huts for the rugged. The locations, facilities, types of service, price structures, and decor in these establishments vary considerably, but I've never inspected an accommodation here that wasn't clean. Most of the architecture of Cortina, incidentally, seems more appropriate to Zell am See, Austria, than to an Italian town.

WHAT TO SEE & DO

The Faloria-Cristallo area in the surroundings of Cortina is known for its 18½ miles of ski slopes and 10 miles of fresh-snow runs.

One of the main attractions in Cortina is to take a cable car "halfway to the stars," as the expression goes. On one of them, at least, you'll be just a yodel away from the pearly gates. It's the **Freccia Nel Cielo** (or "arrow of the sky"). For departure information, phone 0436/5052. Beginning at 9am, departures are every 20 minutes, ending at 5pm in winter, 5:30pm in summer. The cable car operates daily from mid-December to mid-April and from July through September. A round-trip costs 28,000 lire ($22). The first station is Col Druscie at 5,752 feet. The second station, Ra Valles, stands at 8,027 feet, and the top station, Tofana di Mezzo, is at 10,543 feet. At Tofana on a clear day, you can see as far as Venice.

SHOPPING

Good purchases are available at the **Art House,** corso Italia 96 (tel. 863888), which offers the best collection in the area of copper, brass, and pewter fashioned into about a thousand different variations ranging from the most practical to the whimsical. If you're looking for the best cookware available in Italy, you'll find copper saucepans and casseroles that would satisfy Julia Child. You might also find that massive brass door knocker you've been seeking, along with pewter mead glasses. The shop is open Monday through Saturday from 9:30am to 1pm and 3:30 to 8pm.

WHERE TO STAY

The **Tourist Information Office,** piazzetta San Francesco 8 (tel. 0436/3231), has a list of all the private homes in and around Cortina that take in paying guests, lodging them family style for a moderate cost. It's a good opportunity to live with a Dolomite family in comfort and informality. Even though there are nearly 3,500 rooms available, it's best to reserve in advance, especially from August 1 to 20 and December 20 to January 7. The tourist office, however, will not personally book you into a private home. Those arrangements you must make independently.

VERY EXPENSIVE

CRISTALLO PALACE, via Menardi 42, 32043 Cortina d'Ampezzo. Tel. 0436/4281. Fax 0436/868058. 83 rms (all with bath), 8 junior suites. MINIBAR TV TEL **Bus:** Hotel shuttle bus to/from the town center.

$ **Rates** (including half board): 303,000 lire ($237.85) single; 566,000 lire ($444.30) double; from 650,000 lire ($510.25) suite for two. 19% IVA tax extra. AE, DC, MC, V. **Parking:** Free. **Closed:** Apr 8–June 6 and Sept 11–Dec 18.

The Cristallo Palace is a large establishment in the grand tradition of European resort hotels. It offers excellent bedrooms, lots of facilities, and top-notch service (many of the staff are virtually "retainers" of the Cristallo). The managing director keeps the standards high. The good-size bedrooms feature attractive furnishings and picture-window views of the Dolomites. However, the meals produced here are the raison d'être for booking an accommodation. Half board is obligatory in season. Facilities include hard tennis courts, an open-air swimming pool, and terraces for sunning and drinks.

MIRAMONTI MAJESTIC GRAND HOTEL, località Pezzie 103, 32043 Cortina d'Ampezzo. Tel. 0436/4201. Fax 0436/867019. 121 rms (all with bath), 8 suites. MINIBAR TV TEL **Bus:** Hotel shuttle bus to/from the town center.

$ **Rates** (including half board): 240,000–330,000 lire ($188.40–$259.05) per person. AE, DC, MC, V. **Parking:** 25,000 lire ($19.65). **Closed:** Apr–June and Sept–Dec 19.

One of the grandest hotels in the Dolomites, it consists of two ocher-colored buildings with alpine hipped roofs set a short distance from the center of town. There's a gazebo built in the same style as the hotel on the right as you ascend the curved driveway leading up to the dignified facade, and a backdrop of jagged mountains behind the thick stucco walls and the dozens of gingerbread balconies. The rustic interior is filled with warmly appealing colors, lots of exposed timbers, and about the most elegant clientele in Cortina. The well-furnished bedrooms look like the accommodations in a private home, complete with matching wallpaper and bedspreads, built-in closets, and all the modern amenities.

A sports facility is on the premises, with an indoor swimming pool, exercise and massage equipment, a sauna, hydrotherapy, and physical therapy. Other sports facilities for winter and summer exercises are nearby.

MODERATE

ANCORA, corso Italia 62, 32040 Cortina d'Ampezzo. Tel. 0436/3261.
Fax 0436/3261. 71 rms (all with bath). TV TEL **Bus:** 1 or 2.
$ Rates (including half board): 235,000 lire ($184.50) per person. **Parking:** 20,000 lire ($15.70). **Closed:** Sept 15–Dec 19 and after Easter to June.
This "Romantik Hotel" is the domain of that hearty empress of the Dolomites, Flavia Bertozzi, who attracts sporting guests from all over the world and plays host to modern art exhibitions and classical concerts. This "hostess with the mostest" believes in her guests' having a good time. The antique sculptures and objets d'art filling the hotel were gathered from Signora Flavia's trips to every province of Italy. Hers is a revamped hotel flanked on two sides by terraces with outdoor tables and umbrellas—the town center for sipping and gossiping. Garlanded wooden balconies encircle the five floors, and most bedrooms open directly onto these sunny porches. The bedrooms are all well furnished, comfortable, and especially pleasant—many with sitting areas—and you sleep under brightly colored woolen blankets. All is kept shiny clean, the service is polite and efficient, and the food is good.

DE LA POSTE, piazza Roma 14, 32043 Cortina d'Ampezzo. Tel. 0436/4271. Fax 0436/440044. 80 rms (all with bath), 6 suites. TV TEL **Bus:** 1 or 2.
$ Rates (including half board): 180,000–280,000 lire ($141.30–$219.80) per person. AE, DC. **Parking:** 25,000 lire ($19.65). **Closed:** Oct 20–Dec 19.
Built like a Tyrolean mountain chalet, this hotel enjoys a central and sunny position in a pedestrian zone. It has long been a celebrity favorite, attracting such guests as King Hussein and Queen Noor. Its amenities are top rate. Open wooden balconies and terraces encircle the building, giving bedrooms sun porches. All the bedrooms have double windows and French doors, chintz draperies and bedspreads, and built-in wardrobes—many homelike touches. About 45% of the rooms have a minibar. The get-acquainted, woodsy bar, evoking a country tavern, is one of the liveliest spots in town. The hotel, once a postal inn, is the most popular place in Cortina for après-ski drinks.

HOTEL CORONA, via Val di Sotto 12, 32040 Cortina d'Ampezzo. Tel. 0436/3251. Fax 0436/867339. 44 rms (all with bath). TV TEL **Bus:** 1 or 2.
$ Rates: 230,000 lire ($180.55) single or double; 230,000 lire ($180.55) per person with full board. V. **Parking:** Free. **Closed:** Apr–June and Sept 11–Dec 19.
Dating from 1935, the Corona is one of the first hotels built at the resort. Its loyal clients would stay nowhere else during a stopover in Cortina. For anyone interested in modern Italian art, a stopover here is an event. The interior walls are painted a neutral white as a foil for the hundreds of carefully inventoried artworks displayed, acquisitions of Luciano Rimoldi, the athletic manager, over the past 25 years. (He is also a ski instructor who coached Princess Grace in her downhill technique shortly before her death.) He later served as head of the Italian ice-hockey team during the 1988 Winter Olympics at Calgary.

Many of the most important artists of Italy (and a few from France) from 1948 to 1963 are represented here with artwork—not only painting, but sculpture and ceramic bas-reliefs. The hotel doesn't overlook sports either. It was chosen for the World Cup competition by a U.S. ski team just before they headed for the Sarajevo Olympics. The hotel prefers clients to take board in winter.

PARC HOTEL VICTORIA, corso Italia 1, 32043 Cortina d'Ampezzo. Tel. 0436/3246. Fax 0436/440817. 45 rms (all with bath). MINIBAR TV TEL **Bus:** 1 or 2.

$ Rates (including half board): Winter, 260,000 lire ($204.10) per person; mid-July to Sept, 150,000 lire ($117.75) per person. AE, DC, MC, V. **Parking:** Free. **Closed:** Oct–Dec 19 and Apr to mid-July.

The Parc Hotel Victoria is one of the best hotels in the center of town, a modern structure created in the Tyrolean style, with many good-size balconies opening onto views of the mountaintops. It's a successful place, combining the old chalet decor with contemporary, roomy areas, and lots of amenities. In the winter, all the well-furnished rooms have plenty of steam heat. The various living rooms and dining rooms are furnished with reproductions of old country furniture (bare-pine tables, peg-legged chairs). The regional fireplace with a raised hearth is the focal point for after-dinner gatherings.

INEXPENSIVE

HOTEL NORD, via la Verra 10, 32043 Cortina d'Ampezzo. Tel. 0436/4707. Fax 0436/440066. 34 rms (all with bath). **Bus:** 1.

$ Rates (including full board): 82,000–115,000 lire ($64.35–$90.30) per person, double occupancy. V. **Parking:** Free.

Set in the upper reaches of the resort's northern periphery, alongside the road leading to the Brenner Pass, this is one of the most genuinely charming cost-conscious hotels in Cortina. Built like a chalet, and ringed with balconies on three sides, it evokes the mountain buildings of nearby Austria, but with Italian flair. It dates from 1956, with a new wing completed in 1970. Each bedroom contains furniture crafted from local pinewood. TV is available upon request.

MENARDI, via Majon 110, 32043 Cortina d'Ampezzo. Tel. 0436/2400. Fax 0436/862183. 48 rms (all with bath). TEL **Bus:** 1.

$ Rates (including full board): 110,000 lire ($86.35) per person. AE, MC, V. **Parking:** 10,000 lire ($7.85). **Closed:** Mid-Sept to Christmas and Apr 7–June 21.

This eye-catcher in the upper part of Cortina looks like a great country inn, with its wooden balconies and shutters. Its rear windows open onto a meadow of flowers and a view of the rough Dolomite crags. The inn is 100 years old and is run by the Menardi family, who still know how to speak the old Dolomite tongue, Ladino. Decorated in the Tyrolean fashion, each bedroom has its distinct personality. Considering what you get—the quality of the facilities, the reception, and the food—I'd rate this one as the best for the money in Cortina. The living rooms and dining rooms have homelike furnishings: lots of knickknacks, pewter, antlers, spinning wheels.

Should this hotel be full, the family will book you into their second accommodation, containing only eight rooms, each with private bath and a balcony opening onto the Dolomites.

HOTEL AGIP, via Roma 118, 32043 Cortina d'Ampezzo. Tel. 0436/861400. Fax 0436/862140. 42 rms (all with shower). TEL **Bus:** 1 or 2.

$ Rates (including half board): 130,000–140,000 lire ($102.05–$109.90) per person. AE, DC, MC, V. **Parking:** 15,000 lire ($11.80).

Hotel Agip, a member of this popular Italian chain, offers many amenities. It's a good bet if you arrive in Cortina in the off-season, when virtually everything else is closed. Its convenient location on the main road just outside the center of town—coupled with its clean, comfortable, contemporary, and no-nonsense format—have gained increasing favor with its many visitors. The bedrooms are predictably furnished and fairly quiet, the management helpful. The restaurant serves good food, featuring regional specialties.

WHERE TO DINE

EL TOULA, via Ronco 123. Tel. 3339.
Cuisine: ITALIAN/VENETIAN. **Reservations:** Recommended. **Bus:** 2.
$ **Prices:** Appetizers 18,000–24,000 lire ($14.15–$18.85); main courses 28,000–40,000 lire ($22–$31.40). AE, DC, V.
Open: Lunch daily 12:30–2:30pm; dinner daily 8–10:30pm. **Closed:** The day after Easter to July 1 and Sept 15–Dec 19.

The most elegant dining spot in Cortina is this wood-frame structure with picture-window views and an outside terrace. It's perched about a 5-minute drive from the center of town, toward Pocol. The restaurant commands a panoramic view. It is the current Dolomite favorite of the fancy folk and the international set, and there are several other branch establishments throughout Italy. You get excellently prepared dishes here, including squab grilled to perfection and served with an expertly seasoned sauce and veal braised with a white truffle sauce. The filet of beef is also recommended. A complete meal averages anywhere from 80,000 lire to 90,000 lire ($62.80 to $70.65).

RISTORANTE TIVOLI, località Lacadel. Tel. 866400.
Cuisine: ITALIAN. **Reservations:** Required. **Bus:** 1.
$ **Prices:** Appetizers 10,000–18,000 lire ($7.85–$14.15); main courses 20,000–30,000 lire ($15.70–$23.55). AE, DC, MC, V.
Open: Lunch daily 12:30–2:30pm; dinner daily 9–10:30pm. **Closed:** May–June and Oct–Nov.

My favorite restaurant in Cortina, and one of the finest in the area, is this low-slung alpine chalet whose rear seems almost buried in the slope of the hillside. Standing high above the resort, about a mile from the center, it's beside the road leading to the hamlet of Pocol. Vastly popular with a chic and stylishly athletic European clientele, it derives its excellence from the hard-working efforts of the Calderoni family. Their gracious members seem to perform all the services necessary to make this place one of the most fun and interesting at the resort.

Full meals might include stuffed rabbit in an onion sauce, duck filet with bacon and greens, veal filet with basil and pine nuts, or salmon flavored with saffron. The pastas are made in the kitchen the day they are consumed. Examples include ravioli stuffed with spinach, cream, mushrooms, and truffles, or tagliatelle with goose liver. For dessert, you might sample an aspic of exotic fruit. The bustling kitchens are visible from the vestibule as you enter, adding to the warmth and pleasure of the restaurant.

DA BEPPE SELLO, via Ronco 68. Tel. 3236.
Cuisine: ITALIAN. **Reservations:** Recommended. **Bus:** 2.
$ **Prices:** Appetizers 10,000–14,000 lire ($7.85–$11); main courses 14,000–28,000 lire ($11–$22). AE, DC, V.
Open: Lunch Wed–Mon 12:30–2pm; dinner Wed–Mon 7:30–10pm. **Closed:** Apr–May 15 and Sept 15–Oct.

Da Beppe Sello is really a third-class hotel, but habitués of Cortina know it as a village-edge chalet providing regional meals that are generous and tasty. Guests retreat inside the snug Tyrolean dining room. Look for some of these delightful specialties: homemade ravioli, or roast chicken with bay leaves; in season, game is offered. The average meal will cost 38,000 lire ($29.85), unless you order some of the more elaborate specialties, which cost as much as 48,000 lire ($37.70).

RISTORANTE BELLAVISTA–Il MELONCINO, località Gillardon 17. Tel. 861043.
Cuisine: ITALIAN. **Reservations:** Recommended. **Directions:** Follow the signs to Falzarego, stopping in the satellite suburb of Gillardon.
$ **Prices:** Appetizers 8,000–14,000 lire ($6.30–$11); main courses 14,000–18,000 lire ($11–$14.15). No credit cards.
Open: Lunch Wed–Mon 12:30–2:30pm; dinner Wed–Mon 8–11pm. **Closed:** June and Nov.

The sweeping view of Cortina and the mountains beyond it is only one of the attractions of this small, rustic restaurant set at the top of one of the village's easiest ski runs. The building looks like little more than a log hut, although the owners have added wind-sheltered terraces and a nearby barbecue grill on wheels that looks like an adaptation of a Conestoga wagon. You're likely to meet the more experienced members of the Cortina social scene here, all of whom enjoy the unusual Italian specialties prepared in the establishment's tiny kitchen—risotto with fruit (offered from June to September only), homemade liver pâté, scaloppine dishes, roast mountain goat, grilled beef in several variations, ample use of fresh mushrooms, and homemade ice cream.

EVENING ENTERTAINMENT

Like the nightlife scattered through many of the alpine resorts in Europe, the bar and disco scene virtually closes down in the warm months. The popularity rating of any of them is about as fleeting as the mountain snow in June, although, for the record, a few of the more enduring establishments are listed below.

LIMBO, corso Italia 97. Tel. 860026.

This popular disco and restaurant attracts pleasure seekers of all ages. It's closed in summer, but sees winter action when the skiers flock here. The disco is open nightly from 10pm to either 3 or 6am, charging 15,000 lire ($11.80) for your first drink. The restaurant on the premises is open nightly from 8pm to 3am (perhaps the only restaurant in Cortina serving that late). A meal begins at 50,000 lire ($39.25). The cuisine is international.

Admission: Free.

MONKEY CLUB, in the Hotel Cristallo, via Menardi 42. Tel. 4281.

The Monkey Club offers piano music continuing until midnight. Plush, secure, and fashionable, it attracts sophisticated clients, many of whom gather beside a carved limestone fireplace. Drinks start at 12,000 lire ($9.40) or you can have dinner for 70,000 lire ($54.95) and up. Open in winter daily from 9pm to 1am.

Admission: Free.

PIANO BAR, in the Hotel Venezia, corso Italia 209. Tel. 3291.

This popular gathering spot is in the traffic-free center of town. Music is played until midnight. Drinks cost 10,000 lire to 15,000 lire ($7.85 to $11.80). Open Dec–March and July–Aug, Tuesday through Sunday from 9pm to midnight. **Closed:** Apr–June and Sept–Nov.

Admission: Free.

BILBO CLUB, largo Poste. Tel. 861168.

The interior is dark and rustically modern; the crowd, young disco clients from all over Europe and North America. You have to reserve. Open in winter and summer nightly from 11:30pm to 3 or 4am.

Admission: 35,000 lire ($27.50), including your first drink.

AREA, via Ronco. Tel. 867393.

Very modern, it caters to a young set. You enter a bar on street level, but descend to the basement to dance. Open nightly from 11pm to 4am.

Admission: 25,000 lire ($19.65), including the first drink.

IPPO, largo Poste. Tel. 2333.

Ippo caters to the young disco market. You enter a street-level bar, descending to the "cave" to dance. Open nightly from 11pm to 4am.

Admission: 25,000 lire ($19.65), including the first drink.

ENOTECA CORTINA, via del Mercato 5. Tel. 862040.

Enoteca Cortina is said to be the first wine bar to open in Italy, making its debut in 1964. Its interior has been compared to a compartment on the *Orient Express*, although, to some, it suggests an English pub. At least 500 of the finest wines from all major wine districts of Italy are on sale, costing 2,000 lire to 20,000 lire ($1.55 to $15.70) per glass. Locals happily mingle with skiers in winter and mountain climbers in summer. Open all year from 10am to 1pm and 4 to 9pm; it's closed Sunday except during the peak winter ski season. The location is just 200 yards from the town bell tower.

EN ROUTE TO BOLZANO VIA THE GREAT DOLOMITE ROAD

From Cortina d'Ampezzo in the east to Bolzano in the west is a circuitous route of about 68 miles. It ranks among the grandest scenic drives in all of Europe. The first pass you'll cross (Falzarego) is about 11 miles from Cortina. At 6,900 feet above sea level, it offers a panoramic view. The next great pass is called Pordoi, at about 7,350 feet above sea level, loftiest point along the highway (you can take a cable car to the top). You'll find restaurants, hotels, and cafés. In the spring, edelweiss grows in the surrounding fields. After crossing the pass, you'll descend to the little resort of Canazei, then much later pass by sea-blue Carezza Lake.

3. BOLZANO

177 miles NE of Milan, 298 miles N of Rome, 95 miles N of Verona

GETTING THERE By Train Bolzano is a 2½-hour train ride north of Verona; a one-way fare is 8,700 lire ($6.85). The Brenner Pass and Innsbruck are 1½ hours north of Bolzano.

By Bus Bolzano can be reached by bus from Cortina d'Ampezzo (see above). Four buses a day make the 3½-hour trip at a one-way cost of 13,800 lire ($10.85) per person.

By Car From Trent (see below), continue north to Bolzano on A22; or head west from Cortina d'Ampezzo along Route 48 until you reach the signposted junction of Route 241, which covers the final circuitous lap into Bolzano.

ESSENTIALS Bolzano's **telephone area code** is 0471. The **Tourist Information Center** is at piazza Walther 8 (tel. 970660).

The terminus of the Great Dolomite Road (or the gateway, depending on your approach), Bolzano is a town of mixed blood, reflecting the long rule that Austria enjoyed until 1919. Many names, including that of the town (Bozen), appear in German. As the recipient of considerable Brenner Pass traffic (55 miles north), the city is a melting pot of Italians and both visitors and residents from the Germanic lands. The capital of a province of the same name, Bolzano lies in the center of the Alto Adige region. It is traversed by two rivers, the Isarco and Talvera, one of which splits the town into two sections.

Bolzano is a modern industrial town, yet a worthwhile sightseeing attraction in its own right. It has many esplanades for promenading along the river. The most interesting street is the colonnaded via dei Portici. You can begin your stroll down this street of old buildings at either **piazza Municipio** or **piazza delle Erbe**, the latter a fruit market for the orchards of the province.

Bolzano makes a good headquarters for exploring the Dolomites and the scenic surroundings, such as **Renon** (Ritten in German) on the alpine plateau, with its cog train; the village of **San Genesio**, reached by cable north of Bolzano; and **Salten**, 4,355 feet up, an alpine tableland.

WHERE TO STAY

EXPENSIVE

LUNA MONDSCHEIN, via Piave 15, 39100 Bolzano. Tel. 0471/975642.
   Fax 0471/975577. 74 rms (all with bath or shower). TV TEL **Bus:** 1.
$ Rates: 90,000 lire ($70.65) single; 135,000 lire ($106) double. Breakfast 8,000 lire ($6.30) extra. DC, MC, V. **Parking:** 8,000 lire ($6.30).

S Comfortable accommodations are offered in an establishment that combines old-fashioned service with modern amenities. The interior has high ceilings, many of them coffered or adorned with plaster detailing. There's also lots of exposed wood and a combination of up-to-date furniture with copies of the 19th-century accessories. Some rooms contain minibars.

The restaurant, which spills over into a garden section in summer, is one of the best in town. It's closed every Sunday, and full meals begin at 30,000 lire ($23.55) per person.

PARK HOTEL LAURIN, via Laurino 4, 39100 Bolzano. Tel. 0471/ 980500. Fax 0471/970953. 108 rms (all with bath). A/C MINIBAR TV TEL **Bus:** 1.

$ Rates: 145,000 lire ($113.85) single; 195,000 lire ($153.10) double. Breakfast 18,500 lire ($14.50) extra. AE, DC, MC, V. **Parking:** 20,000 lire ($15.70).

★ A choice place to stay, the Park Laurin captures the glamour of the past. It's the only superior first-class hotel in Bolzano, and the large bedrooms are well furnished. The private garden is dominated by old shade trees and a flagstone-enclosed swimming pool. Guests are drawn to the high-beamed and spacious lounge, with its brass chandeliers and its groupings of antiques and reproductions, as well as its baronial fireplace and deeply set windows.

The garden terrace is a sun pocket, ideal for lunches or breakfast. The evening meals are served in the interior dining room to the accompaniment of a softly playing orchestra or in the restaurant in the garden with its comfortable open-air American bar. A lunch or dinner begins at 60,000 lire ($47.10) per person.

GRIFONE-GREIF, piazza Walther 7, 39100 Bolzano. Tel. 0471/977056. Fax 0471/980613. 131 rms (all with bath), 4 suites. MINIBAR TV TEL **Bus:** 1.

$ Rates (including breakfast): 170,000 lire ($133.45) single; 240,000 lire ($188.40) double; from 450,000 lire ($353.25) suite. AE, DC, MC, V. **Parking:** 20,000 lire ($15.70).

Strategically placed on piazza Walther with its Salzburg spirit of ornate buildings and open-air cafés, the Grifone-Greif has a traditional look out front, where there's a sidewalk café under a canopy. In the rear, however, is a garden swimming pool and a revamped modern facade with upper-floor balconies. The rooms vary in size and amenities, although all are comfortable and well maintained.

In fair weather, you can dine in the open-air restaurant, sheltered by a canopy. Excellent South Tyrolean and Italian meals are served in a garden atmosphere.

MODERATE

HOTEL ALPI, via Alto Adige 35, 39100 Bolzano. Tel. 0471/970535. Fax 0471/970535. 110 rms (all with bath). A/C MINIBAR TV TEL **Bus:** 1.

$ Rates (including breakfast): 95,000 lire ($74.60) single; 138,000 lire ($108.35) double. AE, DC, MC, V. **Parking:** 14,000 lire ($11).

The exterior of this tastefully contemporary hotel is dotted with recessed balconies, large aluminum-framed windows, and the flags of many nations. The spacious public rooms are richly covered with paneling, exposed stone, and ceramic wall sculptures, which, with the comfortable upholstered seating areas, make for a pleasant hotel. In the commercial center of town, the hotel has a bar, a restaurant, a well-trained staff, and cozy rooms. Meals begin at 35,000 lire ($27.50) in the hotel's restaurant.

SCALA HOTEL STIEGL, via Brennero 11 (Brennerstrasse 11), 39100 Bolzano. Tel. 0471/976222. Fax 0471/976222. 60 rms (all with bath). **Bus:** 1.

$ Rates: 70,000 lire ($54.95) single; 95,000–105,000 lire ($74.55–$82.45) double. Breakfast 12,000 lire ($9.40) extra. **Parking:** 8,000 lire ($6.30).

The Scala is one of the best of the middle-bracket hotels of Bolzano. Its trilingual staff speaks fluent English, among other languages, and keeps the interior spotless. The neobaroque yellow-and-white facade is well maintained, with plenty of ornamentation scattered symmetrically over its five-story expanse. On the premises is an outdoor pool, plus a summer-garden restaurant specializing in Tyrolean dishes. The hotel affords easy access to the train station and the historic center of town. The rooms are well furnished, and some contain minibars. Meals begin at 32,000 lire ($25.10). The hotel has parking spaces for 50 cars.

WHERE TO DINE

DA ABRAMO, piazza Gries 16 (Grieserplatz 16). Tel. 280141.
   Cuisine: MEDITERRANEAN. **Reservations:** Recommended. **Bus:** 1.
$ Prices: Appetizers 12,000–14,000 lire ($9.40–$11); main courses 18,000–20,000 lire ($14.15–$15.70). AE, V.
   Open: Lunch Mon–Sat 12:30–2:30pm; dinner Mon–Sat 7:30–9:30pm.
The most elegant restaurant in Bolzano took great pains to introduce a chic modern airiness to its physical decor. In a sienna-colored villa across the river from the historic center of town, the restaurant offers a summer garden covered with vine arbors, plus a labyrinthine arrangement of rooms. The accessories include brass lamps. Full meals range upward from 42,000 lire ($32.95) and might include, depending on the mood of the chef, veal in a sauce of tuna and capers, roast quail with polenta, fish soup, spaghetti carbonara, vegetarian antipasti, codfish Venice style, a vast array of shellfish and seafood, tagliatelle with prosciutto, and beefsteak flambé with cognac.

ZUR KAISERKRON, piazza della Mostra 1 (Mustergasse 1). Tel. 970770.
   Cuisine: CENTRAL EUROPEAN. **Reservations:** Recommended at lunch.
   Bus: 1.
$ Prices: Appetizers 9,500–12,500 lire ($7.45–$9.80); main courses 18,000–24,000 lire ($14.15–$18.85). AE, DC, MC.
   Open: Lunch Mon–Sat 12:30–2:30pm; dinner Mon–Fri 7:30–9:30pm.
The food is excellent, the decor appealing, and the management preserves the bicultural ambience for which Bolzano is known. The restaurant is housed in an Austrian yellow-and-white baroque building a block from the cathedral. For warm-weather dining, there's a canopy-covered wooden platform in front surrounded with greenery. You'll be welcomed by a member of the staff and ushered to a table under vaulted ceilings and wrought-iron chandeliers. Favorite dishes include an assortment of alpine dried beef, beef goulash with polenta, trout with salmon, spaghetti with clams, creamy soups, and a range of other frequently changing items.

MARETSCH RESTAURANT, Castel Maretsch. Tel. 979439.
   Cuisine: ITALIAN/CENTRAL EUROPEAN. **Reservations:** Recommended.
   Bus: 1.
$ Prices: Appetizers 8,000–9,000 lire ($6.30–$7.05); main courses 18,000–22,000 lire ($14.15–$17.25). AE, DC, MC.
   Open: Lunch Mon–Sat 9am–3pm; dinner Mon–Sat 5:30–11pm. **Closed:** Jan and Aug.
This restaurant is part of a modern conference complex set in a medieval castle, a 5-minute walk from most of the major hotels in the old town. The location is near the Talfer Promenade in a tranquil setting of vineyards. Lunch and dinner start at 40,000 ($31.40). The food is both traditional Italian and Central European. You might prefer the chef's goulash or a bollito misto, a selection of boiled meats (including tongue), covered with an herb sauce. Guests dine under vaulted ceilings in cooler weather, enjoying the outside tables in the castle courtyard in summer.

CHEZ FREDERIC, via Armando Diaz 12. Tel. 271011.
   Cuisine: INTERNATIONAL. **Reservations:** Recommended. **Bus:** 1.
$ Prices: Appetizers 7,000–10,000 lire ($5.50–$7.85); main courses 15,000–20,000 lire ($11.80–$15.70). AE, DC.
   Open: Lunch Mon–Sat 12:30–2:30pm; dinner Mon–Fri 7:30–9:30pm. **Closed:** July 5–27.
Chez Frédéric is altogether exceptional for the area, serving some of the finest food outside the major hotel dining rooms. Located across the river, it is decorated in an inviting style. In summer, tables are set outside in the courtyard. Everything is cooked to order and served in an efficient manner. To begin your meal, I recommend speck, a

Tyrolean dish of meat sliced razor-thin, the color of dried beef. As a main dish, the pepper steak is also good, or you may prefer the chateaubriand for two people. The chef's recommendation, and I concur, is fegato col uvetta (liver with grapes). Desserts are rich, fattening, and smooth. Depending on your beef selection, the average meal here will range in price from 32,000 lire to 48,000 lire ($25.10 to $37.70).

4. MERANO

18 miles NW of Bolzano, 202 miles N of Milan

GETTING THERE   By Train   Go to Bolzano (see above) and then travel on by bus (see below).

By Bus   From Bolzano, buses run frequently throughout the day northwest to Merano, at a one-way fare of 3,400 lire ($2.65). Buses leave from via Perathoner 4 (tel. 971259) in Bolzano.

By Car   From Bolzano, head northwest along Route 38.

ESSENTIALS   The **telephone area code** for Merano is 0473. The **Tourist Information Center** is at corso della Libertà 45 (tel. 35223).

Once the capital of Tyrol (before Innsbruck), Merano (Meran) was ceded to Italy at the end of World War I, but it retains much of its Austrian heritage. In days gone by it was one of the most famous resorts in Europe, drawing kings and queens and a vast entourage from many countries, who were attracted to the alpine retreat by the grape cure. (The eating of luscious Merano grapes is supposed to have medicinal value.) After a slump, Merano now enjoys popularity, especially in autumn when the grapes are harvested. Before the last war Merano also became known for its radioactive waters, in which ailing bathers supposedly secured relief for everything from gout to rheumatism.

The Passirio River cuts through the town (and along it are many promenades, evoking the heyday of the resorts of the 19th century). In the Valley of the Adige at the foot of Kuchelberg, Merano makes a good base for excursions in several directions, particularly to **Avelengo.** A bus from Sandplatz will deliver you to a funicular connection, in which you can ascend 3,500 feet above sea level to Avelengo, with its splendid vista and mountain hotels and pensions.

Merano is richly endowed with tourist facilities and attractions, such as open-air swimming pools at its Lido, tennis courts, and a race track.

WHAT TO SEE & DO

On the Tappeinerweg promenade, the **Museo Agricolo Brunnenburg,** Ezra Pound Weg 6 (tel. 93533), is housed in a castle owned by the daughter and grandson of Ezra Pound, who lived in Merano from 1958 to 1964. The museum has displays of Tyrolean country life, including a blacksmith's shop and a grain mill. There are also ethnology exhibits, plus a room dedicated to Pound. Open Wednesday through Monday from 9:30 to 11:30am and 2 to 5pm. Admission is 2,000 lire ($1.55) for adults, 1,000 lire (80¢) for children. You can reach the castle by taking bus no. 3 to Dorf Tirol, every hour on the hour from Merano, or by climbing the Tappeinerweg. The house is closed November through March.

WHERE TO STAY
VERY EXPENSIVE

KURHOTEL PALACE, via Cavour 2 (Cavourstrasse 2), 39012 Merano. Tel. 0473/211300. Fax 0473/34181. 124 rms (all with bath), 7 suites. A/C MINIBAR TV TEL **Bus:** 3.
$ Rates (including breakfast): 155,000–185,000 lire ($121.70–$145.25) single;

260,000–320,000 lire ($204.10–$251.20) double; from 380,000 lire ($298.30) suite. Special packages for health and diet available. AE, DC, MC, V. **Parking:** Free. **Closed:** Jan 6–Mar 19 and Nov 10–Dec 18.

This deluxe hotel is a turn-of-the-century re-creation of a baroque palace set into the most beautiful formal gardens in town. The ceilings of the gilt- and cream-colored public rooms are supported by Corinthian columns similar to the ones adorning the yellow-and-white façade. The furniture, in part, seems to be good-quality copies of 18th-century designs, and the crystal chandeliers are massive. From the rear terrace there's a view of the large marble slabs that have been arranged into a chessboard on the lawn. From there you'll be able to see the groupings of small cherubs set onto the hotel's ornate roofline that appear to be squinting down into the gardens. These contain a free-form pool whose waters flow below a tile annex for an indoor extension of the swimming area.

Many of the bedrooms have their own stone or wrought-iron balconies, which look over roses, palms, and palmettos. Although it has been in business for more than 80 years, the hotel has up-to-date comforts. Accommodations vary widely, and rates depend on the size, season, and view.

Dining/Entertainment: Guests gather in the piano bar before going into the Tiffany Grill restaurant, where both a regional and international cuisine are served, with meals costing from 50,000 lire ($39.25).

Services: Room service, baby-sitting, laundry, valet; medical supervision for spa, health, and fitness programs.

Facilities: Fitness equipment, indoor pool, sauna, solarium, hot whirlpool, thermal treatments.

EXPENSIVE

GRAND HOTEL BRISTOL, via Ottone Huber 14, 39012 Merano. Tel. 0473/49500. Fax 0473/49299. 140 rms (all with bath). TV TEL **Bus:** 1A or 1B.
$ Rates (including breakfast): 110,000 lire ($86.35) single; 155,000 lire ($121.70) double. AE, DC, MC, V. **Parking:** 8,000 lire ($6.30). **Closed:** Nov–Feb.

The rooms here are large and well furnished, each with its own private bath or shower (some contain minibars). Some are equipped with ornate pieces, and private balconies envelop the building. While the rooms are comfortable and the baths handsomely tiled (and equipped with bidets), it is the roof garden with the heated swimming pool and view that holds the attraction. A garden with centenary trees surrounds the building. Among its facilities, the hotel offers health cures, spa and cosmetics treatments, and special dietary preparation. The food at the open-air restaurant has been highly praised.

HOTEL MERANERHOF, via Manzoni 1 (Manzinistrasse 1), 39012 Merano. Tel. 0473/30230. Fax 0473/33312. 70 rms (all with bath). A/C TV TEL **Bus:** 1A or 1B.
$ Rates (including breakfast): 103,000 lire ($80.85) single; 200,000 lire ($157) double. AE, DC, MC, V. **Parking:** 12,000 lire ($9.40).

This centrally located, rather fashionable hotel is on the banks of the river, near one of the popular pedestrian promenades of Merano. The hotel contains an elegant bar that curves around one of the sitting rooms. The ceiling of the lobby is supported by stone columns into which elaborately curlicued bas-reliefs have been carved. There's lots of gilding on the ornate Austrian furniture, and modern crystal chandeliers cast a prismatic glow over everything. A swimming pool set into the lawn in back of the hotel beckons, and a series of massage facilities are available upon request. The hotel rents well-furnished bedrooms, each with private bath or shower.

MODERATE

HOTEL AURORA, Kurpromenade 38, 39012 Merano. Tel. 0473/33028. 35 rms (all with bath or shower), 3 suites. TV TEL **Bus:** 1A or 1B.

$ Rates (including breakfast): 62,000–83,000 lire ($48.65–$65.15) single; 108,000–162,000 lire ($84.80–$127.15) double; from 180,000 lire ($141.30) suite. AE, DC, MC, V. **Closed:** Nov 20–Mar 10.

This appealing hotel is set behind a salmon-colored facade on the most popular pedestrian promenade in town. Many rooms have an angled balcony, the better to enjoy river views. Some of the German-speaking guests congregate in a sunny café terrace, or when that's full, in the light-grained sitting room. The most popular place in town, the hotel offers comfortably furnished rooms. The hotel serves good Tyrolean and Italian meals, but only for guests, many of whom opt to take the half-board arrangement.

INEXPENSIVE

HOTEL GARNI SEISENEGG, via Giardini 1 (Gartenstrasse 1), 39012 Merano. Tel. 0473/37212. Fax 0473/37038. 37 rms (26 with bath). TEL **Bus:** 1A or 1B.

$ Rates (including breakfast): 50,000 lire ($39.25) single without bath, 65,000 lire ($51) single with bath; 95,000 lire ($74.60) double without bath, 115,000 lire ($90.30) double with bath. No credit cards. **Parking:** 8,000 lire ($6.30). **Closed:** Nov 5–Mar 15.

The usual way of reaching this family-run hotel is via a narrow walled alley from the center of town. The path will lead you into the private walled garden of a modern hotel set amid towering trees. Bedrooms are comfortably and pleasantly furnished. From the sun terrace, you can see the steeple of a 15th-century church in the nearby commercial part of town, and hear a rushing stream and the chattering of birds. The hotel was built in 1961 on the site of a 17th-century house, whose walls were completely incorporated into the new structure. Breakfast is the only meal served.

WHERE TO DINE

ANDREA, in the Villa Mozart, via Galilei 44. Tel. 37400.
Cuisine: TYROLEAN. **Reservations:** Required. **Bus:** 1A or 1B.
$ Prices: Appetizers 13,000–22,000 lire ($10.20–$17.25); main courses 26,000–35,000 lire ($20.40–$27.50); seven-course menu dégustation 85,000 lire ($66.75). AE, DC, MC, V.
Open: Lunch Tues–Sun 11am–2pm; dinner Tues–Sun 7:30–10pm. **Closed:** Jan 7–Feb 15.

This restaurant is the most outstanding feature of Andreas Hellrigl's sophisticated hostelry, where creative-cookery classes are conducted. It is known to gastronomes on both sides of the Alps as one of the most respected dining spots in the region. The chef's expertise shows in the haute cuisine, based on the dishes of the South Tyrol. His specialties, adapted to modern palates, include fresh asparagus covered with a chervil-flavored cream sauce, beef bordelaise with a purée of fresh parsley, and a ragoût of snails flavored with basil and served with polenta. The menu might also include marinated salmon, Angus beef with parsley purée and red wine sauce, and cheese gnocchi with fruit sauces. Laden with atmosphere, the cozy dining room is directed by Oberrauch Walter and Nothdurfter Pepi. Expect to spend 80,000 lire to 100,000 lire ($62.80 to $78.50) for a meal. The restaurant enjoys a following among locals and visitors alike. Cooking courses are offered for those wishing to learn how an expert does it.

FLORA, via Portici 75. Tel. 33484.
Cuisine: ITALIAN. **Reservations:** Required. **Bus:** 1A or 1B.
$ Prices: Appetizers 10,000–25,000 lire ($7.85–$19.65); main courses 20,000–30,000 lire ($15.70–$23.55). AE, DC, MC, V.
Open: Dinner only Mon–Sat 7pm–midnight. **Closed:** Jan 15–Feb 28.

Flora serves a sophisticated Tyrolean and Italian cuisine of consistently good quality in its conservative, elegant confines. Full meals, 70,000 lire to 90,000 lire ($54.95 to $70.65), are likely to include ravioli stuffed with chicken and exotic mushrooms, pasta blackened with squid ink, rack of lamb cooked in a shell of salt, and marinated trout with fine herbs. The menu changes seasonally.

5. TRENT [TRENTO]

36 miles S of Bolzano, 144 miles NE of Milan

GETTING THERE   By Train   Trent enjoys excellent rail connections. It lies on the Bologna–Verona–Brenner–Munich rail link, and trains pass through here day and night. The trip from Milan takes 2 hours 40 minutes, and to reach Trent from Rome in the south is a 7-hour rail journey. Trains also connect Trent with Bolzano (see above) at the rate of one every hour. Seven trains per day make the 3½-hour run from Venice.

By Bus   It's better to take the train to Trent and then rely on local buses once you get there. The local bus station is on via Pozzo (tel. 983627 for schedules), which has services to such places as Riva del Garda (see Chapter 16). Buses to Riva arrive during the day at the rate of one per hour.

By Car   From Bolzano (see above), head south to Trent along A22. From Verona, continue north to Trent on A22.

ESSENTIALS   The **telephone area code** for Trent is 0461. The **Tourist Information Center** is at via Alfieri 4 (tel. 983880).

A northern Italian city that basks in its former glory, this medieval town on the left bank of the Adige is known throughout the world as the host of the Council of Trent (1545–63). Beset with difficulties, such as the rising tide of "heretics," the Ecumenical Council convened at Trent, a step that led to the Counter-Reformation. Trent lies on the main rail line from the Brenner Pass, and many visitors like to stop off here before journeying farther south into Italy.

WHAT TO SEE & DO

The city has much old charm, offset somewhat by unbridled industrialization. For a quick glimpse of the old town, head for **piazza del Duomo,** dominated by the **Cathedral of Trent.** Built in the Romanesque style and much restored over the years, it dates from the 12th century. It's open daily from 6:30am to noon and 2:30 to 8pm. In the center of the square is a mid-18th-century *Fountain of Neptune,* armed with a trident.

The ruling prince-bishops of Trent, who held sway until they were toppled by the French in the early 19th century, resided at the medieval **Castello del Buonconsiglio** (tel. 233770), reached from via Bernardo Clesio 3. Now the old castle has been turned into a provincial museum, with a collection of paintings and fine art, some quite ancient, including early medieval mosaics. The **Museo del Risorgimento,** also at the castle, is a museum containing mementoes related to the period of national unification between 1796 and 1948. The museums are open Tuesday through Sunday from 9am to noon and 2 to 5:30pm (to 5pm in winter). Admission is 2,000 lire ($1.55) for adults, 500 lire (40¢) for children.

Trent still makes a good base for exploring the sports resort of **Monte Bondone,** with its panoramic view (chair lifts), about 22 miles from the city center; **Paganella,** slightly more than 12 miles from Trent (the summit is nearly 7,000 feet high); and the **Brenta Dolomites.** The latter excursion, which will require at least a day for a good look, will reward you with some of the finest mountain scenery in Italy. From Trent, you'll first pass by **Lake Toblino,** then travel a winding, circuitous road for much of the way, past jagged boulders. A 10-minute detour from the main road is suggested at the turnoff to the Genova valley, with its untamed scenery—at least to the thunderous

Nardis waterfall. A good stopover point is the fast-rising little resort of Madonna di Campiglio.

WHERE TO STAY
EXPENSIVE

ALBERGO ACCADEMIA, vicolo Colico 6, 38100 Trento. Tel. 0461/ 233600. Fax 0461/230174. 43 rms (all with bath), 2 suites. MINIBAR TV TEL **Bus:** 2.
$ **Rates:** 160,000 lire ($125.60) single; 220,000 lire ($172.70) double; from 420,000 lire ($329.70) suite. Breakfast 20,000 lire ($15.70) extra. AE, DC, MC, V. **Parking:** Free on the street.
This is an alpine inn in the center of town made up of three buildings that have been joined to make a comfortable and attractive hostelry. One of the buildings is believed to be of 11th- or 12th-century origin, based on a brick wall similar to the city walls found during renovation work. According to legend, the older part of the Accademia housed church leaders who attended the Council of Trent in the 16th century. The inn stands behind the renaissance Church of Santa Maria Maggiore. The rooms are done in light natural wood. Thirteen rooms are air-conditioned. The suite at the top of the house has a terrace from which you can see the town and the mountains.
The alpine influence is carried out in the bar and the restaurant. You can get a good meal for two, with a bottle of wine, for 60,000 lire ($47.10).

GRAND HOTEL TRENTO, via Alfieri 3, 38100 Trento. Tel. 0461/981010. Fax 0461/981796. 94 rms (all with bath). MINIBAR TV TEL **Bus:** 2.
$ **Rates** (including breakfast): 170,000 lire ($133.45) single; 220,000 lire ($172.70) double. AE, DC, MC, V. **Parking:** 8,000 lire ($6.30).
Part of a chain, this hotel has an L-shaped floor plan with one curved extension stretching toward the city park just across the street. The interior has everything you'd expect in a commercial hotel, including a decor of gray and red marble floors, contemporary furniture, a prominent and comfortable bar, and a restaurant called Al Caminetto, with an adjoining terrace café. Each of the well-furnished rooms contains a radio. The hotel is a 1-minute walk from the station.

HOTEL BUONCONSIGLIO, via Romagnosistrasse 16–18, 38100 Trento. Tel. 0461/980089. Fax 0461/980038. 46 rms (all with bath), 1 suite. A/C MINIBAR TV TEL **Bus:** 2.
$ **Rates** (including breakfast): 130,000 lire ($102.05) single; 180,000 lire ($141.30) double; from 250,000 lire ($196.25) suite. AE, DC, MC, V. **Parking:** 7,000 lire ($5.50).
The Hotel Buonconsiglio is conveniently located on a busy street in the center of town near the railway station. The bigger-than-life-size sculptures (one of which is the hotel's namesake), the abstract modern paintings, and the warmly inviting color scheme contributes to the coziness of the lobby area. The staff speaks English. One of the bigger public rooms contains a bar. The accommodations are comfortable and well decorated.

MODERATE

HOTEL AMERICA, via Torre Verde 50, 38100 Trento. Tel. 0461/983010. Fax 0461/230603. 50 rms (all with bath). TV TEL **Bus:** 2.
$ **Rates:** 83,500 lire ($65.55) single; 118,300 lire ($92.85) double. AE, DC, MC, V. **Parking:** 10,000 lire ($7.85).
This simple, attractive, and centrally located hotel in front of the rail station has iron balconies and a vine-wreathed arbor sheltering the main entrance. Rooms are clean and comfortable. The owner worked in America for a while before naming the hotel after one of his favorite places.

HOTEL MONACO, via Torre d'Augusto 25, 38100 Trento. Tel. 0461/ 983060. Fax 0461/983060. 50 rms (all with bath). TV TEL **Bus:** 2.

$ Rates: 70,000 lire ($54.95) single; 100,000 lire ($78.50) double. Breakfast 7,000 lire ($5.50) extra. V. **Parking:** 7,000 lire ($5.50).

If you look up at the towering cliffs that surround this modern hotel in the center of town, you'll get the idea that you're in the bottom of a rock quarry. That doesn't detract from the comfortable accommodations in this three-story hotel with its prominent balconies and its strong horizontal lines. There is a sidewalk terrace, a bar, a restaurant called La Predara, and ample parking.

WHERE TO DINE

RESTAURANT CHIESA, Parco San Marco. Tel. 238766.

Cuisine: TRENTINE. **Reservations:** Recommended. **Bus:** 2.

$ Prices: Appetizers 10,000–15,000 lire ($7.85–$11.80); main courses 20,000–30,000 lire ($15.70–$23.55). AE, DC, MC, V.

Open: Lunch Mon–Sat 12:30–2:30pm; dinner Mon–Tues and Thurs–Sat 7:30–9:30pm. **Closed:** Aug 11–25.

The Restaurant Chiesa offers the largest array of dishes I've ever seen made with apples. Owners Sergio and Isabella Chiesa recognized that Eve's favorite fruit, which grows more abundantly around Trent than practically anywhere else, was the base of dozens of traditional recipes. After augmenting them with a few creations of their own, they established a popular restaurant in 1974 in what had been the 17th-century home of Count Wolkenstein. The restaurant stands at the back of a large walled garden (you'll have to ring the bell set into the iron gate before gaining access). Once inside, you can choose one of the three large, rustically appointed rooms, with ceiling beams, stone columns, racks of regional pottery, a central serving area, and baskets and barrels filled with the owners' favorite fruit.

Specialties include risotto with apple, apple strudel, liver pâté with apple, apple cocktail Eva (made with beef and spices), filet of perch with apple, and a range of other well-prepared specialties (a few of which, believe it or not, do not contain apples). However, several meat dishes are cooked in cider. A rich dessert might be followed by apple cider.

BIRRERIA FORST, via Oss-Mazzurana 38. Tel. 235590.

Cuisine: TRENTINE. **Reservations:** Recommended. **Bus:** 2.

$ Prices: Appetizers 6,000–7,000 lire ($4.70–$4.50); main courses 8,000–14,000 lire ($6.30–$11). AE, DC, MC, V.

Open: Lunch Tues–Sun noon–2pm; dinner Tues–Sun 7–10pm.

This is a good budget choice set in a redesigned palazzo in the center of Trent near piazza del Duomo. The ground-floor level focuses around a horseshoe-shaped chrome-covered bar behind which beer on tap and varieties of the local wine are served. Below a high ceiling fashioned from half-rounded beams and rough planks, diners enjoy pizzas or meals from 25,000 lire ($19.65). If you don't want to eat in the bar section, there is a separate dining area at the top of a curved staircase at the back of the room. Menu specialties include mixed grill of the house, tripe parmigiana, goulash with potatoes, speck with mushrooms, and typical Italian specialties. After 5:30pm you can order pizzas.

CHAPTER 16

THE LAKE DISTRICT

- **WHAT'S SPECIAL ABOUT THE LAKE DISTRICT**
1. **LAKE GARDA**
2. **LAKE COMO**
3. **LAKE MAGGIORE**

With its flower-bedecked promenades, lemon trees and villas, parks and gardens, and crystal-clear blue waters, a lake-district holiday may sound a bit dated, like a penny-farthing bicycle or an aspidistra in the bay window. But the lakes—notably Garda, Como, and Maggiore—continue to form one of the most enchanting splashes of scenery in northern Italy.

Like the lake district in northwestern England, the Italian lakes have attracted poets and writers, everybody from Goethe to Gabriele d'Annunzio. But after World War II the Italian lakes seemed to be largely the domain of matronly English and German types. In my more recent swings through the district, however, I've noticed an increasing joie de vivre and a rising influx of the 25 to 40 age group, particularly at such resorts as Limone on Lake Garda. Even if your time is limited, you'll want to have at least a look at Lake Garda.

SEEING THE LAKE DISTRICT
SUGGESTED ITINERARIES
Lake Garda

Day 1: Spend the day wandering the streets of the historic old town of Sirmione and overnight here.

Day 2: Head up the western shore of the lake for an overnight visit to Gardone Riviera, which you can use as a base for exploring Vittoriale, the former home of the poet Gabriele d'Annunzio, lover of the great actress, Eleonora Duse.

Day 3: Continue along the western shore of the lake until you reach Riva del Garda, a major resort along Lake Garda and an ideal place to relax or go boating on the lake.

Lake Como

Day 1: Use the city of Como mainly as a transportation hub, especially if your gateway is Milan; then continue along the eastern shore of the lake until you reach Bellagio, where you can overnight. In the afternoon visit Villa Serbelloni.

Day 2: Cross from Bellagio to Tremezzo by boat and spend the night on the western shore. From Tremezzo, visit Villa Carlotta.

Lake Maggiore

Days 1–2: Stresa, on the western shore of the lake, makes the best base. Use it to explore Isola Bella (Beautiful Island), Isola Madre (Mother Island), and Isola dei Pescatori (Fishermen's Island), all of which can be done in one busy day. Spend

WHAT'S SPECIAL ABOUT THE LAKE DISTRICT

Great Towns & Villages

☐ Riva del Garda on Lake Garda, the oldest and most traditional resort along the lake.

☐ Sirmione, jutting out 2½ miles into Lake Garda and noted for its thermal baths.

☐ Bellagio, sitting on a promontory at the point where Lake Como forks, a town rich in aristocratic memories.

☐ Stresa, on the western shore of Lake Maggiore, the best center for exploring this lake of great natural beauty.

Ace Attractions

☐ The Borromean Islands, Lake Maggiore, whose major sight is Isola Bella (Beautiful Island), dominated by a 17th-century palace.

☐ Villa Carlotta, the most visited attraction at Lake Como, dating from 1847 and set in an exotic garden.

Parks & Gardens

☐ Villa Tartanto, Lake Maggiore, a botanical garden spread over more than 50 acres of the Castagnola Promontory.

Museums

☐ Vittoriale, the former home of the poet and military adventurer, Gabriele d'Annunzio, outside Gardone Riviera, on Lake Garda.

most of Day 2 wandering along the acres of plant-filled acres of the Villa Taranto, north of Stresa.

GETTING THERE

The airplane gateway to the region is Milan (see Chapter 17). A car is the best way to tour the lakes, as public transportation is inadequate. Motorists take Route S572 to travel along the western and southern lakefronts of Garda. Route S45bis goes along the northern rim of the western shore, while Route S249 snakes along the eastern side of the lake. To go around Lake Como, follow S340 along the western shore, or S36 on the eastern shore. Route 32 leads north from Novara to the western shore of Lake Maggiore (the highway becomes 33 as it heads for the major center on the lake, Stresa). Route 629 will take you along the less visited eastern shore of Maggiore.

You can reach Como by train. Trains from Milan arrive in Como at the rate of one every 30 minutes, and the one-way fare is 2,100 lire ($1.65). Buses connect Sirmione every 30 minutes with Verona and Brescia; trips take 1 hour from either point, at a one-way fare of 4,000 lire ($3.15).

1. LAKE GARDA

The most easterly of the northern Italian lakes, Garda is also the largest, stretching 32 miles in length and 11½ miles in width at its fattest point. Sheltered by mountains, its scenery, especially the part on the western shore that reaches from Limone to Salo, has often been compared to that of the Mediterranean; you'll see olive, orange, and lemon trees, even palms. The almost transparent lake is ringed with four art cities: Trent to the northeast, Brescia to the west, Mantua (Mantova) to the south, and Verona to the east.

The eastern side of the lake is more rugged, less trampled, but the resort-studded western strip is far more glamorous to the first-timer. On the western side, a circuitous road skirts the lake through one molelike tunnel after another. You can park your car at several secluded belvederes for a panoramic lakeside view. In spring the scenery is splashed with color, everything from wild poppy beds to oleander. Garda is well served by buses, or you can traverse the lake on steamers or motorboats, leaving from a number of harbors.

A WARNING TO MOTORISTS The twisting roads that follow the shores of Lake Garda would be enough to rattle even the most experienced driver. Couple the frightening turns, dimly lit tunnels, and emotional local drivers (who know every bend in the road—and you don't) with convoys of tour buses and trucks that rarely stay in their lane, and you have what might be one of the more frightening drives in Italy.

Be especially careful, and don't be afraid to use your horn around blind curves. Also, be warned that Sunday is an especially risky time to drive, since everyone on the lake and from the nearby cities seems to take to the roads after a long lunch with lots of heady wine.

RIVA DEL GARDA

Some 27 miles southwest of Trent, 105 miles east of Milan, and 124 miles northwest of Venice, astride the narrowing northern point of Garda in the province of Trento, 195 feet above sea level, Riva is the oldest and most traditional resort along the lake. It consists of both an expanding new district and an old town, the latter centered at piazza III Novembre. On the harbor are the **Tower of Apponale,** dating from the 13th century, and the **Rocca,** built in 1124 and once owned by the ruling Scaligeri princes of Verona (it has been turned into a museum).

On the northern banks of the lake, between the Benacense plains and towering mountains, Riva offers the advantages of the Riviera and the Dolomites. Its climate is classically Mediterranean—mild in winter and moderate in summer. Vast areas of rich vegetation combine with the deep blue of the lake. Many come for health cures; others for business conferences, meetings, and fairs. Riva is popular with tour groups from the Germanic lands and from England.

Riva del Garda is linked to the Brenner–Modena motorway (Rovereto Sud/Garda Nord exit) and to the railway (Rovereto station), and is near Verona's Airport Villafranca.

Tourist information is available at the Palazzo dei Congressi, Parco Lido (tel. 554444). The **telephone area code** for Riva del Garda is 0464.

WHERE TO STAY

HOTEL DU LAC ET DU PARC, viale Rovereto 44, 38066 Riva del Garda. Tel. 0464/551500. Fax 0464/555200. 170 rms (all with bath), 8 suites. MINIBAR TV TEL **Bus:** Atesina.

$ Rates: 100,000–120,000 lire ($78.50–$94.20) single; 160,000–250,000 lire ($125.60–$196.25) double; from 280,000 lire ($219.80) suite. Breakfast 15,000 lire ($11.80) extra. AE, DC, MC, V. **Parking:** Free. **Closed:** Oct 20–Apr 1.

This deluxe Spanish-style hotel is the best in town. Set back from the busy road behind a shrub-filled parking lot dotted with stone cherubs, the hotel has several outbuildings closer to the street containing restaurants and additional rooms. The interior of the main building is freshly decorated, with arched windows, lots of spacious comfort, and an enclosed and manicured lawn visible from the lobby. There's a huge dining room, two additional restaurants, an attractive bar, unusual accessories, and a comfortably sprawling format, each corner of which gives the impression of being part of a large private home. It was established as a hotel 100 years ago, though the current structure is from 1953. It was renovated by the Zontini family. The well-trained staff speaks a variety of languages, and seems genuinely concerned with the well-being of their guests. A garden stretches behind the hotel, containing a swimming pool, lakeside beach, and two tennis courts. The bedrooms are well furnished, each with private bath or shower, and 54 are air-conditioned.

LIDO PALACE HOTEL, viale Carducci 10, 38066 Riva del Garda. Tel. 0464/552664. Fax 0464/551957. 62 rms (all with bath). A/C TV TEL **Bus:** Atesina.

$ Rates (including breakfast): 135,000 lire ($106) single; 230,000 lire ($180.55) double. AE, DC, MC, V. **Parking:** Free. **Closed:** Nov–Mar 24.

A first-class choice, the Lido Palace is a grand lakeside retreat, surrounded by gardens and only a 5-minute walk to the town center. The formal tree-lined drive reinforces the feeling of entering a private estate. The hotel was completely renovated and reopened in 1983. It has well-maintained rooms with modern furnishings and private bath or shower. A swimming pool is set on the parklike grounds.

HOTEL SOLE, piazza III Novembre no. 35, 38066 Riva del Garda. Tel. 0464/552686. Fax 0464/552811. 52 rms (all with shower or bath), 3 suites. TV TEL **Bus:** Atesina.

$ Rates: 130,000 lire ($102.05) single or double; 130,000 lire to 180,000 lire ($102.05–$141.30) per person for half board. AE, DC, MC, V. **Parking:** Street parking only. **Closed:** Nov to the day before Easter.

The medium-priced Hotel Sole apparently had far-sighted founders who snared the best position on the waterfront. Although rated second class by the government, and charging second-class prices, the hotel has amenities worthy of a first-class rating. It's an overgrown villa and has a large stack of rooms with arched windows and surrounding colonnades. Its interior has time-clinging traditional rooms. The lounge has a beamed ceiling and centers around a cone-sloped hooded fireplace; clusters of antique chairs sit on islands of Oriental carpets. The character and quality of the bedrooms vary considerably according to their position (most of them have views of the lake). Some are almost suites, with living-room areas; the smaller ones are less desirable. Nevertheless, all rooms are comfortable and spotless, and many of them have a minibar. You can dine in the formal interior room or on the flagstone lakeside terrace.

HOTEL LUISE, viale Roverto 9, 38066 Riva del Garda. Tel. 0464/552796. Fax 0464/552796. 58 rms (all with bath). TEL **Bus:** Atesina.

$ Rates (including half board): 75,000–95,000 lire ($58.90–$74.60) per person, double occupancy. MC, V. **Parking:** Free.

This contemporary hotel is a few hundred yards away from the shore of the lake. It has its own free-form swimming pool as well as a nearby tennis court. The paneled interior contains big windows and comfortable furniture. All units are tastefully restrained, with built-in necessities.

HOTEL VENEZIA, viale Roverto 62, 38066 Riva del Garda. Tel. 0464/522216. Fax 0464/556031. 24 rms (all with bath or shower). TV TEL **Bus:** Atesina.

$ Rates (including breakfast): 65,000 lire ($51) single; 130,000 lire ($102.05) double. DC, MC, V. **Parking:** Free. **Closed:** Nov–Mar 9.

One of the most attractive budget-category hotels in town, the Venezia is housed in an angular modern building whose main section is raised on stilts above a private parking lot. The complex is surrounded by trees on a quiet street bordered with flowers and private homes. The reception area is at the top of a flight of red marble steps. There's an attractively landscaped private pool surrounded by palmettos, and a clean and sunny dining room with Victorian reproduction chairs. The rooms are pleasantly furnished.

WHERE TO DINE

Most guests in Riva del Garda dine at their hotels. However, there are a few good independent eateries, none better than the San Marco.

RISTORANTE SAN MARCO, viale Roma 20. Tel. 554477.
   Cuisine: ITALIAN. **Reservations:** Required. **Bus:** Atesina.
$ **Prices:** Appetizers 8,000–9,000 lire ($6.30–$7.05); main courses 18,000–
   20,000 lire ($14.15–$15.70). AE, DC, MC, V.
   Open: Lunch Tues–Sun 12:30–2:30pm; dinner Tues–Sun 7:30–9:30pm.
   Closed: Feb.
The San Marco lies on one of the main shopping streets of the resort, set back from
the lake. If you arrive early for your reserved table, you can enjoy an apéritif at the bar
up front. The food is classically Italian, and the cookery and service are excellent. You
might begin with a pasta selection, such as spaghetti with clams or tortellini with
prosciutto. Many good fish dishes are presented daily, including sole (prepared several
ways) and grilled scampi. Among the meat selections, try the tournedos opera or the
veal cutlet bolognese. The restaurant charges 38,000 lire to 56,000 lire ($29.85 to
$43.95) for a complete dinner. The owners speak English.

LIMONE SUL GARDA

Leaving Riva, the first resort you'll approach while heading south on the western shore
of Lake Garda is Limone Sul Garda, 6 miles south of Riva, 99 miles northeast of
Milan, and 364 miles north of Rome. Characteristic of the shore is the *limonaie,*
hillside terraces of lemon and orange groves. Taking its name from the fruit of the
lemon tree, Limone is one of the liveliest resorts along the lake.
   Snuggling close to the lake, Limone is reached by descending a narrow, steep road.
The village nestles on a narrow hunk of land. Shopkeepers, faced with no building
room, dug right into the rock (in one such resulting grotto, you can get a cavewoman
coiffure).
   For those seeking recreation, there are 2½ miles of beach from which you can
bathe, sail, or surf. Playing fields, tennis courts, minigolf, soccer, and other sports
activities, as well as discos, are available to the visitor who wants to make Limone a
holiday base. The only way to get about is on foot.
   If you're bypassing Limone, you may still want to make a detour south of the
village to the turnoff to **Tignale,** in the hills. You can climb a modern highway to the
town for a sweeping vista of Garda, one of the most scenic spots on the entire lake.
   From April to September, a **Tourist Information Center** is operated at piazzale
Alcide de Gasperi (tel. 954265). The Limone sul Garda **telephone area code** is
0365.

WHERE TO STAY & DINE

HOTEL CAPO REAMOL, strada Statale, 25010 Limone sul Garda. Tel.
   0365/954040. Fax 0365/954262. 60 rms. TEL
$ **Rates** (including half board): 120,000–150,000 lire ($94.20–$117.75) per per-
   son. MC, V. **Parking:** Free. **Closed:** Nov–Mar.
You won't even get a glimpse of this hotel from the main highway between Riva del
Garda and Limone, because it nestles on the side of the lake well below road level. Be
alert to traffic as you pull into a roadside area indicated by a sign 1¼ miles north of
Limone, and then follow the driveway down a steep and narrow hill into a lower-level
parking lot. Since the hotel is built on a series of terraces stretching down to the edge
of the lake, you'll have to go down, not up, to your freshly decorated bedroom after
registering at the reception desk. The bar, restaurant, and sports facilities are on the
lowest level, sheltered from the lakeside breezes by windbreaks. Many of the public
rooms are painted in pastel shades. Clients can swim in the lake or in the pool, and
rent windsurfers on the graveled beach. There's a disco in a tavern that profits, like
everything else in the hotel, from views of the water. The rooms are well furnished,
each with private bath or shower.

HOTEL LE PALME, via Porto 36, 25010 Limone sul Garda. Tel. 0365/
   954681. Fax 0365/954239. 28 rms (all with bath). TEL

$ Rates (including half board): 72,000–81,000 lire ($56.50–$63.60) per person. No credit cards. **Parking:** Free. **Closed:** Nov–Mar.

Completely renovated, this well-known antique Venetian-style villa, with period furniture, stands in the shade of two centuries-old palm trees in the historic center of Limone, opening directly onto the shores of Lake Garda. Although extensively remodeled for the installation of more private baths, this four-star hotel retains many of its original architectural features. The hotel offers well-furnished bedrooms, each individually decorated, containing a radio. On the second floor is a comfortable reading room with a TV set, while on the floor above is a wide terrace in the open air. On the ground floor is a large dining room with decorative sculpture, opening onto a wide terrace where in fair weather you can order meals and drinks. The cuisine, backed up by a good wine list, is excellent. Because of the popularity of the hotel, it's best to make reservations.

GARDONE RIVIERA

In the province of Brescia, 80 miles east of Milan and 20 miles northeast of Brescia, the western shore of Gardone Riviera is well equipped with a number of good hotels and sporting facilities. Its lakeside promenade attracts a wide range of predominantly European tourists for most of the year. When it used to be chic for patrician Italian families to spend their holidays by the lake, many of the more prosperous built elaborate villas not only in Gardone Riviera, but in neighboring Fasano (some of these have been converted to receive guests). The town also has the biggest man-made sight along the lake, which you may want to visit even if you're not lodging for the night.

The **Tourist Information Office** is at corso della Repubblica 35 (tel. 20347). Gardone Riviera's **telephone area code** is 0365.

WHAT TO SEE & DO

Vittoriale (tel. 20130) was once the private home of Gabriele d'Annunzio (1863–1938), the poet and military adventurer, another Italian who believed in *La Dolce Vita,* even when he couldn't afford it. Most of the celebrated events in D'Annunzio's life occurred before 1925, including his love affair with Eleonora Duse and his bravura takeover as a self-styled commander of a territory being ceded to Yugoslavia. In the remaining years of his life and up until he died in the winter before World War II, the national hero lived the grand life at his private estate on Garda.

North of the town, Vittoriale is open March to October, Tuesday through Sunday from 8:30am to 12:30pm and 2 to 6pm (to 5pm in spring and autumn). Admission to the grounds is 5,000 lire ($3.95), or 15,000 lire ($11.80) to the house and grounds. The furnishings and decor passed for avant garde in their day, but evoke the Radio City Music Hall of the '30s when viewed now. D'Annunzio's death mask is of morbid interest, and his bed with a "Big Brother" eye adds a curious touch of Orwell's *1984* (over the poet's bed is a faun casting a nasty sneer). The marble bust of Duse seems sadly out of place, but the manuscripts and old uniforms perpetuate the legend. In July and August, d'Annunzio plays are presented at the amphitheater on the premises. To sum up, it's a bizarre museum to a dated hero of yesteryear. To reach it, head out via Roma, connecting with via Colli.

WHERE TO STAY

GRAND HOTEL, via Zanardelli 72, 25083 Gardone Riviera. Tel. 0365/20261. Fax 0365/22695. 180 rms (all with bath). MINIBAR TV TEL **Bus:** SIA.

$ Rates (including half board): 165,000 lire ($129.55) single; 280,000 lire ($219.80) double. AE, DC, MC, V. **Parking:** Free. **Closed:** Nov–Mar.

When it was built in 1881, this was the most fashionable hotel on the lake and one of the biggest resort hotels of its kind in Europe. Its massive tower is visible for miles around. In World War II the elegantly proportioned bedrooms served as hospital accommodations, first for the Germans and then for the Americans. Later the hotel's reputation as a glamorous resting place convinced Churchill to stay for an extended period in 1948, where he fished, wrote letters, and recovered from his end-of-the-war defeat in the British elections. Today the establishment still boasts a distinguished clientele, including Fiat owner Agnelli, plus habitués who return year after year.

The hotel is one of northern Italy's great reminders of turn-of-the-century grandeur. It isn't difficult to get lost in the almost-endless high-ceilinged corridors, although the focus of your visit will usually bring you back to the main salon, whose sculpted ceilings, parquet floors, and elegantly comfortable leather chairs make it an ideal spot for reading or watching the lake. The dining room offers the kind of good food and old-time splendor that could easily be imagined on a movie set. In fact, an Italian historical film, *Mussolini and I,* was shot here.

All the rooms face the lake, avoiding the roadside noise. A series of garden terraces, a private beach, and a swimming pool are scattered throughout the extensive gardens.

MONTE BALDO HOTEL, 25083 Gardone Riviera. Tel. 0365/20951. 45 rms (all with bath). TEL **Bus:** SIA.
$ Rates (including half board): 75,000–85,000 lire ($58.90–$66.75) per person. AE, DC, MC, V. **Parking:** Free. **Closed:** Oct 21–Apr 19.
This hotel is composed of both an old and a new building separated from one another by a lakeside garden dotted with trees and an oval swimming pool. The older building is adorned with baroque detailing, such as stone demigoddesses looking benignly out over the water and elaborately crafted balustrades. The newer building, clean and attractive in its own right, has recessed balconies and shutters fastened to the white stucco walls. The location is 200 yards from the very heart of town, overlooking the lake.

PARKHOTEL VILLA ELLA, viale dei Colli 32, 25080 Gardone Riviera. Tel. 0365/21030. Fax 0365/290230. 44 rms (all with bath or shower). TEL **Bus:** SIA.
$ Rates (including half board): 70,000–90,000 lire ($54.95–$70.65) per person. AE, DC, MC, V. **Parking:** Free.
This isolated hotel is set amid trees, copies of Roman statues, and lots of flowers. It's on a hillside above the lake, at the end of a winding series of country roads that take you past ruins of older buildings. The architecture is a combination of new and old, and the earliest sections date from 1910. A swimming pool is on the premises, and some units are available in the nearby annex. Rooms are comfortable and well furnished.

BELLEVUE HOTEL, via Zanardelli, 25083 Gardone Riviera. Tel. 0365/20235. Fax 0365/20235. 34 rms (all with bath or shower). **Bus:** Cosino.
$ Rates (including breakfast): 55,000 lire ($43.20) single; 93,000 lire ($73) double. V. **Parking:** Free. **Closed:** Oct 11–Mar.
In the budget range, this villa perched up from the main road has many terraces surrounded by trees and flowers—and an unforgettable view. You can stay here, enjoying the advantages of lakeside villa life. The furnishings in the bedrooms are modern, and everything is kept shipshape. The lounges are comfortable, and the dining room affords a view through the arched windows. The quality of the meals is excellent (no skimpy helpings here).

A Nearby Place to Stay

Fasano del Garda is a satellite resort of Gardone Riviera, lying 1¼ miles to the north. Many prefer it to Gardone.

HOTEL VILLA DEL SOGNO (Villa of Dreams), via Zanardelli, Fasano del Garda, 25080 Gardone Riviera. Tel. 0365/290181. Fax 0365/290230. 34 rms (all with bath), 4 suites. A/C TV TEL **Bus:** Cosino.

$ Rates (including breakfast): 150,000 lire ($117.75) single; 260,000 lire ($204.10) double; from 310,000 lire ($243.35) suite. AE, DC, MC, V. **Parking:** Free. **Closed:** Nov–Apr 14.

This 1920s re-creation of a Renaissance villa offers sweeping views of the lake and a series of spaciously comfortable old-fashioned bedrooms. Set a few hundred yards above the water, with easy access to its private beach, the hotel also has a pool and is ringed with terraces filled with café tables and pots of petunias and geraniums, which combine with bougainvillea and jasmine to brighten and scent the surroundings. The baronial stairway of the interior, as well as many of the ceilings and architectural details, were crafted from wood. The bedrooms are well furnished, each with private bath or shower. Nine rooms are air-conditioned.

WHERE TO DINE

Most visitors to this resort take their meals at their hotels; however, there are some good independent dining selections.

VILLA FIORDALISO, via Zanardelli 132. Tel. 20158.
   Cuisine: ITALIAN. **Reservations:** Required. **Bus:** SIA.
$ Prices: Appetizers 12,000–15,000 lire ($9.40–$11.80); main courses 25,000–30,000 lire ($19.65–$23.55); fixed-price menu 45,000 lire ($35.35) for three courses, 75,000 lire ($58.90) for seven courses. AE, DC, MC, V.
   Open: Lunch Tues–Sun 12:30–2:30pm; dinner Tues–Sat 7:30–9:30pm.
   Closed: Jan–Feb.

This deluxe establishment is a Liberty-style (art nouveau) villa with gardens stretching down to the edge of the lake. It is cited for serving some of the best food in the area at a good price. The chef's cuisine is personalized, likely to include a terrine of eel and salmon in a herb-and-onion sauce, a timbale of rice and shellfish with curry, and several succulent fish and meats grilled over a fire. Not including wine, the bill ranges from 70,000 lire to 75,000 lire ($54.95 to $58.90). This little citadel of fine food has impeccable service to match.

RISTORANTE LA STALLA, strade per il Vittoriale. Tel. 21038.
   Cuisine: INTERNATIONAL. **Reservations:** Recommended. **Bus:** SIA.
$ Prices: Appetizers 10,000–15,000 lire ($7.85–$11.80); main courses 10,000–20,000 lire ($7.85–$15.70). AE, DC, MC, V.
   Open: Lunch Wed–Mon 12:30–2:30pm; dinner Wed–Mon 7:30–9:30pm.
   Closed: Jan.

This charming restaurant is frequented by local families, who sometimes drive for miles just to dine here. In a handcrafted stone building with a brick-columned porch, outdoor tables, and an indoor ambience loaded with rustic artifacts and crowded tables, the restaurant is set in a garden ringed with cypresses on a hill above the lake. To get there, follow the signs up il Vittoriale, as if you were going to d'Annunzio's former home, to a quiet street with singing birds and residential houses. Sunday afternoon is the most crowded time to visit.

Specialties will be recited by one of the uniformed waiters. Depending on the shopping that day, they might include a selection of freshly prepared antipasti, risotto with cuttlefish, or crêpes fondue. Polenta is served with Gorgonzola and walnuts, or you may prefer filet of beef in a beer sauce. Meals cost 38,000 lire to 65,000 lire ($29.85 to $51).

SIRMIONE

Perched at the tip of a narrowing strip of land 80 miles east of Milan and 25 miles east of Brescia, Sirmione juts out for 2½ miles into Lake Garda. Noted for its thermal baths (used in the treatment of deafness), the town is a major resort that blooms in spring and wilts in late autumn. It's reached by heading north after veering from the autostrada connecting Milan and Verona.

The resort was a favorite of Giosue Carducci, the Italian poet who won the Nobel Prize for literature in 1906. In Roman days it was frequented by still another poet, Catullus. Today the **Grotte di Catullo** is the chief sight, an unbeatable combination of Roman ruins and a panoramic view of the lake. You can wander at leisure through the remains of this once-great villa. At the far end of town, the archeological site is open from 9am to an hour before sunset; closed Monday. The admission is 6,000 lire ($4.70) for adults, 3,000 lire ($2.35) for children. For more information, phone 916157. To reach the grotto, take via Catullo.

At the entrance to the town stands the moated 13th-century **castle** that once belonged to the powerful Scaligeri princes of Verona. Architecturally, the medieval castle is distinguished by its crenellated battlements. You can climb to the top and walk the ramparts. It is open (admission free) from 9am to 6:30pm (9am to 4pm in winter); closed Monday.

The **Tourist Information Center** is at viale Marconi 2 (tel. 916245). The **telephone area code** for Sirmione is 030.

WHERE TO STAY

During the peak summer season, motorists have to have a hotel reservation to take their vehicles into the crowded confines of the town. However, there is a large parking area at the entrance to the town. Accommodations are plentiful. The only way to visit Sirmione is on foot. All the hotels below are in the center of town.

Very Expensive

VILLA CORTINE PALACE, via Grotte 12, 25019 Sirmione. Tel. 030/ 916021. Fax 030/916390. 53 rms (all with bath), 2 suites. A/C TV TEL **Bus:** SAIA.

$ Rates (including breakfast): 200,000–240,000 lire ($157–$188.40) single; 310,000–370,000 lire ($243.35–$290.45) double; from 600,000 lire ($471) suite. AE, DC, MC, V. **Parking:** Free. **Closed:** Nov–Mar.

This first-class choice is luxuriously set apart from the town center, surrounded by imposing, sumptuous gardens. The century-old grounds have a formal entrance through the fluted columns of a colonnade. There are winding lanes lined with cypress trees, wide-spreading magnolias, and flower-bordered marble fountains with classic sculpture. Through the trees merges a partial view of the lake and the nearby private waterside beach area. A newer structure with well-furnished rooms and private baths adjoins the mellow and pillared main building. In comfort and convenience, the bedrooms are unequaled in Sirmione. Each has a private bath or shower, and some offer a minibar. The interior has one formal drawing room, with much gilt and marble—palatial.

Expensive

GRAND HOTEL TERME, viale Marconi 1, 25019 Sirmione. Tel. 030/ 916261. Fax 030/916568. 58 rms (all with bath or shower), 1 suite. A/C MINIBAR TV TEL **Bus:** SAIA.

$ Rates (including half board): 250,000–310,000 lire ($196.25–$243.35) per person. AE, DC, MC, V. **Parking:** Free. **Closed:** Oct–Mar.

This rambling, three-story hotel at the entrance of the old town is on the lake next to the Scaligeri Castle. The wide marble halls and stairs lead to well-furnished, balconied bedrooms. Constructed in 1948, the hotel has contemporary furnishings, plus a number of spa and physical-therapy facilities and a swimming pool. The food served in the indoor-outdoor dining room is excellent, with such offerings as prosciutto and melon, risotto with snails, fettuccine with fresh porcini, and a wide choice of salads and fruits. Meals begin at 65,000 lire ($51).

HOTEL CONTINENTAL, punta Staffalo 7–9, 25019 Sirmione. Tel. 030/ 916031. Fax 030/916278. 53 rms (all with bath). A/C MINIBAR TV TEL **Bus:** SAIA.

$ Rates (including half board): 115,000–140,000 lire ($90.30–$109.90) per person. AE, DC, MC, V. **Parking:** Free. **Closed:** Dec–Feb.

The Continental lies in a lakeside building with spacious recessed balconies. Its gardens are well maintained and include evergreens and a large rectangular swimming pool. The interior contains polished stone floors and low-slung chairs. The rooms have balconies and easy access to the spa facilities.

HOTEL SIRMIONE, piazza Castello, 25019 Sirmione. Tel. 030/916331.
Fax 030/916558. 75 rms (all with bath). A/C MINIBAR TV TEL **Bus:** SAIA.
$ Rates (including half board): 135,000–140,000 lire ($106–$109.90) per person. AE, DC, MC, V. **Parking:** Free. **Closed:** Nov 25–Mar 1.

This hotel is set near the castle at the water's edge, behind an ocher facade with awnings and shutters. A swimming pool juts out on a narrow strip of land just above the lake, within sight of a small marina loaded with sailing craft. The functionally furnished bedrooms often have private balconies.

Moderate

FLAMINIA HOTEL, piazza Flaminia 8, 25019 Sirmione. Tel. 030/916078. Fax 030/916193. 48 rms (all with bath). TV TEL **Bus:** SAIA.
$ Rates (including breakfast): 93,000 lire ($73) single; 137,000 lire ($107.55) double. AE, DC, MC, V. **Parking:** Free. **Closed:** Nov 2–Mar 15.

This is one of the best second-class hotels in Sirmione, with a number of facilities and amenities, including air conditioning in some of the rooms. One of the more modern accommodations, it lies near the town center right on the lakefront, with a terrace extending out into the water. The bedrooms are made attractive by French doors opening onto private balconies. The lounges are furnished in a functional modern style. Breakfast is the only meal served.

HOTEL BROGLIA, via Piana 36, 25019 Sirmione. Tel. 030/916172. Fax 030/916586. 34 rms (all with bath). TV TEL **Bus:** SAIA.
$ Rates (including breakfast): 106,000 lire ($83.20) single; 168,000 lire ($131.90) double; 110,000–135,000 lire ($86.35–$106) per person for half board. AE, DC, MC, V. **Parking:** 20,000 lire ($15.70). **Closed:** Oct 20–Easter.

Located near the spa facilities, this modern building has a contemporary interior with big windows and light-grained paneling, while the gardens have a flagstone-covered terrace and a swimming pool set into the hillside. The bedrooms are comfortably furnished.

HOTEL EDEN, piazza Carducci 18, 25019 Sirmione. Tel. 030/916481. Fax 030/916483. 33 rms (all with bath). A/C TV TEL **Bus:** SAIA.
$ Rates (including breakfast): 98,000 lire ($76.95) single; 142,000 lire ($111.45) double. AE, MC, V. **Parking:** 15,000 lire ($11.80). **Closed:** Nov–Jan.

This hotel opened in 1984 in a totally renovated format that required 4 years of labor. The exterior, whose foundations date from the 12th century, is covered with pink stucco with stone trim around each of the big windows. The awning-covered entrance opens into a beautifully polished hall, where the gray and pink marble covering the floors came from India. Breakfast or drinks can be enjoyed on a flagstone-covered terrace surrounded with flowers. A winding stone staircase leads to the tastefully contemporary bedrooms. Each of the units is outfitted with pastel shades, and has its own marble-trimmed bath and radio—these are among the most up-to-date bedrooms in Sirmione. Fifteen rooms have a minibar. The location is in the center of the old city.

OLIVI, via San Pietro 5, 25019 Sirmione. Tel. 030/916110. Fax 030/916472. 60 rms (all with bath). A/C TV TEL **Bus:** SAIA.
$ Rates (including half board): 130,000–140,000 lire ($102.05–$109.90) per person. AE, MC, V. **Parking:** Free. **Closed:** Jan.

In the medium-priced range, this hotel is the creation of its sun-loving owner, Cerini Franco. Each room is oriented toward the light and view. Furthermore, its location is excellent, on the rise of a hill in a grove of olive trees, at the edge of town. The all-glass walls of the major rooms never let you forget you're in a garden spot of Italy. Even the compact and streamlined bedrooms have walls of glass leading out onto open balconies. In high season, it's best to take the full-board assignment.

WHERE TO DINE

LA RUCOLA, vicolo Strentelle 5. Tel. 916326.
   Cuisine: ITALIAN. **Reservations:** Recommended. **Bus:** SAIA.
$ **Prices:** Appetizers 11,000–12,000 lire ($8.65–$9.40); main courses 20,000–
   22,000 lire ($15.70–$17.25). AE, MC, V.
   Open: Lunch Fri–Wed 12:15–2:30pm; dinner Fri–Wed 7:15–10:30pm. **Closed:**
   Jan 7–Feb 7.
In the heart of town, this restaurant lies on a small alley a few steps from the main gate
leading into Sirmione. The building looks like a vine-laden, sienna-colored country
house. Full meals, served in a modernized interior, range from 65,000 lire ($51) and
could include fresh salmon, langoustines, mixed grilled fish, and a more limited meat
selection. Meats are most often grilled or flambéed, including Florentine beefsteak
and Venetian calves' liver. Good pasta dishes include spaghetti with clams and several
local varieties. Many of the desserts are made for two diners, including crêpes Suzette
and banana flambé.

RISTORANTE GRIFONE DA LUCIANO, via delle Bisse 5. Tel. 916097.
   Cuisine: INTERNATIONAL. **Reservations:** Not needed. **Bus:** SAIA.
$ **Prices:** Appetizers 8,000–15,000 lire ($6.30–$11.80); main courses 10,000–
   30,000 lire ($7.85–$23.55). AE, DC, MC, V.
   Open: Lunch Thurs–Tues noon–1:30pm; dinner Thurs–Tues 7–10:30pm.
   Closed: Oct to mid-Mar.
One of the most attractive restaurants in town is separated from the castle by a row of
shrubbery, a low stone wall, and a moat. From your seat on the flagstone terrace,
you'll have a view of the crashing waves and the plants that ring the dining area. The
headquarters of this establishment is technically an old stone house surrounded with
olive trees. Many of the diners gravitate toward the low-lying glass-and-metal
extension stretching toward the lake. The tables inside are covered with candles and
flowers. Food items include many varieties of fish and many of the standard dishes of
the classic Italian kitchen.

A Nearby Place to Dine

RISTORANTE AL POZZO DA SILVIO, via Statale 15. Tel. 919138.
   Cuisine: ITALIAN. **Reservations:** Recommended Sat–Sun. **Bus:** SAIA.
$ **Prices:** Appetizers 6,500–10,000 lire ($5.10–$7.85); main courses 12,000–
   18,000 lire ($9.40–$14.15). V.
   Open: Lunch Fri–Tues 12:30–2:30pm; dinner Thurs–Tues 7:30–9:30pm.
   Closed: July.
This restaurant is located outside Sirmione at Colombare, some 2 miles away, but it's
worth the trip. It offers family-style dining and a country Italian decor. You can enjoy
savory culinary specialties of the owner and chef. You can try samplings from their
antipasti table, to be followed by dried codfish Lake Garda style (with polenta), osso
buco, perhaps rabbit stew cacciatore.

SAN VIGILIO

Those who'd like to avoid the crowded western shore can drive to San Vigilio on the
southeastern shore. It's uncrowded and relatively unknown, but an easy and short
drive from either Verona or our last stopover at Sirmione.

WHERE TO STAY

LOCANDA SAN VIGILIO, 37016 San Vigilio, Garda. Tel. 045/7256688.
   Fax 045/7256551. 10 rms (all with bath). A/C MINIBAR TV TEL **Directions:**
   Head east from Sirmione along Route 249.
$ **Rates:** 290,000–320,000 lire ($227.65–$251.20) double. AE, DC, MC, V.
   Parking: Free.
   The best hotel in town, the Locanda San Vigilio has been a cherished address to
   the cognoscenti. Prince Charles stayed here for 2 nights, perhaps following in
   the footsteps of Sir Winston Churchill who came here to paint near the rocks of

the horseshoe-shaped harbor. The great actress Vivien Leigh also came here seeking a retreat, but the owner tossed "Miss Scarlett" out when she brought home a "common" fisherman for a whisky. The hotel rents only simply furnished bed-rooms—all doubles—with modern baths, but the rooms definitely play second fiddle to the view of the lake from the windows. Meals, which cost extra, are good tasting. The hotel lies at an isolated point along the lake in a 17th-century house at the end of San Vigilio Point. Architectural critic John Julius Norwich called it "the loveliest small hotel in the world."

2. LAKE COMO

Everything noble, everything evoking love—that was how Stendhal characterized fork-tongued Lake Como. Others have called it "the looking glass of Venus." More than 30 miles north of Milan, it is, next to Garda, the most visited of Italian lakes. A shimmering deep blue, the lake spans 2½ miles at its widest point. With its flower-studded gardens, its villas built for the wealthy of the 17th and 18th centuries, its mild climate, Larius (as it was known to the Romans) is among the most scenic spots in all of Italy.

For a short, but still fairly comprehensive, 1-day motor tour, I suggest going first to Como at the southern tip of the lake. From there, you can travel up the eastern shore of the west branch to Bellagio, the best-known resort. From Bellagio, you can either stop over or traverse the lake by car-ferry to Villa Carlotta and Tremezzo on the western shore, then head south down the strip to Milan again. I've found this to be a more scenic routing than along the eastern branch of Como, called the Laga di Lecco.

COMO

This is both the name of the lake and its principal city. At the southern tip of the lake, 25 miles north of Milan and 388 miles north of Rome, Como is known for its silk industry. Most visitors will pass through here to take a boat tour of the lake. If you do so, you'll cross **piazza Cavour,** the lakeside square and the center of local life.

Because Como is also an industrial city, I have generally shunned it for overnighting, preferring to anchor into one of the more attractive resorts along the lake, including Bellagio. However, train passengers who don't plan to rent a car may prefer Como (the city, that is) for convenience.

For centuries the destiny of the town has been linked to that of Milan. This means that Como prospered along with Milan, but also shared many of its misfortunes.

Como is called the world capital of silk, the silkmakers of the city joining communal hands with the fashion designers of Milan. Como has been making silk since Marco Polo first returned with silkworms from China. However, Como today isn't engaged in mulberry and worm cultivation, and hasn't been since the end of World War II. Those arduous labors, including the spinning of raw silk, are done in China. Como imports its thread from China.

Designers such as Giorgio Armani and Bill Blass pass through Como, discussing the patterns they want with silk manufacturers.

The **Tourist Information Center** is at piazza Cavour 17 (tel. 274064). Como's **telephone area code** is 031.

WHAT TO SEE & DO

Before rushing off on a boat for a tour of the lake, you may want to look at the **Cathedral of Como,** piazza del Duomo, which dates from the 14th century when the master builders of the city began its construction in the Lombard-Gothic style. Before it was finished the Renaissance was in flower, and it wasn't until the 1700s that the Duomo was officially "crowned." The exterior of the cathedral, frankly, is more interesting than the interior. Dating from 1487, it is lavishly decorated with statues, including those of Pliny the Elder (A.D. 23–79) and the Younger (A.D. 62–113), whom one writer once called "the beautiful people of ancient Rome." Inside, look for the 16th-century tapestries depicting scenes from the Bible.

WHERE TO STAY

HOTEL BARCHETTA EXCELSIOR, piazza Cavour 1, 22100 Como. Tel. 031/3321. Fax 031/302622. 82 rms (all with bath), 3 suites. A/C MINIBAR TV TEL **Bus:** 1 or 2.

$ **Rates** (including breakfast): 175,000 lire ($137.40) single; 220,000 lire ($172.70) double; from 324,000 lire ($254.35) suite. AE, DC, MC, V. **Parking:** 30,000 lire ($23.55).

This first-class hotel is set at the edge of the main square in the commercial section of town. Major additions have been made to the hotel, including the alteration of its restaurant and an upgrading of the bedrooms, which are comfortably furnished, often with a balcony overlooking this heartbeat square and the lake. All accommodations have radios, among other amenities, and most have lake views. There's a parking lot behind the hotel, plus a covered garage just over 50 yards away.

METROPOLE & SUISSE, piazza Cavour 19, 22100 Como. Tel. 031/ 269444. Fax 031/300808. 71 rms (all with bath), 2 suites. TV TEL **Bus:** 1 or 2.

$ **Rates:** 100,000–115,000 lire ($78.50–$90.30) single; 135,000–155,000 lire ($106–$121.70) double; from 200,000 lire ($157) suite. Breakfast 12,000 lire ($9.40) extra. AE, DC, MC, V. **Parking:** 18,000 lire ($14.15). **Closed:** Dec.

This hotel offers good value in clean, convenient accommodations. Near the cathedral on this major lake-fronting square, it's composed of three lower floors dating from around 1700, plus upper floors that were added about 60 years ago. The hotel began life as a waterfront store at the edge of what was then part of the lake (the square you see today is a landfill dating from 1850). The Swiss creator of the hotel was photographed with the staff in 1892, a picture that still hangs behind the reception desk. Each of the bedrooms is different, rich with character for the most part. Many repeat clients have staked out their favorite rooms. A parking garage and the city marina are nearby. A popular restaurant, Imbarcadero, under separate management, fills most of the ground floor of the hotel.

WHERE TO DINE

RISTORANTE IMBARCADERO, piazza Cavour 20. Tel. 277341.
   Cuisine: INTERNATIONAL. **Reservations:** Recommended. **Bus:** 1 or 2.
$ **Prices:** Appetizers 10,000–12,000 lire ($7.85–$9.40); main courses 18,000–30,000 lire ($14.15–$23.55). AE, DC, MC, V.
   Open: Lunch daily 12:30–2:30pm; dinner daily 7:30–10pm. **Closed:** Jan 1–8.
Established more than a decade ago in a 300-year-old building near the edge of the lake, this restaurant is filled with a pleasing blend of carved Victorian chairs, panoramic windows with marina views, and potted palms. You'll be greeted near the long, streamlined bar area by a member of the uniformed staff. The outdoor terrace set up on the square in summer is ringed with shrubbery and illuminated with evening candlelight. The chef makes his own tagliatelle, or you may want to order spaghetti with garlic, oil, and red pepper. Main courses include steak tartare, veal cutlet milanese, trout with almonds, and whitefish. Desserts are often lavish productions, including banana flambé and crêpes Suzette.

CERNOBBIO

Cernobbio, 3 miles northwest of Como, 391 miles north of Rome, and 33 miles north of Milan, is a small, fashionable resort frequented by the wealthy of Europe because of its deluxe hotel, the 16th-century Villa d'Este. But its idyllic anchor on the lake has also attracted a less affluent tourist, who'll find a number of third- and even fourth-class accommodations as well.

   The **Tourist Information Center** is at via Regina 33B (tel. 510198). The **telephone area code** for Cernobbio is 031.

WHERE TO STAY

GRAND HOTEL VILLA D'ESTE, 22010 Cernobbio. Tel. 031/511471. Fax 031/512027. 158 rms (all with bath). A/C MINIBAR TV TEL **Bus:** 6.

$ Rates (including breakfast): 269,000–340,000 lire ($211.15–$266.90) single; 470,000–530,000 lire ($368.95–$416.05) double. 19% IVA tax extra. AE, DC, MC, V. **Parking:** Free. **Closed:** Nov–Mar.

⭐ The Villa d'Este is a kingdom unto itself. This historic and splendid palace, surrounded by what must be the finest hotel gardens in Italy, has roots deep in the past. Built in 1557 by Cardinal Tolomeo Gallio, it has in turn been the Italian refuge for a number of celebrated figures, including Maria Feodorovna, empress of Russia (wife of Tsar Nicholas I) and Caroline Amalia of Brunswick, Princess of Wales and later the wife of England's George IV (her parties were the scandal of Europe). The ancestors of the villagers grew accustomed to the arrival of golden coaches. Today's residents settle for a parade of Rolls-Royces. A hotel since 1873, the villa is a romantic, unusual establishment for a select group of international guests. The interior lives up to its reputation: Each room is unique. The Salon Napoleone with its frescoed ceiling has silken wall draperies made especially for the little Corsican's visit. Queen Caroline's boudoir is a miniature stuccoed salon, now an intimate reading room. The Canova Room contains a statue of Venus attributed to Canova. The Grand Ballroom is mostly for banquets; the entrance lobby is graced with a vaulted ceiling and marble columns; the Canova Bar, all white and gold, offering piano music, opens onto the terrace; and, finally, the dining room is a kind of garden salon. Most splendid of all are the old gardens, with their wide-sweeping avenues of pointed trees, opening onto long vistas, highlighted by bits of architectural ruins and sculpture.

To all this splendor one adds the beauty of the bedrooms—each has its own distinction, and each is furnished with antiques or reproductions. In other days the favorite room of the Duke of Windsor and his duchess used to adjoin the personal choice of Prince Rainier and Princess Grace. The corner rooms or bed-sitting rooms are among the most expensive. The recreation facilities are "fit for a king"—a "floating" filtered swimming pool on Lake Como and one of the finest 18-hole golf courses (at Montofano) in Italy.

Dining/Entertainment: The cuisine is a culinary celebration. The head chef, presiding over a staff of nearly 50, is an artist, known for tantalizing the palate of the gourmet. If you're stopping by just for dinner, expect to pay 80,000 lire ($62.80) and up for a complete meal. In the evening there is dancing on an octagonal floor, with lakeside garden tables for drinks, plus a private disco club.

Services: Room service, baby-sitting, laundry, valet, hairdresser.

Facilities: Swimming pool, golf course, sailing, motorboating, fishing, eight top-grade red-clay tennis courts.

HOTEL ASNIGO, via Noseda 2, 22012 Cernobbio. Tel. 031/510062. Fax 031/510249. 30 rms (all with bath), 3 suites. MINIBAR TV TEL **Bus:** 6.

$ Rates (including breakfast): 128,000–141,000 lire ($100.50–$110.70) single; 162,000–194,000 lire ($127.15–$152.30) double; from 250,000 lire ($196.25) suite. AE, DC, MC, V. **Parking:** Free.

Ⓢ The Asnigo, 1 mile northeast of the center of Cernobbio, calls itself *un piccolo Grand Hotel.* Commanding a view of Como from its hillside perch at piazza Santo Stefano, this is a good little first-class hotel set in its own garden. Its special and subtle charms have long been known to a lake-loving set of British visitors as it dates from 1914.

An Englishwoman writes: "Last summer I did something not recommendable to your readers: I went on a trip to Italy with my nephew and his wife from America, who quite frankly patronize a higher type of establishment than I do. Naturally, they were lured to the Villa d'Este on Como. I, fortunately, was able to find a splendid little hotel in the hills, the Asnigo. The proprietor was most helpful, the meals flawless and beautifully served, the room spotlessly clean and comfortable. After being a dinner guest one night at the Villa d'Este, I returned the hospitality the following evening by inviting my relatives for a most enjoyable meal at my hotel. At least they learned that good food and comfort are not the sole domain of a deluxe hotel." I echo her sentiments.

BELLAGIO

Sitting on a promontory at the point where Lake Como forks, 48 miles north of Milan and 18 miles northeast of Como, Bellagio is with much justification given the label of "The Pearl of Larius." A sleepy veil hangs over the town's arcaded streets and its little shops. Bellagio is rich in memories, having attracted fashionable, even royal visitors, such as King Leopold I of Belgium, who used to own the 18th-century Villa Giulia. Bellagio is a 45-minute drive north from Como.

The **Tourist Information Center** is at piazza della Chiesa 14 (tel. 950204). The Bellagio **telephone area code** is 031.

WHAT TO SEE & DO

To reach many of the places in Bellagio, you must climb streets that are really stairways. Its lakeside promenade blossoms with flowering shrubbery. From the town, visitors can take tours of Lake Como and enjoy several sports such as rowing and tennis, or else they can lounge at Bellagio Lido.

If time allows, try to explore the gardens of the **Villa Serbelloni,** piazza della Chiesa (tel. 950204, same as the tourist office), the Bellagio Study and Conference Center of the Rockefeller Foundation (not to be confused with the Grand Hotel Villa Serbelloni by the waterside in the village). The villa is not open to the public, but the park can be visited on guided tours starting at 11am and 4pm, and lasting for 1½ hours. Tours are conducted daily except Monday from mid-April to mid-October at a cost of 4,000 lire ($3.15) per person, the proceeds going to local charities.

The most important tourist attraction of Bellagio is the garden of the **Villa Melzi** museum and chapel, at lungolario Marconi. The villa was built in 1808 for Duke Francesco Melzi d'Eril, vice-president of the Italian republic founded by Napoleon. Franz Liszt and Stendhal are among the illustrious guests who have stayed here. The park has many well-known sculptures, and if you're here in the spring, you can enjoy the azaleas. Today it is the property of Duke Gallarati Scotti, who opens it from April to the end of October, daily from 9am to 6pm. Admission is 4,000 lire ($3.15).

Nearby Attractions

From Como, car-ferries ply back and forth across the lake to Cadenabbia on the western shore. Cadenabbia is another lakeside resort, with hotels and villas, the most important of which you'll surely want to visit is the Villa Carlotta.

Directly south of Cadenabbia on the run to Tremezzo, the ✪ **Villa Carlotta** (tel. 0344/40405) is the most-visited attraction on Lake Como—and with good reason. In a serene setting, the villa is graced with gardens of exotic flowers and blossoming shrubbery, especially rhododendrons and azaleas. Its beauty is tame, cultivated, much like a fairytale that recaptures the halcyon life available only to the very rich of the 19th century. Dating from 1847, the estate was named after a Prussian princess, Carlotta, who married the Duke of Sachsen-Meiningen. Inside the villa are a number of art treasures including Canova's *Cupid and Psyche,* and a number of neoclassical statues by Bertel Thorvaldsen, the Danish sculptor who died in 1844. Also displayed are neoclassical paintings, furniture, and a stone-and-bronze table ornament that belonged to Viceroy Eugene Beauharnais. From March 15 to March 31 and in October, it is open daily from 9am to noon and 2 to 4:30pm; from the first of April through September, daily from 9am to 6pm. Admission is 6,000 lire ($4.70) for adults, 2,500 lire ($1.95) for children.

WHERE TO STAY & DINE

Good choices are available in a number of categories, in hotels that have appealed to everyone from Napoleon to Mark Twain.

GRAND HOTEL VILLA SERBELLONI, 22021 Bellagio. Tel. 031/950216.
Fax 031/951529. 95 rms (all with bath), 5 suites. MINIBAR TV TEL **Bus:** Bellagio bus from Como.

$ **Rates** (including breakfast): 240,000 lire ($188.40) single; 330,000–430,000 lire ($259.05–$337.55) double; from 640,000 lire ($502.40) suite. DC, MC, V. **Parking:** Free. **Closed:** Oct 21–Apr 15.

⭐ This lavish old hotel is for those born to the grand style of life. Prominently placed, it stands proud and serene at the edge of town against a backdrop of hills. Surrounded by its own gardens of flowers and semitropical plants, it is perched on the lakefront, and guests sunbathe on the waterside terrace or doze under a willow tree. Inside, the public rooms rekindle the spirit of the baroque: the grand drawing room with a painted ceiling, marble columns, a glittering chandelier, and ornate gilt furnishings and the mirrored neoclassical dining room. The bedrooms are wide-ranging, from elaborate suites with a recessed tile bath, baroque furnishings, and lake-view balconies to more chaste quarters. Rooms are priced according to view, the most expensive of which open onto the lake. Thirteen rooms are air-conditioned. The hotel is surrounded by a beautiful lakeside garden and park that are often visited by the general public.

HOTEL DU LAC, piazza Mazzini, 22021 Bellagio. Tel. 031/950320. Fax 031/951624. 48 rms (all with bath or shower). TEL **Bus:** Bellagio bus from Como.

$ **Rates** (including breakfast): 80,000 lire ($62.80) single; 115,000–122,000 lire ($90.30–$95.75) double. MC, V. **Parking:** 14,000 lire ($11). **Closed:** Nov-Mar.

The Hotel du Lac was built 150 years ago, when the waters of the lake came directly up to the front door of the ocher facade. Today there's a generous terraced expanse of flagstones in front, on which are café tables and an arched arcade. The hotel is imbued with conservative comfort, with an adjoining bar, a large glassed-in restaurant with a terrace, and a rooftop garden where guests can bask in the sun or relax in the shade while enjoying a view over the lake. The well-furnished bedrooms contain hairdryers. The proprietors are hospitable, and the hotel is in the center of town.

HOTEL FLORENCE, piazza Mazzini, 22021 Bellagio. Tel. 031/950342.
Fax 031/951722. 40 rms (34 with bath). TEL **Bus:** Bellagio bus from Como.

$ **Rates** (including breakfast): 47,000 lire ($36.90) single without bath, 75,000 lire ($58.90) single with bath; 107,000 lire ($84) double without bath, 112,000 lire ($87.90) double with bath. MC, V. **Closed:** Mid-Oct to mid-Apr.

Ⓢ The entrance to this green-shuttered 19th-century villa is under a vaulted arcade near the ferryboat-landing stage. Wisteria climbs over the iron balustrades of the lake-view terraces. The Florence is one of the most charming middle-bracket choices in the resort. The reception desk is at one end of an entrance hall whose ceilings are supported by massive timbers, old vaulting, and Doric columns made of granite. There's even a Tuscan fireplace, with finely chiseled carving and a globelike wrought-iron chandelier. The main section of this hotel was built around 1720, although most of what you see today was added around 1880. For 150 years the hotel has been run by a member of the Ketzlar family, who originally acquired it as a private villa, turning it into one of the artistic centers of the lake area. Today you'll probably be welcomed by the beautiful and charming Roberta Ketzlar (who studied foreign languages and worked for a short time as a Milanese radio announcer), her brother, Ronald, and their mother, Friedl. The bedrooms are scattered amid spacious upstairs sitting and dining areas, and often have high ceilings, antiques, and lake views.

TREMEZZO

Reached by frequent ferries from Bellagio, Tremezzo, 48 miles north of Milan and 18 miles north of Como, is another popular west-shore resort that opens onto a panoramic view of Lake Como. Around the town is a district known as Tremezzina, with luxuriant vegetation that includes citrus trees, palms, cypresses, and magnolias. Tremezzo is the starting point for many excursions. Its accommodations are much more limited than those in Bellagio.

From May to October, there is a **Tourist Information Center** at piazzale Trieste 3 (tel. 40493). The **telephone area code** for Tremezzo is 0344.

WHERE TO STAY

GRAND HOTEL TREMEZZO PALACE, via Regina 8, 22019 Tremezzo. Tel. 0344/40446. Fax 0344/40201. 100 rms (all with bath), 2 suites. MINIBAR TV TEL **Transportation:** Ferry from Bellagio or hydrofoil from Como.
$ **Rates** (including breakfast): 152,000 lire ($119.30) single; 227,000 lire ($178.20) double; from 377,000 lire ($295.95) suite. AE, DC, MC, V. **Parking:** Free. **Closed:** Dec–Jan.

The Tremezzo Palace was built at the beginning of this century, but has seen much modernization since then. This grand old hotel rests on a lakeside ledge, surrounded by spacious terraced gardens and keeping good company with the neighboring Villa Carlotta. Its situation is ideal, especially under palm trees by the open-air swimming pool or on the lakeside lido. The bedrooms for the most part are spacious, with private bath or shower and satellite TV. All rooms that face the lake contain private balconies. Some are air-conditioned. You're given a choice of a lakeside or a park view.

Dining/Entertainment: The hotel also has three restaurants with excellent service and an international regional cuisine, with meals costing from 55,000 lire ($43.20). You can enjoy meals on an open-air terrace overlooking the lake. The private Club l'Escale, with a disco and piano bar, a billiard room, landing stage, heliport, and a congress area, complete the facilities.

Services: Room service, baby-sitting, laundry, valet.

Facilities: In the hotel's large park are two swimming pools, a tennis court, a lido on the lake, and a jogging track.

HOTEL BAZZONI AND DU LAC, via Regina 26, 22019 Tremezzo. Tel. 0344/40403. Fax 0344/41651. 123 rms (all with bath). TEL **Transportation:** Ferry from Bellagio or hydrofoil from Como.
$ **Rates** (including breakfast): 75,000 lire ($58.90) single; 130,000 lire ($102.05) double. AE, DC, MC, V. **Parking:** Free. **Closed:** Oct 15–Mar 1.

There was an older hotel on this spot during Napoleon's era, although it was bombed by the British 5 days after the official end of World War II. Today the reconstructed hotel is a collection of glass-and-concrete walls, with prominent balconies at the edge of the lake. It is one of the best hotels in a resort town filled with hotels with grander formats but much less desirable accommodations. The main restaurant on the ground floor has a baronial but unused fireplace, contemporary wall frescoes of the boats on the lake, and scattered carvings. The pleasantly furnished sitting rooms include antique architectural elements from older buildings. A summer restaurant near the hotel's entrance is constructed like a small island of glass walls.

A Nearby Place to Stay in Menaggio

GRAND HOTEL VICTORIA, lungo lago Castelli 7, 22017 Menaggio. Tel. 0344/32003. Fax 0344/32992. 49 rms (all with bath), 4 junior suites. A/C MINIBAR TV TEL **Transportation:** Ferry from Bellagio or hydrofoil from Como.
$ **Rates:** 110,000–115,000 lire ($86.35–$90.30) single; 160,000–170,000 lire ($125.60–$133.45) double; from 220,000 lire ($172.70) suite. Breakfast 19,000 lire ($14.90) extra. AE, DC, MC, V. **Parking:** Free.

This is one of the best hotels on the lake, and one that is moderate in price considering its grand format. The hotel was built in 1806 along a quiet lakeside road bordered with chestnut trees. It was renovated in 1983 into a format almost as luxurious as the original, with attention paid to the preservation of ornate plasterwork whose tendrils and curlicues entwine the ceiling vaults. Architectural details include lavish use of marble, big windows, and carving on the white facade that resembles the heads of what looks like water sprites.

Some sections of the establishment have been purchased for private use by vacationing individuals, but the majority of the rooms are available to rent. The modern furniture and amenities in the bedrooms include a radio, plus plushly appointed private bath with wall tiles designed by Valentino. As many members of the staff will tell you, the beach in front of the hotel is the best spot on Lake Como for windsurfing, especially between 3 and 7pm.

Dining/Entertainment: Guests enjoy drinks on the outdoor terrace near the stone columns of the tree-shaded portico, or in the antiques-filled public rooms. The restaurant has well-prepared food, art nouveau chandeliers, and an embellished ceiling showing all the fruits of an Italian harvest scattered amid representations of lyres and mythical beasts. Menu specialties include saltimbocca, steak tartare, turtle soup, homemade ravioli, veal cutlet milanese, filet of sole, and crêpes Suzette. Expect to spend 58,000 lire ($45.55) and up for a full meal.

Services: Room service, baby-sitting, laundry, valet.

Facilities: Swimming pool, beach, tennis court, private boats.

WHERE TO DINE

AL VELUU, Rogaro di Tremezzo. Tel. 40510.

Cuisine: LOMBARD/INTERNATIONAL. **Reservations:** Recommended. **Bus:** 10.

$ Prices: Appetizers 10,000–15,000 lire ($7.85–$11.80); main courses 20,000–22,000 lire ($15.70–$17.25). AE, V.

Open: Lunch Wed–Mon 12:30–2pm; dinner Wed–Mon 7:30–10pm. **Closed:** Oct 30–Feb 28.

Al Veluu, 1 mile north of the resort in the hills, is an ideal stopover for visitors looking for a regional restaurant with plenty of charm and lots of personalized attention. Owner Carlo Antonini is an important element in the relaxed and sophisticated format of this excellent restaurant. "Al Veluu" (which means "the sail" in the local dialect) is a reminder to him of the time he spends with his friends sailing his boat on Lake Como, which is visible in a panoramic sweep from one of the terrace's well-prepared tables. The rustic dining room with its fireplace and big windows is a welcome refuge in inclement weather. But in summer, the terrace lures all.

Most of the vegetables and produce come freshly picked from the garden, which lies just across the curving road leading up from the lake. Even the butter is homemade, and the best cheeses come from a local farmer whose home is visible among the rocks and trees of a nearby mountain. Menu items include gamberoni (giant shrimp) and fresh fish prepared in several different ways, plus pasta with salmon or in a pesto sauce, carpaccio, grilled beef, veal cutlet milanese or piccata style, and a series of luscious desserts that might include banana flambé, zabaglione, or crêpes Suzette. On weekends the menu is augumented with lakefish and meats in many varieties from the outdoor grill. Meals usually range from 45,000 lire to 72,000 lire ($35.35 to $56.50).

3. LAKE MAGGIORE

The shores of this lake wash up on the banks of Piedmont and Lombardy in Italy, but its more austere northern basin (Locarno, for example) lies in the mountainous region of Switzerland. At its longest point it stretches a distance of more than 40 miles, and it's 6½ miles at its widest stretch.

A wealth of natural beauty awaits the visitor: mellowed lakeside villas, dozens of gardens with lush vegetation, sparkling waters, panoramic views. A veil of mist seems to hover at times, especially in the early spring and late autumn.

Maggiore is a most rewarding lake to visit from Milan, especially because of the Borromean Islands in its center (most easily reached from Stresa). The fortunate visitor will be able to motor around the entire basin. But those on a more limited schedule may find the western, resort-studded shore the most scenic. From Milan, a drive northwest for about 51 miles will take you to Stresa, the major resort on Lake Maggiore.

STRESA

On the western shore, 407 miles north of Rome and 51 miles northwest of Milan, Stresa has skyrocketed from a simple village of fisherfolk to a first-class international resort. Its vantage on the lake is almost unparalleled, and its level of hotel accommodations is superior to that of the other Maggiore resorts of Italy. Scene of sporting activities and an international **Festival of Musical Weeks** (beginning in late August), it swings into action in April, then dwindles in popularity at the end of October. Depending on traffic, Stresa is reached in 1 hour from Milan on the Simplon Railway. There are no buses for getting about town, but Stresa is small and can easily be walked.

The **Tourist Information Center** is at via Principe Tomaso 70–72 (tel. 30150). Stresa's **telephone area code** is 0323.

WHERE TO STAY

Very Expensive

HOTEL DES ILES BORROMEES, corso Umberto I no. 67, 28049 Stresa. Tel. 0323/30431. Fax 0323/32405. 145 rms (all with bath), 12 suites. A/C MINIBAR TV TEL

$ Rates: 243,950–267,750 lire ($191.50–$210.20) single; 362,950–398,650 lire ($284.90–$312.95) double; from 737,800 lire ($579.20) suite. Breakfast 23,900 lire ($18.75) extra. AE, DC, MC, V. **Parking:** Free.

⭐ Set on the edge of the lake in a flowering garden, this hotel has an ornate facade looking over the water. The Borromean Islands are visible from many of the bedrooms. All the accommodations have been furnished in an Italian/French Empire style, including rich ormolu, burnished hardwoods, plush carpets, and pastel color schemes. Each room has a private bath or shower, which look as if every quarry in Italy has been scoured for matched marble. The hotel opened its doors for the first time in 1863, attracting titled notables. Alexandra, the grand duchess of Russia, carved her name into one of the hotel's windowpanes with a diamond ring in 1870. But it wasn't until the opening of the Sempione Tunnel in 1906 that the hotel (and Stresa) could profit from the beginning of mass tourism. Famous guests of yesterday have included J. P. Morgan and Eleanora Duse. Hemingway ordained that the hero of *A Farewell to Arms* should stay here to escape from World War I.

The public rooms, elegantly capped with two-tone ornate plasterwork and crystal chandeliers, were even the scene of a top-level meeting among the heads of state of Italy, Great Britain, and France in an attempt to stave off World War II. Today all this splendor can be part of your vacation, but it won't come cheaply. The restaurant is as dignified as you'd expect. Full meals cost upward from 90,000 lire ($70.65) per person. The hotel also has a medically supervised health-and-exercise program. In the Centro Benessere, you could not be in better hands: A specialized medical team will help you relax, give you a thorough checkup, and get you back into fine shape with personalized exercise schedules and carefully planned diets.

In addition, the hotel also operates the Residenza, with 47 rooms in a building separate from the main hotel. Prices here are 20% less than those charged in the hotel. Each room in the Residenza is decorated in a modern style, with air conditioning, TV, minibar, and private bath or shower.

Moderate

HOTEL ASTORIA, corso Umberto I no. 31, 28049 Stresa. Tel. 0323/ 32566. Fax 0323/30259. 100 rms (all with bath). MINIBAR TV TEL

$ Rates (including breakfast): 142,000 lire ($111.45) single; 195,000 lire ($153.05) double. AE, DC, MC, V. **Parking:** Free. **Closed:** Oct 26–Apr 6.

This medium-priced establishment is expressly for sun-seekers who want a modern hotel with its own heated swimming pool, Turkish bath, small gym, roof garden, and Jacuzzi. Standing right on the lake, it features triangular balconies—one to each bedroom—jutting out for the view. The bedrooms are streamlined and spacious. The public lounges have walls of glass opening toward the lake view and the garden. The portion of the dining room favored by most guests is the wide-paved, open-air, front terrace, where under shelter you dine on good cuisine while enjoying Maggiore as the chef d'oeuvre.

HOTEL MODERNO, via Cavour 33, 38049 Stresa. Tel. 0323/30468. Fax 0323/31537. 53 rms (all with bath or shower). TEL

$ Rates (including breakfast): 65,000 lire ($51) single; 100,000 lire ($78.50) double. AE, DC, MC, V. **Parking:** Free. **Closed:** Nov–Feb.

True to its name, this is a contemporary hotel a block from the lake and boat-landing stage. It has been completely modernized, with good beds and phones for direct dialing and automatic wakeup calls. The rooms are each personalized, and TV and minibar are available upon request. In addition to its regular dining room, the Moderno also offers two open-air restaurants, the candlelit veranda, Gazebo, in one of the most characteristic streets of Stresa, and La Damigiana in the rear patio shaded by wisteria. In all, the Moderno is one of the best hotels for value in Stresa.

HOTEL LA PALMA, corso Umberto I, 28049 Stresa. Tel. 0323/32401. Fax 0323/32404. 128 rms (all with bath), 6 suites. A/C MINIBAR TV TEL

$ Rates (including breakfast): 100,000–140,000 lire ($78.50–$109.90) single; 180,000–220,000 lire ($141.30–$172.70) double; from 280,000 lire ($219.80) suite. AE, DC, MC, V. **Parking:** Free. **Closed:** Nov 20–Mar 10.

The designs crafted into the wrought-iron balconies of this tasteful hotel reflect the palms for which the hotel is named. Built in 1964, the hotel is set into gardens across a road from the lake and boasts an azalea-covered terrace in front, a private swimming pool, and comfortably furnished bedrooms. About 90% of them face the lake and have a private balcony. All units contain a hairdryer.

REGINA PALACE, corso Umberto I no. 27, 28049 Stresa. Tel. 0323/30171. Fax 0323/30176. 175 rms (all with bath). MINIBAR TV TEL

$ Rates (including breakfast): 186,000 lire ($146) single; 272,000 lire ($213.50) double. AE, DC, MC, V. **Parking:** Free. **Closed:** Jan.

The Regina Palace was built in 1908 in a boomerang-shaped design whose central curve faces the lakefront. The hotel looks almost like the spinnaker of a sailboat running downwind. Foremost among its architectural features are art deco illuminated-glass columns (lit from within) that are capped with gilded Corinthian capitals. A wide marble stairwell is flanked with carved oak lions, while the elaborately patterned ceiling of the main lobby is illuminated with natural light. There's a swimming pool in the rear, and a guest roster that has included George Bernard Shaw, Ernest Hemingway, King Umberto I of Italy, Princess Margaret, and Gina Lollobrigida. Lately, about 90% of the guests are American, many of them with tour groups that stream through Stresa. Tennis courts are on the premises, and there is ample parking. Bedrooms are equipped with all the modern comforts, and many have views of the Borromean Islands, so famous in Italian romantic novels.

Inexpensive

ALBERGO ARISTON, corso Italia 60, 28049 Stresa. Tel. 0323/31195. 12 rms (all with bath).

$ Rates: 48,000 lire ($37.70) single; 75,000 lire ($58.90) double. Breakfast 6,000 lire ($4.70) extra. AE, DC, MC, V. **Parking:** Free. **Closed:** Dec 10–Mar 20.

Here is a good bargain. The hotel is listed as third class, but its comfort is superior. The rooms are well kept and attractively furnished. It's possible for nonresidents to stop for a meal, ordering a lunch or dinner with wine for 35,000 lire ($27.50) and up. The food is served on the terrace, which has a beautiful view of the lake and gardens. Your hosts are the Balconi family.

HOTEL ITALIE ET SUISSE, piazza Marconi 1, 28049 Stresa. Tel. 0323/ 30540. Fax 0323/32621. 28 rms (all with bath). TEL

$ Rates (including breakfast): 53,000–68,000 lire ($41.60–$53.40) single; 76,000–102,000 lire ($59.65–$80.05) double. AE, DC, MC, V. **Parking:** Free. **Closed:** Nov–Mar.

This is considered one of the best bargains at the resort. The rooms are spacious and overlook Lake Maggiore, with bath and toilet and a small balcony. Some of the comfortably furnished rooms have a queen-size bed.

MEUBLE PRIMAVERA, via Cavour 39, 28049 Stresa. Tel. 0323/31286.
Fax 0323/33458. 32 rms (all with bath or shower). TEL
$ Rates (including breakfast): 50,000–62,000 lire ($39.25–$48.65) single; 65,000–92,000 lire ($51–$72.20) double. AE, DC, MC, V. **Parking:** 5,000 lire ($3.95).

The owner, Signor Maurizio Ferraris, has the happy and relaxed temperament you expect from a host. His family-run, year-round hotel is kept immaculately clean. Tiled floors and wood furniture are used throughout. Some of the front bedrooms have windows over via Cavour, facing an old church. They also have balconies of red geraniums. TV and minibar are available upon request. Breakfast is served in the first-floor lounge, where you may chat with Signor Maurizio at night over a glass of grappa.

WHERE TO DINE

RISTORANTE EMILIANO, corso Italia 48. Tel. 31396.
Cuisine: EMILIANA. **Reservations:** Essential.
$ Prices: Appetizers 20,000–22,000 lire ($15.70–$17.25); main courses 30,000–32,000 lire ($23.55–$25.10). AE, DC, MC, V.
Open: Lunch Thurs–Mon 12:30–2:30pm; dinner Wed–Mon 7:30–10pm. **Closed:** Jan 20–Mar 1.

As its name suggests, the cuisine comes directly from the Emilia-Romagna region of Italy. Directed by Romano Felisi, the restaurant is filled with a kind of decor that makes it the most elegant nonhotel restaurant in Stresa. It also serves the best food on Lake Maggiore. The entrance is sheltered from cloudbursts by a wrought-iron and glass canopy, which even extends partially over the tops of the outdoor tables with their view of the lake. Inside, the half-paneled walls are accented with candlelight. Menu specialties feature a frequently changing array of delicacies, which on any given day might include pasta with smoked salmon, rack of spring lamb with rosemary, risotto with scampi, or fried squash blossoms and truffles. Ever had macaroni with fresh asparagus and liver? Surely you've never tasted their adaptation of an ancient Emilian peasant dish of tortelloni stuffed with a combination of potatoes and mushrooms. Meals cost 75,000 lire to 130,000 lire ($58.90 to $102.05).

PETIT PAM PAM, piazza San Michele 4. Tel. 311177.
Cuisine: PIEDMONTESE/INTERNATIONAL. **Reservations:** Preferred.
$ Prices: Appetizers 8,500–15,000 lire ($6.65–$11.80); main courses 12,000–29,000 lire ($9.40–$22.75). AE, DC, MC, V.
Open: Lunch Fri–Wed noon–3pm; dinner Fri–Wed 6pm–midnight. **Closed:** Jan.

This cozy, rustic restaurant is at the top of a short flight of stairs a few blocks from the lake. The decor includes autumnal colors, wrought-iron accents, an array of original paintings, and so many bottles stacked in every available nook that a meal here is a lot like dining in a wine cellar. You'll hear an international medley of languages, and you'll be able to sample a mainly Italian menu that includes pizzas. There is also a large fish menu, including antipasti di mare, large grilled shrimp, sole in butter, and various fruits of the sea. You might also prefer grilled beefsteak, spaghetti with prawns and pink peppercorns, or fondue bourguignonne (the latter served only for two people).

TAVERNA DEL PAPPAGALLO, Principessa Margherita 48. Tel. 30411.
Cuisine: ITALIAN. **Reservations:** Not needed.
$ Prices: Appetizers 5,000–9,000 lire ($3.95–$7.05); main courses 8,000–16,000 lire ($6.30–$12.55). No credit cards.
Open: Lunch Thurs–Mon noon–2:30pm; dinner Thurs–Mon 7pm–midnight.

This informal little garden restaurant and tavern is operated by the Ghiringhelli brothers, who turn out some of the least-expensive meals in Stresa. Specialties of the house include gnocchi (semolina dumplings), many types of scaloppine, scalamino allo spiedoe fagioli (grilled sausage with beans), and saltimbocca alla romana (a veal-and-ham dish). At night pizza is king (try the piazza Regina). A complete meal will range in price from 35,000 lire ($27.50). The tavern service has a personal family touch.

THE BORROMEAN ISLANDS

The heart of Lake Maggiore is occupied by this chain of tiny islands, which were turned into sites of lavish villas and gardens by the Borromeo clan. From the harbor at Stresa, you can buy an excursion ticket on a boat that will take you to the three major islands. Boats leave about every 30 minutes in summer, and the trip takes 3 hours. The navigation offices at Stresa's center port (tel. 46651) are open daily from 8am to 8pm. The best deal is to purchase an excursion ticket for 8,000 lire ($6.30), entitling you to go back and forth during the day.

The **telephone area code** for the islands is 0323.

WHAT TO SEE & DO

The major stopover is on the ✪ **Isola Bella** (Beautiful Island), which should be visited if you have time for only 1 sight. Dominating the island is the 17th-century **Borromeo Palazzo** (tel. 30556). When approached from the front, the figurines in the garden evoke the appearance of a wedding cake. On conducted tours, you are shown through the light and airy palace, from which the views are remarkable. Napoleon slept here. A special feature is the six grotto rooms, built piece by piece like a mosaic. In addition, there is a collection of quite good tapestries, with gory cannibalistic animal scenes. Outside, the white peacocks in the garden enchant year after year. The palace and its grounds are open March to October, daily from 9am to 5pm; annual closing is October 25 to March 26. To visit the palace and its gardens costs 9,000 lire ($7.05) for adults, 4,000 lire ($3.15) for children 6 to 15.

The largest of the chain, ✪ **Isola Madre** (Mother Island), is visited chiefly because of its botanical gardens. You wander through a setting ripe with pomegranates, camellias, wisteria, rhododendrons, bougainvillea, hibiscus, hydrangea, magnolias, even a cypress tree from the Himalayas. The 17th-century **palace** on the grounds may also be visited. It contains a rich collection of 17th- and 18th-century furnishings. Of particular interest is a collection of 19th-century French and German dolls belonging to Countess Borromeo. Livery of various kinds belonging to the House of Borromeo is also exhibited. The unique 18th-century marionette theater of the House of Borromeo, complete with scripts, stage scenery, and devices for sound, light, and other special effects, is on display. Peacocks, pheasants, and other birds live and roam freely on the grounds. Visiting hours are 9am to 5:30pm daily from March 27 to October 24. Admission to both palace and grounds is 8,000 lire ($6.30) for adults, 4,000 lire ($3.15) for children 6–15.

Isola dei Pescatori (Fishermen's Island) is without major sights or lavish villas, but in many ways it is the most colorful. Less a stage setting than its two sisters, it's inhabited by fisherfolk who live in cottages. Good walks are possible in many directions.

THE VILLA TARANTO

Back on the mainland near the resort of Pallanza, north of Stresa, the ✪ **botanical gardens** at Villa Taranto, via Vittorio Veneto III, Verbania-Pallanza (tel. 0323/556667), are spread over more than 50 acres of the Castagnola Promontory, which juts out into Lake Maggiore. In this dramatic setting between the mountains and the lake, more than 20,000 species of plants from all over the world thrive in a well-tended and cultivated institution, begun in 1931 by a Scotsman, Capt. Neil McEacharn. Plants range from rhododendrons and azaleas to specimens from such faraway places as Louisiana and Canada. Seasonal exhibits include fields of Dutch tulips (80,000 of them), Japanese magnolias, giant water lilies, cotton plants, and rare varieties of hydrangeas. The formal gardens of the villas are carefully laid out with ornamental fountains, statues, and reflection pools. Among the more ambitious creations of the gardens is the elaborate irrigation system that pumps water from the lake to all parts of the gardens, and the Terrace Gardens, complete with waterfalls and swimming pool.

The villa gardens are open April 1 through October 31, every day from 8:30am to 7:30pm. Professional guides will take you on tours, which last more than an hour. You may also take a round-trip boat ride from Stresa, which docks at the Villa Taranto pier adjoining the entrance to the gardens. You pay an admission of 7,000 lire ($5.50) for adults, 6,000 lire ($4.70) for children 6 to 14.

CHAPTER 17

MILAN & LOMBARDY

1. MILAN
- **WHAT'S SPECIAL ABOUT MILAN & LOMBARDY**
2. BERGAMO
3. CREMONA
4. MANTUA (MANTOVA)

The vicissitudes of Italy's history are reflected in Lombardy as perhaps in no other region. All conquerors from barbarians to Napoleon have marched across its plain. Even Mussolini came to his end here. He and his mistress—both already dead—were strung up in a square in Milan as war-weary residents vented their rage upon the two bodies.

Among the most progressive of all the Italians, the Lombards have charted an industrial empire unequaled in Italy. Often the dream of the underfed and jobless worker in the south is to go to "Milano" for the high wages and the good life.

But Lombardy isn't all manufacturing. Milan, as we'll soon see, is filled to the brim with important attractions, and nearby are old Lombard art cities—Bergamo, Cremona, and Mantua (Mantova), as well as the Carthusian Monastery of Pavia, to cite only a few.

SEEING MILAN & LOMBARDY
SUGGESTED ITINERARY

Days 1–2: Take in the panorama sweep of Milan, an industrial city and artistic center, and with only 2 days you'll be very busy indeed.
Day 3: Head east to Bergamo for the night, and spend what remains of the day exploring its upper town.
Day 4: From Bergamo, cut south for an overnight in the art city of Cremona.
Day 5: For a final look at Lombardy, continue east to Cremona, famous for its Duomo and its stringed instruments.

GETTING THERE

Milan is the gateway to Lombardy, with two major airports, Malpensa and Linate. Planes from not only Italy, but all over the world, especially European capitals, fly into these airports. Motorists will find that virtually all major roads in northern Italy seem to lead to Milan, and it is also a major rail network, not only for major cities of Italy, such as Rome, but from continental European destinations as well (see "Getting There" under Milan).

The bus is the least attractive way to reach Milan on an intercity route, since bus travel is not fast, cheap, or more convenient than the rails. However, once in Milan, you can use local buses to reach neighboring towns or visit some of the resorts in the lake district.

1. MILAN
355 miles N of Rome, 87 miles NE of Turin, 88 miles N of Genoa

GETTING THERE   By Plane   Milan ranks with Rome as one of the easiest cities in Italy to reach by public transportation. It is serviced by two airports, the

☑ WHAT'S SPECIAL ABOUT MILAN & LOMBARDY

Great Towns & Villages
☐ Milan, the major city of northern Italy, with a history going back 2,500 years.
☐ Mantua, ancient seat of the Gonzagas, hometown of Virgil; the great Mantegna was court painter here for 50 years.
☐ Bergamo, acclaimed for its Città Alta or upper town, fortified by the Venetians during their long centuries of control.
☐ Cremona, on the Po River, the city of the violin, birthplace of Monteverdi and Stradivari.

Religious Shrines
☐ The Duomo of Milan, begun in 1386, a marvel of white marble loaded with belfries, gables, statues, and pinnacles.
☐ The Duomo, at Cremona, a magnificent Lombard building begun in the Romanesque style and famed for its Torrazzo, a beautiful campanile, the tallest in Italy.

Museums & Galleries
☐ Brera Palace and Picture Gallery, at Milan, rich in the works of Lombard and northern Italian painters.
☐ Poldi Pezzoli Museum, Milan, with three major galleries filled with masterpieces, devoted to the Renaissance Lombard school.

Palaces
☐ The Ducal Palace, at Mantua, with luxuriously and sumptuously decorated apartments from the 16th to the 18th century.

Ace Attractions
☐ La Scala, at Milan, acclaimed by some as the world's greatest opera house, with a season lasting from mid-December to May.

Aeroporto di Linate, 4½ miles east of the inner city, and the **Aeroporto della Malpensa,** 31 miles to the northwest. In general, the Malpensa airport is used for most transatlantic flights, whereas Linate is for flights within Italy and Europe. For general flight information about both airports, call 74852200. Buses for Linate leave from the Porta Garibaldi station every 20 minutes between 5:40am and 8:40pm (stops are made at the Stazione Centrale). Buses for Malpensa leave from the Stazione Centrale every 2½ hours before international and intercontinental flight departures. This, I assure you, is much cheaper than taking a taxi.

By Train Milan is also serviced by the finest rail connections in Italy. The main rail station for arrivals is Mussolini's mammoth **Stazione Centrale,** where you'll find the National Railways information office (tel. 67500), open daily from 7am to 10:30pm. One train per hour arrives from either Genoa or Turin (trip time: 1½ to 2 hours from either city); a one-way fare from either point is 8,000 lire ($6.30). Twenty trains arrive per day from Venice (trip time: 3 hours), at a one-way fare of 15,000 lire ($11.80), and one train per hour arrives from Florence (trip time: 3 hours), with a one-way fare of 18,000 lire ($14.15).

By Bus ATM, whose offices are in the piazza del Duomo MM station (tel. 875495 for schedules and information), services the local area. As mentioned, service from other Italian cities isn't the best way to travel. However, one bus per hour arrives at or departs from piazza Castello in Milan to Turin; the trip lasts 2 hours and a one-way ticket costs 12,000 lire ($9.40). Buses might be convenient for going to Pavia or Bergamo (see below) from Milan.

By Car The A4 autostrada is the principal east-west route for Milan, with the A8 coming in from the northwest, the A1 from the southeast, and the A7 from the southwest. The A22 is another major north-south artery, running just east of Lake Garda.

Italians in the south, perhaps resentful of the hard-earned prosperity of the north, sometimes declare that the Milanese are not unlike their nearby neighbors, the no-nonsense Swiss. With two million inhabitants, Milan doesn't evoke the languor and garrulousness of the rest of Italy, it doesn't muck about with excessive manners, and it doesn't snooze somnolently in the midday heat. It works, it moves, and it bustles. It's Italy's window on Europe, its most sophisticated showcase, devoid of the dusty and musty history that sometimes seems to paralyze modern developments in Rome or Florence, or the watery rot that seems to pervade the sublimely beautiful Venice with an inevitable sense of decay.

Part of the work ethic that has catapulted Milan toward the 21st century may have been partly based on the Teutonic origins of the Lombards (originally from northwestern Germany) who occupied Milan and intermarried with its population after the collapse of the Roman Empire. Later, the Teutonic influence was strengthened during the 18th-century occupation by the Austrians.

Today, however, Milan is a chic and sophisticated powerhouse and, partly because of the 400 banks and the major industrial companies headquartered here, the most influential city in Italy. It is the center of the Italian publishing industry, the Italian silk industry, the Italian TV and advertising industries, the Italian design industry; and it lies very close to the densest collection of automobile-assembly plants, rubber and textile factories, and chemical plants in Italy. It also boasts La Scala, one of the most prestigious opera houses in Europe, a major commercial university (the alma mater of most of Italy's corporate presidents), and the site of several world-renowned annual trade fairs.

Since its beginning Milan has, with unashamed capitalistic style, purchased more art than it has produced, and lured to its borders what is probably the most energetic and hard-working group of creative intellects in all of Italy. To make it in Milan, in either business or the arts, is to have made it to the top of the pecking order in modern Italy. Milan is, in effect, the New York of Italy. If you miss the sun-flooded piazzas and the somnolent afternoons of your dreams, you probably won't find them amid the fogs and rains of Milan. You will, however, have placed your finger on the pulse of modern Italy.

Part of Milan's success is because of its need throughout history to succeed by its wits. Set on one of the most fertile plains in Europe, with few natural defenses other than the skill of its diplomats and traders, the Milanese have always more or less successfully negotiated through the labyrinth of European politics. Since the A.D. 313 proclamation by Constantine the Great of the Edict of Milan (which declared the Roman Empire officially Christian), Milan has been in the center of events.

In the 14th century the Visconti family, through their wits, wealth, and a series of astute marriages with the royal families of England and France, made Milan the strongest state in Italy. Realizing its dependence on agriculture early in its history, Milan initiated a continuing campaign of drainage and irrigation of the Po Valley that helped to make it one of the most lavishly fertile regions in the world.

Later, in the 1700s, Milan was dominated by the Hapsburgs, a legacy that left it with scores of neoclassical buildings in its inner core and an abiding appreciation for music and (perhaps) work. In 1848 Milan was at the heart of the northern Italian revolt against its Austro-Hungarian rulers. To buttress its claims of legitimacy, Milan encouraged the development of a pan-Italian dialect (through the novelist Manzoni) which could be understood by everyone in Italy, regardless of their native dialects. Milan (with neighbor Piedmont) was at the center of the 19th-century nationalistic passion that swept through Italy and laid the groundwork for the country's eventual unification. By the turn of the century thousands of workers had immigrated to Milan from the south; they swelled its rosters and raised its industrial output to envied figures.

Milan both elected and then helped to destroy Mussolini, who, after being shot

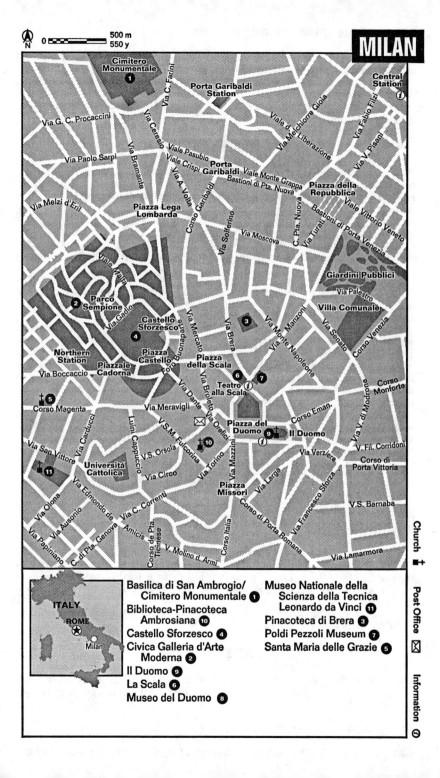

repeatedly by Milanese partisans, was hung by his heels on a meat hook, with his mistress, in the town's main square.

Today Milan is the only Italian city other than Rome that receives transatlantic flights. The city is elegant and prosperous; its inhabitants often chic and sophisticated, very tuned in to developments in Paris, London, and New York, and very proud of their dynamic and unusual city.

ORIENTATION

Piazza del Duomo lies in the heart of historical Milan. This square, which contains the Milan cathedral, is also the geographical heart of the ever-growing city. Milan is encircled by three "rings," one of which is the **Cerchia dei Navigli,** a road that more or less follows the outline of the former medieval walls. The road runs along what was formerly a series of canals—hence the name *navigli.* The second ring is known both as **Bastioni** or **Viali,** and it follows the outline of the Spanish Walls from the 16th century. It is now a tram route (take no. 29 or 30). A much more recent ring is the **Circonvallazione Esterna,** which connects you with the main roads coming into Milan.

If you're traveling within the Cerchia dei Navigli, which is relatively small, you can do so on foot. It is not recommended that you attempt to drive within this circle unless you're heading for a garage. All the major attractions, including Leonardo's *Last Supper,* La Scala, and the Duomo, lie within this ring.

One of Milan's most important streets, **via Manzoni,** begins near the Teatro alla Scala, and will take you to piazza Cavour, a key point for the traffic arteries of Milan. The **Arch of Porta Nuova** marks the entrance to via Manzoni. This *archi,* as they call it in Italian, is a remnant of the medieval walls. To the northwest of piazza Cavour lie the Giardini Pubblici, and to the northwest of these important gardens is **piazza della Repubblica.** From this square, via Vittorio Pisani leads into **piazza Duca d'Aosta,** site of the cavernous Stazione Centrale.

Back at piazza Cavour, you can head west along via Fatebenefratelli into the **Brera** district, whose major attraction is the Accademia di Brera at via Brera 28. This district in recent years has become a major center in Milan for offbeat shopping and after-dark diversions.

GETTING AROUND

A special 3,500-lira ($2.75) one-day **travel pass,** good for unlimited use on the city's tram, bus, and subway network, is available in Milan at the tourist office, Ente Provinciale per il Turismo, at via Marconi 1 (tel. 02/809662). A 2-day pass costs 6,000 lire ($4.70).

The city **bus** system covers most destinations in Milan, at a cost of 1,000 lire (80¢), as does the **subway** at the same fare. Some subway tickets are good for continuing trips on city buses at no extra charge, but they must be used within 75 minutes of purchase. These fares are presented only for your general guidance, and may go up in the lifetime of this edition.

To phone a **taxi,** dial 6767; fares start at 4,000 lire ($3.15). A nighttime surcharge of 4,000 lire ($3.15) is imposed.

FAST FACTS

American Express There is an American Express bank at via Brera 3 (tel. 72003694), open Monday through Friday from 9am to 5:30pm and on Saturday from 9am to 12:30pm.

Area Code The telephone area code is 02.

Consulates The **U.S. Consulate** at largo Donegani 1 (tel. 02/652841) is open

Monday through Friday from 9am to noon and 2 to 4pm. The consulate of **Canada** is at via Vittorio Pisani 19 (tel. 6697451), open Monday through Friday from 9am to noon and 2 to 4pm. Citizens of the **United Kingdom** will find their consulate at via San Paolo 7 (tel. 8693442), open Monday through Friday from 9am to 1pm and 2 to 5pm. **Australia** has a consulate at via Borgogna 2 (tel. 76013330), open Monday through Thursday from 8:30am to 1pm and 1:30 to 5pm, and on Friday from 8:30am to 1:15pm. Citizens of **New Zealand** need to go to their consulate in Rome.

Emergencies For the **police,** call 62261; to report a **fire,** 34999; and to seek **first aid,** 3883, or an **ambulance,** 7733.

Hospital About a 5-minute ride from the Duomo of Milan, **Ospedale Maggiore Policlinico,** Francesco Sforza 35 (tel. 581655), should answer your medical needs.

Laundry Try **Self-Service Lavanderia Automatica,** via Botticelli 7 (tel. 2663300), or **Aqua Secco,** via Betti 426 (tel. 306380).

Library The **U.S. Information Service** is at via Bigli 11A (tel. 795051), in the vicinity of piazza San Babila. It is open Monday through Wednesday from 9:30am to 1pm and 2:30 to 6pm, and on Thursday from 9:30am to 1pm and 2:30 to 7pm.

Newspapers Foreign newspapers, including the *International Herald Tribune,* can be found at all major newsstands, among them those at the Stazione Centrale and piazza del Duomo. If you read Italian (even just a little bit), you can pick up information about present attractions and coming events, such as cinema and theater schedules, by buying the daily *La Repubblica,* a useful newspaper. If you're seeking secondhand bargains, you can learn about sales in *Secondamano,* which comes out only on Monday and Thursday.

Pharmacies If you need a drugstore, you can find an all-night pharmacy by phoning 192 for information. A pharmacy (tel. 6690735) at the Stazione Centrale never closes.

Post Offices Most branches are open from 8:30am to 1:30pm Monday through Saturday. The **Central Post Office** is at via Cordusio 4 (tel. 8056582), and is open Monday through Friday from 8:15am to 8pm and on Saturday from 8:15am to 2pm. To reach it, take the subway to the Cordusio stop.

Religious Services Catholic services in English are conducted at Santa Maria Annunciata, piazza del Duomo 18 (tel. 804441).

Telephone If you need to make long-distance calls, try, if possible, to avoid going through your hotel switchboard, which imposes staggering surcharges. The best place is the Central Post Office (see above), where telephone booths and operators maintain a 24-hour service.

Tourist Offices One of the first things you may need in Milan is some information. If so, you'll find the **Azienda di Promozione Turistica del Milanese,** on piazza del Duomo at via Marconi 1 (tel. 870016), particularly helpful, dispensing free maps and whatever advice they can. There is a branch at the Stazione Centrale (tel. 6690532) for arriving train passengers.

WHAT TO SEE & DO

THE TOP ATTRACTIONS

Despite its modern architecture and industry, Milan is a city of great art. The serious sightseer will give the metropolis at least 2 days for exploration. If your schedule is frantic, see (1) the Duomo, (2) Da Vinci's *Last Supper* at the Santa Maria della Grazie, and (3) the important Brera Picture Gallery.

IL DUOMO, piazza del Duomo. Tel. 870907.

⭐ In the very center of Milan, opening onto the heart of the city's life, is piazza del Duomo. Its impressive lacy Gothic cathedral ranks with St. Peter's in Rome and the cathedral at Seville, Spain, among the largest in the world. It's 479 feet long and 284 feet wide at the transepts. The church, which dates from 1386, has seen numerous architects and builders. The conqueror of Milan, Napoleon, even added his own decorating ideas to the facade in the early years of the 19th century. The imposing structure of marble is the grandest and most flamboyant example of the Gothic style in Italy.

Built in the shape of a Latin cross, the cathedral is divided by soaring pillars into five naves. The overall effect is like a marble-floored Grand Central Terminal—that is, in space—with far greater dramatic intensity. In the crypt rests the tomb of San Carlo Borromeo, the cardinal of Milan. To experience the Duomo at its most majestic, you must ascend to the roof, either by elevator for 4,000 lire ($3.15) or by steps for 2,000 lire ($1.55), from which you can walk through a "forest" of pinnacles, turrets, and marble statuary—like a promenade in an early Cocteau film. The gilded Madonna towers over the tallest spire.

Admission: Free.

Open: June–Sept, daily 7am–7pm; Oct–May, daily 9am–4:30pm. **Subway:** Duomo. **Tram:** 1, 4, or 8.

MUSEO DEL DUOMO, in the Palazzo Reale, piazza del Duomo 14. Tel. 860358.

Across the square, the Museo del Duomo is housed in the Palazzo Reale (Royal Palace). It's like a picture storybook of the cathedral's 6 centuries of history. The museum has exhibits of statues and decorative sculptures, some of which date from the 14th century. Also shown are antique art objects, stained-glass windows (some from the 15th century), and ecclesiastical vestments, many as old as the 16th century.

Admission: 5,000 lire ($3.95).

Open: Tues–Sun 9:30am–12:30pm and 3–6pm. **Subway:** Duomo.

SANTA MARIA DELLE GRAZIE [*The Last Supper*], piazza Santa Maria delle Grazie. Tel. 4987588.

⭐ Off corso Magenta, on piazza Santa Maria delle Grazie, this Gothic church was erected by the Dominicans in the mid-15th century. A number of its more outstanding features, such as the cupola, were designed by the great Bramante. But "trippers" from all over the world flock here to gaze upon a mural in the convent next door. In what was once a refectory, the incomparable Leonardo da Vinci adorned one wall with *The Last Supper*. Commissioned by Ludovico the Moor, the painting was finished about 1497. The gradual erosion of the painting makes for one of the most intriguing stories in art. It narrowly escaped being bombed in 1943, and is now being restored. What remains today, however, is Leonardo's "outline"—and even it is suffering badly. As one Italian newspaper writer put it: "If you want to see 'Il Cenacolo,' don't walk—run!" A painting of grandeur, the composition portrays Christ at the moment he announces to his shocked apostles that one of them will betray him. Vasari called the portrait of Judas "a study in perfidy and wickedness."

Admission: 5,000 lire ($3.95).

Open: Sun–Mon 9am–1:15pm, Tues–Sat 9am–1:30pm and 2–6:15pm. **Subway:** Conciliazione.

PINACOTECA DI BRERA, via Brera 28. Tel. 808387.

⭐ The Pinacoteca di Brera, one of Italy's finest art galleries, contains an exceptionally good collection of both Lombard and Venetian masters. Like a Roman emperor, Canova's nude Napoleon—a toga draped over his shoulder—stands in the courtyard (fittingly, a similar statue ended up in the Duke of Wellington's house in London).

Among the notable artworks, a *Pietà* by Lorenzo Lotto is a work of great beauty, as is Gentile Bellini's *St. Mark Preaching in Alexandria* (it was finished by his brother, Giovanni). Seek out Andrea Mantegna's *Virgin and the Cherubs,* a great work from the Venetian school. Two of the most important prizes at the Brera are Mantegna's *Dead Christ* and Giovanni Bellini's *La Pietà,* as well as Carpaccio's *St. Stephen Debating.*

Other paintings include Titian's *St. Jerome,* as well as such Lombard art as Bernardino Luini's *Virgin of the Rose Bush* and Andrea Solarion's *Portrait of a Gentleman.* One of the greatest panels is Piero della Francesca's *Virgin and Child Enthroned with Saints and Angels and the Kneeling Duke of Urbino in Armor.* Seek out, in addition, the *Christ* by Bramante. One wing, devoted to modern art, offers works by such artists as Boccioni, Carrà, and Morandi. One of my favorite paintings in the gallery is Raphael's *Wedding of the Madonna,* with a dancelike quality. *The Last Supper at Emmaus* is another moving work, this one by Caravaggio.

Admission: 5,000 lire ($3.95).
Open: Mon 9am–1pm, Tues–Sat 9am–2pm. **Subway:** Lanza.

MORE ATTRACTIONS

POLDI PEZZOLI MUSEUM, via Manzoni 12. Tel. 794889.

✪ This truly fabulous museum is done in great taste and is rich with antique furnishings, tapestries, frescoes, and Lombard wood carvings. It also displays a remarkable collection of paintings by many of the old masters of northern and central Italy, including Andrea Mantegna's *Madonna and Child,* Giovanni Bellini's *Cristo Morto,* and Filippo Lippi's *Madonna, Angels, and Saints* (superb composition). One room is devoted entirely to Flemish artists, and there is a collection of ceramics and also one of clocks and watches. The museum grew out of a private collection donated to the city in 1871.

Admission: 5,000 lire ($3.95).
Open: Tues–Sat 9:30am–12:30pm and 2:30–6pm, Sun 9:30am–12:30pm and 2:30–7:30pm. **Closed:** Apr–Sept Sun 2:30–7:30pm. **Subway:** Manzoni. **Tram:** 1 or 4.

MUSEO D'ANTICA, in Castle Sforzesco, piazza Castello. Tel. 62083943.

Castle Sforzesco, the Castle of Milan, is an ancient fortress rebuilt by Francesco Sforza, who launched another governing dynasty. It is believed that both Bramante and Leonardo da Vinci contributed architectural ideas to the fortress. Following extensive World War II bombings, it was painstakingly restored and continued its activity as a Museum of Ancient Art. Displayed on the ground floor are sculpture from the 4th century A.D., medieval art mostly from Lombardy, and armor. The most outstanding exhibit, however, is Michelangelo's *Rondanini Pietà,* on which he was working the week he died. In the rooms upstairs, besides a good collection of ceramics, antiques, and bronzes, is the important picture gallery, rich in paintings from the 14th to the 18th century, including works by Lorenzo Veneziano, Mantegna, Lippi, Bellini, Crivelli, Foppa, Bergognone, Cesare da Sesto, Lotto, Tintoretto, Cerano, Procaccini, Morazzone, Guardi, and Tiepolo.

Admission: Free.
Open: Tues–Sun 9:30am–7pm. **Closed:** Jan 1, Easter, May 1, Aug 15, and Dec 25. **Subway:** Cairoli.

BIBLIOTECA-PINACOTECA AMBROSIANA, piazza Pio XI no. 2. Tel. 800146.

✪ Near the Duomo, the Ambrosiana Picture Gallery and Library were founded in the early 17th century by Cardinal Federico Borromeo. On the second floor, the Pinacoteca contains a remarkable collection of art, mostly from the 15th through the 17th century. Among the notable works are a *Madonna and Angels* by Botticelli; works by Brueghel (which have impressive detail, and are among the best art in the gallery); paintings by Lombard artists, including Bramantino's *Presepe,* in earthy, primitive colors; plus a curious miniature *St. Jerome with Crucifix* by Andrea Solario, along with works by Bernardino Luini. The museum owns a large sketch by Raphael on which he labored before painting *The School of Athens* for the Vatican. The most celebrated treasures are the productions of Leonardo da Vinci's *Codice*

Atlantico. (In Milan, the master had as a patron the powerful Ludovico Sforza, known as "The Moor.") After seeing the sketches (in facsimile), you can only agree with Leonardo's evaluation of himself as a genius without peer. Attributed to him is a portrait of a musician, believed to have been Franchino Gaffurio. The Library contains many medieval manuscripts, which are shown for scientific examination only.

Admission: 5,000 lire ($3.95).
Open: Sun–Fri 9:30am–5pm. **Subway:** Cordusio.

MUSEO NAZIONALE DELLA SCIENZA E DELLA TECNICA LEONARDO DA VINCI, via San Vittore 21. Tel. 48010040.

If you're a devotee of Leonardo da Vinci, as I am, you may want to drop by this vast museum complex where you could practically spend a week devouring the exhibits. For the average visitor the most interesting section is the Leonardo da Vinci Gallery, which displays copies and models from the Renaissance genius.

Another exhibit traces the rail industry in Italy, and presents 20 real locomotives. There is a reconstruction pharmacy from a convent, along with a monastic cell, even a sewing-machine collection. You'll also see antique carriages plus exhibits relating to astronomy, telecommunications, watchmaking, goldsmithery, motion pictures, and the subjects of classic physics.

Admission: 5,000 lire ($3.95).
Open: Tues–Sun 9:30am–8:30pm. **Subway:** Ambrogio.

CIVICA GALLERIA D'ARTE MODERNA, via Palestro 16. Tel. 76002819.

The Civica Galleria d'Arte Moderna (Civic Modern Art Gallery) used to be known as the royal villa before its name was changed to the Villa Comunale. Constructed between 1790 and 1793, it was designed by the architect Leopold Pollack. For a short time it was the residence of Napoleon and Eugène de Beauharnais. The gallery has a large collection of works from the Milanese neoclassical period, along with many paintings that show the development of Italian Romanticism. It is predictably rich in Lombard artists. Important collections that have been donated are those of Carlo Grassi and the Vismara art accumulation. Also important is the Marino Marini Museum, which was opened in 1973. Marini, a famous Italian sculptor, has some 200 works displayed, including not only sculpture, but paintings and graphics, all a gift of the artist himself. You'll recognize the names of many celebrated artists on parade: Picasso, Matisse, Rouault, Renoir, Modigliani, Corot, Millet, Manet, Cézanne, Bonnard, and Gauguin.

Admission: Free.
Open: Wed–Mon 9:30am–noon and 2:30–5:30pm. **Subway:** Palestro.

BASILICA DI SAN EUSTORGIO, piazza San Eustorgio 1. Tel. 8351583.

The bell tower of the 9th-century Basilica of San Eustorgio dates from the 13th century; it was built in the Romantic style by patrician Milanese families. It has the first tower clock in the world, made in 1305. Originally, this was the tomb of the Three Kings (4th century A.D.). Inside, its greatest treasure is the Capella Portinari, designed by the Florentine Michelozzo in the style of the Renaissance. The chapel is frescoed and contains a bas-relief of angels at the base of the cupola. In the center is an intricately carved tomb, supported by marble statuary of the 13th century by Balduccio of Pisa. Inside are the remains of St. Peter Martyr. The basement has a Roman crypt.

Admission: 500 lire (40¢).
Open: Daily 8am–noon and 3–7pm. **Bus:** 50 or 54.

BASILICA DI SAN AMBROGIO, piazza di San Ambrogio 15. Tel. 872059.

This was originally erected by St. Ambrose in the later years of the 4th century A.D. The present structure was built in the 12th century in the Romanesque style. The remains of St. Ambrose rest in the crypt. The church, entered after passing through a quadrangle, is rather stark and severe, in the style of its day. The atrium is its most distinguishing architectural feature. In the apse are interesting mosaics from the 12th century. The Lombard tower at the side dates from 1128, and the facade, with its two tiers of arches, is impressive.

Admission: 3,000 lire ($2.35).
Open: Daily 8am–noon and 3–7pm. **Closed:** Aug. **Subway:** San Ambrogio.
Bus: 50 or 54.

CIMITERO MONUMENTALE, piazzale Cimitero Monumentale 1. Tel. 6599938.

The Cimitèro Monumentale (Monumental Cemetery) has catered for more than 100 years to the whims of Milan's elite society. Actually, the only requirements for burial in the cemetery are, first, that you are dead, and second, that you can buy your way into a plot. Some families have paid up to 200 million lire just for the privilege of burying their dead here. The graves are marked not only with brass plates or granite markers, but also with Greek temples, elaborate obelisks, or such original works as an abbreviated version of Trajan's Column.

This outdoor museum has become such an attraction that a superintendent has compiled an illustrated guidebook—a sort of "Who *was* who." Among the cemetery's outstanding sights are a sculpted *The Last Supper.* Several fine examples of art nouveau sculpture dot the hillside, and there's a tasteful example of Liberty-style architecture (Italy's version of art nouveau) in a tiny chapel designed to hold the remains of Arturo Toscanini's son, who died in 1906. Among the notables buried here are Toscanini himself and novelist Alessandro Manzoni. In the Memorial Chapel is the tomb of Salvatore Quasimodo, who won the 1959 Nobel Prize in literature. Here also rest the ashes of Ermann Einstein, father of the scientist. In the Palanti Chapel is a monument commemorating the 800 Milanese citizens slain in Nazi concentration camps. (A model of this monument is displayed in the Museum of Modern Art in New York.) The location is a few blocks east of Stazione Porta Garibaldi.

Admission: Free.
Open: Apr–Sept, Tues–Sun 8:30am–6pm; Oct–Mar, Tues–Sun 8:30am–5pm.
Tram: 4, 8, 12, or 14.

WHERE TO STAY

In the city are some deluxe as well as a super-abundance of first- and second-class hotels, most of which are big on comfort but short on romance. In the third- and fourth-class bracket and on the pensione (boarding house) level there are dozens of choices—many of which rank at the bottom of the totem pole of comparably classed establishments in all of Italy's major cities, with the exception of Naples. Some places are outright dangerous, and others so rock-bottom and unappealing as to hold little interest for the average visitor. In several places, men sit around in the lobby in their bathrobes watching soccer games on the one TV set.

My recommendation is—if you can afford it—to stay in a better grade of hotel in Milan, and to leave your serious budgeting to such tourist meccas as Rome, Florence, and Venice, which have clean, comfortable, and often architecturally interesting third- and fourth-class hotels and pensioni. However, for the serious economizer I have included some budget recommendations for Milan, which, I am told, represent the best of the lot. They are presented as safe and (hopefully) clean shelters, but with no particular enthusiasm on my part.

Hotels judged "Very Expensive" charge more than 360,000 lire ($282.60) for a double room; "Expensive," 200,000 lire to 360,000 lire ($157 to $282.60); "Moderate," 125,000 lire to 200,000 lire ($98.15 to $157), and "Inexpensive," anything under 125,000 lire ($98.15). These prices are for a standard double room for two people, including tax and service. Sometimes breakfast is included too, but often it's extra.

VERY EXPENSIVE

EXCELSIOR GALLIA, piazza Duca d'Aosta 9, 20124 Milano. Tel. 02/ 6785. Fax 02/656306. 252 rms (all with bath). 10 suites. A/C MINIBAR TV TEL
Tram: 1, 2, 4, 5, or 9.
$ Rates: 250,000–375,000 lire ($196.25–$294.40) single; 420,000–475,000 lire ($329.70–$372.90) double; from 700,000 lire ($549.50) suite. Breakfast 25,000

lire ($19.65) extra. AE, DC, MC, V. **Parking:** 15,000–35,000 lire ($11.80–$27.50), depending on the size of your car.

Originally completed in 1933 by members of the Gallia family, the Excelsior Gallia was enlarged in the 1960s. Its decor is more art nouveau than its year of construction suggests. The hotel lies near the main railway station and is one of the most expensive in Milan. The bedrooms fall into two categories: modern and comfortable in the newer wing and more graciously old-fashioned in the original core. Some units open onto private balconies that front a busy square.

Dining/Entertainment: The hotel has a noted restaurant, Gallia's, serving regional and international dishes. Meals begin at 85,000 lire ($66.75). There is also a piano bar.

Services: Room service, baby-sitting, laundry, valet.

Facilities: Fitness club with a massage center, gym, whirlpool tub, and sauna.

GRAND HOTEL DUOMO, via San Raffaele 1, 20121 Milano. Tel. 02/8833. Fax 02/86462027. 160 rms (all with bath), 20 suites. A/C MINIBAR TV TEL **Subway:** Duomo.

$ Rates: 280,000 lire ($219.80) single; 390,000 lire ($306.15) double; from 530,000 lire ($416.05) suite. Breakfast 20,000 lire ($15.70) extra. MC, V.

The Grand Hotel Duomo, a former palace, is on a traffic-free side street leading directly up to the stone lacework of the side of the cathedral. The lobby is modern, with tall ceilings and a gilded mural showing flute players cavorting in a zoological garden. The low velvet chairs and the chrome and glass accents add an unusual perspective on the many older buildings that abound in this section of town. Businesspeople from many countries seem to prefer this hotel, patronizing its restaurant. The side of the hotel that faces piazza del Duomo is built in a style similar to the arches and arcades of the 19th-century Galeria a few steps away. It is also within walking distance of La Scala. The bedrooms have been renovated into a warmly tinted modern format with all the conveniences.

JOLLY PRESIDENT, largo Augusto 10, 20122 Milano. Tel. 02/7746. Fax 02/783449. 220 rms (all with bath). A/C MINIBAR TV TEL **Subway:** San Babila.

$ Rates (including breakfast): 350,000 lire ($274.75) single; 420,000 lire ($329.70) double. AE, DC, MC, V. **Parking:** 15,000–20,000 lire ($11.80–$15.70).

The Jolly President adds contemporary glamour to this popular chain. In the heart of the city, the Milan Jolly is slick and attractive. The decor throughout, although not daring or unconventional, is in good taste. Each of the well-furnished bedrooms, renovated in 1987, has picture windows and built-in furnishings. Bedside tables have gadgets to operate music and lights. All rooms have an adjoining lounge area with desks.

Dining/Entertainment: Its lounges, dining rooms, and cocktail bar successfully blend the modern with the traditional. Its restaurant, Il Verziere, offers a first-class cuisine. Meals begin at 65,000 lire ($51).

Services: Room service, baby-sitting, laundry, valet.

Facilities: Limited facilities for the disabled.

MILANO HILTON, via Galvani 12, 20124 Milano. Tel. 02/69831. Fax 02/66710810. 322 rms (all with bath), 18 suites. A/C MINIBAR TV TEL **Subway:** Stazione Centrale.

$ Rates: 320,000 lire ($251.20) single; 420,000 lire ($329.70) double; from 480,000 lire ($376.80) suite. Children stay free in parent's room. AE, DC, MC, V. **Parking:** 30,000 lire ($23.55).

The Milano Hilton is a modern glass-and-steel cube a few blocks from the main railway station. Its comfortably furnished bedrooms contain everything you'd expect in terms of high-quality accommodations, as well as many extras. This all-purpose hotel could suit either a tourist or a businessperson, and the mix of clients in the London Bar, with its richly upholstered chairs, contains a comfortable collection of both. The marble-trimmed lobby has four elevator banks.

Dining/Entertainment: The hotel spent millions of lire renovating the upstairs restaurant, Da Giuseppe, whose warmly chosen shades of gilt and brown, along with its Belle Epoque accessories, recall the era of Verdi, whose portrait hangs behind a frequently used grand piano. A portrait of Verdi's mistress, Giuseppina Strepponi, hangs on the opposite wall. Their juxtaposition helps to create the kind of intimacy that goes well with the Italian and international dishes that are the specialties of the house. The London Bar is like an elegant English pub.

Services: Room service, baby-sitting, laundry, valet.
Facilities: Facilities for the handicapped.

PALACE HOTEL, piazza della Repubblica 20, 20124 Milano. Tel. 02/ 6336. Fax 02/654485. 220 rms (all with bath), 6 suites. A/C MINIBAR TV TEL **Subway:** Repubblica. **Tram:** 1, 4, 11, 29, or 330.
$ **Rates:** 260,000–320,000 lire ($204.10–$251.20) single; 320,000–470,000 lire ($251.20–$368.95) double; from 700,000 lire ($549.50) suite. 19% IVA tax extra. Breakfast 26,500 lire ($20.80) extra. AE, DC, MC, V. **Parking:** 30,000 lire ($23.55). **Closed:** Aug.

The Hotel Palace, blithely ignoring the pell-mell commercial world around it, stands aloof on the slight rise of a hill near the railway station; it has a formal car entrance and a facade of 11 floors with tiers of balconies. Primarily a business hotel catering to some of Europe's most prominent figures, the Palace also welcomes tourists and occasional entertainers (Gina Lollobrigida has been a guest here). The bedrooms are furnished with pastel upholstery and carpeting, and reproductions of Italian antiques. Modern conveniences include heated towel racks and minibars concealed behind mahogany chests.

Dining/Entertainment: The hotel bar attracts a sophisticated international clientele, and the Grill Casanova is acclaimed as one of the finest in Milan, offering both regional and international dishes, with meals costing 90,000 lire ($70.65) and up.

Services: Room service, baby-sitting, laundry, valet.
Facilities: Fitness center.

PLAZA GRAND HOTEL (Grande Albergo Plaza), piazza Diaz 3, 20123 Milano. Tel. 02/8058452. Fax 02/867240. 120 rms (all with bath), 5 suites. A/C MINIBAR TV TEL **Bus:** 50, 54, 60, or 65.
$ **Rates** (including breakfast): 287,000–315,000 lire ($225.30–$247.30) single; 363,000–400,000 lire ($284.95–$314) double; from 500,000 lire ($392.50) suite. AE, DC, MC, V. **Parking:** 25,000 lire ($19.65).

The Plaza Grand Hotel is a dramatically angular hotel set on a square centered around a modern metallic sculpture a few blocks from the Duomo. The hotel's severe stone facade opens into a gray-and-white marble-covered lobby divided with mirrors and curved walls into a series of sunlit seating areas, one of which contains a bar. An aquarium bubbles in one corner of the lobby, softening the almost hi-tech ambience of the stylish decor. Each bedroom contains a radio and soundproofing. Breakfast is the only meal served.

PRINCIPE DI SAVOIA, piazza della Repubblica 17, 20124 Milano. Tel. 02/6230. Fax 02/6595838. 150 rms (all with bath), 18 suites. A/C MINIBAR TV TEL **Subway:** Repubblica. **Tram:** 1, 4, 11, 29, or 30.
$ **Rates:** 260,000–340,000 lire ($204.10–$266.90) single; 380,000–500,000 lire ($298.30–$392.50) double; from 850,000 lire ($667.25) suite. 19% IVA tax extra. Breakfast 23,000 lire ($18.05) extra. **Parking:** 25,000 lire ($19.65).

The Hotel Principe was built in 1927 to fill the need for a luxurious hotel in the vicinity of the Stazione Centrale. Substantial and luxurious, it offers good solid comfort in an overscale atmosphere that includes crystal, detailed plasterwork, fine carpets, and polished marble. The bedrooms are spacious and modernized. Many are paneled in hardwoods, and all contain leather chairs, stylish furniture, and modern bath with all the accessories. The Principe, whose elaborately ornamented wings date from 1947 and 1954, has housed what might be a "Who's Who" of modern Western society. Notable guests have included Luciano Pavarotti, Ingrid Bergman, Alexander Haig, Julio Iglesias, Henry Ford, a wide assortment of the Rockefellers, Evita Peron, Maria Callas, Jerry Lewis, and the Duke of Windsor.

Dining/Entertainment: The spacious bar area off the main lobby is the social focal point of the hotel. The hotel has a notable restaurant, serving both regional and international dishes with meals beginning at 85,000 lire ($66.75).

Services: Room service, baby-sitting, laundry, valet.

Facilities: Limited facilities for the disabled.

EXPENSIVE

CARLTON HOTEL SENATO, via Senato 5, 20121 Milano. Tel. 02/798583. Fax 02/785300. 79 rms (all with bath). A/C MINIBAR TV TEL **Subway:** San Balila.

$ Rates: 200,000 lire ($157) single; 250,000 lire ($196.25) double. Breakfast 17,500 lire ($13.75) extra. **Parking:** 45,000 lire ($35.35).

The facade of this hotel appears like a collection of private ocher-fronted villas joined into a single unit behind an iron fence. The modernized interior is set up to receive the dozens of traveling businesspeople who check in weekdays from other sections of Europe and from America. Each of the well-furnished bedrooms contains wall-to-wall carpeting and a high-ceilinged format. The hotel has a restaurant and bar on the premises, and also has a parking garage.

CAVOUR HOTEL, via Fatabenefratelli 21, 20121 Milano. Tel. 02/6572051. Fax 02/6592263. 113 rms (all with bath). A/C MINIBAR TV TEL **Subway:** Palestro.

$ Rates: 190,500 lire ($149.55) single; 214,500 lire ($168.40) double. Breakfast 15,000 lire ($11.80) extra. AE, DC, MC, V. **Parking:** 25,000 lire ($19.65).

This is a leading first-class hotel. The modern decor is far better than average—in fact, it's rather elegant. The hotel is spotlessly clean, offering good service and an excellent location, a short walk from the Duomo and La Scala. Rooms are attractively and comfortably furnished.

HOTEL EXECUTIVE, viale Don Luigi Sturzo 45, 20154 Milano. Tel. 02/6294. Fax 02/29010238. 420 rms (all with bath). A/C MINIBAR TV TEL **Subway:** Garibaldi.

$ Rates (including breakfast): 310,000 lire ($243.35) single; 360,000 lire ($282.60) double. AE, DC, MC, V. **Parking:** 13,000 lire ($10.20).

The Hotel Executive, inaugurated in 1973, is one of Milan's largest hotels. The modern furnishings in the bedrooms are in good taste, and the service is efficient. Its Gibigiana Restaurant, with some of the best meat dishes in Milan, is well known. You can have an excellent meal for 60,000 lire ($47.10). Public facilities include a bar and a garage for 500 cars.

WINDSOR, via Galileo Galilei 2, 20124 Milano. Tel. 02/6346. Fax 02/6590663. 114 rms (all with bath). A/C MINIBAR TV TEL **Subway:** Repubblica.

$ Rates (including breakfast): 194,000 lire ($152.30) single; 242,000 lire ($189.95) double. AE, DC, MC, V. **Parking:** 14,000 lire ($11).

The Windsor, which was erected and furnished in 1968, is an accomplishment. In spite of its "moderno," it maintains a warm ambience. A generous use of vibrant colors, plus a wise selection of traditional furnishings, with an accent on comfort, have made the Windsor a satisfactory hotel in its price range. A corner building of sienna-colored marble, it was built midway between the railway station and the Duomo on a tree-lined boulevard. The accommodations contain wall-to-wall draperies and built-in headboards and chests. Public facilities include a cozy bar, as well as a breakfast room, with tall panels of wood and walls of curtained glass. It's located near piazza Repubblica; there's a parking garage.

MODERATE

ALBERGO BOLZANO, via Boscovich 21, 20124 Milano. Tel. 02/6691451. Fax 02/6691455. 35 rms (all with bath or shower). A/C MINIBAR TV TEL **Subway:** Stazione Centrale.

$ Rates: 105,000 lire ($82.45) single; 156,000 lire ($122.45) double or twin. Breakfast 15,000 lire ($11.80) extra. AE, DC, MC, V. **Parking:** 15,000 lire ($11.80).

This hotel, about 500 feet from the main railway station, has been considerably renewed and upgraded. English is spoken, and the hotel has a helpful management, which makes this a welcome oasis. Ideal for families, some triple and quadruple units are also rented. The hotel has a patio and a comfortable lounge as well.

CASA SVIZZERA, via San Raffaele 3, 20121 Milano. Tel. 02/8692246.
Fax 02/3498190. 45 rms (all with bath). A/C MINIBAR TV TEL **Subway:** Duomo.
$ Rates (including breakfast): 155,000 lire ($121.70) single; 171,000 lire ($134.25) double. AE, DC, MC, V. **Parking:** 25,000 lire ($19.65).

Caza Svizzera, right off piazza del Duomo, is one of the most modern hotels in the city center, now that it has been rebuilt. Two elevators service five floors of rooms. Features include paneled double windows and soundproofing to keep out the noise. The bedrooms, furnished in a homelike fashion, have air conditioning that can be independently regulated.

HOTEL AUGUSTUS, via Napo Torriani 29, 20124 Milano. Tel. 02/66988271. Fax 02/6703096. 56 rms (all with bath or shower). A/C MINIBAR TV TEL **Subway:** Stazione Centrale.
$ Rates (including breakfast): 130,000 lire ($102.05) single; 195,000 lire ($153.05) double. AE, DC, MC, V. **Parking:** 25,000 lire ($19.65).

The Hotel Augustus is just far enough away from the railway station to miss the commotion, yet close enough for convenience. Throughout this medium-size hotel is a blending of marble, wood paneling, and contemporary furnishings. The rooms are compact, modern, and well furnished.

HOTEL GRAN DUCA DI YORK, via Moneta 1A, 20123 Milano. Tel. 02/874863. Fax 02/8690344. 33 rms (all with bath). TV TEL **Subway:** Cordusio.
$ Rates: 100,000 lire ($78.50) single; 143,000 lire ($112.25) double. Breakfast 12,000 lire ($9.40) extra. AE, V. **Parking:** 20,000 lire ($15.70). **Closed:** 3 weeks in Aug (dates vary).

⑤ When it was built by the Catholic church in the 1890s, this Liberty-style palace was used as a residence for dozens of priests who staffed the nearby Duomo. Among them was the cardinal of Milan, who later became Pope Pius XI. Today visitors can rent one of the pleasantly furnished and well-kept bedrooms, each with a private bath sheathed with patterned tiles. Breakfast costs extra. Behind the ocher-and-stone facade, visitors will find a bar in an alcove of the severely elegant lobby, where a suit of armor and leather-covered armchairs contribute to the restrained tone.

HOTEL MANZONI, via Santo Spirito 20, 20121 Milano. Tel. 02/76005700. Fax 02/784212. 52 rms (all with bath). TEL **Subway:** San Babila.
$ Rates: 105,000 lire ($82.45) single; 150,000 lire ($117.75) double. Breakfast 14,000 lire ($11) extra. No credit cards. **Parking:** 20,000 lire ($15.70).

⑤ The Hotel Manzoni charges reasonable prices considering its location near the most fashionable shopping streets of Milan. It lies behind a facade of stone slabs on a fairly quiet one-way street. Each of its bedrooms is outfitted with comfortable functional furniture and carpeting, which are color coordinated. A brass-trimmed winding staircase leads from the lobby into a bar and TV lounge. The cooperative English-speaking staff will point the way to the hotel's garage.

HOTEL STAR, via dei Bossi 5, 20121 Milano. Tel. 02/801501. Fax 02/861787. 30 rms (all with shower). A/C TV TEL **Subway:** Duomo.
$ Rates: 80,000–93,000 lire ($62.80–$73) single; 110,000–135,500 lire ($86.35–$106.35) double. Breakfast 15,000 lire ($11.80) extra. AE, MC, V.

The major drawback to this family-run hotel is its location on a narrow street that the

Milanese seem to consider their private racetrack. Despite that, its position a few blocks from La Scala and the Duomo make it an acceptable low-cost hotel. The dimly lit lobby contains comfortable armchairs, a TV, a bar, and marble floors. The Ceretti family rents simple, clean rooms.

INEXPENSIVE

ANTICA LOCANDA SOLFERINO, via Castelfidardo 2, 20121 Milano. Tel. 02/656905. Fax 02/656460. 11 rms (all with bath). TV TEL **Subway:** Moskova.
$ Rates: 70,500 lire ($55.35) single; 105,000 lire ($82.45) double. Breakfast 12,000 lire ($9.40) extra. V.

When Curzio Castelli established his country-style hotel in 1976, the surrounding neighborhood was considered a depressed backwater of downtown Milan. Since then, however, the location has improved into an avant-garde community of actors, writers, and poets, and this inn deserves some of the credit for the transformation. Castelli, a former road-construction engineer in the jungles of Central and South America, believed the time was right for a personalized approach to innkeeping. He got off to a fortuitous beginning soon after the hotel opened when members of the editorial staff of *Gentleman's Quarterly* stayed here for one of their fashion investigations in Milan. Since then, Lindsay Kemp and Marcello Mastroianni have been among the fashionable clients who either stay in one of the old-fashioned bedrooms or who dine at the ground-floor restaurant (see my recommendation in "Where to Dine," below).

Each bedroom is different, which reflects the floor plan of the 19th-century building that houses it. The furnishings include Daumier engravings, art nouveau or late 19th-century bourgeois pieces, and various armoires purchased from a nearby hotel that went out of business. Staying between the white walls whose doors are surrounded with handcrafted moldings is like lodging in a room 50 years ago. If you didn't know you were in the heart of the most industrialized city of Italy, you'd think you were in a small village. But the baths are modern. Breakfast is extra. Since the hotel is small and often fully booked, it's wise to make reservations as far in advance as possible.

HOTEL KENNEDY, viale Tunisia 6, 20124 Milano. Tel. 02/29400934. 12 rms (5 with shower). TV **Subway:** Porta Venezia.
$ Rates: 40,000 lire ($31.40) single without bath, 45,000 lire ($35.35) single with bath; 60,000 lire ($47.10) double without bath, 80,000 lire ($62.80) double with bath. Breakfast 5,000 lire ($3.95) extra. MC, V. **Parking:** 16,000 lire ($12.55).
The Hotel Kennedy, on the sixth floor of an office building (reached by elevator), is an immaculate accommodation with pleasant rooms. The units are small but comfortable, and the owners watch out for the well-being of their guests. After midnight the door is locked, but they will give you a key.

LONDON HOTEL, via Rovello 3, 20121 Milano. Tel. 02/872988. Fax 02/8057037. 29 rms (15 with bath and shower). A/C TEL **Subway:** Cordusio.
$ Rates: 42,000 lire ($32.95) single without bath, 62,500 lire ($49.05) single with bath; 64,500 lire ($50.65) double without bath, 96,000 lire ($75.35) double with bath. Breakfast 10,000 lire ($7.85) extra. MC, V.
This is a pleasant little hotel near the center of town, convenient for sightseeing and shopping. It's just off via Dante between Miravegli and Foro Buonaparte, a brief walk to piazza del Duomo. Francesco Gambino, who heads this family-operated establishment, speaks English. Rooms are simple, but clean and comfortable.

WHERE TO DINE

The distinctive cooking of Lombardy, which relies heavily on country butter, reaches its finest levels of accomplishment in Milan. Even the minestrone tastes different here from the way it does in other parts of Italy. The specialty is risotto, rice cooked in consommé and flavored with saffron. The vines of Lombardy yield tender grapes, and the grapes are transformed into such aromatic wines as Barbagallo, Buttafucco, and something called "Inferno." The wide economic levels of the population—from textile manufacturer to factory worker—are reflected in the prices in the restaurants, which range from the haute-cuisine type to the pizza parlor.

VERY EXPENSIVE

EL TOULA, piazza Paolo Ferrari 6. Tel. 29517670.
Cuisine: ROMAN/LOMBARD. **Reservations:** Required. **Subway:** Duomo.
$ Prices: Appetizers 15,000–32,000 lire ($11.80–$25.10); main courses 30,000–44,000 lire ($23.55–$34.55). AE, DC, MC, V.
Open: Lunch Mon–Sat noon–2:30pm; dinner Mon–Sat 8–10:30pm. **Closed:** Aug 3–26.

El Toulà, right behind La Scala in the business district, draws the VIP crowd at lunch, and the opera-goers—the cream of Milanese society—in the evening. It is smart, fashionable, elegant, and also expensive. But the service and food are impeccable, as the owners of this "Hayloft" run El Toulà in Rome, one of that city's best restaurants. Popular before and after the theater, El Toulà offers flawless service and a superb wine cellar. Some specialties, particularly veal and beef dishes, are served in its Roman counterpart, but there are variations unique to Lombardy.

GALLIA'S RESTAURANT, in the Hotel Excelsior Gallia, piazza Duca d'Aosta 9. Tel. 6785.
Cuisine: INTERNATIONAL. **Reservations:** Required. **Subway:** Stazione Centrale.
$ Prices: Appetizers 20,000–30,000 lire ($15.70–$23.55); main courses 32,000–45,000 lire ($25.10–$35.35); fixed-price menu 70,000 lire ($54.95). AE, DC, MC, V.
Open: Lunch daily 12:30–2:30pm; dinner daily 7:30–10:30pm.

This is one of the best—perhaps *the* best—of the hotel restaurants of this highly competitive city. Its chef, Nicola Magnifico, has been widely acclaimed. *Il Giornale*, the Milanese daily, wrote that Mr. Magnifico is today the most famous chef in Italy after Gualtiero Marchesi. Decorated with a sumptuous flourish, this stylish dining room lies within the previously recommended hotel (see "Where to Stay," above). Your repast might include smoked swordfish, spaghetti with zucchini flowers and shrimp, succulent slices of braised foie gras, and risotto with porcini mushrooms. For the most part, the cooking is a very Italian modern cuisine, influenced by the kitchens of both Milan and Naples.

GIANNINO, via Amagore Sciesa 8. Tel. 5452948.
Cuisine: MILANESE. **Reservations:** Required. **Tram:** 29 or 30.
$ Prices: Appetizers 18,000–20,000 lire ($14.15–$15.70); main courses 30,000–35,000 lire ($23.55–$27.50). AE, DC, MC, V.
Open: Lunch Mon–Sat noon–2:30pm; dinner Mon–Sat 8–10:30pm. **Closed:** Aug.

Giannino continues to enchant its loyal patrons and to win new adherents every year who sing its praises. Rightly, it's considered one of the top restaurants in all of Lombardy, and has been since its founding in 1899. It has a chef who approaches every day as if he must make his reputation anew. Diners have a choice of several attractively styled rooms, but eyes rivet on the tempting underglass offerings of the *specialità gastronomiche milanesi* from the behind-the-glass kitchen. The choice is excellent, including such characteristic Lombard dishes as the tender, breaded veal cutlet and the risotto simmered in broth and coated with parmesan cheese. It's difficult to recommend any specific dish, as everything I've ordered, or even seen going by, piqued my taste. However, I have special affection for the tagliolini con scampi al verde, fresh homemade noodles with prawn tails in green herb sauce. Also superb are the cold fish and seafood salad and the beautifully seasoned orata al cartoccio (a European fish). This fish is baked in a brown paper bag with shrimp and butter along with fresh herbs.

GUALTIERO MARCHESI, via Bonvesin de la Riva 9. Tel. 741246.
Cuisine: ITALIAN. **Reservations:** Required. **Tram:** 1. **Bus:** 60 or 73.
$ Prices: Appetizers 24,000–60,000 lire ($18.85–$47.10); main courses 40,000–

60,000 lire ($31.40–$47.10); fixed-price menus 90,000–140,000 lire ($70.65–$109.90). AE, DC, MC, V.
Open: Lunch Tues–Sat 12:30–2pm; dinner Mon–Sat 7:30–11:30pm. **Closed:** Sat in July and all of Aug.

The namesake of this restaurant has been cited for years as the patron saint of the *cucina nuova* in Italy. The most creative chef in Italy, Signor Marchesi has invented more original dishes than any competitor in Milan. In fact, *Time* magazine has rated him among the top 10 chefs in the world. Many consider his establishment the finest restaurant in the entire country. A piece of futuristic sculpture sits on each of the limited number of tables in this coolly dignified restaurant where, it is said, the bland decor lights up as soon as the owner, a consummate showman, enters the dining room. The menu may have changed radically by the time you arrive, depending on Signor Marchesi's inspiration. However, you are likely to find rice with herbs and scampi, twice-cooked filet of red mullet (first sautéed, then braised), ragoût of kidneys, cold spaghetti with chives and caviar, and lobster with a purée of sweet peppers. You might also try the crayfish, cooked very al dente, with cucumbers and olive oil, or sample an unusual form of half-opened ravioli. The kitchen uses only super-fresh ingredients. Meals run 100,000 lire to 150,000 lire ($78.50 to $117.75), but could cost twice as much. A jacket and tie are required.

SAVINI, Galleria Vittorio Emanuele II. Tel. 8058343.
　　Cuisine: LOMBARD. **Reservations:** Required. **Subway:** Duomo.
$ **Prices:** Appetizers 20,000–22,000 lire ($15.70–$17.25); main courses 35,000–60,000 lire ($27.50–$47.10). AE, DC, MC, V.
　　Open: Lunch Mon–Sat noon–3pm; dinner Mon–Sat 7:30–11pm. **Closed:** Aug 9–26 and Dec 20–Jan 7.

Savini provides a heavenly introduction to the aromatic cookery of Lombardy and has attracted everybody from Puccini to Pavarotti. Perched in the heart of the great glass-enclosed arcade opposite the Duomo, this "classico" restaurant, which dates from 1867, draws the elite, including both the out-of-towner and the discriminating local who wants some of the most savory viands in the city. Guests sit on the terrace outside, or dine in the old-world main room, with its crystal chandeliers and glittering silverware. Waiters in black jackets hover over you to see that you enjoy every mouthful. Many of the most memorable dishes are unassuming, for example, the specialty of Lombardy—costoletta alla milanese, the most tender veal coated with an egg batter and breadcrumbs, then fried a rich brown. The pièce de résistance of Milan, most often ordered before the main course, is risotto alla milanese—that is, rice simmered in a broth and dressed with whatever the artiste in the kitchen selects that night. Savini is excellently stocked with a wide range of wines (the staff will gladly assist you).

ST. ANDREWS, via Sant'Andrea 23. Tel. 76023132.
　　Cuisine: INTERNATIONAL. **Reservations:** Required. **Bus:** 65, 96, or 97.
$ **Prices:** Appetizers 15,000–35,000 lire ($11.80–$27.50); main courses 30,000–45,000 lire ($23.55–$35.35). AE, DC, MC, V.
　　Open: Lunch Mon–Sat 12:30–3:30pm; dinner Mon–Sat 7pm–1am. **Closed:** Aug.

This restaurant has given much pleasure to many people for many years. It offers one of the finest kitchens in Lombardy, preparing both international and regional food. The cuisine is superior. Try, for example, marinated salmon, sea-bass pie with a potato crust, or the apple tart. At lunch it has somewhat the atmosphere of a private club, and is apt to be filled with businesspeople talking about the affairs of Italy. The armchairs are covered in black leather, the paneling is dark wood, and the lighting is discreet from hooded lamps. Formally attired waiters give superb service.

EXPENSIVE

A SANTA LUCIA, via San Pietro all'Orto 3. Tel. 76023155.
　　Cuisine: ITALIAN/SEAFOOD. **Reservations:** Recommended. **Subway:** San Babila.

$ Prices: Appetizers 10,000–15,000 lire ($7.85–$11.80); main courses 15,000–45,000 lire ($11.80–$35.35). No credit cards.
Open: Dinner only, Tues–Sun 8pm–2am. **Closed:** Aug.

A Santa Lucia pulls out hook, line, and sinker to lure you with some of the best fish dinners in Milan. A festive place at which to dine, the restaurant is decked out with photographs of pleased celebs, who attest to the skill of its kitchen. You can order such specialties as a savory fish soup, which is a meal in itself; fried baby squid; or good-tasting sole. Spaghetti alle vongole evokes the tang of the sea with its succulent clam sauce. Pizza also reigns supreme. Try either the calzone of Naples or the pizza napoletana, the classic dish of the city on the bay. Both are made with mozzarella.

ALFIO-CAVOUR, via Senato 31. Tel. 780731.

Cuisine: ITALIAN/INTERNATIONAL. **Reservations:** Recommended. **Subway:** San Babila.
$ Prices: Appetizers 10,000–20,000 lire ($7.85–$15.70); main courses 20,000–38,000 lire ($15.70–$29.85). AE, DC, MC, V.
Open: Lunch Mon–Fri 12:30–3pm; dinner Sun–Fri 7:30–11pm. **Closed:** Aug 6–20.

There's a luminous quality to the lavish displays of antipasti served with relish at this family-run restaurant. It stems partly from the Tahitian-style decor, where trees grow through the glass panels of a greenhouselike roof and vines entwine themselves among bamboo lattices. You'll be seated in the clear light of what used to be a private garden. The restaurant is best known for its serve-yourself display of antipasti, where the polite but sharp-eyed staff bills you for what you select. A pasta specialty is the flavorful spaghetti pescatore, with bits of seafood. You might follow with large grilled shrimp or a "gran misto" fish fry, or else one of the many excellent beef or veal dishes.

AL PORTO, piazzale Generale Cantore. Tel. 8321481.

Cuisine: SEAFOOD/ITALIAN. **Reservations:** Required. **Subway:** S. Agostino.
$ Prices: Appetizers 12,000–25,000 lire ($9.40–$19.65); main courses 22,000–30,000 lire ($17.25–$23.55). AE, DC, MC, V.
Open: Lunch Tues–Sat 12:30–2:30pm; dinner Mon–Sat 7:30–10:30pm. **Closed:** Aug.

Al Porto, another seafood restaurant, is located in a customs house from the 18th century. It offers one of the best seafood menus in town, and all dishes are well prepared and beautifully served. Specialties include risotto di frutti di mare (seafood), scampi alla livornese, and orata (dorado) al cartoccio. For dessert, I'd suggest the gelato (ice cream) with whisky.

ANTICO BOEUCC, piazza Belgioioso 2. Tel. 76020224.

Cuisine: INTERNATIONAL. **Reservations:** Essential. **Subway:** Duomo.
$ Prices: Appetizers 14,000–16,000 lire ($11–$12.55); main courses 25,000–28,000 lire ($19.65–$22). AE.
Open: Lunch Mon–Fri 12:30–2:30pm; dinner Sun–Fri 7:30–10:30pm. **Closed:** Aug.

This restaurant, established in 1682, is a trio of rooms in a severely elegant old palace, within walking distance of the Duomo and the major shopping streets of Milan. Throughout you'll find soaring stone columns and modern art. In summer, guests gravitate to a terrace for open-air dining. The hearty specialties, the standard of the kitchen, come from different regions of Italy. You might enjoy a spaghetti in clam sauce, a salad of shrimp with arugula and artichokes, or grilled liver, veal, or beef with aromatic herbs. In season, sautéed zucchini flowers accompany some dishes.

LA SCALETTA, piazza Stazione Porta Genova 3. Tel. 58100290.

Cuisine: ITALIAN. **Reservations:** Required. **Subway:** Stazione Genova.
$ Prices: Appetizers 15,000–16,000 lire ($11.80–$12.55); main courses 28,000–30,000 lire ($22–$23.55). No credit cards.
Open: Lunch Tues–Sat noon–1:15pm; dinner Tues–Sat 8–9:30pm. **Closed:** Aug.

La Scaletta emerges near the top in the highly competitive world of Milanese restaurants. Here, modern Italian cuisine is practiced by the chefs with a certain flair. In an elegant setting, which some diners have likened to a small and exclusive London club, the restaurant serves in two rooms. Because this place is so popular with the business community of the city, reservations are essential, as far in advance as possible. The quality of the ingredients is superb. The chefs demand that every item be fresh, whether it be fish or vegetables. The veal dishes are heavenly. You might begin with a tripe terrine in gelatin or a scampi salad, before giving serious attention to your main course.

OSTERIA DEL VECCHIO CANNETO, via Solferino 56. Tel. 6598498.
   Cuisine: ABRUZZESE/SEAFOOD. **Reservations:** Recommended. **Subway:** Moskova.
   $ Prices: Fixed-price dinner 60,000 lire ($47.10). AE, V.
   Open: Lunch Tues–Sat 12:15–2pm; dinner Mon–Sat 7–10:30pm. **Closed:** Aug.
This restaurant is the sibling of the also-recommended Gran Sasso (see below). What the Gran Sasso does with regional cookery, Canneto achieves with the denizens of the deep. For a fixed price you're given a staggering seafood dinner, 16 courses if you want it. You can order pasta, but nearly everything else is from the sea. The cellar location, where you're greeted by a foghorn, is as crowded as its seafood platter. Go here only if you have a gargantuan appetite and are in the mood for noisy, good fun.

PECK'S BOTTEGA DEL VINO, via Victor Hugo 4. Tel. 876774.
   Cuisine: MILANESE/ITALIAN. **Reservations:** Required. **Subway:** Duomo.
   $ Prices: Appetizers 14,000–15,000 lire ($11–$11.80); main courses 28,000–30,000 lire ($22–$23.55). AE, DC, MC, V.
   Open: Lunch Mon–Sat noon–2:30pm; dinner Mon–Sat 7–10:30pm. **Closed:** Sun July 1–20.
   Peck's is owned by the famous delicatessen of Milan, which many gastronomes consider the Milanese equivalent of Fauchon's in Paris. In an environment filled with shimmering marble and modern Italian paintings, an alert staff will serve you an elegant cuisine. The fresh specialties include a classic version of risotto milanese, rack of lamb with fresh rosemary, ravioli alla fonduta, and lombo di vitello (veal) with artichokes, followed by chocolate meringue for dessert.

MODERATE

AL CHICO, via Sirtori 24. Tel. 29406883.
   Cuisine: TUSCAN. **Reservations:** Recommended. **Subway:** Porta Venezia.
   $ Prices: Appetizers 8,000–24,000 lire ($6.30–$18.85); main courses 18,000–25,000 lire ($14.15–$19.65). AE, DC, MC, V.
   Open: Lunch Tues–Sat noon–2:30pm; dinner Mon–Sat 7–10:30pm. **Closed:** Aug 3–27.
Al Chico is a good neighborhood restaurant, which specializes in such fare as onion soup and fondue bourguignonne. Tuscan specialties such as Florentine beefsteak are also featured, and portions are tasty and satisfying. The place is usually crowded, but it's worth the wait for a table. The service is good, and the basic materials that go into the dishes are fresh and well selected at the market. Of course, you'll want to order chianti, that most typical of all Italian wines, to go with your meal. Good house wines from Tuscany are stocked. In summer, you can eat in a garden.

BIFFI, Galleria Vittorio Emanuele. Tel. 8057961.
   Cuisine: MILANESE/ITALIAN. **Reservations:** Recommended. **Subway:** Duomo.
   $ Prices: Appetizers 15,000–18,000 lire ($11.80–$14.15); main courses 25,000–30,000 lire ($19.65–$23.55). AE, DC, MC, V.
   Open: Lunch Mon–Sat noon–2:30pm; dinner Mon–Sat 7–10pm.
Biffi is located in the most popular shopping arcade of Milan. The decor tries to re-create the nostalgic era of the gallery's construction, with its Belle Epoque globe lights, bentwood chairs, and polished brass. Despite the glass canopy high above the heads of the sidewalk diners, there's a striped awning over the pavement in front, with

uniformed waiters who hover in the background. The interior contains a self-service buffet one floor above ground level, while the small tables of the ground floor offer such Italian specialties as roast veal and risotto parmigiana. A la carte meals can be as simple or as elaborate as you want. A fixed-price buffet menu in the restaurant costs 31,000 lire ($24.35), but only 13,000 lire ($10.20) for a full meal in the self-service section.

LA MAGOLFA, via Magolfa 15. Tel. 8321696.
Cuisine: MILANESE/LOMBARD. **Reservations:** Required. **Subway:** Porta Genova.
$ Prices: Appetizers 10,000–15,000 lire ($7.85–$11.80); main courses 15,000–20,000 lire ($11.80–$15.70); fixed-price meal 55,000 lire ($43.20). AE, DC, MC, V.
Open: Dinner only, Mon–Sat 8pm–midnight. **Closed:** Aug.

La Magolfa, one of the city's dining bargains, offers a gargantuan fixed-price meal. The building is a country farmhouse with checkered cloths. It's likely to be crowded, as is every other restaurant in Milan that offers such value. If you don't mind its location away from the center of town, in Zona Ticinese in the southern part of the city, you'll be treated to some very good regional cookery which emerges fresh from battered pots and pans. A general air of conviviality reigns. There is music of local origin nightly.

MANHATTAN, via Verri 3. Tel. 76023566.
Cuisine: MILANESE. **Reservations:** Required at dinner. **Subway:** San Babila.
$ Prices: Appetizers 15,000–20,000 lire ($11.80–$15.70); main courses 18,000–28,000 lire ($14.15–$22). AE, DC, MC, V.
Open: Lunch Mon–Sat noon–2:30pm; dinner Mon–Sat 7:30pm–1am or later.
The view from the dining room is of a charming garden, which at night is skillfully illuminated. This is a good choice for an uncomplicated meal. The cuisine is traditional Milanese, and in the evening, piano music from the adjacent bar is likely to soothe your nerves.

OPERA PRIMA, via Rovello 3. Tel. 865235.
Cuisine: MILANESE. **Reservations:** Recommended. **Subway:** Duomo.
$ Prices: Appetizers 8,000–12,000 lire ($6.30–$9.40); main courses 22,000–30,000 lire ($17.25–$23.55). AE, DC, MC, V.
Open: Lunch Mon–Fri 12:30–2pm; dinner Mon–Sat 8–10:30pm. **Closed:** Aug 5–25.
This is an excellent choice in the center of the city, just a short walk from the Duomo. Francesco Gambino specializes in a classic Milanese cuisine. His establishment is smartly decorated in the Liberty style (Italian art nouveau), with old furniture and candlelit tables. His house specialties include such dishes as taglionlini Opera Prima (noodles with chicken, vegetables, cream, and chili sauce), followed by a traditional veal cutlet milanese. For dessert, he suggests crespelle alla vaniglia e al cioccolato (chocolate and vanilla crêpes). In air-conditioned comfort, guests have the choice of two dining rooms.

PECK, via Victor Hugo 4. Tel. 876774.
Cuisine: MILANESE/LOMBARD. **Reservations:** Required. **Subway:** Duomo.
$ Prices: Appetizers 8,000–10,000 lire ($6.30–$7.85); main courses 12,000–15,000 lire ($9.40–$11.80). AE, DC, MC, V.
Open: Lunch Mon–Sat noon–2:30pm; dinner Mon–Sat 7–10:30pm. **Closed:** July 1–20.

Peck offers one of the best mealtime values in Milan, served in a glamorous cafeteria associated with the most famous delicatessen in Italy (a high-priced restaurant is in the basement where meals cost from 70,000 lire ($54.95). Only a short walk from the Duomo, Peck has a stand-up bar in front, and, in the rear, well-stocked display cases that contain specialties fresh from the establishment's treasure trove of produce. Armed with a plastic tray, you can sample such Italian-cuisine tempters as artichoke-and-parmesan salad, seafood salads, marinated carpaccio, slabs of tender veal in a herb sauce, risotto marinara, and selections from a carving table laden with a juicy display of roast meats.

RISTORANTE SOLFERINO, via Castelfidardo 2. Tel. 6599886.

Cuisine: MILANESE. **Reservations:** Recommended. **Subway:** Moskova.

$ **Prices:** Appetizers 10,000–15,000 lire ($7.85–$11.80); main courses 18,000–25,000 lire ($14.15–$19.65). AE, DC, MC, V.

Open: Lunch Mon–Fri noon–2pm; dinner Mon–Sat 7–11pm. **Closed:** Aug 10–20.

This is a country-style inn with all the accoutrements you'd expect to find in an agrarian community on the outskirts of town rather than in the center of a busy city. Below a beamed ceiling, next to racks of wine bottles and among the fashion stars, you can dine on such specialties as risotto Grande Milano, Milanese veal with vegetables, gnocchi with salmon, carpaccio, and tagliata Solferino, and follow with a dessert known as "Milanese custard." The establishment maintains a limited number of bedrooms upstairs (see "Where to Stay," above), as well as a less formal and much less expensive buffet-style restaurant just around the corner.

TAVERNA DEL GRAN SASSO, piazza Principessa Clotilde 10. Tel. 6597578.

Cuisine: ABRUZZI. **Reservations:** Not needed. **Tram:** 29 or 30.

$ **Prices:** All-you-can-eat dinner 50,000 lire ($39.25); lunch 30,000 lire ($23.55). AE, MC, V.

Open: Lunch Mon–Thurs and Sat noon–1:45pm; dinner Mon–Sat 7:45–10:30pm. **Closed:** Aug.

This old tavern provides regional meals, and a visit here is a joyride as well. Filled with lots of sentimental baubles, its walls are crowded ceiling to floor with copper molds, ears of corn, strings of pepper and garlic, and cart wheels. A tall open hearth burns with a charcoal fire, and a Sicilian cart is laden with baskets of bread, dried figs, nuts, and kegs of wine. As you enter, you'll find a mellowed wooden keg of wine with a brass faucet (you're to help yourself, using glass mugs). The cuisine features a number of specialties from the Abruzzi district in the south of Italy—regional dishes such as maccheroni alla chitarra, a distinctively shaped macaroni with a savory meat sauce. The first course offers at least 10 choices; the second, two; the third, four; the fourth, five; and there are six or seven desserts to choose from for the final selection. The waiters and waitresses wear folk apparel, and they join in the spirit of the place—often by singing folk songs.

TRATTORIA BAGUTTA, via Bagutta 14. Tel. 76002767.

Cuisine: INTERNATIONAL. **Reservations:** Required. **Subway:** San Babila.

$ **Prices:** Appetizers 15,000–16,000 lire ($11.80–$12.55); main courses 28,000–32,000 lire ($22–$25.10). AE, DC, MC, V.

Open: Lunch Mon–Sat 12:30–2:30pm; dinner Mon–Sat 7:30–10:30pm. **Closed:** Aug.

Patronized by artists, this restaurant is the most celebrated of the trattorie in Milan. A venerable-looking establishment, which dates from 1927, it is slightly hard to find in its side-street location. The Bagutta is known for the caricatures—framed and frescoed—that cover its walls. Of the many large and bustling dining rooms, the rear one with its picture windows is most enticing. The lushly tempting food draws on the kitchens of Lombardy, Tuscany, and Bologna for inspiration. Assorted antipasti are offered. Main-dish specialties include fried squid and scampi, lingua e pure (tongue with mashed potatoes), and scaloppine alla Bagutta. The Bagutta enjoys a vogue among out-of-towners, who consider it chic to patronize the sophisticated little trattoria, as opposed to the more deluxe restaurants.

INEXPENSIVE

AL TEMPIO D'ORO, via delle Leghe 23. Tel. 26145709.

Cuisine: ITALIAN. **Reservations:** Not needed. **Subway:** Pasteur.

$ Prices: Appetizers 3,000–5,000 lire ($2.35–$3.95); main courses 6,000–16,000 lire ($4.70–$12.55). No credit cards.
Open: Mon–Sat 8pm–3am. **Closed:** Aug.

This restaurant, near the central railway station, offers inexpensive and well-prepared meals in an ambience similar to what you might have found if an ancient Greek temple had decided to serve beer on tap along with international food specialties. The crowd scattered among the ceiling columns is relaxed, and they contribute to an atmosphere that is somewhat like that of a beer hall. No one will mind if you stop by just for a drink.

L'ACERBA, via Orti 4. Tel. 5455475.

Cuisine: ITALIAN. **Reservations:** Recommended. **Subway:** Porta Romana.
$ Prices: Appetizers 8,000–9,000 lire ($6.30–$7.05); main courses 16,000–18,000 lire ($12.55–$14.15). No credit cards.
Open: Lunch Tues–Fri 12:30–2:30pm; dinner Tues–Sun 8pm–1am; brunch Sun 10am–2:30pm.

Many of the clients who come here are local residents who stock up on the herbal ingredients that are sold from the establishment's small shop. Most of them choose to stay, however, for one of the flavorful and healthy dishes that the kitchen produces with great flair. Scattered among a handful of antiques, in a handsome room with a stone floor and the accoutrements of a café, are a collection of dining tables where food is served.

The menu is not strictly vegetarian, although many vegetarian dishes are featured. Specialties are made with biologically grown vegetables, extra-virgin olive oil, whole-wheat pasta, natural fruit juices, and meat derived from natural breeding methods, with no traces of hormones, vitamins, or chemical products. The establishment serves teas and tisanes, pastries, and late suppers for the after-theater crowd. Brunch consists of a normal Italian breakfast plus all the American breakfast extras. A fixed-price lunch costs 17,000 lire ($13.35); a fixed-price brunch (Sunday only), 32,500 lire ($25.50).

Tip: If you're still hungry after a meal here, add even more nutrition to your diet by asking for a portion of soya ice cream.

PIZZERIA GASPARE, via Piero della Francesca 52. Tel. 48006409.

Cuisine: PIZZA/SEAFOOD. **Reservations:** Recommended. **Subway:** Wagner.
$ Prices: Appetizers 5,000–12,000 lire ($3.95–$9.40); main courses 15,000–20,000 lire ($11.80–$15.70). V.
Open: Lunch Thurs–Tues noon–3pm; dinner Thurs–Tues 7pm–midnight.

Gaspare is an excellent pizza and seafood restaurant that serves the kind of pies you would otherwise have to go to Naples to find. A richly aromatic fish antipasto could precede a pasta and a meat dish, which would be served to you for around 40,000 lire ($31.40), with wine included. Pizzas alone start at 27,000 lire ($21.20).

BUDGET

BURGHY, piazza del Duomo. Tel. 871129.

Cuisine: BURGERS/PIZZA. **Reservations:** Not needed. **Subway:** Duomo.
$ Prices: Appetizers 3,500–4,000 lire ($27.75–$3.15); main courses 2,000–5,000 lire ($1.55–$3.95). No credit cards.
Open: Sun–Tues and Thurs–Fri 10:30am–midnight, Sat 10:30am–1am.

This is a Milanese copy of McDonald's set at the far end of the square facing the cathedral. The colorful Formica and wood-grained decor will remind you of every other fast-food place you've ever been in, except for the ancient granite columns that support the ceiling near the cashiers. There's ample seating, the hamburgers are well prepared and thicker than you'd expect, and perhaps best of all, the staff refuses tips. A large cheeseburger costs 2,200 lire ($1.75). The coffee, unlike other American-inspired items on the menu, comes Italian style, served like espresso in a polystyrene cup. Downstairs, only hamburgers and salads are served. If you want something more substantial, go upstairs to a self-service restaurant, La Piazza, where meals begin at 20,000 lire ($15.70) and are served daily except Wednesday from 11:30am to 10pm.

I PANINI DELLA BAGI, corso Vercelli 23. Tel. 4814032.
   Cuisine: ITALIAN. **Reservations:** Not needed. **Subway:** Pagana.
$ **Prices:** Appetizers 5,000–6,500 lire ($3.95–$5.10); main courses 11,000–13,000 lire ($8.65–$10.20). AE, DC, MC, V.
   Open: Mon–Sat 7:30am–8pm.

Signora Bagi, the owner, runs what is one of the neighborhood's most popular bars and restaurants, mostly because of the excellent food she makes and sells.
   The establishment occupies a cozy, not-very-large space that's almost completely filled with a stand-up bar and a handful of tables. Tagliatelle is homemade fresh every day, but, then, so are the sauces, the pâtés, the bread (panini) that envelopes the deliciously tasty sandwiches, and the desserts. No one will mind if you order only something to drink and a sandwich at the bar, but you can also sit down Sandwiches cost 5,000 lire to 6,000 lire ($3.95 to $4.70) each.

ITALY & ITALY, via Torino at via Stampa. Tel. 8692994.
   Cuisine: ITALIAN. **Reservations:** Not needed. **Subway:** Duomo.
$ **Prices:** Appetizers 3,800–4,100 lire ($3–$3.20); main courses 5,100–6,000 lire ($4–$4.70). No credit cards.
   Open: Mon–Sat 11:30am–11pm.

This is one of the Milan branches of a fast-food empire that stretches across Italy. It operates in a ritual that you've grown used to at hamburger stands throughout North America: Order your food at the counter, pay for it, and carry it to one of the tables on a plastic tray. The array of culinary possibilities here, however, is very Italian, including a variety of pizza called *pizzotto,* sandwiches, meat dishes, or three kinds of spaghetti. They also have the eternal international favorite, hamburgers and cheeseburgers. Sandwiches range from 2,200 lire to 4,800 lire ($1.75 to $3.75); spaghetti is around 4,000 lire ($3.15).

LA CREPERIE, via Cesare Correnti 21. Tel. 8377124.
   Cuisine: CREPES. **Reservations:** Not accepted. **Subway:** Sant'Ambrogio.
$ **Prices:** Crêpes 2,000–6,000 lire ($1.55–$4.70). No credit cards.
   Open: Daily noon–12:30am.

This is an upscale version of a fast-food joint, the difference being that the specialty here is crêpes, those thin pancakes that are curled around a variety of different fillings. You can make a full meal out of one of the carrot and celery-juice "shakes," which will give you lots more nutrition than the fattening dairy product you knew and loved as a child. Many patrons order a salted crêpe (stuffed with Gorgonzola and walnuts, or ham, cheese, and peppers) as a main course, followed by a sweet dessert crêpe filled with, perhaps, chocolate sauce and bananas.

SAVVY SHOPPING

London has Harrods, Paris has all the big-name boutiques you can think of, and Rome and Florence instill an acquisitional fever in the eyes of anyone who even window-gazes. Milan, however, is blessed with one of the most unusual concentrations of shopping possibilities in Europe. Most of the boutiques are infused with the style, humor, and sophistication that has made Milan the dynamo of the Italian fashion industry, a place where the sidewalks sizzle with the hard-driving entrepreneurial spirit that has been part of the northern Italian textile industry for centuries.
   One well-heeled shopper from Florida recently spent the better part of her vacation in Italy shopping for what she called "the most unbelievable variety of shoes, clothes, and accessories in the world." A walk on the fashion subculture's focal point, **via Montenapoleone,** one of Italy's three great shopping streets, a mile-long strip that has become a showcase for famous (and high-priced) makers of clothes and shoes, with excursions into the side streets, will quickly confirm that impression.
   Note carefully that beauty does not come cheaply in the garment industry, and the attention you receive will often be based directly on the salesperson's impression of how much money you plan to spend. But as a handful of American models, along with design imitators from around the world, know, there are indeed riches to be discovered.

Early-morning risers will be welcomed only by silent streets and closed gates. Most shops are closed all day Sunday and Monday (although some open on Monday afternoon). Some stores open at 9am unless they're very chic, and then they are not likely to open until 10:30am. They remain open, for the most part, until 1pm, reopening again between 3:30 and 7:30pm.

BED & BATH

MIROBELLO, via Montebello at the corner of via San Marco. Tel. 6599733.

Many clients of this store come in for the mattresses, quilts, and eiderdowns imported from North America or France. This will probably not be your priority. Instead, look for the embroidered sheets, towels, pillowcases, and blankets whose designs and handwork might not be readily available outside Italy. Open on Monday from 3 to 7:30pm and Tuesday through Saturday from 9:30am to 1pm and 3 to 7:30pm.

BOOKS

AMERICAN BOOKSTORE, largo Cairoli 16. Tel. 870944.

There are bigger and flashier bookstores in Rome, but this one will probably stock that trashy novel you always wanted to read, or the scholarly exegesis of Milanese artwork you should have reviewed before your trip and never did. Only English-language books are stocked, as well as an assortment of periodicals. Open on Monday from 3 to 7pm, Tuesday through Friday from 9am to 7pm, and on Saturday from 10am to 1pm and 3 to 7pm.

DEPARTMENT STORES

LA RINASCENTE, piazza del Duomo. Tel. 89521.

La Rinascente bills itself with accuracy as Italy's largest fashion department store. In addition to clothing, the basement carries a wide variety of giftware for the home, including handwork from all regions of Italy. The information desk on the ground floor will answer your questions. On the establishment's seventh floor a new area has been opened that comprises a bank, a travel agency, Rolando hairdresser, Estée Lauder Skincare Center, a coffee-bar, and the Brunch and Bistrot restaurants operated by the famous Italian chef Gualtiero Marchesi.

Incidentally, the name of the store was suggested by the poet Gabriele d'Annunzio, for which he received a compensation of 5,000 lire. The store was officially opened right before Christmas in the closing year of World War I, but it burned down on Christmas Eve. Rebuilt, it later met total destruction in an Allied bombing in 1943. But it has always rallied back from disaster and now is better than ever, particularly in its choice of merchandise. Open on Monday from 3 to 7:30pm and Tuesday through Saturday from 9:30am to 7:30pm.

FABRICS

GALTRUCCO, piazza del Duomo 2. Tel. 876256.

In some Italian cities, its name is associated with men's fashion (see below), but in Milan it carries one of the city's largest collections of yard goods. A seamstress's delight, it contains wools, silks, linens, and cottons stacked up to the ceiling, in a wide array of patterns, colors, weights, and textures. If you plan on taking up sewing after your trip to pay off your Italy-generated bills, this is the place for you. The collection of silk is especially appealing. Also on the premises is a clothing shop that sells garments for both men and women. Open on Monday from 3 to 7:30pm and Tuesday through Saturday from 9:30am to 7:30pm.

FASHION

For Men

BORSALINO, corso Vittorio Emanuele II no. 5. Tel. 8690805.

There's more to Borsalino than just the famous low-slung hats, although these alone make a visit worthwhile. There's also a collection of stylishly informal men's clothes that evoke a trip to Capri or a jaunt on a friend's yacht. Examples include casually elegant shirts and sweaters, and pants made of such resortwear fabrics as softened canvas in appropriately attractive colors. Open on Monday from 3 to 7:30pm and Tuesday through Saturday from 10am to 7:30pm.

MILA SCHON, via Montenapoleone 6. Tel. 701333.

The sophisticated men's line of the successful female designer is inventoried here. The look is casually chic, hip, and expensive. If you're male, thin, and relatively muscular, you'll probably look terrific in Mila Schön. Mila's women's line is nearby, at no. 2 on the same street (same phone). Even the somewhat flippant accessories are stratospherically expensive. Open on Monday from 3 to 7pm and Tuesday through Saturday from 10am to 1pm and 3 to 5pm.

GIORGIO ARMANI, via San Andrea 9. Tel. 76022757.

Giorgio Armani is housed with the style we've come to expect from Armani, in a large showroom vaguely reminiscent of a very upscale aircraft hangar. Armani's trademark is a look that incorporates loosely fitting, unstructured, and unpadded clothing draped loosely over firm bodies. Though there's a bit more structure to the clothes since Richard Gere made the look popular in *American Gigolo,* Armani still creates elegant upholstery for elegant people. Open on Monday from 3:30 to 5pm and Tuesday through Saturday from 10am to 1:30pm and 3:30 to 5pm.

GALTRUCCO, via Montenapoleone 27. Tel. 7600978.

This store is a two-floor collection of elegant men's suits, shirts, and knitwear. The ready-to-wear clothes are well made and attractively conservative. Also available are a battalion of tailors prepared to create a custom-made suit, laden with details that a discerning eye will pick up immediately, complete with a label by Brioni. Open on Monday from 3 to 7pm and Tuesday through Saturday from 10am to 7pm.

KASHIYAMA, via Sant'Andrea 14. Tel. 798327.

Kashiyama represents the alliance of a Japanese merchandiser with some of the most avant-garde men's clothes in Europe, and the result could outfit practically any male with a *Gentlemen's Quarterly* look. Clothes are expensively informal, often black, and iconoclastic. The ideal client of these stores would be in his 20s, very thin, and rich. Other designers whose men's clothes are for sale here include Bill Kaiserman, Helmut Lang, Dolce e Gabbana, and the Bikkimbergs (each of which is presumably a household word on the new wave haute-couture circuit). Open on Monday from 3 to 7:30pm and Tuesday through Saturday from 9:30am to 1:30pm and 3 to 7:30pm.

GEMELLI, corso Vercelli 16. Tel. 433404.

This store sells well-made clothes for men and women, which, while stylish and serviceable, are neither as glamorous nor as chillingly expensive as some of the city's more famous clothiers. Everything here is off the rack; there is no custom-tailoring service. Open on Monday from 3 to 7pm and Tuesday through Saturday from 9:15am to 1pm and 3 to 7pm.

ERMENGILDO ZEGNA, via Pietro Verri 3. Tel. 795521.

Ermengildo sells some of the best-regarded men's clothing in Italy from a three-story shop loaded with all the accoutrements of male sartorial splendor. As for sizes, they are not well inventoried for large, well-built, or tall men. If you're thin and of short or medium height, however, you'll find a cornucopia of (extremely expensive) riches to choose from. Open on Monday from 3 to 7pm and Tuesday through Saturday from 9:30am to 7pm.

RENCO, corso Venezia 29. Tel. 760-00235.

Many of the taller, broader, bigger, and better-developed men and women of North America used to hunt in vain for Italian clothing that would fit them properly. In many Italian stores, any men's jacket bigger than a "44 Long" is considered almost freakish. Not so at Renco. The sartorial skills of Italy can be appreciated even by tall and full-figure sizes, thanks to this well-stocked, two-level store where even designer clothes come in sizes considered "larger than normal" in Italy. Although its strength is its collection of men's clothes, there is also a collection for tall and/or voluptuous women. Open on Monday from 3:30 to 7pm and Tuesday through Saturday from 10am to 1pm and 3 to 7pm (closed August).

For Women

KRIZIA, via della Spiga 23. Tel. 76008429.

It's the flagship boutique—the most prominent in all of Italy—of a designer whom many sophisticated women know very well. The name behind the legend is Italian entrepreneur Maiuccia Mandelli, whose trademark black panther stalks menacingly (in image only) across the all-white floor of the showroom. The best description for Krizia is that the clothes are fun, and somehow, women who wear them become more fun, too. The inventory includes evening dresses, jeans, sportswear, and a smaller collection for men and children. Krizia will also sell you accessories to go with their voiles and see-through blouses. Open on Monday from 2:30 to 7pm and Tuesday through Saturday from 10am to 1:30pm and 2:30 to 7pm.

MISSONI, via Montenapoleone 1. Tel. 700906.

Missoni is famous for unusual knits, mostly for women (occasionally for men), in geometric patterns remotely inspired by tribal designs, and in gemlike tones inspired by the colors of the prism. Garments are chic, vaguely futuristic, and dauntingly expensive. Open on Monday from 2:30 to 7pm and Tuesday through Saturday from 10am to 1pm and 2:30 to 7pm.

SPIGA 31 DI R. BILANCIONI, via della Spiga 31. Tel. 76023502.

The inventory here includes an unusual look that the casually elegant night owl might like. Styles are flamboyant, sometimes in gold lamé and/or silk, and predictably expensive. Once you return home, if you choose to show it off at the country club, you probably won't need to worry that another woman will be wearing the same dress. Open on Monday from 3:30 to 7:30pm and Tuesday through Saturday from 10am to 1pm and 3:30 to 7:30pm.

GIANFRANCO FERRE, via della Spiga 11. Tel. 76000385.

This is the only outlet in Milan for a famous designer whose women's fashions include avant-garde leather dresses, which are unzipped by one daring pull from neckline to kneecap, and a salmon-colored silk moiré blazer that costs more than most round-trip airfares to Italy. Some of the styles are stunning, especially if your social life requires such attire. Next door to the women's shop is an outlet for men's clothing by the same designer, with the same telephone and hours. Open on Monday from 2:30 to 7:30pm and Tuesday through Saturday from 10am to 1pm and 2:30 to 7:30pm.

FENDI, via San Andrea 16. Tel. 76021617.

Fendi contains a small collection of furs, a chic clientele, and a spacious format of women's purses, shoes, and a small rack of expensive, well-tailored dresses. Leather goods and the next best thing—elegantly offhand accessories made from suddenly fashionable vinyl—are also showcased. Open on Monday from 3 to 7:30pm and Tuesday through Saturday from 10am to 1pm and 3 to 7:30pm.

COMME DES GARCONS, via San Andrea 10A. Tel. 76000905.

This is one of the most unusual stores in the district, designed in a monochromatic combination of Japanese simplicity and avant-garde clothes, many of which are made from linen. Rei Kawakubo is the female designer who produces many of these garments that appeal to the ultra-chic and the obsessively hip. Open on Monday from 2:30 to 7pm and Tuesday through Saturday from 10am to 1pm and 2:30 to 7pm.

HATS

BORSALINO, Galleria Vittorio Emanuele 9. Tel. 874244.

The place is famous for men's hats, but it sells more than just the classic, low-slung fedora made famous by movie heroes in the 1930s. It also carries women's headgear suitable for a polo match or garden party, driver's caps, and something they call a trilby, fittingly decorated with silk ribbons. Open on Monday from 3 to 7:30pm and Tuesday through Saturday from 10am to 7:30pm.

JEWELRY

MARIO BUCCELLATI, via Montenapoleone 4. Tel. 799944.
    Mario Buccellati offers the best-known—and probably the most expensive—silver and jewels in Italy. The designs of the cast-silver bowls, tureens, and christening cups are nothing short of rhapsodic, and the quality is among the finest in the world. You'll be ushered into the tastefully appointed showroom within what turns out to be a formidable security system. Open on Monday from 3 to 7pm and Tuesday through Saturday from 10am to 1pm and 3 to 7pm.

MERU, via Solferino 3. Tel. 864-60700.
    Meru sells consciously avant-garde jewelry, rumored to have been worn and privately publicized by young and beautiful European film stars. Many of the pieces are set into enameled backgrounds and often include unusual types of gemstones such as rose quartz, coral, and amber. All pieces are made by Meru themselves, in a style quite different from the usual traditional jewelry sold in many other stores. Open on Monday from 3:30 to 7:30pm and Tuesday through Saturday from 9:30am to 1pm and 3:30 to 7:30pm (closed August to September 10).

LACE

JESURUM, via Verri. Tel. 76015045.
    This is the Milanese outlet of a Venice-based company which has been famous since 1870 for making and selling lace in many different applications. Set on a very short street where none of the buildings has an obvious street number, it sells all-lace or lace-edged tablecloths, lace doilies, and all the handmade textiles that a bride might like to add to her trousseau. They also sell lace blouses, even a swimming suit (which might be better suited to a photo session than to a game of water polo) and lace by the meter for trimming curtains or whatever. Open on Monday from 3 to 7pm and Tuesday through Saturday from 9am to 1pm and 3 to 7pm.

LEATHER GOODS & SHOES

BELTRAMI, via Montenapoleone 16. Tel. 76002975.
    Prices are chillingly high, but the leather goods for men and women are among the best you'll find anywhere. The showroom is appropriately glamorous, the merchandise appropriately chic. Beltrami has another shop, which has the same hours, at piazza Santa Babila 4A (tel. 76000546). Open on Monday from 3:30 to 7:30pm and Tuesday through Saturday from 10am to 1pm and 3:30 to 7:30pm.

SALVATORE FERRAGAMO, via Montenapoleone 3. Tel. 76006660.
    The label is instantly recognizable, and the quality high at this shop which has created and designed shoes since the 1930s for the fashion goddesses and gods of Europe and Hollywood. The establishment, which is rigidly controlled by a large and extended second generation of the original founders, is still a leader in style and allure. The store contains inventories of shoes, luggage, and accessories for women and men. Also for sale are Ferragamo leather jackets, pants, and a small selection of clothing. Open on Monday from 3 to 7pm and Tuesday through Saturday from 10am to 7pm.

GUCCI, via Montenapoleone 2. Tel. 760-13050.
    Gucci is the Milanese headquarters for the most famous leather goods distributor in Italy. Its shoes, luggage, and wallets for men and women, handbags, and leatherware accessories usually have the colors of the Italian flag (olive and crimson) stitched in the form of a more-or-less discreet ribbon across the front of most of the company's merchandise. At the neighboring store (no. 5 on the same street), Gucci sells its clothing lines for men and women. Open on Monday from 3:30 to 7:30pm and Tuesday through Saturday from 10am to 7:30pm.

TANINO CRISCI, via Montenapoleone 3. Tel. 76021264.

Its showroom evokes the interior of a private club in London because of its oiled paneling and conservative leather chairs. Its inventory includes elegantly conservative footwear for men and women, but its most famous products are the leather boots which will make you look like an ace equestrian, polo player, or stalker of big game—even if they haven't been your lifelong hobbies. Open on Monday from 3:30 to 7:30pm and Tuesday through Saturday from 10am to 7:30pm.

SEBASTIAN, via Borgospesso 18. Tel. 780532.

Sebastian sells excellent shoes for men and women from a ready-made stockpile of fashionable models, which Sebastian makes in its own factories. For almost the same price (if you don't mind waiting 2 months or more) you can order custom-made shoes, which will be shipped to whatever address you specify. This is a boon for clients with wide, narrow, large, or small feet, who consider Sebastian something of a sartorial and orthopedic blessing. Open on Monday from 3 to 7:30pm and Tuesday through Saturday from 9:30am to 7:30pm.

FRATELLI ROSSETTI, via Montenapoleone 1. Tel. 76021650.

Its less expensive line of men's and women's shoes has been dubbed "Made in Italy" by the establishment's marketing experts. More distinctive (and more expensive) are their tastefully conservative shoes suitable for boardrooms and bankers. These will probably (with care) look as wonderful in 10 years as they will next month. Open on Monday from 3 to 7pm and Tuesday through Saturday from 10am to 7pm.

ALFONSO GARLANDO, via Madonnina 2. Tel. 874665.

The prices on the merchandise here range up to the very expensive, but the shop's size and lack of concern with a stylish showroom almost guarantees a reasonable choice of merchandise for a reasonable price. They sell shoes for men, women, and children. Open on Monday from 3 to 7:30pm and Tuesday through Saturday from 10am to 7:30pm.

LINGERIE

DONINI, via Montenapoleone 7. Tel. 76002568.

Donini sells the kind of women's lingerie that might fulfill a Joan Collins fantasy. Available in a variety of colors, including the perennial favorite, basic black lace, the wispily provocative garments will help you weave whatever web your heart might desire. Also for sale is a more mundane, highly serviceable array of garments your mother might have referred to discreetly as "foundations." Open on Monday from 3 to 7pm and Tuesday through Saturday from 10am to 2pm and 3 to 7pm.

B. FINZI, Galleria Vittorio Emanuele. Tel. 872345.

Styles of underwear have changed since this shop was established in 1859, but the Milanese demand for both practical and frivolous "unmentionables" has continued unabated. (The polite Italian word for these is *biancheria intima*.) Most of the stock here is for all kinds and types of women (look especially for the satin-trimmed silk camisoles), but there's also a selection of underwear for men (most of which is bought for them by their wives or companions). Open on Monday from 3 to 7:30pm and Tuesday through Saturday from 9:30am to 1pm and 3 to 7:30pm.

MALLS

CAFFE MODA, via Durini 14. Tel. 76021188.

Despite the implications of its name, this is actually a shopping complex filled with the deliberately informal offshoots of some of the most renowned clothing designers in Italy. Its focal point is the ground-floor café and bar that gives the complex its name, around which all the gossip of the neighborhood seems to ebb and flow. Radiating outward, and stretching over three different levels, are at least 20 different shops. These include jeans outlets of both Valentino and Gianfranco Ferré, and informal (but still expensive) outlets for Missoni, Valentino Uomo, and Krizia Poi. Each boutique maintains its own hours, but most of them are open nonstop Monday through Saturday from 10am to 7pm. A few of the smaller shops might close briefly for lunch. The complex is located about a block behind the Palazzo Reale.

PAPER

I GIORNI DI CARTA, corso Garibaldi 81. Tel. 6552514.

This is one of the city's most unusual outlets for writing paper and stationery, with dozens of different colors, textures, and weights. Much of the inventory is made from ecologically conscious recycled paper. The establishment also sells briefcases to carry your letters, pens and ink, and ornamental paperweights. Open Monday through Saturday from 9am to 1pm and 3:30 to 7:30pm.

PERFUMES

PROFUMO, via Brera 2. Tel. 72023334.

Profumo sells some of Italy's most exotic perfumes, and all the biggest names in Europe. Some Italian scents are exclusively distributed here near the American Express office. Open on Monday from 3 to 7pm and Tuesday through Saturday from 10am to 7pm.

PORCELAIN & CRYSTAL

RICHARD-GINORI, corso Buenos Aires 1. Tel. 29516611.

Since 1735 the company has manufactured and sold porcelain to dukes, duchesses, and ordinary bourgeois consumers. Considered a household word in Italy, Ginori sells oven-proof porcelain in both modern and traditional themes, as well as crystal and silverware that they either make themselves or which they inventory from other manufacturers like Baccarat. There is another branch at via Dante 9 (tel. 800811). Open on Monday from 3 to 7:30pm and Tuesday through Saturday from 9am to 12:30pm and 3 to 7:30pm.

PRINTS & ENGRAVINGS

PETTINAROLI-RAIMONDI, corso Venezia 6. Tel. 76002412.

This is considered the finest shop in Milan for prints, engravings, and antique maps. It was originally established in 1776, a date dear to the heart of many U.S. readers. Of particular interest are the engravings of Italian cityscapes during the 19th century, and the many treasures worth framing after you return home. Open on Monday from 3 to 7pm and Tuesday through Saturday from 9:30am to 12:30pm and 3 to 7pm.

TOYS

TORRIANI, via Mercato 1. Tel. 866519.

A purchase here will usually assuage at least some of your guilt if you've omitted your children from your itinerary through Italy. It's one of the oldest and best-known toy stores in Milan, loaded with childhood distractions that are sometimes equally intriguing to adults. Open on Monday from 3 to 7pm and Tuesday through Saturday from 10am to 12:30pm and 3 to 7pm.

EVENING ENTERTAINMENT

As in Rome, many of the top nightclubs in Milan shut down for the summer, when the cabaret talent and the bartenders pack their bags and head for the hills or the seashore. However, Milan is a big city, and there's always plenty of after-dark diversions. This sprawling metropolis is also one of the cultural centers of Europe.

THE PERFORMING ARTS

The most complete list of cultural events appears in the large Milan newspaper, the left-wing *Repubblica*. If you're in town, try for a Thursday edition, as it usually has the most complete listings.

TEATRO ALLA SCALA, piazza della Scala. Tel. 72003744.

⭐ If you have only a night for Milan and are here between mid-December and May, try to attend a performance at the world-famous Teatro alla Scala. Built to the designs of Piermarini, the neoclassic opera house was restored after World War II bomb damage. The greatest opera stars appear here, and the Milanese first-night audience is considered among the hardest to please in the world. Tickets are also extremely hard to come by and are sold out weeks in advance. However, you do stand a chance of getting gallery tickets, seats so far up they should be called "celestial." The box office is open Tuesday through Sunday from 10am to 1pm and 3:30 to 5:30pm.

Opera lovers will also want to visit the **Museo Teatrale alle Scala** (tel. 8053418) in the same building. Launched in 1913, it contains a rich collection of historical mementoes and records of the heady world of opera. Among them are busts and portraits of such artists as Beethoven, Chopin, Donizetti, Verdi, and Puccini. Two halls are devoted to Verdi alone, with objects including scores written in his own hand and the spinet on which he learned to play. Rossini's eyeglasses and his pianoforte tuning key are in a vitrine, and there are many other such treasures, including a death-cast of Chopin's left hand. A small gallery honors Toscanini, with his batons, medals, and pince-nez on display. One of the greatest thrills for opera lovers who may not be in Milan at the time of a performance at La Scala—or may not be able to get tickets—will be the view from the third floor. From here, you can look down on the theater's ornate auditorium with its velvet draperies. Charging 5,000 lire ($3.95) for admission, it's open Monday through Saturday from 9am to 11:45pm and 2 to 5:45pm. Subway: Duomo.

Prices: Tickets, 20,000–200,000 lire ($15.70–$157).

CONSERVATORIO, via del Conservatorio 12. Tel. 76001755.

The finest in classical music is performed at the Conservatorio, in the San Babila sector. Year round, a high-quality program of classical concerts—widely varied—is showcased here for a cultured Milanese audience. Subway: San Babila.

Prices: Tickets, 15,000 lire ($11.80).

PICCOLO TEATRO, via Rovello 2. Tel. 877663.

Piccolo Teatro, in the vicinity of via Dante, became a socialist theater in the years after World War II, but now the city of Milan is the landlord. Programs are very varied today, and performances are in Italian. Its director, Giorgio Strehler, is acclaimed as one of the most avant garde and talented in the world. The theater lies between the Duomo and the Castle of the Sforzas. It's sometimes hard to obtain seats here. No shows are presented on Monday. Subway: Cordusto or Cairoli. Closed: August.

Prices: Tickets, 24,000–35,000 lire ($18.85–$27.50).

THE CLUB & MUSIC SCENE

CA'BIANCA CLUB, via Lodovico il Moro 117. Tel. 8135260.

Ca'Bianca has a changing venue of live music, which ranges—depending on the availability of the musicians—from folk music to cabaret to jazz concerts. Technically, this is considered a private club, but no one at the door will prevent you from entering if you aren't a member. The show—whatever it may consist of on the night of your visit—begins at 11pm. The club is open Monday through Saturday from 8:30pm to 1am.

Admission: 25,000 lire ($19.65) including show and one drink, 90,000–100,000 lire ($70.65–$78.50) with dinner.

ISOLA FIORITA, Ripa Ticinese 83. Tel. 89402060.

This club contains a winter garden with glassed-in walls and verdant plants; a very large "summer garden," with tables and chairs; a bar; and a restaurant with its own stage upon which appear some of the most popular and successful musical groups in Milan. Each area of this entertainment-related labyrinth is somewhat separate from its neighbor, so there are many different ambiences. (The bar, for example, has recorded music independent of whatever concert is being performed at the moment.) A drink in the bar will cost around 10,000 lire ($7.85); a meal in the restaurant costs 50,000 lire to 75,000 lire ($39.25 to $58.90). The establishment is open Tuesday through Sunday from 8pm to 1am.

Admission: Free.

FACSIMILE, via Tallone 11. Tel. 7380635.

This is a popular rendezvous point where rock-conscious Milanese can commune with their favorite video stars in living color. The decor is almost entirely gray and red, and the rock videos might be the same kinds of images a New Yorker might view on a lonely Friday night. There are outdoor tables for star-gazing. Drinks range from 1,000 lire (80¢) and beyond. The bar is open Friday through Wednesday from 6:30pm to 2am.

Admission: Free, but first drink obligatory.

CLUB ASTORIA, piazza Santa Maria Beltrade 2. Tel. 86463710.

This popular nightclub is one of the most frequented in town, especially by the expense-account junket crowd. When there's a performance, a drink might cost around 40,000 lire ($31.40), which takes the place of a cover charge. Otherwise, drinks begin at 25,000 lire ($19.65). Open daily from 10:30pm to 4am.

Admission: Free.

ZELIG, viale Monza 140. Tel. 2551774.

This is the foremost comedy club in Milan, filled with the young and hopeful talent of the Italian comedy circuit. If you don't speak fluent Italian, you may be reduced to simply watching the audience reaction and smiling wanly when they applaud. If you miss too many of the jokes, there is a separate bar only for drinking and the projection of rock concert videos. Admission to the video bar is free, but drinks there cost 6,000 lire to 7,000 lire ($4.70 to $5.50) each. The comedy club has two shows every night, whose hours change with the number of comedians performing that night. All sections of the establishment are open Tuesday through Sunday from 9:30pm to 2am (till 3am on Friday and Saturday). Closed: August.

Admission: 18,000 lire ($14.15), including one drink.

CLUB DUE, via Formentini 2. Tel. 873533.

Club Due is a basement jazz club that charges 12,000 lire to 18,000 lire ($9.40 to $14.15) per drink when you attend the live concerts that attract the jazz cognoscenti of the city. On street level, a more sedate and relaxing piano bar charges around 8,000 lire to 12,000 lire ($6.30 to $9.40) for a whisky with soda, and around 50,000 lire ($39.25) if you want dinner. Both floors of this establishment are open every day from 9pm to 3am.

Admission: Free.

ROLLING STONE, corso XXII Marzo no. 32. Tel. 7381000.

This club features heavy-metal rock and a difficult-to-define ocean of aggressively energetic exhibitionists in their teens and 20s. Members of the crowd often include visiting rock stars from many nations who have business of one kind or another in Milan. The club is open from 10:30pm to 3am on Friday and Saturday night only. Closed in July and August.

Admission: 20,000 lire ($15.70), including one drink.

Gay Clubs

NUOVA IDEA INTERNATIONAL, via de Castiglia 30. Tel. 6892753.

This is the largest and most popular gay disco in Milan—in fact, it's one of the most famous in northern Italy, drawing a patronage of the young and not-so-young. Many celebrated actors in the Italian film industry and in the theater frequent this place. There's a large video screen, and sometimes live entertainment is presented. It's open on Thursday and Friday from 9pm to 1am and on Saturday from 9pm to 2am; closed Monday through Wednesday. Subway: Gioia.

Admission: 10,000–15,000 lire ($7.85–$11.80).

CONTATTO, corso Sempione 126. Tel. 3314904.

This is another leading gay disco. Technically, membership is necessary and you need to be introduced by another member, but most foreigners are allowed to go in upon presentation of a passport. The disco swings from 11pm to 7am nightly, but it reaches its peak in the hours between 3 and 5am. The *club privato* also has a Turkish bath and a cafeteria open 24 hours a day. Take tram no. 1, 19, or 33; the location is in back of Castello Sforzesco.

Admission: Free, but a 10,000-lira ($7.85) first drink is obligatory.

THE BAR SCENE

AL TEATRO, corso Garibaldi 16. Tel. 864222.

Decorated a bit like the bohemian parlor of one of your unmarried aunts, this is a popular bar set across the street from one of Milan's most visible theaters, the Teatro Fossati. It opens for morning coffee every day except Monday at 7am, and closes (after several changes of ambience) at 2am. At night there is sometimes some kind of musical entertainment, but most of the time clients seem perfectly happy to drink their drinks, gossip, and flirt. Cocktails cost 5,000 lire to 9,000 lire ($3.95 to $7.05). In addition to coffee and drinks, the establishment serves sandwiches and pastries. In fine weather tables are sometimes set outside on corso Garibaldi.

BABOON BAR, in the Excelsior Hotel Gallia, piazza Duca d'Aosta 9. Tel. 6785.

Even if you aren't staying here, a drink at this sophisticated bar will give you a chance to see what might be Milan's most glamorous hotel, the Excelsior Hotel Gallia. Its bar is named after the painting of a baboon by American artist John Ratner, which hangs prominently within its precincts. Barman Francesco Frigerio will mix you any cocktail you ask for, or one of the drinks he created, a "Cisco Splash" or a "Passion Flower." Drinks cost from 12,000 lire ($9.40) each, and have been served to Marcello Mastroianni, Ava Gardner, Sophia Loren, Henry Kissinger, and Albert Sabin. The bar is open daily from 10am to 1am.

BAR GIAMAICA, via Brera 32. Tel. 876723.

The place is loud and bustling, and seats its potential diners with a no-nonsense kind of gruff humor. That, however, is part of the allure of a bar that has attracted writers and artists for many years, and that today is considered one of the mainstays of the Milanese night scene. The personalities who work here haven't changed in many years. If you want only a drink, you'll have lots of company among the office workers who jostle around the tiny tables, often standing rather than sitting because of the lack of room. Tavola calda meals are served from noon to 3pm and 7pm until midnight, and cost 35,000 lire to 45,000 lire ($27.50 to $35.35). Reservations are not accepted in advance, but you won't lack company while waiting at the bar for a table. The bar opens at 9am every day except Sunday, and remains open until around 12:30am or later, depending on the crowd.

LE NAVE, via Maggi 6. Tel. 3490459.

This is a stylish and fashionable bar, where clients jostle to be seen accompanied by the perfect companions, holding the perfect cocktail. It's open Wednesday through Monday from 9pm to 2am. Drinks range from 5,000 lire to 10,000 lire ($3.95 to $7.85).

PONTE DE BRERA, via Brera 32. Tel. 876723.

Ponte de Brera, one floor above the Bar Giamaica, provides a quiet corner to escape to when the noise downstairs gets too intense. A piano will probably be producing relaxing music when you arrive. A drink usually costs around 15,000 lire ($11.80), which the affluent crowd here seems very willing to pay. The bar opens at 10pm, and closes at 2am Monday through Saturday.

THE OLD FOX PUB, piazza Sant'Agostino. Tel. 89402622.

The decor here might remind you of something you might have enjoyed in Britain, layered as it is with the necessary paneling, leather upholstery, and horse brasses. Many clients come here just to drink from the array of beers and whiskies that are freely available, but others view the place as a restaurant. Full meals cost 20,000 lire to 40,000 lire ($15.70 to $31.40), and might include the pub grub you discovered in

London, as well as pastas and Milanese dishes. It's open Monday through Friday from 12:30 to 3pm and Monday through Saturday from 8pm to 12:30am.

GRAND HOTEL PUB, via Ascanio Sforza 75. Tel. 89511586.

In summer, when the audience spills from the bar/theater into the garden, it almost doubles the establishment's capacity. There's some kind of live entertainment every night: Depending on the venue for the night you arrive, this might be either vocal or instrumentalist music, or cabaret/comedy. In a restaurant on the premises, full dinners cost 35,000 lire ($27.50); most visitors, however, come only for a drink, which is priced between 2,000 lire ($1.55) for coffee and 8,000 lire ($6.30) for a long drink. It's open Tuesday through Sunday from 8pm to 2am.

THE CAFE SCENE

Every city in Italy seems to have a café filled with 19th-century detailing and memories of Verdi or some such famous person. It usually offers a wide variety of pastries and a particular kind of clientele who gossip, sip espresso, munch in-between-meals snacks, and compare notes on comparative shopping values in the area. In Milan, the establishments listed below are popular for this activity.

CAFE COVA, via Montenapoleone 8. Tel. 76000578.

Amid a chic assemblage of garment-district personnel, along with the shoppers who support them, the café follows a routine it established back in 1817. This involves concocting gallons of the heady espresso to keep everyone's nerves jumping. They also dispense staggering amounts of pralines, chocolates, brioches, and sandwiches from behind a glass display case. The more elegant sandwiches contain smoked salmon and truffles. Clients drink their espresso from fragile gold-rimmed cups at one of the small tables in an elegant inner room or while standing up at the prominent bar. Most of the action takes place at the bar, so you really don't need a table unless you're exhausted from too much shopping. Coffee at the bar begins at 1,500 lire ($1.20). Most drinks range from 3,000 lire to 5,000 lire ($2.35 to $3.95). Open Tuesday through Sunday from 8am to 8pm; closed in August.

TAVEGGIA, via Visconti di Modrone 2. Tel. 76021257.

Taveggia offers the kind of old-world ambience that is a rarity now in the hustle-bustle atmosphere of modern Milan. Behind ornate glass doors set into the 19th-century facade, Taveggia is reputed to make the best cappuccino and espresso in town. To match this quality, a variety of brioches, pastries, candies, and tortes is offered. Freshly made on the premises, they can be enjoyed while standing at the bar or seated in the Victorian tea room. All service at the tables is slightly more expensive, as is the rule in Europe. A cappuccino costs 1,500 lire ($1.20). Taveggia is open Tuesday through Sunday from 7:30am to 9pm.

BERLIN CAFE, via Gian Giacomo Mora 9. Tel. 8394336.

As its name implies, the decor emulates a café in turn-of-the-century Berlin; the ambience is enhanced with etched glass and marble-top tables. No one will mind if you come just for coffee or a drink (available Tuesday through Sunday from 8am to 2am), but if you want a meal, the establishment serves lunch from noon to 3pm and dinner from 6pm to 2am. Food is predominantly vegetarian, using very little meat or fish (perhaps a bit of ham for flavor). A meal might include platters of pasta, a torte de verdura, rice pilaf, pastries, and ice cream. A fixed-price lunch costs around 15,000 lire ($11.80); an à la carte dinner, around 20,000 lire ($15.70); and a Sunday brunch (served on Sunday from 8am to 1pm) costs 25,000 lire ($19.65). The establishment is also the occasional setting for an exhibition of paintings by local artists.

CAFFE MILANO, via Montebello 7. Tel. 29003300.

In summer, the crowd sometimes spills outside onto the small plaza, turning the pavement in front of the establishment into an extension of the interior. Most visitors consider it a pleasant mixing pot and rendezvous point, with relaxing music and flattering lighting. Drinks cost 2,000 lire to 10,000 lire ($1.55 to $7.85).

The establishment also has a restaurant that serves classic Milanese cuisine, such as risotto, fresh pasta, and veal dishes. Full meals cost 55,000 lire ($43.20), including wine, and are served from noon to 2:30pm and 7:45pm to 1am. The bar is open from 10:30am to 3pm and 5pm to 2am. Both the bar and the restaurant are closed on Sunday.

RESINTIN CAFE, via Mercato 24. Tel. 875923.

The decor is alpine and rustic, true to the northern Italian origins of the establishment's owner. If you love grappa, the acidic liquor distilled from the dregs of wine and brandy barrels, this establishment stocks more than 30 varieties of it, each guaranteed to give you a colossal morning headache. Otherwise, cocktails cost 6,000 lire to 8,000 lire ($4.70 to $6.30) each at a table, slightly less if you stand at the bar. It's open Monday through Saturday from 4pm to 1:30am.

TECOTECA, via Magolfa 14. Tel. 58104119.

Tecoteca's specialty is tea, which is available in an amazing array of flavors. Each is imported directly from Japan, India, China, or Thailand, and is prepared and served with respect for the tea-drinking rituals of the Orient. If you're not in the mood for a cuppa, the establishment also serves pastries, fruit-flavored milkshakes, beer, wine, and a small selection of all-natural foodstuffs. The decor is almost completely black and yellow, and it occasionally welcomes temporary art exhibitions and poetry readings. Tea costs around 6,000 lire ($4.70); liquor, around 10,000 lire ($7.85) a drink. The establishment is open Tuesday through Sunday from 4:30pm to 1am (closed July 15 to August 30).

MOVIES

ANGELICUM, piazza San Angelo 2. Tel. 6551712.

English-language films are shown in their original version at this movie theater. The cinema has showings on Wednesday and Thursday at 5pm, on Friday and Saturday at 5 and 9:15pm, and on Sunday at 2:30, 5, and 9:15pm.

Admission: 8,000 lire ($6.30).

EASY EXCURSIONS

The ✪ **Certosa** (Charter House) of Pavia (tel. 0382/925613) marks the pinnacle of the Renaissance statement in Lombardy. The Carthusian monastery is 5 miles north of the town of Pavia, and 19 miles south of Milan. Gian Galeazzo Visconti founded the Certosa in 1396, but it was not completed until years after. The result is one of the most harmonious structures in Italy.

The facade, studded with medallions and adorned with colored marble and sculptural work, was designed in part by Amadeo, who worked on the building in the latter 15th century. Inside, much of its rich decoration is achieved by frescoes reminiscent of an illustrated storybook. You'll find works by Perugino (*The Everlasting Father*) and Bernardino Luini (*Madonna and Child*). Gian Galeazzo Visconti, the founder of the Certosa, is buried in the south transept.

Through an elegantly decorated portal you enter the cloister, noted for its exceptional terra-cotta decorations. In the cloister is a continuous chain of elaborate "cells," attached villas with their own private gardens and loggia. Admission is free, but donations are requested. The charterhouse keeps its longest hours from May to August when it's open daily from 9 to 11:30am and 2:30 to 6pm. In March and April and again in September and October, it's open from 9 to 11:30am and 2:30 to 5pm. From November through February, its hours are 9 to 11:30am and 2:30 to 4:30pm. Closed on Monday.

Buses run between Milan and Pavia every hour from 5am to 10pm daily, taking 50 minutes and costing 3,300 lire ($2.60) for a one-way ticket. Trains leave Milan bound for Pavia at the rate of one every hour, at a one-way fare of 2,400 lire ($1.90). Motorists can take Route 35 south from Milan or take A7 to Binasco and continue on Route 35 to Pavia and its Certosa.

2. BERGAMO
31 miles NE of Milan, 373 miles N of Rome

GETTING THERE   By Train   Trains arrive from Milan at the rate of one every hour. The trip itself takes an hour, costing 3,500 lire ($2.75) for a one-way ticket. For information about rail connections in Bergamo, call 247624.

By Bus   The bus station in Bergamo is across from the train station. For bus information or schedules in the area, call 248150. Buses arrive from Milan at the rate of one every 30 minutes, a one-way ticket costing 4,700 lire ($3.70).

By Car   From Milan, head east on the autostrada A4.

ESSENTIALS   The **telephone area code** is 035. The **Tourist Information Office** is at viale Vittorio Emanuele 20 (tel. 213185).

A two-in-one city, Bergamo is crowned by the hilltop Città Alta, the old walled town fortified by the Venetians during their long centuries of dominance. The Bergamesque Alps in the background make for a Lombard setting of dramatic intensity, which earned the praise of Stendhal. At its base is the more modern lower town, which has wide streets and shops.

WHAT TO SEE & DO
THE UPPER TOWN

For the sightseer, the higher the climb the more rewarding the view. The ✪ **Città Alta** is replete with narrow circuitous streets, old squares, splendid monuments, and imposing and austere medieval architecture that prompted d'Annunzio to call it "a city of muteness." To reach the upper city, take bus no. 1 or 3, then a 10-minute walk up viale Vittorio Emanuele.

The heart of the upper town is **piazza Vecchia,** which has witnessed most of the town's upheavals and a parade of conquerors ranging from Attila to the Nazis. On the square is the Palazzo della Ragione, the town hall; an 18th-century fountain; and the Palazzo Nuovo of Scamozzi, the library of Bergamo.

A vaulted arcade connects piazza Vecchia with piazza del Duomo. Opening onto the latter is the cathedral of Bergamo, which has a baroque overlay. An interesting church on this square is the **Basilica di Santa Maria Maggiore.** D'Annunzio (roughly translated) said it seemed "to blossom in a rose-filtered light." Built in the Romanesque style, the church was founded in the 12th century. Much later it was baroqued on its interior, and given a disturbingly busy ceiling. There are exquisite Flemish and Tuscan tapestries displayed that incorporate such themes as the Annunciation and the Crucifixion. The choir dates from the 16th century, and was designed by Lotto. In front of the main altar is a series of inlaid panels depicting such themes as Noah's Ark and David and Goliath. It is open daily from 8:30am to noon and 2 to 5pm.

Also opening onto piazza del Duomo is the ✪ **Colleoni Chapel,** which honors the already-inflated ego of the Venetian military hero. The Renaissance chapel, with an inlaid marble facade reminiscent of Florence, was designed by Giovanni Antonio Amadeo, who is chiefly known for his creation of the Certosa in Pavia, south of Milan. For the *condottiere*, Amadeo built an elaborate tomb, surmounted by a gilded equestrian statue (Colleoni, of course, was the subject of one of the most famous equestrian statues in the world, which now stands on a square in Venice). The tomb sculpted for the soldier's daughter, Medea, is much less elaborate. Giovanni Battista

Tiepolo painted most of the frescoes on the ceiling. It is open daily from 9am to noon and 3 to 6pm. Admission is free.

Facing the cathedral is the baptistery, which dates from the mid-14th century and was rebuilt at the end of the 19th century. The original architect of the octagonal building was Giovanni da Campione.

THE LOWER TOWN

CARRARA ACADEMY, piazza Giacomo Carrara 81A. Tel. 399425.

⭐ Filled with a wide-ranging collection of the works of home-grown artists, as well as Venetian and Tuscan masters, the academy draws art lovers from all over the world. The most important works are on the top floor—so head there first if your time is limited. The Botticelli portrait of *Giuliano di Medici* is well known, and another room contains three different versions of Giovanni Bellini's favorite subject, the *Madonna and Child*. It's interesting to compare his work with that of his brother-in-law, Andrea Mantegna, whose *Madonna and Child* is also displayed, as is Vittore Carpaccio's *Nativity of Maria,* which was seemingly inspired by Flemish painters.

Farther along you encounter a most original treatment of the old theme of the "Madonna and Child"—this one the work of Cosmé Tura of Ferrara. Also displayed are three tables of a predella by Lotto; a portrait of the *Holy Family with St. Catherine* (wonderful composition) by Lotto, and Raphael's *St. Sebastian.* The entire wall space of another room is taken up with paintings by Moroni (1523–78), a local artist who seemingly did portraits of everybody who could afford it. In the salons to follow, foreign masters, such as Rubens, van der Meer, and Jan Brueghel, are represented, along with Guardi's architectural renderings of Venice and Longhi's continuing parade of Venetian high society.

Admission: 3,000 lire ($2.35).
Open: Wed–Mon 9:30am–12:30pm and 2:30–5:30pm. **Bus:** 2, 9, 12, or 14.

WHERE TO STAY

HOTEL EXCELSIOR SAN MARCO, piazza della Repubblica 6, 24100 Bergamo. Tel. 035/232132. Fax 035/223201. 180 rms (all with bath). A/C MINIBAR TV TEL **Bus:** 1, 3, 7, or 9.

$ Rates (including breakfast): 180,000 lire ($141.30) single; 240,000 lire ($188.40) double. AE, DC, MC, V. **Parking:** 30,000 lire ($23.55).

This is a modern establishment at the edge of a city park dotted with flowers. It's actually about midway between the old and new towns, both of which might be visible from the balcony of your room. The lobby area contains a small bar, reddish stone accents, and low-slung leather chairs. The most prominent theme of the ceiling frescoes is that of the lion of St. Mark. The bedrooms are attractively furnished and comfortable.

HOTEL CAPELLO D'ORO, viale Papa Giovanni XXIII no. 12, 24100 Bergamo. Tel. 035/242606. Fax 242946. 104 rms (all with bath). TEL **Bus:** 1, 3, 7, or 9.

$ Rates: 55,000 lire ($43.20) single; 85,000–120,000 lire ($66.75–$94.20) double. Breakfast 15,000 lire ($11.80) extra. MC, V. **Parking:** 25,000 lire ($19.65).

The Hotel Capello d'Oro is a renovated corner building on a busy street in the center of the newer section of town. The 19th-century facade has been covered with stucco, and the public rooms and the bedrooms are functional, high-ceilinged, and clean, and might be suitable for an overnight stopover. Rooms are adequately furnished but not air-conditioned, and TV is available for a supplement. Breakfast is extra. The hotel is at Porta Nuova in front of the railway station.

AGNELLO D'ORO, via Gombito 22, 24100 Bergamo. Tel. 035/249883. Fax 035/235612. 20 rms (all with bath or shower). TV TEL **Bus:** 1 or 3.

$ Rates: 38,000 lire ($29.85) single; 64,000 lire ($50.25) double. Breakfast 10,000 lire ($7.85) extra. AE, DC, MC, V.

The Agnello D'Oro is an intimate, old-style country inn right in the heart of the Città

Alta, facing a handkerchief square with a splashing fountain. It's an atmospheric background for good food or an adequate bedrooms, circa 1960, but bring a set of earplugs. The bedrooms could use some refurbishing. When you enter the cozy reception lounge, you should ring an old bell to bring the owner away from the kitchen. You dine at wooden tables, and sit on carved ladderback chairs. Among the à la carte offerings are three worthy regional specialties. Try casoncelli alla bergamasca, a succulent ravioli dish, or quaglie farcite (quail stuffed and accompanied by slices of polenta). If you choose the risotto al profumo di bosco (with mushrooms and truffle cream), you'll be presented with a dish painted by the manager. A complete meal costs 46,000 lire to 78,000 lire ($36.10 to $61.25). The room becomes the tavern lounge between meals. Wine is served in unusual pitchers. The restaurant is closed Monday and in January.

WHERE TO DINE

RISTORANTE DA VITTORIO, viale Papa Giovanni XXIII no. 21. Tel. 218060.

Cuisine: INTERNATIONAL. **Reservations:** Recommended. **Bus:** 1, 3, 7, or 9.

$ **Prices:** Appetizers 25,000–30,000 lire ($19.65–$23.55); main courses 30,000–40,000 lire ($23.55–$31.40); menu dégustation 90,000 lire ($70.65). AE, DC, MC, V.

Open: Lunch Thurs–Tues 12:30–2:30pm; dinner Thurs–Tues 7:30–9:30pm.
Closed: Aug.

This is a well-known and popular restaurant on the main boulevard of the newer section of town. Set on a corner, the establishment lights its entrance with lanterns. You enter a long and narrow hallway, which is richly paneled with dark wood and, in summer, lined with tables laden with all the fruits of the Italian harvest. The menu is amazingly complete; it offers more than a dozen kinds of risotto, more than 20 kinds of pasta, and around 30 meat dishes, as well as just about every kind of fish that swims, somewhere, in the waters around Italy. The service is efficient, all of it directed by members of the Cerea family who by now are among the best-known citizens of Bergamo.

ANTICO RISTORANTE DELL'ANGELO, via borgo Santa Caterina 55. Tel. 237103.

Cuisine: ITALIAN/SEAFOOD. **Reservations:** Required. **Bus:** 2.

$ **Prices:** Appetizers 15,000–20,000 lire ($11.80–$15.70); main courses 26,000–28,000 lire ($20.40–$22). AE, DC, MC, V.

Open: Lunch Tues–Sun 12:15–3pm; dinner Tues–Sun 7:30–11pm. **Closed:** Aug.

Don't be misled by the "antico" in the restaurant's title. It may suggest that it's old fashioned; the cuisine here, however, leans strongly toward the kinds of nouvelle creation that can turn traditional Italian recipes into unusual treats with undeniable flair. Owner Pierangelo Cornaro and his staff turn out such specialties as tortelloni stuffed with sea bass and served with a fresh basil sauce, filet of sea bass with olive oil and an essence of tomatoes, savarin of rice and sole, baby partridge cooked in grappa, and what the chef has named a "violin" of calves' brains with grapes. Each of the dessert pastries is made in-house and might be the perfect way to end a big meal here.

TAVERNA DEI COLLEONI, piazza Vecchia 7. Tel. 232596.

Cuisine: INTERNATIONAL/LOMBARD. **Reservations:** Recommended. **Bus:** 1 or 3.

$ **Prices:** Appetizers 14,000–20,000 lire ($11–$15.70); main courses 20,000–40,000 lire ($15.70–$31.40). AE, DC, MC, V.

Open: Lunch Tues–Sun 12:30–2:30pm; dinner Tues–Sat 7:30–9:30pm.
Closed: Aug.

In the heart of the Città Alta, this restaurant is known to many a gourmet who journeys here to try regional dishes of exceptional merit. Architecturally it continues the design concept of the square. The sidewalk tables are popular in summer, and the view is part of the reward for dining there. Inside, the decor suggests medievalism, but with a fresh approach. The ceiling is vaulted, the chairs are leather, and there's a low-floor dining room with a wood-burning fireplace. Specialties include gioielli alla Colleoni, tagliatelle alla Colleoni, and filetto di bue (beef filet) all Colleoni.

3. CREMONA

59 miles SE of Milan, 61 miles S of Bergamo

GETTING THERE By Train At least 11 trains per day run between Milan and Cremona (trip time: 1½ hours), at a one-way fare of 5,300 lire ($4.15). Train information is available at the rail station in Cremona on via Dante 68 (tel. 22237).

By Bus Seven buses a day make the run from Milan to Cremona, at a one-way fare of 4,700 lire ($3.70). The bus station is on via Dante (tel. 29212 for schedules and information).

By Car From Milan, take Route 415 southeast of Milan.

ESSENTIALS The **telephone area code** is 0372. The **Tourist Information Office** is at piazza del Comune 5 (tel. 23233).

This city of the violin is found on the Po River plain. Music lovers from all over the world flock here, as it was the birthplace of Monteverdi (the father of modern opera), and of Stradivari (latinized to Stradivarius), who made violin-making an art. Born in Cremona in 1644, Antonio Stradivari became the most famous name in the world of violin-making; he far exceeded the skill of his teacher, Andrea Amati. The third great family name associated with the craft, Guarneri, was also of Cremona.

WHAT TO SEE & DO

Most of the attractions of the city are centered on the harmonious ✪ **piazza del Comune.** The Romanesque cathedral dates from 1107, although its actual consecration was in 1190. Over the centuries, Gothic, Renaissance, even baroque elements were incorporated. In the typical Lombard style, the pillars of the main portal rest on lions, an architectural detail matched in the nearby octagonal baptistery from the 13th century. Surmounting the portal are some marble statues in the vestibule, with a Madonna and Bambino in the center. The rose window over it, from the 13th century, is inserted in the facade like a medallion.

Inside, the cathedral consists of one nave flanked by two aisles. The pillars are draped with Flemish tapestries. Five arches on each side of the nave are admirably frescoed by such artists as Boccaccio Boccaccino (see his *Annunciation* and other scenes from the life of the Madonna, painted in the early 16th century). Other artists who worked on the frescoes were Gian Francesco Bembo (*Adoration of the Wise Men* and *Presentation at the Temple*), Gerolamo Romanino (scenes from the life of Christ), and Altobello Melone (a *Last Supper*). It's open Monday through Saturday from 7am to noon and 3 to 7pm, and on Sunday from 7am to 1pm and 4 to 7pm. Admission is free.

Beside the cathedral is the **Torrazzo,** which dates from the latter 13th century and enjoys a reputation as the tallest campanile (bell tower) in Italy. The tower soars to a height of 353 feet. It is open Monday through Saturday from 10am to noon and 3 to 6:30pm, and on Sunday from 10am to 12:30pm and 3 to 7pm; from December to mid-March, however, it is open only on Sunday and holidays. Admission is 5,000 lire ($3.95) for adults and 3,000 lire ($2.35) for children. From the same period, and also opening onto the piazza, are the **Loggia dei Militi** and the **Palazzo Comunale** in the Gothic style as uniquely practiced in Lombardy.

ANTONIO STRADIVARI MUSEUM, via Palestro 17. Tel. 29349.

At this museum you can see a collection of models, designs, and shapes and tools of Stradivari (1644–1737). This Italian violin maker produced more than 1,000 string instruments, many of which are considered among the best ever made. He learned his craft from Niccolò Amati.

Admission: 1,000 lire (80¢).
Open: Tues–Sat 9:30am–12:15pm and 3:15–5:45pm, Sun 9:30am–12:15pm. **Bus:** 1 or 2.

WHERE TO STAY

HOTEL CONTINENTAL, piazza della Libertà 26, 26100 Cremona. Tel. 0372/434141. Fax 0372/434141. 57 rms (all with bath). A/C MINIBAR TV TEL **Bus:** 1 or 2.

$ Rates (including breakfast): 100,000 lire ($78.50) single; 150,000 lire ($117.75) double. AE, DC, MC, V. **Parking:** Free street parking.

Roads from many parts of northern Italy converge on the busy square on which the comfortably contemporary Hotel Continental stands. There isn't that much of a difference between this hotel and scores of other pleasantly up-to-date hotels in Italy, except for the obvious pride in the musical history of Cremona that is displayed by the staff. They will be eager to point out the illuminated glass cases built into the lobby walls. These contain a copy of a violin made by Stradivarius and an original by Amati. There are also instruments made by master luthiers of Cremona, some of whom seem to be on a first-name basis with the management. A bronze bust of Verdi looks out over the lobby and a restaurant that can seat 500 people is on the premises. Each of the hotel's comfortably furnished bedrooms has sound-insulated windows.

HOTEL AGIP, località San Felice, 26100 Cremona. Tel. 0372/450490. Fax 0372/451097. 77 rms (all with bath). A/C MINIBAR TV TEL **Directions:** Motorists take autostrada A21 to the Casello exit for 1½ miles.

$ Rates (including breakfast): 109,000 lire ($85.55) single; 150,000 lire ($117.75) double. AE, DC, MC, V. **Parking:** Free.

This motel, part of a nationwide chain, is at the San Felice exit of the superhighway between Piacenza and Brescia. Many a late-night traveler in this part of Italy has been rescued by the availability of a room here. Checking in has a certain ease. The motel is a modern establishment with comfortable bedrooms outfitted with hairdryers and soundproofed against the noise of the nearby highway. A good restaurant on the premises serves copious amounts of food, with meals beginning at 30,000 lire ($23.55). Parking is also easy here.

WHERE TO DINE

ANTICA TRATTORIA DEL CIGNO, via del Cigno 7. Tel. 21361.
Cuisine: ITALIAN. **Reservations:** Recommended. **Bus:** 1 or 2.
$ Prices: Appetizers 8,000–10,000 lire ($6.30–$7.85); main courses 15,000–18,000 lire ($11.80–$14.15). AE, DC, MC, V.
Open: Lunch Mon–Sat noon–2:30pm; dinner Mon–Sat 7:30–10pm.

This is a popular restaurant that attracts a crowd of local residents who appreciate the historic atmosphere and well-prepared Italian meals. Specialties include risotto with kiwi and small shrimp, veal with pineapple, and filet of beef with pink peppercorns. Ask for marubini, a sort of Cremonese ravioli. The location is in the very center of Cremona, in front of Torrazzo, the admirable late 13th-century bell tower (near piazza del Comune).

CERESOLE, via Ceresole 4. Tel. 23322.
Cuisine: ITALIAN. **Reservations:** Required. **Bus:** 1 or 2.
$ Prices: Appetizers 12,000–14,000 lire ($9.40–$11); main courses 24,000–28,000 lire ($18.85–$22). AE, DC, MC, V.
Open: Lunch Tues–Sat 12:30–2:30pm; dinner Tues–Sat 7:30–9:30pm. **Closed:** Aug 1–20.

Near the Duomo, Ceresole is an elegant and well-known culinary institution of the city. Behind a masonary facade on a narrow street, the establishment has windows covered with elaborate wrought-iron grills. Specialties include rice with rhubarb, a wide array of delicately seasoned fish (some of them served with fresh seasonal mushrooms and truffles), whiting with a green-peppercorn-flavored cream sauce, and grilled baby piglet. Some of the dishes are based on long-standing and time-honored recipes of the region, including spaghetti alla marinara and ravioli with radicchio.

4. MANTUA (MANTOVA)

25 miles S of Verona, 95 miles E of Milan, 291 miles N of Rome

GETTING THERE By Train Mantua has excellent rail connections, lying on direct lines to such cities as Milan, Cremona, Modena, and Verona. Six trains a day arrive from Milan, taking 2¼ hours, a one-way ticket costing 9,300 lire ($7.30). From Cremona, trains arrive every hour (trip time: 1 hour), a one-way ticket costing 4,100 lire ($3.20). The train station is at piazza Don Leoni (tel. 321647).

By Bus Most visitors arrive by train, but Mantua has good bus connections with Brescia, with 16 buses a day making the 4-hour journey at a cost of 5,400 lire ($4.25) for a one-way ticket. The bus station is at piazza Mondadori (tel. 327237).

By Car From Cremona (see above), continue east along Route 10.

ESSENTIALS The **telephone area code** is 0376. The **Tourist Information Center** is at piazza Andrea Mantegna 6 (tel. 350681).

Once a duchy, Mantua had a flowering of art and architecture under the ruling Gonzaga dynasty that held sway over the town for nearly 4 centuries. Originally an Etruscan settlement, later a Roman colony, it has known many conquerors, including the French and Austrians in the 18th and 19th centuries. Virgil, the great Latin poet, has remained its most famous son (he was born outside the city in a place called Andes).

Mantua is an imposing, at times even austere city, despite its situation near three lakes, Superior, di Mezzo, and Inferiore. It is very much a city of the past and is easily reached from a number of cities in northern Italy.

The historic center is traffic free, but there are buses outside the rail station. Take bus no. 3 to the center.

WHAT TO SEE & DO

MUSEO DI PALAZZO DUCALE, piazza Sordello 40. Tel. 320283.

At piazza Sordello, the ducal apartments of the Gonzagas may be visited. With more than 500 rooms and 15 courtyards, the group of palaces is considered by many to be the most remarkable in Italy—certainly when judged from the standpoint of size. Like Rome, the compound wasn't built in a day, or even in a century. The earlier buildings, erected to the specifications of the Bonacolsi family, date from the 13th century. The later 14th and early 15th centuries saw the rise of the Castle of St. George, designed by Bartolino da Novara. The Gonzagas also added the Palatine Basilica of St. Barbara by Bertani.

Over the years the historic monument of Renaissance splendor has suffered the loss of many of the art treasures collected by Isabella d'Este during the 15th and 16th centuries, in her efforts to turn Mantua into "La Città dell'Arte." Her descendants, the Gonzagas, sold the most precious objects to King Charles I of England in 1628, and 2 years later most of the remaining rich collection was looted during the sack of Mantua. Even Napoleon did his bit by carting off some of the objects still there.

The painting collection is rich, including works by Tintoretto and Sustermans, and a "cut-up" Rubens. The display of classical statuary is impressive, gathered mostly from the various Gonzaga villas at the time of Maria Teresa of Austria. Among the more inspired sights are the Zodiac Room, the Hall of Mirrors with a vaulted ceiling constructed at the beginning of the 17th century, the River Chamber, the Apartment of Paradise, the Apartment of Troia with frescoes by Giulio Romano, and a scale reproduction of the Holy Staircase in Rome. The most-interesting and best-known room in the castle is the Camera degli Sposi (bridal chamber), frescoed by Andrea Mantegna. Winged cherubs appear over a balcony at the top of the ceiling. Look for a curious dwarf and a mauve-hatted portrait of King Christian I of Denmark. There are many paintings by Domenico Fetti, along with a splendid series of nine pieces of tapestry woven in Brussels and based on cartoons by Raphael. A cycle of frescoes on the age of chivalry by Pisanello has been recently discovered. A guardian takes visitors on a tour to point out the many highlights.

   Admission: 10,000 lire ($7.85) adults, free for children under 18.
   Open: Mar–Sept, Sun–Mon 9am–1pm, Tues–Sat 9am–1pm and 2:30–5pm; Oct–Feb, Tues–Sat 9am–1pm and 2:30–3:30pm. **Bus:** 3.

BASILICA OF SANT' ANDREA, piazza Mantegna. Tel. 328504.
   Built to the specifications of Leon Battista Alberti, this church opens into piazza Mantegna, just off piazza delle Erbe, where you'll find fruit vendors. The actual work on the basilica, started in the 15th century, was carried out by a pupil of Alberti's, Luca Fancelli. However, before Alberti died in 1472, it is said that—architecturally speaking—he knew he had "buried the Middle Ages." The church was finally completed in 1782 after Juvara crowned it with a dome. As you enter, the first chapel to your left contains the tomb of the great Mantegna (the paintings are by the artist's son, except for the *Holy Family* by the old master himself). The sacristan will light it for you. In the crypt you'll encounter a representation of one of the more fanciful legends in the history of church relics: St. Andrew's claim to possess the blood of Christ, "the gift" of St. Longinus, the Roman soldier who is said to have pierced his side. Beside the basilica is a campanile (bell tower), which dates from 1414.

   Admission: Free.
   Open: Daily 7am–7pm. **Bus:** 3.

PALAZZO TE, viale Te. Tel. 323266.
   This Renaissance palace, built in the 16th century, is known for its frescoes by Giulio Romano and his pupils. At the edge of the city, it is reached on viale Te. Federigo II, one of the Gonzagas, ordered the villa built as a place where he could slip away to see his mistress. The name is said to have been derived from the word *Tejeto,* which in the local dialect means "a cut to let the waters flow out." This was once marshland drained by the Gonzagas for their horse farm. The frescoes in the various rooms, dedicated to everything from horses to Psyche, rely on mythology for subject matter. The Room of the Giants, the best known, has a scene that depicts heaven venting its rage on the giants who have moved threateningly against it.

   Admission: 5,000 lire ($3.95).
   Open: Tues–Sun 10am–5:30pm. **Bus:** 3.

WHERE TO STAY

RECHIGI HOTEL, via P. F. Calvi 30, 46100 Mantua. Tel. 0376/320781.
   Fax 0376/220291. 50 rms (all with bath), 6 suites. A/C TV TEL **Bus:** 3.
$ Rates: 105,000 lire ($82.45) single; 140,000 lire ($109.90) double; from 175,000 lire ($137.40) suite. Breakfast 13,000 lire ($10.20) extra. AE, DC, MC, V. **Parking:** 15,000 lire ($11.80).
Near the center of the old city stands the Rechigi, a comfortable modern hotel, one of the best in Mantua. Its lobby is warmly furnished, with an alcove bar. The owners maintain the property well, and they have decorated the attractively furnished rooms in good taste. There's a parking garage and a restaurant on the premises.

MANTEGNA HOTEL, via Fabio Filzi 10, 46100 Mantua. Tel. 0376/350315. Fax 0376/367259. 37 rms (35 with bath). A/C TV TEL **Bus:** 3.
$ Rates: 63,000 lire ($49.45) single with bath; 60,000 lire ($47.10) double without bath, 100,000 lire ($78.50) double with bath. Breakfast 12,000 lire ($9.40) extra. AE, DC, MC, V. **Parking:** Free.
The Mantegna is in a commercial section of town, a few blocks from one of the

entrances to the old city. This six-story hotel has bandbox lines and a facade of light-gray tiles. The lobby is accented with gray and red marble slabs, along with enlargements of details of paintings by (as you probably guessed) Mantegna. About half the units look out over a sunny rear courtyard, although the rooms facing the street are fairly quiet as well. The hotel is a good value for the rates charged.

HOTEL DANTE, via Corrado 54, 46100 Mantua. Tel. 0376/326425. Fax 0376/221141. 40 rms (all with bath). TV TEL **Bus:** 3.
$ Rates: 63,000 lire ($49.45) single; 95,000 lire ($74.60) double. Breakfast 9,500 lire ($7.45) extra. AE, DC, MC, V. **Parking:** 15,000 lire ($11.80).

Built in 1968, this boxily modern hotel was constructed with a parking area under the recessed entrance area and a marble-accented interior, parts of which look out over a flagstone-covered courtyard. The hotel's location on a narrow street assures peaceful lodging. Some of the rooms have air conditioning and a minibar.

WHERE TO DINE

RISTORANTE II CIGNO (The Swan), piazza Carlo d'Arco 1. Tel. 327101.
   Cuisine: MANTOVANO. **Reservations:** Recommended. **Bus:** 3.
$ Prices: Appetizers 14,000–16,000 lire ($11–$12.55); main courses 28,000–30,000 lire ($22–$23.55). DC, MC, V.
   Open: Lunch Wed–Sun 12:30–2:30pm; dinner Wed–Sun 7:30–9:30pm.
   Closed: Jan 7–14 and Aug 13–23.

One of the best restaurants in town, Ristorante II Cigno is the kind of establishment that gastronomes would drive miles out of their way to enjoy. Its entrance lies under a terra-cotta plaque of the restaurant's namesake, a swan, which looks over a cobblestone square in the old part of Mantua. The exterior of the building is a faded ocher, with wrought-iron cross-hatched window bars within sight of easy parking on the piazza outside. After passing through a large entrance hall studded with trompe-l'oeil frescoes, gray and white cherubs cavorting in the ceiling coves, and Renaissance antiques, you'll come into the elegant dining room whose clear light and dozens of framed artworks make a meal here a rare celebration. Many recipes are based on dishes served in Mantua in the 17th century. Appetizers are likely to include a liver pâté, and you might follow that with the tortelli di zucca, an egg pasta with a filling of puréed pumpkin. Other dishes from which to choose are filet of eel in basil, a homemade terrine of duck and white truffles, sautéed liver with grapes, duck in duck-liver sauce lightly flavored with orange, a savory concoction of risotto with about six seasonal vegetables, and a juicy capon. Lamb is available in autumn and winter only.

L'AQUILA NIGRA (The Black Eagle), vicolo Bonacolsi 4. Tel. 350651.
   Cuisine: MANTOVANO/ITALIAN. **Reservations:** Recommended. **Bus:** 3.
$ Prices: Appetizers 12,000–14,000 lire ($9.40–$11); main courses 20,000–22,000 lire ($15.70–$17.25). DC, MC, V.
   Open: Lunch Tues–Sat noon–2:30pm; dinner Tues–Sat 7:30–9:30pm. **Closed:** Aug 4–20.

This restaurant is in a Renaissance mansion on a narrow passageway by the Bonacolsi Palace. Among the excellent food served in the elegant rooms, which may come as a surprise after going through the more mundane entrance hall, you can choose from such dishes as pike from the Mincio River, called luccio, served with salsa verdi (green sauce) and polenta, as well as other specialties of the region. You might order a pasta or the gnocchi alle ortiche (potato dumplings tinged with puréed nettles) as part of your meal.

RISTORANTE ROMANI, piazza delle Erbe 13. Tel. 323627.
   Cuisine: MANTOVANO. **Reservations:** Recommended. **Bus:** 3.
$ Prices: Appetizers 8,000–10,000 lire ($6.30–$7.85); main courses 12,000–15,000 lire ($9.40–$11.80). AE, DC, MC, V.
   Open: Lunch Fri–Wed 12:30–2:30pm; dinner Fri–Tues 7:30–9:30pm. **Closed:** July.

The Ristorante Romani has the advantage of being located under an ancient arcade on what might be the most beautiful square in Mantua. It's a cozy, intimate family-run establishment whose decor consists of hundreds of antique copper pots hanging randomly from the single barrel vault of the plaster ceiling. A well-stocked antipasti table is placed near the door, and it's loaded with delicacies. In summer, tables spill out into the square, offering guests a chance to drink in the surrounding architecture as well as the aromas from the kitchen. Specialties include agnolotti (a form of Mantovano tortellini) with meat, cheese, sage, and butter, as well as risotto alla mantovana (with pesto). Other palatable dishes include noodles with mushrooms or salmon, roast filet of veal (deboned and rolled), and a well-made blend of fagioli (white beans) with onions.

CHAPTER 18

PIEDMONT & THE VALLE D'AOSTA

1. TURIN (TORINO)
• WHAT'S SPECIAL ABOUT PIEDMONT & THE VALLE D'AOSTA
2. AOSTA
3. COURMAYEUR & ENTREVES

Towering, snow-capped alpine peaks; oleanders, poplars, and birch trees; sky-blue lakes; river valleys and flower-studded meadows; the chamois and the wild boar; medieval castles; Roman ruins and folklore; the taste of vermouth on home ground; Fiats and fashion—northwest Italy is a fascinating area to explore.

Piedmont is largely agricultural, although its capital, Turin, is one of Italy's front-ranking industrial cities (with more mechanics per square foot than in any other location in Europe). The influence of France is strongly felt, both in the dialect and in the kitchen.

The Valle d'Aosta (really a series of valleys) has traditionally been associated with Piedmont, but in 1948 it was given wide-ranging autonomy. Most of the residents (in this least-populated district in Italy) speak French. Closing in the Valle d'Aosta to the north on the French and Swiss frontiers are the tallest mountains in Europe, including Mont Blanc (15,780 ft.), the Matterhorn (14,690 ft.), and Monte Rosa (15,200 ft.). The road tunnels of Great St. Bernard and Mont Blanc (opened in 1965) connect France and Italy.

SEEING PIEDMONT & THE VALLE D'AOSTA
SUGGESTED ITINERARY

Day 1: Explore Turin and its many attractions. Overnight there.
Day 2: Journey to Aosta and acquaint yourself with its surrounding scenic valley.
Day 3: Continue to Courmayeur and take the cable-car lift over Mont Blanc.

GETTING THERE

For air travelers, Turin's Caselle International Airport is the gateway to the region. Train connections are relatively easy, especially at Turin. Turin is also on the main Rome–Paris express line. For those going on to the Valle d'Aosta, the capital at Aosta is connected with the main Turin–Milan rail line at Chivasso, through Ivrea and St. Vincent.

It's better to use buses once you actually reach the region instead of trying to get one to go there (see the individual destination listings for more details).

The autostrada (express highway) network of Italy links Piedmont and the Valle d'Aosta with the rest of the country and with neighboring France. Travelers from France can go through the Mont Blanc Tunnel outside Chamonix. From the south of Italy the A21 autostrada cuts northwest into Turin.

---

1. TURIN (TORINO)

140 miles W of Milan, 108 miles NE of Genoa, 414 miles NW of Rome

GETTING THERE By Plane Alitalia and ATI fly into the **Caselle Airport**

WHAT'S SPECIAL ABOUT PIEDMONT & THE VALLE D'AOSTA

Great Towns & Villages
- ☐ Turin, home of the Fiat auto works, and the great industrial and cultural center of northwestern Italy.
- ☐ Aosta, the major town of one of Italy's most beautiful valleys, with a history going back to the 1st century B.C.
- ☐ Courmayeur, Italy's best all-around ski resort, but a prime target for mountain exploration in summer.

Ace Attractions
- ☐ Cable-car lift, Courmayeur, taking you across Mont Blanc all the way to Chamonix, France, for the ride of a lifetime.
- ☐ Skiing at Courmayeur, not the most challenging in Europe, but the stunning alpine backdrops of Mont Blanc are almost unequaled.
- ☐ Valle d'Aosta, a series of valleys, semi-autonomous in government, that are rich in scenery, folklore, regional food, and handcrafts.

Architectural Highlights
- ☐ Piazza San Carlo, in Turin, considered the loveliest and most unified square in northern Italy, covering some 3½ acres.

Museums
- ☐ The Egyptian Museum, in Turin, rated second only to that of Cairo, including a famed statue of Ramses II.

Religious Shrines
- ☐ Chapel of the Holy Shroud, Cathedral of San Giovanni, in Turin, where the life-size image of a crucified body (was it Christ?) has mystified the world for ages.

(tel. 57781), about 9 miles north of Turin. This important airport receives international-al flights as well, from such cities as London, Paris, and Frankfurt.

By Train   Turin is a major rail terminus, with arrivals at Stazione di Porta Nuova or Stazione Centrale (central station), corso Vittorio Emanuele II (tel. 517551), in the heart of the city. It takes 1½ hours to reach Milan by train from Turin, but anywhere from 9 to 11 hours to reach Turin from Rome, depending on the connection.

By Bus   It's possible to catch a bus in Chamonix (France) and go to Turin. Three buses a day run through the Mont Blanc Tunnel, taking 3½ hours and costing 22,500 lire ($17.65) for a one-way ticket. There are also 15 buses a day arriving from Milan, taking 2 hours and costing 11,000 lire ($8.65) one way.

By Car   If you're coming from France via the Mont Blanc Tunnel, you can pick up the autostrada at Aosta. You can also reach Turin by autostrada from both the French and Italian Rivieras, and there is an easy link from Milan.

In Turin, the capital of Piedmont, the Italian Risorgimento (unification) was born. During the years when the United States was fighting its Civil War, Turin became the first capital of a unified Italy, a position it later lost to Florence. Turin was once the capital of Sardinia. Much of the city's history is associated with the House of Savoy, a dynasty that reigned for 9 centuries, even presiding over the kingdom of Italy when Victor Emmanuel II was proclaimed king of Italy in 1861. The family ruled, at times in name only, until the monarchy was abolished in 1946.

In spite of having been subject to extensive bombings, Turin found renewed prosperity after World War II, largely because of the Fiat manufacturers based there.

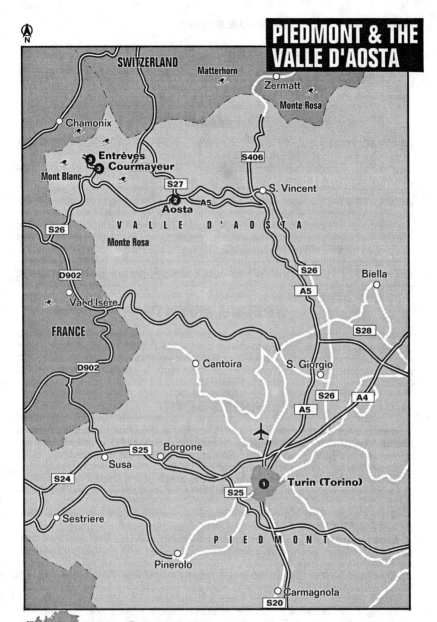

PIEDMONT & THE VALLE D'AOSTA

N

SWITZERLAND

Matterhorn

Zermatt

Monte Rosa

Chamonix

3 Entrèves
3 Courmayeur

Mont Blanc

S406

S27

S. Vincent

A5

2 Aosta

V A L L E   D ' A O S T A

S26

Monte Rosa

S26

D902

Biella

A5

Val d'Isère

FRANCE

S28

D902

Cantoira

S. Giorgio

S26

A4

A5

S25

Borgone

S24

Susa

1 Turin (Torino)

S25

Sestriere

P I E D M O N T

Pinerolo

Carmagnola

S20

Piedmont & The Valle
d'Aosta

ITALY

★ ROME

1 Turin (Torino)
2 Aosta
3 Courmayeur & Entrèves

The city has been called the Detroit of Italy. Many buildings were destroyed, but much of its 17th- and 18th-century look remains. Turin is well laid out, with wide streets, historic squares, churches, and parks. For years it has had a reputation as the least-visited and least-known of Italy's major cities. Easily reached, Turin (Torino in Italian) is on the Po River.

ORIENTATION

INFORMATION If you're seeking specific information about Turin, go to the office of **A.P.T.,** via Roma 222 (tel. 535901), open Monday through Friday from 8am to 7pm and on Saturday from 8am to 12:30pm. There is another office at the train station, Porta Nuova (tel. 531327), open the same hours.

CITY LAYOUT The Stazione di Porta Nuova is in the very center of town. The **Po River,** which runs through Turin, lies to the east of the station. One of the main arteries running through Turin is **corso Vittorio Emanuele II,** directly north of the station. Turin is also a city of fashion, with excellent merchandise in its shops, and you'll want to walk along the major shopping street, **via Roma,** which begins north of the station, leading eventually to two squares that join each other, piazza Castello and piazza Reale. In the middle of via Roma, however, is **piazza San Carlo,** which many consider the heartbeat of Turin.

SPECIAL EVENTS

Turin stages two major cultural fêtes every year, including the **Sere d'Estate** festival in July, with programs devoted to dance, music, and theater. Classical music reigns supreme in September at the month-long **Settembre Musica** with performances at various parts of the city. For details about these festivals, contact Assesorato per la Cultura, piazza San Carlo 161 (tel. 5765573).

FAST FACTS

American Express The representative of American Express in Turin, **Malan Viaggi,** is at via Accademia delle Scienze 1 (tel. 513841). It's closed Saturday afternoon and all day Sunday. Some services are not available on Saturday.

Area Code Turin's telephone area code is 011.

Consulate You'll find the **U.S. Consulate** at via Pomba 23 (tel. 011/517437). There is also a consulate for the **United Kingdom** at corso d'Azeglio 60 (tel. 687832).

Drugstore If you need an all-night drugstore, try **Pescarmona,** via Nizza 65 (tel. 6699259).

Emergencies In a life-threatening emergency, dial 113. To seek first aid or to call an ambulance, phone 5747. A major police station is at via Avogrado 41 (tel. 533853).

Medical Care For a medical problem, call **Unità Samitaria,** via San Domenico 22 (tel. 5747).

Post Office The main post office is at via Alfieri 10; closed on Sunday.

Religious Services English-language evangelical services are conducted at the **Chiesa Evangelica di Lingua Inglese,** via San Pio V 15 (tel. 682838).

Taxis To summon a taxi, phone 5730.

Telephone Public telephones are at via Roma 18 bis, via Arsenale 13, and the Stazione di Porta Nuova.

WHAT TO SEE & DO

Begin your explorations at ✪ **piazza San Carlo;** although heavily bombed during World War II, it is still the loveliest and most unified square in the city. It was designed by Carlo di Castellamonte in the 17th century, and covers about 3½ acres. The two churches are those of Santa Cristina and San Carlo. Some of the most prestigious figures in Italy once sat on this square, sipping coffee and plotting the unification of Italy.

EGYPTIAN MUSEUM, Science Academy Building, via Accademia della Scienze 6. Tel. 544091.

You'll find the most interesting museums housed in the Guarini-designed, 17th-century Science Academy Building. The Egyptian Museum's collection is so vast that it's rated second only to the one at Cairo. Of the statuary, that of Ramses II is the best known, but there is one of Amenhotep II as well. A room nearby contains a rock temple consecrated by Thutmosis III in Nubia. In the crowded wings upstairs, the world of the pharaohs lives on (one of the prize exhibits is the "Royal Papyrus," with its valuable chronicle of the Egyptian monarchs from the 1st through the 17th Dynasty). The funerary art is exceptionally rare and valuable, especially the chapel built for Maia and his young wife, and an entirely reassembled tomb (that of Kha and Merit, 18th Dynasty), discovered in good condition at the turn of the century.

Admission: 3,000 lire ($2.35).
Open: Tues–Sun 9am–2pm. **Bus:** 1 or 4.

SABAUDA (SAVOY) GALLERY, Science Academy Building, via Accademia della Scienze 6. Tel. 547440.

In the same building as the Egyptian Museum, you can see one of the richest art collections in Italy, acquired over a period of centuries by the House of Savoy. The gallery's largest exhibition is of the Piedmontese masters, but it has many fine examples of Flemish art as well. Of the latter, the best-known painting is Sir Anthony van Dyck's *Three Children of Charles I*. Other important works include Botticelli's *Venus*, Memling's *Passion of Christ*, Rembrandt's *Sleeping Old Man*, Duccio's *Virgin and Child*, Mantegna's *Holy Conversation*, Jan van Eyck's *The Stigmata of Francis of Assisi*, Veronese's *Dinner in the House of the Pharisee*, Balotto's *Views of Turin*, intriguing paintings by Brueghel, and a section of the royal collections between 1730 and 1832.

Admission: 3,000 lire ($2.35).
Open: Tues–Sun 9am–2pm. **Bus:** 1 or 4.

CAPELLA DELLA SANTA SINDONE, Cathedral of San Giovanni, piazza IV Marzo. Tel. 5662101.

The Renaissance Cathedral of San Giovanni, dedicated to John the Baptist, is of major interest to visitors since it contains Guarini's **Chapel of the Holy Shroud.** The chapel, crowned by a baroque dome, is only a short walk from the entrance to the Royal Palace. Acquired by Emanuele Filiberto (the subject of the equestrian statue in piazza San Carlo), the shroud is purported to be the one that Joseph of Arimathea wrapped around the body of Christ when he was removed from the cross. Detailed charts in front of the holy relic claim to show evidence of a hemorrhage produced by the crown of thorns. Scientific testing has not been able to confirm or refute the claim.

The shroud, which rests in a silver box behind bulletproof glass, has always been the subject of controversy. When it was first exhibited in 1354, a French bishop denounced it as a fraud. The life-size image of a crucified body looks like a photographic negative; since photography had not yet been invented, how the image was imprinted remains a mystery. You can rest assured that the final word has not been sounded in this matter.

Admission: Free.
Open: Tues–Sat 8:30am–noon and 3–5pm, Sun 9:45–10:30am and 11:30am–noon. **Bus:** 1 or 4.

PALAZZO REALE (Royal Palace), piazza Castello. Tel. 5661455.

The palace that the Savoys called home was begun in 1645. The halls, the columned ballroom by Palagi, tea salon, and "Queen's Chapel" are richly baroque in style. The original architect was Amedeo de Castellamonte, but numerous builders supplied ideas and effort before the palazzo was finally complete. As in nearly all ducal residences of that period, the most bizarre room is the one bedecked with flowering chinoiserie. The Throne Room is of interest, as is the tapestry-draped Banqueting Hall. Le Nôtre, a Frenchman, mapped out the gardens, which may also be visited. In the building you can also visit the Royal Armory (Ameria Reale), with its large collection of arms and armor and many military mementoes.

Admission: 3,000 lire ($2.35).
Open: Tues–Sun 9am–1:30pm. **Bus:** 1 or 4.

CARLO BISCARETTI DI RUFFIA AUTOMOBILE MUSEUM, corso Unità d'Italia 40. Tel. 677666.

Outside the heart of the city in this colossus of a modern exhibition hall, historic "buggies" are handsomely displayed. The exhibitions span the years—ranging from a model of Valturio's "wind machine" (made 20 years before Columbus sailed for America) to the first Fiat car (turn of the century), to a pre–World War II Mercedes-Benz, to the latest Ferrari F1.

Admission: 7,000 lire ($5.50) adults, 2,000 lire ($1.55) children.
Open: Tues–Sun 10am–6:30pm. **Bus:** 34 from via Nizza.

WHERE TO STAY

Like Milan, Turin is an industrial city first and a tourist center second. Most of its hotels were built after the war with an eye toward modern comfort but not necessarily style. Generally the hotels lack distinction, except in the expensive range.

VERY EXPENSIVE

JOLLY HOTEL PRINCIPI DI PIEMONTE, via Gobetti 15, 10123 Torino. Tel. 011/532153. Fax 011/510270. 107 rms (all with bath), 8 suites. A/C MINIBAR TV TEL **Bus:** 1 or 4.

$ Rates (including breakfast): 264,000 lire ($207.25) single; 340,000 lire ($266.90) double; from 545,000 lire ($427.85) suite. AE, DC, MC, V.

A favorite choice of Fiat tsars, this hotel is in the center of the city, near the railway station. Owned by the country's Jolly chain, it employed some of Italy's finest architects and designers in its wholesale revamping. In general, a variety of styles has been used, utilizing antiques and reproductions, as well as modern items. The public rooms are grand in style and furnishings, with bas-relief ceilings, gold wall panels, silk draperies, Louis XVI–style chairs, and baroque marble sideboards.

Dining/Entertainment: There are several dining rooms, both formal and informal, as well as a fashionable drinking lounge.

Services: Room service, baby-sitting, laundry, valet.

TURIN PALACE HOTEL, via Sacchi 8, 10128 Torino. Tel. 011/515511. Fax 011/5612187. 125 rms (all with bath), 2 suites. A/C MINIBAR TV TEL **Bus:** 9.

$ Rates: 275,000 lire ($215.90) single; 330,000 lire ($259.05) double; from 530,000 lire ($416.05) suite. Breakfast 26,000 lire ($20.40) extra. AE, DC, MC, V.
Parking: 30,000 lire ($23.55).

This graceful hotel, with glass doors and a white marble facade, has a tradition of attentive service in plush surroundings. It is convenient to the center of town; its entrance is across from the Porta Nuova train station. Its fashionable address prompted Empress Elizabeth of Austria to stay here in 1893, accompanied by a baron, a countess, three friends, and eight servants. Today the clientele is likely to include top-level management from the General Motors headquarters in Detroit on business trips to Turin. The public rooms contain a scattering of full-size oil portraits as well as opulent chairs and console tables of massively carved and gilded woods. These have been supplemented with an assortment of tasteful contemporary furniture as well. The upper hallways have wide expanses of carved oak detailing, often in a shell motif, along with recessed and illuminated glass cases containing gilded Oriental statues. The bedrooms and baths are soundproof, with conveniences that include radios.

Dining/Entertainment: Guests, mostly businesspeople, gather in the American Bar for drinks before heading for the hotel restaurant where a Piedmont and international cuisine is served with meals ranging from 55,000 lire to 100,000 lire ($43.20 to $78.50). The restaurant closes from August 5 through the 25th.

Services: Room service, baby-sitting, laundry, valet.
Facilities: A garage is on the premises, as are facilities for the disabled.

VILLA SASSI, via Traforo del Pino 47, 10132 Torino. Tel. 011/890556.
Fax 011/890095. 18 rms (all with bath). A/C MINIBAR TV TEL **Bus:** 61.
$ Rates: 240,000 lire ($188.40) single; 340,000 lire ($266.90) double; 340,000 lire ($266.90) per person with half board. AE, DC, MC, V. **Parking:** Free.

This classic 17th-century-style estate is at the edge of the city, surrounded by park grounds and approached by a winding driveway. It was converted long ago into a top-grade hotel and restaurant. The original, impressive architectural details are still intact, including the wooden staircase in the entrance hall. The drawing room features an overscale mural and life-size sculpted baroque figures holding bronze torchiers. Each bedroom has been individually decorated (the furniture is a combination of antiques and reproductions). The manager sees that it is run in a personal way, with "custom-made" service.

Dining/Entertainment: The intimate drinking salon is elegantly decorated with its draped red-velvet walls, bronze chandelier, black dado, and low seat cushions. See "Where to Dine" for a recommendation of the hotel restaurant.

EXPENSIVE

HOTEL CONCORD, via Lagrange 47, 10122 Torino. Tel. 011/5576756.
Fax 011/5576305. 139 rms (all with bath). A/C MINIBAR TV TEL **Bus:** 1 or 4.
$ Rates (including breakfast): 215,000 lire ($168.80) single; 270,000 lire ($211.95) double. AE, DC, MC, V. **Parking:** 26,000 lire ($20.40).

The Concord is across from the hysterical traffic of a street that runs alongside the Porta Nuova train station. Its large facade is decorated with bas-reliefs, and dotted with cast-iron balconies. The entire hotel was modernized in 1982, and many of the guests here are business travelers. The lobby is covered in marble. The comfortable rooms feature individually controlled air conditioning, and double-glazed, sound-proof windows.

Dining/Entertainment: A bank of elevators leads to a stylish bar and restaurant one floor above street level.

Services: Room service, baby-sitting, laundry, valet.
Facilities: Facilities for the disabled.

MODERATE

HOTEL BRAMANTE, via Genova 2, 10126 Torino. Tel. 011/697997. Fax 011/634592. 42 rms (all with bath). A/C MINIBAR TV TEL **Bus:** 1, 18, or 15.
$ Rates (including breakfast): 110,000 lire ($86.35) single; 151,000 lire ($118.55) double. AE, DC, MC, V. **Parking:** 18,000 lire ($14.15).

Built in 1960, the Hotel Bramante, near the Museo dell'Automobile, may not be centrally located, but it's one of the best reasonably priced hotels in Turin. The hotel has a bar-lounge but no restaurant. A cappuccino with brioche is included in the price of the room; a complete continental breakfast will cost extra. The hotel is in the Zona Valentino sector of Turin, 1 mile from the rail station.

HOTEL GENIO, corso Vittorio Emanuele II no. 47, 10125 Torino. Tel. 011/6505771. Fax 011/6508264. 90 rms (all with bath). MINIBAR TV TEL **Bus:** 1, 9, 52, or 67.
$ Rates (including breakfast): 105,000 lire ($82.45) single; 150,000 lire ($117.75) double. AE, DC, MC, V.

This centrally located hotel has a conservatively modern decor that includes a high-ceilinged reception area. The bedrooms contain a comfortable blend of contemporary and late 19th-century pieces, and have double windows for sound-proofing. Half of them are air-conditioned. Only breakfast is served.

HOTEL STAZIONE E GENOVA, via Sacchi 14, 10128 Torino. Tel. 011/545323. Fax 011/519896. 40 rms (all with bath), 2 suites. TV TEL **Bus:** 1, 4, 9, or 12.

$ Rates (including breakfast): 130,000 lire ($102.05) single; 180,000 lire ($141.30) double; from 220,000 lire ($172.70) suite. AE, DC, MC, V. **Parking:** 20,000 lire ($15.70).

The Hotel Stazione is near the Porta Nuova train station, under the same 19th-century arcade as the far more expensive Hotel Turin Palace. The hotel was renovated in 1984, and the bedroom interiors are attractively Italian in style. This hotel is, in my opinion, the best medium-priced hotel in Turin, with a location that's difficult to match and an English-speaking staff. Breakfast is the only meal served.

INEXPENSIVE

HOTEL GOYA, via Principe Amedeo 41, 10123 Torino. Tel. 011/874951. Fax 011/874952. 26 rms (all with bath). A/C MINIBAR TV TEL **Bus:** 1 or 4.
$ Rates: 90,000 lire ($70.65) single; 115,000 lire ($90.30) double. Breakfast 10,000 lire ($7.85) extra. AE, DC, MC, V. **Closed:** Aug.

This hotel, like many others in the Turin chain that owns it, is named after a famous artist. Located on a quiet street in the city center, the Hotel Goya has a modern beige brick facade. Breakfast is the only meal served, but the lobby contains a small bar area just behind the reception desk. You can get air conditioning in the rooms for an extra 10,000 lire ($7.85). There's no garage on the premises, so parking on the street might be a problem.

HOTEL LUXOR, corso Stati Uniti 7, 10128 Torino. Tel. 011/531529. Fax 011/518324. 64 rms (all with bath). A/C MINIBAR TV TEL **Bus:** 1 or 4.
$ Rates (including breakfast): 105,000 lire ($82.45) single; 150,000 lire ($117.75) double. AE, DC, MC, V. **Parking:** 20,000 lire ($15.70).

The Luxor, near the Porta Nuova train station, was completely renovated in 1981. The stylish lobby is accented with oak trim, fresh flowers, and well-placed mirrors; there's also a bar. The bedrooms are comfortable, though less stylish than the public rooms. Rooms facing the back are quieter on summer nights than those opening onto the street. Only breakfast is served.

HOTEL PIEMONTESE, via Berthollet 21, 10125 Torino. Tel. 011/ 6698101. Fax 011/6690571. 35 rms (all with bath), 5 suites. A/C MINIBAR TV TEL **Bus:** 1, 17, 18, 34, 35, or 67.
$ Rates (including breakfast): 80,000–110,000 lire ($62.80–$86.35) single; 150,000 lire ($117.75) double; from 180,000 lire ($141.30) suite. AE, DC, MC, V. **Parking:** 7,000 lire ($5.50).

The Hotel Piemontese is in a 19th-century building near the historical center and the Central Station. The facade is covered with iron balconies and ornate stone trim. The restructured interior is well maintained, and the comfortable bedrooms and public places have undergone a complete restoration. Breakfast, the only meal served, is taken in an airy, sunny room. There is also a bar.

HOTEL VICTORIA, via Nino Costa 4, 10123 Torino. Tel. 011/553710. Fax 011/5611806. 65 rms (all with bath), 3 suites. MINIBAR TV TEL **Bus:** 61.
$ Rates (including breakfast): 109,000 lire ($85.55) single; 145,000 lire ($113.85) double; from 230,000 lire ($180.55) suite. AE, DC, MC, V.

This small but substantial hotel has better accommodations than its second-class designation would lead one to expect. The bedrooms are simply designed, and each one has a different monochromatic color scheme. Graceful furniture and large stained-glass windows contribute to a feeling of luxury in the public rooms. Breakfast is the only meal served.

WHERE TO DINE

The Piedmont kitchen is a fragrant delight, differing in many respects from the Milanese, especially in its liberal use of garlic. What it lacks in subtlety is often made up in large portions of hearty fare. (Turin also gave the world vermouth, for which martini drinkers have been in the eternal debt of the Carpano family.)

EXPENSIVE

DEL CAMBIO, piazza Carignano 2. Tel. 546690.
   Cuisine: PIEDMONT/FRENCH. **Reservations:** Recommended. **Bus:** 1 or 4.
$ **Prices:** Appetizers 10,000–22,000 lire ($7.85–$17.25); main courses 25,000–35,000 lire ($19.65–$27.50). AE, DC, MC, V.
   Open: Lunch Mon–Sat 12:30–3pm; dinner Mon–Sat 7:45–10:30pm. **Closed:** July 26–Aug 26.

Del Cambio is a classic, traditional restaurant of old Turin. Here, you can dine in comparative grandeur, in an old-world setting of white-and-gilt walls, crystal chandeliers, and gilt mirrors. The restaurant was founded in 1757; it is the oldest restaurant in Turin, and possibly in all of Italy. The statesman Camillo Cavour was one of its loyal patrons, and his much-frequented corner is immortalized with a bronze medallion.

The white truffle of Piedmont is featured in many specialties of the chef, who has received many culinary honors. To begin with, the assorted antipasti are excellent; the best pasta dish is the regional agnolotti piemontesi. Among the main dishes to be singled out for special praise are fondue with truffles from Alba and beef braised in Barolo wine. Fresh vegetables are always available. Rounding out the repast is a homemade tart.

DUE LAMPIONI, via Carlo Alberto 45. Tel. 8397409.
   Cuisine: PIEDMONT/INTERNATIONAL. **Reservations:** Required.
$ **Prices:** Appetizers 18,000–50,000 lire ($14.15–$39.25); main courses 25,000–50,000 lire ($19.65–$39.25); fixed-price menus 80,000–100,000 lire ($62.80–$78.50). AE, V.
   Open: Lunch Mon–Sat 12:30–2:30pm; dinner Mon–Sat 7:30–10:30pm. **Closed:** Aug.

Giovanni Agnelli, the head of Fiat, has a gift for finding the best restaurants in Turin; that's why he has been known to patronize this elegant 17th-century palace in the heart of the city, run by chef Carlo Bagatin. Specialties are from the Piedmont district, and only the finest of ingredients go into the tasty dishes. The antipasto selection is among the very best in Turin, and you can follow with a choice of agnolotti, stuffed with duck and cooked with white truffles of the region, or perhaps tournedos with olive purée. If it's featured, be sure to order a magnificent quenelle of artichoke with a fondue of white truffles. Men are required to wear a jacket and tie.

RISTORANTE VECCHIA LANTERNA, corso Re Umberto 21. Tel. 537047.
   Cuisine: PIEDMONT/INTERNATIONAL. **Reservations:** Required. **Bus:** 1 or 4.
$ **Prices:** Appetizers 20,000–22,000 lire ($15.70–$17.25); main courses 30,000–35,000 lire ($23.55–$27.50). AE, DC, MC, V.
   Open: Lunch Mon–Fri noon–3pm; dinner Mon–Sat 8pm–midnight. **Closed:** Aug 10–20.

This is one of Turin's most popular upper-bracket restaurants, and it usually proves to be a rewarding gastronomic experience. The bar area near the entrance has Belle Epoque lighting fixtures, heavy gilt mirrors, ornate 19th-century furniture, and Oriental rugs over carpeting. The dining room reminds guests of old Venice. Most of the furnishings were completed during the reign of the king whose name also supplies the street address.

The antipasti selection is a treat—king crab Venetian style, asparagus flan, pâté de foie gras, grilled snails on a skewer, and marinated trout. This could be followed by ravioli stuffed with duck and served with a truffle sauce, your choice of risotto, or snail soup. Main courses change seasonally, but often include goose-liver piccata on a bed of fresh mushrooms, sea bass Venetian style, garnished frogs' legs, and many other tempting dishes.

EL TOULA–VILLA SASSI, via Traforo del Pino 47. Tel. 8990703.
   Cuisine: PIEDMONT. **Reservations:** Required. **Bus:** 61.

$ Prices: Appetizers 12,000–14,000 lire ($9.40–$11); main courses 28,000–30,000 lire ($22–$23.55). AE, DC, MC, V.
Open: Lunch Mon–Sat noon–2pm; dinner Mon–Sat 8–10:30pm. **Closed:** Aug.

⭐ This spacious 17th-century villa is on the rise of a hill at the edge of the city, 4 miles from the center on the road to Chieri. The stylish, antique-decorated establishment has seen the addition of a modern dining room, with glass walls extending toward the gardens (most of the tables have an excellent view). Some of the basic foodstuff is brought in from the villa's own farm—not only the vegetables, fruit, and butter, but the beef as well. For an appetizer, try the frogs' legs cooked with broth-simmered rice, or fonduta, a Piedmont fondue, made with fontina cheese and the white truffles of the region. Another local dish is agnolotti, a meat-stuffed pasta like ravioli. If it's featured, you may want to try the prized specialty of the house: camoscio in salmi—that is, chamois (a goatlike antelope) prepared in a sauce of olive oil, anchovies, and garlic, laced with wine and served with polenta.

MODERATE

CAFFE TORINO, piazza San Carlo 204. Tel. 545118.
Cuisine: ITALIAN. **Reservations:** Not needed. **Bus:** 72 to piazza Castello.
$ Prices: Appetizers 10,000–15,000 lire ($7.85–$11.80); main courses 13,000–22,000 lire ($10.20–$17.25). AE, DC, MC, V.
Open: Mon and Wed–Sun 7am–1am.

⭐ This famous coffeehouse is the best re-creation in Turin of the days of Vittorio Emanuele. There's a brass inlay of a bull set into the flagstone under the sheltering arcade in front. Inside, the beautiful decor includes frescoed ceilings embellished with depictions of wines and flowers, along with crystal chandeliers. Throughout the establishment is a 19th-century kind of formality worthy of the elegant square in which the café is located.

There are about as many seating areas as there are different colors of marble set into the floor and walls. You can select snacks from a case by the deli-style counter, which is surrounded with cabriole-legged stools. You have to sit on one of the stools, however, since an arbitrary rule prohibits eating at one of the sit-down tables in the adjacent café area. A sit-down beer at the counter costs 6,500 lire ($5.10); a sit-down coffee, 4,000 lire ($3.15). If you want only a quick caffeine fix or a gulp of midafternoon wine, there's a stand-up bar near the entrance. If you want a full meal, a uniformed waiter will serve it to you in an elegantly decorated side room.

DA GIUSEPPE, via San Massimo 34. Tel. 8122090.
Cuisine: PIEDMONT. **Reservations:** Required. **Bus:** 9.
$ Prices: Fixed-price menu 50,000 lire ($39.25). AE, MC, V.
Open: Lunch Tues–Sun 12:30–2:30pm; dinner Tues–Sun 7:30–10pm. **Closed:** Aug.

Ⓢ At Da Giuseppe, you can feast to your stomach's content. There is no menu, but you can partake of various Piedmont dishes brought to you hot or cold, as the temperature and available ingredients of the day dictate. Eggplant, spinach flan, steak tartare alla Alba, lamb piedmontese, and luscious profiteroles are all among the offerings.

RISTORANTE C'ERA UNA VOLTA, corso Vittorio Emanuele II no. 41. Tel. 655498.
Cuisine: PIEDMONT. **Reservations:** Essential. **Bus:** 1, 9, 18, 52, or 67.
$ Prices: Fixed-price dinner 46,000 lire ($36.10). AE, DC, MC, V.
Open: Dinner only, Mon–Sat at 8:30pm.

Ⓢ Near the Porta Nuova Stazione, this restaurant is entered from the busy street through carved oak doors; you take an elevator to one floor above ground level. Many clients are faithful devotees. The decor is in the typical Piedmontese style with hanging copper pots and thick walls of stippled plaster. Fixed-price meals feature an apéritif, a choice of seven or eight antipasti, and two first and two main courses, with vegetables, dessert, and coffee. Typical regional fare includes polenta, crêpes, rabbit, and guinea fowl. The translation of the restaurant's name is "Once upon a time."

TRATTORIA OSTU BACU, corso Vercelli 226. Tel. 264579.
 Cuisine: PIEDMONT. **Reservations:** Recommended. **Bus:** 51.
$ **Prices:** Appetizers 8,000–9,000 lire ($6.30–$7.05); main courses 15,000–25,000 lire ($11.80–$19.65). DC, MC, V.
 Open: Lunch Mon–Sat noon–3pm; dinner Mon–Sat 8–11pm. **Closed:** Aug.

This small restaurant is owned by the Barla family, who prepare the regional specialties that have made the place so popular. These include agnolotti (ravioli stuffed with spinach and beef[hs]), rolled veal, and other savory main dishes. There is also a full array of homemade pastries. The ambience attracts some of the better-heeled diners of Turin, who might show up when they want to avoid the formality of deluxe citadels such as Villa Sassi. The wines are excellent vintages from Piedmont.

INEXPENSIVE

DA MAURO, via Maria Vittoria 21. Tel. 8397811.
 Cuisine: ITALIAN/TUSCAN. **Reservations:** Not accepted. **Bus:** 61.
$ **Prices:** Appetizers 7,000–8,000 lire ($5.50–$6.30); main courses 9,000–18,000 lire ($7.05–$14.15). No credit cards.
 Open: Lunch Tues–Sun noon–2:30pm; dinner Tues–Sun 7:30–10pm. **Closed:** July.

Within walking distance of piazza San Carlo, the best of the low-cost trattorie is generally packed (everybody loves a bargain). The food is conventional, but it does have character; the chef borrows freely from most of the gastronomic centers of Italy, although the cuisine is mainly Tuscan. An excellent pasta specialty is cannelloni. Most main dishes consist of well-prepared fish, veal, and poultry. Desserts such as Italian cheesecake and ice cream are consistently enjoyable.

EVENING ENTERTAINMENT

This city of Fiat is also the cultural center of northwestern Italy. Turin is considered a major stopover for concert artists performing between Genoa and Milan. The daily newspaper of Piedmont, *La Stampa,* will list complete details of any cultural events occurring during your stay.

Classical music concerts are presented at **Auditorium della RAI,** via Rossini 15 (tel. 5710), throughout the year, although mainly in the winter months.

One of the country's leading opera houses, **Teatro Regio,** piazza Castello 215 (tel. 548000), is in Turin. Concerts and leading ballets are also presented here. The box office is open Tuesday through Saturday from 10am to noon and 3:30 to 7pm, and on Sunday from 10am to noon and 2 to 6:30pm.

Opera and other classical productions are presented in summer outside the gardens of the **Palazzo Reale.**

---

2. AOSTA

114 miles NW of Milan, 78 miles N of Turin, 463 miles NW of Rome

GETTING THERE   By Train   Ten trains per day run directly from Turin to Aosta (trip time: 2 hours), a one-way ticket costing 7,800 lire ($6.15). From Milan, the trip involves a change of trains at Chiuasso, takes 4½ hours, and costs 13,400 lire ($10.50) for a one-way ticket.

By Bus   Twelve buses a day travel between Turin and Aosta, taking 2½ hours, and either four to six buses a day arrive from Milan (trip time: 4 hours).

By Car   From Turin, continue north along A5. The autostrada comes to an end just to the east of Aosta.

ESSENTIALS   The **telephone area code** is 0165. The **Tourist Information Center** is at piazza Chanoux 3 (tel. 40526).

In the capital of the Valle d'Aosta stands the **Arch of Augustus,** built in 24 B.C., the date of the Roman founding of the town. Via Sant'Anselmo, part of the old city from the Middle Ages, leads to the arch. Even more impressive are the ruins of a **Roman theater,** reached by the Porta Praetoria, a major gateway that dates from the 1st century B.C. and was built of huge blocks. A **Roman forum** is today a small park with a crypt, lying off piazza San Giovanni near the cathedral. Both the ruins of the theater and the forum are open June through September, daily from 9:30am to noon and 2 to 6pm; off-season, daily from 9:30am to noon and 2 to 4:30pm. Admission is free to either site.

The town is also enriched by its medieval relics. The Gothic **Church of Sant'Orso,** founded in the 12th century, is characterized by its landmark steeple designed in the Romanesque style. You can explore the crypt, but the cloisters, with capitals of some three dozen pillars depicting biblical scenes, are more interesting. The church lies directly off via Sant'Anselmo, and is open Tuesday through Sunday from 9:30am to noon and 2 to 6pm. Admission is free.

Lying as it does on a major artery, Aosta makes for an important stopover point, either for overnighting or as a base for exploring the Valle d'Aosta or taking the cable car to the Conca di Pila, the mountain that towers over the town.

WHERE TO STAY

HOTEL VALLE D'AOSTA, corso Ivrea 146, 11100 Aosta. Tel. 0165/ 41845. Fax 0165/236660. 104 rms (all with bath). MINIBAR TV TEL **Bus:** 2.

$ Rates: 65,000–120,000 lire ($51–$94.20) single; 100,000–170,000 lire ($78.50–$133.45) double. Breakfast 9,000 lire ($7.05) extra. AE, DC, MC, V. **Parking:** Free.

This modern hotel with its zigzag concrete facade is the leading choice in Aosta. Located on a busy road leading from the old town to the entrance of the autostrada, it's a prominent stopover for motorists using the Great Saint Bernard and Mont Blanc tunnels into Italy. The sunny lobby has beige stone floors, paneled walls, and deep leather chairs. All bedrooms have double windows and views angled toward the mountains. Breakfast is available at an extra cost.

Dining/Entertainment: A restaurant is on the premises, under a different management (see "Le Foyer" in "Where to Dine," below). The lobby contains an oversize bar area.

Services: Room service, baby-sitting, laundry.

Facilities: Garage.

LE PAGEOT, via Giorgio, Carrel 31, 11100 Aosta. Tel. 0165/32433. Fax 0165/361377. 18 rms (all with bath). TV TEL **Bus:** 2.

$ Rates (including breakfast): 61,000 lire ($47.90) single; 108,000 lire ($84.80) double. AE, DC, MC, V. **Parking:** 10,000 lire ($7.85).

Built in 1985, this is one of the best-value hotels in town. It has a modern, angular facade of brown brick with big windows, and floors crafted from carefully polished slabs of mountain granite. Bedrooms are clean and functional, and the well-lit public areas include a breakfast room and TV room. The hotel's name translates from an antiquated local dialect into the word for bed. It has no restaurant.

HOTEL ROMA, via Torino 7, 11100 Aosta. Tel. 0165/40821. Fax 0165/ 32404. 32 rms (all with bath). TEL **Bus:** 2.

$ Rates: 50,000–58,000 lire ($39.25–$45.55) single; 76,000–90,000 lire ($59.65–$70.65) double. Breakfast 8,000 lire ($6.30) extra. AE, DC, MC, V. **Parking:** 8,000 lire ($6.30).

Silvio Lepri and Graziella Nicoli are the owners of this hotel, which is on a peaceful alleyway behind a cubist-looking white stucco building; it is surrounded by the balconies and windows of what appear to be private apartments. The entrance is at the top of an exterior concrete stairwell. The public rooms include a warmly paneled bar area, big windows, and a homelike decor filled with bright colors and rustic accessories. There's a garage on the premises, plus public parking a short distance away.

WHERE TO DINE

RISTORANTE LE FOYER, corso Ivrea. Tel. 32136.
Cuisine: VALLE D'AOSTAN/INTERNATIONAL. **Reservations:** Recommended. **Bus:** 2.
$ Prices: Appetizers 8,000–12,000 lire ($6.30–$9.40); main courses 15,000–30,000 lire ($11.80–$23.55). AE, DC, MC, V.
Open: Lunch Wed–Mon 12:15–2:15pm; dinner Wed–Mon 7:15–9:30pm. **Closed:** Jan 5–20 and July 5–20.

This restaurant sits beside a busy traffic artery on the outskirts of town. The full Valdostan meals you get here are both flavorful and cost-conscious. In a wood-paneled dining room that is illuminated by a wall of oversize windows, you can dine on specialties like carpaccio of salmon with three peppers, a salad of smoked trout with orange, fondue valdostana (made with the local Fontina cheese), and grilled fresh fish such as salmon.

RISTORANTE PIEMONTE, via Porte Pretoriane 13. Tel. 40111.
Cuisine: VALLE D'AOSTAN/INTERNATIONAL. **Reservations:** Accepted but not needed. **Bus:** 2.
$ Prices: Appetizers 8,000–10,000 lire ($6.30–$7.85); main courses 15,000–18,000 lire ($11.80–$14.15); fixed-price dinner 30,000 lire ($23.55). AE, DC, MC, V.
Open: Lunch Mon–Sat noon–3pm; dinner Mon–Sat 7–10pm. **Closed:** Jan and June.

On a relatively traffic-free street lined with shops, this family-run place is one of the best of the low-cost trattorie inside the walls of the old town. In a setting of vaulted ceilings and tile floors, you can savor bagna cauda, cannelloni of the chef, risotto with roast pork, good roast beef, and an array of refreshing desserts, which could include fresh strawberries with lemon.

VECCHIA AOSTA, piazza Porte Pretoriane 4. Tel. 361186.
Cuisine: VALLE D'AOSTAN/INTERNATIONAL. **Reservations:** Recommended. **Bus:** 2.
$ Prices: Fixed-price menus 25,000–30,000 lire ($19.65–$23.55) AE, DC, MC, V.
Open: Lunch Thurs–Tues noon–3pm; dinner Thurs–Tues 7:30–10pm. **Closed:** June 5–20 and Oct 15–30.

What is probably the most unusual restaurant in Aosta lies in the narrow niche between the inner and outer Roman walls of the Porta Pretoriane. It is in an old building which, although modernized, still bears evidence of the superb building techniques of the Romans, whose chiseled stones are sometimes visible between patches of modern wood and plaster. Full meals are served on at least two different levels in a labyrinth of nooks and isolated crannies, and might include homemade ravioli, stuffed turkey, pepperoni flan, eggs with cheese fondue and truffles, and a cheese-laden version of Valdostan fondue.

RISTORANTE AGIP, corso Ivrea 138. Tel. 44565.
Cuisine: ITALIAN. **Reservations:** Not needed. **Bus:** 2.
$ Prices: Appetizers 7,500–8,500 lire ($5.90–$6.65); main courses 13,000–15,000 lire ($10.20–$11.80); fixed-price menu 19,000 lire ($14.90). AE, DC, MC, V.
Open: Sept–June, lunch Tues–Sun noon–2:30pm; dinner 7:30–9:30pm; July–Aug, lunch daily noon–2:30pm; dinner daily 7:30–9:30pm.

Normally you think of the gasoline chain Agip as a place to get gas or perhaps to secure motel lodgings for the night. However, in Aosta, next to a garage on the main highway, they operate a restaurant (no rooms), which attracts motorists going to and from the Mont Blanc Tunnel. The location is on a major artery, and you might want to stop here if you're rushed and don't have time to go into the old town of Aosta. Some tables are placed outside in summer, and there is generally adequate parking. In addition to classic Italian recipes, you get specialties here from the Valdostan kitchen, and the helpings are generous.

3. COURMAYEUR & ENTREVES

COURMAYEUR

Courmayeur, a 22-mile drive northwest from Aosta, is Italy's best all-around ski resort, with a "high season" attracting the alpine excursionist in summer, the ski enthusiast in winter. Its popularity was given a considerable boost with the opening of the Mont Blanc road tunnel, feeding traffic from France into Italy (estimated time for the trip, 20 minutes). The cost for an average car is 23,000 lire ($18.05) one way, 30,000 lire ($23.55) round-trip.

With Europe's highest mountain in the background, Courmayeur sits snugly in a valley. Directly to the north of the resort is the alpine village of Entrèves, sprinkled with a number of chalets (some of which receive paying guests).

In the vicinity, you can take a ✪ **cable-car lift**—one of the most unusual in Europe—across Mont Blanc all the way to Chamonix, France. It's a ride across glaciers that is altogether frightening, altogether thrilling, but for steel-nerved adventure seekers only. This is a spectacular achievement in engineering. Departures on the Funivie Monte Bianco are from La Palud, near Entrèves. The three-stage cable car heads for the intermediate stations, Pavillon and Rifugio Torino, before reaching its peak at Punta Helbronner at 11,254 feet. At the latter, you'll be on the doorstep of the glacier and the celebrated 11¼-miles Vallée Blanche ski run to Chamonix (France), which is most often open at the beginning of February every year. The round-trip price for the cable ride is 30,000 lire ($23.55) per person. Departures are every 20 minutes, and service is daily from 8am to 4:20pm. At the top is a terrace for sunbathing, a bar, and a snack bar. Panoramic views unfold of 40 alpine peaks. Bookings are possible at Esercizio Funivie, Franzione La Palud 22 (tel. 0165/89925).

ORIENTATION

GETTING THERE   Proceed to Aosta by rail. In Aosta at the bus terminal, piazza Narbonne (tel. 362027), in front of the train station, you can take 1 of 10 buses leaving daily for Courmayeur. Trip time is 1 hour, and a one-way ticket costs 3,000 lire ($2.35). Motorists should continue west from Aosta on Route 26 heading for Mont Blanc. Courmayeur lies on the way there.

ESSENTIALS   The **telephone area code** for Courmayeur and Entrèves is 0165. The **Tourist Information Center** for Courmayeur is at piazzale Monte Bianco (tel. 842060).

Once you arrive in the center of Courmayeur, you walk, as the resort is rather compact. However, if you're going somewhere in the environs, such as Entrèves or La Palud (to catch the cable car for Mont Blanc), then the buses will be labeled with the geographic destination. The tourist office (see above) has a complete schedule, and buses depart from just outside the office.

WHERE TO STAY

Courmayeur has a number of good and attractive hotels, many of which are open seasonally. Always reserve in high season, either summer or winter.

HOTEL PAVILLON, strada Regionale 60, 11013 Courmayeur. Tel. 0165/ 842420. Fax 0165/844984. 50 rms (all with bath), 8 suites. MINIBAR TV TEL
$ Rates (including full board): 150,000–250,000 lire ($117.75–$156.25) per

person. AE, DC, MC, V. **Parking:** 10,000 lire ($7.85). **Closed:** mid-May to June and Oct–Nov.

⭐ A selection of the prestigious Relais & Châteaux, this is easily the swankiest and most important hotel at the resort, in spite of its small size. Many of the clients warming themselves around the stone fireplace are from England, Germany, and France, which adds a continental allure. Built in 1965, and designed like a chalet, the hotel is located on the outskirts. The bedrooms, which are entered through leather-covered doors, feature built-in furniture and a comfortably conservative decor; all but two have private balconies. The hotel is only a short walk to the funicular that goes to Plan Checrouit.

Dining/Entertainment: One of my favorite restaurants in town is Le Bistroquet, found on these premises.

Services: Room service, baby-sitting, laundry, valet.

Facilities: In the basement is a full array of hydrotherapy facilities; there's also a covered swimming pool which is visible from the entrance vestibule.

PALACE BRON, località Plan Gorret 41, 11013 Courmayeur. Tel. 0165/ 842545. Fax 0165/844015. 26 rms (all with bath), 1 suite. TV TEL **Bus:** Plan Gorret.

$ Rates: 120,000–160,000 lire ($94.20–$125.60) single; 200,000–290,000 lire ($157–$227.65) double; from 480,000 lire ($376.80) suite; 145,000–215,000 lire ($113.85–$168.80) per person for half board. Breakfast 18,000 lire ($14.15) extra. MC, V. **Parking:** Free. **Closed:** May–June and Oct–Dec 19.

⭐ About 1¼ miles from the heart of the resort, this tranquil oasis is one of the plushest addresses in town. The white-walled chalet is the most noteworthy building on the pine-studded hill, and it has a commanding view over all of Courmayeur and the mountains beyond. Guests are often made to feel like members of a baronial private household rather than patrons of a hotel.

The bedrooms are handsomely furnished and well maintained. Summer guests have use of an outdoor pool which has been dug into the side of the steeply sloping mountain, while winter visitors appreciate its proximity to the many ski lifts in the area. Walking from the chalet to the center of town is a good way to exercise after dining on the kitchen's filling cuisine. There's a nearby parking lot for motorists who prefer to drive the long, steep distance.

Dining/Entertainment: The piano bar of the hotel is especially lively in winter, with skiers from all over Europe and America. The restaurant has a refined international cuisine, with formal service; meals cost 55,000 lire to 65,000 lire ($43.20 to $51).

Services: Room service, baby-sitting, laundry, valet.

Facilities: Outdoor pool.

GRAND HOTEL ROYAL E GOLF, via Roma 87, 11013 Courmayeur. Tel. 0165/843621. Fax 0165/842093. 92 rms (all with bath), 4 suites. A/C MINIBAR TV TEL **Bus:** Hotel shuttle transports guests about.

$ Rates (including breakfast): 180,000–300,000 lire ($141.30–$235.50) single; 290,000–510,000 lire ($227.65–$400.35) double; 570,000–980,000 lire ($447.45–$769.30) suite; 188,000–278,000 lire ($147.60–$218.25) per person with half board. AE, DC, MC, V. **Parking:** 18,000 lire ($14.15). **Closed:** Mid-Apr to June 30 and Oct–Nov.

Built in 1950, this hotel is in a dramatic location above the heart of the resort between the most fashionable pedestrian walkway and a thermally heated outdoor swimming pool. Much of its angular facade is covered with rocks, so that it fits in neatly with the surrounding mountainous landscape. Rooms are generally large, with built-in furnishings and streamlined bathrooms.

Dining/Entertainment: The hotel's social center is a large and comfortable lounge, flanked on one side by a bar and on another by a dais where a pianist provides nightly entertainment in season. One of the resort's pockets of posh, Il Grill dell'Hotel Royal e Golf is on the lobby level and will be previewed later.

Services: Room service, baby-sitting, laundry, valet, hydromassage.

Facilities: Swimming pool, sauna, Jacuzzi.

HOTEL COURMAYEUR, via Roma 158, 11013 Courmayeur. Tel. 0165/ 842323. Fax 0165/845125. 25 rms (all with bath or shower). TV TEL

$ **Rates:** 40,000–54,000 lire ($31.40–$42.40) single; 70,000–88,000 lire ($54.95–$69.10) double; 85,000–130,000 lire ($66.75–$102.05) per person with full board. Breakfast 15,000 lire ($11.80) extra. V. **Closed:** Oct–Nov.

The Hotel Courmayeur, right in the center of the resort, was constructed so that most of its rooms would have unobstructed views of the nearby mountains. A number of the bedrooms, furnished in the mountain chalet style, also have wooden balconies. Regional food is served.

HOTEL DEL VIALE, viale Monte Bianco 74, 11013 Courmayeur. Tel. 0165/842227. Fax 0165/844513. 25 rms (all with bath or shower). MINIBAR TV TEL

$ **Rates** (including half board): 80,000–140,000 lire ($62.80–$109.50) per person. AE, DC, MC, V. **Parking:** 8,000 lire ($6.30). **Closed:** May 5–June 14 and Oct 6–Christmas.

This old-style mountain chalet at the edge of town is a good place to enjoy the indoor-outdoor life. There's a front terrace with tables set out under trees in fair weather, and the rooms inside are cozy and pleasant in the chillier months. In the winter, guests can gather in the taproom to enjoy après-ski life, drinking at pine tables and warming their feet before the open fire. The house is filled with such pieces as a large wooden pillar rescued from a wine press, hanging copper kettles, a grandmother's clock, pewter, exposed beams, and pots of flowers in the window. The clean and comfortable bedrooms, with natural wood, have a rustic air about them.

BOUTON D'OR, strada Statle 26 (off piazzale Monte Bianco), 11013 Courmayeur. Tel. 0165/842380. Fax 0165/842152. 35 rms (all with bath or shower). TV TEL

$ **Rates** (including breakfast): 70,000–75,000 lire ($54.95–$58.90) single; 110,000–120,000 lire ($86.35–$94.20) double. AE, DC, MC, V. **Parking:** Free. **Closed:** May and Nov.

Named after the buttercups that cover the surrounding hills in summer, this hotel is owned by the Casale family. It features an exterior painted a deep mustard yellow, stone trim, and a flagstone roof. French windows lead from the clean, comfortable bedrooms onto small balconies. Each of the rooms has a radio, among other amenities. The hotel is about 100 yards (in the direction of the Mont Blanc Tunnel to France) from the most popular restaurant in Courmayeur, Le Vieux Pommier, which is owned by the same family. The hotel also has a garage, a sauna, a solarium, and a garden.

WHERE TO DINE

IL GRILL DELL'HOTEL ROYAL E GOLF, in the Grand Hotel Royal e Golf, via Roma 87. Tel. 843621.
   Cuisine: INTERNATIONAL/ITALIAN. **Reservations:** Required in winter.
$ **Prices:** Appetizers 20,000–40,000 lire ($15.70–$31.40); main courses 40,000–60,000 lire ($31.40–$47.10). AE, DC, MC, V.
   Open: Dinner only, Tues–Sun 7:30–10pm. **Closed:** May–June and Oct–Dec.

On the lobby level of this previously recommended hotel is the most fashionable—and certainly the most expensive—restaurant in town. It has only 30 places for diners interested in the cultivated cuisine inspired by the legacy of "Harry" Cipriani, of Harry's Bar fame. It is sparely decorated, with a carved Gothic screen from an English church standing against one wall. The relatively simple but fresh and well-prepared dishes include pasta e fagioli, carpaccio, risotto with radicchio, and rosettes of veal Cipriani style. The menu changes daily.

LE BISTROQUET, in the Hotel Pavillon, strada Regionale 60. Tel. 842420.
   Cuisine: VALLE D'AOSTAN. **Reservations:** Required.
$ **Prices:** Appetizers 12,000–15,000 lire ($9.40–$11.80); main courses 22,000–25,000 lire ($17.25–$19.65). AE, DC, MC, V.

Open: Dinner only, Tues–Sun 8pm–midnight. **Closed:** Apr 20–Dec 20.
In the cellar of the best and most intimate hotel in town, Le Bistroquet is an understated replica of an Argentine steakhouse. Dozens of cowhides are draped over wooden banquettes; beneath vaulted ceilings, and within view of a theatrically exposed grill, you can enjoy specialties such as bagna cauda piemontese, several kinds of air-dried beef, risotto flavored with red radishes and Asti Spumante, two kinds of fondue, filet of trout perfumed with thyme, and many different steaks and grills.

CADRAN SOLAIRE, via Roma 122. Tel. 844609.
   Cuisine: VALLE D'AOSTAN. **Reservations:** Required.
$ **Prices:** Appetizers 12,000–15,000 lire ($9.40–$11.80); main courses 25,000–28,000 lire ($19.65–$22); fixed-price menus 28,000–48,000 lire ($22–$37.70). MC, V.
   Open: Lunch Wed–Sun 12:30–3pm; dinner Tues–Sun 7:30–11pm. **Closed:** May and Oct–Nov.

In the center of town is the most interesting restaurant in Courmayeur. Named after the sundial (*cadran solaire*) that embellishes the upper floor of its chalet facade, it is owned by Leo Garin, whose also-recommended Maison de Filippo is the most popular restaurant in the Valle d'Aosta. The restaurant is as unusual architecturally as it is gastronomically. Try to come for a predinner drink in the vaulted bar; its massive stones were crafted into almost alarmingly long spans in the 16th century using construction techniques which the Romans perfected. A few steps away, the rustically elegant dining room has its own stone fireplace, a beamed ceiling, and wide plank floors.

Specialties change with the season, but might include fresh asparagus covered with tuna sauce, a warm salad of smoked trout, spaghetti with zucchini and prosciutto, pappardelle with exotic mushrooms, and rack of mountain lamb. Desserts are sumptuous.

LEONE ROSSO, via Roma 73. Tel. 842324.
   Cuisine: VALLE D'AOSTAN. **Reservations:** Recommended.
$ **Prices:** Appetizers 10,000–15,000 lire ($7.85–$11.80); main courses 16,000–25,000 lire ($12.55–$19.65). MC, V.
   Open: Lunch Fri–Wed noon–2:30pm; dinner Fri–Wed 7:30–11pm. **Closed:** Mid-May to mid-June and mid-Sept to mid-Oct.

Leone Rosso is in a stone- and timber-fronted house in a slightly isolated courtyard, a few paces from the busy pedestrian traffic of via Roma. It serves well-prepared and seasoned Aostan specialties, including fondues, a thick and steaming version of regional minestrone, tagliatelle with mushrooms en papilotte, and an array of rich, creamy desserts. Some meats are grilled right at your table. This place is not to be confused with the Red Lion pub, which is recommended separately.

LE VIEUX POMMIER, piazzale Monte Bianco 25. Tel. 842281.
   Cuisine: VALLE D'AOSTAN. **Reservations:** Recommended.
$ **Prices:** Appetizers 12,000–15,000 lire ($9.40–$11.80); main courses 20,000–25,000 lire ($15.70–$19.65). AE, DC, MC, V.
   Open: Lunch Tues–Sun noon–2pm; dinner Tues–Sun 7–9:30pm. **Closed:** Oct.

The apple tree that was cut down so that construction on the restaurant could begin is now the focal point of this establishment, which is located on the main square of town. One of its guests was filmmaker Ingmar Bergman, who, like everyone else, appreciated the exposed stone, the copper-covered bar, the heavy ceiling beams, and thick pine tables arranged in an octagon around the heavily ornamented tree.

Today Alessandro Casale, the son of the woman who established the restaurant, directs the kitchen. He is assisted by his wife, Lydia, and they have traveled on tours of Europe, teaching the technique of their regional cuisine. Your meal might consist of three kinds of dried alpine beef, followed by noodles in a ham-studded cream sauce, and an arrangement of three kinds of pasta or four types of fondue, including a regional variety with Fontina, milk, and egg yolks. Then it's on to chicken suprême en papillote or four or five unusual meat dishes that are cooked mountain style, right at your table. Six kinds of grilled meats are also offered, all of them tasty and flavored with aromatic herbs. Desserts are refreshingly sweet, especially the chocolate-cream parfait. Your meal is usually finished off by coffee served in the style of the Valle d'Aosta.

EVENING ENTERTAINMENT

The life expectancy of the average disco in an alpine resort such as Courmayeur is about that of a snow crystal in July. They can be fun, however, and might offer a chance to meet someone. As of this writing, the après-ski crowd is attracted to the electronic rhythms at the following establishments.

AMERICAN BAR, via Roma 43. Tel. 842126.

Not to be confused with a less desirable bar with the same name at the end of the same street, this is one of the most popular bars on the après-ski circuit. It's rowdy and sometimes outrageous, but most often a lot of fun. You might want to peruse the message board for notes from long-departed friends, but most guests end up in one of the duet of rooms, beside either an open fireplace or a long, crowded bar. The place is open in winter daily from 9am to 1am; it is sometimes closed on Tuesday, but never in ski season. A medium-size beer costs 3,500 lire ($27.50); a glass of white wine goes for 2,500 lire ($1.95) and up.

CAFE POSTA, via Roma 51. Tel. 842272.

The Café Posta is as sedate as its neighbor, the American Bar, is unruly. Many guests prefer to remain in the warmly decorated bar area, never venturing into the large and comfortable salon with a glowing fireplace in an adjacent room. A piano provides live entertainment nightly in season from 8:30pm to 1:30am. The place changes its stripes throughout the day, opening as a morning café at 8:30am. A whisky and soda costs 6,000 lire to 8,000 lire ($4.70 to $6.30).

RED LION, via Roma 54. Tel. 843704.

In a warmly paneled English atmosphere, you'll encounter an array of skiers, foaming mugs of beer, and bar snacks. Open daily from 10:30am to 1:30am, it charges 5,000 lire ($3.95) for a big beer, 4,000 lire to 7,000 lire ($3.15 to $5.50) for whisky.

ABAT JOUR, via Regionale. Tel. 842990.

Abat Jour is popular with a young, sometimes teenage clientele; it boasts a rustic decor and loud new wave music. The admission price includes one drink. After that, drinks cost 7,000 lire ($5.50) and up. The club rocks from 10pm to 1:30am daily in season. Closed: Monday from May to June and in November.

Admission: 12,000–15,000 lire ($9.40–$11.80), including one drink.

LE CLOCHARD, Frazione Dolonne. Tel. 843053.

This is probably the most sophisticated and mature disco in town; it caters to an over-25 crowd. All kinds of recorded music is played here; popular, rock, English, Italian, jazz. Inside are plenty of couches on which to relax, along with a blazing fireplace and lots of exposed stone. Hard drinks start at 7,000 lire ($5.50) each. It's open daily from 9:30pm to 1:30am.

Admission: Sun–Thurs 10,000 or 15,000 lire ($7.85 or $11.80), Fri–Sat 20,000 lire ($15.70).

ENTREVES

Even older than Courmayeur, Entrèves is an ancient community that is small and compact, really a mountain village of wood houses. Many discriminating clients prefer its alpine charm to the more bustling resort of Courmayeur. It is reached by a steep and narrow road. Many gourmets book in here just to enjoy the regional fare, for which the village is known.

Just outside Entrèves on the main highway lies the **Val Veny cable car,** which skiers take in winter to reach the Courmayeur lift system.

Entrèves is located 2 miles north of Courmayeur (signposted off Route 26). Buses from the center of Courmayeur run daily to Entrèves.

There is no local tourist office (ask at the tourist office in Courmayeur for information; see above). The telephone area code is the same for both resorts: 0165.

WHERE TO STAY

Note that one of the restaurants under "Where to Dine," below, also offers accommodations.

LE GRANGE, 11013 Courmayeur-Entrèves. Tel. 0165/89274. Fax 0165/89316. 23 rms (all with bath). MINIBAR TV TEL
$ **Rates:** 88,000 lire ($69.10) single; 95,000 lire ($74.60) double. Breakfast 10,000 lire ($7.85) extra. AE, DC, MC, V. **Parking:** Free. **Closed:** Apr–June and Sept–Nov.

This will be one of the first buildings you'll see as you enter this rustic alpine village, a short distance from Courmayeur, toward the Mont Blanc Tunnel. A few stones of the foundation probably date from as early as the 1300s, when the building was used as a barn for the cows that grazed on the neighboring slopes. What you'll see today is a stone building whose balconies and gables are outlined against the steep hillside into which it is built. The Berthod family transformed a dilapidated property into a rustic and comfortable hotel in 1979, surrounding the establishment with summer flowerbeds. Today it's managed by Bruna Berthod Perri and her nephew, Stefano Pellin, whose youth and enthusiasm are evident. The unusual decor includes a grandfather clock in the lobby, along with a collection of antique tools and a rhythmic series of thick timbers, stucco, and exposed stone walls. Music is played in the bar, which is open only to residents of the hotel. There is also an exercise room and a sauna. A rich breakfast is the only meal served, but you can choose your menu in different restaurants cooperating with La Grange. Facilities include a solarium, sauna, and gym.

WHERE TO DINE

LA MAISON DE FILIPPO, Frazione Entrèves di Courmayeur. Tel. 89968.
Cuisine: VALLE D'AOSTAN. **Reservations:** Required.
$ **Prices:** Fixed-price menu 45,000 lire ($35.35). V.
Open: Lunch Wed–Mon 12:30–2:30pm; dinner Wed–Mon 8–10:30pm.
Closed: June and Nov.

Since 1965, this restaurant has offered the complete gastronomic experience of the regional kitchen in a typical atmosphere. A colorful tavern, it is the creation of Leo Garin, who has been featured in both *Playboy* magazine and *Town & Country*. His establishment is for those who enjoy a rustic, festive atmosphere and bountiful regional food. Many French people ride through the Mont Blanc Tunnel just to dine here. Inside, the three-story open hallway seems like a rustic barn, with an open worn wooden staircase leading to the various dining nooks. You pass casks of nuts, baskets of fresh fruits, window ledges with bowls of salad, fruit tarts, wooden boxes spilling over with spices, onions, gourds, and loaves of freshly baked bread. It's one of the most charming inns in all the valley.

The fare is served either in the mellowed rooms inside, or in the beer garden in summer, which has a full view of Mont Blanc. Mr. Garin features local specialties on an all-you-can-eat basis. Some call his mansion the "Chalet of Gluttony." A typical meal? It might begin with a selection of antipasti, followed by a 2-foot-long platter of about 60 varieties of sausage, with a cutting board and knife. Then there will be a parade of pasta dishes. For a main course, you can pick everything from fondue to camoscio (chamois meat) to trout with an almond-and-butter sauce, to roast duck with an orange glaze. You may even prefer the local boiled dinner, with pungent hamhock, cabbage, and potatoes. Accompanying are huge hunks of coarse country bread from a wicker basket (the size of a laundry bin). For dessert, crêpes Suzette are an ever-popular favorite, along with a selection of regional cheeses.

LA BRENVA, Frazione Entrèves di Courmayeur, 11013 Courmayeur-Entrèves. Tel. 0165/89285.

Cuisine: VALLE D'AOSTAN/ITALIAN. **Reservations:** Recommended
$ Prices: Fixed-price menus 43,000–70,000 lire ($33.75–$54.95). DC, MC, V.
Open: Lunch daily 12:30–1:30pm; dinner daily 7:30–10:30pm.

Many skiers from Courmayeur make a special trek to Entrèves just to have a drink at the old-fashioned bar area of this hotel and restaurant, where a copper espresso machine is topped by a brass eagle, and many of the decorative accessories are at least a century old. The core of the building was constructed in 1884 as a rustic hunting lodge for Victor Emmanuel. In 1897 it became the closest hotel to the base of Mont Blanc, and in 1980 the Vaglio family enlarged its stone foundations with the addition of extra bedrooms and a larger eating area.

The restaurant consists of three rooms, each with exposed stone walls, wide flooring planks, hunting trophies, copper pots, and straw-bottomed chairs. Fires burn almost all the time in winter, and many diners prefer an apéritif in the unusual salon, within view of the well-chosen paintings. On any given day the menu could include prosciutto, fonduta for two, carbonada with polenta, scaloppine with fresh mushrooms, Valle d'Aostan beefsteak, and zabaglione for dessert.

Each of the 14 simple and comfortable bedrooms has a private bath, TV, phone, and lots of peace and quiet. Many of them have covered loggias. With half board included, they rent for 110,000 lire ($86.35) per person daily. La Brenva is a Provençal word for the thousands of larches that cover the surrounding mountainside.

CHAPTER 19

GENOA & THE ITALIAN RIVIERA

- **WHAT'S SPECIAL ABOUT GENOA & THE ITALIAN RIVIERA**
- **1. SAN REMO**
- **2. GENOA (GENOVA)**
- **3. RAPALLO**
- **4. SANTA MARGHERITA LIGURE**
- **5. PORTOFINO**

For years the retreat of the wintering wealthy, the Italian Riviera now enjoys a broad base of tourism. Even in winter (the average temperature in January hovers around the 50° Fahrenheit mark) the Riviera is popular, although not for swimming. The protection provided by the Ligurian Apennines that loom in the background makes the balmy weather possible.

The winding coastline of the Rivieras, particularly the one that stretches from the French border to San Remo, is especially familiar to movie-goers as the background for countless flicks about sports-car racing, jewel thieves, spy thrillers, and even off-the-record romances. Over the years the northwestern coast of Italy has seen the famous and the infamous, especially literary figures: Shelley (who drowned off the shore), D'Annunzio, Byron, Katherine Mansfield, George Sand, D. H. Lawrence.

The Mediterranean vegetation is characterized by pines, olives, citrus trees, and cypresses. The Western Riviera—the **Riviera di Ponente,** from the border to Genoa—is sometimes known as the Riviera of Flowers because of its perfumey profusion of blossoms. Starting at the French border, Ventimiglia is the gateway city to Italy. Along the way you'll encounter the first big resort, Bardighera, followed by San Remo, the major center of Riviera tourism.

Genoa, which divides the Riviera into two parts, is the capital of the Ligurian region—a big, bustling port city that has charm for those willing to spend the time to seek out its treasures.

On the **Riviera di Levante** (eastern) is a triumvirate of small, dramatically situated resorts—Rapallo, Santa Margherita, and Portofino (the favorite of the yachting set).

SEEING GENOA & THE ITALIAN RIVIERA

SUGGESTED ITINERARY

Day 1: Enjoy the flower market of San Remo and visit its old town in the afternoon. Overnight there.

Day 2: Cruise the port of Genoa and visit some of the old palaces in its ancient quarter. Dine in a typical seafood restaurant at night.

Days 3–4: Pick whichever resort appeals to you most—Rapallo, Santa Margherita Ligure, or Portofino—and anchor in for a little *La Dolce Vita*, Italian Riviera style. While based at any one resort, you can explore the other two which are nearby.

GETTING THERE

The autostrada (A12), which runs south from Genoa, connects the Riviera with all southern points in Italy, including Rome, which is about a 6-hour drive from Genoa. Many visitors from Nice on the French Riviera head east on A10 for the 2½-hour ride

WHAT'S SPECIAL ABOUT GENOA & THE ITALIAN RIVIERA

Great Towns & Villages

☐ Genoa, still a major port city, although its prominence was between the 11th and 15th centuries.

☐ San Remo, the capital and major resort of the Italian Riviera, made famous by the wintering wealthy of the Belle Epoque era.

☐ Rapallo, overlooking the Gulf of Tiguillio, still a leading resort, although its heyday was before World War II.

☐ Portofino, called the "Pearl of the Riviera," a former fishing village that today is the rendezvous of the rich and famous.

Beaches

☐ Riviera di Ponente, a narrow coastal strip with rocky outcrops between dozens of sandy coves which open onto wide bays.

☐ Riviera di Levante, a wild, rugged coastline that also contains compact bays and inlets for swimming.

Ace Attractions

☐ Mercato dei Fiori, San Remo, most colorful flower market in Italy, active from October to June; known for its roses, carnations, and mimosa.

☐ The Port at Genoa, the largest in Italy, with a sailors' quarter and five major basins; best seen by taking a boat ride.

Architectural Highlights

☐ Città Vecchia (Old Town), San Remo, a maze of winding alleys and staircases that preserve the life of the fisherfolk of yesterday.

☐ Via Garibaldi, Genoa, a street of palaces that form the most important architectural holdover from the days of the Genovese aristocrats.

to San Remo. It takes about 2 hours to go from Milan to Genoa along A7. The major air connection is at Cristoforo Colombo International Airport, at Genoa Sestri, 4 miles from the center of the city. It has air connections to all major European capitals. For flights to the U.S., Nice is the nearest gateway.

Genoa and the Italian Riviera, including San Remo, enjoy fast and frequent rail links with the rest of Italy. Trip time, for example, between Genoa and Milan is 1½ hours, and from Rome to Genoa, 5 hours. The major bus company, SITA (tel. 010/313851 for information and schedules), services the Genoa area and the eastern and western branches of the Riviera.

1. SAN REMO

10 miles E of the French border, 85 miles W of Genoa, 397 miles NW of Rome

GETTING THERE By Train Since San Remo lies on the coast between Ventimiglia and Imperia—6 miles from each—it is a major stop by many trains coming south from Italy or east from France. A train leaves Genoa heading for the French border at the rate of one per hour, stopping in San Remo. Rome is 8 hours by train from San Remo. For train information and schedules in Genoa, call 284081 from 7am to 11pm.

By Bus If you've arrived in Italy from France in the gateway town of Ventimiglia, you'll find a bus leaving for San Remo about every 15 minutes. The trip takes 30 minutes, and a one-way ticket costs 1,600 lire ($1.25). It's also possible to take one of

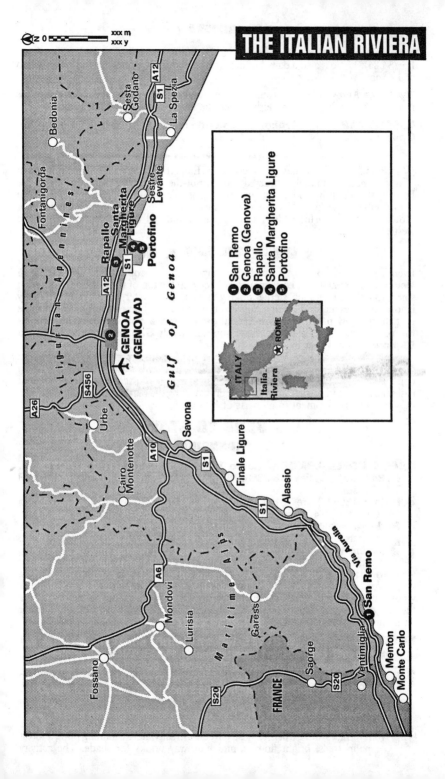

three buses per day from Nice (trip time: 2½ hours), a one-way ticket costing 6,200 lire ($4.85). There is also a daily bus departing Milan at 8am and arriving in San Remo at 1:45pm.

By Car   Autostrada A10 runs east-west along the Riviera, the fastest way for motorists to reach San Remo either from the French border or from Genoa.

ESSENTIALS   The **telephone area code** is 0184. The **Tourist Information Center** is at corso Nuvolon (tel. 571571).

San Remo's reputation has grown ever since Emperor Frederick William wintered in a villa here. It initially attracted the turn-of-the-century wealthy, including the French, the English, and later, the Americans. The flower-filled resort has been considerably updated, and its casino, race track, 18-hole golf course, and deluxe Royal Hotel attract the fashionable. Its climate is considered the mildest on the entire western Riviera.

WHAT TO SEE & DO

Even if you're just passing through, you might want to stop off and visit **La Città Vecchia** (also known as La Pigna), the old city on the top of the hill. Far removed in spirit from the burgeoning, sterile-looking town near the water, old San Remo blithely ignores the present, and its tiny houses on narrow, steep lanes seem to capture the past. In the new town, the palm-flanked **passeggiata dell'Imperatrice** attracts the promenader. For a scenic view, you can reach **San Romolo** and **Monte Bignone** at 4,265 feet by car.

From October to June, you can visit the most famous flower market in Italy, the ✪ **Mercato di Fiori,** open daily from 6 to 8am. It is held in the markethall between corso Garibaldi and piazza Colombo. In this market you'll see some 20,000 tons of roses, mimosa, and carnations which are grown along the balmy climate of the Riviera in winter before shipment to all parts of Europe.

WHERE TO STAY

EXPENSIVE

GRAND HOTEL LONDRA, corso Matuzia 2, 18038 San Remo. Tel. 0184/668000. Fax 0184/668073. 127 rms (all with bath), 7 suites. MINIBAR TV TEL **Bus:** U.

$ Rates: 136,500 lire ($107.15) single; 203,500 lire ($159.75) double; from 350,000 lire ($274.75) suite. Breakfast 18,000 lire ($14.15) extra. AE, DC, MC, V. **Parking:** Free. **Closed:** Oct 10–Dec 20.

Built around 1900 as a two-story hotel, this place was later expanded into the imposing structure you see today. It's within a 10-minute walk of the commercial district, although it is set in a park with a view of the sea. The well-furnished interior is filled with framed engravings, porcelain in illuminated cases, gilt mirrors, and brass detailing. Many of the bedrooms have wrought-iron balconies whose curves are repeated in the art nouveau iron-and-glass canopy that extends over the entryway. Some rooms are air-conditioned. There's also a bar and an outdoor swimming pool.

ROYAL HOTEL, corso Imperatrice 80, 18038 San Remo. Tel. 0184/5391. Fax 0184/61445. 153 rms (all with bath), 17 suites. A/C MINIBAR TV TEL **Bus:** U.

$ Rates: 190,000–230,000 lire ($149.15–$180.55) single; 300,000–480,000 lire ($235.50–$376.80) double; from 500,000 lire ($392.50) suite; 165,000–290,000 lire ($129.55–$227.65) per person with half board. AE, DC, MC, V. **Parking:** 18,000 lire ($14.15). **Closed:** Oct 6–Dec 20.

This place is almost like a mirror reflection of the Beverly Hills Hotel, complete with terraces and gardens, a heated free-form saltwater swimming pool, a forest of palm trees, bright flowers, and hideaway nooks for shade. The activity centers around the garden terrace, since little emphasis is put on the public lounges (decked out in the grand old dowager style). The bedrooms vary considerably—some are of tennis-court size with private balconies, many have sea views, and others face the hills. The furnishings range from traditional to modern. Rooms on the fifth floor—all doubles—are more expensive, because they have the best views and are more luxuriously appointed.

Dining/Entertainment: There's an American bar with piano music nightly. Lunch is served in fair weather on the veranda under an arbor of orange roses. In the more formal restaurant, diners enjoy both a regional and an international cuisine. Meals begin at 75,000 lire ($58.90).

Services: Room service, baby-sitting, laundry, valet.

Facilities: Heated pool, sauna, solarium, minigolf, gym, tennis court, facilities for children, hairdressers, covered and open-air parking areas, a garage with a mechanic, a car wash, and a gas pump.

HOTEL MEDITERRANEE, corso Cavallotti 76, 18038 San Remo. Tel. 0184/571000. Fax 0184/541106. 63 rms (all with bath). A/C MINIBAR TV TEL **Bus:** U.

$ **Rates:** 95,000–128,000 lire ($74.60–$100.50) single; 180,000–216,000 lire ($141.30–$169.55) double; 145,000–165,000 lire ($113.85–$129.55) per person with half board. Children under 12 receive 30% reduction. AE, MC, V. **Parking:** Open parking area, free; garage, 15,000 lire ($11.80) extra.

The traffic in front of this steel-and-glass structure can be profuse, especially in peak season, but once you're inside, or in the rear garden with its Olympic-size pool, you'll scarcely be aware of it. The stylish public rooms contain pleasing color combinations that go well with the many plants, and the generously sized modern sculpture that fills part of the polished floor space. Bedrooms are modernized and well furnished, and also attractively maintained.

Dining/Entertainment: The Aloha restaurant, under a rustic inclined shelter, has a Polynesian theme. There's a drinking area with a metallic ceiling.

Services: Room service, baby-sitting, laundry, valet.

Facilities: Olympic-size pool.

MODERATE

HOTEL MIRAMARE, corso Matuzia 9, 18038 San Remo. Tel. 0184/667601. Fax 0184/667655. 57 rms (all with bath). TEL **Bus:** U.

$ **Rates** (including full board): 130,000–172,000 lire ($102.05–$135) per person. AE, DC, MC, V. **Parking:** Free. **Closed:** Sept 30–Dec 20.

This well-maintained traditional building is set behind semitropical gardens, which border a busy thoroughfare. A curved driveway leads past palmettos to the front entrance, where the lobby is filled with marble floors, gilt-frame mirrors, French portrait busts, 19th-century bronzes, and an art nouveau painting above the reception desk. After passing through the public rooms, you'll discover a seaside garden with sculptures and plenty of verdant hideaways. The bedrooms are clean and comfortable; some are in a neighboring annex with views of the garden. The hotel has a good restaurant. A covered swimming pool is in one of the outbuildings. There's also a sauna, solarium, and gym.

HOTEL PARADISO, via Roccasterone 12, 18038 San Remo. Tel. 0184/571211. Fax 0184/578176. 41 rms (all with bath or shower). MINIBAR TV TEL **Bus:** U.

$ **Rates:** 65,000–72,000 lire ($51–$56.50) single; 85,000–105,000 lire ($66.75–$82.45) double. Breakfast 10,000 lire ($7.85) per person. AE, DC, MC, V. **Parking:** 8,000 lire ($6.30).

The Hotel Paradiso is lodged on a hillside in a former residential sector, now a resort district. Those who visit appreciate the family ownership, the quiet position, the comfort and amenities. The rooms overlook the lower terrace, banked with semitropical vines and flowers. The dining room, where Italian regional specialties are served, has its own airy look, with three walls of glass. The old-fashioned drawing room, on the other hand, is decorated with gilt mirrors and crystal chandeliers. The well-furnished bedrooms are attractively maintained. The seafront rooms all have large balconies with potted geraniums in various colors, the handiwork of the owner Signora Gaiani.

INEXPENSIVE

HOTEL BELSOGGIORNO JUANA, corso Matuzia 41, 18038 San Remo. Tel. 0184/667631. Fax 0184/667471. 43 rms (all with bath or shower). TEL **Bus:** U.
$ Rates: 60,000 lire ($47.10) single; 90,000 lire ($70.65) double; 80,000 lire ($62.80) per person with half board. DC, MC, V. **Parking:** 8,000 lire ($6.30).

This centrally located hotel is near Imperatrice, the main sea promenade, and the beaches. Attractively furnished and inviting, it contains a large reception area, plenty of living rooms for lounging, and TV rooms. Manager Luciana Maurizi De Benedetti has also provided a nice garden in which to sit and enjoy the sun and plants. Because the food is good, many prefer to stay here on the half-board plan. Facilities include a garage.

HOTEL ELETTO, via Matteotti 44, 18038 San Remo. Tel. 0184/531548. 29 rms (all with bath). TEL **Bus:** U.
$ Rates (including breakfast): 60,000 lire ($47.10) single; 90,000 lire ($70.65) double; 75,000 lire ($58.90) per person with half board. MC, V. **Parking:** Free.

This hotel is on the main artery of town, near more expensive hotels. It has a 19th-century facade with cast-iron balconies and ornate detailing. The rear of the hotel is set in a small garden with perhaps the biggest tree in San Remo casting a welcome shade over the flowerbeds. This pleasant stopover point has public rooms filled with carved panels, old mirrors, and antique furniture, as well as windows on two sides. Bedrooms are old fashioned and comfortable, and 15 contain TV. The sunny and well-maintained dining room serves inexpensive meals.

HOTEL MARILUCE, corso Matuzia 3, 18038 San Remo. Tel. 0184/667805. 23 rms (all with bath or shower). TV TEL **Bus:** U.
$ Rates (including breakfast): 81,000 lire ($63.60) single; 125,000 lire ($98.15) double. MC, V. **Parking:** 15,000 lire ($11.80). **Closed:** Nov 1–Dec 20.

As you're walking along the flowered promenade away from the commercial center of town, you'll notice a flowering garden that is enclosed on one side by the neighboring walls of a Polish Catholic church; one of the walls is emblazoned with a gilded coat-of-arms. Behind the garden is the building that until 1945 housed a refugee center that Poles throughout Europe used as a base for finding friends and relatives. Today it's one of the most reasonably priced hotels in the resort, a bargain for San Remo, offering simply furnished but comfortable bedrooms. The furniture in the public rooms is bathed in sunlight from the big windows. From the flowering garden, visitors can see the grounds and facades of surrounding hotels, which are far more expensive. The Mariluce lies 300 yards from the main rail station. A passage under the street leads from the garden to the beach.

WHERE TO DINE

In San Remo you'll be introduced to the Ligurian cuisine, a table characterized by the Genovese style of cooking, with a reliance on seafood dishes. If it's featured on the menu, try the buridda, which is the Ligurian version of Mediterranean bouillabaisse. The white wines from the five villages (the Cinque Terre) are highly valued.

DA GIANNINO, lungomare Trento e Trieste 23. Tel. 504014.
Cuisine: LIGURIAN. **Reservations:** Strongly recommended. **Bus:** U.
$ Prices: Appetizers 18,000–25,000 lire ($14.15–$19.65); main courses 20,000–30,000 lire ($15.70–$23.55). AE, DC, MC, V.
Open: Lunch Tues–Sat 12:30–2:30pm; dinner Mon–Sat 7:30–10pm. **Closed:** June.

The chef, Anna Tiburzio, is the guiding light behind this excellent restaurant, the finest in San Remo. In a conservatively comfortable and elegant setting, you can enjoy such specialties as a changing array of warm seafood antipasti, a flavorful risotto laced with cheese and a pungently aromatic green sauce, and a selection of main courses that change with the availability of ingredients. Some of the more exotic selections are likely to include a marinated cuttlefish gratinée. The wine list includes many of the better vintages of both France and Italy.

PESCE D'ORO, corso Cavalloti 300. Tel. 576332.

Cuisine: PASTA/SEAFOOD. **Reservations:** Recommended. **Bus:** U.
$ Prices: Appetizers 10,000–15,000 lire ($7.85–$11.80); main courses 12,000–20,000 lire ($9.40–$15.70). AE, DC, MC, V.
Open: Lunch Tues–Sun noon–2:30pm; dinner Tues–Sun 7:30–10pm. **Closed:** Feb 15–Mar 15.

Pesce D'Oro serves some of the finest food on the Italian Riviera. The location, in the midst of a mechanics' alley, is so unprepossessing you'll think you're at the wrong address. However, once inside you should place yourself in the hands of Signor Visconti, who is both the chef and the owner. Perhaps he'll suggest a pasta to begin with, the lasagne al pesto (a sauce made with olive oil, garlic, pine seeds, cheese, and fresh basil), or the highly recommendable farfalline al'pizzico—a blending of potatoes, spinach-flavored pasta butterflies, and fresh string beans. Among the seafood dishes, the zuppa di frutti di mare is outstanding, as is the spiedino di scampi. Fresh fish is featured regularly.

LA LANTERNA, via Molo di Ponente al Porto 8. Tel. 506855.

Cuisine: SEAFOOD. **Reservations:** Needed Sat–Sun.
$ Prices: Appetizers 8,000–12,000 lire ($6.30–$9.40); main courses 10,000–15,000 lire ($7.85–$11.80). AE, DC, MC, V.
Open: Lunch Fri–Wed 12:30–2:30pm; dinner Fri–Wed 7:30–10pm. **Closed:** Dec 10–Feb 15.

The smart set goes to this harborside restaurant for top-notch fish dinners and a whiff of local atmosphere. You'll find a good table under parasols, so you can keep an eye trained on the yachting set ("No, darling, we're definitely not going to Hydra this year!"). Most dishes are beautifully cooked and served by an efficient staff. Meals include an excellent fish soup, called brodetto di pesce con crostini, followed by a mixed Ligurian fish fry or a meat course, such as scaloppine in a marsala wine sauce.

IL BAGATTO, via Matteotti 145. Tel. 531925.

Cuisine: LIGURIAN. **Reservations:** Not needed. **Bus:** U.
$ Prices: Appetizers 8,000–15,000 lire ($6.30–$11.80); main courses 18,000–25,000 lire ($14.15–$19.65); fixed-price meal 35,000 lire ($27.50). AE, DC, MC, V.
Open: Lunch Mon–Sat 12:30–3pm; dinner Mon–Sat 7–11pm. **Closed:** June.

Il Bagatto provides good meals in a tavern setting, with dark beams, provincial chairs, and even oversize pepper grinders brought to the tables. The location is in the shopping district of the town, about two blocks from the sea. My most recent dinner began with a choice of creamy lasagne or savory hors d'oeuvres. The scaloppine with artichokes and asparagus was especially pleasing, as was (on another occasion) a mixed grill of Mediterranean fish. All orders were accompanied by potatoes and a choice of vegetables, then followed by crème caramel for dessert. And the pièce de résistance is the Valencian paella—a whopping order with bite-size pieces of fish floating in a sea of rice.

EVENING ENTERTAINMENT

The high life holds forth at the **San Remo Casino,** corso Inglesi, in the very center of San Remo (tel. 534001), which is built in a turn-of-the-century style known as "Liberty," an ornate mixture of classical and art nouveau. For decades, fashionable visitors have dined in high style in the elegant restaurant, reserved tables at the roof garden's cabaret, or tested their luck at the gaming tables. Like a white-walled palace, the pristine-looking casino stands at the top of a steep flight of stone steps above the main artery of town.

Visitors today can attend a variety of shows, fashion parades, concerts, and theatrical presentations staged throughout the year. The entrance fee is 15,000 lire ($11.80) for the French and American gaming rooms, which are open daily from 2:30pm to 3am. A jacket and tie are requested, as is a passport. For the slot-machines section, entrance is free and there is no particular dress code; it's open daily from 11am to 3am. The casino's restaurant is open nightly from 8:30pm to 1am, charging from 70,000 lire ($54.95) per person for dinner, which consists of international specialties. The restaurant has an orchestra playing everything from waltzes to rock music. A roof-garden cabaret is open only from July through September. Shows begin at 10:30pm and 1am nightly. If you visit for drinks only (and not dinner), the cost is from 28,000 lire ($22) per drink.

2. GENOA (GENOVA)

88 miles S of Milan, 311 miles NW of Rome, 120 miles E of Nice (France)

GETTING THERE   By Plane   Alitalia and other carriers fly into **Aeroporto Internazionale de Genova Cristoforo Columbo,** 4 miles west of the city center. For information about flights, call 2415410.

By Train   Genoa has good rail connections with the rest of Italy; it lies only 1½ hours from Milan, 3 hours from Florence, and 1½ hours from the French border.

Genoa has two major rail stations, the **Stazione Principe** and the **Stazione Brignole.** Chances are you'll arrive at the Principe, which is nearest to the harbor and the old part of the city. However, both trains and municipally operated buses run between the two stations. For information about trains, call 284081.

By Bus   SITA buses (tel. 313851), originating in Genoa, service the full length of the Ligurian coast in both directions. It's best to arrive in Genoa by car, plane, or rail, then rely on the bus to take you up or down the coast.

By Car   Motorists will find Genoa right along the main autostrada (A10) that begins its run at the French border, and continues along the Ligurian coastline.

By Ferry   It's highly likely that you'll find yourself in Genoa waiting for a ferryboat to take you to such offshore destinations as Sardinia or Sicily. If so, the number to call for information is the Stazione Marittima (tel. 261466). You can also arrive in Genoa by ferry. There is a 22-hour service to Genoa originating in Palermo (Sicily), costing 82,000 lire ($64.35) per person for a one-way ticket. Ferries also leave from Porto Torres (Sardinia), going to Genoa, at a one-way fare of 45,000 lire ($35.35).

It was altogether fitting that "Genoa the Proud" (Superba) gave birth to Christopher Columbus. Its link with the sea and maritime greatness dates back to ancient times. However, Columbus did his hometown a disservice. By blazing the trail to the New World, he dealt a devastating blow to Mediterranean ports in general, as the balance of trade shifted to newly developing centers on the Atlantic.

Even so, Genoa today is Italy's premier port, and ranks with Marseille in European importance. In its heyday (the 13th century), its empire, extending from colonies on the Barbary Coast to citadels on the Euphrates, rivaled that of Venice. Apart from Columbus, its most famous son was Andrea Doria (the ill-fated ocean liner was named after him), who wrested his city from the yoke of French domination in the early 16th century.

Like a half moon, the port encircles the Gulf of Genoa. Its hills slope right down to the water, so walking is likely to be an up- and downhill affair. Because of the terrain, the Christopher Columbus Airport opened quite late in Genoa's development.

The center of the city's maritime life, the ✪ **harbor of Genoa** makes for an interesting stroll, particularly in the part of the old town bordering the water. Sailors

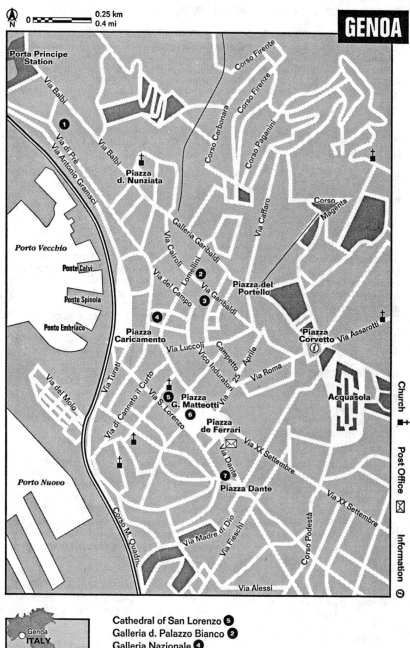

GENOA

0.25 km
0.4 mi

Porta Principe Station

Via Balbi

Via di Prè

Via Antonio Gramsci

1

Via Balbi

Piazza d. Nunziata

Corso Firenze

Corso Firenze

Corso Carbonara

Corso Firenze

Corso Paganini

Galleria Garibaldi

Via Cairoli

Lomellini

Via Caffaro

Corso Magenta

Porto Vecchio

Ponte Calvi

Ponte Spinola

Ponte Embriaco

Via del Campo

2

Via Garibaldi

Piazza del Portello

3

4

Piazza Caricamento

Via Luccoli

Campetto

Vico Indurator

Via 25 Aprile

Via Roma

Piazza Corvetto

Via Assarotti

Acquasola

Via Turati

Via del Molo

Via di Canneto il Curto

Via S. Lorenzo

5

G. Lorenzo

Piazza G. Matteotti

6

Piazza de Ferrari

Via XX Settembre

Via Dante

Porto Nuovo

7

Piazza Dante

Via XX Settembre

Corso Podestà

Corso M. Quadrio

Via Madre di Dio

Via Fieschi

Via Alessi

Church ✝

Post Office ⊠

Information ⓘ

Genoa

ITALY

ROME ★

Cathedral of San Lorenzo **5**
Galleria d. Palazzo Bianco **2**
Galleria Nazionale **4**
House of Columbus **7**
Palazzo Ducale **6**
Palazzo Reale **1**
Palazzo Rosso **3**

IMPRESSIONS

The Genoese manner . . . is exceedingly animated and pantomimic; so that two friends of the lower class conversing pleasantly in the street, always seem on the eve of stabbing each other forthwith, and a stranger is immensely astonished at their not doing it.
—CHARLES DICKENS, LETTER TO JOHN FORSTER, JULY 20, 1844

from many lands search for adventure and women to entertain them in the little bars and cabarets that occupy the back alleyways. Often the streets are merely medieval lanes, with foreboding buildings closing in.

A Word of Warning: The harbor, particularly after dark, is not for the squeamish. It can be dangerous. If you go wandering, try not to be alone, and leave as many valuables in safekeeping as possible. Genoa is rougher than Barcelona, more comparable to Marseille. Not only in the harbor area, but on any side street that runs downhill, a woman is likely to lose her purse.

The present harbor is the result of extensive rebuilding, following massive World War II bombardments that crippled its seaside installations. The best way to view the overall skyline is from a **harbor cruise** which will take you from the Maritime Station at the Ponte dei Mille. The trip lasts 1 hour. Along the way, you pass naval yards, shipbuilders, steelworkers, and warehouses (yachters anchor at Duca degli Abruzzi)—not a pretty picture entirely, but a fascinating landscape of industrial might. Purchase tickets at Cooperativa Battellieri del Porto di Genova (tel. 265712). Tours depart from the Stazione Marittima daily at 10am and 2pm, costing 4,000 lire ($3.10) per person.

ORIENTATION

INFORMATION Visitors can get information at the major office of **Ente Provinciale per il Turismo,** via Roma 11 (tel. 581407). It's open Monday through Thursday from 8am to 2pm and 2:30 to 5pm, on Friday from 8am to 2pm, and on Saturday from 8am to 1pm. Information booths dispensing tourist literature can also be found at the rail stations and at the airport. These are open Monday through Saturday from 8am to 8pm.

CITY LAYOUT Genoa opens onto the Porto di Genova, and most of the section of interest to visitors lies between two main rail stations, **Stazione Prìncipe,** on the western fringe of the town, near the port, and **Stazione Brignole,** to the northeast, which opens onto piazza Verdi. A major artery is **via XX Settembre,** which runs between piazza Ferrari in the west and piazza della Vittoria in the east. **Via Balbi** is another major artery, beginning its run east of the Stazione Prìncipe, off piazza Acquaverde. At the end of Genoavia Balbi you'll come to piazza Nunziata. From there, a short walk along via Cairola leads to the most important touristic street of Genoa, the palazzo-flanked **via Garibaldi** (but more about that later).

FAST FACTS

American Express The representative of American Express in Genoa is **Aviomar S.N.C.,** via Vernazza 48R (tel. 595551). But you should be a client—that is, carry an American Express card or use the company's traveler's checks—before you have your mail sent to them.

Area Code For Genoa, the telephone area code is 010.

Baby-sitters If you need a baby-sitter, get in touch with **Casa della Giovane,** via Galata 38B (tel. 561621), which receives calls only Monday through Friday from 3 to 5:45pm.

Consulate In Genoa, the **U.S. Consulate** is at piazza Portello 6 (tel. 282741), open Monday through Friday from 9am to 5:30pm. A consulate for the **United Kingdom** is at via XII Ottobre no. 2 (tel. 564833), open Monday through Friday from 9am to noon and 2:30 to 4:30pm.

Currency Exchange   To exchange money, you'll find service at **Delfino,** via Balbi 161R. However, both the Brignole and Principe railway stations have exchange offices open daily from 7am to 10pm.

Drugstores   Genoa has several all-night pharmacies, including **Europa,** corso Europa 676R (tel. 380239), and **Ghersi,** corso Buenos Aires 74R (tel. 541661). Need a pharmacy open at night? Dial 192.

Emergency Phone Numbers   Dial 113 for assistance in a **general emergency.** If it's **automobile** trouble, call A.C.I., Soccorso Stradale (tel. 116). For an **ambulance,** call 595951.

Gas Station   If you don't mind self-service, there's an Agip gas station that is open at night, located along viale Brigate Partigiane. You must have the right change.

Lost Property   The lost-and-found office is the Comune, via Garibaldi 9 (tel. 20981).

Medical Care   If you're in need of a doctor, call **A.I.A.D.** (tel. 566158).

Police   Dial 53661.

Post Office   The post office, at via Dante and piazza de Ferrari (tel. 161), has a telex and fax. Hours are Monday through Friday from 8:15am to 8pm and on Saturday from 8am to 1pm.

Religious Services   If you're **Catholic,** you can go into almost any church in Genoa. If you're **Protestant** there's the Chiesa Evangelica Metodista, via Da Persico 40 (tel. 672664), and if you're **Jewish** there's the Tempio Israelitico, on via Bertora (tel. 891513).

Taxi   To call a radio taxi, dial 2696.

Telephone   If you need to make a long-distance call, it's cheapest to go to the office at via XX Settembre no. 139, which is open 24 hours a day (your hotel is likely to impose heavy surcharges). You can also place calls at both the Brignole and Principe railroad stations until 9:30pm.

WHAT TO SEE & DO

In the heart of the city, you can stroll down   ✪ **via Garibaldi,** the street of the patricians, on which noble Genovese families erected splendid palazzi in late Renaissance times. The guiding hand behind the general appearance and most of the architecture was Alessi, who grew to fame in the 16th century (he once studied under Michelangelo).

PALAZZO ROSSO, via Garibaldi 18. Tel. 282641.

This 17th-century palace was once the home of the Brignoles, a local aristocratic family who founded a Genovese dynasty. It was restored after having been bombed in World War II, and contains a good collection of paintings, with such exceptional works as an *Ecce Homo* by Caravaggio and a *Guiditta* by Veronese. Perhaps its best-known exhibit is Sir Anthony van Dyck's portraits of Pauline and Anton Giulio Brignole-Sale from the original collection, and the magnificent frescoes by Gregorio De Ferrari (*Spring* and *Summer*) and Domenico Piola (*Autumn* and *Winter*). There are also collections of old coins, ceramics, and sculpture, and a display of gilded baroque statuary. Across from this red palace is the white palace, the Palazzo Bianco Gallery.

Admission: 2,000 lire ($1.55).

Open: Tues–Sat 9am–2pm, Sun 9am–noon. **Bus:** 18, 19, 20, 35, 39, or 40.

GALLERIA DI PALAZZO BIANCO, via Garibaldi 11. Tel. 291803.

The Duchess of Galliera donated this palace, along with her collection of art, to the city. Although the palace originally dates from the 17th century, its appearance today is the work of later architects. Gravely damaged during the war, the restored palace reflects the most recent advances in museum planning. The most significant paintings—from the Dutch and Flemish schools—include Gerard David's *Virgin of the Pappa* and Van der Goes's *Jesus Blessing the Faithful,* as well as works by Sir Anthony van Dyck and Peter Paul Rubens. A wide-ranging survey of European and local artists is presented—with paintings by Zurbarán and Murillo, and works by

Bernardo Strozzi (a whole room) and Alessandro Magnasco (excellent painting of a scene in a Genovese garden).
Admission: 2,000 lire ($1.55) adults, free for children under 12.
Open: Tues–Sat 9am–7pm, Sun 9am–noon. **Bus:** 18, 19, 20, 35, 39, or 40.

GALLERIA NAZIONALE (National Gallery), in the Palazzo Spinola, piazza della Pellicceria 1. Tel. 294661.

The National Gallery houses a major painting collection. (This palace was originally designed for the Grimaldi family in the 16th century as a private residence, although the Spinolas took it over eventually.) Its notable works include Sir Anthony van Dyck's *Child and His Dog,* Joos van Cleve's *Madonna in Prayer,* Antonello da Messina's *Ecce Homo,* and Giovanni Pisano's *Giustizia.*
Admission: 4,000 lire ($3.15) adults, free for children under 18.
Open: May–Sept, Tues–Sat 9am–7pm, Sun–Mon 9am–1pm; Oct–Apr, Tues–Sat 9am–5pm, Sun–Mon 9am–1pm. **Bus:** 18, 19, or 20.

PALAZZO REALE (Royal Palace), via Balbi 10. Tel. 206851.

The Royal Palace was started about 1650, and work continued until the early years of the 18th century. It was built for the Balbi family, then sold to the Durazzo. It later became one of the royal palaces of the Savoia in 1824. King Charles Albert modified many of the rooms around 1840. As in all Genovese palazzi, some of these subsequent alterations marred original designs. Its Galleria d'Arte is filled with paintings and sculpture, works of art by van Dyck, Tintoretto, G. F. Romanelli, and L. Giordano. Frescoes and antiques from the 17th to the 19th century are displayed. Seek out, in particular, the Hall of Mirrors and the Throne Room.
Admission: 2,000 lire ($1.55).
Open: Mon–Sat 9am–1pm. **Bus:** 18, 19, or 20.

CATHEDRAL OF SAN LORENZO, piazza San Lorenzo (Lawrence). Tel. 3450048.

Although Genoa is noted for its medieval churches, this one towers over all of them. The cathedral is distinguished by its bands of black and white marble adorning the facade in the Pisan style. In its present form it dates from the 13th century, although it was erected upon the foundation of a much earlier structure. Alessi, referred to earlier, designed the dome, and the campanile (bell tower) dates from the 16th century. The Chapel of John the Baptist, with interesting Renaissance sculpture, is said to contain the remains of the saint for whom it is named. The treasury is worth a visit, especially for its Sacred Bowl, thought to be the Holy Grail when Crusaders brought it back from Caesarea in the early 12th century (Eastern traders probably made goodly sums off naïve Christians pursuing relics for the church back home).
Admission: Cathedral, free; treasury, 500 lire (40¢).
Open: Tues–Sat 9–11:30am and 3–5:30pm. **Bus:** 18, 19, or 20.

HOUSE OF COLUMBUS, piazza Dante (off vico Dritto Ponticello).

A last sight that tour buses are fond of pointing out is the so-called House of Columbus, a dilapidated, vine-covered building (not to be visited inside). It is an 18th-century reconstruction at the site of what may have been the house of the explorer.

WHERE TO STAY

Generally, hotels are second rate, but some good finds await those who search diligently. *Warning:* Some of the cheap hotels and pensions in and around the waterfront are to be avoided. My recommendations, however, are suitable even for women traveling alone.

EXPENSIVE

BRISTOL-PALACE, via XX Settembre no. 35, 16121 Genova. Tel. 010/592541. Fax 010/561756. 130 rms (all with bath). A/C MINIBAR TV TEL **Bus:** 18, 37, 46, or 47.

$ Rates (including breakfast): 195,000–220,000 lire ($153.10–$172.70) single; 280,000 lire ($219.80) double. AE, DC, MC, V. **Parking:** 30,000 lire ($23.55).

The Bristol-Palace has a number of features that make one's stay in Genoa special. Its obscure entrance behind colonnades on a commercial street is misleading; the salons and drawing rooms within are furnished nicely with traditional pieces—many antiques are utilized, some of which appear to be of museum caliber. The dining room, in the Louis XVI style, is the most inspired, an ornately carved ceiling highlighting a mural of cloud-riding cherubs in the center. The larger of the bedrooms have an old-fashioned elegance, are spacious and comfortable, and tastefully furnished. The hotel's stairway is one of the most stunning in Genoa. Only breakfast is served, but the English bar is a favorite rendezvous point.

CITY HOTEL, via San Sebastiano 6, 16123 Genova. Tel. 010/5545. Fax 010/586301. 64 rms. A/C MINIBAR TV TEL **Bus:** 41.

$ Rates: 120,000–200,000 lire ($94.20–$157) single; 200,000–300,000 lire ($157–$235.50) double. AE, DC, MC, V. **Parking:** 30,000 lire ($23.55).

One of the best hotels in its category is located in a starkly angular stucco and travertine postwar building, surrounded by a crumbling series of town houses. The convenient location, near piazza Corvetto and via Garibaldi, is one of the hotel's best features. The staff will welcome you upon your arrival in the warm and comfortable wood-and-granite lobby, and usher you to one of the modern rooms. In these, you will find parquet floors, specially designed furniture, and up-to-date amenities. A cocktail bar with snacks is part of the facilities, but there's no restaurant.

HOTEL SAVOIA MAJESTIC, via Arsenale di Terra 5, 16126 Genova. Tel. 010/261641. Fax 010/261883. 120 rms (all with bath), 5 suites. A/C MINIBAR TV TEL **Bus:** 18, 37, 46, or 47.

$ Rates (including breakfast): 178,000 lire ($139.75) single; 260,000 lire ($204.10) double; from 356,000 lire ($279.45) suite. AE, DC, MC, V. **Parking:** 30,000 lire ($23.55).

Across from the train station is the 1887 Hotel Savoia Majestic, which still contains some of its original accessories. It is generally considered the best hotel in town. The clients tend to be overnighters from the European business community. The decor of the high-ceilinged bedrooms ranges from modern to conservatively old fashioned. The lobby and reception area of this hotel is shared with another establishment, the Londra & Continentale.

JOLLY HOTEL PLAZA, via Martin Piaggio 11, 16122 Genova. Tel. 010/893641. Fax 010/891850. 91 rms (all with bath). A/C MINIBAR TV TEL **Bus:** 18, 37, 46, or 47.

$ Rates (including breakfast): 185,000 lire ($145.25) single; 290,000 lire ($227.65) double. AE, DC, MC, V.

This hotel is newer than its modified classic facade suggests. It was actually built in 1950 to replace an older hotel destroyed by an air raid in World War II. Well located, it is just off piazza Corvetto with its equestrian statue, flower-bordered walks, and trees. The interior of the well-run hotel has been completely renewed, providing comfort and convenience. Many have tiny sitting areas and modern, functional furnishings. On the premises are an American bar and a grill room.

MODERATE

ALBERGO VIALE SAULI, viale Sauli 5, 16121 Genova. Tel. 010/561397. Fax 010/590092. 49 rms (all with bath). A/C TV TEL **Bus:** 18.

$ Rates (including breakfast): 80,000 lire ($62.80) single; 120,000 lire ($94.20) double. AE, DC, MC, V. **Parking:** 20,000 lire ($15.70).

On the second floor of a modern concrete office building, the hotel is just off a busy shopping street in the center of town. It is scattered over three floors, each of them reachable by elevator from the building's lobby. The public rooms are a high-ceilinged paneled trio of bar, breakfast room, and reception area, all with big windows and lots of comfort. Enore Sceresini is the opera-loving owner, and his clients usually include businesspeople who appreciate cleanliness and comfort. Each of the units has marble floors and a spacious bath.

HOTEL ASTORIA, piazza Brignole 4, 16122 Genova. Tel. 010/873316.
Fax 010/817326. 75 rms (all with bath). TV TEL **Bus:** 18.

$ **Rates** (including breakfast): 128,000 lire ($100.50) single; 165,000 lire ($129.55) double. AE, DC, MC, V. **Parking:** 25,000 lire ($18.65).

The Astoria was established in 1978 in what was an older hotel, with lots of polished paneling, wrought-iron accents, beige marble floors, and a baronial carved fireplace in one of the public rooms. Rooms are comfortably furnished and the maintainence is high. The hotel sits on an uninspiring square that contains a filling station and whose view encompasses a traffic hub and many square blocks of apartment buildings. There's a bar on the premises, but no restaurant.

HOTEL BRIGNOLE, vico de Corallo 13R, 16122 Genova. Tel. 010/ 561651. Fax 010/565990. 26 rms (all with bath). A/C MINIBAR TV TEL **Bus:** 17, 18, or 37.

$ **Rates:** 75,000 lire ($58.90) single; 110,000 lire ($86.35) double. Breakfast 10,000 lire ($7.85) extra. V. **Parking:** 20,000 lire ($15.70).

This pleasant hotel is on a hard-to-find street near piazza Brignole, from which it takes its name. It's sandwiched between commercial and residential buildings, and you'll see laundry flapping in the wind from the nearby buildings and a storefront on its lower level. After climbing an interior stairwell, you'll find yourself in an unpretentious lobby which leads to the clean and simple rooms. The hotel is scattered over three floors of the building, which doesn't have an elevator. The staff is helpful. Only breakfast is served.

HOTEL LONDRA & CONTINENTALE, via Arsenale di Terra, 16126 Genova. Tel. 010/261641. Fax 010/261883. 50 rms (all with bath). A/C MINIBAR TV TEL **Bus:** 18, 20, 35, 37, or 41.

$ **Rates** (including breakfast): 114,000 lire ($89.50) single; 176,000 lire ($138.15) double. AE, DC, MC, V. **Parking:** 25,000 lire ($19.65).

The lobby and reception personnel of this establishment are shared by another hotel, the Savoia Majestic, which is better rated. The Londra & Continentale, however, maintains its own identity in a modern format with recently renovated rooms. It's only a few steps from the main railway station, and there is parking on the premises. The rooms are neatly and attractively laid out.

INEXPENSIVE

HOTEL AGNELLO D'ORO, vico delle Monachette 6, 16126 Genova. Tel. 010/262084. Fax 010/561124. 38 rms (all with bath). TEL **Bus:** 18, 20, 35, 37, or 41.

$ **Rates:** 55,000 lire ($43.20) single; 85,000 lire ($66.75) double. Breakfast 9,000 lire ($7.05) extra. DC, MC, V. **Parking:** 20,000 lire ($15.70).

⑤ When the Doria family owned this structure and everything around it in the 1600s, they carved their family crest on the walls of the building near the top of the alley, so that all of Genoa would know the point at which their property began. The symbol was a golden lamb, and you can still see one at the point where the narrow street joins the busy boulevard leading to the Stazione Principe. The hotel, which was named after the animal on the crest, is a 17th-century building which includes vaulted ceilings and paneling in the lobby. About half the units are in a newer wing, but if you want the oldest accommodations, ask for no. 6, 7, or 8. Today the hotel is maintained by a family, who have installed a small bar off the lobby.

HOTEL ASSAROTTI, via Assarotti 42, 16122 Genova. Tel. 010/885822.
24 rms (all with bath or shower). TEL **Bus:** 18, 20, 35, 37, or 41.

$ **Rates:** 40,000 lire ($31.40) single; 65,000 lire ($51) double. Breakfast 10,000 lire ($7.85) extra. No credit cards. **Parking:** Free.

Off a busy boulevard, this substantial, well-run establishment—no fuss, no frills—

occupies a floor of a large building with 19th-century ornamentation. Although it has been renovated, the undersize lounges are furnished in a lackluster fashion, with deep leather armchairs. The bedrooms are nondescript in style but functional from the point of view of comfort (the larger, more handsome doubles are parceled out first).

HOTEL VITTORIA ORLANDI, via Balbi 33-45, 16126 Genova. Tel. 010/ 261923. Fax 010/252013. 56 rms (all with bath). TV TEL **Bus:** 18 or 37.
$ **Rates:** 65,000 lire ($51) single; 90,000–110,000 lire ($70.65–$86.40) double. Breakfast 8,000 lire ($6.30) extra. AE, DC, MC, V. **Parking:** 20,000 lire ($15.70).
Since this hotel is constructed on one of the hillsides for which Genoa is famous, its entrance is under a tunnel that opens at a point about a block from the Stazione Principe. An elevator will take you up to the reception area. The establishment welcomes a wide variety of guests, some of them staying for only 1 night, in the simple but clean rooms. Many of the units have balconies. About half the units are air-conditioned and contain a minibar. Best of all, the hotel is quiet because of the way it's sheltered by other buildings from the busy boulevards.

WHERE TO DINE

Genoa, which has been praised for its cuisine, has lots of restaurants and trattorie, many of which are strung along the harbor. The following recommendations will give you several opportunities to judge it for yourself. By ordering anything with *pesto* at the end, you'll be sampling the best-known regional concoction, a sauce made with olive oil, garlic, pine seeds, cheese, and fresh basil.

EXPENSIVE

GRAN GOTTO, via Fiume 11R. Tel. 564344.
Cuisine: SEAFOOD. **Reservations:** Recommended. **Bus:** 17, 18, or 37.
$ **Prices:** Appetizers 13,000–15,000 lire ($10.20–$11.80); main courses 25,000–30,000 lire ($19.65–$23.55). AE, MC, V.
Open: Lunch Mon–Fri 12:30–2:30pm; dinner Mon–Sat 7:30–10pm. **Closed:** Aug 12–31.
Facing a park is this top-notch trattoria, favored by the Genovese for its good atmosphere and fine kitchen. The emphasis is on seafood, but the meat and pasta dishes aren't neglected. In fact, the most typical offering, trenette al pesto, is quite famous, a pasta of paper-thin noodles (depending on the artistry of the chef) that is served with the characteristic pesto. The delicately simmered risotto is also tempting. The main dishes are most reasonably priced and of high standard, including the mixed fish fry or the French baby squid. The zuppa di pesce, like a Mediterranean bouillabaisse, has made many a luncheon for many a gourmet. The rognone al cognac is another superb choice—tender calves' kidneys that have been cooked and delicately flavored in cognac.

RISTORANTE AL PRIMO PIANO, via XX Settembre no. 36. Tel. 540284.
Cuisine: SEAFOOD. **Reservations:** Recommended. **Bus:** 17, 18, or 37.
$ **Prices:** Appetizers 15,000–18,000 lire ($11.80–$14.15); main courses 25,000–28,000 lire ($19.65–$22). AE, DC, MC, V.
Open: Lunch Mon–Fri 12:30–2:30pm; dinner Mon–Sat 7:30–10pm. **Closed:** Aug 10–18 and Dec 24–Jan 7.
As you dine at one of the tables of this elegant establishment one floor above street level, you'll get a discreet view of an Italian family hard at work at their shared goal of running an excellent restaurant. Menu items include a rich assortment of fresh fish, fricassee of lamb, stuffed veal Genovese style, and desserts such as frozen zabaglione.

RISTORANTE SAINT CYR, piazza Marsala 4. Tel. 886897.
Cuisine: GENOVESE. **Reservations:** Required. **Bus:** 18, 20, 35, 37, or 41.

$ Prices: Appetizers 10,000–15,000 lire ($7.85–$11.80); main courses 25,000–30,000 lire ($19.65–$23.55). AE, DC, MC, V.
Open: Lunch Mon–Fri 12:30–2:30pm; dinner Mon–Fri 7:30–10pm. **Closed:** Aug.

My favorite time to come to this restaurant is at night, when some of the most discriminating palates in Genoa might be seen enjoying dishes generously adapted from regional recipes. The food items change every day, although a recent menu featured rice with truffles and cheese, a timbale of fresh spinach, a charlotte of fish, and a variety of braised meats, each delicately seasoned and perfectly prepared. The restaurant is open for lunch, when the clientele is likely to be conservatively dressed businesspeople discussing shipping contracts. There's a good selection of wines to accompany your meal.

RISTORANTE ZEFFIRINO, via XX Settembre no. 20. Tel. 591990.
  Cuisine: LIGURIAN. **Reservations:** Recommended. **Bus:** 17, 18, 20, 29, 31, or 36.
  $ Prices: Appetizers 13,000–15,000 lire ($10.20–$11.80); main courses 25,000–30,000 lire ($19.65–$23.55).
  Open: Lunch Thurs–Tues noon–3pm; dinner Thurs–Tues 7pm–midnight.
In a cul-de-sac just off one of the busiest boulevards of Genoa, this place has hosted celebrities ranging from Frank Sinatra to Luciano Pavarotti. At least 14 members of the Zeffirino family prepare what is said to be the best pasta in the city, from recipes collected all over Italy. These include lesser-known varieties such as quadrucci, pettinati, and cappelletti, as well as the more familiar tagliatelle and lasagne. Following one of these platters, you can select from a vast array of meat and fish, along with 1,000 kinds of wine. Ligurian specialties, including risotto alla pescatore and beef stew with artichokes, are featured.

MODERATE

IL CUCCIOLO, viale Sauli 33. Tel. 546470.
  Cuisine: TUSCAN. **Reservations:** Recommended. **Bus:** 17, 18, or 37.
  $ Prices: Appetizers 10,000–15,000 lire ($7.85–$11.80); main courses 18,000–20,000 lire ($14.15–$15.70). AE.
  Open: Lunch Tues–Sun noon–3pm; dinner Tues–Sun 7:30–10:30pm. **Closed:** Aug.
When you're in Genoa, you may want to dine as the Genovese do. However, if you're going to be around for a while, you may want to vary your diet by dining in one of the best Tuscan restaurants in the city. That is, if you can find it. Go armed with a good map, as it lies on one of those "hidden" squares of the city, with near-impossible parking. Should you go at night, you will find lanterns placed festively outside, adorning this ground-floor restaurant in a 19th-century building. You not only get good Tuscan food, especially beefsteak Florentine, but excellent wines as well. The service is efficient and the reception is gracious.

TRATTORIA DEL MARIO, via Conservatori del Mare 35R, piazza Banchi. Tel. 297788.
  Cuisine: GENOVESE. **Reservations:** Recommended for lunch. **Bus:** 1, 2, 3, 4, 5, 6, or 7.
  $ Prices: Appetizers 10,000–20,000 lire ($7.85–$15.70); main courses 28,000–30,000 lire ($22–$23.55). AE, MC, V.
  Open: Lunch Sun–Fri 12:30–2:30pm; dinner Sun–Fri 7:30–10pm.
This is one of the best dining spots in the old town; what it lacks in atmosphere it makes up for in taste. It may be somewhat hard to find, but the Genovese have been making a trail to its door. It features such specialties as trenette al pesto, which is made with the local, almost perfumed basil. The trenette is a pastalike fettuccine that has been tossed with slices of potato and thin strips of green beans. You might begin your meal with the cold seafood salad known as insalata di pesce. The array of antipasti includes roast sweet yellow peppers, stuffed tomatoes, and mushrooms. An unusual and exciting dish is lettuce leaves that have been stuffed with

a nutmeg-scented ground veal. As an accompanying dish you can order thin slabs of zucchini that have been deep-fried a golden brown.

SPECIALTY DINING

Pasticceria Mangini, via Roma 91R (tel. 564013), is one of the most elegant cafés in town, filled with embellishments from the 19th century. Even the zinc-top bar is supported by what antique connoisseurs would consider a fine piece of furniture. Cappuccino costs 4,000 lire ($31.40) at a table. You can admire the equestrian statue of Victor Emmanuel II in piazza Corvetto while you sip your beverage. Open Tuesday through Sunday from 7:30am to 8:30pm.

3. RAPALLO

296 miles NW of Rome, 17 miles SE of Genoa, 100 miles S of Milan

GETTING THERE   By Train   Trains from Genoa stop off here at the rate of about three per hour, at a one-way fare of 1,800 lire ($1.40). Service is daily from 4:30am to midnight.

By Bus   Buses operated by SITA (tel. 010/313851 in Genoa for information and schedules) link Rapallo with Genoa.

By Car   From Genoa, continue southeast along the A12 autostrada.

ESSENTIALS   The **telephone area code** is 0185. The **Tourist Information Center** is at via Diaz 9 (tel. 51282).

A top seaside resort—known for years to the chic and wealthy crowd who live in villas studding the hillside—Rapallo occupies a remarkable site overlooking the Gulf of Tiguillio. In summer, the crowded heart of Rapallo takes on a carnival air, as hordes of bathers occupy the rocky sands along the beach. In the area is an 18-hole golf course, as well as an indoor swimming pool, a riding club, and a modern harbor. You can also take a cable car to the **Sanctuary di Montallegro,** then walk to **Monte Rosa** for what is considered one of the finest views of the Ligurian coast. There are many opportunities for summer boat trips, not only to Portofino but to the Cinque Terre.

Rapallo's long history is often likened to Genoa's. It became part of the Repubblica Superba in 1229, but Rapallo had existed long before that. Its cathedral dates from the 6th century when it was founded by the bishops of Milan. Walls once enclosed the medieval town, but now only the Saline Gate remains. Rapallo has also been the scene of many an international meeting, the most notable of which was the 1917 conference of wartime allies.

Once you arrive in Rapallo by public or private transportation, you can walk around to the following hotels and restaurants.

WHERE TO STAY

VERY EXPENSIVE

GRAND HOTEL BRISTOL, via Aurelia Orientale 369, 16035 Rapallo. Tel. 0185/273313. Fax 0185/55800. 93 rms (all with bath), 8 suites. A/C MINIBAR TV TEL **Bus:** Buses marked "Zoagli" make the half-mile run from the center of town every 30 minutes.
$ Rates (including breakfast): 210,000–240,000 lire ($164.85–$188.40) single; 280,000–320,000 lire ($219.80–$251.20) double; from 650,000 lire ($510.25) suite. AE, MC, V. **Parking:** 10,000 lire ($7.85).

This hotel, one of the Riviera's grand old buildings, has undergone a sparkling renovation; it is easily one of the most glamorous hotels along the coast. Originally built in 1908, it was reopened in 1984 as the personal brainchild of a multimillionaire who died shortly after its transformation. The turn-of-the-century pink-and-white facade, with surrounding shrubbery and iron gates, was spruced up but basically unchanged during the 5-year rebuilding program. The interior, however, which was mostly gutted, now contains five elegant restaurants in several degrees of formality, and a pool whose inviting waters are visible from many of the bedrooms. The kitchens are about the most modern anywhere, and the polite staff is dressed in formal morning suits. The lush, modern decor includes tasteful colors and stylish accessories. Perhaps best of all, the architects knew what to do with the unused space under the twin Victoria towers on the top floor. There, enclosed within the sloping walls, you'll find an unusual piano bar, complete with live music, plush upholstery, comfortable chairs, and views that stretch up and down the coast.

Some of the bedrooms have private terraces, and all contain electronic window blinds, lots of mirrors, and tree-of-life motifs wallpapered onto the spaces above the oversize beds.

Dining/Entertainment: The most formal of all the hotel's five restaurants, Le Cupole, is outfitted in shades of dusty rose, with massive silver cutlery, an army of waiters, and fixed-price lunches and dinners costing around 70,000 lire ($54.95).

Services: Room service, baby-sitting, laundry, valet.

Facilities: The hotel's free-form swimming pool is one of the biggest in the region. There's also a series of conference rooms.

EXPENSIVE

EUROTEL, via Aurelia Ponente 22, 16035 Rapallo. Tel. 0185/60981. Fax 0185/50635. 65 rms (all with bath), 3 suites. A/C MINIBAR TV TEL

$ Rates (including breakfast): 140,000–155,000 lire ($109.90–$121.70) single; 205,000–235,000 lire ($160.95–$184.50) double; from 265,000 lire ($208) suite. AE, DC, MC, V. **Parking:** Outdoors, free; garage, 18,000 lire ($14.15).

This vivid sienna-colored structure is indented with a series of arched and recessed loggias, plus a curved extension that juts over the front entrance. It's one of the tallest hotels in town, set above the port at the top of a winding road where you'll have to negotiate the oncoming traffic with care. The hotel has a collection of condominiums on the premises that are usually occupied during part of the year by their owners. The lobby has marble floors and a helpful staff. All units overlook the water, and contain built-in cabinets and beds that fold, Murphy style, into the walls. A bar and restaurant, Antica Aurelia, are on the premises, as is a swimming pool.

HOTEL ASTORIA, via Gramsci 4, 16035 Rapallo. Tel. 0185/273533. Fax 0185/274093. 20 rms (all with bath). A/C MINIBAR TV TEL

$ Rates (including breakfast): 146,000 lire ($114.60) single; 216,000 lire ($169.55) double. AE, DC, MC, V. **Parking:** 20,000 lire ($15.70). **Closed:** Dec 8–Jan 10.

On a waterside street near the beach cabañas, you'll find this symmetrical cream-and-white villa with baroque trim. It was one of five turn-of-the-century villas all in a row that have since been turned into hotels. There's a well-maintained rose garden in front. About half the rooms have a sea view, although the rear rooms are much quieter. Breakfast, the only meal served here, costs extra; it can be taken in your room, in the breakfast room, or in the garden.

MODERATE

HOTEL MODERNE & ROYAL, viale Gramsci 6, 16035 Rapallo. Tel. 0185/50601. Fax 0185/50604. 40 rms (all with bath). TEL

$ Rates (including breakfast): 75,000 lire ($58.90) single; 118,500 lire ($93) double; 115,000 lire ($90.30) per person with half board. AE, V. **Parking:** Free.

The Moderne & Royal is a gracious old villa only 50 yards from the harbor, with tables and umbrellas set out on its front terrace. The villa has art nouveau wrought-iron balconies and a carved winged cherub's head capping its uppermost gable. What is now the hotel was originally five units of summer villas; they were united and transformed into a hotel after World War II. Most of the public rooms have high-arched windows with views of the promenade, with its row of palm trees.

Directly across the promenade is Rapallo's swimming beach, with its rows of cabañas and bikini-clad inhabitants. Some of the bedrooms overlook the sea, and TV is available in the rooms upon request for 5,000 lire ($3.95). The restaurant serves both an international and a regional cuisine.

HOTEL RIVIERA, piazza 4 Novembre, 16035 Rapallo. Tel. 0185/50248.
Fax 0185/65668. 20 rms (all with bath). MINIBAR TV TEL
$ Rates (including breakfast): 74,500 lire ($58.50) single; 104,000–122,000 lire ($81.65–$95.75) double. AE, MC, V. **Closed:** Nov 4–Dec 22.

This modernized Victorian-era villa is set on a waterside street corner at the end of a row of villas, all of which contain hotels. There's a big glassed-in terrace where drinks are served in a decor of exposed wood, marble floors, and Italian-modern furniture. The comfortable bedrooms face either the water or a rear garden, the latter of which are much quieter.

INEXPENSIVE

HOTEL BEL SOGGIORNO, via Gramsci 10, 16025 Rapallo. Tel. 0185/54527. 22 rms (all with bath). TEL
$ Rates (including half board): 90,000 lire ($70.65) per person. No credit cards. **Parking:** Free. **Closed:** Nov–Dec 8.

This Victorian building, with ornate gables and green shutters, is in a desirable location near a city park at the edge of the water. The lobby contains photographs from 1904 showing what the street looked like then. The modernized interior has big windows, leather armchairs, and a helpful staff. This is a good budget choice for a stopover, especially because of the garden terrace in front, complete with palmettos and shrubbery.

HOTEL GIULIO CESARE, corso Colombo 62, 16035 Rapallo. Tel. 0185/50685. Fax 0185/60896. 33 rms (all with bath). TV TEL
$ Rates: 45,000 lire ($35.35) single; 80,000 lire ($62.80) double; 80,000 lire ($62.80) per person with half board. AE, MC, V. **Parking:** Free. **Closed:** Nov–Dec 20.

This modernized, four-story villa on the "right" side of Rapallo is a bargain for the Italian Riviera. When the genial owner skillfully renovated the establishment, he kept expenses down to keep room rates lower. The hotel, which lies on the coast road, about 90 feet from the sea, offers bedrooms with a homelike atmosphere, which feature good views of the Gulf of Tiguillo, and are furnished with tasteful reproductions (most of them have sun balconies). Ask for the rooms on the top floor if you want a better view and quieter surroundings. The meals are prepared with flair and fine ingredients (the fish dishes are superb).

HOTEL MIRAMARE, via Vittorio Veneto 27, 16035 Rapallo. Tel. 0185/50293. Fax 0185/273570. 31 rms (all with bath), 6 suites. MINIBAR TV TEL
$ Rates: 60,000 lire ($47.10) single; 100,000 lire ($78.50) double; from 150,000 lire ($117.75) suite; 110,000–130,000 lire ($86.35–$102.05) per person with half board. AE, DC, MC, V. **Parking:** 15,000 lire ($11.80).

On the water near a stone gazebo is this jazz age (1929) re-creation of a Renaissance villa, with exterior frescoes that have faded in the salt air. The gardens in front have been replaced by a glass extension that contains a clean and contemporary restaurant where an aquarium bubbles near the entrance. The accommodations inside are clean and simple, comfortable and high-ceilinged. Many of them have iron balconies that stretch toward the harbor.

WHERE TO DINE

Many guests stay in Rapallo on the half-board plan. However, those who are visiting for the day or who want an extra meal outside their domicile will be interested in the following recommendations.

RISTORANTE DE MONIQUE, lungomare Vittorio Veneto 6. Tel. 50541.
Cuisine: SEAFOOD. **Reservations:** Required.

$ Prices: Appetizers 8,000–12,000 lire ($6.30–$9.40); main courses 8,000–28,000 lire ($6.30–$22). AE, DC, MC, V.
   Open: Lunch Wed–Mon 12:30–2:30pm; dinner Wed–Mon 7:30–10pm.
   Closed: Jan–Feb 7.

This is one of the most popular seafood restaurants along the harbor, especially in summer, when the tavern chairs are almost completely filled. It features nautical decor in a big-windowed setting, which overlooks the boats of a marina. As you'd expect, fish is the specialty, including seafood salad, fish soup, risotto with shrimp, spaghetti with clams or mussels, grilled fish, and both tagliatelle and scampi "Monique."

RISTORANTE ELITE, via Milite Ignoto 19. Tel. 50551.
   Cuisine: SEAFOOD. **Reservations:** Not necessary.
   $ Prices: Appetizers 8,000–12,000 lire ($6.30–$9.40); main courses 18,000–25,000 lire ($14.15–$19.65). AE, DC, MC, V.
   Open: Lunch Fri–Wed 12:30–2:30pm; dinner Fri–Wed 7:30–10pm. **Closed:** Nov.

This establishment is set back from the water on a busy commercial street in the center of town. Mainly fish is served, the offering of which depends on the catch of the day. Your dinner might consist of mussels marinara, minestrone Genovese style, risotto marinara, trenette al pesto, scampi, zuppa di pesci, sole meunière, turbot, or a mixed fish fry from the Ligurian coast. A limited selection of the standard meat dishes is available, too.

4. SANTA MARGHERITA LIGURE

19 miles E of Genoa, 3 miles S of Portofino, 296 miles NW of Rome

GETTING THERE   By Train   Three trains per hour arrive from Genoa daily from 4:30am to midnight, costing 1,800 lire ($14.15) for a one-way ticket. Telephone 286630 in Santa Margherita Ligure for rail information. The station is at piazza Federico Raoul Nobili.

By Bus   Buses run frequently between Portofino and Santa Margherita Ligure daily, costing 1,000 lire (80¢) for a one-way ticket. You can also catch a bus in Rapallo bound for Santa Margherita. During the day one leaves Rapallo every 20 minutes making the 10-minute run.

By Car   Take Route 227 southeast from Genoa.

ESSENTIALS   The **telephone area code** for Santa Margherita Ligure is 0185. The **Tourist Information Center** is at via 25 Aprile 2B (tel. 287485).

A resort rival to Rapallo, Santa Margherita Ligure also occupies a beautiful position on the Gulf of Tiguillio. Its attractive harbor is usually thronged with fun-seekers, and the resort offers the widest range of accommodations in all price levels on the eastern Riviera. It has a festive appearance, with a promenade, flower beds, and palm trees swaying in the wind. As is typical of the Riviera, its beach combines rock and sand. Santa Margherita Ligure is linked to Portofino by a narrow road. It's on the Rome–Genoa rail link. The climate of Santa Margherita Ligure is mild, even in the winter months, when many elderly clients visit the resort.

The town dates back to A.D. 262. The official name of Santa Margherita Ligure was given to the town by King Victor Emmanuel II in 1863. Before that, it had many other names, including Porto Napoleone, an 1812 designation from Napoleon.

You can visit the richly embellished **Basilica of Santa Margherita d'Antiochia,** piazza Carrera, with its Italian and Flemish paintings, along with relics of the saint for whom the town was named.

Santa Margherita Ligure is relatively compact, and once you reach the place—by either public or private transportation—you can walk to the following recommendations.

WHERE TO STAY
VERY EXPENSIVE

**IMPERIAL PALACE, via Pagana 19, 16038 Santa Margherita Ligure.
Tel. 0185/288991.** Fax 0185/271398. 101 rms (all with bath), 15 junior suites.
A/C MINIBAR TV TEL
$ Rates: 195,000–268,000 lire ($153.10–$210.40) single; 420,000–474,000 lire
($329.70–$372.10) double; 200,000–310,000 lire ($157–$243.35) per person
with half board. AE, DC, MC, V. **Parking:** 12,000 lire ($9.40). **Closed:**
Nov–Mar 23.

The Imperial looks like an ornate gilded palace, and many guests like its faded
grandeur to spend their "season on the Riviera." Located at the edge of the resort, it's
built against a hillside and surrounded by semitropical gardens. Bikini-clad women
and men of the international set feel at home here. The public rooms of the Imperial
Palace live up to the hotel's name—old courtly splendor dominates, with vaulted gilt
and painted ceilings, satin-covered antiques, ornate mirrors, and inlaid marble floors.

The bedrooms vary widely—from royal suites to simple singles away from the sea.
Many of the rooms have elaborate ceilings, balconies, brass beds, chandeliers, and
white antiqued furniture. Others are rather rawboned, so your opinion of this hotel
will likely depend on your room assignment.

Dining/Entertainment: The dining room is formal, with white colonnades and
arches and mahogany chairs, an appropriate background for Ligurian and international meals. There's also a two-decker open-air restaurant, and the music room, with its
grand piano and satin chairs, is still enjoyed at teatime.

Services: Room service, baby-sitting, laundry, valet.

Facilities: All along the water edge, a festive recreation center has been created,
with an oval flagstone swimming pool on a terrace, an extended stone wharf for
sunbathing, and cabañas.

EXPENSIVE

**GRAND HOTEL MIRAMARE, via Milite Ignoto 30, 16038 Santa
Margherita Ligure. Tel. 0185/287013.** Fax 0185/284651. 84 rms (all with
bath), 9 suites. A/C MINIBAR TV TEL
$ Rates (including breakfast): 170,000–200,000 lire ($133.45–$157) single;
280,000–340,000 lire ($219.80–$266.90) double; 195,000–260,000 lire
($153.10–$204.10) per person with half board. Reduced rates available for
children under 12 in parents' room. AE, MC, V. **Parking:** Free.

It was on the terrace of this hotel in 1933 that Marconi succeeded in
transmitting for the first time, by means of microwaves, telegraphic and
telephonic signals to a distance of more than 90 miles. Today the building has a
festive confectionary look that is enhanced by the blue shutters and dazzling white
facade. Separated from a stony beach by a busy boulevard, it's a 3-minute walk from
the center of town. The hotel is surrounded by gardens whose meticulously
maintained rear side is visible through huge plate-glass windows. To one side is a
curved outdoor swimming pool with heated sea water. This adjoins a raised sun
terrace dotted with parasols and iron tables. Bedrooms are well furnished.

Dining/Entertainment: The hotel restaurant has many Victorian touches,
including fragile chairs and blue-and-white porcelain set into the plaster walls. Meals
begin at 75,000 lire ($58.90).

Services: Room service, baby-sitting, laundry, valet.

Facilities: Outdoor pool.

MODERATE

**HOTEL CONTINENTAL, via Pagano 8, 16038 Santa Margherita Ligure.
Tel. 0185/286512.** Fax 0185/284463. 76 rms (all with bath). A/C MINIBAR TV
TEL
$ Rates (including breakfast): 107,000–133,000 lire ($84–$104.40) single;

161,000–235,000 lire ($126.40–$104.50) double; 120,000–175,000 lire ($94.20–$137.40) per person with half board. AE, DC, MC, V. **Parking:** 18,000 lire ($14.15).

From the winding road leading into town you'll see this hotel's grandiose facade, with its Doric portico, balustrades, and fancy carvings. After you enter the high-ceilinged and airy public rooms, however, you'll see the terraced gardens that stretch down to a rocky spit where guests can swim if they don't feel like using the pool. The bedrooms are filled with conservative furnishings, and often have tall French windows that lead onto wrought-iron balconies. A nearby annex contains additional lodging. The view from the restaurant encompasses the curved harbor in the center of town, a few miles away. The bedrooms are comfortably furnished.

LIDO PALACE HOTEL, via Andrea Doria 3, 16038 Santa Margherita Ligure. Tel. 0185/285821. Fax 0185/284708. 54 rms (all with bath), 48 junior suites. A/C MINIBAR TV TEL

$ Rates: 134,000–162,000 lire ($105.20–$127.15) single; 178,000–212,000 lire ($139.75–$166.40) double; from 250,000 lire ($196.25) suite. Breakfast 12,500 lire ($9.80) extra. AE, DC, MC, V. **Parking:** 20,000 lire ($15.70). **Closed:** Nov 5–Dec 2.

Set on the harbor in the middle of town, this ornate mustard- and cream-colored building rises imposingly above the palms and the public beach. It was built sometime between 1910 and 1920 and has been kept attractive through restoration ever since. The hotel's accommodations consist of a large number of junior suites for two to four people. All units have views of the Golfo del Tiguillio and are insulated from traffic noise. They are all equipped with kitchenettes. Breakfast is the only meal served.

HOTEL MINERVA, via Maragliano 34, 16038 Santa Margherita Ligure. Tel. 0185/286073. Fax 0185/281697. 33 rms (all with bath). MINIBAR TV TEL

$ Rates (including breakfast): 92,000 lire ($72.20) single; 162,000 lire ($127.15) double; 80,000–105,000 lire ($62.80–$82.45) per person with half board. AE, DC, MC, V. **Parking:** 8,000 lire ($6.30).

Originally built in 1952 as a private villa, this structure was later expanded into this comfortable, sienna-colored hotel owned by the Metaldi family. It's above the resort, at the end of a residential street lined with trees and flowers. You climb a flight of flagstone steps through a private garden to reach the black marble floors, Corinthian columns, and sofas of the sunny public rooms. There's a pleasant bar off the lobby. Rooms are traditionally furnished and comfortable.

PARK HOTEL SUISSE, via Favale 31, 16038 Santa Margherita Ligure. Tel. 0185/289571. Fax 0185/281469. 85 rms (all with bath or shower). TV TEL

$ Rates (including breakfast): 95,000–140,000 lire ($74.60–$109.90) single; 160,000–250,000 lire ($125.60–$196.25) double. AE, DC, MC, V. **Parking:** 8,000 lire ($6.30).

Set in a garden above the town center, the Park Hotel Suisse features a panoramic view of the sea and harbor. It has seven floors, all modern in design, with deep private balconies that are like al fresco living rooms for some of the bedrooms. On the lower terrace is a large, free-form, saltwater swimming pool surrounded by semitropical vegetation. A modernistic water chute, diving boards, a café with parasol tables for refreshments—all give one the advantages of seaside life and then some. The comfortable bedrooms that open onto the rear gardens, without sea view, cost slightly less; the rooms are decked out with contemporary furnishings in bold colors. The hotel lies 800 yards from the rail station above a small harbor about 100 yards from the sea. You have to cross a small street to reach the water, or you can use the outdoor pool.

HOTEL REGINA ELENA, lungomare Milite Ignoto 44, 16038 Santa Margherita Ligure. Tel. 0185/287003. Fax 0185/284473. 94 rms (all with bath). A/C MINIBAR TV TEL

$ Rates (including breakfast): 112,000–130,000 lire ($87.90–$102.05) single; 202,000–224,000 lire ($158.55–$175.85) double. 153,000–171,000 lire ($120.10–$134.25) per person with half board. AE, DC, MC, V. **Parking:** Free.

In a modern boxy building painted in pastel shades, this hotel is separated from a stony beach by the busy thoroughfare that leads to Portofino. Rooms are modern, functionally furnished and well maintained. A nearby annex contains additional rooms. Although the hotel was built in 1908, few of the turn-of-the-century details remain after a renovation.

Dining/Entertainment: The dining room is the most interesting part of the hotel, in a 12-sided structure with walls that are almost entirely made of glass. The half-board plan features some very good cuisine.

Services: Room service, baby-sitting, laundry, valet.

Facilities: Conference center, garden leading to private beach.

INEXPENSIVE

ALBERGO CONTE VERDE, via Zara 1, 16038 Santa Margherita Ligure. Tel. 0185/287139. Fax 0185/284211. 37 rms (all with bath). TEL
$ **Rates** (including breakfast): 60,000 lire ($47.10) single; 100,000 lire ($78.50) double; 60,000–100,000 lire ($47.10–$78.50) per person with half board. AE, DC, MC, V. **Closed:** Nov–Dec 25.

This place offers one of the warmest welcomes in town to the low-budget traveler. Only two blocks from the sea, this third-class hotel has been revamped, and its rooms are simple but adequate. The terrace in front of the hotel has swing gliders, and the lounge has period furnishings, including rockers. All is consistent with the villa exterior of shuttered windows, flower boxes, and a small front garden and lawn where tables are set out for refreshments.

HOTEL JOLANDA, via Luisito Costa 6, 16038 Santa Margherita Ligure. Tel. 0185/287513. Fax 0185/287512. 40 rms (35 with bath). TV TEL
$ **Rates:** 35,000 lire ($27.50) single without bath, 50,000 lire ($39.25) single with bath; 65,000 lire ($51) double without bath, 80,000 lire ($62.80) double with bath; 65,000–85,000 lire ($51–$66.75) per person with half board. Breakfast 7,500 lire ($5.90) extra. AE, V.

This hotel is actually two buildings joined together by a patio that serves as an open-air dining room. It is about two blocks from the sea and piazza Caprera. One of the Siamese halves is an old-style villa, in the semibaroque style; the other is straightforward modern, with rows of balconies. There is no sea view, but the pensione is on a peaceful little street, away from the noise of heavy traffic. The decor is rather jazzy.

WHERE TO DINE

Hotels and boarding houses have the upper hand. However, a few select establishments offer quality meals.

TRATTORIA CESARINA, via Mameli 2C. Tel. 286059.
   Cuisine: ITALIAN. **Reservations:** Recommended, especially in midsummer.
$ **Prices:** Appetizers 20,000–25,000 lire ($15.70–$19.65); main courses 35,000–38,000 lire ($27.50–$29.85). V.
   Open: Lunch Thurs–Tues 12:30–2:30pm; dinner Thurs–Tues 7:30–10pm.
   Closed: Mar 1–15 and Dec 15–31.

This trattoria lies beneath the arcade of a short but monumental street that runs into piazza Fratelli Bandiere. In an atmosphere of bentwood chairs and discreet lighting, you can enjoy the best food in town. Specialties include arrays of meat, vegetable, and seafood antipasti, along with classical Italian dishes such as taglierini with seafood and pappardella in a fragrant sausage sauce, plus seasonal fish, best when grilled, which has been caught off the nearby coast.

RISTORANTE LA GHIAIA, in the Lido Palace Hotel, via Andrea Doria 5. Tel. 283708.
   Cuisine: SEAFOOD. **Reservations:** Recommended.

$ Prices: Appetizers 8,000–24,000 lire ($6.30–$18.85); main courses 15,000–35,000 lire ($11.80–$27.50). AE, DC, MC, V.
Open: Lunch Thurs–Tues 12:30–2pm; dinner Thurs–Tues 8–10pm. **Closed:** Nov.

This establishment's name in translation means "sea rocks," and that is precisely what you'll see from the windows that provide multifaceted views of the water. It's set on the ground floor of one of the town's most centrally located hotels, and the modern decor includes clear colors and paintings throughout the sunny dining rooms. Outdoor tables are shielded from the pedestrian traffic by rows of shrubbery. Your meal might begin with antipasti di mare, tagliolini al salmone, zuppa di pesce (fish soup), risotto di mare (rice with seafood), or spaghetti with lobster. Fresh fish, including turbot, scampi, gamberini, and sea bass, is priced by the gram.

TRATTORIA ALL'ANCORA, via Maragliano 7. Tel. 280559.
Cuisine: SEAFOOD. **Reservations:** Recommended, especially evenings and Sat–Sun.
$ Prices: Appetizers 20,000–22,000 lire ($15.70–$17.25); main courses 35,000–38,000 lire ($27.50–$29.85). AE, DC, MC, V.
Open: Lunch Wed–Mon 12:30–2:30pm; dinner Wed–Mon 7:30–10pm. **Closed:** Jan.

Located about a block from the water, this family-run restaurant with a stone facade is decorated with a rustically nautical decor, many rows of wine bottles, and tavern chairs. Waitresses serve a local clientele that could include a crew of fishermen and electricians taking their midday rest, an extended family with unruly children, or a well-dressed couple celebrating an anniversary. Spaghetti with marinara sauce is proudly presented as one of the specialties of the house. The menu usually features a plate of the day, which most often consists of some kind of fish. Examples include insalata di mare, risotto marinara, minestrone genovese, grilled or fried shrimp, and lasagne and tagliatelle di Portofino served with various sauces, including pesto genovese.

5. PORTOFINO

22 miles E of Genoa, 106 miles S of Milan, 301 miles N of Rome

GETTING THERE **By Train** Go first to Santa Margherita Ligure (see above), then continue the rest of the way by bus.

By Bus Tigullio buses leave Santa Margherita Ligure at the rate of one every 30 minutes, bound for Portofino. The one-way fare is 1,000 lire (80¢), and you can purchase tickets aboard the bus.

By Car From Santa Margherita Ligure, continue south along the only road, which hugs the promontory until you reach Portofino. In summer traffic is likely to be heavy.

ESSENTIALS The **telephone area code** is 0185. The **Tourist Information Center** is at via Roma 35 (tel. 269024).

About 4 miles south of Santa Margherita Ligure along one of the most beautiful coastal roads in all of Italy is Portofino.

Elizabeth Taylor used to make her way from boutique to boutique here, with a "page boy" supplying fresh iced drinks and village mothers thrusting bambini in her face (they'd read in the tabloids that she liked to adopt children). Later, a speedboat whisked Taylor Inc., to a palatial yacht moored off the peninsula.

Back then, and still today, you're likely to see anybody and anything in Portofino—and usually do.

Favored by the yachting set, the resort is in an idyllic location on a harbor, where the water reflects all the pastel-washed little houses that run along it. In the 1930s it enjoyed a reputation with artists; later, a chic crowd moved in—and they're still there, occupying villas in the hills and refusing to surrender completely to popsicle-eating "trippers" who pour in during the day. Then the expatriate, well-heeled habitués flee, only to reemerge at the martini hour when the last tour bus has pulled out.

The thing to do in Portofino: During the day—but preferably before sunset—start on a walk that leads toward the tip of the peninsula. You'll pass the entrance to an old castle (where a German baron once lived), old private villas, towering trees, and much vegetation, until you reach the lighthouse. Allow an hour at least. When you return to the main piazza, proceed to one of the two little drinking bars on the left side of the harbor that rise and fall in popularity.

Once Portofino was a sleepy fishing village, but its history goes back to Roman times. Pliny called it "Portus Delphini." It was the private domain of Benedictines before it was incorporated into the Republic of Genoa in 1414, becoming, in 1815, a part of the Kingdom of the Two Sicilies.

Before beginning that walk to the lighthouse, as mentioned, you can climb steps from the port leading to the little parish Church of St. George. A panoramic view of the port and bay is possible from the terrace here. In summer, you can also take boat rides around the coast to such points as San Fruttuoso.

Portofino is tiny and you can walk to where you want to go.

WHERE TO STAY

Portofino is severely limited in hotels, and in July and August you may be forced to book a room in nearby Santa Margherita Ligure or Rapallo.

ALBERGO SPLENDIDO, viale Baratta 13, 16034 Portofino. Tel. 0185/ 269551. Fax 0185/269614. 63 rms (all with bath), 15 suites. A/C MINIBAR TV TEL

$ Rates (including half board): 315,000–360,000 lire ($247.30–$282.60) single; 630,000–720,000 lire ($494.55–$565.20) double; from 750,000 lire ($588.75) suite for two. AE, DC, MC, V. **Closed:** Oct 23–Apr 6.

This Relais & Châteaux selection provides a luxury base for those who moor their yacht in the harbor below, or have closed down their Palm Beach residence for the summer. The Duke and Duchess of Windsor were the first people to sign the guest lists, only to be followed by such loving couples as Humphrey Bogart and Lauren Bacall, Richard Burton and Elizabeth Taylor, along with Clark Gable, Catherine Deneuve, Liza Minnelli, and Rex Harrison. For decades, the name Splendido has cropped up at every mention of Portofino. The hotel might well have been a monastery; it is reached from the village by a steep and winding road that is flanked by twisting, silvery olive trees and banks of flowers growing against stone walls. From one of the hotel's pergola verandas, you can enjoy a panorama of the sea and rugged Riviera coastline. There are many tile terraces with arbors of wisteria and roses, and many flagstone paths lined with pink geraniums, rhododendrons, and palms.

Inside, a refreshing, informal country-house flavor prevails. The villa is rambling, with several levels of public rooms, terraces, and "oh, that view" bedrooms. Each private room is furnished in a personal way—no two alike. Traditional old pieces include antique desks and comfortable sofas and armchairs in small sitting areas. Prices are high, and vary according to the room assigned.

Dining/Entertainment: The bilevel dining room is divided by a row of arches and furnished with Biedermeier chairs, flower bouquets, and a fine old tapestry. The restaurant terrace not only enjoys a view but also serves traditional dishes of typical Ligurian cooking.

Services: Room service, baby-sitting, laundry, valet, massage.

Facilities: Hotel speedboat, saltwater swimming pool, beauty center, solarium, sauna.

ALBERGO NAZIONALE, 16034 Portofino. Tel. 0185/269575. Fax 0185/ 269578. 2 rms and 11 suites (all with bath). MINIBAR TV TEL

$ Rates: 167,000 lire ($131.10) double; from 325,000 lire ($255.15) suite. Breakfast 16,500 lire ($12.95) extra. MC, V.

At stage center, right on the harbor, this old villa with many roof levels is modest, yet well laid out. The suites here are tastefully decorated, and the little lounge has a brick fireplace, coved ceiling, antique furnishings, and good reproductions. Most of the bedrooms, furnished in a mixture of styles (hand-painted Venetian in some of the rooms), have a view of the harbor. There are no singles.

HOTEL EDEN, 16034 Portofino. Tel. 0185/269091. Fax 0185/269091. 9 rms (all with bath). TV TEL

$ Rates (including breakfast): 85,000 lire ($66.75) single; 160,000 lire ($125.60) double; 90,000–130,000 lire ($70.65–$102.05) per person with half board. AE, DC, MC, V. **Closed:** Dec 1–20.

Just 150 feet away from the harbor in the heart of the village is a little albergo, a budget holdout in an otherwise high-fashion resort. Set in a garden (hence its name), it's a good place to stay. While there is no view of the harbor, there is a winning vista from the front veranda, where breakfast is served. The hotel is run by Mr. Ferruccio, and life here is decidedly casual. The Ristorante da Ferruccio is well known in the area, and many nonresidents visit to sample the Ligurian specialties.

HOTEL SAN GIORGIO, 16034 Portofino. Tel. 0185/269261. Fax 0185/269262. 19 rms (all with bath). MINIBAR TV TEL

$ Rates: 85,000 lire ($66.75) single; 135,000 lire ($106) double. Breakfast 13,000 lire ($10.20) extra. AE, MC, V. **Closed:** Jan–Feb.

This good, family-owned hotel is set on a hill above the port. The bedrooms are clean, not very elaborate, and comfortable, all with radios. There is private parking. Breakfast is the only meal served.

WHERE TO DINE

IL PITOSFORO, Molo Umberto I no. 9. Tel. 269020.
   Cuisine: INTERNATIONAL. **Reservations:** Required.
$ Prices: Appetizers 15,000–50,000 lire ($11.80–$39.25); main courses 30,000–75,000 lire ($23.55–$58.90). AE, DC, MC, V.
   Open: Lunch Thurs–Mon noon–2:30pm; dinner Wed–Mon 7:30–11pm.
   Closed: Jan–Feb; lunch July–Aug.

Reached by climbing steps, Il Pitosforo draws a raft of raves and, most likely, cries of protest when the tab is presented. While not blessed with an especially distinguished decor, its position right on the harbor gives it all the native chic it needs, and has ever since Bogey and Bacall or Taylor and Burton came this way long ago. The food is worthy. Zuppa di pesce is a delectable Ligurian fish soup, or you may prefer the bouillabaisse, which is always reliable here. The pastas are especially recommendable, and include lasagne al pesto, wide noodles prepared in the typical Genovese sauce. Fish dishes include mussels alla marinara and paella valenciana for two, saffron-flavored rice studded with sea fruit and chicken. Men should wear jackets.

DELFINO, piazza Martiri delli Olivetta 40. Tel. 269081.
   Cuisine: SEAFOOD. **Reservations:** Recommended Sat.
$ Prices: Appetizers 10,000–25,000 lire ($7.85–$19.65); main courses 25,000–35,000 lire ($19.65–$27.50). AE, DC, MC, V.
   Open: Lunch Tues–Sun noon–3pm; dinner Tues–Sun 7–11pm. **Closed:** Nov 1–26.

Right on the village square that fronts the harbor is Delfino, Portofino's most fashionable dining spot (along with Il Pitosforo). It's located in a harborside, sienna-colored building with forest-green shutters. It is both nautically rustic and informally chic. Less expensive than Il Pitosforo, it offers virtually the same type of food, such as lasagne al pesto. Again, the fish dishes provide the best reason for lifting your fork: zuppa di pesce (a soup made of freshly caught fish with a secret spice blend), risotto with shrimp, and a mixed fish fry. The latter is exceptional, a whole platter loaded with shrimp, sole, squid, and other sea creatures. If you can't stand fish but are trapped into dining with those who do, then know that the chef at Delfino prides himself on his sage-seasoned vitello all'uccelletto, a roast veal with a gamey taste. Depending on your choice of fish dishes, expect a final tab ranging from 90,000 lire ($70.65) and up. Try to get a table near the front so as to enjoy the parade of visitors and villagers.

DA U'BATTI, vico Nuovo 17. Tel. 269379.
   Cuisine: SEAFOOD. **Reservations:** Recommended.
$ Prices: Appetizers 10,000–15,000 lire ($7.85–$11.80); main courses 28,000–40,000 lire ($22–$31.40). AE, MC, V.
   Open: Dinner only, Tues–Sun at 8 and 9:30pm. **Closed:** Dec–Jan.
Informal, chic, and colorful, this place is on a narrow cobblestone-covered piazza a few steps above the port. A pair of barnacle-encrusted anchors, hanging above the arched entrance, hint at the seafaring specialties that have become this establishment's trademark. Owner and sommelier Giancarlo Foppiano serves delectable dishes, which might include trenette with pesto sauce, a soup of "hen clams," spaghetti with olives, rice with shrimp or crayfish, or fish all Battista. It has a good selection of grappa, as well as French and Italian wines.

RISTORANTE DA PUNY, piazza Martiri delli Olivetta. Tel. 269037.
   Cuisine: SEAFOOD. **Reservations:** Required.
$ Prices: Appetizers 8,000–23,000 lire ($6.30–$18.05); main courses 20,000–35,000 lire ($15.70–$27.50). No credit cards.
   Open: Lunch Fri–Wed noon–3pm; dinner Fri–Wed 7–11pm. **Closed:** Jan–Feb.
This place is becoming better known as it competes with the established leaders of Portofino's portside restaurants. The Puny is set up on the stone square that opens onto the harbor. Because of its location, it's practically in the living room of Portofino, within sight of the evening activities that make the town famous as a hangout for the chic and tan yachting set. Green-painted tables are set under trees at night on a slate-covered outdoor terrace. Inside, the nautical decor includes walls of stippled stucco, with a zodiac theme inlaid in brass above the bar area. The menu includes pappardelle Portofino, antipasto of the house, spaghetti with clams, grilled sole, carne pizzaiola, and an array of freshly caught fish.

EVENING ENTERTAINMENT

LA GRITTA AMERICAN BAR, calata Marconi 20. Tel. 269126.
   La Gritta vies for business with its rival a few storefronts away. Between the two of them, they have attracted the biggest names in show business and elsewhere: from Onassis to Frank Sinatra to John Wayne. It is said that Rex Harrison, while drinking in this bar with the Duke of Windsor, excused himself to go and purchase a package of cigarettes. He never came back. On the way for the cigarettes, he ran into actress Kay Kendal and the two eloped. These celebrities have intermingled with dozens of tourists and a collection of U.S. Navy personnel in this small, well-appointed restaurant. As James Jones, author of *From Here to Eternity*, noted: "This is the nicest waterfront bar this side of Hong Kong." That is true, but it's always wise to check your bar tab carefully before you stagger out looking for a new adventure. La Gritta means "The Crab" in Genovese dialect. Long drinks cost 10,000 lire to 12,000 lire ($7.85 to $9.40) apiece. Hours are daily from 9am to 3pm.

SCAFANDRO AMERICAN BAR, calata Marconi 10. Tel. 269105.
   This is one of the village's chic rendezvous points, a place that has attracted an array of yachting guests. The seating arrangements inside contribute to the general feeling of well-being, since they're three-quarter-round banquettes, pulled up to teakwood tables with brass detailing. The members of your party will be illuminated by hanging dome lights, while in a corner sits a brass-and-copper headset removed from a 19th-century diver's costume. If one of the world's celebrities doesn't happen to come in while you're there, you can always study one of the series of unusual nautical engravings adorning the walls. A whisky begins at 10,000 lire ($7.85); a beer, 6,000 lire ($4.70). Open Wednesday through Monday from 8:30am to 3am.

CHAPTER 20

NAPLES & POMPEII

- **WHAT'S SPECIAL ABOUT NAPLES & POMPEII**
1. **NAPLES (NAPOLI)**
2. **THE ENVIRONS OF NAPLES**
3. **POMPEII**

Campania is in many ways the most eerie, memorable, and beautiful region of Italy, sociologically different from anything else in Europe—haunting, confusing, and satisfying, all at the same time. Campania forms a fertile crescent around the Bays of Naples and Sorrento, and stretches inland into a landscape of limestone rocks dotted with patches of fertile soil. It was off the shores of Campania that Ulysses ordered his crew to tie him, ears unstopped, to the mast of his ship, so that he alone would hear the songs of the sirens without throwing himself overboard in an attempt to sample their pleasures. Today the siren song of Campania still lures, with a sun-flooded, highly scented beauty, and a chemistry that some visitors insist is an aphrodisiac.

The geological oddities of Campania include a smoldering and dangerous volcano (already famous for having destroyed Pompeii and Herculaneum), sulfurous springs that belch steam and smelly gases, and lakes that ancient myths refer to as the gateway to Hades. Its seaside highway is the most beautiful in the world (and probably the most treacherous); it combines danger at every hairpin turn with some of Italy's most reckless drivers. Despite such dark images, Campania is one of the most captivating regions of Italy, sought out by native Italians and visitors alike for its combination of earth, sea, and sky. Coupled with this are what might be the densest collection of ancient ruins in Europe, each celebrated by classical scholars as among the very best of its kind.

The ancient Romans dubbed the land Campania Felix, which may reflect their satisfaction with the district that inspired the construction of hundreds of private villas for their rulers. In some ways the beauty of Campania contributed to the decay of the Roman Empire, as Caesars, their senators, and their courtiers spent more and more time pursuing its pleasures and abandoning the cares of Rome's administrative problems.

Even today, seafront land in Campania is so desirable that hoteliers have poured their life savings into foundations of buildings that are sometimes bizarrely cantilevered above rock-studded cliffs. Despite their numbers, these hotels tend to be profitably overbooked in summer.

Although residents of Campania sometimes stridently extoll the virtues of its cuisine, it is not the most sophisticated or renowned in Italy. Its produce, however, is superb, and its wine heady.

Today Campania typifies the conditions that northern Italians label "the problem of the south." Although the inequities are the most pronounced in Naples, the entire region, outside the resorts along the coast, has a lower standard of living and education, and higher crime rates, plus less developed standards of health care, than the more affluent north.

WHAT'S SPECIAL ABOUT NAPLES & POMPEII

Great Towns & Villages
☐ Naples, Italy's third most populated city, is one of the world's most beautiful seaports.
☐ Pompeii, an archeological treasure trove, unearthed from volcanic ash, rates as one of the top sights of the ancient world.

Ace Attractions
☐ Herculaneum, an archeological site smaller than Pompeii, but in many ways even more interesting; it, too, was buried under volcanic ash.
☐ Vesuvius, a volcano that has struck terror across the Campania, looming menacingly over the Bay of Naples.

Ancient Monuments
☐ The Phlaegrean Fields (Campi Flegrei), an explosive land of myth and legend, lying in the environs of Naples.

☐ Lago d'Averno, 10 miles west of Naples, a lake in an extinct volcanic crater that the ancients called the Gateway to Hades.

Museums
☐ National Archeological Museum, Naples, offering one of Europe's most valuable collections—many treasures removed from long-buried Pompeii.
☐ Museo e Gallerie Nazionali di Campodimonte, Naples, one of Italy's best collections of paintings from the 14th through the 16th century.

Television has contributed to leveling regional differences. Nevertheless, Campania is still rife with superstitious myths, vendettas, and restrictive traditions. It is also home to a people who can sometimes overwhelm you with kindnesses and spontaneity. Despite, or perhaps because of, these tendencies, it is worth investing your vacation time in Campania. In some way, it captures the soul and soulfulness of southern Italy.

SEEING NAPLES & POMPEII
SUGGESTED ITINERARY

Days 1–2: Spend a full day visiting the many attractions within the city limits of Naples. While still based at a hotel in Naples, spend Day 2 exploring the Phlaegrean Fields, west of the city, including Solfatara, Pozzuoli, Baia, Lago d'Averno, and Cuma.
Day 3: You can continue to be based at Naples or else can move south to a hotel at Pompeii (although the choices are very limited). On Day 3, visit Herculaneum in the morning and Pompeii in the afternoon. It would be better to spend an entire day at each site if you can afford the extra time.

GETTING THERE

The fastest way to get there is to fly into Capodichino, 4 miles north of the center of Naples. Flights from all major Italian cities, including Rome and Florence wing into this airport. Naples is also the railway hub of Campania, as the city lies on the major north-south line from Milan down Italy's western coastline to Reggio di Calabria and Messina. There are two routes from Rome—one going via Latina and Formia, the other going via Frosinone and Caserta. Use the bus once you get in Naples for fanning out to explore the region. Motorists find that the quickest route from Rome is the Rome–Naples A2 autostrada, which passes Caserta 18 miles north of Naples, or the Naples–Reggio di Calabria A3, which goes by Salerno, 33 miles south of Naples.

1. NAPLES (NAPOLI)
136 miles S of Rome, 162 miles W of Bari

GETTING THERE By Plane The quickest way to get to Naples from Rome and other major Italian cities, including Milan, is to fly there on a domestic flight, which will put you into **Capodichino Airport,** 4 miles north of the city. A city ATAN bus (no. 14) makes the 25-minute run between the airport and Naple's piazza Garibaldi in front of the main rail terminus. The bus fare is 800 lire (65¢), or about 18,000 lire ($14.15) if you take a taxi. Domestic flights are available on Alitalia, Alisarda, and Ati. Flying time from Milan is 1 hour 20 minutes; from Palermo, 1 hour 15 minutes; from Rome, 50 minutes; and from Venice, 1 hour 15 minutes. For flight information, call 081/5415222.

By Train Frequent trains connect Naples with the rest of Italy. For example, one or two trains per hour arrive from Rome, taking 2½ hours and costing 12,800 lire ($10.05) for a one-way passage. It's also possible to reach Naples from Milan in about 7 hours, costing 46,400 lire ($36.40) for a one-way ticket. Trains also run back and forth to the port city of Brindisi on the Rome–Leone line, taking 6½ hours and costing 26,200 lire ($20.55) for a one-way ticket. This line is used by visitors taking ferries for Greece. The city has two main rail terminals, **Stazione Centrale** at piazza Garibaldi and **Stazione Margelliana** at piazza Amadeo. If you want rail information, call 5534188.

By Bus Take either private or public (airlines, rail) transportation to reach Naples. Once there, various provincial bus companies service all the towns and villages through the region. The SITA buses, departing from via Pisanelli 3 (tel. 616080), are your best bet, as they run to such popular tourist spots as Amalfi, Pompeii, Ravello, and Salerno.

By Car In the old days the custom was to sail into the Bay of Naples, but today's traveler is more likely to drive there, heading down the autostrada from Rome. The Rome–Naples autostrada (A2) passes Caserta 18 miles north of Naples and the Naples–Reggio di Calabria autostrada (A3) runs by Salerno, 33 miles south of Naples.

By Ferry If you're already in Sicily, you can go on a ferry to Naples from Palermo on Tirrenia Lines, Palazzine Stella Maris within the port area of Palermo (tel. 6061111 for information about schedules). A one-way fare costs 61,100 lire ($47.95) per person for the 10½-hour boat trip to Naples.

I ts city government is reportedly corrupt, many of its businesses dominated by the Mafia; it has undisputedly the worst air pollution and traffic in Italy, and its hordes of street children make it the juvenile delinquent capital of Europe. Naples is Italy's most controversial city: You'll either love it or hate it. It is louder, more intense, more unnerving, but perhaps ultimately more satisfying and offering richer insights for the traveler than almost anywhere else in Italy.

Naples has changed a lot since the cholera outbreak of 1973, when the world

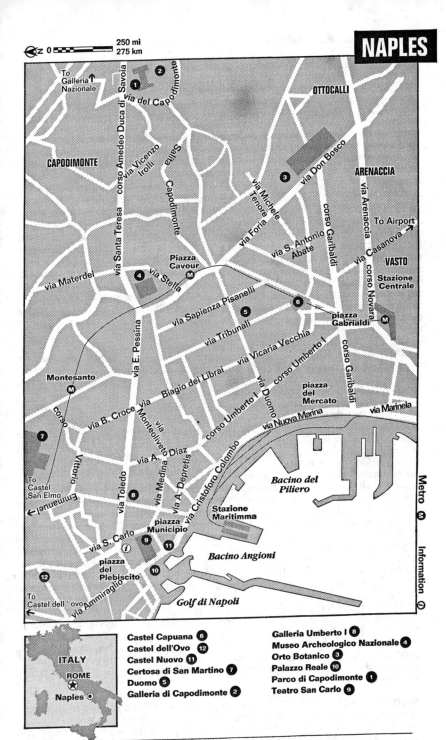

NAPLES

250 mi
275 km

To Galleria Nazionale

via del Capodimonte

corso Amedeo Duca di Savoia

via Vicenzo Irolli

OTTOCALLI

via Don Bosco

CAPODIMONTE

Salita Capodimonte

via Santa Teresa

via Michele Tenore

via Foria

via S. Antonio Abate

corso Garibaldi

via Arenaccia

ARENACCIA

To Airport

via Casanova

VASTO

corso Novara

Stazione Centrale

via Materdei

Piazza Cavour

via Stella

via E. Pessina

via Sapienza Pisanelli

via Tribunali

piazza Gabrialdi

corso Umberto I

Montesanto

via B. Croce

Biagio dei Librai

via Vicaria Vecchia

via Duomo

corso Garibaldi

corso Vittorio

via Montoliveto

piazza del Mercato

via Marinela

To Castel San Elmo

via A. Diaz

via Medina

via A. Depretis

via Nuova Marina

via Cristoforo Colombo

Bacino del Piliero

via Toledo

Stazione Maritimma

Emmanuel

via S. Carlo

piazza Municipio

Bacino Angioni

piazza del Plebiscito

via Ammiraglio

To Castel dell' ovo

Golf di Napoli

Metro ⓜ   Information ⓘ

ITALY

ROME

Naples

Castel Capuana ❻
Castel dell'Ovo ⓬
Castel Nuovo ⓫
Certosa di San Martino ❼
Duomo ❺
Galleria di Capodimonte ❷

Galleria Umberto I ❽
Museo Archeologico Nazionale ❹
Orto Botanico ❸
Palazzo Reale ❿
Parco di Capodimonte ❶
Teatro San Carlo ❾

IMPRESSIONS

[Naples] is a country of fiddlers and poets, whores and scoundrels.
—HORATIO LORD NELSON, DISPATCH TO LORD ST. VINCENT, SEPTEMBER 20, 1798

The museum is full, as you know, of lovely Greek bronzes. The only bother is that they all walk about the town at night.
—OSCAR WILDE, LETTER TO ERNEST DOWSON, OCTOBER 11, 1897

discovered that the city has no sewers and was basking on the edge of a picturesque but poisoned bay. New civic centers have been planned, and some of the city's baroque palaces have been restored. But to the foreigner unfamiliar with the complexities of the multifarious "Italys" and their regional types, the Neapolitan is still the quintessence of the country—easy to caricature ("O Sole Mio," "Mamma Mia," bel canto). If Sophia Loren (a native who moved elsewhere) evokes the Italian woman for you, you'll find more of her look-alikes here than in any other city. Perhaps more visible are the city's children. In one of the most memorable novels to come out of World War II, *The Gallery* by John Horne Burns, there is this passage: "But I remember best of all the children of Naples, the *scugnizzi*. Naples is the greatest baby plant in the world. Once they come off the assembly line, they lose no time getting onto the streets. They learn to walk and talk in the gutters. Many of them seem to live there."

A LOOK AT THE PAST   Neapolitan legends claim that the city was founded after the body of Parthenope (a nymph who committed suicide after being spurned by Ulysses) washed ashore in the nearby bay. Archeological evidence suggests that it was founded by Greek colonists late in the 5th century B.C.

During the height of the Roman Empire, Naples was only one of dozens of important cities that surrounded the famous bay. Roman emperors, especially Nero, perhaps in order to show that they appreciated the finer (Greek-inspired) things in life, treated Naples as a resort, away from the pressure of imperial Rome. They also used it as a departure point for their nearby villas on Capri. It was visited by poets (Virgil wrote the *Georgics* here) and sybarites alike. Under the Byzantine administration of the remnants of the Roman Empire, Naples actually grew and prospered—unlike many of its Italian neighbors. This was in part because of its excellent harbor, and in part because many of its competitors (Pompeii and Herculaneum, for example) were destroyed by economic stagnation or by cascades of molten lava and ash.

Over the centuries Naples has known many conquerors, and lived in constant fear of the potential for a volcanic eruption that might annihilate the city. These facts might help to explain its "live for today" philosophy. Among its conquerors and leaders have been everyone from the Normans in 1139, Charles of Anjou in 1266, the Aragonese of Spain under Alfonso V in 1435, Archduke Charles of Austria in 1707, French Bourbons in 1734, the pan-Italian nationalist armies of Garibaldi in 1861, and, after the fiasco of Mussolini's brand of Fascism during World War II, the Americans.

During the 18th and 19th centuries, French, English, and German tourists visited the Bay of Naples as an essential part (perhaps the highlight) of their grand European tour. They flooded the northern European consciousness with legends and images of Naples as the most beautiful and carefree city in the world. "See Naples and die," the popular wisdom claimed. Some historians write that the unabashed sexual permissiveness of 18th- and 19th-century Naples was more of a lure to northern Europeans than the region's archeology.

AND ON TO THE PRESENT   Today the only "dying" you're likely to experience is being run over by a car. Each of the city's 2.2 million inhabitants seems to have a beat-up Fiat, battalions of which speed erratically and incessantly over hopelessly narrow roads originally laid out more than 2,000 years ago. To add to the confusion, hordes of Neapolitan children will blithely throw lit firecrackers into moving traffic, stop traffic to beg or smear your windshield with a soiled towel, or (sometimes more or less endearingly) try to pick your pocket.

Surely, the Neapolitans are the most spontaneous people on earth, wearing their emotions on the surface of their skin. No Neapolitan housewife gets overheated running up and down the steps to convey a message to someone on the street—she handles the situation by screaming out the window.

Both arguments and love happen spontaneously, and are sometimes just as quickly forgotten. The Neapolitan dialect is considered one of the most distinctive and difficult in all of Italy, with an almost alarming number and diversity of words (a source of pride) for describing intimate body parts and functions. This richness of expression might have been grudgingly respected by Dante. Naples even bears the dubious honor of having introduced syphilis to the world in 1495 (history's first recorded version), the outbreak of which was immediately blamed upon a group of French soldiers quartered there at the time.

Today Naples is a city to be savored in bits and pieces, like the city's zuppa di pesce (fish soup). It comes at you like a runaway car, with tour-ticket sellers, car thieves, hotel hawkers, and pimps, and a series of human encounters that seesaw between extraordinary warmth and kindness and a kind of surrealistic nightmare.

With its almost total absence of parks, its lack of space (it has the highest population density of any city in Europe), and the constant and unrelieved perception that it will disintegrate into total anarchy at any moment, it's not a destination for queasy palates and weak hearts. Add to this the 35% unemployment rate, the unending prevalence of both major and minor larceny, the highest infant-mortality rate in Italy, the heat, and the pollution, and you have a destination many visitors rush through quickly on their way to somewhere else.

Still, the tattered splendor of baroque palaces (whose charm is enhanced by shrubs and bushes growing from cracks in their cornices), the sense of history, and the unalloyed spectacle of humanity struggling, with humor and perseverance, to survive, makes Naples one of the most memorable places you'll visit in Italy. Only thing is, *don't show up on Monday* when most attractions are closed.

Naples is a fantastic adventure. The best approach, from its bay, is idyllic—a port set against the backdrop of a crystal-blue sky and volcanic mountains. The rich attractions inside the city and in the environs (Pompeii, Ischia, Capri, Vesuvius, the Phlaegrean Fields, Herculaneum) make Naples one of the five top tourist meccas of Italy. The inexperienced may have difficulty coping with it. The seasoned explorer will find it worthy ground, and might even try venturing down side streets, some of which teem with prostitutes and a major source of their upkeep: the ubiquitous sailor.

ORIENTATION

ARRIVING   If you arrive by train at the Stazione Centrale, in front of piazza Garibaldi, you'll want to escape from that horror by taking one of the major arteries of Naples, **corso Umberto,** in the direction of the Santa Lucia district. Along the water, many boats, such as those heading for Capri and Ischia, leave from **Porto Beverello.**

INFORMATION   Visitors can ask for information at the **Ente Provinciale per il Turismo** at the Stazione Centrale (tel. 268779). There is another office at piazza dei Martiri (tel. 405311). They're open Monday through Saturday from 9am to 8pm and on Sunday from 9am to 1:30pm.

CITY LAYOUT   Many visitors to Naples confine their visit to the bayside **Santa Lucia** area, and perhaps venture into another section to see an important museum. Most of the major hotels lie along **via Partenope,** which looks out not only to the Gulf of Naples but the Castel dell'Ovo. To the west is the **Margellina** district, site of many restaurants and dozens of apartment houses. The far western section of the city is known as **Posillipo.**

One of the most important squares of Naples is **piazza del Plebiscito,** north of

Santa Lucia. The Palazzo Reale opens onto this square. On a satellite square, you can visit **piazza Trento e Trieste,** with its Teatro San Carlo and entrance to the famed Galleria Umberto I. To the east is the third most important square, **piazza Municipio.** From piazza Trento e Trieste, you encounter the main shopping street of Naples, **via Toledo/via Roma,** on which you can walk as far as piazza Dante. From that square, take via Enrico Pessina to the most important museum in Naples, located on piazza Museo Nazionale.

GETTING AROUND

BY TRAIN   If you're planning to rely on public transportation, chances are you'll use the suburban rail line, the **Circumvesuviana,** to reach the major towns in the environs, including Pompeii (the chief target of sightseers), Sorrento, and Herculaneum.

BY SUBWAY   The **Metropolitana** (subway) line will deliver you from the Stazione Centrale in the west, all the way to the Stazione Margellina. Get off at piazza Amadeo if you wish to take the funicular to Vómero. Fares are reasonable on public transportation, and will probably cost 800 lire (65¢) per trip at the time of your visit.

BY BUS OR TRAM   It's dangerous to ride buses at rush hours. Never have I seen such pushing, shoving, and jockeying for position. On one recent trip, I saw a middle-aged woman fall from a too-crowded bus, injuring her leg. I was later told that this was a routine occurrence. If you're a linebacker, take your chances. Many prefer to leave the buses to the battle-hardened Neapolitans and take the subway or tram no. 1 or 4, which run from Stazione Centrale to Margellina.

BY TAXI   If you survive the reckless driving (someone once wrote that all Neapolitans drive like the anarchists they are), you'll only have to do battle over the bill. You will inevitably be overcharged. Many cab drivers claim that the meter is broken, and they then proceed to assess the cost of the ride, always to your disadvantage. Some legitimate surcharges are imposed, including night drives and extra luggage. However, many taxi drivers deliberately take you "the long way there" to run up your costs. In repeated visits to Naples, I have never yet been quoted an honest fare. I no longer bother with the meter; instead, I estimate what the fare would be worth, negotiate with the driver, and take off into the night. If you want to take a chance, you can call a radio taxi at 5564444.

BY CAR   Getting around Naples can be a nightmare! Motorists should pay particular attention, as Neapolitans are fond of driving the wrong way on one-way streets and speeding hysterically along lanes reserved for public transportation, sometimes cutting into your lane without warning. Red lights seem to hold no terror for a Neapolitan driver. In fact, you may want to park your car and walk. There are two dangers in that. One is that your car can be stolen, as mine once was, even though apparently "guarded" by an attendant in front of a deluxe hotel. The other danger is that you are likely to get mugged (nearly a third of the city is unemployed, and people have to live somehow).

BY FUNICULAR   Funiculars take passengers up and down the steep hills of Naples. The **Funicolare Centrale,** for example, connects the lower part of the city to Vómero. Departures are from piazzetta Duca d'Aosta, just off via Roma. Cable cars run daily from 9am to 7pm. Watch that you don't get stranded by missing the last car back.

BY TRAM   You can take a tram (no. 1 or 4), which will transport you from the Stazione Centrale to the Margellina station. It will also let you off at the quayside points where the boats depart for Ischia and Capri.

BY HORSE & BUGGY   Another means of transport, more expensive but far more romantic than the taxi, is a horse and buggy. They are still in service, most often taking visitors along the waterfront in Santa Lucia. Fares are to be negotiated.

TOURS

If you want to visit points of interest, **Tourcar,** piazza Matteotti 1 (tel. 5520429), has several tours of Naples and its environs. Prices of the trips include transportation from your hotel to the Tourcar offices or to the quay where you take the hydrofoil to Capri, the services of a knowledgeable guide who speaks English, and entrance fees to the attractions; you will be returned to your hotel at the end of the trip.

A whole-day excursion to Capri and Anacapri, excluding the Blue Grotto, takes from about 10am to 6:45pm via hydrofoil, costing 74,000 lire ($58.10), and is available from June 1 to September 30; lunch is included. A whole-day trip to Sorrento and Pompeii is offered daily, and costs 79,000 lire ($62) per person, including lunch in Amalfi.

FAST FACTS

Area Code   For Naples and its environs, the **telephone area code** is 081.

Consulate   You'll find the **U.S. Consulate** on piazza della Repubblica (tel. 7614303). The staff has long ago grown weary of hearing about another stolen passport. It's open Monday through Friday from 8am to 12:30pm and 3 to 5:30pm. The consulate of the **United Kingdom** is at via Crispi 122 (tel. 663511), open in summer, Monday through Friday from 7 to 11am and 1 to 4pm, and in winter, Monday through Friday from 8am to noon and 2 to 5pm. Citizens of **Canada, Australia,** and **New Zealand** will need to go to the embassies and consulates of their home countries in Rome (see Chapter 3).

Drugstore   If it's a drugstore you want, get in touch with **Di Donna,** piazza Cavour 119 (tel. 294940), or call 192 to see what's open. Di Donna is open Monday through Saturday from 9am to 1pm and 4:30 to 8:30pm.

Emergency Phone Numbers   If you have an **emergency,** dial 113. To reach **police or carabinieri,** call 112. For an **ambulance,** call 7520696.

Medical Care   If you are in need of medical services, try the **Guarda Medica Permanente,** piazza del Municipio (tel. 7513177).

Post Office   The main post office is on piazza G. Matteotti (tel. 5511456). Look for the POSTA TELEGRAFO sign outside. It's open Monday through Saturday from 8am to 8pm and on Sunday from 8am to noon.

Telephone   If you need to make a long-distance call, you can do so at the Stazione Centrale, where an office is open 24 hours; if you make calls from your hotel, you'll be hit with an excessive surcharge.

WHAT TO SEE & DO

Before striking out for Pompeii or Capri, you should try to see some of the sights inside Naples. If you're hard-pressed for time, then settle for the first three museums of renown.

MUSEO ARCHEOLOGICO NAZIONALE, piazza Museo 19. Tel. 440166.

With its Roman and Greek sculpture, this museum contains one of the most valuable archeological collections in Europe—the select Farnese acquisitions are notable in particular, as are mosaics and sculpture excavated at Pompeii and Herculaneum. The building dates from the 16th century, and was turned into a museum some 2 centuries later by Charles and Ferdinand IV Bourbon.

On the ground floor is one of the treasures of the Farnese collections: The nude statues of Armodio and Aristogitone are the most outstanding in the room. A famous bas-relief (from an original of the 5th century B.C.) in a nearby salon depicts Orpheus and his wife, Eurydice, with Mercury.

The nude statue of the spear-bearing *Doryphorus,* copied from a work by Polyclitus the Elder and excavated at Pompeii, enlivens another room. Also see the gigantic but weary *Hercules,* a statue of remarkable boldness; it's a copy of an original by Lysippus, the 4th-century B.C. Greek sculptor for Alexander the Great, and was discovered in the Baths of Caracalla in Rome. On a more delicate pedestal is the decapitated but exquisite *Venus* (Aphrodite). The *Psyche of Capua* shows why Aphrodite was jealous. The *Group of the Farnese Bull* presents a pageant of violence from the days of antiquity. A copy of either a 2nd- or 3rd-century B.C. Hellenistic statue—one of the most frequently reproduced of all sculptures—it was also discovered at the Baths of Caracalla. The marble group depicts a scene in the legend of Amphion and Zethus, who tied Dirce, wife of Lycus of Thebes, to the horns of a rampaging bull. After this, you will have seen the best of the works on this floor.

The galleries on the mezzanine are devoted to mosaics excavated from Pompeii and Herculaneum. These include scenes of cock fights, dragon-tailed satyrs, an aquarium, and the finest one of all, *Alexander Fighting the Persians.*

On the top floor are some of the celebrated bronzes, which were dug out of the Pompeii and Herculaneum lava and volcanic mud. Of particular interest is a Hellenistic portrait of Berenice, a comically drunken satyr, a statue of a *Sleeping Satyr,* and *Mercury on a Rock.*

Admission: 8,000 lire ($6.30) adults, free for children under 12.

Open: July–Sept, Mon–Sat 9am–7:30pm, Sun 9am–1pm; Oct–June, Mon–Sat 9am–2pm, Sun 9am–1pm. **Metropolitana:** Piazza Cavour.

CAPODIMONTE NATIONAL GALLERY AND MUSEUM, Parco di Capodimonte (off Amadeo di Savoia). Tel. 741-3102.

The gallery and museum are in the 18th-century Palace of Capodimonte (built in the time of Charles III), which stands in a park, haughtily removed from the squalor of Naples. It houses one of Italy's finest picture galleries (an elevator takes visitors to the top floor).

On display are seven Flemish tapestries, which were made according to the designs of Bernart van Orley, and show grand-scale scenes from the Battle of Pavia (1525), in which the forces of Francis I of France—more than 25,000 strong—lost to those of Charles V. Van Orley, who lived in a pre-*Guernica* day, obviously didn't consider war a horror, but a romantic ballet.

One of the pinacoteca's greatest possessions is Simone Martini's *Coronation* scene, which depicts the brother of Robert of Anjou being crowned king of Naples by the bishop of Toulouse. You'll want to linger over the great Masaccio's *Crucifixion,* a bold expression of grief. The most important room is literally filled with the works of Renaissance masters, notably an *Adoration of the Child* by Luca Signorelli, a *Madonna and Child* by Perugino, a panel by Raphael, a *Madonna and Child with Angels* by Botticelli, and—the most beautiful of all—Filippino Lippi's *Annunciation and Saints.*

Look for Andrea Mantegna's *St. Eufemia* and his portrait of Francesco Gonzaga, his brother-in-law Giovanni Bellini's *Transfiguration,* and Lotto's *Portrait of Bernardo de Rossi* and his *Madonna and Child with St. Peter.*

In one room is Raphael's *Holy Family and St. John,* and a copy of his celebrated portrait of Pope Leo X. Two choice sketches include Raphael's *Moses* and Michelangelo's *Three Soldiers.* Displayed farther on are the Titians, with Danae taking the spotlight from Pope Paul III.

Another room is devoted to Flemish art: Pieter Brueghel's *Blind Men* is an

---

IMPRESSIONS

Whoever it was who said (I believe it was Nelson), "See Naples and die," perpetrated one of the greatest hoaxes in history. Or perhaps I am unlucky when I go there.
—GEOFFREY HARMSWORTH, *ABYSSINIAN ADVENTURE,* 1935

outstanding work, and his *Misanthrope* is devilishly powerful. Other foreign works include Joos van Cleve's *Adoration of the Magi*. You can climb the stairs for a panoramic view of Naples and the bay, a finer landscape than any you'll see inside.

The state apartments downstairs deserve inspection. Room after room is devoted to gilded mermaids, Venetian sedan chairs, ivory carvings, a porcelain chinoiserie salon (the best of all), tapestries, the Farnese armory, and a large glass and china collection.

Admission: 8,000 lire ($6.30) adults, free for children under 12.

Open: July–Sept, Tues–Sat 9am–7:30pm, Sun 9am–1pm; Oct–June, Tues–Sat 9am–2pm, Sun 9am–1pm. **Bus:** 110 or 127 from the rail station.

MUSEO NAZIONALE DI SAN MARTINO, largo San Martino 5 (in the Vómero residential district). Tel. 5781769.

Magnificently situated on the grounds of the Castel Sant'Elmo, this museum was founded in the 14th century as a Carthusian monastery, but fell into decay until the 17th century, when it was reconstructed by architects in the Neapolitan baroque style. Now a museum for the city of Naples, it displays stately carriages, historical documents, ship replicas, china and porcelain, silver, campagna paintings of the 19th century, military costumes and armor, and the lavishly adorned crib by Cuciniello. A balcony opens onto a fabulous view of Naples and the bay, as well as Vesuvius and Capri. Many come here to the museum just to stand on this belvedere in space and drink in the view. The colonnaded cloisters have curious skull sculpture on the inner balustrade.

Admission: 3,000 lire ($2.35) adults, free for children under 18.

Open: Tues–Sat 9am–2pm, Sun 9am–1pm. **Bus:** 49 or 42. **Funicular:** Centrale from via Toledo.

MORE ATTRACTIONS

PALAZZO REALE (Royal Palace), piazza del Plebiscito. Tel. 413888.

This palace was designed by Domenico Fontana in the 17th century. The eight statues on the facade are of Neapolitan kings. Located in the heart of the city, the square is one of the most architecturally interesting in Naples, with a long colonnade and a church, San Francesco di Paolo, that evokes the style of the Pantheon in Rome. Inside the Palazzo Reale you can visit the royal apartments, lavishly and ornately adorned in the baroque style with colored marble floors, paintings, tapestries, frescoes, antiques, and porcelain. Charles de Bourbon, son of Philip IV of Spain, became king of Naples in 1734. A great patron of the arts, he installed a library in the Royal Palace, one of the greatest of the south, with more than 1,250,000 volumes.

Admission: 3,000 lire ($2.35).

Open: Tues–Sat 9am–2pm, Sun 9am–1pm. **Tram:** 1 or 4.

CASTELNUOVO (New Castle), piazza del Municipo.

The New Castle, which houses municipal offices and is not open to visitors, was built in the late 13th century on orders from Charles I, king of Naples, as a royal residence for the House of Anjou. It was badly ruined, and virtually rebuilt in the mid-15th century by the House of Aragon. The castle is distinguished by a trio of three round imposing battle towers at its front. Between two of the towers, and guarding the entrance, is an arch of triumph designed by Francesco Laurana to commemorate the expulsion of the Angevins by the forces of Alphonso I in 1442. It has been described by art historians as a masterpiece of the Renaissance. The Palatine Chapel in the center dates from the 14th century, and the City Commission of Naples meets in the Baron's Hall, designed by Segreta of Catalonia.

Tram: 1 or 4.

CASTEL DELL'OVO (Castle of the Egg).

This 2,000-year-old fortress overlooks the Gulf of Naples. The site of the castle was important centuries before the birth of Christ, and was fortified by early settlers. In time, a major stronghold to guard the bay was erected and duly celebrated by Virgil. In one epoch of its long history, it served as a state prison. The view from here is magnificent. It is not open to the public except for special exhibits.

Directions: Follow via Console along the seafront from piazza del Plebiscito to the port of Santa Lucia; Castel dell'Ovo is at the end of the promontory there. **Tram:** 1 or 4.

PRINCE OF ARAGONA PIGNATELLI CORTES MUSEUM, Riviera di Chiaia 200. Tel. 669675.

This neoclassical villa is in a public park, the Villa Pignatelli. The mansion is filled with a collection of mostly 18th-century porcelain and china, and there's also an impressive collection of antiques. A coach museum can also be visited in a pavillion.

Admission: 2,000 lire ($1.55).

Open: Tues–Sat 9am–2pm, Sun 9am–1pm. **Funicular:** Chiaia lower station.

ACQUARIO, Villa Comunale, via Caracciolo. Tel. 5837111.

The Aquarium is in a municipal park, Villa Comunale, between via Caracciolo and the Riviera di Chiaia. Established by a German naturalist in the 1800s, the Aquarium is the oldest in Europe. It is said to display about 200 species of marine plants and fish, all found in the Bay of Naples (they must be a hardy lot).

Admission: 2,000 lire ($1.55).

Open: Tues–Sat 9am–6pm, Sun 10am–7pm. **Tram:** 1 or 4.

CATACOMBS OF SAN GENNARO (St. Januarius), in the Chiesa del Buon Consiglio, via di Capodimonte.

A guide will show visitors through this two-story underground cemetery, which dates back to the 2nd century and has many interesting frescoes and mosaics. You enter the catacombs on via di Capodimonte (head down an alley going alongside the Madre del Buon Consiglio Church).

Admission: 3,000 lire ($2.35).

Open: Tours Sat–Sun at 9:30, 10:15, 11, and 11:45am. **Tram:** 1 or 4.

SANSEVERO CHAPEL, via Francesco de Sanctis 19. Tel. 416201.

Located north of piazza San Domenico Maggiore, near the Church of San Domenico Maggiore, this chapel is visited mainly by those who wish to view its collection of 18th-century sculpture. The most remarkable piece of work is the *Veiled Christ* by Sammartino. There are also two extraordinary human skeletons of the 18th century, with metal venous apparatus.

Admission: 2,000 lire ($1.55).

Open: Mon–Tues and Thurs–Sat 10am–1:30pm, Sun 10:30am–1:30pm. **Tram:** 1 or 4.

The Churches of Naples

CHURCH OF SANTA CHIARA (Clare), via Santa Chiara 49. Tel. 5526186.

On a palazzo-flanked street, this church was built on orders from Robert the Wise, king of Naples, in the early 14th century. It became the church for the House of Anjou. Although World War II bombers heavily blasted it, it has been restored somewhat to its original look, a Gothic style as practiced by Provençal architects. The altarpiece by Simone Martini is displayed at the Capodimonte Galleries (see above), which leaves the Angevin royal sarcophagi as the principal art treasures, especially the tomb of King Robert in back of the main altar. The Cloister of the Order of the Clares was restored by Vaccaro in the 18th century and is marked by ornate adornment, particularly in the tiles.

Admission: Free.

Open: Daily 7am–noon and 4–7pm. **Tram:** 1 or 4.

IL DUOMO, via del Duomo 147. Tel. 449097.

The Duomo of Naples may not be as impressive as some in other Italian cities, but it is visited nevertheless. Consecrated in 1315, it was Gothic in style, but the centuries have witnessed many changes. The facade, for example, is from the 1800s. A curiosity of the Duomo is that it has access to the Basilica of St. Restituta, which was the earliest Christian basilica erected in Naples and goes back to the 4th century. But an even-greater treasure is the chapel dedicated to St. Januarius (San Gennaro), which is

entered from the south aisle. In a rich 17th-century baroque style, it contains ampullae with the saint's blood, the subject of many religious legends.
Admission: Free.
Open: Daily 8am–noon. **Tram:** 1 or 4.

COOL FOR KIDS

Children can enjoy the **Aquarium** in a city park called Villa Comunale, and the **Giardino Zoologico,** which is in the Mostra d'Oltremare at the entrance to viale Kennedy. And, to cap it off, take them to the **Edenlandia Amusement Park,** also in the area of Mostra d'Oltremare (entrance on viale Kennedy). It's open all year. Call 081/611182 for information.

In the Naples area, children delight in wandering through the ruins of **Pompeii** as much as their parents do.

WHERE TO STAY

With some exceptions, the accommodations in Naples are a sad lot. Most of the large hotels are in the popular (also dangerous) district of Santa Lucia. Many of the so-called first-class establishments line via Partenope along the water. In and around the central railway station are other clusters, many built in the late '50s (and some that seemingly haven't been changed since that faraway time).

Regardless of the price range in which you travel, there's a bed waiting for you in Naples. Regrettably, that bed often isn't clean or comfortable. I'll present a selection of what are generally conceded to be the "best" hotels in Naples, but know that with an exception or two, none of the other candidates leaves me with much enthusiasm. Many of the innkeepers I've encountered seem an indifferent lot.

Hotels considered "Very Expensive" charge 430,000 lire ($337.55) and up for a double room with private bath, those judged "Expensive" ask 255,000 lire to 340,000 lire ($200.20 to $266.90) for a double, and "Moderate" hotels ask for 180,000 lire to 230,000 lire ($141.30 to $180.55) for a double. Anything 140,000 lire ($109.90) or below is considered "Inexpensive." All prices include tax and service.

VERY EXPENSIVE

HOTEL EXCELSIOR, via Partenope 48, 80121 Napoli. Tel. 081/417111.
Fax 081/411743. 114 rms (all with bath). A/C MINIBAR TV TEL **Tram:** 1 or 4.
$ Rates: 296,000 lire ($232.35) single; 430,000 lire ($337.55) double. 19% IVA tax extra. Breakfast 23,000 lire ($18.05) extra. AE, DC, MC, V. **Parking:** 30,000 lire ($23.55).

The Excelsior is situated in a most dramatic position right on the waterfront, with views of Santa Lucia and Vesuvius. It has been restored and refurbished. There are many elegant details, such as Venetian chandeliers, Doric columns, wall-size murals, and bronze torchiers. This same sophistication prevails in the bedrooms, where Oriental rugs blend with traditional elements. Most of them are, in reality, bed/sitting rooms. Each room contains a well-maintained private bath.

Dining/Entertainment: When you dine at the Excelsior, expect to pay 80,000 lire ($62.80) and up for a meal. The cuisine is both Neapolitan and international.

Services: Room service, baby-sitting, laundry, valet.
Facilities: 24-hour garage, solarium.

EXPENSIVE

JOLLY HOTEL AMBASSADOR, via Medina 70, 80133 Napoli. Tel. 081/416000. Fax 081/5518010. 278 rms (all with bath). A/C MINIBAR TV TEL **Tram:** 1 or 4.
$ Rates (including breakfast): 190,000 lire ($149.15) single; 250,000 lire ($196.25) double. AE, DC, MC, V. **Parking:** 25,000 lire ($19.65).

This hotel is a skyscraper, Italian style. Neapolitans call it Il Grattacielo. A few blocks up from the central harbor, this landmark bills itself as the tallest hotel in Italy. The bedrooms occupy the upper part of the building and afford views of the city and the sea. The refurbished rooms are of medium size, and each has built-in furniture with large desk surfaces and an automatic wake-up system.

Dining/Entertainment: The top-floor restaurant is remarkable; you can admire most of the sights of Naples through its all-glass walls, while enjoying regional and international specialties. Breakfast is also served in this 30th-floor restaurant.

HOTEL MIRAMARE, via Nazario Saura 24, 80132 Napoli. Tel. 081/ 427388. Fax 081/416775. 31 rms (all with bath). A/C MINIBAR TV TEL **Bus:** 106 or 150.

$ Rates (including breakfast): 206,000 lire ($161.70) single; 295,500 lire ($231.95) double. AE, DC, MC, V. **Parking:** 22,000 lire ($17.25).

In a superb location, seemingly thrust out toward the harbor on a dockside boulevard, the Miramare is central and sunny. Its lobby evokes a little Caribbean hotel, with a semitropical look. The bedrooms have been renewed, and now are pleasantly furnished and well maintained by the management. The lower rooms are much too noisy (the curse of most Neapolitan hotels), so request a quieter one upstairs. On the premises is an American bar, a restaurant-tavern, and a roof garden.

HOTEL ROYAL, via Partenope 38, 80121 Napoli. Tel. 081/7644800. Fax 081/7645707. 273 rms (all with bath), 14 suites. A/C MINIBAR TV TEL **Bus:** 106, 140, or 150.

$ Rates (including breakfast): 170,000–233,000 lire ($133.45–$182.90) single; 255,000–340,000 lire ($200.20–$266.90) double; from 533,000 lire ($418.40) suite. AE, DC, MC, V. **Parking:** 26,000 lire ($20.40).

The Hotel Royal is in a desirable location on this busy street, which runs beside the bay in Santa Lucia. You park in an underground garage, then enter a greenery-filled vestibule, where the stairs that lead to the modern lobby are flanked by a pair of stone lions. Each of the bedrooms has a balcony and contemporary furniture. Some, but not all, offer a water view. A saltwater pool with an adjacent flower-dotted sun terrace is on the hotel's roof.

HOTEL SANTA LUCIA, via Partenope 46, 80121 Napoli. Tel. 081/ 416566. Fax 081/416566. 130 rms (all with bath). A/C MINIBAR TV TEL **Tram:** 1 or 4.

$ Rates (including breakfast): 194,000 lire ($152.30) single; 285,500 lire ($224.10) double. AE, DC, MC, V. **Parking:** 25,000 lire ($19.65).

The Santa Lucia's imposing neoclassical facade overlooks a sheltered marina that extends off the Bay of Naples. From the windows of about half the bedrooms you can watch motorboats and yachts bobbing at anchor, fishermen repairing nets, and all the waterside life that Naples is famous for. The interior has undergone extensive renovations, and it is decorated in a family-conscious Neapolitan style, with terrazzo floors, and lots of upholstered chairs scattered throughout the lobby. The bedrooms are large and high ceilinged, with French doors that open onto tiny verandas. The noisier rooms overlook the traffic of via Santa Lucia. There's an American-inspired bar on the premises.

HOTEL VESUVIO, via Partenope 45, 80121 Napoli. Tel. 081/417044. Fax 081/417044. 180 rms (all with bath). A/C MINIBAR TV TEL **Tram:** 1 or 4.

$ Rates (including breakfast): 210,000 lire ($164.85) single; 300,000 lire ($235.50) double. AE, DC, MC, V. **Parking:** 30,000 lire ($23.55).

Originally built in 1880, the Vesuvio was restored about 50 years later and features a marble- and stucco-sheathed facade evocative of art deco. When it was constructed, it was the first and foremost hotel along the fabled bay, and many aristocratic members of English society flocked here. Curved balconies extend toward the Castel dell'Ovo (the Castle of the Egg). The overhauled hotel remains one of the best in Naples. Today, each of its rooms has a lofty ceiling, rich cove moldings, parquet floors, a renovated tiled bathroom with lots of space, and large closets. You'll also find a scattering of antiques throughout the echoing hallways.

Dining/Entertainment: The hotel also has a first-class restaurant and a comfortable bar that evokes the most stylish decor of the 1950s. Meals begin at 60,000 lire ($47.10).

MODERATE

ALBERGO SAN GERMANO, via Beccadelli 41, 80125 Napoli. Tel. 081/ 5705422. Fax 081/5701546. 105 rms (all with bath). A/C MINIBAR TV TEL **Bus:** 102 or 152.

$ Rates (including breakfast): 125,000–135,000 lire ($98.15–$106) single; 190,000–215,000 lire ($149.15–$168.80) double. AE, DC, MC, V. **Parking:** 16,000 lire ($12.55).

Designed like an Italian version of a Chinese pagoda, this brick-and-concrete hotel is ideal for late-arriving motorists who are reluctant to negotiate the traffic of Naples. A terraced swimming pool and garden are welcome respites after a day in Naples. The hotel's bedrooms are clean, and each has a tile bath. The hotel serves meals only to residents. There is a lobby bar, along with a modern restaurant.

From the autostrada, follow the signs to Tangenziale Napoli (direction Napoli); exit 8 miles later at Agnano Terme. After paying the toll, drive less than a mile toward Naples, where you'll see the hotel on your right. You can park your car here and take bus no. 102 or 152 into the center of Naples, a distance of about 4 miles.

HOTEL BRITANNIQUE, corso Vittorio Emanuele 133, 80121 Napoli. Tel. 081/7614145. Fax 081/669760. 90 rms (all with bath), 10 suites. **Bus:** 118, 120, or 128.

$ Rates: 173,000 lire ($195.80) single; 230,000 lire ($180.55) double; from 275,000 lire ($215.90) suite. Breakfast 11,000 lire ($8.65). AE, DC, MC, V. **Parking:** 15,000 lire ($11.80).

This remake of a former aristocratic villa has a hillside view of the Bay of Naples. The Britannique is on the curve of a wide hillside boulevard, away from the harbor; it has a panoramic view of the harbor from a distance. Each room contains some antique furnishings. Tropical flowers and plants are found in the hotel's garden. The hotel's restaurant specializes in a continental cuisine. There's also a cocktail lounge and bar.

HOTEL MAJESTIC, largo Vasto a Chiaia 68, 80121 Napoli. Tel. 081/ 416500. Fax 081/416500. 130 rms (all with bath). TV TEL **Metropolitan:** Piazza Amedeo.

$ Rates (including breakfast): 140,000 lire ($109.90) single; 235,000 lire ($184.50) double. AE, DC, MC, V. **Parking:** 20,000 lire ($15.70).

This is one of Naples's finest four-star hotels. Built in 1959 on 10 floors, this renovated hotel is now one of the most up-to-date hostelries in a city too often filled with decaying mansions. A favorite with the conference crowd, it lies in the antique district of Naples. At your doorstep will be dozens of fashionable boutiques. Some rooms have a minibar. Reservations are important, as this hotel is often fully booked. There's a cozy American bar and a restaurant, Magic Grill, which serves both Neapolitan dishes and international specialties.

HOTEL PARADISO, via Catullo 11, 80122 Napoli. Tel. 081/7614161. Fax 081/7613449. 74 rms (all with bath), 2 suites. A/C MINIBAR TV TEL **Bus:** 23, 106, or 140.

$ Rates (including breakfast): 120,000–150,000 lire ($94.20–$117.75) single; 180,000–230,000 lire ($141.30–$180.55) double; 250,000–330,000 lire ($196.25–$259.05) suite. AE, DC, MC, V. **Parking:** 20,000 lire ($15.70).

This hotel might be paradise, but only after you reach it. If you arrive at the central station and head for this address in the Posillipo section, the distance is some 3½ miles. One irate driver claimed that it took about the same amount of time—3½ hours, that is—to reach this address. Once there, however, your nerves are soothed by the view, one of the most spectacular of any hotel in Italy. The Bay of Naples unfolds before you, and in the distance Mount Vesuvius looms menacingly. On a clear day you can even see the promontory of Sorrento. The hotel is one of the best in Naples, with well-furnished and comfortably equipped bedrooms. When you take your breakfast, you may want to linger here before facing the traffic of Naples again.

Should you elect not to go out at night, you can patronize the fine restaurant at the

Paradiso, which serves both Neapolitan and Italian specialties, with meals costing from 45,000 lire ($35.35).

INEXPENSIVE

HOTEL REX, via Palepoli 12, 80132 Napoli. Tel. 081/416388. Fax 081/416919. 40 rms (all with bath). A/C TV TEL **Bus:** 106 or 150.

$ **Rates:** 91,000 lire ($71.45) single; 151,000 lire ($118.55) double. Breakfast 7,000 lire ($5.50) extra. AE, DC, V. **Parking:** 18,000 lire ($14.15).

The most famous budget hotel in Santa Lucia, the Hotel Rex has played host to lira-watchers around the world. Some like it and others don't (the mail tends to be mixed). Nevertheless, proof of its popularity is that its bedrooms are often fully booked when other hotels have many vacancies. The building itself is lavishly ornate architecturally, but the bedrooms are simple. Breakfast is the only meal served.

HOTEL SERIUS, viale Augusto 74, 80125 Napoli. Tel. 081/614844. Fax 081/614844. 69 rms (all with bath). A/C MINIBAR TV TEL **Tram:** 1 or 4.

$ **Rates** (including breakfast): 87,000 lire ($68.30) single; 140,000 lire ($109.90) double. AE. **Parking:** Free in hotel garage.

Built in 1974 to provide well-organized comfort, this hotel is on a palm-lined street of a relatively calm neighborhood known as Fuorigrotto. The paneled split-level lobby contains an intimate bar and several metal sculptures of horses and birds. The bedrooms are simply furnished with boldly patterned fabrics and painted furniture. In addition to the bar, there's a pleasant, contemporary dining room.

A NEARBY PLACE TO STAY

MOTEL AGIP, at Secondigliano, 80144 Napoli. Tel. 081/7540560. Fax 081/7548235. 57 rms (all with bath). A/C MINIBAR TV TEL **Directions:** Take the Secondigliano exit north of the city.

$ **Rates:** 87,000 lire ($68.30) single; 144,000 lire ($113.05) double. AE, DC, MC, V. **Parking:** Free.

Lying 4½ miles to the north of Naples, this place will appeal to motorists who don't want to risk driving into the city and coping with impossible parking problems. At an Agip you know what you get: standardized rooms and good value. In all parts of Italy, the Agip kitchen emphasizes regional cookery. In its restaurant here, Neapolitan dishes are featured, and a complete meal begins about 35,000 lire ($27.50). There is no restaurant service for Saturday lunch or on Sunday.

WHERE TO DINE

A mixed reaction. Naples is the home of pizza and spaghetti. If you're mad for either of those items, then you'll delight in sampling the authentic versions. However, if you like subtle cooking and have an aversion to olive oil or garlic, you'll not "fare" as well.

One of the major problems is overcharging. It is not uncommon for four foreign visitors to have a dinner in a Naples restaurant, particularly those once-famous ones in Santa Lucia, and be billed for five dinners. Service in many restaurants tends to be poor. Again, as in the hotels, I will attempt to pick out the best of the lot.

EXPENSIVE

LA CANTINELLA, via Cuma 42. Tel. 404884.
Cuisine: SEAFOOD. **Reservations:** Required. **Tram:** 1 or 4.

$ **Prices:** Appetizers 18,000–20,000 lire ($14.15–$15.70); main courses 28,000–35,000 lire ($22–$27.50). AE, DC, MC, V.
Open: Lunch Mon–Sat noon–3pm; dinner Mon–Sat 7pm–midnight. **Closed:** Aug.

You get the impression of Chicago in the '20s as you approach this place, and speakeasy-style doors open after you ring. The restaurant is on a busy street that skirts the bay in Santa Lucia, with a terrace overlooking the sea. Inside, in a room sheathed with Tahiti bamboo, you'll find a well-stocked antipasto table and—get this—a phone on each table. The menu includes four different preparations of risotto (including one with champagne), many kinds of pasta (including penne with vodka, and linguine with scampi and seafood), and most of the classic beef and veal dishes of Italy. Best known for its fish, Cantinella serves grilled seafood at its finest.

LA SACRESTIA, via Orazio 116. Tel. 7611051.
Cuisine: PASTA/SEAFOOD. **Reservations:** Required. **Funicular:** From Mergellina.
$ Prices: Appetizers 12,000–20,000 lire ($9.40–$15.70); main courses 29,000–40,000 lire ($22.75–$31.40). AE, DC, V.
Open: July–Aug, lunch Mon–Sat 12:30–4:30pm, dinner Mon–Sat 7:40–10pm; Sept–June, lunch Thurs–Tues 12:30–4:30pm, dinner Thurs–Tues 7:40–10pm.

The trompe-l'oeil frescoes in this establishment's two-story interior, as well as the name La Sacrestia, vaguely suggest something ecclesiastical. But that's not the case here. Reputed to be the best restaurant in Naples, La Sacrestia is a bustling place, sometimes called "the greatest show in town." It's perched near the top of one of the belvederes of Naples, and is reached by going along a seemingly endless labyrinth of winding streets from the port. In summer, an outdoor terrace with its flowering arbor provides seating with a view over the lights of the harbor. Meals emphasize well-prepared dishes often with strong doses of Neapolitan drama. You might, for example, try what is said to be the most luxurious macaroni dish in Italy ("Prince of Naples"), concocted with truffles and mild cheeses. The fettuccine alla Gran Caruso is made from fresh peas, mushrooms, prosciutto, and tongue. Less ornate selections include a full array of pastas and dishes composed of octopus, squid, and shellfish. Main courses include carpaccio and veal. Food is served "until the last diner finishes." The place is best reached by taxi.

ROSOLINO, via Nazario Sauro 5-7. Tel. 415873.
Cuisine: SEAFOOD. **Reservations:** Required. **Tram:** 1 or 4.
$ Prices: Appetizers 9,000–15,000 lire ($7.05–$11.80); main courses 18,000–40,000 lire ($14.15–$31.40). AE, DC, MC, V.
Open: Lunch Mon–Sat 12:30–3:30pm; dinner Mon–Sat 8pm–midnight.

This stylish, expensive place is not defined as a nightclub by its owners, but rather as a restaurant with dancing. Set on the waterfront, it is divided into two distinct areas; there's a piano bar near the entrance, where you might have a drink before passing into a much larger dining room. There, in interiors ringed with stained glass set into striking patterns, you can dine within sight of a bandstand reminiscent of the Big Band era. The food is good, but much of what you'll pay for an evening here will be the music, the decor, and the fun. Dishes include rigatoni with zucchini and meat sauce, an impressive array of fresh shellfish, and such beef dishes as tournedos and veal scaloppine. There are three different wine lists, including one for French wines and champagne.

MODERATE

DON SALVATORE, strada Mergellina 5. Tel. 681817.
Cuisine: SEAFOOD. **Reservations:** Recommended. **Metropolitana:** Mergellina.
$ Prices: Appetizers 10,000–12,000 lire ($7.85–$9.40); main courses 18,000–20,000 lire ($14.15–$15.70). AE, DC, MC, V.
Open: Lunch Thurs–Tues 1–4pm; dinner Thurs–Tues 8pm–1am.

This is no simple, lowly pizzeria, but the creative statement of a serious restaurateur, who directs his waterfront establishment with passion and dedication. Antonio Aversano takes his wine as seriously as his food. The latter is likely to include linguine with shrimp or with squid, or a linguine facetiously named "Cosa Nostra," another name for the Mafia. There's also an array of fried fish served daily, along with a marvelous assortment of fresh Neapolitan vegetables grown in the surrounding countryside. Rice comes flavored in a delicate fish broth, and you can get a reasonably priced bottle from the wine cellar, said to be the finest in Campania. The location is on the seafront near the departure point of hydrofoils for Capri.

GIUSEPPONE A MARE, via Ferdinando Russo 13. Tel. 769-6002.

Cuisine: SEAFOOD. **Reservations:** Required. **Bus:** 140.

$ Prices: Appetizers 12,000–15,000 lire ($9.40–$11.80); main courses 25,000–30,000 lire ($19.65–$23.55). AE, DC, MC, V.

Open: Lunch Mon–Sat 12:30–3:30pm; dinner Mon–Sat 7:30–11:30pm.

This restaurant by the sea offers you a chance to dine in Neapolitan sunshine on an open-air terrace with a view of the bay. The restaurant at Capo Posillipo is known for serving the best and the freshest seafood in the campagna. Diners make their selections from a trolley in the center of the dining room, which is likely to include everything from crabs to eels. You might precede your fish dinner with some antipasti, such as fritters (a batter whipped up with seaweed and fresh squash blossoms). Naturally, there is linguine with clams, a dish familiar enough in restaurants in North America, except that the chef here adds squid and mussels. Much of the day's catch is deep fried a golden brown. The pièce de résistance is an octopus casserole (try it if you dare!). If the oven's going, you can also order a pizza. Some fine southern Italian wines are served too, especially those from Ischia and Vesuvio.

IL GALLO NERO, via Torquato Tasso 466. Tel. 643012.

Cuisine: PASTA/NEAPOLITAN. **Reservations:** Required. **Metropolitana:** Margellina.

$ Prices: Appetizers 15,000–20,000 lire ($11.80–$15.70); main courses 18,000–25,000 lire ($14.15–$19.65). AE, DC, MC, V.

Open: Lunch Sun 12:30–3pm; dinner Tues–Sat 6–11:30pm. **Closed:** Aug.

Dinner here is almost like a throwback to the mid-19th century. Gian Paolo Quagliata is the owner who, with a capable staff, maintains the hillside villa with its period furniture and accessories. In summer, the enthusiastic clientele is served on an elegant outdoor terrace. Many of the dishes are based on 100-year-old recipes from the classical Neapolitan repertoire, although a few are more recent inventions of the chef himself. You might enjoy the Neapolitan linguine with pesto, rigatoni with fresh vegetables, tagliatelle primavera, or macaroni with peas and artichokes. Fish dishes are usually well prepared, whether grilled, broiled, or sautéed. Meat dishes include slightly more exotic creations such as prosciutto with orange slices, veal cutlets with artichokes, and a savory array of beef dishes.

RISTORANTE LA FAZENDA, calata Marechiaro 58A. Tel. 769-7420.

Cuisine: SEAFOOD. **Reservations:** Required. **Bus:** 32.

$ Prices: Appetizers 7,000–11,000 lire ($5.50–$8.65); main courses 10,000–23,000 lire ($7.85–$18.05). AE, DC, MC, V.

Open: Lunch Tues–Sun 1–4pm; dinner Tues–Sun 7:30pm–12:30am. **Closed:** Aug 10–25.

It would be hard to find a more typically Neapolitan restaurant than this one, offering a panoramic view that, on a clear day, can include the island of Capri. The decor is rustic, loaded with agrarian touches and filled with an assortment of Neapolitan families, lovers, and visitors who have made it one of their preferred dining locales. In summer the overflow from the dining room spills onto the terrace. Menu specialties include linguine with scampi, an array of fresh grilled fish, sautéed clams, a mixed Italian grill, several savory stews, and many chicken dishes, along with lobster with fresh grilled tomatoes.

INEXPENSIVE

DANTE E BEATRICE, piazza Dante 44. Tel. 349905.

Cuisine: PASTA/SEAFOOD/MEATS. **Reservations:** Recommended. **Tram:** 1 or 4.

$ Prices: Appetizers 7,000–10,000 lire ($5.50–$7.85); main courses 8,000–15,000 lire ($6.30–$11.80). No credit cards.

Open: Lunch Thurs–Tues 12:30–3:30pm; dinner Thurs–Tues 7:30–11pm. **Closed:** Aug 24–31.

At this modest restaurant, the prices are almost as unpretentious as the clientele. Foods are simple, flavorful, and served without fuss to the many workaday clients who seek it out. Menu choices are limited but well prepared, and might include pasta fagiole Naples style, or a range of pasta, meat, and fish dishes.

LA BERSAGLIERA, borgo Marinari 10. Tel. 7646016.

Cuisine: SEAFOOD. **Reservations:** Recommended. **Tram:** 1 or 4.

$ Prices: Appetizers 11,000–12,000 lire ($8.65–$9.40); main courses 15,000–18,000 lire ($11.80–$14.15). AE, DC, MC, V.

Open: Lunch Wed–Mon 12:30–3:30pm; dinner Wed–Mon 7:30–11pm.

You'll find this restaurant between the bay and via Partenope. In rustic waterfront surroundings, to the sound of accordion and guitars during dinner, you can select from a menu that offers a wide range of fish and other seafoods, veal cutlets milanese or bolognese, tournedos Bersagliera, chicken diavolo and roast chicken, and a complete medley of pasta in all sizes and forms.

UMBERTO, via Alabardieri 30. Tel. 418555.

Cuisine: NEAPOLITAN. **Reservations:** Required. **Bus:** 106 or 150.

$ Prices: Appetizers 4,000–13,000 lire ($3.15–$10.20); main courses 5,000–18,000 lire ($3.95–$14.15). AE, DC, V.

Open: Lunch Thurs–Tues 12:30–3:30pm; dinner Thurs–Tues 7:30–10:30pm. **Closed:** Aug.

Located off piazza dei Martiri, Umberto might be one of the most atmospheric places to dine in all of Naples. The tasteful dining room has been directed for many a year by the same interconnected family. There's likely to be an evening dance band playing. The excellent Italian specialties served here include pizzas, gnocchi with potatoes, and grilled meats and fishes, as well as savory stews and a host of pasta dishes. The bel canto aria lives on here.

VINI E CUCINA, corso Vittorio Emanuele 761. Tel. 660302.

Cuisine: NEAPOLITAN. **Reservations:** Not accepted. **Metropolitana:** Mergellina.

$ Prices: Appetizers 6,000–7,000 lire ($4.70–$5.50); main courses 7,000–15,000 lire ($5.50–$11.80). No credit cards.

Open: Lunch Mon–Sat noon–4:30pm; dinner Mon–Sat 7pm–midnight. **Closed:** Aug.

The best ragú sauce in all of Naples is said to be made at this trattoria, which has only 10 tables and is known for its home-cookery. You can get a really satisfying meal here, but I must warn you—it's almost impossible to get in. Dedicated diners might do as I do: Arrive early and wait for a table. The cooking is the best home-style version of the Neapolitan cuisine I have been able to find in this tricky city. The spaghetti, along with that fabulous sauce, is served *al dente*. The restaurant is in front of the Mergellina station.

SPECIALTY DINING

Pizzerie

PIZZERIA BELLINI, via Santa Maria di Costantinopoli 80. Tel. 459774.

Cuisine: ITALIAN/PIZZA. **Reservations:** Not needed. **Tram:** 1 or 4.

$ Prices: Appetizers 12,000–14,000 lire ($9.40–$11); main courses 20,000–26,000 lire ($15.70–$20.40). No credit cards.

Open: Mon–Sat 9am–2am.

With its cramped interior, this place may look like a pizzeria, but actually it's a full-fledged restaurant. Of course, an array of pizzas is offered, but many clients equally prefer one of the savory pasta selections, including lasagne, bucatini, or vermicelli with clams. You can also order the fresh fish of the day, even roast goat cooked in the style of the campagna. Any of these dishes can be accompanied with a selection of fresh Neapolitan vegetables. You can get by with spending much less than the price quoted above if you come here for just a pizza or perhaps pasta and a salad.

CIRO A SANTA BRIGIDA, via Sant Brigida 71–73. Tel. 5524072.

Cuisine: ITALIAN/PIZZA. **Reservations:** Recommended. **Tram:** 1 or 4.

$ Prices: Appetizers 8,000–16,000 lire ($6.30–$12.55); main courses 8,000–23,000 lire ($6.30–$18.05). AE, DC, V.

Open: Lunch Mon–Sat 12:30–2:30pm; dinner Mon–Sat 7:30pm–1:30am. **Closed:** Aug 9–25.

Every Neapolitan has his or her favorite pizzeria. Many are on narrow, crooked streets, called *vicoli* in Italian, and are the domain of pickpockets, stray cats, hordes of scugnizzi, and blackmarket cigarette vendors. Should you wisely not seek out that secret address some Neapolitan has given you, you'll find some of the best pizzas in town near the San Carlo Opera House, at the address given above. It has been turning out not only pizzas but excellent trattoria food for hordes of faithful customers since 1932, with a few interruptions caused by such catastrophes as world wars when certain ingredients became almost impossible to secure. Those ingredients, at least in Naples, include good olive oil, fresh tomatoes, and mozzarella. This place has not been caught up in the worldwide craze of putting everything but the kitchen sink on top of a pizza.

This pizzeria and trattoria is almost always crowded with hungry diners. Many guests settle just for the basic pizza Margherita, while others prefer more elaborate concoctions such as pizza with fruits of the sea and mushrooms. Pizzas are baked over a wood fire, but, mercifully, the dining rooms are air-conditioned. Fresh fish and good-tasting pastas also appear in the menu.

FRATELLI LOMBARDI, via Bendetto Croce 59. Tel. 5520780.

Cuisine: PIZZA. **Reservations:** Required. **Bus:** 40.

$ Prices: Appetizers 8,000–15,000 lire ($6.30–$11.80); main courses 10,000–20,000 lire ($7.85–$15.70). V.

Open: Lunch Mon–Sat noon–2:30pm; dinner Mon–Sat 7:30pm–midnight.

If you're in a hurry when you come to Lombardi's, you'll stand at a counter, jostled by virtually every student in Naples, to order your pizza or pizza slices. Most clients, however, prefer to sit down at one of the tables and have pizza brought to them. The menu lists 10 different kinds, each made in the traditional Neapolitan way. If you don't want pizza, there is also the typical Italian repertoire of pasta dishes, veal dishes, and chicken dishes.

BRANDI, Salita Sant'Anna di Palazzo 1. Tel. 416928.

Cuisine: NEAPOLITAN. **Reservations:** Recommended. **Tram:** 1 or 4.

$ Prices: Appetizers 5,000–12,000 lire ($3.95–$9.40); main courses 6,000–10,000 lire ($4.70–$7.85). AE, DC, MC, V.

Open: Lunch Tues–Sun noon–3pm; dinner Tues–Sun 6:30pm–1am or 2am.

Considered the most historic pizzeria in Italy, Brandi was established by Pietro Colicchio in the 19th century. His successor, Raffaele Esposito, who enjoyed the reputation that his hard work had earned, was requested one day to prepare a banquet for Margherita di Savoia, the queen of Italy. So successful was the reception of the pizza made with tomato, basil, olive oil, and mozzarella, that the queen accepted the honor of having it named after her. Thus was pizza Margherita born from the kitchens of Naples's Restaurant Brandi.

Today you can order the pizza that pleased a queen, as well as such other specialties as linguine with scampi, fettuccine "Regina d'Italia," and a full array of seafood dishes.

TRIANON, via Pietro Colletta 46. Tel. 5539426.

Cuisine: PIZZA. **Reservations:** Not needed. **Bus:** 106 or 150.

$ Prices: Pizza 5,000–12,000 lire ($3.95–$9.40). No credit cards.

Open: Lunch Mon–Sat 10:30am–3:30pm; dinner daily 6:15pm–midnight.

This unpretentious place is one of the preferred pizzerie in a neighborhood that during the day is populated with the employees of the city's municipal offices. Set in front of the Porta Capuano, near the central railway station, it serves pizza (and only pizza). A *pizza cappricciosa*—suitable as a meal for one or a satisfying snack for two—is a specialty.

Snacks & Fast Food

CALIFORNIA, via Santa Lucia 101. Tel. 421752.
  Cuisine: FAST FOOD/AMERICAN. **Reservations:** Not needed. **Bus:** 106 or 150.
$ **Prices:** Appetizers 8,000–10,000 lire ($6.30–$7.85); main courses 18,000–22,000 lire ($14.15–$17.25). AE, DC, V.
  Open: Mon–Sat 9am–1am. **Closed:** Aug 9–26.

This place bills itself as "the original American luncheonette in Naples." It provides an oasis for those homesick and hankering for banana splits, ice-cream sundaes, ham and eggs, and pancakes. It's both a counter and a table affair, with a glassed-in sidewalk area. Offered are such typical items as chocolate cake, a hamburger steak, or a hot roast beef sandwich. For the Texan, there's chili con carne. The breakfast specials draw a lively clientele who order plates of bacon and eggs, as well as "authentic" Kellogg's corn flakes.

GNAM!, via San Giacomo 11. Tel. 5522564.
  Cuisine: FAST FOOD. **Reservations:** Not needed. **Tram:** 1 or 4.
$ **Prices:** Meal 9,000 lire ($7.05). AE, DC, MC, V.
  Open: Daily 10am–midnight.

Gnam! describes itself as a Neapolitan copy of McDonald's, because of its fast-food format of sandwiches, hamburgers, German-style sausages (*wurstel*), and sodas. Your order, which you place at a counter in typical fast-food style, will cost around 9,000 lire ($7.05) for a sandwich or burger and a drink. Gnam! translates into English as something like "Yum!"

REMY CHEF/REMY GELO, via Galiani 30. Tel. 667304.
  Cuisine: HAMBURGERS/ICE CREAM. **Reservations:** Not needed. **Tram:** 1 or 4.
$ **Prices:** Hamburger 2,800 lire ($2.20). No credit cards.
  Open: Mon–Fri 10am–11pm, Sat–Sun 5pm–midnight.

They occupy different storefronts next door to each other, but the standard procedure in Naples seems to be to order your burgers at Remy Chef, then to saunter next door to Remy Gelo for ice cream. Both are owned by the same entrepreneurs, and both require that you buy your food at the counter and take it out, in typical fast-food style.

The Grand Cafés

The decor of the **Gran Caffè Gambrinus,** via Chiaia 1 (tel. 417582), the oldest café in Naples (about 150 years old), would fit easily into a grand Bourbon palace. Along the vaulted ceiling of an inner room, Empire-style caryatids spread their togas in high relief above frescoes of mythological playmates. The café is known for its espresso and cappuccino, as well as pastries and cakes whose variety dazzles the eye. These pastries are probably the most famous in Naples. You can also order potato and rice croquettes and fried pizzas for a light lunch. Tea costs 3,500 lire ($2.75); cappuccino goes for 3,000 lire ($2.35) at a table. The café is open Wednesday through Monday from 7am to 1am. It is near the Galeria Umberto.

  Caflish, via Toledo 253 (tel. 412466), near the Galeria Umberto, welcomes shoppers who come in for a quick glass of orange-flavored brandy, grappa, sambucca, amaretto, a cup of espresso, or whatever. In the back room, self-service fast food is available. The place is also known for its rich desserts and ice creams. If you stand, coffee begins at 900 lire (70¢). Caflish is open from 8am to 9pm, but closed on Saturday. It is reached by bus C4 or C22.

A Sweet Shop

Scaturchio, at piazza San Domenico Maggiore 19 (tel. 5516944), offers what might be the most voluptuously caloric collection of pastries in Naples, and is famous for both satisfying and fattening local residents since around 1900. Representative pastries include the entire selection of Neapolitan sweets, cakes, and candies, including brioches soaked in liqueur, pound cake (cassate) filled with layered ricotta,

Moor's heads, and cheesy-ricotta pastries known as sfogliatelle, dear to the heart of most Neapolitans, who fondly remember them from childhood. There are tables where you can sit. Pastries cost 1,500 lire ($1.20) and up. It's open Monday and Wednesday through Saturday from 7:30am to 8:30pm.

SHOPPING

Naples is hardly the shopper's paradise that Milan, Venice, Florence, and Rome are, to mention a few of Italy's other big cities. Nevertheless, there are some good buys here for the inveterate shopper willing to invest the time and energy to seek them out. The finest shopping area lies around **piazza dei Martiri** and along such streets as via dei Mille, via Calabritto, and via Chiaia. There's more commercial shopping between piazza Trieste e Trento and piazza Dante along **via Toledo/via Roma.**

Coral is much sought-after by collectors. Much of the coral is now sent to Naples from Thailand, but it is still shaped into amazing jewelry at one of the workrooms at Torre del Greco, on the outskirts of Naples, off the Naples–Pompeii highway. Cameos are also made there.

ANTIQUES

ARTE ANTICA, via Domenico Morelli 6. Tel. 7643704.
Considered one of the finest antique stores in Naples, Arte Antica has been at this address since 1900. The Falanga family, the owners, specialize in Italian antiques. Their specialty is the kind of florid and exquisitely detailed porcelain that has always been prized in Naples. Open on Monday from 4:30 to 8pm and Tuesday through Saturday from 9am to 1:30pm and 4:30 to 8pm.

SALVATORE IERMANO, via Domenico Morelli 30. Tel. 7643913.
The specialty here is antiques, particularly antique versions of an art form practiced in southern Italy for hundreds of years, the crèche. Usually sold as a set of wood or terra-cotta figures that represent all the important characters at the birth of Jesus, they are sought-after as antiques. Open on Monday from 4:30 to 8pm and Tuesday through Saturday from 10am to 1:30pm and 4:30pm to 8pm (closed Saturday afternoon in summer).

BOOKS

DE PERRO, via dei Mille 17. Tel. 418687.
All the books here are in Italian. Many deal with the art and architecture of southern Italy, with photographs that might be considered souvenirs in their own right. Open Monday through Friday from 9am to 1:30pm and 4:30 to 8pm, and on Saturday from 9am to 1:30pm.

TREVES, via Toledo 250. Tel. 415211.
Treves stocks a fine collection of Italian-language books, many of them dealing with art. Open on Monday from 4:30 to 8pm and Tuesday through Saturday from 9am to 8pm.

DEPARTMENT STORES

LA RINASCENTE, via Toledo 343. Tel. 411511.
This is the Neapolitan branch of Italy's most interesting department-store chain. Open on Monday from 4 to 7:45pm and Tuesday through Saturday from 9am to 1:30pm and 4 to 7:45pm.

COIN, via Alessandro Scarlatti 100. Tel. 5780111.
Coin is a department store that is known to virtually everybody in Naples. It sells everything from housewares to clothing. Open on Monday from 4:10 to 8pm and Tuesday through Saturday from 9:15am to 1:15pm and 4:10 to 8pm.

UPIM, via Diaz (corner of piazza Matteotti). Tel. 5523354.

There are seven different branches of this department store in Naples, but this is one of the largest, along with the branch on via dei Mille 59 (tel. 417520). Upim is a large and important department store, not very upmarket, but reasonably priced and interesting for the view of Neapolitan sociology that a promenade down its aisles will give you. Open Monday through Saturday from 9:15am to 1:15pm and 4:15 to 8:15pm.

FABRIC

LA TIENDA, via dei Mille 63. Tel. 415249.

La Tienda is one of the best-known fabric shops in Naples. If you've ever been tempted to take up sewing, you'll find all the ingredients you'll need right here. Some of the fabrics are the same as those used by Italy's well-known designers. Open Monday through Saturday from 9am to 1:30pm and 4:30 to 8pm (closed Monday morning in winter and Saturday afternoon in summer).

FASHION

For Women

EDDY MONETTI, piazza Santa Catarina 7. Tel. 403229.

This is the women's branch of a fine clothing empire still owned by Signor Eddy Monetti. Open on Monday from 4:30 to 8pm and Tuesday through Saturday from 9am to 1:30pm and 4:30 to 8pm.

GABRIELLA SPATARELLA, via Filangieri 23. Tel. 401703.

This store specializes in women's knitwear, especially sweaters, for the discerning woman. Open on Monday from 4:30 to 8pm and Tuesday through Saturday from 9am to 1:30pm and 4:30 to 8pm.

STEFANEL, via Chiaia 195. Tel. 407562.

Stefanel sells fun and informal sports clothes and casual clothes in bright colors for women and men. Open on Monday from 4 to 8pm and Tuesday through Saturday 9am to 1:30pm and 4 to 8pm.

For Men

LONDON HOUSE, via Filangieri 26. Tel. 403908.

London House sells a tasteful and conservative collection of men's clothing— everything that signor would need to consider himself well dressed. There is a less extensive selection of women's clothing, too. Open on Monday from 4:30 to 8pm and Tuesday through Saturday from 9am to 1:30pm and 4:30 to 8pm.

EDDY MONETTI, via dei Mille 45. Tel. 407064.

The men's branch of Eddy Monetti sells elegant men's clothing, well tailored and well selected. Open on Monday from 4:30 to 8pm and Tuesday through Saturday from 9am to 1:30pm and 4:30 to 8pm.

SALVATORE BALBI, via Chiaia 258. Tel. 418551.

Here you can get underwear, nightshirts, socks, and shirts for men, in a shop filled with colorfully artistic underwear displays, and crowds of women making their selections. Many of their garments, especially the bathrobes, are very elegant. Open on Monday from 4:30 to 7:30pm and Tuesday through Saturday from 9am to 1:30pm and 4:30 to 7:30pm.

FOOD

CODRINGTON & CO., via Chiaia 94. Tel. 418257.

Codrington & Co. was founded about a century ago by a British family, and has a reputation in Naples as a purveyor of mostly English foodstuffs, sold and displayed from a briskly English-inspired shop near the Ponte di Chiaia. There are food and spices from throughout the world, as well as Devonshire marmalade, Stilton cheese, and old-fashioned chutney, but along with these edibles you'll find an array of small household objects, kitchen utensils, soap, and those gadgets that—once you discover them—you might not want to do without. Open on Monday from 4:30 to 8pm and Tuesday through Saturday from 9am to 1:30pm and 4:30 to 8pm.

GIFTS

BOTTEGA DELLA CARTA, via Cavallerizza a Chiaia 22. Tel. 421903.

The specialty here is party supplies, carnival masks, and writing supplies. Scattered among their inventory, you'll find possibilities for unusual gifts to take back home. Open on Monday from 4:30 to 8pm and Tuesday through Saturday from 9am to 1:15pm and 4:30 to 8pm.

HERBAL ESSENCES

LA BOTTEGA DELL'ERBORISTA, via Bellini 68. Tel. 219702.

Everything sold here is somehow derived from herbs and flowers. This includes soaps, shampoos, body oils, medications, foodstuffs such as honey and whole grains, and spices. The staff is able to point out which teas will help you sleep and which will help you wake up, which foods will make you beautiful inside and which oils will make you beautiful outside. Open Monday through Friday from 9am to 1:30pm and 4:30 to 8pm, and on Saturday from 9am to 1:30pm.

JEWELRY

THEO BRINKMANN, piazza Municipio 21. Tel. 5520555.

Theo Brinkmann is one of the leading jewelers of Naples, a strictly local, Naples-based establishment with a long history and no other branches. Open on Monday from 4:30 to 8pm and Tuesday through Saturday from 9am to 1:30pm and 4:30 to 8pm.

DEL PORTO, via Santa Lucia 165. Tel. 415093.

The specialty here is jewelry made from coral, much of which is carved into beautifully intricate designs. These include cameos, rings, necklaces, and ear ornaments. Open Monday through Friday from 9am to 1pm and 4:30 to 7:30pm, and on Saturday from 9am to 1pm.

LEATHER & SHOES

SALVATORE SPATARELLA, via Calabritto 1. Tel. 7643794.

Here you can inspect a full array of well-made leather goods such as purses, luggage, shoes, handbags, and wallets. It's run by the Rubinacci family, who also have a carefully selected array of women's clothing. Open on Monday from 4:30 to 8pm and Tuesday through Saturday from 9:30am to 1:30pm and 4:30 to 8pm.

D'ARIA, via dei Mille 71. Tel. 415309.

This is a large and well-stocked shoe outlet that sells Italian and other shoes for both men and women. Open on Monday from 4:30 to 8pm and Tuesday through Saturday from 9am to 1:30pm and 4:30 to 8pm.

LINENS

D'ANDREA, via Santa Brigida 34. Tel. 5510621.

D'Andrea is a well-stocked outlet for tablecloths, napkins, and towels, a few of which are hand-embroidered, though most are machine-made. The establishment also sells undergarments for men, women, and children. Open on Monday from 4:30 to 8pm and Tuesday through Saturday from 9:30am to 1:30pm and 4:30 to 8pm.

SLIPPERS

IORIO, via Chiaia 86. Tel. 416115.
Iorio stocks only slippers, thousands of them, in dozens of different styles and colors, a sort of icon to domesticity and the changing values of the 1990s. The store is quick to stress that slippers are more than just something comfortable to wear after a long day at the office: They save wear and tear on your carpets, help its wearer to let down his/her guard on the home front, and generally celebrate the fine art of enjoying one's home. Open on Monday from 4:30 to 7:30pm and Tuesday through Saturday from 9:30am to 1:30pm and 4:30 to 7:30pm.

WAX

L'ARTE DELLA CERA, via Bellini 13. Tel. 349582.
Whether you're buying candles to illuminate a seance or a romantic tryst, this is the store where you'll find the biggest selection. Some are designed to ward off the evil eye, others just to be beautiful. Open on Monday from 4 to 7pm and Tuesday through Saturday from 9am to 2:30pm and 4 to 7pm.

EVENING ENTERTAINMENT

A sunset **walk through Santa Lucia** and along the waterfront never seems to dim in pleasure, even if you've lived in Naples for 40 years straight. Visitors are also fond of riding around town in one of the *carrozzelle* **(horse-drawn wagons).**

Or you can stroll by the glass-enclosed **Galeria Umberto,** off via Roma in the vicinity of the Theater of San Carlo. The 19th-century gallery, which evokes many a memory for a G.I., is still standing today, although a little the worse for wear. It's a kind of social center for Naples. John Horne Burns used it for the title of his novel *The Gallery,* in which he wrote: "In August 1944, everyone in Naples sooner or later found his way into this place and became like a picture on the wall of the museum."

On its nightclub and cabaret circuit, Naples probably offers more sucker joints than any other port along the Mediterranean (American sailors are the major objects of prey). If you're starved for action, you'll find plenty of it, and you're likely to end up paying for it dearly and regretting it (maybe even worse).

THE PERFORMING ARTS

A performance at the **Theater of San Carlo,** via San Carlo (tel. 416305), is an event to be savored. Summer productions are likely to include Puccini's *Madame Butterfly* or Verdi's *Aïda.* Ticket prices range from 20,000 lire to 80,000 lire ($15.70 to $62.80). And if you want to see just the theater, you can visit it Tuesday through Saturday from 9am to noon, although this will not be possible during rehearsals. The theater was originally built in the baroque style for the Bourbon king Charles III, using such trappings as marble from Siena and crystal from Bohemia. It was rebuilt following an 1816 fire, and was largely restored again after having been bombed extensively in World War II.

A PIANO BAR

DENIRO, via Vito Fornari 15. Tel. 422334.
There's a workaday café and bar near the entrance of this place, where coffee costs

around 1,000 lire (80¢). Two inner rooms however, are more interesting and far more plush, and include both a piano bar and a restaurant. The first drink will cost around 20,000 lire ($15.70); the second, 10,000 lire ($7.85); and on Saturday, a first drink costs 25,000 lire ($19.65). A meal in the restaurant costs around 50,000 lire ($39.25). It's open daily from 10am to midnight.

NIGHTCLUBS

MY WAY, via Cappella Vecchia 30. Tel. 7644735.

This place may have gotten its name from the old, egocentric Sinatra song (no one here seems to remember), or perhaps from the fact that only one road (via Cappella Vecchia) leads to it from the nearby piazza dei Martiri. To enter, you'll descend into a natural cave set deep inside a mountain, similar to the catacombs used by the ancient Christians. There's nothing particularly pious about this place, however, where danceable music reverberates among the rocks every Saturday from 10pm to at least 3am. Entrance costs 25,000 lire ($19.65). The crowd tends to be young.

CHEZ MOI, via del Parco Margherita 13. Tel. 407526.

This is considered one of the city's best-managed nightclubs, with a strict policy of refusing entrance to anyone who looks like he or she might cause trouble inside. This is appreciated by the designers, government ministers, and visiting socialites who seem to enjoy the place. Clients tend to be over 25 years old, and have included the mayor of Naples. You'll be ushered to a table in an interior with a decor of soft blues and greens, where you'll order your first drink. This will cost around 25,000 lire ($19.65). The place is open every night except Monday from 10:30pm until "as long as people continue to enjoy themselves." Occasionally the management will present a cabaret act or a live pianist at the bar, but more frequently the music is highly danceable disco.

DISCOS

IL TONGUE, via Manzoni 207. Tel. 7690800.

The young crowd here pours into this hyper-modern space, sometimes spilling over into the establishment's open-air garden. This new wave environment, studded with mirrors and unusual paintings, is open on Friday, Saturday, and Sunday night from 10pm to 3am.
Admission: 20,000 lire ($15.70).

KISS KISS, via Sgambati 47. Tel. 5466566.

Kiss Kiss is huge—probably the largest disco in Naples. The youngish crowd, which is usually between 18 and 25, mingle and dance and generally have an uninhibited good time. There is a surprisingly small percentage of punk rockers because, in the words of an employee here, "Loud punk rock and loud hard rock isn't popular in Naples." If you tire of the human melee going on at the several bars or on the dance floor, you can watch video movies or videotaped rock concerts on one of several different screens. There's a restaurant and piano bar on the premises, called the Kiss Kiss Café, set up in a separate (and quieter) room. The place is open only on Friday and Saturday from 10pm to 3am and on Sunday from 8pm to 2am. The Friday-night crowd tends to be older and slightly more sophisticated and/or sedate.
Admission: 20,000 lire ($15.70).

2. THE ENVIRONS OF NAPLES

THE PHLAEGREAN FIELDS

One of the bizarre attractions of southern Italy, the Campi Flegrei, as they are known, form a backdrop for a day's adventure of exploring west of Naples and along its bay.

An explosive land of myth and legend, the fiery fields contain a semi-extinct volcano (Solfatara), the cave of the Cumaean Sibyl, Virgil's gateway to the "Infernal Regions," the ruins of thermal baths and amphitheaters built by the Romans, deserted colonies left by the Greeks—and lots more.

If you're depending on public transportation, the best center for exploring the area is **Pozzuoli,** which is reached by Metropolitana (subway) from the Stazione Centrale in Naples. The fare is 800 lire (65¢). Once in Pozzuoli, you can take one of the SEPSA buses at any bus stop, which will take you to places such as Baia in 20 minutes. You can also go to Cumae on one of these buses, or to Solfatara or Lago d'Averno.

SOLFATARA About 7½ miles west of Naples, in the vicinity of Pozzuoli, is the ancient ✪ **crater of Solfatara.** It hasn't erupted since the final year of the 12th century, but it has been threatening to ever since. It gives off sulfurous gases and releases scalding vapors through cracks in the earth's surface. In fact, the activity—or inactivity—of Solfatara has been observed for such a long time that the crater's name is used by Webster's dictionary to define any "dormant volcano" emitting vapors.

The crater may be visited daily from 9am to sunset for 3,500 lire ($2.75) admission. For information, telephone 8672341. To reach it, you can take the Metropolitana line from the Stazione Centrale to Solfatara. Once you get off at the train station, you can board one of the city buses that go up the hill, or you can walk to the crater in about 20 minutes.

POZZUOLI Located a mile and a half away from Solfatara, the seaport of Pozzuoli opens onto a gulf of the same name, and is screened from the Bay of Naples by a promontory. The ruins of the **Anfiteatro Flavio,** built in the last part of the 1st century A.D., testify to past greatness. Considered one of the finest surviving examples of the arenas of antiquity, it is particularly distinguished by its "wings"—which, considering their age, are in good condition. You can see the remains where exotic beasts from Africa were caged before being turned loose in the ring to test their jungle skill against a gladiator. The amphitheater (tel. 8676007), which may be visited daily from 9am to 2 hours before sunset, is said to have entertained 40,000 spectators at the height of its glory. An admission fee of 2,000 lire ($1.55) is charged.

In another part of town, the **Temple of Serapis** was really the "Macellum," or market square, and some of its ruined pillars still project upward today. It was erected during the reign of the Flavian emperors.

Pozzuoli can be reached by subway leaving from the Stazione Centrale in Naples.

BAIA In the days of Imperial Rome, the emperors—everybody from Julius Caesar to Hadrian—came here to frolic in the sun while enjoying the comforts of their luxurious villas and Roman baths. Nero is said to have murdered his mother, Agrippina, at nearby Bacoli, with its Pool of Mirabilis. (The ancient "Baiae" was named for Baios, helmsman for Ulysses.) Parts of its illustrious past have been dug out. Ruins of scope and dimension were revealed, including both the Temple of Baiae and the Thermal Baths, said to have been among the greatest erected in Italy.

You can explore this archeological district from 9am to 2 hours before sunset. It is closed Monday. Admission is 2,000 lire ($1.55). The town is reached in 15 minutes by rail from Cumana Station.

LAGO D'AVERNO Ten miles west of Naples, a bit to the north of Baia, is a lake occupying an extinct volcanic crater. Known to the ancients as the Gateway to Hades, it was for centuries shrouded in superstition. Its vapors were said to produce illness and even death, and Averno could well have been the source of the expression "still waters run deep." Facing the lake are the ruins of what has been known as the Temple of Apollo from the 1st century A.D., and what was once commonly identified as the Cave of the Cumaean Sibyl. According to legend, the Sibyl is said to have ferried Aeneas, son of Aphrodite, across the lake, where he traced a mysterious spring to its source, the River Styx. In the 1st century B.C., Agrippa turned it into a harbor for Roman ships by digging out a canal.

From Baia, the site is reached by bus on the Napoli–Torre Gaveta line.

CUMA Ancient Cumae was one of the first outposts of Greek colonization in what is now Italy. Twelve miles west of Naples, it is of interest chiefly because it is said to have contained the cave of the legendary Cumaean Sibyl. The **cave of the oracle,** really a gallery, was dug by the Greeks in the 5th century B.C. and was a sacred spot to them. Beloved by Apollo, the Sibyl is said to have written the *Sibylline Oracles,* a group of books of prophecy purchased, according to tradition, by Tarquin the Proud. You may visit not only the caves, but also the ruins of temples dedicated to Jupiter and Apollo (later converted into Christian churches), from 9am to 2 hours before sunset, for 2,000 lire ($1.55) admission. It is closed on Monday. On via Domitiana, to the east of Cuma, you'll pass the **Arco Felice,** an arch about 64 feet high, built by Emperor Domitian in the 1st century A.D.

The Ferrovia Cumana train line runs here.

HERCULANEUM

The builders of Herculaneum, ✪ **Ercolano** in Italian, were still working to repair the damage caused by an A.D. 62 earthquake when Vesuvius erupted on that fateful August day in A.D. 79. Herculaneum, a much smaller town (about one-fourth the size of Pompeii), didn't start to come to light again until 1709 when Prince Elbeuf launched the unfortunate fashion of tunneling through it for treasures. The prince was more intent on profiting from the sale of objets d'art than in uncovering a dead Roman town.

Subsequent excavations have been slow and sporadic. In fact, Herculaneum is not completely dug out today. One of the obstacles has been that the town was buried under lava, which was much heavier than the ash and pumice stone that piled onto Pompeii. Of course, this formed a greater protection for the buildings buried underneath—many of which were more elaborately constructed than those at Pompeii, as Herculaneum was a seaside resort for patrician families. The complication of having the slum of Resina resting over the yet-to-be-excavated district has further impeded progress and urban renewal.

Although all the streets and buildings of Herculaneum hold interest, some ruins merit more attention than others. The baths (*terme*) are divided between those at the forum and those on the outskirts (Terme Suburbane, in the vicinity of the more elegant villas). The municipal baths, which segregated the sexes, are larger, but the ones at the edge of town are more lavishly adorned. The Palestra was a kind of sports arena, where games were staged to satisfy the appetites of the spectacle-hungry denizens.

The typical plan for the average town house was to erect it around an uncovered atrium. In some areas, Herculaneum possessed the forerunner of the modern apartment house. Important private homes to seek out include the "House of the Bicentenary," the "House of the Wooden Cabinet," the "House of the Wooden Partition," and the "House of Poseidon (Neptune) and Amphitrite," the last containing what is perhaps the best-known mosaic discovered in the ruins.

The finest example of how the aristocracy lived is provided by a visit to the "Casa dei Cervi," named the House of the Stags because of sculpture found inside. Guides are fond of showing their male clients a statue of a drunken Hercules urinating. The best of the houses are locked and can only be seen by permission of the gatekeepers, who expect tips for their services.

The ruins may be visited daily except Monday from 9am to 1 hour before sunset, for 5,000 lire ($3.95) admission. To reach the archeological zone, take the regular train service from Naples on the Circumvesuviana Railway, a 20-minute ride leaving about every half hour from corso Garibaldi 387; or take bus no. 255 from piazza Municipio. Otherwise, it's a 4½-mile drive on the autostrada to Salerno (turn off at Ercolano).

VESUVIUS

A volcano that has struck terror in Campania, Vesuvius looms menacingly over the Bay of Naples. The date—August 24, A.D. 79—is well known, for it was then that Vesuvius burst forth and buried Pompeii, Herculaneum, and Stabiae under its mass of lava and volcanic mud. Many fail to realize that Vesuvius has erupted periodically ever since (thousands were killed in 1631): The last major spouting of lava occurred in this century (it blew off the ring of its crater in 1906).

The approach to Vesuvius is dramatic, with the terrain growing forlorn and foreboding as you near the top. Along the way you'll see villas rising on its slopes and vineyards (the grapes produce an amber-colored wine known as Lacrimae Christi; the citizens of Pompeii enjoyed wine from this mountainside, as excavations revealed). Closer to the summit, the soil becomes the color of puce and an occasional wildflower appears.

Although it may sound like a dubious invitation to some (Vesuvius, after all, is an active volcano), it is possible to visit the rim—or lips, so to speak—of the crater's mouth. As you look down into its smoldering core, you may recall that Spartacus, in a century before the eruption that buried Pompeii, hid in the hollow of the crater, which was then covered with vines.

To reach Vesuvius from Naples, you can take the Circumvesuviana Railway, or (in summer only) a motor-coach service from piazza Vittoria, which hooks up with bus connections at Pugliano. You get off the train at the Ercolano station, the 10th stop. A bus goes up the mountain several times a day from just outside the station, and costs 2,000 lire ($1.55) round-trip. The bus schedule can be obtained at the Tourist Information Office on the right-hand side of the street connecting the railway station with the Herculaneum excavations. Get off the bus at the beginning of the footpath and walk up the mountain to the rim, about 25 minutes of brisk walking. It's obligatory to hire a guide for 3,500 lire ($2.75) to take you to the top.

---

3. POMPEII

15 miles S of Naples, 147 miles S of Rome

GETTING THERE   By Train   The Circumvesuviana Railway in Naples departs every half hour from piazza Garibaldi. A round-trip fare is 3,000 lire ($2.35) (trip time: 45 minutes each way).

By Bus   At the railway station in Pompeii, bus connections take you to the entrance to the excavations. There is an entrance about 50 yards from the railway station at Villa Misteri.

By Car   To reach Pompeii from Naples, take the 13½-mile drive on the autostrada to Salerno.

ESSENTIALS   The **telephone area code** is 081. The **Tourist Information Center** is at via Sacra 1 (tel. 8631041).

When Vesuvius erupted in A.D. 79, Pliny the Younger, who later recorded the event, thought the end of the world had come. For our next adventure, we head south from Naples to the scene of the long-ago excitement.

The ruined Roman city of Pompeii (Pompei in Italian), dug out from the inundation of volcanic ash and pumice stone rained on it by Vesuvius in the year A.D. 79, has sparked the imagination of the world. At the excavations, the life of 19 centuries ago is vividly experienced.

Numerous myths have surrounded Pompeii, one of which is that a completely intact city was rediscovered. Actually the Pompeiians—that is, those who escaped—returned to their city when the ashes had cooled and removed some of the most precious treasures from the thriving resort. They were the forerunners of the later archeologists. But they left plenty behind to be uncovered at a later date and carted off to museums throughout Europe and America.

After a long medieval sleep, Pompeii was again brought to life in the late 16th century, quite by accident, by the architect Domenico Fontana. However, it was in the mid-18th century that large-scale excavations were launched. Somebody once remarked that Pompeii's second tragedy was its rediscovery, that it really should have been left to slumber for another century or two, when it might have been taken better care of. The comment was prompted by the sad state of some of the present ruins and the poor maintenance in general.

WHAT TO SEE & DO

The most elegant of the patrician villas, the ○ **House of Vettii** has an Etruscan courtyard, statuary (such as a two-faced Janus), paintings, and a black-and-red Pompeiian dining room frescoed with cupids. The house was occupied by two brothers named Vettii, both of whom were wealthy merchants. As you enter the vestibule, you'll see a painting of Priapus resting his gargantuan phallus on a pair of scales. The guard (that is, for a tip) will reveal other erotic fertility drawings and statuary, although most such material has been removed from Pompeii to the Archeological Museum in Naples. This house is considered the best example of a villa and garden that have been restored. The house is also known for its frescoes of delicate miniature cupids.

The second important villa, in the vicinity of Porto Ercolano (Herculaneum Gate), lies outside the walls. The **House of Mysteries** (Villa dei Misteri) is reached by going out viale alla Villa dei Misteri. What makes the villa exceptional, aside from its architectural features, are its remarkable frescoes, depicting scenes associated with the sect of Dionysus (Bacchus), one of the cults that was flourishing in Roman times. Note in some of the backgrounds the Pompeiian red. The largest house, called the **House of the Faun** (Casa del Fauno) because of a bronze statue of a dancing faun found there, takes up a city block and has four different dining rooms and two spacious peristyle gardens. It sheltered the celebrated Battle of Alexander the Great mosaic, which is now in a museum in Naples.

In the center of town is the **Forum**—though rather small, it was the heart of Pompeiian life, known to bakers, merchants, and the wealthy aristocrats who lived luxuriously in the villas. Parts of the Forum were severely damaged in an earthquake 16 years before the eruption of Vesuvius and had not been repaired when the final destruction came. Three buildings that surround the Forum are the **basilica** (the largest single structure in the city) and the temples of Apollo and Jupiter. The **Stabian Thermae** (baths)—where both men and women lounged and relaxed in between games of knucklebones—are in good condition, among the finest to come down to us from antiquity. Here you'll see some skeletons. In a building called Lupanare, erotic paintings are displayed. These frescoes are the source of the fattest tips to guides.

In the **Antiquarium** is a number of objects used in the day-to-day life of the Pompeiians, including kitchen utensils and pottery, as well as mosaics and sculpture. Note the cast of a dog caught in the agony of death.

The excavations may be visited Tuesday through Sunday from 9am until about 1 hour before sunset for an admission fee of 5,000 lire ($3.95). At the entrance you can hire a guide at a prescribed rate.

WHERE TO STAY

Accommodations appear to be for earnest archeologists only. The best of the lot follow.

HOTEL VILLA LAURA, via della Salle 13, 80045 Pompei. Tel. 081/ 8504893. Fax 081/8504893. 26 rms (all with bath). A/C MINIBAR TV TEL
$ Rates: 85,000 lire ($66.75) single; 105,000 lire ($82.45) double. Breakfast 8,000 lire ($6.30) extra. AE, DC, MC, V. **Parking:** 7,000 lire ($5.50).
The Villa Laura is the best hotel in town. Actually, this is a good little discovery,

located on a tranquil, somewhat-hidden street near the rail station in this bustling, traffic-filled town. The hotel is air-conditioned, and offers comfortably furnished bedrooms, mostly with balconies. In the basement of the hotel is a breakfast room and bar. The hotel also enjoys a garden, and garage facilities are available.

HOTEL DEL SANTUARIO, piazza Bartolo Longo 2–6, 80045 Pompei. Tel. 081/8506165. Fax 081/8503310. 52 rms (all with bath). TEL
$ Rates (including breakfast): 55,000 lire ($43.20) single; 80,000 lire ($62.80) double. AE, MC, V. **Parking:** 10,000 lire ($7.85).

The second best hotel in town is in the very center of the town of Pompeii, and opens onto the major square. The entrance faces a small park. The hotel rents simply furnished bedrooms, each clean and well kept. Across from the major basilica of Pompeii, the hotel also offers a ristorante, pizzeria, gelateria, and tea room. Good and reasonably priced meals begin at 22,000 lire ($17.25). You can enjoy such dishes as beefsteak pizzaiola or a mixed fry of shrimp and squid. Limited car parking is available.

HOTEL EUROPA, piazza Santuario 30, 80045 Pompei. Tel. 081/8632190. Fax 081/8633342. 27 rms (all with bath or shower). TEL
$ Rates (including breakfast): 65,000 lire ($51) single; 87,000 lire ($68.30) double. AE, DC, MC, V. **Parking:** 10,000 lire ($7.85).

This hotel of modest dimensions, one of the newest in Pompeii, is within walking distance of the main entrance to the ruins. Every comfortably furnished bedroom has a balcony. The hotel has a rooftop terrace with a panoramic view.

MOTEL VILLA DEI MISTERI, via Villa dei Misteri 8, 80045 Pompei. Tel. 081/8613593. 40 rms (all with shower). **Transportation:** From the Pompeii rail station, take Sorrento train and get off at the Villa dei Misteri stop.
$ Rates: 55,000 lire ($43.20) double. Breakfast 4,000 lire ($3.15) extra. No credit cards. **Parking:** Free.

Located 250 yards from the Vesuviana Station, this place is suitable for motorists. About a mile and a half from the center of town, it features a swimming pool, a little garden, and a place to park your car. The welcome of the owner and staff may compensate for a certain lack of facilities and amenities. The place could stand a facelift, but many readers have expressed their fondness for it. Only doubles are rented.

WHERE TO DINE

IL PRINCIPE, piazza Bartolo Longo 8. Tel. 8633342.
Cuisine: ITALIAN/INTERNATIONAL. **Reservations:** Required.
$ Prices: Appetizers 10,000–18,000 lire ($7.85–$14.15); main courses 15,000–30,000 lire ($11.80–$23.55). AE, DC, V.
Open: Lunch Tues–Sun 12:30–3pm; dinner Tues–Sun 7:30–11:30pm. **Closed:** Aug 1–15.

The leading restaurant of Pompeii, Il Principe is also acclaimed as one of the best restaurants in Campania. Elegant in decor, it offers refined service and an impeccable cuisine. Guests can dine inside its beautiful interior, or select a sidewalk table at the corner of the most important square in Pompeii, with views of the basilica. For your first course, you might start with carpaccio or a salad of porcini (mushrooms); then follow with one of the pasta dishes, perhaps spaghetti vongole (with baby clams). Superb fish dishes, such as sea bass and turbot, are served, and you can also order saltimbocca (sage-flavored veal with ham) or steak Diane.

ZI CATERINA, via Roma 16-22. Tel. 8631263.
Cuisine: SEAFOOD/NEAPOLITAN. **Reservations:** Recommended.
$ Prices: Appetizers 7,000–8,000 lire ($5.50–$6.30); main courses 10,000–12,000 lire ($7.85–$9.40). AE, DC, MC, V.

Open: Wed–Mon noon–11pm.

This good choice for dining is conveniently located in the center of town near the basilica, with two spacious dining rooms. The antipasto table might tempt you with its succulent seafood, although the pasta fagiole with mussels might also be what you'd want to start your meal with. The chef's special rigatoni, with tomatoes and prosciutto, is tempting, as is the array of fish or one of the live lobsters fresh from the tank.

CHAPTER 21

THE AMALFI COAST & CAPRI

- **WHAT'S SPECIAL ABOUT THE AMALFI COAST & CAPRI**
1. **SORRENTO**
2. **POSITANO**
3. **AMALFI**
4. **RAVELLO**
5. **PAESTUM**
6. **CAPRI**

English-speaking people use the phrase "see Naples and die" when referring to the bay and Vesuvius in the background. The Germans reserve the saying for the Amalfi Drive. A number of motorists do see the Amalfi Coast and die, as the road is dangerous—not designed for its current stream of traffic, such as summer tour buses that almost sideswipe each other to pass. It's hard to concentrate on the road for the sights. That eminent traveler André Gide called the drive "so beautiful that nothing more beautiful can be seen on this earth."

Capri and Sorrento have long been known to an international clientele. But the popularity of the resort-studded Amalfi Drive has been a more recent phenomenon. Perhaps it was discovered by German officers in World War II, then later by the American and English servicemen (Positano was a British rest camp in the last months of the war). Later, when the war was over, many returned, often bringing their wives. The little fishing villages in time became major tourism centers, with hotels and restaurants in all categories, even nightclubs honky-tonking their attractions. Sorrento and Amalfi are in the vanguard, with the widest range of facilities; Positano has more snob appeal and remains popular with artists; Ravello is still the choice of the discriminating few, such as Gore Vidal, who desire relative seclusion. To cap off an Amalfi Coast adventure, you can take a boat from Sorrento to Capri, which needs no advance billing. Three sightseeing attractions in this chapter—in addition to the towns and villages—are worthy of a special pilgrimage: the Green Grotto between Amalfi and Positano, the Blue Grotto of Capri, and the Greek temples of the ancient Sybarite-founded city of Paestum, south of Salerno.

SEEING THE AMALFI COAST & CAPRI
SUGGESTED ITINERARY

Day 1: Spend the time enjoying the clifftop resort of Sorrento and take an elevator down to its beach.

Day 2: Continue along the Amalfi Drive to Positano for a day climbing its narrow streets. Cap the evening at one of the waterfront restaurants.

Day 3: Continue to Amalfi stopping outside the city to explore the Emerald Grotto. Overnight in Amalfi.

Day 4: Transfer to the hilltop resort of Ravello and enjoy the rest of the day exploring its attractions and absorbing its panoramic vistas.

Days 5–6: Return to Sorrento or Naples and take a hydrofoil to Capri, which will be the highlight of the trip and the place you'll surely want to spend the most time. If you're rushed, see at least the Blue Grotto.

WHAT'S SPECIAL ABOUT THE AMALFI COAST & CAPRI

Great Towns & Villages

☐ Capri, a tiny jewel of an island in the Bay of Naples that attracts some two million tourists a year.

☐ Positano, a holiday town that for decades has been the retreat of celebrities such as director Franco Zeffirelli.

☐ Amalfi, a once-great maritime power, now a holiday resort known for its Duomo.

☐ Ravello, a tiny town with spectacular panoramas filled with narrow "step streets," a retreat of the rich and famous.

☐ Sorrento, the subject of song, story, and legend, the former "home of the Sirens" with a clifftop position overlooking the Bay of Naples.

Ace Attractions

☐ Emerald Grotto, outside Amalfi, a millennia-old chamber of stalagmites and stalactites.

☐ Blue Grotto, at Capri, known to the ancients, a grotto visited for its stunning cerulean waters.

☐ Amalfi Coast, a corniche road following a rocky coast between Sorrento and Salerno, with innumerable bends and wild landscape.

Ancient Monuments

☐ The ancient Sybarite city of Paestum, 25 miles south of Salerno, known for its impressive Greek ruins and Temple of Neptune.

GETTING THERE

The only commercial airport is at Naples, from which all the resorts along the Amalfi Coast can be reached by bus. Of the resorts, Sorrento enjoys express train service from Naples, taking one hour. From Sorrento, buses continue all around the coast to Salerno. Capri is best reached by hydrofoil from Naples or Sorrento.

---

1. SORRENTO

31 miles S of Naples, 159 miles S of Rome, 31 miles E of Salerno

GETTING THERE   By Train   Sorrento is served by frequent express trains from Naples (trip time: 1 hour). The high-speed train, called *Ferrovia Circumvesuviana,* leaves from one floor underground at the Stazione Centrale; a one-way fare is 2,900 lire ($2.30). For information about schedules to Sorrento, call 5534188 in Naples.

By Bus   From Naples, take the *Ferrovia Circumvesuviana* (see above), which is the fastest and cheapest way to get to Sorrento. Once at the Sorrento train station, you will find SITA buses servicing the Amalfi Coast. Buses depart from the Circumvesuviana station. Take any blue bus headed for Amalfi or Salerno. For information about schedules, call 8782708 in Sorrento.

By Car   From Naples, head south on Route 18, cutting west at the junction with Route 145.

ESSENTIALS   The **telephone area code** is 081. The **Tourist Information Office** is at via De Maio 35 (tel. 8782104), which winds down to the port where ships to Capri and Naples anchor.

Borrowing from Greek mythology, the Romans placed the legendary abode of the Sirens—those wicked mermaids who lured seamen to their deaths with their sweet songs—at Surrentum (Sorrento). Ulysses resisted their call by stuffing the ears of his crew with wax and having himself bound to the mast of his ship. Perched on high

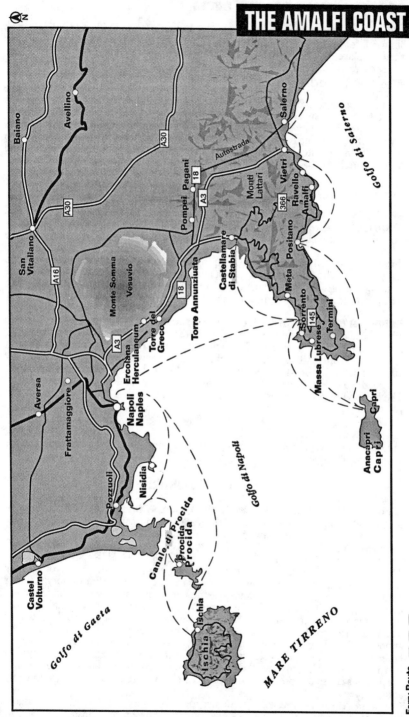

THE AMALFI COAST

N

Ferry Route — — —

MARE TIRRENO

Golfo di Salerno

Golfo di Napoli

Golfo di Gaeta

Salerno

Vietri
Ravello
Amalfi
366
Positano
Monti Lattari
Pagani
Pompei
18
A3
Meta
Sorrento
145
Termini
Massa Lubrense
Castellammare di Stabia
Torre Annunziata
Torre del Greco
Ercolana Herculaneum
Vesuvio
Monte Somma
A3
Napoli Naples
Nisidia
Pozzuoli
Frattamaggiore
Aversa
A16
San Vitaliano
A30
Avellino
Baiano
Autostrada
A30

Anacapri Capri
Capri

Procida
Canale di Procida
Procida

Ischia
Ischia

Castel Volturno

cliffs, overlooking the Bays of Naples and Salerno, Sorrento has been sending out its siren call for centuries—luring everybody from Homer to Lord and Lady Astor. It is the birthplace of Torquato Tasso, author of *Jerusalem Delivered.*

The streets in summer tend to be as noisy as a carnival. The hotels on the "racing strip," corso Italia, need to pass out earplug kits when they tuck you in for the night. Perhaps you'll have a hotel on a cliffside in Sorrento with a view of the "sea of the sirens." If you want to swim in that sea, you'll find both paths and private elevators that take guests down.

To enjoy the beauty of the Amalfi Drive, whose perils are noted above, don't drive it yourself. Take a blue bus marked "SITA," which runs between Sorrento and Salerno or Amalfi. In Sorrento, bus stations with timetables are outside the railway station and in the central piazza.

WHAT TO SEE & DO

SHOPPING   An interesting stop is **A Gargiulo & Jannuzzi,** piazza Tasso (tel. 8781041), the best-known maker of marquetry furniture in the region. Demonstrations of the centuries-old technique are presented in the basement, where an employee will combine multihued pieces of wood veneer to create patterns of arabesques and flowers. The sprawling showrooms, right in the heart of town, feature an array of card tables, clocks, and partners' desks, each inlaid with patterns of elmwood, rosewood, bird's-eye maple, and mahogany. Upstairs is a collection of embroidered napery and table linen. It is open daily from 8am to 10pm.

EVENING ENTERTAINMENT   La Mela, corso Italia 263 (tel. 8781917), is an all-purpose club that begins its evening of festivities with a folkloric show at 9pm. It lasts for 2 hours, and includes a Tarentella program of regional songs and dancing. A fee of 24,000 lire ($18.85) gives you entrance to the show as well as a first drink. After 10:30pm, the price of admission goes down to 15,000 lire ($11.80), when dancing to recorded music is presented. The club closes at 2, 3, or 4am, depending on business. The location is in the center of Sorrento in front of the post office.

WHERE TO STAY

In its first- and second-class hostelries, Sorrento is superior to almost any resort in the south, and offers accommodations in all price ranges.

VERY EXPENSIVE

GRAND HOTEL EXCELSIOR VITTORIA, piazza Tasso 34, 80067 Sorrento. Tel. 081/8071044. Fax 081/8072344. 106 rms (all with bath), 12 suites. A/C MINIBAR TV TEL **Bus:** SITA.

$ Rates (including breakfast): 220,000 lire ($172.70) single; 305,000 lire ($239.45) double; from 480,000 lire ($376.80) suite. AE, DC, MC, V. **Parking:** Free.

This place, built between 1834 and 1882, on the edge of a cliff, and surrounded by semitropical gardens with lemon and orange trees, combines 19th-century glamour with modern amenities. The grounds were designed and planted when grandeur was a prerequisite for a resort hotel. The terrace theme predominates, especially on the water side where you can enjoy the cold drinks served at sunset while gazing at Vesuvius across the bay. Three elevators take bathers down to the harbor. Inside, the atmosphere is old worldish, especially in the mellow dining room (see below). The hotel has 12 luxury suites, including the one named for Enrico Caruso, who stayed in it in 1921. The bedrooms have their own drama, some with balconies that open onto the perilous cliffside drop. The rooms have a wide mixture of furnishings, with many antique pieces.

Dining/Entertainment: The dining room is festive and formal, with ornate, hand-painted ceilings that depict clouds, sprays of flowers, and clusters of cherubs. You'll sit in ivory and cane provincial chairs while you enjoy a top-notch Sorrento cuisine. But the panoramic view makes dining here memorable. Meals begin at 60,000 lire ($47.10). Live entertainment is presented twice a week.

Services: Room service, baby-sitting, laundry, valet.

Facilities: Large swimming pool.

PARCO DEI PRINCIPI, via Rota 1, 80067 Sorrento. Tel. 081/8784644.
Fax 081/8783786. 172 rms (all with bath). A/C MINIBAR TV TEL **Bus:** SITA.

$ Rates (including breakfast): 200,000 lire ($157) single; 300,000 lire ($235.50) double. AE, DC, MC, V. **Parking:** Free. **Closed:** Nov–Easter.

This first-class hotel provides some of the best living in Sorrento, by combining an integrated contemporary design with the past. The core of this cliffside establishment is the 18th-century villa of Prince Leopold of Bourbon Sicily. Milan's distinguished architect, Gio Ponti, conceived the present building, a well-coordinated hotel unit. Both houses are in the parkland—acres of semitropical trees and flowers, a jungle with towering palms, acacia, olive, scented lemon, magnolias.

A private elevator takes swimmers down the cliff, which affords fantastic views of the Bay of Naples and Vesuvius, to the private beach. There is a mooring pier for yachts and motorboats, and for waterskiing. The public rooms are generous and spacious, with blue-and-white herringbone tile floors and slickly designed cerulean-blue furniture. The bedrooms continue the sky-blue theme, with striped floors, walls of glass leading to private balconies, and built-in furniture.

Dining/Entertainment: The hotel restaurant has both a formal dining room and a terrace with a view of the water. Both regional and international dishes are offered. Meals begin at 55,000 lire ($43.20).

Services: Room service, baby-sitting, laundry, valet.

Facilities: Swimming pool.

EXPENSIVE

GRAND HOTEL AMBASCIATORI, via Califano 18, 80067 Sorrento. Tel. 081/8782025. Fax 081/8071021. 103 rms (all with bath), 6 suites. A/C TV TEL **Bus:** SITA.

$ Rates (including breakfast): 130,000–170,000 lire ($102.05–$133.45) single; 210,000–260,000 lire ($164.85–$204.10) double; from 320,000 lire ($251.20) suite; 175,000–205,000 lire ($137.40–$160.95) per person with half board. AE, V. **Parking:** Free.

The heavily buttressed foundation that prevents this cliffside hotel from plunging into the sea looks like something from a medieval monastery. Built in a style reminiscent of a private villa, it was landscaped to include several rambling gardens whose edges conform to the edge of the precipice. A set of steps and a private elevator lead to the wooden deck of a bathing wharf. A barbecue is also available in this area. Inside, a substantial collection of Oriental carpets, marble floors, and well-upholstered armchairs provide plush enclaves of comfort.

Dining/Entertainment: The main restaurant offers both regional and international specialties, with meals beginning at 55,000 lire ($43.20). There is also a snack bar by the pool. Twice a week a live music program of Neapolitan songs is presented.

Services: Room service, baby-sitting, laundry, valet.

Facilities: A garage on the premises provides much-needed parking; there is also a heart-shaped swimming pool. An elevator takes guests down the cliff to the beach.

HOTEL BRISTOL, via del Capo 22, 80067 Sorrento. Tel. 081/8784522.
Fax 081/8071910. 132 rms (all with bath). A/C TV TEL **Bus:** SITA.

$ Rates (including breakfast): 145,000 lire ($113.85) single; 235,000 lire ($184.50) double; 155,000 lire ($121.70) per person with half board. AE, DC, MC, V. **Parking:** Free.

The Bristol is built pueblo style on a hillside at the edge of town, and every room has a view of Vesuvius and the Bay of Naples. The hotel lures with its contemporary decor and spaciousness, and with well-appointed public and private rooms. The bedrooms are warm and inviting, with bright covers and built-in niceties. Most have balconies that overlook the sea, and some contain minibars.

Dining/Entertainment: The attraction of the dining room with its terrace and all-glass facade is really the bay and view. There's an outer sun-shaded terrace for afternoon drinks from the winter-garden bar. A disco, Chez Nino, is near the large pool.

Services: Room service, baby-sitting, laundry, valet.

Facilities: Swimming pool, Finnish sauna.

HOTEL IMPERIAL TRAMONTANO, via Vittorio Veneto 1, 80067 Sorrento. Tel. 081/8782588. Fax 081/8072344. 105 rms (all with bath). A/C MINIBAR TV TEL **Bus:** SITA.

$ Rates (including breakfast): 144,000 lire ($113.05) single; 250,000 lire ($196.25) double; from 180,000 lire ($141.30) per person for half board. AE, V. **Parking:** Free. **Closed:** Jan–Feb.

When approached by boat from Naples, this hotel seems like an integral part of the high cliff on which it sits. In an imperious location right in the center of town, this villa-style establishment offers rooms with view balconies, and some of its public lounges open onto garden patios. The spacious drawing room, with English and Italian antiques, is made cozy by the informal arrangement of its furnishings. The bar and drinking lounge are graced with period pieces—many of them mahogany, Victorian style. The tile-floor bedrooms were designed for long stays. Some have arched French doors and balconies where you can have morning coffee. Furnishings include both antiques and reproductions. All rooms have a private bath, with a bidet and shower. In the garden, you can inhale the aroma of sweet-smelling trees and walk down paths of oleanders, hydrangea, acacia, coconut palms, and walls of glass that lead to private balconies, built-in desks, and headboards with accessories. The rooms have individually controlled air conditioning. Note the swimming pool, designed so as not to disturb the century-old trees. The hotel lies 500 yards from the railroad station.

MODERATE

HOTEL BELLEVUE SYRENE, piazza della Vittoria 5, 80067 Sorrento. Tel. 081/8781024. Fax 081/8781024. 59 rms (all with bath), 4 suites. TEL **Bus:** SITA.

$ Rates (including breakfast): 140,000 lire ($109.90) single; 200,000 lire ($157) double; from 350,000 lire ($274.75) suite; 140,000–180,000 lire ($109.90–$141.30) per person with half board. AE, MC, V. **Parking:** Free. **Closed:** Feb.

Only a short walk from the central square, this hotel is perched at the edge of a cliff, at the end of a shaded walkway lined with vines and flowers. It was built in the 18th century as a private villa. A private elevator carries sun worshipers to the beach. Because this was a private home, the size and shape of the bedrooms vary widely, but each is comfortable and clean. Furnishings are traditional.

INEXPENSIVE

HOTEL REGINA, via Marina Grande 3, 80067 Sorrento. Tel. 081/8782722. Fax 081/8782721. 36 rms (all with bath). A/C TEL **Bus:** SITA.

$ Rates (including breakfast): 72,000 lire ($56.50) single; 124,000 lire ($97.35) double. AE. **Parking:** 5,000 lire ($3.95). **Closed:** Nov–Mar 15.

Evenly spaced rows of balconies jut out over the Regina's well-tended garden. On its uppermost floor, a glassed-in dining room and an outdoor terrace encompass views of the Mediterranean extending as far as Naples and Vesuvius. Only breakfast is served. The clean, functional bedrooms have tile floors and private terraces.

VILLA DI SORRENTO, via Fuorimura 4, 80067 Sorrento. Tel. 081/8781068. 20 rms (all with bath or shower). TEL **Bus:** SITA.

$ Rates (including breakfast): 90,000 lire ($70.65) single; 150,000 lire ($117.75) double. AE, DC, MC, V.

This is a pleasant villa right in the center of town. Architecturally romantic, it attracts travelers with petite wrought-iron balconies, tall shutters, and vines climbing the facade. The rooms have such small niceties as bedside tables and lamps, and some accommodations have terraces. There is an elevator as well.

BUDGET

HOTEL DESIREE, via del Capo 31, 80067 Sorrento. Tel. 081/8781563.
22 rms (all with bath or shower). TEL **Bus:** SITA.
$ Rates (including breakfast): 45,000 lire ($35.35) single; 75,000 lire ($58.90) double. No credit cards. **Parking:** Free. **Closed:** Nov–Mar.

The Désirée is half a mile from the center of town at the beginning of the Amalfi Drive. This tranquil hotel is directed by Mr. and Mrs. Silvio Gargiulo, both of whom speak English. The establishment is ringed with terraces, whose flowered masonry overlooks the Bay of Naples and nearby trees. This used to be an upper-class private home before it was transformed into the good-value hotel it is today. Many of the attractive personal touches remain in the bedroom decor. Only breakfast is served, although there are many good restaurants nearby. You'll recognize the hotel by its green glass lanterns in front and the welcoming awning stretched over the front entrance. A private beach can be reached by elevator.

LA TONNARELLA, via del Capo 31, 80067 Sorrento. Tel. 081/8781153.
17 rms (all with bath or shower). **Bus:** SITA.
$ Rates (including half board): 70,000 lire ($54.95) per person. AE, DC, MC, V. **Parking:** Free. **Closed:** Dec 10–Mar 15.

This is an old-fashioned villa on the outskirts of Sorrento, 800 yards from the rail station, on a cliff-edge projection of garden terraces that opens toward the sea. It's a popular place for dining, but welcomes guests who want sea-view rooms as well. The best feature here—apart from economy and the good meals—is the gardens with oleander, lemon, and eucalyptus trees. There is a bathing beach at the foot of the cliff, with elevator service provided. Four rooms are air-conditioned units, which are simple but comfortable, and the view is magnificent. All is operated by the Gargiulo family, who are proud of their kitchen. Meals are served daily and cost from 35,000 lire ($27.50).

WHERE TO DINE

RISTORANTE IL GLICINE, via Sant'Antonio 2. Tel. 8772519.
Cuisine: CAMPANIA/ABRUZZI. **Reservations:** Not needed. **Bus:** SITA.
$ Prices: Appetizers 8,000–15,000 lire ($6.30–$11.80); main courses 10,000–20,000 lire ($7.85–$15.80). AE, DC, MC, V.
Open: Lunch daily noon–3pm; dinner daily 7pm–midnight. **Closed:** Jan–Feb.

Il Glicine has an unimpressive facade between a nursery and a modern apartment building. You'll find it above the main commercial district of town, on a winding road that leads to the Sorrento Palace Hotel. A pair of affable partners prepare such specialties from the Abruzzi as green ravioli with an almond sauce, linguine with seafood, penne (a pasta) with a pepperoni sauce, a mixed grill of beef and veal, and unusual preparations of turkey, as well as flavorful homemade pastries.

O PARRUCCHIANO, corso Italia 71. Tel. 8781321.
Cuisine: NEAPOLITAN. **Reservations:** Required Sat–Sun. **Bus:** SITA.
$ Prices: Appetizers 4,500–13,000 lire ($3.55–$10.20); main courses 8,000–13,500 lire ($6.30–$10.60). V.
Open: Lunch daily noon–4pm; dinner daily 7pm–midnight. **Closed:** Wed Oct 15–June 15.

This is a good choice on the busiest street in Sorrento. The building is like an old tavern, with an arched ceiling in the main dining room. On the terrace in the rear you can dine in a garden of trees, rubber plants, and statuary. Among the à la carte dishes, classic Italian fare is offered, including ravioli Caprese (filled with fresh cheese and covered with a tomato sauce), cannelloni, a mixed fish fry from the Bay of Naples, and a veal cutlet milanese. The chef will also prepare a pizza for you.

A NEARBY PLACE TO DINE

ANTICO FRANCISCHIELLO, via Partenope 27, 80061 Massa Lubrense. Tel. 081/8771171.

Cuisine: CAMPANIA. **Reservations:** Required. **Bus:** Massa Lubrense bus from Sorrento.

$ **Prices:** Appetizers 8,000–15,000 lire ($6.30–$11.80); main courses 15,000–18,000 lire ($11.80–$14.15). AE, DC, V.

Open: Lunch daily noon–3pm; dinner daily 7–11pm. **Closed:** Wed Oct–May.

The best table for the "fruits of the campagna" won't be found in Sorrento but at Masa Lubrense, about 3½ miles away. This restaurant was founded around 1850 by a famous cook whose legend still lives on in gastronomic circles around Sorrento. Today the establishment is directed by a relative of the founder, Signor Gargiulo (known as Signor Peppino to his clients and friends). With his wife, Pina de Maio, he concocts original recipes and serves such large portions that his establishment has been called a "gourmand's paradise."

The restaurant, with a panoramic view, is doubled in size by an outdoor veranda, which on the hottest days might be too bright even for the most avid sun worshiper. In the center is the antipasto table, crowned with sculpted swans, colored lights, foil decorations, and dozens of antipasti made from virtually every fish and vegetable in the region. The several kinds of bread are homemade, usually from some ancient family recipe. A recent version contained salami, prosciutto, several kinds of cheese, raisins, and red peppers folded into an egg batter. The cannelloni Peppino is prepared with a wholesome and flavorful simplicity. Other specialties include gnocchi Sorrento style, risotto pescatore, grilled or baked fish, mixed meats alla spiedino, and at least two kinds of house wine, products of the family vineyards.

Signor Peppino also rents eight rooms, each simply but comfortably furnished, costing 75,000 lire ($58.90) per person daily with half board. Each room has a private bath, air conditioning, and TV.

Be alert to the road's numbering system, since it seems to follow a logic all its own.

2. POSITANO

35 miles S of Naples, 10 miles E of Sorrento, 165 miles S of Rome

GETTING THERE By Bus Positano has no rail connections, but is reached by a rather thrilling bus ride from Sorrento. SITA buses leave from Sorrento frequently throughout the day, moreso in summer than in winter, and a one-way fare is 1,400 lire ($11). For information about schedules in Sorrento, call SITA at 8782708.

By Car Positano lies along the Amalfi Drive (Route 145, which becomes Route 163 at the approach to the resort).

ESSENTIALS The **telephone area code** is 089. The **Tourist Information Center** is at via del Saracano 2 (tel. 875067).

A hillside, Moorish-style village—traversed by only one road—on the southern strip of the Amalfi Drive, Positano opens onto the Tyrrhenian Sea with its legendary islands of the sirens. The Sirenuse Islands, mentioned in the *Odyssey* by Homer, form the mini-archipelago of Li Galli. Still privately owned, these islands were once purchased by Leonid Massine, the Russian-born choreographer. It is said that the town was "discovered" in the aftermath of World War II when Gen. Mark Clark stationed troops in nearby Salerno. When the U.S. soldiers went on holiday, they learned of the glories of Positano. It has jackrabbited along the classic postwar route of many a European resort: a sleeping fishing village that was visited by painters and writers (Paul Klee, Tennessee Williams), and then was taken over by bohemia-sampling main-drag visitors.

Once Positano was part of the powerful Republic of the Amalfis, a rival of Venice as a sea power in the 10th century. Today smart boutiques dot the village, and bikinis add vibrant colors to the mud-gray beach where you're likely to get pebbles in your sand castle. Prices have been rising sharply over the past few years. The 500-lire-a-night rooms popular with sunset-painting artists have gone the way of your baby teeth.

The topography of the village, you'll soon discover, is impossible. If you learn to climb the landscape with relative ease, you'll be qualified to hire out as a "scab" during the next donkey sit-down strike. John Steinbeck once wrote: "Positano bites deep. It is a dream place that isn't quite real when you are there and becomes beckoningly real after you have gone."

WHERE TO STAY

VERY EXPENSIVE

LE SIRENUSE, via Colombo 30, 84017 Positano. Tel. 089/875066. Fax 089/811798. 58 rms (all with bath), 2 suites. A/C MINIBAR TV TEL **Bus:** 3.

$ Rates (including breakfast): 420,000–480,000 lire ($329.70–$376.80) double; from 620,000 lire ($486.70) suite. AE, DC, MC, V. **Parking:** Free.

Le Sirenuse offers an atmosphere in which taste reigns supreme. Everything exists for its sophisticated clientele, which includes numerous artists and writers. The hotel, an old villa only a few minutes' walk up from the bay, is owned by the aristocratic Sersale family. The marchesa personally selects all the furnishings, which include fine carved chests, 19th-century paintings and old prints, a spinet piano, upholstered pieces in bold colors, and a Victorian settee. A typical touch: The drinking lounge has a polished wooden 16th-century cabinet, taken from an old jewelry shop. The double bedrooms, all with private bath and many with Jacuzzi, are varied, and all have terraces that overlook the village. Your room may have a iron bed, high and ornate and painted red, as well as a carved chest and refectory tables. Only doubles are rented.

Dining/Entertainment: Meals are well served on one of the three terraces, and the chef caters to the international palate with a sophisticated cuisine. Meals start at 65,000 lire ($51).

Services: Room service, baby-sitting, laundry, valet.

Facilities: Swimming pool.

SAN PIETRO, via Laurito 2, 84017 Positano. Tel. 089/875455. Fax 089/811449. 60 rms (all with bath), 5 suites. A/C MINIBAR TV TEL **Bus:** 3.

$ Rates (including breakfast): 400,000 lire ($314) single; 400,000–550,000 lire ($314–$431.75) double; from 700,000 lire ($549.50) suite; 330,000–450,000 lire ($259.05–$353.25) per person with half board. (3-day minimum stay required for half board). AE, DC, MC, V. **Parking:** Free. **Closed:** Nov 4–Mar 27.

A mile from Positano in the direction of Amalfi, San Pietro has only a miniature 15th-century chapel, which projects out on a high cliff, for identification. A behind-the-scenes elevator takes you down to the cliff ledges of what is the chicest resort along the Amalfi Coast. By changing elevators at the reception lounge, you can descend even farther to the swimming and boating cove, where you can sunbathe and enjoy the water in seclusion. The suitelike bedrooms are super-glamorous, and many have a picture window beside the bathtub (there's even a huge sunken Roman bath in one suite). Bougainvillea from the terraces reaches into the ceilings of many of the living rooms. The collection of antiques or reproductions fills the living room. San Pietro neither advertises nor posts signs, and the privacy of guests is zealously guarded. Many have been distinguished, including Lord Laurence Olivier, Rudolf Nureyev, and Gregory Peck.

Dining/Entertainment: Guests gather at sunset in the piano bar. A dining room has been cut into the cliff, and features picture windows the length of the room. A refined international cuisine is featured, but only for guests registered at the hotel.

Services: Room service, baby-sitting, laundry, valet.

Facilities: Swimming pool, private beach, tennis court.

EXPENSIVE

ALBERGO RISTORANTE COVO DEI SARACENI, 84017 Positano. Tel. 089/875059. Fax 089/875878. 58 rms (all with bath). A/C MINIBAR TV TEL **Bus:** 3.

$ Rates (including breakfast): 250,000 lire ($196.25) double; 180,000 lire ($141.30) per person with half board. AE, DC, MC, V. **Parking:** 25,000 lire ($19.65). **Closed:** Oct 28–Easter.

You'll find this rambling pink-and-ocher building a few steps above the port. It's a desirable choice for those who want to be in the swim of the summer action. The side closest to the water culminates in a rounded tower of rough-hewn stone, inside of which is an appealing restaurant open to the breezes and a firsthand view of the crashing waves. Meals begin at 35,000 lire ($27.50). The hotel rents comfortably furnished bedrooms, doubles only.

MODERATE

ALBERGO MIRAMARE, via Trara Genoino 31, 84017 Positano. Tel. 089/875002. Fax 089/875219. 18 rms (all with bath), 4 suites. TEL **Bus:** 3.

$ Rates (including breakfast): 90,000–140,000 lire ($70.65–$109.90) single; 180,000–260,000 lire ($141.30–$204.10) double; from 300,000 lire ($235.50) suite. AE, MC, V. **Parking:** Free. **Closed:** Jan 5–Mar 10.

This is one of the most charming accommodations in Positano, suitable for those who like the personalized touch that only a small, individualized inn can provide. The hotel was converted from a private mansion, which is now well on its way toward a century of life. Located in the heart of town on a cliff, the hotel attracts a discriminating clientele who appreciate the terraces, both public and private, where one can sip Campari and soda and contemplate the sea. Guests, who reach the hotel after a steep climb, are housed in one of two tastefully furnished buildings in a setting of citrus trees, with lots of flamboyant bougainvillea. Your bed will most likely rest under a vaulted ceiling, and the white walls will be thick. Even the bathrooms are romantic. Some rooms have air conditioning and TV.

The conversation piece of the hotel is a glass bathtub on a flowery terrace. What might seem like questionable taste in Los Angeles—a pink porcelain clamshell serving as a wash basin—becomes charming at the Miramare, even when the water rushes from a sea-green ceramic fish with coral-pink gills. The hotel lies about a 3-minute walk from the beach. You reach it by going down a series of stairs.

BUCA DI BACCO E BUCA RESIDENCE, via Rampa Teglia, 84017 Positano. Tel. 089/875699. Fax 089/875731. 54 rms (all with bath). MINIBAR TV TEL **Bus:** 3.

$ Rates (including breakfast): 100,000 lire ($78.50) single; 190,000 lire ($149.15) double. AE, DC, MC, V. **Parking:** 20,000 lire ($15.70). **Closed:** Oct 20–Mar 22.

This is one of the best moderately priced hotels at the resort, also housing one of the best restaurants in the area (see "Where to Eat," below). On the main beach of Positano, it often draws guests who patronize only its bar, one of the best-known rendezvous points along the Amalfi Drive. A large terrace opens onto the beach, and you can enjoy a Campari and soda while still in your bathing suit. The oldest and more expensive part, the Buca Residence, was an old seaside mansion constructed at the dawn of the 19th century. Rooms are well furnished, with many facilities, including balconies that face the sea. Air conditioning is available upon request for 6,000 lire ($4.70).

PALAZZO MURAT, via dei Mulini 23. Tel. 089/875177. Fax 089/811419. 28 rms (all with bath). MINIBAR TV TEL **Bus:** 3.

$ Rates (including breakfast): 180,000–200,000 lire ($141.30–$157) double. AE, DC, MC, V. **Parking:** 20,000 lire ($15.70). **Closed:** Nov–Easter.

For nostalgic atmosphere and baroque style, this place has no equal in all of Positano. The jasmine and bougainvillea are so profuse in its garden that they spill over their enclosing wall onto the arbors of the narrow street outside. Once this was the sumptuous retreat of Napoleon I's brother-in-law, the king of Naples. Considered the most dashing cavalry leader of his age, he was eventually court-martialed and shot. Today, shell designs cap the villa windows, which look out over a cluster of orange trees and the wrought-iron tendrils of the gate that leads into the garden. To enlarge the property, a previous owner erected a comfortable annex in a style compatible with the original villa. Only breakfast is served to occupants of the double bedrooms (there are no singles). Nineteen rooms are air-conditioned.

INEXPENSIVE

ALBERGO l'ANCORA, via Colombo, 84017 Positano. Tel. 089/875318.
Fax 089/811784. 18 rms (all with bath). MINIBAR TV TEL **Bus:** 3.
$ Rates: 155,000 lire ($121.70) double; 110,000–125,000 lire ($86.35–$98.15) per person with half board. AE, DC, MC, V. **Parking:** Free. **Closed:** Oct 21–Easter.

This is a stand-out choice in its classification. A hillside villa turned hotel, it has the atmosphere of a private club. It's fresh and sunny here, with each room like a bird's nest on a cliff. All rooms are doubles, and 10 are air-conditioned. Designed to accommodate the maximum of sun terraces and sheltered loggias for shade, the hotel is a 5-minute climb from the beach (maybe longer if you're past 35). Its main lounge has clusters of club chairs, tile floors, and teardrop chandeliers. But the bedrooms—which cater to couples only—are the stars, with their individualized treatments. Well-chosen antiques, such as fine inlaid desks, are intermixed with more contemporary pieces. The bathrooms in each of the double rooms are tiled and contain a bidet, and each room opens onto a private terrace. Meals are served on the informal outdoor terrace, under a vine-covered sun shelter, but only to clients registered at the hotel.

CASA ALBERTINA, via Tavolozza 4, 84017 Positano. Tel. 089/875143.
Fax 089/811540. 21 rms (all with bath), 3 suites. A/C MINIBAR TV TEL **Bus:** 3.
$ Rates (including breakfast): 100,000 lire ($78.50) single; 180,000 lire ($141.30) double; 250,000 lire ($196.25) junior suite; 130,000–170,000 lire ($102.05–$133.45) per person with half board. AE, DC, MC, V.

This villa guesthouse is reached by climbing a steep and winding road. It offers a view of the coastline from its perch on the side of a hill. Each bedroom is a gem, color coordinated in either mauve or blue. The rooms are furnished with well-selected pieces, such as gilt mirrors, fruitwood end tables, and bronze bed lamps. Each accommodation has wide French doors that lead out to a private balcony. You can have breakfast on the terra-cotta-tile terrace on your own garden furniture. A few rooms have a Jacuzzi. A total of 17 doubles are rented, and 3 junior suites for two, but only one single. The hotel also has a good restaurant that specializes in fresh grilled fish. Laundry service and a baby-sitter are available on request, and the hotel has both a bar and a solarium.

WHERE TO DINE

CHEZ BLACK, via del Brigantino. Tel. 875036.
Cuisine: SEAFOOD. **Reservations:** Required in summer. **Bus:** 3.
$ Prices: Appetizers 12,000–15,000 lire ($9.40–$11.80); main courses 15,000–20,000 lire ($11.80–$15.70). AE, DC, MC, V.
Open: Lunch daily 12:30–3pm; dinner daily 7:30–11pm. **Closed:** Nov 20–Dec 26.

The owner of this sophisticated place is Salvatore Russo, but for his restaurant ne uses the suntan-inspired name that his friends gave him in college. Founded after World War II, the restaurant occupies a desirable position near the beach. In summer, it is in the "eye of the hurricane" of action. Its varnished ribbing, glowing sheath of softwood and brass, and yacht-inspired semaphore symbols make it one of the most beautiful restaurants in town. A stone-edged aquarium holds fresh lobsters, while rack upon rack of local wines give diners a choice. Seafood is the specialty, as well as a wide selection of pizzas fresh from a circular oven. Most diners order substantial meals. The best-known dish is the spaghetti with crayfish, but you might also be tempted by linguine with fresh pesto, grilled swordfish, sole, or shrimp, along with an array of veal, liver, chicken, and beef dishes.

BUCA DI BACCO, via Rampa Teglia 8. Tel. 875699.
Cuisine: CAMPANIA/ITALIAN. **Reservations:** Required. **Bus:** 3.
$ Prices: Appetizers 8,000–14,000 lire ($6.30–$11); main courses 10,000–30,000 lire ($7.85–$23.55). AE, DC, MC, V.
Open: Lunch daily 12:30–3:30pm; dinner daily 8–11pm. **Closed:** Nov–Mar.

Right on the beach you'll find one of Positano's top restaurants. Guests often stop for a before-dinner drink in the bar downstairs, then head for the dining room on a big covered terrace that faces the sea. The tone of the *buca* is apparent as you enter. On display are various fresh fish, special salads, and fruit, including luscious black figs and freshly peeled oranges soaked in caramel. An exciting opener is a salad made with fruits of the sea, or you may prefer the zuppa di cozze (mussels), prepared with flair in a tangy sauce. Pasta dishes are homemade, and meats are well prepared with fresh ingredients.

LA CAMBUSA, Sulla Spiaggia. Tel. 875432.
Cuisine: SEAFOOD. **Reservations:** Not needed. **Bus:** 3.
$ Prices: Appetizers 8,000–14,000 lire ($6.30–$11); main courses 12,000–30,000 lire ($9.40–$23.55). AE, DC, MC, V.
Open: Lunch daily 12:30–3pm; dinner daily 7:30pm–midnight.

You'll have to navigate multiple series of steps and ramplike streets to reach the small square where this attractively intimate restaurant sits. There's a veranda for drinks or dining, as well as a pleasant interior. Your meal might include risotto pescatore (fisherman's rice), spaghetti with clams, linguine with shrimp, or a specialty of the village, pasta with zucchini. The wide array of meats and fish are well prepared and savory, while desserts are homemade and satisfyingly sweet (chocolate mousse or crème caramel would be a good choice).

3. AMALFI

38 miles S of Naples, 21 miles W of Salerno, 169 miles S of Rome

GETTING THERE   By Bus   SITA buses run every 2 hours during the day from Sorrento, for a one-way fare of 2,400 lire ($1.90). There are also SITA bus connections from Positano, a one-way ticket costing 1,200 lire (95¢). Information about schedules is available in Sorrento by calling SITA at 8782708. In Amalfi, the bus terminal is at the waterfront on piazza Flavior Gioia (tel. 871016 for information about schedules).

ESSENTIALS   The **telephone area code** is 089. The **Tourist Information Center** is at corso della Repubbliche Marinare 25-27 (tel. 871107).

From the 9th to the 11th century, the seafaring Republic of Amalfi rivaled those great maritime powers, Genoa and Venice. Its maritime code, the *Tavole Amalfitane*, was used in the Mediterranean for centuries. But raids by Saracens and a flood in the 14th century devastated the city. Its power and influence weakened, until it rose again in modern times as the major resort on the Amalfi Drive.

From its position at the slope of the steep Lattari hills, it overlooks the Bay of Salerno. The approach to Amalfi is most dramatic, whether you come from Positano or from Salerno. Today Amalfi depends on tourist traffic, and the hotels and pensions in dead center are right in the milling throng of holiday makers. The finest and most highly rated accommodations are on the outskirts.

WHAT TO SEE & DO

Evoking a rich past is the **Duomo** (cathedral), piazza del Duomo, named in honor of St. Andrew (Sant'Andrea), whose remains are said to be buried inside the crypt. Reached by climbing steep steps, the cathedral is characterized by its black-and-white facade and its mosaics. Inside, the one nave and two aisles are all richly baroqued. The cathedral dates back to the 11th century, although the present structure has been rebuilt. Its bronze doors were made in Constantinople, and its campanile (bell tower) is from the 13th century, erected partially in the Romanesque style. The Duomo, reached after climbing a flight of stairs, is open daily from 7am to 1:30pm and 3 to 8pm. You can also visit the **"Cloister of Paradise" (Chiostro Paradiso),** to the left of the cathedral, originally a necropolis for members of the Amalfitan "establishment." This graveyard dates from the 1200s and contains the broken columns and statues, as well as sarcophagi, of a long-gone civilization. The cloister is open daily from 9am to 1:30pm and 3 to 8pm and charges 1,000 lire (80¢) for admission.

For your most scenic walk in Amalfi, start at piazza del Duomo and head up via Genova. The classic stroll will take you to the **Valle dei Mulini** (the Valley of the Mills), so called because of the paper mills along its rocky reaches. (The seafaring republic is said to have acquainted Italy with the use of paper.) You'll pass by fragrant gardens and scented citrus groves.

And for the biggest attraction of all, head west to the ✪ **Emerald Grotto (Grotta della Smeraldo).** This ancient cavern, known for its light effects, is a millennia-old chamber of stalagmites and stalactites. Three miles west of Amalfi, the grotto is reached from the coastal road via a descent by elevator, which costs 4,000 lire ($3.15), including the boat ride. Then you board a boat that traverses the eerie world of the grotto. The stalagmites, unique in that some are under water, rise up in odd formations. Visits are possible daily from 9am to 5pm in March and April, from 8:30am to 6pm May through September, and from 10am to 4pm from October through February. Take the SITA bus in Amalfi going toward Sorrento.

WHERE TO STAY
VERY EXPENSIVE

SANTA CATERINA, strada Amalfitana, 84011 Amalfi. Tel. 089/871012.
Fax 089/871351. 70 rms (all with bath), 6 suites. A/C MINIBAR TV TEL **Bus:** SITA.

$ Rates (including breakfast): 220,000–380,000 lire ($172.70–$298.30) double; from 480,000 lire ($376.80) suite; 170,000–230,000 lire ($133.45–$180.55) per person for half board. AE, DC, MC, V. **Parking:** 15,000 lire ($11.80).

✪ Perched on top of a cliff, the Santa Caterina has an elevator that will take you down to a private beach. This "saint" is one of the most scenic accommodations. You are housed in the main structure or in one of the small "villas" in the citrus groves along the slopes of the hill. The accommodations are furnished in good taste, with an eye toward the comfort of all guests. Most of the rooms—all doubles—have a private balcony that faces the sea, a sea that was once filled with the powerful fleet of the Amalfi Republic when it was a formidable sea power. The furniture respects the tradition of the house, and in every room there is an antique piece. The bathrooms are spacious, with luxurious fittings, and all of them have a hairdryer.

Dining/Entertainment: The food here is among the best at the resort, so the boarding arrangement is no hardship. Many of the vegetables are grown in the hotel's own garden, and the fish tastes so fresh that I suspect the chef has an arrangement with local fishermen to bring in the "catch of the day" earmarked for the pampered guests of Santa Caterina. A buffet luncheon is served daily at the open-air restaurant by the swimming pool. Also, once or twice a week, a special evening buffet accompanied by music is held. Nonresidents can order lunch or dinner, which costs 60,000 lire to 80,000 lire ($47.10 to $62.80).

Services: Room service, baby-sitting, laundry, valet.
Facilities: Saltwater pool.

EXPENSIVE

EXCELSIOR GRAND HOTEL, via Pogerola, 84011 Amalfi. Tel. 089/871344. Fax 089/830255. 97 rms (all with bath). TEL **Bus:** SITA.

$ Rates (including breakfast): 135,000 lire ($105.95) single; 250,000 lire ($196.25) double. AE, DC, MC, V. **Parking:** Free. **Closed:** Nov–Mar.

Three miles from Amalfi at Pogerola, the Excelsior is a modern first-class hotel on the coast. This extravaganza on a high mountain perch outdoes the positions of the nearby cliff-hanging monasteries, and all its rooms are angled toward the view. You get the first glimmer of sunrise and the last rays of golden light. The social center is the 100-foot terrazzo-edged swimming pool filled with filtered mountain spring water. For the lazier folk, there's a nearby garden shaded by umbrellas. The hotel structure is unconventional; the core is a high octagonal glass tower that rises above the central lobby, with exposed mezzanine lounges and an open staircase that leads to the view.

The bedrooms are individually designed, with plenty of room, and the furnishings are chosen with flair. The many good reproductions, some antiques, king-size beds, and tile floors all contrast with the white walls. The private balconies, complete with garden furniture, are the most important feature. For those who want a sea experience, the hotel has a private beach.

Dining/Entertainment: The dining room, with mirrored pillars and ornate blue-and-white tile floors, is a dignified place in which to sample the Italian cuisine with Gallic overtones. Several spots were especially created for a festive stay, notably Bar del Night, where an orchestra plays for dancing on weekends.

Services: Transportation to and from the beach is provided by boat and bus for 10,000 lire ($7.85).

Facilities: Swimming pool.

HOTEL LUNA E TORRE SARACENA, via Comite 19, 84011 Amalfi. Tel. 089/871002. 45 rms (all with bath). TV TEL **Bus:** SITA.

$ **Rates:** 120,000 lire ($94.20) single; 170,000 lire ($133.45) double; from 170,000 lire ($133.45) per person with half board. AE, DC, MC, V. **Parking:** 15,000 lire ($11.80).

This hotel boasts a 13th-century cloister said to have been founded by St. Francis of Assisi. Now converted into a modern hotel, it is a sun trap. The long corridors, where monks of old used to tread, are lined with sitting areas, which are used by the most unmonastic guests. The bedrooms have sea views, terraces, and modern furnishings.

Dining/Entertainment: The rather formal dining room has a coved ceiling, high-backed chairs, arched windows that open toward the water, and good food (Italian and international) served in an efficient manner. The hotel also has a nightclub that projects toward the sea. In summer, an orchestra plays for dancing.

Services: Room service, baby-sitting, laundry, valet.

Facilities: A free-form swimming pool is nestled on the rocks, near the sound of the surf and sea gulls.

MODERATE

HOTEL BELVEDERE, Conca dei Marini, 84011 Amalfi. Tel. 089/831282. Fax 089/831439. 36 rms (all with bath). TEL **Bus:** SITA.

$ **Rates:** 85,000 lire ($66.75) single; 140,000 lire ($109.90) double. Breakfast 15,000 lire ($11.80) extra. 150,000 lire ($117.75) per person with half board. AE, MC, V. **Parking:** Free. **Closed:** Nov–Mar.

Lodged below the coastal road outside Amalfi on the drive to Positano, the aptly named Belvedere possesses one of the best swimming pools in the area. It is in a prime location, hidden from the view and noise of the heavily traveled road, and thrust out toward the sea. Rooms have terraces that overlook the water. Signor Lucibello, who owns the hotel, sees to it that guests are content, and provides, among other things, parking space for your car (a bus takes you into Amalfi). The facilities are serviceable and comfortable.

Dining/Entertainment: Well-prepared Italian meals are served either inside (where walls of windows allow for views of the coast) or on the wide front terrace, with its garden furniture. There is also a cocktail bar.

Services: Room service, baby-sitting, laundry, valet.

Facilities: Swimming pool, outdoor parking space.

HOTEL DEI CAVALIERI, strada Amalfitana, 84011 Amalfi. Tel. 089/831333. Fax 089/831354. 60 rms (all with bath). TEL **Bus:** SITA.

$ Rates (including breakfast): 65,000 lire ($51) single; 130,000 lire ($102.05) double. AE, DC, MC, V. **Parking:** Free.

On a rocky hillside above the busy road between Amalfi and Positano, the Cavalieri was built in an angular design of jutting columns and simple detailing in 1976, but it contains so many antiques that when you enter the lobby you'll get the impression it's much older. My favorite piece is the reception desk, whose massive top is supported by a sextet of growling lions. Upstairs, each bedroom has a tile floor in sparkling patterns and a modern bath. About 20% of the guest rooms contain turn-of-the-century bedroom suites, while the furnishings in the other units are neutral but pleasant. Lunch and dinner are also served, but only to residents.

HOTEL MIRAMALFI, via Quasimodo 3, 84011 Amalfi. Tel. 089/871588. Fax 089/871588. 43 rms (all with bath or shower), 3 suites. MINIBAR TV TEL **Bus:** SITA.

$ Rates: 65,000 lire ($51) single; 121,000 lire ($95) double; from 160,000 lire ($125.60) suite; 95,000 lire ($74.60) per person with half board. AE, DC, MC, V. **Parking:** Free.

On the western edge of Amalfi, the Miramalfi lies below the coastal road and beneath a rocky ledge on its own beach. The rooms at this family-owned and -managed hotel are wrapped around the curving contour of the coastline, and have unobstructed views of the sea. The stone swimming pier—used for sunbathing, diving, and boarding motor launches for waterskiing—is reached by a winding cliffside path, past terraces of grapevines. A space saver is the rooftop parking area. The dining room has glass windows and a few semitropical plants; the food is good and served in abundant portions. Breakfast is provided on one of the main terraces or on your own balcony. Each bedroom is well equipped, with built-in headboards, fine beds, cool tile floors, and efficient maintenance. There is a swimming pool and an elevator to the beach.

INEXPENSIVE

HOTEL LIDOMARE, largo Piccolomini 9, 84011 Amalfi. Tel. 089/ 871332. 13 rms (all with bath). TEL **Bus:** SITA.

$ Rates: 55,000 lire ($43.20) single; 70,000 lire ($54.95) double. Breakfast 10,000 lire ($7.85) extra. AE, DC, MC, V. **Parking:** 12,000 lire ($9.40).

⑤ This pleasant, small hotel is just a few steps from the sea, and its building dates from the 13th century. The high-ceilinged bedrooms are airy and clean, and contain a scattering of modern furniture mixed with Victorian-era antiques. The Camera family are the owners, and they extend a warm welcome to their never-ending stream of foreign visitors. They offer 12 double bedrooms (there is only one single), 7 of which have air conditioning. Breakfast is extra and is the only meal served, but you can order it until 11:30am. This hotel is considered one of the best bargains in Amalfi.

MARINA RIVIERA, via Comite 9, 84011 Amalfi. Tel. 089/871104. Fax 089/871351. 50 rms (all with bath or shower). MINIBAR TV TEL **Bus:** SITA.

$ Rates (including breakfast): 50,000 lire ($39.25) single; 90,000 lire ($70.65) double. AE, DC, MC, V. **Parking:** 10,000 lire ($7.85). **Closed:** Oct 31–Mar 31.

Fifty yards from the beach, this hotel offers rooms with terraces that overlook the sea. Directly on the coastal road, it rises against the foot of the hills, with side verandas and balconies. There is a gracious dining room with high-backed provincial chairs, but meals in the open air are preferred. Two adjoining public lounges are traditionally furnished, and a small bar provides drinks whenever you want them. The refurbished rooms are comfortable, with a balcony and such amenities as a hairdryer. Half the rooms are air-conditioned. The hotel consists of both an older section and a newly built section (rooms in the latter building contain air conditioning).

WHERE TO DINE

DA GEMMA, via Cavalieri di Malta. Tel. 871345. **Cuisine:** SEAFOOD. **Reservations:** Required. **Bus:** SITA.

$ Prices: Appetizers 10,000–14,000 lire ($7.85–$11); main courses 20,000–25,000 lire ($15.70–$19.65). AE, DC, MC, V.
Open: Lunch daily 1–3pm; dinner daily 8pm–midnight. **Closed:** Wed Sept–June.

One of the best restaurants in town, Da Gemma takes inspired liberties with the regional cuisine and gives diners a strong sense of the family unity that makes this place popular. The kitchen sends out plateful after plateful of savory spaghetti, sautéed clams, codfish with fresh tomatoes, or sautéed mixed shellfish, fish casserole, and a full range of other "sea creature" dishes. In summer, the intimate dining room more than doubles with the addition of an outdoor terrace.

IL TARI', via Capuano 9. Tel. 871832.
Cuisine: SEAFOOD. **Reservations:** Not needed. **Bus:** SITA.
$ Prices: Appetizers 8,000–12,000 lire ($6.30–$9.40); main courses 8,000–15,000 lire ($6.30–$11.80). AE, MC, V.
Open: Lunch Wed–Mon noon–3pm; dinner Wed–Mon 7–10pm. **Closed:** Nov.

This is a very small, family-run establishment where diners can see the busy goings-on in the tiny kitchen. The unpretentious restaurant is on the main street of town. The menu items are prepared simply and with flavor. They might include spaghetti with clams, mixed seafood grill, seafood salad, and an array of fish. A specialty is scialatelli alla saracena (pasta with seafood).

LA CARAVELLA, via Matteo Camera. Tel. 871029.
Cuisine: CAMPANIA. **Reservations:** Required. **Bus:** SITA.
$ Prices: Appetizers 10,000–12,000 lire ($7.85–$9.40); main courses 12,000–15,000 lire ($9.40–$11.80). AE, V.
Open: Lunch Wed–Mon 12:30–2:30pm; dinner Wed–Mon 7:30–10:30pm. **Closed:** Nov.

La Caravella is a leading restaurant and, happily, it's inexpensive. A grottolike, air-conditioned place, it's off the main street next to the road tunnel, only a minute from the beach. You get well-cooked, authentic Italian specialties, such as spaghetti Caravella with a seafood sauce. Scaloppine alla Caravella is served with a tangy clam sauce, and a healthy portion of zuppa de pesce (fish soup) is also ladled out. You can have a platter of the mixed fish fry, with crisp, tasty bits of shrimp and squid, followed by an order of fresh fruit served at your table in big bowls.

4. RAVELLO

171 miles S of Rome, 41 miles SE of Naples, 18 miles W of Salerno

GETTING THERE   By Bus   Buses from Amalfi leave for Ravello every hour from 7am to 10pm. Buses leave from the terminal at the waterfront at piazza Flavio Gioia (tel. 871016 for schedules and information). The one-way fare to Ravello is 800 lire (65¢).

By Car   From Amalfi, take a circuitous mountain road north of the town (the road is signposted to Ravello).

ESSENTIALS   The **telephone area code** is 089. The **Tourist Information Center** is at piazza del Duomo 10 (tel. 857096).

Known to personages ranging from Richard Wagner to Greta Garbo, Ravello is the choice spot along the Amalfi Drive. Its reigning celebrity at the moment is Gore Vidal, who purchased a villa as a writing retreat. The village seems to hang 1,100 feet between the Tyrrhenian Sea and some celestial orbit. From Amalfi, 4 miles to the southwest, the sleepy (except for summer tour buses) village is approached by a wickedly curving road that cuts through the villa- and vine-draped hills that hem in the Valley of the Dragone. Celebrated in poetry, song, and literature are Ravello's major attractions, two villas.

WHAT TO SEE & DO

VILLA CIMBRONE, via Santa Chiara 26. Tel. 857138.

A long walk past grape arbors and private villas takes you to the Villa Cimbrone. After ringing the bell for admission, you'll be shown into the vaulted cloisters (on the left as you enter); note the grotesque bas-relief. Later, you can stroll (everybody "strolls" in Ravello) through the gardens, past a bronze copy of Donatello's *David*. Along the rose-arbored walkway is a tiny, but roofless, chapel. At the far end of the garden is a cliffside view of the Bay of Salerno, a scene that the devout might claim was the spot where Satan took Christ to tempt him with the world.

Admission: 4,000 lire ($3.15) adults, 2,000 lire ($1.55) children.
Open: Daily 9am–sunset.

VILLA RUFOLO, piazza Vescovado. Tel. 857866.

Located near the Duomo, Villa Rufolo was named for the patrician family who founded it in the 11th century. Once the residence of kings and popes, such as Hadrian IV, it is now remembered chiefly for its connection with Wagner. He composed an act of *Parsifal* here in a setting he dubbed the "Garden of Klingsor." Boccaccio was so moved by the spot that he included it as background in one of his tales. The Moorish-influenced architecture evokes the Alhambra at Granada. The large tower was built in what is known as the "Norman-Sicilian" influence. You can walk through the flower gardens that lead to lookout points over the memorable coastline.

Admission: 2,000 lire ($1.55).
Open: June–Aug, daily 9:30am–1pm and 3–7pm; Sept–May, daily 9:30am–1pm and 2–5pm. **Bus:** SITA.

WHERE TO STAY

The choice of accommodations at Ravello is limited in number, but large on charm.

VERY EXPENSIVE

HOTEL PALUMBO, via San Giovanni del Toro 28, 84010 Ravello. Tel. 089/857244. Fax 089/857347. 20 rms (all with bath), 3 suites. A/C MINIBAR TV TEL **Bus:** SITA.

$ Rates (including breakfast): 423,000–500,000 lire ($332.05–$392.50) double; from 621,000 lire ($487.50) suite. AE, DC, MC, V. **Parking:** 20,000 lire ($15.70).

This elite retreat on the Amalfi Coast, a 12th-century palace, has been favored by the famous ever since Richard Wagner (who did a lot of composing here) persuaded the Swiss owners, the Vuilleumier family, to take in paying guests. If you stay here you'll understand why Max Reinhardt, Rossano Brazzi, Humphrey Bogart (filming *Beat the Devil*), Henry Wadsworth Longfellow, Ingrid Bergman, Zsa Zsa Gabor, Tennessee Williams, Richard Chamberlain, Gina Lollobrigida, and a young John and Jacqueline Kennedy found its situation in the village ideal. D. H. Lawrence even wrote part of *Lady Chatterley's Lover* while staying here.

The hotel offers gracious living in its series of drawing rooms, furnished with English and Italian antiques. Most of the snug but elegantly decorated bedrooms have a tile bath and their own terrace. Some of the bedrooms are in an annex across the street.

Dining/Entertainment: Meals begin at 60,000 lire ($47.10), and are served in a 17th-century dining room with baroque accents and a dining terrace opening to the panoramic outdoors. "Fill-in" bookings are accepted. The cuisine, the finest in Ravello, shows the influence of the Swiss-Italian ownership. It would be worth it to come here just to enjoy the hotel's lemon and chocolate soufflés. The selection of dishes is likely to vary, but, chances are, you'll be offered crêpes with five cheeses, spaghetti with Gorgonzola, locally caught sole, succulent fresh anchovies, and striped bass stuffed with herbs. The Palumbo also produces its own Episcopio wine, served on the premises. The wine originated in 1860 and is stored in 50,000-liter casks in a vaulted cellar.

Services: Room service, baby-sitting, laundry, valet.
Facilities: Solarium overlooking the Gulf of Salerno.

EXPENSIVE

HOTEL CARUSO BELVEDERE, via San Giovanni del Toro, 84010 Ravello.
Tel. 089/857111. Fax 089/857372. 24 rms (all with bath). TEL **Bus:** SITA.
$ Rates (including half board): 196,000–236,000 lire ($153.85–$185.25) per person. AE, DC, MC, V. **Parking:** 2,000 lire ($1.55).

This spacious clifftop hotel, built into the 11th-century remains of what was once the d'Afflitto Palace, is now operated as a hotel by the Caruso family. It has semitropical gardens and a belvedere that overlooks the Bay of Salerno. From here, you can look down the terraced mountain slopes and see the rows of grapes used to make the "Grand Caruso" wine on the premises. The atmosphere is gracious. The bedrooms have character, some with paneled doors, some with antiques, and some with a private terrace. You'll never forget the arcaded walks, the Gothic arches, the pots of geraniums, the orange and purple bougainvillea, and the wine press with its large vats.

Dining/Entertainment: The indoor dining room has the original coved ceiling, plus tile floors. It opens onto a wide terrace where meals are also served under a canopy. The cuisine is special here. Naturally, the locally produced wines are served: red, white, or rosé.

Services: Room service, baby-sitting, laundry, valet.
Facilities: Garden.

HOTEL RUFOLO, via San Francesco 3, 84010 Ravello. Tel. 089/857133.
Fax 089/857035. 30 rms (all with bath or shower), 2 suites. MINIBAR TV TEL
Bus: SITA.
$ Rates (including breakfast): 85,000 lire ($66.75) single; 130,000–150,000 lire ($102.05–$117.75) double; from 190,000 lire ($149.15) suite. AE, DC, MC, V.
Parking: 5,000 lire ($39.25).

This little gem, run by the hospitable Schiavo family, housed D. H. Lawrence for a long while in 1926. The view from the sundecks is superb, and chairs are placed on a wide terrace and around the swimming pool. The bedrooms are cozy and immaculate, some with air conditioning. Recently enlarged and modernized, the hotel lies in the center between cloisters of pine trees of the Villa Rufolo, from which the hotel takes its name, and the road that leads to the Villa Cimbrone. Mr. Schiavo and his family take good care of their guests.

Dining/Entertainment: Food served in the restaurant is quite good, and the service is efficient. Meals begin at 40,000 lire ($31.40).

Services: Room service, baby-sitting, laundry.
Facilities: Swimming pool

MODERATE

HOTEL GIORDANO E VILLA MARIA, piazza del Duomo, 84010 Ravello.
Tel. 089/857170. Fax 089/857071. 26 rms (all with bath or shower). TEL **Bus:** SITA.
$ Rates (including half board): 110,000 lire ($86.35) single; 130,000 lire ($102.05) double. AE, MC, V. **Parking:** Free.

These two treasures of the Amalfi Coast lie in tranquil groves between Villa Rufolo and Villa Cimbrone. Villa Maria, in an old and charming building that has been decorated tastefully with high-quality antiques, overlooks the sea and has a restaurant set in a garden. The more contemporary Giordano has a swimming pool (heated in winter) just a few feet from the rooms. Guests use the facilities of both places, which includes a solarium, music room, and a dance floor. In season pizza parties are popular. The Villa Maria's restaurant serves quality meals with regional specialties not likely to be available elsewhere. Its wine cellar is excellent, and the chef prepares delectable meals with fresh vegetables taken from the garden. The ambience is magnificent, and you can enjoy one of the most spectacular views along the coast. Even if you're not a guest, you may want to dine here, at a cost of 40,000 lire ($31.40) and up for a meal. In 15 minutes, guests can reach the beach by walking along old paths or by public buses that leave every hour from the central square. Plenty of parking is available.

HOTEL PARSIFAL, via G. D'Anna 5, 84010 Ravello. Tel. 089/857144.
Fax 089/857972. 19 rms (all with bath or shower). TEL **Bus:** SITA.
$ Rates: 70,000 lire ($54.95) single; 95,000 lire ($74.60) double; 125,000 lire ($98.15) per person with half board. AE, DC, MC, V. **Parking:** Street parking only.

This little hotel incorporates portions of the original convent, founded in 1288 by Augustinian monks who had an uncanny instinct for picking the best views, and the most inspiring situations in which to build their retreats. The cloister, with stone arches and a tile walk, has a multitude of potted flowers and vines, and the garden spots, especially the one with a circular reflection pool, are the favorites of all. Chairs are placed for guests to watch the setting sun and fiery lights that illuminate the twisting shoreline. Dining is preferred on the trellis-covered terrace where bougainvillea and wisteria scents mix with that of lemon blossoms. The living rooms have bright and comfortable furnishings, set against pure white walls. The bedrooms, while small, are tastefully arranged. A few rooms have a terrace.

VILLA AMORE, via dei Fusco 5, 84010 Ravello. Tel. 089/857135. 15 rms (all with bath). TEL **Bus:** SITA.
$ Rates (including breakfast): 88,000 lire ($69.10) double; 68,000 lire ($53.40) per person with half board. AE, DC, MC, V. **Parking:** Street parking only.
This is a small converted villa like the Albergo Toro (see below). From some of its pleasantly furnished bedroom windows there is a view of the coastline. Only doubles are rented. Good-tasting regional meals are served every day but Monday.

INEXPENSIVE

ALBERGO TORO, viale Wagner 3, 84010 Ravello. Tel. 089/847211. 9 rms (8 with bath). TEL **Bus:** SITA.
$ Rates (including breakfast): 38,000 lire ($29.85) single without bath, 43,500 lire ($34.15) single with bath; 79,000 lire ($62) double with bath; 76,000 lire ($59.65) per person with full board. AE, MC, V. **Closed:** Nov–Mar 15.

This place is a real bargain. It is a small, charming villa that has been converted to receive paying guests. The Toro—entered through a garden—lies just off the village square with its cathedral. It has semimonastic architecture, with deeply set arches, long colonnades, and a tranquil character. The rooms are decent, and the owner is especially proud of the meals he serves.

WHERE TO DINE

Most guests take meals at their hotels. But try to escape the board requirement at least once to sample the goods at the following establishments.

CUMPA' COSIMO, via Roma. Tel. 857156.
Cuisine: CAMPANIA. **Reservations:** Recommended. **Bus:** SITA.
$ Prices: Appetizers 3,000–5,000 lire ($2.35–$3.95); main courses 8,000–10,000 lire ($6.30–$7.85). AE, V.
Open: Lunch daily 12:30–3pm; dinner daily 7:30–10pm. **Closed:** Mon Nov–Mar.

This restaurant's clientele is likely to include everyone from the electrician down the street to a well-known movie star searching for the best home-cooking in town. The kitchen turns out food items sometimes based on old recipes. Try the house version of tagliatelle, followed perhaps by a mixed fish grill, giant prawns, or roast lamb well seasoned with herbs. Many other regional dishes are offered as well. For dessert, try one of several flavors of homemade ice cream. In summertime, part of the premises is transformed into a pizzeria.

RISTORANTE GARDEN, via Boccaccio 4, 84010 Ravello. Tel. 089/857226.

Cuisine: CAMPANIA. **Reservations:** Not needed. **Bus:** SITA.
$ Prices: Appetizers 6,000–8,000 lire ($4.70–$6.30); main courses 7,000–9,000 lire ($5.50–$7.05). MC, V.
Open: Lunch Wed–Mon 12:30–3pm; dinner Wed–Mon 7:30–10pm.

Perhaps this pleasant restaurant's greatest claim to fame occurred in 1962 when Jacqueline Onassis, then the wife of President Kennedy, came from a villa where she was staying to dine here with the owner of Fiat. Today some of that old glamour is still visible on the verdant terrace, which was designed to cantilever over the cliff below. The Mansi family offers well-prepared meals, which might include one of four kinds of spaghetti, cheese crêpes, and an array of soups, a well-presented antipasto table, brochettes of grilled shrimp, a mixed fish fry, and sole prepared in several ways. One of the local wines will be recommended.

On the premises are 10 well-scrubbed rooms, each with its own bath and terrace. Doubles cost 95,000 lire ($74.60), including breakfast. Half board is 85,000 lire ($66.75) per person.

5. PAESTUM

25 miles S of Salerno, 62 miles S of Naples, 189 miles S of Rome

GETTING THERE By Train Paestum is within easy reach of Salerno, an hour away. Both buses and trains service the route. You can catch a southbound train, which departs Salerno with a stop at Paestum about every 2 hours. For schedules, call 231415 in Salerno. A one-way fare is 2,000 lire ($1.55).

By Bus You can also take a bus in Salerno from piazza Concordia (near the rail station); one leaves for Paestum about every 30 minutes. The bus station in Salerno is at corso Garibaldi 117 (tel. 226604). A one-way fare is 2,000 lire ($1.55).

By Car From Salerno, take Route 18 south.

ESSENTIALS The **telephone area code** is 0828. The **Tourist Information Center** is on via Magna Grecia (tel. 811016), in the archeological zone.

The ancient Sybarite city of Paestum (Poseidonia) dates back to 600 B.C. It was abandoned for centuries and fell to ruins. But the remnants of its past, excavated in the mid-18th century, are glorious—the finest heritage left from the Greek colonies that settled in Italy. The roses of Paestum, praised by the ancients, bloom two times yearly, splashing the landscape of the city with a scarlet red, a good foil for the salmon-colored temples that still stand in the archeological garden.

WHAT TO SEE & DO

The **basilica** is a Doric temple that dates from the 6th century B.C., the oldest temple from the ruins of the Hellenic world in Italy. The basilica is characterized by 9 columns in front and 18 on the sides. The Doric pillars are approximately 5 feet in diameter. Walls and ceiling, however, have long given way to decay. Animals were sacrificed to gods on the altar.

The **Temple of Neptune** is the most impressive of the Greek ruins at Paestum. It and the Temple of Haphaistos ("Theseum") in Athens remain the best-preserved Greek temples in the world, both dating from around 450 to 420 B.C. Six columns in front are crowned by an entablature, and there are 14 columns on the sides. The **Temple of Caeres,** from the 6th century B.C., has 34 columns still standing and a large altar for sacrifices to the gods.

The temple zone may be visited Tuesday through Sunday from 9am to 5pm for an admission fee of 3,000 lire ($2.35). Using the same ticket, you can visit the **archeological museum** (tel. 811023), across the road from the Caeres Temple. It displays the metopes removed from the treasury of the Temple of Hera (Juno). It is open from 9am to 2pm (until 1pm on Sunday). The museum is closed Monday, which is a bad day to head south in general because of the closings around Naples and Pompeii.

New discoveries have revealed hundreds of Greek tombs, which have yielded many Greek paintings. Archeologists have called the find astonishing. In addition, other tombs excavated were found to contain clay figures in a strongly impressionistic vein.

WHERE TO STAY

STRAND HOTEL SCHUHMANN, via Laura Mare, 84063 Paestum. Tel. 0828/851151. Fax 0828/851183. 28 rms (all with bath or shower). TEL **Bus:** Paestum bus from Salerno.

$ Rates (including half board): 100,000 lire ($78.50) per person. AE, DC, MC, V. **Parking:** Free.

If you'd like to combine serious looks at Italy's archeological past with the first-class amenities of a beachside resort, try the Strand Hotel Schuhmann, a delightful choice for a holiday. From a base here, you can make trips to Amalfi, Sorrento, Pompeii, Capri, Herculaneum, and Vesuvius—let the crowds fight it out on the overcrowded Amalfi Coast. Set in a pine grove removed from traffic noises, the hotel has a large terrace with a view of the sea and a subtropical garden that overlooks the Gulf of Salerno and the Amalfi Coast to Capri. Its bedrooms are well furnished and maintained, and each has a balcony or terrace. Guests get use of the beach facilities and deck chairs. The Italian cookery is first rate, and even if you're visiting Paestum only on a day trip, consider having a meal here, which will cost 32,000 lire ($25.10) and up.

WHERE TO DINE

NETTUNO RISTORANTE, Zona Archeologica. Tel. 811028.

Cuisine: CAMPANIA. **Reservations:** Not needed. **Bus:** Paestum bus from Salerno.

$ Prices: Appetizers 8,000–10,000 lire ($6.30–$7.85); main courses 15,000–18,000 lire ($11.80–$14.15). AE, DC, MC, V.

Open: Lunch (May–June and Sept–Oct) daily 12:30–3pm; dinner (July–Aug only) daily 7:30–10pm. **Closed:** Mon Nov–Feb.

While at Paestum, you may want to take time out for lunch. If so, you'll find the Nettuno a special place at which to dine. It stands in a meadow just at the edge of the ruins, like a country inn or villa. The interior dining room has vines growing over its arched windows, and from the tables there is a good view of the ruins. The ceilings are beamed, the room divided by three Roman stone arches. Outside, there is a terrace for dining that faces the temples—like a stage for a Greek drama. Under pine trees, hedged in by pink oleander, you can order such a typical selection as beefsteak or roast chicken, a vegetable or salad, plus dessert. Menu suggestions include spaghetti with filets in tomato sauce, veal cutlet, and crème caramel.

6. CAPRI

3 miles off the tip of the Sorrentine peninsula

GETTING THERE **By Boat** You can go from Naples by **hydrofoil** in just 45 minutes with boats departing from Molo Beverello. The hydrofoil (*aliscafo*) leaves several times daily (some stop at Sorrento). A one-way trip costs 13,400 lire ($10.50). It's cheaper but longer (about 1½ hours) to go by regularly scheduled **ferryboat,** with a one-way ticket costing 7,300 lire ($5.75). For schedules, call 081/8377577 in Naples.

ESSENTIALS There is no need to have a car in tiny Capri, and they are virtually impossible to drive on the hairpin roads anyway. The island is serviced by funiculars, taxis, and buses. Many of Capri's hotels are remotely located, especially those at

Anacapri, and some are inaccessible by car. I strongly recommend that visitors to the island arrive with as little luggage as possible. However, with even minor baggage, you may need the services of a porter. You'll find the headquarters of the island's union of porters in a building connected to the jetty at Marina Grande. There you can cajole, coddle, coerce, or connive your way through the hiring process where the only rule seems to be that there are no rules.

One positive aspect to the business is that your porter will know where to find the hotel among the winding passageways and steep inclines of the island's arteries. Your best defense during your pilgrimage might be a sense of humor.

The **telephone area code** is 081.

The broiling dog-day July and August sun that beats down on Capri illuminates a circus of humanity. The parade of visitors would give Ripley's "Believe It or Not" material for months. In the upper town, a vast snakelike chain of gaudily attired tourists promenades through the narrow quarters (many of the lanes evoke the casbahs of North Africa).

The Greeks called Capri (pronounced *Cap*-ry, not Ca-*pree*, as in the old song) "the island of the wild boars." Before the big season rush, which lasts from Easter to the end of October, Capri is an island of lush Mediterranean vegetation (olives, vineyards, flowers) encircled by emerald waters, an oasis in the sun even before the days of that swinger Tiberius, who moved the seat of the empire here. Writers such as D. H. Lawrence have in previous decades found Capri a haven. Some have written of it, including Axel Munthe (*The Story of San Michele*) and Norman Douglas (*Siren Land*). The latter title is a reference to Capri's reputation as the "island of the sirens," a temptation to Ulysses. Other distinguished visitors have included Gide, Mendelssohn, Dumas, and Hans Christian Andersen.

Don't visit Capri, incidentally, for great beaches, as there aren't any. The mountainous landscape doesn't make for long sandy beaches. There are some spots for bathing, and many of these have been turned into clubs called *stabilimenti balneari,* which you must pay to visit.

Touring the island is relatively simple. You dock at unremarkable **Marina Grande,** the port area. From there, you can take the funicular to the town of **Capri** above, site of the major hotels, restaurants, cafés, and shops. From Capri, a short bus ride will deliver you to **Anacapri,** at the top of the island near Monte Solaro. The only other settlement you might want to visit is **Marina Piccola,** on the south side of the island. The major beach is here. There are also beaches as Punta Carnea and Bagni di Tiberio. The tourist office will pinpoint these locations on a map for you.

MARINA GRANDE

The least attractive of the island's communities, Marina Grande is the port, and it bustles with the coming and going of hundreds of visitors daily. It has a little sand-cum-pebble beach, on which you're likely to see American sailors—on shore leave from Naples—playing ball, occasionally upsetting a Coca-Cola over mamma and bambino.

If you're just spending the day on Capri, you should leave at once for the island's biggest attraction, the ✪ **Grotto Azzurra (Blue Grotto),** open daily from 9am till 1 hour before sunset. In summer, boats that leave frequently from the harbor at Marina Grande transport passengers to the entrance of the grotto for 6,650 lire ($5.20) round-trip. Once at the grotto, you'll pay 7,750 lire ($6.10) for the small rowboat that traverses the water. Admission is another 4,000 lire ($3.15).

You'll have to change boats to go under the low entrance to the cave. The toughened boatmen of the Campania are usually skilled at getting heavier passengers from the big boat into the skimpy craft with a minimum of volcanic spills.

The Blue Grotto is one of the best-known natural sights of the region, although the way passengers are hustled in and out of it makes it somewhat of a tourist trap. It is beautiful, however, but because of all the shabby commercialism that surrounds it, many passengers opt to miss it. Known to the ancients, it was later lost to the world until an artist stumbled on it in 1826. Inside the cavern, light refraction (the sun's rays entering from an opening under the water) achieves the dramatic Mediterranean cerulean color. The effect is stunning, as thousands testify yearly.

If you wish, you can take a trip around the entire island, passing not only the Blue Grotto, but the Baths of Tiberius, the "Palazzo al Mare" built in the days of the empire, the Green Grotto (less known), and the much-photographed rocks called the Faraglioni. The motorboats circle the island in about 1½ hours at a cost of 14,550 lire ($11.40) per person.

Connecting Marina Grande with Capri (the town) is a frequent-running funicular that charges 3,000 lire ($2.35) round-trip. However, should you arrive off-season, the funicular, really a cog railway, doesn't operate. Instead, you can take a bus from Marina Grande to Capri at a one-way cost of 1,500 lire ($1.20).

For information, get in touch with the **Tourist Board,** piazza Umberto I no. 19 (tel. 8370686), at Capri, open daily from 8am to 2pm.

CAPRI

The main town is the center of most of the hotels, restaurants, and elegant shops—and the milling throngs. The heart of the resort, piazza Umberto I, is like a grand living room.

WHAT TO SEE & DO

One of the most popular walks from the main square is down via Vittorio Emanuele, past the deluxe Quisisana, to the **Gardens of Augustus.** The park is the choice spot in Capri for views and relaxation. From this perch, you can see the legendary Faraglioni, the rocks, one inhabited by the "blue lizard." At the top of the park is a belvedere that overlooks emerald waters and Marina Piccola. Nearby you can visit the **Certosa,** a Carthusian monastery erected in the 14th century in honor of St. James. The monastery is open daily except Monday from 9am to 2pm and charges no admission.

Back at piazza Umberto I, head up via Longano, then via Tiberio, all the way to Monte Tiberio. Here is **Villa Jovis,** the splendid ruin of the estate from which Tiberius ruled the empire from A.D. 27 to 37. Actually, the Jovis was one of a dozen villas that the depraved emperor erected on the island. Apparently Tiberius couldn't sleep, so he wandered from bed to bed. From the ruins there is a view of both the Bay of Salerno and the Bay of Naples, as well as of the island. The ruins of the imperial palace may be visited daily from 9am to 1 hour before sunset for 2,000 lire ($1.55) admission.

Shopping

Capri has a collection of the chicest boutiques in all of southern Italy. The following is only a brief preview to get you started—there are dozens more.

LA PARISIENNE, piazza Umberto I. Tel. 8370283.

This place is passed by everybody at least once on a visit, as it stands right at the heartbeat center. Fashions have changed a lot since it first opened in 1906, and, except for a wartime slump, it still keeps abreast of what is current in the fashion world. Clothes sold in this store are made right on the island by local women. Open Monday through Saturday 9am to 9pm.

MODA CAPRESE, via Camerelle 61. Tel. 8378732.

Moda Caprese is known for its selection of Capri knitwear. Colors are bright and vibrant, like the island itself. Open Monday through Saturday from 9 or 9:30am to 10pm.

CHANTECLER, via Vittorio Emanuele 51. Tel. 8370544.

This place opened right after World War II and has been going strong ever since. It is the leading jewelry store on the island, and its jewelry is imaginative in design and style. Many items are very expensive, but if you hunt carefully there is some real value here. Another branch at via Camerelle 45 (tel. 8370067) keeps the same hours. Open Monday through Saturday from 10am to 9pm.

CARTHUSIA, via Camerelle 10. Tel. 8370529.

This little shop specializes in perfume made on the island. The scents are unique, and many women consider Capri perfumes to be collector's items. Open daily from 9am to 9:30pm.

WHERE TO STAY

Finding your own bed for the night can be a real problem if you arrive in July or August without a reservation. There is a far greater demand for rooms than there is a supply. Capri is also an exclusive enclave of the wealthy, and even the cheaper accommodations are able to charge high prices. Many serious economizers return to the mainland for the night, unable to pay the steep tariffs of Capri.

Very Expensive

LA SCALINATELLA [Little Steps], via Tragara 8, 80073 Capri. Tel. 081/8370633. Fax 081/8378291. 30 rms (all with bath), 8 suites. A/C MINIBAR TV TEL **Transportation:** Capri funicular.

$ Rates (including breakfast): 250,000 lire ($196.25) single; 370,000 lire ($290.45) double; from 450,000 lire ($353.25) suite. No credit cards. **Closed:** Nov 15–Mar 15.

One of the most delightful hotels in Capri is constructed above terraces that offer a magnificent view of the water and of a nearby monastery. The ambience is one of unadulterated luxury; rooms include a phone beside each of the bathtubs, beds set into alcoves, elaborate wrought-iron accents that ring both the inner stairwell and the ornate balconies, and a sweeping view over the establishment's surrounding gardens and its swimming pool.

QUISISANA & GRAND HOTEL, via Camerelle 2, 80073 Capri. Tel. 081/8370788. Fax 081/8376080. 150 rms (all with bath), 15 suites. A/C MINIBAR TV TEL **Transportation:** Capri funicular.

$ Rates (including breakfast): 250,000–320,000 lire ($196.25–$251.20) single; 390,000–530,000 lire ($306.15–$416.05) double; from 650,000 lire ($510.25) suite. AE, DC, MC, V. **Closed:** Dec–Mar.

The deluxe choice is the Quisisana & Grand Hotel, the favorite nesting place for a regular international clientele. Opened as a small hotel around the turn of the century, the Quisisana was enlarged and became the foremost of the resort hotels here after World War II. More spacious than its central location would indicate, its private garden is shut off form the crisscross tourism outside its front entrance. A large, rather sprawling, but imposing, structure, its bedrooms range from cozy singles to spacious suites—all of which open onto wide arcades with a view of the seacoast. They vary greatly in decor, with both traditional and conservatively modern furnishings. In the main lounge the furnishings are in antique gold. Capri's social center, the terrace of the hotel, is where everybody who is anybody goes for cocktails before dinner.

Dining/Entertainment: There is a formal dining room, with an entire wall of glass that provides views of the park, but a preferred luncheon spot is in the courtyard, where meals are served under a suspended canopy. The head chef is proud of his fresh-tasting and attractively displayed fish dishes, as well as his lush fruits and vegetables. The American bar (which seems appropriate to Berkeley Square, London) is the second-most-frequented spot on the premises, and overlooks the swimming pool on the lower terrace.

Services: Room service, baby-sitting, laundry, valet.

Facilities: Sauna and massage facilities, indoor and outdoor swimming pool, beauty shop.

Expensive

HOTEL FLORA, via Federico Serena 26, 80073 Capri. Tel. 081/8370211. Fax 081/8378949. 24 rms (all with bath). A/C MINIBAR TV TEL **Transportation:** Capri funicular.

$ Rates (including breakfast): 165,000 lire ($129.55) single; 310,000 lire ($243.35) double. AE, DC, MC, V. **Closed:** Nov–Mar.

The Hotel Flora overlooks the Monastery of St. James and the sea, and features terraces edged with oleander, bougainvillea, and geraniums. There are several tile courtyards with garden furniture, pots of tropical flowers, and spots where you can either sunbathe or be cooled by the sea breezes. The public and private rooms are a wise blend of the old and new. The bedrooms are well furnished. There is an annex across the street.

HOTEL LA PAZZIELLA, via P. R. Giuliani 4, 80073 Capri. Tel. 081/ 8370044. Fax 081/8370085. 20 rms (all with bath), 3 suites. A/C MINIBAR TV TEL **Transportation:** Capri funicular.

$ Rates (including breakfast): 200,000 lire ($157) single; 300,000 lire ($235.50) double; from 350,000 lire ($274.75) suite. AE, DC, MC, V.

This place, with walls of white concrete, is set behind a small garden and located only a few pedestrian minutes from the center of Capri. Inside, an expanse of patterned tiles supports the scattering of antique and modern furniture, as well as a handful of plants. Each bedroom has cool white walls and tile floors.

HOTEL LUNA, viale Matteotti 3, 80073 Capri. Tel. 081/8370433. Fax 081/8377459. 44 rms (all with bath). A/C MINIBAR TV TEL **Transportation:** Capri funicular.

$ Rates (including breakfast): 165,000 lire ($129.55) single; 250,000–360,000 lire ($196.25–$282.60) double; 175,000–210,000 lire ($137.40–$164.85) per person with half board. AE, DC, MC, V. **Closed:** Oct 31–Easter.

This first-class hotel stands on a cliff overlooking the sea and the rocks of Faraglioni. It's almost between the Gardens of Augustus and the Carthusian Monastery of St. James. The building, however, is nondescript. The furnishings are reproductions of antiques. Architecturally, the tile designs for the floor set the pace. The bedrooms, a mixture of contemporary Italian pieces and a Victorian decor, incorporate wood and padded headboards and gilt mirrors over the desk, all consistently in good style. Some of the bedrooms have arched, recessed private terraces that overlook the garden of flowers and semitropical plants. There's a clubby drinking lounge, and the dining room lures with good cuisine.

HOTEL PUNTA TRAGARA, via Tragara 57, 80073 Capri. Tel. 081/ 8370844. Fax 081/8377790. 33 rms (all with bath), 35 suites. A/C MINIBAR TV TEL **Transportation:** Capri funicular.

$ Rates (including breakfast): 295,000 lire ($231.60) double; 345,000 lire ($270.85) junior suite for two. Half board 50,000 lire ($39.25) per person extra. AE, DC, MC, V.

This former private villa stands at the tip of the most desirable panorama in Capri, but that isn't all it has in its favor. Its sienna-colored walls and Andalusian-style accents are designed so that each of the apartment accommodations is subtly different from its neighbors. Outfitted with mottled carpeting, big windows, substantial furniture, and all the modern comforts, each unit opens onto a private terrace or a balcony studded with flowers and vines. On the premises are two swimming pools, one of which is heated, plus multibranched cactus plants in oval terra-cotta pots, quiet retreats near a baronial fireplace, and a grotto disco.

LA PALMA, via Vittorio Emanuele 39, 80073 Capri. Tel. 081/8370133. Fax 081/8376966. 80 rms (all with bath). A/C MINIBAR TV TEL **Transportation:** Capri funicular.

$ Rates (including breakfast): 230,000 lire ($180.55) single; 346,000 lire ($271.60) double; 220,000–260,000 lire ($172.70–$204.10) per person with half board. AE, DC, MC, V.

La Palma is a gem. Right in the center of Capri, this heartbeat hotel caters to guests who seek first-class amenities and comforts—and who are willing to pay the piper for the privilege. Restored and renovated in an appealing style that blends modern and

IMPRESSIONS

Capri is not the place for moralizing.
—NORMAN DOUGLAS, *FOOTNOTE ON CAPRI*, 1952

traditional styles, the hotel has a white-walled exterior, and a forecourt with palms and potted shrubs. Each bedroom is handsomely furnished.

Dining/Entertainment: Its restaurant, Relais la Palma, is one of the finest dinner choices in Capri if you'd like to make a reservation in the evening. Meals cost 40,000 lire to 75,000 lire ($31.40 to $58.90).

LA PINETA, via Tragara 6, 80073 Capri. Tel. 081/8370644. Fax 081/8376445. 54 rms (all with bath), 10 suites. A/C MINIBAR TV TEL **Transportation:** Capri funicular.

$ Rates (including breakfast): 180,000 lire ($141.30) single; 275,000 lire ($215.90) double; from 400,000 lire ($314) suite. AE, DC, MC, V.

This is that rare hotel in Capri that remains open all year. Built in 1952, it has been receiving visitors ever since. A four-star hotel, it's on one of the most enchanting walks on the island. A terraced hotel, it lures with its contemporary decor and swimming pool where you can enjoy lunch daily from noon to 5pm. The swimming pool is heated during spring and autumn. Most of the well-furnished bedrooms are air-conditioned.

Moderate

LA CERTOSELLA, via Tragara 15, 80073 Capri. Tel. 081/8370713. Fax 081/8370541. 12 rms (all with bath). MINIBAR TEL **Transportation:** Capri funicular.

$ Rates (including breakfast): 75,000 lire ($58.90) single; 140,000 lire ($109.90) double. AE, V. **Closed:** Nov 15–Easter.

This little three-star hotel is one of the best on the island for value. For years it has been a haven for artists and writers, many of whom call it "Azunta's," after its owner, who has been dubbed "Queen of Capri." Actors from Rome as well as discerning people from all over the world have made their way to its doorstep to enjoy the bloom of its jasmine, wisteria, and hydrangea, as well as its swimming pool. The rooms have been renovated and are well kept and comfortable; some contain TV. The view is outstanding. The hotel also has a handsome garden. La Certosella is mainly known for its restaurant, which some critics consider the best in Capri.

LA VEGA, via Occhio Marino 10, 80073 Capri. Tel. 081/8370481. Fax 081/8370550). 23 rms (all with bath). A/C TEL **Transportation:** Capri funicular.

$ Rates (including breakfast): 110,000 lire ($86.35) single; 180,000 lire ($141.30) double. AE, DC, MC, V. **Closed:** Oct 31–Easter.

This little sun-pocket hotel with a clear view of the sea is nestled against the hillside. Each of the oversize rooms of this four-level building has a shower, and a private balcony that overlooks the water. Below the rooms is a garden of flowering bushes, and on the lower edge is a free-form swimming pool with a grassy border for sunbathing and a little bar for refreshments. The rooms have decoratively tiled floors and the beds have wrought-iron headboards. Some contain TV. All rooms are doubles, but when there is space, singles are booked in here at the rate given above. Breakfast is served on a terrace surrounded by trees and large potted flowers.

REGINA CRISTINA, via Serena 20, 80073 Capri. Tel. 081/8370744. Fax 081/8370550. 55 rms (all with bath), 5 suites. A/C MINIBAR TV TEL **Transportation:** Capri funicular.

$ Rates (including breakfast): 130,000 lire ($102.05) single; 220,000 lire ($172.70) double; from 314,000 lire ($245.50) suite; 150,000–170,000 lire ($117.75–$133.45) per person with half board. AE, DC, MC, V.

The pale-azure facade of the Regina Cristina rises four stories above one of the most imaginatively landscaped gardens in Capri. It was built in 1959 in a sun-flooded design of open spaces, sunken lounges, cool tiles, and *la dolce vita* armchairs. Each accommodation has its own balcony, and lots of calm.

Inexpensive

PENSIONE VILLA BIANCA, via Belvedere Casina 9, 80073 Capri. Tel. 081/8378016. 8 rms (all with bath). **Transportation:** Capri funicular.

$ Rates (including breakfast): 50,000 lire ($39.25) single; 90,000 lire ($70.65) double. No credit cards. **Closed:** Dec–Feb.

The Pensione Villa Bianca is one of the best bargains at the resort. It's run by English-speaking Augusto Ferraro, who has been most helpful to readers in the past. Rooms without a sea view have the use of a roof terrace. A kitchen is available. All is comfortably old fashioned.

VILLA KRUPP, via Matteotti 12, 80073 Capri. Tel. 081/8370362. 15 rms (all with bath), 4 suites. TEL **Transportation:** Capri funicular.

$ Rates (including breakfast): 85,000 lire ($66.75) single; 140,000 lire ($109.90) double; from 150,000 lire ($117.75) suite. V.

This place is a sun-pocket villa-turned-guesthouse, which overlooks the Gardens of Augustus. Surrounded by shady trees, it offers a splendid view of the sea from its lofty terraces. A family-run place, it has the advantage of intimacy. The front parlor is all glass; it has views of the seaside, and semitropical plants set near Hong Kong chairs, all intermixed with painted Venetian-style pieces. Your bedroom may be large, with a fairly good bathroom. Many of the rooms have a terrace. Breakfast is the only meal offered.

VILLA SARAH, via Tiberio 3A, 80073 Capri. Tel. 081/8377817. 20 rms (all with bath). TEL **Transportation:** Capri funicular.

$ Rates (including breakfast): 80,000–90,000 lire ($62.80–$70.65) single; 140,000–160,000 lire ($109.90–$125.60) double. AE. **Closed:** Oct 15–Easter.

The Villa Sarah, although far removed from the day "trippers" over from Naples, is still very central. A steep walk from the main square, it seems part of another world with its Capri garden and good views. All it lacks is a swimming pool. Considered one of the bargains of the island, it is often fully booked, so reservations are needed if you arrive in summer. The view of the sea is only from the upper floors. An old private house stands on the grounds, but it is no longer in use as a hotel—the hotel section of bedrooms is in a modern building. Some bedrooms have terraces, and others contain TVs. Only breakfast is served.

WHERE TO DINE

Expensive

AL GERANIO, Giardini Augusto, viale Matteotti 8. Tel. 8370616.
Cuisine: SEAFOOD/MEDITERRANEAN. **Reservations:** Required Fri–Sat. **Transportation:** Capri funicular.

$ Prices: Appetizers 10,000–12,000 lire ($7.85–$9.40); main courses 16,000–18,000 lire ($12.55–$14.15). AE, DC.

Open: Lunch Wed–Mon 12:30–3pm; dinner Wed–Mon 7:30–10pm. **Closed:** Oct 30–Easter.

One of the most scenically located restaurants in Capri, Al Geranio stands in the Gardens of Augustus en route to the Villa Krupp. It can be easily reached from two of the leading hotels of Capri, the Quisisana and the Luna. You can arrive early to enjoy an apéritif in the piano bar, furnished in a modern style. The earlier you arrive in summer, the better chance you have of getting an outdoor table. The kitchen turns out a good Mediterranean cuisine which is likely to include such dishes as fish soup, fried shrimp, swordfish, crêpes with cheese, and cannelloni. A savory dish to order is zuppa di cozze (mussel soup). You might also try Capri-style ravioli. Look for the daily specials.

I FARAGLIONI, via Camerelle 75. Tel. 8370320.
   Cuisine: SEAFOOD/CONTINENTAL. **Reservations:** Required. **Transportation:** Capri funicular.
$ **Prices:** Appetizers 15,000–20,000 lire ($11.80–$15.70); main courses 20,000–30,000 lire ($15.70–$23.55). AE, V.
   Open: Lunch Tues–Sun 12:30–3pm; dinner Tues–Sun 7:30pm–midnight.
   Closed: Nov–Mar.

Some of the wits of the island say that the food is only a secondary consideration to the social ferment that usually seems to be part of this popular restaurant. In any event, the kitchen turns out a well-prepared collection of European specialties, which is usually based on seafood from the surrounding waters. Examples might include linguine with lobster, seafood crêpes, rice Créole, spaghetti with clams, grilled or baked fish of many different varieties, and a wide assortment of meat dishes. Desserts might be made of one of the regional pastries mixed with fresh fruit.

LA CERTOSELLA, via Tragara 13. Tel. 8370713.
   Cuisine: SEAFOOD. **Reservations:** Required. **Transportation:** Capri funicular.
$ **Prices:** Appetizers 14,000–18,000 lire ($11–$14.15); main courses 12,000–20,000 lire ($9.40–$15.70). AE, DC, MC, V.
   Open: Lunch daily 12:30–2:30pm; dinner daily 7:30–10pm. **Closed:** Oct–May.

La Certosella is considered the best on the island. In a garden setting of hydrangea, wisteria, and bougainvillea, you can enjoy the cuisine of a place its bohemian clientele decades ago labeled "Azunta's," after the owner. Its little hotel has already been previewed, but La Certosella is known mainly for its restaurant. It's the choice of many a discriminating palate, which includes the designer Emilio Pucci when he's on the island. The cuisine is not elaborate but it's good, well prepared, and not disguised so that you can't recognize what you are eating. You get some of the freshest fish on the island, and most customers prefer it grilled. You might begin with a tasty risotto or one of the pasta dishes such as spaghetti with zucchini. The house wine is a delectable Tiberio. Guests dine around a pool.

Moderate

CASANOVA, via Le Botteghe 46. Tel. 8377642.
   Cuisine: NEAPOLITAN/ITALIAN. **Reservations:** Required at dinner in summer.
   Transportation: Capri funicular.
$ **Prices:** Appetizers 6,000–12,000 lire ($4.70–$9.40); main courses 12,000–15,000 lire ($9.40–$11.80); fixed-price menu 30,000 lire ($23.55). AE, DC, MC, V.
   Open: Lunch Fri–Wed noon–3pm; dinner Fri–Wed 7pm–midnight. **Closed:** Nov 4–Mar 15.

Run by the D'Alessio family, and only a short walk from piazza Umberto I, this is one of the finest dining rooms in Capri. Its cellar offers a big choice of Italian wines, with most of the favorites of the Campania, and its cooks turn out a savory blend of Neapolitan and Italian specialties. You might begin with a cheese-filled ravioli, then go on to veal Sorrento or even red snapper "crazy waters" (with baby tomatoes). The seafood is always fresh and well prepared. A large and tempting buffet of antipasti is at hand.

DA GEMMA, via Madre Serafina 6. Tel. 8370461.
   Cuisine: REGIONAL/SEAFOOD. **Reservations:** Required. **Transportation:** Capri funicular.
$ **Prices:** Appetizers 6,000–12,000 lire ($4.70–$9.40); main courses 10,000–20,000 lire ($7.85–$15.70). AE, DC, MC, V.
   Open: Lunch Tues–Sun 12:30–3pm; dinner Tues–Sun 7:30–midnight. **Closed:** Nov.

Long a favorite with painters and writers, this place is reached from piazza Umberto I by going up an arch-covered walkway, reminiscent of Tangier, Morocco. Some tables are arranged for the view. Everything's cozy and atmospheric. The cuisine is provincial, with a reliance on fish dishes. The best beginning is the mussel soup, and pizzas are also featured in the evening. The best main dish to order is the boiled fish of the day with creamy butter, priced according to weight. Desserts are mouth-watering. It has an annex across the street that remains open in winter.

LA CAPANNIA, via Le Botteghe 14. Tel. 8370732.

Cuisine: CAMPANIA/ITALIAN. **Reservations:** Required for dinner. **Transportation:** Capri funicular.

$ Prices: Appetizers 10,000–15,000 lire ($7.85–$11.80); main courses 15,000–25,000 lire ($11.80–$19.65). AE, MC, V.

Open: Lunch Thurs–Tues (daily in Aug) 12:30–3pm; dinner Thurs–Tues (daily in Aug) 7:30–10:30pm. **Closed:** Nov 10–Mar 15.

This restaurant is not pretentious, although it is patronized by a host of famous people, ranging from film actresses to dress designers to royalty. A trio of inside rooms is decorated in a sophisticated tavern manner, although the main draw in summer is the inner courtyard, with its ferns and hanging vines. At a table covered with a colored cloth, you can select the finest meals on the island. Wine is from vineyards owned by the restaurant. If featured, a fine opener is Sicilian macaroni. Main-dish specialties include pollo (chicken) alla Capannina and scaloppine Capannina. However, the most savory skillet of goodies is the zuppa di pesce, a soup made with fish from the bay. Some of the dishes, however, were obviously inspired by the nouvelle cuisine school.

LA CISTERNA, via Madre Serafina 5. Tel. 8377236.

Cuisine: SEAFOOD. **Reservations:** Recommended. **Transportation:** Capri funicular.

$ Prices: Appetizers 5,000–7,000 lire ($3.95–$5.50); main courses 7,000–10,000 lire ($5.50–$7.85). AE, DC, MC, V.

Open: Lunch Fri–Wed 12:30–3pm; dinner Fri–Wed 7:30pm–midnight.

This excellent, small restaurant is run by two brothers, Francesco and Salvatore Trama, who keep it open all year. The warm welcome extended by the owners sets the atmosphere in which to enjoy the fine food. Ask what the evening specials are. They might be mama's green lasagne, or a fish main dish of whatever was freshest at the dock that afternoon, marinated in wine, garlic, and ginger, and broiled. The lightly breaded and deep-fried baby squid and octopus, a mouth-watering saltimbocca, spaghetti with clams, and a filling zuppa di pesce are usually on the menu. The prices listed above include antipasto, a first course, a second course with one or two side dishes, a dessert, and at least two bottles of Capri wine—I guarantee you'll have had a banquet. La Cisterna lies only a short walk from piazza Umberto I and is reached via a labyrinth of covered "tunnels."

LA PIGNA, via Roma 30. Tel. 8370280.

Cuisine: NEAPOLITAN. **Reservations:** Recommended. **Transportation:** Capri funicular.

$ Prices: Appetizers 10,000–13,000 lire ($7.85–$10.20); main courses 15,000–23,000 lire ($11.80–$18.05). AE, DC, MC, V.

Open: Lunch Wed–Mon (daily in Aug) noon–3pm; dinner Wed–Mon (daily July–Sept) 8pm–2am. **Closed:** Oct–Easter.

A short walk from the bus station, La Pigna serves the finest meals for the money on the entire island, outside of the hotel dining rooms. Dining here is like attending a garden party in Capri, and this has been true since 1875. The owner loves flowers almost as much as good food. The ambience is one of a greenhouse, with purple petunias, red geraniums, bougainvillea, and lemon trees that flourish in abundance. Much of the produce comes from the restaurant's gardens in Anacapri. The food is excellent, regardless of what you select, but try in particular the pasta specialty, penne (noodles) tossed in a sauce made of eggplant, and the chicken suprême with mushrooms, the house specialty. Another dish I can recommend is the rabbit, which was raised on the farm; it's stuffed with herbs. The dessert specialty is an almond-and-chocolate torte. Another feature of the restaurant is homemade liqueurs, one of which is distilled from local lemons. The waiters are courteous and efficient, and the atmosphere nostalgic, as guitarists stroll by singing sentimental Neapolitan ballads.

LA SCERIFFA, via Provinciale Marina Grande 86A. Tel. 8377953.
Cuisine: CAPRESE. **Reservations:** Required. **Transportation:** Capri funicular.

$ **Prices:** Appetizers 7,000–10,000 lire ($5.50–$7.85); main courses 11,000–20,000 lire ($8.65–$15.70). AE.
Open: Lunch Wed–Mon noon–2:30pm; dinner Wed–Mon 7:30pm–midnight.
Closed: Nov–Apr.

Near the main piazzetta of town, La Sceriffa is ringed with tables on its outdoor veranda. This restaurant offers good food—one of the culinary inventions is a form of linguine "Terra Felice," made with fresh basil, capers, tomatoes, and a healthy shot of cognac. Other dishes might include spaghetti with mussels and clams, fettuccine house style (with eggplant and peppers), a regional form of ravioli, several tasty chicken dishes, and homemade desserts, many of them laden with cream. No one will mind if you order a carafe of the house wine.

LA TAVERNETTA, via La Palazzo 23. Tel. 8376864.
Cuisine: ITALIAN/INTERNATIONAL. **Reservations:** Required. **Transportation:** Capri funicular.

$ **Prices:** Appetizers 8,000–15,000 lire ($6.30–$11.80); main courses 11,000–32,000 lire ($8.65–$25.10). AE, DC, MC, V.
Open: Lunch Tues–Sun noon–2:30pm; dinner Tues–Sun 7:30–11:30pm.
Closed: Jan–Feb.

This establishment's chef was formerly the chef at the prestigious Hotel Quisisana. But here you can enjoy the "secrets" of the deluxe establishment far more cheaply, although more elaborate repasts can run the tab up to 60,000 lire ($47.10). Specialties include such dishes as torciglioni alla moda (that is, ziti with zucchini which is flavored with fresh basil and served in a cream sauce). Try also his ravioli in a green sauce. For a main dish, the chef recommends entrecôte Café de Paris. Desserts are sumptuous, particularly those made with the citrus of Capri. If you call for a table and the weather's right, ask to be seated outdoors. Service is excellent.

Inexpensive

RISTORANTE DA TONINO AL GROTTINO, via Longano 27. Tel. 8370584.
Cuisine: SEAFOOD/NEAPOLITAN. **Reservations:** Not needed. **Transportation:** Capri funicular.

$ **Prices:** Appetizers 6,000–8,000 lire ($4.70–$6.30); main courses 9,000–10,000 lire ($7.05–$7.85). AE, V.
Open: Lunch Wed–Mon noon–3pm; dinner Wed–Mon 7–11pm. **Closed:** Nov–Mar.

Favored by many of the rich and famous—from Vittorio Gassman to Princess Soraya, Ted Kennedy to Ginger Rogers—it draws a constant crowd. To reach it, you walk down a narrow alleyway that branches off from piazza Umberto I to an establishment not unlike a bistro in North Africa. The chef knows how to rattle his pots and pans. Bowing to the influence of the nearby Neapolitan cuisine, he offers four different dishes of fried mozzarella cheese, any one highly recommended. A big plate of the mixed fish fry from the seas of the Campania is a favored main dish. The zuppa di cozze (clam soup) is a savory opener, as is the ravioli alla caprese. Truly succulent is a plate of crayfish in homemade mayonnaise.

SPECIALITY DINING

One of the major pastimes in Capri is to occupy an outdoor table at one of the cafés on the heartbeat piazza Umberto I. Each arriving visitor picks his or her favorite, although they're all about the same. Even some permanent residents (and this is a good sign) patronize **Bar Tiberio**, piazza Umberto I (tel. 8370268), which is open daily from 7am to midnight, sometimes until 3 or 4am if business merits it. Larger and a little more comfortable than some of its competitors, this café has tables both inside and outside that overlook the busy life of the square where virtually every visitor to

Capri shows up at one time or another. A cappuccino costs 3,500 lire ($2.75) if you're sitting, but you can order many other types of drinks as well. Whisky begins at 9,000 lire ($7.05).

ANACAPRI

Capri is the upper town of Marina Grande. To see the upper town of Capri, you have to get lost in the clouds of Anacapri—more remote, secluded, and idyllic than the main resort, and reached by a daring 3,000-lira ($2.35) round-trip bus ride, more thrilling than any roller coaster. One visitor once remarked that all bus drivers to Anacapri "were either good or dead." At one point in its history Anacapri and Capri were connected only by the Scala Fenicia, the Phoenician Stairs.

When you disembark at piazza della Victoria, you'll find a Caprian Shangri-la, a village of charming dimensions.

To continue your ascent to the top, you then hop aboard a chair lift to **Monte Solaro,** the loftiest citadel on the entire island at its lookout perch of 1,950 feet. The ride takes about 12 minutes, operates daily from 9:30am to sunset, and charges 5,500 lire ($4.30) for a round-trip ticket. At the top, the spectacular panorama of the Bay of Naples is spread before you.

You can head out to **Villa San Michele** on viale Axel Munthe (tel. 8371401). This was the home of Axel Munthe, the Swedish author (*The Story of San Michele*), physician, and friend of Gustav V, king of Sweden, who visited him several times on the island. The villa is as Munthe (who died in 1949) furnished it, in a harmonious and tasteful way. From the rubble and ruins of an imperial villa built underneath by Tiberius, Munthe purchased several marbles, which are displayed inside. You can walk through the gardens for another in a series of endless panoramas of the island. Tiberius used to sleep out there al fresco on hot nights. The villa, which is open daily, may be visited from 9am to 6pm from May to September, from 9:30am to 5pm in April and October, and from 9:30am to 4:30pm in March; in winter, hours are 10:30am to 3:30pm. Admission is 3,000 lire ($2.35). Villa San Michele is a 5-minute walk from piazza Monumento in Anacapri.

WHERE TO STAY

EUROPA PALACE, via Capodimonte 2, 80071 Anacapri. Tel. 081/ 8370955. Fax 081/8373191. 100 rms (all with bath), 20 junior suites. A/C MINIBAR TV TEL **Transportation:** Anacapri bus.
$ Rates (including half board): 240,000 lire ($188.40) single; 380,000 lire ($298.30) double; from 450,000 lire ($353.25) suite for two. AE, DC, MC, V. **Closed:** Oct 15–Easter.

On the slopes of Monte Solaro, the first-class Europa sparkles with *moderne,* and turns its back on the past to embrace the semiluxury of today. Its designer, who had bold ideas, obviously loved wide-open spaces, heroic proportions, and vivid colors. The landscaped gardens with palm trees and plenty of bougainvillea have a large heated swimming pool, which most guests use as their outdoor living room. Each of the bedrooms is attractively and comfortably furnished. Special features are four junior suites, each with a private swimming pool.

Dining/Entertainment: The hotel's restaurant, Alexandre, is known for the fine cuisine with Mediterranean specialties, even with some nouvelle cuisine. Meals begin at 50,000 lire ($39.25). In the swimming-pool area is a snack bar where light lunches and barbecue dishes are served.

Services: Room service, baby-sitting, laundry, valet.

Facilities: Swimming pool, fitness center.

HOTEL SAN MICHELE DI ANACAPRI, viale Axel Munthe, 80071 Anacapri. Tel. 081/8371427. Fax 081/8371420. 56 rms (all with bath). TV TEL **Transportation:** Anacapri bus.
$ Rates (including breakfast): 90,000 lire ($70.65) single; 150,000 lire ($117.75) double; 100,000–115,000 lire ($78.50–$90.30) per person with half board. AE, DC, MC, V. **Closed:** Jan 5–Easter.
This hotel has spacious cliffside gardens and unmarred views, as well as enough shady

or sunny nooks to please everybody. It also has the largest swimming pool in Capri. Guests linger long and peacefully in its private and well-manicured gardens, where the green trees are softened by splashes of color from hydrangea and geraniums. The position of this contemporary, well-appointed hotel is just right: near Axel Munthe's Villa San Michele. The view for diners includes the Bay of Naples and Vesuvius. The lounges are furnished in an older, more traditional vein, much like the appearance of a country house in France. The bedrooms carry out the same theme, with a respect for the past, but also with sufficient examples of today's amenities, such as a tile bath in most rooms, good beds, and plenty of space.

HOTEL BELLAVISTA, via Orlandi 10, 80071 Anacapri. Tel. 081/ 8371463. Fax 081/8370957. 15 rms (all with bath). TEL **Transportation:** Anacapri bus.

$ Rates (including half board): 88,000 lire ($69.10) per person. No credit cards. **Closed:** Oct 31–Easter.

Only a 2-minute walk from the main piazza, this is a modern holiday retreat with a panoramic view. Lodged into a mountainside, the hotel is decorated with primary colors, has large living and dining rooms, and terraces with a view of the sea. The breakfast and lunch terrace has garden furniture and a rattan-roofed sun shelter, and the cozy lounge has an elaborate tile floor and a hooded fireplace on a raised hearth, ideal for nippy nights. The bedrooms are pleasingly contemporary (a few have a bed mezzanine, a sitting area on the lower level, and a private terrace). The restaurant is closed on Monday.

HOTEL LORELEY, via Orlandi 12, 80071 Anacapri. Tel. 081/8371440. 18 rms (all with bath). TEL **Transportation:** Anacapri bus.

$ Rates (including breakfast): 65,000 lire ($51) single; 110,000 lire ($86.35) double. AE, DC, MC, V. **Closed:** Nov–Easter.

The Loreley has more to offer than economy: It's a cozy, immaculately kept accommodation, with a homelike, genial atmosphere. Opened in 1963, it features an open-air veranda with a bamboo canopy, rattan chairs, and of course, a good view. The rooms overlook lemon-bearing trees that have (depending on the season) either scented blossoms or fruit. The bedrooms are quite large, with unified colors and enough furniture to make for a sitting room. Each room has a balcony. The hotel is approached through a white iron gate, past a stone wall. It lies off the road toward the sea, and is surrounded by fig trees and geraniums.

MARINA PICCOLA

A little fishing village and beach on the south shore, Marina Piccola can be reached by bus (later you can take a bus back up the steep hill to Capri). The village opens onto emerald-and-cerulean waters, with the Faraglioni rocks of the sirens jutting out at the far end of the bay.

WHERE TO DINE

LA CANZONE DEL MARE, Marina Piccola. Tel. 8370104. **Cuisine:** CAMPANIA/ITALIAN. **Reservations:** Needed Sat–Sun. **Transportation:** Marina Piccola bus.

$ Prices: Appetizers 15,000–22,000 lire ($11.80–$17.25); main courses 20,000–35,000 lire ($15.70–$27.50). AE, V.

Open: Daily 12:30–5pm. **Closed:** Oct–Easter.

This is a memorable place to spend an afternoon in Marina Piccola. You dine here at a terrace restaurant, then later go for a swim in the luxurious free-form seaside pool. There are shaded dining areas on several levels. This little compound of poshness was created by the late Gracie Fields, the English mill girl with the golden voice who became a star. After a full and dynamic career, starring in many films, countless vaudeville shows, and endless radio and television shows, Miss Fields (the wartime sweetheart of the British) fulfilled a goal by finding the loveliest spot she could in the Mediterranean. She opened this exclusive little restaurant and settled back to enjoy the leisurely life before her death. It is still going strong. Seafood dishes are specialties.

CHAPTER 22

SICILY

- **WHAT'S SPECIAL ABOUT SICILY**
1. **PALERMO**
2. **SEGESTA**
3. **SELINUNTE**
4. **AGRIGENTO**
5. **SYRACUSE [SIRACUSA]**
6. **TAORMINA**

Sicily is an ancient land of myth and legend. On a map, the toe of the Italian boot looks as if it was at any moment going to kick Sicily like an unruly delinquent as far away from the mainland as possible. Located 80 miles from the coast of Africa, the island is swept by winds that dry its fertile fields every summer, crisping the harvest into a sun-blasted palette of browns. The largest of the Mediterranean islands, Sicily is a hypnotic island of dramatic turbulence, as absurdly emotional and intense as a play by native son Luigi Pirandello.

For centuries its beauty and charm have attracted the greedy eye of foreigners: the Greeks, Romans, Vandals, Arabs, Normans, Swabians, the fanatically religious house of Aragon, and the French Bourbons. Homer, author of the ancient epic *The Odyssey,* recorded ancient myths about cannibalistic tribes (the Laestrygones) living near the site of modern Catania.

Centuries later, legends grew about the island's patron saint, Saint Agatha, martyred by having her breasts cut off. The island still teems with partly mythological, partly believed stories about curative powers of water from certain caves, the damaging powers of the evil eye, and tales shrouded in primeval legend. Given the fertile material for both natural and political disasters, it's not surprising that a host of bizarre images have sprouted out of Sicilian lore and legend.

Throughout the ages, a series of plagues, ferocious family vendettas, volcanic eruptions, earthquakes, and economic hardship has threatened many times to destroy the interwoven cultures of Sicily. Always, the island has persevered. Its archeology and richly complex architecture are endlessly fascinating, and the masses of almond and cherry trees in bloom in February makes it one of the most beautiful places in Italy.

Too long neglected by travelers wooed by the art cities of the north, Sicily is today attracting greater numbers of foreign visitors. This land of volcanic islands is full of sensual sights and experiences: skiing on the slopes of volcanically active Mount Etna, a sirocco whirling out of the nearby Libyan deserts, horses with plumes and bells pulling gaily painted carts, vineyards and fragrant citrus groves, Greek temples and classical dramas performed in ancient theaters, and the aromatic fragrance of a glass of marsala.

Today the Sicilians are an intriguing and fiercely proud racial mix, less Latin than the Italians, spiritually akin in many ways to North Africa and the wild wastelands of the Sahara. Luigi Barzini, in *The Italians,* wrote, "Sicily is the schoolroom model of Italy for beginners, with every Italian quality and defect magnified, exasperated, and brightly colored. . . . Everywhere in Italy, life is more or less slowed down by the exuberant intelligence of the inhabitants: In Sicily it is practically paralyzed by it."

There are far too many cars in Palermo, a sometimes-unpleasant reflection of the new (sometimes drug-related) prosperity that seems to have encouraged everyone on the island to buy a car. Parts of the island are heavily polluted by industrialization, but the age-old poverty still remains in the streets, home to thousands of children who seemingly grow up there.

Geologically, Sicily broke away from the mainland of Africa (not Europe) millions of years ago. Even today, the 2½-mile channel separating it from the tip of the Italian peninsula is still a dangerously unstable earthquake zone, making hopes for the eventual construction of a bridge unfeasible. The ancient Greeks claimed that the

WHAT'S SPECIAL ABOUT SICILY

Great Towns & Villages

☐ Taormina, one of the world's loveliest resorts, set on the blue Ionian Sea, looking out at snow-capped Mount Etna.

☐ Palermo, capital of Sicily, opening on the Tyrrhenian Sea, founded by seafaring Phoenicians in the 6th century B.C.

☐ Agrigento, known to the Greeks, one of ancient Sicily's most beautiful and prosperous cities.

☐ Selinunte, ancient Selinus, founded in 682 B.C. and today one of Sicily's most important archeological sites.

Ancient Monuments

☐ Valley of the Temples, Agrigento, a panoramic sweep of surviving Greek temples, including the Temple of Concord (450 B.C.), the second-best-preserved Greek temple in the world.

☐ Segesta, with a Doric temple from 430 B.C. with a peristyle of 36 columns.

☐ The archeological zone of Syracuse, with a Greek theater from the 5th century B.C., one of the largest and best preserved of the ancient world.

Ace Attractions

☐ Mount Etna, the highest point on the island, still active, the largest and most famous volcano in Europe.

Religious Shrines

☐ Montreale, outside Palermo, containing a Duomo known for its dazzling 12th-century mosaics.

busy strait was the lair of deadly sea monsters, Charybdis and Scylla, who, according to legend, delighted in wrecking Greek ships and devouring the flesh of the sailors aboard.

Today Sicily has a relatively stable population of around five million inhabitants. Its resorts, ancient temples, and distinctive cuisine are bringing it increasingly into the world's consciousness. Even Goethe, who traveled widely here, commented on the sometimes bizarre, always captivating, symbols he saw, but concluded, "To have seen Italy without having seen Sicily is not to have seen Italy at all, for Sicily is the clue to everything."

HISTORY

Other than the Paleolithic and Neolithic tribes (whose cave drawings remain in the Palermo grottoes of Monte Pellegrino), the first migrants to Sicily were Iberians from the west and Bronze Age settlers from the eastern Mediterranean. The combinations of these distinctly different peoples began a pattern of cultural intermingling that has continued ever since. Homer frequently mentioned the Greeks' desire to colonize Sicily and use it as a base for the export of Greek culture throughout the western Mediterranean. The Phoenicians, who had expanded their empire in present-day Lebanon into the powerful city-state of Carthage, engaged the Greeks in battle over dominance of the increasingly valuable territory of Sicily, but were defeated in 480 B.C. Greek dominance of the Mediterranean helped to make the Sicilian city of Syracuse one of the most powerful in the Greek-speaking world, causing jealous tremors as far away as Athens. (One of the city's famous sons was Archimedes, whose definitions of the physical world are still taught to schoolchildren today.) Today the Greek ruins of Sicily are among the finest in the Mediterranean, and were the source of inspiration for many of the English Romantic poets.

None of this withstood, however, the growing power of Rome. During the Punic Wars of Rome against Carthage, the Greek colonies of Sicily unwisely sided with Carthage. The Romans razed Carthage into the earth (and sowed the fields with salt so they'd never produce again), then wreaked vengeance upon Sicily, stealing its riches and plunging it into a political obscurity that lasted until the Middle Ages. The Christianization of Sicily is credited to St. Paul himself.

In the 900s the Arabs founded Palermo, encouraged citrus production, and traded heavily with other Muslim communities in southern Spain and northern Africa. After the bloodshed of the initial invasion, they basically left the Christians alone to pursue their farming and pay their very heavy taxes.

The Norman invasion of southern Italy was more the result of inspired adventurism by a handful of mercenaries than it was a concentrated invasion by an organized army. Tancred de Hauteville, a minor landowner from northern France, some of whose forebears had been Viking invaders, produced 12 pugnacious sons, who headed south for whatever gain they could get. The two prizes they eventually gained—through diplomacy, intimidation, and bloodshed—were southern Italy and Sicily.

Southern Italy was conquered by Robert Guiscard (1015–85), who crowned himself the Duke of Apulia, while his youngest brother, Roger Guiscard (1031–1101), crowned himself the Count of Sicily. Sicily today contains a bizarre number of buildings heavily influenced by the early Gothic architecture of northern France, whose contrast with the architecture of the Italian mainland is striking. Sicily also has its share of blue-eyed blondes, a less-well-publicized legacy of the virile northmen. The thousands of Norman colonizers that Roger hoped would arrive never did, however, requiring increasing degrees of assimilation of the Normans with the local Arab, Greek, and Byzantine population. A descendant of Roger, William II (1166–89), arranged a marriage for himself to Joan of England, the sister of the Crusade-obsessed Richard the Lionhearted. This unlikely importation from faraway London helped Sicily continue to meld north European influences with the native Greek and Arab motifs. (The architecture that resulted is unique in Europe.) The cultural stewpot that emerged reached its zenith during most of the 1100s, and is considered one of the golden ages of Sicily.

Upon his death, William II left no heir, and a contested lineage led to the importation of a German prince, Henry of Hohenstaufen. His son, Frederick of Hohenstaufen, the product of Norman and Swabian bloodlines, created one of the most spectacular courts in contemporary Europe, translating the Arabic and Greek classics, bringing Sicily firmly into the European orbit, encouraging the development of mathematical theories, and battling with the voraciously greedy Roman popes at every opportunity.

When he and his heir died within a short span of time, the lineage of the royal family became impossibly blurred. The most likely candidate for the throne was the French-born brother of the king of France, one Charles of Anjou. So unpopular was his imposition of French customs and French taxes that the Sicilian dukes, with the local population, massacred every French person in Sicily in 1282 during the War of the Sicilian Vespers. The French lineage was replaced, after an agreement among the Sicilian nobles, with allegiance to Aragon (Spain), partly as a reaction against the meddling power of the Roman popes.

During the 1400s Sicily was politically joined by the Spanish to Naples, and ruled (and bled) from afar. Sicily was virtually ignored by everyone, except for the Moorish pirates who led periodic raids on coastal cities. The flowering of the Italian Renaissance, unfortunately, never really took hold in Sicily, largely because of the stifling hold placed on it by the Spanish Inquisition.

After a brief dominance during the 18th century by the Austrians, then by the House of Savoy, then again by the Spanish, Sicily joined a unified Italy under the king of Savoy, Vittorio Emmanuele, in 1861. Unity with Italy, however, did not erase the enormous problems between northern and southern Italy. The more prosperous north, except for the energies of Garibaldi, would have probably preferred that a newly defined Italy end somewhere north of Naples. Once again Sicily sank into a backwater, rampant with plagues, hunger, and superstitious domination by the Mafia and the church.

During the early 20th century thousands of Sicilians immigrated to the Americas and Australia. Mussolini poured more money into Sicilian irrigation and roadbuilding projects than any other Italian leader, and made enormous strides in almost eradicating the Mafia.

In 1943 Sicily was the first region of Europe to fall to the Allied reconquest of Europe, under the joint leadership of Gen. George Patton and the less competent British General Montgomery. Their combined forces wiped out Nazi resistance in Sicily, an event broadcast as a message of hope and propaganda throughout the world. Many of the Sicilian survivors, though embattled by local Communists and Mafiosi alike, worked to achieve a political status independent from the rest of Italy. Although their dream fell short of the mark, Italy granted Sicily partial autonomy, which it retains to this day.

SEEING SICILY

SUGGESTED ITINERARY

Day 1: Either by air or ferryboat from Naples, arrive in Palermo, the capital of Sicily, and see some of its attractions, saving time in the afternoon for Monreale in the environs.

Day 2: From Palermo, head southwest to Segesta to see the temple there before proceeding to Selinunte for the night.

Day 3: After exploring Selinunte in the morning, continue east along the coast to Agrigento. Explore the Valley of the Temples at dusk.

Day 4: Continue east to Syracuse for the night, allowing time to explore its archeological zone in the afternoon.

Days 5 & 6: The best for last. Proceed north through the industrial city of Catania to the resort of Taormina. You'll spend the best part of the day getting there and you'll need Day 6 to wind down and enjoy the beauty of Taormina. Those with yet another day for Sicily can explore Mount Etna to the southwest.

GETTING THERE

HEADING SOUTH BY CAR When you head south toward Sicily today, you won't have the transportation headache that plagued Goethe. The Autostrada del Sole stretches all the way from Milan to Reggio di Calabria, sticking out on the "big toe," the gateway to Sicily.

One day a bridge is supposed to connect Sicily with the mainland. The project, it is estimated, would take at least 8 years and cost at least a billion dollars. A major problem is that the span is to stretch across the Strait of Messina, a prime earthquake zone.

At present, one way to reach Sicily is to take a ferryboat from Villa San Giovanni or Reggio di Calabria to Messina, costing 1,000 lire (80¢) per passenger. Departures are daily on this state railway ferryboat; vessels leave from 5am to 10pm, and it takes less than an hour to cross. It costs 18,000 lire ($14.15) and up to take your car on the ferry. Much quicker, shaving at least 22 minutes off the crossing time, is an *aliscafo* (hydrofoil) leaving from Reggio di Calabria. You'll pay 5,000 lire ($3.95) one way. However, the aliscafo is recommended because usually the higher price means fewer passengers—hence, less crowding. You cannot take your vehicle on a hydrofoil. Call 0965/97957 for information.

Near Reggio di Calabria, incidentally, is a much smaller community, Scilla, famous in Homeric legend. Mariners of old, such as Ulysses, crossed the Strait of Messina from here, and faced the double menace of the two monsters Charybdis and Scylla.

FROM NAPLES TO SICILY BY SEA One way to reach Palermo is by night ferry from Naples. The ferry leaves Naples at 8:30pm, arriving in Palermo the next morning at 7am. On Friday there is another departure at 10pm. The service is run by **Tirrenia S.A.** For information about this service, call the company's office in Naples at 081/5512181. However, if you're already in Palermo and want to take the ferry service back to Naples, dial 091/333300. Unfortunately, you will not always find

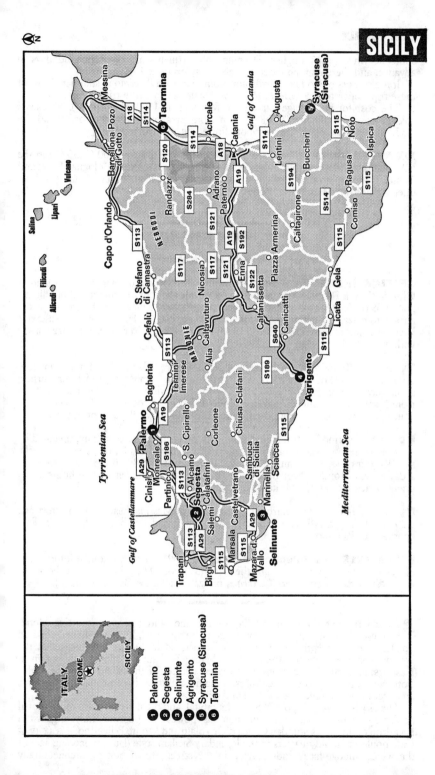

someone who speaks English. Sleeping compartments are often booked days in advance, and there may be space available only on deck.

It is also possible to take a hydrofoil from Naples to Palermo in summer. Most of these trips, operated by **S.N.A.V.,** leave Naples at 3pm, the trip taking 5 hours.

The cost for an average car on the ferryboat is 110,800 lire ($87). First-class passage costs 99,200 lire ($77.85) per person for a one-way ticket or 68,700 lire ($53.95) in second class. Cars are not allowed on the hydrofoil.

FLYING TO SICILY   There are daily **Alitalia** (tel. toll free 800/2235730 in the U.S.) flights to Palermo from Milan, Naples, Venice, Pisa, Genoa, Bologna, Turin, and Rome. There are around six flights a day from Rome. Flights go to Catania at least once a day from Milan, Pisa, Rome, and Turin.

1. PALERMO

145 miles W of Messina

GETTING THERE   By Plane   If you fly from Rome or Naples, you'll land at **Cinisi–Punta Raisi,** some 19 miles west of Palermo. For information about flights, phone 591690. It's best to catch a local airport bus, which runs hourly from the airport to piazza Castelnuovo; the fare is 3,600 lire ($2.85). For the same trip a taxi is likely to charge at least 45,000 lire ($35.35)—more if the driver thinks he can get away with it.

By Train   Trains arrive in Palermo at piazza Cesare (tel. 6161806 for information) on the eastern side of town. It's possible to take a train from Rome, a 15-hour journey; a one-way ticket goes for 50,300 lire ($39.50). Most visitors, however, take the train from Naples, a 13-hour journey, a one-way ticket going for 42,600 lire ($33.45). Of course, a water crossing from the mainland to Sicily is involved in both trips.

By Bus   Palermo has bus connections with other major cities in Italy, operated by Autoservizi Segesta, via Balsamo 26 (tel. 6167919). For example, 16 buses a day make the 2½-hour trip from Catania, a one-way ticket costing 15,800 lire ($12.40). One bus a day arrives Monday through Saturday from Syracuse; the trip lasts 4 hours and a one-way ticket costs 19,200 lire ($15.05).

By Car   After your arrival from mainland Italy at Messina, head west on autostrada A20 which becomes Route 113, then A20 again, and finally A19 before its final approach to Palermo.

ESSENTIALS   The **telephone area code** is 091. There are tourist information offices at strategic points, including the Palermo airport. The principal office, however, is the **Azienda Autonoma Turismo,** piazza Castelnuova 34 (tel. 583847).

As the ferryboat docks in the Bay of Palermo, and you start spotting blond, blue-eyed bambini all over the place, don't be surprised. If the fair-haired children don't fit your conception of what a Sicilian should look like, remember that the Normans landed here in 1060, 6 years before William the Conqueror put in at Hastings, and launched a campaign to wrest control of the island from the Arabs. Both elements were to cross cultures, a manifestation still seen today in Palermo's architecture—a unique style, Norman-Arabic.

The city is the largest port of Sicily, its capital, and the meeting place of a regional parliament granted numerous autonomous powers in postwar Italy. Against a backdrop of the citrus-studded Conca d'Oro plain and Monte Pellegrino, it is a city of wide boulevards, old quarters in the legendary Sicilian style (laundry lapping against the wind, smudge-faced kids playing in the street), town houses, architecturally harmonious squares, baroque palaces, and modern buildings (many erected as a result of Allied bombings in 1943). It also has the worst traffic jams in Sicily.

Palermo was founded by the Phoenicians, but it has known many conquerors, some of whom established courts of great splendor (Frederick II), others of whom brought decay (the Angevins).

GETTING AROUND

Most municipally operated **buses** in Palermo charge 700 lire (55¢) for a ticket, which is a cheap way of getting about. Most passengers purchase their tickets at tobacco shops (*tabacchi*) throughout the city before getting on. Otherwise, you'll need some 100-lira coins handy. If you plan to use the buses at least three times during the day, you might want to purchase a **day ticket,** costing 1,500 lire ($1.20), allowing you unlimited rides on the city's bus network. These tickets are sold at the main bus station in front of the train station at piazza Cesare. For information about the city buses (AMAT), call 222398.

FAST FACTS

American Express   The agent for American Express is **Palermois Rugieri,** via Emerico Amari 40 (tel. 587144), which is open Monday through Friday from 9am to 1pm and 4 to 6pm, and on Saturday from 9am to 1pm.

Consulate   You'll find the **U.S. Consulate** at via Vaccarini 1 (tel. 091/343532), open Monday through Friday from 9am to 1pm and 3 to 5pm. Take bus no. 14 or 15.

Crime   Be especially alert. Some citizens here are the most skilled pickpockets on the continent. Keep your gems locked away (in other words, don't flaunt any sign of wealth). Women who carry handbags are especially vulnerable to purse-snatchers on Vespas. Don't leave valuables in your car. In fact, I almost want to say don't leave your car alone, even knowing how impossible that is. Police squads operate mobile centers through the town to help combat street crime.

Emergencies   In order to call police, report a fire, or summon an ambulance, dial **113.**

Post Office   The major post office is on via Roma (tel. 320926) and is open Monday through Friday from 8:30am to 7:30pm and on Saturday from 8:30am to noon.

WHAT TO SEE & DO

THE TOP SIGHTS

"The four corners" of the city, the   ✪ **Quattro Canti di Città,** is in the heart of the old town, at the junction of corso Vittorio Emanuele and via Maqueda. The ruling Spanish of the 17th century influenced the design of this grandiose baroque square, replete with fountains and statues. From here you can walk to **piazza Bellini,** the most attractive of the plazas of the old city. In an atmosphere reminiscent of the setting for an operetta, you're likely to hear strolling singers with guitars entertaining pizza eaters. Opening onto it is the **Church of Santa Maria dell'Ammiragli** (also known as "La Martorana"), piazza Bellini 3 (tel. 6161692), erected in 1143 with a Byzantine cupola by an admiral to Roger II. Its decaying but magnificent bell tower was built from 1146 to 1185. It is open Monday through Saturday from 8am to 1pm and 3:30 to 7pm, and on Sunday from 8am to 1pm. Admission is free.

Also fronting the square are the **Church of San Cataldo,** erected in 1160 in the Arab-Byzantine style with a trio of faded pink cupolas, and the **Church of Santa Caterina,** from the 16th century.

Adjoining the square is **piazza Pretoria,** dominated by a fountain designed in

Florence in 1554 for a villa, but acquired by Palermo about 20 years later. A short walk will take you to the cathedral of Palermo.

CATHEDRAL OF PALERMO, corso Vittorio Emanuele. Tel. 334373.

This cathedral is a curious spectacle where East meets West. It was built in the 12th century on the foundation of an earlier basilica that had been converted by the Arabs into a mosque. The cathedral—much altered over the centuries—was founded by an English archbishop known as Walter of the Mill. The "porch," built in the 15th century on the southern front in the Gothic style, is an impressive architectural feature. But the cupola, added in the late 18th century, detracts from the overall appearance, and the interior was revamped unsuccessfully at the same time, resulting in a glaring incongruity in styles. The "pantheon" of royal tombs includes that of the Emperor Frederick II, in red porphyry under a canopy of marble.

Admission: Free.

Open: Daily 7am–noon and 4–6pm. **Bus:** 3 or 24.

SAN GIOVANNI DEGLI EREMITI, via dei Benedettini Bianchi 3. Tel. 296238.

The other church worthy of note is Saint John of the Hermits. Perhaps in an atmosphere appropriate for the recluse it honors, this little church with its twin-columned cloister is one of the most idyllic spots in all of Palermo. A medieval veil hangs heavy in the gardens, with their citrus blossoms and flowers, especially on a hot summer day as you wander around in its cloister. Ordered built by Roger II in 1132, the church adheres to its Arabic influence, surmounted by pinkish cupolas, while showing the Norman style as well. The Palace of the Normans is in the vicinity.

Admission: Free.

Open: Daily 9am–2pm. **Bus:** 3 or 24.

PALAZZO DI NORMANNI, piazza del Parlamento. Tel. 6561879.

★ This Palace of the Normans contains one of the greatest art treasures in Sicily, the **Cappella Palatina (Palatine Chapel).** Erected at the request of Roger II in the 1130s, it is considered the finest example of the Arabic-Norman style of design and building. The effect of the mosaics inside is awe-inspiring. Almond-eyed biblical characters from the Byzantine art world in lush colors create a panorama of epic pageantry, illustrating such Gospel scenes as the Nativity. The overall picture is further enhanced by inlaid marble and mosaics and pillars made of granite shipped from the East. For a look at still more mosaics, this time in a more secular vein depicting scenes of the hunt, you can visit the **Hall of Roger II** upstairs, the seat of the Sicilian Parliament, where security is likely to be tight. Visitors are taken through on guided tours.

Admission: Free.

Open: Palace, Mon and Fri–Sat 9am–12:30pm; chapel, Mon–Fri 9am–noon and 3–5pm, Sat–Sun 9am–noon. **Bus:** 3 or 24.

MUSEUMS

GALLERIA REGIONALE DELLA SICILIA, via Alloro 4. Tel. 6164317.

The Palazzo Abbatellis was built in the Gothic and Renaissance styles. Today it houses the Regional Gallery, with important collections of traditional and modern art, including works by local 15th-century painters. On the ground floor is a good collection of medieval sculpture. The gallery's second most famous work is a 15th-century fresco *Triumph of Death,* in all its gory magnificence. A horseback-riding skeleton, representing death, tramples his victims under hoof. Francesco Laurana's slanty-eyed *Eleonora d'Aragona* is worth seeking out, as are seven grotesque *Drôleries* painted on wood. Of the paintings on the second floor, *L'Annunziata* by Antonello da Messina, a portrait of the Madonna with depth and originality, is one of the most celebrated paintings in Italy.

Admission: 2,000 lire ($1.55) adults, free for children under 18.

Open: Tues and Thurs 9am–1:30pm and 3–4:30pm, Wed and Fri–Sat 9am–1:30pm, Sun 9am–12:30pm. **Bus:** 3 or 24.

MUSEO REGIONALE ARCHEOLOGIC, piazza Olivella. Tel. 587825.

⭐ Located in a former convent, this is one of the greatest archeological collections in southern Italy, where the competition's stiff. Many works displayed here were excavated from Selinunte, once one of the major towns in Magna Graecia (Greater Greece). See, in particular, the Sala di Selinunte, displaying the celebrated metopes that adorned the classical temples, as well as slabs of bas-relief. The gallery also owns important sculpture from the Temple of Himera. The collection of bronzes is exceptional, including the athlete and the stag discovered in the ruins of Pompeii (a Roman copy of a Greek original) and a bronze ram that came from Syracuse, dating from the 3rd century B.C. Among the Greek sculpture is *The Pouring Satyr,* excavated at Pompeii (a Roman copy of a Greek original by Praxiteles).
Admission: 2,000 lire ($1.55).
Open: Mon–Sat 9am–2pm and 3–10pm, Sun 9am–1pm. **Bus:** 3 or 24.

CATACOMBS

CATACOMBE CAPPUCCINI, piazza Cappuccini 1. Tel. 212117.

⭐ The final attraction in the city is the most bizarre of all. Located on the outskirts of Palermo, the catacombs evoke the horrors of the Rue Morgue. The fresco *Triumph of Death* dims by comparison to the real thing. The catacombs, it was discovered, contained a preservative that helped to mummify dead people. Sicilians, everyone from nobles to maids, were buried here in the 19th century, and it was the custom on Sunday to go and visit Uncle Luigi to see how he was holding together. If he fell apart, he was wired together again or wrapped in burlap sacking. The last person buried in the catacombs was placed to rest in 1920—a little girl almost lifelike in death. But many Sicilians of the 19th century are in fine shape, considering—with eyes, hair, clothing fairly intact (the convent could easily be turned into a museum of costume). Some of the expressions on the faces of the skeletons take the fun out of Halloween—a grotesque ballet. The catacombs may be visited on guided tours.
Admission: Free (donations accepted).
Open: Tours given Mon–Sat 9am–noon and 3:30–5pm, Sun and hols 9am–noon. **Bus:** 27 from piazza Castelnuovo.

WHERE TO STAY

Generally you'll find a poor lot of hostelries, aided by a few fine choices that prove the exception to the rule. Hunt and pick carefully, as many hotels of Palermo are not suitable for the average international wayfarer.

VERY EXPENSIVE

VILLA IGIEA GRAND HOTEL, salita Belmonte 1, 90142 Palermo. Tel. 091/543744. Fax 091/547654. 117 rms (all with bath), 6 suites. A/C MINIBAR TV TEL **Bus:** 3 or 24.
$ Rates (including breakfast): 290,000 lire ($227.65) single; 450,000 lire ($353.25) double; from 680,000 lire ($533.80) suite. AE, DC, MC, V. **Parking:** Free.

⭐ This deluxe hotel was originally built at the turn of the century as one of Sicily's great aristocratic estates, and today it's one of the top two luxury hotels on the island. The exterior resembles a medieval Sicilian fortress whose carefully chiseled walls include crenellated battlements and forbidding watchtowers. It was constructed of the same buff-colored stone that Greek colonists used during the Punic wars when they erected a circular temple which, although heavily buttressed with modern scaffolding, still stands in the garden. Nearby, nestled amid a grove of pines and palms, is an art nouveau statue of Igiea, goddess of flowers. Everywhere are clusters of antiques. Accommodations vary from sumptuous suites with private terraces to rooms of lesser size and glamour. The hotel, reached by passing through an industrial portside of Palermo, sits on a cliff with a view of the open sea and a nearby shipyard.

Dining/Entertainment: The hotel's bar is baronial, with a soaring stone vault. You dine in a grand and glittering room against a backdrop of paneled walls, ornate ceilings, and chandeliers. Meals, both Sicilian and classic Italian, begin at 80,000 lire ($62.80).

Services: Room service, baby-sitting, laundry, valet.

Facilities: Terrace overlooking the water, swimming pool, tennis court.

EXPENSIVE

JOLLY HOTEL DEL FORO ITALICO, Foro Italico 22, 90133 Palermo. Tel. 091/6165090. Fax 091/6161441. 290 rms (all with bath). A/C MINIBAR TV **Bus:** 3 or 24.

$ Rates (including breakfast): 145,000 lire ($113.85) single; 190,000 lire ($149.15) double. AE, DC, MC, V. **Parking:** Free.

Off a busy boulevard (the Foro Italico, facing the Gulf of Palermo), this hotel invites with shafts of pale blue supporting triangular balconies. Try for the bedrooms on the upper floors or at the rear, which are quieter. One of the best of the modern hotels (and popular for Sicilian wedding receptions), it offers a contemporary atmosphere and good accommodations. The public rooms have bright colors and serviceable furnishings. In the bedrooms all is well organized, with lots of built-in pieces and comfortable beds. Open all year, the hotel boasts 290 rooms, making it the largest hostelry in the city. The Jolly also has a garden.

Dining/Entertainment: On the premises are a restaurant and an American bar. The food is both Sicilian and Italian, beginning at 40,000 lire ($31.40).

Services: Room service, baby-sitting, laundry, valet.

Facilities: Swimming pool, parking lot.

MODERATE

GRANDE ALBERGO SOLE, corso Vittorio Emanuele 291, 90133 Palermo. Tel. 091/581811. Fax 091/6110182. 150 rms (all with bath). A/C MINIBAR TV TEL **Bus:** 3 or 24.

$ Rates (including breakfast): 80,000 lire ($62.80) single; 130,000 lire ($102.05) double. AE, DC, MC, V. **Parking:** 8,000 lire ($6.30).

This pleasant second-class hotel is in the center of town. All rooms, comfortable and fresh-looking, come with a radio, among other amenities. Extras include a television room, day and night restaurants, and a roof garden and terrace for sunbathing.

HOTEL PONTE, via Francesco Crispi 99, 90133 Palermo. Tel. 091/583744. Fax 091/581845. 137 rms (all with bath). A/C MINIBAR TV TEL **Bus:** 3 or 24.

$ Rates: 75,000 lire ($58.90) single; 102,000 lire ($80.05) double. Breakfast 7,000 lire ($5.50) extra. AE, DC, MC, V. **Parking:** 8,000 lire ($6.30).

This modern building on the main dockside boulevard is one of the best of the second-class hotels near the city center. Its lobby invites with marble floors, large mood-setting murals, deep comfortable lounge chairs, and a sense of style. All rooms have contemporary furnishings, and many offer a balcony. You'll find numerous details usually associated with first-class hotels, including a bidet and shower in the bath, bedside lamps, and a little sitting-room area. In the dining room you'll be served good, generous meals.

MOTEL AGIP, via della Regione Siciliana 2620, 90145 Palermo. Tel. 091/552033. Fax 091/408198. 105 rms (all with bath). A/C MINIBAR TV TEL **Bus:** 3 or 24.

$ Rates (including breakfast): 110,000 lire ($86.35) single; 147,000 lire ($115.40) double. AE, DC, MC, V. **Parking:** 8,000 lire ($6.30).

The Motel Agip provides a modern accommodation for those who want up-to-date amenities. Typical of the Agip chain (owned by a gasoline company), this entry on the Palermo hotel scene offers moderate prices for comfort and value. It's on a wide boulevard at the edge of the city, which makes it more suitable for motorists. The rooms are compact, with well-planned features, furnished in the traditional motel style, and with comfortable beds. There is air conditioning, on low voltage. On the premises is a restaurant, dispensing the standard Italian dishes with Sicilian variations.

PRESIDENT HOTEL, via Francesco Crispi 230, 90133 Palermo. Tel. 091/580733. Fax 091/6111588. 130 rms (all with bath). A/C TV TEL **Bus:** 9.
$ **Rates** (including breakfast): 115,000 lire ($90.30) single; 160,000 lire ($125.60) double. AE, DC, MC, V. **Parking:** 7,000 lire ($5.50).
Its eight-story concrete-and-glass facade rises above the harborfront quays where ferryboats dock before sailing to Naples. This is one of the better and more up-to-date of the middle-bracket hotels in town. You'll pass beneath the facade's soaring arcade before entering the informal stone-trimmed lobby. One of the most appealing coffee shop/bars in town lies at the top of a short flight of stairs next to the reception area. There's a panoramic restaurant on the uppermost floor, plus a guarded parking garage in the basement. The bedrooms are comfortably furnished, each with a radio and TV.

INEXPENSIVE

ALBERGO CAVOR, via Manzoni 11, 90133 Palermo. Tel. 091/6162759. 9 rms (3 with bath or shower). **Bus:** 3 or 24.
$ **Rates:** 20,000 lire ($15.70) single without bath; 28,000 lire ($22) double without bath, 40,000 lire ($31.40) double with bath. No credit cards. **Parking:** 10,000 lire ($7.85).
The Albergo Cavor is on the fifth floor of an old building conveniently located in front of the central station. The rooms are spacious, and the manager sees to it that they are well kept and pleasantly furnished, with comfortable mattresses on the beds.

HOTEL SAUSELE, via Vincenzo Errante 12, 90127 Palermo. Tel. 091/6161308. 36 rms (all with bath or shower). TEL **Bus:** 3 or 24.
$ **Rates** (including breakfast): 48,000 lire ($37.70) single; 75,000 lire ($58.90) double. AE, DC, MC, V. **Parking:** 12,000 lire ($9.40).
This modern hotel near the railway station is the best in a run-down area. It's owned and managed by Swiss-born Monsieur Sausele, who has created a clean establishment in the tradition of his native land. Run efficiently, it is a modest but quite pleasant albergo, with bedrooms adequate for a good night's rest. The hotel has an elevator, garage, bar, and TV room. The lounges are air-conditioned.

MODERNO ALBERGO, via Roma 276, 90133 Palermo. Tel. 091/588260. 38 rms (all with bath). TV TEL **Bus:** 1, 2, 7, 14, or 15.
$ **Rates:** 40,000 lire ($31.40) single; 70,000 lire ($54.95) double. AE, DC, MC, V. **Parking:** 8,000 lire ($6.30). **Closed:** Nov.
Located on the upper floor of an old-fashioned building right in the center of the city, this albergo has an elevator to take you to the reception lounge. The hotel has a bar and TV room, and all bedrooms have good beds. Breakfast is extra. It's 400 yards from the main railway station, and all buses from the station pass by the hotel.

HOTEL LIGURIA, via Mariano Stabile 128, 90133 Palermo. Tel. 091/581588. 16 rms (4 with bath). TV TEL **Bus:** 3 or 24.
$ **Rates:** 40,000 lire ($31.40) single or double without bath, 55,000 lire ($43.20) single or double with bath. Breakfast 5,000 lire ($3.95) extra. AE, DC.
This well-scrubbed family-run hotel has won several awards for its quality accommodations. At the upstairs reception desk, Signora Lidia Grosso de Grana will register you into one of her tile-floored accommodations, each of which is suitable for one or two people. Born in Genoa, she named the property after the region of her birth. Many of the rooms are awash with sunlight from the big windows, and each has a clothes press and comfortable bedding. The rooms are scattered over two floors.

WHERE TO DINE

EXPENSIVE

CHARLESTON, piazzale Ungheria 30. Tel. 321366.
Cuisine: SICILIAN/INTERNATIONAL. **Reservations:** Required. **Bus:** 3 or 24.
$ Prices: Appetizers 12,000–15,000 lire ($9.40–$11.80); main courses 20,000–26,000 lire ($15.70–$20.40). AE, DC, MC, V.
Open: Lunch Mon–Sat 1–3 or 4pm; dinner Mon–Sat 8–11:30pm.

For years Charleston was regarded as the finest restaurant in Sicily, although today there is far more competition for that title. Nevertheless, it remains a national culinary monument of Sicilian hospitality and old-fashioned virtues, an appealing choice in Palermo. Co-owners Carlo Hassan and Rinto Tantillo create a refined and perfect milieu for their presentation of Sicilian dishes, which naturally concentrate on fresh fish. The kitchen prepares a number of international dishes as well.

GOURMAND'S, via della Libertà 37E. Tel. 323431.
Cuisine: SICILIAN. **Reservations:** Recommended. **Bus:** 3 or 24.
$ Prices: Appetizers 12,000–16,000 lire ($9.40–$12.55); main courses 16,000–20,000 lire ($12.55–$15.70).
Open: Lunch Mon–Sat 1–3pm; dinner Mon–Sat 8–11pm. **Closed:** Aug 5–25.

Gourmand's is the best restaurant in Palermo for an introduction to the rich, aromatic cookery of Sicily. A corner restaurant in the most elegant commercial district of town, it is a light and airy room filled with original paintings and Chinese-red ceiling lattices. You'll admire the richly laden antipasto table before you're ushered to your table. For a first course, I'd suggest spaghetti Gourmand's or an involtini of eggplant. Fresh fish is always available, and you might prefer it grilled as a main course. However, the chef does many Italian dishes well, including veal escalope in the Valdostan style and pepper steak or, if available, roast quail. Risotto with salmon is often featured on the menu, as is rigatoni Henry IV. Meals begin at about 50,000 lire ($39.25).

L'APPRODO DA RENATO, via Messina Marina 28. Tel. 6302881.
Cuisine: SICILIAN. **Reservations:** Essential Fri–Sat. **Bus:** 31.
$ Prices: Appetizers 12,000–18,000 lire ($9.40–$14.15); main courses 15,000–20,000 lire ($11.80–$15.70). AE, DC.
Open: Lunch Thurs–Tues 12:30–3pm; dinner Thurs–Tues 8–11pm. **Closed:** Aug 10–25.

This restaurant is housed in a former aristocratic residence with a collection of antiques. Run by a husband-and-wife team, it is infused with gaiety. Some visitors are invited to explore the wine cellar, whose contents are said to rival the best in all of Italy, certainly in all of Sicily. For your food selection, consider fish marinated in refined olive oil and flavored with herbs, crêpes filled with seafood, a savory fish soup, swordfish in a mandarin orange sauce, or roast goat flavored with Sicilian herbs. Meals cost from 50,000 lire ($39.25).

LA SCUDERIA, viale del Fante 9. Tel. 520323.
Cuisine: ITALIAN. **Reservations:** Recommended. **Bus:** 1.
$ Prices: Appetizers 12,000–18,000 lire ($9.40–$14.15); main courses 14,000–25,000 lire ($11–$19.65). AE, DC, MC, V.
Open: Lunch daily 12:30–3pm; dinner Mon–Sat 8:30pm–midnight.

Dedicated professionals direct this appealing restaurant, which is surrounded by trees at the foot of Monte Pellegrino. The inside section is augmented in summer with one of the prettiest flowering terraces in town, a place sought after by everyone from erstwhile lovers to extended families to glamour queens in for a holiday. The sound of falling water, followed by the tunes of a piano player, greets you as you enter. The imaginative cuisine includes a mixed grill of fresh vegetables with a healthy dose of a Sicilian cheese called caciocavallo, along with stuffed turkey cutlet, a wide array of beef and veal dishes, involtini of eggplant, risotto with seafood, veal spiedino, and many tempting desserts, one known as pernice all'erotica. Full meals start at 55,000 lire ($43.20).

MODERATE

FRIEND'S BAR, via Brunelleschi 138, Borgo Nuovo. Tel. 201401.
   Cuisine: SICILIAN. **Reservations:** Required. **Bus:** 29 or 72.
$ **Prices:** Appetizers 8,000–10,000 lire ($6.30–$7.85); main courses 15,000–18,000 lire ($11.80–$14.15).
   Open: Lunch Tues–Sun 1–3pm; dinner Tues–Sun 8–10pm. **Closed:** Aug 10–20.

The name, in English no less, might sound like a place run by Archie Bunker in a small town in New Jersey. In spite of that incongruity, it is one of the finest restaurants in Palermo, located in a suburb called Borgo Nuovo. A meal here is considered an event by many Sicilians. Friend's Bar has become one of the sought-after places on the island, one where a reservation for one of the garden seats is almost essential to get past the bar. There is indeed a bar on the premises, although most of the emphasis is on the viands served in the dining room or on the terrace. First, you might enjoy a few of the many delicacies from the antipasto table, followed by one of the many regional specialties such as subtly flavored pastas, and an array of steamed or grilled fish dishes or one of the meat dishes that have made this place so well known locally. The house wine (red) is a good accompaniment for most any meal, which will usually cost about 35,000 lire to 50,000 lire ($27.50 to $39.25).

REGINE, via Trapani 4A. Tel. 586566.
   Cuisine: ITALIAN/INTERNATIONAL. **Reservations:** Required. **Bus:** 3 or 24.
$ **Prices:** Appetizers 10,000–15,000 lire ($7.85–$11.80); main courses 20,000–22,000 lire ($15.70–$17.25). AE, DC.
   Open: Lunch Mon–Sat 1–2:45pm; dinner Mon–Sat 8–10:45pm.
Regine sits about a block off via della Libertà, behind a wood and beveled-glass facade. Its menu features a selection of Italian and international dishes, including spaghetti carbonara, a mixed grill, tournedos with madeira sauce, Cuban-style rice pilaf, game in season, and trenette (a type of pasta) with pesto sauce. Full meals cost 30,000 lire to 42,000 lire ($23.55 to $32.95).

INEXPENSIVE

AL FICO D'INDIA, via Emerico Amari 64. Tel. 324214.
   Cuisine: SICILIAN. **Reservations:** Recommended. **Bus:** 8 or 9.
$ **Prices:** Appetizers 6,000–7,000 lire ($4.70–$5.50); main courses 7,000–8,000 lire ($5.50–$6.30). AE, MC, V.
   Open: Lunch Sat–Thurs 12:30–3:30pm; dinner Sat–Thurs 7–11:30pm.

This regional restaurant, frankly, deserves more acclaim than it traditionally receives. Al Fico d'India dispenses savory viands in a rustic tavern setting. The building dates from the 18th century, and has been enhanced with typically Sicilian decor. The table of antipasti, displayed on an old wagon, is about the best I've encountered in Sicily, each item succulent. On my recent rounds, one diner kept going back for more and more until the waiter pleaded, "But, sir, you should order a main dish." The roast kid (capretto o furnu) is the chef's specialty, as is a tournedos accompanied by a sauce that contains, among other ingredients, prosciutto. About the cheapest you can get by for is 25,000 lire ($19.65). The location is 200 yards from the harbor.

EVENING ENTERTAINMENT

I always like to begin my evening by heading to **Caffè Mazzara,** via Generale Magliocco 15 (tel. 321366), where you can sample Sicilian ice cream—among the best in the world—and order coffee that is the densest in all the country. Or perhaps you'll prefer to sit quietly, sipping one of the heady Sicilian wines and enjoying the piano bar. At this café you can anchor in the corner where Giuseppe di Lampedusa in the late '50s wrote a great many chapters of *The Leopard,* one of the finest novels to come out of Italy. Besides an espresso bar and pastry shop on the first floor, there's a so-called American grill on the second floor as well the prestigious Restaurant Charleston. If you can't find a place to eat in Palermo on a Sunday, when virtually everything is shut, the Mazzara is a good bet. It's open Tuesday through Sunday from 8am to 11pm. Cappuccino costs 1,500 lire ($1.20) at the bar.

The world-famed **Teatro Massimo,** opened in 1897, continues to be closed, with no announced date of reopening. In the meantime, operatic performances are given at **Politeama Garibaldi,** piazza Settimo (tel. 584334), which was constructed in 1874. I recently saw a performance of Donizetti's *Lucia di Lammermoor* here. It's best to have the concierge of your hotel call for seats, which (unless a superstar is appearing) generally range from 48,000 lire to 90,000 lire ($37.70 to $70.65) in the orchestra or 18,000 lire to 35,000 lire ($14.15 to $27.50) in the gallery.

One of the most elegant discos in town, **Speak Easy,** viale Strasburgo 34 (tel. 518486), is open Tuesday through Sunday nights from 10:30pm to 2:30am. Cover ranges from 10,000 lire to 20,000 lire ($7.85 to $15.70) per person, depending on the night of the week and including the cost of your first drink. The disco lies on the northern edge of Palermo (at night it's better—certainly safer—to come here by taxi).

EASY EXCURSIONS
MONREALE

The town of Monreale is 5 miles from Palermo, up Monte Caputo and on the edge of the Conca d'Oro plain. If you don't have a car, you can reach it by taking tram 8 or 9 from piazza Indipendenza in Palermo. The Normans under William II founded a Benedictine monastery at Monreale some time in the 1170s. Near the ruins of that monastery a great cathedral was erected.

As with the Alhambra in Granada, Spain, the ✪ **Church of Monreale** has a relatively drab facade, giving little indication of the riches inside. The interior is virtually covered throughout with shimmering mosaics, illustrating scenes from the Bible, such as the story of Adam and Eve or Noah and the Ark. The artwork provides a distinctly original interpretation to the old, rigid Byzantine form of decoration. The mosaics make for an Eastern look despite the Western-style robed Christ reigning over his kingdom. The ceiling is ornate, even gaudy. On the north and west facade of the church are two bronze doors in relief depicting biblical stories. The cloisters should also be visited. Built in 1166, they consist of twin mosaic columns, every other pair an original design (the lava inlay was hauled from the active volcano, Mount Etna). The church and cloisters are open April to September, Monday through Saturday from 9am to 7pm and on Sunday from 9am to 1pm; October to March, Monday through Saturday from 9am to 2pm and on Sunday from 9am to 1pm. Admission is 2,000 lire ($1.55).

It is also possible to visit the treasury and the terraces, each costing another 2,000 lire ($1.55). They are open from 7:30am to 12:30pm and 3 to 6:30pm. The terraces are actually the rooftop of the church, from which you'll be rewarded with a view of the cloisters.

Where to Stay

PARK HOTEL CARRUBELLA, corso Umberto I, 90046 Monreale. Tel. 091/6402187. Fax 091/6402189. 30 rms (all with bath). A/C TEL **Tram:** 8 or 9 from Palermo.

$ Rates: 50,000 lire ($39.25) single; 77,000 lire ($60.45) double. Breakfast 10,000 lire ($7.85) extra. AE, DC, MC, V. **Parking:** Free.

The Park Hotel is one of the tallest buildings in town, its terraces providing a sweeping view over the famous church, the surrounding valleys, and the azure coastline of faraway Palermo. To reach it, follow a one-lane road originating at the plaza near the church, which takes you along a serpentine series of terraces; the hotel is 800 yards from the cathedral. The hotel's spacious interior is filled with semiluxurious touches, including a black-marble bar built into the rocks of a cliff, gilt-framed mirrors, and deep and comfortable armchairs, along with scattered pieces of sculpture. In the public rooms, as well as in the bedrooms, the floors are covered with rows of Sicilian tiles hand-painted into flowery designs. The genial partners who own this place offer comfortably furnished accommodations, each with its own balcony. Breakfast costs extra. Well-prepared meals are served in the establishment's conservatively elegant dining room.

Where to Dine

LA BOTTE, contrada Lenzitti (S.S. 186) 416. Tel. 414051.
   Cuisine: SICILIAN/ITALIAN. **Reservations:** Essential Sat–Sun. **Tram:** 8 or 9 from Palermo.
 $ Prices: Appetizers 12,000–18,000 lire ($9.40–$14.15); main courses 15,000–20,000 lire ($11.80–$15.70). AE, DC, V.
   Open: Dinner only, Tues–Sun 8:30–10:45pm. **Closed:** July–Aug.
Most of the dishes served here are derived from ancient recipes of Palermo whose origins have long been forgotten. Perhaps you'll begin with an aromatic antipasto of such local ingredients as artichokes, tuna, and shrimp. Main courses include freshly grilled shrimp and traditional Sicilian meat dishes, with full meals costing 40,000 lire to 50,000 lire ($31.40 to $39.25).

MONDELLO LIDO

When the summer sun burns hot and old men on the square seek a place in the shade, and bambini tire of their games, it's beach weather. For the denizen of Palermo, that means Mondello, 7½ miles to the east. Originally, before this beachfront started attracting the wealthy class of Palermo, it was a fishing village (it still is), and you can see rainbow-colored fishing boats bobbing up in the harbor. A sandy **beach,** a good one, stretches for about a mile and a half, and it's filled to capacity on a July or August day. You might call it a Palermitan seaside experience. Some women traveling alone have found Mondello more inviting and less intimidating than downtown Palermo, which, for some, has a rough quality. In summer, an express bus (no. 6, "Beallo") goes to Mondello, leaving from the central train station in Palermo.

Where to Stay

MONDELLO PALACE HOTEL, viale Principe di Scalea 2, 90151 Mondello. Tel. 091/450001. Fax 091/450657. 83 rms (all with bath), 10 suites. A/C MINIBAR TV TEL **Bus:** 6 from Palermo.
 $ Rates: 145,000 lire ($113.85) single; 190,000 lire ($149.15) double; from 277,000 lire ($217.45) suite. AE, MC, V. **Parking:** Free.
   This first-class hotel is set behind a garden of palms and semitropical shrubs in the geographical center of the resort. Only a road separates it from the beach, yet many clients prefer the swimming pool, whose waters reflect the hotel's contemporary design of rounded corners and prominent balconies. This is the biggest hotel at the resort, and its accommodations are also the finest. Each room is well furnished.

SPLENDID HOTEL LA TORRE, via Piano di Gallo 11, 90151 Mondello. Tel. 091/450222. Fax 091/450033. 179 rms (all with bath), 9 suites. A/C TV TEL **Bus:** 14.
 $ Rates: 89,000 lire ($69.85) single; 134,000 lire ($105.20) double; from 191,000 lire ($149.95) suite. AE, MC, V. **Parking:** Free.
From your comfortable bed you can get up and walk out onto your private terrace overlooking the sea from which the Normans came to invade. Like any Mediterranean resort hotel, La Torre is crowded during the peak summer months so reservations are important. It offers well-furnished chambers, some quite spacious. All are well maintained (at least the 14 units I recently inspected with a maid who wanted to show me everything, including the linen closet). During the day there are many sports and recreational activities to occupy your time, including swimming pools, a tennis court, a garden, and plenty of games for children. La Torre is very much a family resort instead of a romantic retreat.
   It attracts some heavy drinkers as well—the bar opens at 9am, staying open till

1am. The place is not a gourmet haven, but I've enjoyed my meals here, especially the pasta and fish dishes. The cookery is quite good, the choice is ample, and the waiters take good care of you. Expect to spend 38,000 lire to 60,000 lire ($29.85 to $47.10).

Where to Dine

CHARLESTON LE TERRAZZE, viale Regina Elena. Tel. 450171.
   Cuisine: SICILIAN/INTERNATIONAL. **Reservations:** Required. **Bus:** 6 from Palermo.
$ Prices: Appetizers 12,000–15,000 lire ($9.40–$11.80); main courses 20,000–26,000 lire ($15.70–$20.40). AE, DC, MC, V.
   Open: Lunch daily 1–3pm; dinner daily 8–11pm. **Closed:** Oct–May.

The best food in Mondello is served at this restaurant, a buff-colored seaside fantasy of art nouveau, with spires and gingerbread detailing. It fronts the sands. The kitchen, fortunately, matches the delights of the eye. The Sicilian staff who work here add to the sense of luxury and refinement. However, it's expensive, so bring lots of money—at least 50,000 lire to 70,000 lire ($39.25 to $54.95) per person. The chef specializes in many dishes, including such favorites as melanzana (eggplant) Charleston (in my modest opinion, the Sicilians do the best eggplant dishes in the world). Try also the pesce spada (swordfish) al gratin and scaloppe Conca d'Oro. For dessert, you can have a spectacular finish to a worthy meal by ordering a parfait di caffee. For a wine, I recommend a Corvo, which comes both "blanco" and "rosso." Of course, with a name like Le Terrazze it's got to deliver the mandatory terrace with a view.

GAMBERO ROSSO, via Piano di Gallo 30. Tel. 454685.
   Cuisine: SICILIAN/SEAFOOD. **Reservations:** Not necessary. **Bus:** 6 from Palermo.
$ Prices: Appetizers 7,000–10,000 lire ($5.50–$7.85); main courses 10,000–15,000 lire ($7.85–$11.80).
   Open: Lunch Tues–Sun noon–3:30pm; dinner Tues–Sun 7:30–11:30pm. **Closed:** Jan 7–27.

This restaurant is cheaper than Le Terrazze, but also good. Some establishments depend on their owners for their identities and creative force, and this terraced restaurant with its panoramic sea view is one of them. Rosolino Gulizzi is the energetic force, personally supervising everything from the flavoring of the sauces to the table arrangements. Your meal might consist of an appetizer of lobster and shrimp, followed by paella, several stews, shrimp flambé, or other well-seasoned meats. A full list of local wines is available. Full meals, which are served to an appreciative audience, begin at 45,000 lire ($35.35).

BAGHERIA

Take a side trip east from Palermo to Bagheria, about 20 miles away, to see the **Villa Palagonia,** at piazza Garibaldi (tel. 934543). Built by an eccentric, deformed nobleman at the beginning of the 18th century, it has a garden full of grotesque statuary. Atop the garden wall are stone dwarfs and other freaks, some of them playing musical instruments. One of the rooms of the villa has a ceiling with mirrors creating a bizarre illusion. If you have an interest in the strange and grotesque, the villa will intrigue you. Goethe has an interesting passage about it in his travel diary. It can be visited from 9am to 6pm daily. Admission is 2,000 lire ($1.55).

CEFALÙ

For another day's excursion, I recommend a trek east from Palermo for 43 miles to this fishing village, which is known all over Europe for its Romanesque cathedral, an outstanding achievement of the Arab-Norman architectural style. Two SAIS buses a day connect Palermo to Cefalù.

What to See & Do

IL DUOMO, piazza del Duomo (off Corso Ruggero). Tel. 21293.

Resembling a military fortress, the Duomo was built by Roger II to fulfill a vow he made when faced with a possible shipwreck. Construction began in 1131, and in time two square towers dotted the landscape of Cefalù, curiously placed between the sea and a rocky promontory. The architectural line of the cathedral has a severe elegance, and inside are some outstanding Byzantine-inspired mosaics. Seek out especially *Christ the Pantocrator* in the dome of the apse. Capitals in the Sicilian-Norman style are supported by columns.

Admission: Free.
Open: Daily 9am–noon and 3:30–7pm.

MUSEO MANDRALISCA, via Mandralisca. Tel. 21547.

Before leaving town, be sure to visit this museum opposite the cathedral, with its outstanding collection of art, none more notable than the 1470 *Portrait of a Man* by Antonello de Messina. Some art critics have journeyed all the way down from Rome just to stare at this handsome work.

Admission: 1,500 lire ($1.20).
Open: Mon–Sat 9:30am–noon and 3:30–6pm.

Where to Dine

After the sights, the restaurants in town, frankly, dim in comparison, but you can still eat reasonably well.

AL GABBIANO DA SARO, viale Lungomare 17. Tel. 21495.

Cuisine: SICILIAN. **Reservations:** Recommended Sat–Sun.
$ Prices: Appetizers 5,000–10,000 lire ($3.95–$7.85); main courses 10,000–25,000 lire ($7.85–$19.65). AE, DC, V.
Open: June 15–Sept 15, lunch daily noon–3pm; dinner daily 7pm–midnight. Sept 16–June 14, lunch Thurs–Tues noon–3pm; dinner Thurs–Tues 7pm–midnight.
Closed: Mid-Jan to mid-Feb.

I've found the best food here. Fresh fish is the item to order at this rustic trattoria on the seaside, making your way through a list of unpronounceable sea creatures. You might begin with zuppa di cozze, a savory mussel soup. The vegetables and pastas are good too, especially pennette alla Norma (with eggplant). The cookery is consistent, as is the service. If you speak a little Italian, it helps. Expect to spend at least 35,000 lire ($27.50).

DA NINO AL LUNGOMARE, viale Lungomare 11. Tel. 22582.

Cuisine: SOUTHERN ITALIAN/SICILIAN. **Reservations:** Necessary.
$ Prices: Appetizers 7,000–8,000 lire ($5.50–$6.30); main courses 10,000–20,000 lire ($7.85–$15.70). AE, DC, MC, V.
Open: June–Sept, lunch daily noon–3pm; dinner daily 7–11pm. Oct–May, lunch Wed–Mon noon–3pm; dinner Wed–Mon 7–11pm. **Closed:** Jan–Feb.

This is a reasonably good choice for southern Italian and Sicilian cuisine. That means that the kitchen is in no way influenced by trends or food fads. Time-tested recipes are served here, including a delectable risotto marinara or "fisherman's rice." Fresh fish is the featured item. Full meals begin at 38,000 lire ($29.85).

2. SEGESTA

41 miles SW of Palermo, 91 miles NW of Agrigento

GETTING THERE **By Train** Two trains daily run from Palermo to Segesta. For information, call 6161806 in Palermo. A one-way fare is 9,900 lire ($7.75).

By Bus If you're going to see one of the classical plays (see below) you can take a bus leaving from piazza Politeama in Palermo approximately 2 hours before the show is presented. You should purchase your ticket in advance in Palermo, however; most travel agents sell such tickets, costing from 10,000 lire ($7.85).

By Car Continue west from Palermo along autostrada A29.

ESSENTIALS Consult the Tourist Information Office in Palermo (see above).

Segesta was the ancient city of the Elymi, a people of mysterious origin, although they have been linked by some to the Trojans. As the major city in western Sicily, it was brought into a series of conflicts with the rival power nearby, Selinus (Selinunte). From the 6th through the 5th century B.C. there were near-constant hostilities. The Athenians came from the east to aid the Segestans in 415 B.C., but the expedition ended in disaster, forcing the city to turn eventually for help to Hannibal of Carthage.

Twice in the 4th century B.C. it was besieged and conquered, once by Dionysius and again by Agathocles, the latter a particularly brutal victor who tortured, mutilated, or made slaves of most of the citizenry. Recovering eventually, Segesta in time turned on its old (but dubious) ally, Carthage. Like all Greek cities of Sicily, it ultimately fell to the Romans.

WHAT TO SEE & DO

Today Segesta is visited for its remarkable Doric ✪ **temple,** dating from the 5th century B.C. Although never completed, it is in an excellent state of preservation (the entablature still remains). The temple was far enough away from the ancient town to have escaped leveling during the "scorched earth" days of the Vandals and Arabs.

From its position on a lonely hill, the Doric temple commands a majestic setting. Although you can scale the hill on foot, you're likely to encounter Sicilian boys trying to hustle you for a donkey ride. From mid-July until the first week of August, classical plays are performed at the temple. Ask at the Tourist Information Office in Palermo for details. Local travel agents in Palermo sell tickets.

In another spot on Mount Barbaro, a **theater,** built in the Greek style into the rise of the hill, has been excavated. It was erected in the 3rd century B.C.

In the car park leading to the temple is a café for refreshments. Otherwise, Segesta is bereft of dining or accommodation selections.

---

3. SELINUNTE

76 miles SW of Palermo, 70 miles W of Agrigento

GETTING THERE By Train From Palermo, Trapani, or Marsala, you can make rail connections to Castelveltrano. Once at Castelveltrano, you must board a bus for Selinunte. Most passengers reach Selinunte from Palermo (call 6161806 in Palermo for more information).

By Bus Buses (about five per day) depart from in front of the rail terminal at Castelveltrano, heading for Selinunte. A one-way fare is 1,800 lire ($1.40).

By Car Selinunte is on the southern coast of Sicily and is best explored by car, as public transportation is awkward. From Segesta, continue south on autostrada A29 until Castelveltrano. From there, follow the signposted secondary road marked "Selinunte" which leads south to the sea.

ESSENTIALS There are no tourist offices in the area. The **telephone area code** for Selinunte is 0924.

One of the lost cities of ancient Sicily, Selinunte traces its history to the 7th century B.C. when immigrants from Megara Hyblaea (Syracuse) set out to build a new colony. They succeeded, erecting a city of power and prestige adorned with many temples. But that was like calling attention to a good thing. As earlier mentioned, much of Selinunte's fate was tied up with seemingly endless conflicts with the Elymi people of Segesta. Siding with Selinunte's rival, Hannibal virtually leveled the city in 409 B.C. Despite an attempt, the city was never to recover its former glory, and fell into ultimate decay.

Today it is an ❂ **archeological garden,** its temples in scattered ruins, the mellowed stone, the color of honey, littering the ground as if an earthquake had struck (as one did in ancient times). From 9am to dusk daily, you can walk through the monument zone, exploring such relics as the remains of the Acropolis, the heart of old Selinunte. Parts of it have been partially excavated and reconstructed, as much as is possible with the bits and fragments remaining. Admission is 2,000 lire ($1.55).

The temples, in varying states of preservation, are designated by alphabetical lettering. Temple E, in the Doric style, contains fragments of an inner temple. Standing on its ruins before the sun goes down, you can look across the water that washes up again on the shores of Africa, from which the Carthaginian fleet emerged to destroy the city. The temples are dedicated to such mythological figures as Apollo and Hera (Juno). Most of them date from the 6th and 5th centuries B.C. Temple G, in scattered ruins, was one of the largest erected in Sicily, and was built in the Doric style.

NEARBY PLACES TO STAY & DINE IN MARINELLA

The little seafront town of Marinella lies only a mile east of Selinunte, reached by going along a winding country road lined in part with stone walls.

HOTEL ALCESTE, via Alceste 23, 91020 Marinella di Selinunte. Tel. 0924/46184. Fax 0924/46143. 30 rms (all with bath). TEL
$ Rates (including breakfast): 40,000 lire ($31.40) single; 60,000 lire ($47.10) double; 60,000–68,000 lire ($47.10–$53.40) per person with half board. AE, V.
Parking: Street parking free. **Closed:** Dec–Feb.
After they erected the concrete walls of this hotel, the builders painted it a shade of sienna and filled its three-sided courtyard with dining tables and plants. This seasonal hotel is about a 15-minute walk of the ruins. The simple bedrooms each have private bath or phone. Most visitors, however, stop only for a meal, enjoying a regional dinner costing 25,000 lire to 35,000 lire ($19.65 to $27.50).

4. AGRIGENTO

80 miles S of Palermo, 109 miles SE of Trapani

GETTING THERE   By Train   Fifteen trains per day arrive from Palermo, taking 3 hours, a one-way ticket costing 12,200 lire ($9.55). For information about schedules, call 6161806 in Palermo. If you're already on the east coast of Sicily, the best connections are through Catania, with six trains per day arriving at Agrigento. Trip time is 3¾ hours, and a one-way ticket costs 12,200 lire ($9.55). In Catania, call 531625 for information.

By Bus   From Selinunte (see above), take the bus to Castelveltrano, at a one-way cost of 1,300 lire ($1), then transfer on to another bus bound for Agrigento. There is frequent service throughout the day from Castelveltrano to Agrigento. The trip takes 1¼ hours, and a one-way ticket costs 5,000 lire ($3.95).

By Car   From Palermo, cut southeast along Route 121 which becomes 188 and 189 before it finally reaches Agrigento and the Mediterranean.

ESSENTIALS   The **telephone area code** for Agrigento is 0922. The **Tourist Information Center** is at viale della Vittoria 255 (tel. 401352).

Greek colonists from Gela (Caltanissetta) named it Akragas when they established a beachhead here in the 6th century B.C. In time their settlement grew to become one of the most prosperous cities in Magna Graecia (Greater Greece). A great deal of that growth is attributed to the despot Phalaris, who ruled from 571 to 555 B.C. and is said to have roasted his victims inside a brazen bull, eventually meeting the same fate himself.

Empedocles, the Greek philosopher and politician (also credited by some as the founder of medicine in Italy), was the most famous son of Akragas, born around 490 B.C. He formulated the four-elements theory (earth, fire, water, and air), modified by the agents love and strife. In modern times the town produced Luigi Pirandello, the playwright (*Six Characters in Search of an Author*), who won the Nobel Prize in 1934.

Like nearby Selinunte, the city was attacked by war-waging Carthaginians, the first assault in 406 B.C. In the 3rd century B.C. the Carthaginians and Romans played Russian roulette with the city until it finally succumbed to Roman domination by 210 B.C. The city was then known as Agrigentium.

The modern part of the present town (in 1927 the name was changed from Girgenti to Agrigento) occupies a hill site. The narrow streets—casbahlike—date back to the influence of the conquering Saracens. Heavy Allied bombing in World War II necessitated much rebuilding.

Below the town stretch the long reaches of "La Valle dei Templi," containing some of the greatest Greek ruins in the world.

WHAT TO SEE & DO

THE VALLEY OF THE TEMPLES ✪ Writers are fond of suggesting that Greek ruins be viewed at either dawn or sunset. Indeed, their mysterious aura is heightened then. But for details you can search them out under the bright cobalt-blue Sicilian sky. The backdrop for the temples is idyllic, especially in spring when the striking almond trees blossom into pink. Riding out strada Panoramica, you'll first approach (on your left):

The **Temple of Juno** (Giunone): With many of its Doric columns restored, this temple was erected sometime in the mid-5th century B.C., at the peak of a construction boom that skipped across the celestial globe honoring the deities. As you climb the blocks, note the remains of a cistern as well as a sacrificial altar in front. There are good views of the entire valley from the perch here.

The **Temple of Concord,** next, ranks along with the Temple of Hephaistos (the "Theseum") in Athens as the best-preserved Greek temple in the world. Flanked by 13 columns on its side, along with 6 in front and 6 in back, the temple was built in the peripteral hexastyle. You'll see the clearest example in Sicily of what an inner temple was like. In the late 6th century A.D. the pagan structure was transformed into a Christian church, which may have saved it for posterity, although today it has been stripped down to its classical purity.

The **Temple of Hercules** is the most ancient, dating from the 6th century B.C. Badly ruined (only eight pillars are standing), it once ranked in size with the Temple of Zeus. At one time the temple sheltered a celebrated statue of Hercules. The infamous Gaius Verres, the Roman magistrate who became an especially bad governor of Sicily, attempted to steal the image as part of his temple-looting tear on the island.

The **Temple of Jupiter** (Zeus) was the largest in the valley, similar in some respects to the Temple of Apollo at Selinunte. In front of the structure was a large altar. The giant on the ground was one of several telamones (atlases) used to support the edifice.

The so-called **Temple of Dioscuri,** with four Doric columns intact, is a *pasticcio*—that is, it is composed of fragments from different buildings. At various times it has been designated as a temple honoring Castor and Pollux, the twin sons of Leda, and deities of seafarers; and Demeter (Ceres), the goddess of marriage and of the fertile earth; and Persephone, the daughter of Zeus who became the symbol of spring.

The temples can usually be visited daily from 9am till 1 hour before sunset. City bus nos. 8 and 9 leave from piazza Marconi in Agrigento, taking you to the site of the temples.

IN TOWN The **Museo Regionale Archeologico** stands near the Church of

Saint Nicholas, on contrada San Nicolà (tel. 29008), and is open daily from 9am to 6pm, charging no admission. Its single most important exhibit is a head of the god Telamon from the Temple of Jupiter. The collection of Greek vases is also impressive. Many of the artifacts on display were dug up when Agrigento was excavated.

WHERE TO STAY

Only a fair lot of hostelries is offered, but they are compensatingly inexpensive, the best choices falling in the medium-priced range.

JOLLY HOTEL DEI TEMPLI, Parco Angeli, Villagio Mosè SS 115, 92100 Agrigento. Tel. 0922/606144. Fax 0922/606685. 146 rms (all with bath), 2 suites. A/C MINIBAR TV TEL **Bus:** 9.
$ **Rates** (including breakfast): 125,000 lire ($98.15) single; 190,000 lire ($149.15) double; from 210,000 lire ($164.85) suite. AE, DC, MC, V. **Parking:** Free.
Located in a commercial section, this modern structure boasts a swimming pool and well-furnished accommodations with balconies. On the premises are a bar and a restaurant where meals begin at 35,000 lire ($27.50). Sicilian and international cuisines are featured.

HOTEL VILLA ATHENA, via dei Templi, 92100 Agrigento. Tel. 0922/596288. Fax 0922/402180. 40 rms (all with bath). A/C MINIBAR TV TEL **Bus:** 8, 9, 10, or 11.
$ **Rates** (including breakfast): 115,000 lire ($90.30) single; 180,000 lire ($141.30) double. AE, DC, MC, V. **Parking:** Outdoor parking free.
This 18th-century former private villa, set in the Valley of the Temples less than 2 miles from town, rises from the Sicilian landscape. The grounds around it have been planted with fruit trees that bloom in January. During the day, guests sit on the paved courtyard, enjoying a drink and the fresh breezes. At night from one of the villa's windows, a view of the floodlit temples, a string of Doric ruins, can be seen. In a setting of gardenia bushes and flowers, a swimming pool has been installed. The dining room is in a separate building, serving both regional specialties and international dishes. In summer, make a reservation about 2 weeks in advance. Rooms are modern, with Italian styling. Room 205 frames a perfect view of the Temple of Concord.

HOTEL TRE TORRI, Viallagio Mosè 115, 92100 Agrigento. Tel. 0922/606733. Fax 0922/607839. 118 rms (all with bath). A/C TEL **Bus:** 8 or 9.
$ **Rates** (including breakfast): 75,000 lire ($58.90) single; 110,000 lire ($86.35) double. AE, V. **Parking:** Free.
On the eastern approach to Agrigento, this hotel lies near the better-known Jolly Hotel in an unattractive commercial district, yet some consider it the best hotel in town. Sheltered behind a mock-medieval facade of white stucco, chiseled stone blocks, false crenellations, and crisscrossed iron balconies, the hotel is a favorite with the Italian business traveler. A swimming pool in the small, terraced garden is visible from a restaurant. There's also a bar, sometimes with live piano music, plus an indoor pool, a sauna, and a disco. The bedrooms are comfortable, and some contain TV. Furnishings are modern.

WHERE TO DINE

TRATTORIA DEL VIGNETO, via Cavalieri Magazzeni 11. Tel. 414319.
Cuisine: SICILIAN. **Reservations:** Not needed but accepted. **Bus:** 9.
$ **Prices:** Appetizers 7,000–10,000 lire ($5.50–$7.85); main courses 8,000–15,000 lire ($6.30–$11.80). AE.
Open: Lunch Wed–Mon 12:30–3pm; dinner Wed–Mon 8–10pm. **Closed:** Nov.
This is a fine place to go for a Sicilian meal after a visit to the Valley of the Temples, just a short distance away. Menu items include a mixed Sicilian grill, loaded with many kinds of meat, along with lamb cutlets and a flavor-packed beefsteak laced with cheese and local herbs. The welcome is sincere, and the cost of the meal will range upward from 35,000 lire ($27.50).

LE CAPRICE, strada Panoramica dei Templi 51. Tel. 26469.
   Cuisine: SEAFOOD/ITALIAN. **Reservations:** Required. **Bus:** 9.
$ **Prices:** Appetizers 7,000–10,000 lire ($5.50–$7.85); main courses 15,000–30,000 lire ($11.80–$23.55). AE, DC, MC, V.
   Open: Sept–June, lunch Sat–Thurs 12:30–3pm; dinner Sat–Thurs 7:30–11pm. Aug, lunch daily 12:30–3pm; dinner daily 7:30–11pm. **Closed:** July.

A loyal clientele return to this well-directed restaurant for special celebrations as well as for everyday fun. Specialties of the house include an antipasto buffet, a mixed fish fry from the gulf, along with rolled pieces of veal in a savory sauce. Full meals cost 32,000 lire to 45,000 lire ($25.10 to $35.35).

5. SYRACUSE (SIRACUSA)

35 miles S of Catania

GETTING THERE   **By Train**   From other major cities in Sicily, you'll find Syracuse best reached by train: 1½ hours from Catania (coming up), 2 hours from Taormina (also coming up), and 5 hours from Palermo (already previewed).

By Bus   If you're in Catania, you can continue south by SAIS bus for Syracuse. Eight buses make the 1½-hour trip per day, costing 5,300 lire ($4.15) one way. Phone SAIS in Syracuse at 66710 for information and schedules.

By Car   **From Catania, continue south along Route 114.**

ESSENTIALS   The **telephone area code** for Syracuse is 0931. The **Tourist Information Center** is at via San Sebastiano 43 (tel. 67710), facing the Church of San Giovanni, with a branch office at the entrance to the archeological park, on largo Teatro Greco (tel. 60510).

Of all the Greek cities of antiquity that flourished on the coast of Sicily, Siracusa was the most important, a formidable competitor of Athens in the West. In the heyday of its power, it dared take on Carthage, even Rome. At one time its wealth and size were unmatched by any other city in Europe.

On a site on the Ionian Sea, colonizers from Corinth founded the city in about 735 B.C. Much of its history was linked to despots, beginning in 485 B.C. with Gelon, the "tyrant" of Gela who subdued the Carthaginians at Himera. Siracusa came under attack from Athens in 415 B.C., but the main Athenian fleet was destroyed and the soldiers on the mainland captured. They were herded into the Latoma di Cappuccini at piazza Cappuccini, a stone quarry. The "jail," from which there was no escape, was particularly horrid, as the defeated soldiers weren't given food and were packed together like cattle and allowed to die slowly.

Dionysius I was one of the greatest despots, reigning over the city during its particular glory in the 4th century B.C., when it extended its influence as a sea power. But in 212 B.C. the city fell to the Romans who, under Marcellus, sacked its riches and art. Incidentally, in this rape Siracusa lost its most famous son, the Greek physicist and mathematician Archimedes, who was slain in his study by a Roman soldier.

Before you go, you might want to read Mary Renault's *The Mask of Apollo,* set in Syracuse of the 5th century B.C. As one critic put it, "It brings the stones to life."

WHAT TO SEE & DO

THE ARCHEOLOGICAL GARDEN

West of the modern town (take viale Rizzo) is the archeological garden, peppered with the three most important sightseeing attractions. The archeological park, charging 2,000 lire ($1.55) for admission, is open daily from 9am to 2 hours before sunset all year; closed New Year's Day, April 25, May 1, August 15, and Christmas.

On Temenite Hill, the ✪ **Greek theater** was one of the great theaters of the classical period. Hewn from rocks during the reign of Hieron I in the 5th century

B.C., the ancient seats have been largely eaten away by time. You can, however, still stand on the remnants of the stone stage where plays by Euripides were presented. In the time of Hieron II in the 3rd century B.C.—a "term" that lasted through a golden jubilee—the theater was much restored. In spring the Italian Institute of Ancient Drama presents classical plays, works by Euripides, Aeschylus, and Sophocles. In other words, the show hasn't changed in 2,000 years.

The **Roman amphitheater** was erected at the time of Augustus. It ranks among the top five amphitheaters left by the Romans in Italy. Like the Greek theater, part of it was carved from rock. Unlike the Greek theater and its classical plays, the Roman amphitheater tended toward more "gutsy" fare. Gladiators—prisoners of war and exotic blacks from Africa—faced each other with tridents and daggers, or naked slaves would be whipped into the center of a to-the-death battle between wild beasts. Either way, the victim lost. If this combatant, man or beast, didn't do him in, the crowd would often scream for the ringmaster to slice his throat. The amphitheater is near the entrance to the park, but it can also be viewed in its entirety from a belvedere on the panoramic road.

The most famous of the ancient quarries, the **☼ Latomia del Paradiso** is one of four or five latomies from which stones were hauled to erect the great monuments of Siracusa in its day of glory. On seeing one of the caves, Michelangelo de Caravaggio is reputed to have dubbed it "The Ear of Dionysius," because of its unusual shape like that of a human ear. But what an ear! It's nearly 200 feet long. You can enter the inner chamber of the grotto where the tearing of paper sounds like a gunshot. It is said that the despot Dionysius used to force his prisoners into the "ear" at night, where he was able to hear every word they said. But this story, widely reported, is dismissed by some scholars as fanciful. Nearby is the Grotta dei Cordari, where ropemakers plied their ancient craft.

OTHER SIGHTS

MUSEO PAOLO ORSI, viale Teocrito 66. Tel. 66222.

One of the most important archeological museums in southern Italy, the Museo Paolo Orsi made its debut in 1988, replacing an early archeological museum. Here, in these modern quarters, you can survey the Greek, Roman, and early Christian epochs in sculpture and fragments of archeological remains. The museum also has a rich coin collection. Of the statues here (and there are several excellent ones), the best known is the headless *Venus Anadyomene* (arising from the sea). This work of art dates from the Hellenistic period in the 2nd century B.C. One of the earliest-known works is of an earth mother suckling two babes, from the 6th century B.C. The pre-Greek vases have great style and elegance. The museum stands in the gardens of Villa Landolina in Akradina.

Admission: 2,000 lire ($1.55) adults, free for children under 18.
Open: Tues–Sun 10am–noon and 3–6pm. **Bus:** 1.

CATACOMBE DI SAN GIOVANNI (St. John), at the end of viale San Giovanni.

These honeycombed tunnels of empty coffins evoke the catacombs along the Appian Way in Rome. The world down below is approached from the Chiesa di San Giovanni, from the 3rd century A.D., and the present building is of a much later date. Included in the early Christian burial grounds is the crypt of St. Marcianus, which lies under what was reportedly the first cathedral erected in Sicily.

Admission: 2,000 lire ($1.55).
Open: Mar–Nov, Thurs–Tues 9:30am–12:30pm and 3:30–5:30pm; Dec–Feb, Thurs–Tues 9:30am–12:30pm and 3–5pm. **Bus:** 1.

The Island of Ortygia

Its beauties praised by Pindar, the island, reached by crossing the Ponte Nuova, was the heart of Siracusa, having been founded by the Greek colonists from Corinth. In Greek mythology, it is said to have been ruled by Calypso, daughter of Atlas, the sea nymph who detained Ulysses (Odysseus) for 7 years on the island. The island is about a mile long and half again as wide.

Heading out the Foro Italico, you'll come to the **Fountain of Arethusa,** also famous in mythology. Alpheius, the river god, son of Oceanus, is said to have fallen in love with the sea nymph Arethusa. The nymph turned into this spring or fountain, but Alpheius became a river and "mingled" with his love. According to legend, the spring ran red when bulls were sacrificed at Olympus.

At piazza del Duomo, the **Cathedral of Syracuse,** with a baroque facade, was built over the ruins of the Temple of Minerva, and employs the same Doric columns. The temple was erected after Gelon the Tyrant defeated the Carthaginians at Himera in the 5th century B.C. The Christians converted it into a basilica in the 7th century A.D.

The **Palazzo Bellomo,** fronting via Capodieci, off Foro Vittorio Emanuele II, dates from the 13th century, with many alterations, and is today the home of the **Museo Nazionale.** Not only is the palace fascinating, with its many arches, doors, and stairs, but it has a fine collection of paintings. The most notable is an *Annunciation* by Antonello da Messina from 1474. There is also a noteworthy collection of antiques, porcelain, and paintings. It is open Tuesday through Saturday from 9am to 2pm and on Sunday from 9am to 1pm, charging an admission of 2,000 lire ($1.55).

WHERE TO STAY

HOTEL AGIP, viale Teracati 30-32, 96100 Siracusa. Tel. 0931/66944. Fax 0931/67115. 87 rms (all with bath). A/C MINIBAR TV TEL **Bus:** 2, 8, or 11.
$ Rates (including breakfast): 120,000 lire ($94.20) single; 160,000 lire ($125.60) double. AE, DC, MC, V. **Parking:** 8,000 lire ($6.30).
Each of the rooms is comfortably furnished and well maintained, and contains several streamlined modern comforts. The restaurant is often visited by residents of Syracuse who consider the generous portions and flavorful specialties worth the trip. Menu items include a wide array of Sicilian and international dishes, including pastas, stuffed veal, tournedos American style, and a changing variety of fish. Full meals begin at 35,000 lire ($27.50). Open every day, the establishment lies near the archeological zone.

JOLLY, corso Gelone 43, 96100 Siracusa. Tel. 0931/64744. Fax 0931/461111. 100 rms (all with bath). A/C MINIBAR TV TEL **Bus:** 1.
$ Rates (including breakfast): 145,000 lire ($113.85) single; 190,000 lire ($149.15) double. AE, DC, MC, V. **Parking:** Free.
The best place to stay is the Jolly, a member of a chain that is the Holiday Inn of Italy. You get no surprises here—clean, modern, functional rooms, short on soul but good on comfort. Each room is equipped with a bath or shower. The hotel restaurant offers lunch or dinner for 40,000 lire ($31.40).

HOTEL BELLAVISTA, via Diodoro Siculo 4, 96100 Siracusa. Tel. 0931/36912. Fax 0931/37927. 45 rms (all with bath or shower). TV TEL **Bus:** 1.
$ Rates (including breakfast): 56,000 lire ($43.95) single; 90,000 lire ($70.65) double. AE, DC, MC, V. **Parking:** Free.
Family owned and run, this hotel is hidden on a lane in a quiet residential section, surrounded by flowering trees and vines. There is an annex in the garden for overflow guests. The main lounge has a sense of space, with leather chairs and semitropical plants. The bedrooms are informal and comfortable, often furnished with traditional pieces. Most of the rooms have their own sea-view balcony.

PANORAMA, via Necropoli Grotticelle 33, 96100 Siracusa. Tel. 0931/32122. 51 rms (all with bath or shower). TV TEL **Bus:** 1.
$ Rates: 48,000 lire ($37.70) single; 66,000 lire ($51.80) double. Breakfast 6,000 lire ($4.70) extra. V. **Parking:** Free.
Near the entrance to the city, on a rise of Temenite Hill, is this bandbox-modern hotel, built on a busy street, about 5 minutes from the Greek theater or Roman amphitheater. It is not a motel, but does provide parking space. Inside, a contemporary accommodation awaits you. The bedrooms are pleasant, and up-to-

date with comfortable but utilitarian pieces. On the premises is a hotel dining room serving only a continental breakfast (not included in the room prices).

WHERE TO DINE

ARLECCHINO, via dei Tolomei 5. Tel. 66386.
   Cuisine: SEAFOOD. **Reservations:** Recommended. **Bus:** 1.
$ **Prices:** Appetizers 10,000–15,000 lire ($7.85–$11.80); main courses 15,000–30,000 lire ($11.80–$23.55). AE, DC, V.
   Open: Lunch Mon–Sat 12:30–3pm; dinner Mon–Sat 8–10pm. **Closed:** Aug 10–Sept 10.

Despite its understated decor, Arlecchino is considered by some gourmets the best restaurant in town. Many specialties emerge from this fragrant kitchen. These include a wide array of homemade pastas, a cheese-laden crespelline of the house, pasta with sardines, spiedini with shrimp, and a selection of pungent beef, fish, and veal dishes. Full meals range from 40,000 lire to 60,000 lire ($31.40 to $47.10).

DARSENA DA IANUZZO, riva Garibaldi 6. Tel. 66104.
   Cuisine: SEAFOOD. **Reservations:** Required. **Bus:** 1.
$ **Prices:** Appetizers 6,000–15,000 lire ($4.70–$11.80); main courses 8,000–18,000 lire ($6.30–$14.15). AE, DC, MC.
   Open: Lunch Thurs–Tues 12:30–3pm; dinner Thurs–Tues 8–10pm.

S This might not differ all that much from dozens of other seafood restaurants in town, except that the food here seems to be exceptionally good and the welcome warm. Specialties include fresh shellfish, spaghetti with clams, a wide collection of fresh grilled and baked fish, and the ever-present fish soup. A full meal ranges from 35,000 lire to 58,000 lire ($27.50 to $45.55).

RISTORANTE JONICO E RUTTA E CIAULI, riviera Dionisio il Grande 194. Tel. 65540.
   Cuisine: SICILIAN. **Reservations:** Recommended. **Bus:** 1.
$ **Prices:** Appetizers 8,000–9,500 lire ($6.30–$7.45); main courses 18,000–20,000 lire ($14.15–$15.70). AE, DC, V.
   Open: Lunch Wed–Mon 12:30–3pm; dinner Wed–Mon 8–10pm.

This is one of the best restaurants on the island for serving the typical cuisine and local wines of Sicily. The restaurant offers a veranda and garden setting right on the sea, with a panoramic view (the location is about 100 yards from the Latomia dei Cappuccini). The decoration is in the typical Sicilian style. The antipasto array alone is dazzling. Superb homemade pasta dishes are served (ask one of the English-speaking waiters to explain some of the many variations or settle for spaghetti with caviar). One of the most interesting fish dishes I recently sampled was spada a pizzaiola (a swordfish in a savory, garlic-flavored sauce). Meat specialties include polpettone (rolled meat) alla siracusana, and a delectable stew made of various fish. The dessert specialty is a cassatine siciliana. Expect to pay 45,000 lire to 55,000 lire ($35.35 to $43.20).

RISTORANTE ROSSINI, via Malta 37. Tel. 24317.
   Cuisine: MEDITERRANEAN. **Reservations:** Recommended. **Bus:** 1.
$ **Prices:** Appetizers 8,500–9,000 lire ($6.65–$7.05); main courses 12,000–15,000 lire ($9.40–$11.80). AE, DC, MC, V.
   Open: Lunch Sun–Fri 12:30–3:30pm; dinner Mon–Sat 8–10pm.

S Ristorante Rossini is a homelike and comfortable enclave of regional gastronomy, offering meals to 50 fortunate diners a night, from 35,000 lire ($27.50) for a complete meal. You might begin with an assortment from the amply stocked buffet table of antipasti, then select one of many main dishes, including a mousse of fish with fresh shrimp, perhaps a shellfish risotto with roast peppers and tomato purée. A twice-roasted swordfish is also a specialty. For food of the region, this place deserves a visit.

RISTORANTE BANDIERA—DA LINO, via Eritrea 2. Tel. 68546.
   Cuisine: SICILIAN/MEDITERRANEAN. **Reservations:** Recommended. **Bus:** 1.

$ Prices: Appetizers 6,000–10,000 lire ($4.70–$7.85); main courses 12,000–18,000 lire ($9.40–$14.15). AE, V.
Open: Lunch Fri–Wed 12:30–3pm; dinner Fri–Wed 8–10pm.

Ideal for those who want to dine at an old tavern, this restaurant is near the entrance to the bridge leading to the Città Vecchia (old town). Restored, it is a mellow building, close to the fishing boats. It has a certain charm, and the cuisine is dedicated to the best of Sicilian dishes. A reliable dish is the zuppa di pesce (fish soup). An alternative choice is the zuppa di cozze, a plate brimming with fresh mussels in a savory marinade. Among the *asciutte,* the Sicilian cannelloni is good. The meat dishes feature a number of choices from the kitchens of Latium, Tuscany, and Emilia-Romagna. A complete meal will cost 35,000 lire to 45,000 lire ($27.50 to $35.35).

6. TAORMINA

33 miles N of Catania, 33 miles S of Messina, 155 miles E of Palermo

GETTING THERE **By Train** You can make rail connections on the Messina line to Syracuse. Telephone 51511 in Taormina for schedules. The train station at Taormina, however, is a mile from the heart of the resort, but buses waiting there will take you up a hill.

By Bus Most visitors arrive in Messina, their "gateway" to Sicily. There they can board a Taormina-bound bus, nearly 20 leaving per day, taking an hour and 30 minutes. More details are available in Messina by calling SAIS, the bus company, at 771914.

By Car From Messina, head south along autostrada A18. From Catania, continue north along A18.

ESSENTIALS The Taormina **telephone area code** is 0942. From June to September, the city operates a **Tourist Information Center** in the Palazzo Corvaja, largo Santa Caterina (tel. 23243).

Once you arrive in the center of Taormina, you can walk to the following recommendations. If you arrive at the train station, you'll find a bus taking you up to the center of Taormina every 15 to 45 minutes (schedules vary throughout the year). Service is daily from 9am to 9pm; a one-way ticket costs 1,200 lire (95¢).

Runaway bougainvillea, silvery olive branches, a cerulean sky, cactuses adorning the hills like modern sculpture, pastel plastered walls, garden terraces of geraniums, trees laden with oranges and lemons, ancient ruins—all that and more is Taormina, Sicily's most desirable oasis.

Dating from the 4th century B.C., Taormina hugs close to the edge of a cliff overlooking the Ionian Sea. Writers for English Sunday supplements rave of its unspoiled charms and enchantment. The sea, even the railroad track, lie down below, connected by bus routes. Looming in the background is Mount Etna, the active volcano. Noted for its mild climate, the town enjoys a year-round season.

A lot of people contributed to putting Taormina on the tourist map. Since it was first inhabited by a tribe known as the Siculi, it has known many conquerors, including Greeks, Carthaginians, Romans, Saracens, French, and Spanish. Its first tourist was said to have been Goethe, who arrived in 1787. He recorded his impressions in his *Journey to Italy.* Other Germans were to follow in the centuries to come, including a red-haired Prussian, Otto Geleng. Arriving at the age of 20 in Taormina, he recorded its beauties in his painted landscapes. These were exhibited in Paris and caused much excitement—people had to go themselves to find out if Taormina was all that beautiful.

Another German, Wilhelm von Gloeden, arrived to photograph not only the town, but nude boys crowned with laurel wreaths. These pictures sent European high society flocking to Taormina. Von Gloeden's photographs, some of which are even printed in official tourist literature to this day, form one of the most enduring legends of Taormina. Souvenir shops still sell his pictures, which, although considered scandalous in their day, would be tame, even innocent, by today's X-rated standards.

Following in the footsteps of von Gloeden came a host of international celebrities hoping to see what all the excitement was about: Truman Capote, Tennessee Williams, Marlene Dietrich, Joan Crawford, Rita Hayworth, and Greta Garbo, to name only some of the more stellar personalities of yesterday. Always in disguise, sometimes as Harriet Brown, Ms. Garbo used Taormina as a vacation retreat from 1950 until her last mysterious arrival in 1979. Many of these stars, including Garbo, stayed at a villa on the road to Castel Mola owned by Gayelord Hauser, the celebrated dietician to Hollywood stars back in the golden age. In time another wave of stars were to arrive: Taylor and Burton, Cary Grant, and the woman who turned him down, Sophia Loren.

The rich and famous still come here, along with a lot of middle-class visitors as well. Taormina remains chic.

WHAT TO SEE & DO

The ✪ **Greek and Roman theater,** via Teatro Greco (tel. 23220), is the most visited monument, offering a view of rare beauty of Mount Etna and the seacoast. At an unrecorded time the Greeks hewed the theater out of rock on the slope of Mount Tauro, but the Romans remodeled and modified it greatly for their amusement. The conquering Arabs, who seemed intent on devastating the town in the 10th century, slashed away at it. On the premises is an antiquarium, containing not only artifacts from the classical period but early Christian ones as well. The theater is open daily from 9am to 2 hours before sunset. Admission is 2,000 lire ($1.55) for adults; children under 18 are admitted free.

The other thing to do in Taormina is to walk through the **Giardino Pubblico,** via Bagnoli Croce, a flower-filled garden overlooking the sea, a choice spot for views as well as a place to relax. At a bar in the park, you can order drinks. Take bus no. 1 or 2 to reach these attractions.

WHERE TO STAY

The hotels in Taormina are the best in Sicily—in fact, the finest in southern Italy after you head south of Amalfi. All price levels and accommodations are offered, from sumptuous suites to army cots once you arrive.

VERY EXPENSIVE

SAN DOMENICO PALACE, piazza San Domenico 5, 98039 Taormina. Tel. 0942/23701. Fax 0942/625506. 101 rms (all with bath), 8 suites. A/C MINIBAR TV TEL **Bus:** 1 or 2.

$ Rates (including breakfast): 320,000 lire ($251.20) single; 560,000 lire ($439.60) double; from 1,560,000 lire ($1,224.60) suite; 325,000–425,000 lire ($255.15–$333.65) per person for half board. AE, DC, MC, V. **Parking:** 30,000 lire ($23.55).

✪ This is one of the great old hotels of Europe, converted from a 14th-century Dominican monastery, complete with cloisters. Overhauled, it almost begrudgingly boasts air conditioning and a flower-edged swimming pool. Its position is legend to discriminating travelers—high up from the sea coast, on several different levels surrounded by terraced gardens of almond, orange, and lemon trees. In the 19th century it blossomed as a hotel, with no expense spared, and was a favorite of the elite: kings, artists, writers, statesmen.

The large medieval courtyard is planted with semitropical trees and flowers. The encircling enclosed loggia, the old vaulted-ceilinged cloister, is decorated with potted palms and ecclesiastical furnishings (high-backed carved choir stalls, wooden angels and cherubs, religioso paintings in oil). Off the loggia are great refectory halls turned into sumptuously furnished lounges. While antiques are everywhere, the atmosphere is not museumlike, but gracious, with traditional upholstered chairs and sofas. Ornate ceilings climb high, and arched windows look out onto the view. Dining in the main hall is an event.

The bedrooms, opening off the cloister, would surely impress a cardinal. One-of-a-kind furniture has been utilized, including elaborate carved beds, gilt, Chinese red, provincial pieces, Turkish rugs, Venetian chairs and dressers.

Dining/Entertainment: The cuisine, a combination of Sicilian and Italian dishes, is the most refined in Taormina. Dining in the main hall is an event. The cuisine is supervised by a masterful chef.

Services: Room service, baby-sitting, laundry, valet.

Facilities: Swimming pool.

EXPENSIVE

BRISTOL PARK HOTEL, via Bagnoli Croce 92, 98039 Taormina. Tel. 0942/23006. Fax 0942/24519. 55 rms (all with bath), 2 suites. A/C MINIBAR TV TEL **Bus:** 1 or 2.

$ Rates: 125,000 lire ($98.15) single; 218,000 lire ($171.15) double; from 243,000 lire ($190.75) suite; 110,000–160,000 lire ($86.35–$125.60) per person for half board. AE, DC, MC, V. **Parking:** 10,000 lire ($7.85). **Closed:** Jan 10–Feb and Dec 1–20.

This is one of the all-out comfort hotels built high on the cliffside at the edge of Taormina. Close to the public gardens of Duca di Cesaro, it offers a spectacular view of the coastline and Mount Etna from most of its private sun balconies. The interior decor is amusing: with tufted satin, plush and ornate. In contrast, the bedrooms are traditional, with private bath. Meals, ordered separately, begin at 50,000 lire ($39.25). The dining room, with arched windows framing the view, offers international meals, with an occasional Sicilian dish. There's a private beach with free deck chairs and parasols, plus bus service to the beach from June 1 to September 30. The hotel also has a swimming pool, and there's a private garage.

EXCELSIOR PALACE, via Toselli 6, 98039 Taormina. Tel. 0942/23975. Fax 0942/23978. 89 rms (all with bath). A/C TV TEL **Bus:** 1 or 2.

$ Rates (including breakfast): 132,000 lire ($103.60) single; 210,000 lire ($164.85) double. AE, DC, V. **Parking:** Free.

The Excelsior seems like a Moorish palace, lost on the end ridge of the mountain fringe of Taormina. As foreboding as a fortress on two sides, the severity dissolves inside into style and comfort. The gardens at the back have terraces of scented semitropical flowers, date palms, yucca, and geraniums. The view of Etna and the seacoast below is of a rare enchantment. Renovated successfully, the hotel is managed so that superior facilities and service await all guests. The bedrooms have plenty of space and are decorated in a traditional manner. You can swim at the hotel's seaside annex, and the kitchen staff will pack you a picnic lunch.

HOTEL MONTE TAURO, via Madonna delle Grazie 3, 98039 Taormina. Tel. 0942/24402. Fax 0942/24403. 30 rms (all with bath), 40 junior suites. A/C MINIBAR TV TEL **Bus:** 1 or 2.

$ Rates (including half board): 140,000–175,000 lire ($109.90–$137.40) per person. AE, DC, MC, V. **Parking:** 10,000 lire ($7.85).

Engineering skills and tons of poured concrete went into the construction of this dramatic hotel built into the side of a scrub-covered hill rising high above the sea, within view of the coastline. Each bedroom has a circular balcony, often festooned with flowers. The social center is the many-angled swimming pool, whose cantilevered platform is ringed with a poolside bar, dozens of plants, and comfortable deck chairs. The velvet-covered chairs of the modern, tile-floored interior are upholstered in the same blues, grays, and violets of the sunny bedrooms where Mondrian-style rectangles and stripes decorate the bedspreads and accessories. The hotel rents well-furnished bedrooms and suites, each with private bath or shower. Guests stay here on half-board terms.

JOLLY HOTEL DIODORO, via Bagnoli Croce 75, 98039 Taormina. Tel.

0942/23312. Fax 0942/23391. 102 rms (all with bath). A/C MINIBAR TV TEL **Bus:** 1 or 2.

$ Rates (including breakfast): 160,000 lire ($125.60) single; 210,000 lire ($164.85) double; 140,000–189,000 lire ($109.90–$148.40) per person with half board. AE, DC, MC, V. **Parking:** Free.

The Jolly is one of the most luxurious of the first-class hotels. Actually it was built and designed privately, and then taken over by the Jolly chain. The design of everything— the public lounges, the bedrooms—is well coordinated, on a high taste level. The dining room, with tall windows on three sides, is projected toward the sea and Mount Etna. If there's sun in Taormina, you'll find it here. The outdoor swimming pool is also a sun trap; you can bathe, swim, and enjoy the view of mountains, trees, and flowers. The bedrooms are tasteful and comfortable, with well-designed furniture and the latest gadgets. Each has a private bath or shower. Many of the rooms are angled toward the sea, with wide-open windows.

MODERATE

ARISTON, via Bagnoli Croci 128, 98039 Taormina. Tel. 0942/23428. Fax 0942/21137. 22 rms (all with bath). A/C MINIBAR TEL **Bus:** 1 or 2.

$ Rates (including breakfast): 67,000 lire ($52.60) single; 119,000 lire ($93.40) double. V. **Parking:** Free.

Ariston, opened in 1975, and standing near the Greek and Roman theater, enjoys a convenient and tranquil position. The landscape has been enhanced with vegetation, and guests stroll about enjoying the scenery. Inside, a decorator has made a statement with bold fabrics. Everything is beautifully maintained and run, and you're made to feel at home. All bedrooms have a terrace, and the view from many of the windows is stunning.

VILLA BELVEDERE, via Bagnoli Croce 79, 98039 Taormina. Tel. 0942/ 23791. Fax 0942/625830. 48 rms (all with bath). TEL **Bus:** 1 or 2.

$ Rates (including breakfast): 80,500 lire ($63.20) single; 148,000 lire ($116.20) double. MC, V. **Parking:** 5,000 lire ($3.95). **Closed:** Nov–Feb.

This is a gracious old villa bathed in Roman gold near the Giardino Pubblico. In its garden is a heated swimming pool. From the cliffside terrace in the rear—a social center for guests—is that view: the clear blue sky, the gentle Ionian Sea, the cypress-studded hillside, and menacing Mount Etna looking as if it's about to blow its top. It's the same view, incidentally, enjoyed by clients at the more expensive first-class hotels nearby. The formal entrance is enhanced by potted plants and wall-covering vines, and the interior living rooms of this generations-old, family-run establishment would captivate Elizabeth Barrett Browning. The bedrooms have been restored, and 15 of them are air-conditioned. Only breakfast is served, although there are two bars.

VILLA FIORITA, via Pirandello 39, 98039 Taormina. Tel. 0942/24122. Fax 0942/625967. 24 rms (all with bath). A/C MINIBAR TV TEL **Bus:** 1 or 2.

$ Rates (including breakfast): 95,500 lire ($74.95) single; 103,000 lire ($80.85) double. AE, DC, MC, V. **Parking:** 10,000 lire ($7.85).

One of the most charming hotels in its category, Villa Fiorita stretches toward the town's Greek theater from its position beside the road leading up to the top. Designed in 1976, its imaginative decor includes a handful of ceramic stoves, which the owner delights in collecting. A well-maintained garden is bordered by an empty but ancient Greek tomb whose stone walls have been classified as a national treasure. The bedrooms are arranged in a steplike labyrinth of corridors and stairwells, some of which bend to correspond to the rocky slope on which the hotel was built. Each unit contains some kind of antique, as well as a tile bath, radio, and usually a flowery private terrace. There are no single rooms, although one person occupying a double is quoted a special rate.

VILLA PARADISO, via Roma 6, 98039 Taormina. Tel. 0942/23922. Fax 0942/625800. 33 rms (all with bath or shower). A/C TV TEL

$ Rates (including half board): 125,000–150,000 lire ($98.15–$117.75) per person. AE, DC, MC, V. **Parking:** 20,000 lire ($15.70). **Closed:** Nov–Dec 20.

This charming five-story hotel is at one end of the main street of town, in the vicinity of the Greek theater and overlooking the public gardens and tennis courts. The creation of Signor Salvatore Martorana, it is a moderately priced center for those who want to live well. He loves his establishment, and that attitude is reflected in the personal manner in which the living room is furnished, with antiques and reproductions. Each of the bedrooms is individually decorated, containing a balcony. Guests spend many sunny hours on the rooftop solarium, or in the informal drinking bar and lounge where wallflowers are rare. There's also a television room for guests, plus two elevators. Prices include transportation to and from the Paradise Beach Club in Letojanni, use of sun umbrellas, deck chairs, and showers, plus changing cabins, swimming pool, hydromassage, and garden. The beach is private. Guests can play tennis free year round.

INEXPENSIVE

LA CAMPANELLA, via Circonvallazione 3, 98039 Taormina. Tel. 0942/23381. 12 rms (all with bath). TEL **Bus:** 1 or 2.
$ Rates (including breakfast): 52,000 lire ($40.80) single; 90,000 lire ($70.65) double. No credit cards.
This hotel offers an environment rich in the aesthetics of gardening, painting, and hospitality. It sits at the top of a seemingly endless flight of stairs, which begin at a sharp curve of the main road leading into town. You climb past terra-cotta pots and dangling tendrils of a terraced garden, eventually arriving at the house. The owners maintain clean and uncluttered bedrooms, each with its own bath.

HOTEL ELIOS, via Bagnoli Croci 98, 98039 Taormina. Tel. 0942/23431. Fax 0942/23431. 18 rms (all with bath). **Bus:** 1 or 2.
$ Rates: 58,000 lire ($45.55) single; 86,000 lire ($67.50) double. AE, MC, V.
The Hotel Elios is built into the side of its more glamorous neighbor, the Bristol Park. Its white stucco facade juts above a narrow street a short distance below the commercial center of town, just opposite the entrance to the public gardens. The bedrooms are clean but offer no frills, each with conservative furniture. One of the most sweeping views of Mount Etna stretches far away to the distance, a view amplified from a position on the rooftop terrace where members of the Bambara family set out iron tables and chairs.

PENSIONE SVIZZERA, via Pirandello 26, 98039 Taormina. Tel. 0942/23790. Fax 0942/625906. 20 rms (all with bath).
$ Rates (including breakfast): 33,000 lire ($25.90) single; 58,000 lire ($45.55) double. AE, DC, MC, V. **Parking:** Free. **Closed:** Jan–Feb.
This is a pleasant place to stay, about an eighth of a mile from the center of town. The pensione is owned and operated by Antonino Vinciguerra and his German-born wife, both of whom speak English. Try to get a room that overlooks the sea and Isola Bella. All bedrooms have a shower and toilet. There is also a garden with shady palm trees. The funicular going down to the beach at Mazzaro is a little over 100 yards from the pensione, as is the bus terminal.

VILLA NETTUNO, via Luigi Pirandello 33, 98039 Taormina. Tel. 0942/23797. 13 rms (all with bath). **Bus:** 1 or 2.
$ Rates: 43,000 lire ($33.75) single; 69,000 lire ($54.15) double. Breakfast 4,000 lire ($3.15) extra. AE. **Parking:** 5,000 lire ($3.95).
What's probably my favorite budget-priced accommodation in town is in a geranium-colored villa with Renaissance-style stone trim. Visitors are obliged to climb several flights of steps after leaving the traffic of the main street leading into town. They pass beneath an archway whose keystone is carved with a grotesque stone face. The villa was acquired by the Sciglio family in 1887 and converted into a pensione by the warm-hearted but highly discerning Maria Sciglio in 1953. Guests enjoy breakfast in a garden with hibiscus and night-blooming jasmine. The dining room is like the rococo living quarters of an elegant Sicilian family. Each of the

attractive, well-scrubbed bedrooms contains its own modernized bath and panoramic terrace (all but two of the terraces look out to sea).

PLACES TO STAY IN NEARBY MAZZARO

If you arrive in Taormina in summer, you may prefer to stay at Mazzaro, which is about 3 miles from the heart of the more famous resort (same telephone area code). This is the major beach of Taormina, and has some fine hotels, as reflected by those previewed below. A cable car goes back and forth between the two resorts.

MAZZARO SEA PALACE, 98030 Mazzaro. Tel. 0942/24004. Fax 0942/626237. 87 rms (all with bath), 4 suites. A/C MINIBAR TV TEL
$ Rates (including breakfast): 225,000 lire ($176.65) single; 450,000 lire ($353.25) double; from 480,000 lire ($376.80) suite; 225,000–275,000 lire ($176.65–$215.90) per person with half board. **Parking:** 20,000 lire ($15.70). **Closed:** Nov–Mar.

The Sea Palace is the only deluxe hotel in this little satellite resort of Taormina. It opens onto what is said to be the most beautiful bay in Sicily. Its modern design was completed in the early 1970s, and graced with enough big windows to let in cascades of light, as well as offer views of the coastline. Candlelight dinners are served beside the pool and a variety of folkloric shows presented for the entertainment of many guests, who are picked up at the airport in the hotel limousine. The food is served on fine china and crystal, and guests are pampered by the staff. The piano bar is a popular nighttime rendezvous point. There is also a private beach for guests. The rooms are well furnished, opening for the most part onto beautiful views. It is customary to stay here on the half-board plan.

GRANDE ALBERGO CAPO TAORMINA, via Nazionale, 98039 Mazzaro. Tel. 0942/24000. Fax 0942/625467. 207 rms (all with bath), 1 suite. A/C MINIBAR TV TEL
$ Rates (including half board): 276,000 lire ($216.65) single; 452,000 lire ($354.80) double; from 512,000 lire ($401.90) suite for two. AE, DC, MC, V. **Parking:** 15,000 lire ($11.80). **Closed:** Jan 1–Easter.
The Grande Albergo is a world unto itself, nestled atop a rugged cape projecting into the Ionian Sea. It was designed by one of Italy's most famous architects, Minoletti. There are five floors on five wide sun terraces, plus a saltwater swimming pool at the edge of the cape. Elevators take you through 150 feet of solid rock to the beach below. Bedrooms are handsomely furnished and well proportioned, with wide glass doors opening onto private sun terraces. There are two bars—one intimate, the other more expansive with an orchestra for dancing. The lobby blends the cultures of Rome, Carthage, and Greece, and an open atrium reaches skyward through the center. The food is lavishly presented, and is effectively enhanced by Sicilian wines.

VILLA SANT'ANDREA, via Nazionale, 98030 Mazzaro. Tel. 0942/23125. Fax 0942/24838. 59 rms (all with bath or shower). A/C MINIBAR TV TEL
$ Rates (including breakfast): 195,000 lire ($153.10) single; 270,000 lire ($211.95) double; 200,000 lire ($157) per person with half board. AE, DC, MC, V. **Parking:** 20,000 lire ($15.70).
This hotel stands at the base of the mountain, directly on the sea, where you can swim off its own private beach. A villa was converted into a first-class hotel. A cable car, just outside the front gates of the hotel, will whisk you to the heart of Taormina. The villa receives guests year round. You'll feel like part of a house party. The rooms are informal, with a homelike prettiness, and there is a winning dining terrace where you can enjoy good food.

WHERE TO DINE
MODERATE

RISTORANTE LA GRIGLIA, corso Umberto 54. Tel. 23980.
Cuisine: SICILIAN/INTERNATIONAL. **Reservations:** Recommended. **Bus:** 1 or 2.

$ **Prices:** Appetizers 8,000–15,000 lire ($6.30–$11.80); main courses 12,000–24,000 lire ($9.40–$18.85). AE, DC, MC, V.

Open: Lunch Wed–Mon 12:30–3pm; dinner Wed–Mon 7:30–11pm. **Closed:** Nov.

Opened in 1974, this restaurant is one of the best in town. The vestibule that funnels visitors from the main street of the old city into the interior contains a bubbling aquarium and a menagerie of carved stone lions. The masses of plants inside almost conceal the terra-cotta floors and big-windowed views over the feathery trees of a garden. Your meal might include a selection from the antipasto display, a carpaccio fresh fish, and an involtini of spaghetti and eggplant.

GIOVA ROSY SENIOR, corso Umberto 38. Tel. 24411.

Cuisine: SICILIAN. **Reservations:** Recommended. **Bus:** 1 or 2.

$ **Prices:** Appetizers 10,000–20,000 lire ($7.85–$15.70); main courses 15,000–30,000 lire ($11.80–$23.55). AE, DC, V.

Open: Lunch Tues–Sun 12:30–3pm; dinner Tues–Sun 8–10:30pm. **Closed:** Jan 6–Feb 1.

This rustically old-fashioned place serves a variety of local specialties, including, for example, an array of linguine, risotto dishes, and a spiedini with shrimp and lobster dosed with a generous shot of cognac. You might also enjoy Sicilian antipasti or eggplant with ricotta. You'll have a view of the ancient theater, while giving your order to a member of the staff. Full meals range from 35,000 lire to 55,000 lire ($27.50 to $43.20).

RISTORANTE LURALEO, via Bagnoli Croce 27. Tel. 24279.

Cuisine: SICILIAN/INTERNATIONAL. **Reservations:** Recommended. **Bus:** 1 or 2.

$ **Prices:** Appetizers 5,000–10,000 lire ($3.95–$7.85); main courses 10,000–40,000 lire ($7.85–$31.40).

Open: Lunch Thurs–Tues noon–3pm; dinner Thurs–Tues 7–11pm. **Closed:** Jan.

Defended by a handful of the city residents as being the best eating establishment in town, Ristorante Luraleo is eager to offer excellent value for an attractive price. Many diners prefer the flowering terrace, where pastel tablecloths are shaded by the vine-covered arbor overhead. Of course, if you prefer to dine indoors, there's a not-very-large country-rustic dining room with tile accents, flowers, evening candlelight, racks of wine bottles, and a richly laden antipasto table. The grilled fish is good here, as are the pastas, regional dishes, and herb-flavored steak. Risotto with salmon and prosciutto is a specialty, as is the house tortellini and involtini siciliana. Full meals, including wine and all the extras, can come to around 45,000 lire ($35.35) per person, but many manage for much less.

RISTORANTE DA LORENZO, via Michele Amari 4. Tel. 23480.

Cuisine: SICILIAN/ITALIAN. **Reservations:** Required. **Bus:** 1 or 2.

$ **Prices:** Appetizers 8,000–14,000 lire ($6.30–$11); main courses 14,000–28,000 lire ($11–$22). V.

Open: Lunch Wed–Mon noon–3pm; dinner Wed–Mon 6:30–11pm. **Closed:** Jan–Feb.

Lorenzo Maffei is the owner of this clean and bright restaurant on a quiet street near the landmark San Domenico Hotel. The restaurant has a terrace shaded by an 850-year-old tree. You can enjoy meals which might include a fresh selection of antipasti, spaghetti with sea urchins, scaloppine mozzarella, grilled swordfish, filet of beef with Gorgonzola, and bean soup. Some of the oil paintings that decorate the white walls add an aesthetic element to your dinner. Full meals cost 35,000 lire to 45,000 lire ($27.50 to $35.35). The restaurant is in front of the town hall.

INEXPENSIVE

RISTORANTE U' BOSSU, via Bagnoli Croce 50. Tel. 23311.

Cuisine: SICILIAN. **Reservations:** Required. **Bus:** 1 or 2.
$ **Prices:** Appetizers 5,000–7,000 lire ($3.95–$5.50); main courses 10,000–20,000 lire ($7.85–$15.70). AE, DC, MC, V.
Open: Lunch Tues–Sun 12:30–3pm; dinner Tues–Sun 7:30–10pm.

Vines are entwined around the facade of this small and crowded restaurant in a quiet part of town. Amid a pleasing decor of fresh flowers, wagon-wheel chandeliers, prominently displayed wine bottles, and burnished wooden panels, you can enjoy a meal pungent with all the aromas of a herb garden. Specialties include antipasti from the buffet, pasta with sardines, homemade ravioli, grilled shrimp, fish soup, and grilled swordfish. Full meals begin at 35,000 lire ($27.50).

CICLOPE, corso Umberto. Tel. 23263.
Cuisine: SICILIAN/ITALIAN. **Reservations:** Recommended. **Bus:** 1 or 2.
$ **Prices:** Appetizers 7,000–9,000 lire ($5.50–$7.05); main courses 10,000–18,000 lire ($7.85–$14.15). AE, MC, V.
Open: Lunch Thurs–Tues 12:30–3pm; dinner Thurs–Tues 7:30–10pm. **Closed:** Jan 7–Feb 5.

This is one of the best of the low-priced trattorie of Taormina. Set back from the main street, it opens onto the pint-sized piazzetta Salvatore Leone. In summer, try for an outside table if you'd like both your food and yourself inspected by the passing parade. Meals are fairly simple but the ingredients are fresh, the dishes well prepared. Try, for example, the fish soup or Sicilian squid. If that doesn't interest you, then go for the entrecôte Ciclope, or perhaps the grilled shrimp. Most diners begin their meal, costing from 30,000 lire ($23.55), with a selection from the antipasti di mare, a savory collection of seafood hors d'oeuvres.

PLACES TO DINE IN NEARBY MAZZARO

RISTORANTE ANGELO A MARE–IL DELFINO, via Nazionale, Mazzaro. Tel. 23004.
Cuisine: MEDITERRANEAN/ITALIAN. **Reservations:** Not needed. **Transportation:** Cable car.
$ **Prices:** Appetizers 8,000–15,000 lire ($6.30–$11.80); main courses 12,000–16,000 lire ($9.40–$12.55). AE, DC, MC, V.
Open: Lunch daily noon–3pm; dinner daily 7pm–midnight. **Closed:** Nov–Feb.
Located in Mazzaro, about 3 miles from Taormina, this restaurant offers a flowering terrace with a view over the bay. Both the decor and the menu items are inspired by the sea, and carefully supervised by the chef and owner. Mussels are a specialty, as well as house-style steak, along with involtini of fish, cannelloni, and risotto marinara (fishermen's rice). Complete meals cost 35,000 lire to 45,000 lire ($27.50 to $35.35).

EVENING ENTERTAINMENT

CAFFE WUNDERBAR, piazza IX Aprile, corso Umberto. Tel. 625302.
During the years he came to Taormina, this popular spot was a favorite watering hole of Tennessee Williams and his companion, Frank Merlo. It's in two areas of the most delightful square in town. Beneath a vine-entwined arbor, the outdoor section is perched as close as is safely possible to the edge of the cliff. I prefer one of the Victorian armchairs of the elegant interior, where an impressionistic pair of sculpted figures fill symmetrical wall niches beneath chandeliers. There's also a well-stocked bar, as well as a piano bar. An espresso costs 3,100 lire ($2.45), and a cappuccino, 3,800 lire ($3) if you sit. Open Wednesday through Monday from 8:30am to 2:30am.

TIFFANY, van San Pancrazio 5 (Porto Messina). Tel. 625430.
A gridwork of illuminated lattices stretches above the glossy dance floor of this underground air-conditioned disco, in the historic center of Taormina. Open daily from 10pm to 3:30 or 4am. The disco stands at the entrance to town.
Admission: 10,000 lire ($7.85), including the first drink.

EASY EXCURSIONS
CASTEL MOLA

Once this little hamlet, 3 miles northwest of Taormina, rivaled the resort itself in importance. But it long ago retired to a happy slumber. Castel Mola is reached only from Taormina. Many visitors walk the entire goat-climbing distance, enjoying spectacular sea views and making a day of it. Five buses a day run between Taormina and Castel Mola.

Castle walls surround Castel Mola, and all the medieval fortification commands today is a view of the coast, Taormina, and formidable Etna, that repository of a thousand fearsome myths.

Even if it weren't for that view, it would be worth coming to Castel Mola to enjoy the superb food at Il Faro.

Where to Dine

IL FARO, contrada Petralia (via Rotabile Castel Mola). Tel. 28193.
Cuisine: SICILIAN. **Reservations:** Recommended.
$ **Prices:** Appetizers 5,000–6,000 lire ($3.95–$4.70); main courses 12,000–15,000 lire ($9.40–$11.80). No credit cards.
Open: Lunch Thurs–Tues 12:30–3pm; dinner Thurs–Tues 7:30–10pm.

The proprietor is handsome and charming, and inquiring if everything is pleasing. You'll see him going between the dining terrace and the inside room, filling glasses of wine, whatever. At his ristorante/bar, half a mile before Castel Mola, homemade Sicilian cookery is the specialty of the kitchen, and it's done with consummate skill. The food seems to reflect the rugged character of the people who inhabited this part of Sicily. Aromatic sauces cover the pastas, and the stews are complicated. Of course, everyone overindulges in the wine. Etna has both red and white wines. Expect to spend 25,000 lire to 35,000 lire ($19.65 to $27.50) per person for a complete meal, including wine. Never make the excursion on Wednesday, when Il Faro is closed.

MOUNT ETNA

Looming menacingly over the coast of eastern Sicily, Mount Etna is the highest and largest active volcano in Europe. The peak changes in size over the years, but is currently listed somewhere in the neighborhood of 10,800 feet. Etna has been active in modern times (in 1928 the little village of Mascali was buried under its lava), and eruptions in 1971 rekindled the fears of Sicilians.

Etna has figured in history and in Greek mythology. Empedocles, the 5th-century B.C. Greek philosopher, is said to have jumped into its crater as a sign that he was being delivered directly to Mount Olympus to take his seat among the gods. It was under Etna that Zeus crushed the multiheaded, viper-riddled dragon Typhoeus, thereby securing domination over Olympus. Hephaestus, the god of fire and blacksmiths, was believed to have made his headquarters in Etna, aided by the single-eyed Cyclopes.

The Greeks warned that whenever Typhoeus tried to break out of his "jail," lava erupted and earthquakes cracked the land. Granted that, the monster must have nearly escaped on March 11, 1669, the date of one of the most violent eruptions recorded, destroying Catania about 17 miles away.

By road, the approach from below is idyllic, past orange and lemon trees, as well as the vineyards from which both a red and a white wine known as Etna are made. As you near Rifugio Sapienza, the landscape becomes more rugged and bleak. Check with the tourist office in Catania at largo Paisiello 5 (tel. 317720), about the most convenient means of transportation for viewing Etna. These change, depending on conditions at the time of your visit. It is possible, for example, to take a bus departing at 8am from in front of the Stazione Centrale in Catania, taking you to Sapienza. There you can usually share the cost of a Jeep or minibus which will take you within a half hour's walk of the top. But it's cheaper to take a SITAS bus from Sapienza to various stops that will put you only a half hour's walk from the top. Others, more athletic, will often make the 4- to 5-hour hike from Sapienza to the top of Etna. The grounds around the station evoke the setting of a science-fiction film of Earth people landing on Mars.

Because of Etna's more than 3½ miles of ski tracks and snow-covered slopes at 8,700 feet above sea level, it is frequented by skiers in winter. But even in July and August the weather will be cold, so dress accordingly.

SAT buses also visit Mount Etna from Taormina. Trips are possible in April and May on Monday, Wednesday, and Friday, and from June through October on Monday and Wednesday. The cost is 25,000 lire ($19.65) per person for the ride there, plus 53,000 lire ($41.60) for the final trip to the crater. Call SAT at 50198 in Taormina to make a reservation and secure bus departure details.

APPENDIX

A. BASIC VOCABULARY

ENGLISH	ITALIAN	PRONUNCIATION
Good morning or Good afternoon	Buon giorno	bwohn djor-*noh*
Good evening	Buona sera	bwohn-ah say-*rah*
Good night	Buona notte	bwohn-ah not-*tay*
How are you?	Come sta?	koh-may stah?
Very well	Molto bene	mohl-toh bay-*nay*
Thank you	Grazie	grah-*tsyeh*
Good-bye	Arrivederci	ah-reev-ay-dehr-*chee*
Please	Per piacere	payr pee-yah-chay-*ray*
Yes	Si	see
No	No	noh
Excuse me	Scusi	skoo-*zee*
Where is? . . .	Dov'è? . . .	doh-*vay*? . . .
the station	la stazione	lah stah-tsee-oh-*nay*
a hotel	un albergo	oon ahl-bayr-*goh*
a restaurant	un ristorante	oon rees-toh-rahn-*tay*
the toilet	il gabinetto	eel ga-bee-nay-*toh*
To the right	A destra	ah dess-*trah*
To the left	A sinistra	ah see-nee-*strah*
Straight ahead	Avanti	ah-vahn-*tee*
How much is it?	Quanto costa?	kwahn-*toh* kaw-stah?
The check, please	Il conto, per piacere	eel kohn-*toh, payr pee-yah-chay-ray*
When?	Quando?	kwahn-*doh*?
Yesterday	Ieri	ee-yay-*ree*
Today	Oggi	aw-*djee*
Tomorrow	Domani	doh-mah-*nee*
Breakfast	Colazione	koh-lah-tzyoh-*nay*
Lunch	Pranzo	prahn-*tsoh*
Dinner	Cena	chay-*nah*
What time is it?	Che ore sono?	kay oh-*ray* soh-noh?
What day is it today?	Che giorno è oggi?	kay djor-*noh ay* aw-djee?
Monday	Lunedi	loo-*nay*-dee
Tuesday	Martedi	mahr-*tay*-dee
Wednesday	Mercoledi	mehr-koh-lay-*dee*
Thursday	Giovedi	djoh-vay-dee
Friday	Venerdi	vay-nehr-*dee*
Saturday	Sabato	sah-*bah*-toh
Sunday	Domenica	doh-may-neek-*ah*

1 **uno** (oo-*noh*)
2 **due** (doo-*ay*)
3 **tre** (tray)
4 **quattro** (kwah-*troh*)

5 **cinque** (cheen-*kway*)
6 **sei** (say)
7 **sette** (set-*tay*)
8 **otto** (au-*toh*)

9 **nove** (noh-*vay*)
10 **dieci** (dee-ay-*chee*)
20 **venti** (vayn-*tee*)
30 **trenta** (trayn-*tah*)

40 **quaranta**	**(sehss-ahn-***tah***)**	90 **novanta**
(kway-rahn-*tah*)	70 **settanta**	(noh-vahn-*tah*)
50 **cinquanta**	(seht-tahn-*tah*)	100 **cento** (chayn-*toh*)
(cheen-kwan-*tah*)	80 **ottanta**	1,000 **mille** (mee-*lay*)
60 **sessanta**	(oh-tahn-*tah*)	

B. ITALIAN MENU SAVVY

Abbacchio Roast haunch or shoulder of lamb baked and served in a casserole and sometimes flavored with anchovies.

Agnolotti A crescent-shaped pasta shell stuffed with a mixture of chopped meat, spices, vegetables, and cheese; when prepared in rectangular versions, the same combination of ingredients is identified as ravioli.

Amaretti Crunchy, very sweet, almond-flavored macaroons.

Anguilla alla veneziana Eel cooked in sauce made from tuna and lemon.

Antipasti Succulent tidbits served at the beginning of a meal (before the pasta), whose ingredients might include slices of cured meats, seafood (especially shellfish), and what critics sometimes claim is the most succulent collection of cooked and seasoned vegetables in the Italian repertoire. Typical examples might include: *carciofi alla guidia* (flattened and deep-fried baby artichokes), *carciofi sott' olio* (artichoke hearts in olive oil), *funghi trifolati* (mushrooms with garlic, anchovies, and lemon), *gamberi al fagiolino* (shrimp with white beans), and *prosciutto con melone* (melon garnished with slices of raw cured ham).

Aragosta Lobster.

Arrosto Roasted meat.

Baccalà Dried and salted codfish.

Baccalà alla vicentina Codfish simmered in a broth of milk, onions, anchovies, parsley, and (sometimes) cinnamon.

Bagna cauda Hot and well-seasoned sauce, heavily flavored with anchovies, designed for dipping raw vegetables; literally translated as "hot bath."

Bistecca alla fiorentina Florentine-style steaks, coated before grilling with olive oil, pepper, lemon juice, salt, and parsley.

Bocconcini Veal layered with ham and cheese, and fried.

Bollito misto Assorted boiled meats served on a single platter.

Braciola Pork chop.

Bresaola Air-dried spiced beef.

Bruschetta Toasted bread, heavily slathered with butter and garlic and topped with tomatoes.

Bucatini Hollow, coarsely textured spaghetti.

Busecca alla milanese Tripe (beef intestines) flavored with herbs and vegetables.

Cabretto ripieno al forno Oven-roasted stuffed baby goat.

Cacciucco all livornese Seafood stew.

Calzone Pizza dough rolled with the chef's choice of sausage, tomatoes, cheese, etc., then baked into a kind of savory turnover.

Cannelloni Tubular dough stuffed with meat, cheese, or vegetables, then baked in a creamy white sauce.

Cappellacci alla ferrarese Pasta stuffed with pumpkin.

Cappelletti Small ravioli ("little hats") stuffed with meat or cheese.

Carciofi Artichokes.

Carpaccio Thin slices of raw cured beef, sometimes in a piquant sauce.

Cassatta alla siciliana A richly caloric dessert combining layers of sponge cake, sweetened ricotta cheese, and candied fruit, bound together with an icing of chocolate buttercream.

Cervello al burro nero Brains in black-butter sauce.

Cima alla genovese Baked filet of veal rolled into a tube-shaped package containing eggs, mushrooms, and sausage.

Coppa Cured morsels of pork filet encased in sausage skins, served in slices.

Costoletta alla milanese Veal cutlet dredged in breadcrumbs, fried, and sometimes flavored with cheese.

Cozze Mussels.

Fagioli White beans.

Fave Fava beans.

Fegato alla veneziana Thinly slived calves' liver fried with salt, pepper, and onions.

Fettuccine Flat noodles.

Foccacia Ideally, concocted from potato-based dough left to rise slowly for several hours, then garnished with tomato sauce, garlic, basil, salt, and pepper drizzled with olive oil; similar to a high-pan, deep-dish pizza most popular in the deep south, especially Bari.

Fontina Rich cow's-milk cheese.

Frittata Italian omelet.

Fritto misto A deep-fried medley of whatever small fish, shellfish, and squid are available in the marketplace that day.

Fusilli Spiral-shaped pasta.

Gelato (produzione propria) Ice cream (homemade).

Gorgonzola One of the most famous blue-veined cheeses of Europe; strong, creamy, and aromatic.

Gnocchi Dumplings usually made from potatoes (*gnocchi alla patate*) or from semolina (*gnocchi alla romana*), often stuffed with combinations of cheese, spinach, vegetables, or whatever combinations strikes the chef's fancy.

Granita Flavored ice, usually with lemon or coffee.

Insalata di frutti di mare Seafood salad (usually including shrimp and squid) garnished with pickles, lemon, olives, and spices.

Involtini Thinly sliced beef, veal, or pork, rolled, stuffed, and fried.

Lasagne An oven-baked pasta dish which incorporates thin layers of green (*lasagne verde*) or white dough alternating with sausage or ground meat, grated cheese, and white sauce; in certain regions this dish is laced with ricotta.

Minestrone A rich and savory vegetable soup usually sprinkled with grated parmesan cheese and studded with noodles.

Mortadella Mild pork sausage, fashioned into large cylinders and served sliced; probably the closest thing in Italy to the U.S. concept of lunchmeat, "bologna."

Mozzarella A nonfermented cheese, made from the fresh milk of a buffalo (or, if unavailable, from a cow), boiled and then kneaded into a rounded ball, served fresh.

Mozzarella con pomodori Fresh tomatoes with fresh mozzarella, basil, papper, and olive oil.

Nervetti A northern Italian antipasto concocted from chewy pieces of calves' foot or shin.

Osso buco Beef or veal knuckle slowly braised until the cartilage is tender, and then served with a highly flavored sauce.

Pappardelle alle lepre Pasta with rabbit sauce.

Pancetta Herb-flavored pork belly, rolled into a cylinder and sliced.

Panettone Sweet yellow-colored bread baked in the form of a brioche.

Panne Heavy cream.

Pansotti Pasta stuffed with greens, herbs, and cheeses, usually served with a walnut sauce.

Parmigiano Parmesan, a hard and salty yellow cheese usually grated over pastas and soups but also eaten alone; also known as *granna*.

Peperoni Green, yellow, or red sweet peppers.

Pesci al cartoccio Fish baked in a parchment envelope with onions, parsley, and herbs.

Pesto A flavorful green sauce concocted from basil leaves, cheese, garlic, marjoram, and (if available) pine kernels.

Piccata al marsala Thin escalope of veal braised in a pungent sauce flavored with marsala wine.

Piselli al prosciutto Peas with strips of ham.

Pizza Italy's most popularized culinary export, it's probably the dish most immediately associated with Italy. Specific varieties include: *capricciosa* (its ingredients depend on the whim of the chef and can vary widely depending on his or her culinary vision and the ingredients at hand), *margherita* (incorporates tomato sauce, cheese, fresh basil, and memories of the first queen of Italy, Marguerite di Savoia, in whose honor it was first concocted by a Neapolitan chef), *napoletana* (includes ham, capers, tomatoes, oregano, cheese, and the distinctive taste of anchovies), *quattro stagione* (translated as "four seasons" because of array of fresh vegetables in it, it also contains ham and bacon), and *siciliana* (contains black olives, capers, and cheese).

Pizzaiola A process whereby something (usually a beefsteak) is covered in a tomato-and-oregano sauce.

Polenta Thick porridge or mush made from cornmeal flour.

Polenta de uccelli Assorted small birds roasted on a spit and served with polenta.

Polenta e coniglio Rabbit stew served with polenta (see above).

Pollo alla cacciatore Chicken with tomatoes and mushrooms cooked in wine.

Pollo alla diavola Highly spiced grilled chicken.

Ragù Meat sauce.

Ricotta A soft and bland cheese, often used in cooking, made from cow's or sheep's milk.

Rigatoni Large macaroni designed with ridges to more effectively absorb sauce.

Risotto Italian rice.

Risotto alla milanese Rice with saffron and wine.

Salsa verde "Green sauce," made from capers, anchovies, lemon juice and/or vinegar, and parsley.

Saltimbocca Veal scallop layered with prosciutto and sage; its name literally translates as "jump in your mouth," a reference to its tart and savory flavor.

Salvia Sage.

Scaloppina alla Valdostana Escalope of veal stuffed with cheese and ham.

Scaloppine Thin slices of veal coated in flour and sautéed in butter.

Semifreddo A frozen dessert; usually ice cream with sponge cake.

Seppia Cuttlefish (a kind of squid); its black ink is used for flavoring in certain sauces for pasta, and also in risotto dishes.

Sogliola Sole.

Spaghetti A long, round, thin pasta, variously served: *alla bolognese* (with ground meat, mushrooms, peppers, etc.), *alla carbonara* (with bacon, black pepper, and eggs), *al pomodoro* (with tomato sauce), *al sugo/ragù* (with meat sauce), and *alle vongole* (with clam sauce).

Spiedino Pieces of meat grilled on a skewer over an open flame.

Strangolaprete Small nuggets of pasta, usually served with sauce; the name is literally translated as "priest-choker."

Stufato Beef braised in white wine with vegetables.

Tagliatelle Flat egg noodles.

Tiramisu Richly caloric dessert containing layers of triple-crème cheeses and rum-soaked sponge cake.

Tonno Tuna.

Tortelli Pasta dumplings stuffed with ricotta and greens.

Tortellini Rings of dough stuffed with minced and seasoned meat and served either in soups or as full-fledged pasta covered with sauce.

Trenette Thin noodles served with pesto sauce and potatoes.

Trippe alla fiorentina Beef tripe (intestines).

Vermicelle Very thin spaghetti.

Vitello tonnato Cold sliced veal covered with tuna-fish sauce.

Zabaglione/zabaione Egg yolks whipped into the consistency of a custard, flavored with marsala, and served warm as a dessert.

Zampone Pig's trotter stuffed with spicy seasoned pork, boiled and sliced.
Zuccotto A liqueur-soaked sponge cake, molded into a dome and layered with chocolate, nuts, and whipped cream.
Zuppa inglese Sponge cake soaked in custard sauce and rum.

C. GLOSSARY OF ARCHITECTURAL TERMS

Ambone A pulpit, either serpentine or simple in form, erected in an Italian church.
Apse The half-rounded extension behind the main altar of a church; Christian tradition dictates that it be placed at the eastern end of an Italian church, the side closest to Jerusalem.
Atrium A courtyard, open to the sky, in an ancient Roman house; the term also applies to the courtyard nearest the entranceway of an early Christian church.
Baldacchino (also ciborium) A columned stone canopy, usually placed above the altar of a church; spelled in English as baldachin or baldaquin.
Basilica Any rectangular public building, usually divided into three aisles by rows of columns; in ancient Rome, this architectural form was frequently used for places of public assembly and law courts; later, Roman Christians adapted the form for many of their early churches.
Caldarium The steam room of a Roman bath.
Campanile A bell tower, often detached, of a church.
Capital The top of a column, often carved and usually categorized into one of three different orders: Doric, Ionic, or Corinthian.
Castrum A carefully planned Roman military camp, whose rectangular form, straight streets, and systems of fortified gates quickly became standardized throughout the Roman Empire; modern cities that began as Roman camps and that still more or less maintain their original forms include Chester (England), Barcelona (Spain), and such Italian cities as Lucca, Aosta, Como, Brescia, Florence, and Ancona.
Cavea The curved row of seats in a classical theater; the most prevalent shape was that of a semicircle.
Cella The sanctuary, or most sacred interior section, of a Roman pagan temple.
Chancel Section of a church containing the altar.
Cornice The decorative flange that defines the uppermost part of a classical or neoclassical facade.
Cortile Courtyard or cloisters ringed with a gallery of arches or lintels set atop columns.
Crypt A church's main burial place, usually located below the choir.
Cupola A dome.
Forum The main square, and principal gathering place, of any Roman town, usually adorned with the city's most important temples and civic buildings.
Duomo: Cathedral.
Grotesques Carved and painted faces, deliberately ugly, used by everyone from the Etruscans to the architects of the Renaissance; they are especially amusing when set into fountains.
Hypogeum Subterranean burial chambers, usually of pre-Christian origins.
Loggia Roofed balcony or gallery.
Lozenge An elongated four-sided figure which, along with stripes, was one of the distinctive signs of the architecture of Pisa.
Narthex The anteroom, or enclosed porch, of a Christian church.
Nave The largest and longest section of a church, usually devoted to sheltering and/or seating worshippers, and often divided by aisles.

Pietra Dura Richly ornate assemblage of semiprecious stones mounted on a flat decorative surface, considered to have been perfected during the 1600s in Florence.

Pieve A parish church.

Portico A porch, usually crafted from wood or stone.

Pulvin A four-sided stone that serves as a substitute for the capital of a column, often decoratively carved, sometimes into biblical scenes.

Putti Plaster cherubs whose chubby forms often decorate the interiors of baroque chapels and churches.

Stucco Colored plaster composed of sand, powdered marble, water, and lime, either molded into statuary or applied in a thin, concretelike layer to the exterior of a building.

Telamone Structural column carved into a standing male form; female versions are called *caryatids*.

Thermae Roman baths.

Transenna Stone (usually marble) screen separating the altar area from the rest of an early Christian church.

Travertine Known as the stone from which ancient and Renaissance Rome was built, it's known for its hardness, light coloring, and tendency to be pitted or flecked with black.

Tympanum The half-rounded space above the portal of a church, whose semicircular space usually showcases a sculpture.

D. METRIC MEASURES

LENGTH

1 millimeter (mm)	=	.04 inches (*or* less than 1/16 inch)
1 centimeter (cm)	=	.39 inches (*or* just under 1/2 inch)
1 meter (m)	=	39 inches (*or* about 1.1 yards)
1 kilometer (km)	=	.62 mile (*or* about 2/3 mile)

To convert kilometers to miles, multiply the number of kilometers by 0.62. Also use to convert speeds from kilometers per hour (kmph) to miles per hour (m.p.h.).

To convert miles to kilometers, multiply the number of miles by 1.61. Also use to convert speeds from m.p.h. to kmph.

CAPACITY

1 liter (l)	=	33.92 ounces	=	2.1 pints	=	1.06 quarts
	=	0.26 U.S. gallons				
1 Imperial gallon	=	1.2 U.S. gallons				

To convert liters to U.S. gallons, multiply the number of liters by 0.26.

To convert U.S. gallons to liters, multiply the number of gallons by 3.79.

To convert Imperial gallons to U.S. gallons, multiply the number of Imperial gallons by 1.2.

To convert U.S. gallons to Imperial gallons, multiply the number of U.S. gallons by 0.83.

WEIGHT

1 gram (g)	=	0.035 ounces (*or* about a paper clip's weight)
1 kilogram (kg)	=	35.2 ounces
	=	2.2 pounds
1 metric ton	=	2,205 pounds = 1.1 short ton

To convert kilograms to pounds, multiply the number of kilograms by 2.2.

To convert pounds to kilograms, multiply the number of pounds by 0.45.

AREA

1 hectare (ha)	=	2.47 acres
1 square kilometer (km²)	=	247 acres = .39 square miles

To convert hectares to acres, multiply the number of hectares by 2.47.
To convert acres to hectares, multiply the number of acres by 0.41.
To convert aquare kilometers to square miles, multiply the number of square kilometers by 0.39.
To convert square miles to square kilometers, multiply the number of square miles by 2.6.

TEMPERATURE

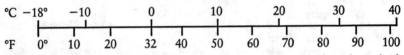

To convert degrees Celsius to degrees Fahrenheit, multiply °C by 9, divide by 5, and add 32 (example: 20°C × 9/5 + 32 = 68°F).
To convert degrees Fahrenheit to degrees Celsius, subtract 32 from °F, multiply by 5, then divide by 9 (example: 85°F − 32 × 5/9 = 29.4°C).

GENERAL INFORMATION

Accommodations, 63–5
  see also Destinations *index*
ACI (Automobile Club d'Italia), 59
Adventure/alternative travel, 46–8
Air travel to Italy:
  APEX (advance purchase excursion) fares, 51
  bucket shops, 52
  charters, 52–3
  courier, 53
  major airlines, 50
  money-saving tips, 54
  rebators, 53
  regular fares, 51
  standbys, 53
Air travel within Italy, 57
Alcohol, 27–8
  liquor laws, 70
Alpine huts, 64
American Express, 68
ANAC (bus network), 58
APEX (advance purchase excursion) fares, 51
Architectural terms, 696–7
Art and architecture, 14–16, 29
Automobile Club d'Italia (ACI), 59

Banks, 68
Bed and breakfast, 64
Beverages, 26–8
  liquor laws, 70
  water, 71
Bicycle races, 22
Boat travel, in Italy, 58
Books about Italy, 28–31
Breakdowns/assistance, automobile, 61
BTLC Pass (Italian Railpass), 57–8
Business hours, 68
Bus travel:
  to Italy, 55
  in Italy, 58–9
Calendar of events, 38–40
Camera/film, 68
Cars and driving:
  in Italy, 59–61
  rentals, 59–60
  traveling to Italy, 55
Carta d'Argento (Senior Citizen's Silver Card), 57
Cigarettes, 68
Climate, 37–8
Clothing, 43–4
Consulates, 69
Cooking classes, 49
Cuisine, 24–6
Currency, 35–7
  exchange, 36
Customs, 69

Dining, 65–7
  see also Destinations *index*
Disabled travelers, tips for, 44
Driving rules, 61
Drug laws, 69
Drugstores, 69
Dry cleaning, 70

Educational and study travel, 49
Electricity, 69
Embassies and consulates, 69.
Emergencies, 69
Engraving and ceramics, courses, 49
Entry requirements, 34
Etiquette, 69
Eurailpass, 54–5

Families, tips for, 45–6
Fax, 71
Ferries, 61–2
Festivals, 38–40
Film/camera, 68
Films, 31–2
Folklore, 21–2
Food, 24–6
Football (soccer), 22

Gasoline, 60–1
Geography, 1–6
Glossary, 692–7
Gratuities, 71

Health concerns and precautions, 42
History of Italy, 6–14
Hitchhiking, 62
Holidays, 38
Home exchanges, 47, 64–5

Information sources, 34
Insurance, 42–3
International understanding, promoting, 46–7
Italian Flexirail Card, 58
Italian Railpass (BTLC Pass), 57–8
Itineraries, suggested, 62–3

Kilometric Ticket, 58

Language, 19–20, 70
  learning, 49
Laundry and dry cleaning, 70
Legal aid, 70
Liquor, 27–8
Liquor laws, 70
Lira, 35
Literature, 16–17
Lost and found, 70

Magazines, 70

Mail, 70
Maps, 4–5
Menu terms, 693–6
Money, 35–7
  currency exchange, 36
Money-saving tips, air travel, 54
Movies, 31–2
Music, 17–19
  recordings, 32–3

Newspapers and magazines, 70

Opera tours, 47
Organized tours to Italy, 55–7

Packing for your trip, 43–4
Pensiones, 64
Petrol, 60–1
Pets, 70
Photographic needs, 68
Planning and preparing for your trip:
  adventure/alternative travel, 46–9
  calendar of events, 38–40
  climate, 37–8
  disabled travelers, 44
  entry requirements, 34
  families, 45–6
  getting around Italy: *see* Transportation
  getting to Italy: *see* Traveling to Italy
  health concerns and precautions, 42
  holidays, 38
  information sources, 34
  insurance, 42–3
  money, 35–7
  senior citizen travelers, 44–5
  single travelers, 45
  special events and festivals, 38–40
  student travelers, 46
Police, 70
Politics, 14
Post office, 70

Radio and TV, 70
Recordings, 32–3
Recreation, 23–4
Regions, 3, 6
Relais & Chateaux, 65
Religion, 20–1
Restaurants, 65–7
  see also Destinations *index*
Restrooms, 71
Road maps, 61

Safety, 71
Senior Citizen's Silver Card (Carta d'Argento), 57

Senior citizen travelers, tips for, 44–5
Senior-citizen vacations, 47–8
Shopping, 67–8
Single travelers, tips for, 45
SITA (bus network), 58–9
Soccer (football), 22
Special events and festivals, 38–40
Sports, 22
Student travelers, tips for, 46

Taxes, 71
Taxis, 59
Telegram/telephone/telex/fax, 71
Television, 70
Temperatures, average monthly, 38
Time, 71

Tipping, 71
Tourist information, 34
Tours, organized, to Italy, 55–7
Train travel:
 to Italy, 54–5
 within Italy, 57–8
Transportation:
 bus, 58–9
 car, 59–61
 ferry, 61–2
 hitchhiking, 62
 plane, 57
 ship, 58
 taxi, 59
 train, 57–8
Travel books, 30–1
Traveler's checks, 35–6

Traveling to Italy:
 by bus, 55
 cars and driving, 55
 package tours, 55–7
 by plane, 51–4
 by train, 54–5

Vocabulary, 692–7

Water, 71
Weather, 37–8
Wine, 26–7
 liquor laws, 70

Yellow Pages, 72
Youth hostels, 65

DESTINATIONS

AGRIGENTO, 675–8
AMALFI, 636–40
accommodations, 637–9
restaurants, 639
sights and attractions, 636–7
tourist information, 636
traveling to, 636
AMALFI COAST, 623–56
Amalfi, 636–40
Capri, 645–6
map, 627
Paestum, 644–5
Positano, 632
Ravello, 640–4
Sorrento, 626, 628–32
suggested itineraries, 623
traveling to, 626
what's special about, 626
see also specific places
ANACAPRI, 655–6
ANZIO, 201
AOSTA, 557–60
ARDEA, 205
ASSISI, 317–21
accommodations, 319–20
restaurants, 320–1
sights and attractions, 318–19
tourist information, 317
traveling to, 317

BAGHERIA, 672–3
BAIA, 619
BELLAGIO, 495–6
BERGAMO, 538–41
BOLOGNA, 326–38
accommodations, 331–4
map, 327, 329
restaurants, 334–8
sights and attractions, 328, 330–1
suggested itineraries, 325
tourist information, 328

transportation, 328
traveling to, 326
what's special about, 326
BOLZANO, 472–5
BORROMEAN ISLANDS, 502–3
BURANO, 434–5

CAERE (CERVETERI), 202
CAMPI FLEGREI (PHI-LAEGREAN FIELDS), 618–19
CAPRI (ISLAND), 625–6, 645–56
Anacapri, 655–6
Capri (town), 647–55
Marina Grande, 646–7
Marina Piccola, 656
suggested itineraries, 623
traveling to, 626, 645
what's special about, 626
see also specific places
CAPRI (TOWN), 647–55
accommodations, 648–51
restaurants, 651–5
shopping, 647–8
sights and attractions, 647
CASTELGANDOLFO, 198
CASTELLI ROMANI, 198–200
CASTEL MOLA, 690
CERNOBBIO, 493–5
CERVETERI (CAERE), 202
COMO (TOWN), 492–3
COMO, LAKE, 492–3
Bellagio, 495–6
Cernobbio, 493–5
Como (town), 492–3
Tremezzo, 496–8
see also specific places
CORTINA D'AMPEZZO, 466–72

accommodations, 467–9
entertainment and nightlife, 471–2
restaurants, 470–1
sights and attractions, 467
tourist information, 466
traveling to, 466
COURMAYEUR, 560–4
accommodations, 560–2
entertainment and nightlife, 564
orientation, 560
restaurants, 562–4
CREMONA, 541–3
CUMA, 619–20

DOLOMITES, THE, AND SOUTH TYROL, 457–80
Bolzano, 472–5
Cortina d'Ampezzo, 466–72
map, 459
Merano, 475–8
scenic routes, 472
suggested itineraries, 457–8
traveling to, 458
Trent, 478–80
what's special about, 458
see also specific places

EMILIA-ROMAGNA, 325–54
map, 327
suggested itineraries, 325
traveling to, 326
what's special about, 326
see also specific places
ENTRÈVES, 564–6
ERCOLANO (HERCULANE-UM), 620

FERRARA, 338–42
accommodations, 340
restaurants, 341–2
sights and attractions, 339–40

KEY TO ABBREVIATIONS: *B* = Budget; *E* = Expensive; *I* = Inexpensive; *M* = Moderate; *VE* = Very Expensive; *$* = Special Value; *** = an Author's Favorite

FERRARA (cont'd)
tourist information, 338
traveling to, 338
FIESOLE, 291–3
FLORENCE (FIRENZE),
  206–93
accommodations, 216–39, 292–3
  maps, 218–19, 222–3
  money-saving tips, 217
airports, 207
American Express, 213
arriving in, 207–10
babysitters, 213
barbers, 213
bars, 290
books about, 31
business hours, 213
cafes, 290–1
car rentals, 212
cars and driving, 212
consulates, 213
contemporary music and nightclubs,
  289–90
currency exchange, 213
discos, 289–90
doctors and dentists, 213
drugstores, 213
dry cleaning, 213
emergencies, 213
entertainment and nightlife, 288–91
excursion areas, 291–3
eyeglasses, 213
fax, 214
free and special events, 280–1
for gay men and lesbians, 215, 291
getting around, 212
hairdressers and barbers, 213
hospitals, 213
information sources, 210
laundry and dry cleaning, 213
layout of, 210–12
libraries, 213–14
lost and found, 214
luggage storage/lockers, 214
maps, 208–9
  accommodations, 218–19,
    222–3
  restaurants, 242–3
  sights and attractions, 260–1
  walking tours, 274–5, 278–9
money-saving tips:
  accommodations, 217
  restaurants, 240
movies, 291
neighborhoods, 211–12
newspapers and magazines, 214
nightclubs and contemporary music,
  289–90
performing arts, 288–9
photographic needs, 214
police, 214
post office, 214
radio, 214
religious services, 214
restaurants, 239–55
  for children, 239, 254
  map, 242–3
  money-saving tips, 240
  picnic supplies, 254–5
FLORENTINE
  Bar Ristorante la Loggia (M),
    251–2
  Buca dell'Orafo (M$), 247
  Buca Mario (M), 250

Da Ganino (M), 245
Da Pennello (M$), 245–6
Giannino in San Lorenzo (M),
  244–5
La Carabacia (I), 241, 244
Ristorante Natale (M), 247
Ristorante Otello (M), 241
Sabatini (M*), 240–1
Sostanza (M$), 241
Trattoria Coco Lezzone (M),
  245
Vecchia Firenze (I$), 245
FRENCH
  Doney (M), 244
GELATO
  Gelateria Vivoli (B*), 253
IN HOTELS
  Il Cestello (E), 252
INTERNATIONAL
  La Nandina (M), 247–8
  Ristorante Leo in Santa Croce
    (M), 248
  Toula-Oliviero (E), 248–9
ITALIAN
  Caffè Voltaire (I), 253
  Da Pennello (M$), 245–6
  Harry's Bar (E*), 246–7
  Il Cavallino (M$), 246
  Le Bistro (I), 253–4
  Paoli (M), 246
  Ristorante Leo in Santa Croce
    (M), 248
LIGHT FARE
  Caffè Voltaire (I), 253
  Kenny (B), 253
  Le Bistro (I), 253–4
  Snack Bar and Ristorante La
    Borga (B), 254
MEDITERRANEAN
  Cibreo (M), 248
  Il Cestello (E), 252
MOLISIAN
  Le Fonticine (M*), 240
PIZZA
  Giannino in San Lorenzo (M),
    244–5
RUSSIAN
  Al Lume di Candela (M), 249
SANDWICHES/SALADS
  Kenny (B), 253
SARDINIAN
  Trattoria Garga (M$), 249
SEAFOOD
  Pierot (M), 250
  Trattoria Vittoria (M), 250–1
TUSCAN
  Al Lume di Candela (M), 249
  Buca Lapi (M), 249–50
  Cantinetta Antinori (M), 250
  Da Ganino (M), 245
  Il Cavallino (M$), 246
  Il Cestello (E), 252
  La Nandina (M), 247–8
  Le Lance at San Domenico,
    Fiesole (M), 293
  Le Mossacce (I$), 244
  Mamma Gina (M), 251
  Paoli (M), 246
  Snack Bar and Ristorante La
    Borga (B), 254
  Toula-Oliviero (E), 248–9
  Trattoria Antico Fattore (I), 251
  Trattoria Cammillo (I–M), 252
  Trattoria Garga (M$), 249

Trattoria Le Cave di Maiano,
  Fiesole (M), 293
VEGETARIAN
  Centro Vegetariano Fiorrentino
    Almanacco (B$), 252–3
WITH VIEWS
  Bar Ristorante la Loggia (M),
    251–2
restrooms, 214
safety, 214
for senior citizens, 215
shoe repair, 214
shopping, 282–8
sights and attractions in or near,
  257–80, 291–2
  Bandini Museum (Fiesole),
    291–2
  Baptistery, 277
  Campanile,* 258–9
  Cappelle Medici,* 262–3
  Casa Buonarroti, 272–3
  Casa di Dante, 272
  Casa Guidi, 272
  churches, 267–9
  Florence American Cemetery and
    Memorial, 273
  Frommer's favorite experiences,
    282
  Galleria degli Uffizi,* 263–4, 273
  Galleria dell'Accademia, 262,
    277
  gardens, 271–2
  Giardini di Boboli, 271–2
  Horne Museum, 271
  of literary interest, 272
  Loggia della Signoria,* 258
  map, 260–1
  Medici chapels, 276
  Medici Palace, 280
  Museo Archeologico, 270
  Museo Bardini, 271
  Museo del Duomo, 276
  Museo Missionario Frances
    Cano Fiesole (Fiesole), 292
  Museo Nazionale del Bargello,*
    265, 277
  Museo dell'Opera del Duomo,
    270–1
  Museo di San Marco, 265–6
  Museo Stibbert, 271
  museums and galleries, 270–1
  New Sacristy, 280
  Ospedale degli Innocenti, 267
  palaces, 269–70
  Palazzo Bargello, 276
  Palazzo Medici-Riccardi,
    269–70
  Palazzo Vecchio, 269
  Pitti Palace, 264–5, 273
  Ponte Vecchio, 266–7
  Roman Theater and Archeologi-
    cal Museum (Fiesole), 292
  San Giovanni, Battistero di,* 259
  San Lorenzo, Basilica of, 268,
    276
  San Lorenzo, church of, 280
  Santa Croce, Basilica of, 267, 276
  Santa Croce, church of, 277
  Santa Maria del Carmine, 268–9
  Santa Maria del Fiore, Cathedral
    of,* 259, 262
  Santa Maria Novella, Basilica di,
    267–8
  suggested itineraries, 257

FERRARA (cont'd)
Synagogue of Florence, 269
for visiting Americans, 273
special and free events, 280–1
sports and recreational activities,
281–2
for students, 215
taxes, 214
telegrams/telex/fax, 214
television, 215
tourist information, 210
transit information, 215
transportation, 212
walking tours:
in the footsteps of Michelangelo,
277–80
heart of Florence, 273–7
map, heart of Florence, 274–5
map, in the footsteps of Michelangelo, 278–9
weather, 215
what's special about, 207
for women, 215
shopping, 282–8
antiques, 283
art, 283
books, 283
children's wear, 283–4
department stores, 284
embroidery, 284
fabrics, 284
fashion, 284
gifts, 285
handcrafts, 285
jewelry, 285
leather, 285–6
markets, 286
mosaics, 287
paper and stationery, 287
prints and engravings, 287
shoes, 287–8
silver, 288
straw and raffia goods, 288
FRASCATI, 199–200
FREGENE, 201–2

GARDA, LAKE, 482–92
Gardone Riviera, 486–8
Limone sul Garda, 485–6
Riva del Garda, 483–5
San Vigilio, 491–2
Sirmione, 488–91
travelers' advisory, motorists, 483
see also specific places
GARDONE RIVIERA, 486–8
GENOA (GENOVA), 574–83
accommodations, 578–81
map, 575
orientation, 576–7
restaurants, 581–3
sights and attractions, 577–8
suggested itineraries, 567
traveling to, 574
what's special about, 568
GIUDECCA, 417–18

**HERCULANEUM
(ERCOLANO)**, 620
HILL TOWNS, THE, 294–324
Assisi, 317–21
map, 296–7
Perugia, 312–17
San Gimignano, 305–8
Spoleto, 321–4

suggested itineraries, 294
what's special about, 295
see also specific places

ITALIAN RIVIERA, 567–93
Genoa, 574–5
map, 569
Portofino, 590–3
Rapallo, 583–6
San Remo, 568–74
Santa Margherita Ligure, 586–90
suggested itineraries, 567
traveling to, 567–8
what's special about, 568
see also specific places

LAGO D'AVERNO, 619
LAKE DISTRICT, 481–503
Lake Como, 492
Lake Garda, 482–92
Lake Maggiore, 498–503
suggested itineraries, 481–2
traveling to, 482
what's special about, 482
see also specific places
LIMONE SUL GARDA, 485–6
LOMBARDY, 504–46
Bergamo, 538–41
Cremona, 541–3
Mantua, 543–6
Milan, 504–38
suggested itineraries, 504
traveling to, 504
what's special about, 505
see also specific places

MAGGIORE, LAKE, 498–503
Borromean Islands, 502–3
Stresa, 499–502
MANTUA (MANTOVA),
543–6
MARINA GRANDE, 646–7
MARINA PICCOLA, 656
MARINO, 198
MERANO (MERAN), 475–8
MILAN, 504–38
accommodations, 513–18
airports, 505
American Express, 508
bars, 535–6
cafes, 536–7
consulates, 508–9
drugstores, 509
emergencies, 509
entertainment and nightlife, 532–7
bars, 535–6
cafes, 536–7
movies, 537
nightclubs and contemporary
music, 533–5
performing arts, 532–3
excursion areas, 537–8
gay nightlife, 534–5
hospitals, 509
information sources, 509
laundry and dry cleaning, 509
libraries, 509
map, 507
movies, 537
music, contemporary, 535
newspapers and magazines, 509
nightclubs and contemporary music,
533–5
opera, 532–3
orientation, 508

performing arts, 532–3
post office, 509
religious services, 509
restaurants, 518–26
shopping, 526–32
bed and bath, 527
books, 527
department stores, 527
fabrics, 527
fashion, 527–9
hats, 529–30
jewelry, 530
lace, 530
leather goods and shoes, 530–1
lingerie, 531
malls, 531
paper, 532
porcelain and crystal, 532
toys, 532
sights and attractions, 509–13
Biblioteca-Pinacoteca
Ambrosiana,* 511–12
Cimitèro Monumentale, 513
Civica Galleria D'Arte Moderna,
512
Il Duomo,* 510
Museo D'Antica, 511
Museo del Duomo, 510
Museo Nazionale della Scienza e
Della Tecnica Leonardo da
Vinci, 512
Pinacoteca de Brera,* 510–11
Poldi Pezzoli Museum,* 511
San Ambrogio, Basilica di, 512
San Eustorgio, Basilica di, 512
Santa Maria delle Grazie,* 510
suggested itineraries, 504
telephone, 509
tourist information, 509
transportation, 508
traveling to, 504–6
what's special about, 505
MODENA, 342–5
MONDELLO LIDO, 671–2
MONREALE, 670–1
MOUNT ETNA, 690–1
MURANO, 432, 434

NAPLES (NAPOLI), 594–621
accommodations, 605–8
airport, 599
arriving in, 599
consulates, 601
cost of everyday items, 37
drugstores, 601
emergencies telephone numbers,
601
entertainment and nightlife, 617–18
environs of, 618–21
Herculaneum, 620
Phlaegrean Fields (Campi
Flegrei), 618–20
Vesuvius, 620–1
funicular, 600
history, 598
information sources, 599
layout of, 599–600
map, 597
orientation, 599–600
post office, 601
restaurants, 608–14
shopping, 614–17
sights and attractions, 601–5
Acquario, 604

NAPLES (NAPOLI) (cont'd)
  Capodimonte National Gallery
    and Museum, 602
  Castel dell'Ovo, 603
  Castelnuovo, 603
  Catacombs of San Gennaro, 604
  for children, 605
  Il Duomo, 604
  Museo Archeologico Na-
    zionale,* 601–2
  Museo Nazionale di San
    Martino, 603
  Palazzo Reale, 603
  Prince of Aragona Pignatelli Cor-
    tes Museum, 604
  Sansevero Chapel, 604
  Santa Chiara, Church of, 604
  subways, 600
  suggested itineraries, 595
  telephone, 601
  tourist information, 599
  tours, 601
  transportation, 600
  traveling to, 595
  what's special about, 595
NEMI, 199
NETTUNO, 201

ORTYGIA, 679–80
OSTIA, 197–8

PADUA (PADOVA), 447–52
  accommodations, 449–50
  map, 439
  restaurants, 450–2
  sights and attractions, 447–9
  suggested itineraries, 436
  tourist information, 447
  traveling to, 436, 447
  what's special about, 438
PAESTUM, 644–5
PALERMO, 662–73
  accommodations, 665–7
  entertainment and nightlife, 669–70
  excursion areas, 670–3
  orientation, 663
  restaurants, 668–9
  sights and attractions, 663–5
  tourist information, 662
  transportation, 663
  traveling to, 662
PALESTRINA, 200
PARMA, 345–9
  accommodations, 347–8
  restaurants, 348–9
  sights and attractions, 346–7
  tourist information, 345
  traveling to, 345
PERUGIA, 312–17
  accommodations, 314–15
  restaurants, 315–17
  sights and attractions, 313–14
  tourist information, 313
  traveling to, 312–13
PESCATORI ISOLA DEI, 502
**PHLAEGREAN FIELDS
    (CAMPI FLEGREI),**
    618–19
**PIEDMONT AND THE
    VALLE D'AOSTA,**
    547–66
  Aosta, 557–60
  Courmayeur, 560–4
  Entrèves, 564–6

  map, 549
  suggested itineraries, 547
  traveling to, 547
  Turin, 547–57
  what's special about, 548
  see also specific places
PISA, 308–12
  accommodations, 310–11
  map, 296–7
  restaurants, 311–12
  sights and attractions, 308–10
  suggested itineraries, 294
  tourist information, 308
  traveling to, 308
  what's special about, 295
POMPEII, 595–6, 621–4
  accommodations, 622–3
  restaurants, 623–4
  sights and attractions, 622
  suggested itineraries, 595
  tourist information, 621
  traveling to, 595–6, 621
  what's special about, 595
PORTOFINO, 590–3
POSITANO, 632–6
  accommodations, 633–5
  restaurants, 635–6
  tourist information, 632
  traveling to, 632
POZZUOLI, 619

RAPALLO, 583–6
RAVELLO, 640–44
  accommodations, 641–3
  restaurants, 643–4
  sights and attractions, 641
  tourist information, 640
  traveling to, 640
RAVENNA, 349–50
  accommodations, 352–3
  restaurants, 353–4
  sights and attractions, 350–2
  tourist information, 349
  traveling to, 349
RIVA DEL GARDA, 483–5
ROCCA DI PAPA, 198–9
ROME, 73–205
  accommodations, 86–108
    map, 88–9
    money-saving tips, 87
  addresses, locating, 78
  airport, 73, 75
  American Express, 81
  arriving in, 73–5
  ATAC (buses), 80
  babysitters, 81
  ballet and dance, 186
  barbers, 82
  bicycle, motorscooter and motor-
    cycle transportation, 81
  business hours, 81
  bus pass, tourist, 80
  bus/tram, 80
  calendar of events, 41–2
  car rentals, 80
  cars and driving, 80–1
  cemeteries, 148
  for children, 109, 129
  churches, 148–50
  consulates, 82
  cost of everyday items, 36–7
  currency exchange, 81–2
  dance and ballet, 186
  doctors and dentists, 82

  drugstores, 82
  dry cleaning, 82
  embassies and consulates, 82
  emergencies, 82
  entertainment and nightlife, 185–93
    ballet and dance, 186
    bars and cafes, 190–93
    Brazilian music, 189
    dance and ballet, 186
    dinner theater, 186
    films, 193
    gay clubs, 189–90
    Irish pubs, 193
    jazz, soul, funk, 188–9
    movies, 193
    nightclubs and cabaret, 186–8
    opera, 186
    performing arts, 185–6
  excursion areas, 193–205
    Anzio and Nettuno, 201
    Ardea, 205
    Castelli Romani, 198–200
    Etruscan historical sights, 202–3
    Fregene, 201–2
    map, 195
    Ostia, 197–8
    Palestrina, 200–1
    Tivoli, 194, 196–7
    Viterbo, 203–5
  eyeglasses, 82
  fax, 84
  galleries and museums, 151–5
  gardens and parks, 154
  for gay men and lesbians, 84
  hairdressers and barbers, 82
  hospitals, 82
  hotlines, 82
  information sources, 75
  laundry and dry cleaning, 82
  layout of, 75, 78–9
  libraries, 82
  lost and found, 82–3
  luggage storage and lockers, 83
  magazines, 83
  mail, 83
  maps, 76–7, 110–11, 136–7
    accommodations, 88–9
    excursion areas, 195
    sights and attractions, 136–7
    walking tours, 157, 161, 167, 171
  Metropolitana (Metro), 79
  money-saving tips, 113
    accommodations, 87
    restaurants, 113
  museums and galleries, 151–5
  music, 186–9
    Brazilian, 189
    cabaret, 188
    classical, 186–7
    jazz, soul, funk, 188–9
    opera, 186
  neighborhoods, 78–9
  newspapers and magazines, 83
  orientation, 73–9
  Papal audiences, 135, 138
  parking, 80–1
  parks and gardens, 154
  post office, 83
  radio and TV, 83
  religious services, 83
  restaurants, 108–32
    picnic supplies, 132
  ABRUZZI
    Abruzzi (!$), 122

ROME (cont'd)
Ambasciata d'Abruzzo (M$), 120–1
La Maiella (M), 116
AMERICAN
The Cowboy (B), 132
ANGLO-AMERICAN
Babington's Tea Rooms (M), 128–9
BOLOGNESE
Dal Bolognese (E), 123
BREAKFAST
Bibo Astoria '73 (M), 131
CALABRIAN
Le Maschere (I), 117
EMILIANA ROMAGNOLA
Colline Emiliane (M), 122–3
FAST FOOD
Birreria Viennese (B), 129–30
Cose Fritte (B), 129
McDonald's (B), 129
FRENCH
L'Eau Vive (M), 119–20
Le Cabanon (E), 124
Sans Souci (VE), 113
GELATO
Tre Scalini (I), 129
IN HOTELS
Massimo D'Azeglio (M-E), 131
INTERNATIONAL
Alfredo Alla Scrofa (E), 115
Alvaro Al Circo Massimo (E), 126–7
Bibo Astoria '73 (M), 131
George's (VE), 113
La Pergola (VE), 130
L'Eau Vive (M), 119–20
Passeto (M), 116
Ristorante Ranieri (M), 112
Ristorante Ulpia (I), 130–1
Taverna Flavia Di Mimmo (E), 126
ITALIAN
Al Ceppo (M), 121
Aurora 10 da Pino Il Sommelier (M), 114
Bibo Astoria '73 (M), 131
Birreria Viennese (B), 130
The Cowboy (B), 132
La Pergola (VE), 130
Le Cabanon (E), 124
Patrizia e Roberto del Pianeta Terra (VE*), 127
Vecchia Roma (E), 125
Montevecchio (E), 115
Trattoria Elettra (I), 118
LATE-NIGHT SNACKS
The Cowboy (B), 132
La Casa del Tramezzino (B), 132
MIDDLE EUROPEAN
Birreria Viennese (B), 130
MOLISIAN
Ristorante Giardinaccio (I), 119
NEAPOLITAN
Scoglio di Frisio (M$), 117
NORTH AFRICAN
Le Cabanon (E), 124
ROMAN
Alfredo Alla Scrofa (E), 115
Angelino A Tormargana (M), 125
Babington's Tea Rooms (M), 128–9
Da Giggeto (M), 126

El Tartufo (M), 121
El Toulà (VE*), 109
Hostaria l'Archeologia (M), 128
Il Barroccio (I), 120
Il Domiziano (I$), 116–17
Il Matriciano (M), 118
Il Ristorante 34 (also Al 34) (M), 112
La Cisterna (E), 124
Massimo d'Azeglio (M-E), 131
Monte Arci (I$), 117–18
Montevecchio (E), 115
Osteria Margutta (M), 112
Papa Giovanni (VE), 115
Passeto (M), 126
Quirino (M), 126
Relais le Jardin (VE*), 120
Ristorante da Pancrazio (M), 127–8
Ristorante del Giglio (I), 118
Ristorante del Pallaro (I$), 128
Ristorante Mastrostefano (M), 130
Ristorante Pierdonati (M), 118–19
Romolo (E), 124–5
Sabatini I (E), 124
Satyricon (I), 118
Sora Lella (M), 127
Taverna Flavia di Mimmo (E), 126
Taverna La Mejo Pastascuitta der Monno (I), 119
Trattoria Elettra (I), 118
Trattoria l'Albanese (I), 121–2
Tre Scalini (I), 129
SANDWICHES
La Casa del Tramezzino (B), 131–2
SARDINIAN
Monte Arci (I$), 117–18
Il Drappo (M), 116
SEAFOOD
Alberto Ciarla (VE*), 123
Piccolo Abruzzo (M), 114–5
Sabatini I (E), 124
Trattoria Vincenzo (I), 125
TEA ROOM/BRUNCH
Babington's Tea Rooms (M), 128–9
TUSCAN
Giarrarrosto Toscano (M), 114
Ristorante Nino (M), 112
VEGETARIAN
Margutta Vegetariano (I), 131
Vecchia Roma (E), 125
VENETIAN
Il Canto del Riso (E), 122
WITH VIEWS
La Pergola (VE), 130
Ristorante Mastrostefano (M), 130
Ristorante Ulpia (I), 130–1
restrooms, 83
safety, 83
for senior citizens, 84–5
shoe repair, 83–4
shopping, 173–85
antiques, 175
areas, 174–5
art, 175–6
beauty centers, 176
bookstores, 176
department stores, 176–7

discount, 177
eyeglasses, 177
fabrics, 177–8
fashion, 178–80
food, 180
gifts, 180
gloves, 180–1
hats, 181
jewelry, 181
knitwear, 181–2
leather, 182
lingerie, 182–3
liquors, 183
markets, 183
mosaics, 183
religious art, 183–4
shoes, 184
silver, 184
toys, 184–5
wines, 185
sights and attractions, 133–72
Antoninus and Faustina, Temple of, 163
Appian Way, 144–5
Arte Ebraico della Comunità Israelitica di Roma, Museo di, 154
Augustus, Forum of, 158
Basilica Emilia, 160, 162
Basilica Julia, 162–3
Borgia Apartments, 139
Caesar, Julius, Forum of, 159
Caesar, Julius, Temple of, 163
Capitoline Hill, 143
Capitoline Museum,* 152
Castel Sant'Angelo, 143–4
the Castors, Temple of, 163
The Catacombs, 144–5
Cecilia Metella, Tomb of, 145
Chiaramonti Museum, 139
for children, 155
Cimitero Monumentale dei Padri Cappucini, 148, 166
Circus Maximus, 160
Città Romana, Museo della, 154
The Colosseum, 142–3
Conservatori, Palace of the,* 152
Constantine, Basilica of, 163–4
Curia, 162
Domus Augustana, 142
Egyptian-Gregorian Museum, 138
Emanuele (Vittorio) Monument, 159
Ethnological Museum, 140
Etruscan-Gregorian Museum, 138–9
Farnese Gardens, 142
Flavian Palace, 164–5
Flavii, Palace of, 142
Fontana di Trevi (Trevi Fountain),* 146–7
Foro Italico, 156
Fortuna Virile, Temple of, 159–60
Fountain of Neptune, 146
Fountain of the Bees, 147
Fountain of the Four Rivers,* 146
Fountain of the Moor, 146
Fountain of the Triton, 147
Frommer's favorite experiences, 147
Fun Fair (Luna Park), 155
Galleria Borghese,* 151–2

ROME (cont'd)
  Galleria Nazionale D'Arte
    Antica, 154
  Giardino del Lago, 155
  Hippodrome, 142
  Historical-Artistic Museum, 135
  History Museum, 140
  Janiculum Hill, 151
  Keats-Shelley Memorial, 155
  Lapis Niger, 162
  Livia, House of, 142
  Milizie, Tower of the, 158
  Modern Art, Museum of,
    139–40
  National Gallery of Modern Art,
    152–3
  National Museum of the Villa
    Giulia,* 151
  Nazionale Romano, Museo,*
    151
  Nerva, Forum of, 158
  Orti Farnesiani, 165–6
  Palatine Hill, 141–2
  Palazzo dei Congressi, 156
  Palazza dei Conservatori, 143
  Palazzo della Sport, 156
  Palazzo Doria Pamphilj, 153
  Palazzo Venezia, Museum of the,
    153–4
  The Pantheon, 145–6
  Phocas, Column of, 163
  Pinacoteca, 138
  The Pincio, 168
  Pius Clementinus Museum, 139
  Porta Pinciana, 168
  Protestant Cemetery, 155–6
  Pyramid of Caius Cestius, 148
  Roman Forum,* 141
  Romulus, Temple of, 163
  Rostra, 162
  St. Calixtus, Catacombs of, 145
  St. Clemente, Basilica di, 150
  St. Peter's Basilica, 134–5, 138
  St. Peter's tomb, 135
  St. Sebastian, Tomb of, 144–5
  San Giovanni in Laterano, Basili-
    ca of, 148–9
  San Paolo Fuori Le Mura, 149
  San Pietro in Vincoli, Chiesa di,
    149–50
  Santa Maria D'Aracoeli, 150
  Santa Maria degli Angeli, 150
  Santa Maria in Cosmedin, 150
  Santa Maria Maggiore, Basilica
    di, 149
  Senatorium, 143
  Severus, Septimius, Arch of, 162
  Sistine Chapel, 140
  Spanish Steps (Scalinata di
    Spagna), 169
  suggested itineraries, 133–4
  Teatro di Marcello, 159
  Terme di Caracalla, 147
  Titus, Arch of, 164
  Trajan, Forum of, 158–9
  Trajan's Column, 159
  Trajan's Market, 158
  The Vatican, 138–9
  Vatican Gardens, 140–1
  Vatican grottoes, 135
  Vatican Library, 139
  Vesta, Temple of, 163
  Villa Borghese, 154–5
soccer (football), 172

sports and recreational activities,
  172–3
street maps, 78
for students, 84
subway, 79
taxes, 84
taxis, 80
telegrams/telex/fax, 84
television, 83
theater, dinner, 186
tourist information, 75
tours, organized, 172
tram/bus, 80
transit information, 84
transportation, 79–81
  bicycle, motorscooter, motor-
    cycle, 81
  bus/tram, 80
  cars and driving, 80–1
  on foot, 81
  subway, 79
  taxi, 80
walking tours:
  Imperial Rome, 156–60
  Piazza Barberini to Piazza del
    Popolo, 166–9
  Roman Forum and Palatine Hill,
    160–6
  Spanish Steps to Quirinale,
    169–72
water, 84
what's special about, 74
for women, 84

SAN GIMIGNANO, 305–8
SAN REMO, 568–74
accommodations, 570–2
entertainment and nightlife, 573–4
restaurants, 572–3
sights and attractions, 570
traveling to, 568–70
**SANTA MARGHERITA LI-
  GURE,** 586–90
accommodations, 587–9
area code, 586
restaurants, 589–90
sights and attractions, 586
tourist information, 586
traveling to, 586
SAN VIGILIO, 491–2
SEGESTA, 673–4
SELINUNTE, 674–5
SICILY, 657–91
Agrigento, 675–8
history, 658–60
map, 661
Palermo, 662–73
Segesta, 673–4
Selinunte, 674–5
suggested itineraries, 660
Syracuse, 678–82
Taormina, 682–91
traveling to, 660, 662
what's special about, 658
see also specific places
SIENA, 294–305
accommodations, 300–4
map, 296–7
restaurants, 304–5
sights and attractions, 298–300
special events, 295
suggested itineraries, 294
tourist information, 295
traveling to, 294–5

what's special about, 295
SIRACUSA: see SYRACUSE (SI-
  RACUSA)
SIRMIONE, 488–91
SOLFATARA, 619
SORRENTO, 626, 628–32
restaurants, 631–2
sights and attractions, 628
tourist information, 626
traveling to, 626
SOUTH TYROL, 457–80
SPOLETO, 321–4
STRESA, 499–502
SYRACUSE (SIRACUSA),
  678–82
accommodations, 680–1
restaurants, 681–2
sights and attractions, 678–9
tourist information, 678
traveling to, 678

TAORMINA, 682–91
accommodations, 683–7
entertainment and nightlife, 689
excursion areas, 690–1
restaurants, 687–8
sights and attractions, 683
tourist information, 682
traveling to, 682
TARQUINIA, 202–3
TIVOLI, 194, 196–7
TORCELLO, 435–6
TREMEZZO, 496–8
TRENT (TRENTO), 478–80
TRIESTE, 457–66
accommodations, 462–3
map, 459
restaurants, 463–6
sights and attractions, 460–2
suggested itineraries, 457–8
tourist information, 460
traveling to, 458, 460
what's special about, 458
TURIN (TORINO), 547–57
accommodations, 552–4
entertainment and nightlife, 557
festivals, 550
orientation, 550
restaurants, 554–7
sights and attractions, 550–2
special events and festivals, 550
traveling to, 547–8

VENICE, 355–436
accommodations, 365–84
airport, 356
air travel, 356
American Express, 362
  organized tours, 421
arriving in, 355–7
babysitters, 362
barbers, 363
bars, 429–30
books about, 31
bookstores, 362
buses, 357
cafés, 430–1
car rentals, 362
cars and driving, 357
churches and schools, 413–16
consulates, 363
currency exchange, 362–3
doctors and dentists, 363
drugstores, 363

VENICE (cont'd)
dry cleaning, 363
embassies and consulates, 363
emergencies, 363
entertainment and nightlife, 428–32
  bars, 429–30
  cafes, 430–1
  gambling, 431–2
  nightclubs and contemporary
    music, 429
  performing arts, 428–9
excursion areas, 432–6
  Burano, 434–5
  map, 433
  Murano, 432, 434
  Torcello, 435–6
eyeglasses, 363
fax, 364
festivals, 421–2
free and special events, 421–2
galleries and museums, 409–13
gambling, 431–2
for gay men and lesbians, 364
gondolas, 362
hairdressers/barbers, 363
hospitals, 363
information sources, 357
lacemaking, 434
laundry and dry cleaning, 363
layout of, 357–61
libraries, 363
lost and found, 363
luggage storage/lockers, 363
magazines, 363
maps, 358–9
  accommodations, 368–9
  excursion areas, 433
  restaurants, 386–7
  sights and attractions, 404–5
  walking tour, 419
money-saving tips
  restaurants, 385
museums and galleries, 409–13
music, contemporary, 429
neighborhoods, 360–1
newspapers and magazines, 363
nightclubs and contemporary music,
  429
organized tours, 421
performing arts, 428–9
post office, 363
radio, 363
religious services, 363
restaurants, 384–401
  for children, 400
  map, 386–7
  money-saving tips, 385
  picnic fare, 400–1
FRENCH
  Les Deux Lions (E-VE), 398
INTERNATIONAL
  Al Gambero (M$), 390–1
  All'Angelo (M), 390
  Club del Doge (M-VE), 397–8
  Do Forni (E), 389
  Harry's Dolci, La Giudecca (M*),
    397
  Il Cortile (VE), 388–9
  La Caravella (VE*), 385
  Locanda Montin (M$*), 396
  Ristorante da Raffaele (M), 391
  Ristorante Noemi (E), 389
  Taverna la Fenice (VE), 388
  Trattoria alla Colomba (E),

    389–90
ITALIAN
  Al Teatro (I$), 391–2
  Arcimboldo (M), 392
  Locanda Montin (M$*), 396
LIGHT FARE
  Alfredo, Alfredo (B), 398–9
  Alla Vedova (B), 399
  Bar Torino (B), 399
  Da Patata (B), 399
  Le Chat Qui Rit (B), 398
  Maddalena (B), 399
  Osteria alle Botteghe (B), 399–
    400
  Tiziano Snack (B), 399
SEAFOOD
  Da Ciccio (B$), 393
  Al Barbacani (VE), 388
  "Al Graspo de Ua" (E*), 393–4
  Hostaria da Franz (M), 392–3
  La Furatola (M), 395–6
  Nuova Rivetta (I$), 392
  Ostaria ai Pescatori, Burano
    (M-E$), 435
  Osteria da Fiore, San Polo (M-E),
    396
  Ristorante a la Vecia Cavana (E),
    389
  Ristorante Corte Sconta (E), 395
  Trattoria Busa alla Torre, Mura-
    no (M), 434
  Trattoria Madonna (I$), 395
TUSCAN
  Dalvo (M), 390
VENETIAN
  Al Corallo, Murano (M), 434
  Al Gambero (M$), 390–1
  Al Vetrai, Murano (M), 434
  Alfredo, Alfredo (B), 398–9
  Alla Vedova (B), 399
  Antica Martini (VE*), 384–5
  Arcimboldo (M), 392
  Cantina do Spade (B$), 398
  Club del Doge (M-VE), 397–8
  Da Ciccio (B$), 393
  Fiachetteria Toscana (M), 394
  Harry's Bar (VE*), 385, 388
  Il Cortile (VE), 388–9
  Le Chat Qui Rit (B), 398
  Locanda Cipriani, Torcello (E*),
    436
  Maddalena (B), 399
  Restaurant da Bruno (I), 394
  Ristorante Belvedere (M), 393
  Ristorante da Raffaele (M), 391
  Ristorante Noemi (E), 389
  Rosticceria San Bartolomeo (I$),
    394–5
  Taverna la Fenice (VE), 388
  Trattoria alla Colomba (E),
    389–90
  Trattoria Antica Besseta, San Polo
    (M), 396–7
  Trattoria De Romano, Burano (I),
    435
  Vini da Arturo (M), 391
WITH VIEWS
  Club del Doge (M-VE), 397–8
restrooms, 363
safety, 364
schools and churches, 413–16
for senior citizens, 364
shoe repair, 364
shopping, 423–8

antiques, 423–4
brass objects, 424
carnival masks, 424
fashions, 424–5
gifts, 425
glass, 425–6
graphics, 426
jewelry, 426
Jewish handicrafts, 426
lace, 426
leather, 426–7
markets, 427
paper, 427
shoes, 427–8
sights and attractions in or near,
  402–21
  Accademia,* 409–10
  Ca' D'Oro, 411
  Cattedrale di Torcello (Torcello),
    436
  Ca' Rezzonico, 411
  Chiesa Madonna Dell'Orto,
    414–15
  for children, 416–17
  Collezione Peggy Guggenheim,*
    412
  Duomo (Burano), 435
  Frommer's favorite experiences,
    413
  Gallerie Dell'Accademia, 418
  The Ghetto, 416
  Ghiesa dei Gesuiti, 418
  glass-manufacturing works, 417
  gondola ride, 416–17
  Grand Canal,* 408–9
  The Lido, 408
  map, 404–5
  Museo Correr, 410–11
  Museo Fortuny, 412–13
  Museo Israelitico, 416
  Museo Navale and Arsenale, 412
  Museo Vetrario di Murano (Mu-
    rano), 432
  Palazzo Ducale,* 406–7
  Ponte Rialto, 412
  SS. Giovanni e Paolo, Church of,
    416
  San Giorgio Degli Schiavoni,
    Scuola di, 414
  San Giorgio Maggiore, Basilica
    di, 415
  San Marco, Basilica,* 403, 406
  San Marco, Campanile di, 407
  San Marco, Piazzetta, 408
  San Pietro Martire, Church of
    (Murano), 432
  San Rocco, Scuola di,* 413–14
  San Sebastiano, Church of, 415
  Santa Maria Dei Frari, 414
  Santa Maria Della Salute, 415–16
  Santi Maria e Donato (Murano),
    432, 434
  San Zaccaria, Church of, 415
  Scola Tedesca, 416
  Scuola Merietti (Burano), 435
  suggested itineraries, 402–3
  Torre Dell'Orologio, 407–8
special and free events, 421–2
sports and recreational activities,
  422–3
for students, 364
taxes, 364
telegrams/telex/fax, 364
television, 364

VENICE (*cont'd*)
tourist information, 357
tours, organized, 421
train travel, 357
transit information, 364
transportation, 361–2
useful telephone numbers, 364
walking tour, 417–21
   map, 419
what's special about, 356
for women, 364

VERONA, 436–47
accommodations, 443–5
map, 439
restaurants, 445–7
sights and attractions, 440–3
suggested itineraries, 436
tourist information, 438
traveling to, 436–7
what's special about, 438
VESUVIUS, 620–1

VICENZA, 452–6
accommodations, 454–5
map, 439
restaurants, 455–6
sights and attractions, 452–4
suggested itineraries, 436
tourist information, 452
traveling to, 436, 452
what's special about, 438
VITERBO, 203–5

NOW, SAVE MONEY ON ALL YOUR TRAVELS!
Join Frommer's™ Dollarwise® Travel Club

Saving money while traveling is never easy, which is why the **Dollarwise Travel Club** was formed 32 years ago to provide cost-cutting travel strategies, up-to-date travel information, and a sense of community for value-conscious travelers from all over the world.

In keeping with the money-saving concept, the annual membership fee is low— $25 for U.S. residents and $35 for residents of Canada, Mexico, and other countries—and is immediately exceeded by the value of your benefits, which include:

1. Any TWO books listed on the following pages;
2. Plus any ONE Frommer's City Guide;
3. A subscription to our quarterly newspaper, *The Dollarwise Traveler;*
4. A membership card that entitles you to purchase through the Club all Frommer's publications for 33% to 40% off their retail price.

The eight-page **Dollarwise Traveler** tells you about the latest developments in good-value travel worldwide and includes the following columns: **Hospitality Exchange** (for those offering and seeking hospitality in cities all over the world); and **Share-a-Trip** (for those looking for travel companions to share costs).

Aside from the various Frommer's Guides, the Gault Millau Guides, and the Real Guides you can also choose from our Special Editions, which include such titles as *Caribbean Hideaways* (the 100 most romantic places to stay in the Islands); and *Marilyn Wood's Wonderful Weekends* (a selection of the best mini-vacations within a 200-mile radius of New York City).

To join this Club, send the appropriate membership fee with your name and address to: Frommer's Dollarwise Travel Club, 15 Columbus Circle, New York, NY 10023. Remember to specify which single city guide and which two other guides you wish to receive in your initial package of member's benefits. Or tear out the pages, check off your choices, and send them to us with your membership fee.

FROMMER BOOKS
PRENTICE HALL TRAVEL   Date_____
15 COLUMBUS CIRCLE
NEW YORK, NY 10023

Friends: Please send me the books checked below.

FROMMER'S™ COMPREHENSIVE GUIDES
(Guides listing facilities from budget to deluxe, with emphasis on the medium-priced)

☐ Alaska $14.95	☐ Italy $19.00
☐ Australia $14.95	☐ Japan & Hong Kong $17.00
☐ Austria & Hungary $14.95	☐ Morocco $18.00
☐ Belgium, Holland & Luxembourg $14.95	☐ Nepal $18.00
☐ Bermuda & The Bahamas $17.00	☐ New England $17.00
☐ Brazil $14.95	☐ New Mexico $13.95
☐ California $18.00	☐ New York State $19.00
☐ Canada $16.00	☐ Northwest $16.95
☐ Caribbean $17.00	☐ Puerta Vallarta (avail. Feb. '92) $14.00
☐ Carolinas & Georgia $17.00	☐ Portugal, Madeira & the Azores $14.95
☐ Colorado (avail. Jan '92) $14.00	☐ Scandinavia $18.95
☐ Cruises (incl. Alaska, Carib, Mex, Hawaii,	☐ Scotland (avail. Feb. '92) $17.00
Panama, Canada & US) $16.00	☐ South Pacific $20.00
☐ Delaware, Maryland, Pennsylvania &	☐ Southeast Asia $14.95
the New Jersey Shore (avail. Jan. '92) . . $19.00	☐ Switzerland & Liechtenstein $19.00
☐ Egypt $14.95	☐ Thailand $20.00
☐ England $17.00	☐ Virginia (avail. Feb. '92) $14.00
☐ Florida $17.00	☐ Virgin Islands $13.00
☐ France $15.95	☐ USA $16.95
☐ Germany $18.00	

0891492

FROMMER'S CITY GUIDES

(Pocket-size guides to sightseeing and tourist accommodations and facilities in all price ranges)

☐ Amsterdam/Holland	$8.95	☐ Minneapolis/St. Paul	$8.95
☐ Athens	$8.95	☐ Montréal/Québec City	$8.95
☐ Atlanta	$8.95	☐ New Orleans	$8.95
☐ Atlantic City/Cape May	$8.95	☐ New York	$12.00
☐ Bangkok	$12.00	☐ Orlando	$12.00
☐ Barcelona	$12.00	☐ Paris	$8.95
☐ Belgium	$7.95	☐ Philadelphia	$11.00
☐ Berlin	$10.00	☐ Rio	$8.95
☐ Boston	$8.95	☐ Rome	$8.95
☐ Cancún/Cozumel/Yucatán	$8.95	☐ Salt Lake City	$8.95
☐ Chicago	$9.95	☐ San Diego	$8.95
☐ Denver/Boulder/Colorado Springs	$8.95	☐ San Francisco	$12.00
☐ Dublin/Ireland	$10.00	☐ Santa Fe/Taos/Albuquerque	$10.95
☐ Hawaii	$12.00	☐ Seattle/Portland	$12.00
☐ Hong Kong	$7.95	☐ St. Louis/Kansas City	$9.95
☐ Las Vegas	$8.95	☐ Sydney	$8.95
☐ Lisbon/Madrid/Costa del Sol	$8.95	☐ Tampa/St. Petersburg	$8.95
☐ London	$12.00	☐ Tokyo	$8.95
☐ Los Angeles	$8.95	☐ Toronto	$8.95
☐ Mexico City/Acapulco	$8.95	☐ Vancouver/Victoria	$7.95
☐ Miami	$8.95	☐ Washington, D.C.	$12.00

FROMMER'S $-A-DAY® GUIDES

(Guides to low-cost tourist accommodations and facilities)

☐ Australia on $40 a Day	$13.95	☐ Israel on $40 a Day	$13.95
☐ Costa Rica, Guatemala & Belize on $35 a Day	$15.95	☐ Mexico on $45 a Day	$18.00
		☐ New York on $65 a Day	$15.00
☐ Eastern Europe on $25 a Day	$16.95	☐ New Zealand on $45 a Day	$16.00
☐ England on $50 a Day	$17.00	☐ Scotland & Wales on $40 a Day	$18.00
☐ Europe on $45 a Day	$19.00	☐ South America on $40 a Day	$15.95
☐ Greece on $35 a Day	$14.95	☐ Spain on $50 a Day	$15.95
☐ Hawaii on $70 a Day	$18.00	☐ Turkey on $40 a Day	$22.00
☐ India on $40 a Day	$20.00	☐ Washington, D.C., on $45 a Day	$17.00
☐ Ireland on $40 a Day	$17.00		

FROMMER'S CITY $-A-DAY GUIDES

☐ Berlin on $40 a Day	$12.00	☐ Madrid on $50 a Day (avail. Jan '92)	$13.00
☐ Copenhagen on $50 a Day	$12.00	☐ Paris on $45 a Day	$12.00
☐ London on $45 a Day	$12.00	☐ Stockholm on $50 a Day (avail. Dec. '91)	$13.00

FROMMER'S FAMILY GUIDES

☐ California with Kids	$16.95	☐ San Francisco with Kids	$17.00
☐ Los Angeles with Kids	$17.00	☐ Washington, D.C., with Kids (avail. Jan '92)	$17.00
☐ New York City with Kids (avail. Jan '92)	$18.00		

SPECIAL EDITIONS

☐ Beat the High Cost of Travel	$6.95	☐ Marilyn Wood's Wonderful Weekends (CT, DE, MA, NH, NJ, NY, PA, RI, VT)	$11.95
☐ Bed & Breakfast—N. America	$14.95		
☐ Caribbean Hideaways	$16.00	☐ Motorist's Phrase Book (Fr/Ger/Sp)	$4.95
☐ Honeymoon Destinations (US, Mex & Carib)	$14.95	☐ The New World of Travel (annual by Arthur Frommer for savvy travelers)	$16.95

(TURN PAGE FOR ADDITONAL BOOKS AND ORDER FORM)

0891492

| ☐ Paris Rendez-Vous . . . . $10.95 | ☐ Travel Diary and Record Book . . . . $5.95 |
| ☐ Swap and Go (Home Exchanging) . . . . $10.95 | ☐ Where to Stay USA (from $3 to $30 a night) . . . . $13.95 |

FROMMER'S TOURING GUIDES

(Color illustrated guides that include walking tours, cultural and historic sites, and practical information)

☐ Amsterdam $10.95	☐ New York $10.95
☐ Australia $12.95	☐ Paris $8.95
☐ Brazil $10.95	☐ Rome $10.95
☐ Egypt $8.95	☐ Scotland $9.95
☐ Florence $8.95	☐ Thailand $12.95
☐ Hong Kong $10.95	☐ Turkey $10.95
☐ London $12.95	☐ Venice $8.95

GAULT MILLAU

(The only guides that distinguish the truly superlative from the merely overrated)

☐ The Best of Chicago $15.95	☐ The Best of Los Angeles $16.95
☐ The Best of Florida $17.00	☐ The Best of New England $15.95
☐ The Best of France $16.95	☐ The Best of New Orleans $16.95
☐ The Best of Germany $18.00	☐ The Best of New York $16.95
☐ The Best of Hawaii $16.95	☐ The Best of Paris $16.95
☐ The Best of Hong Kong $16.95	☐ The Best of San Francisco $16.95
☐ The Best of Italy $16.95	☐ The Best of Thailand $17.95
☐ The Best of London $16.95	☐ The Best of Toronto $17.00

☐ The Best of Washington, D.C. $16.95

THE REAL GUIDES

(Opinionated, politically aware guides for youthful budget-minded travelers)

☐ Amsterdam $9.95	☐ Mexico $11.95
☐ Berlin $11.95	☐ Morocco $12.95
☐ Brazil $13.95	☐ New York $9.95
☐ California & the West Coast $11.95	☐ Paris $9.95
☐ Czechoslovakia $13.95	☐ Peru $12.95
☐ France $12.95	☐ Poland $13.95
☐ Germany $13.95	☐ Portugal $10.95
☐ Greece $13.95	☐ San Francisco $11.95
☐ Guatemala $13.95	☐ Scandinavia $14.95
☐ Hong Kong $11.95	☐ Spain $12.95
☐ Hungary $12.95	☐ Turkey $12.95
☐ Ireland $12.95	☐ Venice $11.95
☐ Italy $13.95	☐ Women Travel $12.95
☐ Kenya $12.95	☐ Yugoslavia $12.95

ORDER NOW!

In U.S. include $2 shipping UPS for 1st book; $1 ea. add'l book. Outside U.S. $3 and $1, respectively.

Allow four to six weeks for delivery in U.S., longer outside U.S. We discourage rush order service, but orders arriving with shipping fees plus a $15 surcharge will be handled as rush orders.

Enclosed is my check or money order for $_____

NAME _____

ADDRESS _____

CITY _____ STATE _____ ZIP _____

0891492

The

Singing

and Dancing

Daughters

of God

The

Singing

and Dancing

Daughters

of God

TIMOTHY SCHAFFERT

UNBRIDLED BOOKS

Unbridled Books
Denver, Colorado

Copyright © 2005 Timothy Schaffert

Library of Congress Cataloging-in-Publication Data

Schaffert, Timothy.
The singing and dancing daughters of God / Timothy Schaffert.
p. cm.
ISBN 1-932961-12-7 (alk. paper)
1. Divorced men—Fiction.   2. Single fathers—Fiction.   3. Country musicians—Fiction.   I. Title.
PS3619.C325S56 2005
813'.6—dc22
2005015899

1   3   5   7   9   10   8   6   4   2

Book Design by SH • CV

First Printing

For

Rodney Rahl

and my parents,

Larry and Donita

ACKNOWLEDGMENTS

Thanks to Alice Tasman and Jean Naggar, and Greg Michalson and Fred Ramey, for their commitment to my work. Also thanks to those who have read this book in various stages or have otherwise contributed to its development: Judy Slater, Gerry Shapiro, Leslie Prisbell, Justin Wolta, Janet Lura, Maud Casey, and Ladette Randolph. A few of the characters in this novel first appeared, in a somewhat different guise, in a short story that was published in issue 11 of the literary journal *Press*.

PART ONE

1 .

§§§§

T O get through the afternoons that wound into early evenings,
driving a school bus along long country roads and driveways,
Hud kept slightly drunk. He sipped from an old brown root-
beer bottle he'd filled with vodka. There'd been a few times in
the past when he'd gotten too drunk, when he'd swerved too
much to avoid a raccoon, and even once a sudden hawk
swooping too low. He made himself sick to think how he'd
once nearly driven the rickety bus in all its inflammability
into an electrical pole. He knew what an ugly notoriety such
an accident would bring him. *The whole world,* Hud thought,
likes to mourn together and hate together when it can.

There was a man in town named Robbie Schrock, who,
like some fairy-tale hag, had murdered his own two boys
with rat-poisoned candied apples he'd dropped into their
Halloween sacks. When the children died, Robbie Schrock
cried on the TV news and blamed the neighbors, and the
whole little town cried with him, shocked by the inhumanity

of some people. Robbie Schrock eventually confessed, and shocked the town all over again. The state tried and sentenced him and gave him the chair.

Today was the afternoon of the execution, and some of the children on Hud's bus celebrated by dressing up in Halloween costumes, though it was only early September. One boy wore a bandanna and a pirate's eye patch pushed up on his forehead. Another boy wore an Indian headdress and a breastplate made of sticks and feathers. A little girl was a Belgian nun in a pale blue habit and a winged wimple folded from newspaper.

Hud, disturbed by what he thought to be morbid spectacle, took a last shot-back of vodka from the root-beer bottle. He looked in the rearview mirror to the two boys sitting behind him. Both were dressed up in churchy blue suits, their faces painted a pale gray.

"What are you supposed to be?" Hud asked.

"We're the murdered Schrock boys," they said, their voices in tired and rehearsed unison.

"You're the worst of them all," Hud mumbled. He felt compelled to write a song for Robbie Schrock, though he'd hardly known the man and, of course, did not condone his crime. Whistling, Hud drove with one hand, and with the other he wrote down key words to the song coming together in his head. He wrote "lonesome" and "divorce" and "weakly" in ink on the leg of his jeans.

He understood something of Robbie Schrock's circumstances. Hud's newly ex-wife, Tuesday, at times was full of vindictiveness. For a short while she had conspired to keep

Hud's daughter away from him, judging him a drunk and a misfit and unworthy of even the few decent things this worthless world offered him. Robbie Schrock, his babies taken away, probably in an ugly divorce, probably left with only an occasional weekend or an occasional holiday with his children, wanted the whole world to know what loss can really do to a person. Hud could sympathize.

Though he would never hurt his own eight-year-old, his adorable Nina, he had thought about stealing her away, about painting his car a different color and driving and driving until they found some suitable no-place. They'd wear fake glasses, and when they spoke to the people at the gas stations and grocery stores, they'd cover their mouths with handkerchiefs to disguise their voices. He'd change the part in his hair and go by the name of some other Paul Newman character—Luke, maybe. Maybe Butch. Nina could choose her own name, would probably choose "Jessie"; that was what she named all her dolls.

Whenever with Nina, and only with Nina, Hud felt calm and attentive, and he thought if she was his all the time, he'd be a better man. A few weeks before, Tuesday had let Hud have Nina for an afternoon in his apartment above the shoe repair shop on the town square. Hud and Nina went up on the flat roof and harvested the tomatoes he'd grown in pots. Afterward, after eating some, Nina lay back to nap, seeds on her cheeks, and asked him to sing a song about her. He sat so his shadow kept the vicious sun from her skin, and he plucked a tune from his guitar. He called it "Nina Is All I Need, Really," and as she drifted off, he sang about every aspect of her face, giving her nose, her pink lips, the red freckle on her neck, each its own separate piece of melody. *This could be why people have children in the first place,* he thought.

Hud and Tuesday had one other child, a seventeen-year-old boy named Gatling, a real retro hipster with a slick pompadour, cuffed jeans, and dice tattooed on his bicep. Or at least, that was how he looked when last they saw him. Since he'd vanished on the first hot day in May, they'd received only postcards; he was touring with a band called the Daughters of God, playing guitar and singing backup at revivals and fairs.

Gatling was the reason Hud and Tuesday had married so young, and he'd been a handful for years. Once last winter, practicing some new brand of discipline she had learned about at a seminar, Tuesday had locked Gatling out of the house for a few days for giving Nina a drink of his Windsor Canadian. "I knew she wouldn't like it," he'd said, and though it was only a tiny sip that had dribbled mostly down Nina's chin, it had been the last bit of badness Tuesday would allow. And that was when he had started spending so much time at the Lutheran church, hanging out with a group of Jesus freaks and driving into Omaha with them to hand out pamphlets in front of rock concerts.

Gatling had also taken to scarring and cutting himself, had even carved all nine letters of his ex-girlfriend's name across his chest in an act so romantically psychotic it had almost won him Charlotte back.

All Hud knew for sure was that so much had stopped seeming possible that afternoon in May when Gatling left.

Hud remembered driving into the driveway, only seconds after Gatling had gone off for good on his Vespa, some ice cubes in the grass not yet melted despite the day's uncommon heat.

After dropping off the last of his costumed passengers, Hud went home to sit alone and compose some lyrics. Robbie Schrock's life seemed perfectly lived for a country song. Country songs, to Hud, were chronicles of destitution, haunted by beaten-dead wives and abandoned children. The key to an authentic country song, he thought, was to tell the story of a life lived stupidly and give it pretty strains of remorse.

Hud wrote: "He had the cheap kind of heart that broke when you wound it too tight." Then he wrote: "He got all turned around on what was supposed to be wrong and what was supposed to be right." Hud had spent many of the summer's days, the days following the finalization of his divorce, at his kitchen table writing songs and drinking Mogen David red like it was soda pop.

Hud climbed out through his window and up to his roof. The town square was usually quiet at night, but people continued to celebrate the execution of Robbie Schrock. The costumed children strung toilet paper in the trees on the courthouse lawn and knocked on doors for handfuls of candy. There were costumed adults on their way to parties: a man in a cape and top hat and white gloves alongside a woman wearing only a long red magician's box, her head and arms and feet sticking out, a saw stuck through the middle. A woman dressed as a nurse in blue jacket and white stockings pushed a pram jingling with bottles of liquor.

Hud, not amused, began to sing one of his more mournful songs, about a girl stung to death by wasps. He strummed a purple guitar. People passed in the street, but no one stopped to listen. No one wept for the man in the song sad about the death of his girl. No one even offered a knowing, sympathetic nod.

My neighbors hate me, Hud thought. They all knew and loved his wife. Tuesday taught art at the grade school, taught the town's children how to make tongue-depressor marionettes and abstract paintings using slices of old potato. *And they hate me now,* Hud thought, *only because I'm without her.*

2 .

AFTER his rooftop performance, Hud suddenly remembered he was supposed to help Tuesday's dad at the drive-in; they were showing a movie with bloodsuckers and prom queens to further celebrate this mock Halloween, and they expected a late-night crowd. The Rivoli Sky-Vue was one of only a handful of drive-ins in the state, and one of only a few in the nation that still showed classic drive-in movie fare. All the spaghetti Westerns and the dirty wet-bikini flicks and the souped-up back-road racing movies were part of a private collection owned by Hud's ex-father-in-law. He even had a few out-and-out pornos that they showed from time to time after midnight. The Rivoli made little money, but it was the town's only tourist attraction and had been featured in *People* magazine and *Film Comment.*

Though the movie had started, Hud stood at the front gate taking admission for Tuesday's dad, who they all called Red though his head of thick curls had turned gray years before.

Red had a longtime girlfriend, the Widow Bosanko, the town's librarian. Hud remembered, from when he had checked out Zane Grey Westerns as a kid, how she always wore a bracelet of wooden cherries that knocked together with a pleasant click.

Alone in the drive-in's entryway, Hud collected a few of the summer's last fireflies, trapping them in an olive jar to bring to Nina, who enjoyed bugs. He was interrupted when Junior, a boy Gatling's age, drove up. You wouldn't know from Junior's piercings up and down both ears and his black-eye that he was the zealot responsible for Gatling's religious conversion. Now that Gatling was off touring with the Daughters of God, Junior dated Charlotte, Gatling's pensive ex-girlfriend.

Hud had always had a harmless crush on Charlotte that had been helped along a few nights before when he had seen her selecting songs at the jukebox at the Steak and Black Coffee, an all-night diner on the highway, her tongue at her lips in concentration. She wore a tight t-shirt pulled over the top of a sundress. After selecting a few dollars' worth of old country ballads like "Crazy" and "Cold, Cold Heart," she sat down with Junior, who bowed his head in prayer over his New York strip and hash browns. But Charlotte didn't pray along, involved as she was in the music, her coffee cup held still just beneath her lips as Hank Williams sang about the robin's lost will to live.

"Looking awfully lonely there tonight," Hud said. He peered inside the car to where Junior sat alone.

"Well, I tell ya, old man," Junior said, handing Hud $5 and shrugging, winking, "I think I scare all the pretty little girls away."

Hud leaned in more, looking beneath the steering wheel. He reached in to push the button to pop the trunk. "Ah, come on, man . . ." Junior protested. "You can't . . ."

Hud walked to the back to open the trunk lid, where he found Charlotte curled up. "Some date," he told her, taking her hand to help her step out. She wore a slick red robe patterned with bluebirds sitting on the branches of spindly trees. Her fine hair was knotted up atop her head and stuck through with black lacquered chopsticks.

"We're broke," she said, leaning back against the car, fanning herself with a fragile paper fan that featured faceless geishas fanning themselves.

"I would've let you in anyway," Hud said. He tapped a knuckle against her cheek. "I still like you some." Hud just barely kept himself from giving Charlotte a short kiss, just on the cheek or the forehead, just something friendly and fatherly. "Here," he said, handing Charlotte a pair of pink plastic fangs he'd been giving out to the children.

"If you were smart you'd get back with Tuesday," Charlotte said, moving the fangs between her fingers, pretending they were doing the talking.

"I happen to know that," Hud said. Just last Fourth of July, Hud and Tuesday had had a momentary truce, a few nights of reunion that involved popping off fireworks in the front yard. When night fell, Hud lit the expensive ones, the ones with all the color and noise, but he didn't watch the sky; he couldn't take his eyes off Tuesday, who sat with Nina on her lap, holding a parasol above their heads to protect them from the burnt shrapnel that fell from the sky. The summer had been dangerously dry, and they all looked a little nervously to the leaves of the trees, which rattled as the hot pieces of the spent fireworks rained through the branches.

Junior called out, "Lottie," a name Hud thought only he and his son called Charlotte, and Charlotte slipped away. As Hud walked to the side of the car, he saw Charlotte taking a drag off Junior's cigarette, the pink teeth loose in her mouth.

Hud became desperate to see his daughter, as he thought ahead, of her growing up only to become confused and lost and learning too much too fast. He hoped to God Nina never crawled into the trunk of a car at the request of a cheap boy.

Hud wanted to wake Nina up and pull her out of bed and rock her back to sleep. He wanted to count all her fingers and toes, and all the hairs on her head. He'd sneak in through the window, and he'd tell Nina, "Nobody else is worried about you. Just me. Everyone else sleeps through the night."

Hud drove quickly to the house and let himself in to find Tuesday sleeping on the sofa, the still hot coal of her cigarette burning a hole in the velveteen of the cushion. Hud sat on the coffee table and took the cigarette from her fingers. He leaned back, took a drag, examined Tuesday's costume—she wore a 1970s-style shirtdress, her hair swept up in a fresh beehive slightly crushed by the sofa pillow, a false eyelash dangling from one eyelid. A fake yellow bird with synthetic feathers sat perched in a small birdcage at the foot of the sofa. Hud couldn't figure out who she was supposed to be.

Tuesday had always slept the deadest sleep he'd ever witnessed—her body didn't move at all, not even with her breath. She usually stayed up late painting desert scenes on the skulls of cows and horses, then fell into her bed. Hud could too easily imagine all sorts of things happening in the night of Tuesday's deep sleep—a terrible storm, or a kidnapping, or a fire engulfing the entire house long before she choked awake on a single breath of smoke. *That's the only reason I drink,* he thought, crossing his legs, crossing his arms, blowing cigarette smoke toward Tuesday's face to test her as she slept. She didn't flinch. *I drink because I worry myself sick about my girls,* he thought.

He started to snuff the cigarette out in a glass ashtray, then recognized it as a souvenir from a family trip of years before. He picked it up and spat in it, then rubbed his thumb at the black. After rubbing some of the ash away, he could see the bare feet of Fred and Wilma Flintstone. Hud and Tuesday had taken the kids, with Nina practically just born, up to South Dakota one summer, where they had walked through Flintstone Village, taken a tour of a cave, and eaten in a cafeteria with a view of Mount Rushmore. Hud had bought Tuesday a locket of Black Hills gold that she had promptly lost when they went swimming in a naturally warm pool in Hot Springs. Tuesday had cried about it at the motel that night, upsetting Gatling a little, but Hud had loved it. He'd loved holding her and telling her they'd go back to the pool to search, or that he'd buy her another, cooing at her like she was a kid. He'd been glad she'd wanted the necklace so much because even back then, especially back then, they'd had many fights and troubles.

Hud got up and stuck the dirty ashtray in the saggy back pocket of his jeans as he walked through the kitchen, flicking the cigarette into the sink. A nightlight near Nina's bed lit the room enough for Hud to see Nina sleeping, still in a cowgirl costume, still even in boots and prairie skirt and Western shirt printed with yellow roses. A straw hat hung on the bedpost. Hud tugged on Nina's skirt, and she woke peacefully, too peacefully, Hud thought. "You shouldn't be sleeping next to an open window," he whispered, and Nina sat up in bed and puckered her lips for a kiss. Hud kissed her, then said, "Any creep could come along. Aren't you afraid of creeps?"

"Oh, sure," she said, shrugging her shoulders.

"Let's go for a drive someplace," Hud said. He opened the window and lifted the torn flap of the screen.

"OK," Nina said, standing up in the bed, "but first, don't you like my costume? We went to a party."

"It's nice," he said.

"I'm Opal Lowe," she said, and Hud was touched that she had dressed up like Opal Lowe, his favorite country singer. He'd taken Nina to a county fair a few weeks before to see Opal singing in the open-air auditorium. They'd had to sit far in the back on a bale of hay, had to strain to hear above the bleats and clucking of the animals judged in nearby pens, but Nina had loved it and had hummed along as Opal Lowe sang about her man's habits, how he liquored her up on Wild Turkey, lit her Old Golds, made her need him like water.

Nina said, "Can I bring my purse?" and she picked up a clear plastic purse from the end of the bed. Inside was a tube of lipstick, a little box, a comb, and a plastic baby doll's head with wild yellow hair.

"Sure, bring your purse," Hud said. He jotted a note in crayon: "I'll be back with her before sunlight, before you even read this," and left it atop the rumpled covers of the bed. Nina crawled onto his back, and they slipped through the torn window screen. He imagined never returning with her, imagined his picture next to hers on fliers sent through the mail.

"We'll go anywhere you want to go," Hud said, helping her into the car. "Should we go to some ocean far away? Go smoke a friendly cigarette with the fishies?" Nina laughed, and Hud said, "Go to Mexico for some cow-tongue soup?"

"No," Nina said. "Disgusting."

"We could go to Disneyland and ride a roller coaster," Hud said. "Just be careful not to spill your beer," and Nina laughed at the idea of having beer to spill.

Hud drove off toward the highway. "We could run away together for good," he said.

"I live with my mom, and you have to drive the school bus," Nina said, almost scolding.

"We'd write songs for a living," he said. "Our first song could be called 'Two Fugitives.' It'll go . . . um . . . 'We're fugitives from a bad life. Breaking free from . . .' From what . . . 'From the chains and shackles of separation and loss.'"

Nina sighed with disapproval. She'd become an expert fan of country music ever since Hud had taken her to see Opal Lowe. She turned on the radio now, as they drove to the edge of town, listening, hoping for an Opal Lowe. But instead they heard Chief Kentucky Straight, a man one-sixteenth Ogalalla

Sioux who sang of the pain of life on the reservation. They heard a choir of hard-living rednecks called the Widowmakers. Then there was Rose-Sharon and her Lilies of the Valley. Rose-Sharon was a woman with cancer who sang gospel. Nina sang along to her song called "I'm So Full of Jesus."

"What was your mom dressed up as?" Hud asked.

"A mermaid," Nina said.

"No," Hud said, but he thought a second, thinking of the bird, remembering Catherine Deneuve's canary in a cage at the beginning of *Mississippi Mermaid,* one of Tuesday's favorite movies they'd watched many times together. Deneuve hadn't had a beehive in that movie, he was almost certain, but rather a tall straw hat. He wondered if Tuesday had missed having him at her side at the party, someone who would truly appreciate the charm of her costume. He could have gone as her Jean-Paul Belmondo, but he would've preferred to be Belmondo in *Breathless* in fedora and sharp suit, puffing on a French cigarette.

It was Tuesday who had first called him Hud; when they were dating in high school, they stayed up late to watch the movie, just long enough for them both to be impressed by Newman's cantankerousness. "You've got his snarl and skinny legs," she said, then they nodded off to sleep long before Newman raped Patricia Neal.

Hud asked Nina, "Do you know why you even wore that costume today?"

"Well, you see," Nina said, "you see . . . there was this guy . . . and he was somebody's dad . . . and there were these boys . . . and the dad hurt the boys so bad that they were killed. And everybody dressed up because . . . um . . . there's going to be a funeral soon."

"Jesus," Hud said, sighing and shaking his head with frustration, "nobody even told you much about it, did they? They just let you get dressed up for their own perverted god-damn reasons."

Nina said, "I do so know everything about it." She looked out the car window. "And I hate it when you swear." She normally enjoyed when he let some swearing slip in front of her.

Hud took off down the unlit gravel roads, squinting into the dark, looking for the sign to tiny Rhyme, Nebraska. Behind a grocery store there lay an old Happy Chef, the thirty-foot-tall fiberglass statue that had once towered in front of a highway café. The store's owner had bought the statue long before, and it now rested flat on its back in the tall grass. Hud had brought Nina there last summer, and she had liked sitting in the Happy Chef's spoon.

Nina, not speaking to Hud, combed her long, white-blond hair. A strand flew in Hud's face, and he plucked it away and let it fly out the open window. They drove past a mailbox and a spooky crooked iron weather vane. Hud imagined Nina's strand of hair finding its way into an old house where a man lived alone, a man who had maybe killed his wife in silence and buried her in a small patch of his miles of untrespassed-upon land. Hud imagined the old man waking with the long hair on his pillow or finding it in his soup and from then on living in terror of what he'd done.

"What's the name of your doll there in your purse?" Hud asked, to get Nina talking again.

Nina looked down at her clear plastic purse and tapped her finger at the doll head inside. "It's not a doll," Nina said. "It's just a head. Heads don't have names," and she returned her stare back out the window.

Hud now felt entirely sober, and very tired. He wished he had just peeked in on Nina, had just watched her sleep undisturbed. *A good father,* Hud thought, *lets his children sleep through the night.* This was what Hud didn't like about being sober. He didn't like coming to his senses. Good sense can prevent a man from taking what he should have.

When Hud's car began to sputter, he stomped on the gas pedal, and the car went a little farther before sputtering again, then stopping. It wouldn't start back up. The needle of the gas gauge had been stuck on empty for years, and the odometer had read 138,323 for several hundred miles, but the old Pontiac and its habits had become so familiar to Hud over time that he'd thought he knew well how far he'd get on a full tank.

Before turning off onto the country roads, Hud had taken a deserted back highway, with no traffic across its broken pavement. They wouldn't make it back tonight on foot even if he could find the way. He tried to think of what else might be wrong with the car, something he could easily fix. He turned the key again and listened closely to the engine as it still refused to turn over. He became frightened, and he worried over all the destruction that was about to befall him. By not returning his daughter to that bed next to that wide-open window, in that house with the weak locks, where his wife slept through everything, everything for him could change.

He might be arrested. He might not be allowed to take Nina out again. He might lose his job.

"Goddamnit!" he practically screamed. "That bitch!" He pounded his fists against the steering wheel. He punched the horn at the center of the steering wheel, then drove his fists into it, holding the horn down to blare. The muscles in his arms were tight, and he thought if he pushed harder, he'd make the noise louder, deafening.

When he let up on the horn, the hollow silence of the night fell again, and he could hear Nina sobbing. Her face was turned away from him, and she held both her hands tight at her mouth, like she was trying to keep herself quiet. Hud gently pushed the hair from Nina's face and behind her ears. "Nina," he said, "I'm sorry. I should have just let you sleep." He should have just taken her out trick-or-treating, to collect some sweets and heave some bad eggs, like everybody else was doing.

"It's all right," Nina said, still crying.

Hud wiped her tears with his thumb. She swallowed hard, then wiped her face with her sleeve. She took from her purse a little hinged box and opened it. "I haven't shown you this," she said, her voice still all chokey. She displayed her collection of dead desert bugs, identifying each one—the brown recluse, the palo verde beetle, the tarantula hawk. When she touched her finger to a brittle scorpion's back, its hooked stinger broke off. When Tuesday and Hud first tried a trial separation almost a year ago, the fall before Gatling left, Tuesday had taken Nina with her to Arizona, where her mother lived in a cool, square cottage painted blue. Tuesday had even talked about moving there but had been concerned about the bugs in the house. She wanted to know which ones to fear, to learn about poisons and toxins and antidotes. She'd heard that scorpions climbed up walls and flung themselves into children's beds, that wasps caught in sheets on the laundry line and stung in the night. "I need to know what to be scared of," she'd told him on the phone. She'd used a playing card to knock a black widow into a Dixie cup. She'd freeze the bugs, then take them in a little tin that used to be a sewing kit to Poison Control, where she'd have them identified.

"I caught some fireflies for you tonight, but I guess I forgot them at the drive-in," Hud said. He thought of them dying, slowly losing their flicker in the olive jar. "Nina . . . we're out of gas, I guess. And I'm not real sure where we are. But see that dot of light over there?" He pointed to someplace far up the road. "I think we can walk over there, and maybe there'll be a phone."

Nina shrugged, and said nonchalantly, "Mom won't be mad. It could happen to anybody."

Hud took a flashlight from the glove compartment. Outside the car, he squatted so that Nina could crawl onto his back. She wrapped her legs around his waist, clasped her hands at his chest. With her warm breath on his neck, he thought he could walk for hours and hours. And he thought he might have to—the small dot of light was not growing. When Hud nearly tripped on some barbed wire at the edge of a cornfield, it was as if he could feel the danger in his ankles then, a tenseness, and he kept the beam of the flashlight low to the ground. After a while, Nina's grip loosened, and she was slipping, and he asked if she'd like him to carry her in his arms so she could sleep. He felt her nod her head against his.

In his arms, she was much heavier, and he tired quickly. He sat down to rest on the edge of a ditch. When he looked up for the light, it was gone; the family in the house had simply turned out their lights and gone to bed.

Let it happen, he thought. *Let's stay lost.* The summer sun could wear their skin away and bleach their bones. Experts would have to unlock their rib cages and untangle their skeletons. Then, in memory and punishment, the town could celebrate Halloween again, no matter what season of the year, dressing up in skull masks and glow-in-the-dark bone suits.

Nina scratched her ear in her sleep. As Hud ran his finger along her cheek, the bridge of her nose, her lips, he welcomed all the misery that would come in the morning for having kept her in his arms in the middle of nowhere. He felt brave only because Nina felt safe and protected enough to rest.

3 .

iiiiiiiiiii

TUESDAY woke on the sofa,, blinking at the morning light, her shirtdress drenched in sweat. Scratching her head, which itched from the thick Aqua Net in her unraveling beehive, she stood and put her bare foot over the floor vent. She felt only a gust of tepid air. Twice in five days the air conditioner repairman had claimed to have fixed a Freon leak. She got a stomachache thinking of the expense of replacing the unit, and she began to list in her mind all the other fallibilities of her house. The unkempt branches of a tree would soon enough be scratching threateningly against the windows with any gust of winter wind. And the faulty wiring kept the house only halfway electrical.

This was something Tuesday did—she would stop a minute to concentrate on the most decrepit circumstances of her life. She'd close her eyes and immerse herself in the misery until she was druggy with unhappiness, until every obstacle seemed hazy with the impossibility of solution, and she'd drop, tired, into her sofa cushions. If it was just her, Tuesday wouldn't care about a house hot like an oven. If she was all alone, all she'd need was a tiny corner of a cold-water flat.

When she opened the window to glance outside at the air conditioner, she saw a girl's legs poking out from the thicket of mums planted alongside the house. Though the legs were long and thin, entirely un-Nina-like, Tuesday felt certain for a second that she'd just happened upon her daughter dead in the grass. Part of her had always been prepared for Nina to go suddenly and absolutely from her life. Some nights she'd be startled awake by the complete silence of the house, and she'd have to wake Nina with a soft shake and crawl into bed with her. Nina would stroke Tuesday's hair and whisper-sing a new song she'd memorized.

A butterfly landed on the leg blotchy with sunburn, and the girl, not dead after all, slapped at the startlingly sea-blue bug as if it was as useless as a mosquito. Tuesday stepped out-side. "Millie," she said, seeing that the legs belonged to the girl who lived in the country but was always tumbling around town, the twelve-year-old with perpetually dirty knees who would sometimes sneak into the backyard to play with Nina and strip her Barbies naked. Millie wore a yellow tutu and ballerina slippers, and she lay next to candy spilled from a plastic, pumpkin-shaped bucket.

"Did you take Nina's candy?" Tuesday said. She noticed Nina's open window and recognized the bucket and its con-tents from when Tuesday took her trick-or-treating around the block before the costume party. Millie sat up then, her eyes heavy-lidded, her head bobbing on her neck. She seemed startled out of some stupor, looking all caught-in-the-act.

"Nina's not in her room," Millie said. Her skin was the white-blue of skim milk, her breath smelling slightly of chemicals. "This was on her bed." She handed Tuesday a crumpled piece of paper, then stood, her tutu droopy, and stumbled away, nearly tripping over the loose laces of her slippers.

Before Tuesday even read the note, she knew it was from Hud, recognized the skinny, spiky letters of his serial-killer scrawl. Tuesday rushed to the open window, anxious to touch Nina, to feel Nina's back minutely rise and fall with her slow breath as she slept so late. She reached into the window and, pushing at the empty puff of the goose-down duvet on the bed, she realized how easily any passing stranger could grab Nina by the hair and whisk her away with nothing much more than a flick of the wrist.

Deep in her heart, she knew Hud would never vanish with their daughter, though he wouldn't be throwing away much of a life, as she saw it. All he loved about the town was the flea market on the courthouse lawn on Saturdays. Trashy teen-aged girls gathered in the grass at the steps of the bandstand where he sat to play his guitar and sing the songs he'd originally written for Tuesday. Tuesday sometimes worked a face-painting table at the flea market, painting unicorns and daisies on the cheeks of the children, and these girls, their dirty hair stinking with smoke, would walk up in their ratty tube tops and request that Tuesday paint little hearts and daggers, or their boyfriends' names in gothic letters, on their chests and skinny upper arms. They'd sit giggling as Tuesday worked her brush begrudgingly across their baby-pink skin, the girls tipsy off whatever soft booze—the melon liqueur or wine cooler—they drank from a lunch-box thermos, using a Twizzler for a straw.

When I get Nina back, Tuesday thought, picking up a Tootsie Pop from the ground, unwrapping it, and tapping it against her teeth, *I'll let her have the run of the place.* She would let Nina drink Pepsi for breakfast, let her sleep naked in the sandbox. "Why would I go anywhere with you?" Nina would tell Hud as she painted her toenails any color, even a garish hooker-red.

I hate him, she thought. Walking quickly toward the town square, where the flea market would already be under way, she ducked the toilet paper hanging from some of the trees and twisting in the hot breeze like streamers. Even when she loved Hud madly, she would fantasize about his death. Maybe not fantasize, but she would imagine what it would be like. *He put her through a lot,* people would say, marveling at her stoicism, *but she was so devoted.* They'd all call her the Young Widow Smith and would feel a thump of sympathy when they'd catch sight of her in the months after, wearing sunglasses in the winter and polyester scarves over her hair, resembling Barbara Stanwyck on her way to an illicit encounter.

As Tuesday approached the courthouse lawn, chewing on the hard candy of the Tootsie pop, she saw that Hud's small but regular audience had already gathered at the bandstand steps. One of the girls wore curlers and distractedly pulled at a piece of frayed thread at the edge of the American flag draped across a rail of the gazebo. "Where is he?" Tuesday asked, and the girl shrugged. This was the one who loved Hud the most—Tuesday had watched her once. She had rested her head on another girl's shoulder as she listened to Hud sing. Later, she had come to Tuesday's table and asked her to paint on her throat as many words as she could fit from the lyric, "I taste the tart wild plum on your lips," which Tuesday knew from a song Hud had written about a summer afternoon they'd spent at a lake years before, back when they were a couple of love-struck babies.

"When he sings," the girl had said as Tuesday painted, the stretched skin of her neck twitching as she spoke, causing the blue letters to smear, "his voice is so strong, I can feel it shiver my chest." But that wasn't enough for the girl. Tuesday could tell she was thinking deep by the way her tongue clicked a little, her whistle wet with more to say. "It's so strong in my chest, he can change the beat in my heart, make it beat to the beat of the song." *Ridiculous,* Tuesday thought. Hud's singing voice was weak and full of cracks. It would break at a song's most emotional moment, obscuring key words, sometimes obliterating all meaning.

"Have you seen Hud? Or Nina?" Tuesday asked Ozzie Yates, who sold peaches from the back of the pickup he backed up to the edge of the lawn. Tuesday and Ozzie were old friends, and Tuesday's son, Gatling, had loved Ozzie's daughter, Charlotte.

"No," Ozzie said, winking, "I've not seen Hud. And I'm damn near close to tears about it." Ozzie and Hud shared a notorious animosity for each other, a friendly hatred that bordered on the sexy. Ozzie, in his dirty, loose-fit Levis and Western shirt all unsnapped down the front of his hairy chest, had been the one she had imagined being alone with when she was still lying next to Hud every night, scheming ways to ruin everything.

Ozzie took a pale yellow, nearly white peach from a basket and held it to Tuesday's cheek, touching the gentle fuzz to her skin. "How much for it?" she said. She took the fruit, running her thumb across its light bruises and its few patches of orange freckles.

"It's on the house," he said, and Tuesday smiled and walked away. Ozzie depressed her terribly sometimes, even when they just stood there negotiating the price of peaches. He'd once had a pretty wife who died of a swift illness, leaving him to raise Charlotte alone. Though Ozzie was not at all judgmental, she sensed something pleading in his wet eyes, like he wanted to scold her for so blindly letting her family fall apart.

Tuesday walked on down the rows of tables of castoff notions and novelties, still asking about Hud and Nina. She stopped at Lily Rollow's table and dipped her fingers into the teacups full of jewelry. Lily and her sister ran an antique shop in the country; the sister, Mabel, gave better bargains. Lily was cranky—she was pregnant and freshly divorced and only twenty years old. She sat in a fragile-looking lawn chair with a broken weave, a handheld battery-operated fan blowing her bangs up. "Who are you supposed to be?" Lily asked.

Tuesday touched at her hair, remembering she was still in last night's costume. "Catherine Deneuve in *Mississippi Mermaid*," she said.

"You're so funny," Lily said with a chuckle.

People often said that to Tuesday. But Tuesday didn't think of herself as funny at all, hadn't told so much as a tired joke in years. "Yeah," she told Lily. "I'm a regular Henny Youngman."

If anything, she was completely unfunny. She used to be funny, but she hadn't liked it. A woman wants to be thought mysterious and tragic. *I cry my eyes out most nights,* she wanted to object. *I listen to Roberta Flack and get sauced on hard cider and conk out, useless, around midnight.*

"It's adjustable," Lily pointed out as Tuesday watched the glass of a mood ring on her pinky cloud over from a peacock-feather blue. "Fifty cents."

Tuesday wanted to buy the ring for Nina, but she only had a quarter in the pocket of her dress. As she dug for more change, her fingers ran across a few hexagonal happy pills the Widow Bosanko had pressed into the palm of her hand the other afternoon during Nina's birthday party. She'd been carrying them around ever since. While a group of neighborhood brats had batted at a Raggedy Ann piñata, Hud had sauntered in holding a beer bottle at his side, with a girl's rabbit-fur coat he'd ordered from a catalog. Nina had worn the coat outside all day, stumbling, nearly fainting from the heat, her fair hair dark with sweat. "Mother's little helper," the Widow had whispered, administering the pills to Tuesday in a handshake, the wooden cherries of her bracelet rattling.

Tuesday wanted to swallow the pills now, but she remembered how a psychiatrist had put Gatling on prescriptions once, mood drugs that made him dopey and sluggish and trembled his hands. But for a while it had been a relief having Gatling so docile and curled up on her sofa watching afternoon reruns of *The Rockford Files* and *McMillan and Wife*.

Lily accepted the quarter as payment for the ring, and Tuesday walked on to Hud's building. The buzzer, she knew, didn't buzz, so she picked up some crumbled pieces of brick on the sidewalk and tossed them up to tap against the upstairs windows. *Where is my family?* she thought, noticing her reflection in the window of the defunct shoe repair shop. She pulled the one remaining false eyelash from her lid, then ran her long press-on nails through her hair, combing out her beehive. *When you're all alone in the world, you only have yourself to worry about,* she thought. *But when you have people, their tragedies are your tragedies. Your potential for misery is doubled, tripled, quadrupled.*

Then she looked past her reflection to the shoes that remained on a shelf. The shop owners had just up and closed one day, after committing their thirty-year-old autistic son to an institution. They retired to Oregon, leaving behind some repaired shoes still uncollected, others still unrepaired. Tuesday saw one of her own strappy sandals that she'd forgotten she owned. The thin black ankle strap that had broken loose was now perfectly reattached, and the shoe sat waiting to step off into an elegant evening, high-heeled and pristine, its toe scuffs polished away. It wasn't the type of shoe she'd wear, so she hadn't even missed it, didn't even know where its match was. She'd bought the shoes a few years before, when she and Hud were trying to save their marriage. Every other weekend or so, they would dress up and drive to the casinos across the river from Omaha. While Hud played blackjack after dinner with loosened necktie, Tuesday, in her black cocktail dress, would sit alone at a table in the lounge sipping chocolate martinis and listening to a woman who impersonated Barbara Streisand, Tina Turner, and Karen Carpenter. Those evenings, Tuesday thought, weren't as bad as they sounded. They were nice, actually.

Tuesday rubbed at the glass of her mood ring as she headed back home, hoping to work its mud-colored froth into a shade of pink. As she turned the corner onto her street, she slowed her steps, giving Hud a better chance to sneak Nina back into her bed. Ghosts knotted together from pillow cases hung from porch eaves. A scarecrow, its stuffing beaten out of it, lay in a heap in the middle of the street.

In her driveway now were her father's Caddy and her sister's VW bug. When she saw Mrs. Katt, the neighbor, walk up to the porch, she began to panic. Mrs. Katt would show up at any moment of despair with a can of Folgers, and she'd scrub your kitchen while you convalesced with your family in another room. You'd sit in your pajamas, you'd play rummy, waiting for some news or some fever to break, and become somewhat eased by the heavy scent of cinnamon as Mrs. Katt heated an offering in the stove. Tuesday had a cupboard full of Mrs. Katt's plates and tureens she needed to return, all with the woman's name on a piece of masking tape on the bottom.

Tuesday quit worrying when she heard the loud discord of the out-of-tune piano as somebody tumbled their fingers across the keys. Hud was the only one who ever played the piano, which had been shoved onto the screened-in back porch, and she began to hear his voice rising above the whir of the broken air conditioner. She didn't want to be, but she was glad to hear him singing in her house. She thought of one beautiful song Hud had played for her on the piano on a wet October night. As the rain *tip-tipped* against the screens, she rocked a sleeping Nina in the old chair they'd had since their first apartment. The joints of the rocking chair squeaked and quivered, and Hud sang softly a song he made up on the spot, about what it felt like to dream at night about a girl like Tuesday.

Pressing her forehead against the screen of the porch door, Tuesday watched Hud entertain her father and the Widow and her older sister, Rose, named for the shock of her father's red hair she'd been born with, and Mrs. Katt. They all stood or sat sipping coffee from Tuesday's best cups, swaying to Hud's song, which seemed to be about a brokenhearted father putting his children to bed. Rose and Red sat in the nearly wrecked wicker chairs, small plates of Mrs. Katt's crumb cake balanced on their knees. Everyone's eyes were on Nina, who did an interpretive dance in the middle of the small room, just behind the piano bench. Nina linked her fingers above her head, closed her eyes, and turned on the ball of one foot in an approximation of a pirouette. She then quickly and awkwardly moved into a jazz singer's slo-mo hip shimmy and snaked her arms around in front of herself. Nina's dancing was silly and pretty all at once, and Tuesday closed her eyes, mesmerized by her daughter.

Then Nina screamed, startled out of her hypnotic dance by the sight of Tuesday's dark shadow at the screen. Nina stood there, both hands tight at her mouth. Hud stopped playing, and everyone looked, alarmed, toward the door.

"Mommy!" Nina said when she realized it was only Tuesday. She ran to the screen and opened it, then hugged Tuesday's legs. "Oh, you won't believe what happened," Nina said, speaking in a rush. "It's not Daddy's fault, really it's not," she said. "Really it's not. The car. It's the car's fault. The car just up and took a shit on him."

Tuesday finger-thumped the top of Nina's head. "You know I don't want you talking like that," she said. She looked around the room as everyone avoided her eyes. They looked into their coffee cups, or out the windows of the porch, suddenly embarrassed for having enjoyed Hud's company. Hud just sat hunched at the piano, pushing down slowly on this key, then that, making no music. Rose pinched at a run in the ankle of her stocking. *Stockings,* thought Tuesday. *Now, how about that. Practically crack-of-dawn Saturday morning and there she sits in pricey shoes and her best light-yellow summer dress.* Rose always did have a thing for Hud. Tuesday could smell the stench of Rose's perfume, some designer knockoff she ordered by the vat on the Internet.

"Honeycomb," Tuesday said to Nina, bending over to kiss the top of her head, "would you go to your room and wait for Mommy? I'll be in in a minute to tell you how much you worried me."

"OK," Nina said, walking away with her head lowered.

"So how'd everyone hear about Hud's little party this morning?" Tuesday said. "His little party here in my house?"

"We were up at the flea market," the Widow said. "People said your hair was a mess and you were looking for Nina."

"Don't make a federal case, Day," Rose said, sharing a smirk with Hud and crossing her legs. "Everything's fine."

"You stink," Tuesday said, feeling mean toward everyone there. "Where the hell did you get that cologne? Truck stop?"

"Oh, girls," Red said. "Let's be sweet."

Rose laughed through her nose, rolled her eyes. "Shows you how much you know," she said. "It's Shoot the Moon you're smelling."

"Oh, is that what that is?" the Widow said, clearly impressed. "I thought maybe that's what."

"Got it at Marshall Field's that last time in Chicago," Rose told the Widow, uncrossing her legs, then recrossing them. "I'll get you some the next time I go back."

"Oh, honey, I'd kiss you all over," the Widow said.

Rose would never have paid the $100 a bottle for Shoot the Moon, Tuesday knew. She probably just tore an ad from a fashion magazine and rubbed the scented page against her throat in the car on the way over.

When Hud began tapping out "Chopsticks" on the piano, Tuesday reached over to slam down the lid over the keys. Hud snapped his hands back just in time and jumped at the loud noise of the fallen lid. "Damn, Day," he said, looking up at her with that baffled, what-the-hell-did-I-ever-do-to-you? look he'd mastered years before. With that look, so carefully maneuvered he must have practiced in a mirror, he always effectively made Tuesday feel like the biggest bitch that'd ever walked upright. In his lovely blue eyes, with that look, were kindness and a boy's gentle confusion. Gatling had in-herited Hud's counterfeit innocence, had started working that same look way too young.

"One of these days I'll run away with her myself," Tuesday said, remembering the peach in her pocket. She pulled it out and pressed at a soft part of the fruit, trying to keep from cry-ing again. "I'll drop a match on this whole house of sticks as I leave. You'll lose everything. The piano, your songbooks, all the crap you left behind. And we'll be nowhere to be found."

"You were just inches from setting the place on fire last night," Hud said, whispering just loudly enough for every-one in the room to hear. "You had fallen asleep with a cigarette still smoking, burning a hole in the sofa. Who knows how big a fire you would've made if I hadn't shown up? I, for one, don't particularly want a little burn victim for a little girl."

"Cigarettes," the Widow Bosanko said, sighing, shaking her head. Mr. Bosanko had died of lung cancer.

Tuesday put the peach back in her pocket and left the room. She didn't feel on the verge of tears anymore. Hud al-ways took an argument just one step too far. He could so eas-ily have her in the palm of his hand, right there along with Rose and the Widow, but then he'd say something too god-awful. If he'd just left it at "Who knows how big a fire . . ." But then he had to turn Nina into a burn victim, erasing away all her darling features, her tiny, perfect nose and soft lashes and those lips of pale, pale pink.

In the bathroom she took off her dress and leaned her head over the side of the tub to rinse out her stiff hair. When she turned the water off, she heard that Hud had gone back to performing the rest of his song. Tuesday wrapped her wet head in a towel, stepping into the hallway wearing only the matching silk bra and underwear patterned with blue bunnies that Rose had given her last Christmas.

After pulling on a short tartan skirt and a t-shirt and grabbing her face-painting kit, Tuesday went to Nina's room. Nina sat on the bed dressing her paper doll in a paper ball gown, and Tuesday sat beside her. She touched the fringe of Nina's faux-leather vest. "You can wear this today too if you want," Tuesday said.

"Good," Nina said.

"Don't ever leave me in the middle of the night, please," Tuesday said. "Not even with your father. He's full of evil schemes. I hate him."

"No, you don't," Nina said, taking the tiny comb from her plastic purse, then running it through Tuesday's hair.

"Yes, I do. Ouch. My hair's all snaggy." She took the comb from Nina and did it herself. "I hate him, and so will you someday. And you'll hate me too, someday, I suppose."

"No, I won't," Nina whined, scrunching up her nose and chin with offense. "You don't know."

Tuesday lifted the torn screen of the window. "Let's go," she whispered, and together they crept out onto the lawn as Hud got to an emotional part of the song that involved a kind of pained bellowing. Tuesday lifted Nina into the handlebar basket of her bicycle, hooked the face-painting kit to the back, and rode away, the bike shaky on its wheels. Nina sat high in the basket in her cowgirl suit, the fresh peach cradled in the cup of her two hands.

4 .

‖‖‖‖

H I S thumb in a thimble, Ozzie sat on the open tailgate of his pickup. He sewed to distract himself these days, repairing years of tears in old trousers and shirts and moth-eaten sweaters. He had taught himself embroidery from a book, and he stitched a rose into the point of a collar of one of Charlotte's childhood blouses.

When he had left his house that morning with his few baskets of peaches collected from the tiny orchard in his backyard, Charlotte had yet to come home from the drive-in. Her staying out all night wasn't all that unusual anymore, but she claimed complete innocence, spoke of all-night prayer meetings and spiritual sweats at midnight and meditation in country ditches. "Junior's a good boy," she told him, "not like Gatling." Charlotte spent most of her late afternoons lying sullen and lanky on the living room sofa, letting Junior kneel beside her and talk in her ear. In a hard whisper, the boy seduced her easily with preaching of biblical catastrophe and plague. She was at an age to be prone to any sort of depravity, Ozzie's neighbors said. A girl Charlotte's age, they said from their front porches and window perches, a girl so long without a mother, looks for divine undoing, for the kind of violent, snaky salvation a boy like Junior promises.

Ozzie's fingers were a bit too big for the delicate embroidery, and he stopped a moment and rested his hands in his lap. Ozzie worked with stained glass, repairing church windows from county to county. His burned and scarred hands, with the grooves in the skin, were lately beginning to resemble his windows of glass shards. He used to be much more careful handling the melted lead for the soldering.

Though the death of Jenny, Charlotte's mother, three years before, was certainly one of the reasons for Charlotte's newfound religion and her skanky, psalm-reciting boyfriend, Ozzie recognized his own blame. For years he'd brought Charlotte along to the churches old and new, country and city, to remove the damaged stained-glass windows. As she waited, she stood at the pulpits and pounded her fists, faking blustery sermons, or baptized her rag dolls, dipping their yarn hair into the fonts. Then the windows, for weeks, sat in his studio as he intricately pieced back together a broken glass Jesus or nameless saint. When the sun was at the back windows, the powdery colors filled the room, touching Charlotte's cheeks and hands as she played on the floor with the cat.

"Charlotte's on the other side of the square," said a neighbor as she purchased a sackful of peaches. The neighbor had teenagers of her own and spoke with a conspiratorial hush.

Ozzie poked his needle into the cuff of his shirt and walked through the flea market, scanning the crowd. He found Charlotte, still in her geisha-girl costume and wearing what looked to be pink fangs in her open mouth, lying in the grass and sleeping with her head on Junior's chest. Junior slept as well, his hand in Charlotte's hair. Junior was certainly not unlikable. He was as handsome as a drowned-rat kind of a boy could be, with thick black hair greased back. He carried a clarinet around with him, saying that he was teaching himself complicated jazz tunes like "So What" and "Undecided." Charlotte met him when he worked as an apprentice at an ironworks. Above the garage door of the building was a plaster statue of Christ in an iron cage wrought with curlicues and spikes. Ozzie could just see Charlotte penitent in the doorway watching the boy stand among sparks and blue flame.

Charlotte and Junior slept next to a quilt—for the previous few flea markets, Charlotte had been selling off the stuff of her childhood. All the long-abandoned dolls and books of fairy tales and framed photos of childhood friends had been spread out across the quilt and marked with bottom-barrel prices, and Ozzie had been her best customer—last week he'd bought a tin bird he'd bought for her years before, and some faded candy necklaces. Now, next to the few things she had yet to sell, was a sign that said, "Take whatever you want. It's all FREE."

Ozzie recalled the words of Charlotte's high school guidance counselor, who he had visited one recent afternoon: *Don't worry much*, the woman had said, *until she starts to give her things away*. A sign of suicidal tendencies, it seemed.

Ozzie kicked gently at Charlotte's side—he could almost imagine his daughter and Junior sleepy from poison-spiked Kool-Aid.

"Daddy," Charlotte said, unalarmed, sitting up to stretch.

Ozzie grabbed the box next to the quilt and collected the few things that remained. "Pickup's parked over there," Ozzie said. "We're going home."

"I'm glad you're here, Mr. Yates," Junior said, standing and brushing the dried grass off his jeans. Ozzie saw Junior give Charlotte a wink and a nod, granting her permission to obey her father. The gesture turned Ozzie's stomach. "I'd like to discuss something with you," Junior said, his eyes on Charlotte as she walked away.

Though Junior was soft-spoken, Ozzie knew there was no refusing him. Junior had no knives, no gun, and was too slight in build to pose any physical threat. His command of the family was simply the result of Charlotte's devotion. Charlotte's fast love for him had turned her feral and easily spooked, and Ozzie was afraid if he made one wrong move, she'd dart.

"Actually, I want to talk to you too," Ozzie said before Junior spoke again. Ozzie picked up a Slinky from the box and let it coil and uncoil in his hand. "I don't want you to see my daughter so much anymore." He looked deeper into the box, his weak demand dropping off. A spark of sunlight glinted off the tip of the boy's cowboy boot.

"Oh, Mr. Yates," Junior said, smiling, shrugging. "'The glory of young men is their strength, and the honor of old men is their gray hair.'"

"I'll call the authorities," Ozzie said. He pushed back the bangs of his hair, none of it gray that he had ever noticed. "There's a thing called statutory rape, and it's very illegal."

"I don't think you will, Mr. Yates." Junior stepped in and put his hand to the back of Ozzie's head. He leaned over, whispering, "'For you bear with anyone if he enslaves you, if he devours you, if he takes advantage of you, if he exalts himself, if he hits you in the face.'" Just the sound of Junior's voice brought to Ozzie's mind scratchy black woodcut images of hordes of children, their eyes lidded with pestilence, of screaming angels with burnt wings, of buzzards and dead lions, all of which the boy had described to Charlotte as his picture of the end of the world.

Ozzie looked up again, his eyes only inches from the boy's. "Don't you have any words of your own?" he said. But he understood something about Junior. Ozzie had had his own brief bout with religion in the months after Jenny's death—he'd wanted to sink into the open arms of the church and become disoriented by the archaic recitations of proverbs and creeds. The congregation, their Bibles and hymnals held to their faces, spoke a dark language of rapture and damnation. Ozzie had wanted no ease with the world, or easeful words to speak with. He'd wanted to be ruined for life.

Junior smiled with only half his mouth, a wicked smile, you'd call it, and he snapped a flame from his open Zippo. He lit a hand-rolled cigarette and said, "We're getting married, Mr. Yates. That's what I wanted to tell you. And don't go thinking that she's too young, because she's not." He leaned in again, and Ozzie felt his hot breath on his cheek. "'Her lips drip honey,'" he said. "'Honey and milk are under her tongue.'" As he slipped a card into the chest pocket of Ozzie's shirt, Ozzie shoved Junior's shoulders. Junior stumbled backward, his arms flailing for balance, until he fell into the tall base of a memorial statue that the Chamber of Commerce had installed on the courthouse lawn in honor of soldiers who'd fought in Vietnam.

"Mr. Yates," Junior said, getting back up, a spot of blood blooming just beneath his eye from the scratch of the tip of an angel's stone wing, "we're told, 'A tranquil heart is life to the body, but passion is rottenness to the bones.'"

"Rotten bones," Ozzie mumbled. He turned and walked away with the cardboard box of Charlotte's things.

Ozzie took from his pocket what Junior had put in: a picture of Christ, a very contemporary representation of him as pretty as a blue-eyed young girl with his long hair partly braided. He was entirely nude and nailed to the cross, blood flowing along the sinewy muscle of his arms, his godly schlong mostly hidden by shadow. *His Pain, Your Gain* was written at the bottom of the card. Ozzie wondered where the boy had even come across such a picture; perhaps priests handed them out in the street to seduce young people into church.

Charlotte sat in the truck, waiting, reading a tiny green Gideon's Bible with a magnifying glass. Ozzie got in with the box, then drove away without closing the tailgate. He ignored the light thumping of the peaches as they spilled and rolled across the truck bed.

At a stop sign, he leaned toward Charlotte and smelled something sugary on her breath. Didn't they used to say that if a baby's breath smelled sweet, it portended a terrible sickness? As new parents, Ozzie and Jenny had been forewarned of all sorts of infanticides. When Charlotte was first born, Jenny banished Simp, the old tom, to the studio out back. Ozzie had never heard of a cat's attraction to a sleeping child's breath, but Jenny had been warned by all the old ladies up and down the street of the danger of such suffocation.

"Did you know," Charlotte said, barely looking up from her little green book, "that you can break a snake's back if you don't handle it correctly? And there are whole churches of people who mix themselves strychnine drinks because the Bible says, 'Drink poison and ye shall live.' They call it a salvation cocktail." Lightly, she delivered this information, this hint at how deeply a religious fervor had infected her.

"On my way back to the truck just now," Ozzie said, "I remembered that afternoon we found that bat in the house. The one we had in the attic. Remember that? Your mom made me catch it in a coffee can so we could let it out in the country. So the three of us drove a few miles down a road . . . the bat crying all the way."

Charlotte, clearly bored by the fact that he didn't make more of her mention of snake handling and poison drinking, rolled her eyes and returned to the New Testament.

Ozzie saw that Charlotte's lips and fingertips were berry-stained, skeletons of dry leaves caught in her hair. Her scent of sweetness had dissolved into the smell of smoke, but not cigarette smoke, smoke like from twigs and bark. She seemed weakened by her thinking about the night. *Keep a tranquil heart,* he wanted to warn her. *Passion is rottenness to the bones.*

On the corner of Elm and Oak sat one of the older churches in town, a squat, homely thing of gray stone, but with a few majestic windows depicting intricate biblical scenes. Ozzie had long wanted to get his hands on the glass of Grace Lutheran—the windows looked to have been shoddily repaired in the past, and poorly maintained, with some of the lighter-colored pieces—like the opalescent skirts of an angel—having grown dim with years of dust. And if he wasn't mistaken, the belly of the whale was made of what looked to be rotten ruby—a rare antique red.

Ozzie pulled around the corner and stopped the truck a fair distance from the church. He opened the truck door, then picked up a library copy of *Franny and Zooey* from the box. He dropped the book into Charlotte's lap.

"I've read this," she said, pushing the book aside.

"And you love it," he shouted, seethed, really. "Read it again." He then took from the box the paper-thin plastic Halloween mask Charlotte had worn three years before, when she'd trick-or-treated as Spider-Man. That fall, the first after Jenny's death, he'd put together an elaborate Rapunzel costume for her for a junior high party—gold and silver thread stitched into a blue velvet cloak, a blond wig with a thick braid that wrapped around her waist and fell to her feet. But at the last minute Charlotte refused the Rapunzel costume, and Ozzie took her to the grocery store, where she bought the Spider-Man mask with matching plastic smock, the only costume left on the shelf, and went off to the party looking like some hopeless urchin.

Walking back to the church, keeping close to the row of trees that lined the street, Ozzie put the mask over his face, pulling the little string of elastic over his head. With his other hand, he picked up a pumpkin from the edge of someone's yard and carried it by its stem. His heavy breaths were noisy against the flimsy mask. He squinted to see through the slim eyeholes.

The damage he intended to do wouldn't be serious, he told himself. And it would cost the church nothing—Ozzie had every intention of volunteering his services for the repairs, and footing the bill for any replacement glass. The church would chalk it all up to vandals, and Ozzie could finally drive by the old place with a sense of peace. He'd no longer have to see all that sunlight muddied by dirt trapped in the glass, or see how the window sagged and chipped from its own weight.

Crouching in a deep shadow, Ozzie lifted the pumpkin above his head and aimed for a warped sash in order to do minimal harm. The pumpkin crashed against the window, shattering just enough of the glass to require careful repair, and Ozzie bolted from the site before the broken rind and guts of the pumpkin even hit the ground.

Once back inside the truck, he pushed the mask up off his face to rest atop his head. As he drove off, Charlotte, who had seen none of her father's destruction, reached into the box and picked up some x-ray specs. "You know Mrs. diFanta from down the street?" she said, putting on the glasses. "She witnessed a sun miracle. That's when you look in the sky and see the sun dancing. That's how she went blind." She wiggled her hands in front of her face, as if she could see through her skin.

Ozzie looked straight ahead but watched his daughter in the rearview mirror. For years Ozzie had been looking at Charlotte, studying her, certain there'd come a time when he'd never see her again. Her absence from his life had always seemed just seconds away. And now it was as if he couldn't see her at all, not even when looking right at her. Instead, he saw her clearly, so clearly, at thirteen years old, in the moments just before he told her that her mother had died. He had waited for her in front of the house and, with both dread and relief, watched her approach. It had begun to rain, and Charlotte struggled and rushed down the street on her roller skates, her open umbrella flailing about as she tried to keep her balance.

5.

᪥

I N all the years Tuesday had been smitten with Ozzie Yates, she'd only ever kissed him on the stage of the community theater. She'd played Frankie to his Johnny in *Frankie and Johnny in the Clair de Lune* a few summers before Jenny took sick. Tuesday particularly remembered one evening's late rehearsal when they'd waited out a hailstorm, backstage, sipping too-strong coffee, sitting on the lumpy poppy-print sofa that had been used in the theater's every living room stage set of the last twenty years. Tuesday and Ozzie had known each other since high school, but that night was the first he'd heard that her father had named her after Tuesday Weld. "Ah, the Marlon Brando of women," Ozzie had said. He had to tell her he was quoting from *The Motel Chronicles* by Sam Shepard, and after the first show, Ozzie gave her a copy of the Shepard book as a gift, wrapped in the colorful print of the previous Sunday's funnies. Hud hadn't even given her a single rose on opening night.

So she knew Ozzie, despite his Spider-Man mask, by his long legs and the dark curls that just touched the top of his collar, by the way he kept the cuffs of his shirt sleeves unsnapped. She had been on her way back to the flea market, with Nina in the basket of her bicycle, but stopped the bike at the curb by the church when she saw the pumpkin flung. She didn't even realize she was giggling until Nina looked back, her eyes wide with shock, after Ozzie dashed away. "What's funny?" Nina scolded.

"Nothing," Tuesday said.

"Then why are you laughing?" Nina said.

"Sometimes I laugh at things that aren't funny," she said. What explanation was there? She had caught sight of an old friend so down for so long with heartache and grief, doing something sudden and dumb. It was hilarious. *You should be laughing your head off,* she wanted to tell Nina.

"He broke the angel with blue feathers," Nina said, her voice hushed with reverence. A few years before, on the courthouse lawn, Nina had tensed at the sight of the sculpture of a stone angel on a podium kneeling in remorse, its enormous gray wingspan casting a long, thin, late-afternoon shadow across the grass. Nina had shrieked, as if the angel were poised to swoop down and scoop her up. In the days that followed, Tuesday took her out to seek angels—they spotted one painted on the side of a barn, another carved into a tombstone turning to dust in an abandoned cemetery, a glass one with a gold trumpet in Rose's china cabinet. Nina's fears abated, she and Tuesday picnicked beneath the stained-glass angel with blue-tinted wings in the church window, stuffing themselves with fried chicken legs and macaroni.

They rode directly to Ozzie's house, and Charlotte answered the door, pushing back her cuticles with an orange stick. She wore a t-shirt and pajama bottoms, her face scrubbed clean, leaving her looking pudgy-cheeked and babyish. It was funny for Tuesday to think of all the damage this raggedy thing did to her home only months before, when her son used to date her. Tuesday missed seeing Ozzie regularly, when he'd come to the house distraught over Charlotte kept out too late. Tuesday had secretly loved his midnight arguments with Hud, when he'd threaten to have Gatling arrested if his motherless little girl wasn't soon returned to the safety of her pink canopy bed. Once Ozzie had even bloodied Hud's nose, and as Hud, too drunk to stand that night, tried to pick himself up from the porch floor, Ozzie whispered to Tuesday, "I'm not mad at *you.*" She blushed at the satisfying absolution, feeling as if she somehow conspired against the errant men of her home.

"Nin, darling," Charlotte said, faux demure, bending at the waist, pinky lifted, to kiss Nina on the cheek.

"Lot," Nina said, kissing back. She mimicked Charlotte's tea-party snootiness, but Tuesday could tell Nina wanted to leap like a wild child into Charlotte's arms. When she dated Gatling, Charlotte took Nina out for sisterly afternoons shopping thrift stores in Grand Island, and Nina would come home looking a fright in a faded, powder-blue Hello Kitty baby tee, her little-girl paunch peeking out the bottom of it, or shaky-legged on a pair of platform clogs three sizes too big.

"I've missed you," Charlotte told Nina, and she reached into a cardboard box on the floor next to the door. She took from it a barrette with a cloth daisy and clipped it into Nina's hair. "I want you to have that."

"Tell her thank you," Tuesday said.

"I love it," Nina said, trying to see it through the tops of her eyes, reaching up to touch the daisy's frayed petals.

"Dad's upstairs," Charlotte told Tuesday. "Go on up. He just got in the tub, and he'll be in it for hours. He just sits there crying, drinking pink Andre, and turning pruney." She tapped her orange stick on the top of Nina's head. "You and me are going to go wash that dirty, dirty hair of yours. I have a recipe for some shampoo that I clipped from an old *Cosmo* I found at the Salvation Army. It calls for beer and egg."

"Ick," Nina said happily.

Her hair was dirty, it was true; Tuesday hadn't washed it for her in days. Nina normally hated to have her head touched, so she went through life with rats and tangles and natural curls that sagged like she was some gutter-drunk Shirley Temple. *I should be turned in to Social Services,* Tuesday thought, plucking a nettle from Nina's hair, charmed by Nina's messiness. *I should be denied all motherly privileges.*

Nina handed Tuesday the peach, its skin damp and warm from Nina's palms, then followed Charlotte into the kitchen. Upstairs, Tuesday stopped to listen at the bathroom door. She knocked gently. "I saw what you did," she said.

"Come on in," Ozzie said. "Most of myself is behind the shower curtain."

Ozzie soaked in the soapy water, the Spider-Man mask pushed up to the top of his head, his body halfway concealed by the once-clear shower curtain now opaque from mildew and water stain. Tuesday had seen Ozzie naked once, when he was eighteen and she was sixteen. They had all gone skinny-dipping at the river. Tuesday and her sister, Rose, nude, sunned themselves self-consciously on an inflatable raft, their arms carefully placed, legs carefully crossed, positioning themselves to cast modest shadows. They pretended not to stare at Ozzie and the way his muscles moved, the way drops caught and glistened in the hair of his body. He stood waist-high in the river, trying to lift his laughing Jenny in his arms to dunk her, headfirst, into the drink.

"You didn't see what you think you saw," Ozzie said, writing Tuesday's name in the steam on the shower curtain.

Tuesday had a seat on the closed toilet lid and took a swig from Ozzie's bottle of pink champagne gone flat, then another swig. "What do I think I saw?"

"Wipe the steam from the TV screen, would you, doll face?" Ozzie asked, handing her a dry washcloth. A tiny portable black-and-white with tinfoil on its antenna sat in the sink. "That cougar's about to rip the big wings off that ugly bird."

Tuesday offered him the peach, and Ozzie took his straight razor from the edge of the tub and sliced at the fruit. He held the razor and a piece of peach up to Tuesday's lips, and she ate the fruit off the blade. She felt a little dizzy, and her eyes watered, just from her few sips of Andre, the steaminess of the room, and the heavy scent of Ozzie's soap. And from the lush of the peach, she guessed. The soap had a wet-wood smell that made her nostalgic and that she could taste on her tongue, reminding her of her grade school band practice and the reeds of her alto sax.

"You think you saw me ruining something, but, see, I was actually saving that window," he said. "They've just been letting it crack and warp. I've offered several times to work on it, but they don't care enough."

"Hud took Nina in the middle of the night," Tuesday said, anxious to cast aspersions on her ex. Ozzie had always been willing to hear the worst about Hud, even back when everybody was everybody's friend. "While I slept. Didn't bring her back until after daylight."

Ozzie rolled his eyes and muttered. "But I wasn't all that worried," she said, suddenly feeling guilty. Steam hot on her cheek, Tuesday remembered a Christmas morning of a few years before, Gatling and Nina off in Phoenix with their grandmother, as Hud and Tuesday worked at their marriage. They'd had a moody bath together, Tuesday lying back against Hud's chest, drinking a beer at 10 A.M. They listened to a scratchy bootleg of Lucinda Williams singing a Hank Williams song. "It wasn't like he didn't leave a note. I knew he'd bring her back. It was just kind of unnerving. The poor guy's still in love with me after all, I think."

"Love," Ozzie said. "That's all the motivation a guy needs to wreck everything." He rubbed his bar of soap against the stubble of his chin, working up a lather, then picked up a shard of broken mirror from a tray of aftershaves and hair tonics at the side of the tub. In the little bit of mirror, Tuesday could see Ozzie's eye and his long black lashes. She loved the sound of the scratch of the blade against his chin, and, for a minute, she missed having men in her house.

Tuesday licked at sweat that dripped down her cheek to her lip and watched the wildlife show on the TV—two chee-tah kittens wrestled and hissed. "Everybody's air conditioner is breaking down," she said. "I saw two repair trucks just on the short ride over here."

"The kids are huffing," Ozzie said. "They like to unscrew the valve with the Freon to get a whiff of it. Sometimes they pass out from it. But what the hell else do the little addicts have to do around here?"

Poor Millie, Tuesday thought, thinking of what a fright that girl would grow up to be. But she was actually relieved that there might not be anything seriously wrong with her air conditioner. She considered what she would buy with the money she would save from not having to get a new one. Maybe something very frivolous—a $100 bottle of Shoot the Moon. Or a pair of ostrich-skin cowboy boots for Nina that she would quickly outgrow.

"There's a guy in this support group I go to," Ozzie said, "who said his daughter is addicted to sniffing the gas out of cans of whipped cream."

"Support group," Tuesday said, standing. "How did all my friends get so old and confused?" Ozzie had finished shaving, and Tuesday pulled his Spider-Man mask back down to cover his face. She put her lips to the lips of the mask for a tiny kiss, then turned to leave.

"I tell you what we're going to do," Ozzie said, taking off the mask. "You're going to go home, pack a few suitcases, then we're going to steal our children away before somebody else does it. We can throw the girls in the back of my pickup. We'll drive from town to town, busting church windows at night, repairing them during the day. Then we'll move on."

"That's sweet," Tuesday said, closing the door behind her as she left the bathroom. Walking down the hall, she daydreamed about a runaway afternoon with Ozzie in a motel room, drinking pink champagne and playing gin, while Charlotte combed out weeks' worth of snarls from Nina's hair.

PART TWO

ⅈⅈⅈⅈⅈⅈⅈⅈ

A F E W weeks after the execution of her husband, Nanette Schrock returned to her house on Plum Street. She'd been living in Lincoln with her aunt for several months, and no one in town had seen anything of her except on the television news, briskly climbing courthouse steps, shading her eyes, bumping the shoulders of reporters and ignoring their requests for comment. Her hair was cut in a severe shag with a fresh drug-store dye job, in a shade called "mink," according to the women around town, and she always gripped in her gloved hand a can of Whooptydoo, a grocery-store brand of cola.

A college literature professor who had been conducting poetry workshops at the prison had fought for Robbie Schrock's life in its final days. The professor had had to walk past picketers and protesters calling for the head of the killer, and he was joined in his efforts by a pair of frail nuns with long jail records for their years of peaceable, anti-death-penalty demonstrations. The governor, with shoe-polish-black hair that resembled the dip and weave of a toupee, presided lazily over a hearing during which the professor read some of Robbie Schrock's poems about God and forgiveness, about wrenching regret, about his boys playing cowboys and Indians with cap guns and slingshots in the clouds of heaven.

The professor wept as he described how Robbie Schrock was teaching himself lullabies on a plastic piccolo, and that was when everyone remembered how they recognized the professor. Only months before he had been on the news defending his selection of a gay man's AIDS memoir for his freshman lit class, a selection that a few of his fundamentalist students were denouncing. *Of course,* people began to realize, *the man is in love.* Some could sympathize; though Robbie was a child killer, he had a full head of curly hair, freckles on his cheeks, and honey-colored eyes. There were a few women in town who joked in hushed tones that they would have happily sacrificed their brats to have such a handsome husband to visit in prison.

Nanette Schrock attended every hearing, saying nothing, seemingly so confident her ex-husband would fry for poisoning her boys that she chewed on a pencil, puzzling over the newspaper's crossword. A victims' advocacy group spoke on Nanette's behalf, and she had provided them with ample ammunition in the fight against her ex-husband's reprieve— the advocacy group's leader, a plump, grandmotherly woman, stood in front of the governor, her old friend. She held up a pair of tiny, fuzzy, footed pajamas patterned with cows leaping over moons, and she read a prayer that one of the boys had written for a Sunday school class. In it the boy asked God to bless Mommy, Daddy, Grammy, Grampy, the president, the wild dog that lived beneath the back church steps, and the little girl in the news who had fallen in a frozen lake and had had to have all her fingers and toes cut off.

A writer for the editorial page of the *Lincoln Journal Star*, a columnist opposing capital punishment, complained of the manipulation in the next day's newspaper, pointing out that the boys would have outgrown the footed pajamas years before. But it was so weak, this writer's argument that the very young boys had not been such babies, that he apologized profusely in the next edition, as did the newspaper's publisher.

The people of Bonnevilla had at first left their scarecrows and jack-o'-lanterns on their porches in the days after their early-September celebration of the execution, seeing no reason to box them up, only to unbox them come October. But when they started noticing that the lights of the house on Plum Street were lit in these encroaching fall evenings that were growing cold, they began to take down their Halloween decorations, worried about their effect on Nanette Schrock. Nanette was suddenly always in her backyard, wearing a wide-brimmed straw hat, cutting away the dried bramble and dead thicket of her neglected garden.

Then, within the first few days of October, Nanette taped in her window a child's drawing of a red-eyed black cat in mid-hiss, its back arched, its hackles raised in the shape of the teeth of a saw. Everyone then returned their Halloween decorations to their trees and eaves and front lawns, taking the child's drawing as a statement from the silent Nanette that she just wanted everything to be normal.

♨♨♨♨♨

7

H U D rested his neck on the cracking red leather of the barber's chair, indulging in an old-fashioned professional shave, complete with a fat stogie smoldering between his fingers that he couldn't stomach to actually smoke. He'd grown out his sideburns and would stop in weekly to have Wilson trim them to a trendy point.

It was early October, and Hud hadn't had a drink since September 20, a Jack and Pepsi with a maraschino cherry. He was proud of the ease with which he'd given up the hooch. He hadn't been a drunk at all, he decided, or he'd be constantly itching for a shot, wouldn't he?

On September 20, he'd been invited to Steak and Black Coffee by Tuesday and her family to celebrate Nina's casting as the lead lemon drop in her dance class recital. He had wanted to propose a toast but had worried that he would look even more like an alcoholic if he raised only his glass of cola, so he allowed himself the shot of whiskey and went home mostly sober, feeling a buzz only from the moment that Tuesday had kissed him on the cheek to thank him for wearing a necktie. She had then wiped the trace of lipstick away with her thumb.

Beneath the plastic cape covering Hud in the barber's chair, he wore the uniform for his new job—a secondhand tuxedo for playing piano in the lounge of an interstate Ramada Inn. It was a twenty-mile drive every evening to the hotel, and the tips weren't always fantastic, but some nights they were. The hotel entertained conventioneers, and the career women with nametags pinned to their silk blouses would get sauced on mango margaritas, the house specialty, and they'd group at the table next to the piano requesting tunes like "Love on the Rocks" and "Islands in the Stream." Hud would wink and smile, make his voice as smoky as it would go, and he'd unbow his tie and undo a few buttons of the ruffle of his tuxedo shirt. Sometimes he'd sneak in a few of his own songs—"Penny," named after a fictional lover with copper-colored eyes, was particularly popular. The ladies would buy him drinks that lined up, undrunk, across the top of his baby grand.

After paying the barber, Hud stepped outside into the autumn evening, pulling his jacket tighter around him.

A few doors down from the barbershop, in the doorway of the long-defunct Hotel Juliet, stood Charlotte in a trench coat and a polka-dot headscarf. She was bent a little, scratching her calf through a rip in her dark nylon stocking.

"Don't you ever stay home with your daddy?" Hud asked, blowing on the coal of his cigar to spark it back up, then holding it toward Charlotte. She held her hands open over the cigar, warming her palms with the smoke and its puff of heat. "You look like a goddamn hobo," he said. The front of her coat was missing most of its buttons.

"I've been divesting myself of my worldly goods," she said, and at first Hud thought she said *whirly* goods, which he liked the sound of. "All My Whirly Goods" would make a nice song title.

In the crook of her arm was a small pink-and-white-striped paper bag from Victoria's Secret that she used as a purse. She reached into it and took out a few sour-cherry candies, offering one to Hud. As he took the candy, he noticed a red dot drawn on her palm—he'd been seeing these mock stigmata on the wrists and palms of some of the girls around town. One of the girls who gathered on the lawn at the flea market to hear him sing had taken a marker to the hands of her two younger sisters as he performed, and afterward she had made them bow their heads and recite some prayer about wounds and virgins. The other night, as the skinny waitress at the Steak and Black Coffee gave him his change, Hud saw she had red dots on both the front and the back of her left hand.

Hud licked his thumb and grabbed Charlotte's wrist to try to rub the mark away. "Don't, you crazy bastard," Charlotte said, pulling her hand back. "It's taken me days to get it that red."

"There's something wrong with you," Hud sighed. "There's something wrong with all of you. It's not even the color of blood. It's too red."

"It's better than blood," she said. She pressed her fingertip against the dot.

"And you don't even know your stuff," Hud said. "A nail in the palm wouldn't have been enough to keep him stuck to the cross. They would've had to hammer it in his wrist, or he would've slipped right the hell off. Your little stigmata dot needs to be on your wrist."

"A nun in Bolivia named Constance bled from her palms every Thursday and Friday. A stigmatic in Italy bleeds from her shoulders in her sleep." Charlotte walked away from Hud, away from the Hotel Juliet. "My point being: you bleed where you bleed," she called back. The high heels of her yellow shoes clicked noisily against the sidewalk—the shoes had little vinyl bows at their backs, rhinestones at their centers. Even in her castoff clothes, all mortified for Jesus, Charlotte was still the fanciest girl in town, Hud thought.

"Join me for supper," Hud said, flinging the cigar into the street and nodding toward the Waffle Iron, where he often ordered from the breakfast menu at 6 P.M. "I don't know what you're doing out here in the cold night alone, anyway. Your nose is runny already."

Charlotte brushed away his offer of a handkerchief, and she looked forlornly up and down the quiet street as she wiped her nose with the sleeve of her trench. "Junior was supposed to pick me up here. He was going to take me to some church youth group square dance tonight," she said softly, with what seemed to Hud a pathetic pinch of longing in her voice. "Some country chapel near Gothenburg. But sometimes he gets these crippling migraine headaches, and he just has to fall into bed and put a washcloth across his eyes."

"Macho type, eh?" Hud joked, but Charlotte didn't smile. "And I suppose you're madly in love with him."

"Yeah," she said, "sort of, I am."

Hud put his arm in hers and walked her toward the diner on the corner. "Why are you all gussied up anyway?" Charlotte said, plucking some lint from his velveteen lapel. "You're not working the drive-in like that, are you?"

"I quit the drive-in," Hud said. "Word of advice: don't ever work for ex-in-laws." But Red had been good to him since the divorce, too good really, padding every other paycheck with an extra $50 or so and lending Hud his reliable old Caddy a time or two to take Nina to hockey matches in Kearney. The Widow Bosanko would often invite Hud to join her and Red for supper in the office in the back of the concession building. They'd sit around the desk, balancing their plates atop books and stacks of paper, cutting into the T-bones the Widow cooked on the grill behind the projection booth. After eating, they'd all lean back with glasses of thick raspberry wine Red had bottled himself and stare contentedly at the walls papered with faded movie posters. Even as his teeth ached with the sweet of the wine and his stomach still grumbled from the undercooked steak, he felt nostalgic for that very minute, at the very moment he lived it. Hud couldn't bear to think of Tuesday with a new husband, or himself with a new wife, Nina suddenly the stepchild of strangers.

"Oh, take me with you tonight," Charlotte said when Hud told her about his new job. She sat in the booth, removing her headscarf, promising to sit silently in a corner of the lounge drinking baby bellinis. "I'll be utterly peepless."

Hud felt a jolt of pain in his side, some phantom twinge from an old sucker punch to the kidneys. Once, Gatling drove Charlotte to Kansas City on the back of his Vespa for a five-day drunk in a highway motel room. The night the kids left, Ozzie came out to the house calling it a kidnapping, and Hud had stupidly put up his dukes. Hud now touched his ribcage gently through his tuxedo jacket. Gatling's teenaged rebellion had somehow seemed precious to Hud then, and worth defending.

"I'm still recovering from your daddy's wrath of months ago," Hud said. He could just picture it, him taking Charlotte home in the A.M., Oz on the porch with a baseball bat, accusing Hud of getting Charlotte snockered on sugar water to molest her in a ditch.

Hud could always have taken Oz easy, or at least gotten in a jab or two, but he actually thought he was somehow comforting his old friend. The fighting had felt like an intimate exchange, a step toward reconciliation. They hadn't seen much of Ozzie right after Jenny's death, except in a rumpled coat at the grocery store, so it had been good to have him back up and swinging.

The menu for the Waffle Iron was a lit-up contraption at the side of the booth, wired with a red telephone, the offerings unaltered since the 1950s. Hud always ordered the Protein Special, a piece of fatty New York strip with scrambled eggs and a slice of Texas toast buttered to sopping. "Just a bowl of chicken broth for me," Charlotte told Hud as he dialed up the waitress. "With some oyster crackers."

"Christ," Hud muttered, and he ran his finger down the menu. "The lady will have the french toast and a hot chocolate," he said before hanging up as Charlotte complained. "I know, I know," he said. "You're all through with the whirly goods."

Looking across at Charlotte's cheeks, still pink from the wind, Hud thought of his son, and he began to feel weepy. Like some schoolgirl, Hud had once imagined a wedding for the two children, complete with church bells and fat bridesmaids. He pictured Ozzie, handsome as hell in a crappy tuxedo, drunk on bubbly, giving a toast that would bring all the guests to tears as he said worshipful things about Charlotte's dead mother.

"Do you ever think about him?" Hud asked. "About Gatling? Do you ever hear from him?"

"No," she said. She poured sugar into the hot chocolate the waitress brought.

"Here," he said, reaching into the inside pocket of his jacket for the postcard Tuesday had passed on to him about a month before. The picture was of a pink Victorian house with gingerbread woodwork, the sun setting in the ocean in the background. Tiny print at the top of the picture described the house as having been the birthplace of the Rev. Manny Hamlet, famed child evangelist. *We perform on the beach,* Gatling wrote. *Rev. Manny Hamlet even came to one of our shows. He's 94, but everybody around here still calls him the Child Evangelist. He sits in his wheelchair and whispers when he speaks so that the girls have to lean in. He rubbed his thumb against Harmony's nipple. He put his hand on Sunny's hip. I hope I'm someday such a respected dirty old man. xxoo, Gat.*

This was the first, since his conversion, that Gatling had shown even a speck of delight in the sinful. When he first ran away to play guitar for the singing and dancing Daughters of God, he sent Hud and Tuesday magazine clippings with pictures of the band, the four twenty-year-old innocents in elaborate gowns they built themselves on a secondhand electric Singer, according to their publicity. The gowns were white and flouncy, strangely bridal, with bras that pushed their cleavage up and out, but whenever Gatling wrote of Sunny, Harmony, Dolly, and June, he spoke of them as if they were as sexless as nuns. But this postcard suggested that Gatling's life was more than day-and-night piety and restraint. Reading between the lines of the short letter, Hud could sense the beating of Gatling's rebel heart and felt confident that the boy was just inches from entirely defiling that quartet of foolish virgins.

He hoped Charlotte would take the card, would be charmed by Gatling's words, and spend the rest of the night pining for him. But she pushed the postcard away without a glance. "You keep it," she said.

What had happened between Charlotte and Gatling to damage them both? he wondered. Maybe it had been nothing, or close to nothing; all these children were such weaklings. And while a father agonizes about his children done in by things like drugs and liquor and sex without rubbers, along comes religion. Religion, it seemed to Hud, got passed around in town like something infectious. He'd known too many perfectly fine people who, upon falling in love with someone full of faith, quit drinking, quit cussing, suddenly knew nothing but compassion for every living goddamn thing.

8 .

iiiiiiiiii

B E F O R E stepping into the Ramada Inn lounge, Tuesday checked her lipstick in the mirror of her compact. The curl at her forehead had wilted in the night's light drizzle, so she gave it a twist with her finger to give it more spring. She wouldn't be there at all, she told herself, if she wasn't still buzzing from the most of a bottle of red she had sipped with Oz earlier that evening at the Wiggle Room, a lifeless honky-tonk where the dance floor gave you slivers. Had it not been for the wine, she would never have messed with putting up her hair, with pressing the clingy blue dress that had fallen off its hanger to wrinkle on the closet floor.

"Let me see," Nina said, reaching up for the compact. Tuesday held the mirror before her, and Nina straightened the limp orchid tucked behind her ear. Tuesday had let Nina pluck the flower from the plant near death on the back porch.

"Sophisticated ladies," Tuesday said, snapping the compact shut and swinging her hips, a swing that Nina quickly mimicked. Nina was in her bliss. She had been begging Tuesday for days to take her to hear Hud play piano; Hud had promised a mellow rendition of Opal Lowe's classic country-funk tune, "Snake Eyes and Alligator Shoes." Slowed way down, Hud had explained to Nina, the song's precious melody, and its sentiments about lousy luck and addiction, showed through nicely. Nina had been intrigued.

Inside the lounge, Hud played an Al Green song to a small crowd of lonely zombies. Most everyone sat singly, stirring around their ice cubes with swizzle sticks. The only noise rose from a raucous table of businessmen in mussed comb-overs, the men happy with self-congratulation and stubby cigars.

Nina crawled up into a vinyl seat at the bar, and the bartender gave her a maraschino cherry. "You have ID, little miss?" the woman said.

"This is Nina Smith," Tuesday said, sitting next to her, putting her counterfeit Kate Spade atop the bar. Her sister, Rose, had hosted a purse party during which a representative with rhinestone-studded, dragon-lady fingernails had demonstrated the click and clack of the gilded clasps of a wide selection of designer knockoffs. Tuesday bought the Kate Spade and a Gucci and got slightly soused off the pitcher of fuzzy navels Rose had mixed up.

"Hud's daughter," the woman said with a wink, placing cocktail napkins atop the bar. "I hear you're a little musical too. Maybe we can get you to sit on top of the baby grand later and belt out a few tunes." Nina blushed from the bartender's attention. Then, when the woman said, "You must be Tuesday," Tuesday blushed too.

The woman introduced herself as Augustine, then offered to buy them both a drink. "I make a mean virgin sex-on-the-beach," she said, winking at Nina again.

"She'll have that," Tuesday said, loosening the knot on her scarf. "And I'll have . . . well, y'know what, I'm going to have a martini. A Sapphire martini, on the rocks, very very dry."

"Olives?"

"Um, do you happen to have those little cocktail onions? I'll have three of those."

"And this ant will have a grasshopper," Nina said, flicking the insect that had fallen onto her sleeve from her orchid. Nina had been teaching herself the names of drinks in a bartender's manual she'd found at the flea market.

Hud had apparently noticed their arrival, as he'd begun to play "Scar Baby," a song of his own he'd written about the afternoon he first proclaimed his love to Tuesday, when they were both only seventeen. "You wouldn't love me once you got me naked," she had told him as they creaked down the Platte River in an old rowboat. "I'm covered in horrible scars. My father tried to dissolve me with battery acid when I was a baby." Hud then stripped her teasingly, slowly, lifting an inch of blouse here, pushing down an inch of underwear there, looking for some hint of any kind of scar. All he found, once she was entirely naked, was a white crescent moon next to her belly button, from when she rolled over onto a piece of glass while sunning herself in the backyard when she was fourteen.

"I think I'll order martinis when I'm older," Nina said as Augustine swished some vermouth around in the bottom of a glass before pouring the liquid into the sink. "It comes with something to eat. Does it come with one of those little umbrellas?"

"No," Tuesday said, not looking back at Hud as he sang but feeling as if he stared at her, as if he stood right at her back, his breath on her neck. "You'll have to drink a Singapore sling to get one of those." *Skin milk-white in the moonlight/me counting new scars and old freckles.*

Tuesday took a sip of the gin, hoping to stave off the sobriety she felt creeping up on her tipsiness.

"Go make a request," she told Nina, handing her a dollar. As Hud played the Opal Lowe all slow for her, Nina sat next to him on the bench. Tuesday picked up their drinks and her handbag and scooted into a corner banquette. Hud had kicked off his shoes, working the pedals of the piano in stocking feet. After Nina's request, he dipped into his own collection of original songs, playing some of the more melodic ones—"A Lovely Afternoon for a Crying Jag," "Secondhand Go-Go Boots," "A Broken Heart and Crazy Glue."

He sang about going to New Orleans with Tuesday on their second honeymoon. In the song, Tuesday stands in a street in the French Quarter, shading herself with a $2 umbrella and clutching a paper sack of souvenir voodoo dolls made in Taiwan. *I'm crooning about my voodoo honeymoon,* he sang with a witchy zing, Screamin' Jay Hawkins–like, *my tired bride waiting for a jazz funeral in the hot rain.*

Tuesday thought about how easy they'd had it back when they'd thought everything so impossible. Practically every Saturday night, Hud and Tuesday and Gatling had shown up at Oz and Jenny's back door for what they all considered an evening out. One night in the fall, Charlotte and Gatling, only about six and seven years old and in their pajamas before dark, rolled out their sleeping bags beneath the piano in the sunroom, the coldest room in the house. The adults had cocktails in the brightly lit kitchen, and they indulged Hud as he played a new composition on the plastic strings of Charlotte's toy ukulele. As he strummed out "The Rain Puddle Waltz," Tuesday and Jenny, the only two in the room who knew a proper two-step, danced in the cramped kitchen, giggling, bumping their hips against the stove and fridge and table, tripping along.

Hud announced to the club that he was taking a short break, then picked up Nina from the piano bench to carry her to Tuesday's banquette. "Did I ever tell you," Hud asked Tuesday as he tickled Nina's ribs, "about how this child was born with nothing but bleach-blond fuzz on top of her bald head?"

"I was there when it happened," Tuesday said. Hud wore a potent aftershave, though his chin was stubbly, at least two days this side of seeing the business end of a razor blade. But knowing Hud, the sloppy look—the crooked tie, the stocking feet—was probably calculated. He liked to make women want to baby him. It even still worked on her, and she had been seeing through him for years.

"Your head looked like a peach," Hud said, "so your mommy wanted to call you Georgia. But your pappy wanted to call you Peaches."

Tuesday smiled at this fiction. They had decided on Nina's name hours before they saw her head bristled with peach fuzz; they had named her after Al Hirschfeld's daughter. Tuesday had been enrolled in a correspondence caricature class at the time and, too hot and heavy to move an inch that last summer month of her pregnancy, she spent her hours puzzling over Hirschfeld's drawings in a book, scanning them for the name of his daughter hidden among the scribbles of a can-can dancer's skirts, or in the lines of the brilliantined hair of a movie actor. Lying in bed, a cold rag at her forehead, she'd been pleasantly hypnotized by counting Ninas.

"Can I change my name to Peaches?" Nina said, lying down in the booth, resting her head on Hud's leg, her feet in Tuesday's lap.

"Not until you're older," Hud said. "When you're an emancipated minor."

"A fancy-panted what?" Nina said.

"An eman-ci-pa-ted mi-nor," Hud exaggerated, faking sign language, fluttering his fingers in front of Nina's face. "Somebody call Miracle Ear. This girl needs to schedule a fitting."

"I wish I *was* deaf," Nina said, covering her ears. "Because you talk too much," and Hud tickled her more in retaliation. Tuesday sat idly by, mildly amused, stoking her drunk with her martini refill. This was a familiar role for her: an audience for Hud's little vaudeville act with his children. She had often come across as the sourpuss in the family, sitting at the kitchen table playing solitaire, drinking supermarket sherry, as Hud worked his children into a slaphappy frenzy. Even as the marriage fell apart, Hud remained Nina's comic foil, filling the house with laughter that turned Tuesday gloomy. Because once Nina conked out for the night, Hud would fade away, bored with the notion of simply loving his wife. *You have a man who's madly in love with his children,* Rose had told Tuesday as she had first contemplated divorce. *You're the luckiest idiot I know.*

"Speaking of emancipated minors," Hud said, taking Gatling's postcard from his jacket pocket, "you can have this back." Gatling sometimes sent the postcards to Hud's address, sometimes to Tuesday's, which Tuesday hoped was some sort of nonverbal effort to make his parents visit each other, some gesture of concern. It hurt Tuesday that Gatling never asked after anyone in the family, not even Nina, whom he so adored. Tuesday glanced at the postcard, but then returned it to Hud's pocket. "I want him back, Mother," Hud said. "Let's go on TV and cry our eyes out. Let's say they brainwashed him."

"We were the ones who kicked him out of the house once or twice," Tuesday said. "We sent him away to camps. Facilities. He was giving you gray hairs in your sideburns," and she touched his sideburn. He reached up to take her hand, and she let him hold it for a few seconds before pulling it away.

"Well, then, we'll say that *we* were brainwashed. What, we're the only two goddamn losers in the world who aren't allowed to unmake a mistake?"

"Don't swear in front of Mommy," Nina mumbled, halfway to falling asleep.

"Our Nina, always the pope," Hud said. "We'll do things differently with this one," he said to Tuesday, pointing his thumb at Nina. "We oughta at least make some money off her when we cast her off. Sell her to the circus, or to a carny." He leaned closer to Tuesday. "You smell pretty," he told her.

"No," she said, "my sister smells pretty. She borrowed this scarf and stank it up with her perfume." Tuesday didn't hate the idea of Hud being in love with her again, she had to confess. But wouldn't everything be easier if he just skulked off like a wounded mutt? Wouldn't it almost be better if he was relentlessly bitter, wishing her the worst? "What about Augustine over there?" Tuesday said. "Don't tell me you haven't even asked her out. Don't tell me you haven't even stolen a kiss. She's a beaut. Stunning baby blues. She's very statuesque, I'd say." She found herself leaning toward him as she spoke, her voice low.

"You and me," Hud whispered in her ear. "We'll get a room in the hotel. We'll just sleep, nothing else. We'll keep our clothes on. I'll be good. Nina can sleep in the bed between us." *Pat my head,* Tuesday thought, leaning her head on his shoulder. *Tell me I'm too drunk. Tuck me in like the gentleman you ain't.* "Let's try it out, Day. I don't care what happens. I don't care if you kick me to the side again. Mess me up, if that's what's got to happen, I don't care. All messed up by you is about a hundred times better than nothing."

"Where was all this sweep-me-off-my-feet shit a year ago?" Tuesday said.

"You can't convince me that you're happy," Hud said, his fingers soft at the back of her neck.

"I'm happy as hell," she said. "There are things I definitely don't miss."

"What don't you miss?" He kissed her cheek.

"I don't miss that," she said, "for one thing," as she leaned in for another. "I don't miss those patronizing little kisses whenever I tried to talk seriously about things."

"Then don't let me do it," Hud said, kissing her again. He put two fingers on her chin and brought her lips to his. "Stop me," he said. Tuesday closed her eyes, eased by the familiarity. *A kiss by the catacombs of witches long undead,* Hud had sung in the song about their second honeymoon. Tuesday remembered the tour they took of a cramped New Orleans graveyard with its crumbling mausoleums and stone angels streaked with pollution. As they stood in line to peek through the cracked lid of a marble sepulchre at the skeleton of a dead stranger, Hud whispered in Tuesday's ear, "Don't kiss me."

That was a little thing they had. During some unromantic moment, or moment inappropriate, during a dull church service or in the hallway of the grade school, Hud would whisper, "Don't kiss me," and Tuesday would look around, then swiftly steal a kiss.

As she kissed Hud now, she recalled another honeymoon, a fourth or fifth, to a seaside town in Florida. They were forever leaving their children with the grandparents, escaping in efforts to revive their marriage, declaring any vacation a honeymoon in order to treat themselves to champagne and suites, while the shingles of their house decayed and the termites became legion. Still winter, Tuesday had lain on the beach in long sleeves and long pants as Hud ran the cool, smooth edges of a piece of pink sea glass across her cheek, her throat. Later they walked too far, watching the tide, and had to lean into the strong ocean wind as they walked back, Tuesday's eyes tearing up. The skies were overcast, with just one strip of clear blue, one thin line cut through the clouds like the exhaust trail of a plane. "Don't kiss me," Hud had said when he'd sensed she was angry. And she had been, blaming him for some reason for the cold and the wind, so she hadn't kissed him.

What did I have to be angry about? she thought now. A long walk along the beach? Why hadn't she just kissed him? she wondered. What would it have cost her, that little kiss?

"Get a room," Augustine said, winking, setting down another martini.

"Oh, take it away," Tuesday said, too softly and too late, as Augustine returned to the bar. She remembered she'd been eating onion after onion. "My breath, I suppose," she said, putting her hand to her mouth.

"Nothing wrong with your breath," Hud said. He lifted the glass to hold it to Tuesday's lips. She took a sip, then pushed his hand away. Tuesday had never been much of a drinker before the divorce; she'd even verged on the holier-than-thou about it, trotting off alone to Al-Anon meetings to yack about the bad habits of her husband and teenaged son. She didn't get much comfort from the meetings—she would glaze over from the store-bought crullers and the oversugared Sanka and the hard-luck scenarios that made her own life seem only troubled and not at all wrecked. But she liked writing, "Gone to Al-Anon, Back at 6" in big letters in black marker on a full page of notebook paper she would stick to the fridge with a magnet shaped like a strawberry.

When Hud took a drink of her martini, Tuesday said, "I thought you were on the wagon."

"Well, I don't think I've been on the wagon since I started kissing you five minutes ago," he said, "inhaling all that hooch."

Tuesday knew she was too drunk to do the smart thing. She sat up straight, picked up her phony Kate Spade, clutched it to her chest. She held the scarf to her nose and breathed in the scent of Shoot the Moon. She wished she was more like Rose. Despite being completely unlucky in love and lousy at keeping a job, Rose was always utterly cool. Rose made all the wrong moves with real aplomb.

Tuesday took her keys from her purse. "This is no good," she said. "I shouldn't be out drunk with Nina."

"So stay here," he said, tugging at her keys.

"Yeah, I can just see us," she said, picturing herself and Hud, drunk, x's for eyes, in a hotel room, the bed filled with empties. She picked up Nina, then began to scoot from the banquette. Hud grabbed Nina's ankle, making Nina groan and wake a little.

"Let go," Tuesday said, and Hud did, causing Tuesday to stumble as she stood. Hefting Nina up and out the door was awkward; Nina was too big to be carried these days. *I'm no kind of mother,* Tuesday thought, dreading the next day and the long, sober afternoon. She would spend it in bed with pots of tea, wracked with guilt, worshipping God just long enough to thank him repeatedly for sparing her from some drunken car crash. *I'll start going to church again,* she thought now, already praying and negotiating.

As Hud followed her from the lounge and to her car, he said, "Give me the keys" a few times in what sounded to Tuesday, annoyingly, like a threatening, fatherly tone that he never deigned to use on his own darling children. She shifted Nina in her arms to unlock the back door of the car, then laid her down across the seat. When Tuesday turned to Hud, he took hold of her right hand, gripping hard. Her fist tight in his grip, she felt the keys digging into her skin.

"Give them to me," he said. "I'm not letting you drive drunk with my daughter."

"Oh, I'm not the drunk in this picture," she said, though quite clearly she was. She knew she shouldn't be driving. One more martini and she would have been blind with double vision. There was an old motel just down the highway; she could see, as a speck of green light, its lit sign featuring a girl in a swimsuit poised to dive, advertising the heated pool that had long since been filled in. She would inch down the highway, as slowly as she could, and check in there for the night.

"What happened?" Hud said.

"Hud, you've asked that a million times, and I've answered a million times, and I don't have any more . . . words to . . ."

"No, no," Hud said. "I mean just now. What happened tonight? It was really nice there for a minute or two." He sniffled, either from the cold drizzle of rain or from disappointment. She couldn't quite tell, even looking right into his wet eyes. "And you got all dressed up. And the pretty hairdo."

"Hud," she said, "something like this, whatever this is, you know, it would take time. It took me years to get up the gumption to finally divorce you to begin with. I move slowly." Tuesday leaned back against the car, and the pressure of Hud's grip built. "That hurts," she said.

"Then drop the keys."

"I can't drop them," she said, "until you let go."

"Grow up, Day," Hud said. "Give me the keys."

"*You* grow up." *Why can't you chuckleheads refuse to speak to each other like other parents do?* Gatling scolded one morning when he was fifteen, interrupting some lazy spat of Tuesday and Hud's. *Or just stab each other in the throat, and put us all out of our misery.* Then, miraculously, Gatling wept, his feet up on the kitchen table, as he ate peanut butter from the jar with a steak knife. Tuesday and Hud just sat there, stunned to silence, fumbling with their coffee spoons and Sugar Twin as everyone pretended that Gatling wasn't soaking his dirty t-shirt with tears. Tuesday cried a little then too, embarrassed, but mostly relieved. It had been wonderful to see her son, already at that point out of reach and out at all hours, showing signs that he gave a damn.

"I'm serious," Tuesday said, feeling some pain work up her arm. "Let go."

"Give me the keys then."

Tuesday just looked at Hud, and Hud looked back, the hard pressure of his hand steady. *What was I thinking?* she thought. *There's something so wrong with us.* Then she felt him squeeze just a pinch tighter, but enough to make the pain unendurable. "Fine, have the keys, you psycho," she said, giving him a kick in the ankle, "but you're breaking my freakin' hand." She only meant to be melodramatic when she said it, but when Hud let go, and she felt the weight of the keys, she recognized the pain of fractured bone. In the sixth grade, she'd fallen trying to walk down the basement stairs in roller skates, intending to practice her figure eights on the concrete floor.

"Shit," she said, dropping the keys to the pavement. She tried to close her fist and wiggle her fingers. "Oh, great. Great."

"What?" Hud said.

"I think it *is* broken."

"I didn't break your hand," he said, rolling his eyes, reaching out for her elbow.

Just snapping back her wrist, stepping away from Hud, gave her another jolt of pain. "No, you did. It's like, it feels like funny-bone pain, like when you bump your funny bone, except kind of worse." But maybe it wasn't broken, she thought. Maybe it was only sprained, or just out of joint. *Please, just be out of joint.* "I can't believe this," she said, cradling her wounded hand in the other. Hud tentatively put his fingers to her elbow, and she allowed it.

"Are you . . . are you crying because it hurts, or . . ." Hud said.

"I'm not crying," she said. "It doesn't hurt that bad." She stood there, looking intently at the palm of her hand, searching for the letters of her daughter's name among the crisscross of the hundreds of lines.

"I should take you to the emergency room," he said.

"No. No," she said. She wiped her eyes with the back of her good hand. "I'll go to the doctor's office tomorrow."

"You know that I didn't mean to hurt you, right?" Hud said, gently taking her wrist, tracing his finger softly across her open palm.

"I know," she said. She had to leave without another word or she knew she would end up cradling his head to her chest, pitying him for his clumsiness. But when she bent over to pick up the keys she'd dropped on the pavement, she stumbled and had to grab hold of Hud's leg to steady herself.

Hud squatted next to her, leaning over to whisper in her ear. "I really can't let you drive," he said. "Just stay here at the hotel, please. I won't bother you. You can check in under an assumed name."

"Like what?" she said, letting him kiss her neck.

"Mrs. Smith?" he said.

"I'm already Mrs. Smith," she said. "That'd be a dead giveaway. You'd be on to me in a second."

"Mrs. Jones?"

"OK," she said, standing, "I'm Mrs. Jones." Anxious to get out of the wet and the cold, and to put her aching wrist in a bucket of ice, she walked off, leaving Hud to collect Nina from the backseat. "And I don't want to see you for a while," she said, though she suspected, from the sound of the clop of his boots, that Hud was too far behind to hear her. "There's something wrong with us. We're lousy for each other."

A little later, in a motel room that smelled of a mix of stale cigarette smoke and the pine-tree air fresheners that hung from rearview mirrors in cars, Tuesday sat on the floor next to the credenza to call her sister. As she spoke, she struggled to peel off her pantyhose with only her left hand.

"Maybe I'll get my hand in a cast, and all the kids in my art classes can doodle on it," Tuesday said. "'What happened, Mrs. Smith?' 'Ah, well, you know, I got shit-house on gin, then when I went to drive my daughter home, my ex-husband, who I had been making out with in the bar, broke my hand because I wouldn't sleep with him.' I mean, what kind of white-trash shit is that?"

"I'll come get you," Rose said, yawning.

"No," she said, "I'm too tired to do anything about it tonight."

"If it's a fracture, you could make it worse," Rose said. "By sleeping on it wrong. It could get twisted around. Remember Ann-Margret's toothache."

"Remember Ann-Margret's toothache" was an old family warning from when Rose and Tuesday were little girls visiting their grandmother. Bored on the farm, lazy in the rockstone branches of a fallen tree in the pasture, the girls would drink fresh lemonade so gritty with sugar the sweat bees would hover above their lips, and they'd read their grandmother's Hollywood tabloids. Though mostly scandal and gossip, the papers occasionally featured a story of celebrity ill health. For some reason, one article had haunted the sisters for years: Ann-Margret, or someone like her, had ignored a simple toothache for a few days, resulting in an infection that coursed through her body, provoking a fever that nearly killed her. Over the years, Ann-Margret's toothache had been invoked mostly as a metaphor for leaving things too long unsaid.

"I'm not going to sleep wrong," Tuesday said. "I probably won't sleep at all."

"Well, whatever. Just don't tell Dad that I didn't rush right up to get you. Or I'll be the one in big trouble."

"I don't plan on telling Dad much of anything," Tuesday said. "I'll just say I fell off my roller skates again." Nina, in the room's one double bed, began to snore, exhausted from her perfect evening on her father's piano bench. "I'm so glad that Nina slept through the whole thing."

"Yeah, she's usually such a light sleeper," Rose said. "Are you sure she was asleep, or was she just playing possum?"

"OK, this conversation has ceased to bring me comfort; I'm hanging up."

"Call me if you want me to come get you," Rose said.

When she got off the phone, Tuesday turned on an old movie channel and sat up in the bed, still in her blue dress. She rested her hand, throbbing some, on a pillow in her lap, and with the other she gently rubbed Nina's back. A foreign movie played, black and white, one she didn't recognize; its white subtitles were washed out by the white tablecloth of a scene in a café. An occasional word would reach past the tablecloth and spill onto the black skirt of the woman drinking from a tiny cup. *Place. Red. Lost. Winter.*

Closing her eyes, Tuesday listened, lulled by the French conversation. Her father had worshipped Jean-Paul Belmondo and, while working for a movie distributor, had collected some prints of his films as well as an original poster for *Une Femme Est une Femme,* with Belmondo's signature scrawled just beneath Anna Karina's pout. After Red moved his family to Bonnevilla to buy and refurbish the defunct drive-in, when Tuesday and Rose were teenagers, he would show his favorites on winter nights, the theater closed, the girls wrapped in blankets next to the drafty window of the concession booth that looked out onto the screen. Tuesday would rest her head on Rose's shoulder, swooning from watching the handsome Belmondo through a flurry of snow, the French dialogue crackling on the office's antique speakers.

One Saturday night Rose had even consented to chop Tuesday's hair short, like Jean Seberg's in *Breathless*. It wasn't long after that that she first spoke to Hud at a keg party in somebody's basement. Hud had just had his heart stomped by a girl named Kitty, and he wore a jean jacket she had left behind in his car. This Kitty had bedazzled her name across the front pocket, and the jacket was too tight on him, too short in the sleeves.

"From *À Bout de Souffle*," Tuesday had said, explaining the inspiration for her haircut and using the movie's French title in an effort to sound brilliant and strange. Hud confessed he didn't know the movie, but he sang a few lines from a song he'd written about a French foreign exchange student he had once dated who had worn a wristwatch that ran fast. That night Tuesday sat with him in his car, resting her head against his shoulder, scratching off the sequins spelling out Kitty's name.

Huddling into the sheets of the motel bed, Tuesday imagined the life she might have had, had she not gotten pregnant and married so young. She conjured up a one-room flat in Paris and a meager life of scrimping, working days selling newspapers and peppermints, spending nights painting until morning. The particulars of Tuesday's life fell away as she condensed her belongings to all that would fit in an attic apartment. Falling asleep, she peopled the place with favorite objects—her grandmother's hand-painted teapot on the windowsill, a Japanese lantern over the light bulb, the upright piano she never learned to play, pushed into a corner, leaving just enough room to open the door a crack. She saw herself alone in the room only a little uneasy, only mildly distracted with regret for having never had babies.

9 .

AUGUSTINE put her hand in Hud's, telling him to squeeze as hard as he had. She had locked up the lounge, and she and Hud sat together at the bar.

"No," Hud said, still holding her hand, taking a sip of the splash of Jack she had poured for him in a cordial glass. *Just a few gulps to unrattle your nerves,* she had said. "I don't want to put your arm in a sling too."

"I just can't imagine that you broke any bones," she said. "You probably just pinched a nerve in her hand. I'll prove it to you. Squeeze. It won't even hurt."

Hud wanted to. He wanted to squeeze as hard as he could, just so Augustine would continue to sit there smiling, batting her eyelashes, convincing him she didn't feel a damn thing.

He turned her wrist to read her watch. Almost 2:15 A.M. Upstairs, Tuesday was likely fast asleep. Hud considered renting a room across the hall from her, then joining her and Nina in the morning so they could sit around in rented terrycloth robes eating room-service eggs over easy. He would allow Nina to stunt her growth with a cup of coffee just the way she liked it—nearly white with sugar and milk.

"I'll get you some more," Augustine said, picking up the glass.

"Thanks, but no," Hud said. Augustine was usually stingy with the liquor after last round. She had been the one to convince him to give up drinking in the first place, though he'd never believed himself to be half the drunk some of his friends were. But she'd been right in her preaching about how a man of thirty-five, a father of two, should have a certain respectability.

Hud thought of his own father, unbelievably likable, but no one you'd admire. In old Polaroids, Nicky Smith had been handsome in red denim leisure suits and glittery tie clips, in sharp contrast to Hud's stringy-haired mother, who'd had ill-fitting false teeth ever since a teenaged car wreck. Before he'd left his family for another woman, Nicky had had a short-lived business as a photographer, going up in crop dusters to take aerial shots of area farms. He'd then print the pictures and frame them and go door to door, coercing the farmers into buying the blurry, overblown photos of their own property. Most of the farmers, happy to please such a pleasant man, and vain about their houses and fields, bought the photos, but some didn't. Hud, who hadn't seen his father in well over twenty years, had found all the failed sales attempts in a box in an attic after his mother died. Hud had hung them in the sunroom of his house, above the piano, sometimes losing himself in the photos of the roofs of farmhouses somewhere, of fields thickly green with summer, thin creeks sparkling with reflected sun.

Augustine set more whiskey before Hud, as well as an open tin box. At the lip of the box, Augustine's parakeet, Lucinda, perched. Lucinda's wings had been clipped so she could hang out in the lounge without taking flight up into the ceiling fans. Hud whistled at her to make her trill a little.

"She knows over six thousand songs," Augustine said, mocking Hud's claim on his resume. It was a number he'd plucked out of nowhere to get the job, and the powers that be had worked it into the newspaper advertisements for the club along with a photo of Hud looking contemplative and holding an unlit cigar.

Hud wondered if he'd ever do anything at all inspired before the end of his life. Years ago, when newly wed, it hadn't seemed so far-fetched to fantasize about being discovered playing his guitar for the grim happy-hour crowd of the Cocktail Cherry, the bar down the alley between L and M Streets. Talent scouts were supposed to haunt the hopelessly out-of-the-way. Tuesday, who read the gossip rags while working the register at 12th Street Package, had told Hud that people like Sam Shepard and Jessica Lange and Debra Winger and Lisa Marie Presley thought it hip to skulk, unrecognized, in narrow Nebraska dives.

"You want to know what's sick?" Hud asked Augustine. "What's sick is that I may just want Gatling back in order to ruin his life. To keep him close to nowhere, so he can accomplish nothing, just like his dear old dad, and his dear old dad before him. That's probably what I want more than anything."

"You haven't accomplished nothing," she said. "And you love Gatling. You want him back because you want him back."

Augustine put her hand on his arm, and Hud realized he was only flirting now. He thrived on the tender sympathy she offered whenever he fell morose—a hand on his knee here, a peck on the cheek there. Actually, he wanted the best for Gatling; he admired how his son, at seventeen, saw nothing but misdirection when he looked ahead at a life in Bonnevilla. Though Hud hadn't seen Gatling leave, he had an image of his son running away, fleeing his mistakes on his Vespa, his blue guitar strapped to his back. When Hud had been Gatling's age, he'd wasted hours in his bedroom listing the songs that he'd have on his first, second, and third albums, songs he had yet to write or to hear in his head, that existed only as titles—"Marlboro Reds and Pink Lemonade," "The Johnny Cash Blues," "Salty Wounds," "I Knew You When."

A year later Hud was married, Tuesday pregnant. Neither had even been drunk the night they conceived Gatling. The two had been in Hud's bedroom, stunned dumb with true love, a box of rubbers left in the nightstand drawer. Afterward they'd spooned naked, both shivering despite the heat of the room, the sheets kicked to the floor. They'd already started to worry.

Some nights Hud stayed over at Augustine's duplex, her bachelorette pad, as she called it, sparsely furnished with a few zebra-print beanbag chairs and a sofa shaped like a woman's red kiss. Hud would sack out for the night on the cushions of the lower lip.

Augustine got him to down another shot of whiskey at the lounge, and she insisted he was too sleepy for the twenty-mile drive back to Bonnevilla. Hud liked the idea of sticking near the Ramada Inn so he could check on Tuesday in the morning. As he lay alone on Augustine's sofa, his tux in a pile in the middle of the living room floor, he tried to convince himself that Tuesday's hand remained unbroken. He put his own left hand in his right, squeezed, evaluated the pain. What the hell was he supposed to have done? Hud wondered. Let Tuesday drive away drunk, their daughter unbuckled in the backseat? What kind of father would just shut his eyes to such a thing?

"Stop worrying," Augustine said, suddenly there in the room. In the lamplight from the open door of the bedroom, Hud could see Augustine in only pink underwear and a V-neck t-shirt, her makeup scrubbed away, leaving her eyes looking baggy and tired. "Sleep with me tonight," she said.

Hud sat up on the sofa and patted the cushion, gesturing for Augustine to sit. She did, and he leaned toward her, his shoulder against hers, his arms across his naked chest. He wore only his boxers, and the room was a little too cold. "I'm going to tell you why we can't do that," he said. "We work together, for one. But the main thing is that, somewhere along the line, I fell back in love with my ex-wife. And I still hope that, once I . . . you know . . . stop breaking her bones and shit, that . . . you know . . . ."

Augustine laughed, pushing her shoulder into him. "I know all that. But I just had in mind a little tussle. Nothing serious. But you're probably right." She stood up, shaking her head, sighing. "I happen to be in love with my ex, too. I'm the one who threw him out, but here I am, a year later, pining away."

Hud wished she wasn't giving up her lazy seduction so easily; he wanted her to talk him into it. He hadn't had sex since July, when he took Tuesday out to toast the finalization of their divorce. They had been leaning slightly toward reconciliation for a few days, and he thought it would be sophisticated and charming to take her to a riverside seafood place for $35 lobster. They got dressed up, and he gave her a gift of a book about famous divorces—Cary Grant and Barbara Hutton's, Liz Taylor and Richard Burton's.

Augustine leaned against the bedroom door. "Tuesday didn't seem so dumb," she said, "but she's just as big a joke as I am. What is it that we're thinking when we think we'll be better off? How do we manage to tell ourselves with a straight face that we can improve our lives? What a big, fat joke."

After Augustine returned to her bedroom, Hud heard her put on some soft music—jangly and foreign with a kind of synth zither sound. Not sleeping with Augustine solved nothing, Hud decided. He would wait for his dick to soften up, then he would go to Augustine's bed—he didn't want to swagger in there with his erection peeking out through the fly of his boxers.

He went into the bathroom and put some Pepsodent on his finger, then ran it over his teeth and tongue. He patted down his rooster tail with some tap water. He'd looked young for his age for years, but that was beginning to change, some acne scars stark on his cheeks and gray stubble in his permanent 5 o'clock shadow. But he liked how he was looking a little bit ragged these days—up until he was fourteen years old or so, people had mistaken him for a girl because of his soft features and long, curly hair.

He used to be as slight as a girl too, and had stressed over the Charles Atlas ads in his comic books that depicted a ninety-eight-pound weakling incapable of defending his girlfriend from a bully. Hud, only twelve, would sit with his copy of *Ghost Rider* open in his lap, afraid that he'd never be able to protect a wife and children. He imagined a world in which stronger men than you lurked around every corner, poised to thieve everything that's yours.

Hud tried to think of all the possible worst-case scenarios, all the repercussions for breaking Tuesday's hand. A restraining order; maybe a change in visitation rights. Tuesday's father would be further disappointed, and Rose would raise her hackles. It was like a flu or a fever, all this worry. Hud would just have to wait for it to ease away on its own.

Hud went to Augustine's room, where she rested against pillows, flipping through a magazine. The room smelled of vanilla from the candles that burned on the windowsill. He sat on the edge of the mattress, his back to Augustine.

"I went to the doctor last spring because of some allergies," he said, "and he told me he'd just been reading an article in a medical journal about some breakthrough inoculation that would allow people to live to be two hundred years old. The science is almost there, he said. But you'd have to be a baby for the inoculation to work. So you and I will be eighty years old, five minutes from death, while these kids have two hundred years ahead of them. When my doctor told me that, I thought, *How shitty*. I thought, *How unfair*. But then I thought about how fearful you'd be, you know, of accidental death. Dying young would be that much more tragic, because instead of losing sixty years, or whatever, you'd lose more than a hundred and sixty. Then I thought, Is that something we should even want? To live to be two hundred? We don't cherish our every day now. We get it into our head that we'll just go on and on and on. Imagine what it'll be like if you think you have some mini-eternity on earth. If you think you'll have all the time in the world to do what you want. You'd never get anything done."

Augustine kissed Hud's neck, touching her fingertips to his spine. "Hopefully it will only be for the rich," she said. "Who wants to be poor for two hundred years?"

Hud's insomnia, usually fueled by too much late-night coffee, sometimes lent itself easily to morbid fantasy. Some nights Nina was the dead one, tempted into a car with lollipops, then left in a ditch with a broken neck. But most often it was Gatling's death he expected to hear described by some stranger on the phone. He could imagine the Daughters of God gone up in smoke after a church bombing, or assassinated while plucking banjos at a prolife rally. And it didn't matter when a night passed without a dreadful word of news, because it could just as well come the next night, or the night after that, or really at any minute of the day. There was no time that a father could reasonably take a breath of relief.

"Ooooh, boy, you're way off someplace else," Augustine said, flopping back on the pillows. She dug a Benson & Hedges from a crumpled pack on the windowsill next to the bed and lit it with the flame from a votive.

"I'm sorry," Hud said. "It's just been a weird night." He lay down beside her, and they passed the cigarette back and forth, both staring at the smoke that rose to the ceiling.

"You shouldn't smoke," he said.

"It's OK," she said. "I drink green tea all day. It has antioxidants."

"Huh?"

"The antioxidants neutralize free radicals. Stops cancer."

"Gotcha," he said. He decided he'd wait for Augustine to finish her cigarette and fall asleep, then he'd go back to the sofa and give some thought to the song coming together in his head. "A Tea Party with Radicals," he might call it, and it might be about how he hadn't kissed any woman other than Tuesday in eighteen years.

But Hud fell asleep before Augustine did, with longing for the suit he hadn't bought from a vintage shop when he was young. It had been a shiny blue-green thing with skinny lapels, very Steve McQueen, and it had been only thirty bucks. For years Hud had regretted not buying it, the suit showing up in some of his songs as a symbol of tawdry dreams lost. It was what he had pictured himself wearing for the cover of his third album, *Late Afternoon on the Moon*.

̇̇̇̇̇̇̇̇̇

O Z Z I E , hungover, lay on the concrete floor of his studio drinking yesterday's espresso. He'd spent the early evening before at the Wiggle Room with Tuesday, guzzling the wine they sold for cheap, doing some shots, until she'd left him behind to go listen to Hud play piano.

The church window Oz had broken with a pumpkin days and days before leaned against a wall of the studio, mostly untouched, far from repair. He could barely look at the broken window and all its dizzying biblical allusion. There was much too much of what there should be, all the disparate characters too intimate with each other. Jesus stepped lithely atop a frothy curl of a Red Sea wave freshly parted by Moses. Mary Magdalene, her loose robe revealing an infinitesimal peek of pink nipple, looked to be doing a table dance at the Last Supper.

Though Noah's wife, who had appeared to be adrift not on an ark but on a rib of Jonah's whale, had not been damaged by the pumpkin, Ozzie had delicately broken her away with a small hammer. He took the shard from his pocket now and touched the jagged edge to a cut on his forearm, a cut that started minor from when he knocked a bottle of aftershave into the sink. In the days since breaking Noah's wife from the window, he'd kept his wound fresh, sometimes reopening it and making it bleed a thick drop of dark blood. Oz liked the idea of regressing, his old grief manifesting itself in some new, twisted manner. The act of slicing his skin with Noah's wife felt a private abuse, made him blush with the thought of it, as if with some adolescent sexual shame. He put the cut to his mouth now, tasting, as part of the ritual.

He began to drift off to sleep, still on the hard floor, the room dark with a brewing storm. Oz remembered his wife one spring in a lawn chair, a bird above her jumping from branch to branch on the flowering crabapple, rattling the leaves, sending the blossoms petal by petal to carpet the ground and the lap of Jenny's robe. With a swatter of torn wire mesh, she batted lazily at the fat flies that bobbed and wove above her. It had been during a brief, deceptive spurt of health, when all could convince themselves she still might live. Jenny uncorked a bottle of red peach nectar Oz had brewed himself, and she reclined to reread *Marjorie Morningstar,* a book she had loved as a girl.

Oz woke after only a minute to the sound of silverware jingling against a plate, and to footsteps on the brick walk that wound from the kitchen to the studio. Every morning Charlotte left a breakfast of grapes and French bread and fresh espresso outside Oz's studio door, then skittered away without knocking. Lately, for maybe the last few weeks, she'd been leaving peculiar little gifts on the plate, like a ballerina broken off a music box and a matchbook from a defunct club called the Blithe Spirit on some street in Kansas City. She'd once left him a half-smoked Havana cigar that he smoked the rest of the way while flipping through an antique *Playboy* she had left the day before that.

Oz stood to peek out the window, to watch Charlotte leave the plate, then duck beneath the dried trumpet vine on her way out the back gate.

Her palm up and out to check for raindrops, Charlotte stopped to open an umbrella, baby-blue and see-through, Oz had never noticed before. She wore a new secondhand white denim jacket, a flurry of butterflies appliquéd all up the back. She had taken to accumulating junk again, Oz was pleased to see. He was anxious to go up and snoop in her room, to search for all the signs of life.

Charlotte had been a fat baby but had grown much too thin, Oz worried. As he watched her step into the back alley, he ticked off in his mind all of her frailties.

Oz had spent years assuring himself that most people survived into old age, that the odds of losing Charlotte too were too slim to fret over. Some days he could even convince himself that Jenny's early death guaranteed a long life for his little girl. Because of those lovely odds. Fate, cruelty, even disease, had some decorum. But then darkness would settle in his mind, the cold certainty of disorder reasserting itself.

"It is not ours to question God's intentions," the nearly decrepit minister had intoned at Jenny's funeral, his hands trembling with palsy against the onionskin pages of his Bible. Above him was the stained glass, and the gold-checked pattern of the long blue dress of Noah's wife that Jenny had always admired. "No matter how mysterious, how seemingly heartless, sad, vicious." He practically spat the last word, maybe fed up with comforting the victims of God's childish wrath. Maybe the minister felt he'd grown old enough to scold the Lord.

During the church service for Jenny's funeral, the sun shone just at the other side of the stained-glass window, sending all the confusion of colors to speckle the white of the lilies and the silvery alabaster of the casket closed at the altar.

Why a white box? Oz wondered then, looking away from the altar, away from the lilies. *Why did we choose a white box?* It was the absolutely wrong color, wasn't it? Why a box at all? Oz imagined a fairy-tale burial, preparing Jenny's ruined body himself with perfumes and oils, and rose petals for the bed of her grave beneath a peach tree. He would have gently put her in the ground, just her body in a simple summer dress, her wedding ring on her finger.

Charlotte had sat next to Ozzie in the front pew but rested her head against the breast of Jenny's sister, Ellie. Ellie held her arm around Charlotte, pressing her cheek to the top of Charlotte's head. Oz cleared his throat, sniffled quick, lifted his finger to wipe away a tear with a movement he hoped was inconspicuous. His finger scratched against stubble—no one had even told him to shave, and he hadn't shaved for days. Had he even combed his hair? Oz didn't want Charlotte to know he was crying, but in seconds his body and breath shook with sobbing. He slouched forward, his tears quickly soaking the cuffs of his shirtsleeves. He felt Charlotte's hand on his, but he couldn't look her way.

Oz's weeping grew so loud that even the ancient minister, who'd likely witnessed every conceivable variety of grief, went silent with shock. Oz felt his daughter draw her hand away, and he leaned forward to press his forehead against the wood railing in front of him.

"Scootch," Hud said, having come up the side aisle from somewhere in the back. He knocked his hip against Ozzie, making him make room at the end of the pew. Hud, in a black suit and blue tie, put one arm around Oz's shoulder, pulling Oz up to sit straight, and with his other hand he made a fist that he pounded lightly against Oz's chest. Hud squeezed his shoulder so hard, Oz had a fat bruise for a week. "Cry your eyes out, kiddo," Hud whispered in Oz's ear. Hud whispered some other things too, but Oz couldn't really hear the words; he was comforted nonetheless by the movement of his friend's breath on his ear and his cheek.

Oz opened the studio door and knelt next to the plate of breakfast Charlotte had left him. Before he could even nibble on a corner of toast, he was startled at the sound of a crash behind him. The noise was so loud, he stumbled out the door, his hands covering his head, certain the whole feeble studio was tumbling to the ground. He looked down to see a softball roll out the door and knock over the dented espresso pot. *The church window,* he thought, afraid to look back. But when he did turn around, and he saw the softball had broken only the back studio window facing the alley, he was somewhat disappointed. In the few seconds after the crash, he had pictured the window mercifully beyond repair. He could have claimed to the church board to have been near completion. He could have held the softball up as evidence.

Ozzie heard fast footsteps in the alley, and he ran to the fence. A wood bat had been abandoned to lie on the pavement. Oz looked up and down the alley, seeing no one, then noticed a skinny girl trying to hide behind an even skinnier tree in a neighboring yard. He saw her scraped knee and her laceless basketball sneaker, her boy's tube sock bunched around her ankle.

"Come on out from there," Oz said, trying to conceal the angry shake in his voice. "I'm not mad. You're not in trouble. I just want to give you your ball back, you little asshole." That slipped out, that *little asshole*, and the child, frightened, leapt from behind the tree and sped off. It was Millie, the terrible girl who had spent her summer huffing Freon from people's air conditioners. One of her braided pigtails had unraveled.

Ozzie jumped over his fence and took off after her. But he stopped abruptly when Millie's summer dress caught on a protruding nail at the end of the alley. She frantically but gently tugged at her dress, trying to release herself from the corner of a shed without tearing the light fabric. The dress looked to be brand new, still bright yellow with a pattern of apples still bright red. If she tore it, her mother would be furious. But who was her mother? Who was her father? Millie was ubiquitous about town, but for all he knew, she lived in that ramshackle house in the country all alone.

Ozzie approached Millie, slowly tossing the ball up, then catching it, slick as a schoolyard bully. He had no idea what to do or say, or what exactly he wanted. But it felt like a fatherly instinct, this cornering her and toying with her nerves.

"Did you act alone?" he asked. "Did someone pitch the ball to you? Or did you just throw it up and aim for my window?"

"I was aiming for that dog," Millie said, pointing across the street to a pit bull resting in the grass. The dog had seemed so old even when it was young that its owners had named it Methuseleh. He lay too lethargic to snap at the flies that mistook him for dead and hovered around his snout.

Millie's intentions disturbed Oz but also intrigued him. If only Charlotte's treachery had ever been so simple. Charlotte longed to float from reach, to teach Oz of her irretrievability, while here stood Millie, caught on a nail, dumb and unrepentant, confessing to plots of animal cruelty. Millie's delinquency was an age-old cliché; there were millions of books and pamphlets on how to crush the spirit of a child like her, any number of pills to coax her into a manageable pliancy.

Just as Oz was about to counsel the girl, to ask, *What did you hope to gain from braining a near-dead dog?* Millie loosened herself from the nail and darted around the corner. Though Oz, long-legged, should have been able to outrun her, Millie was wily and seemed to know all the neighborhood's avenues of escape. She ducked through a rip in chain link, crawled beneath the broken picket of a fence. When Oz would stop, bent, puffing, certain he'd lost her, he'd catch a glimpse of her down the street disappearing behind a hedge or rolling beneath a parked car and out the other side.

Oz kept running, but he had lost any interest in grabbing hold of Millie's one pigtail. Millie held no answers of any kind. There was no recompense he could seek from such a wild-haired, undomesticated thing. He kept running because he hadn't run that much, that far, in years.

Oz had mostly forgotten about Millie by the time he'd reached the town square, by the time the clouds had grown blacker and the wind had worked up. He was still running, but others were running too, hurrying to get to their cars as the clouds broke. He could hear the flat brass of the high school band trumpeting and trombone-ing in the gazebo; their sheet music blew across the lawn. The flea-market merchants folded their tables and stands, boxing up their wares. A woman who sold antique Christmas ornaments hurriedly wrapped the blown glass in tissue, the wind knocking a few off her tabletop to the grass.

Tuesday must be here, he thought, when he saw a few children, the first raindrops of the storm smearing their face painting, their little unicorns and daisies dripping down their cheeks. He stopped running, his sides aching, and he forced the softball that he'd held tight in his fist into the pocket of his jacket. He saw Tuesday already across the street, beneath an awning. She wasn't watching the chaos of the flea market but rather looking in through the window of the storefront. As

Oz approached, he saw that, inside, several girls of various heights and sizes spun in amateur pirouettes.

"I thought we all quit smoking years ago," Oz said, holding out his hand for Tuesday's cigarette. He took a drag, then gave it back. "After Jenny died."

"We all quit *everything* when Jenny died," Tuesday said. "Wave at Nina," and Oz did, and Nina waved back, beaming, hopping up and down in her leotard, her short ponytail bouncing. She was all in yellow, with some feathery thing in her hair, looking quite duckish. Ozzie adored Nina, and she seemed to like him—she giggled whenever he tugged on her earlobe and when he called her Swee'pea. But whenever Tuesday and Oz got together, they abandoned Nina to a relative, and they slunk off to someplace out of the way to drink scotch and watch motley strangers try to pick each other up. Sometimes Oz and Tuesday kissed, but they had yet to make it to bed together.

"Let me buy you ladies a breakfast steak at the Waffle Iron," Oz said. "After Nina's little dance lesson. They have a special till noon on Saturdays."

"We're just going to go home," Tuesday said, dropping the cigarette, then rubbing her forehead. Oz longed to follow her back to her house, for the three of them to play Go Fish at the kitchen table as they drank hot chocolate and the rain fell loudly on the roof. This secret fling, or whatever it was, had started only a few weeks before, with Tuesday in a miniskirt, her bare legs goose-bumped, filling the cab of his pickup with soft perfume and nervous laughter, but it was beginning to seem a little dark and a little desperate. After every date, after dropping Tuesday off at her house, Oz went home feeling slightly nauseated from having drunk one too many, and from the bar's smokiness caught in his clothes and in his hair and in the beard he'd been letting grow thick.

Oz was about to suggest that he could get the steaks to go, but suddenly Tuesday held up her right hand from where she'd been hiding it behind her back. She had a plastic cast over it and partway up her forearm. "Last night, when I took Nina to hear Hud at the club, I guess I got . . . well, I *know*, I don't *guess*, I *know* I got a little hammered. And Hud tried to get my keys from me, and I ended up breaking . . . just fracturing, my hand. I went to the doctor early this morning. He said six weeks with this."

"How the hell did you fracture . . ."

"I wouldn't let go of the keys, and Hud squeezed too hard, I guess."

"That piece of shit," Oz muttered, looking up the street, trying to remember where on the square Hud now lived.

"You don't get to defend me, Ozzie," Tuesday said matter-of-factly, crossing her arms, leaning back against the window. As the storm worked up, the fluorescent lights of the dance studio were all that lit the sidewalk where they stood. "The only reason I'm telling you all about it is because I don't want to be secretive and weird, like some battered wife protecting her husband. I'm not an idiot who has a warped perspective on things. I'm as much to blame as Hud is. I mean, more so. I mean, Hud's not to blame at all. And aren't you tired of fighting him anyway? You two have been duking it out since you were fifteen. And Hud can't stand to fight back anymore, because he's heartsick about you."

"Jesus," Oz said. "Sorry." The cigarette on the sidewalk still smoldered, so Oz picked it up, wiped the filter on his jacket, and took another drag. He looked inside to where Nina intently followed the moves of her instructor demonstrating some kind of cha-cha-cha. True, Ozzie and Hud had fought an awful lot over the years, and had often gone months without speaking, but their disappointment in each other had always been brotherly. Even after they both got married and had kids too young, they would get together alone in Hud's basement and have liquor-fueled discussions about the things they suspected they might be missing out on. Oz had thought even then that Hud should be happier with Tuesday. For years Hud's discontent had made Oz want to clock him in the jaw, and from time to time he'd done just that.

"What's he heartsick about?" Oz asked.

"Don't tell me you don't know," Tuesday said, taking the cigarette for a drag, then giving it back. "You don't know that you've been a wreck for years?"

"Not a wreck," Oz said softly. "Not for years." Months ago, when Tuesday's son dated Oz's daughter, Ozzie would sit in his living room alone late at night, jealous of his own child for having a semblance of a life. Some nights he went so far as to keep an alarm clock in his hand for when he nodded off in his easy chair, woozy from his after-dinner nips of whiskey. When he woke he'd go to Hud and Tuesday's house in a sleepy rage. It had calmed him to disrupt their home in the middle of the night, to shove Hud around. He'd loved how Tuesday, usually in a pair of men's pajamas, would gently but firmly demand quiet and order, reminding them all that Nina still slept. Hud, mad, would go back to bed, but Oz and Tuesday would wait up together, drinking decaf and watching a movie.

"I don't have any room to talk," Tuesday said. "I'm probably a wreck these days too. I didn't want to get all depressed at home this morning and just stew in my hangover, so I brought Nina to dance lessons and sat on the square thinking I could do some face painting." She kicked at her little green toolbox at her feet. "But I have to use my left hand, so all these kids ended up with ugly splotches on their faces. They'd look in the mirror, so excited, then, just, this look of horror."

Oz chuckled, taking her good hand in his, running his thumb over her fingers.

"Probably shouldn't hold my hand here," Tuesday said, not pulling her hand away.

"I won't break it," Oz said.

"Very funny," she said, not smiling, still not pulling her hand away. "I don't want Nina to see us like this."

"That's dumb," he said. "Why the hell not?"

"Because, you know, maybe Nina will get upset, and maybe she'll tell Hud, and maybe he'll get upset. Then maybe in the middle of the night some night, he'll just steal her. He'll run away with her. He's threatened to do it. And what has he got to lose, really? Nothing."

"Hud wouldn't do that. Would he?"

"He would love to go MIA. To go underground. Sounds perfect to him, I bet." Tuesday took her hand from Ozzie's. "When you have kids, you have to work at a divorce just like you have to work at a marriage."

"So get back together with him," he said. He mostly meant to taunt, but he did believe Tuesday and Hud had a kind of melancholy love affair that could easily have lasted them into old age, if they'd only bothered to get to know each other better.

The door to the dance studio swung open, with girls and their mothers stepping out into the rain, lifting their jackets up to cover their heads. Oz looked inside and saw that Nina sat on the floor intently fussing with a buckle on her dance shoe. He took Tuesday's face in his hands then and kissed her, and kept kissing her, and she kissed back. Some smart-aleck girl in a pink leotard wolf-whistled as she passed, causing another girl to burst out laughing.

Oz stepped away from Tuesday, winked at her, then ran into the rain. He kept running until he ran out of breath, until his clothes became too sopping wet, his jeans weighing down his legs. He didn't think about anything but getting home and the ache of his muscles. Back in his studio, panting, he peeled off all his clothes as quickly as he could, desperate to feel dry. As he stood there entirely naked, his long, wet hair and beard dripped water down his chest. He suddenly felt the symptoms of a cold cloud his head, so he dug beneath his workbench for a bottle of VSOP he'd gotten one Christmas from an aunt. He started a fire in the wood-burning stove in the corner, tearing out pages of the old *Playboy* and wadding them up for kindling. As a page burned, a model in a bubble bath, with bubblegum-pink skin, sizzled away. The magazine was from the early 1960s, and the woman wore thick eye shadow and a piled-high hairdo and an expression of wholesome delight. There was nothing come-hither about her.

"Life goes so quickly," Ozzie's father had once said in a kindly tone. But the old man was wrong. When you lose something you care about with every bit of your being, every day after feels endless.

Ozzie bent over and took the softball from the pocket of his jacket on the floor. He stood, looking at the stained-glass window, tossing the ball up, then catching it. With the light of the fire flickering in the glass, Oz thought he saw something not quite right among all the biblical goings-on—a little red devil slipping up the skirt of an angel, the tongue of a glowing-eyed serpent lapping at Adam's fig leaf. Sodom and Gomorrah flashed and glittered with a promising and inviting Vegas neon.

The whole beautiful, sinful spectacle, as quick and as practically invisible as it was, made the window almost worth saving. But not quite. Ozzie wound up and pitched the softball. The ball crashed through the glass, hit the back wall, then bounced back to Oz. He picked it up again and threw it at what remained.

You need closure, everyone had said when Jenny died. *Once you find closure, you'll move on.* He had never before wanted any such thing.

11.

💧💧💧💧💧💧💧💧

A FEW nights after Tuesday's wrist got cracked, Hud was at the house, picking up Nina for the evening. Tuesday hadn't blamed Hud for what had happened, but she nonetheless made a little spectacle of her injury, wincing whenever she lifted her fractured hand off the pillow in her lap.

Nina decided to wear her kimono in honor of Hud's gift of a boxful of drink parasols he'd snagged for her from the club. On the back of the slick black robe, Tuesday had hand-painted a coiling, red-eyed dragon with several handlebar moustaches. It held a lit firecracker in one of its many fists.

"Go find your shoes," Tuesday said, drinking coffee from a thermos lid.

"In China," Nina told Hud, popping open and closed a puny paper umbrella, "they used to bend babies' feet so they could fit into teensy shoes. People there have feet like dolls," she said, cheerful, as if she thought them lucky.

"And run a comb through that rat nest," Tuesday said, sighing. "Do I have to do all your thinking for you?"

With Nina in her bedroom selecting socks and shoes, Hud said, "Why don't you come with us to the drive-in, Day? It'll be nice. I have the bus, we'll sit on the roof." Ever since Hud's car had given up the ghost on that back highway weeks before, he'd been driving the school bus everywhere, with the bus manager's tentative OK.

"You are not taking that child up on the roof of that bus," Tuesday said, rolling her eyes like she was so bored from her years of correcting him.

"I hate you, Mommy," Nina objected, shouting from down the hall.

"You better hope to God that's not true," Tuesday yelled back. Then she said, quieter, mostly just to Hud with a little laugh, "Because if it is, you've got some long, hard years of misery ahead of you."

Hud snickered and put the stick of a drink parasol between his teeth and chewed on it, like chewing a toothpick. "So let's say we talk about what we're not talking about," he said.

"What aren't we talking about?" she said.

"I think things went real easy-like the other night," Hud said, "up until I broke your hand. We did kiss a little, you know."

"Hud, I was so . . ."

"Yeah, drunk, so drunk, I know. But I wasn't drunk at all."

"Yeah," she said. "And a person might say you took advantage of me."

"Might say that, I guess." They just looked at each other for a few beats, then Tuesday took another sip of her coffee. "And it felt pretty right," he said. "Felt so right that now

I'm feeling inclined to leaning over and kissing you some more."

"Don't kiss me," she said, and she meant it, and Hud thought that was kind of a dirty trick, her taking his old line, *Don't kiss me,* and turning it around on him. But he could tell, from the way she started gnawing nervously on her thumbnail, that she hadn't meant any real harm by saying it. She just simply didn't want to kiss him.

None of these things were his anymore, Hud thought, looking around the room. He touched his fingers to the top of a cigar box on the end table, a box that had held the Churchills he'd handed out at Nina's birth. He closed his eyes, as if divining. "A pocket knife with a picture of Marilyn Monroe in a pink swimsuit and high heels that I bought at a gas station just down the hill from Mount Rushmore," he said. "The glass eye from a teddy bear you had when you were a kid. A snap-on ribbon Nina wore when she was a baby, when her hair was thin. A piece of red string from who knows what." He opened his eyes and smiled at Tuesday, not bothering to check the inside of the box. "Ask me anything," he said, slouching, resting his head against the back of the sofa. "Ask me what's under your bed, why don't you. What's in the hall closet. Looking for something? I'll tell you where it is."

Tuesday cringed as she moved her wrist again, as she turned back to yell, "Nina, hurry up. It'll be dark soon. They're going to start the movie."

"I'm changing again," Nina yelled back.

Tuesday rolled her eyes, then rested her head too against the sofa.

"I'm not going to kiss you," Hud said, "so don't worry. I don't even *want* to kiss you now."

"Hud, I'm sorry, I . . . that I . . . I mean, if I . . . oh, I don't know." She said, pulling at a stitch in a sofa cushion, "I should have my head examined," half under her breath, as if Hud wasn't sitting right there. "What business did I have, for example, getting all dolled up and going to see you play piano? Taking Nina out so late? I don't want us to fall back into something just because it's easier than doing something else. I don't want to ever kiss you again, and I don't ever want to sleep with you anymore. We shouldn't end up back together just because we don't want to be bothered with improving our lives."

"Never another kiss?" Hud asked with a wink, a bluesy tune coming together in his mind, a song he'd call "I Should Have My Head Examined." Though Tuesday was telling him that there was no longer any chance for them, Hud really didn't mind it as a topic of discussion. Talking about how they wouldn't be having sex was somehow sexually satisfying.

Hud and Nina didn't go to the top of the bus, but they did crawl onto the hood, and they looked up at the stars instead of at the movie—one of their favorites, *Your Cheatin' Heart,* with George Hamilton as Hank Williams. Nina, looking like an Eskimo in her hooded parka with its fur trim, lay flat on her back, popping Hot Tamales.

"We're a lot alike, you and me," Nina said, sounding pensive.

"Why do you say that?" Hud asked. Some dried corn-husks from a neighboring field caught a twist of wind and fluttered off like birds.

"Lots of reasons," was all Nina said then.

"Maybe we're Siamese twins separated at birth," Hud said, pushing down his pale blue Foster Grants and looking at Nina over the tops of them. He had put on the sunglasses to look cute for the new concessions girl who had mixed Hud and Nina some hot cocoa. Her name was Dot, and she wore baby-chick-yellow nail polish. Every time Hud saw her, she was holding a wrapped bomb pop to her forehead and complaining of a migraine. "Siamese twins born years apart to different mothers," he said. "Stranger things have happened."

"You ever going to move back in with us?" she said.

"Probably not," Hud said. From his pocket he took the dried bud of a hibiscus bloom he'd picked from a plant on Tuesday's porch, its closed petals as soft as a powdery moth. He opened Nina's fist and placed the bud in her palm. Nina, tiny, seemed barely to ever grow. Gatling had needed bigger clothes constantly; every few months some shirt or pair of pants was packed away practically new. But Nina had been wearing that same parka winter after winter.

"Look," Nina said, tapping at the glass of her mood ring as she closed her fist around the soft bloom, "it's turning green. That means I want you to marry Mom and not Dot."

"I'm not going to marry Dot," Hud said.

"Grandpa says Dot is as mean as a cockfight," Nina said. "Do you ever think about getting a dog?"

"Dogs make me sad," Hud said. "They have sad faces. Even when they're happy to see you, they seem lonely. I don't think they like not being human."

When Nina finally fell asleep, softly snoring, her head on his leg, Hud sat up, his back against the bus's front window, and counted the parked cars—far too few to make the night even nearly profitable for Red. In an El Camino, alone, was Chet Blake, the officer who'd been the one to investigate the murder of the Schrock boys. He'd seen the boys poisoned and blue in their pj's, tucked into their racing-car sheets, on the first morning of November.

Hud began to feel sleepy too, the music of the movie working into his brief dream about him and Nina on a creaking Ferris wheel. When he snapped back awake, his sleepy vision adjusting to the blue tint of his sunglasses, he thought he spotted two watery, weeping figures on the steps of a basement saloon. When Hud squinted, the figures flickered away entirely, the shadows lifting to merge with the haze of cigarette smoke. Though he saw nothing else extraordinary, by the end of the movie Hud had turned the image around and around in his head, determining that he'd seen the figures in Halloween costumes, masks in their hands, their heads bowed in deadly remorse.

PART THREE

♫♫♫

A S word circulated that the Schrock boys, smudgy but clearly miserable, would occasionally flicker across the screen of the Rivoli Sky-Vue during *Your Cheatin' Heart,* people drove in to catch a glimpse of what might be a holy sight. Some brought their binoculars and opera glasses and sat on the hoods of their cars, attentive to every unfocused corner of every frame. They all wanted to be haunted.

By the end of the week business had tripled, and Red took to showing *Your Cheatin' Heart* on a continual loop from dusk until dawn. A reporter for the county newspaper managed to randomly snap a shot of the movie that, once run on pulpy newsprint with its bleeding ink, fueled speculation further—in a scene in the Opry, two tiny specters could almost be deciphered among the shadows of the band.

Hud had no faith in the supernatural, but he expertly orchestrated the whole spectacle, manipulating everything with an ease that inspired him. Maybe there was a profession to be had in designing miracles, he thought. For example, say a slumlord's property is about to be condemned. You simply hire someone to spot a vision, to see the contours of the Virgin in a streak of rust or Christ in a bloodstain on the hallway carpet, call one of the local unethicals at the daily rag, and in days the state diocese gives the dump its seal of authenticity and the slumlord is swimming in donations and offers to buy.

The first night of Hud's sighting, he went to the dinged-up pink Cadillac that old Mrs. Winter had once won for power-selling Mary Kay. Mrs. Winter was a regular at the Rivoli, lonely and long husbandless, and Hud asked her if she had seen what he had seen. Convinced she had, Mrs. Winter was moved to speak of her discovery during her daily community news report on the town's AM radio broadcast.

Later Hud sneaked one of those silk-flower memorial wreaths with a stuffed teddy bear at its center, intended for the decoration of the graves of children, into the dirt at the base of the drive-in movie screen. By Wednesday of that week, a few other wreaths had popped up, but it wasn't until Thursday, when Hud conceived his pièce de résistance, that the shrine really caught on—he sprinkled some candy among the wreaths, seeding the shrine with a couple handfuls of gummy bears, jawbreakers, Cherry Clan, Lemonhead. By Friday, still a few weeks before Halloween, all the stores in town had been nearly depleted of their stock of sweets, and the ground beneath the screen glittered with the foil wrappers of chocolate bars and the cellophane of hard candy.

"A genius gimmick," said Dot, the concession-stand worker with the migraines, who turned out not to be mean at all, despite Nina's report. She was merely sullen, having lost her own little girl in a custody battle. After her divorce Dot had taken up with a drug dealer and gotten sent to the York women's prison for two months; her ex, a successful drywall contractor who had remarried, had snagged a pricey lawyer, and Dot now only had limited visitation rights. But she'd had some intensive rehab and was now clean as a whistle.

"Genius," the Widow Bosanko scoffed. "The whole thing gives me the willies." Hud had once again been invited back into the office for dinner, and they all sat around the desk eating a roasted chicken and some fries made from the sweet potatoes the Widow had dug from her backyard garden. "We're capitalizing on a tragedy," she said, leaning forward to refill everyone's coffee cup. "We should at least not charge at the gate. It's like blood money, really, isn't it?"

Dot began rubbing her temples, another headache apparently tapping at her brain, and Hud, his hand out of sight of Red and the Widow, wormed a finger through the rip at the calf of her fishnet stocking. With his peripheral vision, Hud could see Dot meekly smiling at him. Hud had yet to ask Dot out, but he had stolen a quick kiss a few days before as they both leaned in to examine the insides of the Slush Puppy machine to determine the source of its rattling. Her lips were sticky and sour-appley from the lollipop she'd been licking.

Ever since hearing her story about losing her girl, Hud had felt the little tug of an infatuation developing. He would entertain notions of running off with Dot, the two of them getting hitched in a quickie midnight ceremony. Sometimes, in a certain state of mind, Hud could convince himself that he could live without Nina. He'd imagine a life sunny without Tuesday's moodiness and her back-and-forth affection, without her using Nina as retaliation for whatever she thought he'd ever done that was so terrible.

"It's not as bad as all that," Red said. But for the Widow's benefit, Red acted sheepish, concealing his enthusiasm for the recent upturn in business. Hud knew Red was thrilled to have a captive audience of sorts, to have an opportunity to conduct a citywide cinematic education. He had plans to play, in between showings of *Your Cheatin' Heart*, others from the vast library he'd accumulated from his years of working as a movie distributor on the West Coast—that night he had scheduled *Paris, Texas* and *Rocco and His Brothers*. Tomorrow night he'd sneak in *Mikey and Nicky* and *Pickup on South Street*.

The Widow stopped complaining of bad karma a few days later when the long, deluxe tour bus of the Daughters of God squeezed down the narrow brick streets of the town square. Hud had contacted them via an address he'd found on their website. In a letter (signed only "A Good Citizen") to Sunny, Harmony, Dolly, and June, Hud explained the circumstances surrounding the murder of the Schrock boys. He described the celebration on the night of Robbie Schrock's state execution and the Sunday-night miracle of the boys' appearance on the movie screen. "They were sorrowful there in *Your Cheatin' Heart*," Hud wrote. "We should do what we can to deliver those angels to heaven." He sugared his letter with a Christian zeal, turning the Daughters' own words back on them—he used a line from their song "The Lord's Lovely Lips" about the healing properties of heartfelt music in order to appeal to their vanity and to their sense of obligation as missionaries.

Though the tour bus of the Daughters of God growled loudly on the street just below his bedroom window, the noise of the engine shimmying a teacup of cigarette butts off the sill to shatter on the wood floor, Hud slept through the singers' arrival. He wasn't even allowed a moment of excitement upon seeing the bus, not a second of fast heartbeat in antici-pation of putting his arms around his son again—he slept un-til the Widow called to tell him that the Daughters of God were now parked on the drive-in lot, but Gatling was not among them.

"It seems he's run away from them too," the Widow said.

13.

ᛁᛁᛁᛁᛁ

T H E Saint Ignatius Methodist Church put up the Daughters of God in an old sanctuary of blood-red brick.

"Nobody's supposed to know that's where they're stay-ing," Junior told Charlotte the night after the tour bus pulled into town. "I was sworn to secrecy."

"By who?" Charlotte asked, but Junior didn't answer. They sat on the hood of Junior's car, in a harvested cornfield next to the Rivoli Sky-Vue, waiting for the Daughters of God to take to their makeshift stage near the drive-in's screen. They'd brought binoculars and parked far from the gathering crowd to avoid paying for a ticket, but they could still smell the rancid sweetness thick in the air. An unseasonal heat had spent all afternoon melting the candy that the locals in their pilgrimages had sprinkled in the dead grass of the drive-in.

It wasn't quite dark yet. Junior leaned back against the car's front window as Charlotte assisted with his horror-show makeup. In the basement of the Holy Three Church, the youth group staged a nightly haunted house, every vignette some mean, grisly sermon. Before the guide pulled back each sheet, he'd describe the agony of the person behind the curtain—the suicide among the orange-cellophane flames of hell; the drug abuser pincushioned head to toe with needles and syringes. Ever since the first of October Junior had played the part of an AIDS patient most nights until midnight, the lines and sexy hollows of his face darkened for gauntness, putty applied to his chest and arms for mock flesh-rot.

"Don't you feel like a complete asshole doing that haunted-house thingie?" Charlotte asked. "It's kind of cruel, don't you think? Especially since so many of those church boys are probably gay. Soft voices. Sweet to their moms. Infatuated with Jesus. A bunch of closet cases. But maybe that's what you are. A closet case."

As Charlotte carefully penciled in a pair of crow's feet that spider-legged down the sides of his face, Junior read an unauthorized biography called *The Brides of Jesus: The Divine Maidenhood of the Daughters of God*. He looked up from the book to wink at Charlotte. "You know," he said, "I wouldn't be surprised if I was," then returned to reading.

But Charlotte knew he wasn't remotely gay. The other day one of the youth group girls told Charlotte that she spotted Junior crawling into the backseat of Imagine Baxter's white Olds parked in the alley behind the church. They'd both been still in makeup, Junior riddled with painted-on lesions, Imagine's face whitewashed a bloodless skim-milk blue—in her skit Imagine was a teenager driven mad by the ghost of her aborted baby.

Charlotte shaded Junior's pout with gray lipstick. She freckled his throat with a bruise-colored rouge. Though Junior was on the bony side, he always looked shockingly healthy, his skin a hearty pink.

"I think you're losing a little interest in me, Junior," Charlotte said. At that Junior put down his book and tenderly kissed her throat, then unbuttoned her blouse to kiss her nipple, flicking his tongue pretty expertly for such a goody-good Jesus freak. She was falling completely out of love with Junior, she suspected. She'd spent weeks ridding herself of all the tiniest things—she'd even sold her half-used lipsticks and eye shadows. But lately she'd been haunting the thrift shops again, wasting her money on junk like costume jewelry with chipped rhinestones and party dresses with missing sequins. She'd even permed her hair, though the curls had already gone limp from all the recent rainy days.

"I've heard rumors about you and Imagine Baxter," Charlotte said, only slightly aroused by his running his fingers over the skin of her stomach. She'd been nervous about bringing the rumor up to Junior, for fear he'd readily confess. But Charlotte guessed she needed something dramatic like that to either break them up or set them into that slow, painful start of collapse.

"Imagine's a mess," Junior said. "We've only talked to each other. I've only given the girl a tiny, little bit of advice." He took Charlotte's hand to hold it against his chest. She wondered if this was a trick he'd read about somewhere—make your girl feel your beating heart as you tell her your lies, and she'll believe them more easily. It wasn't entirely ineffective.

"I'm a mess too," Charlotte said, whining in a way she instantly wished she hadn't. "She's not half the mess I am." *I'm falling back in love with Gatling,* she was tempted to say. *How's that for a mess?* But Junior wouldn't care; no one knew where Gatling was. Word had quickly gotten around that Gatling had abandoned the Daughters of God somewhere along the way.

As Junior slipped his fingers into her jeans to touch the lacy waist of her underwear, his easy, smooth, precise moves only made her miss Gatling more. Gatling had never been so graceful with her when they fooled around in the back of the Pontiac Gatling borrowed from Hud. He lumbered around, pinching and bruising her in the process, knocking his teeth against hers when he kissed. He sucked on her tongue too hard, and tried to jimmy himself into her too soon and too fast.

"Why have you stopped asking me to marry you all the time?" Charlotte asked as Junior kissed his way down to her stomach.

"I got tired of fighting your dad," he said. But Charlotte knew that wasn't true. In the last few weeks Ozzie had stopped noticing Junior at all. Had stopped noticing Charlotte, for that matter. In the middle of any night, she could look from her bedroom window to the studio still blazing with fluorescent light. *I could be raped and left for dead,* Charlotte would think, sleepless in a threadbare negligee, brushing her hair, watching her father's shadow stretch and shift across the back lawn. *I could be nabbed and sold into white slavery, and he wouldn't know.* Charlotte would be lulled to sleep with thoughts of all the various ways she could be stolen away and violated.

But even at his most possessive, Oz was little more than a ghost—things would be moved around, there'd be noises, but no one would really be there. Her father was far too weak to save her from herself.

When applause broke out among the crowd, and sharp whistles, Charlotte grabbed the binoculars and stood on the hood of the car. The Daughters of God stepped out on stage wearing short white dresses as clingy as lingerie that shimmered with iridescence. Harnessed to their backs were elaborate wings, fantastical contraptions that flapped to the beat of the music, the girls operating the rigging of their own wings with pull cords on each side. With each flap, feathers fell into the light breeze to flow above the crowd, and everyone raised their arms in hopes of snagging one, jumping up and down, like reaching for a pop fly. Men held their children above their heads, and the boys and girls plucked the feathers from the sky.

The Daughters of God were tarted up in silver stiletto heels, their hair teased into neo-beehives, their lips a slutty wine-red, their eyes shadowed in 1970s blue.

"I was a stranger and you did not invite me in," the girls sang to a disco thumpety-thump that could be heard for miles, flapping the hell out of their wings. "Naked and you did not clothe me/Sick and in prison, and you did not visit me." The song was "Weeping and Gnashing," their first stab at a dance tune.

"Sunny's not with them," Charlotte said. "I hope she's all right."

"This book says Sunny has collapsed on stage eighteen times," Junior said. "She's the bad Daughter of God." He turned the page to a tabloid shot of Sunny in a leather mini and sequined tube top, stumbling from a nightclub.

Looking again through the binoculars, Charlotte followed the path of an errant feather floating away from the crowd, off to the side, rocking slowly to land in the ruffle of Hud's tuxedo shirt. Hud stood there, suited up for his piano-club gig, his bow tie undone, as usual. He didn't seem to notice the feather on his shirt, or anything else going on around him, his hands sunk in his trouser pockets.

Maybe she could buy a sparkly gown, upsweep her hair, and accompany Hud at the lounge. She could slink around the tables as she sang on a cordless mike, running her fingers through old men's toupees for tips. She didn't have much of a voice, but she didn't think she needed one. She and Hud could take their show on the road and seek Gatling together.

Charlotte and Junior stayed through only one costume change—the Daughters of God doffed their wings for hoop-skirted black robes and white tunics that resembled the getups of acolytes. "We dedicate this song to the lost souls of the Schrock boys," Harmony whispered into a microphone. Holding candles, the tiny flames fluttering with their breath, the girls sang of their hearts in anguish. When they got to the part about wanting to fly away from the stormy wind and tempest, they lifted their skirts in unison, and ten or fifteen doves flew out from between their legs, frantically thrashing their wings to rise above the stage and the crowd.

Sunny's absence had been only briefly explained ("She's having shin splints"), but Charlotte had become preoccupied by it, thinking even that she could hear Sunny's missing voice echoing among the others. The Daughters' dance steps seemed slightly off, as if they needed Sunny's feet to keep the kinks from the choreography.

Charlotte drove to the church so that Junior could stay wrapped in a sheet to prevent smudging his body paint. With the Daughters of God performing, the youth group didn't expect much of a crowd, but Junior and his people saw their horror show as a ministry, there to aid every last lost soul who stumbled by. When Charlotte saw the pamphleteers at the door to the basement, waiting for sinners to come up the stairs disturbed and on the verge of being converted, she was tempted to go down herself and touch a matchstick to the papier-mâché stalactites, to torch the whole flammable hell. Though Junior would certainly condemn her for such an act, her father wouldn't. Ozzie would love it if she became a young hellion under house arrest. He'd allow her to devote her whole life to just being his orphan.

But Charlotte got out of Junior's Trans-Am and left the churchyard, stepping through the chill October wind that had returned with nightfall, toward the Saint Ignatius sanctuary. Willow Ave., the street leading to the church where the Daughters of God were rumored to be staying, echoed slightly with electronic noise, the wind tripping the triggers of Halloween decorations. Plastic ghouls bobbed and whimpered in the trees; black cats with glowing green eyes hissed and shrieked. All the amusement fell on an empty street.

Charlotte stepped around to the back of the church, to the tall wood fence surrounding the sanctuary. She hoped to at least catch sight of Sunny at the window, convalescing. Charlotte peeked between the slats and the dried tendrils that still held shriveled deep-red grapes, out onto a yard messy with yellow leaves. Light from an upstairs room rested on a fountain's stone cherub, a little boy mossy with a few broken curls. Charlotte moved along slowly, rubbing warmth into her bare arms, looking for any line in the fence to see through. When she got to the closed gate, her eye met someone else's, and she jumped.

"Who's there?" came a voice.

"I'm Charlotte."

"Not *his* Charlotte?"

"Not whose Charlotte?" Charlotte asked.

"Gatling's," she said.

"Has he talked about me?" Charlotte asked.

"I don't remember him ever really mentioning you," Sunny said. She leaned in closer to the gate, cigarette smoke rising with her words. "But I've run my hands across your name many times."

The previous spring, Easter Sunday afternoon, Gatling called her bawling, distraught over their breakup. She agreed to go to his house to keep him from doing anything drastic, where she found him leaning over the bathroom sink, dripping blood across the porcelain, every last letter of her long first name carved with a penknife into the skin of his chest.

The "c" and the "h" and the "a" and the "r" had been large, but the rest of her name had shrunk letter by letter as the pain of it got the best of him. The last "t" had been left uncrossed, and the ending "e" was just one little line to the left of his nipple. After pouring him a shot of tequila, Charlotte dabbed iodine on his wounds, and she felt foolish for feeling impressed with herself. Though she knew, even as she ran a cotton ball over the lines of damage in his skin, that she couldn't see him anymore, she loved the idea of him going through life with her name forever scarring his flesh.

"Where is he?" Charlotte asked, suddenly Sunny's intimate.

"Last I heard," she said, "he was wandering around Nashville." Sunny leaned into the fence to whisper. "I'd invite you in, Charlotte, but I'm under suicide watch. One of the old church ladies here is supposed to be looking after me. She fell asleep needlepointing. Everybody's worried that if I off myself, too many girls would follow suit. That's something, huh?"

"Do you *want* to kill yourself?" Charlotte whispered.

"No," Sunny said. "No, that's nothing I want to do. But if I did, I'd do it big. I'd do a double flip off the Golden Gate. Or dive under the hooves of a bucking bronco at a rodeo." Sunny chuckled and threw a dry grape up and over the tall gate and it hit the toe of Charlotte's boot. Charlotte plucked it from the ground and stuck it in her pocket to keep as a souvenir of their conversation.

"Sounds terrible," Charlotte said, wistfully, imagining what it might be like to be so beloved as to inspire copycat suicides far and wide. "Can I ask you something?" Charlotte asked. "Why did Gatling quit your band?" She thought back to one 3 A.M., Gatling naked on the end of her bed with his blue guitar, his thumbnail purple-black from a hammer blow from building canvases for his mom. "Please Mister Please," he played, because Charlotte had been on an Olivia Newton-John jag. She'd bought a wobbly turntable at a library fire sale in order to play the records her mother had collected as a child, and she'd coerced Gatling into learning some of the songs she remembered her mother returning the needle to again and again. Even back when her mother had played them, the records had been old and nearly worn out, popping and skipping with every hair-thin scratch.

"He lost his religion a few months in, I think," Sunny said a little cheerfully. "Gatling's a fine one. You must have really twisted him up good to get him to run so far away from you."

"No," Charlotte said, not offended. Gatling had been with the Daughters of God only a handful of months, so all Sunny probably got was the beautifully morose part of the boy, not the useless fits of fever and agony. "I saw him fall apart all the time, about anything," Charlotte said. "Whatever I did to him . . . it wasn't anything special." Gatling had been blessed with the lovingest family she knew, but he just picked at the seams of it.

Charlotte wished Sunny would follow her to her house, where she would describe a life she'd never led. *Here I fell from the steps and had to get five stitches in my broken head,* Charlotte would lie. *Here I threw a fit and kicked a hole in the wall. I tried to hang myself from that chandelier.* She'd describe a girl of fragility and devastating weakness, someone poorly, poorly composed.

14.

ᎥᎥᎥᎥᎥᎥᎥᎥᎥᎥ

"I LOVE this song," Nina said, beginning some frantic shag to the echoing thump and warble from the distant speakers. Nina and Tuesday stayed far away from the crowd, viewing the Daughters of God through antique opera glasses. Tuesday lowered her gaze to Nina, the opera glasses magnifying Nina's wide china-doll eyes and long, soft lashes, the crooked line of her bangs, a single cheek dimple.

When Nina turned sixteen, Tuesday would escort her to Paris, and maybe Nina would be smart enough to get lost, to disappear into the crunch of a crowd in the Metro and not resurface for years, not until after she'd had some detrimental love affairs and had modeled in the altogether for an artist brilliant and a touch psychotic.

"You feed this girl sugar out of the bag?" Hud said, suddenly there, lifting Nina, making her giggle as he tickled her neck with his lips. He took a seat in a lawn chair across from Tuesday, keeping Nina in his lap, and he asked Tuesday, "What's going on in that cute skull of yours?"

Whatever happened to that? she wanted to say. When they were first in love, Hud would notice Tuesday's every shift of mood. They could be with a group, out, and he'd lean in to say softly, "What's wrong?" before she even realized she was down.

"I was just thinking about what a sour old lady I'll be," Tuesday said. "And how Nina will have to look after me when I can't look after myself. When my wigs droop, she'll be the only one around to give 'em a shot of Aqua Net."

"I'll be too busy being in love with my husband to undroop your wigs," Nina said. "And I'll have a boy and girl of my own. Gatling and Nina, Jr."

"What kind of name is Gatling, anyway?" Hud said, gruff. "You would think a couple of kids named that child." He gave Tuesday a wink, a half smile, and she remembered an afternoon when she was newly pregnant. She lay in her bed, feeling blue and melodramatic, still in her pj's at 3, plucking the petals from the last of the roses in a quickly wilted winter bouquet. Hud, come down with a cold, read to Tuesday from a beat-up comic book his dad had had as a kid, a Western with a black-hatted cowboy named Gatling. Tuesday was soothed by his low, sickly, scratchy voice, by his boyish sniffle and his cartoon sound effects for the popping of guns and the rumble of horse hooves.

"Are you terribly sad that Gatling's still gone?" Tuesday said, peering again through her opera glasses, focusing on the ice blue of one of Hud's eyes.

"Yes. You're not?"

"I am," she said, though she wasn't, not terribly. She blamed him, though somewhat unfairly, she realized, for her and Hud getting to know each other less and less. Gatling had been a misery from the minute of his difficult birth. And now he was nowhere, it seemed, his postcards only fraudulent evidence—a good life not lived. "Of course I'm sad," she said. "What kind of mother would I be if I wasn't?"

"I've got twenty bucks," Hud said, exaggerating patting at the sewn-shut breast pockets of his tuxedo jacket, doing a goof on a guy looking for a misplaced money clip when it came time to pony up at happy hour. "Draw me. Capture a father's heartbreak."

Tuesday's right hand was still in its cast, and would be for weeks, but she had recently discovered that, with her left, she could doodle distinctive cartoons that somehow resembled her subjects—the shaky lines and oblong circles tumbling together into a twisty fun-house reflection. Before, Tuesday had always struggled with sketching people, arms and legs uneven and noses and eyes unintentionally lopsided. But with just an extra bit of scribble, at twenty bucks a caricature, she had made over $500 from the people who had flocked to the drive-in to line up for the Daughters of God.

"Forget it," she said. "I've just retired. And you might object to my interpretation."

"Just be kind," he said, shrugging. He stretched his leg out to tap the toe of his boot against the side of her transparent pumps. "Because girls in glass slippers shouldn't kick rocks at people."

"They're plastic," she said, lifting her foot to rest it on his knee. He held her heel in his hand and looked at the clear sole—"Seven ninety-eight," he said, reading the price that had been felt-tipped on at the thrift shop.

"Please draw him, Mommy," Nina said. "I want to see what he looks like."

Tuesday took her foot back, then took the charcoal pencil from behind her ear. Performing nights had bagged his eyes, Tuesday thought as she sketched, but she'd always been a patsy for his sleepy demeanor. Late in the day after every late-night drunk, he'd practically whisper each word he spoke. That and his moving slow, and his lazy affection, had seemed like the best tenderness. Sunday nights had been spent on the sofa, the two of them entangled, watching old movies, and sipping some hair of the dog.

"I almost forgot," Hud said, reaching into his pocket. "Hold out your hand, Neen. It's a piece of a bone of a martyr." Nina examined the yellowish chip. A traveling priest, freshly defrocked, peddled the bone chips and the threads of holy garments at spiritual sites across the country; for the last few days he'd set himself up across the road from the drive-in, his van an elaborate mural of a smiling Mexican Jesus, and a Virgen de Guadalupe in hair ribbons, and skeletons dancing in their holes in the ground. Tuesday had bought a 3D picture of a dark, seductive Joan of Arc; by tilting the picture up and back, she could make the flames lick and Joan's full lips part in an expression of pain. In among the Saint Christopher's medals and plastic dashboard virgins and Spanish novenas for sale were some chihuahuas dressed up in neckerchiefs and kept in birdcages. The priest sat outside the van in a tan suit and Panama hat, reading Harold Robbins, next to a sloppily painted sign: DOGS AND ARTIFACTS.

"*Saint Andy was dragged through brambles and thorns in punishment for kicking over a jug of wine in a pagan temple,*"

Hud read from a tiny slip of paper. *"But from his wounds arose a perfume fragrant with apples and honey."*

"You get a haircut?" Tuesday asked.

"Cut it myself," he said.

"Really? Yourself? I'm impressed. It looks like you could have spent seven, eight bucks on it." Hud smiled wide and Tuesday sketched in his lips as a wavy line. She remembered him singing, every Friday night at the tavern, ten years or so before. He had affected a strangled croon in order to sound agonized, and would let a hand-rolled cigarette smolder, un-smoked, in an ashtray on the floor at his feet. A few of the easy songs he'd play with a longneck held between the fingers of his left hand. Tuesday would get dressed up but sit toward the back, ordering manhattans with extra cherries, feigning mystery though everyone in the bar knew she was Hud's wife.

Tuesday had only just stopped wearing her wedding ring the night before. She stuck it in a jewelry box when she went to bed, and dreamt that a bird ate her fingers.

Hud's fingers were ringless too, Tuesday noticed. She added the wedding ring to the drawing anyway, a hard, dark chicken-scratch on a finger of his long left hand. Where *was* his ring? she wondered. Hocked or tucked away? Rumor had it that Hud had been spending time with the trashy concession-booth girl who wore disco-blue shadow on her droopy, come-do-me eyelids. *I'll tell you this much,* Tuesday wanted to tell him now, *I'll suffocate Nina with a pillow before I'll let that druggie start stepmothering my girl.*

"I hear you've been dating," Tuesday said, to stir things up.

"Then your hearing must not be so hot," he said.

"Sure it is," she said. "The gal who works the concession counter. The one whose bra is always showing because she doesn't button her shirt up enough. You know . . . whatever her name is."

"Yeah, I know who you're talking about," Hud said, grinning at Tuesday like he thought he knew her so goddamn inside out. "She's not my girlfriend. And as far as I'm concerned, that's all I've got to say on the subject."

"She has a little girl too, doesn't she?" Tuesday asked, penciling a ukulele into his fist. "I just read in the newspaper about a study. Seems that more people who have daughters get divorced than people who have only sons. Guess we're both a bit hobbled."

Hud covered Nina's ears and cast Tuesday a squint of disapproval. "That comment should resurface nicely in about ten years or so," Hud said, "when she's yacking her brain out to some shrink." Like a coconspirator, Nina sat passively, seemingly happy to not listen, even putting her hands over Hud's at her ears. "I thought this is what you wanted," Hud said.

"What? What did I want?"

"To never kiss me again, is what you said," he said, his voice low. She half wanted him to whisper, exactly that, in her ear. Tuesday knew she could so easily make a mess of everything by breathing just a few immature words. "Come back" or something equally reckless.

"Well, let's not fight about it," she said.

"Fight about what?" Hud said. "We're not fighting."

"Are we not fighting, or are we just not admitting that we're fighting?" she said, adding to the ukulele a curling, snapped string. "Or are we just not talking about the things that'll make us fight?" If there was nothing at all to scrap about, she thought, then why was he so coy about the whole Dot thing, when Rose had most definitely spotted them picking tunes together at the jukebox at the Steak and Black Coffee? They'd played some Merle Haggard, Rose had reported, and Norah Jones doing a Dolly Parton. Hearing about it hadn't bothered Tuesday much, but that had been before she'd seen his wedding ring gone.

Tuesday tore the drawing from her sketchpad. "Read it and weep," she said, handing it over.

"Well, I don't know about you, Nina," Hud said, uncovering Nina's ears, "but I think that may be the handsomest son of a bitch I've ever laid eyes on. If I didn't know better, I'd think your mom had a crush on me, making me look so goddamn drop-dead."

"I just think you can do a little better than Dot, is all," Tuesday said.

Hud sighed and lifted Nina from his lap, sitting her on the ground at his feet. He took a tiny bottle of aspirin from his inside jacket pocket, then popped a few, swallowing without water. "I've *done* better," he said. "Prettier. Smarter. Look where it's got me."

"Look where it's got you?" Tuesday said. She stuck her pencil into the thumbhole of her cast to scratch at some sudden, psychosomatic itch. "It got you to not such a bad place. It got you a beautiful daughter. A beautiful son. A few good years of marriage here and there." She guessed she truly was sad over Gatling's absence, and the fact that he had not shown up with the Daughters of God. Every piece of her broken home could have piled in the car and gone to the diner to treat Gatling to his favorite—a slice of the chocolate meringue, preferably day-old and muddy, the way he loved it back when he was a pretty-faced brat. "What else would you have been doing all these years if you hadn't been spoiling your babies?"

"I know, precious," Hud said. "I was just kind of joking."

Tuesday paused, waiting for Nina to get fully involved in the Daughters of God who'd struck up a dirgelike number. Nina, balancing on one leg, eyes closed, holding the saint's bone chip tight in her fist, did another of her graceless interpretive dances. Watching, Tuesday knew how much she'd hate not having Nina every evening, not hearing her tiny, tuneless voice as she sang along to the most maudlin of country. *Look where it's got me,* she thought.

"I know that it must seem like I never know what I want," Tuesday said softly, leaning forward, "or maybe it seems like I want a lot. I don't know. I just know I want things to get easy between us, for her sake mostly. I want us to have one of those, what do they call them, amicable splits." Hud clucked his tongue, nodded, looked up at the sky, and Tuesday assumed he was thinking of how he could slip "amicable split" into one of his many bitter divorce ballads. "I just want us to be able to talk about things, without anybody getting mad," Tuesday said.

"So you go first," Hud said, leaning forward too. "Spill your guts if you're so gung-ho about being chummy. Seeing somebody new? I know nothing. Because that little girl over there tends to keep her big flap shut too much."

Tuesday could smell the shampoo he'd used for years, some store brand that smelled like sugared strawberries. When Hud had first moved out, Tuesday had used the last of the bottle he'd left in the shower, giving herself some nasty frizz for days. But the scent it left on her pillow had helped her sleep.

"Nobody," Tuesday said. "Just Ozzie, you know, coming around to fix some things. And, you know, we've had a drink or two." Tuesday could have sworn she'd told Hud that Oz had fixed the latch on Nina's bedroom window and had tended to the echoing drip of the bathroom faucet that had kept Tuesday awake for weeks. Surely she'd mentioned Ozzie coming around, if for no other reason than to be wicked, to remind Hud of his negligence in ignoring the house's need for repair.

But Hud leaned back, scowling. He again reached into his jacket pocket and this time took out a closed drink parasol, the stick of which he chewed on with agitation. "Ozzie," Hud said. "The Ozzie who used to come into my very own house, uninvited, and slug me. That Ozzie, you're talking about."

"Of course that Ozzie," Tuesday said.

"So, OK, since we're all chummy here, all amicable, tell me more," Hud said. "You and Oz. You've had a few drinks, a few friendly happy hours or some such. What else?"

What was there to confess? That she and Ozzie got together from time to time to get drunk, and that he got drunk quick, and had a nifty disappearing act a few shots in? Oz, so handsome and tragic, would vanish in plain sight, sitting still but completely gone, as foggy as a phantom.

"I feel like you're getting mad, and I didn't mean for . . ."

"I'm not mad," Hud snapped. He crossed his arms across his chest and spat his parasol off to the side. "So, what is it? You've kissed him? Worse?"

The last time Ozzie had taken her to the Wiggle Room, only a few nights before, she'd sipped a single glass of their lousy screw-top red as Oz had slammed back double bourbon after double bourbon. As she watched discreet lovers two-step slow, she felt such relief from the lack of possibility. Ozzie was lost to all, but that was what she liked about getting sloshed with him, it was what made their kissing so nicely inconsequential. *I had love once*, she thought. *Look where it's got me.*

"Nothing serious is happening," Tuesday told Hud.

"So, what, exactly, isn't happening? Kissing isn't happening? Sex isn't happening?"

"Shhh," Tuesday said, rolling her eyes in Nina's direction.

"I don't think I like the idea of Ozzie being around my daughter," Hud said, standing, shoving his hands in the pockets of his trousers. "My jaw still clicks from when he popped me one just because Gatling had Charlotte out after 10." He leaned in so Tuesday could hear the noise his jaw made when he opened his mouth extra wide. "He's not a reasonable son of a bitch. And look at the shape that miserable Charlotte is in. Before her mom died, that girl was the queen of the spelling bee. She spelled 'loquacious' or some goddamn thing. She played Jane Fonda in a sixth grade production of *Barefoot in the Park*. Now Oz has let her become an out-and-out freak."

"But you've always liked Charlotte."

"I'm just trying to tell you, Day, that I want Nina to have a shot at being happier than the rest of us. I really should just steal her away so she doesn't have to grow up listening to all our dumb back-and-forth." Hud tossed his caricature in her lap. "You might need this portrait to put next to Nina's on the milk cartons. Because what have I got to lose, really? You might want to pencil in some glassy drunk's eyes. Give me some stringy hair, make my teeth crooked. Make sure everybody can see I'm the worst kind of skunk."

"You're so lucky I don't take you seriously," Tuesday said.

Nina had paused in her dance to watch Hud and Tuesday's dustup, her blue crayon once again a mock cigarette between her lips. "Those things'll kill you," Hud said, going to Nina to give her a kiss on the top of her head. He then grabbed a handful of Nina's hair. "Exhibit A," he said, pointing at the crayon. "She's already picking up our bad habits." He then walked away, even his strut a part of his angry song and dance.

Nina shot Tuesday a scarily adult *What's up with him?* look. "He's just crabby because he was hoping to see your brother," Tuesday said.

Nina leaned her head against Tuesday's shoulder and studied the bone chip in her palm. "I want to be a martyr," Nina said.

"Perfect," Tuesday said. "We could use one of those in the family."

1 5 .

AUGUSTINE'S mother, who filled in at the lounge on the nights Augustine was off, stood on a ladder to hang a crepe-paper jack-o'-lantern above the bar. In between blending strawberry margaritas for a book club of middle-aged women, Blanche twisted little ghosts from Kleenex and tucked them into the bouquets of ratty silk roses throughout the lounge; she'd dusted off a stuffed witch and propped it on top of Hud's piano.

The members of the book club were intoxicated and forgiving. Some of the ladies had kicked off their shoes and clinked glasses with every new round of cocktails, but they kept their good cheer at a respectable hush as Hud played terribly. They scribbled their requests—Celine Dion and Bacharach songs—on tens and twenties and passed them up. They didn't even seem to mind that Hud kept getting lost midsong, forgetting what he was singing in the middle of a lyric and letting the tune shuffle off, note by note, into silence. The women would applaud when the music stopped, then wait for him to stumble through the next selection.

Hud was distracted by thoughts of Tuesday and Oz alone, perhaps alone at that minute. Hud had let Oz, that bastard, weep all over his best suit the afternoon of Jenny's funeral. Oz had moaned and wailed, making a general spectacle, and Hud had been the only one with the nuts to get up and go to him, to get him to shut the hell up. It should have meant something to Oz, Hud thought, something significant that he had a friend who loved him to pieces and cared about his dignity. Instead, Ozzie vanished, too determined to be inconsolable. Now here he was, the ingrate, horning in on Hud's new ex.

"What's new?" a woman asked, with a twenty for his oversized brandy snifter stuffed with tips.

"Not much," Hud said. His rendition of "Do You Know the Way to San Jose" slipped his mind and left his fingers. "Just doing my little organ-grinder's-monkey routine."

"No," the woman said, giggling in a way she probably thought seductive. "I mean the old song, 'What's New?' Do you know it?"

"Oh, yeah, yeah, I think so," Hud said, giving it a shot. Her request seemed slightly shopworn, her giggle a little rehearsed, as if she dragged out her ol' "What's New?" bit every time she sidled up to a piano man. The woman, whose soda-can curls were piled high atop her head in an outdated mode, lingered there, leaning into the baby grand, tapping her turquoise ring against her rocks glass. Hud knew the words to "What's New?" but he decided not to sing, because he didn't want it to seem that he was singing to her. It wasn't unusual for him to chat up the clientele, but he didn't go in for going all gigolo just for extra tips. "Here for the book club?" he asked.

"No. I'm the concierge at a Sheraton up in Gary, Indiana," she said. "I'm driving to a convention in Denver. To accept an award. Just a little, tiny, nothing award, really. Nothing worth mentioning."

"Have a speech?" Hud asked. He hoped so, so he could ask her to recite it, so he could ignore her and wallow more in his disgust over Tuesday and Oz. He just wanted to sit and stew, to picture them cozy in Hud's house, listening to Hud's dad's jazz records, drinking the last of the booze from the bottoms of the bottles Hud had left behind in a kitchen cabinet.

"No speech," she said. "I'll just wing it. I'll talk about how I worked as a maid for years and years at a broken-down bed and breakfast. And how I had an epiphany while feather-dusting a bowl of glass fruit."

Hud lost his place in "What's New?" so he moved into the middle of "If I Had You," one of his favorites. "I've had an epiphany or two," he said. "Some pretty useless ones. They're difficult to sustain."

"Oh, don't I know it," she said. "When did I ever think that I'd someday be traveling. And in a bar in a silk dress. Getting tipsy on chilled Southern Comfort. About to make a jackass of myself by asking the piano player if I can buy him a drink."

Then "If I Had You" fell apart too, and Hud got caught up thinking about a song of his own he'd been writing, a tune he thought would be perfect for a crooner like Chick Magnum, the pinup boy with the trademark red felt hat. On his album covers, Chick wore Wranglers that looked so tight as to be painful; he sang songs about teddy bears bought in truck-stop gift shops, and babies abandoned in Salvation Army donation bins, and mommies with cancer, and 9/11 widows on Christmas day.

"I'm sorry," Hud said, standing and picking up his brandy snifter of tips. "I'm going to close up shop early tonight. I've had a pretty bad day."

"Just let me buy you one little sip," she said, back to anxiously tapping her ring against her glass. "I'm a good listener, I'm told."

"I wouldn't be good company," Hud said. "I'll tell you what it is. I just found out that my wife is having some kind of something with my oldest friend."

"Your wife," she said. "I didn't see a wedding ring, so I thought . . ."

"No," Hud said, scratching at his bare finger. He'd put the ring in its velvet-lined box the week before, when he'd toyed with the idea of seducing Dot. The night he'd decided to put the ring up, he'd dreamt it had spun off his finger during a raucous rendition of "Jambalaya."

"Actually, she's my ex-wife," Hud said. "And actually, he's my ex-friend. What's *not* ex with me, I guess, huh?" He stuck the snifter in the crook of his arm. "I should give you your tip back."

"Don't be silly," she said. She pulled a business card from her leopard-print pocketbook. "Look me up if you ever get to Gary," she said.

If you ever get to Gary, look me up. He liked the rhythm of that. It would make for a catchy refrain. Two travelers, dressed up for no reason, lonely in a hotel lounge, wedding rings secreted away. *It's raining outside, but the martinis are dry,* or lyrics halfway sophisticated like that. He'd call it "Straight up, Two Olives."

After saying good-night to (a quick peek at the business card) Ms. Eve M. Flannery, Hud slunk from the lounge looking not unlike a gentlemen thief, he thought, when he caught his reflection in the lobby doors, seeing himself with the snifter full of cash, his tux rumpled, his red cowboy boots scuffed away to a shade of pink. He sure did wish he stood up straighter, but he didn't mind imagining himself as a minor outlaw. As he walked to the bus on the other end of the parking lot, he ran his fingers through the bills, estimating. There had to be a good couple hundred in the snifter, he thought. That, along with the small roll of fifties he kept tucked away in a piggy bank, could easily book transport for himself and his daughter to some godforsaken back acre.

Who am I kidding? Hud thought. It killed him to think of Tuesday lonely in the old house, Nina's noise nowhere around. She'd go batty while Hud and Nina, happily on the lam, sunned themselves poolside at some off-the-map motel. *Because Tuesday,* Hud thought, *she's the real weakling of the two of us.*

Nearing the bus, wishing he'd at least kept the caricature Tuesday had drawn, Hud heard footsteps quick behind him. He felt something heavy hit his back, dropping him to his knees, his kneecaps cracking loud against the pavement. The parking lot seemed to buckle and lift beneath him. In the split second before Hud fell forward to hit his cheek on the cement, he thought he could easily get back on his feet and keep the snifter from tumbling from his arms.

Hud remained conscious as the snifter rolled away unbroken, his sense of smell overwhelmingly powerful. Though he was on the ground looking up, he felt like he was above looking down on the man in the parka and ski mask. Hud could smell something chemically evergreen, and cinnamon gum, and the antiseptic burn of the hard liquor the gum was meant to conceal. He could smell stale smoke on the man's parka. In the rush of wind as the man ran off with the snifter full of cash, Hud got a strong whiff of the faint remains of aftershave, a dime-store menthol brand. The culprit, Hud concluded when he caught the hint of baby powder in the air, was a freckled, redheaded housekeeper everybody called Howie; Howie, not much more than a kid, had just fathered a welfare brat.

Then Hud could smell nothing, not the reek of the nearby dumpster nor of the wet leaves at his cheek. And as the pictures in his head floated and shook, he couldn't smell his young father now towering above him, whose breath was thick with the three Jack-and-Cokes he'd drunk at lunch. He couldn't smell the hairspray his mother used to stiffen her 'do, a spray that had always reminded Hud of watermelon and that he had long thought was his mother's perfume. The rubber boots she wore over her dress shoes squeaked as she squatted next to Hud, the back of her hand against his forehead. Hud wasn't ill—he had slipped on the ice as he skidded and playfully spun down the sidewalk pretending to be a hockey player—but checking for a fever was probably the only motherly gesture she could think of at the moment. Hud's mother often seemed so lost in her own thoughts that the out-side world could only just barely intrude.

"Well, that's what you get," Hud's father said, "for horsin' around."

But that's what kids do, you cranky son of a bitch, Hud said now, scolding his old man some twenty-five years later. *They horse around and get hurt.* He wished he had faked paralysis as he lay there flat on his back, or had rolled his eyes up, mock comatose, so his father's black heart might have been tricked into skipping a beat.

Hud's father had brought them all along in his truck—he'd had to haul a load of something to somewhere—and they'd stopped in Omaha for some Christmas shopping. The gift Hud had chosen for his mother now sat shattered in the bag at his side, a tea set painted with bumblebees and pansies, though Hud had only ever seen his mother drink Pepsi. Hud had often traveled with his father in those months that he made his living with a dented Peterbilt, shimmied to sleep in the sleeper by the rattle and shake of the truck. Hud sniffed the air, hoping. To this day, he found comfort in the reek of diesel.

Hud woke, his cheek still against the parking-lot pavement. Picking himself up from the ground, he felt like his every bone was popping harshly back into its socket, his entire skeleton slightly askew. Once behind the wheel of the bus, he leaned forward to sniff at the air freshener hanging from the rearview; he could smell nothing, but he was slightly congested from having been out in the cold night air. He drove home, worrying all the way that he might fall asleep at the wheel, wondering if he'd made a mistake in not going to the emergency room. He could at least have wakened Tuesday with a 2 A.M. call from his hospital bed, working her into a fit by telling her not to worry.

He passed the drive-in as its marquee lights went dark. From the highway, he could see the stage still lit, though the Daughters of God had likely long since finished their concert. One of the last cars of the night pulled out in front of Hud from the drive-in's driveway to putt along. Hud didn't pass the car; he was in no hurry to get home and to try to keep from sleeping. He remembered how, a few years before, one of Tuesday's cousins took a capful of over-the-counter cough medicine after having been out doing shots at her own bachelorette party. The girl, nineteen or something ridiculous like that, died in her sleep from the mix.

When the car in front of him slowed down more and pulled onto the shoulder of the highway, Hud was happy that somebody else was up so late and troubled. He pulled along the shoulder too, then walked to the driver's side to tap at the glass. The woman, alone in the car, ignored Hud, her head in her hand as she rubbed her temples. Hud tapped again, and this time startled her. "Do you need a jump?" he shouted, though her engine still purred. What he really wanted was to invite her to the all-night for a bottomless pot of their undrinkable coffee. Maybe she was on the edge of some fascinating state of defeat, and he could talk her through it. But when she rolled down her window, he recognized her, Mrs. Schrock, the woman with the dead kids. The dead *everything*, he realized, seeing her alone in the green light from the speedometer. At one time she'd had a normal life, had had every reason to believe she always would.

"Is your car broken down?" Hud said, not bothering to attempt to reintroduce himself. He'd only known her vaguely, as the woman who'd taken the driver's-license photos at the courthouse, in the years before her tragedy. But Hud was vain enough to be disappointed that she didn't recognize him, since she used to gently flirt with him whenever he renewed. *With that smile you don't seem so innocent,* she'd said once, looking through the lens. *If I was a cop pulling you over, I'd slap on the cuffs.*

"Can I give you a ride?" Hud asked.

Nanette put both her hands on the steering wheel to grip it tightly, and looked straight ahead. "I forgot where I live," she said.

"Oh," Hud said. "Well. You know, maybe I could help . . ."

"It's so funny," she said, interrupting. "My little boy predicted it. My youngest. One day, when they were both pretty little, I was driving us home from the grocery store, and he asked, 'Mommy, what would you do if you forgot how to get home?' And I said, 'Well, I guess you'd have to find our way,' and then he said, 'What if *I* forgot?' And I said, 'Well, then your brother would have to find our way.' Then he said, 'What if *he* forgot?' And I· said, 'Then I guess I'd drive around and around until we recognized our house.' But I was wrong, wasn't I? I didn't do that at all. I just stopped."

"I, I, I think," Hud said, stuttering, wracked with guilt for his spiritual fraud. *I'm the one,* he wanted to confess, *the one to conjure your boys out of the blurry backdrops of* Your Cheatin' Heart. Maybe she would forgive him when he explained that it was only an effort to bring his own son home. He and Nanette Schrock could be friends, he thought. They could commiserate. *A child who loses a parent is called an orphan,* Hud wanted to tell her, quoting from an earnest psychologist on a talk show, a grief counselor with a big black bow at the back of her head. *A wife who loses a husband is a widow.* "Where's our word, Mrs. Schrock?" Hud said, so tired he could barely stand. His eyes blinked rapidly with the effort of staying open.

"Those weren't my boys," she said. She put on a pair of sunglasses despite the pitch dark of the unlit highway ahead. "In the movie. I don't know who those children were, but they weren't my boys." Then, "2212 Plum Street," she said, just above her breath, gasping with remembrance. She inched the car forward, seeming to forget that Hud stood there. "2212 Plum Street, 2212 Plum Street," she quietly recited.

I didn't wake up, he thought for a moment, just dizzy enough to think he was wandering around in some dumb purgatory. *Why didn't I just have a drink with Eve M. Flannery of Gary, Indiana?* She probably would've let him talk about himself for hours, he thought. Then Howie and his welfare brat wouldn't be sitting at home, blood on their hands, lighting their fatso stogies with his tip money.

It wasn't until Hud was back in his apartment, standing in the light of his open refrigerator, holding a bottle of beer to the pain at the back of his neck, that he noticed the damage to his tuxedo. His trousers were bloody at the knees and the lapel of his jacket was ripped and hung flapped over. The suit had long been on its last legs anyway, he realized as he stripped down to his boxers. His clothes and boots strewn across the kitchen floor, Hud still worried about drifting off into a fatal sleep.

Hud seemed to remember a snazzy sports coat of reddish-orange velour, with a Western cut, that had been among his father's suits. Hud's dad, upon taking the job of selling aerial photos to area farmers, had invested in a new wardrobe. Hud remembered spending all of one day in the executive dressing room of Rushmore Winslow's, a spiffy men's store once on the town square; an old clerk in shirtsleeves had fussed and tape-measured. "Soak it all in, pipsqueak," Hud's father said, watching himself in the full-length mirror unwrapping the flashy silver foil from a peppermint. "A quality shop like this is on its way to dinosaur. When *you* finally go to buy a suit, Susie Q, you won't get treated like a goddamn king." (Hud's father sometimes called him Susie Q on account of his head of girlish gold curls.) "All these bastards will be long dead, god rest their souls. No offense, Patschky." The old man, on his knees, muttered something unintelligible, his lips puckered around straight pins as he tucked up the trouser cuffs. "Stroke the sleeve of that topcoat, son," Hud's father said, gesturing to the long green coat draped across the back of a leather wing chair. "That's what 10 percent cashmere feels like, case you were wondering."

Rushmore Winslow himself, dandruff snowy against his gently hunched back, brought Hud's father a cup of strong coffee in a tiny china cup. Though Hud's dad's check turned out to be rubber, leading to Old Man Winslow turning ungentlemanly ("Little boy, you tell your dad," he said on the phone once, "that unless he pays for that apparel, I know a guy who'll ram him so hard that he'll never stop shitting crooked"), and though his father was fired from the sales job within a year, those suits always represented to Hud the zenith of elegance.

When his mother died, Hud found the suits, still zipped into their gold-colored vinyl bags, at the back of her closet; Hud's father had taken little with him when he abandoned them for another family. The suits now hung on an exposed pipe in the basement of Tuesday's house.

Hud poured himself a cup of coffee, stirred in some slightly soured milk and several heaping spoonfuls of sugar, then went to the phone in his bedroom. He punched in his old number with some indignation, certain Tuesday would sleep through its ringing, would be oblivious to the possibility of dire emergency. She had never even bothered to replace the answering machine that had recently quit working. "I could be the police, Sleepyhead," Hud whispered into the receiver, counting the rings, *eight, nine, ten.* "I could have abducted Nina again. There could have been a chase, and I could have driven the bus off a bridge. Wake up, Mrs. Smith, you need to identify the remains of your family. Time to wake up and get the bejesus scared out of you." He whistled. "Yoo-hoo."

After about the sixteenth ring, Nina answered. Hud said, "What are you doing up, for God's sake?"

"I'm *not* up," she said. "I'm halfway not awake."

"Where's your mother?" Hud asked. "No, let me guess. She's out like a light, snoring her life away, while you wander around the house, getting into the household poisons. Or while you open the door to strangers. Am I right?"

"I'm about two seconds away from popping you one," Nina said, yawning. "And not softly either. Hard."

"Honestly. Who talks to their father that way?" Hud asked. "I'll tell you who talks to their father that way: dirty orphans who grow up in the street."

"Dirty orphans," Nina repeated, chuckling. "I put my bone chip in my locket."

"Which one?"

"The saint's bone chip."

"No, dummy, I mean which locket."

"Oh, the one that came with the little doll in it that had pink hair that smelled like dog."

Even in the months before Nina was born, Hud had been buying her jewelry. Nina had delicate silver and gold necklaces, and adjustable rings with precious stones and mother of pearl, but most often she dripped with the fifty-cent pieces of junk—the plastic ruby clip-on earrings, the diamonds that blinked in different colors—sold in the checkout aisles of the grocery store.

"I'm falling asleep," Nina said. "I'm hanging up."

"No, no, wait," Hud said. "Hey, kid, try to remember to tell your mom something for me in the morning. Tell her I need those suits of my dad's. I wrecked my tux."

Hud pressed at the pain at the back of his neck, wincing. He remembered the splotchy line of black-and-blue up and down his back from when he had fallen on the sidewalk that day years before when he'd horsed around on the ice. His father moved out before Hud's bruises faded; he threw his shaving kit and a deck of cards into the sleeper of his semi a few days before Christmas and made a beeline for his new love, a wheelchair-bound woman in Iowa who sold Bibles over the phone and had three girls. Hud's dad had first taken up with the woman on the CB radio, having intense evangelical dialogue over one of the lesser-used channels. Hud had learned all the details in an unrepentant letter of explanation, riddled with Bible verses, his father sent a few months later.

Hud's father had even left behind the Christmas gifts Hud and his mother had bought for him and had put beneath the tree. When Hud emptied the house after his mother died years later, he found the gifts, still wrapped and ribboned, on a shelf in a utility closet, and he stood there, ripping into them—a Norelco and some aftershave in a bottle shaped like a mallard and a novelty necktie hand-painted with a pinup girl in a miniskirted Santa suit. For a second Hud had pitied the kid he'd been, remembering how he'd chosen the aftershave and the sexy necktie because he'd always thought of his dad as more of a bachelor uncle, a slim, sophisticated ladies' man who listened to scratchy jazz records and joked about how he was always a sucker for a funny brunette and a well-shook gin martini. *My children will never be strangers to me,* Hud had vowed right then, Nina still only an infant and Gatling still a boy, as he slapped some of his dad's abandoned aftershave onto his cheeks.

"Neen, can I ask you a question? And will you promise not to tell your mom that I asked?"

"Mommy says I'm not supposed to keep secrets."

"No, no, no," Hud said, "no, she means if somebody molests you or something, and tells you not to tell, that's the kind of secret she means. So this isn't really a secret, don't think of it as a secret, just think, y'know, it's me and you just flapping our gums about nothing she needs to know about."

"Whatever."

"So, I just wanted to ask, is Ozzie there?"

"No," Nina said with a convincing tone of confusion.

"Does he ever spend the night?"

"No," she said.

Hud kept silent for several seconds, thinking if he shut up for a bit, she'd break if she was fibbing. "Did your mom tell you not to tell me if Oz stays over? Because that's a secret too, you know. If you don't tell me, you're keeping a secret, and you're not supposed to keep secrets."

"I'm on the kitchen floor now," Nina said. "That's how tired I am."

"Do you like Ozzie?" Hud asked.

"Yeah," she said. "He's nice. Do you like him?"

"I'm not particularly fond of him at this point in time," Hud said. "But the poor guy's had a string of really, really lousy luck; he probably shouldn't be expected to ever do the right thing."

"Mmm-hmmm," Nina mumbled.

"You're falling asleep on me, Neen."

"Call me tomorrow, Daddy."

"OK," Hud said. "Oh, and don't forget to tell your mom to leave the back door unlocked so I can pick up those suits. But if you can figure out some way to tell her that without telling her that I called in the middle of the night, that'd be fantastic-o."

"Good-bye, Daddy. I love you."

"Sweetie, I love you and I love you and I love you. Did you hear that?"

"Yes."

"So you'll never be able to say that your father never told you that he loved you, will you? Because I'm telling you that I love you," he said, but Nina had already hung up. It didn't matter; she'd eased his delirium.

¡¡¡¡¡¡¡

E V E N as he picked up the brats on his crack-of-dawn bus route, Hud wondered drowsily, punchy from downing a thermos-full of coffee, if he'd died in his sleep. What would they put in, and what would they leave out, of his obituary? *A man who falsely claimed to know six thousand songs was found in his bed, having bought the farm, as stripped as the day he clawed his way out into the world.* "He was going nowhere fast *for years," said his unsympathetic ex-ball-and-chain. "Guess he finally got there, poor bastard."*

"You're ten minutes late, Hud," said Millie, the girl Hud most longed to send through the front window of the bus with a sudden stomp of the brakes. "What I got on my two little toothpicks is as flimsy as nothing." She pinched at the hot pink tights, giving the snug material a sassy snap.

A few minutes after settling into the front seat directly behind Hud, Millie said, "This is what I'm going as on Halloween." He looked in the rearview to see that she'd already dismantled the sandwich from her lunchbox—she'd chewed two eyeholes and a mouth into a slice of bologna and draped it across her face like a mask. "Tell me that you love it, poopsie-woopsie, or I scream 'rape.'"

"Christ," Hud said, gnawing faster on the licorice whip that dangled from his lips and coiled in his lap. "You're twelve years old. The things that come out of you people's mouths." She stuck out her tongue through the mouth hole and buzzed him a raspberry, then peeled the bologna from her face. Looking at Millie's reflection in the rearview, at her chronic freckles and high forehead, Hud realized there was nothing exceptional about her wickedness. Millie dressed every morning as if three sheets to the wind. Her pink tights, her gingham skirt, her bright-orange down vest—it was the pure ugly of her that nagged at him. Meanwhile, he had no idea what kind of cute duds Nina had selected for herself that morning.

Waiting at the end of a weedy lane was a girl named Belinda, her face a raw pink from psoriasis, her eyes blood-shot from too little sleep. Belinda was everything Millie was not—mousy, pleasant, plump, and she always took a seat at the far back of the bus to read preachy, religious versions of Archie comics—the ones where Betty and Veronica never wore bikinis.

Posted in the middle of the fallow field of Belinda's family's farm was a peeling billboard, an ancient and vague antiabortion message with fading pastel butterflies, not quite visible to the interstate traffic that rumbled through the farmland a mile away.

"Every life is precious," Millie said, reading its message aloud.

"Don't be so naïve," Hud said.

A few minutes after stepping on, Belinda returned to the front. "Mr. Smith?" Belinda said, tapping Hud so softly on the shoulder he didn't feel it at first. "There's a girl in the back. I poked at her, but I think she might be dead."

Excited by the possibility of something tragic, Millie stood on her seat and shrieked. "Oh, no, there better not be nothin' dead on this bus," Millie practically sang. "I better not get traumatized by this."

I could power-staple steak to Millie's flesh, then toss her in with a pack of junkyard dogs, Hud thought as he slowed the bus to a stop in the middle of the dirt road.

The sun was only just up, and the bus still mostly empty. Millie, Belinda, and the two others—a white-haired boy and his teenaged sister, who wore beaded fringe and too much blush—followed Hud to the back. Hud saw that someone lay on the seat, her feet in the aisle, little dirty red bows atop her beat-up dressy shoes, but he doubted Belinda's forensics. He even thought he could hear the corpse snoring.

The feet belonged to Charlotte, as it turned out, the girl fast asleep, cigarette butts on the floor around her, her trench coat open to reveal only a satiny red slip with old torn lace that had turned brownish. She must have snuck in during the early morning hours, while the bus sat blocking the alley behind Hud's apartment.

Hud bent over to pick up the cigarette butts. For the first time since getting clocked on the back of the head the night before, Hud caught a scent—he could smell the booze that had spilled from a bumpy bottle shaped like grapes, and he felt a rush of relief, his nerves settling.

"Why don't you guys all go up front," Hud said, and even Millie obeyed without a peep. Charlotte, looking a bit demented with dried blood on her chapped lips, her hair flyaway with static, seemed to disturb the children more than if she'd turned out to be a stiff.

Hud took Charlotte's hand in his. "Yoo-hoo," he whispered.

"Where am I?" she said, waking tranquilly.

"Good question," Hud said. He picked up the bottle from the floor.

"That shit's treacherous," she said. "It's homemade. One of the church ladies brewed it and gave it to Daddy to knock him out after Mom died. It's been sitting in a cupboard all this time, working itself into a frenzy." She sat up, took a compact from her coat pocket, and flipped up its mirror. She flinched at her reflection, then licked her fingertips to try to smooth down her mussed hair. "I've run away from home," she said. "Not that anybody would notice."

"You're not going to get far in the back of my bus," Hud said.

"That's where you're wrong," she said. She crossed her legs and reached down to straighten the bow on her shoe. "You're going to kidnap me. Leave these monsters in the ditch there, and let's take off."

"I can't think of a worse idea," he said, sitting in the seat across from her. He picked up a toy pistol one of the kids had forgotten, and he popped a few shots in the air. He deeply inhaled the burnt smell of the spent cap.

"We're going to go find Gatling," Charlotte said. "He's in Nashville."

"Gatling's not in Nashville," Hud said, though he had no idea where along the road the Daughters of God had abandoned his boy. He'd snuck backstage to get a message to one of the Daughters as she'd stood in a stark-white choir robe, a roadie plucking her towering platinum wig from her head with one hand, powder-puffing her sweaty cheeks with the other. The girl was practically naked before Hud, wearing only underwear with elaborate belts and trusses, her breasts and butt cleverly hoisted and cantilevered. Hud stammered something about looking for his son, but before he could finish a sentence, a bouncer a full head taller than Hud grabbed him by the neck. "I got half a mind to yank out your peepers, ya perv," the bouncer said before literally kicking him through a curtain back into the crowd.

"I tried to find out where he was," Hud told Charlotte, "but the Daughters of God wouldn't let me get a word in. They wouldn't even accept the song I wrote for them." Hud patted the pocket of his torn tuxedo jacket, which he'd grabbed from the kitchen floor on his rush to the bus that morning. Inside was still the notepaper on which he'd composed a ditty with a few lines that sounded Bible-ish—about lambs and lilies and glossolalia, a word he'd learned from the defrocked priest who'd sold him the saint's bone chip.

"I happened to meet the bad Daughter of God," Charlotte said. "Have you ever just run into someone famous? It's like that chill you get when you almost step on a snake, but in a good way."

Hud was trying to imagine Gatling on the streets of Nashville. He felt a mix of pride and disgust. He loved picturing Gatling toiling around the town peddling his precious little tunes about tragically pretty girls. Gatling's voice wasn't much, but it was tense in a sexy way, and he had just the right look for an alternative-country album cover—filthy blue jeans hanging off his skinny hips, obscenely big belt buckles commemorating old rodeo championships, secondhand t-shirts with peeling iron-ons. Top it off with that silly, shoe-polish-black Elvis Lives hairdo and you've got yourself a phenomenon, Hud thought. Gatling could be the champion heartthrob of a cable talent show Hud occasionally watched on a lonely Saturday night, a contest for country-music hopefuls who perform their do-it-yourself songs for a panel of has-beens in the industry. *But,* Hud thought, *wouldn't it have been nice if I could've just up and left when I was so wet behind the ears, back when nothing frightened the hell out of me?* Instead he'd been saddled with the responsibility of trying not to be as shitty a father as his own had been.

Charlotte said, "Sunny said Gatling was headed for Nashville, last she knew. And she said he'd been religious, but then lost it. Lost his religion." She yawned, then lay back again, getting dreamy. "So I propose to go save his soul."

Hud's first instinct was to get all fatherly on her, to remind her that she was only sixteen years old and too young to be preoccupied with anyone's lousy soul but her own. But all summer he'd thought she might marry the Jesus freak and be folded into a lunatic congregation. She'd become one of those snaggle-toothed country wives who ended up in the news after doing something like dangling her firstborn into a pit of sacred rattlers.

"You and Gatling both could afford to fall a little," Hud said, relieved to hear that Gatling had given up on being born again. *You need to put the fear of God in him,* Tuesday's father had said when Gatling had his first semi-serious brush with the law. At thirteen Gatling had snuck behind the drugstore counter to thieve a *Hustler,* a pack of Sen-Sen, some cherry pipe tobacco, and a box of luxury sheepskin rubbers; only a year later he got sauced on a bottle of grocery-store Beaujolais and drove the Nova of his then-girlfriend (an older woman at seventeen) into an ice machine outside a gas station. Red foot the bill to send Gatling to a Christian camp for hopeless cases, and the boy returned after a month having turned almost deliriously good and madly in love with the Lord; but he also seemed embarrassed by Hud and Tuesday, who often overslept on the weekends and preferred their own ritual of long, leisurely breakfasts of waffles and omelets and the Sunday funnies. Hud secretly hoped for the devil to inch up into Gatling just a bit—and when Tuesday found a freshly rolled joint in the back pocket of Gatling's black churchgoing pants a few months after the Christian retreat, she and Hud celebrated by getting naked in their bedroom and smoking it while listening to a Jackie Gleason record Tuesday had just picked up for a nickel at a garage sale.

Gatling didn't have another bout with religion until just before he left, after Charlotte decided to no longer be his girl.

He'd tried to convince everyone that cutting her name into the skin of his chest was a kind of holy mortification.

"Don't you eat?" Hud asked Charlotte, noticing the bump of her ribs in the thin slip. He whistled toward the front of the bus. "Millie, bring me your lunch." Hud gave Millie five bucks, then put the tin pail on Charlotte's knees. The other children had wandered back too, and they all stared at Charlotte as she devoured the buttered bread that had once held bologna, and as she scooped chocolate pudding onto her finger and into her mouth. She tore into Millie's bag of gummy bears.

"Here," Millie said, taking the wilting cloth rose from the front of her dress and safety-pinning it to the lapel of Charlotte's trench. The pale boy's sister scooted in to sit on the other side of Charlotte, a plastic comb in her hand. She licked the teeth, then went to work on the tangles of Charlotte's hair.

Getting kidnapped would be the best thing that could happen to her, Hud thought as he watched Charlotte dig for the raisins at the bottom of a tiny box. All Ozzie's moping made his home a mausoleum. A neglectful daddy like Oz should be locked up, he thought, no matter what the man's dismal circumstances. But no, if Hud were to simply rescue the girl, buy her a dress and a steak, then drive her to Nashville to keep her from hitchhiking and getting meat-cleavered by a trucker gone psycho, Hud would be the one fingerprinted and mugshot.

Sitting in the seat across from Charlotte, Hud pressed his cheek to the cold window and looked out across the field. The four strapping sons of Vance Maxwell slogged their way toward the bus, apparently tired of waiting. One of the boys practiced his tuba and his marching-band goosestep. And coming down the road was Hilary Meek, the next stop on his route, on a pair of stiletto heels too old for her. *There's no escaping them,* he thought. Even when stopped in the middle of a desolate road, Hud drew every miserable wretch of a child to him, like a backward Pied Piper.

♦♦♦♦♦♦♦♦♦

I GOT *frisky in Frisco,* a mermaid declared in a dialogue balloon on the front of an illustrated postcard. She sunned herself, bare-chested and red-nippled, on the rocks of Alcatraz. In the week since he'd received the card, Hud had read and reread the writing on the back, comforted by his son's sloppy penmanship. But it wasn't until the evening after Charlotte's talk of Nashville, as Hud sat at his kitchen table conducting an amateur handwriting analysis, discerning a tendency toward rage in the severe slant of Gatling's *Jesus loves you* and a pronounced homesickness in the loops of his *God bless all,* that he noticed the postcard's curious postmark.

The card had not been mailed from San Francisco, nor from Nashville, but from Hot Springs, South Dakota, a small spa town just on the other side of the state line. Hud then checked the postmark of another card he'd recently received from his son, one with a picture of a row of Las Vegas slots spinning lemons and cherries. Gatling's latest stories about life with the Daughters of God, his musical ministry in cities of sin, were pieces of fiction conjured practically under Hud's nose—a measly four hours north.

Though late for his piano gig, Hud stuck the postcard in his back pocket, slapped on some aftershave, and headed off to Tuesday's to stitch together that amicable split they had discussed.

"Hey, darlin', I'm just sorry as hell," Hud rehearsed in his head as he stopped at the corner grocery store to grab a fistful of half-price, half-wilted daisies. Tonight he needed desperately to be welcomed into the house he'd often been kicked out of, to sit, have a cigarette, be poured a shot from a squat bottle of scotch. Hud dreaded returning to the Ramada Inn lounge. He'd never been bullied as a child—he'd been scrawny, so he'd affected a delinquent's squint on the playground that scared people off—but the thought of crossing paths with the punk who had stolen his tips gave Hud a kid's case of butterflies.

Red's yellow Cadillac stretched across most of Tuesday's driveway, with Rose's bug crammed in behind it, nipping at the Caddy's bumper. Hud parked the school bus across the street, then crept across the lawn to peep through the dining room window. *Rose's birthday,* he remembered when he saw what remained of a white cake on a plate, a few candles still burning and dripping their wax onto the frosting. Rose leaned forward to light a slim, ladylike cigar from one of the candles, while Tuesday did a Kentucky foxtrot with her father at the back of the room. Charlotte sat tearing a paper napkin to confetti in her lap, looking defeated despite her effort to gussy herself up—a spot of lipstick, a bent bobby pin.

Ozzie stood at the table's end to uncork a bottle of wine with the manner and ease of the man of the house. Criminal, Hud thought, that Ozzie could be at all comfortable in a place he'd so many nights disrupted.

Hud stepped close enough to the window for his breath to fog the glass. Suddenly Nina was on the other side, having snuck away from the table unnoticed. She breathed on the same spot of windowpane, then wrote "i c u" in the fog.

Hud winked, put his finger to his lips, and moved away to the back door. In the darkness of the screened-in back porch, depressed about not being invited to Rose's fling, he sat at the piano to quietly tap out a few bars of "Do Not Fold, Spindle, or Mutilate," Opal Lowe's suicide ballad that Nina liked to sing in the tub.

Hud stood to open the lid of the piano bench, where Tuesday kept much sentimental junk among the sheet music, then plucked from it a dried white rosebud from an old please-forgive-me bouquet. He put it behind his ear. From a yellowing envelope, he sprinkled some lost baby teeth into the palm of his hand and stuck them in his shirt pocket. Hud then took from the bench a tiny, undrunk bottle of mini-bar cognac saved from a night in a casino hotel suite he and Tuesday had won in a radio trivia contest. ("Patsy Cline's daughter has a name that might give you a cavity," the morning DJ had announced, then asked, "What is it?" Hud had been the first to phone in with "Julie Fudge.") Hud now twisted off the bottle's lid and downed the liquor, psyching himself up to storm into the dining room and wet-blanket the whole merry shebang.

From the bench, Hud took the first pack of cigarettes Tuesday had ever confiscated from Gatling, when the boy was only twelve, some soft-pack Marlboro reds she'd kept all these years.

"Hey, Ozzie, switch the record to something with some kick," Hud heard Rose say, though they were listening to Dinah Washington's perfectly kicky "Me and My Gin."

As Hud lit a stale cigarette, he heard Ozzie bump into the record player, knocking the needle to screech across the vinyl. With only a few puffs, the dried-up tobacco and cigarette paper burnt down to the filter, filling Hud's lungs with a ghastly black smoke that choked him.

He hacked as he stumbled down the hall, into the dining room, past the domestic bliss of the birthday party, and right up to Oz. He grabbed Ozzie's shoulders and shoved him into the china cabinet where the record player was awkwardly propped, sending the needle skipping forward into the middle of a maddening bossa nova. "If you're going to play my dad's old LPs on a shitty thrift-store turntable, at least show respect," Hud said through teeth still clenched on the cigarette's filter.

"Aw, sugar," Rose said, her cloud of eau de cologne thick in the air, "let's not have conniptions on my birthday." Hud had always cherished Rose, and just feeling the soft weight of her hand on his shoulder, hearing "sugar" on her tongue, almost compelled him to turn away from Ozzie. But it annoyed Hud how Oz stood so still, his arms limp at his sides, looking as polite as a door-to-door Mormon in his white shirt and black tie, as if he believed his lack of fight somehow made him the better man.

Hud spat the filter aside. "Don't pity me, you pathetic son of a bitch," Hud whispered, his lips just inches from Ozzie's ear. "You're worse off than I am, don't forget it." Hud gave Oz another shove against the cabinet, and the record skipped ahead into "Come Rain or Come Shine," and a few teacups tumbled forward to bust on the floor.

Oz had no business being at all confident or keeping company with another man's wife. Hud inched his hands back to touch the jut of Ozzie's shoulder blades, and he concentrated on his old friend's freak-show skinniness. It would never be a fair fight, Hud knew. Ozzie, and his lost little girl, were a tabloid tragedy in the works. You'd read about them someday, father and daughter, starved away to *Guinness Book* levels of invisibility.

Tuesday knelt on the floor, collecting the shattered pieces of teacup, clucking her tongue as if they'd ever owned anything other than mismatched china bought for nickels and dimes at this and that garage sale. "Go home, Hud," Tuesday said, tugging on his pant leg with her fractured hand, "or I'll call the police."

Rose said, "Oh, for God's sake, Day." She had poured some whiskey into a wine glass, which she now held up for Hud to see. She swirled the liquor around in the glass, letting it catch and release some sparkle of light in the dim room. "Nobody's inviting the cops over. Here, Hud, drink this. Drink more. Get drunk. A girl doesn't turn thirty-eight every day, you know."

The cognac and the dry smoke still burned in Hud's throat, so he shook his head at Rose's whiskey, trying to think of something mature and profound-sounding to mutter about the lack of comfort in hooch and cigarettes. Maybe he only drank and smoked because he liked the props, holding a glass by its stem, a bottle by its neck. He loved the cold, sharp snap of the lid of his steel lighter, and rubbing his thumb over the lighter's scratched decal of a Vargas girl in a slinky baby-doll. He hoped to grow up to be one of those men who could enjoy a proper happy hour, who took ease from the routine of one martini, then dinner, then TV, then sleep.

Hud unhanded Ozzie and took a step back to straighten the knot of Oz's necktie. Oz had wise, wide-open, gray-blue eyes that had always made him look old when he was young but would probably make him look young when he was old. "You're the rottenest dad around, kid," Hud said, tapping a finger at Ozzie's rib cage. He leaned in to whisper again. "Get to know your little girl a little better," he said, "or she'll run off. She'll be hitchhiking, blowing truck drivers, just to get as far away from you as she can."

At that Ozzie put his hand to Hud's chest to forcefully, but calmly and slowly, push him away. The blowing-truck-drivers bit was likely what finally provoked him, and even Hud realized it was a cheap shot. Hud knew he had no business dragging Charlotte, angelic enough and a long way from resorting to sucking off truckers, into his redneck effort to aggravate her father.

But instead of punching, Oz again acted the gentleman, stepping aside, taking Rose's glass of whiskey for only one sip.

"Who am I, anyway?" Hud mumbled, turning to look at the others in the room. They all feigned distraction, as if they hadn't even noticed he'd stopped their party. The Widow Bosanko brushed some crumbs off the tabletop. Rose swayed to music, though the music had ended. When he looked at Charlotte and saw her chewing, childlike, on the ends of her hair, he nearly apologized to her.

Hud took a candy letter from Charlotte's plate, the "s" from Rose's name on the cake, and ate it while admiring Nina. Nina stood on her chair wearing a dress not only too old for her, but *way* too old for her; with its leopard print and mangy fur collar and cuffs, she looked to be dressed like a hot-to-trot retiree. But Nina, a downright funny girl, somehow pulled it off.

"I'm sorry, have we met?" Hud said, winking at Nina. She giggled, then reached down to scratch at the back of her knee, bagging her loose tights in the process. The itch was quick, but enough to remind Hud of the spider bites she'd shown him the other day. She'd run her finger over the few small bumps on her leg and ankle as if they were something to be proud of. The girl had venom in her skin, Hud thought, because Tuesday never bothered to dust away cobwebs.

At the thought of spiders in Nina's sheets, their fangs in her leg, he reached out and grabbed his daughter around the waist with one arm, picking her up as she kicked for balance. Before he'd even stolen out of the room with her, everyone had begun yelping. Barreling toward the front door, Nina held in his arms awkwardly (his one hand at her hip, his other at her neck), he saw the reflection in the front picture window of the entire party in pursuit: Red rapping his ankle on the ottoman, the Widow sloshing her cocktail, Rose knocking over a floor lamp and sending clumsy shadows rushing across the walls.

Hud made it to his school bus even before the others had stumbled down the porch steps, but it was Nina who slowed his easy getaway. She had begun to whimper as he set her gently on the seat. "Aw, Neen," he said, with a tone of disappointment he hoped she didn't notice. Then he said, "I didn't hurt you, did I, Petunia?" Though her lips trembled, she squeaked out a "Nuh-uh," then, "My name's not Petunia." He pressed his thumb to a tear on her cheek. He considered, for a split second, that it might not be too late to undo the last rash few minutes. He could come out of the bus, swaggering and winking, dangling Nina by the ankle. *It's just a teensy-weensy party prank, you cranky sons of bitches! I'm the birthday clown!* The evening could still end pleasantly, couldn't it? With everyone gathered around the piano as Hud pounded out a polka with ribald lyrics?

But as Tuesday approached the bus, Hud's desire to punish returned, and he gave Nina a quick kiss on the top of her head, then got behind the wheel and closed the door. The old bus, not built for escape, putt-putted, backfiring, inching away from the curb. Tuesday kept pace alongside, pounding at the bus with both her hands. The thought of it—his wife desperate at the door as he ran off with their weeping little girl—gave him a sharp pain at his temples, a pain that worked down to tighten his stomach.

He braked and opened the door. Tuesday stood there in the street, in the flashing red light of the bus's stop sign.

"Don't beat the vehicle with your broken hand, dummy," he said. "You're just going to jack your fist up more, and guess what poor bastard you're going to blame it on." Tuesday's eyes were wet, her breathing hard from the running. She put one foot on the step up. "Look at the postmark," he said, handing her the San Francisco postcard. "Gatling's got to be in South Dakota," Hud said. "We can get there by, I don't know, just past midnight."

Hud wasn't sure if it was Gatling's proximity that lured Tuesday into the bus or the sound of Nina's crying, but he didn't ask and she didn't say. As Tuesday sat behind him to cradle their daughter in her arms, Hud simply closed the door and drove off, leaving the birthday party spoiled on the lawn.

PART FOUR

1 8 .

"**NASHVILLE,**" Charlotte uttered, with a sigh, after having been silent all evening. Everyone lingered on Tuesday's front lawn, looking off into the dark in the direction of the bus's disappearance. Oz undid his tie, his hands still jittery from the evening's confrontation. The Widow dug the muddled fruit from the bottom of her old-fashioned and chewed at the pulp of an orange slice. Rose fussed with the clasp on her wristwatch as Red's comb-over collapsed and fluttered in the gusts of a winterlike wind that had picked up.

"That's where they've gone, maybe," Charlotte told Oz. "That's where Gatling is, in Nashville." Speaking Gatling's name seemed to drop her deeper into her romantic funk. She fingered through her long string of flapperesque plastic pearls like she was counting off prayers on a rosary. Since when had Gatling been back on Charlotte's mind? Oz wondered. Wasn't it only days ago that she'd given away every dumb little gift Gatling had ever given her?

"I thought you thought Gatling was, you know, a little cuckoo for Cocoa Puffs," Oz said. "He cut your name into his skin, for God's sake."

"Right above his heart," she said, her lips in a pout, as she ran her fingers over the skin of her chest. She snapped out of her daze long enough to say, in a whisper of accusation, "Are you in love with Hud's wife?"

"Do you mean, Am I in love with Hud's *ex*-wife?" he said.

Charlotte sighed, then mumbled, "Why do we even bother?" She turned to go back into the house.

When it became apparent that the bus would not be immediately returning, Tuesday's family began to leave the yard, abandoning their initial plans to raise a toast at the strike of 11:53 (the exact minute in the night that Rose had been born back in nineteen-sixty-whatever). Ozzie volunteered to stay and clean up, and the Widow handed him her highball on her way to the Cadillac. Then Rose walked over and took the highball to get at the smashed maraschino among the ice cubes. "Sorry you got all roughed around tonight," she told Ozzie, chewing on the cherry as she handed the glass back. "My entire family is just out-and-out toxic," she said. "We should be avoided at all possible costs." The way she said it, with a wink and a foxy smile, it was clear to Oz there wasn't a speck of regret to her apology. Rose adored her family's failings and its civilized hostility to outsiders.

Ozzie returned to the dining room, where Charlotte sat eating from a puddle of melted ice cream with a soupspoon.

"What if I said yes?" Ozzie asked, though he wasn't in love with Tuesday; he didn't think so, anyway. All he knew for sure was that he loved how being with Tuesday felt both covert and perfectly logical. Back when both of them were married, he used to flirt with her—or he thought he was flirting (a wink, an aside half-whispered in her ear), but it was possible she never noticed. He and Tuesday, when alone now, rarely reminisced about the days before Jenny died, even though, some nights, old times were all he wanted to talk about.

"What if you said yes?" Charlotte said. "To what?"

"To what you just asked me out there. What if I said, Yes, I'm in love with Tuesday?"

"What if *I* said, You're answering a question with a question and that that's not a very good answer?" This time Oz was the one to sigh and shrug. He drank the dregs of the spice tea at the bottom of a cup.

"I'm embarrassed," Oz said. He put on another of Hud's dad's old albums, a scratched Peggy Lee so familiar that he knew exactly on which verse the record skipped—whenever he heard "Is That All There Is?" in his head, he heard the bump in the music too. Hud had been wrong in at least one regard: Ozzie did treat the records with respect. Hearing a song he hadn't heard in years could rush Oz back and settle him gently among the hundreds of simple evenings he'd spent in this very house, when they'd play round after round of card games they taught themselves from the Book of Hoyle. When Charlotte was little, in the years before Nina, the only girly toys Tuesday had for her was a blue buggy from her own childhood, containing a plastic doll bald from having had all its hair loved off. Oz could remember Charlotte clutching the doll to her chest as she lay in Jenny's arms, Jenny somehow, all at once, rocking Lottie, winning at cards, and sipping her white zin without spilling.

"Hud seems to think I don't know my own girl," Oz said.

"Do you want the honest-to-God truth?" Charlotte asked.

"No," he said, then he chuckled, as if he was only joking. "No, go ahead. What is it?"

"I slept in Hud's school bus last night," she said, her voice almost sing-song. It was the same voice she'd used only weeks before to taunt him with hints of her sordid religious awakenings. "Then when he found me this morning I begged him to kidnap me. I tried to talk him into taking me to Nashville. Doesn't that scare the living daylights out of you, Ozzie?"

"Yes," Oz said, but actually what he felt was a complicated relief. Thank Jesus that Hud was such a good man deep down. There'd actually been something reassuring about the evening's dustup, a camaraderie with his old friend that Oz had desperately missed. "And since when have you called me Ozzie?"

"Only for, like, the last, I don't know, two years," Charlotte said. Suddenly, for a second that was breathtaking, Charlotte sounded like the newly motherless 13-year-old she'd been, her soft voice breaking with an inarticulate and fragile anger. "In case you haven't noticed," she said, "I have terrible habits."

"Your mother would have done so much better with you," Ozzie said. He was thinking of Jenny's easy demeanor, how impossible it had been to discourage her. By the time Jenny turned 32, she'd had short-lived careers as a piano instructor, arts-and-craft director at a nursing home, a jewelry store clerk, and a librarian's assistant. "You'd been better off," Oz said, "if I'd been the one to . . . you know. And she'd been the one to . . ."

"What does any of that matter?" Charlotte said, raising her voice and hitting her fist against the table, rattling the spoon on the plate. "You just say things like that to get sympathy. I'm supposed to feel sorry for you because *you* feel bad for making *me* feel bad?" She took a cigarette from a pack left atop the table. Ozzie's instinct was not to nag her for lighting up in front of him, but to egg her on, to say all the wrong things and keep her defiant. She'd been so weak in the knees from Junior's wicked and prayerful influence, that Oz welcomed any sign of revolt. If *he* were to give *her* the honest-to-God truth, it would be that he'd been afraid for her for weeks. He'd caught himself obsessively squinting at her pupils, worrying they'd shrunk to pinpoints like a drug addict's; he thought her skin looked splotchy at times, and that her stomach pooched, her hair gone dull, signs of conditions he couldn't bear to know about.

In avoidance of his daughter, Ozzie had spent most recent nights hiding in the studio, the doors locked, the windows blacked-out with trash bags. Since shattering the church window, he'd been immersed in refashioning it into his own rebellion. Word of his crime, his destruction, would quickly spread. Who again would ever trust him with something delicate like the repair of a trumpet played by a glass Gabriel, or the replacement of the broken fold of a saint's robe? But at least this window, if it were his last, would be noticed.

"What if I took you to Nashville myself?" Ozzie said.

"Now, why would you want to do a thing like that?" Charlotte asked, blowing smoke out haughtily.

He didn't want to tell her that Charlotte's mother had spoken, at her sickest, about the three of them taking a trip to Nashville where the country star Rose-Sharon (backed by a trio of chubby women in white pantsuits called the Lilies of the Valley) performed nightly in her own mini-Opry. Rose-Sharon, at the height of her career, had been temporarily silenced by tongue cancer. When she did again sing, with the aid of a prosthesis, it was mostly a high-pitched hum drowned out by the killer pipes of the Lilies of the Valley; nonetheless the ailing flocked from around the world, convinced they'd be healed just from hearing what few peeps they could from the blessed survivor. Jenny mostly joked about such devotion, but Oz could see how enraptured she'd become by the idea of quick-fix miracles. Ever since, he couldn't listen to a Rose-Sharon song on the car radio without having to pull over and blubber.

"We could hunt for Gatling together," Oz told Charlotte.

"You hate Gatling," she said, dismissively, standing, grabbing her purse and snuffing her cig in a slice of birthday cake.

Maybe, when his window was put into place, he'd be declared a heretic, and he and Charlotte would be chased far from town. He was attracted to the idea of a new life somewhere strange. It could conceivably save them, his act of destroying church property.

"Where are you going?" Oz asked.

"Home," she said, leaving the room.

"But I said I would clean up," he called after her.

"So, clean up," she said. The front screen door squeaked open, then slammed shut.

Ozzie walked to the sideboard to splash more bourbon over the fruit in the Widow's glass. As he sipped his drink, he picked up a studio portrait of Tuesday and her family, taken only a few years before, she and Hud and Gatling and Nina sitting stiff-backed in their Sunday garb. Though so much about the portrait seemed forced—from their postures, to their pressed suit jackets and fresh haircuts—Ozzie was jealous. Hud's family looked indestructible. They could all walk out on each other and still never disentangle.

Someone knocked at the front door. "Trick or treat," came a girl's voice, though Halloween was not for another few nights. Ozzie happened to know that Tuesday had a serious sweet tooth for Hot Tamales—for years she'd been buying boxes in bulk from the drive-in's concession stand supplier. As he looked for her stash in the kitchen pantry, he thought of all the elaborate costumes Jenny had sewn for Charlotte's childhood, based on fairy tale characters and historical figures—powdered wigs, endless ruffles, puffy skirts. Charlotte had often wanted to go dressed simply—as a daisy or a bumblebee—but she indulged Jenny, who had always wanted a precocious daughter.

"I don't got all night," came the voice again from the front porch. When Oz went to the door with the box of Hot Tamales, the child gasped. It was Millie, goose-pimpled in a polka-dot bikini and flip-flops, who he hadn't seen since she'd hit the softball through his studio window. Millie dropped her pillowcase of loot and ran into the street, nearly getting sideswiped by a gangly teenaged boy riding a Huffy too small for him. The boy tinkled the bike's bell at her, she called him a faggot, and she wriggled under a row of rosebushes and vanished. It's not too late to accuse her, he thought, to lie and say that it was her stray ball that had shattered the stained glass. Maybe her sudden appearance on the porch, begging for sugar, was a celestial sign of his last chance at salvation. *She doesn't even know she didn't do it,* whispered the little devil in Oz's left ear.

Oz dismissed the temptation, but not because of any sympathy for Millie. No, he wouldn't pass blame, because then he'd have to give up his plot of rebuilding the window himself—he'd likely have to relinquish all its worthless pieces to the church.

Ozzie sorted through Millie's candy on the porch floor, picking out a few lollipops and some Bazooka, then set the bag inside the front door. He couldn't wait another minute to introduce Charlotte to the wreckage in his studio. Driving home, he pulled up to the sidewalk when he saw her; her long loop of pearls hung down her back, almost reaching the zigzaggy seams of her loose vintage nylons. Charlotte had an artist's spirit, he thought with both pleasure and disappointment.

"I broke the church window," he told her before she'd even closed the pickup door. He handed her a lollipop. "Shattered it. Ruined it."

"How?" she said, gasping, her surprise authentic. *I've got her,* he thought.

"Threw a ball at it."

"On purpose?"

"On purpose," he said. "Kind of on purpose, anyway. But I don't think I was quite in my right mind."

"What are you going to do?"

"Want me to show you?" he asked. Charlotte nodded, and they drove in silence the few blocks to the house. He could tell from the way she chewed on the lollipop, cracking the candy hard on her teeth, that she was nervous. But once they were in the studio, she took on the brisk manner of a woman in charge. She walked to Ozzie's work area, her arms crossed, the authoritative click of her heels echoing.

On a plank of plywood on the floor, Ozzie had begun to jigsaw together his design, meticulously arranging the salvaged shards alongside new pieces of glass. He was working from the bottom up, and had only so far positioned a field of lilies with abstract blooms. Two of the lilies had as their stems the long speckled necks of the giraffes that had originally poked up from the stern of Noah's ark. Another bloomed from the cotton-candy-pink leg that had broken off the biblical stripper Salome. "There had been a choir of angels at the top originally, remember?" he said, kneeling next to the plywood. "But their robes were such a thick white, the morning sunlight would get lost. So I'm using the white glass down here at the bottom." He said nothing of how the flowers suggested Rose-Sharon's loud Lilies of the Valley, or of the other personal references he planned to make. He certainly wouldn't yet tell her about the significance of elevating modest-faced Noah's wife, in the iridescent dress Jenny had so admired, to the very top of the window, graven-image-like, to the red clouds of the revised heaven.

"Where's the cartoon?" Charlotte asked, tapping her foot and glancing around the room before seeing it taped to the wall behind her. Just hearing her use, so unselfconsciously, an inside term like "cartoon"—a stained-glass artist's blueprint, a rendering on paper of a window's design—set Ozzie to picturing Charlotte as his apprentice. As she appraised the drawing, scratching her chin with concentration, Ozzie invented a rosy future for them: Yates & Yates they'd call themselves, or The Oz and Lottie Glass Co.

"Mine is actually a tribute to the original," Oz said, picking up some Polaroids from his workbench. He pointed out to Charlotte the first window's subversive worship—the forked tongue of the snake tickling Eve's naked toes, for example, and the leer of a juggler unicycling through the alleyways of Sodom.

Charlotte only glanced at the photos, and returned her attention to Ozzie's cartoon. He couldn't wait to see her standing in the varied light of the finished window and mesmerized by his Apocrypha—the severed and scattered limbs of biblical figures in turmoil like from the dreams of a fevered priest: Adam's apple on Eve's head; the mummified Lazarus stepping up from the blowhole of Jonah's whale.

"Do you think it's ridiculous?" Oz asked her.

"Yeah," she said, giggling. "Yeah. It's totally ridiculous."

"Well, sure, yeah, it's definitely playful," Oz said. "But I don't know if I, you know, like the idea of it being ridiculous. But yeah, you're probably right, it's maybe too . . . peculiar.

I was afraid of that. It's too ridiculous. What should I change?"

"Oh, no, nothing," Charlotte said. "Nothing at all. It's just crazy. And it's sweet. And you're never going to get away with it."

Then Charlotte, with a spirit he hadn't seen in her in months, maybe years, said, "What if we did go to Nashville?" She picked up a piece of glass that had once been part of a burning bush, and she smoothed her thumb over it. Ozzie intended the flame for the wings of an angel singed by the Apocalypse. "You could open up a shop and sell your own stuff. Not just windows, but lamps. Or sun catchers, and that kind of crap." She glanced back at the cartoon. "Noah's wife at the top. Because Mom liked her dress?"

"How did you know about that?" he said.

"You've told me a million times," she said.

If she were his apprentice, she could convince a congregation of anything, he was certain. She could stand at the altar and articulate that the new window was no act of blasphemy, but rather the exact opposite. *My father has never felt closer to God,* she'd tell them with the gentle fervor of a girl evangelist.

"Sometimes I still have arguments with your mom," Ozzie said. "In my head. Or even out loud sometimes, when I'm alone. I'll think of things we should have fought about more. Like, I still get mad at her for that time she left the back gate open and Darling Clementine ran away. She was always leaving the back gate open. She was so careless a lot of the time." Whenever the gate was open, Clementine, as dumb a dog as any there was, would wander off. And though she was a Great Dane and 120 pounds, she one day just vanished into thin air. Jenny took it the worst, standing in the front of the house in 30-degree cold until midnight, whistling, pacing, like a sailor's wife on the shore gone lunatic. She ended up blaming Oz though, for jinxing the dog, for naming it irresponsibly after the old song that seemed a foretelling: "My darling Clementine, you are lost and gone forever."

"Isn't that stupid?" Oz said. "Old arguments from years ago."

"Ridiculous," Charlotte said, in a voice as tiny as the snap of a twig.

ᗅᗅᗅᗅᗅᗅᗅ

N I N A bawled nonstop, at the top of her puny lungs, for approximately seventy miles. In the first seat of the school bus, she rested her head on Tuesday's lap and petted the mangy fur collar of her dress in an effort to comfort herself, loosening tiny wild hairs that Tuesday had to occasionally pluck from her own tongue.

Hud tried what he could to quiet her as he drove—he sang a song he composed off-the-cuff, a thing called "Nina's Got No Reasons to Weep," in which he literally sang her praises. Tuesday thought the song was darling but endless.

But, truth be told, for the first fifteen miles or so Tuesday had no interest in calming Nina; had Nina cried herself to sleep too soon, she would have had to pinch the girl to keep her riled up. Hud deserved the guilt. Usually Nina was a too-willing accomplice in Hud's schemes—Tuesday could imagine Nina easily escaping with Hud to Hot Springs and composing her own misleading postcards chronicling her renegade life. It was actually a relief to have Nina so done in by this kidnapping.

Eventually Nina's crying worked to settle Tuesday's anger; as she and Hud suffered together through Nina's noisy nervous breakdown, she found herself needing to exchange exhausted looks in the rearview—they would glance up at each other, smile consolingly, keeping eye contact in the mirror for a moment or two. They didn't share a word, but she knew that he was thinking what she was thinking: of those many long middle-of-the-nights when Nina was newborn and colicky. The squalling baby in his arms, Hud walked in circles in the bedroom, adorable in only his saggy pj bottoms, his hair sticking straight up as he leaned forward to uselessly whisper some coo-cooing in Nina's ear. The infant Nina had been such a brat that Tuesday had gone to the drive-in that first Halloween as Mia Farrow in *Rosemary's Baby*—she'd taken scissors to a blond wig to mimic Mia's Vidal Sassoon hack job and zipped Nina into red terry-cloth jammies on the hood of which she'd sewn little horns.

Tuesday took Nina's mood ring from her finger and put it on her own pinky. At the birthday party they'd all passed the ring around the table, trying it on to watch the clouds in the glass stir into murky telltale colors.

"What does bluish-greenish-yellowish mean?" Tuesday shouted above Nina. "Like a light bruise?" She reached forward and tapped her hand on Hud's arm for him to see. She could have refused to speak to him, or complicated things in any number of ways. She felt she was being generous by not staying in a snit.

"It means you're miserable," Hud shouted back. "Lost. Confused. On the verge in a big way."

Tuesday took her hand back to watch the colors shift again, some pink bubbling up. "I'm not miserable at all," she said, and it was mostly true. She was, in large part, happy, somehow.

"What?" Hud asked, Nina's crying finally lowering to a whimper.

"Nothing," she said. She didn't want him to know that she wasn't miserable. She was surprised by how pleased she was at the thought that she might see Gatling soon. In the days before he left, Gatling had only looked at her with disappointment and pity, seemingly seeing a woman far too inept to keep her son in line. And a crooked glance from one of her children was often all it took to sweep her into insecurity. Even Nina's fits, when she'd accuse Tuesday of cruelty for making her put on a jacket or take a bath, sometimes worked to convince her that she was inept at motherhood. It was foolish, but she couldn't deny it: her children could tell her anything about herself, cast a judgment no matter how skewed, and she'd almost always, at least partly, believe them.

Tuesday was careful to keep still so as not to disturb Nina, who had finally stopped crying, whose lips puffed with soft, congested-sounding snores. She leaned over to rest her forehead against the window as the bus's headlights swept across a salvage yard of junked vehicles. She should have stayed furious with Hud, she knew. If Nina had just gone silently along with the snatch-and-grab, Hud would have ignored Tuesday's banging her fists against the bus. He wouldn't have stopped; he wouldn't have shared his discovery of the South Dakota postmark. She should not mistake any of this, she told herself, for something romantic.

"Do you remember that time," Tuesday said, "when we only had Gatling, and we'd been to South Dakota, and we were driving back along this highway after dark? We saw that guy or that kid or whatever he was, on the shoulder of the highway? He was trying to wave us down, and he had a flashlight."

"Ohhhh yeah," Hud said, "I think so. He was stepping up out of the ditch, I think. But he was holding the flashlight in front of himself, wasn't he? Lighting himself up so we could see him? He was either a short man or a tall boy."

"I don't think he was crawling up out of the ditch," Tuesday said. "He was standing there, standing still, waving one arm really slowly. And I think he was smiling. You know, now that I think about it, *that's* what was so creepy about him. I think that's why we didn't stop." That upsetting smile, sudden and brightly lit, had lingered in the car with them that night, for hours disrupting their sense of safety. "Why do you think he was there?"

"To murder us and steal our damn car," Hud said, too loud.

"Shhh," Tuesday said as Nina shifted on her lap and blinked her eyes open. Tuesday held as still as she could and bit her lip, hoping for Nina to just drift back off. When Nina did close her eyes again, Tuesday said softly, "Or maybe he lived in one those houses out there in the middle of nowhere and needed a ride to the next town. There could have been an emergency. Maybe he wasn't smiling at all and just looked like he was smiling. We drove by so quickly."

"Nah," Hud said. "He had a straight razor in his back pocket that he intended on holding to some poor sucker's throat, I guarantee. Or his junkie girlfriend was crouching in the ditch with a pistol. And we had borrowed your dad's Caddy for the trip, which was pretty new at the time. Leather seats. That fancy climate control that it's got. If we'd have been the ones to be good Samaritans, we'd still be rattling around in that trunk."

"Wouldn't you want someone like us to stop for Gatling if he crawled up out of a ditch? Wouldn't you feel better knowing that respectable people don't just drive by, afraid, when they see some kid needing help?"

"Sure," Hud said. "But I also feel pretty good knowing that I didn't read in the paper the next morning about me and my little family being disemboweled by a hitchhiker. Obviously, if we'd stopped for the kid, and he'd offed us all, Gatling would never have even had a chance to grow up and run away from us. And to crawl up out of a ditch himself someday."

"Ack," Tuesday said, shaking her head at him in the mirror. "The way your brain works." But Tuesday, against her better sense, felt somewhat relieved by Hud's logic and his certainty about the hitchhiker's psychosis and threat. She even felt a little blessed at the thought of having cheated death that night by simply ignoring a gesture for help.

ﻟﻟﻟﻟﻟﻟﻟ

S N O W fell in Hot Springs in the early morning. Tuesday and Nina sat on the deck of the hotel spa on a teak bench, their legs wrapped with a frayed electrical blanket that popped and sizzled as it heated up. They looked like pampered dowagers, both in terry-cloth robes, dryer-fresh towels twisted around the tops of their heads. A creek, busy with ducks, ran in front of the deck, and wisps of steam rose from the warm water. Tuesday held above herself and Nina an umbrella she had borrowed from the concierge; she concentrated to listen to the hiss of the heavy flakes as they touched the water's surface, a sound like the snuffing of a matchstick.

"Why did you and Daddy get a D-V-I-T-O-R-T?" Nina asked, annoyed.

Tuesday squinted, putting the letters together in her head. "Where'd you learn how to almost spell that word?" she asked.

"Daddy and I sing that song sometimes," she said. "You know," then she sang, off-key, "D-R-O-R-I-T-E."

"No," Tuesday said, then corrected, singing, "D-I-V-O-R-C-E." Nina had wanted them all to strike out together that morning—Hud's plan was to poke around in coffee shops, to question the town's old coots who likely knew everybody. But Tuesday's back and neck ached from the bus ride, so when she saw the list of deluxe services offered in the hotel's spa, it had been too tempting to be a little neglectful. Nina had been mollified some by the lemon wedge the spa specialist had given her to suck on (Nina loved things sour enough to make her nose run), but she was still fidgety with disgust.

For all of Tuesday's frustrations with Gatling, she had faith that his return to their lives would restore the old warped order. From the time that Nina was an infant, she and Hud had sided together in family disputes. Hud would get angry with Gatling for some dumb bit of rebellion, and as punishment, he'd lavish all his attention on his little girl. Tuesday sometimes actually felt nostalgic for those days when Hud barely spoke to Gatling, and she and her son would steal moments alone to lament all the dysfunction of their tiny house as they snuck cigarettes in the mudroom or rocked slowly on the backyard swing set. They'd sit there, the chains creaking, staring at the house, at the reflections of the trees in the windows, and inventorying all Hud's failings. All the while they'd be secretly hoping for him to step outside and smile and wave, or bring them some cold bottles of root beer, signaling the end of his fit of bad temper. Hud was not at all cruel, only childish, and stubbornly distant at his worst. And when he was at his worst, everyone around him fell hostage to his mood.

A spa lady in pink scrubs appeared with a mortar and pestle. "So what brings you to Hot Springs?" she asked. The woman began to putty the crushed fruit onto Tuesday's cheeks with a tongue depressor.

"I'm looking for my son," Tuesday told her. She said it like a woman might say it in an English mystery, giving it a tenor of hope and exhaustion and propriety. "His name is Gatling Smith."

Tuesday had already left a message with her school's secretary explaining that she had to attend to a family emergency. As she looked up at the former veteran's hospital on the hillside that towered, abandoned, over the village like a fairy-tale castle, she considered quitting her job. She could become an art therapist in a spa town, she thought. In her years as a grade school art teacher, she'd interpreted hundreds of telling works in crayon and pencil, feeling privy to the children's most deep-seated psychoses. She'd seen stick figures exact bloody violence on father types in neckties, and pretty, chimney-topped houses painstakingly drawn brick by brick only to then be scribbled over with a swirling tornado. Boys had articulated the intricacies of complicated guns, every trigger and switch, while girls had rendered themselves entirely without faces in family portraits.

"Do you have a picture of your son?" the woman asked, obscuring Tuesday's vision by placing a few thin slices of cucumber over her eyes.

Before leaving to comb Hot Springs, Hud had given Tuesday one of the two outdated wallet-sizes of Gatling that he always carried around with him. Both pictures were creased and water-speckled. Hud took Gatling age seven, front teeth missing, stubborn cowlick, suede vest. Tuesday took Gatling age twelve with a bowl-like haircut he'd probably never forgive her for.

"I've got it," Nina said. She had kept it at hand all morning.

"But imagine him almost eighteen now," Tuesday said, lifting a cucumber slice to watch for the woman's reaction.

"They have computer programs that can, you know, do a time-lapse thingie," she said, handing it back. "You know. Make them look like they might look. Did his dad run off with him?"

"No," Tuesday said, though she was tempted to say *yes* so she wouldn't have to admit that she had simply let Gatling slip away. "Gatling's tall. Pretty blue eyes. And these long, dark lashes I'd kill for. And he has this kind of pompadour, I guess you'd call it?" She smoothed her fingers over the top of her head, as if signing the international symbol for "pompadour." "I've always hated that haircut," Tuesday added. She laughed. "He'd look so much better with it just normal. Oh, and he has a tattoo on his arm. Dice." She didn't tell the woman about the scars across his chest; she didn't want her to judge.

"A friend of my sister's," the woman said, nodding, and Tuesday's pulse sped up.

"Gatling's a friend of your sister's?" she asked.

"Oh, no, no, sorry, dear," she said. "A friend of my sister's got her kid snatched." She took a file to the fingernails of Tuesday's broken hand. "A little boy named . . ." She *hmmm*ed, twisting her lips around in semi-deep thought. "Freddie?

Frankie? Anyway, it's been, like, four years. The boy's dad took him on a hunting trip and didn't bring him back, and now who the hell knows? About a year later, there was a message on my sister's friend's answering machine that might have been from the kid, but all it was was a tiny little voice saying a single word—what sounded like 'Mommy?' We all sat there and listened and listened, and one of us would think we heard it clearly, so we'd play it back, then play it again, then we'd start to think it wasn't even a voice at all, but like the squeak of a bedspring. Or a bird tweeting. It was like when a word's at the tip of your tongue. It was like at the tip of your ear, you know? The tip of your hearing. But before she could even bring the answering machine to the police, she lost the message. It was just on one of those microchips, and it got recorded over when her boyfriend called to yell at her for not coming over to walk his dog. Can you believe it? Trash."

Her eyes shut behind the cuke slices, Tuesday instinctively reached a pinky out, just to feel Nina beside her. "Did your sister's friend ever suspect that her ex would run off with Freddie? Frankie?" Tuesday asked.

"I don't think so," she said. "He had a cushy job. He'd just bought new boobs for his fiancée. Things were looking up for him."

All morning Tuesday's patience with Hud had wavered—when he'd brought her a change of clothes from a hardware store, she'd at first been flattered that the Levis didn't fit, implying that he thought she was much thinner in the hips than she actually was. But then she'd gotten miffed, wishing he knew her better, that he'd ever bothered to notice that she wasn't the same insanely petite thing he'd married. Then, as they'd headed around the corner to a café with lace drapes to have cinnamon bear claws, she'd put her arm in his in front of a place called Mad Hattie's Haberdashery. In the window, on a mannequin, was a dress of crushed blue velvet.

"I might go as Isabella Rossellini this year," Tuesday speculated. "You could go as Dennis Hopper. You could wear an oxygen mask; that might be cute." She knew she shouldn't encourage any hope for a return to old times, but something about seeing her breath in the cold morning air made her nostalgic. For years the drive-in had played its last movie of the season on Halloween, people showing up in costume to sit through a wretched horror flick from Red's collection. Hud had once chosen to go in t-shirt and cuffed jeans as Paul Le Mat, an actor he regarded as underrated, in *American Graffiti,* with Tuesday as his Mackenzie Phillips. After sending the kids to the drive-in's office to play Monopoly with the Widow, Hud and Tuesday, though having barely touched their thermos full of grape juice and vodka, kissed and heavy-petted in the backseat.

Dressing up as movie couples had become one of their own traditions, and Hud had always longed for tradition, Tuesday knew. He'd admired how Tuesday's family was so close-knit and shut off, with their own words for things and their own odd habits on holidays. Standing in front of Mad Hattie's Haberdashery, wrapping her arms around Hud for warmth, she'd realized how much she'd probably upset him by not inviting him to Rose's stupid party. And in the chill and the slow snowfall, in this town with its healthful waters, she felt like forgiving him, and overlooking for the moment his capacity for making a hash of everything. If he ended up agreeing to go as Dennis Hopper to her Isabella Rossellini, she thought she might even be able to entertain the idea of inching toward reconciliation.

DESPITE flashing Gatling's old school picture around and offering explicit description, down to the chicken-pock mark to the left of his left eye and the oval burn scar on his ankle from once touching against the hot muffler of a refurbed moped when he was eleven, Hud gathered nothing from the coffee-shop gossips. But he was buoyed by the attention the strangers gave him, and their sympathetic gestures of buying him cup after cup of bitterly strong joe as he sat right down at their tables to tell them the story of losing his family.

The only person to offer a clue of where to begin to look was a woman who sat on the porch of a bed and breakfast, with an easel and paints, wearing a yellowed white-fur coat. Though the woman cast her gaze down the street and up a cliff, she painted an old boat abandoned to a lake.

"Try Mad Hattie's Haberdashery," the woman said upon hearing about the postcards Gatling had been sending. "She has a collection of postcards from all over. I bought one once—a nifty holograph of a pagoda. When you moved it a little, Japanese girls stood and bowed."

When Mad Hattie's finally opened at noon, Hud, who'd been waiting on a bench, stepped in feeling ice-cold, his head filled with the noise of his teeth clacking. "I want to buy that dress in the window," he told the only person inside. The woman stood adjusting the coat-hanger rabbit ears of a black-and-white TV in an effort to bring in a soap opera—the noise in the room moved back and forth between syrupy violin strings and static.

"I'll tell you right now it's not going to fit," the woman deadpanned. Though she wore a baseball jersey with Evel Knievel on it, and pajama bottoms patterned with cacti and coiled rattlesnakes, Hud mistook her for a serious person.

"It's not for me," he said.

The woman sighed and moved toward the window display. "I know," she said, not pleasantly. "I'm a little bit of a comedian." The zipper on the blue velvet dress stuck, so she ended up dismantling the mannequin, unscrewing the hands from the wrists, the waist from the hips. The woman cussed up a storm as she struggled with the parts of the dummy.

Hud refused to let the woman's sourness affect his temper. There'd been no sign yet of Gatling in Hot Springs, but in the hours since sunup Hud had been nearly delirious with contentment. When Tuesday slipped her arm in his in front of the window of Mad Hattie's, when she'd proposed going out on Halloween as another sick movie couple, it had been all he could do to keep an ounce of cool. In his enthusiasm, he'd nearly ruined the moment by rattling off other costume suggestions—Hud had always preferred to go as someone who looked good, like James Dean in *Giant*, with Tuesday as Liz Taylor, in the scene where Dean serves her tea in his shack.

"You want the velvet shoes too?" the woman asked.

"Why not?" Hud said. "So are you Hattie, or what?"

"People call me Trish," she said. She took the dress and shoes to a roll-top desk, where she stapled a rip in a seam, then began to color in scuff marks on the shoes with a mascara brush. "Hattie was just the name already on the window when I bought the place."

Hud saw the spinning rack of postcards across the room; he went to thumb through them, picking up one featuring a cartoon 'gator in a tux wishing greetings from the Florida Everglades, and a naughty one with a naked lady in a beret sitting at a sidewalk bistro in Paris. Just as he was about to ask Trish if a boy named Gatling frequented Mad Hattie's, he saw the guitar—midnight blue with Nina's name in yellow in quotation marks painted along a curve.

"Oh my God," Hud said, more relieved than shocked, picking the guitar up from where it sat perched in the bowl of a dry stone birdbath. The beaded strap held the scent of Gatling's skin, a mix of Brut cologne and sweat. Hud put the strap around his shoulder and strummed a few chords, then tightened the strings to tune. "How the hell'd you get this?" he asked.

"Oh," Trish said, "Charlotte." In a split second Hud conjured up a whole conspiracy, Charlotte tiptoeing up to Hot

Springs for weekends on the sly, inventing theories of Nashville to throw everyone off. "That's what we call him, anyway," she said, "because that's what it says on the poor thing's chest. He works as an afternoon lifeguard over at the indoor Plunge. He doesn't talk to anyone much, so I don't think anyone even knows his real name."

Hud hugged his son's guitar to his chest and ran his cheek against the neck of it. No wonder no one had responded to Hud's description of the boy—he'd left off the scars, he realized. He'd totally forgotten. He'd been simply describing a big-eyed, misguided youth likely making a living as a street musician. A nomadic troubadour.

"This might interest you too," Trish said, opening a drawer in a curio cabinet. "I keep these out of sight. I'm not sure what to charge for them." She held up a plastic baggy containing a pair of white panties. "Used," she said. "And even signed by the bad Daughter of God, believe it or not." She opened the baggy and took from it a Polaroid that she held up for Hud to see. In it, the Daughter of God named Sunny, with a dirty grin, lifted her choir robe to show the very same white panties now preserved at Mad Hattie's Haberdashery. "Can't ask for more authentication than that," she said. She touched her fingertip to the photo, to Sunny's privates.

"Just add this guitar to the dress and shoes, please," he said with a strum.

"What's your interest in it, anyway?" she asked.

"The guy you call Charlotte is my son," he said. He played a few chords of "A Boy Named Sue."

After putting the dress and shoes in a grocery sack, Trish lit up a cigarette and crossed her legs. She seemed to study Hud's face a moment. He thought she might be seeking a resemblance. "I have a fifteen-year-old daughter who won't even get her curls wet at the Plunge," she said, "though your boy doesn't look in her direction. Thank God. My Sylvie would escape with him in a second if he said a word. It's bad enough that he's kind of pretty, but he's got that precious-innocent look on his face. And with that girl's name gouged into his chest? Forget it. He could be lethal to a dumb kid like mine."

"Well, whatever," Hud said, with pride in his son's aura of mystery and trouble. "I'll be taking him away. He'll be going home with me."

"Don't sneak up on him, for God's sake," she said. "You don't want to spook him, so don't go waltzing to the Plunge expecting a big 'Good to see ya.' Leave him a note. Tell him where you are. Let him come to you."

Hud was tempted to take her advice—Trish had silver hairs and dark circles beneath her eyes, and had begun to speak in the grave voice of a woman who'd seen more than a few things through to their worst possible conclusions.

GATLING slouched in a low lifeguard's chair at the edge of the indoor pool, looking not at all like the devil-may-care, soulful-eyed boy Hud had been describing around town. When Hud saw that he'd buzzed his thick hair to the skin of his skull and that he'd grown thinner in the seven or so months since running off, he nearly turned and snuck out.

"If I was a drowning man," Hud called out, "I'd have to call for a priest. Look at yourself." Gatling appeared unfit to rescue even himself if forced to leap into the deep end—he was lucky if he weighed a good 130 pounds soaking wet. Hud had intended for his greeting to sound kind of slap-on-the-back, all buddy-buddy, unceremonious. But his voice trembled and echoed off the walls.

Gatling looked up, smiling, not a flicker of shock on his face. "Hey, Pops," he said with a wink. He too seemed to want to come across as the king of smooth, but then he bit his lip and looked back down toward the water, his shoulders beginning to shake. Hud stopped at the sound of Gatling's sniffling, still several steps from the lifeguard's chair. He clenched his teeth and rubbed his tongue against the roof of his mouth, then remembered you did that to keep from sneezing, not to keep from crying.

"I didn't mean it, Gup," he said, resurrecting an old nickname, short for "Guppy," he hadn't used in years. The few times Hud had brought his family to Hot Springs for vacation, they'd spent most of their days in the 80-degree waters of the Plunge, Gatling the most content to abolish all plans of sightseeing the Badlands and Mount Rushmore and even the Reptile Gardens, where Nina had hoped to rub elbows with defanged vipers. More than once, in the thick air of the indoor pool, Gatling had upset them all with his talent for dead-man-floating so convincingly.

"Nah, come on, kid, you look svelte," Hud said, sniffling now himself. "The girls go for scrawny these days, right?" He didn't want Gatling to feel too bad, but he certainly didn't want him to feel too good. After all, he hoped to convince Gatling to move into his bachelor pad with him, where he could fatten him up with steaks and beer as dark as molasses.

Gatling tipped himself forward and dropped into the water with a splash that rocked a toddler in her turtle-shaped inner tube, sending her slightly, merrily floating away from her mother, who leaned against a wall of the pool immersed in a paperback. Hud walked to the edge and squatted to watch Gatling gently kick his legs to keep beneath the surface. Hud remembered the afternoon at the Plunge when Tuesday lost a heart-shaped locket he'd just bought for her from a souvenir shop that sold Black Hills gold. Inside the tiny thing, she'd put Nina's lips, cut from a photo she'd had in her purse, and Gatling's right eye. Hud and Gatling had taken deep breaths and plumbed the shallow depths, running their hands along stones and turning them over, hoping to feel the locket's gold chain catch in their fingers like thin strings of seaweed.

Hud now put his hand in the water. Gatling reached up and touched Hud's fingertips with his own. After a moment, Hud took hold of Gatling's hand and tugged. Gatling floated, face first, to the surface, his eyes shut. He then crossed his arms on the edge of the pool and rested his chin on one elbow. Hud ran the flat of his hand over Gatling's buzz cut, then gave his boy's head a light rub with his knuckles. He wanted to wrap him in a towel and cradle him in his arms until he stopped shivering.

"How'd you know where I was?" Gatling asked. Hud touched Gatling's earlobe, then the freckled skin of his shoulder, then the back of his neck.

"The postmarks on your notes from your so-called travels," Hud said. "Then some woman named Trish at that Mad Hattie's sold me this." He reached behind himself to thump the guitar he carried there. "I got it back for you."

"Ack," Gatling said. He lowered his head, hiding his eyes in his arms. "Do me a big favor and smash the hell out of it. Rip it apart string by string. Prolong its agony."

"That's not what you want." Hud hoped he'd never been the type of father to discourage his son's ambitions, though he knew he'd never been one to fuss, like a father probably ought to fuss, over the dippy soft-country songs Gatling wrote. Gatling's writing, in Hud's opinion, tended toward greeting-card sentiment—too many sunsets, too much moonlight. But sometimes something more would rise above the clutter of love stuff. His best song, one he wrote for Charlotte called "A Girl in a Tire Swing Eating a Pear," seemed to capture something exact about the girl's sadness. Gatling had only ever sung it once for Hud.

"I barely know how to even play a guitar right," Gatling said. "Take it back to Mad Hattie's. Some knucklehead can pick it up and start his own crappy band."

"See, that just kills your old dad. To hear that tone in your voice. What didn't I do for you, Gup? Why did you come here instead of coming home?"

"I'm a failure," Gatling said.

"You're not a failure," Hud said. "Not one bit of a failure. I admire you. I want to be you. Y'know? When I grow up, I guess." He laughed, but Gatling said nothing for a moment. He just rubbed his thumb against the toe of Hud's boot.

"The Daughters of God gave me my walking papers up in Fargo," Gatling said. "We'd stopped to do a concert for a woman who got shot in the head twice and lived. She shows off her bullet holes and people freak. Stella, that's the manager, she didn't like it that I'd been messing around with Sunny, so she gave me the heave-ho. But I shouldn't complain, I suppose. They were good to me, while things were fine."

Hud ran his hand down to touch the scars on Gatling's chest. He closed his eyes, hoping that he wouldn't be able to feel the letters if he wasn't looking right at them.

"Get out of the pool," Hud said, his voice shivery again. Then he felt a shot of almost otherworldly strength and energy, maybe that superhuman adrenaline rush you sometimes read about, when men find themselves capable of pushing cars off the tops of their broken wives, or jumping into frozen-over river rapids to rescue a little girl. Hud felt compelled to knock Gatling unconscious and drag him away by the nape of the neck if he had to. "Your mom and Nina are back at the hotel. They'll croak when they see you walk in. Come on. Out."

Gatling giggled, tickled, as Hud put his hands beneath his arms in an effort to pull him up. He slapped Hud's hands away. "Stop, Pops. Cool it." He pushed himself off the wall of the pool and floated on his back a few feet away, serene ripples lifting and lowering his body. "I've got to finish my shift. They've been good to me here. I don't want to leave them in the lurch. I'll meet you guys at your hotel in a couple of hours."

Hud was frightened to let Gatling out of his sight for even a second now that he'd found him, but then Gatling swam back to the edge, muscles moving beneath the skin of his shoulders. "I'm not going to ditch you, Pops," Gatling said, reaching up to offer a painfully hard handshake that belied his new frailty. "Why would I do that, old man? I'm no worthless kid at heart."

TUESDAY cranked up the heat of the hotel room to a fever-ish peak, and she allowed everyone wine, even Nina, who drank a few sips from Gatling's glass. They'd all dressed up to go out, but when Gatling arrived so pencil-thin, strangled by a gaudy necktie with a crooked knot, Tuesday cried just enough to make a mess of her little bit of makeup. The weep-ing was unexpected, but she welcomed it. It felt like maternal instinct.

They'd decided to cancel their reservations and splurge on room service; the floor was now littered with empty bottles, and plates with picked-clean T-bones.

"My glass is filthy," Gatling said, squinting, in his tipsi-ness, at the gray ghost of a lipstick print. He held the glass up to the glow of the lamp—Tuesday had dimmed way down the room's light.

"Nah, it's that stay-on lipstick the girls wear now," Hud said. "It's a serious problem for Augustine at the lounge. You could scrub at that glass for hours and get nowhere." Hud lay alone on the other bed in a laughably yellow suit he'd picked up at Mad Hattie's on his way back to the hotel, the only suit in the shop that had fit decent.

"I'm wearing Mom's lipstick," Nina said, puckering up.

"Just for tonight," Tuesday said.

"Gimme a smudge," Gatling said, tapping a finger against his cheek. Nina hadn't left his side since he arrived, her head now next to his on a pillow. She kissed him lightly, then harder, neither kiss leaving much of a mark. Then everyone devoted their attention to getting Nina's lip print on Gatling's cheek, with Tuesday painting Nina's lips and Hud advising on smooching technique. Finally Nina had covered both Gatling's cheeks with expert lipstick splotches.

"Here's a place for you, Mom," Nina said, pointing at a naked spot on Gatling's forehead.

But Tuesday just put the lid on the tube and dropped it into the nightstand drawer. "Lipstick ain't cheap, honey," she said, though she'd only paid 79 cents for it at the drugstore next to the hotel, and had had to make do with an orangey tint of coral, the only shade left.

She noticed Hud drifting off to sleep, the glass of wine in his hand beginning to teeter. Tuesday carefully lifted the glass from his fingers, then returned to sitting on the edge of the other bed, to drink the rest of his wine.

Gatling, Nina's head now resting on his stomach, played with the loose thread of a seam up the side of Tuesday's blue velvet dress, and she held still, pretending not to notice. She was afraid if she noticed, he might stop.

"Please tell me I'm not the reason you're staying away from home," Tuesday told Gatling.

Gatling shook his head and smiled sympathetically, running his finger over Nina's sweat-soaked bangs. "Nobody's the reason," he said. Nina's eyes blinked rapidly, then she was asleep too.

"I know I can be vindictive sometimes, maybe, but that's not anything I like about myself," Tuesday continued. "That's not even me. It's just my mother coming through in me. That's the way *she* is. Unforgiving. Punishing." She refilled Gatling's glass, though his eyes were wet and heavy-lidded. This felt like the thump of maternal instinct too, this need to drug her family with wine and warmth, to keep them all asleep in this cramped room in winter.

"Are you and Dad back together?" Gatling asked.

"No," Tuesday said. "He has the room across the hall." Hud had rolled over, his back to them, fetaled up and breathing slow. For years Tuesday had worried about herself in old age, were Hud to go first, and what it would be like to wake all alone every day, in your terrible last years when you needed your husband the most. But now they were divorced, and all those worries were replaced with others. She missed that old anxiety, with an ache in her stomach.

"What really happened to your hand?" Gatling asked. Though Tuesday had all along been entirely opposed to lying about how her hand broke, when Gatling had first asked, only moments after seeing her again, she'd found herself stuttering, claiming to have tripped into a wall. Even Nina kept silent, Nina, who lived for ratting out people who fibbed.

"I don't want to get into it," she said. "It's complicated. You know, you can't leave, then just show up out of nowhere, expecting answers."

"I didn't show up out of nowhere," he said. "You came to me. Here I was, minding my own business."

"Come home with us, baby," she said. She took a tissue and licked it, then began to dab at Gatling's cheeks to wash away Nina's sloppy kisses. Gatling laughed and gently pushed her hand away. "Charlotte misses you too. I know she does."

"That sucks for Charlotte," Gatling said. "Because I don't miss her. I've got other girls to miss now."

Tuesday was relieved to hear the touch of spite in his voice. "It's for the best, maybe," she said. "It's probably good when you can leave young love behind you. It doesn't age well."

Gatling rolled his eyes, clucked his tongue. He spoke softly, almost whispering. "You love to say things that I don't want to hear, don't you?"

"What did I say that you don't want to hear?" she said, whispering now too.

"I don't know," he said. He gently lifted Nina away from him so that he could sit upright next to Tuesday. "When I was a kid. I mean, the things you thought were OK to say to me . . ." He shook his head, disapproving.

"I know there was stuff I did wrong," she said, "but you have to know that my heart was in the right place."

"Well, sometimes it seems to me that maybe your heart was, really, just nowhere even near where it needed to be. Do you remember this one time, I was, like, five, or six, and I don't think I was even doing anything, I mean, I don't think I was being a brat, or anything, I was just sitting there eating a cookie, and you said to me, out of nowhere, I can hear it, you said, 'Honey, I almost gave you up for adoption when you were born. I don't want there to be any secrets. So I'm telling you right now, I had every intention of giving you up for adoption. And as much as I love you, and I love you to death, that probably would've been the best thing for all of us. We probably both would've had a better life.' It was just like that. I mean, goddamn, Mom. I was *five*."

Tuesday had no recollection of it. She could barely picture Gatling at five years old. It seemed he'd always been a surly teen. But even if she had said exactly that, hadn't she said she loved him to death? She looked over at Hud, who either slept soundly or feigned sleep to avoid taking a stand. She was tempted to wake him and demand that he defend her. He owed her big for the night before; when she had seen him lift Nina from the dining room chair during Rose's party, her heart had sped up with fear and filled with certainty that he and Nina would never return.

"Maybe I didn't always say the right things," Tuesday said, "but cut me some slack, why don't you? I was barely older than you are now."

"Yeah, well, if I had a kid of my own now, I'd never let him know how miserable I am."

"You'll be a great father someday," she said, not wanting to bicker. She put her hand on his chest, pleased to feel the lines of scars beneath his shirt. The name cut into his skin, damage so self-inflicted, was a living sign that Tuesday and Hud weren't responsible for all the boy's injury. He was far too sensitive.

"Come home with us," Tuesday said again. "We'll talk it all out."

Gatling smiled wide and shook his head. "What is home, anyway? Where would I stay? With you? Dad? You'd probably fight about it." Gatling gave his mother a hug and a kiss on the cheek. "Besides, I have a girl here in town, and I want it to work out. Speaking of being a father. She's got a two-year-old who's kind of getting attached to me."

"How long have you even . . ."

"We've been hanging out for about a month. The kid's a doll-baby. Talks all the time but doesn't know a word. Jabbers his own little language."

"A month."

He took a folded-up snapshot from his wallet, a picture of him with the boy on his knee, sitting on the back of a rusty white Pinto with vanity plates that said *SPOIL ME*. "That's Jasmine's shadow stretching across the ground there," Gatling said. "She was taking the picture. That's her car. I'd say you could meet her, but she's even more of a chatterbox than her kid. We'd never get a word in edgewise." Now that Gatling was talking about the chatty Jasmine and her son, he no longer seemed sleepy or drunk, or even morose or angry. He hopped over onto the other bed to shake his father awake, then to kiss his dad's neck and wrap his arms around him.

"Sorry to bore you right to sleep, Pops," Gatling said.

"No," Hud said. "No. It's just been a long couple of days. Why'd you let me drift off?"

"It's fine," Gatling said, standing and plucking the photo from Tuesday's hand, and sticking it back in his pocket. "Me and the mother of your children have just been doing a little catching up." He winked at Tuesday as he stepped backward toward the door, nervously clapping his hands together, looking like a man flat broke trying to weasel away from a poker game gone awry.

"Should we meet for breakfast?" Hud asked. "You still have a chocolate doughnut and Pepsi every morning?"

"Nah," he said. "Jasmine's a health nut. Just hot cereal and banana mush for me these days. Besides, we're actually going out of town tomorrow. True story, honest to God. Leaving at the crack of dawn. Taking her kid down to see her mom and twin sister in Boulder, Colorado." He looked at his watch, but he didn't seem to see the time at all. "Matter of fact, Jazzy and the kid are probably watching the clock right now, waiting for me. Tell Nina there that I kissed her while she slept. You know me, never had the stomach for good-byes."

"Now wait a minute, Gup," Hud said as both he and Tuesday stood.

Gatling opened the door. Smiling, he reached out to slap Hud's shoulder. "Pops, you know where to find me now. You'll come up and you'll check on me from time to time. I'm not going anywhere, I swear to God. I'm staying put. Not moving an inch. I promise." With that, he was gone with a skip into the hall.

Hud sat on the end of the bed, and after a quiet minute or two picked up Gatling's guitar from the floor. "Should I chase after him and give him this?" he asked. "Or go get him and drag him back? Kicking. Screaming." He then began to hum and mumble the words *kicking* and *screaming,* stretching them out, and he played a few pleasing notes. "Who's Jasmine? Who's her kid?"

"New people," Tuesday said. She rumpled Hud's hair as she passed. At the window, she watched the snow fall like rain in the light of a streetlamp. She worried about Gatling out in such weather. Then she dreaded another winter in her little drafty house with its ice-cold walls. When she had first married Hud, she'd fretted that neither of them was resourceful enough to keep their old house from falling down around them all. Even as a little girl she'd wondered if she would have been as clever as Gretel, capable of tricking the witch into her own stove.

2 4 .

⁋⁋⁋⁋⁋

H U D dropped off a disposable camera for one-hour developing late the next morning, Nina having been a frenzied shut-
terbug the night before, snapping shots of Gatling even as he
gnawed on his steak and spilled wine on his pants.

During the wait Hud and Tuesday and Nina toured a fos-
sil excavation site; still tired and preoccupied, they moved
sluggishly across scaffolding along the edge of a pit where
mammoths had perished eons before. The beasts had stepped
out of the cold winds of an ice age into a pool of hot spring
water for a luxurious soak, a guide explained, only to find
themselves unable to scale back up the muddy walls. Now
this mass grave was bone dry and covered and climate controlled, and spotlit for anthropologists.

Nina walked between Hud and Tuesday, holding both
their hands, as they moved along the path, glancing down at
the men and women below dusting off tusks and pelvic gir-
dles lodged in silt. "Is Gatling coming home with us?" Nina

asked. She wore a black fright wig with streaks of white that Hud had bought for her from a bin of quick-discount Halloween costumes at the drugstore.

"Nope," Tuesday said. "You know," she said to Hud, "he told me I told him too much when he was a kid. Revealed too much. And maybe I did. Before Nina came along, we were alone together a lot. I probably did confide in him."

Hud, however, thought Tuesday held her tongue too often for her own good. If she'd spoken up more during their marriage, maybe he would have better understood her unhappiness. Instead she would use up her fight, hushed, on the kitchen phone with her sister, Rose, guzzling coffee or cotton-balling old polish from her nails.

"Shhh, you're rude," Nina said, dropping their hands and stepping forward to be nearer the guide. And it was rude, Hud supposed, to be talking; there were only two other people in the group, the place practically a ghost town in the off season.

"I wonder if I'll get fired for taking that rattletrap of a bus," Hud whispered close to Tuesday's ear. He took her hand. Her fingers were loose in his at first, but then he felt them tighten, and he felt her lean against him. "I wonder how the kids got to school this morning," he said. "By spring I want to be in a better position. I want Nina to be able to rely on me for things. I'm going to look into this freelance gig one of the other bus drivers was telling me about. He's making forty bucks a phone call to tell farmers that their health insurance is tripling."

As the guide described how hunters would follow the migration of their prey, erecting huts built from the rib cages and hides of giant bears and woolly mammoths, Nina scrambled ahead, then tried to pull herself up to see better over the railing. "Pssst," Hud hissed in her direction, snapping his fingers at her, gesturing for her to get down. He could just imagine her tumbling over and into the pit. Cracking her head open on a skull bone. "I wouldn't have run off with Nina alone the other night," Hud told Tuesday. "I would've just driven around the block until I cooled off."

"I know," Tuesday said.

"I would never take Nina away from you," he said.

"I know," she said. She squeezed his hand a few times before letting go. He was fairly certain she believed him.

Before leaving Hot Springs that afternoon, Hud paid what he considered a rather cruelly exorbitant price for the rest of Gatling's belongings at Mad Hattie's. They then stopped at the Plunge, to call Gatling's bluff, but the boy had indeed taken some days off, they were told, and Nina left him a plea to come home, in her sloppy handwriting, all her "i's" dotted with hearts.

The weather worsened, and they drove a few long hours in snow and sleet, the roads frightening and slick. All the nervous breath in the bus fogged the window, requiring that Hud often lean forward to wipe at the window with the end of his sleeve. "Ease up on the breathing, girls," he said, to make light, but Tuesday and Nina were too anxious to laugh. When the stretches of snow on the land gave way to the return of the yellows and wines and reds of autumn, and the start of the sunset riddled the clouds with shots of light, the mood in the bus lifted. It lifted so much that Tuesday ended up in the aisle teaching Nina a dusty old line dance from the days when she and Hud would drive up the highway to the now-defunct Swift Kick Saloon where, in the parking lot, Mexican strippers peddled hot car stereos and VCRs.

But, to their surprise, as they neared home, they drove back into snow and ice. Though it wasn't unusual for South Dakota to see winter before the end of fall, it had snowed in October in their Nebraska town only a few times that Hud could remember. Tuesday and Nina sat behind Hud, clicking their tongues with shock at the sight of all the ravaged trees. The branches had not yet dropped all their leaves and couldn't bear the additional weight of the icicles and heavy snow.

The drive-in's marquee promoted its annual Halloween costume party and a double bill of schlock, *She-Freak* and *Shriek of the Mutilated*, but the place sat dark and unplowed, its gate padlocked. Some of the residential streets of the town were closed, blocked off by broken branches or snapped power lines or whole trees that had split down their middles. It was early evening, after dark, but there were no trick-or-treaters around, only Millie steering her bike in the street around branches and patches of ice and snow; she wore a toy tiara and a pink gown that looked made of paper. One of the few porch lights lit was Nanette Schrock's. Hanging in front of the light was a puppetlike witch decoration. With her loosely hinged joints, the witch did an impromptu soft-shoe in the night wind, casting quivering shadows across the drifts on Nanette's lawn.

Hud pulled up in front of the home of Ozzie and Charlotte, the photos from the night before in his back pocket. He wanted to offer Charlotte proof, and to tempt her toward Hot Springs with a sight of Gatling's skin-and-boniness, to appeal to her sense of drama. Though Gatling had another girl now, there was simply no denying an old love whose name was splayed, like a bloody crime, across your flesh.

A note was taped over the doorbell. "Gone to Nashville," it said, and it was signed by both Oz and Charlotte. Hud was skeptical, though all the lights of the house were out and the pickup gone from the drive. Hud selected a photo in which Gatling looked the perfect mix of lost lamb and rebel soul, and he slipped it beneath the door.

"The mayor canceled Halloween earlier today," Tuesday explained as Hud got back on the bus. Tuesday sat in the driver's seat, having tuned the AM radio to a local station. "A lot of people are still without electricity."

Nina moped with the fright wig in her lap. "Well, I'm not so sure the mayor has the authority to cancel Halloween," Hud said. "What's to cancel? You knock on people's doors and they either give you candy or they don't. I say we act in defiance of the mayor! It's revolution!" He put Nina's wig back on her head.

Their revolution consisted only of going back to the house for their own private Halloween party. Tuesday put her blue velvet dress and shoes back on. Nina decided to be one of the teenaged tramps that loitered at the drive-in in the summer, so she put on a tube top and some cutoffs and sparkled her cheeks with spray-on glitter. Hud just put on one of his dad's old suits, musty from having been abandoned in the basement. When they discovered a mysterious pillowcase containing a scant amount of sweets, just sitting atop the trunk by the front door, they couldn't have been more tickled if the bag had been filled with something useful. Nina divvied up the candy, and Hud told a ghost story about a disembodied eyeball, but he found himself unable to remember the ending of it.

After a dinner of microwave popcorn and Hot Tamales, Hud gentlemanly excused himself, pinching Nina's shimmering cheek, then kissing it. Tuesday walked him to the front door.

"Did I tell you I got blackjacked coming out of the lounge the other night?" Hud asked. He turned the back of his neck to Tuesday, and she pushed down on his collar. She pressed his bruise, and he cringed from the jolt of pain.

"Sorry," she said, snapping her hand back with a little laugh. "A lot of bad luck in that parking lot," she said, waving her cast. Tuesday crossed her arms and shivered from the cold let in by the open door. "Thanks for getting us home safely tonight. Those roads were tricky. I could tell you were really white-knuckling it."

"I was nervous," he said. He wanted to kiss her quick, but instead reached up to push some fine strands of hair from her cheek.

"Come back in the morning early and shovel the walk," Tuesday said. "I'll fix you breakfast after."

"It'll have to be early early," Hud said. "I've got to get all those kids to school."

"Early early's good," she said, and there was that pause when there could've been a kiss, but Hud thought it more gallant to simply wink.

It was funny to Hud, as he drove back to his apartment, that he could be so looking forward to a morning so dismal, to breaking his back scooping snow in the cold, especially when he recalled all the years of battle over such things—the squabbling over leaky faucets and cracks in windows, over who dressed what kid last, who drove who where, all the empty whats and whens that had slowly turned him and Tuesday against each other.

Hud drove past the church with a panel of wood covering its missing window—across the wood someone had spray-painted *JESUS IS WITH YOU* in black, and the sight of it was startling in a way the stained glass never had been.

Then Hud's headlights swept across a kid dressed in the red long johns of some superhero, his sleeves stuffed to simulate bulging muscles. The kid tossed toilet paper into a severed tree limb on the ground, stringing the paper among icicles, then disappeared around a corner. As Hud drove slowly toward the town square, he caught glimpses of other covert trick-or-treaters, children without their coats, ignoring the mayor's proclamation, got up as ninjas and wizards, as disco queens and evil clowns and robots of cardboard and foil.

Hud drove into the pitch dark of Cherry Ave., the power still out in that part of town; even the streetlamps remained unlit. Then, just as a boy in a vampire's cape and widow's peak ran in front of the bus to egg its front window with a splat that made Hud's stomach jump, the houses along the row lit up all at once, their power restored. Plastic jack-o'-lanterns began to glow yellow, as did the eyes of an electric mummy on someone's front lawn. The cauldron of a witch on a roof flickered with purple and green, and from somewhere came the recorded bellowing of the undead. Hud had to park a moment and take it all in. Witnessing such a sudden return to life as usual lifted his spirit. He knew that what he was feeling was the next best thing to faith.